PUBLIC PAPERS OF THE PRESIDENTS

OF THE UNITED STATES

Jimmy Carter

1979

(IN TWO BOOKS)

BOOK I—JANUARY 1 TO JUNE 22, 1979

UNITED STATES GOVERNMENT PRINTING OFFICE

WASHINGTON : 1980

Published by the
Office of the Federal Register
National Archives and Records Service
General Services Administration

For sale by the Superintendent of Documents, U.S. Government Printing Office
Washington, D.C. 20402

Stock No. 022-003-01037-8

Foreword

Alexis de Tocqueville once wrote that historians and politicians are "equally deceived" by their differing perspectives on public events. Historians, he wrote, tend to overemphasize the extent to which broad, impersonal forces shape events, neglecting the sometimes decisive role of specific, day-to-day developments.

Politicians, he remarked, suffer from the opposite handicap. "Living in the midst of disconnected daily facts, they are prone to imagine that everything is attributable to particular incidents, and that the wires they pull are the same as those that move the world."

This collection of Presidential papers, covering the first half of 1979, documents a number of landmark events—the historic Middle East peace treaty, ending thirty years of war between Israel and Egypt; the successful conclusion of the Multilateral Trade Negotiations; the first overhaul of the Federal civil service in a century. Together with earlier volumes, it chronicles each major event not as an isolated moment but as the culmination of a sustained effort.

These papers do something more. They permit the historian to see these breakthroughs as they occurred—in the context of the daily business of government. And they allow public officials like myself to see our actions not as a set of discrete steps, but as part of an historical continuum. In this way, these papers should enhance the view from both perspectives.

Jimmy Carter

Preface

This book contains the papers and speeches of the 39th President of the United States which were issued by the White House Press Office during the period January 1–June 22, 1979. A second Public Papers book completing President Carter's third year in office will be printed later in 1980. The material has been compiled and published by the Office of the Federal Register, National Archives and Records Service, General Services Administration.

The material is presented in chronological order within each week, and the dates shown in the headings are the dates of the documents or events. In instances when the release date differs from the date of the document itself, that fact is shown in the textnote. Every effort has been made to ensure accuracy. Tape recordings are used to protect against errors in transcription of Presidential remarks, and signed documents are checked against the original to verify the correct printing. Textnotes, footnotes, and cross references have been provided by the editors for purposes of identification or clarity. Speeches were delivered in Washington, D.C., and other documents released there, unless indicated. All times noted are local times.

All materials have been fully indexed. In addition to the usual subject-matter entries in the index, the material has been classified in categories reflecting the type of Presidential activity or document. For example, a reader interested in the President's speeches will find them listed in the index under "Addresses and Remarks." An index accounting for all the materials for 1979 will be included in Book II.

The Public Papers series was begun in 1957 in response to a recommendation of the National Historical Publications Commission. An extensive compilation of messages and papers of the Presidents covering the period 1789 to 1897 was assembled by James D. Richardson and published under congressional authority between 1896 and 1899. Since then, various private compilations have been issued, but there was no uniform publication comparable to the Congressional Record or the United States Supreme Court Reports. Many Presidential papers could be found only in the form of mimeographed White House releases or as reported in the press. The Commission therefore recommended the establishment of an official series in which Presidential writings, addresses, and remarks of a public nature could be made available.

The Commission's recommendation was incorporated in regulations of the Administrative Committee of the Federal Register, issued under section 6 of the Federal Register Act (44 U.S.C. 1506), which may be found in Title 1, Part 10, of the Code of Federal Regulations.

A companion publication to the Public Papers series, the Weekly Compilation of Presidential Documents, was begun in 1965 to provide a broader range of Presidential materials on a more timely basis to meet the needs of the contemporary reader. Beginning with the administration of Jimmy Carter, the Public Papers series expanded its coverage to include all material as printed in the Weekly Compilation. That coverage provides a listing of the President's daily schedule and meetings, when announced, and other items of general interest issued by the White House Press Office. Also included are lists of the President's nominations submitted to the Senate, materials released by the Press Office which are not printed full-text in the book, and acts approved by the President. This information is compiled on a weekly basis and appears at the end of each week's coverage.

Volumes covering the administrations of Presidents Hoover, Truman, Eisenhower, Kennedy, Johnson, Nixon, and Ford are also available.

This series is under the direction of Ernest J. Galdi, Acting Director, Office of the Federal Register, and is produced by the Presidential Documents Division, Robert E. Lewis, Director, and Richard L. Claypoole, Deputy Director. Editors of this book were Katherine A. Mellody, Kenneth R. Payne, Brian L. Hermes, and Gwendolyn J. Henderson.

White House liaison was provided by Patricia Y. Bario, Deputy Press Secretary. The frontispiece and photographs used in the portfolio were supplied by the White House Photo Office.

The typography and design of the volume were developed by the United States Government Printing Office under the direction of John J. Boyle, Public Printer.

JAMES E. O'NEILL
Acting Archivist of the United States

R. G. FREEMAN III
Administrator of General Services
January 1980

Contents

	PAGE
FOREWORD	v
PREFACE	vii
PUBLIC PAPERS OF JIMMY CARTER, JANUARY 1–JUNE 22, 1979	1
INDEX	A–1

Administration of Jimmy Carter

1979

PRESIDENTIAL DOCUMENTS

Premier Hua Guofeng of the People's Republic of China

New Year's Message From the President. January 1, 1979

Today, after a generation of isolation from each other, the United States of America and the People's Republic of China establish full diplomatic relations between our governments. The cause of world peace will be served by this historic act of reconciliation.

The estrangement of our peoples has sometimes produced misunderstanding, confrontation and enmity. That era is behind us. We can now establish normal patterns of commerce, and scholarly and cultural exchange. Through common effort, we can deepen the new ties of friendship between our peoples, and we can jointly contribute to the prosperity and stability of Asia and the Pacific region.

Precisely because our two countries have different traditions, cultures, and political and economic systems, we have much to gain from each other. The United States prizes the great variety of opinions and origins among its own citizens. Similarly, the United States desires a world of diversity in which each nation is free to make a distinctive contribution to express the manifold aspirations, cultures, traditions, and beliefs of mankind.

The American people value the enormous contributions the Chinese people have made to the achievements of humanity. And we welcome the growing involvement of the People's Republic of China in world affairs. We consider China as a key force for global peace.

We wish to cooperate closely with the creative Chinese people on the problems that confront all people.

Your Excellency, in our country, the first day of the New Year is a time of rededication and resolve. In that spirit, we pledge during the coming years:

—to continue as an enlightened Asian and Pacific power, determined to help maintain peace and stability in the region;

—to enrich the lives of our peoples, both spiritually and materially, through expanded trade, tourism, and student and cultural exchanges, and cooperation in the sciences, all on a basis of equality and mutual benefit; and

—to extend our hands across the Pacific to you in friendship and peace.

Vice Premier Deng Xiaoping of the People's Republic of China

New Year's Message From the President.
January 1, 1979

On this New Year's Day, I welcome the establishment of full diplomatic relations between the United States of America and the People's Republic of China.

New tasks now await us. The new Sino-American relationship offers great potential benefit to the welfare of our peoples, to the promotion of peace and prosperity of the Asia-Pacific region, and to stability throughout the world.

The American people—and I personally—look forward to your forthcoming visit to the United States. In Washington, we can talk seriously with each other about both global and bilateral matters.

Together, we can seize the opportunity your visit affords us to foster a constructive and enduring relationship between our two peoples. To that end, Mrs. Carter joins me in wishing you and Madame Cho Lin a Happy New Year, and we look forward to greeting you in the United States.

Meeting With Prime Minister J. Malcolm Fraser of Australia

White House Statement.   January 2, 1979

President Carter met with the Prime Minister of Australia, the Right Honorable J. Malcolm Fraser, in the Cabinet Room at the White House at 11 a.m., Tuesday, January 2, 1979, for an hour. Prime Minister Fraser was accompanied by Australian Foreign Minister Andrew Peacock, Ambassador to the United States Alan Renouf, and Mr. Geoffrey Yeend,

Secretary of the Department of the Prime Minister and Cabinet. Vice President Mondale, Secretary of State Cyrus Vance, Assistant to the President for National Security Affairs Zbigniew Brzezinski, and other U.S. officials also were present.

In the context of the close U.S.-Australian friendship and alliance, President Carter and Prime Minister Fraser discussed a broad range of gobal and regional topics of importance to Australia and the United States, including developments in Iran and the Middle East, the need for cooperation among the developed nations to combat inflation and restore economic health and stability throughout the world, and the recent United States decision to normalize relations with the People's Republic of China.

Following the meeting with the President, Secretary of State Vance hosted a luncheon for Prime Minister Fraser and his party at the State Department.

Office of Personnel Management; Merit Systems Protection Board

Recess Appointment of Members.
January 2, 1979

The President today announced four recess appointments to positions created by the civil service reorganization plan, effective January 1, 1979. They are:

ALAN K. CAMPBELL, previously Chairman of the Civil Service Commission, is appointed Director of the Office of Personnel Management;

JULE M. SUGARMAN, previously Vice Chairman of the Civil Service Commission, is appointed Deputy Director of the Office of Personnel Management;

RUTH T. PROKOP, previously General Counsel of the Department of Housing and Urban Development, is appointed as Chairman of the Merit Systems Protection Board; and

H. PATRICK SWYGERT, previously General Counsel of the Civil Service Commission, is appointed Special Counsel of the Merit Systems Protection Board. Swygert, 35, a graduate of Howard University Law School, was a professor of law at Temple University before joining the Civil Service Commission.

Executive Schedule

Executive Order 12111. January 2, 1979

LEVELS IV AND V OF THE EXECUTIVE SCHEDULE

By the authority vested in me as President of the United States of America by Section 5317 of Title 5 of the United States Code, and in order to place the position of Counselor on Labor Management Relations, Department of Commerce, in level IV of the Executive Schedule, Executive Order No. 12076, as amended, is further amended by deleting "Assistant to the Secretary and Land Utilization Adviser, Department of the Interior." from Section 1–102(g) and inserting "(s) Counselor on Labor Management Relations, Department of Commerce." in alphabetical order in Section 1–101 thereof.

JIMMY CARTER

The White House,
January 2, 1979.

[Filed with the Office of the Federal Register, 2:01 p.m., January 2, 1979]

Seal for the Office of Administration

Executive Order 12112. January 2, 1979

By the authority vested in me as President by the Constitution of the United States of America, it is hereby ordered as follows:

1–101. There is established for the Office of Administration in the Executive Office of the President an official seal described as follows:

On a blue seal, the Arms of the United States proper above the inscription "OFFICE OF ADMINISTRATION," in gold raised letters, all within a white border edged gold and inscribed "EXECUTIVE OFFICE OF THE PRESIDENT OF THE UNITED STATES," in blue raised letters. Dark blue suggested by the Seal of the President denotes the direct organizational link with the Presidential office.

1–102. The seal shall be of the design which is attached hereto and made a part of this Order.

JIMMY CARTER

The White House,
January 2, 1979.

[Filed with the Office of the Federal Register, 2:02 p.m., January 2, 1979]

NOTE: The seal of the Office of Administration is printed in the FEDERAL REGISTER of January 4, 1979.

American Bolt, Nut, and Large Screw Industry

Proclamation 4632. January 4, 1979

TEMPORARY DUTY INCREASE ON THE IMPORTATION INTO THE UNITED STATES OF CERTAIN BOLTS, NUTS AND SCREWS OF IRON OR STEEL

By the President of the United States of America

A Proclamation

1. Pursuant to section 201(d)(1) of the Trade Act of 1974 (the Trade Act) (19

3

U.S.C. 2251(d)(1)), the United States International Trade Commission, hereinafter referred to as the USITC, on November 3, 1978, reported to the President (USITC Report 201–37) the results of its investigation under section 201(b) of the Trade Act (19 U.S.C. 2251(b)). The USITC determined that certain bolts, nuts and screws of iron or steel provided for in items 646.49, 646.54, 646.56, and 646.63 of the Tariff Schedules of the United States (TSUS) are being imported into the United States in such increased quantities as to be a substantial cause of serious injury, or the threat thereof, to the domestic industry producing articles like or directly competitive with the imported articles. The USITC recommended the imposition of additional duties on imports of the above specified articles.

2. On December 22, 1978, pursuant to section 202(b)(1) of the Trade Act (19 U.S.C. 2252(b)(1)), and after taking into account the considerations specified in section 202(c) of the Trade Act (19 U.S.C. 2252(c)), I determined to prevent or remedy the injury or threat thereof found to exist by the USITC through the proclamation of a temporary duty increase different from that recommended by the USITC. On December 22, 1978, in accordance with section 203(b)(1) of the Trade Act (19 U.S.C. 2253(b)(1)), I transmitted a report to the Congress setting forth my determination and intention to proclaim a temporary duty increase and stating the reasons why my decision differed from the action recommended by the USITC.

3. The bolts and nuts provided for in items 646.54 and 646.56 of the TSUS are currently eligible for duty-free treatment under the Generalized System of Preferences (GSP), and section 503(c)(2) of

the Trade Act (19 U.S.C. 2463(c)(2)) provides that no article shall be eligible for purposes of the GSP for any period during which such article is the subject of any action proclaimed pursuant to section 203 of the Trade Act (19 U.S.C. 2253).

4. Section 203(e)(1) of the Trade Act (19 U.S.C. 2253(e)(1)) requires that import relief be proclaimed and take effect within 15 days after the import relief determination date.

5. Pursuant to sections 203(a)(1), 203(e)(1), and 503(c)(2) of the Trade Act (19 U.S.C. 2253(a)(1), 2253(e)(1), and 2463(c)(2)), I am providing import relief, as hereinafter proclaimed, through the temporary increase of import duty on, and, where applicable, the removal from eligibility for duty-free entry under the GSP, of the bolts, nuts and screws of iron or steel covered by the affirmative finding of the USITC.

Now, THEREFORE, I, JIMMY CARTER, President of the United States of America, acting under the authority vested in me by the Constitution and the statutes of the United States, including General Headnote 4 of the TSUS (19 U.S.C. 1202), sections 203, 503 and 604 of the Trade Act (19 U.S.C. 2253, 2463, and 2483), and in accordance with Articles I and XIX of the General Agreement on Tariffs and Trade (GATT) (61 Stat. (pt. 5) A12 and 61 Stat. (pt. 5) A58; 8 UST (pt. 2) 1786), do proclaim that—

(1) Part I of Schedule XX to the GATT is modified to conform to the action taken in the Annex to this proclamation.

(2) Subpart A, part 2 of the Appendix to the TSUS is modified as set forth in the Annex to this proclamation.

(3) GSP eligibility is removed for the bolts and nuts covered by items 923.51

and 923.52 of the Annex to this proclamation.

(4) This proclamation shall be effective as to articles entered, or withdrawn from warehouse, for consumption on or after January 6, 1979, and before the close of January 5, 1982, unless the period of its effectiveness is earlier expressly modified or terminated.

IN WITNESS WHEREOF, I have hereunto set my hand this fourth day of January, in the year of our Lord nineteen hundred and seventy-nine, and of the Independence of the United States of America the two hundred and third.

JIMMY CARTER

[Filed with the Office of the Federal Register, 12:56 p.m., January 4, 1979]

NOTE: The annex is printed in the FEDERAL REGISTER of January 8, 1979.

International Trade Agreements

Memorandum From the President.
January 4, 1979

Memorandum for the Special Representative for Trade Negotiations

I have today sent the attached notices to the Speaker of the U.S. House of Representatives and the President of the Senate. These notices shall be published in the FEDERAL REGISTER.

JIMMY CARTER

Dear Mr. Speaker: (Dear Mr. President:)

We have an important opportunity this year to build a new and better approach to international trade. The first important step depends on acceptance and implementation by the Congress of the agreements reached in the Tokyo Round of multilateral trade negotiations. We are now within sight of a successful conclusion to these negotiations. I am confident that the results will embody the U.S. objectives outlined by the Congress in the Trade Act of 1974 and developed in close consultation with members of the Congress, their staffs, and our private-sector advisors. Neither Bob Strauss, my Special Trade Representative, nor I will accept anything less on behalf of the United States.

The progress of the negotiations is such that I can notify the Congress at this time of our intention to enter into several international agreements dealing mainly with non-tariff trade matters. These agreements, to which Congress gave a high priority in its mandate for the negotiations, are intended primarily to ensure that the international trading system is both fair and open. The agreements are listed and identified below and are described more fully in an attachment to this letter.

• An agreement on *subsidies and countervailing duties* will limit trade-distorting subsidy practices and will enunciate more clearly the right of the United States and others to counteract such practices. The agreement may provide for a number of conforming changes in the international Anti-dumping Code.

• An agreement on *safeguards* in response to a specific Congressional directive, will ensure that countries observe international trading rules when temporarily limiting imports that are injuring domestic industries.

• An agreement on *technical barriers to trade* or *standards* will require countries to use fair and open procedures in the adoption of product standards and related practices that affect international trade.

• An agreement on *government procurement* will increase opportunities for

American and other exporters to bid for sales to foreign governments.

• An agreement on *licensing* will reduce the extent to which unnecessary or unduly complicated import licensing requirements impede trade.

• An agreement on *customs valuation* will encourage more uniform methods of appraising imports for the purpose of applying import duties.

• An agreement on *commercial counterfeiting* will promote cooperation and uniform approaches for this growing trade problem.

• An agreement on *aircraft* will provide a basis for fairer trade in this important U.S. export sector.

• Agreements to *improve the international trading framework* will tighten the handling of international trade disputes, respond to needs of developing countries in a fair and balanced manner, modernize the international rules applicable to trade measures taken in response to balance-of-payments emergencies, and provide a basis for examining the existing international rules on export and import restraints, while currently strengthening those rules through improvements in the dispute-settlement procedures.

Several other agreements on tariff and non-tariff matters have been negotiated in response to specific requests that were made by the United States or other countries. These agreements are described in the attachments.

In addition, members of the Administration will be consulting with the Congress about the implementation of several agreements on *agricultural trade* that we intend to enter into at about the time the

Tokyo Round is concluded. These agreements will provide for a fairer international sharing of the burdens in international wheat trade, and will encourage consultations and cooperation on international trade in coarse grains, meat, and certain dairy products. The agricultural agreements are also expected to improve the application of accepted international trading rules to agricultural trade.

In accordance with procedures specified in the Trade Act, the United States will not enter into the agreements outlined above for the next 90 calendar days. After the agreements have been signed, they will be submitted for Congressional approval, together with whatever legislation and administrative actions may be needed to implement the agreements in the United States. The agreements will not take effect with respect to the United States, and will have no domestic legal force, until the Congress has specifically approved them and enacted any appropriate implementing legislation.

During Congressional consideration of these agreements, we will also supply information on the related negotiations to reduce, harmonize, or eliminate tariff barriers, and on the recent establishment of an International Steel Agreement in the Organization for Economic Cooperation and Development.

The success of the Tokyo Round and its implementation will be the product of a good working relationship among the Congress, the Administration, and the American public. Through these agreements and their domestic implementation, we can construct trade policies and institutions that advance our national interest and enhance the prosperity of our people.

I look forward to our working together to complete this effort.

Sincerely,

JIMMY CARTER

[Filed with the Office of the Federal Register, 4:07 p.m., January 4, 1979]

NOTE: The notices are printed in the FEDERAL REGISTER of January 8, 1979.

Deputy Assistant to the President

Appointment of William Simpson. January 4, 1979

The President announced today that Mr. William Simpson of Gulfport, Miss., will join the White House staff immediately as Deputy Assistant to the President. In this capacity, Mr. Simpson will be working with Hamilton Jordan and his staff on the priority goals and programs of the administration.

Simpson was born in Gulfport on July 29, 1923. He attended the Marion Military Institute, Marion, Ala., and the University of Mississippi before graduating from the U.S. Merchant Marine Academy at Kings Point, N.Y. He saw combat service as a naval midshipman and officer in the Pacific Theater in World War II.

From 1947 to 1965, he was associated with his father and brother in operating the family shrimp and oyster canning facility in Gulfport. From 1965 to 1968, he was special assistant to Mississippi Governor Paul B. Johnson, Jr. Simpson also served as first chairman of the Mississippi Marine Conservation Commission and as president of the State Port Authority at Gulfport.

From 1968 through 1978, Simpson was administrative assistant to Senator James

O. Eastland of Mississippi, who served as President pro tempore of the Senate from 1972 until his recent retirement.

Federal Pay and the Anti-Inflation Program

Memorandum From the President. January 4, 1979

Memorandum for the Heads of Executive Departments and Agencies

Subject: Federal Pay and the Anti-inflation Program

The success of our anti-inflation effort is critical to the economic well-being of the nation. To achieve this success, it is vital that the Government, in managing its own affairs, join with the rest of the nation in a positive commitment to reducing inflationary pressures. Accordingly, I have determined that it would be inconsistent with the public interest for any category of Federal pay rates to be increased by more than 5.5 percent during fiscal year 1979.

To this end, this Administration and the Congress have frozen Federal executive pay altogether, and have placed a 5.5 percent ceiling on pay increases for most Federal workers—those under the General Schedule and related pay systems, the members of the uniformed services, and most Federal wage employees.

However, there are substantial numbers of nonappropriated fund employees and other workers employed by entities of the Federal Government who are not covered by these Government-wide actions, since they are under a variety of relatively small pay systems over which you have pay setting authority. In order to ensure that proposed pay increases for other pay systems do not exceed the maximums for

Federal pay that the Congress and I have set, the policy of this Administration is:

In the public interest to control inflation, each officer or employee in the executive branch who has administrative authority to set rates of pay for any Federal officers or employees should exercise such authority, to the extent permissible under law, treaty, or international agreement, in such a way as to ensure that no rate of pay for any category of officers or employees is increased more than 5.5 percent during fiscal year 1979. Specifically excluded from this limitation are rates of pay for foreign nationals authorized under the Foreign Service Act of 1946 as amended (22 U.S.C. 889) and increases in rates of pay to implement the minimum wage provisions of the Fair Labor Standards Act of 1938, as amended, as authorized under currrent agency policies.

The Chairman of the Civil Service Commission, until January 1, 1979, and the Director of the Office of Personnel Management, on and after January 1, 1979, will provide you with any further advice or assistance you may need in complying with this policy.

JIMMY CARTER

Independent Water Project Review

Executive Order 12113.   January 4, 1979

By the authority vested in me as President by the Constitution and laws of the United States of America, in furtherance of the Water Resources Planning Act (79 Stat. 244; 42 U.S.C. 1962 *et seq.*), and in order to ensure coordinated planning and independent review of Federal water resource programs and projects, it is hereby ordered as follows:

1–101. The Water Resources Council shall ensure that it has established a current set of principles, standards, and procedures for Federal participants in the preparation of comprehensive regional or river basin plans and for the formulation and evaluation of Federal water and related land resources projects (42 U.S.C. 1962a–2).

1–102. The Council shall ensure that an impartial technical review is performed on preauthorization reports or proposals and preconstruction plans for Federal and Federally assisted water, and related land resources, projects and programs, as they are defined in the Council's principles and standards.

1–103. The Council shall develop a planning manual for use by each agency (a) in calculating benefits and costs by using the best available techniques and (b) in applying the principles and standards in a consistent manner.

1–104. The impartial technical review shall evaluate each report, proposal, or plan for compliance with (a) the Council's principles and standards, (b) the planning manual or, pending issuance of the manual, established agency procedures, (c) other Federal laws, regulations and guidelines relevant to the planning process, and (d) the goal of wide public participation in the development of project plans, including adequate opportunity for public comment and adequate consideration of those views.

1–105. (a) Beginning April 1, 1979, all agencies shall submit, prior to their approval by the head of the agency, preauthorization reports or proposals and preconstruction plans for Federal and Federally assisted water, and related land resources, projects and programs to the Council at least 90 days prior to the scheduled time for their submission to the

Office of Management and Budget in support of authorization or funding requests for those activities in fiscal year 1981 and subsequent years.

(b) An agency shall not submit to the Council more than one-third of the total reports, proposals, and plans scheduled for review in any fiscal year during any quarter of that fiscal year.

(c) Within 60 days of the submission by an agency of a report, proposal, or plan, the Chairman of the Council shall transmit the results of the impartial technical review to the appropriate agency head, including identification of any specific variations from Council approved procedures and manuals and the steps necessary to bring the plan into conformance therewith.

1–106. (a) All agency reports, proposals and plans submitted to the Council for review shall include sufficient information to allow an adequate technical review. In particular, this information shall include:

(1) Sufficient documentation to allow a technical review of the analysis by the agency of the ratio of the benefit to the cost.

(2) Evidence that an adequate evaluation has been made of reasonable alternatives, including nonstructural ones, for addressing the water-related problems of the affected regions and communities.

(3) An explanation of the relationship of the plan to any approved regional water resource management plans.

(4) A summary of the consideration given to water conservation measures and a listing of those measures incorporated into the plan.

(5) Evidence that there has been compliance with relevant environmental and other laws and requirements.

(6) Evidence that the public and State and local officials have been involved in the plan formulation process.

(b) If the documents and information necessary for the review are not initially submitted, the Chairman may extend the review period by not more than 30 days. If the documents and information submitted do not demonstrate compliance, a finding detailing the areas of noncompliance will be transmitted to the agency head.

1–107. Before any agency submits to the Congress, or to any committee or member thereof, a report relating to, or affecting in whole or in part its advance programs, or the public works and improvement projects comprising such programs, or the results of any plan preparation for such programs or projects, such report or plan shall be submitted to the Office of Management and Budget for advice as to its relationship to the program of the President. When such report or plan is thereafter submitted to the Congress, or to any committee or member thereof, it shall include a statement of the advice received from the Office of Management and Budget.

1–108. Agency submissions to the Office of Management and Budget of the reports, proposals or plans reviewed pursuant to this Order shall be accompanied by a statement of the findings transmitted to the agency head.

1–109. Executive Order No. 9384 of October 4, 1943, as amended, is revoked.

JIMMY CARTER

The White House,
   January 4, 1979.

[Filed with the Office of the Federal Register,
   3:37 p.m., January 5, 1979]

NOTE: The text of the Executive order was released on January 5.

Independent Water Project Review

Memorandum From the President.
January 4, 1979

Memorandum for the Chairman and Members of the Water Resources Council

In my Water Resources Policy Reform Message of June 6, 1978, I stated that an independent project review unit would be created in the Water Resources Council to ensure water projects have been planned in accordance with the Principles and Standards and other planning requirements. Today I have signed an Executive Order which establishes this independent water project review function in the Water Resources Council.

I look forward to your speedy organization of the independent review unit. As described in my Water Policy Message, I expect the review function will be performed by a professional staff of about 30 and will be operational in time for the 1981 budget cycle. Rules, regulations and procedures necessary to implement the independent review function should be published in proposed form in the FEDERAL REGISTER within six weeks and in final form within the following six months.

JIMMY CARTER

NOTE: The text of the memorandum was released on January 5.

Environmental Effects Abroad of Major Federal Actions

Executive Order 12114.   January 4, 1979

By virtue of the authority vested in me by the Constitution and the laws of the United States, and as President of the United States, in order to further environmental objectives consistent with the foreign policy and national security policy of the United States, it is ordered as follows:

SECTION 1.

1–1. *Purpose and Scope.* The purpose of this Executive Order is to enable responsible officials of Federal agencies having ultimate responsibility for authorizing and approving actions encompassed by this Order to be informed of pertinent environmental considerations and to take such considerations into account, with other pertinent considerations of national policy, in making decisions regarding such actions. While based on independent authority, this Order furthers the purpose of the National Environmental Policy Act and the Marine Protection Research and Sanctuaries Act and the Deepwater Port Act consistent with the foreign policy and national security policy of the United States, and represents the United States government's exclusive and complete determination of the procedural and other actions to be taken by Federal agencies to further the purpose of the National Environmental Policy Act, with respect to the environment outside the United States, its territories and possessions.

SEC. 2.

2–1. *Agency Procedures.* Every Federal agency taking major Federal actions encompassed hereby and not exempted herefrom having significant effects on the environment outside the geographical borders of the United States and its territories and possessions shall within eight months after the effective date of this Order have in effect procedures to implement this Order. Agencies shall consult with the Department of State and the Council on Environmental Quality concerning such procedures prior to placing them in effect.

2–2. *Information Exchange*. To assist in effectuating the foregoing purpose, the Department of State and the Council on Environmental Quality in collaboration with other interested Federal agencies and other nations shall conduct a program for exchange on a continuing basis of information concerning the environment. The objectives of this program shall be to provide information for use by decisionmakers, to heighten awareness of and interest in environmental concerns and, as appropriate, to facilitate environmental cooperation with foreign nations.

2–3. *Actions Included*. Agencies in their procedures under Section 2–1 shall establish procedures by which their officers having ultimate responsibility for authorizing and approving actions in one of the following categories encompassed by this Order, take into consideration in making decisions concerning such actions, a document described in Section 2–4(a) :

(a) major Federal actions significantly affecting the environment of the global commons outside the jurisdiction of any nation (e.g., the oceans or Antarctica) ;

(b) major Federal actions significantly affecting the environment of a foreign nation not participating with the United States and not otherwise involved in the action;

(c) major Federal actions significantly affecting the environment of a foreign nation which provide to that nation:

(1) a product, or physical project producing a principal product or an emission or effluent, which is prohibited or strictly regulated by Federal law in the United States because its toxic effects on the environment create a serious public health risk; or

(2) a physical project which in the United States is prohibited or strictly regulated by Federal law to protect the environment against radioactive substances.

(d) major Federal actions outside the United States, its territories and possessions which significantly affect natural or ecological resources of global importance designated for protection under this subsection by the President, or, in the case of such a resource protected by international agreement binding on the United States, by the Secretary of State. Recommendations to the President under this subsection shall be accompanied by the views of the Council on Environmental Quality and the Secretary of State.

2–4. *Applicable Procedures*. (a) There are the following types of documents to be used in connection with actions described in Section 2–3:

(i) environmental impact statements (including generic, program and specific statements) ;

(ii) bilateral or multilateral environmental studies, relevant or related to the proposed action, by the United States and one or more foreign nations, or by an international body or organization in which the United States is a member or participant; or

(iii) concise reviews of the environmental issues involved, including environmental assessments, summary environmental analyses or other appropriate documents.

(b) Agencies shall in their procedures provide for preparation of documents described in Section 2–4(a), with respect to actions described in Section 2–3, as follows:

(i) for effects described in Section 2–3 (a), an environmental impact statement described in Section 2–4(a) (i) ;

(ii) for effects described in Section 2–3 (b), a document described in Section 2–4(a) (ii) or (iii), as determined by the agency;

(iii) for effects described in Section 2–3(c), a document described in Section 2–4(a) (ii) or (iii), as determined by the agency;

(iv) for effects described in Section 2–3(d), a document described in Section 2–4(a) (i), (ii) or (iii), as determined by the agency.

Such procedures may provide that an agency need not prepare a new document when a document described in Section 2–4(a) already exists.

(c) Nothing in this Order shall serve to invalidate any existing regulations of any agency which have been adopted pursuant to court order or pursuant to judicial settlement of any case or to prevent any agency from providing in its procedures for measures in addition to those provided for herein to further the purpose of the National Environmental Policy Act and other environmental laws, including the Marine Protection Research and Sanctuaries Act and the Deepwater Port Act, consistent with the foreign and national security policies of the United States.

(d) Except as provided in Section 2–5 (b), agencies taking action encompassed by this Order shall, as soon as feasible, inform other Federal agencies with relevant expertise of the availability of environmental documents prepared under this Order.

Agencies in their procedures under Section 2–1 shall make appropriate provision for determining when an affected nation shall be informed in accordance with Section 3–2 of this Order of the availability of environmental documents prepared pursuant to those procedures.

In order to avoid duplication of resources, agencies in their procedures shall provide for appropriate utilization of the resources of other Federal agencies with relevant environmental jurisdiction or expertise.

2–5. *Exemptions and Considerations.*
(a) Notwithstanding Section 2–3, the following actions are exempt from this Order:

(i) actions not having a significant effect on the environment outside the United States as determined by the agency;

(ii) actions taken by the President;

(iii) actions taken by or pursuant to the direction of the President or Cabinet officer when the national security or interest is involved or when the action occurs in the course of an armed conflict;

(iv) intelligence activities and arms transfers;

(v) export licenses or permits or export approvals, and actions relating to nuclear activities except actions providing to a foreign nation a nuclear production or utilization facility as defined in the Atomic Energy Act of 1954, as amended, or a nuclear waste management facility;

(vi) votes and other actions in international conferences and organizations;

(vii) disaster and emergency relief action.

(b) Agency procedures under Section 2–1 implementing Section 2–4 may provide for appropriate modifications in the contents, timing and availability of documents to other affected Federal agencies and affected nations, where necessary to:

(i) enable the agency to decide and act promptly as and when required;

(ii) avoid adverse impacts on foreign relations or infringement in fact or appearance of other nations' sovereign responsibilities; or

(iii) ensure appropriate reflection of:

(1) diplomatic factors;

(2) international commercial, competitive and export promotion factors;

(3) needs for governmental or commercial confidentiality;

(4) national security considerations;

(5) difficulties of obtaining information and agency ability to analyze meaningfully environmental effects of a proposed action; and

(6) the degree to which the agency is involved in or able to affect a decision to be made.

(c) Agency procedures under Section 2–1 may provide for categorical exclusions and for such exemptions in addition to those specified in subsection (a) of this Section as may be necessary to meet emergency circumstances, situations involving exceptional foreign policy and national security sensitivities and other such special circumstances. In utilizing such additional exemptions agencies shall, as soon as feasible, consult with the Department of State and the Council on Environmental Quality.

(d) The provisions of Section 2–5 do not apply to actions described in Section 2–3(a) unless permitted by law.

Sec. 3.

3–1. *Rights of Action.* This Order is solely for the purpose of establishing internal procedures for Federal agencies to consider the significant effects of their actions on the environment outside the United States, its territories and possessions, and nothing in this Order shall be construed to create a cause of action.

3–2. *Foreign Relations.* The Department of State shall coordinate all communications by agencies with foreign governments concerning environmental agreements and other arrangements in implementation of this Order.

3–3. *Multi-Agency Actions.* Where more than one Federal agency is involved in an action or program, a lead agency, as determined by the agencies involved, shall have responsibility for implementation of this Order.

3–4. *Certain Terms.* For purposes of this Order, "environment" means the natural and physical environment and excludes social, economic and other environments; and an action significantly affects the environment if it does significant harm to the environment even though on balance the agency believes the action to be beneficial to the environment. The term "export approvals" in Section 2–5(a)(v) does not mean or include direct loans to finance exports.

3–5. *Multiple Impacts.* If a major Federal action having effects on the environment of the United States or the global commons requires preparation of an environmental impact statement, and if the action also has effects on the environment of a foreign nation, an environmental impact statement need not be prepared with respect to the effects on the environment of the foreign nation.

Jimmy Carter

The White House,
January 4, 1979.

[Filed with the Office of the Federal Register,
3:38 p.m., January 5, 1979]

Note: The text of the Executive order was released on January 5.

Digest of Other White House Announcements

The following listing includes the President's public schedule and other items of general interest announced by the White House Press Office and not included elsewhere in this issue.

January 1

The President returned to the White House from Camp David, Md.

January 2

The President met at the White House with Zbigniew Brzezinski, Assistant to the President for National Security Affairs.

January 3

The President met at the White House with:

—Vice President Walter F. Mondale, Charles L. Schultze, Chairman of the Council of Economic Advisers, James T. McIntyre, Jr., Director of the Office of Management and Budget, Alfred E. Kahn, Advisor to the President on Inflation and Chairman of the Council on Wage and Price Stability, Barry P. Bosworth, Director of the Council on Wage and Price Stability, and Stuart E. Eizenstat, Assistant to the President for Domestic Affairs and Policy;

—Dr. Brzezinski;

—Ambassador Andrew J. Young, U.S. Representative to the United Nations;

—Secretary of Energy James R. Schlesinger.

January 4

The President met at the White House with Dr. Brzezinski.

The President left the White House for a trip to Guadeloupe.

NOMINATIONS SUBMITTED TO THE SENATE

NOTE: The Congress having adjourned *sine die* on Sunday, October 15, 1978, no nominations were submitted during the period covered by this issue. The first session of the 96th Congress will begin on Monday, January 15.

CHECKLIST OF WHITE HOUSE PRESS RELEASES

The following listing contains releases of the White House Press Office which are not included in this issue.

Released January 1, 1979

Text: New Year's message from Secretary of State Cyrus R. Vance to Foreign Minister Huang Hua of the People's Republic of China

Released January 5, 1979

Fact sheet: on Executive Order 12114, concerning environmental effects abroad of major Federal actions

ACTS APPROVED BY THE PRESIDENT

NOTE: The President completed his consideration of acts and joint resolutions passed during the second session of the 95th Congress on November 10, 1978.

Editor's Note

Note Concerning the Closing Time of This Issue

On Friday, January 5, the President was in Guadeloupe. Releases issued there, but not received in time for inclusion in this week's issue, will be printed next week.

PRESIDENTIAL DOCUMENTS

Saint-François, Guadeloupe

Remarks to Reporters Following the Conclusion of Meetings Between the President and Western European Leaders.
January 6, 1979

PRESIDENT GISCARD D'ESTAING. I will now give you the results of our talks. First, I would like to emphasize the personal and trusting nature of our conversations. We have, in fact, stuck to the initial objective of this meeting, which was to have a political and global consideration of the situation, and in particular, we did not go into such matters as economic and monetary considerations.

For me—and like my colleagues, I've taken part in a number of international meetings—I would like to say that I consider that our discussions went into considerable substance and depth. We found no divergence among us concerning the assessment of the situation. Naturally, there were differences in the stresses placed on certain features, but there was no divergence.

Our talks have brought to light a dual objective, which is, first, to increase security and, secondly, to reduce tension in the world.

We considered that the legitimate recognition of the realities of the present-day world should be accompanied by the pursuit of efforts designed to improve the world situation and, in particular, the pursuit of the efforts towards détente and the efforts towards limitations of armaments and, in particular, expressing the hope for an early conclusion of the SALT agreement. Finally, special attention was devoted to the development of the North-South relations.

Now, if you want me to engage in the usual exercise of trying to find appropriate adjectives to qualify a meeting, I would say that the adjectives that come to mind would be as follows: The meeting has been frank, friendly, and useful.

PRIME MINISTER CALLAGHAN. I would like to begin by thanking President Giscard for his initiative in calling us together and inviting us for what has been a very valuable and informal occasion. And, also, I'm sure I'm allowed to say our thanks to the people of Guadeloupe for entertaining us in this most delightful and beautiful island.

I think I can almost forgive the French for recovering it from the British, although, no doubt, though, the occasion will come when we shall have to call for it back again. [*Laughter*]

Secondly, I'd like to echo what President Giscard said about the nature of the discussions. They have been conducted between four of us who trust each other, who have confidence in each other, and who, I think it is fair to say, are friends. And that makes a very great deal of difference to the quality of the discussion and to the way in which it's conducted. And, as President Giscard said, the discussions have been direct; they have been frank; they have been open. But I think we've all been working towards the same common objectives. And when you are friends, discussing matters with each other, there can be differences of emphasis or nuance which are slight in relation to the attitudes between ourselves but which, if we were not talking as friends, if we were talking elsewhere, would be regarded as very substantial. That has not been the case here, and I want to emphasize this, because so often, differences of emphasis are written up as though they are very great differences of objective. That is simply not true.

And I think this has been a most valuable meeting, as far as I am concerned. It certainly added to our knowledge of each other's point of view. I've heard from my three colleagues their analysis of the world scene in many different facets, and that in itself is an invaluable help in enabling Britain to formulate its own analysis. I think we have, in certain circumstances, been able to comment on each other's analysis and to, perhaps, modify our own positions as a result of it.

But as the President said, we were not reaching decisions here. But the effect will be felt in the discussions that we shall have with all our partners and the various organizations, international organizations, to which we belong.

I'm sorry—[*turning to interpreter*]—did you want to translate that? You're quite happy, are you? [*Laughter*] That's good. It's well known that everybody speaks very good French.

Now, just two things, if I may. First of all, we heard from President Carter about the SALT agreement. It is reaching its final stages now. He gave us his analysis of the position. Of course, during the whole process there has been continuous consultation. I would like to urge—speaking as someone who is on the other side of the Atlantic—I would like to urge the speedy ratification, the conclusion of the agreement and speedy ratification on both sides, that is, on the United States side and on the Soviet Union.

I think it would be a very sad day if this agreement were not ratified, and the administration will have our support in their efforts when they place it before the American people. And we look forward to the development of a SALT III negotiation, which we believe will be of benefit to us.

I'd like to say just, I think, two other words. First of all, we did review some of the trouble spots of the world. And they are deeply disturbing. Nevertheless, I think it would not be unfair to say that there's a general conclusion that if you take out these highlights that are deeply disturbing, that perhaps the general position of our part of the world is rather more satisfactory—I qualify it in that sense—is rather more satisfactory than it was 2 or 3 years ago, and we met against that atmosphere. And I say that in order to put the matter in perspective.

Finally, I'd like to say that we spent a considerable amount of time on our relations with China. We welcome them into the comity of nations. We do so because she is a great country, but we do not improve our relations with China at the expense of any other country.

Our relations with the Soviet Union are as important to us as our relations with China, and indeed, our relations with the Soviet Union are central to the development of détente, which is so important to us in Europe.

So, I conclude by thanking President Giscard again very much, and thank my colleagues for helping me to get a better understanding of the world during the last 48 hours.

PRESIDENT CARTER. First, I'd like to add my voice of thanks to Valéry Giscard d'Estaing, the people of France, and particularly those of Guadeloupe, who have made our visit so delightful, enjoyable, and profitable. Because of the unstructured agenda and the informality of the discussions and the almost unprecedented harmony that exists among us, I have never attended a conference which was more beneficial to me, nor more substantive in nature.

One of the dearest and most valuable assets of the American people, and perhaps even most of the world, is the close harmony, the easy communication, and the common purpose of those peoples who are represented here by myself, by Chancellor Helmut Schmidt, by President Giscard d'Estaing, and by Prime Minister Callaghan.

Most of our discussions were about regional problems and about global issues, because the differences which exist among us bilaterally are very minor and of little consequence.

We have been determined to strengthen even further the valuable ties of friendship and cooperation militarily—for common defense and for peace—politically, culturally, and economically.

Our commitment is to contribute to global peace. And we have observed with interest and gratification that in the last few years, there has been an enhancement in the normalization of relationships among the nations of the world. Former enemies have become friends; potential enemies have sought to avoid violence by close consultation and negotiations; and existing friendships have been strengthened.

We're all in agreement that the emergence of the People's Republic of China toward the outside world, the Western World, has been one of constructive development. And we are all determined to enhance this development and to assure that it never becomes an obstacle to détente, and that it might possibly be used in the future, we hope, as an avenue of even strengthening our ties of friendship and harmony with the people of the Soviet Union.

We discussed the potential trouble spots of the world, and we tried to capitalize upon the unique opportunity that one or several of us have to alleviate tension, to let the people of those regions find for themselves, with our assistance on occasion, an avenue toward peace, so that stability and development of a better quality of life and enhanced human rights might be continuing throughout those regions where our influence might be felt.

And finally, I would like to thank these experienced leaders for their advice and counsel for me and their constructive support for the efforts in the SALT negotiations and other important international measures in which the American people have taken the lead. This is always of great benefit to me and to my people. And I'm deeply grateful for the relationships that we have enjoyed and, I pray, will continue to enjoy in an enhanced degree in the years to come.

Thank you.

CHANCELLOR SCHMIDT. To speak as the last in a row of four, it's not so very easy to add anything new to what my colleagues already have said, especially when, as it is the case, I'm in full agreement with the remarks you already have heard.

Now I would like—in dealing with the cordiality, the directness, the cooperative friendship in which our discussions have been led—I would like to concede that we

19

made one mistake. We should have had the press invited for at least one session, in order to let it be witnessed by yourselves how friendly the atmosphere really was. [*Laughter*]

Representing nations who belong to the same alliance, it was, of course, natural that we at some length dealt with security questions, among which, of course, was of great importance the report that we were given by the American President, by Jimmy Carter, on the progress of SALT II. And I would like to join my British colleague here in stressing that in our view, SALT II is going to be a very important contribution toward stabilizing world peace.

I do hope for early conclusion and, also, for swift ratification thereafter. And as far as my country is concerned, we will take the appropriate opportunity to make this very clear to everybody in the world.

President Giscard d'Estaing already indicated that we also talked about other matters in the field of arms control, which was a chance for me to express my desire to bring about progress also in the field of mutual balanced force reductions. And in this context, of course, we also dealt with the French proposal for a European conference on arms limitation.

Naturally, France, Great Britain, and Germany, having had diplomatic relations with the People's Republic of China already, all of us considered it to be a contribution to normalization in the world that there now should also be diplomatic relationships between the United States and the People's Republic of China.

I think one could sum up this part of our deliberations in telling you that we did agree on the global necessity to stabilize the equilibrium of the world and to carry on détente with the Soviet Union, of course, especially so, including limitation of armaments.

In confirming that we have talked about a number of trouble spots in the world of today, I would, as well, wish to stress what already has been said by two previous speakers, namely, that we all are confident on the present stability of the world, which we consider to be improved as compared with the situation a couple of years ago.

Stability of the world did, of course, include the relationship between industrialized and developing countries, which gave me a chance to directly report to the other three gentlemen about a conference which I recently was participating in, not far away from here, on the invitation of Prime Minister Manley of Jamaica.

In concluding, I wish to express my gratitude to the host of this meeting, my friend, the French President, especially for his hospitality, especially for the initiative which has been taken by him, which has led us here. I would express my personal gratitude to the two Presidents and the British Prime Minister for this very personal exchange of views, of judgments, of information, which I'm quite certain will improve the foundations for decisions which one will have to take in the later course of 1979.

I must confess that I've learned a lot in this meeting, would like to thank the host, to thank the other participants and, in the end, like to thank the people on this wonderful island for the hospitality they have shown to all of us.

Thank you very much.

NOTE: President Valéry Giscard d'Estaing of France spoke at 1:15 p.m. at the Meridien Hotel. He spoke in French, and his remarks were translated by an interpreter. Also speaking were Prime Minister James Callaghan of the United Kingdom, President Carter, and Chancellor Helmut Schmidt of the Federal Republic of Germany.

The 2-day series of meetings was held at the Hamak, a resort located on the southern coast of Grand Terre, Guadeloupe.

Department of State

Nomination of K. Mathea Falco To Be Assistant Secretary for International Narcotics Matters. January 8, 1979

The President today announced that he will nominate K. Mathea Falco, of Washington, D.C., to be Assistant Secretary of State for International Narcotics Matters.

Falco was born October 15, 1944, in Montgomery, Ala. She received a B.A. from Radcliffe College in 1965 and a J.D. from Yale Law School in 1968.

From 1968 to 1969, Falco was law clerk to the Chief Judge and Administrator of the Criminal Justice Act in the Juvenile Court of the District of Columbia. From 1969 to 1971, she was assistant to the Director of the National Office of Legal Services at the Office of Economic Opportunity.

From 1971 to 1973, Falco was chief counsel and staff director of the U.S. Senate Subcommittee on Juvenile Delinquency. From 1973 to 1977, she was special assistant to the president of the Drug Abuse Council. Since 1977 she has been senior adviser to the Secretary of State and Director for International Narcotics Control Matters. She is the author of several articles on drug abuse.

American Heart Month, 1979

Proclamation 4633. January 10, 1979

By the President of the United States of America

A Proclamation

More than 40 million Americans suffer from some form of heart or blood vessel disease. During 1979, these diseases and their complications will claim more than 980,000 lives and partially or completely disable several million other Americans. The total economic cost in disability payments, medical expenses and lost wages and productivity will exceed $50 billion.

The picture would be darker had not the Nation launched a concerted effort against cardiovascular diseases more than thirty years ago. Since 1948, this effort has resulted in greatly increased support for cardiovascular research; for training thousands of new research workers and clinicians; for health education and information programs; and for community service programs concerned with preventing, diagnosing, and relieving cardiovascular disorders. Over this period, we have learned more about the cardiovascular system and its diseases than during all previous medical history. The application of this knowledge has enabled us to decrease the mortality rate for all cardiovascular diseases combined by 30 percent.

Our successes in combatting cardiovascular diseases have accelerated since 1968. I am particularly gratified that the mortality rate of the two major killers among this family of diseases—coronary heart disease and stroke—has decreased nearly 20 and 25 percent respectively.

If present trends continue during 1979, there will be at least 170,000 fewer deaths from cardiovascular disease in the U.S. than if the mortality rates of ten years ago still prevailed.

Two organizations have been in the forefront of the national effort against the cardiovascular diseases: the National Heart, Lung and Blood Institute—a Federal agency—and the American Heart Association, supported by private contributions. But it has been a cooperative effort involving a great many agencies and groups—Federal and private, national and local. Our continued success must rest, as always, on the support and participation of the American people.

21

Recognizing the need for all Americans to help in the battle against cardiovascular disease, the Congress, by joint resolution approved December 30, 1963 (77 Stat. 843; 26 U.S.C. 169b)[1] has requested the President to issue annually a proclamation designating February as American Heart Month.

Now, THEREFORE, I, JIMMY CARTER, President of the United States of America, do hereby proclaim the month of February, 1979, as American Heart Month. I invite the Governors of the States, the appropriate officials of all other areas subject to the jurisdiction of the United States and the American people to join with me in reaffirming our commitment to the search for new ways to prevent, detect and control cardiovascular disease in all its forms.

IN WITNESS WHEREOF, I have hereunto set my hand this tenth day of January, in the year of our Lord nineteen hundred seventy-nine, and of the Independence of the United States of America the two hundred and third.

JIMMY CARTER

[Filed with the Office of the Federal Register, 4:59 p.m., January 10, 1979]

Anniversary of the Birth of Martin Luther King, Jr.

Message of the President.
January 11, 1979

January 15, 1979, marks the fiftieth anniversary of the birth of Dr. Martin Luther King, Jr. Let us make it an occasion of national rebirth by rededicating ourselves to the principles for which he lived and by reaffirming our determina-

[1] EDITOR'S NOTE: The correct citation is (77 Stat. 843; 36 U.S.C. 169b).

tion to reach the goals for which he struggled and died.

Dr. King taught us the peaceful way to bring down human barriers and to build up human opportunities. In a very short time he showed us the power of love to change men's hearts and to overcome differences that decades of conflict could not resolve. In a tense and trying era he was a symbol of hope and a voice of reason.

In America and throughout the world he stands tall among the greatest champions of human rights. And we are stronger as a nation and as a world community because he made us more sensitive as individuals to the dignity and worth of others.

JIMMY CARTER

United States Fire Administration

Nomination of Gordon Vickery To Be Administrator. January 11, 1979

The President today announced that he will nominate Gordon Vickery, of Seattle, Wash., to be Administrator of the United States Fire Administration.

Vickery, 58, was with the Seattle Fire Department from 1946 to 1972, beginning as a line firefighter and finally serving as fire chief for the city of Seattle. Since 1972 he has been superintendent of the Seattle Department of Lighting.

Vickery is on the board of directors of the International Association of Fire Chiefs. He has received numerous awards, including the Municipal League of Seattle Award for Outstanding Public Official of 1972.

Federal Service Impasses Panel

Announcement of Terms of Seven Members. January 11, 1979

The President has signed commissions which set the terms of seven members of the Federal Service Impasses Panel whom he appointed on February 21, 1978. This action is necessary under the law implementing civil service reorganization, which requires that members of the Panel be appointed for set terms, with the initial terms staggered.

The commissions provide for 5-year terms for Howard G. Gamser (also appointed Chairman of the Panel), Charles J. Morris, and Beverly K. Schaffer; 3-year terms for James E. Jones, Jr., and Arthur Stark; and 1-year terms for Irving Bernstein and Jean T. McKelvey.

National Commission on Social Security

Recess Appointment of Four Members. January 11, 1979

The President today announced the recess appointments of four persons as members of the National Commission on Social Security. Three of these persons were nominated for these positions on October 11, 1978, but were not confirmed before the Senate adjourned. They are:

JAMES J. DILLMAN, a Sheboygan, Wis., attorney, vice chairman of the Wisconsin Retirement Fund board of trustees, and a member of the Wisconsin Retirement Research Committee;

MILTON S. GWIRTZMAN, of Newton, Mass., an author on tax policy and economic policy and a practicing attorney, who is also designated Chairman of the Commission;

DAVID H. RODGERS, of Spokane, Wash., deputy commissioner of insurance for eastern Washington, formerly manager of the employee benefits office of the Aetna Life Insurance Co.

The fourth person appointed today had not been previously nominated. He is:

DONALD S. MACNAUGHTON, of Nashville, Tenn., chairman and chief executive officer of Hospital Corporation of America, formerly chairman of the board and chief executive officer of Prudential Insurance Co.

Endangered Species Committee

Appointment of Three Members. January 11, 1979

The President today announced the appointment of three persons as members of the Endangered Species Committee. This Committee was established by the Endangered Species Act Amendments of 1978. The persons appointed are:

GOVERNOR ED HERSCHLER of Wyoming;

PAUL W. SNYDER, assistant attorney general of Nebraska;

WILLIAM WILLIS, a Nashville, Tenn., attorney interested in environmental education.

John F. Kennedy Center for the Performing Arts

Appointment of Six Members of the Board of Trustees. January 11, 1979

The President today announced the appointment of six persons as members of the Board of Trustees of the John F.

23

Kennedy Center for the Performing Arts. They are:

K. LeMoyne Billings, president of the Park Foundation, a trustee of the Robert F. Kennedy Memorial, and a member of this Board from 1960 to 1972;

Frances H. Breathitt, of Hopkinsville, Ky., active in civic affairs, wife of former Kentucky Governor Edward T. Breathitt;

Marshall B. Coyne, builder and owner of the Madison Hotel in Washington, D.C., and a number of other buildings;

Marjorie M. Lawson, a Washington, D.C., attorney and former associate judge of the D.C. Juvenile Court; now chairman of the board and president of WYCB, the first commercial broadcaster in the Washington area under minority ownership;

Lois M. Ribicoff, of Hartford, Conn., active in civic and community affairs, the wife of Senator Abraham Ribicoff;

Franklin D. Roosevelt, Jr., former Under Secretary of Commerce and the first Chairman of the Equal Employment Opportunity Commission, now active in civic affairs and chairman of the board of Fiat-Roosevelt Motors.

Federal Labor Relations Authority

Recess Appointment of Two Members.
January 11, 1979

The President today announced the recess appointments of two persons as members of the Federal Labor Relations Authority, created under civil service reorganization. They are:

Henry B. Frazier III, of Alexandria, Va. Frazier, 44, has been Executive Director of the Federal Labor Relations Council (the agency replaced by this Authority) since 1973. He joined the Council as Chief of the Program Division in 1970 and then served as Deputy Executive Director. He had previously spent 11 years in personnel

management work with the Department of the Army.

Ronald W. Haughton, of Grosse Pointe Farms, Mich., who will also be designated Chairman of the Authority. Haughton, 62, is codirector of the Institute of Labor and Industrial Relations of the University of Michigan and Wayne State University. He is also vice president for urban affairs and professor of management at Wayne State University. He has served as an arbitrator for many labor disputes and is a member of numerous arbitration and mediation professional associations.

United States Postal Service

Recess Appointment of William J. Sullivan
as a Governor. January 12, 1979

The President today announced the recess appointment of William J. Sullivan, of Bangor, Maine, to be a Governor of the United States Postal Service for a term expiring December 8, 1984.

Sullivan, 47, has been vice chancellor for administration at the University of Maine since 1976. From 1964 to 1976, he was with the Post Office Department and Postal Service, serving as Staff Assistant to the Postmaster General; Assistant Staff Director of the President's Commission on Postal Organization; Director of Planning for the Postal Service from 1968 to 1971; Postmaster-District Manager of the U.S. Postal Service in Cleveland, Ohio, from 1971 to 1973; and Western Regional Postmaster General from 1973 to 1976.

Sullivan holds an MBA from Harvard University Graduate School of Business Administration and has attended the Woodrow Wilson School of Public and International Affairs at Princeton University.

Digest of Other White House Announcements

The following listing includes the President's public schedule and other items of general interest announced by the White House Press Office and not included elsewhere in this issue.

January 4

Following his arrival in Guadeloupe, the President met in the evening with President Valéry Giscard d'Estaing of France, Prime Minister James Callaghan of the United Kingdom, and Chancellor Helmut Schmidt of the Federal Republic of Germany.

January 6

In the evening, the President attended a reception for elected officials from Guadeloupe at the residence of the Prefect of Guadeloupe, where he stayed during the remainder of his visit to Guadeloupe.

January 7

In the evening, the President attended a reception hosted by Prime Minister and Mrs. Callaghan aboard the *Scylla*.

January 9

In the evening, the President returned to the White House from Guadeloupe.

January 10

The President met at the White House with:

—Zbigniew Brzezinski, Assistant to the President for National Security Affairs;
—Vice President Walter F. Mondale, Stansfield Turner, Director, and Robert R. Bowie, Deputy, National Intelligence, Central Intelligence Agency, and Dr. Brzezinski;
—Vice President Mondale;

—James T. McIntyre, Jr., Director of the Office of Management and Budget.

January 11

The President met at the White House with:

—Vice President Mondale, Secretary of the Treasury W. Michael Blumenthal, Charles L. Schultze, Chairman of the Council of Economic Advisers, Alfred E. Kahn, Advisor to the President on Inflation and Chairman of the Council on Wage and Price Stability, Barry P. Bosworth, Director of the Council on Wage and Price Stability, Stuart E. Eizenstat, Assistant to the President for Domestic Affairs and Policy, John N. Gentry, Deputy Adviser on Inflation and Counselor on Labor-Management Relations, and Mr. McIntyre;
—Dr. Brzezinski;
—Mayor Marion S. Barry, Jr., of the District of Columbia;
—Wilma Rudolph, former Olympic champion;
—Mrs. Carter, for lunch;
—Attorney General Griffin B. Bell.

In a ceremony in the Oval Office, the President received diplomatic credentials from Ambassadors Nicolas Mondjo of the People's Republic of the Congo, Jose-Joseph Amiar of the Gabonese Republic, Jose Antonio Bermudez-Milla of Honduras, Francisco Augusto Lora Gonzales of the Dominican Republic, and Ephraim Evron of Israel.

January 12

The President met at the White House with:

—Vice President Mondale, Secretary of State Cyrus R. Vance, Secretary of Defense Harold Brown, Hamilton Jordan, Assistant to the President, and Dr. Brzezinski;

—Dr. Brzezinski;

—Dr. Schultze;

—George Meany, president, and executive council members of the AFL–CIO;

—members of the National Advisory Committee for Women.

The White House announced that the President has decided to relieve Bella S. Abzug of her responsibilities as Cochairperson and member of the National Advisory Committee for Women.

NOMINATIONS SUBMITTED TO THE SENATE

NOTE: The Congress having adjourned *sine die* on Sunday, October 15, 1978, no nominations were submitted during the period covered by this issue. The first session of the 96th Congress began on Monday, January 15.

CHECKLIST OF WHITE HOUSE PRESS RELEASES

The following listing contains releases of the White House Press Office which are not included in this issue.

Released January 5, 1979

News conferences: on meetings between the President, President Valéry Giscard d'Estaing of France, Prime Minister James Callaghan of Great Britain, and Chancellor Helmut Schmidt of the Federal Republic of Germany, in Guadeloupe—by Pierre Hunt, spokesman for the Elysee (two releases)

ACTS APPROVED BY THE PRESIDENT

NOTE: The President completed his consideration of acts and joint resolutions passed during the second session of the 95th Congress on November 10, 1978.

National Advisory Committee for Women

White House Statement.   *January 13, 1979*

The commitment of this administration to issues important to the women of the country is strong and permanent. Each member of the National Advisory Committee for Women was personally selected by the President, and they are individuals for whom he has great respect and in whom he continues to have confidence. We hope that the members of the Committee will continue to serve in this work, which is so important to gain the legitimate rights of women.

The President feels that the Committee can and will be more productive on behalf of women, and individual members on behalf of their constituencies, if there is a harmonious working relationship between the administration and the Committee's leadership.

The President reached his decision to appoint a new Chairperson after concluding that new leadership is necessary to achieve the goals he shares with the members of the Committee and the women of the country.

We are contacting members of the Committee to offer the continued cooperation of the administration and to urge them to work even more effectively with the President and with other Government leaders toward these important goals.

Atlanta, Georgia

Remarks Accepting the Martin Luther King, Jr. Nonviolent Peace Prize.
January 14, 1979

Prime Minister Ullsten, Foreign Minister Frydenlund, members of the diplomatic corps from throughout the world, Senator Talmadge, Congressman Levitas, my good friend and mentor, Dr. Benjamin Mays, my friend Daddy King, Coretta King, Chairman Jesse Hill, Reverend Dr. Roberts, ladies and gentleman:

I'm indeed glad to be back in this historic church where I have attended many inspirational and delightful services.

I would say two or three things. First of all, that I would like to donate this money, if Coretta has no objection, to the Martin Luther King, Jr. Center for Social Change, and I appreciate it very much.

Coretta referred to things that don't change and the proper correlation of them

27

with values which change. Today I had lunch with my own family, many of whom live in Georgia—my sons, my daughter, my three grandchildren. During lunch, I held my new granddaughter, Sarah. Daddy King, I looked at her very closely. She looks like me. I'm sure she's authentic. [*Laughter*] It did take me a few minutes to get my suit cleaned before I could come to this meeting, but those kinds of close, personal family relationships do not change. And the worldwide family that has already been described by Jesse Hill as a family of Martin Luther King, Jr., changes only in its dynamic growth and inspiration. But its basic principles don't change.

I've been President now almost exactly 2 years. I'm delighted to come back to Georgia. I was reading a 2-year analysis of my own personal character this morning in the newspaper. It reminded me somewhat of Daddy King. First of all, the commentator said I was getting older. He said I was getting grayer. He said I was getting wiser. And he said I was getting leaner. [*Laughter*] At least I heard three amens. [*Laughter*]

I come here grateful, and I accept this award not as an honor that I have earned, but as an affirmation, publicly, that I share the hopes and dreams of Martin Luther King, Jr., and I recognize the tremendous progress still left to be made. And together, you and I, millions of people around the world will continue to make that progress, and we will also realize those hopes and dreams.

Martin Luther King, Jr., looked about him in his young life and saw great injustice. Many others before him had seen, and some—too few—had deplored racial prejudice, which resulted in deprivation of some and hatred among many. But for generations, little of that had changed. He looked about him and saw many of his own people who couldn't sit down at a

lunch counter, who couldn't drink from a water fountain, some of whom were afraid to register and to vote in the self-professed greatest democracy on Earth. He saw a people without power or influence who were branded as inferior by both law and custom.

But when he looked at his own people, he saw not powerlessness or weakness, he saw potential. And he believed in the great power of ordinary people who combine together to fight for what they know to be right.

He showed all of us that we are not powerless if we care enough and if we are willing to sacrifice enough and if we are willing to risk public failure and disappointment and condemnation and criticism and, sometimes, humiliation, and if we are always ready to come back and fight again and try again.

Martin remembered the words of Jesus, "Blessed are they which are persecuted for righteousness' sake, for theirs is the kingdom of heaven." And he was able to inspire the quiet and the timid folks by the truth of these words, proven by his own courageous actions.

We remember him marching on as people spat on him, emerging triumphant time after time from jail, having defeated his enemies with his simple and his peaceful refusal either to stop what he was doing, to yield to pressure, or to descend to the violence of those who persecuted him.

We remember him moving great crowds and even an entire nation with his eloquent words.

But it's important for us to remember that he tasted defeat as well as he tasted victory. When he said, "How long, O Lord, how long?", it was not just a rhetorical flourish. It was an anguished cry of a heart that knew too much suffering in between those rare victories.

He called out to the best in people, even those who looked the other way at the time. He called out to courage that many people did not know they had. He called upon their endurance and their patience and their simple goodness. He spoke of the America that had never been, but he spoke of the America that we hope in the future will be.

We have survived as an increasingly free people now for 200 years, and we will prevail in the struggle for human rights, because men and women like Daddy King, Martin Luther King, Jr., Coretta King, Andy Young, and all those in the civil rights movement will never stop believing in the promise of our democracy, even in its darkest days. And others like me have learned from you; together we will prevail.

We can speak out now as a nation with one voice on the sensitive issue of human rights all around the world, because Martin Luther King, Jr., and the civil rights movement helped to liberate all Americans from the chains of official racism here at home.

Had he not lived, had his voice not been heard, had his actions not prevailed, it would now be an embarrassment for the United States to mention the words "human rights" in international councils.

Daddy King spoke the truth when he said, "Too many people think Martin frees only black people. In truth, he helped to free all people."

Now the challenge facing all of us today, and particularly government, is to stay true to the trust placed in America by the civil rights movement and Martin Luther King, Jr. He trusted our country. He trusted our Government. He trusted our people, even when an objective observer would say in complete truth, there were times when our Government, its laws, and many of its people didn't deserve to be trusted.

Let no one doubt where I stand. My administration and I personally stand with you. We are committed to civil rights. We are committed to equal opportunity. We are committed to equal justice under the law, and you can depend on it.

As President of the United States, representing now 220 million people, I pledge to you that I will continue to strengthen and to enforce the civil rights laws of the land, firmly and without equivocation, not only the letter of the law but the spirit of the law as well.

Many of those responsible for enforcing civil rights laws in our Government today are people who struggled alongside you in the battle for civil rights—people like Eleanor Holmes Norton and Drew Days and Wade McCree and many others. And I pledge to you that they not only have my full support as President, but they have the encouragement of many others who work with me in Government like John Lewis, who's here, Andy Young, in the enforcement of equal opportunity.

I might say that Andy was planning on being here today, but about 2:30 this morning, the Secretary of State had to call Andy for a special assignment, and he's not able to be here. But his spirit is with us. And Jean, his wife, is here.

In our Government, we will not authorize Federal tax money, your tax money, to fund or pay for discrimination. It's difficult to root out, because sometimes it's hard to find, and influential people benefit from different aspects of discrimination—in hiring practices, in promotion of employees, in housing, in redlining bank loans. But we must do more than correct these defects. For too many years we have passed equal rights laws and administered equal rights laws from a city where 700,000 Americans are denied their full right to vote. It's time to give the people of the District of Columbia their full voting rights.

But we must, and we will, do more. We cannot overcome 200 years of discrimination simply by writing the promise of justice into the laws of our land. We must and we will fulfill that promise, not just through administering the law but through vigorous affirmative action programs in all elements of government.

President Lyndon Johnson put it very well in the last public speech he made when he was no longer President. And he said, "To be black in a white society is not to stand on level and equal ground. While the races may stand side by side, whites stand on history's mountain, and blacks stand in history's hollows."

The only way to overcome unequal history, which leaves discrimination when the laws are equal, is to promote and defend and enforce the equal opportunity for all disadvantaged Americans in this land. And that, again, is what we will do.

But we must and we will do more, much more. It's not enough to have a right to sit at a lunch counter if you can't afford to buy a meal. And a ghetto looks the same, even when you're sitting in the front end of a bus.

Martin Luther King, Jr.'s dream lives among us today. But too many individual dreams have died. In rat-ridden slums and decaying homes and rotting neighborhoods, dreams are dying. There are still hundreds of thousands of young people, many of them minority youth, in our country who have never had a chance to hold a decent job. They learn in our streets, not in our schools. And they learn about drugs and alcohol and crime and not about religion or medicine or mathematics or law. We cannot permit another generation of Americans to grow up with no hope.

In the last 2 years, we have been able to add more jobs in this country than any other time in the history of our Nation. But we've still got a long way to go. And I'm proud that we joined together, Coretta King, I, the Members of the Congress, Senator Talmadge, Elliott Levitas, and many others, last year, and wrote the promise of full employment into the laws of our land by passing the Humphrey-Hawkins bill.

We have begun to put our people back to work, but we must do more. We must stop the inflation that's robbing the poor and those who live on a small, fixed income and the aged who are retired and the young people who are still struggling economically to find a future that will make them happy and fulfill their expectations and their potential.

We are blessed in our country with a strong economy, but I want to make it stronger. I want to build an economy so fair and equitable, so creative, so vital, so free, that every able American can have pride and dignity and self-respect that comes from an honest job, doing honest work, with constant growth in that person's life.

For the first time now, we are also expanding to minority-owned businesses a fair share of the benefits of our great free enterprise system, and that progress will continue.

We must and we will continue to provide every child in America a chance to learn and to flower and to grow with the best education we can provide. Last year, we added to the Federal education budget about $12 billion, more than had ever been added before, because we know that what the Negro College Fund brochures say is right: "A mind, a human mind, is a terrible thing to waste." And that's why in a budget that will fight inflation, I have preserved and will fight for new support, increased support to educate disadvantaged children in our Nation, for Headstart, for the handicapped, and for the struggling college student that wants to realize his potential.

Dr. Benjamin Mays reminds me often that in a time of need, this Nation's historically black colleges were a haven of opportunity for all those who were denied their equal chance to learn. Here in Atlanta, the Atlanta University complex was a beacon of light and a beacon of hope when there were not many such beacons in our country. Now, in their time of need—those black colleges—we must and we will use our resources to strengthen and to preserve them and the predominantly black universities throughout our country.

There can be no better investment of limited tax funds than a broader and more productive life for the young people of our Nation who have been deprived so long of the chance for equal opportunity and to use their lives productively.

Martin Luther King, Jr., spoke out also against what he saw as a tragic moral flaw of our country in the Vietnam war. And in a moving address, exactly 1 year before he died, he went beyond advocating an end to the war to demand what he called, and I quote, "a true revolution of values"—a world revolution, peaceful in nature, that he felt America was uniquely qualified to lead. He insisted that we look at both our political and our economic relations with other countries around the world and hold to a standard of justice, both domestic and internationally. And I'm determined, as President, to hold our Nation to a high standard of justice in dealing with other nations, to restore America's leadership in a peaceful world, a revolution that demands freedom and justice and self-determination not just for ourselves but for all people.

To help me in that effort, I've got at the United Nations a man, sometimes quiet and timid, a man as good as any who has ever represented any nation, in any government, my good friend, Andy Young.

For many people around the world, those who are poor, hungry, black, brown, yellow, from little nations, the United States Government is Andy Young. They trust him. And in their trust for him, I gain their trust. And when Andy Young and I gain their trust, the people of this Nation gain their trust. And as I have said many times, it's a delight now to face a session of the United Nations General Assembly, because we're no longer the target of every attack. We are no longer the butt of every joke. We are a people now who reach out a hand of equality and friendship and mutual respect where formerly there was antagonism and a chasm that could not be crossed. And I thank Andy Young for it. And I thank those on the stage with me, and Martin Luther King, Jr., for helping to train Andy Young so well.

This administration is working to restore America's moral authority in the world. As I've said before, human rights is the soul of our country's foreign policy. And as long as I'm President, America will continue to lead the struggle for human rights.

Martin Luther King, Jr., said, "We must lay hands on the world order and say of war, 'This way of settling differences is not just.'"

He said that the crucial political and moral question of our time was the need to overcome oppression and violence without resorting to oppression and violence. It's still a difficult but a crucial question.

I'm trying to perpetuate and to spread the peace which our Nation, thank God, now enjoys, to use our moral force and our good offices to get ancient enemies to lay aside their differences so that the energies and the talents of their people can be used to produce better lives instead of suffering and death.

In southern Africa, we are working with the leaders and the people there, a people long deprived of basic rights, to bring about majority rule, an end to racism and hatred, and to terminate the legal sanctioning of apartheid throughout that great continent. In Nicaragua, we are working with other countries to mediate a dispute and to bring about freedom and democratic principles in one of our neighboring countries.

In the Middle East, we are trying to act as a mediator under the most difficult possible political circumstances to bring about peace between two ancient enemies. We've made a great deal of progress because of a desire of those people for peace. This week, we'll dispatch another delegation of negotiators and mediators to the Mideast to resolve the last elements of differences on language of the peace treaty itself. And then we will address a very major political question of how to carry out the fullest terms of the Camp David accords.

At that moment, it being a political question, I'm sure that this will be elevated at least to the Secretary of State level. And, if necessary, I will not hesitate to invite President Sadat and Prime Minister Begin to meet with me again to get a peace treaty between Israel and Egypt.

A united America, with your support, gives us a strong and a vital voice that can be heard abroad.

In closing, let me say that I was trained in the art of war, but I share this dream of Martin Luther King, Jr., that mankind can find a better way. Our generation knows too much of war. We've seen it as it is. It's thousands of tons of bombs falling in the middle of night. It's misery and death in a wet and lonely foxhole, on a frozen mountainside, or in a steaming jungle—without fanfare and without glory.

The poor who were not able to pay for a college education were the first to go to war and to give their lives to a country that had made it possible for them to be deprived of opportunity. This must never happen again.

War is a little dying child crying in a burning village, an old man burying his only son with a heart that can never be comforted. It's a destruction of the human spirit and of all that we have that's beautiful or valuable. War holds a real threat of massive nuclear annihilation. Only mad men today can believe that war is the solution of anything.

We're trying to reach out a hand of friendship to past enemies, to heal differences, and to provide for world peace. We're in the last stages of negotiating a SALT II agreement that will limit the further spread of nuclear weapons between us and the Soviet Union and will set for the world a clear example that our Nation stands for peace.

This treaty, which I have personally supervised in its negotiation, will protect our Nation's security interests. It will provide the prospect for future progress in the future, in years to come, to cut down further on nuclear weapons. And it will be presented to the Senate for ratification as a treaty as soon as it's concluded.

A rejection of this treaty would deal a severe blow to the prospects for peace around the world. It would deal a severe blow to the control and the containment of nuclear weapons. It would deal a severe blow to the peaceful interrelationships between the world's two greatest military powers. It would deal a severe blow to the opinion held of us by peace-loving people in the small and developing nations around the world. And it would deal a severe blow to the opinion and support of the United States enjoyed now by us among our Western allies and those who join with us in mutual defense treaties. It would deal a severe blow to the reputation of our country as a nation desirous of peace.

Just as Dr. King and Mahatma Gandhi knew that nonviolence was not the course of cowards, so our search for peace is a sign not of weakness, but of strength. We must also demonstrate that our national human values work so well that they are worthy for other nations to adopt, to emulate. We will never purchase a peace that's merely a surrender of our ideals and beliefs, and neither will we seek to force our values on others. That, too, would be a surrender of our commitments and our principles.

Dr. King spoke of two kinds of peace, of negative peace, which meant the absence of fear and tension, and he spoke of a positive peace, which meant the presence of justice.

It's a positive peace that we now seek—peace that keeps alive his audacious dream that all people can have food and health care for their bodies, education and culture for their minds, and dignity, equality, and freedom for their spirits.

It is this ideal America—an America that has not yet been, but that can be, that will be—that we seek for our own children and for children yet to come.

As President, I will follow through on the continuing revolution that our founders started, and that many of you perpetuated, to make our Nation a standard of justice and freedom and opportunity.

Martin Luther King, Jr., his life, has become an inspiration for many people. It must never be forgotten. Tomorrow, we celebrate the 50th anniversary of the birth of Martin Luther King, Jr. I support the Democratic platform call for making his birthday a national holiday, and I will work for it. And I particularly hope that in this 50th anniversary year, that I will be able to sign a bill proclaiming January 15 as a national holiday in honor of Dr. King's principles and accomplishments.

We must never forget his dream. To-gether, Daddy King, me, Coretta, all of you, we can make it come true.

Thank you very much.

NOTE: The President spoke at 2:53 p.m. at the Ebenezer Baptist Church.

Attendees at the ceremony included Prime Minister Ola Ullsten of Sweden, Foreign Minister Knut Frydenlund of Norway, Senator Herman E. Talmadge and Representative Elliott H. Levitas of Georgia, Dr. Martin Luther King, Sr., pastor emeritus, and the Rev. Dr. Joseph L. Roberts, Jr., pastor of the Ebenezer Baptist Church, and Dr. Benjamin E. Mays, chairman, board of trustees, and Jesse Hill, Jr., chairman of the board of directors, Martin Luther King, Jr. Center for Social Change.

Coretta Scott King, widow of Dr. King and president of the Center, presented the award to the President. The award consisted of a citation, a medal, and a cash stipend of $1,000, which the President donated to the Center.

Interview With the President

Question-and-Answer Session With Black Media Representatives.   January 10, 1979

MR. AGURS. Good morning, Mr. President. As I said, I'm Don Agurs of the Mutual Black Network. And I'd like to congratulate you, first of all, on your award of the 1979 Martin Luther King, Jr. Nonviolent Peace Prize and thank you for this opportunity to talk with you today.

THE PRESIDENT. Well, that's a great honor for me, and I look forward to being in Atlanta with Mrs. King and the others who admire not only what Dr. Martin Luther King, Jr.'s life meant while he was with us but what it still means and will mean in the future.

Thank you very much, Don.

UNEMPLOYMENT

MR. AGURS. My first question, Mr. President, is, in the last days of his life, Dr. King became an active campaigner for economic justice in addition to civil rights, as we witnessed the poor people's campaign and his final effort in Memphis. Among his stated goals was a job for everyone willing to work. Now, even with the Humphrey-Hawkins bill on the books, such as it is, it now seems likely that unemployment next year is bound to creep upward again as the economy slows down.

My question is, aside from the allowances in the anti-inflation program, should not there be a greater emphasis on retaining the job-creating measures in the 1980 budget, at least at the current level, if you accept the caucus' premise that unemployment in the black community is already in a crisis state?

THE PRESIDENT. Well, I think our record so far on employment, unemployment, has been very good. In the last 2 years, we've added a net increase of about 7 million jobs in our country and have cut down the unemployment rate by more than 25 percent.

Between the 1978 and 1979 fiscal year budgets, we added about $4 billion to specific programs for the poor. And between this year and next year, the new budget, we'll add about that much more, a little more than $4 billion in increased programs for the poor.

In addition, we've tried to concentrate on job opportunities for minority groups, not just in public service employment, which is temporary and transient at best, but stable, permanent jobs, primarily in the private sector. And we've had especially good support from the Congress so far in providing these job opportunities in minority-owned businesses.

And, of course, for the 1980 fiscal year budget, which has not yet been revealed, I can tell you that we'll have another substantial increase in the allocation of public funds for this purpose. Even in the general areas of bank investments of Federal funds, we've increased those in black and other minority-owned banks.

We have allocated large portions of our total purchases for the Federal Government to minority-owned businesses. And in the $4 billion public works program, between 10 and 15 percent of that total allocation of contracts has gone to minority-owned businesses—I think about 3,500 black-owned businesses have benefited from that.

We are still dedicated to carrying out the purposes espoused by Dr. King, and also we were very eager to help in the passage of the Humphrey-Hawkins bill.

I might say one other thing just in passing. It's equally important to poor people and to minorities not to have their earnings and what they own sapped away by rapidly rising inflation. So, I wouldn't want the anti-inflation program to be characterized as being against poor people. Those who suffer most from rampant inflation are those who have very low incomes and those who are retired or otherwise have a limited income and can't move from one job to another.

So, I think a proper balancing of anti-inflation efforts, to which we are dedicated, with an increase in job opportunities, to which we are dedicated, is the best approach.

MR. AGURS. Our next question will come from Ms. Allen.

MARTIN LUTHER KING, JR.

MS. ALLEN. Mr. President, Vicki Allen from the National Black Network. Does your administration plan to back the bill that will create a national holiday for the late Dr. Martin Luther King?

THE PRESIDENT. Yes. This is in the Democratic National Party platform, and we would very much—I would like to sign a bill, passed by the Congress, to have this done.

Ms. ALLEN. Thank you.

MR. AGURS. Mr. Briscoe.

MINORITY-OWNED PUBLISHING FIRMS

MR. BRISCOE. Mr. President, I'm Sherman Briscoe from the National Newspaper Publishers Association. As you know, the first amendment rights have prohibited the Small Business Administration—that is, it has interpreted it as so in its regulations—not to make insured loans to communications media. That was true with respect to electronic media until recently, but now it does insure loans to electronic media to buy stations, to build towers, to buy and install equipment. What do you think of having the prohibition removed with respect to small newspapers and minority newspapers, where they, too, could obtain loans, insured loans, from the Small Business Administration to buy presses and equipment and this kind of thing?

THE PRESIDENT. In addition to what you've described, we, through the Federal Communications Commission, have encouraged the allocation of radio and television licenses to minority-owned corporations. I think it would be very helpful if we could have small business-type loans made available to the owners or potential purchasers of newspapers, if the courts can work out a way to protect any dominance or unwarranted influence by the Government on those publishers and editors, who ought to have a free right to speak their own voices in the publishing field.

So, if that one concern can be alleviated, I think it would be very helpful to have loans made to either expand black-owned publishing firms or to let black-owned corporations or others buy into the publishing field.

MR. BRISCOE. Would you suggest how the black press might go about obtaining this kind of relaxing of the prohibition?

THE PRESIDENT. Well, there are only two methods that I can think of offhand. One is for a test case to be pursued in the Federal courts to define more clearly where the options are for increased financing for black-owned publishing firms. And the other would be for corrective legislation. My guess is that in your own professional organization, a test case in the courts would be the most rapidly concluded procedure.

MR. AGURS. Mr. Betts.

PEOPLE'S TEMPLE

MR. BETTS. Mr. President, Roy Betts, Johnson Publishing Company, Ebony and Jet magazines. An estimated 600 bodies of victims, mostly black, of the Guyana cult massacre still remain at the Dover Air Force Base in Delaware, as you probably are aware. Residents there are demanding that the Government have mass cremations or burials at sea so that the cult will not build a burial shrine in that State. How can the Government bring a fitting close to this terrible chapter of violence?

THE PRESIDENT. This has been one of the most shocking and disheartening occurrences that I've ever known about. The Government, as you know, played no role in the procedure except, in a humanitarian way, to go in and to recover the bodies, to bring them back to our country. We are now trying to make maximum opportunity available for the families of those deceased persons to identify and to claim the bodies. After that effort has been exhausted and we feel sure that no additional families would come forward, then final decisions would be made on how to have appropriate burial. But at this time, Roy, I just don't know what can be done other than to encourage the families to come forward and to provide every possible opportunity for them to identify the remains of those members of their own families.

MR. BETTS. If I might follow up, Mr. President, in reference to the Government's effort to notify families, do you think that an adequate job is being done to notify families that there could be relatives among this very, very large number of people who were a part of this very tragic situation?

THE PRESIDENT. Well, I can't say that it's adequate, but we're doing the best we can. There's been a great deal of criticism of the Federal Government, by many very conservative Americans and others, for making any attempt to bring the bodies back to our country. But I felt at the time I authorized this action by the Government that it was proper. And we're doing the best we can to provide any possible identification information to the families who are searching for a lost loved one who may have been in Guyana. And although it will never be completely satisfactory, I don't know of anything else that we can do at this time.

MR. AGURS. Mr. Boone.

BLACK JUDGES

MR. BOONE. I am Ray Boone of the Afro-American Newspapers, Mr. President. Mr. President, you have promised that you would name blacks to the Federal judiciary, which remains almost all white still today. Could you give us an idea as to how many blacks you plan to name to the 152 new Federal judgeships, and particularly in the South, where there's only 1 black judge among about 136?

THE PRESIDENT. Well, my goal is to have black judges in Georgia, Florida, the Carolinas, Mississippi, Alabama, Louisiana—indeed, throughout the country. As you know, in some parts of the Nation there are very few blacks who live in those States and an extremely tiny portion of the total members of the bar. We are working, though, with every Senator in the Government to encourage their submission to me of names selected by commissions, which include both women and minority representatives. And I can't give you an exact number yet, but whenever possible we will have a representative number of blacks, those who speak Spanish, and women.

One of the problems in the district judgeships is that the individual Members of the Senate, in effect, have veto power over the appointments. In circuit judgeships, I have set up my own selection panels, and I can guarantee you in the circuit judgeships that you will be well pleased.

In the district judgeships, when the Senators have refused to include in their list of recommended judges those who are black or other minorities and those who are women, then we are delaying any appointments, going back to the Senators and asking them to enlarge their list.

MR. BOONE. I take it that you are referring to Senator Byrd of Virginia, who has disagreed with your position on including minorities or blacks on the list of recommended judges.

THE PRESIDENT. He's one of several, yes.

MR. BOONE. You said you were working with all Senators. Does that include Senator Byrd?

THE PRESIDENT. Yes. The Attorney General is working with Senator Byrd and others to encourage them to expand their list of recommended nominees to include both minority representatives and women, yes.

MR. BOONE. Is he bending?

THE PRESIDENT. You could better get an answer for that from the Attorney General, who's had conversations with Senator Byrd. I've not talked to him directly. But we are making every effort we can in Virginia to encourage the selection of minority members to be judges.

I might say that in several of the Northern States we are also having a problem getting the Members of the Senate to change their longstanding policy and to make it possible for me to appoint black judges. But I'm determined to succeed.

CIA AND FBI; CONGRESSIONAL ASSASSINATIONS INVESTIGATIONS

MR. AGURS. Mr. President, my next question is, are you satisfied that all of the people who are responsible for illegal or unethical acts by the CIA or the FBI are now out of those agencies? And are you convinced that there is no longer a possibility that a government-run campaign could be mounted to destroy or discredit a national leader in our country?

THE PRESIDENT. I'm convinced that the leadership of the CIA and the FBI and the White House are all equally determined that there should never be a repetition of the attack on a minority leader, as was the case with Martin Luther King, Jr. And although I can't guarantee what will happen after I leave the White House, I can guarantee you that while I'm here in the White House as President, there will be no such attack on a leader as there was in the past.

MR. AGURS. In that same connection, are you satisfied that the House assassinations investigation—are you satisfied with their conclusion, and do you feel that the Justice Department now should take a look at these conspiracies that the committee feels might have existed?

THE PRESIDENT. There is no definite answer to whether or not there was a conspiracy. I think the thorough investigation, though, of all new evidence is necessary. And the FBI has publicly stated that they will pursue any new information that's available to them.

MR. AGURS. Ms. Allen.

HOSPITAL COST CONTAINMENT

MS. ALLEN. Mr. President, in view of the fact that health care costs in the past 10 years have been such a high source of inflation, what steps are being taken to reduce the percentage of health care costs in the Federal budget, in terms of the underprivileged especially?

THE PRESIDENT. As you know, health care costs, hospital costs, have been going up—doubled every 5 years for the last 15 or so years. And unless we do something about it, hospital costs are going to double again in the next 5 years.

Last year, we mounted a major campaign in the Congress to have passed hospital cost containment legislation similar to what has already been passed in States like New York and Connecticut, which has proven so successful. Because of the extraordinary influence of the hospital lobby and the medical doctors lobby, we were not able to get this legislation passed in the House, although it did pass the Senate in modified form.

We will make another effort this year, which I believe will be successful. What we need in order to accomplish this goal is to have broad citizen understanding of how much their own best interests are involved in having a strong hospital cost containment bill passed. It would be at the top of our priorities in controlling inflation.

I think these extremely high costs are unnecessary and unwarranted, and I believe that the public is being robbed. And I hope that everyone listening to this broadcast will let their Member of the Congress in the House or Senate know that as citizens themselves, worried about their own families' future, that they join in with me in passing a strong hospital cost containment bill this year.

Ms. ALLEN. Thank you.

MR. AGURS. Mr. Briscoe.

NATIONAL ASSOCIATION FOR THE AD-VANCEMENT OF COLORED PEOPLE

MR. BRISCOE. Mr. President, I'm a life member of the National Association for the Advancement of Colored People, the NAACP. My wife is a subscribing life member. Hundreds of thousands of Americans, black and white, have supported the NAACP. I'm sure you and Mrs. Carter have given substantial support. But as you know now, the NAACP is in a financial crisis. The Mobil Oil Company is placing ads in some of the major newspapers to help solicit funds for the organization, to save it, so it can carry on its vital functions.

What would you think of inviting Mr. Hooks [1] down and making a presentation to him as a symbol of what can be done by all Americans to help save this organization?

THE PRESIDENT. I agree with you about the importance of the NAACP continuing and also continuing as a strong and well-financed organization. Benjamin Hooks was here at this very table last month. And he comes to meet with me often to pursue the goals of the NAACP.

I think one of the things that can be done is, through broadcasts like this, to let the people of our Nation know, both black and white, how important I, as President, believe that a strong NAACP is to the future of our country and the protection of minority rights.

Many people feel that the major battles for civil rights have been won in our country, which is certainly not the case. We need to be constantly vigilant about

---

[1] Executive director of the NAACP.

encroachments on the freedom and quality of life of poor people, in general, and of minority poor who have compounded their problems. And I think that everyone listening to this program can certainly afford the $5 membership fee for the NAACP, and I would encourage them to send in their contribution to make sure this organization is strong and viable.

I've noticed in recent days that the NAACP leadership has begun turning more and more to corporate contributions to support the NAACP. This is obviously necessary to prevent a curtailment of the staffing and the efforts of the organization. But the best source of NAACP funds still remains the small, concerned private member, who only contributes $5 a year but, in that contribution, becomes a part of the NAACP effort. And as President, without violating the nonbiased point of view of the Oval Office, I would like to encourage a stronger membership in the NAACP of all those who are listening.

MR. AGURS. Mr. Betts.

SOUTHERN AFRICA

MR. BETTS. Mr. President, you should be commended for your crusading pledges for human rights and peace throughout the world. However, the racial condition in southern Africa doesn't seem to improve, even though the news media and the Government seem to overlook the circumstances in favor of news in other parts of the world. Do you expect to take a firm stand in improving the racial conditions in southern Africa, beyond what we've seen now?

THE PRESIDENT. I believe that under Andy Young's leadership as a strong and unrestrained vocal leader in the United Nations, we have materially improved our own Nation's position with respect to the majority of citizens who live in Africa, that is, the black citizens. And I think we've been relatively successful, compared to previous records of our own country. We have an immediate prospect for success in having a majority government established in Namibia. And we've exerted every effort, along with other members of the United Nations, particularly the leadership from Canada, Great Britain, France, and Germany, working in harmony, to bring about the move by South Africa to withdraw their own influence from Namibia and let the people who live there choose on a one-person-one-vote basis the majority government.

In addition, working closely with the British, and also through, of course, Andy Young and others, we've tried to bring together the National Front—the present government of Rhodesia and the frontline governments surrounding Rhodesia—to have a majority government established in that country, which would then be called Zimbabwe, based on a one-person-one-vote representation. We haven't made much progress there, although I think all three of those entities that I named are looking for some continued leadership from the United States and, particularly, Great Britain. We deplore apartheid and any sort of racial discrimination, and we strongly support the establishment of majority rule government in South Africa. We have made this clear to the Botha government and continue to pursue that goal.

I think, in general, the progress has been detectable and sound. In my opinion, it's been too slow, but we are determined. And I think we have at least been successful in arousing among the black leaders of Africa an increasing degree of confidence in our own Government when, for decades, even generations, we have stayed aloof from any movement toward majority rule, black rule in Africa.

So, I think we made good progress, slow progress, but we'll be very consistent through Andy Young and other leaders in pursuing these goals that I've described to you.

MR. BETTS. One brief followup. Would you consider a followup trip to your earlier trip to Nigeria or some other part of Africa in the near future?

THE PRESIDENT. Not in the near future, but I'd like very much to go back to Africa again and to travel in countries that I was not able to visit before. In the meantime, of course, we've had many of the top leaders from Africa come here and meet with me. And I think that as a result of this there's been a much better understanding. So, yes, I would like very much to go back to Africa again.

MR. AGURS. Mr. Boone.

PRESIDENTIAL ADVISERS ON BLACK ISSUES

MR. BOONE. Mr. President, I would like to know who is your top adviser on concerns of the black community? I'd like to know whether this person is black. I ask this question, because I have seen a number of lists published which show your top advisers, but never is there a black person. So, could you comment on that, please?

THE PRESIDENT. Well, one thing that I've tried to avoid is any arrangement within the White House or within my Cabinet advisers where only a black person can be responsible for improving the quality of life of the black citizens of our country. Louis Martin works very closely with me here in the White House on matters that relate directly to black persons alone.

But I would like to point out that I consider myself to be a good spokesman for the well-being of black citizens. I think I could not possibly have a better Vice President than Fritz Mondale, whether that Vice President was black or white. And I believe that every member of my domestic and foreign counselors are strongly oriented, as am I, toward the improvement of the life of minority citizens in this country.

If I should ever have any proven allegations that this is not the case with a single Cabinet member or any of my advisers, I would discharge them immediately. And I hope that the minority citizens of our country don't feel that when they have a special problem that relates to the United States Government, that they have to find a black person to listen to them. I'm available, and I hope that every member of my staff, every member of my Cabinet feels the same way.

BLACK SUPPORT FOR THE PRESIDENT

MR. BOONE. Mr. President, a followup. You proved your credibility in the black community 2 years ago when you won 90 percent of the vote. But times change and, of course, the degree of credibility changes.

THE PRESIDENT. Yes.

MR. BOONE. You're in midterm now. My question is, if you decide to run, and I understand you have made a decision to that effect, do you think you could pull a repeat 90-percent performance in an election, considering the heavy criticism that you have received from the black community, particularly in the area of unemployment and the budget? Could I have a response to that, please?

THE PRESIDENT. Mr. Boone, let me say that I think my record on the unemployment and budget is very good. But I don't take anything for granted. Certainly, I don't take for granted an automatic support by the black citizens of our country just because I'm a Democrat or just because I've been in office or just because I got good support 2 years ago. My effort

will be continuing the next 2 years to do a good job, so that whether I am the next President or not, the black citizens of our country would say, "Jimmy Carter was a friend of ours as long as he was in the White House." So, I want to run on my record, if I run, and not based on any sort of assumption that I will get support from the black community just because of who I am or what I've done.

PRESIDENT'S 1980 CANDIDACY

MR. BOONE. One followup, Mr. President. Have you decided whether you would run, and would you share that with us? In 1980, are you going to run?

THE PRESIDENT. I've decided, but I haven't decided when I'm going to announce my decision.

1980 BUDGET

MR. AGURS. The last question, Mr. President, is do you foresee a serious congressional challenge to your budget-making decisions and that is why you've put on additional lobbying strengths? And also, if so, do you think the lawmakers would be more interested in increasing your social and domestic expenditures? What is your assessment?

THE PRESIDENT. I've worked the last 12 months on this 1980 fiscal year budget. And I believe, Mr. Agurs, that it's a good budget. Obviously, it's going to be 5 or 6 months, at least, before the Congress takes final action on the budget I propose. And during that 5 or 6 months or more, economic circumstances will change, estimates of revenue and expenditures will become much more accurate, and there might be some modifications to the budget that I, myself, would propose to the Congress, as I have the 2 preceding years.

But I believe that the Congress will find, in general, this to be a fair budget, a responsible budget, and a very enlightened budget.

As I said earlier, in allocation of funds for civil rights, we will have substantial increases; for minority businesses, substantial increases; for allocations of funds for the poor, substantial increases in 1980, about the same as we had between '78 and '79. And I believe that if the Congress does make any changes, they will be relatively minor.

We'll be monitoring this very closely, because I would not stand idly by and see the Congress take funds away from those who need Federal assistance most and give it to those less worthy. So, we'll be monitoring it closely. But I think it's a good, sound budget and, in general, the Congress will approve.

MR. AGURS. Thank you, Mr. President.

THE PRESIDENT. Thank you. I have enjoyed it very much, Don. I thank all of you for letting me be with you.

NOTE: The interview began at 10:34 a.m. in the Cabinet Room at the White House. It was recorded for later broadcast on the Mutual Black Network and the National Black Network.

The transcript of the interview was released on January 15.

Office of Personnel Management

Recess Appointment of Bernhardt K. Wruble as Director of the Office of Government Ethics. January 15, 1979

The President today announced the recess appointment of Bernhardt K. Wruble, of New York City, as Director of the Office of Government Ethics in the Office of Personnel Management.

Wruble, 36, is a graduate of Williams College and the University of Pennsylvania Law School. He served as a law clerk for the late Judge Phillip Forman of the Third Circuit, U.S. Court of Appeals. From 1967 to 1977, he was an associate and then a partner of the New York law firm of Simpson, Thacher & Bartlett. From August 1977 to the present, he has served as Principal Deputy General Counsel to the Department of the Army.

Wruble will serve as Director of the Office of Government Ethics until a permanent Director is nominated and confirmed.

United States Ambassador to the People's Republic of China

Nomination of Leonard Woodcock. January 15, 1979

The President today announced that he will nominate Leonard Woodcock, of Detroit, Mich., to be Ambassador Extraordinary and Plenipotentiary of the United States to the People's Republic of China.

Woodcock has been Chief of the United States Liaison Office with the People's Republic of China since 1977. He was born February 15, 1911, in Providence, R.I., and attended Wayne State University.

Woodcock was with the United Automobile Workers of America from 1940 until 1977, and served as president from 1970 to 1977.

Commodity Futures Trading Commission

Nomination of James M. Stone To Be Chairman. January 15, 1979

The President today announced that he will nominate James M. Stone, of Boston, Mass., to be Chairman of the Commodity Futures Trading Commission.

Stone was born November 12, 1947, in New York City. He received a B.A. with highest honors in economics from Harvard College in 1969, an M.A. with specialization in monetary theory and fiscal policy in 1970, and a Ph. D. in economics in 1973.

Stone was a teaching fellow at Harvard from 1969 to 1973, and a lecturer in economics from 1973 to 1975, teaching a course on the economics of securities markets. Beginning in 1971, he was a part-time consultant to Fairfield and Ellis, Inc., a Boston insurance brokerage specializing in large industrial accounts. From 1974 to 1975, he was vice president-economist at Fairfield and Ellis.

Since 1975 Stone has been commissioner of insurance for the Commonwealth of Massachusetts. Under his administration, the Insurance Department has initiated publication of a series of guides for insurance consumers, restructured the rating classifications in automobile insurance, and undergone a staff reorganization resulting in an increase in the number of professional employees and a decrease in the budget.

Stone is the author of "One Way for Wall Street," a book on regulatory issues in the securities industry published in 1975.

Department of Housing and Urban Development

Nomination of William B. Welsh To Be an Assistant Secretary. January 15, 1979

The President today announced that he will nominate William B. Welsh, of Annandale, Va., to be Assistant Secretary of Housing and Urban Development for Legislative Affairs and Intergovernmental Relations.

Welsh was born September 18, 1924, in Munfordville, Ky. He received an A.B. from Berea College in 1949 and an M.A. from the University of Kentucky in 1952. He served in the U.S. Army from 1943 to 1946.

Welsh was legislative assistant to U.S. Senator Herbert H. Lehman from 1952 to 1956, and research director of the Democratic National Committee from 1957 to 1958. From 1959 to 1967, he was administrative assistant to U.S. Senator Philip Hart.

In 1967 and 1968, Welsh was administrative assistant to Vice President Hubert Humphrey. From 1969 to 1971, he was executive director of the Democratic National Committee. Since 1972 he has been executive director for governmental affairs of the American Federation of State, County and Municipal Employees.

United States Ambassador at Large

Nomination of W. Beverly Carter, Jr. January 15, 1979

The President today announced that he will nominate W. Beverly Carter, Jr., of Philadelphia, Pa., to be Ambassador at Large. He would have overall responsibility for liaison with State and local governments for the State Department.

Carter, 57, is currently Ambassador to Liberia. He joined the Foreign Service in 1965 and served as a public affairs officer in Nairobi and Lagos. From 1969 to 1972, he was Deputy Assistant Secretary of State for African Affairs.

From 1972 to 1975, Carter was Ambassador to Tanzania. From 1975 to 1976, he was special assistant to the Assistant Secretary of State for African Affairs. Since 1976 he has been Ambassador to Liberia.

and as chairman of the Governor's Highway Safety Commission. Williams also served as secretary of the Florida Department of Administration from 1975 to 1977.

Department of Agriculture

Nomination of James H. Williams To Be Deputy Secretary.   January 15, 1979

The President today announced that he will nominate James H. Williams, of Ocala, Fla., to be Deputy Secretary of Agriculture.

Williams was Lieutenant Governor of Florida until the expiration of his term, earlier this month.

Williams was born June 17, 1926, in Ocala, Fla. He served in the U.S. Army Air Force in 1944 and 1945. From 1943 to 1949, he owned and operated a cattle ranch of approximately 7,000 acres. In 1947 and 1948, he taught veterans on-the-farm training, and from 1948 to 1950, he owned and operated a sawmill and logging operation. From 1950 to 1962, he was joint owner and vice president of Dixie Lime and Stone Co.

In 1962 Williams entered Central Florida Junior College, and in 1966 he received a B.A. in political science from the University of Florida.

Williams was elected to the Florida Senate in 1968, where he served until 1974. He was chairman of the governmental operations committee and received several awards for effectiveness as a legislator.

In 1975 Williams became Lieutenant Governor, elected with Governor Reubin Askew. In this office, he served as chairman of the Governor's Commission on Criminal Justice, Standards, and Goals,

United States Railway Association

Nomination of Thomas P. Salmon To Be a Member of the Board of Directors. January 15, 1979

The President today announced that he will nominate Thomas P. Salmon, of Bellows Falls, Vt., to be a member of the Board of Directors of the United States Railway Association.

Salmon, 46, is an attorney in Bellows Falls. He served as Governor of Vermont from 1972 to 1976 and was chairman of the New England Governors' Conference for 1974 and 1975. He previously served in the Vermont House of Representatives, where he was house minority leader in 1969 and 1970. He is currently on the board of directors of the Council for Northeast Economic Action.

California Debris Commission

Nomination of Brig. Gen. Norman G. Delbridge, Jr., To Be a Member. January 15, 1979

The President today announced that he will nominate Brig. Gen. Norman G. Delbridge, Jr., of the Army Corps of Engineers, to be a member of the California Debris Commission.

Delbridge, 51, is Division Engineer with the U.S. Army Engineer Division, South Pacific. He has been in the Army over 27 years.

The California Debris Commission was formed in 1893 to protect navigable rivers by preventing deposits of debris from mining operations, natural erosion, or other causes.

National Council on Educational Research

Nomination of Helen S. Astin To Be a Member.   January 15, 1979

The President today announced that he will nominate Helen S. Astin, of Los Angeles, Calif., to be a member of the National Council on Educational Research.

Astin, 47, is professor of higher education and head of the higher education program at the University of California at Los Angeles and vice president of the Higher Education Research Institute. She has also served as director of research and education for the University Research Corp. in Washington, and as research associate for the Bureau of Social Science Research. Her primary research interests are in the fields of educational and career development, with special emphases on women, adults, disadvantaged students, and the relationships between education and work.

Mississippi River Commission

*Nomination of Two Members.
January 15, 1979*

The President today announced that he will nominate two persons to be members of the Mississippi River Commission. They are:

Maj. Gen. Louis W. Prentiss, Jr., Corps of Engineers. Prentiss, 51, is Deputy Chief of Staff, Engineer, for the United States

Army Europe and Seventh Army. He was previously Division Engineer for the U.S. Army Engineer Division in Europe.

Maj. Gen. Richard L. Harris, Corps of Engineers. Harris, 50, is Division Engineer with the U.S. Army Engineer Division, North Central, based in Chicago. He was previously Commanding General of the U.S. Army Training Center at Fort Leonard Wood, Mo.

National Institute of Building Sciences

Nomination of Six Members of the Board of Directors.   January 15, 1979

The President today announced six persons whom he will nominate to be members of the Board of Directors of the National Institute of Building Sciences. They are:

GUY O. MABRY, vice president of the insulation operations division of Owens-Corning Fiberglass Corp. in Toledo, Ohio;

LEONARD MILLER, of Miami Beach, Fla., co-owner of Pasadena Homes, Inc., and a director of the National Association of Home Builders;

JOHN P. MILLHONE, director of the Minnesota Energy Agency;

JOSEPH H. NEWMAN, of West Orange, N.J., senior vice president of Tishman Construction and Research Co.;

BLANCA CEDEÑO, a member of the board of directors of the New York City Housing Authority, formerly director of the office of community affairs for that authority;

LOIS A. CRAIG, of Boston, Mass., a former director of the Federal Architecture Project, now on a design project fellowship to write about the relationship between public design and changing ideas of public life.

The National Institute of Building Sciences was created in 1974 to develop and encourage the adoption of performance criteria for building components. The Institute provides technical advice to contractors, local governments, and others, on building regulations and techniques.

National Council on the Arts

Nomination of Six Members.
January 15, 1979

The President today announced six persons whom he will nominate to be members of the National Council on the Arts. They are:

NORMAN B. CHAMP, JR., a St. Louis, Mo., businessman, a trustee of the St. Louis Art Museum, and a member of the Commission for the Preservation of the White House;

MARTIN FRIEDMAN, of Minneapolis, director of the Walker Art Center;

BERNARD B. LÓPEZ, executive director of the New Mexico Arts Commission in Sante Fe, past chairman of the Western States Arts Foundation;

ROBERT L. SHAW, music director and conductor of the Atlanta Symphony Orchestra;

JESSIE A. WOODS, executive director of Urban Gateways in Chicago and a member of the executive committee of the Chicago Council on Fine Arts and the community arts councils panel of the Illinois Arts Council;

ROSALIND W. WYMAN, of Los Angeles, executive chairperson of the Producers Guild of America.

National Council on the Humanities

Nomination of Dave Warren To Be a
Member.   January 15, 1979

The President today announced that he will nominate Dave Warren, of Santa Fe, N. Mex., to be a member of the National Council on the Humanities.

Warren, 46, is Director of the Division of Research and Cultural Studies Development of the Bureau of Indian Affairs'

Institute of American Indian Arts in Santa Fe. He has also served as Acting Director of Education Programs for the Bureau of Indian Affairs. He is the author of numerous articles.

National Commission on Social Security

Nomination of Elizabeth Duskin To Be a
Member.   January 15, 1979

The President today announced that he will nominate Elizabeth Duskin, of Chevy Chase, Md., to be a member of the National Commission on Social Security.

Duskin, 43, is director of research for the National Council of Senior Citizens. She has also served as an economic consultant to the Federal Council on Aging, where she prepared congressionally mandated studies. Her professional background has emphasized programs and policies affecting U.S. income distribution, particularly social and private insurance policies, income-conditioned programs, and health-related financing mechanisms.

Nominations to Government Positions

Announcement of 45 Nominations To Be
Submitted to the Senate.   January 15, 1979

The President today announced that he will nominate the following persons for positions for which they received recess appointments during the last recess:

GEORGE M. SEIGNIOUS II to be Director of the Arms Control and Disarmament Agency;

JOHN W. McGARRY to be a member of the Federal Election Commission;

JOHN PATRICK WHITE to be Deputy Director of the Office of Management and Budget;

RICHARD W. YARBOROUGH to be a member of the Foreign Claims Settlement Commission of the United States;

WILLIAM J. SULLIVAN to be a member of the Board of Governors of the United States Postal Service;

JAMES J. DILLMAN, MILTON S. GWIRTZMAN, DONALD S. MACNAUGHTON, and DAVID H. RODGERS to be members of the National Commission on Social Security;

CHARLES V. HAMILTON, LOUIS J. HECTOR, M. CARL HOLMAN, JACOB NEUSNER, SISTER JOEL READ, LEON STEIN, HARRIET M. ZIMMERMAN, MARY BETH NORTON, and KAY HOWE to be members of the National Council on the Humanities;

ALAN K. CAMPBELL to be Director of the Office of Personnel Management;

JULE M. SUGARMAN to be Deputy Director of the Office of Personnel Management;

RUTH T. PROKOP to be a member and Chairman of the Merit Systems Protection Board;

H. PATRICK SWYGERT to be Special Counsel of the Merit Systems Protection Board;

HENRY B. FRAZIER III and RONALD W. HAUGHTON to be members of the Federal Labor Relations Authority.

Also, the President announced that he will renominate the following persons who were nominated in the last session but not confirmed before the Senate adjourned:

LARRY E. MEIEROTTO to be Assistant Secretary of the Interior;

ANNE P. JONES to be a member of the Federal Communications Commission;

MAX L. FRIEDERSDORF to be a member of the Federal Election Commission;

PHILIP H. ALSTON, Jr., to be Ambassador to the Republic of Nauru (to serve concurrently with his present position as Ambassador to Australia);

PETER H. WOLF to be an Associate Judge of the Superior Court of the District of Columbia;

GEOFFREY COWAN, PAUL S. FRIEDLANDER, KATHLEEN NOLAN, and HOWARD A. WHITE to be members of the Board of Directors of the Corporation for Public Broadcasting;

F. WILLIAM MCCALPIN, MICHAEL KANTOR, ROBERT J. KUTAK, REVIUS O. ORTIQUE, JR., HOWARD R. SACKS, and RAMONA

T. SHUMP to be members of the Board of Directors of the Legal Services Corporation;

EUGENE H. COTA-ROBLES, ERNESTINE FRIEDL, WALTER E. MASSEY, DAVID V. RAGONE, EDWIN E. SALPETER, and CHARLES PENCE SLIGHTER to be members of the National Science Board.

Multilateral Trade Negotiations

Message to the Congress Transmitting Proposed Legislation.   January 15, 1979

To the Congress of the United States:

I am today transmitting to the Congress a proposal for legislation to extend until September 30, 1979, the authority of the Secretary of the Treasury under Section 303(d) of the Tariff Act of 1930 to waive the application of countervailing duties. The Secretary's authority to waive the imposition of countervailing duties expired on January 2, 1979. Expansion of this authority is essential to provide the Congress with time to consider the results of the Tokyo Round of Multilateral Trade Negotiations (MTN). Failure to extend this authority is likely to prevent the reaching of a conclusion to these negotiations and could set back our national economic interests. Accordingly, I urge that the Congress enact the necessary legislation at the earliest possible date.

As stipulated by the Congress in the Trade Act of 1974, negotiation of a satisfactory code on subsidies and countervailing duties has been a primary U.S. objective in the Tokyo Round. We have sought an agreement to improve discipline on the use of subsidies which adversely affect trade. I am pleased to report that in recent weeks our negotiators have substantially concluded negotiations for a satisfactory subsidy/countervailing duty code which includes: (1) new rules on the use of internal and export subsidies which substantially increase protection of United States agricultural and industrial trading interests, and (2) more effective provisions on notification, consultation and dispute settlement that will provide for timely resolution of disputes involving trade subsidies in international trade.

My Special Representative for Trade Negotiations has informed me that negotiations on almost all MTN topics have been substantially concluded, and that those agreements meet basic U.S. objectives. However, final agreement is unlikely unless the waiver authority is extended for the period during which such agreements and their implementing legislation are being considered by the Congress under the procedures of the Trade Act of 1974.

Under current authority, the imposition of countervailing duties may be waived in a specific case only if, inter alia, "adequate steps have been taken to eliminate or substantially reduce the adverse effect" of the subsidy in question. This provision and the other limitations on the use of the waiver authority which are currently in the law would continue in effect if the waiver authority is extended. Thus, U.S. producers and workers will continue to be protected from the adverse effects of subsidized competition.

A successful conclusion to the MTN is essential to our national interest, as well as the continued growth of world trade. If the waiver authority is not extended, such a successful conclusion will be placed in serious jeopardy. Accordingly, I urge the Congress to act positively upon this legislative proposal at the earliest possible date.

JIMMY CARTER

The White House,
January 15, 1979.

Proposed amendment to Section 303 (d) of the Tariff Act of 1930, *as amended,* by Section 331(a) of the Trade Act of 1974, (19 U.S.C. 1303).

At the end of paragraph (d) of Section 303 add the following new paragraph:

(4) Notwithstanding subparagraph (d)(2), the four-year period referred to therein is extended until September 30, 1979, and all determinations reached by the Secretary pursuant thereto prior to the enactment of this subparagraph shall continue in effect until such date, unless the Secretary revokes his determination as provided in subparagraph 303(d)(3). Any other determination by the Secretary to waive countervailing duties as to which an intention to do so was announced prior to the enactment of this subparagraph shall be effective as of the date notice of intent to waive was published in the FEDERAL REGISTER.

Interview With the President

Excerpts From a Question-and-Answer Session With John Chancellor of NBC News. January 13, 1979

MR. CHANCELLOR. I kind of hate to bring this up, but I have to. Do you think your brother, Billy, would be a liability in a campaign?

THE PRESIDENT. Well, you know, family matters and my brother, Billy, are fairly sensitive with me. Billy is an extremely independent person. Any criticism that I might make publicly of Billy would cause, I think, him to react very strongly and to reexert his independence. We have a good personal relationship. It's always been that way.

Billy and I have very strong differences of opinion on many issues. He expresses those differences much more frequently than do I. And I don't look on Billy's actions as a basis for success in future political activities. And I hope the people of the United States realize that I have no control over Billy; he has no control over me.

We are two very independent people. We love each other. But any attempt that I might make to control Billy's words or actions would not be successful at all.

MR. CHANCELLOR. Counterproductive, as they say.

THE PRESIDENT. I think it would be counterproductive, because Billy prides himself on being independent from me. And I think he would show it if I tried to dominate him, and I have no intention to try to do so.

[*The transcript of the above exchange was made available by the White House Press Office on January 13. The transcript of the following exchange was released on January 16.*]

MR. CHANCELLOR. Now, Mr. President, talking about cooperation from the private sector, you've got some big labor contracts coming up. Suppose the Teamsters Union, for example, which is a big and very important union, wants to go beyond your guidelines and suppose a strike should result. A big, bad Teamsters strike would cripple a lot of things in this country. Wouldn't you be tempted to relax your guidelines in that case?

THE PRESIDENT. Well, I hate to answer a conjectural question like that. I believe that the members of the Teamsters Union are very interested in seeing the anti-inflation effort work. They've been forthcoming, without giving me any commitments on what their stance will be when the contract is negotiated. But they are Americans. They're patriotic. They are sound people. They have interest in a stable income. And for them to get very high wage increases that would destroy the efforts to control inflation would not pay dividends for them in the future. They understand that.

I can't think of anything more damaging to the economy than a sustained Teamsters strike. This is a unique union in that they could bring our economy almost to a halt. They've not ever done this. And they have shown, I think, a remarkable degree of responsibility about this in the past. We would not be able to accommodate a strike of that kind. Either I or the Congress would have to act very rapidly to bring to an end a strike of that sort if it should occur. But I don't think that that's going to happen.

We can't write a labor contract and mandate that employers and employees adopt it. The only way we can be successful is to convince the public, employers, employees in all segments of our economy, that it's in their best interests to have a strong American economy with inflation under control. And that's the basis on which we hope we'll have success.

NOTE: The interview began at 9:38 a.m. in the Oval Office at the White House. NBC News broadcast portions of the interview during the following week.

Historically Black Colleges and Universities

Memorandum From the President.
January 17, 1979

Memorandum for the Heads of Executive Departments and Agencies

The approximately one hundred historically black colleges of this Nation have played and continue to play a unique and important role in providing educational opportunities to many thousands of students. They have done so in the past when there were no other avenues open to the overwhelming majority of black students. They do so now by continuing to provide special opportunities for students of all races.

The continuing importance of historically black colleges and universities, not only to students but also to this Nation's social, economic and educational life, cannot be over-estimated. This Administration is committed to enhancing their strength and prosperity.

In moving toward this goal the Department of Health, Education, and Welfare criteria call for efforts to strengthen the historically black public institutions through increased financial support, new and expanded programs, and the elimination of educationally unnecessary program duplication between them and their traditional white counterparts. These efforts are required to ensure that the historically black colleges are able to participate fully in the educational and social progress of our Nation.

I have repeatedly expressed my hope that the historically black colleges will be stronger when I leave office than when my Administration began. I am asking today that you personally join with me in meeting this objective by initiating and overseeing the following actions:

• Conduct a thorough review of the operations within your department or agency to ensure that historically black institutions are being given a fair opportunity to participate in Federal grant and contract programs. Ensure that an affirmative effort is made to inform black colleges of the opportunity to apply and compete for grants and contracts. Particular attention should be given to identifying and eliminating unintended barriers that may have resulted in reduced participation in and benefits from Federal programs by these colleges.

• Identify areas where historically black institutions can participate more effectively in your Department's activities.

Consider, for example, small research contracts or grants which can be let without competition, and new or existing cooperative education programs which facilitate minority student access to Federal employment.

• Where appropriate, establish goals and timetables for increased participation of historically black colleges in the activities of your department or agency. These goals should reflect targets for increased expenditures beyond your fiscal 1978 levels.

• Establish a forum for continuing consultation with representatives from the historically black colleges and universities. Plan visits and other efforts to familiarize appropriate staff in your agency with the unique and indispensable resources at black colleges.

• Appoint a high-level liaison person to oversee these activities.

I am asking Louis Martin, my special assistant, in cooperation with the Secretary of Health, Education, and Welfare, to monitor the implementation of this directive government-wide. I personally plan to review periodically progress made toward increasing access of historically black colleges to all Federal agencies.

In a separate communication, I have asked that Secretary Califano resume publication of the Federal Interagency Committee on Education's annual report on patterns of Federal funding for historically black colleges.

I want to be certain that this Administration's strong commitments to the Nation's historically black colleges and the contents of this directive are thoroughly understood by everyone. Please be certain that copies of this directive are circulated to all appropriate individuals within your department or agency.

JIMMY CARTER

THE PRESIDENT'S NEWS CONFERENCE OF JANUARY 17, 1979

THE PRESIDENT. Good afternoon, everybody. I have a brief opening statement to make.

FISCAL YEAR 1980 BUDGET

Last fall, when I outlined the administration's commitment to control inflation, I set as a goal for ourselves the submission of a budget for 1980 fiscal year with a deficit of less than $30 billion, which would be substantially more than a 50-percent cut compared to the deficit that I inherited.

The budget will be submitted to Congress this coming Tuesday. I have more than met that goal. As a matter of fact, the fiscal year 1976 budget deficit was more than 4 percent of our gross national product. In 1980, we will have cut it down to 1.2 percent of our gross national product. We had an earlier commitment also to reduce total Federal spending down to 21 percent of our GNP by fiscal year 1981. We will have met that commitment 1 year earlier.

This has been a very difficult budget to prepare because of those stringent goals. But I felt it was necessary, and I believe the Nation agrees with me that it is necessary, to restrain Federal spending.

We have not neglected the needs of the disadvantaged Americans, poor Americans, and those who are unemployed. As a matter of fact, the total allocation of funds for the poor will be increased by $4½ billion by 1980 fiscal year, and we will have a total of about $11 billion designed for jobs and job training to sustain the high employment rate in our country.

So, to summarize, the budget commitment will be to control inflation. It will be very austere, stringent, tough, fiscal policy, but fair to the American people and oriented to help those who are most disadvantaged have a better quality of life.

Mr. Cormier [Frank Cormier, Associated Press].

QUESTIONS

IRAN

Q. Mr. President, what will the posture of our Government be now toward the various contending factions in Iran that even continue to vie for power over there?

THE PRESIDENT. We have very important relationships with Iran—past, present, and I hope, in the future—and I expect in the future. They have been good allies of ours, and I expect this to continue in the future.

In accordance with the provisions of the Iranian Constitution, a change in government has now been accomplished. Under Mr. Bahktiar, whose government we do support, the Majles, the lower house of parliament, and the upper house, the Senate, have approved his government and his Cabinet.

We have encouraged to the limited extent of our own ability the public support for the Bahktiar government, for the restoration of stability, for an end of bloodshed, and for the return of normal life in Iran.

As you know, the Shah has left Iran; he says for a vacation. How long he will be out of Iran, we have no way to determine. Future events and his own desires will determine that. He's now in Egypt, and he will later come to our own country. But we would anticipate and would certainly hope that our good relationships with Iran will continue in the future.

Q. Mr. President, a month ago at a news conference, you said the Shah would maintain power. How could you be so wrong, and is it typical of our intelligence elsewhere in the world? And are you in touch with Khomeini in case he winds up at the top of the heap?

THE PRESIDENT. Well, it's impossible for anyone to anticipate all future political events. And I think that the rapid change of affairs in Iran has not been predicted by anyone, so far as I know.

Our intelligence is the best we can devise. We share intelligence data and diplomatic information on a routine basis with other nations. And this is a constant process whenever a problem arises in a country throughout the world.

I have confidence in the Iranian people to restore a stable government and to restore their economic circumstances for the future.

No, we have not communicated directly with Mr. Khomeini. Our views have been expressed publicly that he support stability and an end to bloodshed in Iran and, no matter what his deep religious convictions might be—and I don't doubt their sincerity—that he permit the government that has now been established by the legal authorities in Iran, and under the Constitution, to have a chance to succeed. We do know that the Iranian military and many of the religious and political opponents to the Shah have given their pledge of support to the Bahktiar government. And that's our hope.

And I would like to add one other thing. We have no intention, neither ability nor desire, to interfere in the internal affairs of Iran, and we certainly have no intention of permitting other nations to interfere in the internal affairs of Iran.

Q. If we had had better intelligence in Iran, is there anything that we could have done to save the Shah? And there's a second part to that question. You just referred to Iran as allies. Would you authorize new weapons shipments to the Bahktiar regime?

THE PRESIDENT. Even if we had been able to anticipate events that were going to take place in Iran or other countries, obviously, our ability to determine those events is very limited. The Shah, his advisers, great military capabilities, police, and others couldn't completely prevent rioting and disturbances in Iran. Certainly, we have no desire nor ability to intrude massive forces into Iran or any other country to determine the outcome of domestic political issues. This is something that we have no intention of ever doing in another country. We've tried this once in Vietnam. It didn't work well, as you well know.

We have some existing contracts for delivery of weapons to Iran, since sometimes the deliveries take as long as 5 years after the orders are placed. Our foreign military sales policy is now being continued. We have no way to know what the attitude of the Bahktiar government is. We've not discussed this with them.

After the Iranian Government is stable, after it assuages the present disturbances in Iran, then I'm sure they'll let us know how they want to carry out future military needs of their own country. It is important to Iran, for their own security and for the independence of the people of Iran, that a strong and stable military be maintained. And I believe that all the leaders of Iran whom I have heard discuss this matter agree with the statement that I've just made.

Q. Still on Iran, Mr. Carter, there is a suggestion that if Iranian oil supplies do not begin flowing again, perhaps within 2 months, there may be a shortage and perhaps a price increase for us. Does our intelligence indicate that might happen, or is there such a prospect as you see it?

THE PRESIDENT. We derive about 5 percent of our oil supplies from Iran in recent months—much less than many other countries, as you know, who are more heavily dependent on Iranian oil. I think an extended interruption of Iranian oil shipments would certainly create increasingly severe shortages on the international market.

So far, other oil-producing nations have moved to replace the lost Iranian oil supplies. If this should continue, it would just reemphasize the basic commitment that our Nation has tried to carry out in the last 2 years, that is, to have a predictable energy policy, to reduce consumption of energy in toto, certainly, to reduce dependence on foreign oil, and to eliminate waste of oil.

I don't think there's any doubt that we can cut back consumption of oil by 5 percent without seriously damaging our own economy. And I would hope that all Americans who listen to my voice now would do everything possible within their own capabilities to cut down on the use of oil and the waste of all energy supplies.

I think that this restoration of Iranian oil shipments is a desire by all the religious and political leaders in Iran who have an influence over the future. We have seen since the OPEC price increases, even before the Iranian supplies were interrupted, some shortage of spot shipments of oil.

The present price of oil, even with increased production from other suppliers, is now slightly above the established OPEC price. But our hope is that oil prices will go down, at least to some degree, as Iranian supplies are reintroduced.

NATIONAL ADVISORY COMMITTEE FOR WOMEN

Q. Mr. President, as I think everyone knows, you've had some problems with your women's advisory committee recently. I'm wondering how you can get a new and effective committee in view of the fact that you seem to feel that if they issue public criticism of you, you don't want them on the committee.

THE PRESIDENT. I have no aversion to public criticism. Someone who runs for President and who serves in this office for 2 years becomes acclimated to that environment as a matter of course. And I think there's hardly an interest group in our Nation who doesn't at one time or another severely and publicly criticize the President and the administration. That's not part of it at all.

There were and are about 40 women whom I personally approved to serve on the advisory committee. Their function is to work with me, hopefully in harmony, to achieve mutual goals, goals of enhanced opportunities for women, for the elimination of any discrimination against women, to assure that every decision made by the Government, in the executive branch or Congress, has at least as one factor to be considered how we can best meet the needs of women, and to overcome the suffering that they have experienced because of past legal and other discriminatory actions.

This is a good function for the Committee, and it's a need that I have to continue. I have no quarrel with, no problems with the Committee itself. I did select and appoint Ms. Abzug to serve as the Chairperson of the Committee last year, and it didn't work out well.

The Committee has never been well organized. Their functions have never been clearly expressed to me. There has not been good cooperation between the Committee and the Cabinet members or my advisers or me, and I felt it was necessary to change the Chairperson, whom I had appointed personally.

It's a prerogative of the President. And we'll do everything we can now under a fine, new Chairperson of the Committee to restore its effectiveness and to make sure that I and the women throughout the country, and particularly in this group, work to achieve those mutual goals which we share.

PEOPLE'S REPUBLIC OF CHINA AND TAIWAN

Q. Mr. President, on your negotiations with China over normalization of diplomatic relations, did you at any point ask the Chinese to provide a binding, written pledge that they would not try to seize Taiwan by force? And if you did request that, why didn't you get it? And if you didn't, why didn't you ask for it? [*Laughter*]

THE PRESIDENT. Yes. One of our goals in the negotiation was to get a public commitment on the part of China that the differences with Taiwan would be resolved peacefully. This was not possible to achieve. The final outcome of that was that we would make a unilateral statement that we expect any differences between Taiwan and China to be resolved peacefully, and the agreement was that the leaders in China would not contradict that statement.

Since the announcement of normalization, Vice Premier Deng Xiaoping and others have made public comments that substantiate the statement that I have made. It's a matter internally for the Chinese to resolve, but I think Mr. Deng has made several statements saying that it ought to be resolved peacefully.

We were also insistent upon the fact that the treaty between us and Taiwan would not be peremptorily or immediately canceled or abrogated. The treaty will be terminated in accordance with its own provisions, with a 1-year's notice to Taiwan. The Chinese did not agree with this originally, but they finally accepted that fact.

Another insistence that we had, which was finally agreed to, was that we would

go ahead with normal trade, cultural relationships with Taiwan and also that existing treaties other than the defense treaty would continue in effect.

One point on which we did not agree with the Chinese was that we will, after this year, continue to sell defensive weapons to Taiwan to provide for their security needs. The Chinese leaders do not agree with this policy, but they understand that it is our policy and, knowing that, they went ahead with normalization.

So, there were some differences between us, but I think this is one of the major achievements for peace in the world and, particularly, to cement our relationship with the nations in the Western Pacific. And I think we had a very good outcome for the long negotiations.

THAILAND

Q. Mr. President, next month you are going to meet, supposedly, with the Prime Minister of Thailand, who is the head of a nation that is now threatened by the Vietnamese. I need to know two things, if you could. One, what is the U.S. prepared to offer Thailand to ease their concerns about the Vietnamese? Will it be money, economic aid, military weapons, or American-piloted aircraft? Number two, have you personally been in touch with the leaders of China and the Soviet Union to see what they plan to do to help ease the situation?

THE PRESIDENT. We are very interested in seeing the integrity of Thailand protected, the borders not endangered or even threatened by the insurgent troops from Vietnam in Cambodia. We have joined in with almost all other nations of the world in the United Nations in condemning the intrusion into Cambodia by Vietnamese forces. This obviously involves the adjacent country of Thailand.

Mr. Kriangsak will be coming here to visit with me, and during that time, we will reassure him that our interests are in a stable and secure and peaceful Thailand. We have continuing trade relationships with Thailand. We provide them with some military arms for defensive purposes, as have been negotiated for a long period of time.

We don't detect any immediate threat to the borders of Thailand. In some instances, the invading forces into Cambodia have deliberately stayed away from the border itself. And, of course, the Chinese give Thailand very strong support. The Soviet Union has expressed their support for Vietnam, as you know. And in our efforts, along with others in the United Nations, we have warned both the Vietnamese, and also the Soviets, who supply them and who support them, against any danger that they might exhibit toward Thailand.

FORMER PRESIDENT RICHARD NIXON

Q. You have invited former President Richard Nixon to the White House for the dinner for Chinese leader Deng Xiaoping. During your campaign, you said Mr. Nixon had disgraced this country, and about a year ago, you said that you thought he had indeed committed impeachable offenses. Why are you honoring him in this way now?

THE PRESIDENT. Well, as you know, the consequences of the Watergate actions by President Nixon have already been determined by the Congress and by the actions of Mr. Nixon himself, having been pardoned by President Ford.

In preparing for the upcoming visit by Vice Premier Deng Xiaoping, I felt that it was a fair thing and a proper thing to invite both President Nixon and President Ford to the White House for the banquet at which Mr. Deng will be honored. As you know, as President, one of the major

achievements of President Nixon was to open up an avenue of communications and consultation and negotiation with the Chinese, which resulted ultimately in normal relationships.

I think it's entirely proper that he be there. In addition to that, the Chinese officials, including Vice Premier Deng himself, had asked for an opportunity to meet with President Nixon and to express their thanks personally to him for the role he played in opening up Chinese-United States relationships.

So, I have no apology to make. I think it was a proper thing to do, and I'm very pleased that President Nixon has accepted our invitation.

FISCAL YEAR 1980 BUDGET

Q. Mr. President, in your opening statement you mentioned that you had succeeded in your goal of holding the budget deficit to $30 billion. Some critics of your budget policy say that goal was set rather arbitrarily early in the budget process and that, in fact, if the deficit had been a little higher, say $35 billion, that a lot of the current cutbacks could have been avoided and with only a marginal impact on the war on inflation, maybe, perhaps two-tenths of 1 percent.

How was that figure set? And why did you not choose to make such a decision, knowing that there would be a great deal of opposition to the budget cuts among many constituencies on which you will have to depend next year in the election?

THE PRESIDENT. That commitment that I made, I think in October, to hold the budget deficit down to $30 billion or less was very carefully considered and, as a matter of fact, was hotly debated among us when I was getting ready to present to the American people a program for controlling inflation. The basic argument was roughly between $32 billion as a goal for the deficit versus $30 billion, and I finally decided to choose the most stringent figure.

We will, by the way, exceed that goal by about $1 billion. This budget, when it's examined in its entirety over this coming weekend, for revelation on Monday, the 22d, I think will be seen by any fair person as meeting the legitimate needs of those who are most dependent on government, on meeting the defense needs of our country, on being well-balanced, on being fair, and contributing greatly to controlling inflation.

I think it's important that the Government set an example. We can't ask business, labor, and private Americans to make any sort of sacrifice in• controlling inflation if the Federal Government doesn't set an example. And if I have to err on one side or the other, I would be more likely to set a stringent example than I would to have the allegation made that we were not sincere about controlling inflation.

I might add one other thing. There's an erroneous premise that exists in this country that to control inflation hurts poor people. The ones who suffer most in our Nation from rampant inflation are those who have fixed incomes that can't be changed, those who are unemployed, those who are poor, or those who can't move from one job to another, looking for a better life as circumstances change. So, I think to control inflation is the best thing that I can do for those with relatively low incomes and who are most dependent on government.

So, a combination of those two, controlling inflation and having a fair budget, is a very good goal, and I'm just glad that we were able to make it.

CIGARETTE SMOKING AND TOBACCO PRICE SUPPORTS

Q. Mr. President, in a speech last August 5, in Wilson, North Carolina, you spoke of making the smoking of tobacco even more safe than it now is. This past week the Surgeon General's department came out with a report saying that smoking of tobacco is not safe at all and, in fact, is positively hazardous to health. Will you continue to support Federal price supports for tobacco, and why?

THE PRESIDENT. Yes, I intend to continue to support those Federal price supports.

I think it's a completely legitimate action for the Government to point out the dangers of smoking, and I don't have any way to dispute the arguments, one side or the other, derived from scientific examinations, experiments, and from medical analyses. I think it's important that people know the dangers of smoking. Because of these revelations in the past with the first Surgeon General's report and, hopefully, to be escalated with the recent revelations of dangers of smoking, those who do smoke cigarettes now have safer cigarettes to smoke with less nicotine and less tar. And I think the progress that has been made has been derived primarily from that purpose. There's been some slight reduction in the cigarette consumption per capita in our country.

So, I do intend to continue the program for stabilizing tobacco prices for the farmers who depend upon that for an income. But, at the same time, I have no criticism—in fact, I support the role of the health authorities in our Nation who point out the dangers of smoking.

DOMESTIC OIL PRICES

Q. Mr. President, given your concern over inflation, which you've reemphasized today, it is still your intention this year to propose some variation of the well-head tax or take some other action that would have the effect of raising domestic oil prices?

THE PRESIDENT. Ultimately, domestic oil prices will have to be raised substantially. As you know, the law changes twice, as fixed now: once in May of this year and, again, I believe, in October of 1981, when all controls go off of oil prices. Exactly what schedule that decontrol might take and what compensatory tax assessments might be passed by the Congress—those decisions have not yet been made. And I'm not prepared yet to announce decisions that haven't been made. But we'll be consulting with Congress and trying to assess how we can balance the inevitable increase in oil prices to constrain consumption and, at the same time, to have a minimal adverse impact on inflation.

It's a difficult decision. Those two decisions work against one another. But I'll have to make them eventually, and I will announce them later on when I decide.

INTELLIGENCE SOURCES IN IRAN

Q. Mr. President, do you see any danger of our losing our intelligence listening posts in Iran? And if we do lose those posts, will we have enough backup capability so that you can assure Congress that we can verify a new SALT agreement if you get one?

THE PRESIDENT. There is obviously, in any country where we have intelligence sources, a danger for those sources to be modified or lost. We had this occur, as you know, a few years ago in Turkey, when we had an embargo against the sale of military weapons to Turkey. And this has happened from time to time in an evolutionary way.

We have constantly been able and determined to provide increasing capability for surveillance which would allow us to compensate for those changes that are inevitable in any changing society.

So, I can assure the public and the Congress that no matter what happens to the specific intelligence sources in Iran, we can adequately compensate for their change and provide adequate verification for the compliance by the Soviet Union with SALT agreements.

STRATEGIC ARMS LIMITATION

Q. There seem to be a lot of people who think that the Soviets now are gaining a military edge over us.

THE PRESIDENT. Yes.

Q. Now, isn't this perception basic to the problem of getting a SALT treaty ratified?

THE PRESIDENT. I don't think the perception is accurate. I think that militarily, we are certainly equal to or superior to the Soviet Union in our own capability. Certainly, in addition to that, we have harmony with our neighbors, which the Soviet Union lacks. And our allies are free and independent and tied to us philosophically with a deep commitment, as is the case with NATO and other alliances. The Soviets can't match that dependability and independence among their allies.

Economically, politically, I think our systems are superior to the Soviet Union. There is no doubt, however, that the approval of the SALT treaty by the American people and by the Congress will certainly be influenced by perceptions that we are indeed now and we will indeed in the future be secure and that our military strength and capability in its totality will be adequate to meet any Soviet threat. And there is no doubt that we will be able to meet any such threat now or in the future.

SOVIET REACTION TO U.S.-CHINESE RELATIONS

Q. Mr. President, following up again on China, shortly after your announcement last month, you said in a television interview that President Brezhnev's response in a private message to you had been positive.

THE PRESIDENT. Yes.

Q. TASS then took issue with you, and this week in an interview published in Time, Mr. Brezhnev said that it was like playing with fire to encourage China's militancy. In view of these statements, do you still feel that the Kremlin is positive about your China policy?

THE PRESIDENT. I have reread the original dispatch that I got from President Brezhnev, and I've also read the TASS statements, and happen to have read last night the interview with President Brezhnev in Time. I think my interpretation of Brezhnev's original statement was accurate. He did point out the fact that they had relationships with China that could be contributory to peace. He expressed in his original statement a desire or an intention to monitor future relationships between ourselves and China and expressed some concern about a possibility of our using this new relationship against the Soviet Union.

This is not our intention. We never intend to use our improved relationships with China against the Soviet Union or the relationships with the Soviet Union, which I hope to improve, as a factor to endanger or to threaten China. So, that was a proviso put in his first dispatch.

But I think, still, in balance, it was constructive. It was certainly constructive and positive, compared to the anticipation that I had from the Soviet Union.

PROPOSED CONSTITUTIONAL CONVENTION

Q. Mr. President, Governor Brown of California has called for a constitutional amendment requiring the Federal Government to balance the budget. If Congress rejects the amendment, he says the States should initiate a constitutional convention to get it started. How do you feel, sir, about the wisdom or feasibility of this proposal?

THE PRESIDENT. Well, one of my political philosophies and economic philosophies and one of the commitments of my own administration all have been to reduce the Federal deficit and to work toward a balanced budget.

I think it would be extremely dangerous for a constitutional convention to be assembled for this purpose. Many legal scholars and others believe that such a convention would be completely uncontrollable, that the Constitution could be amended en masse, with multitudes of amendments originating therefrom. It would be a radical departure from the policy of amendment of our Constitution that we've experienced for the last 200 years. And I think an amendment to our Constitution ought to be a very cautious, careful thing.

I personally prefer that amendments be carried out to the Constitution—originating in the Congress, and then ratified by the States—as we have used so well as a policy for the last 200 years.

It would be also a serious matter, a difficult matter, to devise a constitutional amendment prohibiting any deficit spending without adding provisos that would let us deal with unanticipated military or security needs and unanticipated needs when we have a deep depression for keeping our people at work and providing for large numbers of those who might be poor or hungry or needing services.

So, I think this is something that ought to be approached very gingerly, very carefully. And if there is any constitutional amendment, it ought to be done in accordance with practices that we've used in the past.

The final thing I'd like to reemphasize is that I intend to continue to work for a balanced budget, and I believe that this is the best approach to it.

MEXICAN OIL AND NATURAL GAS

Q. Mr. President, with Iran off-line now on oil production, and your worrying about spot shortages, there are a lot of scientists who see Saudi Arabia down there, and Mexico. Yet we seem to be turning our back on natural gas production in Mexico; some question about whether they want to have substantial gas in the American market. How do you reconcile that?

THE PRESIDENT. We are very interested in Mexican oil and natural gas to be purchased by our own Nation. The decisions, however, on how rapidly to produce and to market their oil and natural gas is a decision to be made by Mexico. They are understandably very independent in this respect, and we would not try to encroach on their independence nor try to encourage them to more rapidly produce gas and oil than they themselves desire.

We have immediate needs and also long-range needs, sometimes not quite the same. In the immediate future, the next few months, there is no urgency about acquiring Mexican natural gas. We have at this moment a surplus of natural gas in our own country, and the statements made by the Secretary of Energy were related to that fact.

He has encouraged large users of oil and gas to use gas instead of oil, but, for

instance, new powerplants to be built in the future have to be designed to use coal. And we also have the problem of using efficiently gas produced in the 48 States of our country and, in the future, how to bring the natural gas that is available from Alaska down through Canada to our Nation. It's a very complicated thing. And when I go to Mexico next February, this will obviously be one of the matters that I will discuss.

But I'm not going down there to negotiate the price of natural gas. We'll be talking, myself and President López Portillo, more on long-range strategic approaches on how we might best provide a good market for Mexican oil and gas that they want to sell to us.

MR. CORMIER. Thank you, Mr. President.

THE PRESIDENT. Thank you very much.

NOTE: President Carter's forty-second news conference began at 4 p.m. in Room 450 of the Old Executive Office Building. It was broadcast live on radio and television.

National Prayer Breakfast

Remarks at the Annual Breakfast.
January 18, 1979

Fairly early in my naval career, we moved from Hawaii back to this country, about the time of the advent of television. We had doubts about its value, because the reports said that it was going to destroy the moral fabric of our Nation.

But one of the delights of my life, one of the greatest contributions of this technological miracle was the presentation by Bishop Fulton Sheen, on his regularly scheduled program, of the religious interrelationships in his own life and how they related to a modern world.

And I'm deeply grateful to him for being willing to come this morning to share with us the dynamism and the strength and the sensitivity and commitment of his own life again with us.

Thank you very much, Bishop Sheen. It even boosts my spirits when he refers to me as a "fellow sinner." [*Laughter*]

I listened with great care to him this morning as he talked about the liberty, the love, the duties, responsibilities, the constraints that bind us, as believers in God, and that offer us a guide to the future.

Last year was a year of turmoil. I noticed one public opinion poll that asked news reporters and American citizens what were the three most interesting news events of the year. All three had some religious connotation. One was a story of great tragedy—almost disgrace for the world of believers—where hundreds of people, simple people, searching for an elusive element of truth at Jonestown, perished because of misguided leadership. That was the top story of the year.

Another story in this last year demonstrated a great change in leadership, as a Cardinal from Poland, outside Rome, behind the Iron Curtain, became the leader of a great Christian faith.

And the third most important story to the people of our country was the Camp David discussions between myself, President Sadat, and Prime Minister Begin. We stayed there 13 days. And the first day we agreed, almost as an outpouring of mutual commitment and concern, that we would pray within Camp David and that we would call on the entire world to join us in a common prayer for peace. And we called upon the very same congressional and other leaders who put this breakfast together to coordinate that effort.

For several days, that was the only thing on which we did agree. [*Laughter*] And we made great progress because of

those prayers. But peace is still elusive, and I hope that out of this breakfast can come a reconfirmation that all of you will continue to use your influence to revitalize that prayer for peace in the Middle East and throughout the world.

I would guess that one of the great news stories of 1979 will be the impact around the Persian Gulf, in the Middle East, of religious fervor and the searching for some compatibility between a modern, rapidly changing, technological world on the one hand, and an inclination on the part of devout religious leaders to cling to stability and security predicated on past social and personal habits.

So, as you can well see, in various ways, even in a modern world when we consider it to be highly secular, the great events that move the people here and in other nations are intimately related to religion.

Our Nation requires by law that the church and the state must be separated. The church cannot dominate our government. Our government cannot dominate nor influence religion. But there is no way for a human being to separate in one's own heart and mind those inevitable correlations—responsibilities of a secular life, even in government, on the one hand, responsibilities to God on the other. They combine to form what a person is, what a person thinks, what a person hopes to be. And in international events, no matter how we try to order or separate religious trends, changes, hungers, thirsts, there is no way to sever that from public events.

In Africa, South America, Indonesia, many other nations where a crisis has not reached the tornado stage, those undercurrents of religious people searching for compatibility with the modern world, a changing world, are intense and of profound significance to everyone in this room.

Our own Nation is not impervious to this circumstance. We have suffered severely in the past because we who are Christians, others who are deeply religious in our own Nation have not been willing to accommodate those who have been deprived, who have and do suffer as they struggle for a better life.

We tend to say, "This could only happen in the past. Today, certainly, it's not a factor in our lives." I grew up in a region of the country which has in the past, and still sees quite often—too often—the Christian churches as the last bastion for racial segregation and even discrimination.

This past Sunday I went down to Ebenezer Baptist Church in Atlanta and participated in a program commemorating the 50th birthday of Martin Luther King, Jr. Speakers there—Dr. Benjamin Mays, Daddy King, others—pointed out the progress that has been made, but the emphasis was on the progress yet to be made.

One of the elements that I noticed was the absolute truth that tends to come forward much more vividly in a quiet prayer.

I was honored at that meeting, but when Dr. Benjamin Mays got up to give his prayer, I sat back with the anticipation that somehow in his prayer he would compliment me and help my image with the audience there, the congregation. And as we bowed in prayer, he talked about all the troubles in our country, the poor, deprived, discrimination. And the culmination of his prayer was that at least our President has done a little something about some of these problems. [*Laughter*] And he thanked God for that little something. [*Laughter*]

Truth is a mandatory element of a sound basis for a religious life. But sometimes we cannot accept the truth.

I was intrigued by Bishop Sheen's reference to the "immaculate conception" complex of Americans. It is difficult for us as Americans to think that we might be sinful, that we might be in some ways inferior, that we might have some elements of our life not yet realized, that we might have standards that have been prescribed for us which we have not met. And there's a natural, human inclination to lower those standards to accommodate the very low achievements of our own life.

We must guard against the abuse of our own religious faith. We have seen broad changes in history. In the first few centuries after Christ's life and death on this Earth, it was a crime to be a Christian. I've been reading Barbara Tuchman's delightful history of the 14th century era. And during those days, it was a crime not to be a Christian. And the horrors of the Inquisition, the equation of a Christian commitment with a willingness to be a constant, dedicated warrior, a complete dependence on combat and bloodshed, and the abuses within the Christian Church are vividly expressed. And I'm sure at that time, there was a rationalization among devout religious believers that what we look on now with abhorrence, and sometimes so remotely with amusement, was the true teaching of Christ. And we must avoid a distortion or a rationalization because of materialistic inclinations in our own hearts, of our own religious faith and its beliefs. When any religion impacts adversely on those whom Christ described as "the least of these," it can have no firm foundation in God's sight.

The last point I want to make is the dramatic sense of how our religion pertains to a modern era. Shortly before Christmas, we had Alec McCowen, a great British actor, come to the White House. And he stood there on a bare stage, and he quoted from memory the book of Mark, I think about 16,000 verses, 2½ hours. He didn't use a modern translation; he used the King James version. And there was a sense among those two or three hundred people that here came someone directly from the presence of Christ and told, almost like a newspaper, in the most vivid, moving terms, about the life of the Son of God.

There was nothing stale about it. There was nothing ancient about it. There was nothing removed about it from the existence of those assembled in that room. If you get a chance, I hope you will hear him give that recitation.

Almost everyone in this room is a leader. People have exhibited faith and trust in us not only to carry out the mundane duties of a sometimes confused government responsibility but also to carry out the responsibilities much broader than that, to set an example, to search more fervently for the truth.

Sometimes we lose our confidence. One of the great problems with the modern church is its timidity about self-assertion. We're sometimes fearful not to project ourselves as believers in God into a controversial issue, because we are fearful we might fail, we might be rebuffed. So, it's much more easy for us in the confines of our church or our synagogue to sit back and say, "I'll enjoy those around me whom I know, who trust me, with whom I share limitations and ignore limitations," than it is to project a deep belief in love, compassion, understanding, service, humility, into our broad influence among others.

It's difficult to be bold and gentle at the same time. Peace and gentleness and humility are perhaps the most difficult characteristics of a human being.

In Paul's second letter to the Corinthians, he said, "Since we have hope, we are very bold." And I hope that we believers in God have not lost our hope and will continue to be bold. And later on in the same chapter of Second Corinthians, he says, "Where the spirit of the Lord is, there is freedom." Where the spirit of the Lord is, there is freedom.

There's no incompatibility between gentleness and boldness. There's no incapatibility between the constraints and the shackles on our lives by standards prescribed by God on the one hand, and the ultimate freedom that can come when the spirit of the Lord is present.

NOTE: The President spoke at 8:52 a.m. in the International Ballroom at the Washington Hilton Hotel. The breakfast is sponsored by the United States Senate and House prayer breakfast groups.

Department of Housing and Urban Development

Nomination of Sterling Tucker To Be an Assistant Secretary.   January 18, 1979

The President today announced that he has nominated Sterling Tucker to be Assistant Secretary of Housing and Urban Development for Fair Housing and Equal Opportunity. He would replace Chester C. McGuire, Jr., who has resigned.

Tucker was born December 21, 1923, in Akron, Ohio. He received a B.A. and an M.A. in social psychology from the University of Akron.

Tucker served as assistant executive director of the Akron Urban League and as executive director of the Canton (Ohio) Urban League. In 1956 he became executive director of the Washington Urban League, a position he held until 1974. During that time he also held various positions with the National Urban

League and served as special assistant to the late Whitney Young, Jr.

In 1975 he became the first elected chairman of the Council of the District of Columbia.

Tucker has been active in both local and national affairs in Washington, serving as a consultant to the "War on Poverty" program, the Peace Corps, and President Kennedy's Committee on Juvenile Delinquency and Youth Crime. He is the author of several books and has held a number of teaching and consulting assignments.

United States Participation in the United Nations

Message to the Congress Transmitting a Report. January 18, 1979

To the Congress of the United States:

I am pleased to send Congress this report of United States Government activities in the United Nations and its affiliated agencies during calendar year 1977.

This 32nd annual report strengthens my conviction that the United Nations is of great and growing importance to the conduct of U.S. foreign relations. We cannot effectively advance world peace and our other national interests if we ignore the potential of this global organization.

Ambassador Andrew Young called the 1977 General Assembly the "most constructive session in many years." It was largely free of the wasteful tactics of confrontation that had marred other recent sessions.

The other organs of the United Nations and the various specialized agencies also made progress on many of the difficult issues that humanity faces.

I am proud of the role we played in encouraging this constructive atmosphere.

We are committed to resolving problems through reason and discussion, not confrontation.

Our national interests are best served by such cooperation, and by listening with respect to the problems of all nations, large and small. Our delegations paid particular attention to the views of those developing nations which make up two-thirds of the UN's membership and worked with them to identify points of common concern.

The interests of America and of many other UN members coincided in the search for peace in the Middle East and southern Africa, the promotion of human rights, the Panama Canal Treaties, and economic development to help meet the basic human needs of more than a billion of the world's people.

One of my first acts as President was to invite UN Secretary General Kurt Waldheim to the White House, and I have discussed international issues with him on a number of occasions since then. During 1977, I was also privileged to speak at the United Nations twice— once during March, and again at the opening of the 32nd General Assembly in September. Also while in New York, I took the occasion to sign the two United Nations human rights covenants which for many years had lacked U.S. signature.

Secretary of State Cyrus Vance has taken extraordinary pains—including direct participation in Security Council and General Assembly meetings—to make the United Nations an increasingly vital factor in the conduct of this country's foreign relations. And Ambassador Young has worked with great skill and unusual effectiveness in improving our relationship with the UN and its member states.

Events in the United Nations system

will not always go the way that this country might desire. The changing makeup of these organizations, the increasing diffusion of global power and the growing complexities of all issues make this inevitable. But those occasions should not make us withdraw our support, for the UN reflects the reality of the world in which we must live. We should, instead, feel challenged to develop imaginative and thoughtful new approaches in our diplomacy so as to advance our interests, and to play a constructive role in the world community. In particular, we need to continue demonstrating our faith in the basic purposes of an organization whose strength and effectiveness are essential to us and to the world.

The attached report details U.S. positions and policies on the issues which arose in the UN system during 1977. It includes:

—The extensive conduct of the so-called "North-South" dialogue—the discussion of economic and other issues between industrialized countries and the developing nations;

—Our support for the social and economic development activities—including those of the UN Development Program. Some 90 percent of the funds expended by the UN system benefit these activities;

—U.S. efforts to support new progress on human rights throughout the UN system;

—preparations for the 1978 special General Assembly session devoted to disarmament;

—the adoption by consensus of a General Assembly resolution on aircraft hijacking, to make the world's airways safer for people everywhere;

—the beginning of extensive efforts against great odds to pursue peaceful settlements in Namibia and Rhodesia; and

—U.S. ratification and support of a new UN specialized agency—the International Fund for Agricultural Development—which will provide new resources to improve food production and nutrition in low-income countries and can benefit us by stabilizing the global food market.

Also included in this document is an analysis of the U.S. decision to withdraw from the International Labor Organization in November 1977. I took this decision with regret, since U.S. interests in international organizations are better met through membership and active participation than through withdrawal. Nevertheless, since announcement in 1975 of U.S. intention to withdraw, we believed that insufficient progress had been made in resolving a number of difficulties in operation of the ILO. I still hope that the United States can return to the ILO when its operations clearly return to the organization's basic purposes.

Finally, among the activities of 1977—but not included in this report—was steady work within the Administration on ways that the United States can work to strengthen the United Nations. My report on that topic, sent to the Congress on March 2, 1978, outlines reforms which can make the United Nations even more effective as the world's major forum for discussion and action on global issues.

I welcome the continuing interest of the Congress in U.S. participation in the United Nations, and I urge its increased moral backing and financial support as the United States addresses in the United Nations the increasingly difficult issues that lie ahead.

JIMMY CARTER

The White House,
January 18, 1979.

NOTE: The 335-page report is entitled "U.S. Participation in the UN—Report by the President to the Congress for the Year 1977."

United States Sinai Support Mission

Message to the Congress Transmitting a Report. January 18, 1979

To the Congress of the United States:

I am pleased to transmit, as requested by section 4 of Public Law 94–110 of October 13, 1975, the Sixth Report of the United States Sinai Support Mission, describing operations of the U.S. early warning system in the Sinai Desert. The Mission's activities are an important part of the disengagement arrangements between Egypt and Israel concluded in September 1975.

The cost of operating the Sinai Support Mission during Fiscal Year 1978 was $11.7 million, about a half million dollars less than the amount appropriated. The estimated budget for Fiscal Year 1979 remains at $11.7 million.

At the request of the Subcommittee on Europe and the Middle East of the Committee on International Relations, House of Representatives, this report includes a brief review of the applicability of the United States early warning system concept to other areas of the Middle East. It concludes that the basic approach to early warning employed in the Sinai could be successful elsewhere, provided the parties directly concerned want and are willing to support it.

Talks now under way in Washington between Egypt and Israel are likely to result in substantial changes in the United States' role in the Sinai. I will consult closely with the Congress as these and subsequent talks proceed, in order to insure that the peacekeeping efforts of the United States continue to advance the goal of permanent peace in the Middle East.

JIMMY CARTER

The White House,
    January 18, 1979.

NOTE: The report is entitled "Report to the Congress, SSM, United States Sinai Support Mission" (28 pages plus annexes).

Federal Civilian and Military Pay Increases

Message to the Congress. January 18, 1979

To the Congress of the United States:

In accordance with the provisions of section 5305 of title 5 of the United States Code, I hereby report on the pay adjustment I am ordering for the Federal statutory pay systems in October 1978.

The Secretary of Labor, the Director of the Office of Management and Budget and the Chairman of the Civil Service Commission, who serve jointly as my agent for Federal pay, found that an increase averaging 8.4 percent would be appropriate if comparability with private enterprise salary rates for the same levels of work were to be achieved. The Advisory Committee on Federal Pay recommended that the findings of my agent be implemented.

After considering the findings of my agent and the recommendation of the Advisory Committee on Federal Pay, I determined that an across-the-board increase of 5.5 percent was dictated by economic conditions affecting the general welfare and transmitted to the Congress the alternative plan to that effect called for by section 5305(c) of title 5 of the

United States Code. On October 7, 1978 I signed the Executive order to implement this increase.

I am transmitting herewith copies of the reports of my Pay Agent and the Advisory Committee on Federal Pay, the alternative plan, and the Executive order I promulgated to put this pay adjustment into effect.

JIMMY CARTER

The White House,
     January 18, 1979.

National Health Plan Legislation

White House Statement.   January 18, 1979

The President was briefed today by Secretary Califano on proposals for national health plan legislation to be submitted to the Congress this year, including a number of options for phasing in a national health plan. The President made no decision among the options.

He instructed Secretary Califano immediately to undertake broad consultations with the Congress, with Governors, and with outside groups which have evidenced interest in a national health plan, including the AFL–CIO and the UAW, as well as health-related organizations.

He asked the Secretary to expedite these consultations and to report back to him as soon as possible, hopefully within 4 weeks.

The President will ultimately determine what legislation to submit to the Congress based upon these consultations and upon further internal analysis of the options presented to him.

Present at the meeting were the President, the Vice President, Secretary Califano, Chairman of the Council of Eco-

nomic Advisers Charles Schultze, OMB Director Jim McIntyre, Assistant to the President for Domestic Affairs and Policy Stu Eizenstat, and other staff aides.

The meeting in the Cabinet Room lasted from 2 p.m. until approximately 4 p.m.

White House Conference on Balanced National Growth and Economic Development

Remarks at a White House Ceremony.
January 19, 1979

THE PRESIDENT. Both I and the Nation are very grateful at the results of the White House Conference on Balanced Growth that was held last year. More than a thousand people actually came to Washington to participate in this Conference, representing many other thousands of Americans who are deeply interested in resolving the apparent present and inevitable future conflicts as we see the progress of our Nation economically progress.

Typical of the leaders who came and representative of them are Governor Jay Rockefeller, who was the Chairman, representing State and local officials; Senator Jennings Randolph, representing the Congress; and Secretary Kreps, representing the executive branch of Government.

Today, I'll be sending to the Congress recommendations and also an analysis of the findings of this group. I think they've been very constructive. I and my entire staff and Cabinet have studied with great attention and appreciation the results of the Conference and their recommendations to us.

The recommendations are broad-based. They encompass many elements of decisionmaking which have been made much easier because of their fine work. And I think the messages that I will send, although brief, are certainly worthy of the examination of all those interested in the future of our country.

One of the most important decisions that everyone reached was the necessity for government to do everything it can to strengthen the American private economy and to minimize any adverse effect of government action or regulation which might work counter to a strong free enterprise system.

We have studied with care the need for the continuation of the regional commissions and decided that they are needed. We've analyzed many major programs that the Congress has been considering the first 2 years of my own administration, like energy impact, and made recommendations accordingly.

We are determined to improve the quality of life in our Nation. Foreign exports have not been adequately encouraged in our country. There's not a sense within the business community or the general populace, my administration, or the Congress, even, of the importance of enhanced and increasing exports of American goods.

I think we have made substantial progress in agricultural products. But I asked the chairman of the National Governors' Association, this past year, to consider forming a special committee comprised of Governors, who would work closely with me, with the Secretary of Commerce, with the State Department, and others, to concentrate on improving trade with foreign nations. And this committee has now been established. It's already being briefed and instructed, and I'm sure it will be a new addition to the

American political scene which will be very valuable.

Governor George Busbee has been appointed by the Chairman to head up this committee. We've asked the Governors and mayors and county officials particularly to concentrate on energy conservation and development of our own energy resources, to build up the economic base of individual communities, and also to assure that transportation facilities are adequate, both now and in the future.

We trust that the regional commissions will continue to encourage better coordination of efforts among States who occupy a particular region of our country. Obviously, there will be some competition among States—that's inevitable—for new industry, for jobs, for export opportunities. But the benefits to be derived jointly among States by cooperation and consultation and common planning are substantial.

I think the recommendations of this White House Conference were potentially very divisive, but because of their sound and constructive approach and the close consultation that was held not only in Washington but prior to the conference itself, throughout the country, the recommendations are very sound. They are substantive and aggressive and innovative and helpful. But they're not radical enough to cause a complete aversion among Americans to their recommendations.

The final thing I'd like to say is that we have substantially enhanced the degree of strength of the system of federalism in our country. The mayors and Governors are now playing a much stronger role in their interrelationship with the Federal Government in all its aspects. This has not always been the case in the recent past. But as we evolve programs now that affect the growth of our country, balanced growth, even in the formative stages of legislative proposals, mayors, county officials, Governors are intimately involved.

I think there's a remarkable degree of harmony, which I value very highly. They recognize that there is a difficulty between environmental quality and sustained growth. They recognize that there is a potential conflict between rapidly improving employment opportunities and the control of inflation. And my ability to counsel with these wise and experienced leaders, who are close to the people who receive government services, is certainly very valuable.

Under Jack Watson's leadership here in the White House, the Interagency Coordinating Council will help to bring increasing order out of the chaos that did exist in harmonizing the efforts and the regulations and policies of different Federal agencies who deal with a single subject. And now there's a renewed commitment that these confusing statements, policies, regulations, administrative attitudes will be resolved. And this is an avenue, too, for Governors and others at the local level to feed back into the system, to say, "This program is working well, but it can work better if we make a certain change."

So, I want to express my deep thanks to all those who are assembled here from the Congress, from State and local governments, and from my own administration, for the fine work that they have done. They've brought in a wide range of interested groups of a nongovernmental nature—business, labor, education, and others—and I think this is a wonderful product of a very fine and dedicated effort among these responsible and competent and unselfish individuals who have contributed so much.

And now I'd like to sign my messages to the Congress outlining the recommendations of the White House Conference on Balanced Growth and also recommendations to the Congress on what we can do in the future, together, to carry out these beneficial commendations for congressional action that will help the American people have a better life.

Thank you all very much, and I'm deeply grateful to you.

I might ask Jay Rockefeller if he would respond briefly.

GOVERNOR ROCKEFELLER. Mr. President, I want to thank you for the fact that you did not, as you said you would not, in any way take this White House Conference on Balanced Growth and shelve its recommendations. You have very specifically, in the case of the Title V Commissions, not only taken some of the suggestions from the White House Conference, but also through Jack Watson, the Interagency Coordinating Council, have worked, I think, extraordinarily closely and effectively with the National Governors' Association. Governor du Pont, Governor Judge were on a special task force which dealt with Title V. You worked very closely with them. The resolution of that is partly here before us today.

I think the process of the White House Conference was kind of a declaration of interdependence on the different sections of the country; people realizing that there could not be North, South, East, West; that there are common problems; we will have our differences, but we work to solve them together.

I think the presence of Governors, Senators—Senator Randolph, of course, fundamental to this whole process—so many of your own people—Juanita Kreps' outstanding leadership—helped make this possible. It was a successful conference and one that I might say was the most open process, the most participatory process that either I or most of the others who participated have ever had the chance to be in.

So we thank you, Mr. President.

THE PRESIDENT. I have to say that I approached the Conference with a great deal of trepidation—[*laughter*]—and concern. But the more we got into these analyses, the more we saw that we're all in the same boat together. And the early confrontations that did exist among disputing groups were very quickly resolved in a constructive way, in many instances even before the groups got to Washington, with a broad range of regional conferences throughout the country.

And I think this feeding back of local opinion and local experience into the Federal Government itself has been a single factor among many. But that single factor has made the White House Conference of much more benefit than all the cost and effort that went into it.

Senator Jennings Randolph, please.

SENATOR RANDOLPH. Mr. President, Mr. Chairman, Secretary Kreps, I shall say only that we do believe that the Conference was constructive. The more than 1,000 persons who were there were not only there to listen but to participate and to bring their ideas and convictions and commitments and to form them into recommendations which have helped you, Mr. President, and others, to come now, at this point, not to—as the Governor of West Virginia has said—put something on the shelf, but to put something into being, into action. And in a sense, I speak for the colleagues who are here today, the Senate and House—the chairman over here, Bizz Johnson of California, and of course, Quentin Burdick, who chairs our Subcommittee on Economic Development, Chairman Williams, all who are here, of course, Huddleston, and many others, Applegate—I will not call the roll. But we do feel that what was done was an investment in America, in a coordinated effort of, let's say, moving forward, not to destroy but to build and even to rebuild.

Thank you.

THE PRESIDENT. Thank you very much. I noticed that the key Members of the Congress who helped with the White House Conference, I believe without exception, were reelected last November—[*laughter*]—which is a good indication that participation was at least not politically fatal. [*Laughter*]

Thank you very much, Senator.

SENATOR RANDOLPH. Thank you.

THE PRESIDENT. Secretary Juanita Kreps.

SECRETARY KREPS. Well, it's my function later to sign the agreement for the three new regional commissions. But I would like to say to the members of the White House Conference Committee, and to Jay Rockefeller, in particular, that we are very grateful to them for their hard work, and to say also, Mr. President, that I think you have today written a new chapter in the history of intergovernmental relations. And I shall look forward to working with the Governors and with the White House in pushing ahead these recommendations.

THE PRESIDENT. Anyone assembled on this side of the table could very well make a fine presentation about their own contribution and their own ideas for the future. But I'd like to conclude the statements by saying that this is just the beginning of a long process. This gives us an outline or a plan for the future, and that's the purpose of the White House Conference. It was not to solve all the problems or to even assess the progress that had been made in the past, but to make sure that as we reach for the future, for a greater and more vital and more prosperous America, that every person who lives in our great country could have a better quality of life, not only 2 years in the future but 20 or 30 or even 50 years in the future.

And those long-range trends of transportation development—rail, other surface transportation, water transportation, air transportation—as it relates to economic growth and development, education, environmental quality—these kinds of things, the husbanding of our own natural resources, are so closely intertwined on a long-range basis that this just gives us a blueprint or basis from which we can now make much more substantive progress.

Again, my overwhelming sense of the moment is one of gratitude for all of you who've served with very little public recognition, but served in a way that's vital and very beneficial to our own country.

Thank you again.

NOTE: The President spoke at 9:10 a.m. in the Cabinet Room at the White House.

White House Conference on Balanced National Growth and Economic Development

Message to the Congress Transmitting a Report.   January 19, 1979

To the Congress of the United States:
In fulfillment of a requirement of P.L. 94–487, October 12, 1976, I am transmitting my report on the White House Conference on Balanced National Growth and Economic Development. For many weeks preceding the final Conference, there were State and regional Conferences organized like town meetings, giving citizens and elected officials an opportunity to exchange views on the critical issues of growth and development. Held in Washington on January 29 through February 2, 1978, the Conference was attended by more than 700 individuals from all parts of the country.

An important outcome of the Conference was the general agreement among the delegates that no massive new Federal spending programs were needed. Instead, they called for more effective government, more balanced decisions, and a real partnership among levels of government and the private sector in meeting persistent social and economic problems. This theme has been an invaluable guide in helping shape the growth and development policies of my administration.

We are indebted to those who participated in the Conference. It could have been so controversial or so sterile that no useful purpose was served. Instead, it provided many constructive insights to help shape future growth and development policy in this country.

JIMMY CARTER

The White House,
     January 19, 1979.

"SHARED RESPONSIBILITY FOR GROWTH AND DEVELOPMENT"

The President's Message to Congress on his Recommendations and Findings on the White House Conference on Balanced National Growth and Economic Development

I. INTRODUCTION

The White House Conference on Balanced National Growth and Economic Development involved a broad spectrum of American society in considering and formulating national policy of fundamental concern to our people. At every level of government, such meetings are essential elements of the democratic process, assuring that elected officials remain in touch with those whom we represent.

A White House Conference concerning planning, growth, and economic development could have been either so controversial that its purposes were lost, or so sterile that its function came to no avail. Both extremes were successfully avoided. I commend the Congress, Secretaries Kreps, Harris and Bergland, Governor Rockefeller, members of the Advisory Committee and the 700 individuals and organizations who participated, and I congratulate the Governors who helped design the preparatory state and regional conferences.

As a participant who has already made innumerable decisions affecting balanced growth and economic development, I can say with conviction that this White House Conference has proven invaluable in shaping my Administration's policies. I am in substantial agreement with the philosophies expressed in the Conference reports, and note with satisfaction that the Conference findings closely paralleled many of the major domestic policy initiatives underway or being planned by my Administration. I shall first describe the Conference findings, and then indicate how we have already acted and how we propose to act to implement the Conference recommendations.

II. CONFERENCE FINDINGS

Two overriding principles and growth policy directions arose simultaneously and independently among the Conference participants. They are:

• Effective national growth and development policies must be "balanced," addressing the issues of growth as well as decline, seeking the equitable distribution of economic opportunities among all people and places and capitalizing on local and regional advantages for our collective betterment.

• A "fair and flexible Federalism" is needed. The Federal Government must play a more sensitive role in the Federal system, setting national objectives while recognizing the special characteristics of particular geographic areas, and providing regions, states, and localities greater responsibility for deciding how to attain those objectives.

These principles reflect a significant change in the way America perceives the question of national economic growth. They mark a shift from a predominant concern with the economic health of the Nation as a whole to greater attention to the economic vitality of subnational units, be they regions, states, or localities. The Conference found the question of the distributional impacts of Federal policy to be of critical importance. The Conference urged improvements in the processes by which growth policy is developed. In exercising its responsibility for setting the general directions of such policies, the Federal Government should bring together and involve regions, states, localities and the private sector in a shared responsibility for planning and implementing them.

Consistent with these policy directions, the Conference identified four major issues around which their recommendations clustered. They are: *Employment and Inflation; Governmental Effectiveness; Growth Policy Process;* and *Urban and Rural Policy.*

EMPLOYMENT AND INFLATION

The Conference recognized both the necessity and the limitations of macro-economic policies. Controlling inflation and achieving full employment are national goals of paramount importance. The Conference urged Federal policies to assure a growing economy with an expanding employment base. Although unemployment problems are generally assumed to be the greatest concern of low-income and minority groups, the negative consequences of inflation on low-income families' budgets are also severe.

The Conference also served, however, to remind the Nation that, despite record growth in overall employment and a substantial drop in unemployment since January 1977, there are groups of Americans and places still experiencing Depression levels of joblessness. For these distressed peoples and places, carefully targeted remedies must be applied. The primary emphasis of employment and economic development programs should be on retaining and creating jobs where unemployed people live, although some relocation assistance may be needed for those who desire it.

The private sector must be at the core of any national effort to achieve full employment. Two major points of consensus were expressed:

• permanent, private sector jobs are more desirable than temporary, public service employment, and

• government incentives to business are needed to leverage private expansion of job opportunities for disadvantaged workers.

The Conference recognized that public monies must be used, not simply as expenditures, but as investments, linking Federal programs and local plans to stimulate private action.

EFFECTIVE GOVERNMENT

The Conference participants expressed the view that there is need to take a fresh look at the present roles of the different levels of government to make them more effective and responsive. The "fair and flexible Federalism" proposed by the Conferees will require some reassignment of functions and responsibilities and reexamination of outmoded systems of revenue allocation injurious to distressed communities. The Conference urged the Federal Government to provide incentives to states to assume more responsibility for the problems of their local governments by modernizing local governmental structures and reforming inequitable revenue systems and state expenditure patterns.

The Conference recognized that uniformly applied national practices and rules ignore substantial regional differences. The Federal Government must begin to fine tune national policy and programs, taking into account substantial diversity among regions, states and localities, and encouraging through incentives more shared responsibility in the achievement of national objectives. Thus, a stronger role for states and localities in the design and management of Federally-assisted programs and greater decentralization in their administration is needed. As former Massachusetts Governor Dukakis said: "We cannot leave to chance the role of state governments in the implementation of a national economic policy . . . Unless the states are involved, and involved deeply, it is doomed to failure."

In return for greater state involvement, the Conference recommended that state governments assume increased responsibility for local education costs, while the Federal Government assumes more responsibility for welfare costs.

GROWTH POLICY

The Conference recognized the need for greater coherence in policy-making at all levels of government. Henry Ford said, "We must know how each action affects another, and be willing to change or eliminate those that are counterproductive." The processes that shape energy, environmental, business, community, and economic growth policies in particular

71

must be related to and support one another. The proper role of the Federal Government is to establish a coordinated policy framework to guide regional, state and local planning and decision-making, seeking insofar as possible to anticipate change so as to enable all levels of government as well as private interests to take timely actions.

Conferees asserted that growth policy processes should provide a systematic, consultative forum for the establishment of goals, the analysis of alternative policies and programs, and the reconciliation of conflicting laws, programs and regulations, thereby strengthening the capacity of elected officials to guide growth and development in beneficial ways. State and local governments should continue to have responsibility for planning, assuring participation of governmental and private interests, while responsibility for establishing policy processes, setting goals and reconciling differences should reside at the Federal, regional and state levels.

Many problems of growth and decline, the Conferees noted, are most effectively dealt with in a multi-state context. Effective regional institutions are required to attack problems that transcend state borders and which, if not sensitively handled, serve to exacerbate negative, unproductive sectionalism. The State-Federal Regional Commissions could provide a partnership means of achieving national objectives while respecting regional differences. These institutions should be strengthened to realize their full potential for helping shape Federal growth policies and development programs.

To exhibit "balance," the Conferees thought growth policies should reflect:

- a concern with the problems of rural counties and small towns as well as with metropolitan jurisdictions;

- a recognition of the needs of rapidly growing as well as declining communities; and

- the opportunity to consider simultaneously environmental mandates and economic growth proposals.

Conferees felt that some Federal, State and local regulations and red tape have a dampening effect on economic growth and contribute to our inflation problem. Energy, industrial location, and transportation initiatives have been stalled or thwarted by a maze of procedures and litigation stemming from excessive regulation. The Conference urged that:

- regulations be simplified and coordinated;

- Federal, State and local regulations be periodically reviewed; and

- state and local governments and the private sector have larger roles in shaping Federal regulations.

National energy policy, according to the Conferees, is essential to a balanced growth policy. In order to curtail inflation and expand employment, the Nation needs dependable, affordable energy sources which reduce U.S. dependence on imported oil. Energy conservation and development should create new jobs to help meet our full employment goals.

URBAN AND RURAL POLICIES

National urban and rural policies are also essential components of national growth policy, the Conferees said. The Conference favored selected targeting of Federal and State assistance to areas of greatest need, regardless of region, whether they be central cities or small cities, suburbs, rural counties or areas in decline or impacted by rapid and disorderly growth. Moreover, the Conference urged the resolution of State and local fiscal burdens through selective reassignment of responsibilities within the Federal system.

The Conference affirmed that Federal and State tax policy should help target private investment in distressed communities. Federal aid should, however, be premised on clear-cut national performance criteria concerning economic, fiscal, and employment objectives which reflect national commitments to equal opportunity, housing and jobs.

Finally, the Conference recognized the need for a balance between the national concern for large urban centers and counties, and for rural areas and small towns. It acknowledged that urban and rural development may require different tactics to address the diverse contexts in which similar problems may occur.

III. THE ADMINISTRATION'S INITIATIVES

Many of the recommendations made by the Conference have the same basis as the principles which have guided my Administration in setting new directions. The development of my domestic policy rests upon the recognition of the need for "shared responsibility" among all levels of government, and with the private sector, for the economic health and well-being of all people and places. The Conference came at an excellent time to help us think through the elements of our National Urban Policy, while it also helped launch a badly needed review of the performance of Federal programs in rural counties and small towns, largely in response to Conference recommendations, my Administration has taken the following steps toward a "fair and flexible Federalism."

INFLATION AND EMPLOYMENT

Overall, we have made dramatic gains in the past two years in expanding employment and reducing the number of jobless. In order to strengthen further the Nation's commitment to full employment while guarding against the crippling effects of high inflation I have signed into law the Humphrey-Hawkins Full Employment and Balanced Growth Act. By requiring the more systematic consideration of both concerns in developing national economic policies, it provides a framework for pursuing the more orderly and integrated growth policy process which the Conference endorsed.

The overall economic health of our Nation, however, is also founded on the economic well-being of its individual regions, communities, people and industries. This interdependence means that the distress of some people and places affects all of our people and places. Moreover, a non-inflationary national growth policy requires the efficient use of unemployed and underemployed workers and of underutilized private and community infrastructure. Federal action on the subnational economic development front, therefore, is an important, long neglected component of national economic policy concerned with stemming inflation, reducing unemployment and underemployment and increasing the productivity of our nation's industries.

In a break with past practice, the Federal Government is now deliberately and systematically pursuing "micro-economic" policies to help distressed places as well as people as an essential part of overall economic policy. This Administration has expanded and improved Federal community and economic development programs. We recognize that national development policies must link related development activities such as job creation and training, business assistance, housing and community improvements, human services, and transportation in unified state and locally planned programs. Pursuant to the Conference emphasis on private sector jobs, we have expanded the Comprehensive Employment and Training Act program, adding a new Private Sector Initiative which involves local, private sector councils in designing training and developing unsubsidized jobs. $400 million has been requested to support the new program. We have also developed with the Congress a targeted tax audit which provides a substantial tax incentive to employers to encourage them to hire poor young persons.

My Administration has also:

• Increased funding for HUD's Urban Development Action Grant and Commerce's Economic Development programs to leverage and target job-creating private investments.

• Launched the Air Quality Planning Grant program to help cities comply with the Clean Air Act without reducing needed private sector investments.

• Begun targeting $9 billion in Farmers Home Administration development funds, including over $1 billion in business and industry loans, on the most distressed rural communities and population groups.

• Established for the first time loans to farmers and ranchers for economic distress. This revolving fund of credit will strengthen the rural economy as well as the many segments of our national economy that benefit from a strong agricultural system.

• Develop a new Home Ownership Assistance Plan for very low-income rural residents, which will aid 16,000 families during 1979.

• Better targeted scores of existing programs toward urban and distressed rural areas.

My anti-inflation program includes the first systematic review of Federal regulations to reduce their cost and to eliminate those whose costs are not warranted by their effects. I urge state and local governments to join us periodically in reviewing such regulations as those affecting construction, environmental protection and energy production to speed decisions and reduce burdensome and inflationary costs.

Other elements of my anti-inflation program are:

• A restrained but fair budget.

• Review of existing and proposed regulations through the newly formed Regulatory Council which will develop for the first time a Regulatory Calendar that will present all the major regulations the government will issue in the forthcoming year. A Regulatory Analyses Review Group will review major regulations to insure they are as cost-beneficial as possible.

• Establishment of non-inflationary wage and price standards for both the public and private sectors. State and local governments are asked to comply with these standards.

• Review of health costs, State and local regulation costs, productivity within government, and the inflationary impact of Federal policies on State and local governments.

• Proposal of a program of real wage insurance by which workers who limit their raises to 7% would be eligible for a tax rebate if current prices rise by more than that amount, together with other anti-inflationary proposals such as hospital cost containment.

EFFECTIVE GOVERNMENT

I am determined to make Federal programs fairer, better coordinated, more easily administered and capable of responding to regional, State and local growth strategies in a concerted fashion. Examples of Administration actions supporting Conference recommendations in this area include:

• Congressional passage of all six reorganization proposals I made last year, including civil service reform, which will help provide better incentives for productive work by Federal officials.

• An Executive Order establishing a White House led Interagency Coordinating Council. This is a new mechanism for resolving conflicts among agencies and community programs, providing a comprehensive Administration-wide response to coordinated State and local development strategies.

• The Assistant Secretaries' Working Group on Rural Development to work on major, long-standing rural problems, through links to the White House and the Interagency Coordinating Council.

• Coordination of project investment activities and joint applications among domestic departments. Commerce and HUD are working toward streamlined economic development planning requirements.

• Coordination of Federal programs to target on special rural problems. Some of the results to date are:

—EPA and Agriculture will give priority in existing loan and grant programs to rural towns to comply with the Safe Drinking Water Act.

—HEW and Agriculture have agreed that Agriculture will target a share of its community facilities loans to make possible the construction, renovation and equipping of some 300 rural primary health care clinics. The Department of Labor will support training to enable people to work in these clinics. In all, over 13.5 million previously medically underserved Americans in rural areas will now have greater access to care.

—EPA, EDA, HUD, and FmHA have adopted procedures for improving the coordination and delivery of rural water and sewer services, with emphasis on paperwork reduction (e.g., single applications, consolidated reporting and auditing

requirements), simplified compliance requirements for the host of Federal laws applicable to water and sewer construction, joint agency training seminars and technical assistance materials, a common data base for needs assessments, and joint agency consultation with applicant communities to ensure that proposed facilities are affordable and suited to local needs. A companion agreement between DOL and EPA has resulted in the training of 1,750 workers in the water and wastewater treatment field to meet critical rural shortages in this rapidly expanding job market.

• Agreement between the Department of Transportation and the Environmental Protection Agency on a joint planning and funding process for air quality and transportation planning.

• Joint development and implementation of a public transportation assistance program in rural areas and small cities by the Federal Highway Administration and Urban Mass Transportation Administration.

• A "zero-based" review of Federal planning requirements governing receipt of Federal grants by State and local governments. This has produced:

—Demonstration programs in up to five States permitting a single integrated planning and budgeting process to substitute for HEW's multiple planning procedures.

—Annual program plans required by HUD are being replaced with triennial plans with annual updates.

—Approximately 165 of the more than 300 EPA planning requirements will be consolidated or simplified.

—State/EPA agreements will be negotiated to develop an integrated approach to solving water supply, solid waste, and water pollution control problems.

—Agreement between DOT and Farmers Home Administration to coordinate grants on Branch Line Railroad Investments.

The Conference urged a selected reassignment of fiscal responsibilities. I will soon propose welfare reform proposals which would increase Federal participation in public assistance and moderate the fiscal burden of hard pressed State and local governments. This program will offer jobs to those who need them and income support to families where adults are unable to engage in full-time work. The Administration recognizes the need for reform in the welfare system which is fairer to the recipient and is easier to administer at all levels of government.

This Administration will continue to help improve education, but calls on the States to do more to help meet the educational and other fiscal burdens that fall disproportionately on communities with inadequate tax bases.

GROWTH POLICY

The creation of more effective growth policy processes at all levels of government was among the forward-looking objectives of the late Senator Hubert H. Humphrey. Senator Humphrey co-sponsored the White House Conference legislation, and although he died before it occurred, the Conference strongly reflected his vision and concerns.

The Conference was correct in suggesting that growth policy processes at all levels of government should assist elected decision-makers and the private sector to:

- anticipate economically significant trends, such as sectoral shifts and the energy problems that have grown over the past decade;
- relate sometimes conflicting national objectives, such as regulatory and growth policies, to one another; and
- involve all levels of government and non-governmental interests in priority setting.

We have learned how important it is for business and labor, as well as the public sector, to understand how future industrial and employment changes will affect regions, states and major population centers. Furthermore, in the interest of a strong national economy and a healthier climate for investment, we must reduce to the extent possible the uncertainty and contradictory nature of public decisionmaking.

Elements that could be made part of a more coherent, forward-looking and systematic growth policy process exist now in the Federal Government. Coordinated use should be made, for example, of the policy planning processes affecting Federal energy, employment, regional, and urban and rural community responsibilities that exist in Federal statutes. To provide a basis for coordinated Federal policies, the Secretary of Commerce will oversee the development of a comprehensive information system, including a broad range of demographic and economic indicators of community conditions, along with the technological and trade data and forecasts necessary for State and regional decisionmaking.

Effective national growth policy processes require that regional, state and local growth policy processes be effective, too. Federal planning assistance programs have assisted State and local governments to develop workable systems for sensing public preferences on issues of growth and decline and translating these into long-term growth policies and development programs. In addition, however, Federal programs assisting development, direct Federal investments, and Federal regulatory actions must prove more sensitive to and support regional, state and local planning and investment policies. Therefore,

I am directing the Chairman of the White House Interagency Coordinating Council and the Director of the Office of Management and Budget to work with the Departments and Agencies to accelerate progress toward this objective.

One model will be the Department of Agriculture's invitation to Governors to develop joint investment strategies with its agencies. This has resulted in a rural development cooperation agreement signed by the State of North Carolina and the Farmers Home Administration. Such opportunities will be offered to other states in the months ahead. These initiatives represent a kind of "contract federalism," providing a new predictability of Federal action and a new recognition of state circumstances.

The national energy policy I presented to Congress is another essential element in growth policy. The resulting landmark legislation will help conserve natural resources, encourage exploration for natural gas by phased deregulation, lead to reform of utility rates, and encourage the conversion to coal. I have also proposed a new five-year Energy Impact Assistance Program to increase the capability of State and local governments to manage rapid growth resulting from energy development.

URBAN AND RURAL POLICY

Last spring, this Administration framed the "New Partnership to Conserve America's Communities," the Nation's first comprehensive and unified urban policy. This partnership is being implemented through four new Executive Orders, more than 100 improvements in existing Federal programs, and 19 legislative proposals. The elements include:

• Targeted employment tax credits to encourage private sector businesses to hire unemployed youths from low-income households.

• Location of Federal facilities slated for metropolitan areas in inner cities in order to provide jobs and make those neighborhoods more attractive for redevelopment.

• Purchasing by Federal agencies of more goods and services from areas with high unemployment rates.

• Increased funding for HUD's housing rehabilitation program.

• Revisions in Commerce's Economic Development Administration programs to strengthen minority economic development and to target aid to economically distressed people and places in all regions of the country.

• Allocation of $15 million to neighborhood and voluntary organizations for housing and neighborhood revitalization projects.

• Funding joint transportation and economic development projects.

• A new system for analyzing major new legislative, budgetary or regulatory initiatives in terms of their potential adverse effect on communities, both rural and urban.

This Administration is actively reviewing rural development needs, focusing initially on four areas—health, housing, transportation, and water and sewer systems—identified by Conference participants as particularly significant.

The principles expressed in the Urban Policy have had beneficial effects on overall government operations. This initiative encouraged my Administration to undertake the rural policy review which, taken together, will comprise a balanced community policy.

NEW LEGISLATION

The Administration expects to forward to Congress proposals for legislation which reflect the deliberations of the White House Conference. Moreover, the Administration is currently reviewing major Federal community and economic development programs, including the proper Federal organization to most effectively and efficiently develop the benefits of these programs. This effort is intended to address many of the concerns raised during the Conference—most notably the need for a balanced approach to development, streamlined government processes, and growth policy processes.

REGIONAL FEDERALISM

The legislation authorizing the Appalachian and Title V Regional Commissions expires next year. I am proposing new legislation which builds on the successful elements of the existing State-Federal programs, while providing the Commissions with new opportunities to shape Federal policies and programs to reflect regional differences. The principal elements of this new legislation are:

• The opportunity for all states to participate in multi-state Regional Commissions within boundaries delineated in consultation with the Governors according to minimal Federal guidelines.

• A broad definition of regional development including energy, export, and human and natural resources concerns.

• Incentives to improve the coordination of state and regional development programs.

In addition to the ongoing policy and administration responsibilities of the Department of Commerce for this program, I am expanding the role of the White House Interagency Coordinating Council to provide the Commissions with Administration-wide program and coordination support.

REAUTHORIZATION OF THE ECONOMIC DEVELOPMENT LEGISLATION

The future direction of the Commerce Department's economic development programs was among the primary concerns which led to the enactment of the legislation authorizing the White House Conference. The Public Works and Economic Development Act of 1965 as amended expires next year. The Administration intends to transmit recommendations to Congress concerning these important programs for building jobs and revenues in distressed communities.

CONCLUSION

The roots of this Conference lay in a series of state-organized growth policy processes that occurred over the past decade as well as in the pre-Conference meetings held by the Regional Commissions throughout the country. I commend the Governors and legislators concerned for providing excellent examples of how to make government truly sensitive to the needs and wishes of our people.

The challenge before us is to expand and systematize this process of shared responsibility among the regions, states and localities, involving private interests, and applying the results in framing national growth policies. The intergovernmental partnership must be one of shared concern and shared responsibility for reducing the disparities among people and places in our Nation. The message of the White House Conference was that subnational as well as national policies must address this need. The new urban, regional, and energy policies I have and will continue to propose, are important steps toward that objective.

There are few areas of potentially greater controversy than those that touch upon the varying economic opportunities of peoples and places. The White House Conference addressed those potentially divisive issues in a spirit of constructive accommodation. There was a willingness among those who labored in the workshops to take into account opposing views, framing reports which encourage those of us in elected office to approach these issues in a similar spirit. It is in that spirit that I forward to you my views on the Conference and my recommendations for action.

Regional Commissions

Memorandum From the President.
January 19, 1979

Memorandum for the Heads of Executive Departments and Agencies and Federal Cochairmen of Multistate Regional Commissions

Subject: Regional Commission Support

BACKGROUND AND PURPOSE

The White House Conference on Balanced National Growth and Economic Development found that the varied and changing problems and economic circumstances in the Nation's regions require greater flexibility in the way Federal policies and programs are designed and administered across the country. This variety suggests a need for strong state and local action to develop regional balanced growth policies and to target local, state and Federal funds in accord with these strategies. Multistate regional commissions established under the Appalachian Regional Development Act of 1965 and Title V of the Public Works and Eco-

nomic Development Act of 1965 and strengthened under the Regional Development Act of 1975 are intended to enhance development opportunities and conditions in multistate regions. Through planning and selective management of resources and activities, these commissions also afford a common framework within which the different levels of government can apply their energies to regional problems.

In light of the changing patterns of economic activity across the country, and in order to extend the ability of states and localities to shape Federal policies in behalf of regional concerns, new processes for planning, coordination and policy support are required. To develop and carry them out will require cooperation on the part of the Secretary of Commerce, Federal departments and agencies, the Interagency Coordinating Council, the Federal Cochairmen of the Appalachian and Title V Regional Commissions and the Federal Regional Councils.

By means of this memorandum, I am instituting a regional growth policy process to assist the regional commissions in developing and implementing their multiyear regional development plans and annual investment programs. These plans and, more importantly, the annual investment programs should be developed from the ground up, reflecting substate and state development plans. Through this policy process, the regional commissions will be given an opportunity to prepare recommendations to Federal departments and agencies for solutions to problems of regional growth and decline. In framing these recommendations, the commissions will consult with the Federal departments and agencies affected, taking advantage of the expertise available in the regional headquarters of each agency, as well as with substate, local and private interests.

RESPONSIBILITIES OF FEDERAL PARTICIPANTS

To assure that Federal actions recognize regional differences and facilitate state, local and private initiatives in addressing the special problems of balanced growth which each region faces, I am directing that the following actions be taken by the Secretary of Commerce, the Federal departments and agencies, the Federal Cochairman of the Appalachian and Title V Regional Commissions, the Interagency Coordinating Council and the Federal Regional Councils:

SECRETARY OF COMMERCE

With respect to the Title V Regional Commissions, the Secretary of Commerce is directed to:

1. develop, in consultation with the appropriate parties, guidance for the preparation of regional plans, investment programs and growth policy recommendations. The multi-year regional development plans, annual investment programs, policy recommendations and obstacles to interagency coordination may be presented by the Secretary to the heads of the relevant Federal departments and agencies through the White House Interagency Coordinating Council;

2. assist each Federal Cochairman of a regional commission in presenting the multi-year regional development plan, annual investment program and growth policy recommendations developed from the plan; and

3. institute a mechanism for consultation with Federal Cochairmen regarding policy and administrative improvements in the program.

FEDERAL DEPARTMENTS AND AGENCIES

The head of each Federal department and agency is directed to:

1. assist and cooperate with the Secretary of Commerce, the Federal Cochairmen of the Appalachian and Title V Regional Commissions, and with the Interagency Coordinating Council in performance of their functions with respect to the regional growth policy process;

2. administer planning and development assistance programs so as to facilitate regional and unified state growth policy processes, and to the extent practicable, support multi-year regional development plans and annual investment programs of the regional commissions through financial assistance and direct Federal development activities which are consistent with such plans; and

3. recognize the mutual agreement of the governors in each regional commission that the commission may participate in the current process for evaluation, review and coordination of Federal and Federally assisted projects under Part II of OMB Circular No. A–95. Projects for review should be referred to the commission by State clearinghouses according to procedures jointly prescribed by governors. I am directing the Director of the Office of Management and Budget to propose amendments to OMB Circular No. A–95 to this effect.

INTERAGENCY COORDINATING COUNCIL

The Chairman of the Interagency Coordinating Council is directed to:

1. work with the Secretary of Commerce, the heads of the other federal departments and agencies, and the Federal Cochairpersons to overcome obstacles in carrying out the objectives of this policy; and

2. ensure that, at the request of the Secretary of Commerce and the Federal Cochairman of the Appalachian Regional Commission, the annual investment programs and policy recommendations receive a coordinated high-level analysis and review by relevant federal departments and agencies.

FEDERAL COCHAIRMEN

In addition to the responsibilities defined in existing statutes, regulations and Executive Orders, the Federal Cochairmen of the Appalachian and Title V Regional Commissions, with the concurrence of the affected commission(s), shall become members of each Federal Regional Council which serves all or any portion of his/her region. It is my intention to further amend Executive Order 11647 to this effect.

Each Title V Federal Chairman, working with the regional commission, is directed to:

1. assist the regional commission to participate in the regional growth policy process;

2. present the commission's multi-year regional development plan, annual investment program and growth policy recommendations to the Secretary of Commerce;

3. involve Federal departments and agencies in the activities of the commissions, as appropriate; and

4. participate in the consultative mechanism described under Secretary of Commerce directives, # 3 above on page 3.

FEDERAL REGIONAL COUNCILS

The Federal Regional Councils are directed to work with the Secretary of Commerce and the Interagency Coordinating Council to provide continuing liaison with regional commissions.

JIMMY CARTER

Permanent American Cemetery in the Republic of Panama
Executive Order 12115.   January 19, 1979

By the authority vested in me as President by the Constitution and the laws of the United States of America, including Section 10 of the Act of March 4, 1923 (42 Stat. 1509), as amended (36 U.S.C. 132), and to implement the intent of the United States Senate (124 Cong. Rec. S 3857 of March 16, 1978) as set forth by Reservations (1) and (3) to the Resolution of Ratification of the Treaty Concerning the Permanent Neutrality and Operation of the Panama Canal, it is hereby ordered as follows:

1–101. The Secretary of State shall take all appropriate steps to complete, prior to the date of entry into force of the Treaty Concerning the Permanent Neutrality and Operation of the Panama Canal, hereinafter referred to as the Neutrality Treaty, the negotiations which have begun with the Republic of Panama for an agreement under which the United States of America would, upon the date of entry into force of such agreement and thereafter, administer as a permanent American cemetery such part of Corozal Cemetery as encompasses the remains of citizens of the United States of America.

1–102. Subject to the conclusion of the agreement referred to in Section 1–101 of this Order, the American Battle Monuments Commission shall administer that part of Corozal Cemetery which encompasses the remains of citizens of the

United States of America, in accordance with the terms of the agreement with the Republic of Panama.

1–103. The Governor of the Canal Zone shall, to the extent funds are available, disinter from Mount Hope Cemetery, before entry into force of the Neutrality Treaty, and reinter in Corozal Cemetery the remains of United States citizens, and the remains of members of their immediate family that are buried with them. The Governor shall not remove from Mount Hope Cemetery the remains of any such person whose next of kin timely requests in writing that such remains not be disinterred. The Governor shall transport to the United States for reinterment the remains of any such person whose next of kin timely requests in writing that such remains be transported to the United States for reinterment.

1–104. The Secretary of Defense shall, to the extent funds are available, disinter from Corozal Cemetery and transport to the United States for reinterment the remains of United States citizens, and the remains of members of their immediate family buried with them, whose next of kin requests in writing by April 1, 1982, that such remains be transported to the United States for reinterment.

1–105. Subject to the availability of funds, all the costs incurred in the disinterment, reinterment in Corozal Cemetery, and transportation of remains required by this Order, including the costs of preparation, cremation if requested, and a casket or urn, shall be borne by the United States of America. The costs of reinterment in the United States, including any costs for funeral home services, vaults, plots, or crypts, will be the responsibility of the next of kin making the re-

quest, except to the extent otherwise provided by law, including any unused specific entitlements available pursuant to statute.

1–106. (a) The Governor of the Canal Zone shall identify, to the extent feasible, the closest surviving next of kin of each deceased United States citizen buried in the Mount Hope and Corozal Cemeteries, and of such next of kin of each member of the immediate family that is buried with such United States citizen.

(b) The Governor shall provide notice to the next of kin of such deceased buried in Mount Hope Cemetery that the Government plans to remove the deceased to Corozal Cemetery unless the next of kin requests in writing, not later than three months after the first issuance of such notification, either that the remains not be removed from Mount Hope Cemetery, or that the remains be moved to, and reinterred in, the United States in a cemetery or other burial site designated by the next of kin.

(c) The Governor shall also provide notice to the next of kin of such deceased who are buried in Corozal Cemetery that the Government will disinter and transport such deceased to the United States for reinterment in a cemetery or other burial site designated by the next of kin, if the next of kin so requests in writing not later than April 1, 1982.

(d) The Governor shall publish the notices provided for in subsections (b) and (c) of this Section in appropriate newspapers, magazines and other periodicals, and utilize such other means of communicating with the next of kin that he finds to be practical and effective.

1–107. The Governor of the Canal Zone shall, before the entry into force of the Neutrality Treaty, fully advise the next of kin of all available options, and their implications, in those cases where a request has been made that remains not be removed from Mount Hope Cemetery.

1–108. The Secretary of the Army shall supervise the planned removal of the remains from Mount Hope Cemetery to Corozal Cemetery and shall ensure compliance with the wishes of any next of kin who, within the time specified in clause B(i) to the Third Reservation to the Neutrality Treaty, objects to such removal.

1–109. As used in this Order:

(a) "Next of kin" means the person whom the Governor of the Canal Zone determines to be the nearest living relative, by consanguinity or affinity, of a person buried at Mount Hope Cemetery or Corozal Cemetery.

(b) "Members of their immediate family" means the spouse, children, mother or father of the deceased United States citizen.

JIMMY CARTER

The White House,
    January 19, 1979.

[Filed with the Office of the Federal Register,
    11:03 a.m., January 22, 1979]

Issuance of Food Stamps by the Postal Service

Executive Order 12116.   January 19, 1979

By the authority vested in me as President of the United States of America by Section 11(k) of the Food Stamp Act of 1977 (91 Stat. 974; 7 U.S.C. 2020 (k)),[1] the United States Postal Service is hereby granted approval for post offices in all or

---

[1] EDITOR'S NOTE: The correct citation is (91 Stat. 974; 7 U.S.C. 2012 (k)).

part of any State to issue food stamps to eligible households, upon request by the appropriate State agency, as defined in Section 3(n) of the Food Stamp Act of 1977 (91 Stat. 960; 7 U.S.C. 2012(n)).

JIMMY CARTER

The White House,
    January 19, 1979.

[Filed with the Office of the Federal Register,
    11:04 a.m., January 22, 1979]

Agreement on International Carriage of Perishable Foodstuffs

Message to the Senate Transmitting the Agreement.   January 19, 1979

To the Senate of the United States:

I transmit herewith, for the advice and consent of the Senate to accession, the Agreement on the International Carriage of Perishable Foodstuffs and on the Special Equipment to be Used for Such Carriage (ATP), done at Geneva on September 1, 1970, under the auspices of the Economic Commission for Europe (ECE). For the information of the Senate, I also transmit the report of the Department of State on the Agreement.

The Agreement came into force on November 21, 1976 following ratification by France, the Federal Republic of Germany, Spain, the Union of Soviet Socialist Republics, and Yugoslavia. Since then, Denmark, Austria, Italy, Luxembourg, and Bulgaria have also ratified it.

The Agreement requires that insulated, refrigerated or heated transportation equipment used to move perishable foodstuffs into contracting states be tested, certified and marked to ensure that such equipment is properly insulated and capable of maintaining a prescribed temperature within the equipment.

Article 5 exempts equipment whose movement involves a deep sea voyage of 150 kilometers or more. Thus, traffic in foodstuffs between the United States and Europe is not subject to the ATP. In addition, and in accordance with an option available under Article 10, the United States will not apply the ATP to transport equipment operating within and moving into and out of the United States and its territories.

However, accession to the ATP will ensure that the United States has a voice in ECE deliberations and decisions pertaining to the administration of the ATP, a matter of concern to U.S. exporters of perishable foodstuffs and operators of refrigerated equipment. U.S. participation will be particularly important in relation to the Article 5 exemption of carriage involving a long sea voyage. As a contracting party, the U.S. will be able to preserve this exemption by exercising the power under Article 18 to veto any proposed changes in the ATP.

Moreover, accession will enable manufacturers, owners and operators of U.S. transport equipment to have their equipment tested and certified in the United States with the assurance that the U.S.-issued certificates will be recognized by all of the contracting parties. While parties to the ATP must, under the terms of Article 2, recognize the validity of certificates issued by other contracting parties, they need not recognize certificates issued by non-parties. If the United States does not become a party, U.S. transport equipment which does not qualify for the Article 5 exemption—that is, equipment moving between countries in Europe—will be placed at a competitive disadvantage with respect to equipment owned by nationals of parties to the ATP. Furthermore, the availability of testing and certification services in the United States will enable manufacturers, owners and operators of U.S. transport equipment which may become involved in inter-European transport to test and certify their equipment while it is still on the production line.

I recommend that the Senate give early and favorable consideration to the Agreement and give its advice and consent to accession, subject to the declaration pursuant to Article 10 that the Agreement does not apply to carriage in the United States or its territories.

JIMMY CARTER

The White House,
    January 19, 1979.

Nice Agreement on International Trademarks

Message to the Senate Transmitting the Revised Agreement.   January 19, 1979

To the Senate of the United States:

With a view to receiving the advice and consent of the Senate to ratification, I transmit herewith the revised Nice Agreement Concerning the International Classification of Goods and Services for the Purposes of the Registration of Marks, done at Geneva on May 13, 1977. I also transmit, for the information of the Senate, the State Department report on the Agreement.

The revised Agreement provides that amendments to the classification system may be made by a four-fifths majority of the members present and voting, instead of a unanimous vote, as the present Agreement requires. The other important change is that the Agreement and the classification are to be published in an authentic English text, as well as a French text.

Ratification of the revised Agreement will enable the United States Patent and Trademark Office to do its work more efficiently, and will improve the international system for the protection of trademarks. The revised Agreement would, thereby, benefit American trademark owners and the administration of the United States trademark system. I therefore recommend that the Senate give early and favorable consideration to the revised Agreement and advise and consent to its ratification.

JIMMY CARTER

The White House,
January 19, 1979.

United States-Federal Republic of Germany Treaty on Extradition

Message to the Senate Transmitting the Treaty.   January 19, 1979

To the Senate of the United States:

With a view to receiving the advice and consent of the Senate to ratification, I transmit herewith the Treaty on Extradition Between the United States of America and the Federal Republic of Germany, signed at Bonn on June 20, 1978.

I transmit also, for the information of the Senate, the report of the Department of State with respect to the treaty.

The treaty is one of a series of modern extradition treaties being negotiated by the United States. It expands the list of extraditable offenses to include aircraft hijacking and narcotics offenses, as well as several other offenses not now covered by our existing Extradition Treaty with the Federal Republic of Germany. Upon entry into force, it will terminate and supersede the existing Extradition Treaty between the United States and the Federal Republic of Germany.

This treaty will make a significant contribution to international cooperation in law enforcement. I recommend that the Senate give early and favorable con-

sideration to the treaty and give its advice and consent to ratification.

JIMMY CARTER

The White House,
January 19, 1979.

Convention on Pollution From Ships

Message to the Senate Transmitting a Protocol to the Convention. January 19, 1979

To the Senate of the United States:

I transmit herewith, for the advice and consent of the Senate to ratification, a certified copy of the Protocol of 1978 Relating to the International Convention for the Prevention of Pollution from Ships, with its Annexes I and II, and Protocols I and II, 1973, done at London February 17, 1978 (the MARPOL Protocol). I send along with it, for the Senate's consideration, the State Department's report.

The MARPOL Protocol results from proposals the United States made last year following a series of tanker incidents in or near United States waters. It aims to reduce accidental and operational pollution from tankers. The Protocol applies many new operating and construction standards to more tankers than are covered by the International Convention for the Prevention of Pollution from Ships, 1973 (the MARPOL Convention). The MARPOL Convention has not been ratified by the United States, and has not entered into force.

The MARPOL Protocol incorporates, with modifications, the MARPOL Convention transmitted to the Senate on March 22, 1977 for advice and consent to ratification. Ratification of the Protocol will, therefore, constitute acceptance of the provisions of the Convention, subject to the modifications and additions contained in the Protocol. Accordingly, I request that the Senate give advice and consent to the Protocol in place of the Convention. The MARPOL Convention contains three optional Annexes, Annexes III, IV and V, which deal with pollution from packaged harmful substances, sewage and garbage. I am not now seeking the Senate's advice and consent to these optional annexes.

The entry into force of the MARPOL Protocol will be an important step in controlling and preventing pollution from vessel discharges. I recommend that the Senate give early consideration to this Protocol and advise and consent to its ratification.

                                  JIMMY CARTER

The White House,
    January 19, 1979.

Convention for the Safety of Life at Sea

Message to the Senate Transmitting a Protocol to the Convention. January 19, 1979

To the Senate of the United States:

I transmit herewith, for the advice and consent of the Senate to ratification, the Protocol of 1978 Relating to the International Convention for the Safety of Life at Sea, 1974, done at London, February 17, 1978. The report of the Department of State is enclosed for the information of the Senate.

The Safety of Life at Sea (SOLAS) Protocol is an international response to proposals which we made last year to improve the construction requirements for tankers, and the system for inspecting and certifying them. It deals with measures that, when they take effect, will reduce deficiencies in the physical condition of cargo ships, especially tankers, minimize steering gear failures, enhance the ability to detect collision situations and avoid collisions, and diminish the possibility of explosions.

The SOLAS Protocol, which is a separate treaty, modifies and adds to the 1974 SOLAS Convention, to which the Senate gave its advice and consent to ratification on July 12, 1978. The Protocol requires the deposit of an instrument of ratification distinct from that of the related Convention. The Conference, as advocated by the U.S. delegation, set a target date of June 1979 for the entry into force of the SOLAS Convention and as soon as possible thereafter for the SOLAS Protocol.

The United States has been in the forefront of the drive for the adoption of both the Convention and the Protocol and would like to encourage other countries to act expeditiously on this matter. I therefore recommend that the Senate give prompt consideration to the SOLAS Protocol.

                                  JIMMY CARTER

The White House,
    January 19, 1979.

Maritime Boundary Treaties With Mexico, Venezuela, and Cuba

Message to the Senate Transmitting the Treaties. January 19, 1979

To the Senate of the United States:

I transmit herewith, for the advice and consent of the Senate to ratification, three treaties establishing maritime boundaries: the Treaty on Maritime Boundaries between the United States of America and the United Mexican States, signed at Mexico City on May 4, 1978; the Maritime Boundary Treaty between the United States of America and the Republic of Venezuela, signed at Caracas on March 28, 1978; and the Maritime Boundary Agreement between the United States of America and the Republic of Cuba, signed at Washington, December 16, 1977.

These treaties are necessary to delimit the continental shelf and overlapping claims of jurisdiction resulting from the establishing of a 200 nautical mile fishery conservation zone off the coasts of the United States in accordance with the Fishery Conservation and Management Act of 1976, and the establishment of 200 nautical mile zones by these neighboring countries.

The treaty with Mexico establishes the maritime boundary between the United States and Mexico for the area between twelve and two hundred nautical miles off the coasts of the two countries in the Pacific Ocean and Gulf of Mexico. In this regard, it supplements the Treaty to Resolve Pending Boundary Differences and Maintain the Rio Grande and Colorado River as the International Boundary between the United States of America and the United Mexican States, signed at Mexico November 23, 1970, which establishes maritime boundaries out to twelve nautical miles off the respective coasts. The treaty with Venezuela establishes the maritime boundary between the two countries in the Caribbean Sea, between Puerto Rico and the U.S. Virgin Islands and Venezuela where the 200 nautical mile zones overlap. The treaty with Cuba establishes the maritime boundary between the two countries in the Straits of Florida area and the eastern Gulf of Mexico where the 200 nautical mile zones overlap.

I believe that these treaties are in the United States interest. They are consist-

ent with the United States interpretation of international law that maritime boundaries are to be established by agreement in accordance with equitable principles in the light of relevant geographic circumstances. They will facilitate law enforcement activities, and provide for certainty in resource development.

I also transmit for the information of the Senate the report of the Department of State with respect to each of these treaties.

I recommend that the Senate give early consideration to these treaties and advice and consent to their ratification.

JIMMY CARTER

The White House,
January 19, 1979.

Presidential Medal of Freedom

Announcement of Award to Margaret Mead.
January 19, 1979

The President today announced that he will award the Presidential Medal of Freedom posthumously to Margaret Mead.

The President has asked U.N. Ambassador Andrew Young to present the award to Margaret Mead's daughter, Dr. Catherine Bateson. The presentation will take place on Saturday, January 20, at a special program honoring the contributions of Margaret Mead, sponsored by the American Museum of Natural History in New York City.

The citation accompanying the medal follows:

"Margaret Mead was both a student of civilization and an exemplar of it. To a public of millions, she brought the central insight of cultural anthropology: that varying cultural patterns express an underlying human unity. She mastered her discipline, but she also transcended it.

Intrepid, independent, plain-spoken, fearless, she remains a model for the young and a teacher from whom all may learn."

The Presidential Medal of Freedom is the Government's highest civil award. It may be awarded only by the President to persons who have made especially meritorious contributions to the security or national interest of the United States, to world peace, or to cultural or other significant public or private endeavors.

National Advisory Committee for Women

Designation of Marjorie Bell Chambers as Acting Chair.   January 19, 1979

The President today announced that he will designate Marjorie Bell Chambers as the Acting Chair of the National Advisory Committee for Women. The designation of Chambers was recommended by the Committee on the basis of a poll of its membership.

In this temporary assignment, Chambers' initial task will be to work with Sarah Weddington to expand the access of the Committee to policymaking forums within the administration. The White House anticipates a solid working relationship with the Committee and will continue to consult with it and seek its advice. The Committee will work to effectively fulfill its mandate of assisting the President and the administration in promoting full equality for American women.

The White House will continue to consult with Chambers, the Committee, and former members of the Committee on the selection of a permanent chair and the continuing role of the Committee.

Chambers, 56, of Los Alamos, N. Mex., is president of Bell Chambers Associates,

a consulting firm for government, education, science, and technology, specializing in equity management services. She is national president of the American Association of University Women (AAUW) and president of the AAUW Educational Foundation. She is a former president of Colorado Women's College and has also been a professor of history at several colleges. She has served as chairman of the County Council of Los Alamos.

Digest of Other White House Announcements

The following listing includes the President's public schedule and other items of general interest announced by the White House Press Office and not included elsewhere in this issue.

January 13

The President met at the White House with Zbigniew Brzezinski, Assistant to the President for National Security Affairs.

January 14

Deng Xiaoping, Vice Premier of the State Council of the People's Republic of China, in response to an invitation from President Carter, will visit the United States from January 28 through February 5. Vice Premier Deng is expected to arrive at Washington by air in the afternoon of January 28, and his formal state visit will begin on January 29. He will depart from Seattle by air for the People's Republic of China on the morning of February 5. His itinerary during his stay in the United States is as follows:

—Washington, D.C., January 29, 30, 31

—Atlanta, Ga., February 1 and 2

—Houston, Tex., February 2 and 3

—Seattle, Wash., February 4 and 5

Ambassador Leonard Woodcock, Chief

of the United States Liaison Office in Peking, will accompany the Vice Premier on his travels within the United States as a Personal Representative of the President.

January 15

The President met at the White House with:
—Dr. Brzezinski;
—Frank B. Moore, Assistant to the President for Congressional Liaison;
—the Cabinet;
—John C. White, chairman of the Democratic National Committee.

The President has approved an extension of the time, from January 15 to February 15, within which the Emergency Board to investigate the dispute between Wien Air Alaska and the Air Line Pilots Association must report.

January 16

The President met at the White House with:
—Dr. Brzezinski;
—Mr. Moore;
—the Democratic congressional leaders;
—Vice President Walter F. Mondale, Stansfield Turner, Director of Central Intelligence, Hamilton Jordan, Assistant to the President, and Dr. Brzezinski;
—Mrs. Carter, for lunch;
—James T. McIntyre, Jr., Director of the Office of Management and Budget.

The President declared an emergency for the State of Illinois because of the impact of an abnormal accumulation of snow on vital transportation arteries within the State.

January 17

The President met at the White House with:
—Dr. Brzezinski;

—Senator John C. Stennis of Mississippi;
—Representative James J. Howard of New Jersey.

January 18

The President met at the White House with:
—David L. Aaron, Deputy Assistant for National Security Affairs;
—Prime Minister Ola Ullsten of Sweden;
—Vice President Mondale.

January 19

The President met at the White House with:
—Vice President Mondale, Secretary of State Cyrus R. Vance, Secretary of Defense Harold Brown, Dr. Brzezinski, and Mr. Jordan;
—Mr. Moore;
—Charles L. Schultze, Chairman of the Council of Economic Advisers;
—Representative and Mrs. John M. Murphy of New York;
—Mr. McIntyre and members of the reorganization staff.

The President declared an emergency for the State of Wisconsin because of the impact of an abnormal accumulation of snow on vital transportation arteries within the State.

The President left the White House for a weekend stay at Camp David, Md.

NOMINATIONS SUBMITTED TO THE SENATE

The following list does not include promotions of members of the Uniformed Services, nominations to the Service Academies, or nominations of Foreign Service officers.

Submitted January 18, 1979

JOHN PATRICK WHITE, of California, to be Deputy Director of the Office of Management and Budget, to which office he was appointed during the last recess of the Senate.

NOMINATIONS—Continued

Submitted January 18—Continued

JOHN WARREN MCGARRY, of Massachusetts, to be a member of the Federal Election Commission for a term expiring April 30, 1983, to which office he was appointed during the last recess of the Senate.

HENRY BOWEN FRAZIER III, of Virginia, to be a member of the Federal Labor Relations Authority for a term of 1 year, to which office he was appointed during the last recess of the Senate.

RONALD W. HAUGHTON, of Michigan, to be a member of the Federal Labor Relations Authority for a term of 5 years, to which office he was appointed during the last recess of the Senate.

RICHARD W. YARBOROUGH, of Texas, to be a member of the Foreign Claims Settlement Commission of the United States for a term of 3 years from October 22, 1978, to which office he was appointed during the last recess of the Senate.

RUTH T. PROKOP, of the District of Columbia, to be a member of the Merit Systems Protection Board for the remainder of the term expiring March 1, 1981, to which office she was appointed during the last recess of the Senate.

RUTH T. PROKOP, of the District of Columbia, to be Chairman of the Merit Systems Protection Board, to which office she was appointed during the last recess of the Senate.

JAMES J. DILLMAN, of Wisconsin, to be a member of the National Commission on Social Security for a term of 2 years, to which office he was appointed during the last recess of the Senate.

MILTON S. GWIRTZMAN, of Massachusetts, to be a member of the National Commission on Social Security for a term of 2 years, to which office he was appointed during the last recess of the Senate.

D. S. MACNAUGHTON, of Tennessee, to be a member of the National Commission on Social Security for a term of 2 years, to which office he was appointed during the last recess of the Senate.

DAVID H. RODGERS, of Washington, to be a member of the National Commission on Social Security for a term of 2 years, to which office he was appointed during the last recess of the Senate.

KAY HOWE, of Colorado, to be a member of the National Council on the Humanities for the remainder of the term expiring January 26, 1980, to which office she was appointed during the last recess of the Senate.

NOMINATIONS—Continued

Submitted January 18—Continued

CHARLES V. HAMILTON, of New York, to be a member of the National Council on the Humanities for a term expiring January 26, 1984, to which office he was appointed during the last recess of the Senate.

LOUIS J. HECTOR, of Florida, to be a member of the National Council on the Humanities for a term expiring January 26, 1984, to which office he was appointed during the last recess of the Senate.

M. CARL HOLMAN, of the District of Columbia, to be a member of the National Council on the Humanities for a term expiring January 26, 1984, to which office he was appointed during the last recess of the Senate.

JACOB NEUSNER, of Rhode Island, to be a member of the National Council on the Humanities for a term expiring January 26, 1984, to which office he was appointed during the last recess of the Senate.

MARY BETH NORTON, of New York, to be a member of the National Council on the Humanities for a term expiring January 26, 1984, to which office she was appointed during the last recess of the Senate.

SISTER JOEL READ, of Wisconsin, to be a member of the National Council on the Humanities for a term expiring January 26, 1984, to which office she was appointed during the last recess of the Senate.

LEON STEIN, of New York, to be a member of the National Council on the Humanities for a term expiring January 26, 1984, to which office he was appointed during the last recess of the Senate.

HARRIET MORSE ZIMMERMAN, of Georgia, to be a member of the National Council on the Humanities for a term expiring January 26, 1984, to which office she was appointed during the last recess of the Senate.

ALAN KEITH CAMPBELL, of Texas, to be Director of the Office of Personnel Management, to which office he was appointed during the last recess of the Senate.

JULE M. SUGARMAN, of Virginia, to be Deputy Director of the Office of Personnel Management, to which office he was appointed during the last recess of the Senate.

GEORGE M. SEIGNIOUS II, of South Carolina, to be Director of the United States Arms Control and Disarmament Agency, to which office he was appointed during the last recess of the Senate.

WILLIAM J. SULLIVAN, of Maine, to be a Governor of the United States Postal Service

NOMINATIONS—Continued

Submitted January 18—Continued

for the term expiring December 8, 1984, to which office he was appointed during the last recess of the Senate.

K. MATHEA FALCO, of the District of Columbia, to be Assistant Secretary of State for International Narcotics Matters (new position).

LEONARD WOODCOCK, of Michigan, to be Ambassador Extraordinary and Plenipotentiary of the United States of America to the People's Republic of China.

PHILIP HENRY ALSTON, JR., of Georgia, now Ambassador Extraordinary and Plenipotentiary of the United States of America to Australia, to serve concurrently and without additional compensation as Ambassador Extraordinary and Plenipotentiary of the United States of America to the Republic of Nauru.

W. BEVERLY CARTER, JR., of Pennsylvania, a Foreign Service information officer of Class one, to be Ambassador at Large.

LARRY E. MEIEROTTO, of the District of Columbia, to be an Assistant Secretary of the Interior, vice Ronald G. Coleman, resigned.

JAMES H. WILLIAMS, of Florida, to be Deputy Secretary of Agriculture, vice John C. White, resigned.

GORDON VICKERY, of Washington, to be Administrator of the United States Fire Administration, vice Howard D. Tipton, resigned.

HELEN S. ASTIN, of California, to be a member of the National Council on Educational Research for a term expiring September 30, 1979, vice John C. Weaver, term expired.

WILLIAM BROWNLEE WELSH, of Virginia, to be an Assistant Secretary of Housing and Urban Development, vice David S. Cook, resigned.

DAVE WARREN, of New Mexico, to be a member of the National Council on the Humanities for the term expiring January 26, 1982, vice Arthur L. Peterson, term expired.

BRIG. GEN. NORMAN G. DELBRIDGE, JR., 383–24–5493, United States Army, to be a member of the California Debris Commission, under the provisions of Section 1 of the Act of Congress approved 1 March 1893 (27 Stat. 507) (33 U.S.C. 661), vice Brig. Gen. Richard Martin Connell, reassigned.

LOUIS NUÑEZ, of Maryland, to be Staff Director for the Commission on Civil Rights, vice John A. Buggs, resigned.

The following-named persons to be members of the Board of Directors of the Communi-

NOMINATIONS—Continued

Submitted January 18—Continued

cations Satellite Corporation for the terms indicated:

JESSE HILL, JR., of Georgia, until the date of the annual meeting of the Corporation in 1979, vice Rudolph A. Peterson, term expired.

JOAN FLEISCHMANN TOBIN, of the District of Columbia, until the date of the annual meeting of the Corporation in 1980, vice Frederic G. Donner, term expired.

GEOFFREY COWAN, of California, to be a member of the Board of Directors of the Corporation for Public Broadcasting for a term expiring March 26, 1984, vice Joseph D. Hughes, term expired.

PAUL S. FRIEDLANDER, of Washington, to be a member of the Board of Directors of the Corporation for Public Broadcasting for a term expiring March 26, 1984, vice Gloria L. Anderson, term expired.

KATHLEEN NOLAN, of California, to be a member of the Board of Directors of the Corporation for Public Broadcasting for a term expiring March 26, 1984, vice Amos B. Hostetter, Jr., term expired.

HOWARD A. WHITE, of New York, to be a member of the Board of Directors of the Corporation for Public Broadcasting for the remainder of the term expiring March 26, 1980, vice W. Allen Wallis, resigned.

PETER HENRY WOLF, of the District of Columbia, to be an Associate Judge of the Superior Court of the District of Columbia for a term of 15 years, vice Harold H. Greene, elevated.

ANNE P. JONES, of Massachusetts, to be a member of the Federal Communications Commission for a term of 7 years from July 1, 1978, vice Margareta E. White, term expired.

IRVINE HENRY SPRAGUE, of California, to be a member of the Board of Directors of the Federal Deposit Insurance Corporation for a term of 6 years, vice George A. LeMaistre, resigned.

MAX L. FRIEDERSDORF, of Indiana, to be a member of the Federal Election Commission for a term expiring April 30, 1983, vice William L. Springer, term expired.

MICHAEL KANTOR, of California, to be a member of the Board of Directors of the Legal Services Corporation for a term expiring July 13, 1981, vice Glee S. Smith, Jr., term expired.

NOMINATIONS—Continued

Submitted January 18—Continued

ROBERT J. KUTAK, of Nebraska, to be a member of the Board of Directors of the Legal Services Corporation for a term expiring July 13, 1981 (reappointment).

F. WILLIAM McCALPIN, of Missouri, to be a member of the Board of Directors of the Legal Services Corporation for a term expiring July 13, 1981, vice Roger C. Cramton, term expired.

REVIUS O. ORTIQUE, JR., of Louisiana, to be a member of the Board of Directors of the Legal Services Corporation for a term expiring July 13, 1981 (reappointment).

HOWARD R. SACKS, of Connecticut, to be a member of the Board of Directors of the Legal Services Corporation for a term expiring July 13, 1981, vice J. Melville Broughton, Jr., term expired.

RAMONA TOLEDO SHUMP, of Kansas, to be a member of the Board of Directors of the Legal Services Corporation for a term expiring July 13, 1981, vice Glenn C. Stophel, term expired.

MAJ. GEN. RICHARD LEE HARRIS, 203–22–4382, United States Army, to be a member of the Mississippi River Commission, under the provisions of Section 2 of an Act of Congress, approved 28 June 1879 (21 Stat. 37) (33 U.S.C. 642).

MAJ. GEN. LOUIS WATKINS PRENTISS, JR., 229–26–9023, United States Army, to be a member of the Mississippi River Commission, under the provisions of Section 2 of an Act of Congress, approved 28 June 1879 (21 Stat. 37) (33 U.S.C. 642).

ELIZABETH DUSKIN, of Maryland, to be a member of the National Commission on Social Security for a term of 2 years (new position).

NORMAN B. CHAMP, JR., of Missouri, to be a member of the National Council on the Arts for a term expiring September 3, 1984, vice Henry Cauthen, term expired.

MARTIN FRIEDMAN, of Minnesota, to be a member of the National Council on the Arts for a term expiring September 3, 1984, vice Clint Eastwood, term expired.

BERNARD BLAS LÓPEZ, of New Mexico, to be a member of the National Council on the Arts for a term expiring September 3, 1984, vice Eudora Welty, term expired.

ROBERT LAWSON SHAW, of Georgia, to be a member of the National Council on the Arts for a term expiring September 3, 1984, vice Judith Jamison, term expired.

NOMINATIONS—Continued

Submitted January 18—Continued

JESSIE A. WOODS, of Illinois, to be a member of the National Council on the Arts for a term expiring September 3, 1984, vice Rosalind Russell Brisson, term expired.

ROSALIND W. WYMAN, of California, to be a member of the National Council on the Arts for a term expiring September 3, 1984, vice James D. Robertson, term expired.

The following-named persons to be members of the Board of Directors of the National Institute of Building Sciences for the terms indicated:

For a term expiring September 7, 1979

BLANCA G. CEDEÑO, of New York (new position).

For terms expiring September 7, 1980

GUY O. MABRY, of Ohio, vice Robert J. Brungraber, term expired.

LEONARD MILLER, of Florida, vice Jodie R. Johnson, term expired.

JOHN P. MILLHONE, of Minnesota (new position).

JOSEPH HERBERT NEWMAN, of New Jersey (reappointment).

For a term expiring September 7, 1981

LOIS A. CRAIG, of Massachusetts (new position).

S. LEE KLING, of Missouri, to be a member of the Board of Directors of the National Railroad Passenger Corporation for a term expiring July 18, 1981, vice Donald P. Jacobs, term expired.

EUGENE H. COTA-ROBLES, of California, to be a member of the National Science Board, National Science Foundation, for a term expiring May 10, 1984, vice William H. Meckling, term expired.

ERNESTINE FRIEDL, of North Carolina, to be a member of the National Science Board, National Science Foundation, for a term expiring May 10, 1984, vice Wesley G. Campbell, term expired.

WALTER EUGENE MASSEY, of Rhode Island, to be a member of the National Science Board, National Science Foundation, for a term expiring May 10, 1984, vice T. Marshall Hahn, Jr., term expired.

DAVID V. RAGONE, of Michigan, to be a member of the National Science Board, National Science Foundation, for a term expiring May 10, 1984, vice Joseph M. Reynolds, term expired.

NOMINATIONS—Continued

Submitted January 18—Continued

EDWIN ERNEST SALPETER, of New York, to be
a member of the National Science Board,
National Science Foundation, for a term expiring May 10, 1984, vice William A. Nierenberg, term expired.

CHARLES PENCE SLICHTER, of Illinois, to be a
member of the National Science Board, National Science Foundation, for a term expiring May 10, 1984 (reappointment).

THOMAS P. SALMON, of Vermont, to be a
member of the Board of Directors of the
United States Railway Association for the
remainder of the term expiring July 8, 1982,
vice Richard B. Ogilvie, resigned.

JAMES M. STONE, of Massachusetts, to be a
member of the Commodity Futures Trading
Commission for a term expiring April
13, 1983, vice Read Dunn, Jr., term expired.

JAMES M. STONE, of Massachusetts, to be
Chairman of the Commodity Futures Trading Commission, vice William T. Bagley,
resigned.

STERLING TUCKER, of the District of Columbia,
to be an Assistant Secretary of Housing and
Urban Development, vice Chester Crawford
McGuire, Jr., resigned.

Submitted January 19, 1979

PHYLLIS A. KRAVITCH, of Georgia, to be
United States Circuit Judge for the Fifth
Circuit, vice Lewis R. Morgan, retired.

JOHN G. PENN, of Maryland, to be United
States District Judge for the District of Columbia, vice Joseph C. Waddy, retired.

ABRAHAM D. SOFAER, of New York, to be
United States District Judge for the Southern District of New York, vice Marvin E.
Frankel, resigned.

NOMINATIONS—Continued

Submitted January 19—Continued

CARLON M. O'MALLEY, JR., of Pennsylvania,
to be United States Attorney for the Middle
District of Pennsylvania for the term of 4
years, vice S. John Cottone.

CHECKLIST OF WHITE HOUSE PRESS RELEASES

The following listing contains releases of the
White House Press Office which are not included in this issue.

Released January 14, 1979

Advance text: remarks at the Martin Luther
King, Jr. Nonviolent Peace Prize award
ceremony in Atlanta, Ga.

Released January 19, 1979

Announcement: nomination of Phyllis A.
Kravitch to be United States Circuit Judge
for the Fifth Circuit

Announcement: nomination of John G. Penn
to be United States District Judge for the
District of Columbia

Announcement: nomination of Abraham D.
Sofaer to be United States District Judge
for the Southern District of New York

Announcement: nomination of Carlon M.
O'Malley, Jr., to be United States Attorney
for the Middle District of Pennsylvania

ACTS APPROVED BY THE PRESIDENT

NOTE: No acts approved by the President were
received by the Office of the Federal Register
during the period covered by this issue.

Budget Message

Remarks at the Signing Ceremony.
January 22, 1979

THE PRESIDENT. In about 2 hours, the 1980 fiscal year budget will be presented to the Congress. And my role in this ceremony is to sign the official copies of the budget which will go to the Speaker of the House of Representatives and to the Vice President, who, as you know, is the President of the Senate.

My first inclination, however, is to thank the superb staff in the Office of Management and Budget, under the direction of Jim McIntyre, for the great work they have done on this budget. It has been a very difficult, stringent, severe, and tough budget in its preparation. And I think only with the most careful and constant consultation with those who are not satisfied with having had their own desires met and a realization on their part, after scrutiny, that the budget is indeed fair to everyone in our Nation, has there been an alleviation of the intense criticisms that were evident earlier late last year and would have been so present now. A tough budget that is fair, I believe, is acceptable.

Our most important role, economically speaking, this year, is to control inflation. And this budget meets that requirement. This budget eliminates unnecessary spending. It cuts back drastically on the Federal deficit. It lowers the percentage of our national income that is collected and spent by the Government down to 21 percent, a goal that we never thought we would meet so early.

Obviously, there's no way to please everyone in the preparation of any budget, particularly one designed, as is this one, to be stringent and to control Government spending and to control inflation. We realize, however, that we must live within our means, that we must put restraints on the always-rising demands on Government, and that we must make strong moves to eliminate inefficiency, waste, fraud, and corruption.

This budget, when implemented, will make major strides towards solving the problems of our country forthrightly, fairly, and with compassion and concern for those who depend most heavily on the services of Government.

Controlling inflation is the best policy that we can espouse, and particularly for those who are the poor, the elderly, those who live on small and fixed incomes, those who quite often are inarticulate and lacking in political influence, and who are not mobile enough or well-trained enough to travel around to different places to seek out better jobs and better opportunities.

This is a budget that is good enough so that I am sure that the American people will support it. It's a budget that's good enough that I will fight for it. And it's a budget that's good enough so that I have no doubt the Congress will adopt it.

In closing, let me express my thanks again to the superb professionals in the Office of Management and Budget, to Secretary of Treasury Mike Blumenthal, Secretary Kreps, my own economic advisers under Charles Schultze, and many others who have worked so well with us on the budget. Even though it will be presented officially at noon today, large numbers of key Members of Congress have already been briefed as thoroughly as possible on the elements of this budget document, and I believe at this point it's fair to say that the response has been very encouraging.

So, thank you all for being so effective in your difficult job. And at this point, I'd like to sign the copy of the budget that will go to the Speaker of the House.

And now to sign the copy that will go to the President of the Senate.

And I have already signed, first, a copy of the budget that will go to Jim McIntyre, the Director of the Office of Management and Budget. Jim, thank you.

MR. McINTYRE. Mr. President, thank you very much for the kind words you've had to say about the staff at OMB. I'd like to second the professionalism at OMB, but, most importantly, tell you how dedicated these people are to seeing that your policies are translated into the proper budget documents and into the proper statements and legislation so that they can be carried out by the Congress.

We feel we're very proud to be associated with this budget. It's a good budget; it's a tough budget, but one that does meet the needs of the American people. Thank you for your support in this effort.

THE PRESIDENT. I might say that after these long months of hard work, in some of which I participated, I think it's important that the OMB staff have some well-deserved rest. And I would suggest that in August, when the Congress adopts this budget, that you give some of your people—*[laughter]*——

NOTE: The President spoke at 10:05 a.m. in the Cabinet Room at the White House.

Budget Message

Message to the Congress Transmitting the Fiscal Year 1980 Budget.   January 22, 1979

To the Congress of the United States:

This budget for fiscal year 1980 is lean and austere. It recommends a spending level well below that suggested by the recent momentum of Federal spending. It will disappoint those who seek expanded Federal efforts across the board. It meets my commitment to a deficit of $30 billion or less.

This policy of restraint is not a casual one. It is an imperative if we are to overcome the threat of accelerating inflation. If that threat is realized, it would severely disrupt our economy and the well-being of our society. Americans with low and fixed incomes would suffer the most. Restraint would eventually become an inescapable necessity. But the longer we wait, the more severe and costly the inevitable restraint will be. By contrast, this budget supports a balanced fiscal policy. It is sufficiently restrained to ease inflationary pressures, but it will permit continued economic growth.

The Federal Government cannot overcome inflation by itself. Success will require cooperation from business, from labor, from consumers, from State and local governments—in short, from everyone. I have called for that cooperation as part of my anti-inflation program. However, only through its leadership and its example can the Federal Government secure this cooperation. This budget provides that leadership. It restrains Government's demand on the economy. At the same time, it makes the Federal dollar work harder and better.

The key to effective Federal leadership against inflation, unemployment, and poverty lies in more effective allocation and management of available resources. We must reduce the growth of total Federal spending while protecting the security of our Nation and the well-being of the American people.

This budget provides the necessary discipline over Federal spending by:

—eliminating programs that are unworkable;

—improving programs to make them more effective;

—focusing assistance on the disadvantaged and the poor; and

—reorganizing and consolidating Federal activities to improve efficiency and avoid waste, abuse, or mismanagement.

I believe this discipline represents an opportunity to reassess and build strong foundations for future Government activity, an opportunity to change Government for the better. It is my firm intention to continue these policies in future years, to reduce the size of the deficit, and to achieve a balanced budget as soon as economic conditions permit.

My budget provides for total outlays

THE BUDGET TOTALS

[In billions of dollars]

	1978 actual	1979 estimate	1980 estimate	1981 estimate	1982 estimate
Budget receipts....................	402	456	503	577	653
Budget outlays....................	451	493	532	578	615
Surplus or deficit (−)...............	−49	−37	−29	−1	38
Budget authority..............	502	560	616	651	696

in 1980 of $532 billion, an increase of $38 billion, or 7.7%, over 1979, and receipts of $503 billion. For 1981 and 1982, it provides for total outlays of $578 billion and $615 billion, respectively. Budget outlays will decrease as a share of the Nation's gross national product from 22.1% in 1978 to 21.2% in 1980 and 20.3% in 1982. This reduction in the share of our national product spent by the Federal Government is a fundamental goal of my policy, equally as important as reducing the deficit.

The expenditures I recommend are specifically focused on overcoming our Nation's crucial problems. Through rigorous zero-base analyses, priorities have been established to help us get the best Government possible for the resources we can afford. Careful attention to efficiency and productivity will enable Federal managers to achieve our most important priorities with less money and fewer people.

The spending restraint in this budget means that in some areas the Government will simply not be able to do as much as it has in the past. Inevitably, real sacrifices must be made if we are to overcome inflation. In formulating this budget, I have made every effort to spread that burden fairly and objectively. Restraint has not been applied arbitrarily.

However, there are areas where we cannot make major reductions. I have sought to reconcile the need for extraordinary restrictions on Government spending with the need to maintain a strong defense; to implement a national energy policy; to assist people in need; and to continue important public services and investments.

First, as President, it is my central responsibility to ensure that our defense forces are strong enough to deter aggression. This budget does that.

In May of 1977 I met with our NATO allies and urged that we work together to strengthen our common defense. They are meeting the goal that we agreed upon. We must and will do our share.

In total, the 1980 defense budget provides for growth in outlays in real terms of 3% above the current year's spending. Most of this increase will be for strengthening our NATO forces and maintaining the strategic balance. The budget continues my policy of steady modernization of our strategic forces, and improved combat readiness of our tactical forces. It also emphasizes research and development to meet future challenges to our security. At the same time, however, it restrains defense costs by introducing important economies in purchasing, supply management, and personnel costs and numbers.

Second, the 1980 budget recognizes the vital importance of energy to the Nation. Because of our dependence on foreign oil, we continue to be in danger of having supplies disrupted as they were 5 years ago. It is essential that we continue to move forward with an effective national energy program that will decrease our demand for foreign oil and protect against disruption of foreign oil supplies.

The 1980 budget provides for the continued buildup of the strategic petroleum reserve. It continues to assist in the development of technologies to tap our domestic energy resources more effectively. I have given special emphasis to developing advanced solar power technologies. The budget proposals give increased attention to more efficient use of uranium, to nuclear proliferation and environmental problems, and to effective measures to deal with nuclear waste.

Third, even when budget restraint is essential, we will continue as a compassionate society to meet our commitments to the disadvantaged. Therefore, I have ensured that my budget include adequate funds for programs that help those Americans most truly in need. To make these funds as effective as possible, the budget includes recommendations for adjustments in direct payment programs, better targeting of existing programs, and improved management so that funds are not wasted but go to the people for whom they were intended.

My administration is developing a national health plan. Consistent with the development of that plan, the budget emphasizes programs to address critical health needs. As early steps toward this plan, my proposals extend health services to 2 million more low-income children and pregnant women who cannot afford health care that they need, and bring new health care resources to people who live in medically-underserved areas. The budget includes new and expanded programs to reduce activities that cause ill health, such as drug and alcohol abuse, as well as to protect individuals and communities from pollution and other toxic substances; increased funding for mental health research; and expanded health-related services such as nutrition programs for low-income mothers and children.

I am again proposing legislation to contain the exorbitant nationwide rise in hospital costs. The 320% rise in these costs in the past 10 years has been a major inflationary force and an unacceptable drain on family incomes. The Congress *must* act on this problem.

Curbs on hospital costs will benefit State and local budgets—and those of private citizens—as well as the Federal budget. They will strike directly at inflation in a sector where price increases have been chronically high.

The budget recommends a number of changes in the social security system to streamline it and eliminate unnecessary benefit payments. They will reduce the future costs of this largest of all Federal programs—and, ultimately, hold down the taxes imposed on workers and employers. I will consider future social security tax reductions in conjunction with these savings.

In the past 2 years, total employment in the U.S. has increased by 7.4 million jobs. This is an average rate of 4.1% per year, one of the most rapid expansions in our history. The proportion of our civilian population employed is higher, at almost 60%, than it has ever been before. But despite these gains, unemployment, particularly among the disadvantaged and minorities, remains too high.

Continued high structural unemployment in an inflationary economy requires a redirection of our efforts. Programs targeted to employ the truly disadvantaged are continued at their current high levels as established by this administration. More general employment programs, not directed specifically to those most in need, must be reduced to reflect improvements in the economy and our need to establish priorities. Our youth employment and CETA programs reflect my continued strong commitment to fight unemployment of the needy. The employment tax credit enacted last year is encouraging the private sector to provide increased employment opportunities for the disadvantaged, primarily youth. This incentive will be reinforced by a private sector employment initiative, for which I am requesting a $400 million supplemental appropriation for 1979.

This budget also provides strong support for economic development programs, and again proposes a National Development Bank to help fund these efforts. The budget provides for a 36% increase in assistance to minority business enterprises.

Finally, I believe that the Federal Government must lead the way in investing in the Nation's future. This budget, therefore, continues my policy of providing real growth in Federal support of basic research. This support amounts to a relatively small part of the total budget—$4.6 billion in 1980—but it is vital to the future of our Nation. The knowledge created through basic research holds the potential for breakthroughs to the solution of problems we face or may face in such critical areas as agriculture, health, environment, energy, defense, and the overall productivity of our economy. Higher productivity gains in the future, moreover, will make an important contribution to reducing inflation.

––––––––––

Meeting the essential needs of the Nation, while restraining growth in overall spending, makes efficient management not just desirable, but essential.

In 1977 I proposed—and the Congress approved—a Cabinet-level Department of Energy, a streamlined Executive Office of the President, and a consolidation of our international information activities.

In 1978 I proposed—and the Congress approved—reorganizations of the Federal civil service system, emergency preparedness and disaster relief programs, civil rights enforcement, and the pension plan insurance system in order to make them more responsive and effective.

In 1979 I will resubmit my proposal to establish a Department of Education and propose further reorganization and consolidation in economic development assistance, natural resources management, and surface transportation.

For the second year, my budget reflects detailed, Government-wide, zero-base budgeting. Agency programs were explicitly ranked by priority, and programs were ranked across agencies, in a new interagency, zero-base budgeting process.

For the first time, the budget reflects the 3-year budget planning system I have instituted to gain better control of the longer-range effects and direction of Government policies.

In this budget I am proposing a new system to control the growth of Federal credit activities, particularly federally-guaranteed credit.

Other important steps will be taken to improve the way the Government operates and the way it affects the private sector. To increase the efficiency of the private sector, the administration will eliminate unnecessary regulation where possible, and will minimize the redtape involved in necessary environmental and safety regulation. Further efforts will be made to reduce excessive paper work. State and local governments, private institutions, and citizens will benefit from simplified conditions for receiving Federal assistance. In particular, a number of programs have been consolidated to simplify the grant system, and more will be proposed in the future. The Government's own management will be improved through

more effective cash management, application of the Civil Service Reform Act, and use of new offices of Inspectors General to identify waste and search out fraud and corruption.

Preparing this budget reminds me once more of the overwhelming demands upon the Federal budget and of the limits on our resources.

I believe that we must firmly limit what the Government taxes and spends. We must balance public and private needs. We must set priorities more carefully. We must change some old priorities and establish new ones. We must defer some of our demands if we are to meet adequately today's most critical needs.

These principles have guided my actions in shaping this budget and they will continue to do so in the future:

—the budget must be kept within the bounds of what is appropriate in today's economic circumstances;

—the Government has no resources of its own, its only resources are those it collects from the taxpayer;

—Government action must be limited to those areas where its intervention is more likely to solve problems than to compound them; and,

—we have an obligation to manage with excellence and to maintain proper priorities within the $532 billion proposed in this budget.

I know that the Congress shares these beliefs. You, as well as the executive branch, are sensitive to the American people's concerns about the scope of Government, the burdens of taxes, the needs of our citizens, and the efficiency of public management. Indeed, the Congress in the last few years has taken important steps— in particular, through the establishment of the congressional budget process—to improve its own means of establishing priorities. I have worked closely with the Congress, and will continue in this spirit of cooperation.

I look forward to working with the Congress and its leadership on this budget.

The decisions I have made are difficult ones. They involve, not figures on a balance sheet, but the lives and future of the American people. I have chosen restraint in Government spending because inflation must be controlled. I have tried to be equitable in ordering priorities. Yet I have continued to support those programs that represent our most pressing needs. To do so I have terminated, reduced, or deferred other programs.

It is difficult to maintain a sense of strong national purpose when we do not face a clear and immediate crisis. But it is equally important. These are times when responsible leadership means anticipating those day-to-day actions that enable us to avoid crises and to build toward the future. This has been the fundamental purpose behind the decisions considered here, and that is the intent of this budget.

JIMMY CARTER

January 22, 1979.

NOTE: The President's message is printed in the report entitled "The Budget of the United States Government, Fiscal Year 1980" (Government Printing Office, 605 pages).

United States Ambassador to Bahrain

Nomination of Robert H. Pelletreau, Jr.
January 22, 1979

The President today announced that he will nominate Robert H. Pelletreau, Jr., of Hartford, Conn., to be Ambassador Extraordinary and Plenipotentiary of the United States to the State of Bahrain. He would replace Wat T. Cluverius IV, resigned.

Pelletreau was born July 9, 1935, in Patchogue, N.Y. He received a B.A. from Yale University in 1957 and an LL.B. from Harvard Law School in 1961.

Pelletreau joined the Foreign Service in 1962 and was posted in Tangier, Nouakchott, Beirut, Amman, and at the State Department as an international relations officer. From 1973 to 1975, he was political officer in Algiers, and from 1975 to 1978, he was Deputy Chief of Mission in Damascus.

United States Ambassador to Tunisia

Nomination of Stephen W. Bosworth.
January 22, 1979

The President today announced that he will nominate Stephen W. Bosworth, of Jenison, Mich., to be Ambassador Extraordinary and Plenipotentiary of the United States to the Republic of Tunisia. He would replace Edward W. Mulcahy, resigned.

Bosworth was born December 4, 1939, in Grand Rapids. He received a B.A. from Dartmouth College in 1961 and joined the Foreign Service that year. He was posted in Panama, Colón, and Madrid, and was assistant to the U.S. Special Representative for Panama Canal Negotiations from 1964 to 1967.

From 1974 to 1976, Bosworth was Director of the Office of Fuels and Energy, Bureau of Economic and Business Affairs, at the State Department. Since 1976 he has been Deputy Assistant Secretary of State for International Resources and Food Policy.

Panama Canal Treaties

Letter to the Speaker of the House and the President of the Senate Transmitting Proposed Legislation.   January 23, 1979

Dear Mr. Speaker: (*Dear Mr. President:*)

I am pleased to forward herewith the text of proposed legislation to implement the Panama Canal Treaty of 1977 and its Related Agreements. I would appreciate its urgent consideration and timely passage by the Congress.

Senate approval of the Canal Treaties last April, and the delivery of instruments of ratification in June, marked the beginning of a new and important phase in our relations with the Republic of Panama and other nations of the Hemisphere. Under the Treaties, the United States will retain operational control of the Canal and primary responsibility for its defense until the end of this century. Panama will participate in the operation and defense of the Canal and will assume full responsibility for its operation when the Canal Treaty expires. Under a second treaty approved by the Senate the United States retains, permanently, the right to defend the Canal against any threat to its neutrality.

The constitutional processes of both countries have now been completed, and the treaties will enter into effect on October 1, 1979. Under their terms, on that date the Canal Zone will cease to exist, the United States Government agencies known as the Panama Canal Company and the Canal Zone Government will cease to operate within Panama, and general jurisdiction over the area as well as the performance of a number of important support functions will pass to Panama. Property transfers will become effective in accordance with Treaty provisions.

Under the Treaty, we will acquire extensive obligations and rights with respect to the Canal on October 1. We will not, however, be in a position to exercise these rights in a manner which will fully protect our interests in the Canal unless legislative action is taken promptly. To assure a smooth transition and continued efficient Canal operation once the new Treaties come into force, the legislative framework—in which the agencies responsible for operating and defending the Canal will be operating—must be established well in advance so that they may make the necessary plans and preparations.

Delay in adopting the legislation beyond May 31, 1979, could thus make conversion to the new system of Canal operation and defense less efficient and more costly. Moreover, uncertainty concerning the proposed legislative protection and benefits for Canal employees will increasingly affect employee morale and complicate the process of making necessary personnel adjustments. The consequent disruptive impact on the work force could reduce the efficiency of Canal operations and adversely affect the interests of U.S. shippers and consumers.

Our stewardship of the Panama Canal has been one of the outstandingly successful undertakings of American history. I urge the Congress to consider this legislation as a step toward the completion of another chapter in that history—one in which we will join with Panama to keep the Canal open, efficient and secure. In doing so, I am confident that this Government will maintain a system of management and a standard of performance of which all Americans can continue to be proud.

JIMMY CARTER

NOTE: This is the text of identical letters addressed to Thomas P. O'Neill, Jr., Speaker of the House of Representatives, and Walter F. Mondale, President of the Senate.

Federal Coal Mine Health Activities

Message to the Congress Transmitting a Report. January 23, 1979

To the Congress of the United States:

I transmit herewith the 1977 Annual Report of Health Activities under the Federal Coal Mine Health and Safety Act of 1969.

The Report, prepared by HEW's National Institute for Occupational Safety and Health, Center for Disease Control, Public Health Service, describes the coal mine health research conducted by the Institute, as well as the Institute's medical examination program for coal miners required by the Coal Mine Health and Safety Act of 1969, as amended in 1977.

I recommend that, in order to save HEW staff resources and time, the statutory reporting requirement for this report be changed from once every year to once every three years. All of the information contained in this Report is available to Congress during annual appropriations and oversight hearings, and HEW will inform Congress immediately of any scientific breakthroughs in the field.

JIMMY CARTER

The White House,
    January 23, 1979.

NOTE: The 20-page report is entitled "The Federal Coal Mine Health Program in 1977— Eighth Annual Report of Health Activities Under the Federal Coal Mine Health and Safety Act of 1969."

The State of the Union

Address Delivered Before a Joint Session of the Congress. January 23, 1979

Mr. President, Mr. Speaker, Members of the 96th Congress, and my fellow citizens:

Tonight I want to examine in a broad sense the state of our American Union— how we are building a new foundation for a peaceful and a prosperous world.

Our children who will be born this year will come of age in the 21st century. What kind of society, what kind of world are we building for them? Will we ourselves be at peace? Will our children enjoy a better quality of life? Will a strong and united America still be a force for freedom and prosperity around the world?

Tonight, there is every sign that the state of our Union is sound.

Our economy offers greater prosperity for more of our people than ever before. Real per capita income and real business profits have risen substantially in the last 2 years. Farm exports are setting an all-time record each year, and farm income last year, net farm income, was up more than 25 percent.

Our liberties are secure. Our military defenses are strong and growing stronger. And more importantly, tonight, America—our beloved country—is at peace.

Our earliest national commitments, modified and reshaped by succeeding generations, have served us well. But the problems that we face today are different from those that confronted earlier generations of Americans. They are more subtle, more complex, and more interrelated. At home, we are recognizing ever more clearly that government alone cannot solve these problems. And abroad, few of them can be solved by the United States alone. But Americans as a united people, working with our allies and friends, have never been afraid to face problems and to solve problems, either here or abroad.

The challenge to us is to build a new and firmer foundation for the future—for a sound economy, for a more effective government, for more political trust, and for a stable peace—so that the America

103

our children inherit will be even stronger and even better than it is today.

We cannot resort to simplistic or extreme solutions which substitute myths for common sense.

In our economy, it is a myth that we must choose endlessly between inflation and recession. Together, we build the foundation for a strong economy, with lower inflation, without contriving either a recession with its high unemployment or unworkable, mandatory government controls.

In our government, it is a myth that we must choose between compassion and competence. Together, we build the foundation for a government that works—and works for people.

In our relations with our potential adversaries, it is a myth that we must choose between confrontation and capitulation. Together, we build the foundation for a stable world of both diversity and peace.

Together, we've already begun to build the foundation for confidence in our economic system. During the last 2 years, in bringing our economy out of the deepest recession since the 1930's, we've created 7,100,000 new jobs. The unemployment rate has gone down 25 percent. And now we must redouble our fight against the persistent inflation that has wracked our country for more than a decade. That's our important domestic issue, and we must do it together.

We know that inflation is a burden for all Americans, but it's a disaster for the poor, the sick, and the old. No American family should be forced to choose among food, warmth, health care, or decent housing because the cost of any of these basic necessities has climbed out of reach.

Three months ago, I outlined to the Nation a balanced anti-inflation program that couples responsible government restraint with responsible wage and price restraint. It's based upon my knowledge

that there is a more powerful force than government compulsion—the force created by the cooperative efforts of millions of Americans working toward a common goal.

Business and labor have been increasingly supportive. It's imperative that we in government do our part. We must stop excessive government growth, and we must control government spending habits.

I've sent to this Congress a stringent but a fair budget, one that, since I ran for President in 1976, will have cut the Federal deficit in half. And as a percentage of our gross national product, the deficit will have dropped by almost 75 percent.

This Congress had a good record last year, and I now ask the 96th Congress to continue this partnership in holding the line on excess Federal spending. It will not be easy. But we must be strong, and we must be persistent.

This budget is a clear message that, with the help of you and the American people, I am determined, as President, to bring inflation under control.

The 1980 budget provides enough spending restraint to begin unwinding inflation, but enough support for our country to keep American workers productive and to encourage the investments that provide new jobs. We will continue to mobilize our Nation's resources to reduce our trade deficit substantially this year and to maintain the strength of the American dollar.

We've demonstrated in this restrained budget that we can build on the gains of the past 2 years to provide additional support to educate disadvantaged children, to care for the elderly, to provide nutrition and legal services for the poor, and to strengthen the economic base of our urban communities and, also, our rural areas.

This year, we will take our first steps to develop a national health plan.

We must never accept a permanent group of unemployed Americans, with no hope and no stake in building our society. For those left out of the economy because of discrimination, a lack of skills, or poverty, we must maintain high levels of training, and we must continue to provide jobs.

A responsible budget is not our only weapon to control inflation. We must act now to protect all Americans from health care costs that are rising $1 million per hour, 24 hours a day, doubling every 5 years. We must take control of the largest contributor to that inflation—skyrocketing hospital costs.

There will be no clearer test of the commitment of this Congress to the anti-inflation fight than the legislation that I will submit again this year to hold down inflation in hospital care.

Over the next 5 years, my proposals will save Americans a total of $60 billion, of which $25 billion will be savings to the American taxpayer in the Federal budget itself. The American people have waited long enough. This year we must act on hospital cost containment.

We must also fight inflation by improvements and better enforcement of our antitrust laws and by reducing government obstacles to competition in the private sector.

We must begin to scrutinize the overall effect of regulation in our economy. Through deregulation of the airline industry we've increased profits, cut prices for all Americans, and begun—for one of the few times in the history of our Nation—to actually dismantle a major Federal bureaucracy. This year, we must begin the effort to reform our regulatory processes for the railroad, bus, and the trucking industries.

America has the greatest economic system in the world. Let's reduce government interference and give it a chance to work.

I call on Congress to take other anti-inflation action—to expand our exports to protect American jobs threatened by unfair trade, to conserve energy, to increase production and to speed development of solar power, and to reassess our Nation's technological superiority. American workers who enlist in the fight against inflation deserve not just our gratitude, but they deserve the protection of the real wage insurance proposal that I have already made to the Congress.

To be successful, we must change our attitudes as well as our policies. We cannot afford to live beyond our means. We cannot afford to create programs that we can neither manage nor finance, or to waste our natural resources, and we cannot tolerate mismanagement and fraud. Above all, we must meet the challenges of inflation as a united people.

With the support of the American people, government in recent decades has helped to dismantle racial barriers, has provided assistance for the jobless and the retired, has fed the hungry, has protected the safety, health, and bargaining rights of American workers, and has helped to preserve our natural heritage.

But it's not enough to have created a lot of government programs. Now we must make the good programs more effective and improve or weed out those which are wasteful or unnecessary.

With the support of the Congress, we've begun to reorganize and to get control of the bureaucracy. We are reforming the civil service system, so that we can recognize and reward those who do a good job and correct or remove those who do not.

This year, we must extend major reorganization efforts to education, to economic development, and to the management of our natural resources. We need to enact a sunshine [sunset] law that when government programs have outlived their value, they will automatically be terminated.

There's no such thing as an effective and a noncontroversial reorganization and reform. But we know that honest, effective government is essential to restore public faith in our public action.

None of us can be satisfied when two-thirds of the American citizens chose not to vote last year in a national election. Too many Americans feel powerless against the influence of private lobbying groups and the unbelievable flood of private campaign money which threatens our electoral process.

This year, we must regain the public's faith by requiring limited financial funds from public funds for congressional election campaigns. House bill 1 provides for this public financing of campaigns. And I look forward with a great deal of anticipation to signing it at an early date.

A strong economy and an effective government will restore confidence in America. But the path of the future must be charted in peace. We must continue to build a new and a firm foundation for a stable world community.

We are building that new foundation from a position of national strength—the strength of our own defenses, the strength of our friendships with other nations, and of our oldest American ideals.

America's military power is a major force for security and stability in the world. We must maintain our strategic capability and continue the progress of the last 2 years with our NATO Allies, with whom we have increased our readiness, modernized our equipment, and strengthened our defense forces in Europe. I urge you to support the strong defense budget which I have proposed to the Congress.

But our national security in this complicated age requires more than just military might. In less than a lifetime, world population has more than doubled, colonial empires have disappeared, and a hundred new nations have been born. Mass communications, literacy, and migration to the world's cities have all awakened new yearnings for economic justice and human rights among people everywhere.

This demand for justice and human rights is a wave of the future. In such a world, the choice is not which super power will dominate the world. None can and none will. The choice instead is between a world of anarchy and destruction, or a world of cooperation and peace.

In such a world, we seek not to stifle inevitable change, but to influence its course in helpful and constructive ways that enhance our values, our national interests, and the cause of peace.

Towering over this volatile, changing world, like a thundercloud on a summer day, looms the awesome power of nuclear weapons.

We will continue to help shape the forces of change, to anticipate emerging problems of nuclear proliferation and conventional arms sales, and to use our great strength and influence to settle international conflicts in other parts of the world before they erupt and spread.

We have no desire to be the world's policeman. But America does want to be the world's peacemaker.

We are building the foundation for truly global cooperation, not only with Western and industrialized nations but with the developing countries as well. Our ties with Japan and our European allies are stronger than ever, and so are our friendly relations with the people of Latin America, Africa, and the Western Pacific and Asia.

We've won new respect in this hemisphere with the Panama Canal treaties. We've gained new trust with the developing world through our opposition to racism, our commitment to human rights, and our support for majority rule in Africa.

The multilateral trade negotiations are now reaching a successful conclusion, and congressional approval is essential to the economic well-being of our own country and of the world. This will be one of our top priorities in 1979.

We are entering a hopeful era in our relations with one-fourth of the world's people who live in China. The presence of Vice Premier Deng Xiaoping next week will help to inaugurate that new era. And with prompt congressional action on authorizing legislation, we will continue our commitment to a prosperous, peaceful, and secure life for the people of Taiwan.

I'm grateful that in the past year, as in the year before, no American has died in combat anywhere in the world. And in Iran, Nicaragua, Cyprus, Namibia, and Rhodesia, our country is working for peaceful solutions to dangerous conflicts.

In the Middle East, under the most difficult circumstances, we have sought to help ancient enemies lay aside deep-seated differences that have produced four bitter wars in our lifetime.

Our firm commitment to Israel's survival and security is rooted in our deepest convictions and in our knowledge of the strategic importance to our own Nation of a stable Middle East. To promote peace and reconciliation in the region, we must retain the trust and the confidence both of Israel and also of the Arab nations that are sincerely searching for peace.

I am determined, as President, to use the full, beneficial influence of our country so that the precious opportunity for lasting peace between Israel and Egypt will not be lost.

The new foundation of international cooperation that we seek excludes no nation. Cooperation with the Soviet Union serves the cause of peace, for in this nuclear age, world peace must include peace between the super powers—and it must mean the control of nuclear arms.

Ten years ago, the United States and the Soviet Union made the historic decision to open the strategic arms limitations talks, or SALT. The purpose of SALT, then as now, is not to gain a unilateral advanage for either nation, but to protect the security of both nations, to reverse the costly and dangerous momentum of the nuclear arms race, to preserve a stable balance of nuclear forces, and to demonstrate to a concerned world that we are determined to help preserve the peace.

The first SALT agreement was concluded in 1972. And since then, during 6 years of negotiation by both Republican and Democratic leaders, nearly all issues of SALT II have been resolved. If the Soviet Union continues to negotiate in good faith, a responsible SALT agreement will be reached.

It's important that the American people understand the nature of the SALT process.

SALT II is not based on sentiment; it's based on self-interest—of the United States and of the Soviet Union. Both nations share a powerful common interest in reducing the threat of a nuclear war. I will sign no agreement which does not enhance our national security.

SALT II does not rely on trust; it will be verifiable. We have very sophisticated, proven means, including our satellites, to determine for ourselves whether or not the Soviet Union is meeting its treaty obligations. I will sign no agreement which cannot be verified.

The American nuclear deterrent will remain strong after SALT II. For example, just one of our relatively invulnerable *Poseidon* submarines—comprising less than 2 percent of our total nuclear force of submarines, aircraft, and land-based missiles—carries enough warheads to destroy every large- and medium-sized city in the Soviet Union. Our deterrent is overwhelming, and I will sign no agreement unless our deterrent force will remain overwhelming.

A SALT agreement, of course, cannot substitute for wise diplomacy or a strong defense, nor will it end the danger of nuclear war. But it will certainly reduce that danger. It will strengthen our efforts to ban nuclear tests and to stop the spread of atomic weapons to other nations. And it can begin the process of negotiating new agreements which will further limit nuclear arms.

The path of arms control, backed by a strong defense—the path our Nation and every President has walked for 30 years—can lead to a world of law and of international negotiation and consultation in which all peoples might live in peace. In this year 1979, nothing is more important than that the Congress and the people of the United States resolve to continue with me on that path of nuclear arms control and world peace. This is paramount.

I've outlined some of the changes that have transformed the world and which are continuing as we meet here tonight. But we in America need not fear change. The values on which our Nation was founded—individual liberty, self-determination, the potential for human fulfillment in freedom—all of these endure. We find these democratic principles praised, even in books smuggled out of totalitarian nations and on wallposters in lands which we thought were closed to our influence. Our country has regained its special place of leadership in the worldwide struggle for human rights. And that is a commit-

ment that we must keep at home, as well as abroad.

The civil rights revolution freed all Americans, black and white, but its full promise still remains unrealized. I will continue to work with all my strength for equal opportunity for all Americans—and for affirmative action for those who carry the extra burden of past denial of equal opportunity.

We remain committed to improving our labor laws to better protect the rights of American workers. And our Nation must make it clear that the legal rights of women as citizens are guaranteed under the laws of our land by ratifying the equal rights amendment.

As long as I'm President, at home and around the world America's examples and America's influence will be marshaled to advance the cause of human rights.

To establish those values, two centuries ago a bold generation of Americans risked their property, their position, and life itself. We are their heirs, and they are sending us a message across the centuries. The words they made so vivid are now growing faintly indistinct, because they are not heard often enough. They are words like "justice," "equality," "unity," "truth," "sacrifice," "liberty," "faith," and "love."

These words remind us that the duty of our generation of Americans is to renew our Nation's faith—not focused just against foreign threats but against the threats of selfishness, cynicism, and apathy.

The new foundation I've discussed tonight can help us build a nation and a world where every child is nurtured and can look to the future with hope, where the resources now wasted on war can be turned towards meeting human needs, where all people have enough to eat, a decent home, and protection against disease.

It can help us build a nation and a world where all people are free to seek the truth and to add to human understanding, so that all of us may live our lives in peace.

Tonight, I ask you, the Members of the Congress, to join me in building that new foundation—a better foundation—for our beloved country and our world.

Thank you very much.

NOTE: The President spoke at 9:04 p.m. in the House Chamber at the Capitol. He was introduced by Thomas P. O'Neill, Jr., Speaker of the House of Representatives. The address was broadcast live on radio and television.

Chinese New Year, 1979

Message of the President.   January 24, 1979

New Year's Eve in the Chinese tradition is a time of reunion and reconciliation. It is a time when family quarrels are forgotten and when doors and windows are left open to give access to any beneficent spirits that may be passing.

This tradition takes on a special significance this year as the American and Chinese people build new ties of friendship and mutual cooperation.

Let Americans of Chinese ancestry and, indeed, all our citizens join in a special New Year's prayer that this relationship will blossom for the benefit of all Chinese and American people and of all nations.

Rosalynn and I welcome this opportunity to express our warmest New Year wishes to all Chinese Americans. May this Year of the Ram be remembered for having strengthened the structure of peace and fulfilled the hopes of all mankind for a more tranquil, prosperous and satisfying life.

JIMMY CARTER

Department of the Army

Nomination of Michael Blumenfeld To Be an Assistant Secretary.   January 24, 1979

The President today announced that he will nominate Michael Blumenfeld, of Washington, D.C., to be Assistant Secretary of the Army for Civil Works.

Blumenfeld was born November 10, 1934, in Brooklyn, N.Y. He received a B.A. from Harvard College in 1958 and an M.B.A. from Harvard Graduate School of Business Administration in 1960. He served in the U.S. Army from 1953 to 1956.

From 1960 to 1967, Blumenfeld was an account executive, then vice president and account supervisor, for Benton & Bowles, Inc., Advertising. From 1967 to 1969, he was Director of Public Affairs and Education for the United States Equal Employment Opportunity Commission. From 1969 to 1970, he was assistant to the vice president, public affairs, of Consolidated Edison Co. of New York.

From 1970 to 1973, Blumenfeld was deputy health services administrator of the city of New York. From 1973 to 1977, he was director of public affairs for New York University.

Since March 1977, Blumenfeld has been Deputy Under Secretary of the Army. In this position he oversees the Army's civil works program, a job which has included encouraging effective dialog between the Army Corps of Engineers and environmental groups and formulation of the Army's proposal for a non-Federal dam safety program.

Commodity Credit Corporation

Nomination of James H. Williams To Be a Member of the Board of Directors.
January 24, 1979

The President today announced that he will nominate James H. Williams, of Ocala, Fla., to be a member of the Board of Directors of the Commodity Credit Corporation. Williams was nominated to be Deputy Secretary of Agriculture on January 19, 1979.

Mutual and Balanced Force Reductions Negotiations

Appointment of Jonathan Dean as U.S. Representative.   January 24, 1979

The President today announced the appointment of Jonathan Dean, of New York City, as U.S. Representative for Mutual and Balanced Force Reductions (MBFR) Negotiations. The President also announced that he will nominate Dean for the rank of Ambassador during his tenure as U.S. Representative.

Dean was born June 15, 1924, in New York City. He received a B.A. from Columbia University in 1948 and an M.A. (1954) and Ph. D. (1973) from George Washington University.

Dean joined the Foreign Service in 1950 and served in a number of cities in Europe. From 1966 to 1968, he was special assistant to the Counselor of the State Department, and from 1968 to 1972, he was counselor for political affairs in Bonn.

From 1970 to 1972, Dean was Deputy U.S. Representative to the Berlin negotiations. In 1972 he served as Chairman of the Interagency Coordinating Committee for Mutual and Balanced Force Reductions, and in 1973 he was U.S. Representative to the preparatory talks for MBFR.

From 1973 to 1978, Dean was Deputy U.S. Representative to the MBFR negotiations. Since 1978 he has been Acting U.S. Representative to the MBFR negotiations.

Economic Report of the President

Annual Message to the Congress.
January 25, 1979

To the Congress of the United States:

Two years ago when I took office our economy was still struggling to recover from the deep recession of 1974–75. Unemployment was widespread, and a substantial part of our industrial capacity stood idle.

Today 7 million more Americans are at work, and factories across the country have regained high levels of output. Family incomes, after adjustment for inflation, have risen handsomely and so have business profits.

The task now confronting us is to manage an economy operating at close to its capacity—to sustain prosperity and extend its benefits more widely among our citizens.

Under the best circumstances, designing economic policies to carry out that task calls for restraint and careful choices. Developing such policies has been made more complex by the acceleration of inflation last year and the declining growth of productivity that was partly responsible for it.

My economic and budgetary program deals forthrightly with the economic realities we face today. It is based on four principles.

First, reducing inflation must be our top economic priority. Inflation endangers the gains in employment and income that we have made during the past 2 years. We must act forcefully and effectively to combat inflation, and we must persist until the battle is won.

Second, government must do its job better. Reducing inflation will require budgetary austerity and moderation of economic growth. With productivity growth at a low ebb, living standards will not rise as fast as they have in the past 2 years. In such a climate, waste, inefficiency, or misplaced priorities are particularly intolerable. It is now more essential than ever that our government, in both its budgetary and regulatory programs, make the best use of the resources at its disposal and seek better, less costly means to achieve our national objectives.

Third, we will not reduce inflation at the expense of the most vulnerable members of our society—the poor, the elderly, and those who have difficulty finding jobs even in a high-employment economy. Ours is a compassionate Nation, dedicated to a sense of fairness. We will not lose sight of those who most need our help.

Fourth, our policies must reflect the fact that the United States is a very important part of a closely related world economy. We will continue to pursue domestic policies and undertake other actions as necessary and appropriate to foster a strong and stable dollar, and we will join with other countries to promote an open and growing world economy.

In the months ahead, I will work closely with the Congress to ensure that the pol-

icies adopted by this government are consistent with these four precepts. The budget for 1980 must be very tight, and I intend to make sure that a fiscal policy of firm and measured restraint is maintained. But the budget must continue and strengthen our most essential programs, and I have supported such programs strongly. In order to further the fight against inflation, I will seek prompt adoption of my real wage insurance program and my proposals for hospital cost containment and regulatory reform.

I will continue to seek the cooperation and support of the American people in the fight against inflation. Last October, I proposed to the Nation a program of price and pay standards designed to brake the price-wage spiral that has beset our economy for more than a decade. This program has received substantial support from the American people, and I will make every effort to enlist the broadest possible cooperation with it in the year to come.

The pay and price standards ask every American to exercise restraint. Every American should therefore expect the government to ensure that its own actions will contribute to, not undermine, the voluntary effort to reduce inflation. Steadfast pursuit of fiscal and monetary discipline and limits on the inflationary impacts of other government actions are crucial to the success of the anti-inflation program. Together, the actions of government and the private sector can lay a new foundation for a durable prosperity.

PROGRESS AND PROBLEMS IN 1978

Among my first actions in office were steps to strengthen economic growth and speed the return to a high-employment economy. Those actions paid generous dividends. In 1977 our rate of economic growth increased by nearly a full percentage point over the prior year, and in 1978 the Nation's output of goods and services advanced by a healthy 4¼ percent. Today our Nation is using its industrial capacity more fully than a year ago.

Last year 3 million new jobs were created. A larger proportion of our people is at work now than at any other time in our history. Gains in employment during the past 2 years have been especially strong among women and members of minority groups.

Unemployment declined to less than 6 percent of the labor force during 1978. Nearly 1½-million fewer Americans were unemployed in December 1978 than 2 years earlier. Unemployment among minority groups has also begun to decline from the very high levels that persisted earlier in the recovery, but these groups still bear a disproportionate share of the burden of unemployment.

Gains in employment and output produced strongly rising incomes for most Americans during 1978. Disposable personal income, adjusted for inflation, rose by more than 3 percent over the 4 quarters of last year. The income of our country's farmers, which was severely depressed in 1976 and 1977, showed a marked recovery.

Business profits rose more than 10 percent in 1978, thereby promoting conditions for the continued growth in investment needed for productivity improvement and healthy economic expansion. Business investment in new plant and equipment also strengthened in 1978, raising the proportion of our national output devoted to capital formation to the highest level in 4 years.

On most counts, the prosperity of our Nation rests on a solid base. Our economy at the end of last year was still growing strongly. The momentum of expansion will be sustained early this year by the reductions in taxes on individual incomes and corporate profits that were provided in the Revenue Act of 1978. Last year, as in the earlier years of the recovery, the process of economic expansion remained relatively well balanced. Business inventories are lean. Industrial firms and financial institutions are in good financial condition. Shortages and speculative buying generally are absent. But inflation does pose a serious threat to the Nation's continued economic health. If we make progress in reducing inflation, the prospects are good for a successful transition from a period of economic recovery to a period of moderate but sustained growth.

For more than 10 years, our country, like many other nations, has faced stubborn inflation. During the course of 1978 our inflation problem worsened. Consumer prices rose by about 9 percent, a large acceleration from the 6¾ percent rate of inflation in 1977. Increases in wages also were larger and, since productivity gains declined sharply, costs of production moved up much more strongly.

The anti-inflation effort was given top priority in 1978. In May, I recommended that the Congress reduce by $5 billion and delay 3 months the tax cut that had been proposed earlier. In October, I set forth a strong and comprehensive program to combat inflation. Shortly thereafter, in cooperation with other countries, the Nation undertook a series of measures to strengthen the dollar abroad and further contribute to a reduction of inflation at home.

INFLATION IN 1978

Rising inflation last year stemmed from several sources. Cold winter weather affected food supplies and prices. Depreciation of the dollar in foreign exchange markets added to prices of imports and to prices of goods produced by U.S. firms that compete with imported products. Costs of land and building materials were driven up by exuberant demands for new homes, and the rise of mortgage interest rates added to the costs of buying a home. At the same time, the cumulative effects of government legislation and regulation over recent years gave further impetus to cost pressures.

A large part of the worsening of inflation last year, however, stemmed from poor productivity. Over the past decade or more, the rate of growth in our productivity has been slowing. In late 1977 and throughout 1978, the slowdown in productivity growth reached serious proportions. Last year the productivity of our economy increased by less than 1 percent.

The reasons for the weakening of productivity growth in our country, especially its poor performance last year, are complex and are not fully understood. But the consequences are well known. With slower productivity growth, our living standards individually and as a Nation cannot rise as fast. Slower productivity growth means that the resources available for carrying out governmental programs become scarcer. It means that large increases in wages and other incomes put greater upward pressure on costs and prices. If we ignore the realities of slower productivity growth—if governments continue to press forward with unabated claims on resources, and private citizens continue to demand large gains in money incomes—our inflationary problem will worsen.

DEALING WITH INFLATION

Inflation injures every person in our country. It means that paychecks do not go as far as they once did. It means that savings accumulated for retirement or for a child's education become inadequate. Many poor and elderly persons see prices they pay for food, shelter, and heat rise rapidly while their incomes rise slowly or not at all. These problems are so acute that they demand an all-out effort to reduce inflation. Yet rising prices and costs have additional and very serious effects on our economy as a whole.

Inflation drives up interest rates. It undermines the competitiveness of our industries and the value of our dollar abroad. Confidence of businesses in the future is reduced and investment plans are upset. Consumers' confidence in their own future is sapped. Sooner or later, these effects of inflation will undermine the basis for economic expansion and make sustained prosperity impossible.

Finally, the corrosive effects of inflation eat away at the ties that bind us together as a people. One of the major tasks of a democratic government is to maintain conditions in which its citizens have a sense of command over their own destiny. During an inflation individuals watch in frustration as the value of last week's pay increase or last month's larger social security check is steadily eroded over the remainder of the year by a process that is beyond their individual control. All of us have to plan for the future when we lend or borrow, save for a child's education, change a job, buy a home, or choose a career. The future is uncertain enough in any event, and the outcome of our plans is never fully within our own control. When the value of the measuring rod with which we do our planning—the purchasing power of the dollar—is subject to large and unpredictable shrinkage, one more element of command over our own future slips away. It is small wonder that trust in government and in social institutions is simultaneously eroded.

It is for all of these reasons that reducing inflation must now be the primary concern of economic policy.

POLICIES TO CONTROL INFLATION

Firm, sustained and carefully applied fiscal and monetary restraint must be the first element in our effort to reduce inflation. We have entered a period in which the high rate of economic growth that we experienced when the margin of unused resources was larger no longer is appropriate. We will apply the needed restraint and stick with it.

We will *not* try to wring inflation out of our economic system by pursuing policies designed to bring about a recession. That course of action would be unfair. It would put the heaviest burden of fighting inflation on those who can least afford to bear it. It also would be ineffective. Twice in the past decade inflation has accelerated and a recession has followed, but each recession brought only limited relief from inflation. The underlying pressures behind rising prices and costs continued to be strong, and inflation eventually accelerated again when recovery began. Stop-and-go policies do not work. A successful anti-inflation program must be durable to deal with a long-run inflation problem. Our program meets that test.

When I announced my anti-inflation initiatives last October, I pledged to pursue a restrained budgetary policy in fiscal year 1980. I have kept that pledge. The central element of my fiscal program is tight control over Federal spending:

• Growth in Federal spending will be curtailed. As in 1979, Federal outlays in the next fiscal year will increase in real terms by significantly less than 1 percent.

• The share of the Nation's output accounted for by Federal spending will be reduced to about 21 percent in fiscal 1980,

a full year ahead of the schedule that I had earlier announced.

Restricted growth in Federal spending, combined with the revenues yielded by a moderately growing economy, will reduce the budget deficit to $29 billion in fiscal 1980, less than half its size in the year before I took office. This course of fiscal policy will exert the measured restraint that is needed. Excessive demands upon the Nation's resources will be avoided. Growth in economic activity will slow to a little below the rise in the Nation's economic potential.

These measures of fiscal policy are being complemented by firm and careful monetary restraint on the part of the Federal Reserve Board. In this way, monetary and fiscal policy are supporting each other to combat inflationary pressures and foster a healthy and stable economy.

OTHER GOVERNMENTAL ACTIONS

I am taking other steps to reduce the inflationary effects of government actions. I have directed the agencies of the executive branch to pay special attention to ensuring that the regulations they issue do not impose unnecessary burdens on the public, and I shall continue the efforts that got under way in 1978 to improve the regulatory process.

Last year the deregulation of the airline industry brought American consumers the benefits of substantially lower prices and better service. This year I intend to seek congressional approval of legislation to increase the role of competitive forces in the trucking and railroad industries. I will submit to the Congress legislation to reform the process by which regulations are developed by Federal agencies, and to increase the emphasis on a careful balancing of costs and benefits. And I am taking steps to reduce the burden of paperwork imposed by the government on the private sector.

Government must set a clear example in the fight against inflation. For that reason, I ordered last year that the rate of pay increase for Federal workers be held to 5.5 percent and that sharp limitations be imposed on new Federal hiring.

Although these actions by government will not, by themselves, bring inflation to an end, they are indispensable. They can create an environment that encourages voluntary cooperation with the pay and price standards. Without restraint by government, the pressures of an overheated economy easily could render meaningless the best efforts of businesses and workers to reduce price and wage increases. However, it will take broad cooperation from the private sector if the voluntary effort is to succeed in reducing inflation.

VOLUNTARY WAGE AND PRICE STANDARDS

The voluntary wage and price standards call for an average rate of pay increase of 7 percent or less this year. I also have asked businesses to hold their average rate of price increase to at least one-half percentage point below the average rate of increase in 1976–77. Where such price deceleration is not possible, the standards provide for limitations on profit margins.

To meet these standards both workers and businesses must exercise restraint. But they are fair and flexible standards. If they are widely observed, as I believe they will be, we can reverse the momentum of the price-wage cycle and gradually bring down the rate of inflation.

I recognize that cooperation with this program entails uncertainties for workers who comply with the wage standards. They may lose if others do not comply, or if forces beyond anyone's control cause

prices to rise unexpectedly. In order to provide them some assurance that those who cooperate will not suffer as a result, and thus to motivate wider observance of the standards, I have proposed to the Congress a program of real wage insurance. Under this program, if inflation increases by more than 7 percent this year, groups of workers that meet the 7 percent pay standard will receive a tax credit at a rate equal to the difference between the actual inflation rate and 7 percent. This credit will insure workers' real wages over a range of inflation as high as 10 percent this year, far higher than is expected to occur.

The elements of my anti-inflation program are mutually supportive and designed to mount a sustainable attack on our long-run inflation problem. Voluntary cooperation with the pay and price standards is essential to reversing the momentum of inflation. Government needs to take strong action to avoid contributing to inflationary pressures in order to ensure that the benefits of voluntary restraint are fully realized. Together, these policies offer our best opportunity to win the fight against inflation.

OUTLOOK FOR 1979

My anti-inflation program will support the health of our economy in 1979 in two respects. First, the rate of inflation should slow this year—to about 7½ percent over the year as a whole, and to somewhat below 7 percent by the end of the year. Second, moderation of inflation will help us avoid a recession and improve the prospects for sustained economic growth in 1980 and beyond.

Over the 4 quarters of 1979, the Nation's output should rise by about 2¼ percent, somewhat less than the economy's potential growth. This should create an economic climate in which the wage and price standards have good prospects for success. The labor force will continue to expand strongly and most new workers will find jobs.

Further progress in reducing inflation can be expected in 1980 as the effects of the anti-inflation program begin to cumulate. Moderate growth in the year ahead, combined with substantial progress against inflation, will lay the basis for an enduring prosperity.

In the years beyond 1980, as we are successful in containing the growth in Federal spending and bringing down the rate of inflation, we can look toward reductions in Federal taxes. Rising real income and inflation, even at a reduced pace, push taxpayers into higher tax brackets and thereby raise the average effective tax rate. Both to sustain economic growth and to relieve citizens from unwarranted tax burdens, tax reductions will, from time to time, be highly desirable.

It would be unwise—and, indeed, very dangerous—to commit ourselves now to any mechanical formula for future reductions. No such formula will pass the test of budgetary responsibility. Our knowledge of future economic conditions and developments affecting the rate of inflation is too limited to make such decisions at this time. There is simply no substitute for the difficult process of matching our overall budgetary policies year by year to the economic requirements of the Nation.

POLICIES TO MEET THE NATION'S NEEDS

In a period when the overall growth of budgetary resources must be tightly restrained, budget decisions take on special importance. Some real growth in our defense budget is essential to meet our national security needs and keep our inter-national commitments in the face of the growing military strength of our potential adversaries.

Within the domestic budget I have given special priority to the needs of the poor and the disadvantaged. I have recommended substantial funding for programs that address their needs for assistance in health care, education, employment and training, and basic subsistence. The 1980 budget directs the resources of those programs more carefully toward those most in need. Similarly I have sought to maintain and, in some cases, expand the assistance provided to our financially troubled cities and counties. I have paid particular attention to the need to move ahead with the development of alternative energy sources, including solar energy, and to spur basic research and development, which has been lagging in our country.

We cannot be satisfied with the condition of our economy while many of our disadvantaged citizens, especially among minorities, are unable to find work even in periods of prosperity. In 1978, the Congress enacted with my support the Full Employment and Balanced Growth Act. That act restates and amplifies the responsibilities of economic policy that have faced our Nation in recent decades. The act challenges us to provide the fullest possible opportunities for useful employment, to rely on the private sector as the principal provider of jobs, and to create an environment of price stability that will make it possible to sustain prosperity. These are very ambitious goals that challenge us as a Nation to set our sights high. The act also establishes important new procedures for moving toward the realization of full employment and price stability.

Neither can we rest while large numbers of Americans still live in poverty.

This Nation has made a concerted effort to provide for those in our society who are in need. We have assisted the poor to acquire the basic necessities of life. We have taken steps to assure adequate incomes and medical care for the elderly. And we have helped to assure better health care, nutrition, and education for the young. My budget for 1980 continues to respond to the challenge that poverty sets before our Nation.

Each of these challenges calls for action by the government. In a period of inflation, however, our ability to act is limited. We cannot do everything, but we must do what we can and do it well. That is the framework within which I have constructed my budgetary program for 1979 and 1980. This budget provides a carefully balanced spending plan which will ensure that the activities of the Federal Government are well administered and effective, and that we continue to respond to the important needs of the country.

My 1980 budget provides important building blocks for the future in many areas:

• *Health programs,* which I have expanded substantially during my first 2 years in office, will be maintained at those levels and in some cases increased. In addition, consistent with the development of a National Health Plan, new resources have been provided for the Child Health Assessment Program, which will extend Medicaid benefits to over 2 million low-income children. Funds have also been provided for extending Medicaid coverage to 100,000 low-income pregnant women not now eligible.

• *Authority for new spending for education* is maintained at the level that I provided in my budget last year. This program will support spending nearly 20 percent greater, in real terms, than 2 years ago.

• *Publicly assisted housing* will be provided through subsidies for 325,000 new units for families with low or moderate incomes.

• *Job-related programs* will include funds that will support an average of 546,-000 public service jobs, phasing down to 467,000 jobs by the end of 1980. These jobs have been targeted more tightly to serve the structurally unemployed. Another 424,000 training opportunities also will be provided for the structurally unemployed. Programs to provide employment and training opportunities for youths remain a high priority. More private sector job opportunities will be made available through the new private sector initiative and the targeted employment tax credit.

• *A welfare reform program,* to take effect in 1982, will expand aid to families with dependent children, increase the earned income tax credit for low-wage workers, substantially improve employment opportunities for the Nation's neediest citizens, and provide fiscal relief to State and local governments with severe welfare burdens. Important reforms in the administration of the program will make America's welfare system easier to operate.

• *Aid to our cities and counties* will continue to be provided through revenue sharing, community development block grants, urban mass transit assistance, and urban development action grants. My budget provides new resources for the National Development Bank and requests funding in fiscal 1979 and 1980 for a new program of special fiscal assistance to cities and counties with severe unemployment problems.

This spending program provides for our Nation's vital needs, while remaining within the constraints required by today's inflationary economy.

THE INTERNATIONAL ECONOMY

Developments last year reminded us once again of the interdependence of our economy and those of other nations around the world. Our trading partners are looking at our ability to deal with our economic problems at home as an indicator of the strength and leadership they can expect from the United States. We will not disappoint them.

Nineteen hundred and seventy-eight was a year of significant progress in the world economy. Real output began to pick up in industrial countries other than the United States. Important initiatives in the international arena occurred in trade policy, in balance of payments adjustment, and in financial markets—all influenced by the cooperation shown at the Bonn Summit.

Late 1978 and early 1979 will mark the culmination of the Tokyo round of Multilateral Trade Negotiations. These historic negotiations—which began in 1975 and were intensified in 1977—should lead to the first comprehensive overhaul of the rules of international trade since the 1960s.

The need for a revamping of the trading system is clear. Our large foreign trade deficit stems in part from a loss of American vitality in world markets. But it has also resulted from the tariff and nontariff barriers of our trading partners. Over the coming years, under a final multilateral trade agreement, barriers at home and abroad will be reciprocally dismantled.

During 1979 I will be working closely with the Congress to adopt the final multilateral trade agreement, along with implementing legislation, that will foster robust export growth and free and fair competition in world trade under rules that are both equitable and economically sensible. These measures will provide a framework for trade that will enhance our living standards in the decade to come.

In recent years, the United States has had a serious balance of payments deficit. Our imports surged as we grew rapidly and drew heavily on imported oil. Our exports lagged because of slow economic growth abroad. These factors contributed to a trade deficit rising from about $10 billion in 1976 to an annual rate of almost $45 billion in early 1978. As a result of the sharp increase in our external deficit and the acceleration of inflation in the United States, the value of the dollar in foreign exchange markets fell substantially last year.

We have taken important steps to correct the deficit:

• In late 1978, Congress enacted the National Energy Act, the first comprehensive legislation for dealing with our energy problems. The effect will be to reduce our oil imports in 1985 by 2.5 million barrels per day.

• In 1978, I announced the first phase of a National Export Policy. By setting up a framework to increase support for exports and reduce disincentives to export, we can begin to increase our share of world commerce. Fundamental improvement in our trade position is critical to a healthy dollar.

• A strong and effective anti-inflation program has been put into place. An integral part of that program consists of monetary and fiscal policies that will moderate the rate of economic expansion. These actions will help reduce our large foreign trade deficit.

These policies were beginning to bear fruit by the end of 1978. Exports today are growing more rapidly than the domestic economy. The merchandise trade deficit declined from a $38-billion annual rate in the first half of last year to about $32 billion in the latter half of the year. Narrowing of the deficit should continue and we foresee a marked improvement in the more comprehensive current account measure.

Nineteen hundred and seventy-eight was also a year of unusual instability in international financial markets. In the fall, movements in the exchange value of the dollar became very disorderly, and its decline became clearly excessive.

On November 1, I announced a series of steps to restore order to the foreign exchange markets and to correct the excessive decline of the dollar. Up to $30 billion in foreign exchange resources were assembled by the United States, to be used in coordination with other countries utilizing their own resources, to protect the dollar's value in currency markets. Domestic interest rates were raised significantly to help reduce inflation and strengthen the dollar in exchange markets. And the United States underlined its commitment to deal with its inflation problem and strengthen its underlying economic position.

These actions have improved the tone of the exchange markets and contributed to a rise in the value of the dollar. More importantly for the longer term, they are helping to create more stable conditions in the exchange markets, in which the value of the dollar can better reflect the fundamental strength of the U.S. economy.

Progress also was made in 1978 in achieving closer economic cooperation among the leading industrial nations. I met in Bonn with the leaders of the six major industrial countries to discuss major economic problems facing us. Out of this came a concerted action program to restore greater balance and confidence in the international economy and in world financial markets. Together, we took the necessary steps to achieve those ends—the United States committed itself to combat inflation and reduce oil imports, Germany and Japan to increase growth and reduce

trade surpluses, others to take measures on trade or inflation. Only through continued economic cooperation and sound policies can we attain the goal of full employment and price stability that is our ultimate objective.

BUILDING FOR THE FUTURE

During this coming year, we as a Nation have an opportunity to strengthen our economy and lay the basis for continuing prosperity. The gains of the last 2 years have been notable. We have made great progress at home in recovering from the recession, and we have strengthened the stature of the United States in the world economy. In the year ahead, we can secure and extend those gains by working together to moderate inflation. I am confident that we will rise to the challenge.

JIMMY CARTER

January 25, 1979.

NOTE: The President's message is printed in the report entitled "Economic Report of the President, Transmitted to the Congress, January 1979—Together with the Annual Report of the Council of Economic Advisers" (Government Printing Office, 306 pages).

Council on Environmental Quality

Message to the Congress Transmitting a Report.   January 25, 1979

To the Congress of the United States:

I am pleased to transmit to the Congress the Ninth Annual Report of the Council on Environmental Quality.

The Report contains abundant evidence of progress in meeting our national commitment to protecting our environment. The dimensions of the task still before us also emerge from the Report. For example, the Report cites encouraging evidence that the quality of our streams and lakes is improving in many places. Yet few areas of the country are entirely free of even those water quality problems which we understand best and control most effectively. And we are only on the threshold of comprehending and controlling newer problems of toxic pollution in water supplies.

Our efforts to enhance the quality of urban environments offer another example. We have gained many insights in the past few years into how tax, water, sewer, transportation, and a host of other Federal programs affect the shape of cities and the use of land. Those insights are reflected in my Urban Policy Message of last March and in many new laws and Executive Branch policies. Yet as we find ourselves better able to cope with the problems of urban sprawl, new and unfamiliar problems have emerged with the unprecedented migration from cities to small towns and rural counties in the 1970's. The lesson is that even as we learn more and do better in protecting our environment, new challenges will continue to appear.

We can be proud of our achievements so far. In my 1977 Environmental Message, I promised energetic enforcement of the environmental programs already on the books and asked your collaboration in developing certain new ones. As a result of our partnership, we can point to:

• The first law setting Federal standards for the stripmining of coal;

• a renewal of the Clean Air and Clean Water Acts, with strict but enforceable standards;

• amendment of the 25-year-old Outer Continental Shelf Lands Act to provide orderly development of offshore oil and gas resources with high standards of environmental protection;

• a nuclear non-proliferation law;

• our selection of the environmentally preferable route for shipping Alaskan natural gas to the lower 48 States;

• the permanent protection of nearly 95 million acres of unspoiled lands in Alaska in our park and refuge systems;

• a major expansion of the Nation's park and wilderness systems, including the addition of large acreage to Redwood National Park; and

• effective regulation of fishing in the U.S. 200-mile fishery conservation zone, with a 50 percent reduction of foreign fishing and a total ban on commercial whaling within that zone.

Building on the foundation already laid by Congress and using authority already granted me, I asked agencies of the Executive Branch to undertake a number of broad policy reforms in environmental matters, including:

• a comprehensive new water resource policy that stresses conservation, environmental protection, Federal-State cooperation, cost sharing, and rational economic evaluation;

• an Administration policy that would reduce the risks of plutonium and nuclear weapons proliferation;

• vigorous support for the development of solar energy, continuation of selected solar projects, and a national policy review;

• improved protection of health and safety in the workplace, emphasizing serious health hazards while eliminating trivial regulations;

• a concerted drive by all Federal agencies to design a uniform approach toward the control of cancer-causing, life-altering toxic substances;

• a thoroughgoing reform by EPA of its regulations to minimize costs and delay, welcome outside ideas and participants, and test flexible new approaches, while ensuring adequate protection of health and the environment.

Finally, I directed the Council on Environmental Quality to issue regulations under the National Environmental Policy Act which will help all Federal agencies make well-informed, environmentally sound decisions, with a minimum of paperwork and delay. I asked for new regulations which would improve the government's ability to assess the effects of its actions and encourage the preparation of concise, analytic environmental impact statements. After public hearings and a thorough review by other Federal agencies, the Council drafted regulations to achieve these goals.

I am pleased that the United States has pioneered laws to protect our air, water and land. I believe our leadership has proved its worth. Since the National Environmental Protection Act (NEPA) was passed, at least 25 States have adopted "little NEPAs" patterned after the Federal model, 16 other nations have adopted some form of environmental impact review of governmental activities, and more than 80 nations have incorporated into their governments a ministry with environmental responsibility.

In the years ahead, let us continue our fruitful collaboration and our leadership in environmental protection.

JIMMY CARTER

The White House,
January 25, 1979.

NOTE: The report is entitled "Environmental Quality: The Ninth Annual Report of the Council on Environmental Quality—December 1978" (Government Printing Office, 599 pages).

The State of the Union

Annual Message to the Congress.
January 25, 1979

To the Congress of the United States:

My State of the Union Address was devoted to what I believe are the highest priorities facing our Nation in 1979 as we seek to build a new foundation at home and abroad.

However, my Administration's time and effort this year will also be focused on a significant number of other important initiatives and goals. I am sending this State of the Union Message so that the Members of the 96th Congress are presented with a full picture of my basic legislative program in domestic and foreign affairs for the year.

Over the past two years, my Administration has developed a very cooperative relationship with the Congress. That relationship not only resulted in the extraordinarily productive record of the 95th Congress, but will provide the foundation for a renewed sense of trust and confidence by the American people in their government.

We have an enviable record to match. But with your help, the 96th Congress can meet this challenge. My Administration and I are eager to help in the effort.

Our basic goals will be to continue working with you to build solid foundations for the next century—a solid economic foundation of stable prices and continued growth—a solid foundation for a more efficient, less intrusive Federal government—a solid foundation for world peace and American security.

FOUNDATION FOR PROGRESS

When I took office two years ago, the country faced serious domestic problems:

• the economy had not recovered from a recession;

• unemployment was intolerably high at 7.8%, with 7¾ million Americans out of work;

• the Nation had no sound energy policy and oil imports were rising rapidly;

• the Federal government was operating inefficiently in numerous vital areas;

• trust in the openness and integrity of the government was low;

• major social problems were being ignored or inadequately addressed by the Federal government.

In the ensuing two years, we have tackled these problems head-on. While problems cannot be solved overnight, real progress has been made:

• the economy has strengthened—real Gross National Product has increased 10% and real disposable personal income has increased 8.9%;

• the unemployment rate has decreased by 25% since my election, from nearly 8% to 5.9%; 7.3 million new jobs have been created; total employment has reached a record of 95.9 million;

• a comprehensive national energy policy has been enacted and a Department of Energy created to help implement it;

• the first major reform of Civil Service System in nearly a century was enacted; 6 reorganization plans have been approved and implemented; the Federal paperwork burden has been reduced by 10%; inspectors general are being placed in departments and agencies to help root out fraud and abuse; zero-based budgeting practices have been instituted throughout the government; several hundred million dollars have been saved through sound cash management reforms; regulations are being written in simple English, and a Regulatory Council has been established to develop the Nation's first regulatory calendar and agenda;

• a renewed sense of confidence and faith in the government is gradually being restored;

• long-ignored domestic problems have been attacked aggressively: the Na-tion's first urban policy was developed and its implementation begun; the Social Security System was refinanced to assure its long run solvency; the Humphrey-Hawkins Full Employment Act was passed; aid to education has been expanded by 50%; and a welfare reform program was developed and debated in Congress and will serve as a foundation for our efforts this year to overhaul the welfare system;

• cumbersome regulatory apparatus which deters competition in our economy was dismantled by the deregulation of the airline industry.

DOMESTIC POLICY PRIORITIES

Over the next year, our domestic program will concentrate on further developing a new foundation for progress in each of several areas:

• restraining inflation, while continuing to pursue our employment and other economic and budgetary goals;

• making government more efficient and effective;

• enhancing basic human and social needs;

• protecting and enhancing our rights and liberties; and

• preserving and developing our natural resources.

INFLATION

My Administration's major domestic priority is to reduce the rate of inflation, while maintaining economic growth. That is clearly the major domestic concern of the American people, and it is the problem they are looking to us to help solve. Inflation places a cruel burden on the poor and on those on fixed incomes. It serves as a disincentive to investment. It threatens our continued economic growth and job creation. This is more than an economic challenge. Inflation is the persistent, historic enemy of a free society. It saps our confidence and faith in the future. It undermines our trust.

I am determined to meet the challenge now before us. Last October I announced an anti-inflation program which can aid significantly in the effort to reduce inflation. It is a tough and responsible voluntary program.

Throughout this year, we will be working to implement our anti-inflation program. Part of the program requires new legislation, and we intend to work closely with you in developing and enacting that legislation.

The effort to reduce inflation will be one of the most difficult battles our government has undertaken in many years. But it is not a battle we can afford to lose. Government cannot solve the problem of inflation alone. But we can and must lead the way. With your cooperation, we can and will win.

The 1980 Budget

In announcing my anti-inflation program last year, I made a commitment to the American people to reduce the budget deficit for fiscal year 1980 to $30 billion or less. The budget I submitted to the Congress honors that commitment. The FY '80 budget projects a deficit of $29 billion, which is less than half the deficit the Nation had when I ran for office and represents *the smallest budget deficit in the last six fiscal years.*

The FY '80 budget has $531.6 billion in projected budget outlays, which is an increase of only 7.7% above the previous year. That is the smallest annual increase in Federal spending *in the last seven years.*

The $531.6 billion spending total also means that we will be meeting my goal of reducing Federal spending to about 21% of Gross National Product *one year ahead of schedule.*

The decisions I had to make in restraining spending were difficult. But if we are to succeed in breaking the back of inflation, Federal spending *must* be restrained to set an example for the private sector. If there were easier solutions, they would have been taken by now.

Finally, I want to emphasize that my FY '80 budget does *not* neglect the basic needs of the disadvantaged, the poor, and the unemployed. For instance, the budget will provide $4.5 billion in increased assistance to the poor. It also will provide a total of $11.2 billion for adult and youth employment and training programs, which will be especially targeted to the disadvantaged and long-term unemployed. Moreover there are significant increases for education programs for the disadvantaged and a new fiscal assistance program for our Nation's cities.

In short, this budget *is* austere, but it also maintains our commitment to help those in our country who most need it.

Hospital Cost Containment

One of my highest legislative priorities for this year is hospital cost containment. It will be one of the clearest tests of the seriousness of the Congress in dealing with the problem of inflation. Clearly the most inflationary part of health care costs in recent years has been in the hospital industry. Last year, hospital charges grew at the rate of about 13 percent. Experience in several States has shown that through programs such as the one I will propose, hospitals can save money and reduce costs through sound cost containment practices. I expect to shortly propose hospital cost containment legislation which will build on the proposal passed last year by the Senate.

Real Wage Insurance

I have proposed to the Congress a real wage insurance program to protect employee groups that comply with the 7% voluntary wage standard against losses in purchasing power if inflation exceeds 7%. If inflation exceeds 7%, these employees will receive a tax refund equal to their 1979 income up to $20,000 times the difference between the actual inflation rate (up to 10%) and 7%. This program will give workers a strong economic incentive to cooperate with the voluntary pay standards I have established, thereby helping to break the wage/price spiral that is at the root of the current persistent inflation.

This is a novel approach to the inflation problem. The persistence of high inflation for the past ten years makes clear that new solutions are needed. Innovative approaches must be added to the arsenal if we are to break the back of inflation. Real wage insurance represents the type of innovative approach which is required: it will provide a significant tax benefit for those working people who participate in helping to reduce the inflationary cycle, but without raising taxes for anyone else.

My administration intends to work very closely with Congress in developing and enacting a real wage insurance law.

Voluntary Pay and Price Standards

It is vital that our program of voluntary pay-price standards succeed. At stake is the reduced rate of inflation that all Americans demand and deserve. The cooperation of business and labor is obviously essential, and we have already had

clear evidence of their willingness to join in this effort. I have already received assurance from over 200 of the Nation's largest corporations that they will comply with the standards. And just recently the Oil, Chemical, and Atomic Workers Union reached agreement on a contract with the major refineries that met the pay standards.

Throughout this year the pay and price standards will continually be tested. Your cooperation in encouraging voluntary compliance can help ensure the standards' success. The Administration will keep the Congress fully informed and involved as we work to implement this program.

State and Local Governments

If we are to succeed in our anti-inflation efforts, the cooperation and active participation of State and local governments is essential. We will soon announce a program which actively involves the Governors, Mayors, County Executives, and other local officials in a comprehensive approach to restrain inflationary pressures within their control.

The Necessities

In recent years, the greatest inflationary burden on the working men and women has involved necessities of life—food, energy, housing, and medical care. An effective anti-inflation program must involve a series of concerted attacks on the sources of rising prices in these vital sectors.

In each of these areas, the Administration has established task forces to identify existing government policies that unreasonably inflate prices, and to suggest actions that can be taken, at both national and local levels, to combat inflation. In these efforts we will work directly with

Congress, State and local governments, and consumer groups.

Multilateral Trade Negotiations (MTN)

I have already notified the Congress that we expect to sign and submit for Congressional approval a set of trade agreements which we will reach in the Tokyo Round of the Multilateral Trade Negotiations. With these agreements, we expect to achieve major reductions in tariff and nontariff barriers to international trade. These agreements will:

—lead to increased opportunities for U.S. exports;

—ensure that import competition is fair; and

—result in lower prices, increased competition, and greater prosperity for the American people.

Passage of the MTN will be one of my highest legislative priorities this year. It is critical to the health of our domestic and of the world economy.

Countervailing Duties

I have recently sent to the Congress a message urging prompt passage of legislation permitting the waiver of the imposition of countervailing duties on certain imported products. Passage is essential to the successful completion of the Multilateral Trade Negotiations, and therefore, should be one of Congress' highest priorities at the beginning of this session.

Exports

The United States has entered a period where export growth is essential to improve our balance of payments, strengthen the dollar, and thereby help reduce inflationary pressures. To do this, both the private sector and the Federal government must place a higher priority on exports.

With the National Export Policy I announced last year, we are moving to meet this need. First, we are working to reduce domestic barriers to exports so that exporters are not stifled by excessive governmental regulation. Second, we are providing further incentives in the form of better export financing and better government export development programs. Third, we are working with our trading partners in the Multilateral Trade Negotiations to reduce foreign barriers to our exports and to secure a fairer international trading system for all exporters.

These actions should expand our exports in 1979 and help us move toward a reduced trade deficit, although they will not cure our serious balance of trade difficulties overnight. They are the first steps in an essential, long-term effort to strengthen the U.S. position in world trade, while reaffirming the Nation's commitment to maintain an open world trading system and to resist protectionism.

Council on Wage and Price Stability

The Council on Wage and Price Stability is playing a vital role in our anti-inflation efforts. The Council and its staff have the lead responsibility within the Executive Branch for implementing the voluntary wage and price standards that I have announced. Without the Council's continuing role, the anti-inflation effort would have a very slim chance of succeeding.

I therefore believe it is essential that the Council, along with its staff operation, be reauthorized early this year with the additional staff I will request to handle the enormous volume of work under my anti-inflation program. The reauthorization should not contain amendments that interrupt or restrain the necessary work of the Council or its staff.

EMPLOYMENT

The Administration, working closely with Congress, has made significant progress over the last two years in reducing unemployment and creating new jobs:

• The December unemployment rate of 5.9% represents almost a 25% reduction from the December, 1976 rate.

• 7.3 million more people have jobs than they did before the beginning of the Administration. This increase exceeds the employment growth in any other two-year period since World War II.

• Total employment has reached an all-time high of 95.9 million.

• Over the past two years black employment is up by 12%; and black teenage employment is up by 19.7%; adult female employment has increased by 10.5%; teenage employment overall has increased by 11%. Although progress has been made, unemployment remains unacceptably high for these groups. And in inner-city areas unemployment remains much too high for all workers.

Last year, which ended with the lowest unemployment rate in 3 years, a framework for continued progress into the next decade was established:

• the Comprehensive Employment and Training Act (CETA) was reauthorized at high levels for four more years;

• the Humphrey-Hawkins Full Employment Act became law after many years of effort;

• the Administration's demonstration youth programs were extended for two more years;

• a new partnership between the government and the private sector to assist the unemployed was approved by Congress with the passage of a new Title 7 of CETA—the Private Sector Initiatives Program; the targeted jobs tax credit, to encourage private employees to hire our poor young people and others who are hard to employ; and an expanded tax credit for mothers on welfare.

In 1979 this framework will help us continue to improve the employment prospects for America's workers. We especially want to improve the targeting of job creation programs to those who most need these opportunities and to improve the quality of the training and employment assistance for the poor, blacks, Hispanics, youth and women.

We expect to achieve these goals through a number of actions:

First, we will continue working toward achievement of the Humphrey-Hawkins Full Employment Act goals. We will provide an average of 546,000 CETA public jobs, and shift many of them to the long-term or "structurally" unemployed. We will continue to search for the most promising ways to reduce the structural unemployment that denies many the opportunity for full participation in American life.

Second, we will begin implementing the new Private Sector programs, including establishment of Private Industry Councils in communities throughout the country, to encourage business to hire the hard-core unemployed. I am proposing to Congress that this effort be supported at a level of $400 million this year.

Third, we will continue our special efforts to provide jobs and training programs for young workers in cooperation with community-based organizations and the private sector. We must meet our responsibility to provide opportunities for young Americans to learn to work.

Fourth, we will take steps to improve the management and delivery of employment and training services. I will seek a reform of the Wagner-Peyser Act, which authorizes the U.S. Employment Service, to integrate that program more effectively into our employment and training system. My Administration will also implement the CETA amendments, which establish practices and procedures to improve the quality of programs, provide better management and prevent fraud and abuse.

MAKING GOVERNMENT MORE EFFICIENT AND EFFECTIVE

The American people are demanding a Federal government which is effective and efficient. For the past two years, I have worked toward that goal by reorganizing and reforming the government's operation and by uncovering and removing fraud, waste and abuse. Real progress has been made. But the government is still not operating as competently as I want or the American people deserve. In 1979, we must build on the base of the last two years to provide our people with the type of government they deserve. Your help in this effort is essential. We have already begun to build a new foundation of government efficiency and we will do more in the year ahead.

Reorganization

We have begun to reorganize the government through the creation of a Cabinet-level Department of Energy and the changes resulting from the six reorganization plans approved by Congress over the past two years. Those plans helped to reshape and improve the operation of the Executive Office of the President, the international cultural and communications agencies, emergency preparedness agencies, the equal employment opportunity enforcement agencies, the Civil Service Commission, and the administration of the Employee Retirement Income Security Act.

I will again propose to the Congress that a Cabinet-level Department of Edu-

cation be created. This will be a very high priority of this Administration. Education issues deserve far more attention and more accountable management than they can receive in a department as large and complex as HEW. The department would provide a Cabinet-level official devoting full-time attention to education and reporting directly to me. It will also enable the Federal government to be a more responsive and reliable partner with States, localities, and private institutions which have primary responsibility for education.

I will also be proposing to Congress reorganization plans involving economic development and the management of our natural resources development, and will intensively study possible reorganizations in the areas of surface transportation, the Selective Service system and the Alaska natural gas pipeline. The natural resources and economic development reorganizations involve areas where overlap, duplication and unclear authority have hamstrung our efforts. Reorganization here can save money and people. We will be consulting closely with Congress over the next several weeks before submitting these reorganization plans.

Regulatory Reform

Last year we took major steps toward reform of the Federal regulatory system, ranging from improved regulation writing to saving hundreds of millions of dollars through improved cash management techniques. The dramatic reductions in airline prices that occurred when Congress joined with us to lift the heavy hand of Federal regulation illustrate the advantages of letting the competitive market, rather than government, control industry performance. The public will benefit similarly through improved service, increased competition, and lower Federal

127

expenditures, if we reform Federal regulation of surface transportation. I will send to Congress shortly a Surface Transportation Reform Message dealing with the rail, inter-city bus, and trucking industries.

In 1978 I used my authority as Chief Executive to improve the management of the Federal regulatory process. I issued Executive Order 12044, setting standards to ensure that each Executive Branch regulatory agency facilitates public participation and avoids needless costs. A regulatory analysis program was established under an inter-agency Regulatory Analysis Review Group to help ensure that major new regulations are as cost-effective as possible. The Executive Order also established procedures for all Executive Branch agencies to conduct sunset reviews to reevaluate outdated regulations and remove them from the books wherever warranted. Finally, I created a Regulatory Council composed of the Executive Branch regulatory agencies, with voluntary participation by independent agencies, to develop a calendar of all major Federal regulations to be issued or proposed in 1979. The Nation's first Regulatory Calendar will be published next month and will be used to eliminate duplication, overlap, and inconsistent practices.

This year I will propose to Congress a number of legislative actions that can be taken to improve the regulatory process. They will include improvements in specific regulatory programs, as well as a Regulatory Reform Act so that no regulation can be issued unless it is genuinely required, and unless it gets the job done with maximum efficiency and minimum paperwork, costs, and other burdens.

The quality of regulations can also be improved by providing opportunities for all interested parties to participate in regulatory proceedings. Public involvement should be enhanced by providing financial assistance to those whose participation is limited by their economic circumstances. While many agencies have inherent authority to fund participation, we will seek legislation to specifically authorize these programs.

While I will propose a wide-ranging legislative program, I will continue to oppose the legislative veto. This approach is unconstitutional; it increases uncertainty and delay; and it deflects attention from the real solutions.

None of our actions in this area will be taken at the expense of my deep personal commitment to protect health and safety in the environment, the workplace, the highway, and consumer products; and to prevent deception and unfairness to consumers. My regulatory reform program will help make needed programs work better, cost less, and gain support among all sectors of our society.

Civil Service and Pay Reform

Enactment of the Civil Service Reform Act of 1978 by the 95th Congress represented one of the finest examples of cooperation between the Legislative and Executive Branches in recent times. That effort showed a determination to respond to the clear public desire to improve the management of the Federal bureaucracy. Implementation of the Reform Act is well under way. The Office of Personnel Management, the Merit System Protection Board, and the Federal Labor Relations Authority authorized by the Act have been established. In addition, the heads of the Federal departments and agencies have moved promptly to implement the new personnel procedures that will permit a better motivated and more effective civil service.

However, other improvements in management of the government's work force are needed. Our white collar, blue collar, and military systems must be reformed in order to make certain that we neither overpay nor underpay Federal employees. Therefore, I will propose Federal pay reform legislation covering each of these systems to the Congress that is equitable to Federal employees and the public. These pay reforms are an important follow-on to our civil service reform.

Public Financing

The time is long overdue for reforming the way Congressional elections are financed. The current flood of money threatens to pervert our electoral process. We can no longer permit our elections to be open to the highest bidder. The recent elections have clearly demonstrated the kinds of problems caused by uncontrolled campaign spending. It is time to adopt public financing for Congressional elections—before it is too late. Public financing operated successfully in the last Presidential election, and it can do the same in Congressional races. My Administration will work with Congress for passage of a sound Congressional public financing law.

Sunset

My Administration will again work with the Congress to enact a sound sunset bill. Under such a bill, each Federal program would have to be carefully re-examined on a periodic basis to determine whether its continued existence is justified. Through such a procedure, the American people can be assured that unnecessary government programs and agencies will be ended, rather than continued through the force of inertia; and other programs and agencies will be improved.

There are few more important building-stones to the new foundation of government efficiency we seek than passage of sunset legislation. It goes to the heart of making government work.

Lobby Reform

The American people have a right to know what significant influences affect their national legislature. The proliferation of well financed, organizational lobbying activities during recent years has demonstrated the clear need for reform of the outdated and ineffective lobby disclosure law now in effect. This year my Administration will continue to work with Congress to pass a sound lobby law reform bill—one that respects the First Amendment right of all Americans and minimizes paperwork burdens, yet allows meaningful disclosures.

Waste, Fraud, and Inefficiency

Although the vast majority of Federal employees are able, honest and hardworking, we need to continue to be vigilant to ensure that the taxpayers' dollars are not wasted through fraud or abuse. The implementation of civil service reform will lead to improvements in agency management practices and program efficiency. In addition, I am committed to continuing to cut excess paperwork, simplify grants requirements, and evaluate our programs better and more frequently. We have already significantly reduced the paperwork burden and implemented many of the recommendations of the Federal Paperwork Commission. We will continue to do more in 1979.

Early this year I will nominate highly qualified Inspectors General armed with tough new powers to prevent waste and corruption. The Justice Department will increase its already intensive effort to prosecute those few employees and contractors who abuse the public trust. In addition, a new Office of Ethics in the Office of Personnel Management and a Special

Counsel in the Merit System Protection Board will help ensure the integrity of the Federal work force and protect its members from political abuse.

State and Local Government Relations

As the first President in more than thirty years to be elected immediately after service as a Governor, I have made relations with State and local government a high priority of my Administration. During my first two years in office, we have strengthened the Federal system significantly. We have involved the Federal Regional Directors in the management of the government and have reinvigorated the Federal Regional Councils. As a result, the Federal government is now able to respond better and more quickly to State and local needs. In addition, we have involved State and local officials in the development of our policies to a greater degree than any previous Administration.

Since 1977, Federal grants-in-aid to State and local governments have increased to more than $80 billion per year, 25 percent above the level of aid when I first took office. Progress has also been made towards my goal of giving Governors, Mayors, and county officials more flexibility in managing Federal programs. The Federal government is now taking seriously, for the first time, the burdens and costs we impose on State and local governments and all taxpayers when we legislate and regulate from the Federal level.

In this time of limited budget resources we must achieve more cost-effective management of Federal resources and place greater reliance on the experience, knowledge, and ability of State and local governments.

In the future, we must attempt to limit the imposition of new costs on State and local governments, and to avoid where possible prescribing every detail of how they administer Federal programs. We must work together to identify specific ways in which more flexibility can be given to State, city, and county officials in the administration of Federal programs without compromising the national purposes that each program is designed to serve.

Transportation

In 1979 we shall continue the effort begun in the 95th Congress to reduce the regulatory burden on the Nation's transportation industry. Our proposals for surface transportation deregulation will build upon the principles of increased competition that have proven successful for the airline industry.

Shortly, I will propose broad legislation which begins to deregulate the railroad industry. Regulatory reform is a crucial first step toward revitalizing this important transportation mode.

In addition, I will also be proposing significant reductions in the regulation of inter-city bus transportation and certain regulatory changes in the trucking area.

We are also committed to improving the level of safety for our transportation industry. As part of this effort, we intend vigorously to pursue legislation improving equipment and conditions affecting truck drivers, and giving stronger enforcement authority to Federal agencies.

My forthcoming Surface Transportation Regulatory Reform Message will provide the details of these proposals.

Finally, I will propose overdue changes in the Nation's maritime policies. We must improve the ability of our Merchant Marine to win a fair share of our cargo.

No-Fault

The Administration will continue to support legislation to establish Federal minimum standards for state no-fault automobile compensation systems. No-fault systems have proven to be far more efficient in delivering benefits to the victims of automobile accidents than the current tort system, and they also provide greater opportunities to coordinate and reduce overall insurance costs. Too great a percentage of the premiums paid by policy-holders goes for the administration of the current wasteful tort liability system. No-fault would save money and court-time. It deserves Congressional support.

Consumer Representation

My Administration has developed new procedures that will set standards and assess performance for effective public representation within government agencies. These procedures are designed not only to improve the delivery of government services to our citizens, but also to enhance the awareness of government to the health, safety, and economic concerns of all consumers. In 1979, we will direct adequate resources to these procedures, which include complaint handling, training and technical assistance for consumer organizations, advocacy, consumer education and information, and citizen participation.

LEAA

Last year I proposed legislation which would institute significant and long-overdue changes in the structure and programs of the Law Enforcement Assistance Administration. The LEAA has the potential to improve and strengthen State and local law criminal justice programs, but in its present form it has fallen far short of its potential. My Administration will work with the Congress again this year to reform this framework, which includes a National Institute of Justice to enable us to obtain better information and research about crime problems. Once the legislation is enacted, we will make certain that the new agency is efficiently carrying out its mission of providing meaningful Federal law enforcement assistance.

Judgeships

Last year my Administration worked closely with the Congress to enact legislation creating the additional Federal judgeships needed to reduce our court's backlogs and delays. As a result, I will soon be nominating 152 new Federal judges—the largest addition to the Federal judiciary in our history. Some of these judges will still be serving in the next century.

I am determined to nominate judges of the highest quality; our Federal judiciary must be selected on the basis of merit. I am also determined to increase the low representation on the Federal bench of women, blacks, Hispanics, and other minorities. These goals are within our reach, if we work together cooperatively and recognize the importance our country places in the selection of these new judges.

Judicial Reform

Because our Federal courts do not function as well as we have the right to expect, my Administration has made judicial reform one of its goals. During 1978, Congress took major steps toward alleviating the problem by increasing substantially the number of Federal judges and by adopting numerous substantive and procedural reforms in the handling of bankruptcy matters.

Other judicial reforms remain to be made. Some, such as expanding the authority of magistrates and curtailing diversity jurisdiction, were proposed to the last Congress. I will shortly send a message to the Congress urging prompt action on these and several additional proposals designed to improve the responsiveness and efficiency of our system of justice. They merit the attention and approval of the Congress.

In addition, as was indicated in my Consumer Message to Congress, the Administration will continue to support reform of class action procedures. Reform legislation should seek to ease unnecessary burdens and costs of class actions, while at the same time preventing them from being used in a harassing manner.

Antitrust Enforcement and Competition

Free enterprise and competition, protected by the antitrust laws, are the central organizing principles of our economic system. Competition produces powerful incentives for innovation and efficiency, fights inflation, and enhances consumer welfare. Strict enforcement of our antitrust laws are critical to the health of competition and the Nation's economy.

Several important strides were made last year in improving antitrust enforcement. In 1978, the courts imposed over $11 million in corporate fines for antitrust violations and imprisoned 29 individuals for antitrust violations. These fines and sentences are significantly larger than in past years, and are consistent with my strong commitment to vigorous antitrust enforcement.

Last year I appointed the National Commission for the Review of Antitrust Laws and Procedures to suggest ways of expediting antitrust cases and making relief more effective. Its members have recently reported to me, and we will work closely with the Congress and the Judicial Conference to implement many of its recommendations.

Similar progress in improving the effectiveness of antitrust enforcement can be made in the 96th Congress.

I continue to support legislation to allow those who are injured by antitrust violations to recover damages from the antitrust violator, whether the injured person is a direct or indirect purchaser. Under the Supreme Court's decision in the *Illinois Brick Case* only direct purchasers may recover, even though they may have passed on the injury to consumers, who are prevented from suing. This decision undercuts state and private enforcement of the antitrust laws, reduces their deterrent effect, may contribute to higher prices, and often allows the violator to keep his gain at the expense of the injured consumer. This needed legislation would overturn that decision.

Banking

I anticipate receiving shortly the recommendations of the Administration's Task Force studying Regulation Q and the system of deposit interest rate controls, and I expect to make recommendations based upon the Task Force's findings.

My Administration remains supportive of Congressional action to deal with the need to halt the continuing attrition in the percentage of bank deposits subject to the reserve requirements of the Federal Reserve System.

Carryover Basis

Carryover basis was one of the most important reforms passed by Congress in the Tax Reform Act of 1976. This reform would add substantial equity to our tax laws and greater efficiency to our capital markets.

The carryover basis reform has the effect of ending a situation in which many of our wealthiest taxpayers could *permanently* escape paying income tax on their gains from inherited property. Unfortunately, the effective date has been delayed until the end of 1979.

My Administration will strongly oppose any efforts to repeal this reform or further delay its implementation.

ENHANCING BASIC HUMAN AND SOCIAL NEEDS

In the years immediately preceding my Administration, too many of our Nation's basic human and social needs were being ignored or handled insensitively by the Federal government. Over the past two years, we have significantly increased funding for many of the vital programs in these areas; developed new programs where needs were unaddressed; targeted Federal support to those individuals and areas most in need of our assistance; and removed barriers that unnecessarily kept many disadvantaged citizens from obtaining aid for their most basic needs.

The progress over the past two years *has* noticeably moved us forward toward building a new foundation to solve some of the country's fundamental human and social problems. My Administration has vastly expanded assistance in the last twenty-four months in areas of employment, education, housing, community and economic development and health care, which represent an improvement for the American people.

The record of the past two years demonstrates that government can meet our citizens' basic human and social needs in a compassionate way. No longer can there be any doubt that the government is able to treat Americans' problems with sensitivity.

In the coming fiscal year, budget restraints make it more difficult to expand funding significantly for many major domestic programs, though some programs *will* be increased. We will continue to make existing social programs work more effectively; to reduce the waste and fraud and excess bureaucracy which drains tax dollars intended to meet basic human needs. In a period of austerity, efficiency is itself an act of compassion because it unlocks resources needed for health care, education, housing, economic development and other urgent social priorities.

Health Program

One of the highest goals of the 96th Congress should be taking action to provide all Americans with the opportunity to lead a more healthy life. This opportunity has been denied to many in our country because of health care services which are unaffordable, inaccessible, and inefficient. In addition, our current system of health care is focused on the treatment of disease, with too little attention being directed toward its prevention. We need a national health strategy which corrects these inadequacies in the existing system. Some of the elements of this strategy are already in place and need only be strengthened. Others will require new legislation from the 96th Congress.

National Health Plan and Other Improvements

Last year I outlined the principles upon which the National Health Plan I intend to propose will be based. Based on those principles, the Administration has been working to develop a National Health Plan that will enable the country to reach the goal of comprehensive, universal health care coverage. I remain committed to that goal.

133

The need for improved health care coverage is clear:

• About 19 million Americans have no health insurance.

• Another 65 million Americans face potential bankruptcy because they lack insurance protecting them against catastrophic medical expenses.

• The health care system is highly inflationary. Spending in the entire health care industry—has been rising at an annual rate of 12%. These expenditures cannot be successfully contained under current health delivery and financing methods, which produce unnecessary hospitalization, over-reliance on expensive technology and inadequate preventive care.

• Health resources are unevenly distributed across the country, resulting in significant gaps in vital medical services for many residents of rural and inner city areas.

Over the next several weeks, we will be consulting closely with Congress and interested outside groups on the scope and nature of the plan I will propose. I expect to submit a plan later in the year shortly after those consultations have been completed, and I look forward to working with the Congress toward a prompt enactment of that plan.

An essential companion to any plan must be hospital cost containment legislation. As I have indicated earlier in this Message, I will make passage of that legislation one of my highest priorities this year.

Our effort to control health care costs would be further strengthened by the early passage of the Health Planning Act.

We must also continue to promote competition in the health care sector of the economy. Accordingly, the FY '80 budget expands Federal support for Health Maintenance Organizations, which have demonstrated a significant potential for cost saving. I will also continue to press for reforms making it easier for HMO's to obtain equitable reimbursement under Medicare and Medicaid.

Prevention and Accessible Health Services

More health care services alone, however, will not necessarily improve the health status of our Nation—even if these services are affordable, accessible, and efficient. Our national health strategy must direct more attention to health promotion and disease prevention if we are to achieve our goal of improved health status. The Surgeon General will present this year a major report outlining our needs in this area. I will be asking for your help in carrying out many of its recommendations.

We have made great strides in expanding the availability of health care services to rural and low-income urban areas in recent years through the creation of the National Health Service Corps and the establishment of a system of Community Health Centers. If health care is to be accessible to all Americans, these programs must be expanded, and the FY '80 budget provides for such an expansion.

Child Health Assessment

I believe that our health strategy must place high priority on the health of our children. Accordingly, I will submit a revised Child Health Assessment Program to improve the early and preventive screening, diagnosis, and treatment program for lower-income children under Medicaid. This program would cover over 2,000,000 low-income children who are not receiving Medicaid services. An additional 100,000 low-income pregnant women would become eligible for medical services prior to delivery, improving the health of both the mothers and infants.

This should be part of a national health plan.

Mental Health

Based upon last year's recommendations of the President's Commission on Mental Health, I will be proposing comprehensive mental health legislation this year along with a Mental Health Message. A new Community Mental Health System will make new efforts to link mental health, health, and social services for the chronically mentally ill to enable them to live successfully in the community and will provide new community mental health services. We will emphasize efforts to provide improved recognition and treatment of mental health problems in the general health care system. In addition, we will increase support for mental health research to restore our mental health research capacity, which the Commission found had seriously eroded over the past decade.

The First Lady has helped spearhead the Administration's efforts to sensitize the Nation to the problems in the mental health area. She will continue to work directly with me to implement the pertinent recommendations of the Commission.

Drug Abuse

In continuing our efforts to combat drug abuse, my Administration will rely on those programs and initiatives which have proven to be successful in the past year and which serve as building blocks for future programs. Today, in the United States, there are 110,000 fewer heroin addicts than there were in 1975; 1,000 fewer Americans died of heroin overdoses in the twelve-month period ending June 30, 1978 than in the previous twelve months. Seizures of illegal drugs are at their highest level ever. Improved co-ordination and cooperation among Federal agencies have resulted in a more effective drug program without major budget increases. But much remains to be done and the situation remains serious.

In 1979 we will look more to the behavior of the individual who turns to drugs, will stress financial investigations as a means of prosecuting those individuals responsible for the drug traffic, and will rely heavily on enlisting foreign cooperation in the overall drug program. These efforts should further our success in controlling drug abuse both in the United States and abroad.

Drug Regulation Reform

My Administration will continue to work with the Congress to overhaul our current drug regulation laws in order to assure that consumers have prompt access to safe and effective drugs.

Food and Nutrition

Last year, we worked with the Congress to enact the Child Nutrition Amendments, which revamped many of our food programs and greatly expanded the Supplemental Food Program for Women, Infants and Children. This year I will propose further legislation to strengthen these and other food programs by: improving the targeting of school meal programs for the needy; instituting an error sanction scheme to encourage States to reduce costly Food Stamp errors; and eliminating the cap on food stamp expenditures. These reforms will insure that additional nutrition resources are targeted to those truly in need.

Worker Health and Safety

We will continue to fully enforce laws protecting worker health and safety in a sensible and efficient manner. There will be further efforts to eliminate frivolous and unneeded rules while concentrating greater enforcement efforts on the most dangerous and particularly the most unhealthy occupational environments. More efficient management of this program will serve the interest that both labor and management have in better working conditions.

Housing

We are committed to holding down housing construction costs and eliminating unnecessary regulatory burdens, so that the American consumer will have an affordable choice in the housing marketplace. Our efforts will be accelerated this year. We have also supported introduction of the new money market certificates, which have helped the housing industry by maintaining a steady supply of mortgage credit.

The Administration has supported the provision of Federal housing assistance to low-and-moderate income people, including the elderly and the handicapped.

During the period of 1978 through 1980, the Administration will have committed resources for over one million additional units of assisted housing for low-and-moderate income renters and homeowners. This is evidence of our commitment to the goal of a decent home for every American. In 1980, I am recommending 325,000 units of housing for low-and-moderate income persons.

The problems of providing adequate housing in rural areas is especially acute. Lack of available land, high site development costs, widespread substandard, overcrowded housing, and limited credit opportunities continue to plague rural areas. Government attempts to help are often hampered by inappropriate, burdensome regulations and paperwork. This year the Administration will take steps to assure that Federal regulations accommodate locally acceptable housing codes and

that the endless paperwork, inspections, and processing requirements currently mandated by the three major housing agencies, HUD, FHA, and VA, are consolidated and streamlined.

Community Development

My Administration remains committed to a partnership involving Federal, State, county, and local governments, the private sector, and community organizations. The Community Development Block Grant program is a cornerstone of that partnership, and I am proposing in my FY '80 budget that it be funded at the full authorization level. This will be an increase of $150 million in FY '80 above the FY '79 level.

In 1977, we developed the Urban Development Action Grant program and it has already succeeded in leveraging $2.9 billion in private investment and creating or saving 125,000 jobs. I am proposing a continuation of the Action Grant program next year, at the $400 million authorization level.

Neighborhoods

My Administration has been devoted to the preservation of neighborhoods and the development of sound neighborhood self-help projects. This goal has been evident in the emphasis on neighborhoods in my urban policy as well as in the operation of the Department of Housing and Urban Development and other agencies. Last year, as part of our urban policy, we proposed and Congress passed the Livable Cities and Neighborhood Self-Help Development programs to enable neighborhood groups and organizations to rebuild their neighborhoods. In addition, Congressional passage of the National Consumer Cooperative Bank makes available new sources of financing and technical assistance to groups who are engaged in building cooperative enterprises to reduce costs in key consumer goods and services.

This year, my Administration and Congress will receive the final report of the National Commission on Neighborhoods. We look forward to working with the Congress on many of the Commission's recommendations. With your help, we can make the Federal government increasingly more responsive to the needs of neighborhood people who are working together to meet basic needs in housing and community development, health care, nutrition, and energy conservation.

Urban Policy

Last year, I proposed the Nation's first comprehensive urban policy. That policy involved more than one hundred improvements in existing Federal programs, four new Executive Orders and nineteen pieces of urban-oriented legislation. With Congress' cooperation, thirteen of these bills passed last year.

I will again propose to the Congress several important parts of the urban policy not adopted last year. The two principal proposals are: an urban fiscal assistance program, and the National Development Bank.

My fiscal assistance proposal will include two principal components. The first, a standby countercyclical fiscal assistance program, will protect State and local governments against unexpected changes in the national economy. It would trigger into place if the national unemployment rate rises above 6.5 percent and would provide fiscal aid to many needy governments. The second component is a transitional, highly targeted fiscal assistance program that provides fiscal aid to only the most fiscally-distressed local governments. Relatively few cities and counties will be eligible for this highly targeted program; but those eligible will be truly in need. I will seek a $250 million supplemental in FY '79 and $150 million in FY '80 for this targeted fiscal assistance program.

I also will propose a National Development Bank to provide financing for local economic development projects which will aid the revitalization of our Nation's communities. As part of the Bank, I will propose a significant increase in economic development funding—$550 million in new economic development capital grants to business and $2.65 billion in new loan guarantee authority for FY '80.

This Bank will be the central engine for the economic development in the government. We will propose the consolidation of many economic development loan programs into the Bank as part of the economic development reorganization. This will add over $1 billion in additional loan authority.

Social Security Changes

In 1977 the Congress worked with the Administration to take the difficult but necessary action to make the Social Security system financially sound for the next fifty years. In so doing, we helped protect the benefits of current recipients and of those now working. However, the Social Security system from time to time needs adaptation to changing conditions, so the Administration this year will make proposals which will reduce somewhat the cost of the program by trimming the costs of certain benefits. These proposals will be sent to the Social Security Advisory Council, which is representative of the contributing employers, employees and the public, and to the National Commission on Social Security, appointed in part by the Congress and in part by me, so they can have an ample opportunity to review these proposals prior to the submission of the changes to the Congress and the Administration and the Congress can have their recommendations, if any.

If the Administration's proposals for Social Security outlay reductions and hospital cost containment legislation are enacted, it would be possible to consider a reduction in Social Security taxes beginning in 1981. However, such a reduction would have to be considered in light of alternative uses of such savings, including reduction of any budget deficit and funding of high-priority programs.

Beyond the immediate reforms I have proposed, the Administration is committed to review the entire pension system that has developed in our country. I have established a Pension Commission to provide the type of long-range analysis this vital area needs.

Disability Insurance Reforms

I will propose to Congress an integrated package of reforms for the Disability Insurance system, separate from the Social Security changes I have just discussed. These measures will improve incentives for rehabilitation of the disabled, ensure that benefits do not exceed pre-disability disposable income, and make administration of the system simpler and more consistent. We must make certain that those who should receive benefits are not excluded, but that those who are not truly disabled or can otherwise return to work, do so.

Welfare Reform

The Nation's welfare system is inequitable, inefficient and long overdue for serious reform.

I will recommend to the Congress a package consisting of reforms in cash assistance, expansion of the earned income tax credit, an expansion of private and public job opportunities for welfare recipients, and fiscal relief for State and local governments. This package will enable us to develop a welfare system that is more simple, narrows the great differences in the way States help the very poor, that encourages people to work, and that helps eliminate the fraud and abuse currently plaguing parts of our welfare system.

My Administration has already begun to work closely with this Congress to enact welfare reform this year. We must expeditiously move forward with welfare reform this year.

Families

Our major social initiatives and goals for this year will be undertaken with vigor and with a commitment to the security and enhancement of the American family structure. Our government must never impede nor work against the American family, but rather we must design programs and policies that support families and ensure that future generations of American families will thrive and prosper. The White House Conference on the Family will continue and expedite its planning this year with that goal firmly in mind.

Child Welfare Reform

The Nation's present system of overlapping, inadequate child placement programs does a great disservice to parents, foster parents, and children in need of homes. There is too little emphasis on reunification of families and permanent placement of children; the special problems of hard-to-place children often go unattended. I will therefore again propose to Congress major reforms in our foster care and adoption services, and urge prompt Congressional approval. This problem must not be left unattended any longer.

Older Americans

Early in the Administration we moved to correct one of the major concerns of older Americans: the possible bankruptcy of the Social Security Trust Funds. The legislation that was enacted ensures the financial solvency of the funds through the beginning of the next century.

The Administration has also acted to help remove discrimination against senior citizens by supporting the legislation which removed the forced retirement requirement in the Federal civil service and postponed mandatory retirement in the private sector from age 65 to 70. In addition, the Administration worked with the Congress to amend the Older Americans Act in a way that will improve the administration of the Act's social and housing programs, employment provisions, food delivery, and establishment of centers for the elderly.

This year the Administration will continue its efforts to ensure that seniors remain in the mainstream of American life, free from age discrimination and able to receive the assistance and other benefits they have earned.

Veterans

Our Nation has no obligation more basic than providing for those men and women who served us as members of our armed forces.

There are still many veterans who need medical care, employment assistance, and assistance in adjusting to disabilities that resulted from their service.

During the last two years we have made significant improvements in programs to help meet all these needs.

In 1979 my Administration will seek legislation to increase compensation rates for disabled veterans, improve education programs for the disadvantaged under the G.I. Bill, provide special readjustment counseling assistance for those Vietnam Era Veterans who need them, and modernize the VA vocational rehabilitation program. These efforts will help veterans help themselves. In addition, we will continue to provide quality medical care in our VA hospital system by making it more efficient and thus more responsive to the needs of a changing veteran population.

Education

Improving skills and educational opportunities has been one of my Administration's major goals. To aid in this improvement, I have increased the Federal Office of Education budget authority alone by 50% since taking office—from $8 billion in FY '77 to $12.2 billion in the proposed FY '80 budget.

The increased education funding will continue to be targeted at programs which emphasize equal education opportunity, support for local schools, student assistance, basic skills, and the linkages between school and work.

School districts with high concentrations of low income children have extra costs in meeting their commitment to equal educational opportunity. Last year I proposed concentration grants which would give supplemental payments for compensatory education programs in high poverty school districts. This year I am requesting $400 million to fully fund this proposal.

As is stated elsewhere in this Message, I will continue to work with the Congress to create a Cabinet-level Department of Education. Through such a Department we can make certain that education receives the attention at the Federal level that it deserves.

Higher Education

Last year, I signed into law the Middle Income Student Assistance Act, which extends Federal student aid to middle income families facing rising college tuition costs. I propose to fully fund the Basic Grants program and to continue funding for the other college student aid programs. This year I will propose reauthorization of our omnibus higher education legislation—the Higher Education Act and the National Defense Education Act. Through renewal of these acts, we can help enormously to ensure the continuation of strong higher education institutions and equal educational opportunities for all students.

Our Nation owes a debt of gratitude to the historically black colleges, which in the past were the only source of college education for talented blacks, and which today retain a critical importance to the production of college-educated black citizens. One-half of all college-educated blacks earned their degrees at black colleges. I have vowed that I would enhance the role of black colleges during my term in office. I recently directed all Federal agencies to utilize more fully the resources at black colleges. And, in my FY '80 budget I have increased funding for Howard University, and asked for $120 million to fully fund the Developing Institutions Program, which strengthens colleges with high concentrations of minority students.

Science and Technology

When I came into office, I found Federal efforts to promote basic research and development lagging. I was determined to change this situation and develop a sounder scientific and technological foundation for the future. Basic scientific research and development is an investment in the Nation's future, essential for all fields, from health, agriculture, and environment to energy, space, and defense. We are enhancing the search for the causes of disease; we are undertaking research to anticipate and prevent significant environmental hazards; we are increasing research in astronomy; we will maintain our leadership in space science; and we are pushing back the frontiers in basic research for energy, defense and other critical national needs. Despite the severe budgetary constraints this year, we will continue to increase Federal support for basic research with a request for a 13% increase in outlays for FY '80.

Even though Federal funding for basic research is being increased, I believe that the government's role in demonstration and commercialization pilot projects should be more selective, with greater reliance upon private sector financing. We are enhancing our high technology approach to defense to counter the growth of Soviet forces. We have a broad energy research program that emphasizes long-term applications of solar, coal, geothermal, biomass and alternate nuclear technologies. But we will rely on industry to do its full part in the demonstration of new technologies in energy and in other fields.

Rather than government funding of their research and development, companies need more favorable investment climates, better economic growth, better trade prospects, and sound policies about patents, antitrust, procurement, and environmental regulation. Under the direction of the Department of Commerce, we are also engaged in a major Cabinet-level review of these aspects of technological innovation, with participation of numerous individuals from various industrial sectors.

Science and technology are playing an important part in our international relationships as well. Many countries, especially developing countries, look to America for our expertise and problem-solving abilities. I have proposed the establishment of a Foundation for International Technological Cooperation (FITC) to foster collaborative efforts with people and institutions in developing countries. These efforts will be directed to basic human needs in agriculture, nutrition, health, small-scale energy systems, and rural development.

Science and technology also have played a critical part in the dramatic advances of our relationship with the People's Republic of China. These scientific and technological relationships that will be built with China will be parallel to many such relationships we have established and enhanced over the years with other nations and groups of nations.

Space

Last year marked the 20th Anniversary of the National Aeronautics and Space Administration. The 21st year started with the incredible success of the Pioneer missions to Venus. This year we hope to open a new era in space with the first launch of the Space Shuttle.

Under the national civil space policy I announced last fall, we will remain dedicated to ensuring U.S. scientific and technological leadership in space. To further that policy, my budget request for FY '80 includes funding to maintain the Shuttle development and production schedule to continue space science and exploration; to initiate efforts on selected areas of advanced satellite communications techniques; and to enhance remote sensing activities that will bring benefits in areas such as earth resources, climate, weather, pollution and agriculture.

Communications

Last year we worked with Congress to reorganize communications policy-making in the Executive Branch and enact legislation to strengthen public broadcasting. In 1979 our priorities will include:

• continued work with Congress on the important effort to revise the Communications Act to take account of technological changes;

• vigorous pursuit of the program already underway to increase minority ownership of broadcast stations through regulatory actions, government loan guarantees, and private loan and training programs;

• a program to use new communications technologies to improve rural life by delivering education, agricultural, and medical services and by increasing the diversity of radio and TV;

• elimination of unnecessary regulations and paperwork requirements in cooperation with the Federal Communications Commission;

• proposals on the role of the Postal Service in providing electronic mail services; and

• participation in the World Administrative Radio Conference to ensure that increasing demands for radio frequencies are balanced in a reasonable and flexible manner.

Small Business

As a former businessman, I am especially sensitive to the importance of small business in our economy and to the vital role the Federal government can play in assisting small business.

Through a number of actions over the past two years, my Administration has worked to help small business flourish and remain competitive. Under the leadership of the Small Business Administration, we have increased tax incentives significantly for small business; expanded small business loan opportunities; worked to increase small business exports; expanded opportunities for minority-owned small businesses; and initiated programs to increase small business opportunities for women. In addition, we have begun preparations for a White House Conference on Small Business in January of 1980 which will include local and regional conferences throughout the country.

This year, while continuing efforts to prepare for the White House Conference, the Administration will work closely with the Congress to develop legislation to improve the operation and effectiveness of the Small Business Administration.

Cultural Affairs

Over the last decade, the National Endowments for the Arts and the Humanities have made enormous progress in developing projects and materials to enhance our Nation's cultural life. This year, the Endowments will continue their distinguished record of achievement. I am hopeful Congress will provide adequate funds for White House Conferences on the Arts and Humanities. This year we will also strengthen the programs of the International Communications Agency, which present the diversity of American culture to the world and deepen our appreciation of other cultures.

PROTECTING BASIC RIGHTS AND LIBERTIES

Since taking office, I have worked to protect and enhance the basic rights and liberties provided to Americans under the Constitution and our other laws. With the cooperation of the Congress, we have made important progress in this area. Over the next year, though, a great deal

remains to be done if our goal of ensuring equality and basic freedoms for all Americans is to be realized. The dream of equal opportunity remains unfulfilled. I will do everything in my power to bring that dream closer to realization.

Civil Rights

Civil Rights and Equal Opportunity

I take no obligation of my office more seriously than that of striving to secure full civil rights and equal opportunity for all Americans. In the quarter century since the Supreme Court's historic desegregation decision, our Nation's progress in these vital areas of human rights had been significant, but we have more to do. I am determined to use all of my authority to resist any efforts to weaken enforcement of any of our civil rights and equal opportunity laws. Recent actions by some in Congress to impair my Administration's efforts to enforce the law of the land will be forcefully opposed. These laws have made our society more open to equality of opportunity than virtually any on earth, and attempts to weaken them cannot be tolerated or allowed to succeed.

My Administration has taken important steps to make civil rights enforcement more effective. The Justice Department has been diligent in its prosecution of civil rights violations. The Office of Federal Contract Compliance Programs (OFCCP) and the Equal Employment Opportunity Commission (EEOC) has been reorganized and granted increased authority. The OFCCP will vigorously enforce the guidelines of Executive Order 11246, which prohibits employment discrimination by Federal contractors and requires affirmative action by these contractors. In addition the EEOC will continue this year to provide an effective central mechanism to enforce compliance with our equal opportunity laws.

As we have done in recent cases before the Supreme Court, my Administration will continue to strongly support affirmative action programs to help bring minorities into the mainstream of American life, while opposing rigid and inflexible quotas which have no place in our laws.

Beyond existing laws, however, as I state elsewhere in this Message, we need to ratify two Amendments to the Constitution which will significantly clarify and enhance the liberties and rights of Americans: The Equal Rights Amendment and the District of Columbia Voting Rights Amendment.

The Equal Rights Amendment will provide women with equal legal status in our country. We cannot effectively champion human rights throughout the world until we have given to women the full rights they are entitled to as citizens.

We must also work to ratify the amendment that will finally give the citizens of the District of Columbia the rights other Americans have to elect voting representation in Congress.

In addition, we need to correct a weakness in an existing civil rights law. Title VIII of the Civil Rights Act of 1968, which prohibits discrimination in housing, remains largely an empty promise because of the lack of an adequate enforcement mechanism.

I will soon propose to the Congress that this problem be alleviated by providing the Department of Housing and Urban Development with cease and desist powers. That Department, which now investigates and makes findings upon individual complaints, would then be able to enjoin further discriminatory acts and to direct an appropriate remedy. My Administration will work with the Congress to see that this proposal is given prompt and favorable consideration.

Women

One of the overriding concerns of my Administration is ensuring equal opportunity for women. Last year we worked closely with the Congress to extend the deadline for ratification of the Equal Rights Amendment until June 30, 1982. That extension will provide a greater opportunity to ensure ratification of this long-overdue Amendment. I will continue to dedicate myself, as well as the full resources of my Administration, to the ratification effort.

This is not a battle that we can afford to lose. I am determined to win. The opposition to the Amendment cannot be solidly based on an understanding of its legal effect. The Amendment will do nothing more—nor less—than provide equality to more than one-half of America's population. I am confident that with the active support of the members of Congress from States which have *not* yet ratified, we can achieve ratification of ERA. I urge you to join the effort to provide women, at long last, with equal rights under the law.

My Administration has championed, and will continue to champion, the right of women to choose their roles in society. To protect those who have chosen the role of full-time homemaker:

• We have succeeded in enacting legislation that provides assistance for displaced homemakers and we supported the legislation that has now reduced from 20 to 10 years the marriage requirement for a former wife to claim against her husband's social security entitlement.

We are facilitating the choice of many women to combine family and work responsibilities. To accomplish this goal:

• we supported the legislation passed to increase part-time and flexible-hour employment opportunities; and

• we supported the Pregnancy Disability Act that outlaws employment discrimination based upon pregnancy, childbirth, or related conditions.

We are striving to improve women's professional opportunities within the Federal government. To this end:

• women have been appointed in senior positions in the Administration, including two Cabinet officers. About 20% of my senior appointees have been women, and many of them are in areas in which no previous women had served; and

• we have strengthened and increased our equal employment opportunity enforcement.

This year, in addition to continuing our efforts to ratify the Equal Rights Amendment, we will work closely with the Congress to enhance the economic standing of women—particularly the poor, minority, and elderly—by improving their access to housing, health care, and child care for those who choose to work. We will expand additional opportunities this year for women business owners and will create a permanent interagency group to review and help improve the position of women business owners. I will make every effort to select as many women as possible to fill the 152 new Federal judgeships. Their under-representation in the courts cannot be continued. Our country needs and deserves the full participation of women in our society, and I am committed to taking the steps needed to ensure this partnership.

District of Columbia

My Administration worked with the 95th Congress to pass a proposed amendment to the Constitution granting full voting representation to the citizens of our Nation's Capital. The ratification process

for this proposed amendment has begun and I urge the state legislatures which have not ratified the resolution to join with the States of New Jersey, Ohio and Michigan by promptly ratifying the amendment. My Administration will work this year in the effort to ratify this amendment.

My Administration will also work closely with the Congress and the new District Government under Mayor Marion Barry to expand home rule for the District. This includes streamlining the procedures for Congressional review of locally enacted legislation, removal of the Federal government from the District budgetary process by 1982, developing a rational formula for determining the Federal payment to the District, and an equitable Federal sharing of financial responsibility for funding of the District's pension plan for police, firemen, teachers and judges.

I will work with Mayor Barry to make our Nation's Capital city a model for the rest of the Nation to emulate.

Native Americans

The Federal government has a special responsibility to native Americans, and I intend to continue to exercise this responsibility fairly and sensitively. My Administration will continue to seek negotiated settlements to difficult conflicts over land, water, and other resources and will ensure that the trust relationship and self-determination principles continue to guide Indian policy. There are difficult conflicts which occasionally divide Indian and non-Indian citizens in this country. We will seek to exercise leadership to resolve these problems equitably and compassionately.

Handicapped

For Americans with physical disabilities, this year will result in continued improvements in their accessibility to many opportunities those of us who are not disabled take for granted—education opportunities, employment opportunities, and greater access to public facilities and services. We will make further progress in removing obstacles that impede and discriminate against our disabled community. If our Nation is to remove the barriers of discrimination in our society, the Federal government must serve as a model in the successful removal of physical and psychological barriers thrown in the way of our Nation's disabled. The Section 504 Regulations issued by the Department of Health, Education, and Welfare provide a basis for the Federal government to lead the way in ensuring the rights of the handicapped.

Undocumented Aliens

One of the most difficult and sensitive domestic issues facing the country concerns the Federal government's policy toward undocumented aliens.

I continue to believe that effective but humane measures need to be devised which will help relieve the causes and effects of the presence of large numbers of undocumented aliens in this country. I will pursue this issue in my consultations with the government of Mexico during my visit there next month and will make no final decisions until after those consultations.

Martin Luther King, Jr.

Dr. Martin Luther King, Jr. led this Nation's effort to provide all its citizens with civil rights and equal opportunities. His commitment to human rights, peace and non-violence stands as a monument to his humanity and courage. As one of our Nation's most outstanding leaders, it is appropriate that his birthday be commemorated as a national holiday, and I will strongly support legislation to achieve this.

Minority Business

This year we will move vigorously to implement the strong minority business legislation enacted by Congress in 1978; meet my goal of tripling Federal procurement from minority businesses (to a total of $3 billion) ; faithfully implementing the minority set-aside programs of the government and improve the operation of the several programs designed to achieve equal entrepreneurial opportunity and vital minority economic development. We are currently evaluating the adequacy and organization of current minority business development programs, with the commitment to taking whatever action, legislative or administrative, is needed to ensure that their operation is efficient and effective.

Civil Liberties

Privacy

Government and private institutions collect increasingly large amounts of personal data and use them to make many crucial decisions about individuals. Much of this information is needed to enforce laws, deliver benefits, provide credit, and conduct similar, important services. However, these interests must be balanced against the individual's right to privacy and against the harm that unfair uses of information can cause. Individuals should be able to know what information organizations collect and maintain about them; they should be able to correct inaccurate records; and there should be limits on the disclosure of particularly sensitive personal information.

My Administration is developing a comprehensive privacy policy to address these concerns. Last year, legislation was enacted which established restrictions on

145

wiretapping for intelligence purposes and on government access to financial records. Early in 1979, I will propose privacy legislation to cover medical, financial, and other sensitive personal records. I will also take administrative actions to strengthen privacy controls for Federal agencies' records. These measures will go far toward giving all American citizens the privacy protections they need in a modern society.

I recently announced my intention to submit legislation to Congress protecting the rights of the press, and others preparing materials for publication, from searches and seizures undertaken without judicial approval. Under the legislation I will propose, Federal, State and local law enforcement officials will generally be required to obtain a subpoena before conducting a search or seizure against those preparing materials for publication. Such legislation, which would deal with the problems created by the Supreme Court's decision in the *Stanford Daily* case, should serve as a solid protection of the rights of the news media and others under the Fourth Amendment.

Labor Law Reform

The Nation's labor laws are vital to ensuring that a sound labor-management relationship exists in collective bargaining. Efforts to abuse those labor laws, especially by unduly slowing or blocking their implementation, have increased in recent years. As a result, a reform of our labor laws is required in order to guarantee that their intended spirit is fully observed and enforced.

I am again prepared to work with the Congress to develop legislation which improves the fairness and effectiveness of our labor laws. Efforts to defeat this legislation last year were based on emotion and a lack of information about its actual effect. If the will of the majority in Congress is allowed to prevail, we *can* enact sound labor law legislation.

Export Administration/Anti-Foreign Boycott

My Administration will work with the Congress to reauthorize the Export Administration Act, which plays a vital role in ensuring that American trade serves our national interest. We will make particular efforts to reauthorize that part of the Act which prohibits American compliance with the foreign economic boycott of Israel. The anti-boycott amendments passed by the Congress were fair and equitable and must continue to be strenuously enforced.

Intelligence Charters

I will be working closely with the Congress to develop and enact statutory charters for the intelligence community. The charters, for the first time, will define in law the duties and responsibilities of our intelligence agencies and will set forth the authority of those agencies to fulfill those responsibilities. The disclosures of abuses in recent years make clear the need for charters, and my Administration is strongly committed to developing and passing charter legislation that protects our citizens' rights, while permitting our intelligence agencies to perform effectively their essential duties.

Criminal Code

The Federal criminal laws are often archaic, frequently contradictory and imprecise, and clearly in need of revision and codification. My Administration will continue to work with the Congress to develop a Federal criminal code which simplifies and clarifies our criminal laws—as well as protects our basic civil liberties. The criminal code which passed the Senate in the last session can serve as a basis for progress this year.

Hatch Act Reform

We will continue to support efforts to reform the Hatch Act so that Federal employees in non-sensitive positions will have the right to participate in off-the-job political activities while preventing any on-the-job political abuse.

Hunger

We share a growing concern with other Nations and their people over the serious problem of world hunger. While our government and the governments of other Nations and international organizations are working to assure the basic right to food, the problems of hunger and malnutrition are a daily fact of life for millions of people throughout the world. In order to make our own programs more effective and to examine additional efforts that might be undertaken, I have established the Presidential Commission on World Hunger, under the leadership of Ambassador Sol Linowitz, to recommend realistic solutions which we and other Nations might undertake in a prompt and efficient manner. The Commission will report to me this year and will then be involved in the implementation of its recommendations. The Administration will be working closely with Congress on the Commission's recommendation.

Holocaust Commission

Last year I established a Holocaust Commission to recommend to me how our government might officially recognize, for the first time, the tragedy of the Holocaust. The Commission's work is well underway, and I will receive its report this year. I expect to work together with Congress in developing a suitable memorial to the millions who died in the Holocaust.

PRESERVING AND DEVELOPING NATURAL RESOURCES

My highest legislation priority during the 95th Congress was enactment of our first national energy plan. The dedication of many members of Congress made that goal a reality. My Administration is committed to using that legislation as the foundation for further efforts to reduce our dependence on foreign oil; to increase our ability to develop domestic energy sources; and to conserve wasted energy.

Our energy and other development goals can and will be reconciled with the Administration's resolve to clean the Nation's air and water and to preserve our most precious natural resources. We will continue to further the protection of our environment.

We will continue to develop our fertile agricultural land. The Administration is committed to helping our Nation's farmers continue to achieve record yields and exports.

Energy

The Administration remains committed to meeting our future energy needs. Building upon the framework of the National Energy Act, signed last November, we will be addressing key issues such as further developing and commercializing solar and renewable energy resources, making better use of our coal reserves and other abundant energy resources, continuing our emphasis on using energy more efficiently, and improving the manner in which we produce and use conventional sources of energy such as oil, natural gas, and uranium. To minimize the impacts of potential supply disruptions, we will continue the storage of oil in the Strategic Petroleum Reserve, and will be submitting for Congressional approval overall energy contingency plans.

While much remains to be done in the energy area, past investments in improving our energy supplies and our energy use are beginning to pay off: the rate of growth of our industrial energy use has dropped while industrial production has increased. From 1975 to 1977 the growth in domestic energy consumption has been 70% of the growth in GNP Previously, the two growth rates had been roughly equal. With significant improvements in automobile efficiency, gasoline consumption is an estimated 5% lower than it otherwise would have been. Use of heating oil, electricity, and other home energy sources has become much more efficient. Oil consumption grew last year at a rate of only 1.5%.

On the supply side, the new natural gas legislation, whose provisions have just begun to take effect, will ensure new domestic production of this premium fuel and help expedite the delivery of natural gas to the interstate market. Furthermore, due to the addition of Alaska North Slope oil, our domestic production of oil has held steady over the last year, and foreign imports were down in 1978.

In 1979 and the FY '80 budget we are continuing strong investments in energy research and development. The FY 1980 budget provides outlays of $3.7 billion for a wide range of programs to develop energy technologies for the future. Particular emphasis will be given to long-term solar energy research and development, to improvements in the mining and burning of coal, fission and fusion research, to improvements in existing technologies for conservation, oil and gas recovery, and uranium efficiency, and to energy-related basic research. These commitments to technologies for the future, both long and shorter term, are critical to a sound and comprehensive energy policy.

Solar Energy

Within the next few weeks, I will send to the Congress a message on solar energy based on an interagency study under the Domestic Policy Review System. The transition to wide-spread use of solar and renewable resources can and must begin now. Solar, wind energy, and use of biomass resources can contribute significantly in both the short and long run to meeting our Nation's energy needs. Some of these technologies, such as solar heat and hot water, use of biomass for generation of electricity, and wind energy, are available now and are competing with other conventional energy sources. The tax credits in the National Energy Act, along with other commercialization incentives, will help accelerate the use of solar and other renewable technologies in the residential and industrial sectors of our economy.

The FY 1980 Budget increases our government-wide solar research and development programs by 40% over FY 1979. Total expenditures for solar energy will exceed $800 million, including tax credits and important initiatives undertaken by the Department of Energy, the Agency for International Development, the Tennessee Valley Authority, the Department of Agriculture and the Small Business Administration. Application of solar technologies in federally-owned buildings will also increase, thereby providing new markets for our existing solar industry.

In our research and development program, strong emphasis will be given to photovoltaics through which electricity can be produced directly from solar energy. Conversion of organic materials to useable energy forms will also receive increased funding. Funds for the new Solar

Energy Research Institute at Golden, Colorado, will also be increased.

The proposals I will later announce, coupled with the FY '80 budget, will chart a firm and ambitious course for accelerating the use of solar and other renewable energy sources both now and in the future. The time for solar energy has come.

Other Energy Research, Development, and Demonstration

In the coming year, significant investments will be made in the demonstration of technologies which can convert coal to more useable and environmentally acceptable energy forms, continued strong research and development in fusion, development of geothermal energy sources, such as hot underground brines and hot rock resources, and efforts to resolve a range of environmental issues which these and other technologies raise.

Nuclear Energy

A wide range of Administration initiatives, both legislative and administrative, will be proposed to ensure that this country can further use light water reactors for the generation of electricity, safely and efficiently. Of central importance will be the development and implementation of a strong, responsible program to manage and dispose of nuclear wastes. As a result of the work of the Interagency Review Group on Waste Management, I will be making a series of legislative and administrative recommendations to ensure that the necessary schedules, coordination, and legislative authorities are firmly in place. Public discussion and participation in the nuclear waste management area, along with the close cooperation of State and local elected officials, will receive continued high priority. Legislation will also

be proposed to provide interim storage for spent fuel from existing reactors until a permanent waste repository is established.

Enactment of nuclear licensing and siting legislation to shorten the leadtimes required to plan, locate, construct and license nuclear power reactors will again be sought. Design and construction activities for the new centrifuge enrichment plant at Portsmouth, Ohio, will continue to ensure that the U.S. is able to meet the nuclear fuel needs of our domestic industry, as well as our international customers who share our non-proliferation objectives. These activities, coupled with the Administration's waste management program will help ensure that our country can continue to rely on current nuclear technologies to meet power needs.

Looking toward the future, we will seek to improve the efficiency of our existing power reactors by reducing their uranium feed requirements. For the longer run, the Administration will maintain and strengthen the strong research and development program we now have for more advanced nuclear fission technologies such as the fast breeder reactor. We continue to believe that the Clinch River Breeder reactor project is premature, technically inadequate, and should not go forward, but the Administration is committed to keeping the breeder option open for the future.

Domestic Crude Oil Pricing

Provision of adequate incentives for both domestic production of crude oil and for conservation must be carefully weighed in light of our efforts to control inflation. In consultation with the Congress, I will be making my decisions and recommendations on domestic crude oil pricing and related issues later this year.

149

Energy Impact Assistance

As new domestic energy resources are developed, particularly in rural or isolated areas of the country, provision must be made for the needs of rapidly developing communities. The Administration will again seek enactment of legislation establishing an Inland Energy Assistance program, with funding of $150 million per year, to aid those states and local areas which are experiencing a rapid growth in population as a result of new energy supply development. These communities often cannot plan for or meet increased need for new public facilities or services, since the population increases occur before the new energy supply activities are fully developed and producing local revenues. This legislation is essential to ensure that the burdens associated with solving our energy problems are borne equitably by all citizens and regions of the country.

Management of Federal Energy Resources

The last two Congresses passed landmark legislation to reform the management of federally-owned coal, oil and gas resources. These new laws include Federal strip mine controls, and amendments to the Outer Continental Shelf Lands Act and the Mineral Leasing Act. With this new framework, the Administration is proceeding to implement swiftly new programs which will permit increased leasing and development activities while protecting our environment.

Water Policy Legislation

Water is a basic human necessity and its proper management is essential to economic activity, particularly in the arid West. The policies of my Administration are designed to emphasize the more effi-cient use of water as well as the need to provide adequate water supplies. We are particularly sensitive to the interests of the West and other areas in the development of additional water resources, to the importance of water conservation, and to the concerns of many Eastern urban areas about their water systems.

Last year I announced a comprehensive water policy which included many reforms now being implemented administratively. In addition, I will propose legislation to increase the role of the States in water policy, through increased water planning grants and through new grants for state water conservation programs. I will also propose legislation which would provide for states to share in the costs of Federal water projects. This cost sharing proposal will result in direct participation by states in setting water project priorities and will help insure that Federal programs are responsive to the most pressing water-related needs.

Congressional action is also needed on Administration Amendments to modernize the 1902 Reclamation Act to ensure that acreage limitations in federally-funded irrigation projects are equitable and fair.

Environment

My Administration is committed to balancing the needs for development, conservation and preservation of our natural resources. Our Nation has been blessed with an outstanding natural heritage which, if properly cared for, can meet our needs for food and fiber, mineral, energy, recreation, and solitude in a way that is environmentally sound. The Congress and the Administration have worked together over the past two years to achieve this goal. We have enacted the first Federal standards for strip-mining coal; we have improved and extended the Clean Air and

Clean Water Acts; we have created a substantial number of new National Parks and other protected areas. During 1979, protection of Alaska lands, implementation of water policy, resolution of wilderness and nonwilderness designations in the National Forest System and reformed management of Federal energy resources will be major environmental initiatives of my Administration. Efforts to enforce and implement environmental statutes firmly and fairly, to streamline environmental review requirements, to protect public health and to preserve wildlife resources will continue to be pursued vigorously and as cost-effectively as possible.

Alaska

As in the last Congress, passage of legislation designating National Parks, Wildlife Refuges, Wilderness Areas, National Forests and Wild and Scenic Rivers in Alaska is the highest environmental priority of my Administration. To protect these magnificent Alaskan wild lands, I took several actions after the adjournment of the 95th Congress, including the creation of 17 National Monuments covering 56 million acres. These areas, as well as other outstanding parts of Alaska covered in Administration proposals, should be protected promptly by legislation in order to assure that the great national treasures of wildlife, scenery, history and untouched ecosystems can be saved for our children and grandchildren, while permitting appropriate commercial use of certain of the areas.

Roadless Area Designations (Rare II)

The Agriculture Department has released tentative recommendations and nearly completed work on a study which will lead to proposals to resolve the status of most of the remaining roadless areas in the National Forest System. The Administration proposal will involve additional wilderness designations in many States and the release of remaining lands for non-wilderness activities. This initiative will also eliminate uncertainty over land uses in most parts of the National Forest System and will ensure that development uses will be adequately supported, while preserving critical parts of our natural heritage in an unspoiled condition.

Environmental Protection

In recent years, the quality of our environment has improved, but much remains to be done to clean up our air and water, and to control contamination by toxic materials. The Environmental Protection Agency is focussing its efforts on the protection of public health by assessing the effects of substances before they are introduced into the environment, and by ensuring that hazardous wastes are disposed of safely.

At the same time, EPA, and the other health and safety agencies are exercising new care when implementing environmental regulations to avoid imposing unnecessary costs or red tape. A healthy, safe environment need not be incompatible with a healthy economy. We are committed to both.

The Nation's investment in environment cleanup must have the incentives and the flexibility to allow our most important environmental goals to be achieved at the lowest cost. Unnecessary requirements which cause delays and increase costs will be removed. EPA will simplify and consolidate its permit programs to reduce paperwork, red tape and delays.

The Agency is beginning to introduce innovations which allow firms the flexibility to find the lowest cost methods of controlling pollution. I will submit legislation to consolidate Federal funds for environmental programs at the State level, thus giving the States more flexibility to use these funds to deal with their most pressing environmental problems.

These and other changes we are making will assure the American public that the money we spend on environmental controls is the best investment we can make in our future and our children's future.

The State of Food and Agriculture

World food security has been substantially improved in 1978. For the third consecutive year, good-to-record crops were harvested in most parts of the world, pushing supplies to record quantities and creating the opportunity for people all over the world to improve their diets.

For the United States, 1978 was also a year of records. Large food and record feed grain crops were harvested by U.S. producers, re-emphasizing the U.S. farm sector's capability to lead the world in productivity. But despite the record crops which placed downward pressure on prices here and abroad, our farm economy became stronger in 1978 and our agricultural trade reached record levels.

The value of U.S. agricultural exports reached $27.3 billion in fiscal 1978—14 percent above 1977's record. The volume of our farm exports was a record 125 million metric tons—up 18 percent from 1977. Agricultural trade made another record contribution to our balance of payments—$13.4 billion in fiscal 1978. Exports also accounted for one out of every four dollars the U.S. farmer earned.

Net farm income, which was $20.6 billion in 1977, is estimated at over $28 billion for 1978—second highest on record. In constant dollars, this was the best year since 1975. This was achieved while we

met our domestic needs, fulfilled our commitments to our overseas customers and built reserves for future stability protection. This recovery in agriculture has been shared by crop and livestock producers alike. Indeed, American livestock producers can now look forward to several years of good returns to help them recover from the last four years which were marked by poor prices and forced liquidation of herds.

Part of the recovery in the farm sector can be attributed to the programs and policies adopted by my Administration and the Congress—which farmers have used to improve their incomes and stabilize prices.

I am personally proud of the recovery our farmers have made.

International Agricultural Trade

Over the past 2 years, this Administration has worked to reduce barriers to international trade and to develop new markets and encourage increased exports of agricultural products. The Agricultural Trade Act of 1978, for example, provides important new authorities for intermediate credit and the establishment of trade offices in major markets. We have moved to establish new and stronger trade ties with several nations, including Japan and the People's Republic of China. Partly as a result of these efforts, exports of U.S. farm produced goods are expected to reach a record $29 billion in fiscal 1979—21 percent higher than 2 years ago—and contribute $15 billion to our balance of payments.

Unlike previous Multilateral Trade Negotiations, in the current MTN we have placed heavy emphasis on the lessening of restrictions on trade in agricultural products. Our efforts here should have a major impact on U.S. agriculture in the future, by broadening our access to important existing and new international markets.

Crop Insurance

The Federal government now operates several programs to protect farmers from economic losses associated with crop failure. The experience of recent years with these programs has demonstrated their many serious shortcomings—in the breadth of coverage, the equity of program benefits, and the efficiency of program administration.

We will propose again a comprehensive, nationwide all-risk insurance reform bill to the 96th Congress aimed at providing fairer and more effective protection for farmers, and at no additional cost to the taxpayer. Under this proposal, several existing disaster assistance programs would be consolidated into one comprehensive, share-the-cost program to ensure against economic losses resulting from natural disaster and other uncontrollable risks.

International Emergency Wheat Reserve

The cornerstone of our domestic food and agricultural policy is the farmer-owned grain reserve. In little more than a year, we have built this into a 1.3 billion bushel grain reserve—the equivalent of more than a third of our carry-over stocks from the past year. These stocks remain under the ownership of those farmers who produced them rather than in the hands of government or international grain traders. This reserve provides a critical cushion against shocks in the market caused by production shortfalls either here or abroad.

We now need to establish the same sort of protection for our international food aid programs. Accordingly, the Administration will reintroduce legislation to authorize the establishment and management of an international emergency wheat reserve. This reserve will provide developing countries assurance that we will be able to fulfill our food aid commitments. At the same time, it will protect the domestic economy from further inflationary pressures during periods of grain shortages.

Sugar

In the absence of Congressional passage of a domestic sugar program in the last session, the Administration has taken several further steps to assure domestic producers of a fair return and consumers an assured supply at stable prices. To underscore Administration commitment to achieving ratification of the International Sugar Agreement, I directed that sugar imports from countries not party to the agreement be strictly limited to the levels permitted under the agreement for 1979. We have also asked for and received an extension of the deadline for ratifying the ISA to June 30, 1979. In addition, at the end of last year, I issued a proclamation that provides for a new, more flexible system of sugar import fees protecting a domestic raw sugar price of 15 cents per pound.

To help stabilize world sugar prices, to satisfy our international commitments, and to protect our domestic sugar producers, my Administration is committed to working with the Congress to develop an effective, non-inflationary domestic sugar program early in this session, and to achieve ratification of the International Sugar Agreement.

Rural Development

Throughout 1978 my Administration took steps to make existing Federal rural development programs work better. For many rural areas, and for most rural residents, the 1970's have been a period of rapid growth and development. Income levels have risen and large numbers of better jobs have been created in rural communities across the Nation. Rates of population and employment growth for rural areas have been substantially greater than for urban areas—causing problems of unplanned rapid growth in some areas but also reversing decades of rural out-migration and economic stagnation. Nevertheless, rural Americans still experience a disproportionate concentration of pressing human problems:

• two-thirds of all homes lacking complete plumbing are in rural areas;

• rural infant mortality rates are 10 percent higher than urban ones;

• 70 percent of the rural poor and half of the rural elderly have no automobile, causing great hardship because of the distances to travel to get access to basic health care, jobs, and other social services;

• while only a quarter of all Americans live in rural areas, 40 percent of the Nation's poor live there.

For too long the small town mayor, the rural county official and the individual rural American have been frustrated by a maze of Federal grant applications, requirements, eligibility standards, audits and deadlines which have made it virtually impossible to address these rural problems effectively.

For too many years, money and time has been wasted. We are moving to address this chronic problem. In the last year, White House Rural Development initiatives have resulted in:

• a commitment to build 300 rural primary health clinics to serve 1.3 million Americans who lacked access to care;

• major streamlining of the rural water and sewer grant process through which five agencies distribute $2.5 billion in Federal funds each year. The new process permits a single application, single audit, single funding source and single point of Federal contact—at a savings to local government of several hundred million dollars each year along with a reduction in processing time of as much as 15 months; and

• specially targeted rural job training programs for rural disadvantaged in the water and sewer and health support fields.

This effort to address rural problems will continue and be expanded in 1979, addressing the problems of rural transportation, housing, and economic development among others. In addition, during the year I plan to articulate a set of overall rural development principles and goals which will guide the actions of my Administration. These principles will provide focus, direction and priority to the myriad of now separate Federal actions and policies, so that we can more effectively work to:

• overcome the problems of rural isolation;

• promote economic development;

• meet basic human needs;

• protect the quality of rural life;

• assure equity in the administration of Federal programs for which rural Americans are eligible; and

• build a more effective partnership among Federal, State and local governments and the private sector in meeting locally defined rural development priorities.

Furthermore, several other Administration initiatives will have an impact on the conditions in rural America. We will make certain that the rural perspective is considered as initiatives are developed in such areas as welfare reform and a national health plan.

FOREIGN POLICY PRIORITIES

THE CONTINUING CHALLENGES OF
CHANGE

When I took office two years ago this month, I was convinced that America had to pursue a changed course in a world which was itself undergoing vast change.

In the midst of this accelerating change, America's choice lies between facing chaos or building with others a new foundation for a true world community. Our foreign policy accepts the latter responsibility both because of our basic belief, and because of America's critical role in the world.

To this end, we must have four broad objectives:

• to buttress American power on which global security and stability depend;

• to strengthen our relations with other nations throughout the world in order to widen the spirit of international cooperation;

• to deal constructively with pressing world problems which otherwise will disrupt and even destroy the world community we seek;

• to assert our traditional commitment to human rights, rejoining a rising tide of belief in the dignity of the individual.

Progress towards these goals depends first on our ability as a Nation to work together in the common interest. During the coming year, the Congress, the Executive, and the public will be addressing an unusually wide range of international issues. The action taken will have an impact on our Nation's position in the world for many years to come—in establishing a secure nuclear balance, in developing closer relations with the world's most populous Nation; in achieving an historic step towards peace in the Middle East; or in setting the pattern of trade relations during the next decade and beyond.

This report elaborates on my address to the Congress and, in particular, concentrates on the issues in which the role of the Congress will be most important to building a new foundation for peace. In each case, the challenge is clear: to exercise strong American leadership with others to shape change rather than permit change to shape us.

AMERICA'S MILITARY STRENGTH

Elsewhere in this report I have described the domestic programs and policies required for a just, united and productive America. The maintenance of American military strength is an essential foundation for a successful foreign policy that safeguards our freedom, our accomplishments and our friendships. In a world of accelerating change, fraught with potential danger and uncertainty, and marked by a continuing Soviet military buildup, we must have, together with our allies, unsurpassed military capability to deter attack or attempts at political coercion. Moreover, we must have the military force to mount an effective defense at any level of hostilities where our vital interests are jeopardized.

The defense budget which I have presented to the Congress funds a program of prudent investments that will ensure the effectiveness of our strategic and conventional military posture. It will:

• begin full-scale development of a new, more survivable ballistic missile system to enhance the ICBM component of our strategic triad;

• maintain the Trident submarine and missile programs, increasing the security, striking power and the range of our submarine force;

• extend the effectiveness of our bomber force with the addition of air-launched cruise missiles;

155

• pursue a vigorous program of research and development in cruise missiles, aircraft and other systems to ensure the continued technological superiority of America's nuclear deterrent.

In addition, the defense budget I have submitted this week will strengthen our conventional capabilities to fulfill our commitments to our major allies and friends and retain a credible military presence in both the Atlantic and the Pacific. We will continue to add armor and firepower to our infantry and build a more modern, smaller aircraft carrier which, together with more frigates and destroyers, will improve the effectiveness and flexibility of our surface fleet.

In NATO, we have already achieved important progress toward making the Alliance more effective in the changing security environment.

• We helped launch the Alliance's Long-Term Defense Program to offset growing Soviet modernization of its deployment in Europe. The LTDP will increase NATO military capabilities through better coordination of defense efforts, increased investment, and more modern equipment.

• We removed, with the support of Congress, a serious obstacle to strengthening Turkey's defensive capabilities and made further progress toward the reintegration of Greek armed forces into NATO's military structure; both these efforts helped repair a serious deficiency on NATO's southern flank.

• We neared final agreement with the Portuguese on the renewal of our base rights in the Azores.

The provision of adequate military as well as economic assistance to Turkey, Portugal and other allies and friends in need will be a matter of high priority during the coming year.

NATO's strength is growing. In 1979, we can further that encouraging process by standardizing more of the Alliance's equipment and improving Allied readiness. The proposal I will soon put before the 96th Congress calls for the authorization of intergovernmental agreements to simplify logistical problems both in peacetime and during any period of hostilities. Such agreements will permit the U.S. to reinforce NATO more rapidly and provide more effective defense at lower cost.

We also intend to maintain a vigorous American military presence in the Pacific. Successful completion of a revised military base agreement in the Philippines, following ten years of negotiations, provides an essential underpinning for our military capability in Asia.

Congressional authorization for the transfer of military equipment to the Republic of Korea was another contribution to assuring the security of Korea and Japan. Both actions unmistakably signal not only our desire to promote East Asian stability but our intention to remain a concerned, involved and responsible power in the Pacific.

The essential task of improving our military posture must also be accompanied by increased efficiency. I take this opportunity to thank the Congress for its support last year of our actions to reduce waste and needless duplication in our defense budget. Vigorous cost-saving efforts will continue this year in order to assure that the United States will possess strong military forces at the lowest possible cost.

BUILDING THE COMMUNITY OF NATIONS

Military strength is essential to peace but cannot alone guarantee it. The system of cooperation we have with the rest of the world is part of the foundation for our own security. Our best hope for a safer America and a peaceful world resides in the building of closer ties with as many nations as possible.

The Major Allies

Throughout 1978, the North Atlantic Alliance and the growing partnership which links us with both Western Europe and Japan remained at the heart of our foreign policy. The cooperation we share with those whose purposes and traditions are closest to our own is strong and growing stronger.

Through our summit meetings, and through an unprecedented pattern of consultations at other levels of our governments, we are working together on virtually all of today's most critical issues:

• together we are seeking to reduce the risk of nuclear confrontation;

• we are working on ways to strengthen the common defense;

• we are attempting to promote a peaceful transition in southern Africa;

• we are striving to resolve conflicts in the Eastern Mediterranean to support a just and lasting peace in the Middle East and to maintain stability in the Persian Gulf;

• we are contributing to a sounder international economy;

• we are consulting on the issues that confront all our societies: the problems of youth and age, family and community, growth and conservation—in short, advancing our democratic ideals at home in a time of change in each of our countries.

America's role as host for the NATO summit meeting in Washington last spring, and our attendance at the seven-nation economic summit in Bonn last summer, symbolized American commitment to the strength of relations with Europe and Japan. I look forward to meeting these and other allied leaders at the Tokyo Summit next June, where we will continue the essential effort to deepen further the cooperation between us.

A Wider Community

The changing realities of political and economic interdependence require that we strengthen our ties throughout the developing world and seek to improve relations with Communist nations as well.

My trips to Nigeria, India, Saudi Arabia, Iran, Brazil, and Venezuela underlined American sympathy and support for the international roles these countries are playing in the process of world change. Strengthened consultations with the ASEAN nations serve the same end.

My trip to Mexico early next month will be a part of this process; Mexico is important to us not only because it is a neighbor but also because it is one of the most vigorous democracies in this Hemisphere and a leader in the developing world. As neighbors, we share an agenda of common concerns—trade, migration, economic growth and social development—that provides an opportunity to establish a uniquely productive, cooperative relationship.

My trip to Poland and the visits of Secretary Vance and Secretary Blumenthal to Hungary and Romania underscore the importance we attach to better relations with the nations of Eastern Europe. The support of the Congress for our policy toward Eastern Europe has provided a strong foundation for building a stronger economic, cultural and political relationship—a process that will continue to go forward in the coming year.

China

The arrival next week of the first leader of the People's Republic of China to officially visit Washington will give us an early and welcome opportunity in the new year not only to cement the ties of friendship and hospitality between us but to emphasize our expectation that our relationship with China will be a constructive one. It will contribute to diversity in the world and to peace and stability in Asia. It is not directed against the interests of any other country.

To fulfill the promise of this new era in Sino-American relations, we will require legislation and support from the Congress. Such legislation is particularly important to facilitate continued trade and other relations with the people of Taiwan through non-governmental instrumentalities and to assure continued peace and prosperity there. This has very high priority in our legislative program for 1979.

USSR

We seek better relations with both the Soviet Union and the People's Republic of China. Doing so is profoundly in the interests of our Nation and of global security.

I therefore would like also to welcome President Brezhnev to our country in the near future. At that time we would hope to conclude an agreement curbing the strategic arms race. There are other areas where our two nations can work constructively together. These include a comprehensive nuclear test ban treaty; limits on Indian Ocean deployments, and on the transfer of conventional arms; and restraint in areas of turbulence and tension. Such cooperative effort would do much to make the world a safer place for all.

We will never ignore Soviet actions which challenge our interests. We both have a responsibility to our peoples and the world to maintain a pattern of détente which is genuinely reciprocal and broadly defined.

DEALING WITH WORLD PROBLEMS

A true world community cannot be fashioned or endure so long as the weapons of war multiply and spread, so long as ancient disputes fester and the demands for justice are unmet, so long as much of mankind remains impoverished and without hope.

As I emphasized in my State of the Union address, the need to curb the strategic arms race has never been more urgent. It increases the risk of nuclear war. It is a needless competition that draws away scarce resources we need to invest in other areas of our Nation's strength. It undermines America's security.

The conclusion and ratification of a satisfactory SALT II Treaty with the Soviet Union is therefore among our top priorities. It will make a major contribution to enhancing our long-term security, while keeping open our options to carry out needed modernization of our strategic forces and preserve our deterrence.

We will take whatever time is necessary to negotiate a sound, verifiable agreement. I am convinced that once the American people and Congress have had a chance to examine the terms and benefits of this Treaty—and consider the shape of our future without it—they will conclude it serves our vital security interests.

We will continue to consult the Congress as we proceed this year with other important arms control negotiations: on a comprehensive nuclear test ban; the prevention of anti-satellite warfare; mutual and balanced force reductions in Europe; and limits on the rising tide of conventional arms transfers.

The risks inherent in the proliferation of nuclear technology figure prominently among the dangers to the world community. Although we and the rest of the world still have far to go in dealing responsibly with such risks, the United

States took an important step last March with the adoption of the Nuclear Non-Proliferation Act. For the first time in our history we established comprehensive legislation covering international cooperation in the nuclear field and the export of nuclear-related materials. To build on that promising beginning throughout 1979, we need progress in the following areas, both nuclear and non-nuclear:

• The International Nuclear Fuel Cycle Evaluation (INFCE), a 53-nation effort, can help us develop a new international nuclear fuel consensus that will adequately balance energy needs with non-proliferation concerns. We continue to believe that better alternatives exist to the commercialization of dangerous breeder reactors and we will cooperate as fully as possible with other countries in exploring those alternatives.

• We will seek more substantial progress in the problem of managing nuclear waste and in attracting greater international support for the acceptance of nuclear safeguards. I ask the Senate to ratify the treaty on the IAEA Voluntary Safeguards Offer which will provide concrete proof of our belief that international safeguards do not interfere with the successful development and operation of commercial nuclear power.

• I will call for early Senate ratification of Protocol I of the Treaty of Tlatelolco, which will contribute to the lessening of nuclear dangers for our Latin American neighbors; the U.S. and Cuba are now the only countries in our Hemisphere which have not yet ratified that Treaty.

Regional Conflict and Tension

Curbing the means of war cannot in itself remove the threat of war. For that, we must seek to resolve conflicts, ease tension and build trust. The urgency of this task and its importance to the United States and the world is nowhere more clear than in the Middle East. Though there has been great progress, the goal of a just and lasting settlement in that troubled part of the world still eludes us. No one who has looked at Middle East history can harbor any illusion about the difficulties ahead. Yet we have made great strides toward a final peace agreement between the two principal adversaries in the Middle East. The differences which they have overcome far outweigh the issues which still divide them. Israeli and Egyptian commitment to peace will provide an indispensable step toward peace between Israel and all its neighbors and foster the stability and orderly change we favor for the entire Middle East region. Peace will permit us to strengthen our ties with the Arab states in the region and enhance our relationship with Israel, a relationship which will always be special to us.

In 1979 I will count on the continued collaboration of the 96th Congress on behalf of our efforts to gain and maintain peace throughout the region. The support of the Congress and the American people for a purposeful role in that region is particularly important in light of the tumultuous events taking place in Iran. Since the end of the Second World War, the United States has maintained a close relationship with Iran and it has a vital interest in Iran's independence and integrity. The people of Iran should shape their own future without foreign interference. That is the policy of the government of the United States and we expect it to be the policy of all of Iran's neighbors.

Africa

Congressional support for peace, stability, and orderly change are essential in other tense regions, as well.

159

In Southern Africa we are trying to help bring about a peaceful transformation to majority rule which will avoid growing bloodshed between white and black and deeper intervention by the Soviet Union and Cuba.

Together with our European allies, Canada, and African states directly concerned, we are making progress toward the independence and majority rule of Namibia—a step that would have a positive impact on the evolution of events in Rhodesia and elsewhere in Southern Africa. We are heartened by the support of the African leaders who have worked with us in efforts to resolve the Namibian and Rhodesian issues.

Congressional repeal of the Byrd Amendment was essential in enhancing our credibility in the effort to avoid a gathering war and further Soviet and Cuban gains in Southern Africa. We will consult closely with the Congress during the coming months, as we seek the most constructive role we can play. It will be increasingly important to maintain our position of impartiality among the parties so we can help them resolve their differences should they choose the path of peace.

Latin America

In our own Hemisphere, we can point with pride to the cooperative spirit which enabled us to change, in mutually beneficial ways, the basis of our relations with Panama. Senate approval of the two Panama Canal treaties last year has improved the quality of our historic relationship not only with Panama itself but with our friends in every part of Latin America. By that act, our country helped demonstrate its ability both to protect major security interests and to deal with smaller nations with dignity and mutual respect. Congressional action to pass the necessary implementing legislation for these treaties be-

fore the October 1 deadline will ensure that the Canal is efficiently operated during the transition to a new partnership with Panama.

The treaties and implementing legislation, like our efforts to help the people of Nicaragua find an enduring democratic solution to the current crisis there, are important to the future stability of Central America as a whole and the strengthening of our new and mature relationship with the nations of all Latin America.

The International Economy

In our daily lives, we are constantly reminded of the importance of a healthy world economy to the strength of our own. We see this in the wages of our workers who produce goods for export, in the choice of goods for our consumers, in the price of energy.

We must work closely with other countries to ensure that the world economy can steadily develop through non-inflationary growth, while together we manage the use of its resources and protect our environment.

The focus for much of this effort during the past year was the Bonn Economic Summit. We worked out a strategy of cooperation with our partners to improve the world economic situation: within the framework of those Summit decisions, West Germany and Japan have taken measures to stimulate their economies while we are giving top priority to fighting inflation. Our actions, along with those taken by other Summit participants, are leading to a convergence of economic policies that will strengthen the global economy.

We have strengthened the dollar by working out arrangements with other countries to counter speculative disorder in currency markets. Since I announced my dollar stabilization measures last November, we stopped the dollar's decline in value against other currencies and have actually increased the dollar's value by around 10 percent against several major currencies. Moreover, we have announced a multi-faceted program to increase U.S. exports, which will benefit American farmers and workers, while further strengthening the position of the dollar.

We are now close to new agreements with our trading partners to establish a fairer, better operating and more open framework for world trade.

The American people have a vital stake in Congressional approval of these agreements. Ten million American jobs depend on our exports. Every third acre of our farmland produces for sales abroad. Two-thirds of our imports are essential raw materials or goods we cannot readily produce.

At a time of difficult strains in our own economy, there is always an impulse to abandon our commitment to an open world trading system. But the costs of such a course to the American people would be enormous. Each American family would pay more for what it buys and would have less choice in the goods available. Inflation would be fueled. Jobs would be jeopardized, for protectionism against our trading partners breeds protectionism by them against us.

I am convinced that our economy can adapt to changing patterns of world trade in ways that protect the future of our workers. We can compete effectively in the world economy. The new trade agreements give us the opportunity to do so.

Our programs of economic development assistance abroad are also an investment in our own future as well as the future of other nations. Our most rapidly growing markets lie in the developing world. By helping the people of these countries, we not only help extend their opportunities for a better life, we help ourselves. By demonstrating to their governments that we are concerned for the well-being of their people, we encourage their increasing cooperation with the West on a broad range of issues.

I therefore urge Congressional approval of the funding we propose for our bilateral assistance programs and our participation in the work of the multilateral development banks and UN agencies.

My proposal to establish a Foundation of International Technological Cooperation reflects our recognition that scientists in many developing nations are ready to work in collaboration with our technological institutions to solve the great problems of health, nutrition, productivity and other aspects of economic development.

Key commodity agreements can also help us deal with the legitimate needs and interests of the developing countries. Senate ratification of the International Sugar Agreement, which we signed last year, along with price support legislation will stabilize prices for that important commodity. We have pledged a contribution to the International Tin Agreement, and we will conduct negotiations on a rubber accord.

Efforts to build a stronger international economy are directed not simply at managing economic relationships among nations, but at improving the lives of individual people around the world. For it is the lives of individuals which define the success or failure of our foreign policies.

REASSERTING AMERICA'S VALUES

America's future is best secured in a world founded on decency, justice and compassion.

The effort to make human rights a central component of our foreign policy comes from our deepest sense of ourselves as a humane and freedom-loving people.

We do not make our standards the precondition for every relationship we have with other countries; yet human rights can never be far from the focus of our thinking or we violate our own best values.

In the year just passed, some have quarrelled with the timing or the tactics of our emphasis on human rights abroad. Others have pointed to our own imperfect record on human rights at home. Yet few can dispute an important fact of this experience: our concern for human rights has met with great resonance in the world at large. The very term has entered the language and become imbued with an everyday familiarity that was simply unknown little more than two years ago.

We believe our efforts have contributed to a global awakening:

• thousands of political prisoners have been freed;

• in several countries, torture of prisoners has been significantly reduced or eliminated and trials are more often open to the public;

• open advocacy of human rights has occurred in nations where the concept was heretofore forbidden;

• international organizations such as the UN and the OAS now have vigorous human rights commissions for the investigation and airing of human rights violations and the Commission on Security and Cooperation in Europe has helped to make human rights an institutionalized part of the international agenda on both sides of the Atlantic;

• in a number of key nations around the world, democratic institutions are being strengthened as democratic values are reasserted.

Americans can be proud of the leading role their government has played in advancing this process. I now ask the Congress to take action in 1979 which will further strengthen our human rights record. I have signed four important human rights treaties, including the Convention on Racial Discrimination, the International UN Covenants on Economic and Social Rights, and on Political and Civil Rights, and the Inter-American Convention on Human Rights. Senate ratification of these treaties will firmly align our Nation with the growing forces for rule of law and human dignity in this world. Similarly, I call upon the Senate finally to ratify the Genocide Convention. The United States is one of the very few countries which have not yet ratified this convention; this anomaly should be corrected at the earliest possible moment in this Congress.

I am also proud of the efforts we have undertaken this past year to alleviate the plight of refugees from the far corners of the world, particularly those fleeing the troubled Indochinese peninsula. We have done a great deal to reduce suffering among these desperate people and to provide many of them with a possibility of a new home and a new start.

We will continue to do our part and to encourage others to increase their financial assistance and opportunities for resettlement. I hope to cooperate closely with this Congress in the passage of new legislation which will allow us to focus U.S. assistance more efficiently in working toward the solution of this global, human problem.

Our challenges reflect a single fact: the pressure of accelerating change in our century. We need not fear this phenomenon; indeed, we should welcome it. Change has not been merely a challenge in American history; to a very real degree, it has been our Nation's charter. We have not prospered and grown for more than two hundred years by worshipping the status quo. In building our Nation and confronting the many tasks which history has assigned us, we have found change to be our natural element.

We should approach the task of building a new Foundation for a world of change with the confidence of a Nation whose strengths are unmatched. Our military forces are strong and growing stronger. Our technological and industrial capacities are unsurpassed. Our allies are strong and reliable. Our way of life, and what we stand for as a Nation, continue to have magnetic international appeal.

I do not pretend that change comes without cost. I do not pretend that it comes without pain. Neither the visionary men of the 18th Century who founded our Republic, nor the citizens of conscience who opposed slavery in the 19th, nor the men and women of the 20th who led us successfully through two world wars looked upon change as easy. They did, however, look upon it as inevitable.

So it was in the beginning of our country, so it has been through all the stages of our history. The future has always brought Americans to a higher level of national achievement as long as we were willing to invest the time and the energy and the imagination toward shaping that future ourselves.

As we begin a new year, I repledge my Administration to time, energy, and imagination essential to build a new Foundation for a world of peace, prosperity and human justice. Together, America's Congress, its people, and its President cannot only master the many challenges of change, but make them a part of our Nation's purpose in the world. In so doing, we can bring America closer to that "more

perfect union" of Jefferson's dream in a wider and more secure global community congenial to our values, interests and ideals.

JIMMY CARTER

The White House,
    January 25, 1979.

Committee for Purchase From the Blind and Other Severely Handicapped

Appointment of Brig. Gen. Nathaniel R. Thompson, Jr., as a Member.
January 25, 1979

The President today announced the appointment of Brig. Gen. Nathaniel R. Thompson, Jr., as a member of the Committee for Purchase From the Blind and Other Severely Handicapped.

Thompson is Director of Transportation, Energy and Troop Support in the Office of the Deputy Chief of Staff for Logistics, Department of the Army.

Interview With the President

Question-and-Answer Session With Zhao Zhongxiang of Central TV, People's Republic of China. January 25, 1979

MR. ZHAO. Mr. President, first of all, we would like to express our appreciation for giving us this opportunity to have this interview.

THE PRESIDENT. It's a great honor and privilege for me to have a chance to talk to the millions of Chinese people who are once again our very important, very close friends.

MR. ZHAO. Mr. President, you have made positive contributions to the normalization of relations between China and the United States. The Chinese people are most happy about the establishment of diplomatic relations between our two countries. What do you think is the significance of the normalization of Sino-U.S. relations? How would you assess the outlook for our relationship after the normalization?

THE PRESIDENT. The normalization of relations between China and the United States is a development of great historical importance. After long years of estrangement between our people, we now have a new and exciting, very happy opportunity to strengthen the ties of friendship which our people have longed for.

This also opens up opportunities for political discussions between our leaders for improved cultural exchange, better trade relationships, and also, of course, scientific opportunities, where both our nations would have great mutual benefit. This original opening of relations will also permit future growth in all these aspects of a better quality of life for our people and will lay a foundation for the enhancement of peace in the entire Asian region and, indeed, throughout the entire world. It will let our people cooperate with one another on goals of mutual interest to the people of China and the people of the United States of America.

MR. ZHAO. Vice Premier Deng Xiaoping is coming to the United States soon for a friendly official visit at your invitation. This is going to be the first visit by a Chinese state leader to this country. What do you expect from this visit?

THE PRESIDENT. Well, the most important element of his visit, from my perspective, is the extensive and private conver-

sations between Vice Premier Deng Xiaoping and myself. We will have a broad agenda of issues to be discussed of great mutual interest to our people.

We also will have an opportunity to show, through the welcome extended to Vice Premier Deng Xiaoping, his wife, and his entire party of leaders of China, the friendship of the American people for the people of China.

The Vice Premier will have an opportunity, as well, to discuss issues with the Members of the Congress of the United States, and will have a chance to visit some of our very fine cities—Atlanta, Houston, Seattle. This is an important element of the Chinese ability to understand the peace-loving nature of Americans and the common purposes that we obviously share.

So, I believe that this visit will be exciting, enjoyable, and a wonderful opportunity to show the entire world that the new friendship that exists between our countries and our people is important to us and will be of increasing importance in the future.

MR. ZHAO. Mr. President, what is your assessment of the outlook for the world situation in the new year?

THE PRESIDENT. Obviously, there are some very disturbing trouble spots around the world where people are not at peace. And we obviously have a need to extend the beneficial effect of the desire for peace that exists among our people to those troubled areas.

We have great need for an improved quality of life for those who are hungry, who don't have adequate shelter or health care, who are struggling for more freedom, and who desire to expand their range of knowledge of the entire world and, therefore, their beneficial effect.

We have, I think, a good opportunity, however, with the new relations between China and our own country to influence those troubled areas toward a more peaceful existence, to prevent the spread of violence to adjacent areas, and to let people live in harmony, one with another.

So, I think, in general, the world is in a peaceful state. The trouble spots can be brought to peace with our combined efforts. And we'll be working with China and other nations to let this influence be as great as possible for peace.

MR. ZHAO. This is the first opportunity for the Central TV of the People's Republic of China to have an interview with a U.S. President. We would like to express once again our appreciation. Do you have any message to convey to the Chinese TV audience?

THE PRESIDENT. Yes. This is my opportunity to speak to the largest audience I've ever had. And I'm very delighted, on behalf of the 220 million people in our Nation, to extend my personal thanks for the new, friendly relations between our people.

I might point out that this opportunity has not just resulted from the last few weeks of negotiation between myself, as President of our country, and Premier Hua and Vice Premier Deng Xiaoping in China. It's a culmination of years of negotiation between Chairman Mao and Premier Zhou Enlai of China and my predecessors, Presidents Nixon and Ford, in this country. And this represents a broad degree of support from many great leaders and also the people ourselves.

I know there's a great feeling of gratitude in China and the United States for this new, wonderful relationship. And that gratitude is expressed not only from our own people but from the nations around the world who see our new friendship as a basis for increased friendship, harmony, and peace throughout the world.

So, best wishes to all the people of China, and we are very grateful for this new opportunity for increasing friendship and peace in the years ahead.

MR. ZHAO. Thank you.

THE PRESIDENT. Thank you very much.

NOTE: The interview began at 11:45 a.m. in the Cabinet Room at the White House. Mr. Zhao spoke in Chinese, and his remarks were translated by an interpreter. The interview was taped for later broadcast in the People's Republic of China.

The transcript of the interview was released on January 26.

United States Relations With the People on Taiwan

Message to the Congress Transmitting Proposed Legislation. January 26, 1979

To the Congress of the United States:

The United States of America has recognized the Government of the People's Republic of China as the sole legal government of China and is establishing diplomatic relations with that government. The Joint Communique issued by the United States and the People's Republic of China was the culmination of a long process begun by President Nixon and continued by President Ford and me.

I have also announced that, in the future, the American people will maintain commercial, cultural, and other relations with the people on Taiwan without official government representation and without diplomatic relations. In furtherance of that policy, and pending enactment of legislation on the subject, I have directed all departments and agencies to continue unofficially to conduct programs, transactions and other relations with Taiwan.

To authorize legally the permanent implementation of that policy, I am today transmitting to the Congress a bill "to promote the foreign policy of the United States through the maintenance of commercial, cultural and other relations with the people on Taiwan on an unofficial basis, and for other purposes."

This bill will confirm the continued eligibility of the people on Taiwan for participation in programs and activities that under United States law are to be carried out with foreign governments; provide for the carrying out of such programs and activities on an unofficial basis through the American Institute in Taiwan, a non-profit corporation, and the corresponding instrumentality being established by the people on Taiwan; and establish funding, staffing and administrative relationships of the Institute. It also contains other authorizations and provisions relating to the foregoing matters.

I am confident the Congress shares my view that it is in the national interest that these unofficial relations between the American people and the people on Taiwan be maintained. It is highly desirable that this legislation be enacted as promptly as possible. I look forward to working with the Congress on this important project.

JIMMY CARTER

The White House,
   January 26, 1979.

NOTE: The text of the proposed legislation and a section-by-section analysis of the legislation are included in the press release.

Color Television Receiver Imports

Proclamation 4634. January 26, 1979

IMPLEMENTATION OF ORDERLY MARKETING AGREEMENTS—AND THE TEMPORARY QUANTITATIVE LIMITATION ON THE IMPORTATION INTO THE UNITED STATES OF COLOR TELEVISION RECEIVERS AND CERTAIN SUBASSEMBLIES THEREOF

By the President of the United States of America

A Proclamation

1. On March 22, 1977, the United States International Trade Commission (USITC) reported to the President (USITC Publication 808) the results of its investigation under section 201(b) of the Trade Act of 1974 (19 U.S.C. 2251(b)) (the Trade Act). The USITC determined that color television receivers assembled or not assembled, finished or not finished, provided for in item 685.20 of the Tariff Schedules of the United States (TSUS) (19 U.S.C. 1202) are being imported into the United States in such increased quantities as to be a substantial cause of serious injury to the domestic industry producing articles like or directly competitive with the imported articles. By an evenly divided vote, three USITC Commissioners determined serious injury to exist in the monochrome television receiver industry and three Commissioners made no determination of injury with respect to the monochrome receiver industry. The Commissioners also had an evenly divided determination on the question of injury to that portion of the industry producing subassemblies of color television

receivers, also provided for in item 685.20 of the TSUS.

2. On June 24, 1977, in order to remedy the serious injury found to exist by the USITC, I proclaimed (Presidential Proclamation 4511) that the Government of the United States of America and the Government of Japan had entered into an orderly marketing agreement on May 20, 1977, pursuant to section 203(a)(4) of the Trade Act (19 U.S.C. 2253(a)(4)) limiting the export from Japan to the United States of color television receivers and certain subassemblies thereof, for a period of three years beginning July 1, 1977, to 1.75 million units in each annual restraint period.

3. In Proclamation 4511 I delegated my authority under section 203(e)(3) of the Trade Act (19 U.S.C. 2253(e)(3)) to determine that any agreement negotiated pursuant to section 203(a)(4) of the Trade Act (19 U.S.C. 2253(a)(4)) is no longer effective to the Special Representative for Trade Negotiations (hereinafter referred to as the "Special Representative").

4. Pursuant to the authority delegated to the Special Representative in paragraphs 2 and 4 of Proclamation 4511, and after consultation with representatives of member agencies of the Trade Policy Staff Committee, the Special Representative has determined that imports of color television receivers and certain subassemblies thereof from Taiwan and the Republic of Korea have increased in such quantities so as to disrupt the effectiveness of the orderly marketing agreement with Japan with respect to such products and that for the purposes of section 203 (e)(3) of the Trade Act (19 U.S.C. 2253(e)(3)) the orderly marketing agreement with Japan does not continue

to be effective. I concur with that determination.

5. Pursuant to the authority vested in the President by the Constitution and the statutes of the United States, including section 203(a)(5) and 203(e)(3) of the Trade Act (19 U.S.C. 2253(a)(5) and 2253(e)(3)), and in order to restore the effectiveness of the orderly marketing agreement with Japan, and to remedy the serious injury to the domestic industry producing color television receivers and certain subassemblies thereof found to exist by the USITC, orderly marketing agreements were concluded on December 14, 1978, and December 29, 1978, between the Government of the United States of America and the Government of the Republic of Korea and Taiwan respectively.

The orderly marketing agreements limit the export from the Republic of Korea and Taiwan to the United States of color television receivers and certain subassemblies thereof, for the period February 1, 1979, through June 30, 1980, and set forth conditions under which limitations will be placed on the importation into the United States of such articles by the Government of the United States through quantitative restrictions. These restrictions are to be implemented under the authority of sections 203(a) (5), (e)(3), and (g)(2) of the Trade Act (19 U.S.C. 2253(a)(5), (e)(3), and (g)(2)).

6. In accordance with section 203(d) (2) of the Trade Act (19 U.S.C. 2253 (d)(2)), I have determined that the level of import relief hereinafter proclaimed permits the importation into the United States of a quantity or value of articles which is not less than the average annual quantity or value of such articles imported

into the United States, from the Republic of Korea and from Taiwan, in the 1972–75 period, which I have determined to be the most recent representative period for imports of such articles.

Now, THEREFORE, I, JIMMY CARTER, President of the United States of America, acting under the authority vested in me by the Constitution and statutes of the United States, including sections 203 and 604 of the Trade Act (19 U.S.C. 2253 and 2483), and section 301 of Title 3 of the United States Code, do hereby proclaim:

(1) Orderly marketing agreements were entered into on December 14, 1978, and December 29, 1978, between the Government of the United States of America and the Government of the Republic of Korea and Taiwan, respectively, with respect to trade in color television receivers and certain subassemblies thereof, effective February 1, 1979. The orderly marketing agreements are to be implemented according to their terms and by quantitative restrictions as directed in this proclamation, including the Annex thereto.

(2) Subpart A, part 2 of the Appendix to the Tariff Schedules of the United States (19 U.S.C. 1202) is modified as set forth in the Annex to this proclamation.

(3) The President's authority under section 203(e)(2) of the Trade Act (19 U.S.C. 2253(e)(2)) to negotiate orderly marketing agreements with other foreign suppliers of articles subject to this proclamation after any import relief proclaimed pursuant to section 203(a) (1), (2), (3) or (5) of the Trade Act (19 U.S.C. 2253(a) (1), (2), (3) or (5)) takes effect, is hereby delegated to the Special Representative. The President's authority under section 203(e)(3) of the Trade Act (19 U.S.C. 2253(e)(3)) to determine that any agreement negotiated pursuant

to section 203(a) (4) or (5) or 203 (e)(2)) of the Trade Act (19 U.S.C. 2253(a) (4) or (5) or 2253(e)(2)) is no longer effective is hereby delegated to the Special Representative, to be exercised in conformity with paragraph (5) below. In the event of such a determination, the Special Representative shall prepare any proclamations that may be appropriate to implement import relief authorized by section 203(e)(3) of the Trade Act (19 U.S.C. 2253(e)(3)).

(4) The President's authority in section 203 (g) (1) and (2) of the Trade Act (19 U.S.C. 2253(g) (1) and (2)) to prescribe regulations governing the entry or withdrawal from warehouse of articles covered by the orderly marketing agreements and to issue rules and regulations governing entry, or withdrawal from warehouse, for consumption of like articles which are the product of countries not parties to such agreements, has been delegated to the Secretary of the Treasury pursuant to section 5(b) of Executive Order No. 11846. Such authority shall be exercised by the Secretary of the Treasury, upon direction by the Special Representative, on consultation with representatives of the member agencies of the Trade Policy Staff Committee.

(5) In exercising the authority delegated in paragraphs (3) and (4) above, the Special Representative shall, in addition to other necessary actions, institute the following actions.

(a) Statistics on imports from the Republic of Korea and Taiwan and from other sources of articles covered by the agreements shall be collected on a monthly basis. Should the effectiveness of the orderly marketing agreements be disrupted, the Special Representative, after consultation with representatives of member agencies of the Trade Policy Staff Committee, may make a determination that for the purposes of section 203(e)(3) of the Trade Act (19 U.S.C. 2253(e)(3)) the orderly marketing agreements do not continue to be effective.

(b) Beginning on February 1, 1979, if during any restraint period the quantity of imports of the articles covered by the agreements, from countries other than Taiwan and the Republic of Korea, appear likely to disrupt the effectiveness of the provisions of the orderly marketing agreements described in paragraph (1) above, the Special Representative may initiate consultations with those countries responsible for such disruptions and may prevent further entry of such articles for the remainder of that restraint period or may otherwise moderate or restrict imports of such articles from such countries pursuant to section 203(g)(2) of the Trade Act (19 U.S.C. 2253(g)(2)). Before exercising this authority, the Special Representative shall consult with representatives of the member agencies of the Trade Policy Staff Committee.

(c) Should the Special Representative determine, pursuant to this proclamation, to institute import restrictions on articles entered, or withdrawn from warehouse, for consumption from countries other than Taiwan or the Republic of Korea pursuant to this proclamation, such action shall be effective not less than eight days after such determination and any necessary changes in the TSUS have been published in the FEDERAL REGISTER.

(6) The Special Representative shall take such actions and perform such functions for the United States as may be necessary concerning the administration, implementation, modification, amendment or termination of the agreements described in paragraph (1) of this procla-

mation, and any actions and functions necessary to implement paragraphs (3), (4) and (5) of this proclamation. In carrying out his responsibilities under this paragraph the Special Representative is authorized to delegate to appropriate officials or agencies of the United States authority to perform any functions necessary for the administration and implementation of the agreements or actions. The Special Representative is authorized to make any changes in Part 2 of the Appendix to the TSUS which may be necessary to carry out the agreements or actions. Any such changes in the agreements shall be effective on and after their publication in the FEDERAL REGISTER.

(7) The Commissioner of Customs shall take such actions as the Special Representative shall determine are necessary to carry out the agreements described in paragraph (1) of this proclamation and to implement any import relief pursuant to paragraphs (3), (4) and (5) of this proclamation, or any modification thereof, with respect to the entry or withdrawal from warehouse, for consumption into the United States of products covered by such agreements or by such other import relief.

(8) This proclamation shall be effective as of February 1, 1979, and shall continue in force through June 30, 1980, unless the period of its effectiveness is earlier expressly modified or terminated.

IN WITNESS WHEREOF, I have hereunto set my hand this twenty-sixth day of January, in the year of our Lord, nineteen hundred and seventy-nine, and of the Independence of the United States of America the two hundred and third.

JIMMY CARTER

[Filed with the Office of the Federal Register, 12:04 p.m., January 26, 1979]

NOTE: The annex is printed in the FEDERAL REGISTER of January 29, 1979.

National Security Information

*Order Designating an Official To Classify
Information "Top Secret." January 26, 1979*

Pursuant to the provisions of Section 1–201 of Executive Order 12065 of June 28, 1978, entitled "National Security Information," I hereby designate the Director of the White House Military Office to classify information originally as "Top Secret."

This Order shall be published in the FEDERAL REGISTER.

JIMMY CARTER

The White House,
   January 26, 1979.

[Filed with the Office of the Federal Register,
   12:05 p.m., January 26, 1979]

THE PRESIDENT'S
NEWS CONFERENCE OF
JANUARY 26, 1979

THE PRESIDENT. Good afternoon.

Ms. Thomas [Helen Thomas, United Press International].

PEOPLE'S REPUBLIC OF CHINA
AND TAIWAN

Q. Mr. President, the United States has acknowledged that there is one China, and Taiwan is a part of it. And, remembering the Gulf of Tonkin resolution as an underpinning of the Vietnam war, my question is, are you concerned that the congressional resolutions regarding Taiwan's security may infringe on China's sovereignty and, two, may involve us at some future point in Asia again?

THE PRESIDENT. No, I'm not concerned about that. I could not approve any legislation presented to me by Con-gress that would be contradictory or that which would violate the agreements that we have concluded with the Republic of China—the People's Republic of China. I, myself, am committed to a strong and a prosperous and a free people on Taiwan. We intend to carry on our diplomatic relations with the People's Republic of China as the Government of China, but we'll have trade relationships, cultural relationships with the people on Taiwan. And I believe that the legislation that has now been presented to the Congress is a good foundation for this.

But I don't see this as an opening for bloodshed or war. I think the statements made by the Chinese leaders since the announcement of intentions to establish diplomatic relations have been very constructive and have indicated a peaceful intent.

Q. Are you speaking also of the Kennedy resolution, which will be introduced on Monday, or only your own resolution?

THE PRESIDENT. I haven't read the so-called Kennedy resolution. I really don't believe that any resolution is needed. I think our legislative proposal and the announcement made about normalization, the combination of those two is adequate.

STRATEGIC ARMS LIMITATION

Q. Mr. President, on Tuesday you said that we would have a SALT agreement if the Soviet Union continued to negotiate in good faith.

THE PRESIDENT. Yes.

Q. Do you have any slight doubt in your mind on that score?

THE PRESIDENT. No. I've been in office now 2 years, and we've been negotiating with the Soviets almost full-time on a SALT agreement. Prior to that time, 4 additional years of negotiations were conducted with the Soviet Union. My understanding is that prior to the time I came into office, and since I've been in office, they have negotiated in good faith.

They are tough bargainers; we are, too. We have tried to evolve an agreement with the Soviet Union which would, first of all, be verifiable, which would preserve the security of our Nation and even enhance it, which would control nuclear weapons, and which would lay a basis for increased friendship between us and the Soviet Union and let us control or reduce the threat of the proliferation of nuclear explosives to other nations throughout the world. I think that we and the Soviets have those goals in mind. And I hope and expect that our progress will continue.

Now we're negotiating every day at Geneva and supplementing that negotiation through diplomatic channels, both here and in the Soviet Union.

Q. Could you say whether they have hardened their position in the last month or two?

THE PRESIDENT. No, they have not hardened their position in the last month or two. I think their positions, along with ours, have been adequately hard. We have negotiated very firmly, and there has been a steady progress. There has never been one time since I've been in office when we've had a recess in the efforts, nor a retrogressive action when we were discouraged. We've been making steady progress, and we still are.

IRAN

Q. Mr. President, the shipment of 200,-000 barrels of gasoline and diesel fuel to Iran—doesn't that really amount to the interference in Iran's internal affairs that you have said the U.S. will not now be part of? And would you stand for a sim-ilar such action from any other nation? And may I please follow?

THE PRESIDENT. I don't see the shipment of fuel supplies to Iran in any way as an interference in the internal affairs of Iran. These shipments of energy supplies and, I'm sure, food and other goods to let the people of Iran have a better life, I think, are very good and constructive and proper. We do not have any intention of interfering in the affairs of Iran, the internal affairs of their government, and we don't want any other country to do it either.

Q. To what extent do you accept a congressional investigating committee's finding that you and your top foreign policy advisers must share responsibility with the CIA for the downfall of the Shah?

THE PRESIDENT. The situation in Iran now, politically speaking, is very sensitive, and I can't think of anything I could say about it that would contribute to the hopes that we have that Iran would settle their problems peacefully, that bloodshed would be prevented, and that any political change in their government would be conducted in an orderly fashion in accordance with the Iranian Constitution. So, I don't intend to make any statements about the impact of what we have done or will do on Iran.

As I said earlier, we do not interfere in the internal affairs of Iran. We do not want any other government to do it either.

SELECTION OF FEDERAL JUDGES

Q. Mr. President, from your experience so far, sir, with selection committees for Federal judges, do you think they're working out all right? And if you don't, how would you like to change them?

THE PRESIDENT. Well, the ones that we have appointed—I have myself appointed to choose Federal circuit judges—I think have worked fairly well. They've certainly been an improvement over arbitrary selections on a political basis or without adequate assessment of merit.

We have tried to induce the Members of the Senate to do two things: One is to choose a list of potential judge appointees on the basis of merit, but also to take into consideration the fact that for many years there have been discriminatory practices in the appointment of judges—against minority groups, those who speak Spanish, for instance, those who are black, and also against women. And those two, that combination of efforts, merit and a correction of past discrimination, are the bases on which we're trying to make these appointments. I hope that the Senators will cooperate. In some instances they have, not yet enough.

PRESIDENT'S 1980 CANDIDACY; THE
NEW FOUNDATION

Q. Mr. President, a couple of related political questions, since a lot of people are trying to jump in already to run against you in 1980. Will you promise now to debate your Republican opponent in 1980, on television as you did in 1976, assuming you run and that you are the nominee of your party? And second, who thought up the slogan "New Foundation"? [*Laughter*]

THE PRESIDENT. On the first question, I really don't want to get involved in answering questions about the 1980 campaign. I think it's too early for me to do it. I would rather address my attention and the attention on me on my present duties, not some future campaign.

Secondly, I think the new foundations question or basis for the State of the Union speech is a good one. We got into a discussion about what theme we should pursue during the preparation of that speech. Many of the decisions that we have made and are making do not pay off in immediate political benefits, but it's an investment at the present time for future dividends for America. And some of the decisions that Congress has made in approving the programs that I advocated were really difficult for them politically.

Some of the decisions that I am making right now, in having a tough and stringent budget for 1980, may not be politically popular, but I think in the long run the control of inflation will pay rich dividends for our country. And the fact that we are building a foundation for future progress was the reason we chose that as a theme for the speech.

Q. Mr. President, to follow up on the previous question, sir. For 2 years you avoided the use of a slogan similar to New Frontier or Great Society or whatever. And now you've used it often enough this week to indicate that you'd like to make this your motto. Why did you make that change, and, secondly, do you think this slogan will survive the way some of the others did?

THE PRESIDENT. I doubt if it will survive. [*Laughter*] We are not trying to establish this as a permanent slogan. It was the theme that we established because of extreme logic, which I've just described in the previous question, for one State of the Union speech. I think it accurately describes what I wanted to project to the American people. I think we did it very well.

U.S.-SOVIET RELATIONS

Q. Mr. President, have U.S.-Soviet relations been impaired in any way by the Deng visit? Any unhappiness being expressed by the Soviets over the visit?

THE PRESIDENT. No, I don't believe so. My own belief is that the Deng visit and the normalization of relations between ourselves and China will not only help the people of our two countries but will provide for stability and peace in the Western Pacific or the Asian region and, also, the entire world. And my hope and expectation is that the Soviets will agree that that assessment is accurate, that this will not be a destabilizing factor in the future, but a stabilizing factor, and that world peace will be enhanced.

We will be cautious in not trying to have an unbalanced relationship between China and the Soviet Union. And if there has been some concern expressed by some sources—and I'm not familiar with them—I don't think they are well advised.

MINORITY EDUCATION PROGRAMS

Q. Mr. President, in the last few days you have taken on various steps in the area of education, focusing on increasing Federal assistance to black colleges, specifically. I think you have even issued a memorandum to Federal agency heads, and you have also endorsed the new department of education.

My question is two-fold: One, what kind of increases can black colleges expect from the Federal Government in this time of overall restraint in the budget? And secondly, how will you seek to enforce and implement the civil rights laws that exist in the education area?

THE PRESIDENT. I think last year we increased total Federal allocations for education about $12 billion.* This was for the preschool programs, for Title 1 education for disadvantaged students who were in the public schools, and, also, a very large and, I think, well-contrived

---

* NOTE: The President meant to say "*to* about $12 billion." The education budget was increased last year from $10.15 billion to $12.7 billion, an increase of 23 percent. [Printed in the transcript.]

allocation of new funds for student loans. These will, obviously, apply to all students, both black and white, some emphasis on disadvantaged children.

My recent directive to the different agencies of the Federal Government were designed to extract from them advice on how all the multiple group of agencies could best support the historically black colleges. And when I get their reports in, we will assess them, primarily with the Department of Health, Education, and Welfare, and proceed to make sure that those black colleges, predominantly black colleges, are strengthened in the future and not weakened in any way.

So, I can't answer your question about specifically what we will do in the future, except when I get those recommendations from different agencies, we'll decide at that point what ought to be done.

SOCIAL SECURITY BENEFITS

Q. Mr. President, you really got the Democratic establishment in a tizzy over the social security cutbacks, Speaker O'Neill and Senate Majority Leader Byrd. My question is, did you know, when you were proposing these cutbacks, that they primarily affect widows who need the death benefit to pay for funeral expenses and allotments to widows raising teenaged children? Was there discussion among your aides or was this a recommendation of Mr. Califano?

THE PRESIDENT. We had quite a lengthy discussion about this. I might point out that the total of all the changes that we advocated in social security reform only comprise about one-half of 1 percent of the total benefits. In general, I think in its entirety, the recommendations are designed to eliminate duplicating services, where either within the social security system or in other government programs, a given benefit is provided in addition to what we've advocated to be changed.

In the long run, we have got to make sure that within the limited social security funding, which is derived from those who are working now, that the allocation of funds goes to those who need it most, who don't have any other way to derive benefits. And with a limited amount of money, it's imperative that the system be efficient and that benefits go where they are most needed.

This is not a politically popular proposal. I understand that. But I believe that those reform proposals ought to be implemented. They will be assessed by the Social Security Advisory Committees. They will be assessed thoroughly by the Congress. And if they stand those tests, combined with testimony, then they'll be implemented.

I might say that there's an additional factor concerned with disability payments, aside from social security. I think they are much more needed and much less controversial. But the entire package is designed to have a better social security structure.

I might add one other thing, that in the year of a very stringent budget, that is, 1980 fiscal year budget, we have a 12-percent increase in allocation of funds for the elderly in this country. So, we have not in any way overlooked the genuine needs of elderly or retired people in this Nation.

Q. But a key issue is that these benefits are now an entitlement under payroll taxes under social security. Are you going to turn these into welfare programs, when you say "go to the neediest people"?

THE PRESIDENT. No. We're not turning them into welfare programs at all. I think I've already answered the question adequately by saying that these are one-half of 1 percent of the total benefits. They are well-advised reforms. They comprise reforms that need to be done in any instance, and they cover benefits that can be derived from some other source. And we have to have an efficient allocation of funds. It's the best answer I can give you.

VISIT OF VICE PREMIER DENG

Q. Mr. President, Vice Premier Deng arrives in this country on Sunday. And, of course, his major purpose is to get to know this country a little bit better and so that you can have more of an opportunity to discuss a variety of issues. But I wonder if you're shooting for a conclusion of any diplomatic agreements or trade agreements with him, as well as the other things that I've mentioned?

THE PRESIDENT. There are some outstanding ancient claims filed on the part of China against our country and vice versa. We hope to lay the groundwork for the resolution of that difference. We would like to prepare for the future visits to China of some of our key Cabinet officers concerning trade and commerce. Secretary Blumenthal, Secretary Kreps will be going there within the next few weeks. We hope to conclude an aviation agreement with them to provide better transportation to and from our countries. We hope to conclude, in addition, agreements that would encompass technology, scientific exchanges. These are the kinds of bilateral agreements that we will explore.

Perhaps some of them can be resolved while Vice Premier Deng is here. Most of them, I think, would be concluded later on with more detailed technical discussions when an actual legal document can be drafted for signature. But we'll have a very broad agenda of items to be discussed with China. Those are some illustrative examples of the kind of bilateral agreements that will be discussed.

FEDERAL BUDGET DEFICITS

Q. Mr. President, the Congressional Budget Office report, the use of the $41 billion figure by Miss Rivlin and her statement that a balanced budget by 1981 is now virtually impossible in her view—how do you respond to that, sir?

THE PRESIDENT. I think our economic projections are accurate. There are several factors involved which I think might cause some differences in estimates. We took into account the very substantial growth in our national economy that occurred the fourth quarter of 1978, which was unexpected. It shows a vigorous, broad-based strength in our economy that was a pleasant surprise.

Secondly, we anticipate good results from our anti-inflation effort, and this is mirrored in the projections for this year. We have also a good prospect for retaining a stable dollar overseas, which we did not have, as you well know, in 1978. The dollar has proven to be strong recently in several political and economic tests.

In addition, we expect to reduce substantially our trade deficit which we experienced in 1978, which will help. Our own national growth rate in our economy will be much more comparable with those of our major trading partners, whereas in the past couple of years we've had a much higher growth rate in our country than, say, Japan and Germany.

So, there are many factors involved which are the bases for my believing that our projections are accurate. I think that we will reach the goals that I described in the economic summaries.

OIL INDUSTRY

Q. Mr. President, the fourth quarter profits are out for the major oil companies. I won't mention the names, but they read 48 percent, 72 percent, 44 percent, 134 percent. Given the fact that you've asked the country to make sacrifices to prepare for lean and austere years, I was wondering if you'd give us your reaction to those profits, profits that size when American workers are being asked to hold wage increases to 7 percent.

THE PRESIDENT. Well, I would hope and expect that with increases—I guess those are increases in profits?

Q. Fourth quarter profit earnings.

THE PRESIDENT. I guess that's, though, increases, compared to the previous fourth quarter.

Well, in the new energy bill, we've obviously had some bases on which to increase incentives for production of oil and natural gas. We've had a substantial amount of natural gas become available for American consumers as a result of the new energy legislation. And above a certain point in earnings, of course, the income tax levies against even oil companies are partially adequate.

But I would hope that we can continue, with a more stable production rate and with more careful conservation of existing oil supplies, to keep all industrial profits at a reasonable level, with none being exorbitant. As you know, we are faced later this year with a substantial change in the control mechanism for restraining oil prices. And then, I believe, October of 1981, all controls by law will be terminated.

And whether or not the free enterprise system with competition and a rigid application of antitrust laws can induce both increased production and, therefore, more competition and lower prices, I can't anticipate. But I would, obviously, as all Americans would, like to see a good balance between prices and profits.

FORMER PRESIDENT RICHARD NIXON

Q. Mr. President, since former President Nixon will be here during the visit by

Vice Premier Deng, do you have any plans to meet separately with the former President to discuss, say, not solely China, but other subject matters? Or will Mr. Nixon's presence here be purely a social one?

THE PRESIDENT. I think as far as I'm concerned, it would be purely social. I don't have any plans now to meet with him in an extended private way to discuss these issues. We will provide him with appropriate briefings on what has been done in our negotiations with the people of China. And he's been very helpful in giving us information, when asked, about some of the historic interrelationships that he experienced with the Chinese. But I don't anticipate private meetings nor briefings from me to him.

NUCLEAR TEST BAN AGREEMENT

Q. Mr. President, there is a report that the Russians have agreed to allow the United States to put seismic listeningposts inside Russia to make sure that they are not testing nuclear weapons. Is that report accurate, and, if so, does that mean we're very close to a nuclear test ban agreement?

THE PRESIDENT. Well, I think it's inappropriate for me to discuss specific items on which we are negotiating with the Soviet Union now. They agreed not to discuss them publicly. We agreed to do the same. But, obviously, that's one of the items that we are negotiating with them.

As I said about the SALT agreement, I'm not going to sign a SALT agreement unless it's verifiable. And I am not going to sign a comprehensive test ban agreement unless it's vertifiable. Since tests of nuclear explosives can be at a very low level and sometimes perhaps concealed if they are in a very deep depth within the Earth, listening devices, either around the periphery of the Soviet Union or within

the Soviet Union, are, obviously, advantageous.

So, the placement of listening devices within the continental boundaries of our country and the Soviet Union and Great Britain—Great Britain is a partner with us—is one of those items that are being discussed. No final agreement has yet been reached.

DEFENSE BUDGET

Q. Mr. President, Defense Secretary Brown told the Congress yesterday that the U.S. arsenal is far and away superior to that of the Soviet Union. My question is, if that is the case and, realizing, of course, that you're obviously trying to sell the SALT treaty, why did you not see fit to keep your campaign promise to reduce the defense budget instead of raising it at the expense of social programs, which you said you would never do?

THE PRESIDENT. I think we have kept the campaign promise. We, obviously, can't freeze the defense budget at a given figure, but we've had savings that are substantially in excess of the $5 billion that I promised during the campaign.

I have no apology to make for a strong, adequate defense, nor for the allocation of funds necessary to ensure a strong and adequate defense. I think we are able at this point to match any military capability that the Soviets have. I think we are much stronger economically and politically than the Soviet Union is. But in the last 10, 15 years, the Soviets every year have had above and beyond inflationary costs a 4- or 5-percent increase in allocation of funds for defense purposes. In most of those years, we've been decreasing, actually, in the amount of funds allocated for defense.

I have not robbed the poor or the deprived or the social programs in order to provide for defense. The percentage of our budget that goes for defense has been steadily reduced for a number of years.

And it's absolutely imperative that our country always have the ability to defend itself. It's imperative for our people to know that we are safe. It's imperative for our allies to know that we stand with them with an adequate defense. It's imperative that the Soviet Union know that we are capable of defending ourselves. It's a major contribution to peace. I have no apology to make for it at all.

Q. Do you feel then, Mr. President, that you are getting a bum rap from the so-called special interest groups which criticize you for deserting the disadvantaged, abandoning the cities, et cetera?

THE PRESIDENT. I think that we've had a very good budget evolve in the 1980 fiscal year. It's balanced. It provides for the needs of our people. In the social programs, I think when it's examined in detail in the congressional committee hearings, it will stand the test of the most intense scrutiny.

We've had substantial increases for social programs since I've been in office. In 2 years we've increased them more than 20 percent. I mentioned earlier a 12-percent increase for the elderly. In programs dealing specifically with the poor, in the 1980 fiscal year budget, which is very stringent, we'll have a $4½ billion increase in allocation of funds for those purposes.

In repairing the quality of life in our deteriorating downtown urban areas, we've had an unprecedented increase in the allocation of Government programs and also funds for those purposes.

But overall, we have not had to allocate as much increase in money, nor to provide a large number of new Federal programs, because our emphasis has been on making the existing programs more efficient.

So, I don't think there's any basis on which we could be criticized in a year of a tight budget because we've not provided adequately for those who need the services of government most.

Let me add one other thing, and that is that some people erroneously believe and frequently state that an effort to control inflation in some way cheats the poor or the aged or those who live on fixed incomes. Inflation is bad for all Americans. But it's much worse, as I said in my State of the Union speech, a disaster for those who have a very low income, or who have a very low fixed retirement on which to live, or who are not mobile or sometimes who are unemployed. Those are the ones that will be served best by controlling inflation.

FRANK CORMIER [Associated Press]. Thank you, Mr. President.

THE PRESIDENT. Thank you, Frank.

NOTE: President Carter's forty-third news conference began at 3 p.m. in Room 450 of the Old Executive Office Building. It was broadcast live on radio and television.

Digest of Other White House Announcements

The following listing includes the President's public schedule and other items of general interest announced by the White House Press Office and not included elsewhere in this issue.

January 21

The President returned to the White House from Camp David, Md.

January 22

The President met at the White House with:

—Zbigniew Brzezinski, Assistant to the President for National Security Affairs;

—Frank B. Moore, Assistant to the President for Congressional Liaison;

—representatives of the trucking industry;

—Joel W. (Jay) Solomon, Administrator of the General Services Administration;

—Vice President Walter F. Mondale;

—members of the Democratic Steering and Policy Committee of the House of Representatives.

January 23

The President met at the White House with:

—Dr. Brzezinski;

—Mr. Moore;

—Senator Robert C. Byrd of West Virginia;

—Senator Sam Nunn of Georgia;

—Senators Nunn, John H. Glenn, Jr., of Ohio, William S. Cohen of Maine, and Gary Hart of Colorado.

The President transmitted the following reports to the Congress:

—the 12th annual report on the Operation of the Automotive Products Trade Act of 1965;

—the 1977 annual report on Coastal Zone Management;

—the 15th quarterly report on the Activities of the Council on Wage and Price Stability;

—the eighth annual report on Hazardous Materials Control;

—the fifth report of the Director of the National Heart, Lung, and Blood Institute.

January 24

The President met at the White House with:

—a group of new Senators of the 96th Congress;

—Dr. Brzezinski;

—Mr. Moore;

—Vice President Mondale, Stansfield Turner, Director of Central Intelligence, and Hamilton Jordan, Assistant to the President;

—Attorney General Griffin B. Bell and John H. Shenefield, Chairman, and members of the National Commission on Antitrust Laws and Procedures, to receive the report of the Commission;

—James T. McIntyre, Jr., Director of the Office of Management and Budget;

—Senator Abraham A. Ribicoff of Connecticut and a congressional delegation, to discuss the delegation's visit to the Soviet Union;

—Senator Henry M. Jackson of Washington.

Prime Minister Kriangsak Chomanan of Thailand will be visiting the United States from February 4 to 16. During his official stay in Washington, the Prime Minister will call on the President on February 6, and on the Secretary of State on February 7. He will also meet with other senior administration officials and with Members of Congress.

January 25

The President met at the White House with:

—Secretary of the Treasury W. Michael Blumenthal, Charles L. Schultze, Chairman of the Council of Economic Advisers, Alfred E. Kahn, Advisor to the President on Inflation, Stuart E. Eizenstat, Assistant to the President for Domestic Affairs and Policy, Jack H. Watson, Jr., Assistant to the President for Intergovernmental Affairs, and Mr. McIntyre;

—Dr. Brzezinski;

—Mr. Moore and staff members of the Office of Congressional Liaison;

—representatives of the Junior Achievement Program's National Business Leadership Conference;

—Mrs. Carter, for lunch;

—Senator Edmund S. Muskie of Maine and Representative Robert N. Giaimo of Connecticut.

In a ceremony in the Oval Office, the President presented the National Security Medal to Leslie C. Dirks, Deputy Director for Science and Technology of the Central Intelligence Agency.

January 26

The President met at the White House with:

—Vice President Mondale, Secretary of State Cyrus R. Vance, Secretary of Defense Harold Brown, Dr. Brzezinski, and Mr. Jordan;

—Dr. Brzezinski;

—Mr. Moore;

—a group of editors and news directors (transcript will be printed next week).

The President left the White House for a weekend stay at Camp David, Md.

NOMINATIONS SUBMITTED TO THE SENATE

The following list does not include promotions of members of the Uniformed Services, nominations to the Service Academies, or nominations of Foreign Service officers.

Submitted January 22, 1979

ROBERT H. PELLETREAU, JR., of Connecticut, a Foreign Service officer of Class three, to be Ambassador Extraordinary and Plenipotentiary of the United States of America to the State of Bahrain.

STEPHEN WARREN BOSWORTH, of Michigan, a Foreign Service officer of Class one, to be Ambassador Extraordinary and Plenipotentiary of the United States of America to the Republic of Tunisia.

NOMINATIONS—Continued

Submitted January 25, 1979

JONATHAN DEAN, of New York, a Foreign Service officer of Class one, for the rank of Ambassador during the tenure of his service as Representative of the United States of America for Mutual and Balanced Force Reductions Negotiations.

MICHAEL BLUMENFELD, of the District of Columbia, to be an Assistant Secretary of the Army, vice Victor V. Veysey, resigned.

ROBERT E. KEETON, of Massachusetts, to be United States District Judge for the District of Massachusetts, vice a new position created by P.L. 95–486, approved October 20, 1978.

JOHN JOSEPH MCNAUGHT, of Massachusetts, to be United States District Judge for the District of Massachusetts, vice a new position created by P.L. 95–486, approved October 20, 1978.

DAVID SUTHERLAND NELSON, of Massachusetts, to be United States District Judge for the District of Massachusetts, vice a new position created by P.L. 95–486, approved October 20, 1978.

RYA W. ZOBEL, of Massachusetts, to be United States District Judge for the District of Massachusetts, vice a new position created by P.L. 95–486, approved October 20, 1978.

JAMES H. WILLIAMS, of Florida, to be a member of the Board of Directors of the Commodity Credit Corporation, vice John C. White, resigned.

CHECKLIST OF WHITE HOUSE PRESS RELEASES

The following listing contains releases of the White House Press Office which are not included in this issue.

Released January 23, 1979

Advance text: State of the Union address

Released January 24, 1979

Announcement: visit of Prime Minister Kriangsak Chomanan of Thailand to the United States

Released January 25, 1979

News conference: on the Economic Report of the President—by Charles L. Schultze, Chairman of the Council of Economic Advisers

CHECKLIST—Continued

Released January 25—Continued

Announcement: nomination of Robert E. Keeton to be United States District Judge for the District of Massachusetts

Announcement: nomination of John J. McNaught to be United States District Judge for the District of Massachusetts

Announcement: nomination of David S. Nelson to be United States District Judge for the District of Massachusetts

CHECKLIST—Continued

Released January 25—Continued

Announcement: nomination of Rya W. Zobel to be United States District Judge for the District of Massachusetts

ACTS APPROVED BY THE PRESIDENT

Approved January 22, 1979

H.J. Res. 1_____ Public Law 96–1
A joint resolution to extend the time for filing the Economic Report.

Interview With the President

*Remarks and a Question-and-Answer Session
With Editors and News Directors.
January 26, 1979*

THE PRESIDENT. First of all, let me thank
you all for coming to the White House.
Some of you are coming back for a second
visit. This has been one of the most interesting, I think, and productive policies
that we've adopted, is having key news
leaders throughout the Nation come in
every 2 weeks, as a matter of fact, 30 to 40
at the time, to meet primarily with my
staff and key advisers and also to meet
briefly with me.

It's helped us to understand the attitude and the concerns around the Nation.
And I hope it's been helpful in letting the
people of the different communities understand how our White House operated
and what the key issues were at a particular moment.

ADMINISTRATION POLICIES

We've addressed the major domestic
issues recently in a fairly complete form
in the presentation of the budget. In addition to that, we have some key foreign
policy concerns coming up very shortly.
One would be the visit of Vice Premier

Deng, who will arrive here Monday. I'll
spend this weekend at Camp David reviewing all the briefing notebooks and getting ready for his visit.

Equally important to me, however, and
to our country will be the forthcoming
visit that I will pay to Mexico. The first
head of state who came to visit me officially was President López Portillo. And
my wife went to Mexico for his inauguration, and his wife came to my inauguration. And both the Vice President and
Secretary of State have been to Mexico
since I've been President to pursue the
wide range of agenda items which are so
crucial to us and to our very key and
friendly neighbor in the south.

I'll be well prepared to spend as much
time as possible with López Portillo on a
broad range of subjects of very great importance to us, not only bilateral issues
but also the growing beneficial influence
of Mexico on regional and international
questions. They've been one of the key
movers, for instance, in trying to control
the arms traffic throughout this hemisphere. They've been a key spokesman for
the developing nations of the world in key
areas. They've been helpful in trying to
resolve the Belize question with Guatemala, have been very good advisers for
us as we dealt with Nicaragua and other

181

questions, and I look forward to this visit as well.

Later on, we anticipate Crown Prince Fahd will come here, along with Prime Minister Kriangsak from Thailand. So, in the next few weeks I've got a broad combination of both domestic issues to address with the Congress, primarily, and foreign affairs visits, which will help to cement our ties with very important people in other nations.

I think perhaps the best way to spend our time outside of this opening statement would be to turn the questions over to you. I'll try to be brief and, obviously, try to be accurate.

QUESTIONS

RADIOACTIVITY EXPOSURE IN UTAH AND NEVADA

Q. Mr. President, the citizens of Utah, my State, are quite concerned about recent discoveries of extremely high cancer death rates in the southern part of the State due, it appears, to atmospheric nuclear testing in the 1950's and 60's in Nevada. Regarding the Federal Government's role, and your administration, where do we stand now? What can or will the administration do for the victims in southern Utah and Nevada?

THE PRESIDENT. When I was in Utah recently, I discussed this with your Governor, and also with some of the church officials there, and have directed that the Department of Energy and also the Department of HEW proceed with an analysis of the statistics available to see what patterns do exist and what we can do to have an equitable solution of problems that have already occurred there, and obviously to prevent any future recurrences.

No one knows the outcome of these discussions. But I think it's accurate to say that we are working very harmoni-

ously with the Utah officials, and they agreed with my assessment when I was there. But I hope that you will relate—if there is any problem with cooperation as I've outlined, I would like to hear from you directly after you return to Utah, or let the Governor call me directly.

MEXICAN ENERGY SUPPLIES

Q. Mr. President, I'm sure there will be interest here in the Deng visit, but before you get to that, could you talk a little bit about our relationship with Mexico and how it may change in light of the increasing Mexican economic leverage because of their oil discoveries? What kind of a longer range relationship do you see between two countries that are so close together, cheek by jowl along the border, and with Mexico growing so fast?

THE PRESIDENT. I'd say that there are three brief things. First of all, the control of Mexico's natural resources, obviously including oil and gas, is completely up to them. Mexico is highly independent in their resolution of how to proceed with exploration and production, and of course, they have wide options on customers to be served and, also, the prices to be charged. We understand that. We sympathize with it. We certainly have no quarrel with it.

Secondly, we look upon Mexico as a very valuable, present and future source of needed energy supplies for our country. We want to negotiate with them in good faith and provide for ourselves this very valuable source of oil and natural gas in the future. That'll be done by private and official negotiations over a long period of time. I'm not going down to Mexico to negotiate the price, the spot price of natural gas and so forth.

And thirdly, I think we have to distinguish between immediate needs and long-range needs. My understanding of the Mexican recent oil and gas discoveries is that they are the type of deposits which would necessitate a fairly long-range program for exploration and development. And I think the long-range supplies are what we have as a greater need.

At this point, because of various factors, the impact of new energy legislation and enhanced discoveries in our own Nation, we have a surplus at this particular moment of natural gas—a very valuable result, by the way, of the new energy legislation. So, for the immediate next few months or maybe couple of years, there is no high need for us to escalate the acquisition of natural gas.

So, those three basic factors are fairly well correlated, sometimes a little bit anomalous, but I think that they are ones that I'll be discussing in detail with López Portillo.

AIR POLLUTION STANDARDS

Q. Mr. President, outside of inflation, which I am sure is the number one problem with most everybody around the country, in my city of Denver, it's air pollution. It's viewed as a crisis in this city. I'm wondering if you view air pollution as a problem of crisis proportion in some of the major cities of the Nation, and if so, if you have any new program to espouse in the next several months to control it or help out the situation?

THE PRESIDENT. When I was in Denver last year, it became obvious to me that perhaps more than for any other city in the Nation, air pollution has become the key problem in the quality of life of your people. I think also, there's a dramatic difference in air quality now in Denver than what it was in years gone by. The deterioration there has been much more rapid and far-reaching than any place in the country that I know.

We have allocated special funds of an awfully small nature, a few million dollars at the time, to help Denver and State officials with your air pollution efforts. But I think it's primarily a local responsibility.

The standards that we have now established by EPA, Environmental Protection Agency, according to the law, are very stringent. They are so stringent that very few of the major communities can meet them. And today, the EPA will announce very stringent standards still, but that can be enforced, particularly ozone levels, which is one of the measurements of air quality.

Our administration, since I've been in office, has taken several steps to enhance the quality of air pollution by increasing the severity of the standards and also by controlling automobile emissions. But I would say the effectiveness with which automobile emissions are controlled is an area that needs further exploration in Denver and other parts of the country.

And when you have a special problem, as does your city, then I think a high concentration of local and State effort on ensuring that all automobiles do comply would be one of the major elements involved. We are eager to cooperate, particularly with a city like Denver that has a special problem. I'd say your problem is perhaps the worst with which I'm familiar in our country.

UNDOCUMENTED ALIENS

Q. I am Rowland Nethaway from the American-Statesman in Austin. Texas, somehow or other, just elected its first Republican Governor in more than a hundred years, and——

THE PRESIDENT. I heard about that. [*Laughter*]

Q. ——one of his first responses was to fly down to Mexico, ahead of your trip, and discuss some international problems with President López Portillo. And he reported that they agreed that the proposed "tortilla curtain" fence was a bad idea. And is the administration going to go ahead with that fence?

THE PRESIDENT. Well, as you know, the fence has existed for years. And the recent proposals to repair it, I think, were excessive and aggravating, and I called a halt to that immediately.

One of the obvious items that will be on the agenda for discussion between me and President López Portillo will be border problems, including the undocumented aliens who come into our country. The long-range solution, obviously, is a better economic prospect for employment and for prosperity in Mexico, which I think is inevitable now. The good administration there and the discovery of higher quality natural resources will contribute to that.

But we certainly don't want to do anything to aggravate the good relations between ourselves and Mexico. And I think, as I said earlier, the plans for the repair of that fence were unnecessarily aggravating, ill-advised, and I called a halt to them.

ARMS SALES TO CHINA

Q. Mr. President, in regard to Mr. Brezhnev's warning to the West against sale of sophisticated arms to China, as I understand it, the U.S. is not planning to make any such sales. West Germany says it will sell only to its allies, but the attitude is very different in Paris and London. The question is, what is the U.S. attitude toward sale of such weapons by its allies, and secondly, what, if anything, are we doing in support of that attitude?

THE PRESIDENT. We have responded very clearly to President Brezhnev, who contacted me directly about these sales. We will not sell weapons to either China or Russia.

Secondly, our allies are independent, sovereign nations, and they would resent any intrusion by us into their weapons sales policies. We have a very clear understanding among ourselves, particularly Germany, Great Britain, France, and the United States. We discussed this in some depth at Guadeloupe. Our publicly expressed and privately expressed advice to the other nations is that the sale of any weapons should be constricted to defensive weapons—and of course, President Giscard d'Estaing, Prime Minister Callaghan, Chancellor Schmidt would decide with their advisers on what is or is not a defensive weapons sale.

The Soviets need not be concerned about this, in my opinion. They've expressed their opinion to the foreign leaders as well as to myself. And I think my response was basically cast in the posture of reassurance to the Soviets. We certainly have no intention to sell weapons to the Soviet Union or China.

The technologically advanced equipment, computers and so forth, would have to be assessed on the basis of each individual item and whether it could contribute in a substantial way to enhancement of the military capabilities of both the Soviet Union and China. And, in general, we will apply the same restraints of that kind of sale to both countries.

MEXICAN ENERGY SUPPLIES

Q. Mr. President, getting back to your trip to Mexico, you said, of course, that the purpose of your trip was not to go down there and negotiate about oil and gas prices. But is Secretary Schlesinger scheduled to make the trip with you, or could you say at this point?

THE PRESIDENT. I don't believe so. I haven't discussed it with him. My present plans are not to take the Cabinet members along, except perhaps the Secretary of State. But I may change my mind. I really haven't gone into that, exactly who will be in my entourage.

Q. Do you accept Mr. Schlesinger's position that the United States is not willing to pay the world price for oil to Mexico and ties it in with Canada?

THE PRESIDENT. You mean gas?

Q. Yes.

THE PRESIDENT. Yes. I think at this time Mexico is charging at least a dollar more than the world price on oil. But on natural gas, at this time we don't need to bid a very high price for Mexican gas. That's why I said it's so important to distinguish between short-term needs, which are being met by domestic supplies, and long-term needs, looking several years into the future, when we probably will not have adequate supplies in our own country.

We've had an additional complication created by the passage by Congress, the signing of an agreement between myself and the Prime Minister of Canada in constructing a natural gas pipeline to bring our own gas from Alaska down to this country. And the construction of that pipeline and the quantity of gas that's brought through it obviously is dependent upon the price that we can afford to pay. And we cannot afford to pay, any time in the near future, a much higher price for Mexican gas than we pay for our own domestic gas or that gas that's brought from Alaska down here. That's just the facts of the matter.

But I don't want to get involved in deciding exactly what the price levels shall be. It's obviously a factor to be considered. And as the supplies of natural gas become more stringent in the future, we'll have a completely different perspective than we have for the immediate next 24 months or 36 months. But they are interrelated. And I don't think Secretary Kissinger [Schlesinger] insinuated that on a long-term basis

we wouldn't need and value the right to negotiate with Mexico on buying natural gas from them. But the immediate price for Mexican gas is affected, from our point of view, by domestic prices, and also by the price of natural gas projected for the Alaskan sources.

UNDOCUMENTED ALIENS

Q. Mr. President, are you going to resubmit your proposals for dealing with the problem of undocumented aliens, including the amnesty provisions?

THE PRESIDENT. Well, the proposal is in the Congress, in the Judiciary Committees of the House and Senate. And we've not modified those proposals since we sent them up. But I've told several of my advisers that I will refresh my own memory about the details of those proposals, which I helped draft personally, before I go to Mexico. That'll be one of the items that I will discuss with President López Portillo. And there'll be parallel discussions at the Cabinet level that'll be more definitive in nature.

And then if, after that visit to Mexico, we see that some of our recommendations ought to be modified to accommodate Mexican interests without violating the laws of our own country, then we'll certainly recommend those changes to the Congress.

I might say that I'm constrained by my oath, as are all other officials in the Government, to enforce United States law. And we cannot condone a violation of United States law. And the legality or illegality of those who come into our country has to be addressed in those terms. But we want to be humane about it, want to be consistent about it, if possible. We want to meet the subject of real value that we have from Mexican immigrants who come into our country either temporarily or permanently. But we want to make their

185

entry and their egress from our country be consistent, understandable, and legal.

And in some instances, we'll be modifying American law to comply with existing practices. In others, we'll be trying to bring order out of chaos. And we're trying to get the cooperation of the Mexican authorities as well.

All these factors are very complicated. Nobody's been willing, really, in the Congress yet, as you know, to address this sensitive and politically difficult issue. We have addressed it as best we could. And obviously we have an open mind about it. If we think that Mexican opinion, as expressed to me by President López Portillo, would be constructive, that modifications to our proposal will make it more acceptable to the Congress and to the people of our country and to the Mexicans, then we would certainly advocate those changes.

FARM PROGRAMS

Q. Mr. President, many farmers are on their way to Washington in a tractorcade. What type of reception do you feel they will get when they arrive?

THE PRESIDENT. I think as long as they demonstrate their support for our programs—[*laughter*]—or displeasure with some of them legally and peacefully, they'll certainly be welcomed.

I have a background in agriculture, and I meet with many farmers when I go home, both those who register their advice and counsel and criticisms constructively, and the ones who register their advice, counsel, and criticism in a contrary way.

I think that in general, though, the 1977 farm act passed by Congress has been a very beneficial decision made for American farmers. Last year, net farm income went up about 25 percent. The only year that it's ever been that high is 1973, when there were some extraordinary circumstances. And I believe that most of the complaints that originated the American farm movement have now been answered.

We have each year record farm exports. We obviously have not had an embargo against the sale of American products overseas. But I expect farmers—being one of them—always to want better programs, higher parity payments, and so I think they'll be received well.

And I'm sure that there's not the deep sense of indignation and animosity that did exist 18 months ago, because many of those problems that were legitimately described by the American farm movement have now been resolved successfully.

VICE PREMIER DENG OF CHINA

Q. Mr. President, I wonder if you could tell us, Mr. President, what you're likely to say to Deng Xiaoping and what you would like to hear from him.

THE PRESIDENT. That would take a long time to describe all the items. As you know, this will be the end of decades of estrangement between the Chinese and the American people. And I think it's an historic change, all elements of it, for the better.

We'll be talking about how we can enhance political discussions between our two countries, to improve cultural exchange, student exchange, trade, technology, science, agriculture. We'll be demonstrating vividly to Vice Premier Deng Xiaoping, his wife, and his party—here in Washington, with meetings with me and the Congress, with the receptions that I anticipate his receiving in Atlanta, Houston, Seattle—that we, indeed, have a broad base of American friendship toward the Chinese people, that we appreciate the importance of this new move, new relationship. I think we'll be discussing how the new Chinese and American friendship can stabilize further the Western Pacific-Asian region, give a better quality of life for people who live there, enhance peace in that region and, indeed, throughout the world.

We'll be describing to the Chinese leaders and listening to their description of the world political scene from each individual perspective. We'll be exploring areas of compatibility and trying to resolve areas of disparity in approach and opinion. We'll be encouraging the Chinese to help us with some trouble spots.

One obvious item on the agenda would be to see maximum Chinese influence be exerted on North Korea, and in response, we'll exert maximum influence on South Korea to bring those two groups of leaders together to alleviate tension there.

So, I think the agenda is so broad, that's about the best I can do in a brief period of time. I look forward to it.

I've had a chance to study the verbatim transcriptions of the conversations that were conducted on some of Kissinger's trips, on Nixon's trip, Ford's trip, Vance's trip, and also Brzezinski's, and more recently the congressional delegations who've gone there. And from those discussions, I think we've gotten a fairly good picture of the attitude of Mao Zedong, Zhou Enlai, and more recently Chairman Hua Guofeng, and Deng. So, I think I'll be prepared to try to alleviate some of their concerns and to recruit them to join with us in having a more prosperous and peaceful world.

FISCAL YEAR 1980 BUDGET

Q. Mr. President, in the light of your efforts last year to close some of the tax loopholes for those in the upper brackets of wealth, I wonder if you share with Senator Kennedy the sense that it's inappropriate to reduce direct subsidies to the poor and elderly as an inflation measure without trying further to do away with some of the tax exemptions for people in the upper brackets. Do you see a relationship there, and any kind of inappropriateness?

THE PRESIDENT. There's a relationship. I'm hesitant to answer that question, because I don't really understand the particular opinion that you've described as Senator Kennedy's.

Q. Well, his statement, following your State of the Union and budget messages, that we should not, for example, be reducing school milk, school lunch, food stamp programs, until we have closed, for example, the loophole in the three-martini lunch, the other tax exemptions that are granted people of great wealth in this country.

THE PRESIDENT. That's a sore subject you brought up with news people, and I wish you hadn't mentioned it. [*Laughter*] I don't mean the school lunch program; I mean the three-martini lunch. [*Laughter*]

Q. But is there a relationship and inappropriateness there?

THE PRESIDENT. That's a sore subject you brought up with news people, and I Senator Kennedy was critical, he's in error. The balanced presentation in a budget is always a challenge for a President. And I don't know that any President has ever worked harder in having a fair and equitable budget than I did on the 1980 fiscal year budget.

I think it is well balanced. And many of the program changes that are presently criticized, I think, will stand when scrutinized more thoroughly. For instance, summer youth programs—we had an excessive allocation of money for summer youth programs. The money was not used. There was no way to spend that much money on summer youth programs, because the constituency group was not great enough to use all the funds expended. But when you cut back to provide exactly what can be spent under optimum circumstances, the cutback looks as though we're trying to cheat summer youth out of potential jobs.

The same thing applies to the school lunch program, and the same thing applies, by the way, to food stamps. I don't think any administration has done more to enhance the ease with which the food stamps can be used and to serve the poor people better with the food stamp program than have we. The administration of it is going to be much more efficient, much more effective, much more broad-reaching, less paperwork, less expense for administrative purposes, and more easily used by people who formerly did not use the food stamp program.

But, obviously, there has to be a great attention given to closing loopholes for rich and powerful and influential people, as combined with making the effective delivery of services to the poor a very high priority. And this balance is a responsibility constantly on my shoulders and on that of the Congress.

I might say that controlling inflation has erroneously been equated in the past to cheating the poor. But, as I've tried to say in every possible forum, the people who suffer most from inflation are the poor and the unemployed and the minority groups and the aged who are retired on a fixed income, all those who are not well educated and not capable of moving from one job to another to find a better opportunity if they are constrained overly by inflation and can't live on what they've got as an income. And I see that the ones that benefit most from an anti-inflation program, those very constituency groups that Senator Kennedy has effectively defended.

Someone at my income level—I can very well accommodate inflation without my own family suffering. But a person with a very low income cannot. And quite often the most difficult elements of inflation to control are the elements applying directly to the necessities of life—food, clothing, health care, and shelter. And we're trying to concentrate our efforts there.

So, I don't think there's any difference between me and Kennedy in the premise. I just think that I have done the best possible job in evolving a budget to balance those factors that he has described as important.

MR. WURFEL. Thank you, sir.

TAX REFORM

Q. Without a new tax bill to attach it to, will you make another try this year at closing some of those loopholes that you talked so much about last year?

THE PRESIDENT. Yes. The answer is yes, I would like very much to see them passed and will pursue it with every opportunity. But I don't want to open up the entire tax question unless I understand clearly that the Congress is not going to be retrogressive in opening up more tax loopholes than they close.

Last year we were taken aback by the attitude of the Congress. They were much more inclined to create more loopholes for the wealthy than they were to close loopholes in some instances, and I don't want to run that risk. It would put me in a posture of vetoing a bill. I almost vetoed the so-called tax reform bill last year. And only the fact that it reduced taxes overall induced me to sign it, and it was a close call. And this year I don't see any need for a general tax reduction. We need to deal with inflation first before we start talking again about tax reductions.

I've got to go, but I would like to ask you, particularly if you haven't been up here before, to come and let me get a photograph with you individually. And I want to express my thanks again, for your willingness to come.

Have you already met with Brzezinski this morning?

EDITORS. Yes.

THE PRESIDENT. I think this afternoon you'll be meeting with Bob Pastor, who is our specialist in the White House on Latin American affairs, and you can pursue additional questions with him that I was not able to answer because of the press of time. But I appreciate it very much. I understand you'll be attending the press conference this afternoon as well. That's good.

Thank you very much.

NOTE: The interview began at 11 a.m. in the Cabinet Room at the White House. Walter W. Wurfel is a Deputy Press Secretary.

The transcript of the interview was released on January 27.

Nelson A. Rockefeller

Statement on the Death of the Former Vice President. January 27, 1979

Today the Nation mourns one of its most distinguished public men, Nelson Rockefeller. Rosalynn and I extend our deepest sympathy to Mrs. Rockefeller and his family.

Nelson Rockefeller was born to privilege and accepted his privilege as an obligation to serve his State and Nation. He sought the highest service, but willingly and ably performed whatever tasks were asked of him by his country. He was a strong and popular Governor. He served unstintingly under many Presidents of both parties whenever there was a special task to be done.

At a time when our people's trust in their Government had been deeply shaken, he accepted appointment to the Vice Presidency, helping to reassure the Nation with his own integrity and vigorous optimism.

But Nelson Rockefeller did not limit himself to tasks others assigned him. He had special concern for the less fortunate, for the arts, for the processes of government itself, and most of all, for the vision that guided this Nation. When he saw a need, he marshaled the necessary resources and talent to set about meeting it.

A warm and generous friend, he knew how to lose with grace and win with enthusiasm. He drank deeply of life from a full cup.

We knew him by his good works.

NOTE: The President attended memorial services for Mr. Rockefeller at the Riverside Baptist Church in New York City on February 2.

Visit of Vice Premier Deng Xiaoping of the People's Republic of China

Remarks at the Welcoming Ceremony. January 29, 1979

THE PRESIDENT. *Vice Premier Deng, Madame Zhuo Lin, distinguished Chinese guests, fellow Americans, and friends:*

On behalf of the people of my country, I welcome you, Mr. Vice Premier, to the United States of America.

Today we take another step in the historic normalization of relations which we have begun this year. We share in the hope which springs from reconciliation and the anticipation of a common journey.

The United States of America has major interests in the Asian and in the Pacific regions. We expect that normalization of relations between our two countries will help to produce an atmosphere in the Asian and Pacific area in which the right of all peoples to live in peace will be enhanced.

We expect that normalization will help to move us together toward a world of

189

diversity and of peace. For too long, our two peoples were cut off from one another. Now we share the prospect of a fresh flow of commerce, ideas, and people, which will benefit both our countries.

Under the leadership of Premier Hua Guofeng and of you, Mr. Vice Premier, the People's Republic of China has begun to move boldly toward modernization. You have chosen to broaden your cultural, trade, and diplomatic ties with other nations. We welcome this openness. As a people, we firmly believe in open discussion with others and a free exchange of ideas with others.

Our Nation is made up of people of many backgrounds, brought together by a common belief in justice, individual liberty, and a willingness to settle differences peaceably. So, we particularly welcome the opportunity to exchange students and scholars and to improve our trade, technological, scientific, and cultural contacts. We are eager for you and your people to see and to experience our Nation and for our people to experience yours.

There is a Chinese saying that seeing once is worth more than a hundred descriptions. For too long, the Chinese and the American peoples have not been able to see each other for themselves. We are glad that time is past.

China is one of the nations to which a significant number of Americans, our own citizens, trace their ancestry. The American people have warm feelings for the Chinese. From an earlier time when I visited China, 30 years ago, I recall days of close contact and of friendship and hospitality.

But history also teaches us that our peoples have not always dealt with each other wisely. For the past century and more, our relations have often been marred by misunderstanding, false hopes, and even war.

Mr. Vice Premier, let us pledge together that both the United States and China will exhibit the understanding, patience, and persistence which will be needed in order for our new relationship to survive.

Our histories and our political and economic systems are vastly different. Let us recognize those differences and make them sources not of fear, but of healthy curiosity; not as a source of divisiveness, but of mutual benefit.

As long as we harbor no illusions about our differences, our diversity can contribute to the vitality of our new relationship. People who are different have much to learn from each other.

Yesterday, Mr. Vice Premier, was the lunar New Year, the beginning of your Spring Festival, the traditional time of new beginnings for the Chinese people. On your New Year's Day, I am told, you open all doors and windows to give access to beneficent spirits. It's a time when family quarrels are forgotten, a time when visits are made, a time of reunion and reconciliation.

As for our two nations, today is a time of reunion and new beginnings. It's a day of reconciliation, when windows too long closed have been reopened.

Vice Premier Deng, you, your wife, your party are welcome to our great country. Thank you for honoring us with your visit.

THE VICE PREMIER. *Mr. President and Mrs. Carter, ladies and gentlemen:*

First of all, I wish to thank the President and Mrs. Carter for this grand and warm welcome, which we consider to be a token of the American people's friendship for the Chinese people. We, on our part, have brought the American people a message of friendship from the Chinese people.

The history of friendly contacts between our two peoples goes back for nearly 200 years, and what is more, we fought shoulder to shoulder in the war against fascism. Though there was a period of unpleasantness between us for 30 years, normal relations between China and the United States have at last been restored, thanks to the joint efforts of our two governments and peoples. In this respect, President Carter's farsighted decision played a key role.

Great possibilities lie ahead for developing amicable cooperation between China and the United States. In the next few days, we will be exploring with your Government leaders and with friends in all walks of life ways to develop our contacts and cooperation in the political, economic, scientific, technological, and cultural fields.

Normalization opens up broad vistas for developing these contacts and cooperation to our mutual benefit. We have every reason to expect fruitful results.

The significance of normalization extends far beyond our bilateral relations. Amicable cooperation between two major countries, situated on opposite shores of the Pacific, is undoubtedly an important factor working for peace in this area and in the world as a whole. The world today is far from tranquil. There are not only threats to peace, but the factors making for war are visibly growing. The people of the world have the urgent task of redoubling their efforts to maintain world peace, security, and stability. And our two countries are duty-bound to work together and make our due contribution to that end.

Mr. President, we share the sense of being on an historic mission. Sino-U.S. relations have reached a new beginning, and the world situation is at a new turning point. China and the United States are great countries, and the Chinese and American peoples, two great peoples. Friendly cooperation between our two

peoples is bound to exert a positive and far-reaching influence on the way the world situation evolves.

I sincerely thank you for your welcome.

NOTE: The President spoke at 10:12 a.m. on the South Lawn of the White House. The Vice Premier spoke in Chinese, and his remarks were translated by an interpreter.

Following the ceremony, which was broadcast live on radio and television, the President and the Vice Premier went to the Oval Office for the first of two separate meetings held during the day.

The Cyprus Conflict

Letter to the Speaker of the House and the Chairman of the Senate Foreign Relations Committee. January 29, 1979

In accordance with the provisions of Public Law 95–384, I am submitting the following report on progress made during the past 60 days toward the conclusion of a negotiated solution of the Cyprus problem.

During this reporting period, further intensive efforts have been made to bring the two Cypriot communities back to the negotiating table for serious and sustained talks under the auspices of Secretary General Waldheim. The substantive suggestions that the U.S., the U.K. and Canada made available to the two sides and to the United Nations on November 10 appeared to have stimulated the negotiating process and were recognized as constructive by significant (although not all) elements in Cyprus, Turkey and Greece. In the context of recent developments—especially the new atmosphere created by the lifting of the arms embargo on Turkey, the U.S.-Canadian-U.K. suggestions, the United Nations debates, and a growing international consensus for a negotiated settlement—Secretary General Waldheim submitted to the two Cypriot parties a draft United Nations formula

191

for the resumption of negotiations. As of the date of this report, it appeared that both the Greek and Turkish Cypriots were seriously and sympathetically considering the Secretary General's proposal.

The Government of Turkey has taken a constructive attitude towards these efforts to bring about a resumption of the intercommunal negotiations. Prime Minister Ecevit has publicly affirmed that the Turkish Cypriots are prepared to return to the table, and he has indicated that they could accept the suggestions of November 10 as an aid to negotiation if the Greek Cypriots were prepared to do likewise. During a meeting with Deputy Secretary of State Christopher in Ankara on January 11, Mr. Ecevit emphasized his strong interest in seeing a resumption of the intercommunal talks and expressed the hope that some way for doing this could soon be found.

At the time of my last report, the United Nations Security Council was meeting at the request of the Government of Cyprus to consider the Cyprus issue. On November 27, the Council adopted a resolution by consensus that called upon the two Cypriot parties to cooperate in the implementation of Security Council resolutions on Cyprus "within a specific time-frame" and urged that intercommunal negotiations be resumed. The Secretary-General was asked to report on both these aspects by May 30, 1979. The United States fully supports the goals of this resolution.

This Administration warmly welcomes the initiatives that Secretary-General Waldheim has taken and is continuing to take to bring about sustained and productive negotiations on Cyprus. We have been encouraged by recent developments, and hope very much that a resumption of the talks will prove possible in the near future. The U.S.-Canadian-U.K. suggestions of November 10 have served a useful purpose in generating some of this forward movement and in stimulating fresh thinking on the substance of the problem, and it is our expectation that they will be actively considered in the negotiations.

A copy of Secretary-General Waldheim's comprehensive report of December 1 to the Security Council on the United Nations operation in Cyprus is attached.

Sincerely,

JIMMY CARTER

NOTE: This is the text of identical letters addressed to Thomas P. O'Neill, Jr., Speaker of the House of Representatives, and Frank Church, chairman of the Senate Foreign Relations Committee.

Visit of Vice Premier Deng of China

Toasts at the State Dinner.   January 29, 1979

THE PRESIDENT. *Vice Premier Deng, Madame Zhuo Lin, distinguished visitors from the People's Republic of China, President Nixon, my fellow Americans, and friends:*

This house belongs to all Americans, people who are firmly dedicated to a world of friendship and peace. And, Vice Premier Deng, on behalf of all Americans, I welcome you here to our house.

Your visit here, Mr. Vice Premier, is an important milestone in the development of friendly relations between the United States of America and the People's Republic of China. I'm gratified that after too many years of estrangement, that our two countries have now grasped the opportunity to reestablish these vital, formal links that exist between us.

In the past year, more than 120 delegations from the People's Republic of China have come here to the United States to visit us. And an even greater number of American groups have left here and gone to visit China. Exchanges have already begun in the natural sciences, in space, in agriculture, in medicine, in science, in technology, and other fields. And now with the establishment of normal diplomatic relations, the exploratory nature of these many exchanges can give way to a more valuable and a more permanent relationship. This will serve the interests of both our nations and will also serve the cause of peace.

Today, for the first time since the establishment of normal diplomatic relations, the Governments of the United States of America and the People's Republic of China have begun official discussions at the highest level. Our discussions are fruitful and they are constructive, because both of us are keenly aware that what we do now will establish precedents for future peaceful relationships.

We've not entered this new relationship for any short-term gains. We have a long-term commitment to a world community of diverse nations and independent nations. We believe that a strong and a secure China will play a cooperative part in developing that type of world community which we envision. Our new relationship particularly can contribute to the peace and stability of the Asia-Pacific region.

Your nation, Vice Premier Deng, like ours, has been created by the hard work of ordinary men and women. Despite our cultural, political, and economic differences, there's much for us to build on together.

The United States, born out of a revolution for freedom, is a young country with an independent history of only 200 years. But our Constitution is the oldest continuing written constitution in the entire world.

Chinese civilization, with more than 4,000 years of recorded history, is one of the oldest cultures in the world. But as a modern nation, China is quite young. We can learn much from each other.

There are many hundreds of thousands of Americans of Chinese origin, and their contributions to our society have been even greater than their numbers could possibly suggest. Our national life has been enriched by the work of Chinese American architects, artists, and scientists—including three recent winners of the Nobel Prize.

Like you, Mr. Vice Premier, I'm a farmer, and like you, I'm a former military man. In my little farming community, when I grew up, our agricultural methods and our way of life were not greatly different from those of centuries earlier. I stepped from that world into the planning and outfitting of nuclear submarines. And when I later returned to the land, I found that farming had been absolutely transformed in just a few years by new scientific knowledge and by technology.

I know the shocks of change in my own life, and I know the sometimes painful adjustments required when change occurs, as well as the great potential for good that change can bring to both individuals and to nations.

I know, too, that neither individuals nor nations can stifle change. It is far better to adapt scientific and technological advantages to our needs, to learn to control them, and to reap their benefits while minimizing their potential adverse effects.

And I know that the Chinese people and you, Mr. Vice Premier, understand these things about change very well. Your ambitious modernization effort in four different areas of human life attests to that. The American people wish you well in these efforts, and we are looking forward to cooperating with you and with the people of China.

In his final message, the day before he died, Franklin Roosevelt—who would have been 97 years old tomorrow—wrote these words: "If civilization is to survive, we must cultivate the science of human relationships—the ability of people of all kinds to live together and to work together, in the same world and at peace."

In that spirit, Mr. Vice Premier, I would like to propose a toast: To the newly established diplomatic relationships between the United States of America and the people of the republic of China; to the health of Premier Hua Guofeng; to the health of Vice Premier Deng and Madame Zhuo Lin; and to the further development of friendship between the people of China and the people of the United States of America.

THE VICE PREMIER. *Mr. President and Mrs. Carter, ladies and gentlemen:*

We thank the President and Mrs. Carter for hosting this grand dinner in our honor. Allow me to take this opportunity to extend good wishes to the American Government and the people on behalf of the Chinese Government and people, Premier Hua Guofeng, and in my own name.

Our arrival in the United States coincides with the Spring Festival in China. From time immemorial, the Chinese people have celebrated this festival marking "the beginning of the annual cycle and rejuvenation of all things in nature." Here, on this occasion, we share with our American friends present the feeling that a new era has begun in Sino-U.S. relations.

For 30 years, our two nations were estranged and opposed to each other. This abnormal state of affairs is over at last. At such a time we cherish, in particular, the memory of the late Chairman Mao Zedong and Premier Zhou Enlai, who

blazed a trail for the normalization of Sino-U.S. relations.

Naturally, we think also of the efforts made by former President Nixon, former President Ford, Dr. Kissinger, many U.S. Senators and Congressmen, and friends in all walks of life. We think highly of the valuable contributions of President Carter, Secretary of State Cyrus Vance, and Dr. Brzezinski to the ultimate normalization of our relations.

Our two countries have different social systems and ideologies, but both Governments are aware that the interests of our peoples and of world peace require that we view our bilateral relations in the context of the overall international situation and with a long-term strategic perspective. This was the reason why the two sides easily reached agreement on normalization.

Moreover, in the Joint Communique on the Establishment of Diplomatic Relations our two sides solemnly committed themselves that neither should seek hegemony and each was opposed to efforts by any other country or group of countries to establish such hegemony. This commitment restrains ourselves and adds to our sense of responsibility for world peace and stability. We are confident that the amicable cooperation between the Chinese and American peoples is not only in the interest of our two countries' development but will also become a strong factor working for the preservation of world peace and the promotion of human progress.

I ask you to join me in drinking to the health of the President and Mrs. Carter; to the health of the Secretary of State and Mrs. Vance; to the health of Dr. and Mrs. Brzezinski; to the health of all friends present; to the great American people; to the great Chinese people; to friendship between the Chinese and American peoples;

and to the peace and progress of the people of the world.

NOTE: The President spoke at 8:48 p.m. in the State Dining Room at the White House. The Vice Premier spoke in Chinese, and the translation of his remarks follows the White House press release.

Visit of Vice Premier Deng of China

Remarks Following a Performance at the John F. Kennedy Center for the Performing Arts. January 29, 1979

THE PRESIDENT. All of us are fortunate in being able to participate in a truly momentous and historic occasion, the formal cementing of friendship now and permanently in the future between the 220 million Americans and the more than 900 million Chinese. We are grateful for this opportunity to extend our welcome to Vice Premier Deng Xiaoping, to Madame Zhuo Lin, to all the delegation, who've come here from China.

We are grateful for the opening up of new avenues of scientific, trade, cultural exchange. And there could be no better way to demonstrate what our Nation is, what we have to offer, than the wonderful performers who have joined us tonight to give them just a tiny glimpse, but a beautiful glimpse of some of the superb talent of great American performers.

Mr. Vice Premier, it's indeed a great honor for me, as President of a great country, to welcome you, the Vice Premier of another great country, to the people of America. Thank you for coming.

God bless all of you. We thank you for being with us as we join our two nations together on this formal occasion.

Thank you very much.

THE VICE PREMIER. *Mr. President and Mrs. Carter, ladies and gentlemen:*

Thank you, Mr. President and Mrs. Carter, for arranging this magnificent performance by American artists, which gives us an enjoyable evening and leaves on us an indelible impression.

This occasion reminds me of what Lu Xian, the great Chinese thinker, once said. He said, "It would be best if mankind could avoid lack of mutual understanding and show concern for one another."

Art and literature will provide the best means towards that goal.

The art and literature of each nation is unique. International exchanges in this area will contribute to mutual understanding between peoples, to the flourishing of art and literature of each country, and to world peace and human progress.

No doubt there should be active cultural exchanges between China and the United States following normalization. Here I'm happy to inform you that the Boston Symphony Orchestra, as the first cultural exchange item since the establishment of diplomatic relations between China and the United States, will visit China in March.

We hope that more American musicians, dancers, actors, and other artists will come to China on performing tours. We, on our part, will send more Chinese artists here to perform for the American people.

Thank you.

NOTE: The President spoke at 10:35 p.m. in the Opera House. The Vice Premier spoke in Chinese, and his remarks were translated by an interpreter.

The program, entitled "An Evening for the Performance of American Arts," was broadcast live on television.

National Science Board

Nomination of Michael Kasha To Be a Member. January 30, 1979

The President today announced that he will nominate Michael Kasha, of Tallahassee, Fla., to be a member of the National Science Board for a term expiring May 10, 1984.

Kasha, 58, is director of the Institute of Molecular Biophysics and professor of physical chemistry at Florida State University in Tallahassee.

Patent and Trademark Office

Nomination of Sidney A. Diamond To Be an Assistant Commissioner. January 30, 1979

The President today announced that he will nominate Sidney A. Diamond, of Tucson, Ariz., to be an Assistant Commissioner of Patents and Trademarks.

Diamond, 64, is an attorney and is presently counsel to a New York law firm. He is an expert on patent and copyright law and has served as chairman of the American Bar Association's section of patent, trademark, and copyright law. He is vice president of the International Patent and Trademark Association and the author of numerous articles on trademark and patent law in legal and other periodicals.

National Commission on Libraries and Information Science

Nomination of Three Members. January 30, 1979

The President today announced three persons whom he will nominate to be members of the National Commission on Libraries and Information Science. They are:

Francis Keppel, of Cambridge, Mass., director of the Aspen Institute program in education for a changing society and a senior lecturer at the Harvard Graduate School of Education. Keppel is a former dean of the Harvard Graduate School of Education and has also served as Assistant Secretary of Health, Education, and Welfare for Education.

Bessie B. Moore, of Little Rock, Ark., executive director of the Arkansas State Council on Economic Education. Moore has been a classroom teacher, a county and State supervisor of schools, and State coordinator of environmental education for the Arkansas Department of Education.

Philip A. Sprague, of Michigan City, Ind., a consultant to and member of the executive committee of Milton Roy Co., former director of the Foundation for Instrumentation Education and Research, active in community affairs in Michigan City.

National Inventors' Day, 1979

Proclamation 4635. January 30, 1979

By the President of the United States of America

A Proclamation

The founding fathers in Section 8 of Article I of our Constitution provided that the Congress shall have the power to promote the progress of the useful arts by securing for a limited time to inventors the exclusive right to their discoveries.

The first Congress, pursuant to that Constitutional provision, enacted legislation providing inventors with such a right. That legislation became the first United

States patent law when it was signed by President George Washington on April 10, 1790.

With the knowledge that the patent system contributes significantly to technological progress for the benefit of mankind, the United States since then has continually and actively maintained a national patent system even in times of war and rebellion.

This incentive provided inventors has prompted millions of our people to apply great effort and valuable resources, often persevering in the face of seemingly insurmountable odds, to create, perfect and bring to the marketplace many inventions which have made our labors more productive and which have contributed to our health and welfare.

The economic and technological preeminence which our Nation has known for many years and enjoys today is in large part due to the efforts of our inventors. This preeminence can be maintained by giving encouragement to their future efforts.

In honor of the important role played by inventors in promoting progress in the useful arts and in recognition of the invaluable contribution of inventors to the welfare of our people, the 95th Congress, by House Joint Resolution 685, which I signed into law on October 14, 1978 (Public Law 95–463), designated February 11, 1979, as "National Inventors' Day."

February 11, 1979, is especially significant for celebration as National Inventors' Day because it is the anniversary of the birth of Thomas Alva Edison who one hundred years ago perfected and patented the first practical incandescent lamp, an invention which as we all know dramatically changed the way of life all over the world.

Now, THEREFORE, I, JIMMY CARTER, President of the United States of America,

do hereby call upon and urge the people of the United States to honor all inventors by joining me in observing February 11, 1979, National Inventors' Day, with appropriate ceremonies and activities.

IN WITNESS WHEREOF, I have hereunto set my hand this thirtieth day of January, in the year of our Lord nineteen hundred seventy-nine, and of the Independence of the United States of America the two hundred and third.

JIMMY CARTER

[Filed with the Office of the Federal Register, 5:01 p.m., January 30, 1979]

Thomas Edison and the Centennial of Light

Message of the President.   January 30, 1979

This year marks the one hundredth anniversary of Thomas Alva Edison's invention of the incandescent lamp. More than any other invention, the light bulb ushered in the Age of Electricity. When Edison had perfected it, he knew he was ready to bring electric lighting into the streets, homes, factories and offices of America. And he did.

In recognition of this historic feat, a series of events throughout 1979 will be held across the country to honor Edison's inventive genius. These events will offer our people many chances to review and reflect on the numerous important inventions that came from the mind and hands of this unique American.

But Thomas Edison was more than an inventor. He was a true innovator. He pioneered the first industrial research laboratory. He created the industries and institutions to bring his inventions to the people. He brought about change, opportunity and progress for all mankind.

197

As we commemorate the invention of the incandescent lamp and celebrate the accomplishments of this remarkable man, we should all draw new inspiration from him. I hope that the memory of Thomas Alva Edison will help us all to realize, as he did, that with perseverance, hard work, knowledge and imagination we can overcome adversity and achieve new advances from which all can benefit.

JIMMY CARTER

Visit of Vice Premier Deng of China

Remarks to Reporters Following a Meeting. January 30, 1979

THE PRESIDENT. Vice Premier Deng Xiaoping and I will meet again tomorrow afternoon to conclude the signing of agreements that will be worked out between now and then. Our discussions yesterday and today have been far-reaching. They have been very frank and honest. They've been very cordial and harmonious, and they've been extremely beneficial and constructive.

We have, I think, established a relationship for future routine consultation which will bring great benefits to the people of the United States of America and to the People's Republic of China.

Again, we consider this visit one of the most historic events in our Nation's history, and we are grateful for the progress that has been made already and for the prospects of even greater benefits in the future.

THE VICE PREMIER. As for myself, I agree to every word that the President has just said. And I also believe that through these discussions and through this visit, we have enhanced our mutual understanding and friendship. And through this visit, I am even more convinced that China and the United States and the Chinese people and the American people have broad prospects in various fields—politically, economically, in the science and technological fields, and in the cultural field, et cetera.

Of course, the reception which is being accorded to me and my party by the American Government and people has not yet concluded. But up to the present, I would still like to express our sincere thanks and appreciation for the kind reception given to us and given to me personally by the President, Mrs. Carter, and the American Government and people, and for their friendship which they expressed to us.

Let us shake hands once again, a handshake between the two peoples.

THE PRESIDENT. Thank you again. Thank you very much.

NOTE: The President spoke at 10:58 a.m. on the South Grounds of the White House. The Vice Premier spoke in Chinese, and his remarks were translated by an interpreter.

General Services Administration

Nomination of Kurt W. Muellenberg To Be Inspector General.   January 30, 1979

The President today announced his intention to nominate Kurt W. Muellenberg, of Washington, D.C., as Inspector General of the General Services Administration.

Muellenberg, 46, is currently Chief of the Organized Crime and Racketeering

Section of the Criminal Division of the Justice Department.

He was born January 6, 1932, in Jena, East Germany. He came to the United States in 1952. In 1952 and 1953, he worked as a laborer for Western Electric Co. in Buffalo, N.Y. From 1953 to 1957, he served in the United States Air Force.

Muellenberg received a B.A. from the University of Maryland in 1958 and an LL.B. degree from the University of Maryland in 1961. From 1961 to 1965, he was a trial attorney at the U.S. Department of Agriculture. From 1965 to 1968, he served as a trial attorney in the Justice Department's Organized Crime and Racketeering Section, Criminal Division, in Washington.

He was deputy attorney in charge of the Organized Crime Strike Force in Detroit, Mich., from 1968 to 1969, and attorney in charge of the Organized Crime Strike Force in Cleveland from 1969 to 1970.

Muellenberg was Deputy Chief of the Organized Crime and Racketeering Section of the Justice Department in Washington from 1970 to 1976. From February to October of 1976, he served as Chief of the Narcotics and Dangerous Drugs Section, Criminal Division. He was named Chief of the Organized Crime and Racketeering Section in November of 1976.

As Chief of that section, he supervises the Federal Government's efforts against organized crime in the United States. He is chairman of the National Organized Crime Planning Council, a group of management-level representatives from law enforcement agencies that serves as a policy board for the Justice Department's organized crime program.

He is a member of the Maryland and D.C. bar associations.

Carnegie Commission on the Future of Public Broadcasting

Statement on Receiving the Commission's Report. January 30, 1979

I am pleased to receive the report of the Carnegie Commission on the Future of Public Broadcasting.

In 1967 the first Carnegie Commission issued a report that set the course for the public broadcasting system. In the intervening 12 years the system has grown into an important part of our Nation's culture. Now a new Carnegie report proposes a new set of long-term directions.

Public broadcasting's immediate future was assured last year by the Public Telecommunications Financing Act, which increased Federal support, strengthened insulation from political control of program content, mandated extension of coverage to areas not now served, and improved the system's structure.

The new Carnegie report provides a focal point for continued work by government and—most importantly—by the system itself. The report will help deal with such long-run issues as the opportunities for multichannel service provided by satellite; the need to increase creative programing for minorities, children, the elderly, and other groups; the responsibilities that may flow from partial deregulation of commercial broadcasting; and the need to increase resources without excessive dependence on Federal spending.

The Carnegie report represents an 18-month effort by a distinguished group of citizens, under the able leadership of William J. McGill, president of Columbia University. It will make an important contribution to the system's long-term development. My administration will study the recommendations with care, along with the proposals being developed in Congress. I look forward to a year of continued advances for public broadcasting.

Budget Rescissions and Deferrals

Message to the Congress.   January 31, 1979

To the Congress of the United States:

In accordance with the Impoundment Control Act of 1974, I herewith report ten proposals to rescind a total of $914.6 million in budget authority previously provided by the Congress. In addition, I am reporting six new deferrals of budget authority totalling $1,169.8 million and six revisions to previously transmitted deferrals increasing the amount deferred by $28.8 million.

The rescission proposals affect programs in the Departments of Energy, Health, Education and Welfare, Housing and Urban Development, the Interior, and several independent agencies.

The new deferrals and revisions to existing deferrals involve programs of the Departments of Agriculture, Commerce, Defense, Energy, the Interior, Justice, Labor, Transportation, the Treasury, and the Tennessee Valley Authority.

The details of each rescission proposal and deferral are contained in the attached reports.

JIMMY CARTER

The White House,
   January 31, 1979.

NOTE: The attachments detailing the rescissions and deferrals are printed in the FEDERAL REGISTER of February 5, 1979.

Visit of Vice Premier Deng of China

Agreement Between the United States and China on Cooperation in Science and Technology.   January 31, 1979

AGREEMENT BETWEEN THE GOVERNMENT OF THE UNITED STATES OF AMERICA AND THE GOVERNMENT OF THE PEOPLE'S REPUBLIC OF CHINA ON COOPERATION IN SCIENCE AND TECHNOLOGY

The Government of the United States of America and the Government of the People's Republic of China (hereinafter referred to as the Contracting Parties);

Acting in the spirit of the Joint Communique on the Establishment of Diplomatic Relations between the United States of America and the People's Republic of China;

Recognizing that cooperation in the fields of science and technology can promote the well-being and prosperity of both countries;

Affirming that such cooperation can strengthen friendly relations between both countries;

Wishing to establish closer and more regular cooperation between scientific and technical entities and personnel in both countries;

Have agreed as follows:

ARTICLE 1

1. The Contracting Parties shall develop cooperation under this Agreement on the basis of equality, reciprocity and mutual benefit.

2. The principal objective of this Agreement is to provide broad opportunities for cooperation in scientific and technological fields of mutual interest, thereby promoting the progress of science and technology for the benefit of both countries and of mankind.

ARTICLE 2

Cooperation under this Agreement may be undertaken in the fields of agriculture, energy, space, health, environment, earth sciences, engineering, and such other areas of science and technology and their management as may be mutually agreed, as well as educational and scholarly exchange.

ARTICLE 3

Cooperation under this Agreement may include:

a. Exchange of scientists, scholars, specialists and students;

b. Exchange of scientific, scholarly, and technological information and documentation;

c. Joint planning and implementation of programs and projects;

d. Joint research, development and testing, and exchange of research results and experience between cooperating entities;

e. Organization of joint courses, conferences and symposia;

f. Other forms of scientific and technological cooperation as may be mutually agreed.

ARTICLE 4

Pursuant to the objectives of this Agreement, the Contracting Parties shall encourage and facilitate, as appropriate, the development of contacts and cooperation between government agencies, universities, organizations, institutions, and other entities of both countries, and the conclusion of accords between such bodies for the conduct of cooperative activities. Both sides will further promote, consistent with such cooperation and where appropriate, mutually beneficial bilateral economic activities.

ARTICLE 5

Specific accords implementing this Agreement may cover the subjects of cooperation, procedures to be followed, treatment of intellectual property, funding and other appropriate matters. With respect to funding, costs shall be borne as mutually agreed. All cooperative activities under this Agreement shall be subject to the availability of funds.

ARTICLE 6

Cooperative activities under this Agreement shall be subject to the laws and regulations in each country.

ARTICLE 7

Each Contracting Party shall, with respect to cooperative activities under this Agreement, use its best efforts to facilitate prompt entry into and exit from its territory of equipment and personnel of the other side, and also to provide access to relevant geographic areas, institutions, data and materials.

ARTICLE 8

Scientific and technological information derived from cooperative activities under this Agreement may be made available, unless otherwise agreed in an implementing accord under Article 5, to the world scientific community through customary channels and in accordance with the normal procedures of the participating entities.

ARTICLE 9

Scientists, technical experts, and entities of third countries or international organizations may be invited, upon mutual consent of both sides, to participate in projects and programs being carried out under this Agreement.

ARTICLE 10

1. The Contracting Parties shall establish a US–PRC Joint Commission on Scientific and Technological Cooperation, which shall consist of United States and Chinese parts. Each Contracting Party shall designate a co-chairman and its members of the Commission. The Commission shall adopt procedures for its operation, and shall ordinarily meet once a year in the United States and the People's Republic of China alternately.

2. The Joint Commission shall plan and coordinate cooperation in science and technology, and monitor and facilitate such cooperation. The Commission shall also consider proposals for the further development of cooperative activities in specific areas and recommend measures and programs to both sides.

3. To carry out its functions, the Commission may when necessary create temporary or permanent joint subcommittees or working groups.

4. During the period between meetings of the Commission, additions or amendments may be made to already approved cooperative activities, as may be mutually agreed.

5. To assist the Joint Commission, each Contracting Party shall designate an Executive Agent. The Executive Agent on the United States side shall be the Office of Science and Technology Policy; and on the side of the People's Republic of China, the State Scientific and Technological Commission. The Executive Agents shall collaborate closely to promote proper implementation of all activities and programs. The Executive Agent of each Contracting Party shall be responsible for coordinating the implementation of its side of such activities and programs.

ARTICLE 11

1. This Agreement shall enter into force upon signature and shall remain in force for five years. It may be modified or extended by mutual agreement of the Parties.

2. The termination of this Agreement shall not affect the validity or duration of any implementing accords made under it.

DONE at Washington this 31st day of January, 1979, in duplicate in the English and Chinese languages, both equally authentic.

For the Government of the United States of America:

JIMMY CARTER

For the Government of the People's Republic of China:

DENG XIAOPING

Visit of Vice Premier Deng of China

United States Letter Implementing Understandings on Educational Exchange, Agriculture, and Space as Part of the Agreement on Science and Technology. January 31, 1979

Dear Mr. Minister:

With reference to the Agreement Between the United States of America and the People's Republic of China on Cooperation in Science and Technology, signed in Washington today, it is the understanding of the Government of the United States of America that existing understandings in the fields of education, agriculture and space will become a part of the formal specific accords to be concluded in those fields under Article 5 of the Agreement.

Attached as annexes to this letter are the Understanding on the Exchange of Students and Scholars reached in Washington in October 1978, the Understanding on Agricultural Exchange reached in Beijing in November 1978, and the Understanding on Cooperation in Space Technology reached in Washington in December 1978.

If the Government of the People's Republic of China confirms this understanding and the texts of the understandings annexed hereto, this letter and the letter of confirmation of the People's Republic of China will constitute an agreement relating to these fields between our two governments.

Sincerely,

FRANK PRESS
Director, Office of Science and Technology Policy

[His Excellency Fang Yi, Minister in Charge, The State Scientific and Technological Commission, Beijing]

UNDERSTANDING ON THE EXCHANGE OF STUDENTS AND SCHOLARS BETWEEN THE UNITED STATES OF AMERICA AND THE PEOPLE'S REPUBLIC OF CHINA

An understanding on educational exchanges between the United States and China was reached in Washington, D.C. in October 1978 during discussions between the Chinese education delegation headed by Dr. Chou Pei-yuan, Acting Chairman of the PRC Science and Technology Association, and the U.S. education delegation headed by Dr. Richard C. Atkinson, Director of the National Science Foundation, as follows:

1. Both sides agreed they would pursue a program of educational exchange in accordance with and in implementation of the spirit of the Shanghai Communique;

2. There will be a two-way scientific and scholarly exchange which will provide mutual benefit to both countries;

3. The exchanges will include students, graduate students and visiting scholars for programs of research and study in each country;

4. The two sides exchanged lists of fields in which its students and scholars

are interested and lists of institutions where they wish to work. Each side will use its best efforts to fulfill the requests of the other for study and research opportunities. Each side will expeditiously grant visas for such exchanges in accordance with its laws and regulations;

5. The sending side will pay the costs associated with its participants;

6. Both sides may take full advantage of any scholarships which may be offered;

7. Each side will be responsible for the implementation of the program in its territory, including responsibility for providing advice to the other side and relevant information and materials about the universities and research institutions concerned;

8. The two sides agreed that the students and scholars sent by both sides should observe the laws and regulations and respect the customs of the receiving country;

9. The Chinese side indicated it wishes to send a total of 500 to 700 students and scholars in the academic year 1978–1979. The United States side indicated it wishes to send 10 students in its national program in January 1979 and 50 students in its national program by September 1979 as well as such other numbers as the Chinese side is able to receive. Both sides agree to use their best efforts to implement such programs;

10. To set each year the number of students and scholars to be exchanged and to discuss the progress of the program of exchanges, the two sides will meet when necessary. Consultations on important matters may also be held by the governments of the two countries. In addition, both sides will encourage direct contacts between the universities, research institutions, and scholars of their respective countries;

11. Both sides believe that the discussions mark a good beginning and have

opened up the prospect of broadened opportunities for exchanges between the two countries in the fields of science, technology and education as relations between them improve. Both sides also believe that such exchanges are conducive to the promotion of friendship and understanding between their two peoples.

UNDERSTANDING ON AGRICULTURAL EXCHANGE BETWEEN THE UNITED STATES OF AMERICA AND THE PEOPLE'S REPUBLIC OF CHINA

During a visit to China of a delegation led by U.S. Secretary of Agriculture Robert Bergland in November 1978, discussions were held with Chinese officials which resulted in understandings concerning US-PRC agricultural exchange. It was agreed that it would be of mutual benefit to promote cooperation in agricultural technology, economic information, science and education, and trade in agricultural products, and that contacts between organizations and institutions of all types in these fields should be facilitated.

It was noted that study groups had already been exchanged in the fields of science and research, farm machinery, citrus fruits, wheat and vegetables. It was agreed that areas in which further exchanges should occur would include germ plasm (seed research and selection), biological control of pests, livestock and veterinary science, and agricultural education and research management methods. It was also agreed that, within the next two or three years, cooperation would be carried out in the fields of forestry, agricultural engineering, improvement of grasslands and management of pasturelands, cultivation of fruit trees, medicinal plants, and the application of remote sensing and computer technology to agriculture. Such cooperation would include mutual visits of, and joint research by, students, scientists and technicians.

The U.S. side agreed to facilitate contacts between officials of the People's Republic of China and U.S. manufacturers of agricultural equipment and supplies. Each side expressed its interest in the statistical methods of agricultural economics and experience in agricultural management of the other side. It was agreed also that, through the cooperator program of the U.S. Department of Agriculture, further discussions should be held regarding the products and technology best suited to conditions in China and that USDA teams would begin visiting China in early 1979. Reciprocal scientific teams from the PRC will also begin U.S. study visits in 1979.

It was agreed that the development of agricultural trade between the two countries was in the mutual interest and that its prospects were bright.

It was agreed that when study teams or technical trainees are exchanged on a one-for-one basis, the host country would pay in-country costs; and that when the exchange is not reciprocal, the sending country will pay all costs.

UNDERSTANDING ON COOPERATION IN SPACE TECHNOLOGY BETWEEN THE UNITED STATES OF AMERICA AND THE PEOPLE'S REPUBLIC OF CHINA

During a visit to the United States in November and December 1978 by a delegation headed by Dr. Jen Hsin-min, Director of the Chinese Academy of Space Technology, an understanding in principle was reached with a delegation headed by Dr. Robert A. Frosch, Administrator of the National Aeronautics and Space Administration, on U.S.-Chinese cooperation in the peaceful utilization of space technology.

This understanding includes:

1. Cooperation in the development of the civil broadcasting and communica-

tions system of the PRC. The PRC intends, under suitable conditions, to purchase a U.S. satellite broadcasting and communications system, including the associated ground receiving and distribution equipment. The space portion of the system will be launched by NASA and placed in geostationary orbit by a U.S. contractor, with continued operation to be carried out by China; and

2. The intended purchase, under suitable conditions, by the PRC of a U.S. ground station capable of receiving earth resources information from the NASA Landsat remote sensing satellites, including the Landsat now under development.

It was also agreed that, through further discussions and correspondence, both sides would develop the details of the understanding described above and consider other fields of civil space cooperation which could be of mutual interest and benefit.

NOTE: Mr. Press and Vice Premier Fang signed the letters of understanding at the ceremony in the East Room at the White House prior to the signing of the science and technology agreement by the President and the Vice Premier.

Visit of Vice Premier Deng of China

Accord Implementing Cooperation in High Energy Physics Under the Agreement on Science and Technology. January 31, 1979

IMPLEMENTING ACCORD BETWEEN THE DEPARTMENT OF ENERGY OF THE UNITED STATES OF AMERICA AND THE STATE SCIENTIFIC AND TECHNOLOGICAL COMMISSION OF THE PEOPLE'S REPUBLIC OF CHINA ON COOPERATION IN THE FIELD OF HIGH ENERGY PHYSICS

The Department of Energy of the United States of America and the State Scientific and Technological Commission of the People's Republic of China (hereinafter referred to as the Parties), for the purpose of promoting cooperation and collaboration in the field of high energy physics subject to the Agreement Between the Government of the United States of America and the Government of the People's Republic of China on Cooperation in Science and Technology, signed in Washington, D.C. on January 31, 1979, have agreed as follows:

ARTICLE 1

The objective of this Accord is to further the energy programs of the Parties by establishing a framework for cooperation in the field of high energy physics, including theoretical and experimental research, accelerator design and construction techniques; and related technology areas as may be mutually agreed.

ARTICLE 2

Cooperation under this Accord may include the following forms:

1. Exchange and provision of information on scientific and technical developments, activities, and practices;

2. Research and development activities in the form of experiments, tests, and other technical collaborative activities;

3. Exchange of scientists, engineers, and other specialists; including visits by specialist teams or individuals to the facilities of the other Party, and exchange of personnel for training purposes;

4. Exchange and provision of samples, materials, instruments, and components for testing and evaluation;

5. Such other forms of cooperation as are mutually agreed.

ARTICLE 3

Specific undertakings, obligations and conditions with respect to the conduct of each activity under Article 2 including responsibility for payment of costs shall be agreed by authorized entities on a case-by-case basis.

ARTICLE 4

1. For the purpose of coordinating activities pursuant to this Accord, a Committee on High Energy Physics is hereby established, consisting of representatives of the Parties and such other persons from each Party's national research community as it may designate. Each Party shall designate one person to act as its co-chairperson on the Committee.

2. The Committee will encourage contacts between scientists, universities, and laboratories of the two nations.

3. The Committee each year shall develop and maintain a listing of joint activities to be carried out, and, as requested by the participating institutions and scientists, shall assist with arrangements for the listed activities. Items may be listed by consensus at meetings of the Committee, or, between meetings, by agreement of the co-chairpersons.

4. Each Party shall designate its members of the Committee within two months of the effective date of this Accord. The first meeting of the Committee should be held, if possible, within three months thereafter at an agreed site. Subsequently, the Committee shall meet in the United States and the People's Republic of China alternately at intervals of about 12 months or as agreed by the co-chairpersons.

5. The Committee shall be subject to the direction of the US–PRC Joint Commission on Scientific and Technological Cooperation established under the aforesaid Agreement of January 31, 1979, and shall periodically report the Status of its program to that Commission.

6. The Committee may assume other duties as mutually agreed by the Parties.

ARTICLE 5

The application or use of any information exchanged or transferred between the Parties under this Accord shall be the responsibility of the Party receiving it, and the transmitting Party does not warrant the suitability of such information for any particular use or application.

ARTICLE 6

The Parties recognize the need to agree upon provisions concerning protection of copyrights and treatment of inventions or discoveries made or conceived in the course of or under this Accord in order to facilitate specific activities hereunder. Accordingly, the Parties shall appoint experts in these two fields who shall separately recommend to the Parties detailed provisions which, if the Parties agree, shall be made an Annex to this Accord.

ARTICLE 7

Both Parties agree that in the event equipment is to be exchanged, or supplied by one Party to the other for use in cooperative activities, they shall enter into specific understandings on a case-by-case basis.

ARTICLE 8

1. Whenever an attachment of staff is contemplated under this Accord each Party shall ensure that staff with necessary skills and competence are selected for attachment to the other Party.

2. Each attachment of staff shall be the subject of an exchange of letters between the participating institutions, covering funding and other matters of interest not otherwise specified in this Accord.

3. Each Party shall provide all necessary assistance to the attached staff (and their families) of the other Party as re-

gards administrative formalities, travel arrangements and accommodations.

4. The staff of each Party shall conform to the general rules of work and safety regulations in force at the host establishment, or as agreed in separate attachment of staff agreements.

ARTICLE 9

1. All questions related to this Accord or activities carried out hereunder shall be settled by mutual agreement of the Parties.

2. Each Party will accept liability to the extent authorized by its national laws for damages arising from cooperative activities under this Accord.

ARTICLE 10

1. This Accord shall enter into force upon signature, and, unless terminated earlier in accordance with paragraph 2 of this Article, shall remain in force for a five-year period. It may be amended or extended by mutual agreement of the Parties.

2. This Accord may be terminated at any time at the discretion of either Party, upon 6 months advance notification in writing by the Party seeking to terminate the Accord.

3. The termination of this Accord shall not affect the validity or duration of specific activities being undertaken hereunder.

DONE at Washington this 31st day of January, 1979, in duplicate in the English and Chinese languages, both equally authentic.

For the Department of Energy of the United States of America:

JAMES R. SCHLESINGER

For the State Scientific and Technological Commission of the People's Republic of China:

FANG YI

NOTE: Secretary of Energy Schlesinger and Vice Premier Fang signed the texts of the accord at the ceremony in the East Room at the White House prior to the signing of the science and technology agreement by the President and the Vice Premier.

Visit of Vice Premier Deng of China

Cultural Agreement Between the United States and China. January 31, 1979

CULTURAL AGREEMENT BETWEEN THE GOVERNMENT OF THE UNITED STATES OF AMERICA AND THE GOVERNMENT OF THE PEOPLE'S REPUBLIC OF CHINA

The Government of the United States of America and the Government of the People's Republic of China,

Noting with satisfaction that better understanding between the peoples of both countries has been brought about through contacts and exchanges in culture, arts, humanities, journalism, sports, and other fields;

For the purpose of promoting wider contacts between the two peoples in the interest of consolidating and developing friendly relations between the two countries, and enhancing mutual understanding through encouraging and promoting cultural exchanges between the two countries in the spirit of the Joint Communique on the Establishment of Diplomatic Relations between the United States of America and the People's Republic of China and on the basis of the principles of equality, reciprocity and mutual benefit;

Have agreed as follows:

ARTICLE I

The two governments will encourage a deeper knowledge of their respective histories, cultures, literatures, arts, languages, sports and other areas including attention to general knowledge in addition to more specialized study. Through cooperative programs as well as exchanges, the two governments will promote and assist their respective efforts to this end.

ARTICLE II

The two governments will encourage and facilitate further development of contacts and exchanges between the peoples of the two countries, including but not limited to interchanges between representatives of professional groups, cultural organizations, news and public information organizations, radio and television organizations and academic institutions and persons on the basis of shared interests.

ARTICLE III

The two governments will encourage, through mutually agreed programs and exchanges, enhanced understanding between the two peoples. Programs and activities to further this objective may include, but would not be limited to, the publication and distribution of books, magazines, and other printed materials; production and dissemination of films, recordings, and other audio-visual materials; as well as exhibitions relating to history, culture, arts and contemporary life; presentations of musical, dramatic and dance performances; and sports. In order to make such presentations and materials more readily understood in the other country, each government will encourage the development of activities such as translation programs.

ARTICLE IV

The two governments will encourage the broadest participation and support by non-governmental as well as governmental institutions for programs and activities covered by this Agreement.

ARTICLE V

On behalf of the Government of the United States of America, the Executive Agency for this Agreement shall be the International Communication Agency; on behalf of the Government of the People's Republic of China, the Executive Agency for this Agreement shall be the Ministry of Culture of the People's Republic of China.

The two Executive Agencies shall communicate with one another to review and assist in the implementation of this Agreement and may meet periodically as they may agree. They may reach understandings with one another regarding specific programs for agreed periods of time, which will guide the implementation of this Agreement.

The two Executive Agencies will encourage and facilitate, as appropriate, the development of contacts and cooperation between government agencies, institutions of higher learning, research institutes and other entities of the two countries and the conclusion of agreements between such bodies for mutually beneficial activities.

ARTICLE VI

This Agreement shall come into force on the date of signature for a period of five years. It shall be automatically renewed for another five years unless one of the governments gives written notice of termination to the other at least six months prior to the expiration of the period, and shall be renewable accordingly thereafter.

Done at Washington this 31st day of January, 1979, in duplicate in the English and Chinese languages, both equally authentic.

For the Government of the United States of America:

JIMMY CARTER

For the Government of the People's Republic of China:

DENG XIAOPING

Visit of Vice Premier Deng of China

Agreement Between the United States and China on Consular Relations and Consulates General. January 31, 1979

AGREEMENT BETWEEN THE GOVERNMENT OF THE UNITED STATES OF AMERICA AND THE GOVERNMENT OF THE PEOPLE'S REPUBLIC OF CHINA ON THE MUTUAL ESTABLISHMENT OF CONSULAR RELATIONS AND THE OPENING OF CONSULATES GENERAL

The Government of the United States of America and the Government of the People's Republic of China agree to establish consular relations, open consular offices by each side in the other's territory, promote the well-being of each side's citizens in the other's territory, and foster family reunion, tourism, commercial, scientific-technological, cultural and other relations between the peoples of the United States and China. The Government of the United States of America agrees to the opening of Consulates General by the Government of the People's Republic of China in San Francisco and Houston. The Government of the People's Republic of China agrees to the opening of Consulates General by the Government of the United States of America in Guangzhou and Shanghai. For practical arrangements, see Annex. These Consulates General will be opened at mutually agreed times in the future.

DONE at Washington this 31st day of January, 1979, in duplicate in the English and Chinese languages, both equally authentic.

For the Government of the United States of America:

CYRUS R. VANCE

For the Government of the People's Republic of China:

HUANG HUA

ANNEX ON PRACTICAL ARRANGEMENTS

The Government of the United States of America and the Government of the People's Republic of China agree that consular relations will be conducted on a basis of reciprocity and mutual benefit and in accordance with the general principles and practice of international law. In the event of disagreements, both governments undertake to resolve them through consultations in a spirit of mutual understanding and cooperation, drawing on the principles of customary international law embodied in the Vienna Convention on Consular Relations of 1963.

Pending entry into force of a Consular Agreement to be negotiated, the two sides agree to the following interim practical arrangements:

1. The two governments agree to facilitate the reunion of families and will process all applications as quickly as possible under mutually agreed arrangements and in accordance with each side's laws and regulations.

2. The two governments agree to facilitate travel between their respective countries of persons who may claim simultaneously the nationality of the United States of America and the nationality of

the People's Republic of China. Exit formalities and documentation shall be dealt with in accordance with the laws of the country in which the person concerned resides. Entry formalities and documentation shall be dealt with in accordance with the laws of the country to which the person concerned wishes to travel.

3. United States citizens entering the People's Republic of China on the basis of United States travel documents containing Chinese entry visas will, during the period for which their status has been accorded, and in accordance with the visa's validity, be considered United States nationals by the appropriate Chinese authorities for the purpose of ensuring consular access and protection. Such persons shall have the right of departure from the People's Republic of China without further documentation, regardless of whether they may also be regarded as citizens of the People's Republic of China, nor shall they lose the right of consular protection or the right of departure without further documentation if the period of validity for which the status has been accorded has expired during the course of judicial or administrative proceedings which prevent their earlier departure.

4. Citizens of the People's Republic of China entering the United States using travel documents of the People's Republic of China containing United States entry visas will, during the period for which their status has been accorded, and in accordance with the visa's validity, be considered nationals of the People's Republic of China by the appropriate United States authorities for the purpose of ensuring consular access and protection. Such persons shall have the right of departure from the United States without

further documentation, regardless of whether they may also be regarded as citizens of the United States, nor shall they lose the right of consular protection or the right of departure without further documentation if the period of validity for which the status has been accorded has expired during the course of judicial or administrative proceedings which prevent their earlier departure.

5. If a citizen of the sending country is arrested or detained in any manner, the authorities of the receiving country shall, without delay, notify the consular post or embassy accordingly of the arrest or detention of the person and permit access by a consular officer of the sending state to the citizen who is under arrest or detained in custody.

6. Persons residing in the People's Republic of China who are entitled to receive financial benefits from the Government of the United States of America shall receive their benefits under mutually agreed arrangements and in accordance with each side's laws and regulations.

7. Persons residing in the United States of America who are entitled to receive financial benefits from the Government of the People's Republic of China shall receive their benefits under mutually agreed arrangements and in accordance with each side's laws and regulations.

8. In addition to consular offices whose opening has already been agreed upon, the two sides agree to discuss the opening of consular offices in other cities as the need arises.

NOTE: Secretary of State Vance and Chinese Foreign Minister Huang signed the texts of the agreement prior to the signing of the cultural and science and technology agreements by the President and the Vice Premier.

Visit of Vice Premier Deng of China

Remarks Following the Signing of Agreements Between the United States and the People's Republic of China. January 31, 1979

THE PRESIDENT. *Mr. Vice Premier, American and Chinese friends:*

What we have accomplished in the last 3 days is truly exceptional. But our aim is to make this kind of exchange between our countries no longer the exception, but the norm; no longer a matter of headlines and historians, but a routine part of the everyday lives of both the Chinese and the American people. With the signing of these agreements, we have begun to do just exactly that.

After too many eras in which one or the other of our nations has sought to dominate the relations between us, China and the United States of America are now meeting on a basis of equality, with full diplomatic relations. We've charted a new and irreversible course toward a firmer, more constructive, and a more hopeful relationship.

I have come to know Vice Premier Deng well in the hours we have spent together. He speaks his mind, and he values results. In our conversations about world affairs, we have found that we share many common perspectives. While we pursue independent foreign policies, our separate actions in many places can contribute to similar goals. These goals are a world of security and peace, a world of both diversity and stability, a world of independent nations free of outside domination.

Both our countries have a special interest in promoting the peace and prosperity of the people of East Asia. We have agreed to consult regularly on matters of common global interest. The security concerns of the United States do not coincide completely, of course, with those of China, nor does China share our responsibilities. But a strong and secure China which contributes constructively to world affairs is in our interest, and a globally engaged, confident, and strong America is, obviously, in China's interest.

The agreements that we have just signed for cultural, scientific and technological exchanges, and for consular arrangements will bring the tangible benefits of normalization to increasing numbers of both our peoples. We look forward to an early settlement of the issue of claims and assets, to the reunification of families, to expanded tourism, and to the development of a healthy and a vigorous trading relationship between our countries.

In the near future, because of these agreements, American consulates will open in Shanghai and Guangzhou, and Chinese consulates will open in Houston and San Francisco. Hundreds of American students will study and will learn in China, and hundreds of Chinese students will further their education in the United States.

Our National Aeronautics and Space Administration, NASA, will launch a civilian communications satellite, paid for by China, that will bring color television and expanded communications to all of the people of China for the first time.

Mr. Vice Premier, your stay in Washington is nearly over, but your trip to the United States has just begun. You leave tomorrow for three of the most interesting cities in our country: Atlanta, Houston, and Seattle. You will see something of the way Americans work and live.

And as you travel from one end of our country to the other, I think you will find that the American people are eager to get to know you and to join in building the new relationship between our two countries.

You leave Washington with many new friends, and you will return to China with a great many more. And when you return to your homeland, I hope that you will convey my best wishes to Premier Hua Guofeng and to the people of China.

THE VICE PREMIER. *Mr. President and Mrs. Carter, ladies and gentlemen:*

First of all, allow me to express my thanks to you, Mr. President, for the many friendly words which you have just said with regard to developing the relations of friendship and cooperation between our two countries and two peoples. We have just done a significant job. But this is not the end, but a beginning.

We anticipated that following the normalization of relations, there would be a rapid development of friendly cooperation between our two countries in many broad fields. The agreements we have just signed are the first fruits of our endeavors. There are many more areas of bilateral cooperation and many more channels waiting for us to develop. We have to continue our efforts.

It is my belief that extensive contacts and cooperation among nations and increased interchanges and understanding between peoples will make the world we live in more safe, more stable, and more peaceful.

Therefore, the work we have just done is not only in the interests of the Chinese and American peoples but of the peoples of the world as well. It is with these remarks that I mark the signing of the agreement between China and the United States on scientific and technological cooperation, the cultural agreements, and other documents.

Finally, I would like once again to express sincere thanks to Mr. President and Mrs. Carter for your very warm and kind reception which you have given us in Washington. And I look forward to meeting with Mr. President and Mrs. Carter in the near future in China.

NOTE: The President spoke at 4:40 p.m. at the signing ceremony in the East Room at the White House. The Vice Premier spoke in Chinese, and his remarks were translated by an interpreter.

Visit of Vice Premier Deng of China

Joint Press Communique. February 1, 1979

At the invitation of the President of the United States of America and Mrs. Carter, the Vice-Premier of the State Council of the People's Republic of China Deng Xiaoping and Madame Zhuo Lin are on an official visit to the United States which lasts from January 29 to February 4, 1979. Vice-Premier Deng and President Carter held talks on questions of mutual interest in Washington. Accompanying Vice-Premier Deng in the talks were Vice-Premier Fang Yi, Foreign Minister Huang Hua and others. Accompanying President Carter in the talks were Vice President Mondale, Secretary of State Cyrus Vance, Assistant to the President for National Security Affairs Zbigniew Brzezinski and others.

The talks were cordial, constructive and fruitful. The two sides reviewed the international situation and agreed that in many areas they have common interests and share similar points of view. They also discussed those areas in which they have differing perspectives. They reaffirm that they are opposed to efforts by any country or group of countries to establish hegemony or domination over others, and that they are determined to make a contribution to the maintenance of international peace, security and national independence. The two sides consider that the difference in their social systems should not constitute an obstacle to their strengthening friendly relations and cooperation. They are resolved to work toward this end, and they firmly believe that such cooperation is in the interest of their two peoples and also that of peace and stability in the world and the Asia-Pacific region in particular.

Vice-Premier Deng Xiaoping on behalf of the Government of the People's Republic of China and President Carter on behalf of the United States Government signed an Agreement on Cooperation in Science and Technology and a Cultural Agreement. Vice-Premier Fang Yi and the President's Science Adviser Frank Press signed and exchanged letters of understanding on cooperation between the two countries in education, agriculture and space. Vice-Premier Fang Yi and Secretary of Energy James Schlesinger signed an Accord between the two countries on Cooperation in the Field of High Energy Physics. Foreign Minister Huang Hua and Secretary of State Cyrus Vance signed an Agreement on the Mutual Establishment of Consular Relations and the Opening of Consulates General in each other's country.

Each side agreed to facilitate the accreditation of resident journalists by the other side.

The two sides agreed to conclude trade, aviation, and shipping agreements. These will be discussed during the visits to the People's Republic of China by Secretary of the Treasury Michael Blumenthal and Secretary of Commerce Juanita Kreps.

On behalf of the Chinese Government and Premier Hua Guofeng, Vice-Premier Deng Xiaoping extended an invitation to President Carter to visit China at a time convenient to him. President Carter accepted this invitation. President Carter extended an invitation to Premier Hua Guofeng to visit the United States. Vice-Premier Deng Xiaoping accepted this invitation on behalf of Premier Hua Guofeng. The specific time for these visits by the top leaders of the two countries will be discussed and decided upon at a later time.

Presidential Commission on World Hunger

Appointment of Orville L. Freeman as a Member. February 1, 1979

The President today announced the appointment of Orville L. Freeman, of Ardley-on-Hudson, N.Y., as a member of the Presidential Commission on World Hunger.

Freeman, 60, was Secretary of Agriculture from 1961 to 1969. He is currently chief executive officer of Business International Corp. He is the author of "World Without Hunger" and numerous articles.

Red Cross Month, 1979

Proclamation 4636. February 1, 1979

By the President of the United States of America

A Proclamation

Since its founding in 1881, the American Red Cross has had one basic purpose: The concern for others in distress. Indicative of this concern is the fact that over five million people successfully completed Red Cross safety courses last year. Many of them received instructions in cardiopulmonary resuscitation and first aid techniques for choking. Exemplifying this concern is the Certificate of Merit, which is presented to our fellow Americans who have saved or sustained a human life with the skills learned in a Red Cross first aid, small craft or water safety training program. Since 1928, well over 6,000 persons have received this award.

The Red Cross also operates its Blood Services, which collects and processes half of the supply of blood needed by the Nation's medical facilities. Red Cross is continuously seeking new and more economical uses for blood and blood products. And there is always a need for more volunteer blood donors to meet the ever-increasing need for this lifesaving gift.

The Red Cross serves members of the armed forces, their families and veterans through financial assistance, counselling and emergency communications. Thousands of disaster victims each year receive a variety of Red Cross services, including emergency food, shelter and clothing, first aid and medical help, replacement of occupational tools and other vital services.

And Red Cross volunteers may be found each day performing compassionate, personal tasks to aid the elderly, the handicapped and the homebound. Young people develop leadership skills as they assist in Red Cross programs in their schools and communities.

Each year, March is observed as Red Cross Month. Although the American Red Cross works closely with government, there are no Federal funds appropriated for its support. The Red Cross depends upon the American people for membership and voluntary contributions to carry out the functions of its Congressional Charter.

Now, THEREFORE, I, JIMMY CARTER, President of the United States of America and Honorary Chairman of the American Red Cross, designate March 1979, as Red Cross Month. I urge all Americans to give generous support to the work of their local Red Cross chapter.

IN WITNESS WHEREOF, I have hereunto set my hand this first day of February, in the year of our Lord nineteen hundred seventy-nine, and of the Independence of the United States of America the two hundred and third.

JIMMY CARTER

[Filed with the Office of the Federal Register, 2:31 p.m., February 1, 1979]

Red Cross Month, 1979

Memorandum From the President. February 1, 1979

Memorandum for the Heads of Executive Departments and Agencies

I have just signed a Presidential Proclamation designating the month of March as Red Cross Month.

For almost 100 years the American people have been counting on the Red Cross for disaster relief, the collection and distribution of blood, services to members of the armed forces, their families and veterans, first aid and water safety instruction and a wide variety of community health programs.

There are three things we can do to help the Red Cross during March:

1. Become a Red Cross volunteer

2. Donate blood

3. Support our Red Cross chapter's membership enrollment efforts.

The Red Cross is a part of the Combined Federal Campaign for Federal employees, but more than half of its 3,000 chapters raise all their funds in March. All chapters use the month to inform the public of Red Cross services available to citizens and to recruit new blood donors and volunteers.

As President of the United States and Honorary Chairman of the American Red Cross, I urge all civilian employees of the Federal government and members of the armed forces to support this vital voluntary effort to the best of their ability.

JIMMY CARTER

United States Postal Service

Nomination of Two Governors.
February 1, 1979

The President today announced two persons whom he will nominate as Governors of the United States Postal Service. They are:

Richard R. Allen, of Fayetteville, N.C. Allen, 47, is president of D. R. Allen & Son, Inc., a construction company in Fayetteville. He is a professional engineer and general contractor.

George W. Camp of Roswell, Ga. Camp, 58, worked for the Postal Service from 1957 until his retirement in 1978. He has served as Postmaster of the Atlanta Post Office, District Manager-Postmaster of the Atlanta District, and Regional Director of the Customer Services Department.

United States Ambassador to Malta

Nomination of Joan M. Clark.
February 2, 1979

The President today announced that he will nominate Joan M. Clark, of Great Neck, N.Y., to be Ambassador Extraordinary and Plenipotentiary of the United States to the Republic of Malta. She would replace Lowell B. Laingen, who has been reassigned.

Clark was born March 27, 1922, in Ridgefield Park, N.J. She attended Katherine Gibbs School in New York.

She began her career with the Foreign Service in 1945 as a clerk, then administrative assistant, in Berlin. She was economic assistant in London from 1951 to 1953 and administrative assistant in Belgrade from 1953 to 1957. From 1957 to 1962, she served at the State Department as a placement officer, then administrative officer.

From 1962 to 1968, Clark was administrative officer in Luxembourg. In 1968–69, she was coordinator for administrative training at the State Department's School of Professional Studies. From 1969 to 1971, she was personnel officer, then administrative officer, at the Bureau of Inter-American Affairs at the State Department.

From 1971 to 1977, Clark served in the Bureau of European Affairs, as Deputy Executive Director, then Executive Director. Since 1977 she has been Director of the State Department's Office of Management Operations.

Comprehensive Test Ban Negotiations

Accordance of the Personal Rank of Ambassador to Herbert F. York, Head of the U.S. Delegation. February 2, 1979

The President today announced that he has accorded the personal rank of Ambassador to Dr. Herbert F. York while he serves as Head of the U.S. Delegation to the Comprehensive Test Ban Negotiations which are scheduled to begin February 5 in Geneva.

York was born November 24, 1921, in Rochester, N.Y. He received a B.A. (1942) and M.S. (1943) from the University of Rochester and a Ph. D. from the University of California at Berkeley in 1949.

York was with Berkeley from 1943 to 1958, as a physicist in the radiation laboratory, a professor of physics and, from 1952 to 1958, director of the Lawrence Radiation Laboratory, Livermore.

From 1958 to 1961, York was Director of Defense Research and Engineering in the Office of the Secretary of Defense. Since 1961 he has been with the University of California at San Diego. He has been a professor of physics there since 1964, and has also served as chancellor, as dean of graduate studies, and as director of the program on science, technology and public affairs.

Energy Use by the Federal Government

Memorandum From the President.
February 2, 1979

Memorandum for the Heads of Executive Departments and Agencies

Subject: Reduction of Energy Use by the Federal Government

Because of the world shortfall in oil production resulting from the Iranian situation, I am directing that executive departments and establishments take immediate steps to reduce the use of petroleum fuels. For this purpose, all agency heads should establish goals, prepare plans and issue necessary instructions to implement them. The specific actions that agency heads can take include, but are not limited to, the following:

• Lowering thermostat settings in Federally owned and operated buildings to not more than 65 degrees during the day and 55 degrees during the night.

• Reducing electrical use generally throughout agency activities, particularly lighting.

• Reducing petroleum use by eliminating unnecessary activities and vehicle trips and combining and consolidating the essential ones.

• Reducing agency activities that use large amounts of energy and could be deferred, such as research and experimental activities that involve the use of highly energy intensive equipment.

In addition, I urge all agency heads aggressively to pursue employee awareness programs on energy conservation, and to promote employee use of carpools and mass transit.

Agency heads should submit their goals and instructions for implementation to the Secretary of Energy by February 15, 1979. Agencies which currently submit quarterly reports on energy consumption to the Department of Energy should include in their FY 1979 second quarter report a statement showing energy savings accomplished from this special effort.

Department of Defense operational readiness activities are exempt from this directive.

JIMMY CARTER

Digest of Other White House Announcements

The following listing includes the President's public schedule and other items of general interest announced by the White House Press Office and not included elsewhere in this issue.

January 28

The President returned to the White House from Camp David, Md.

January 29

The President met at the White House with:
—Zbigniew Brzezinski, Assistant to the President for National Security Affairs;
—Frank B. Moore, Assistant to the President for Congressional Liaison;
—Vice President Walter F. Mondale.

The President, acting upon the recommendation of the Department of Justice, commuted the 7-year sentence of Patricia Campbell Hearst to a term of 2 years, 4 months, and 10 days, which will effect her immediate release on February 1, 1979, because of good time allowances earned.

January 30

The President met at the White House with:
—Dr. Brzezinski;
—Mr. Moore;
—A. Daniel O'Neal, Chairman of the Interstate Commerce Commission;
—James T. McIntyre, Jr., Director of the Office of Management and Budget.

In a ceremony in the Oval Office, the President presented the first annual Women's Caucus for Art awards for "Outstanding Achievement in the Visual Arts" to painters Isabel Bishop and Alice Neel and sculptors Louise Nevelson and Selma Burke. The fifth award recipient, painter Georgia O'Keeffe, was unable to attend the ceremony and was honored in absentia.

The President has declared a major disaster for the State of New Mexico as a result of flooding, beginning about December 19, 1978, which caused extensive public and private property damage.

January 31

The President met at the White House with:
—Dr. Brzezinski;

—Mr. Moore;
—the Democratic congressional leadership;
—Marjorie Bell Chambers, Acting Chair of the National Advisory Committee for Women;
—Vice President Mondale, Stansfield Turner, Director of Central Intelligence, Hamilton Jordan, Assistant to the President, and Dr. Brzezinski;
—Representative Jack Brooks of Texas;
—Vice President Mondale and Representative Al Ullman of Oregon.

The President transmitted to the Congress the annual report of the Office of Alien Property, Department of Justice.

February 1

The President met at the White House with:
—Dr. Brzezinski;
—Mr. Moore;
—Mrs. Carter and Gov. and Mrs. George Nigh of Oklahoma, for lunch;
—members of the Oklahoma State Legislature;
—Vice President Mondale and Senator Russell B. Long of Louisiana;
—Senator Richard Stone of Florida.

The President transmitted to the Congress the budget of the District of Columbia for fiscal year 1980.

In the evening the President participated in a foreign affairs briefing for a group of Senators.

February 2

The President met at the White House with Vice President Mondale, Secretary of State Cyrus R. Vance, Secretary of Defense Harold Brown, Dr. Brzezinski, and Mr. Jordan.

Following the memorial service for former Vice President Rockefeller, in New York City, the President went to Camp David, Md., for the weekend.

NOMINATIONS SUBMITTED
TO THE SENATE

The following list does not include promotions of members of the Uniformed Services, nominations to the Service Academies, or nominations of Foreign Service officers.

Submitted January 31, 1979

DALE ERNEST HATHAWAY, of the District of Columbia, to be Under Secretary of Agriculture for International Affairs and Commodity Programs (new position).

SIDNEY A. DIAMOND, of Arizona, to be an Assistant Commissioner of Patents and Trademarks, vice Bernard A. Meany, resigned.

The following-named persons to be members of the National Commission on Libraries and Information Science for terms expiring July 19, 1983:

FRANCIS KEPPEL, of Massachusetts, vice Daniel William Casey, Sr., term expired.

BESSIE BOEHM MOORE, of Arkansas (reappointment).

PHILIP A. SPRAGUE, of Indiana, vice Julia Li Wu, term expired.

MICHAEL KASHA, of Florida, to be a member of the National Science Board, National Science Foundation, for a term expiring May 10, 1984, vice Anna J. Harrison, term expired.

CHECKLIST OF WHITE HOUSE
PRESS RELEASES

The following listing contains releases of the White House Press Office which are not included in this issue.

CHECKLIST—Continued

Released January 29, 1979

List: attendees at the 11 a.m. meeting between the President and Vice Premier Deng Xiaoping in the Cabinet Room

Press announcement: the President's commutation of the sentence of Patricia Campbell Hearst—by Jody Powell, Press Secretary to the President

Announcement: the President's commutation of the sentence of Patricia Campbell Hearst

Advance text: toast of the President at the state dinner for the Vice Premier

Released January 30, 1979

List: attendees at the 9 a.m. meeting between the President and the Vice Premier in the Cabinet Room

Released January 31, 1979

Fact sheet: Rural Elderly Housing program

Advance text: remarks of the President on signing agreements between the United States and the People's Republic of China

---

ACTS APPROVED BY
THE PRESIDENT

NOTE: No acts approved by the President were received by the Office of the Federal Register during the period covered by this issue.

PRESIDENTIAL DOCUMENTS

Week Ending Friday, February 9, 1979

Save Your Vision Week, 1979

Proclamation 4637. February 5, 1979

By the President of the United States of America

A Proclamation

Good eyesight, like so many of life's blessings, is too often taken for granted. Today, millions of Americans must cope with the burden of impaired vision. In many of these cases, visual loss could have been prevented had only simple precautions been taken.

Through periodic eye examinations, for example, certain potentially blinding and disabling eye conditions can often be found in time to be cured or arrested. Regular eye examinations are particularly important for children who may not realize that their vision has been impaired. For some people who have already lost vision, sight can be restored through modern eye care. Special aids and magnifiers can frequently help the partially-sighted make the most of their remaining vision.

Besides taking advantage of professional eye care services, there is much we can do on our own to help save sight. We can protect our eyes from accidents at work and during recreational activities. We can encourage the sensible use of household products, appliances, and cosmetics and avoid abuse of drugs and alcohol. And we can be alert to the signs of eye problems among family and friends. With proper care and attention, more than half of the serious vision problems that affect both young and old can be prevented.

To focus the attention of all Americans on the importance of good vision, the Congress, by joint resolution approved December 30, 1963 (77 Stat. 629, 36 U.S.C. 169a), has requested the President to proclaim the first week of March of each year as Save Your Vision Week.

Now, THEREFORE, I, JIMMY CARTER, President of the United States of America, designate the week beginning March 4, 1979, as Save Your Vision Week. I urge all Americans to observe this period by considering what they can do to take care of their eyes and protect them from disease and injury. I invite vision care professionals, the communications media, educators, and all public and private organizations which support sight conservation to participate in activities which will teach Americans about eye care and encourage them to preserve or make the most of their vision.

IN WITNESS WHEREOF, I have hereunto set my hand this fifth day of February, in the year of our Lord nineteen hundred seventy-nine, and of the Independence of the United States of America the two hundred and third.

JIMMY CARTER

[Filed with the Office of the Federal Register, 2:55 p.m., February 5, 1979]

United States Ambassador to Jamaica

Nomination of Loren E. Lawrence.
February 5, 1979

The President today announced that he will nominate Loren E. Lawrence, of Bethesda, Md., to be Ambassador Extraordinary and Plenipotentiary of the United States to Jamaica. He would replace Frederick Irving, who has retired from the Foreign Service.

Lawrence was born January 26, 1926, in Hamilton, Kans. He attended Washington University. He served in the U.S. Army from 1944 to 1945 and 1947 to 1953.

He entered the Foreign Service in 1954 as special officer of the Refugee Relief Program in Rotterdam. He served as a consular officer in Hong Kong, Macao, and Tel Aviv. From 1966 to 1970, he was at the State Department as a personnel management specialist, then career management officer.

From 1970 to 1973, Lawrence was counselor for consular affairs in Manila. In 1973–74, he attended the senior seminar in foreign policy at the Foreign Service Institute. From 1974 to 1975, Lawrence was Deputy Director of Personnel for Management at the State Department, and from 1975 to 1976, he was

Deputy Administrator of the Bureau of Consular Affairs.

From 1976 to 1977, Lawrence was counselor for consular affairs in London. Since 1977 he has been Deputy Assistant Secretary of State for Passport Services.

Vice President Mondale's Visit to the Nordic Countries and the Netherlands

Statement Announcing the Trip.
February 5, 1979

At the invitation of the Governments of the Nordic countries and the Netherlands, Vice President Mondale will make official visits to Iceland, Denmark, Norway, Sweden, Finland, and the Netherlands in mid-April.

I have asked the Vice President to serve as my personal representative during these visits.

Close and cordial relations with all these nations are very important to us, and the Vice President's visit will reinforce them. We share a great deal in common, not only because we have the same democratic ideals and values but because of close ties of kinship and affection. Four of these nations—Iceland, Denmark, Norway, and the Netherlands—are NATO Allies, while two—Sweden and Finland—are neutral states whose independence we respect and with whom we cooperate on major international issues.

During the course of these visits the Vice President will review our excellent bilateral relations, current developments in Europe, developments in East-West relations, and other international issues of mutual interest.

NOTE: On the same day, the White House announced that Mrs. Joan Adams Mondale will accompany the Vice President on the trip.

Visit of Prime Minister Kriangsak Chomanan of Thailand

Remarks at the Welcoming Ceremony. February 6, 1979

THE PRESIDENT. It's a delight for me, on behalf of the people of the United States of America, to welcome back to our Nation a very distinguished international leader and a friend of our people, Prime Minister Kriangsak of the Kingdom of Thailand.

Our friendly relationships have been historically very important to our country. One hundred and forty-three years ago this month, for the first time with any nation in Asia, our country signed a treaty of peace with the people of Thailand, then known as Siam. This was the first peace treaty that we signed with any peoples of Asia. Since then, we've experienced years, even generations of friendship, growth, and change. And throughout all these years—sometimes years of testing and trial—the friendship between our two countries has been very valuable to the people of the United States.

We've been allies in times of peace and war. Our distinguished visitor fought alongside American troops in Korea. And I understand from one of my staff members who recently visited your home, that on your private home walls, there are photographs of you and American GI's as one of the dear possessions in your personal life.

Our Nation is intensely interested and deeply committed to the integrity and to the freedom and the security of Thailand, that your borders stay inviolate. And as you well know, the bilateral commitment and the multilateral commitments made in the Manila Pact are the bases for our security agreements with you and with your people, Mr. Prime Minister.

You come here at a very important time, when your own region of the world is again witnessing conflict at your very shores and borders, a time of mutual concern. Following the visit of Vice Premier Deng of the People's Republic of China, my conversations with you will be very valuable to me and to the people of the Nation that I represent.

You come not only representing a great country but also the Association of Southeast Asian Nations, ASEAN countries, within which you are an acknowledged and respected leader.

We are very deeply interested in the independence and the security of the people of Southeast Asia. We believe in a stable system of governments, joined in peace, with independence of each nation preserved and inviolate.

So, in politics and in security affairs, our relationships have been of great mutual importance. In addition, economic interrelationships have been dear to our own people and to yours. Heavy American business investments and interests in Thailand have been very profitable for both our people.

We witness under your own benevolent administration, with great appreciation, a strong example of the preservation of human rights. Your country has, through great difficulty, welcomed and helped to care for 140,000 or more refugees. Our country has received a like number. And, as you know, this is important to the people of the United States, because our country is a nation originally formed by and built by refugees.

Later on this spring, in April, democratic elections will be held under your leadership to establish a parliamentary form of government based on the principles of democracy. And the improvements in your judicial system and in the general benevolent attitude toward the

221

rights of individuals have indeed been an inspiration to us all.

So, Mr. Prime Minister, we welcome you, your beautiful wife, your son, your daughter, your political party representatives to our country.

After frequent visits to our Nation, you have made many friends in the past who welcome you here today. And I have no doubt that this visit will let you depart from our Nation, after an extensive tour, with a large number of new friends for you, your family, and the people of your great nation.

Welcome to the United States, Prime Minister Kriangsak.

THE PRIME MINISTER. *Mr. President, Mrs. Carter, friends, ladies and gentlemen:*

This is for us an auspicious day. On behalf of my colleagues, I want to thank you for this warm and generous welcome. It is a special pleasure to return to a country which has so many close ties with Thailand and so many happy associations for me, personally.

We in Thailand look at our relationship with the United States as something special. Like you, we cherish our independence, our freedom, and our way of life. Our nations have worked side by side to advance these cherished beliefs in Southeast Asia and throughout the world. Our ties are based on mutual interest and respect, and our peoples have benefited from our common endeavors. I am confident that they will persist.

But our relations transcend politics. Some 100,000 of my countrymen have attended schools and universities in the United States. Our peoples also retain close ties with Americans through professional associations, business partnerships, and frequent travel.

Throughout these contacts and shared experiences, the links between our peoples are firm and progressive. Most importantly, our peoples get along well together. We Thais enjoy your openness and informality. On our part, while I cannot say we outdo your famous Southern hospitality, Americans seem to feel at home with us.

The nations of Southeast Asia have witnessed many dramatic events during the past few years. I regret that the peace and stability that we long for in Southeast Asia has not yet been established. The killing still goes on. While the present situation has dangers, we are confident that the strength and the resiliency of the Thai people will enable us to withstand all challenges.

We also know that we have the support and encouragement of the United States and most other countries of the world. Both the material and moral strengths of the United States are vital to the peace of the world.

The Thai people are pleased with your continuing recognition that the peace and well-being of Asia is of vital interest to the United States, and with your determination to continue to play an active role in the region. We believe such an active and constructive American presence is essential if we are to achieve peace and continue with our political and economic development.

We appreciate your commitment to the security of Thailand. Your response to the unfortunate developments in Kampuchea is evidence of your concern and your values. For its part, Thailand has tried hard to improve relationships with all our neighbors, based on the principle of mutual respect, territorial integrity, and noninterference.

Elementary prudence requires us to improve our own defenses. We will rely on the strength of our own people, but we will need your cooperation in improving our military deterrent. But we also recognize that the security of Thailand depends on more than weapons. It rests, also importantly, on national unity, based on a just and prosperous society and on long-held Thai values.

We are working hard to move closer to such a society. We will devote major efforts and resources to improving the lot of our poorer farmers. We will protect our unique historical and cultural patterns as we protect the rights of our citizens. We have maintained our humanitarian principles and have granted asylum to large numbers of Indochinese refugees.

My own experience is illustrative of the special relationship which exists between our nations and the warm bonds which mark personal relations between Thais and Americans.

With a number of my colleagues here, I fought with your forces under the united flag in Korea—the United Command Flag in Korea. For 30 years I have worked closely and intimately with the officials of your country in numerous common endeavors. I, personally, am grateful to the doctors and the nurses at Walter Reed Hospital, surely one of the world's great medical centers.

Our ties with America are simply unique. My colleagues and I look forward to our meeting with you, Mr. President. We look forward to renewing old friendships and forging new ones with the American people.

In the years ahead, I am confident that with your encouragement and support, our two countries will build on the strong foundation of friendship to enhance and develop new areas for mutual cooperation. My colleagues and I humbly dedicate our visit to this cause.

Mr. President, thank you for receiving us so warmly. Although this is our first meeting, we feel we are among close friends. We look forward with great anticipation to what I know will be a warm and successful visit.

Thank you.

NOTE: The President spoke at 10:38 a.m. on the South Lawn of the White House.

Convention on the Prevention of Marine Pollution

Message to the Senate Transmitting Proposed Amendments to the Convention. February 6, 1979

To the Senate of the United States:

I transmit herewith, for the advice and consent of the Senate to acceptance, proposed amendments to the Convention on the Prevention of Marine Pollution by Dumping of Wastes and Other Matter, done at Washington, London, Mexico City and Moscow December 29, 1972 (the Convention). These amendments provide procedures for peaceful settlement of disputes arising under the Convention. The report of the Department of State is enclosed for the information of the Senate.

Since entering into force in 1975 this Convention has provided an important focus for international concern about the protection and effective management of our oceans and for practical and constructive actions by Parties in the control of marine pollution. These amendments will make the Convention even more effective. I recommend that the Senate give prompt consideration to them and advise and consent to their acceptance.

JIMMY CARTER

The White House,
February 6, 1979.

Organization for Economic Cooperation and Development

Nomination of John P. Lewis for the Rank of Minister While Serving as Chairman of the Development Assistance Committee. February 6, 1979

The President today announced that he will nominate John P. Lewis, of Princeton, N.J., for the rank of Minister during his service as Chairman of the Development Assistance Committee of the U.S. Mission to the Organization for Economic Cooperation and Development (OECD).

Lewis, 57, has been Chairman of the Committee since 1978. He was a professor of economics and international affairs at Princeton University from 1969 to 1978 and has also served on the faculty of Indiana University. From 1964 to 1969, he was Minister-Director of the USAID Mission to India.

Imports From Uganda

Executive Order 12117. February 6, 1979

By the authority vested in me as President by the Constitution of the United States of America, and in order to provide for the consistent implementation of import restrictions imposed against Uganda by Section 5(c) of the Act of October 10, 1978 (92 Stat. 1051), it is hereby ordered as follows:

1–101. The Secretary of the Treasury shall administer those provisions of Section 5(c) of the Act of October 10, 1978 (Public Law 95–435; 92 Stat. 1051; 22 U.S.C. 2151 note) which prohibit a corporation, institution, group or individual from importing, directly or indirectly, into the United States or its territories or possessions any article grown, produced, or manufactured in Uganda. The Secretary

of the Treasury shall issue such regulations that the Secretary deems necessary to implement those import restrictions. Prior to issuing those regulations the Secretary of the Treasury shall consult with the Secretary of State.

1–102. The Secretary of State shall advise the President whenever the Secretary believes that "the Government of Uganda is no longer committing a consistent pattern of gross violations of human rights" within the meaning of Section 5(c) of the Act of October 10, 1978.

1–103. If the President determines that the Government of Uganda is no longer committing a consistent pattern of gross violations of human rights, he shall so certify to the Congress. Thereafter, the Secretary of the Treasury shall revoke the regulations issued pursuant to this Order.

JIMMY CARTER

The White House,
    February 6, 1979.

[Filed with the Office of the Federal Register, 11:44 a.m., February 7, 1979]

Administration of Security Assistance Programs

Executive Order 12118. February 6, 1979

By the authority vested in me as President of the United States of America by Section 621 of the Foreign Assistance Act of 1961, as amended (22 U.S.C. 2381), and Section 301 of Title 3 of the United States Code, in order to delegate certain responsibilities to the Secretary of State and the Secretary of Defense and to reserve others to the President, it is hereby ordered as follows:

1–101. Section 201(a) of Executive Order No. 10973, as amended, relating to the administration of foreign assistance, is further amended by deleting "(except chapter 4 thereof)" and inserting in lieu thereof "(except chapters 4 and 6 thereof)".

1–102. In Section 201 of Executive Order No. 10973, as amended, a new subsection (c) is added as follows:

"(c) Those functions under Section 634A of the Act, to the extent that they relate to notifications to the Congress concerning changes in programs under Part II of the Act (except chapters 4 and 6 thereof), subject to prior consultation with the Secretary of State.".

1–103. Section 201(d) of Executive Order No. 10973, as amended, is revoked.

1–104. Section 203(a) of Executive Order No. 10973, as amended, is further amended to read as follows:

"(a) Those under Section 502B of the Act.".

1–105. Section 401(c) of Executive Order No. 10973, as amended, is further amended by adding "515(f)," immediately after "506(a)," and by deleting "634(c), 663(a), and 669(b)(1)" and inserting in lieu thereof "633A, 663(a), 669(b)(1), and 670(b)(1)".

1–106. Section 401(g) of Executive Order No. 10973, as amended, is revised to read as follows:

"(g) Those under Section 607 of the Foreign Assistance and Related Programs Appropriations Act, 1979 (92 Stat. 1591), with respect to findings.".

1–107. Executive Order No. 11958 of January 18, 1977, entitled "Administration of Arms Export Controls," is amended in Section 1(a) by deleting "(c)(3) and (c)(4)" and inserting in lieu thereof "(c)(3), (c)(4), and (f)".

JIMMY CARTER

The White House,
    February 6, 1979.

[Filed with the Office of the Federal Register, 11:51 a.m., February 7, 1979]

Visit of Prime Minister Kriangsak of Thailand

Toasts at the State Dinner. February 6, 1979

THE PRESIDENT. *Prime Minister Kriangsak, Mrs. Virat, all the distinguished guests from Thailand, and our friends from throughout our country:*

First of all, let me say that it's a great honor for me to welcome all of you guests to the White House and, particularly, our honored guest, who comes here representing a great nation and a great people.

This is the first time since 1968 that we've had a Prime Minister from Thailand come as an honored and official guest to visit the White House. And I think it was in 1967 that King Phumiphol came here with Her Majesty, the Queen, to visit the President.

So, this is indeed a rare pleasure and a long overdue visit, Mr. Prime Minister, on your part, to the White House, to pay homage to the friendship that has existed between our two countries for more than 150 years.

As I mentioned today in my welcoming remarks, the first nation in Asia with whom the United States signed a treaty of peace was with the people of Thailand, then known as Siam, in 1833, February 1833, 145—146 years ago. And we are very deeply grateful for the tremendous benefits that have accrued to our country from this long relationship between our people.

Thailand has been a country with very sound judgment, wisdom among the leaders—not always perfect, but close to it.

In 1861, for instance, King Rama was not very well advised. He offered to give a fleet of elephants to then President Lincoln to help expedite the end of the War Between the States. [*Laughter*] Fortunately for the South, President Lincoln did not accept the gift—[*laughter*]—

225

otherwise, the North might have won the war—[*laughter*]—and because of the elephants, President Lincoln might even have become a Republican. [*Laughter*]

I want to say that we have enjoyed this visit. And since I've been in office, I've tried to continue the goal of our Nation to establish very close and friendly relationships with the people of Asia.

We've been commenting lately that for the first time, certainly in my memory, we now have a close friendship, personally and officially, with the great nations of Asia—with India, Japan, China, as well as the rapidly growing economic organization known as the ASEAN countries. Thailand is certainly one of those leaders.

But when you travel down the coast of Asia, the Western Pacific, Eastern Asia, we have growing friendships with that extremely important region.

We've recently concluded a new base agreement with the Philippines, and I think that the recent visit of Vice Premier Deng Xiaoping has been, perhaps, one of the most notable occurrences, certainly in my term as President. And the far-reaching historical effects of that change in relationships may, perhaps, be the most important development, historically speaking, during my own term in office.

And Prime Minister Kriangsak very early saw the advantages of this new relationship and expressed his public approval of this change which can help to provide increased opportunities for stability and peace throughout Eastern Asia.

At the same time, as the Prime Minister and I discussed today, we still retain our friendship, our allegiance, our trade, our cultural relationships with the people of Taiwan, and we believe that the security of Taiwan has not at all been weakened and the prospects for their future

peace and security may even have been enhanced.

We have strengthened our ties with Australia, New Zealand. So, I believe that in that region of the world, we have been making excellent progress.

I have benefited greatly from the sound advice and counsel of Prime Minister Kriangsak, both before he came here and obviously during this visit. He's a man who represents the political leadership of a great nation and a people who have long looked upon our country as intimate friends.

During the Korean war, under the auspices of the United Nations, the people of Thailand fought with us, and then Major Kriangsak was a bloodbrother, defending freedom alongside Americans. And this is still looked upon by him as one of the most notable experiences of his life.

We have come to value the principles that have been exemplified, without interruption, among the people of Thailand—a country dedicated to peace, a country dedicated to personal freedom, a country dedicated to the extension of their own beneficial influence among their neighboring nations, a nation that has never tried to dominate others and which has always been using its influence, again, to help preserve the independence of peoples and countries throughout the world.

Even during the time European colonialism was extended almost entirely throughout the Asian world, there was one nation that stayed free, and that was the people of Thailand. This shows a strength founded not on overwhelming military might, but on wisdom, justice, and the principles on which our own Nation was founded.

We are honored because we have found so much in common with the people of Thailand. And the security relationships, the political relationships, the economic relationships that have naturally come to be shared between our two people have been of intense value both to them, as expressed by the Prime Minister to me today, and obviously have been of great value to the people of our own country.

We are concerned about recent developments in Kampuchea, or Cambodia, the invasion of that country by their neighbors, the Vietnamese. We joined with Thailand and the other countries of the ASEAN region in the United Nations, in a proper way, to condemn this violation of international borders, again, not plotting against anyone, but expressing the concern that we feel very deeply and the concern of the overwhelming number of governments throughout the world about this threat to the peace of the region.

But again, Thailand stands like a rock, honored and respected by their historical friends and allies, also honored and respected even by their potential adversaries.

I read the biographies of the leaders of Thailand who came here today with the Prime Minister. And in almost every intimate and, I think, accurate biography that I read in preparation for the visit, there was a phrase that caught my eye, referring to intense, personal honesty or a total absence of fraud and corruption throughout the political career of those who serve Thailand.

So, the cleanness and the decency and the patriotism and the personal commitment to the service of one's fellow human beings is indeed a permeating characteristic of the Prime Minister and those who serve with him in this great country.

The name Thailand itself comes from "the land of freedom." And I'm very deeply honored tonight to share with you other Americans the role of host to the leaders of a great people.

I would like now to propose a toast: To His Majesty the King of Thailand, to Prime Minister Kriangsak, his family, and those who've come with him, and to the great and free people of the land of the free, Thailand.

THE PRIME MINISTER. *Mr. President, Mrs. Carter, distinguished guests and friends:*

We have been warmed and delighted by your welcome for me and my colleagues today, and we all wish to express our profound gratitude for the hospitality and friendliness we have encountered since our arrival. It is indeed a special occasion to be once again in the United States, where we have so many good friends and so many happy associations.

Earlier today, we had an opportunity to discuss together some matters of mutual concern and of vital importance for the future well-being of my country, of Southeast Asia, and, perhaps, of the world.

For the past 40 years, the United States has been the leader of the world. You have been in the forefront of scientific and technical developments. You have led the effort for a peaceful world. You have been a major moral force for human betterment which has intensified under the leadership of President Carter. The United States has been indispensable, Mr. President.

I'm pleased that you share our strong views about the importance of the American presence in Asia and the Pacific and the need for an active and constructive U.S. role in Southeast Asia. Such an American role and presence quite simply is needed if peace is to be strengthened and prosperity expanded. We, for our part, have been grateful for American help in protecting our security and expanding our economy.

I hope that I was able to give you and our American friends and colleagues an accurate picture of Thailand today. We are a proud but peace-loving people who cherish our traditional institutions and our way of life. Monarchy, Buddhism, and nation are all integral parts of the Thai fiber. In most of our domestic and foreign policy, we share with you a wide convergence of views and a strong mutuality of interests.

Our highest priority at home is to build a modern, just, and prosperous society and, at the same time, preserve that culture which defines our national identity. Toward that end, my government is concentrating on helping our poorer farmers and accelerating agricultural growth. I have named this year in Thailand the Year of the Farmer, and my government will do its utmost to give meaning to that phrase.

Like Americans, the Thai people recognize the importance of human rights and the connection between economic prosperity and the development of human potential.

Like you, we favor economic growth spurred by individual initiative. We also want to see American investment in Thailand. We need and welcome your businessmen. They can both serve themselves and serve the people of Thailand as well.

In foreign affairs, we seek to build stable friendships with all nations in Asia, based on mutual respect and noninterference without regard to ideology.

The establishment of relations between the United States and the people of the republic of China will be a major contribution to the peace and stability of Asia. Similarly, although we are small and less directly involved, we welcome your efforts to develop a more constructive relationship with the Soviet Union and to conclude a SALT agreement.

We live in an age where peace is indivisible and where peace is essential among the great powers.

One area of particular concern to Thailand is the continually troubled Indochina. Peace has not yet come. Cambodia, or Kampuchea, with which we have a long common border, remains beset by war. The tragic exodus of Indochina's refugees continues at even higher levels, and the burden has fallen most heavily on Thailand and Malaysia.

But here, also, your country has played an exemplary role. The Thai people do not expect anyone to solve our problems. That is our responsibility. And we are confident we will meet it. But we do need the understanding and cooperation of the international community and, most importantly, the commitment of the United States to help us deal with international problems which start beyond our borders but impact heavily on Thailand.

For this reason, we ask for your continued awareness and support in meeting the challenge to our common humanitarian principles posed by thousands of refugees arriving on our shores and those of other countries in Southeast Asia.

We ask your cooperation in helping us to purchase, on a timely basis, the means we need to defend ourselves. And we look to you as a friend and as the world's most advanced nation for the knowledge and technology to help advance the social welfare of our people. And that is all we ask.

Mr. President, Thailand and the United States have a long history of close friendship, common interests, and shared values. The United States helped Thailand in extraterritoriality, and you have consistently helped us maintain our integrity. No other nation has been as close to us these past 40 years, and no other nation's intentions and values do we hold in such high esteem.

We hope that this visit, together with Vice President Mondale's visit to Thailand in May of last year, will underscore to our people and to the rest of the world the determination of Thailand and the United States to continue to cooperate for peace and stability in Asia.

I and my colleagues wish to express our deepest thanks to you and Mrs. Carter and, through you, to all American people, for your hospitality, graciousness, and thoughtfulness for Thailand.

This is a very special occasion and we want to say simply how pleased my colleagues and I are.

Ladies and gentlemen, I would like you to join me in a toast: To the President of the United States.

NOTE: The President spoke at 9:30 p.m. in the State Dining Room at the White House.

In his opening remarks, he referred to Mrs. Khunying Virat Chomanan, the wife of the Prime Minister.

National Commission on the International Year of the Child, 1979

Appointment of Maria B. Cerda as a Member. February 7, 1979

The President today announced the appointment of Maria B. Cerda, of Chicago, Ill., as a member of the National Commission on the International Year of the Child, 1979.

Cerda, 44, is executive director of the Latino Institute in Chicago. She was a founding member of Aspira of Illinois and a member of the planning committee for the Conference of Puerto Ricans.

Small Business Conference Commission

Appointment of Six Members. February 7, 1979

The President today announced the appointment of six persons as members of the Small Business Conference Commission. They are:

ERNEST M. CAMACHO, of Montebello, Calif., an associate and consultant for Financial Kinetics Corp., a firm dealing with financial planning techniques;

TOM CHAN, of Chicago, president and chief executive officer of Chinese Noodle Co. and Chinese Trading Co. and other Chicago firms dealing with food preparation and restaurant supplies;

SHELDON B. LUBAR, of Milwaukee, president of Lubar & Co., an investment, management, and advisory company, and a former Assistant Secretary of Housing and Urban Development for Housing Production and Mortgage Credit;

LOUISE H. SAUNDERS, of Edina, Minn., a Minneapolis attorney and chairman of the board and president of Charlie's Cafe Exceptionale, Inc., a restaurant which employs over 160 persons;

DALE SIGHTS, of Robards, Ky., chairman and chief executive officer of Ohio Valley National Bank, formerly president of Sani-Clean Services, a family-owned business serving the textile rental industry;

A. MACEO WALKER, SR., of Memphis, Tenn., chairman of the board of Universal Life Insurance Co. and president of Memphis Mortgage Guaranty Co.

Visit of Prime Minister Kriangsak of Thailand

Joint Press Statement. February 7, 1979

At the invitation of the President of the United States of America and Mrs. Carter, the Prime Minister of the Kingdom of Thailand Kriangsak Chomanan and

Madame Khunying Virat Chomanan are visiting the United States officially during the period February 4 to February 16, 1979. In addition to Washington, D.C., the Prime Minister and his party will also extend his official travel to New York City, Los Angeles and Honolulu.

The Prime Minister is accompanied by Deputy Prime Minister Sunthorn Hongladarom, Foreign Minister Upadit Pachariyangkun, Minister of Interior General Lek Naeomali, Minister of Communications General Surakij Mayalarp, Minister Somporn Punyagupta, Minister of Industry Kasame Chatikavanij and other senior civilian and military officials of the Royal Thai Government. In Washington, the President and the Prime Minister met on February 6. Participants on the United States side included Vice President Mondale, Secretary of State Cyrus Vance, Secretary of Defense Harold Brown, Assistant to the President for National Security Affairs Zbigniew Brzezinski and others.

The President's invitation to the Prime Minister was extended last May by Vice President Mondale during his visit to Thailand and Southeast Asia.

PURPOSE AND SIGNIFICANCE

The President welcomed the Prime Minister recognizing particularly the long and close relations between the U.S. and Thailand. The two countries have had diplomatic contact for nearly a century and a half and the fabric of U.S. and Thai relations has been particularly close for over 30 years.

The visit enabled the two leaders to discuss directly recent events in Asia and Southeast Asia and the efforts of the two governments to pursue regional peace and stability. The President was able to hear first-hand views from one of the leaders of ASEAN, a dynamic organization recognized internationally as dedicated to peace, stability and economic growth in Southeast Asia. ASEAN has the active support of the U.S. as well as Japan, Australia, New Zealand, Canada, the EEC and other nations.

THE MEETINGS

The President reviewed the United States role as an Asian and Pacific power and noted recent developments, including the normalization of United States relations with China and the new agreement on U.S. bases in the Philippines, which contribute constructively to the future of the region.

The Prime Minister outlined his view of current developments in Indochina and the policies which the Thai Government is pursuing to support a peaceful system of independent states in the region, a goal which the United States shares. He welcomed U.S. relations with China as a positive contribution. Both the Prime Minister and the President agreed on the importance of an independent Cambodia to regional stability.

The President stated that the United States supports the integrity of Thailand both in terms of the historic US-Thai friendship as well as our interest in Thailand as a stable, secure and peaceful nation in Southeast Asia with an important role in regional peace and cohesion. He confirmed the continuing validity of U.S. commitments in the Manila Pact.

The Prime Minister stressed that Thailand's policies are based on self-reliance and independence. Foreign economic and military assistance are important, but must be complementary to Thailand's own policies and efforts.

Within the context of an ongoing military assistance program, the United States will expedite items of military equipment already ordered by Thailand and has increased military credits (FMS) for FY

1979. The U.S. will consider sympathetically new Thai requests. The President also stated Congressional authorization would be sought for the cost-free transfer to Thailand of $11.3 million of US-owned ammunition currently stored there.

The two leaders noted the success of Thailand's economic policies, its plan to continue rapid and equitable growth policies, and the dynamic aspects of the ASEAN region. The President was particularly impressed by the priority given to rural development during Thailand's 1979 "Year of the Farmer" and confirmed the continuing U.S. supplementary role in supporting the new Thai emphasis.

The Prime Minister welcomed the continuing economic interests of the United States and other nations in Thailand and ASEAN, particularly American investment and other business activities. He noted the favorable business climate offered by Thailand to foreign commerce and investment and discussed plans to improve the situation further. The President welcomed U.S. firms contributing to economic growth and trade with Thailand and hoped our business relations would expand as more American firms become aware of the opportunities in Thailand and the ASEAN region.

The Prime Minister of Thailand stressed the serious burdens in providing temporary shelter and care to Indochinese refugees. He urged the international community to take additional steps to ease the problem. The President appreciated the humanitarian policies of Thailand, outlined his commitment to a long-range systematic U.S. program of resettlement, and reviewed the continuing U.S. efforts with other nations to do more.

The President congratulated the Prime Minister on current progress to combat narcotics production and trafficking in and through Thailand, particularly the creation of innovative crop substitution programs. They agreed on the need for expanded cooperative efforts in this area of such importance to the United States and Thailand as well as other affected countries.

Prime Minister Kriangsak invited President Carter to visit Thailand. The President expressed pleasure and said he would seek a mutually convenient time.

National Council on the Humanities

Nomination of A. D. Frazier, Jr., To Be a Member. February 8, 1979

The President today announced that he will nominate A. D. Frazier, Jr., of Atlanta, Ga., to be a member of the National Council on the Humanities for the remainder of the term expiring January 26, 1982. He would replace John Hope Franklin, resigned.

Frazier, 34, is director of corporate planning for the Citizens and Southern National Bank. He is active in civic affairs in Atlanta and is a member of the National Municipal League Council and Development Committee.

National Poison Prevention Week, 1979

Proclamation 4638. February 8, 1979

By the President of the United States of America

A Proclamation

Since the first Poison Prevention Week was observed in 1962, we have seen a 75 percent drop in childhood accidental fatal poisonings, according to the latest figures from the National Center for Health Statistics.

Ingestions by youngsters of household products sold in safety packaging were down as well. But, because not all substances can be packaged safely, it is up to everyone responsible for child care to guard against these dangers in the way we store, handle, and dispose of potentially hazardous household products.

Accordingly, by joint resolution of September 26, 1961 (75 Stat. 681, 36 U.S.C. 165), Congress has requested the President to issue annually a proclamation designating the third week in March as National Poison Prevention Week.

Now, THEREFORE, I, JIMMY CARTER, President of the United States of America, designate the week beginning March 18, 1979, as National Poison Prevention Week. It is particularly important during this International Year of the Child that we become aware of this specific need for child protection.

IN WITNESS WHEREOF, I have hereunto set my hand this eighth day of February, in the year of our Lord nineteen hundred seventy-nine, and of the Independence of the United States of America the two hundred and third.

JIMMY CARTER

[Filed with the Office of the Federal Register, 4:32 p.m., February 8, 1979]

Domestic Clothespin Industry

Letter to the Speaker of the House and the President of the Senate Transmitting a Report. February 8, 1979

Dear Mr. Speaker: (Dear Mr. President:)

In accordance with section 203(b)(1) of the Trade Act of 1974, enclosed is a report to the Congress setting forth my decision to provide import relief on wood and plastic clothespins in the form of a price-bracketed quota.

Sincerely,

JIMMY CARTER

IMPORT RELIEF ACTION

CLOTHESPINS

As required under section 203(b)(2) of the Trade Act of 1974, I am transmitting this report to Congress setting forth the action I will take with respect to wood and plastic clothespins covered by the affirmative finding on December 12, 1978 of the U.S. International Trade Commission (USITC) under section 201 (d)(1) of the Trade Act.

After considering all relevant aspects of the case, including those considerations set forth in section 202(c) of the Trade Act of 1974, I have decided to authorize import relief which is a variation on the relief recommended by the USITC. Within 15 days, I will issue a Presidential Proclamation authorizing the imposition of a three-year, global quota on wooden and plastic spring clothespins (TSUS 790.05) with a dutiable value of not more than $1.70 per gross. The quota, administered quarterly on a *pro rata* basis, will be broken down as follows:

Category	Yearly quota allocation (gross)
Valued not over 80 cents per gross	500,000
Valued over 80 cents per gross but not over $1.35 per gross	600,000
Valued over $1.35 per gross but not over $1.70 per gross	900,000
Total	2,000,000

During the course of each year, as it becomes apparent that the quota for any price bracket will not be filled for the year, then the remainder of the allocation may be reapportioned among the other brackets whose quotas have been filled.

The relief option I have authorized is slightly less restrictive than the USITC recommended action though it will be effective in limiting imports. The USITC quota was overly restrictive with respect to lowest price producers and too generous with higher price clothespins which are not currently traded in significant volumes. The remedy I have chosen also would have a less distortive impact on the imports of additional suppliers, who have not participated in the surge in imports and should enable domestic producers to expand their capacity utilization rates to more efficient operating levels.

NOTE: This is the text of identical letters addressed to Thomas P. O'Neill, Jr., Speaker of the House of Representatives, and Walter F. Mondale, President of the Senate.

Domestic Clothespin Industry

Memorandum From the President.
February 8, 1979

Memorandum for the Special Representative for Trade Negotiations

Subject: Determination Under Section 202(b) of the Trade Act; Clothespins

Pursuant to section 202(b)(1) of the Trade Act of 1974 (P.L. 93–618, 88 Stat. 1978), I have determined the action I will take with respect to the report of the United States International Trade Commission (USITC), transmitted to me on December 12, 1978, concerning the results of its investigation of import injury which was established on its own motion. The investigation was initiated as an outgrowth of information collected in conjunction with Commission investigations Nos. TA–406–2, TA–406–3, and TA–

406–4, conducted under section 406(a) of the Trade Act of 1974 and concerning clothespins from the People's Republic of China, the Polish People's Republic, and the Socialist Republic of Romania. All four investigations have concerned clothespins imported under items 790.05, 790.07, and 790.08 of the TSUS.

After considering all relevant aspects of the case, including those considerations set forth in section 202(c) of the Trade Act of 1974, I have decided to accept a variation of the injury relief recommendation made by the USITC. Within 15 days, I will issue a Presidential Proclamation authorizing that a three-year global import quota be established on wood and plastic clothespins (TSUS item 790.05) with a dutiable value not over $1.70 per gross in the amount of two million gross pins. The quota, administered quarterly on a *pro rata* basis, will be allocated as follows:

Category	Yearly quota allocation (gross)
Valued not over 80 cents per gross	500,000
Valued over 80 cents per gross but not over $1.35 per gross	600,000
Valued over $1.35 per gross but not over $1.70 per gross	900,000
Total	2,000,000

During the course of each year, as it becomes apparent that the quota for any price bracket will not be filled for the year, then the remainder of the allocation may be reapportioned among the brackets whose quotas have been filled.

Relief is warranted for the following reasons:

1. The social costs of denying relief would be very high, since producers are located in isolated regions in the Northeast where alternative employment is scarce.

2. Assistance will not be costly and will not impose an inflationary burden on the economy. The major clothespin manufacturers have provided commitments to comply with the Administration's anti-inflation program.

3. Major clothespin producers have given their assurances that the relief period will be used to modernize facilities, improve distributional channels and promote their product. These steps should put them in a better competitive position once relief is lifted.

This determination is to be published in the FEDERAL REGISTER.

JIMMY CARTER

[Filed with the Office of the Federal Register, 4:33 p.m., February 8, 1979]

Anti-inflation Program

White House Statement on a Meeting With Government Officials To Discuss Competition Policy. February 8, 1979

President Carter, his chief inflation fighter, Alfred Kahn, and Consumer Adviser Esther Peterson met today with Michael Pertschuk, Chairman of the Federal Trade Commission, and John Shenefield, Assistant Attorney General in charge of the Antitrust Division of the Justice Department, to discuss the role of competition policy in fighting inflation.

Pertschuk and Shenefield reported on actions by the FTC and the Justice Department to keep prices down by challenging private and public restraints on competition. These restraints include collusion, price fixing, and excessive regulation.

Pertschuk indicated that the Commission had established health care, food, housing, transportation, energy, and clothing as priority sectors in which inflation

has taken a heavy toll on consumers. In health care delivery, for example, the Commission has barred publication of medical society fee schedules, "ethical" bans against salaried practices by specialists, and Blue Shield discrimination against health maintenance organizations.

Antitrust Division cases and investigations cover a broad range of industries and commodities affecting the daily lives of consumers, including the construction, energy, mining, paper products, metals, and food industries. Shenefield noted that the civil and criminal cases filed by the Antitrust Division in the last year involved over $9 billion in commerce.

Professional self-regulation and profession-inspired regulation are also undergoing Antitrust Division and Commission scrutiny. Restraints by doctors, lawyers, accountants, and realtors are currently under investigation. Some professional groups, such as veterinarians and psychologists, have recently responded by undertaking voluntary reforms to free up competition.

Additionally, the agencies have been working in close cooperation with concerned State legislators and regulators to enhance procompetitive actions at the State level. The FTC's model State generic drug substitution law (sent last week by President Carter to each State Governor) would allow pharmacists to fill prescriptions with lower cost equivalent drugs unless otherwise specified by the physician.

The President, in his inflation message, noted his support for those regulations "which fight inflation." The Commission's recent eyeglass rule will enable consumers to benefit from price advertising and comparative shopping for eyeglasses. Rules being considered this year would also provide information on insulation and on energy costs of major appliances.

The Justice Department and the FTC are leading advocates for competition in numerous proceedings before Federal regulatory agencies and throughout the Government. The Antitrust Division has participated in regulatory hearings on energy, transportation, banking, securities, international trade and communications matters. The Antitrust Division also participated in several important administrative legislative initiatives concerning competition. The Commission has undertaken a program of competitive advocacy within policymaking councils of the administration, before Congress, and before other agencies, notably the CAB and ICC.

Chairman Pertschuk also told the President that several FTC initiatives illustrate the benefits flowing from a vigorous competition policy. Following the issuance of a complaint alleging that Levi Strauss had fixed retail prices, jeans prices dropped by $4. The FTC eyeglass rule could save consumers $500 million a year.

Without necessarily endorsing each FTC or Antitrust Division initiative, the President and Chairman Kahn expressed broad support for a vigorous national competition policy to be spearheaded by the two agencies.

"Both the FTC and the Antitrust Division," the President said, "are responding vigorously to the call I sounded in the inflation message—to redouble our effort to put competition back into the American free enterprise system."

Interview With the President

Question-and-Answer Session With Jacobo Zabludovsky of Televisa, Mexico.
February 8, 1979

MR. ZABLUDOVSKY. Mr. President, do you agree with those in Mexico who say that relations between our two countries are at a low point?

THE PRESIDENT. No. I believe that the relationships between Mexico and the United States have improved the last 2 years. The fact is that we have concluded new trade agreements, maritime agreements, agreements concerning fisheries, exchange of prisoners. There has been an emerging consultation between myself and President López Portillo, almost of an unprecedented nature.

When he was inaugurated, my wife was there. When I was inaugurated, Mrs. López Portillo was here. My first official visitor was President López Portillo, and of course, the Vice President and my wife have been back to visit Mexico since then.

There is a new relationship because of the emerging greatness of Mexico and the political influence that's now being exerted by Mexico throughout the world. And I think there's a new sense in our country of equality, of the sharing of responsibility for world events and for the control of weapons and the maintenance of peace in this hemisphere.

So, I think a new sense of partnership— and we believe that this inevitably causes challenges, but in my opinion, since I've been in office as President, we have met those challenges very well.

And my visit with President López Portillo will be an additional opportunity for us to resolve even further the differences that still remain and to meet those challenges together.

MR. ZABLUDOVSKY. Mr. President, about oil and gas, do you expect to come to some practical agreement on these and other issues?

THE PRESIDENT. The recent discoveries of enormous quantities of oil and gas in Mexico is very good news indeed, for us and for the people of Mexico. We believe that all decisions about the production and sale of energy supplies in Mexico should be made by the Mexican people. This is not something in which we ought to be involved. We recognize this responsibility as being uniquely on the shoulders of the people and the leaders of Mexico.

We want to be customers, to purchase both oil and natural gas, and we want to be good customers. We want to pay a fair price, and those prices will be negotiated in good faith, with very careful attention paid to the sensitivities and the needs of the people of Mexico and to the needs of our own country as well. I see no reason for this to be anything other than a very good development for Mexico and for the people of our country as well.

Mr. Zabludovsky. Mr. President, regarding illegal immigration, what do you see as the next step in facing this problem?

The President. My knowledge of the Mexican people is that they share our commitment to the honoring of law. And I'm sure they recognize that I, as President, have taken an oath to carry out laws of our country.

What I think we ought to do is to have a legal arrangement, new laws passed by the Congress, that would deal effectively with the problem of illegal immigration. We want to be very careful that all the 20 million Mexican Americans who live here, plus even those who have come into our country in contravention of the law, are treated with respect and treated fairly.

I submitted to the Congress last year a proposal for a new immigration law. That legislation may be resubmitted to me for this new Congress, but before I decide whether to submit the law to Congress again, or the form that the law takes, the specifics of it, I want to consult with President López Portillo first, to be sure that

the advice that he might give to me and the counsel that I might receive from him and other Mexican leaders is fully accommodated in the proposal that I make to Congress.

Mr. Zabludovsky. Are you satisfied with the United States and Mexican efforts to halt the traffic of illegal drugs into the United States?

The President. This has been one of the most exciting and gratifying experiences that I've had since I've been President. The cooperation there has been superb, and there has been a drastic reduction in the trafficking of drugs across the border. Also, we've helped each other by having a much more effective control of smuggling and other violation of border law and customs. This permits a great enhancement of mutual trust, also helps to control crime and, at the same time, promotes the benefits of legitimate trade and commerce. So, I'm very pleased.

Mr. Zabludovsky. As you know, Mr. President, Mexican Americans are one of the fastest growing segments of the United States population. What are your views of the progress as a group? What can you say about the reports of mistreatment and discrimination against them?

The President. I believe that in the past, there have been very serious instances of mistreatment and discrimination. We now have about 20 million Spanish-speaking residents, citizens of our country. They are making a great beneficial impact on the life of America.

As you undoubtedly know, our whole population is made up of immigrants from different countries in the world, sometimes even refugees who came here to save their own lives, including my own ancestors, earlier. So, we are a country that's accustomed to receiving with an open heart and with open arms those who want to come to our country for a different life.

At the same time, I think we're beginning to see, with this large number of Americans who speak Spanish, the benefits of shared history and shared culture, and we can derive the best of the habits and the customs of one another. So, in every possible way that I can detect in our own country, this large number of Mexican immigrants and others who speak Spanish has been very helpful to us.

I have directed our own Attorney General and the law enforcement agencies throughout our country to stamp out instantly and very severely any violation of basic human rights and any discriminatory practices that might formerly have existed in our border States or throughout our country against those who might speak Spanish.

MR. ZABLUDOVSKY. When I interviewed you during your election campaign in 1976, we spoke a little Spanish. How is your Spanish now? Would you comment on the value of the Spanish language TV broadcasting in the United States, too, please?

THE PRESIDENT. In addition to having 20 million Spanish-speaking Americans, we have about 450 TV and radio stations that broadcast, as you know, either full-time or part-time in Spanish.

Mi esposa y yo estudiamos español. No hay mucha oportunidad de practicar español en Washington. Será una grande oportunidad para nosotros visitar al gran país de México y para mí consultar con su Presidente, López Portillo. [My wife and I study Spanish. There is not much opportunity to practice Spanish in Washington. It will be a great opportunity for us to visit the great country of Mexico and for me to consult with your President, López Portillo.]

I hope when I arrive there to have a chance to practice more Spanish. And this is a language that we find to be very precious. We enjoy speaking it, I'm sure, more than the people enjoy hearing us as we learn. But it's a language that I hope to share with many people in the future.

MR. ZABLUDOVSKY. Mr. President, in the name of Televisa, whom I am representing now here, I give you my thank you. And I hope you will have a nice trip to Mexico and a nice time there.

THE PRESIDENT. *Muchas gracias.*

MR. ZABLUDOVSKY. *Gracias, Señor Presidente.*

NOTE: The interview began at 1:30 p.m. in the Map Room at the White House. It was taped for later broadcast in Mexico.

National Defense Transportation Day and National Transportation Week, 1979

Proclamation 4639.   February 9, 1979

By the President of the United States of America

A Proclamation

Transportation is a vital force in our society. It moves the Nation's goods, delivers the products of our farms and factories, and enables us to live and work where we choose and travel where we please. Transportation enriches our economy and strengthens our defense.

Because of transportation's importance, and to encourage greater safety and efficiency in the ways we develop and use it, Congress has requested the President to proclaim annually the third Friday in May as National Defense Transportation Day, and the week in which that day falls as National Transportation Week (71

Stat. 30, 36 U.S.C. 160; 76 Stat. 69, 36 U.S.C. 166).

Now, THEREFORE, I, JIMMY CARTER, President of the United States of America, designate Friday, May 18, 1979, as National Defense Transportation Day, and the week beginning May 13, 1979, as National Transportation Week.

I urge the Governors of our States and other appropriate officials, organizations concerned with transportation, and the people of the United States to join with the Department of Transportation in observing this day and week.

IN WITNESS WHEREOF, I have hereunto set my hand this ninth day of February, in the year of our Lord nineteen hundred seventy-nine, and of the Independence of the United States of America the two hundred and third.

JIMMY CARTER

[Filed with the Office of the Federal Register,
11:41 a.m., February 12, 1979]

United States-France Convention on Taxation and Fiscal Evasion

Message to the Senate Transmitting the Convention.   February 9, 1979

To the Senate of the United States:

I transmit herewith, for Senate advice and consent to ratification, the Convention between the United States of America and the French Republic for the Avoidance of Double Taxation and the Prevention of Fiscal Evasion with Respect to Taxes on Estates, Inheritances and Gifts, signed at Washington, November 24, 1978. For the information of the Senate, I also transmit the report of the Department of State with respect to the Convention.

The Convention would replace the estate tax convention between the United States and France which entered into force on October 17, 1949.

The Convention is the second such convention negotiated since the Foreign Investors Tax Act of 1966. The first such convention was signed with the Netherlands and entered into force in 1971. Others are under negotiation.

A principal feature of this Convention is a rule under which a citizen of one State residing in the other State is not considered domiciled in that other State for purposes of its estate or inheritance tax jurisdiction unless he has lived there for five of the prior seven years. This provision is beneficial to U.S. businessmen living in France.

Another provision exempts, reciprocally, stock and debt obligations of portfolio investors domiciled in the other State. This provision benefits especially French portfolio investors in the United States.

I recommend that the Senate give early and favorable consideration to the Convention and advise and consent to its ratification.

JIMMY CARTER

The White House,
February 9, 1979.

United States-France Convention on Income and Property Taxes

*Message to the Senate Transmitting a Protocol to the Convention.
February 9, 1979*

To the Senate of the United States:

I transmit herewith, for Senate advice and consent to ratification, a Protocol to the Convention between the United States of America and the French Republic with Respect to Taxes on Income and Property of July 28, 1967, as amended by the Protocol of October 12, 1970. The Protocol, together with a related exchange of notes, was signed at Washington on November 24, 1978. For the information of the Senate, I also transmit the related exchange of notes and the report of the Department of State with respect to the Protocol.

The Protocol breaks new ground by providing for the first time that the country of residence (France) and the country of citizenship (United States) share the responsibility to avoid double taxation of expatriate U.S. citizens.

Early ratification of the Protocol is essential as a new French law which takes effect on January 1, 1979, may otherwise subject U.S. citizens living in France to double taxation. The Protocol provides for retroactive effect, upon entry into force, to January 1, 1979.

The accompanying exchange of notes clarifies the treatment by France of certain income and expenses of U.S. citizens resident in France. It also points out certain issues of continuing concern for which no current solution could be found.

I recommend that the Senate give early and favorable consideration to this Protocol and advise and consent to its ratification.

JIMMY CARTER

The White House,
February 9, 1979.

Digest of Other White House Announcements

The following listing includes the President's public schedule and other items of general interest announced by the White House Press Office and not included elsewhere in this issue.

February 4

The President returned to the White House from Camp David, Md.

February 5

The President met at the White House with:

—Frank B. Moore, Assistant to the President for Congressional Liaison;
—the Cabinet;
—Vice President Walter F. Mondale;
—members of the board of directors and officers of the National Association of State Departments of Agriculture;
—Secretary of State Cyrus R. Vance, Secretary of Defense Harold Brown, and General Robert E. Huyser, Deputy Commander in Chief, United States European Command, to discuss the situation in Iran.

The President has named Vice President Mondale to head the U.S. delegations to the inaugurations of President-elect Luis Herrera Campins of Venezuela, in Caracas, on March 12, and President-elect João Baptista de Oliveira Figueiredo of Brazil, in Brasília, on March 15.

February 6

The President met at the White House with:

—Zbigniew Brzezinski, Assistant to the President for National Security Affairs;
—Mr. Moore;
—James T. McIntyre, Jr., Director of the Office of Management and Budget.

The President has accepted with regret the resignation of Manuel D. Plotkin as Director of the Bureau of the Census.

The President transmitted to the Congress the 14th annual report of the Secretaries of Agriculture and the Interior on the status of the National Wilderness Preservation System.

February 7

The President met at the White House with:

—Mr. Moore;

—a group of new Senators of the 96th Congress;

—Dr. Brzezinski;

—Representative Jamie L. Whitten of Mississippi;

—Ralph A. Lyman, president of the Lions Clubs International;

—representatives of the Boy Scouts of America, to receive the Scouts' annual report to the Nation;

—Mrs. Carter and Amy, for lunch;

—Vice President Mondale, Senators Jacob K. Javits and Daniel P. Moynihan and Gov. Hugh Carey of New York, Mayor Edward I. Koch of New York City, Secretary of Health, Education, and Welfare Joseph A. Califano, Jr., W. Michael Blumenthal, Secretary, and Roger C. Altman, Assistant Secretary, Department of the Treasury, Stuart E. Eizenstat, Assistant to the President for Domestic Affairs and Policy, and Jack H. Watson, Jr., Assistant to the President for Intergovernmental Affairs.

At the invitation of the President, Crown Prince Fahd Bin Abd al-Aziz al-Sa'ud of Saudi Arabia will make an official visit to Washington on March 13 and 14.

The White House released manifests listing passengers who have flown on White House authorized military aircraft from July 1 through December 31, 1978. The lists were sent to Representative Jack Brooks, chairman of the House Committee on Government Operations, and were also made available for inspection by the press.

As required by Public Law 95–426, the President transmitted to the Speaker of the House of Representatives and to the chairman of the Senate Foreign Relations Committee reports on "International Journalistic Freedom," "International Communications Policy," and "U.S. Policy Toward Cuba." He also transmitted to the chairman of the Senate Committee on Commerce, Science, and Transportation the report on "International Communications Policy."

In the evening, the President participated in a foreign affairs briefing for a group of Senators.

February 8

The President met at the White House with:

—Vice President Mondale, Secretary Blumenthal, Charles L. Schultze, Chairman of the Council of Economic Advisers, Alfred E. Kahn, Advisor to the President on Inflation and Chairman of the Council on Wage and Price Stability, Barry P. Bosworth, Director of the Council on Wage and Price Stability, Mr. McIntyre, and Mr. Eizenstat;

—Dr. Brzezinski;

—Mr. Moore;

—Vice President Mondale, Stansfield Turner, Director of Central Intelligence, Hamilton Jordan, Assistant to the President, and Dr. Brzezinski;

—Mrs. Carter and Senator and Mrs. Frank Church of Idaho, for lunch.

February 9

The President met at the White House with:

—Vice President Mondale, Secretaries Vance and Brown, Dr. Brzezinski, and Mr. Jordan;

—Dr. Brzezinski;

—Mr. Schultze;

—a group of editors and news directors (transcript will be printed next week).

The President left the White House for a weekend stay at Camp David, Md.

NOMINATIONS SUBMITTED TO THE SENATE

The following list does not include promotions of members of the Uniformed Services, nominations to the Service Academies, or nominations of Foreign Service officers.

Submitted February 5, 1979

JOAN MARGARET CLARK, of New York, a Foreign Service officer of Class one, to be Ambassador Extraordinary and Plenipotentiary of the United States of America to the Republic of Malta.

LOREN E. LAWRENCE, of Maryland, a Foreign Service officer of Class one, to be Ambassador Extraordinary and Plenipotentiary of the United States of America to Jamaica.

GEORGE WATSON CAMP, of Georgia, to be a Governor of the United States Postal Service for the term expiring December 8, 1985, vice William A. Irvine, term expired.

RICHARD R. ALLEN, of North Carolina, to be a Governor of the United States Postal Service for the term expiring December 8, 1986, vice Crocker Nevin, term expired.

Submitted February 6, 1979

JOHN PRIOR LEWIS, of New Jersey, for the rank of Minister during the tenure of his service as Chairman of the Development Assistance Committee of the Organization for Economic Cooperation and Development at Paris, France.

ROBERT M. PARKER, of Texas, to be United States District Judge for the Eastern District of Texas, vice a new position created by P.L. 95–486, approved October 20, 1978.

HAROLD BAREFOOT SANDERS, JR., of Texas, to be United States District Judge for the Northern District of Texas, vice a new position created by P.L. 95–486, approved October 20, 1978.

GARY LOUIS BETZ, of Florida, to be United States Attorney for the Middle District of Florida for the term of 4 years, vice John L. Briggs, resigned.

NOMINATIONS—Continued

Submitted February 9, 1979

MARTIN F. LOUGHLIN, of New Hampshire, to be United States District Judge for the District of New Hampshire, vice a new position created by P.L. 95–486, approved October 20, 1978.

DAVID O. BELEW, JR., of Texas, to be United States District Judge for the Northern District of Texas, vice a new position created by P.L. 95–486, approved October 20, 1978.

A. D. FRAZIER, JR., of Georgia, to be a member of the National Council on the Humanities for the remainder of the term expiring January 26, 1982, vice John Hope Franklin, resigning.

CHECKLIST OF WHITE HOUSE PRESS RELEASES

The following listing contains releases of the White House Press Office which are not included in this issue.

Released February 5, 1979

Announcement: designation of Vice President Walter F. Mondale to head the U.S. delegations to the inaugurations of the Presidents-elect of Venezuela and Brazil

News conference: on the signing of the first Government contract containing the anti-inflation pay and price guidelines, between the National Aeronautics and Space Administration and Rockwell International Corp.'s Space Systems Group of Downey, California—by James T. McIntyre, Jr., Director, and Lester A. Fettig, Administrator of the Office of Federal Procurement Policy, Office of Management and Budget; Alfred E. Kahn, Advisor to the President on Inflation; Alan M. Lovelace, Deputy Administrator of NASA; and Donald R. Beall, executive vice president of Rockwell International Corp.

Released February 6, 1979

Announcement: nomination of Robert M. Parker to be United States District Judge for the Eastern District of Texas

Announcement: nomination of Harold Barefoot Sanders, Jr., to be United States District Judge for the Northern District of Texas

CHECKLIST—Continued

Released February 6—Continued

Announcement: nomination of Gary L. Betz to be United States Attorney for the Middle District of Florida.

List: attendees at the meeting between the President and Prime Minister Kriangsak Chomanan in the Cabinet Room

Released February 7, 1979

Announcement: visit of Crown Prince Fahd Bin Abd al-Aziz al-Sa'ud of Saudi Arabia to Washington, D.C.

Released February 8, 1979

News conference: on the proposed department of education—by Vice President Walter F. Mondale and James T. McIntyre, Jr., Director of the Office of Management and Budget

Fact sheet: proposed department of education

Announcement: nomination of Martin F. Loughlin to be United States District Judge for the District of New Hampshire.

CHECKLIST—Continued

Released February 8, 1979—Continued

Announcement: nomination of David O. Belew, Jr., to be United States District Judge for the Northern District of Texas

News conference: on their meeting with the President to discuss the anti-competition policy and inflation program—by Alfred E. Kahn, Advisor to the President on Inflation, Esther Peterson, Special Assistant to the President for Consumer Affairs, Michael Pertschuk, Chairman of the Federal Trade Commission, and John H. Shenefield, Assistant Attorney General, Antitrust Division, Department of Justice

---

ACTS APPROVED BY THE PRESIDENT

NOTE: No acts approved by the President were received by the Office of the Federal Register during the period covered by this issue.

PRESIDENTIAL DOCUMENTS

Week Ending Friday, February 16, 1979

Interview With the President

*Remarks and a Question-and-Answer
Session With Editors and News
Directors.   February 9, 1979*

THE PRESIDENT. Well, I apologize for
interrupting your meeting. [*Laughter*]

It's a pleasure to have you here. Coincidentally, you comprise a group within
which the 1,000th editor or news executive sits, who've come here since we began
this series shortly after I took this office.
Twice a week* I have a chance to meet
with the national press over here in the
White House area, and twice a week* I
meet with a group like yourselves from
around the country. I'm very grateful that
you could come.

ADMINISTRATION POLICIES

What I'd like to do is to outline, as
quickly as I can, just a few issues that are
affecting me and our people within this
country in domestic and foreign affairs
and spend what time we have available
answering your questions.

I'm preparing this weekend, and have
been for the last couple of weeks, for
a very important foreign trip to Mexico.
We've got a very large number of closely
interrelated subjects to discuss between

---

*Twice a *month*. [Printed in the transcript.]

myself and President López Portillo and
others. I think you know the closeness with
which we have consulted with Mexico
since I've been President. The first thing
that happened when López Portillo was
elected was my wife went to his inauguration. His wife came to mine. My first
visitor who came here representing a foreign country after I became President was
President López Portillo, and I've been
looking forward to this visit as well.

We are continuing our negotiations on
SALT. Every Friday morning when
Vance and I are in town, we have an
early breakfast, and we are pursuing that.

We've invited the Foreign Ministers
of Egypt and Israel to come over here to
this country to meet with Secretary Vance,
and I'll undoubtedly be meeting with
them as well while they are here. We hope
that this will resolve the differences that
still exist on a Mideast peace treaty.

We have ongoing negotiations now with
ourselves and four other of our Western
allies, through the United Nations, to
bring about majority rule and independence for the nation of Namibia.

We've concluded, as you know, in the
last 2 weeks, preparations and the consummation of Vice Premier Deng Xiaoping's
visit. A couple more of our key Cabinet
officers will be going to China very
shortly—Secretary of Commerce, Secre-

tary of Treasury—and the Congress is dealing with legislation to implement the Panama Canal treaties and to continue our trade and cultural relationships with the people of Taiwan. If the Congress does not act on this legislation by the first of March, there will be problems in continuing Eximbank loans and OPIC insurance guarantees and other official functions of our Government with the corporations that we are establishing to represent our two peoples. Those are just a few items that are on the foreign affairs agenda.

I would say the overwhelming problem and question, domestically speaking, is to control inflation. This is a serious challenge. It has been with us for 10 years or more. It is not getting better. Recent price index changes are of deep concern to us and, I think, emphasize dramatically the necessity for the special interest groups and the doubting Members of Congress, the local and State officials, those who represent industry and labor, to cooperate as completely as possible in controlling inflation. It is a burning issue, an important issue, and the overriding issue on the domestic scene.

I think at this time I'll just answer your questions, and I'll try to be as brief as possible.

QUESTIONS

ETHNIC AND MINORITY GROUPS

Q. Mr. President, my name is Mike Krajsa. I publish Slovak-Amerike, which is the oldest Slovak newspaper in the country and very active in ethnic affairs.

The Democratic National Committee did a survey polling 500 ethnic editors last year, which represents a circulation of about 5 million, and frankly, they're quite displeased, myself included, by your elimination of the Office of Ethnic Affairs in the White House, which your predecessors

had, and the attentions that you have paid to the ethnics of this country.

Speaking as a Democrat from Pennsylvania, I was very supportive of your campaign, as well as the heavy ethnic concentration of that State, but in last year's gubernatorial election, the ethnic votes swung dramatically to the Republican side.

As the elections approach, the ethnics again are going to continue to ask you to reestablish that office and, if at all possible, to also establish some sort of council comparable to what you have with the feminists and with the black movement, to begin to advise you and have some input into a lot of the foreign policy that has escalated, especially in your administration, dealing, in my case, particularly with Central Europe.

Do you have any intention of reestablishing that? We would like to be very helpful, frankly. We represent 17 percent of the vote, and there's a number of people—my publication goes abroad, and frankly, the people behind the Iron Curtain look for us to continue to spearhead your human rights issue. And it's becoming increasingly difficult, as the polls have shown.

THE PRESIDENT. Well, as you undoubtedly recognize, our country is a nation of immigrants, and even refugees, including my own ancestors, a couple hundred years or more ago.

Yes, I am deeply concerned, and interested in the special problems that relate to ethnic Americans. I've always taken the position, however, in dealing with any particular group of Americans, whether it be the elderly or blacks or Spanish-speaking or women, that it's better for them to have a President and a Vice President, and a complete Cabinet, and also a complete White House staff, members who are both interested in and sensitive to the needs, than to have a single isolated person through whom you had to channel questions relating to a particular group.

I've met in this room or in the White House with larger groups from the communities whose ancestors came from Hungary, Romania, Poland, Estonia, and many other, both major and smaller countries, and we are continuing that responsibility.

Lately, we have been talking again about how to improve the relationship with ethnics in a more conglomerate group, and not isolated individually as representatives whose families came from a particular country.

Q. Is there someone on your staff that we could talk to about coalescing?

THE PRESIDENT. I think Tim Kraft would probably be the best one to talk to, and Anne Wexler, either one of those. But I'd say Tim Kraft.

ORGANIZATION OF PETROLEUM EXPORTING COUNTRIES

Q. Mr. President, Hank Keezing, Hartford, Connecticut, Herald. On energy, more and more is being written and discussed about why isn't this country trying to break the OPEC cartel price structure. Has any thought been given to that tactical approach?

THE PRESIDENT. As you know, we've got now about half of our oil being imported; very little of our natural gas is imported, because we have an adequate supply now for those special uses that we have for it. A lot of thought's been going into how to minimize the adverse effect of the OPEC price structure.

We presented a comprehensive energy proposal to the Congress in April of 1977, about 65 percent of which was adopted. The part relating to oil pricing, unfortunately, has not yet been adopted.

The best way to deal with this question, I think, is not to have an idle hope that we can destroy the structure of OPEC. I think it's now become such an institutionalized structure that it would be very doubtful that anyone could break it down. Whenever we've challenged the authority of OPEC or tried to influence their pricing habits, we've never found much response from countries that were much more dependent on imported oil than are we. Our European allies—in France, for instance, and Japan, for instance—import sometimes 75, 80, 95 percent of their oil; whereas, we import much less, percentagewise.

I don't think we could mount an international and successful challenge, but we can control the dependence and the adverse effect of OPEC by shifting away from imported oil, by increasing production in our own country, by shifting to coal, to solar energy, to natural gas, where we have a more adequate supply, and also by dealing with countries that are naturally bound to us historically in a spirit of friendship.

When we had the oil embargo in 1973, we got an increasing portion of our oil from countries like Nigeria, Venezuela, Indonesia, that we had to import. And of course, since then we've brought in the Alaska pipeline to start bringing in oil.

I might point out to you that right now we are in the unfortunate position that the OPEC price is not the prevailing price. The spot market price for oil now is $6 or $7 above the OPEC price. Obviously most of the oil is sold on a contract basis at the OPEC price level. But an increasing portion of the total oil in the international markets is being sold now at about $20 to $21 a barrel; whereas, the OPEC price is a little above $14.

That's the best answer I can give you. I don't think it's possible to destroy OPEC. The best way to do it is to cut down on our dependence on imported oil.

DEPARTMENT OF EDUCATION

Q. Mr. President, you have just announced you are planning to form a Cabinet-level department of education. And educators that I've talked to this past week tell me that they think this is going to just be more government control over education and more paperwork for them. What's your thinking behind this?

THE PRESIDENT. That's not the case. Obviously, I wouldn't do that if I thought that. I've been a Governor for 4 years, and before that I was on the local school board, the county school board, for 7 years. I've had a deep interest in education.

I think it's important to have a department in the Federal Government responsible for education and not have it buried in a much larger department that's dominated by interests of a welfare and health nature. I sit around this table and meet with my Cabinet every week or every 2 weeks, and I would say that outside of hotly disputed segregation lawsuits and things of that kind, we don't spend half of 1 percent of our time discussing what we can legitimately do to make education of our children and adults in this country better.

And I believe that it will be very helpful to have a single person that's identified by students, parents, county, State officials as the person responsible for education in this country working with me. We've eliminated enormous quantities of unnecessary paperwork, reports, forms, at the suggestion of and with the cooperation of both college presidents, who have met in this room with me, and the representatives of the States, State school superintendents, who've met over in the larger room with me for that particular purpose. I believe it'll be a much cleaner relationship in eliminating confusion and overlapping and redtape and the duplication of reports if we can have a separate department.

We've been very careful in drafting the legislation. We've not tried to abuse anyone. But for those reasons, I think it would be a step in the right direction, not backwards. As you know, the NEA, the largest organization of teachers, thinks it'd be very good. And although Joe Califano has not been an enthusiastic supporter of it, he agrees with my decision. [*Laughter*]

Q. Do you have anybody in mind to head the department?

THE PRESIDENT. Not yet. But I think the Congress is very likely to pass that legislation, and when they do, I think it'll be a step in having better education for our children. I would certainly never do anything as President to usurp the clear responsibility for the curriculum and for other aspects of education away from the local officials primarily and, obviously, the State officials secondarily. And I would put the Federal Government as a level of educational administration that ought to be removed from decisions concerning the students themselves as much as possible.

GAMBLING

Q. Mr. President, there are now at least five States considering legalized gaming to alleviate their financial conditions. Have you or will you consider a national gaming policy, or would you consider intervening in gaming in any way?

THE PRESIDENT. I'm not in favor of it. When I was Governor, I opposed any form of legalized gambling, and I still have the same conviction that it's not well-advised.

Q. Would you intervene at all in gambling policy?

THE PRESIDENT. No. Obviously, the Federal Government has responsibility through the Internal Revenue Service and through the Justice Department and other agencies to assure that legalities are followed. This is a prerogative of the States, in accordance with constitutional delineations of responsibility. And only when we deal with foreign governments does the Federal Government have a direct influence on gambling.

No, I wouldn't want to sponsor a constitutional amendment giving the Federal Government the authority to prohibit it, but my own personal opinion is that gambling is not good.

INFLATION AND TAXATION

Q. Mr. President, Dave Willmott, Suffolk Life Newspapers, Westhampton, [New York]. Indexing has been brought up as a method of controlling inflation, tying indexing inflation to taxes. Your administration, I understand, has opposed it. Could you tell us why?

THE PRESIDENT. Well, most of the indexing means that you have to do it both ways. If the inflation rate goes up, then all the other prices, payments to retirees, pension payments, and everything go up with it.

I think to have an automatic connection between the inflation rate and the rate of taxation, or the rate of payment of Federal funds for different programs, is ill-advised. Quite often you need some flexibility to decide on an annual basis the best way to expend both tax privileges and also to distribute tax funds once they are collected.

Q. Doesn't indexing give the Federal Government, though, an automatic tax increase on a regular basis every time we have inflation because of the progressive income tax system that we're on?

THE PRESIDENT. The trends are certainly in the right direction. When you have a higher inflation rate at a given— for, if everything else stays the same, people move into a higher income level to get the same real wage, and therefore, they pay a higher rate of taxation. That's what you are talking about, a higher percentage of our income?

Q. Right.

THE PRESIDENT. Yes. And the Congress and the incumbent President, whoever it might be, take that into consideration by modifying the tax laws generally through reductions. But I think it's better since it's done on an annual basis—sometimes it's considered several times during the year—to do it in that respect rather than to have an automatic formula.

U.S. FORCES IN SOUTH KOREA

Q. Mr. President, Virginia Reuss, Gouverneur, New York. Do you have any plans to bring back the troops from Korea in the near future, and if you do, have you an idea where they will be stationed, just what will be considered?

THE PRESIDENT. Over a period of time, I think the troops ought to be brought back from Korea. We've had our troops there for 30 years, and I've made a basic decision that the troops should be brought back.

The rate of returning them to the United States is constantly being assessed. We've already brought back a few. Right now we are holding in abeyance any further reduction in American troop levels until we can assess the new intelligence data on the buildup of North Korean force levels, the impact of the normalization with China, and the new peace proposal or discussions for peace that have been put forward by both the North Korean and the South Korean Governments.

There is hardly a more vigorous and successful economic system in the world than South Korea, and over a period of time they've built up their capacity to both finance and construct their own military weapons systems. But I think that there won't be any rapid withdrawal of troops, and we don't have any plans yet for where they will be placed when they come back.

The major problem that we've had to face since I've been in office has been how to reinvigorate the NATO Alliance and how to make sure that the forces that we do have standing in a reserve capacity on active duty could be deployed rapidly to different parts of the world when they are needed.

So, we are cautiously carrying out a basic policy of withdrawing troops from South Korea, letting South Korea be more self-sufficient in defending themselves, analyzing recent changes in the international situation. And I don't know where the troops will be placed.

U.S. RELATIONS WITH CHINA

Q. Mr. President, Kent Collins, from Quincy, Illinois. The other day on Capitol Hill, Senator Danforth of Missouri warned that the American people and maybe your administration were putting too much faith in what he described as an elderly, twice-purged Vice Premier from China. Is there any validity to that warning? Do you worry that the Vice Premier could be ousted and the tide turned?

THE PRESIDENT. I don't, obviously, predict that that's going to happen; I don't think it's going to happen. It's always inevitable, though, that leaderships will change.

The policy that has been adopted by the People's Republic of China recently, leading toward normalization, is, so far as I know, a unanimous decision among the leadership within China. Premier Hua, who I think is only a little bit older than I am—57, 58—strongly supports this policy. Deng Xiaoping, the Vice Premier, one of the Vice Premiers, is in his early seventies. But I think it's accurate to say that the young leadership and the more elderly leadership are all unanimous in thinking this is a good idea.

There's another facet to it, and that is that their relationship with us has not been unique. They have reached out their influence and also their partnership in trade, peace, normalization, to many other countries around the world in the last couple of years, with Japan. And I noticed in the paper this morning that it was announced that they've now normalized relationships with Portugal. And Portugal will continue the administration of Macao.

But we've got an awareness that it's to China's advantage in their major modernization program which affects every one in China to retain these newly formed diplomatic, political, and trade relationships with countries throughout the world. Ours is perhaps the most important in their eyes. As far as the consequences to us, if they should change their policies in the future, I don't see any serious consequence that could evolve.

If a catastrophe should occur in China or any other country, and the existing government should be changed, then we'd have to reassess our relationships with them anew. But that's a constant responsibility that a President has. We have protected our ability to deal with the people of Taiwan in a continuing, constructive, supportive basis—trade, cultural affairs, and defense. There's nothing to prohibit a future President or a future Congress, if we feel that Taiwan is unnecessarily endangered, from interposing the American Pacific Fleet between the island and the Mainland. And there's certainly nothing to prevent a future President or Congress from even going to war, if they choose, to protect the people of Taiwan, or to protect any other people in the country [world][1] that we look on with favor. So, we still have complete flexibility to deal with that kind of conjectural possibility if we choose.

FARM PRICES

Q. Mr. President, Jeanie Stream, KSIB Radio, Creston, Iowa. Quite obviously, the farmers came to Washington this week. Can you tell me if you think the demands for 90 percent parity are reasonable?

THE PRESIDENT. Obviously, I think the farmers have a right not only to come to Washington but to demonstrate when they disagree with Government policy, or feel that they've been abused in getting an equitable treatment in our economic system.

I think the American Agricultural Movement, a year or two ago, when it was first formed, effectively dramatized the plight of farmers. The new agriculture bill went into effect in October of 1977. It has worked very well. There is no possibility of the Congress or I approving action which would lead to an across-the-board 90 percent of parity payment for all crops.

Did I answer your question?

REGISTRATION FOR THE DRAFT

Q. Mr. President, Howard Kelley from WTLV in Jacksonville, [Florida]. Ten days ago, Secretary Brown indicated that we ought to start considering registering 18-year-old men in case we need them for the military. He said while

_____
[1] Printed in the transcript.

we're at it, we ought to start registering women, too. Do you agree?

THE PRESIDENT. Yes, I think I agree. If we register persons for future use in some form in our country, it would probably be inevitable that we'd register both. But that doesn't mean that women will be drafted, or that men will be drafted to go into the Armed Forces. Secretary Brown gave me a brief memorandum and said that we ought to explore the advisability in some way of having a record for possible drafting during any emergency of people in certain age groups. And I think if we register men, that the women should be registered as well. But I don't anticipate this happening.

FEDERAL AID TO CITIES

Q. Mr. President, Rick Beyer, from Gary, Indiana. Gary and other mid-sized American cities are in an economically depressed time. And they have a feeling that because while their costs rise, they have very little control over taxes and control over their revenues, that they are very dependent upon the Federal Government. And this is particularly true in Indiana, where the State has imposed a tax——

THE PRESIDENT. You're talking about the city government officials now?

Q. Yes, I am—for instance, the mayor and deputy mayor of Gary. They feel it's especially true in Indiana now, where there's a State-imposed tax freeze, and the city cannot raise its income from any sort of taxes. They feel that they are dependent upon the Federal Government and that when the Federal Government gives a lot of money to cities, that they are better off when the money stays the same or increases in real terms, and you still have inflation, that they become somewhat worse off.

I have a two-part question. Given that very strong feeling on the part of the city officials, can you tell me what basis you disagree with that—as you have said that you do in the past—and that your 1980 budget, which includes some of these decreases, will not hurt cities? And the second part of the question is, do you think there might ever come a time in 4, 5, 10 years, when cities would be more independent of the Federal Government, and if so, what would it take? I guess that's about four questions, all in one.

THE PRESIDENT. I noticed that. [*Laughter*]

First of all, I agree that the cities are better off the more Federal funds they get. Secondly, I see the difference between cities and county governments on the one hand, and State governments on the other. State governments have complete flexibility under the Constitution to levy what taxes they choose, very few exceptions involving international trade, for instance. City and county governments can only levy the kinds of taxes that the State legislatures permit them to.

During my campaign years, I advocated—and when I was Governor, as well—that revenue sharing funds should be channeled to cities and local governments and not to State governments. And certainly if there's a choice between them, the cities and counties should get the priority.

We have substantially increased allocation of funds for local governments since I've been in office, including the fiscal year 1980 budget. This includes some—many requests that I've made to the Congress that were carried out, plus some that have not yet been carried out, like countercyclical funds. But there will be another increase next year in things like water and sewage funds, recreation funds, and a continuation of large

amounts of money for CETA jobs, and others that will help the cities directly.

So, the trend has certainly, strongly, in the last few years, been in the direction of increasing Federal aid. There might be an inclination on the part of the Congress to kind of level off the increase, but I don't see any possibility in the future of eliminating Federal aid for the cities.

Q. Is your answer to the second part of my question then that there is probably not a possibility in the next 5 or 10 years of cities becoming more independent from the Federal Government or from the States, even?

THE PRESIDENT. I don't believe so, but I'll have to say that that's a two-way responsibility. If the States should give city governments an unlimited right to levy whatever taxes they choose, I think that would be a serious mistake. I would not do it as Governor. Secondly, the Congress is intensely lobbied by local government officials at the county and city level, and I think the Congress and my predecessors here in the White House have been very sensitive to the needs of local governments.

So, I don't see any prospect at all of the cities having to become more independent of financial aid from the Federal Government. The trend has been just the opposite, an increasing allocation of Federal aid for local governments.

MS. BARIO. Thank you, sir.

THE PRESIDENT. Well, one more question.

EGYPTIAN-ISRAELI PEACE NEGOTIATIONS

Q. Mr. President, a policy question with regard to the upcoming Middle East talks, if I may. On the one hand, it's argued that a separate Israel-Egyptian peace would generate irresistible psychological momentum for a broader, comprehensive settlement, and such that explicit linkage would not be required. The other hand, pragmatists say that a separate peace would so tip the political and military balance in Israel's favor that there would be very little likelihood of progress in the future toward a comprehensive peace.

Which of these approaches would you press upon Israel and Egypt when they come here?

THE PRESIDENT. The United States does not have a position to put forward on a peace treaty. There's not a word or a phrase or a sentence or a paragraph that I want to see put in a peace treaty between Israel and Egypt. What we do is to encourage Israel and Egypt to put forward their ideas.

In 95 percent of the total cases, they have now reached agreement. In those remaining 5, we add our good offices to propose to them, when a deadlock exists between Israel and Egypt, alternative wording and substance, hoping that they'll accept some of our proposals. If they don't, we go back to the drafting board.

But at Camp David, there was evolved a description of a comprehensive peace settlement for Israel, Egypt, Jordan, Lebanon, Syria, and the Palestinians who live on the West Bank and Gaza. That was one document. The other document outlined the basic principles of a peace treaty between Israel and Egypt unilaterally. But the Israel and Egypt treaty terms were also mentioned very clearly within the comprehensive settlement outline.

I think that the commitment of both Begin and Sadat was to a comprehensive peace settlement. And I've heard Prime Minister Begin say several times to President Sadat in my presence, when only the three of us were there, "I am not looking for a separate peace treaty with Egypt."

The way the negotiations have evolved, with the Palestinians and the Jordanians unwilling to participate, this has of necessity led to the bilateral discussions between Israel and Egypt. Egypt is very insistent that Israel comply with the agreement at Camp David that a comprehensive peace settlement be sought, and Israel, on the other hand, is very insistent that the peace treaty that's being evolved between Israel and Egypt not be abrogated because of factors beyond their control—for instance, the refusal of the Palestinians to participate in future negotiations.

So, I think that's where the basic deadlock exists. I, therefore, am very deeply committed to carrying out, if I can, the principles of the Camp David accords, which encompass a comprehensive settlement.

Q. You believe in linkage?

THE PRESIDENT. Well, I think the word "linkage" has become kind of a code word, where Israel says no linkage, Egypt says linkage. I think it's better to talk about the need for a comprehensive settlement. That's language that both sides can accept without violating the honor of their own nation.

We hope that in the privacy of the upcoming discussions at the Foreign Minister level that we can make additional progress. One of the worst ways to negotiate is through the news media, because once a negotiator makes a public statement—"This is our position"—it almost becomes, to repeat myself, a violation of one's word of honor to be flexible and actually to negotiate. And I think the privacy of Camp David was the key factor in the success that we had.

So, when Dayan and Khalil come back over here, maybe around the end of this month, to meet with Secretary Vance, one of the things that we'll try to do is to have the meetings conducted in privacy so that the negotiators don't have to go out and repeat to the news media and to the public every day what their latest negotiating position might be.

I read your articles, by the way, very carefully, relating to the United Nations and other matters, and I enjoy them.

Let me say this in closing: I'm very grateful that you could come. I think the breadth and variety of your own questions is indicative of the kind of decisions that I have to make every day. I've enjoyed the job very much. I've learned in the process.

I think one of the things that gets lost because we deal with daily crises and debates and disharmonies and arguments is the basic strength and soundness of our country militarily, economically, politically, I hope, ethically. There is no country as strong as ours—no other country as strong as ours—and I think that we sometimes lose a sense of the cohesiveness that's so crucial to us.

We've learned a great deal from the visits of editors and other executives from around the country who come here. You have a different perspective from the perspective of news media representatives who stay in Washington full-time, and it's a good educational process for me to have to listen to your questions and to try to think of an accurate answer. But I'm grateful that you could come.

If you have no objection, I would like to get an individual photograph with each one of you. And I see some around the room that I've known for a long time; and I'd like to thank you for coming again. So, if you'd come by, and let me just shake hands, we'll get a photograph. I don't have time for another question as you go by though, that's the only thing.

I think you'll be meeting this afternoon with Barry Bosworth. I think you'll be impressed with him. We hope that when you leave you'll have a little clearer picture of what we do here at the White House for you.

NOTE: The interview began at 1:15 p.m. in the Cabinet Room at the White House. Patricia Y. Bario is an Associate Press Secretary and Barry P. Bosworth is Director of the Council on Wage and Price Stability.

The transcript of the interview was released on February 10.

Interview With the President

Question-and-Answer Session With Joaquin Lopez-Doriga of Channel 13, Government of Mexico Television. February 8, 1979

MR. LOPEZ-DORIGA. Mr. President, in a few days you will be visiting Mexico. In view of developments in Mexico's oil production and the problem of illegal workers, how do you see relations between the two countries?

THE PRESIDENT. I think in the last 2 years, since I've been in office and since President López Portillo has been President, the relations have improved considerably. For a number of decades, there have been strains between Mexico and the United States and a lack of adequate consultation and the sharing of mutual problems. I think President López Portillo and I have both recognized that problem when we became Presidents, and we've made great strides to relieve those challenges.

In the field of trade, border problems, agriculture, fisheries, maritime problems, exchange of prisoners, the control of narcotics, the enforcement of customs laws, the holding down of smuggling, in many other hemispheric problems, the control of arms, the enhancement of peace, the control of nuclear weapons, we have seen the admirable leadership of President López Portillo in working with us to reach agreement on how we can approach these problems as partners.

So, I think the situation is improving rapidly, and I will learn a great deal and my country will benefit very much from my coming visit with your people and your President.

MR. LOPEZ-DORIGA. Mr. President, President López Portillo has said that Mexican oil production is adjusted to the needs of Mexico. Do you expect an increase of oil and gas production to meet the needs of the United States, or some kind of agreement on this issue?

THE PRESIDENT. I expect the rate of exploration and production of oil and gas in Mexico to be decided by the Mexican people only. This is not something that we should try to influence. This should be done with very careful attention to what's best for the Mexican people.

We have been very pleased to see the prospect of new prosperity and new growth in job opportunities and a better quality of life for the people of Mexico because of the new discoveries of this valuable energy source. And we want to be a good customer for the portion of oil and gas that Mexico decides to sell to us as a neighbor. But the price must be fair, and the control of production and distribution must be kept in the hands of the Mexican people.

So, we want to be good customers, and we feel that your people and the people of my country will benefit from these new energy discoveries.

MR. LOPEZ-DORIGA. Turning to the problem of illegal immigration, Mr. President, what do you see as a solution to this problem which our two countries share?

THE PRESIDENT. First of all, I will have to enforce the laws of my country. And I've been very deeply impressed on my visits to Mexico with the desire of Mexican people to live in accordance with the law.

In some ways, the immigration laws that we now have in effect have not been workable, and I have submitted to the last Congress proposals for change in those immigration laws. The Congress did not act on my proposals. Before I decide whether or not to submit new laws to Congress or what form they should take, I want to consult very closely with President López Portillo and other interested Mexican officials so that when we do change our law, it will be one that will be fair and workable and will protect the interests and the basic human rights of even those who have come to our country in the past in violation of our immigration laws.

We want to be fair to all those who've come here, whether they originally came within the bounds of the law or otherwise, and to make sure we have a law that's simple and workable and suitable both to the Mexican people and to the people of my country.

MR. LOPEZ-DORIGA. Mr. President, every United States President since Franklin Roosevelt, I think, has met with his Mexican President and hailed the visit as a breakthrough for both countries. But after the speeches are over, very little really happens. I don't know if you agree with this. Is your visit, Mr. President, merely ceremonial, or can you promise followup actions?

THE PRESIDENT. Well, there will be followup actions. When President López Portillo was inaugurated, even before I was President, my wife went to the ceremonies. When I was inaugurated, Mrs. López Portillo came here to be an honored guest. When I decided who would be my first foreign visitor after I became President, my choice was President López Portillo. And our Vice President has been to Mexico, and we've had constant consultations at the Cabinet level of our top Ministers. And, as I mentioned earlier in the interview, we've already concluded agreements relating to irrigation, agriculture, customs, the control of narcotics, fisheries, maritime law. We've worked out a treaty on exchange of prisoners, and we've laid a good basis for further achievements, both on my upcoming visit and also for the future.

So, the consultations have been very productive so far. I think they'll be much more productive in the future.

One of the things that we see is a rapid improvement in the job opportunities and quality of life of the people of Mexico and my country because of increased trade. Mexico is our most important trade partner in this hemisphere, in Latin America. And our trade level now is about $10 billion a year. We export about the same amount that we import from Mexico. It's an even and mutual benefit.

So, these are the kind of things that we see as great opportunities in the future, even for more rapid progress. We're very excited about this.

MR. LOPEZ-DORIGA. Mr. President, would you tell us, please, which is the main purpose of your visit to Mexico—oil, gas, illegals, or all together?

THE PRESIDENT. Well, all of our relationships with Mexico are very complex and complicated. There will be an agenda for which I'm preparing that consists of literally dozens of different subjects, and I think they are very closely interrelated. You can't isolate just one subject and say this is the most important thing.

We are very grateful for the friendship that exists between Mexico and the United States. I'm also very grateful and have admiration for your leaders and your people, because Mexico has in recent years become one of the most influential countries of the whole world in stabilizing affairs in this hemisphere, in providing a commitment that never changes for the protection of human rights, in promoting democratic principles in all the govern-

ments of the Western Hemisphere, in trying to hold down the spread of weapons and war, in trying to prevent nuclear explosives from spreading throughout the Southern Hemisphere.

We are very interested also in seeing the benefits that come to us and the entire world for Mexico's leadership among the nations that are rapidly developing, and as a regional leader, Mexico's good relationships with us are very valuable to the United States. And I think in a system of mutual respect and equality, partnership, friendship, we benefit greatly, as do the people of your country.

I might add that we now have 20 million American citizens of Mexican ancestry who live among us. And we derive great strength from this sharing of a common background. Our Nation is one of immigrants. And almost everyone who lives in our country, with very few exceptions, immigrated to our Nation. So, we value this strength and this natural tie of kinship and friendship very much.

MR. LOPEZ-DORIGA. *Muchas gracias, Señor Presidente. ¿ Cómo va su español,* your Spanish? [Thank you, Mr. President. How is your Spanish?]

THE PRESIDENT. *No hay mucha oportunidad de practicar aquí en Washington. Será un gran placer para mí estar en México y un grande oportunidad de consultar su Presidente. Muchas gracias a tí, señor.* [There is not much opportunity to practice here in Washington. It will be a great pleasure for me to be in Mexico and a great opportunity to consult with your President. Thank you, sir.]

MR. LOPEZ-DORIGA. *Muchas gracias, Señor Presidente.*

NOTE: The interview began at approximately 1:40 p.m. in the Map Room at the White House. It was taped for later broadcast in Mexico.

The transcript of the interview was released on February 12.

THE PRESIDENT'S NEWS CONFERENCE OF FEBRUARY 12, 1979

THE PRESIDENT. I have two or three brief statements I'd like to make before the questions.

THE SITUATION IN IRAN

First of all, I'd like to say a few words about Iran. Over the past several months, we have observed closely the events unfolding there. Our objective has been and is a stable and independent Iran which maintains good relations with the United States of America. Our policy has been not to interfere in the internal affairs of Iran and to express our firm expectation that other nations would not do so either.

We hope that the differences that have divided the people of Iran for so many months can now be ended. As has been the case throughout this period, we have been in touch with those in control of the Government of Iran, and we stand ready to work with them. Our goals are now, as they have been for the past few months, to ensure the safety of Americans in Iran, to minimize bloodshed and violence, to ensure that Iran is militarily capable of protecting her independence and her territorial integrity, to prevent interference or intervention in the internal affairs of Iran by any outside power, and to honor the will of the Iranian people.

These have been our hopes and our goals, and our involvement there has been, as you know, minimal during the last few months.

The curtailment of Iran's energy supplies is of special interest to the people of our country and to the world. This underscores the vulnerability about which I spoke when I presented our proposal for a comprehensive energy plan to the Congress in April of 1977.

The net shortfall from the curtailment of Iran's energy production is, on a worldwide basis, about 2 million barrels per day and for the United States a curtailment of about one-half million barrels per day. To put this in perspective, it comprises about 2½ percent of the current American consumption.

Most petroleum stocks were fairly high at the beginning of this winter season, and while we are, therefore, in no immediate danger, the stocks here and throughout the world continue to be drawn down.

I want to emphasize and support the call that Secretary Schlesinger made for voluntary conservation of oil within our Nation by all Americans. If we would honor the 55-mile-per-hour speed limit, set thermostats no higher than 65 degrees in homes and buildings, and limit discretionary driving, voluntarily, and shifting to carpools and to rapid transit systems, we could offset the current reduction in Iranian supply of oil to our country.

A prudent public response early and on a broad-scale basis will make sure that any interruption in our economic system will be minimal in the future.

INFLATION

I'd like to make a brief statement about inflation, because last month's increase in the wholesale price index emphasized again a very clear message to our Nation, that we cannot shrink from making tough decisions which are needed to bring inflation under control.

The demands of special interest groups, no matter how legitimate or benevolent, must be resisted. The Congress must hold the line on Federal spending this year. We have steadily reduced the Federal deficit over the past 2 years, and we will continue to reduce the Federal deficit further. The

Congress must act as well to pass long overdue legislation to contain hospital costs.

The American people badly need relief from this punishing, excessive inflation. I said when I announced our wage-price guidelines last fall that inflation might very well get worse in the short run before it got better. The January wholesale price index obviously bears out that prediction. But we do not expect such large increases in the wholesale price index to occur in the months immediately ahead.

All available evidence indicates that the guidelines which we've established are beginning to take hold. The first major wage settlement by the Oil, Chemical and Atomic Workers and by others since then have fallen within the 7-percent guideline figure. The overwhelming majority of major corporations have pledged to comply with the voluntary guidelines, and we expect the others to follow suit.

The staff of the Council on Wage and Price Stability, now well-organized, will vigorously monitor all pricing decisions to ensure compliance. The Congress must do its part in enacting legislation that we have proposed, real wage insurance. American workers who have restrained their own wage demands deserve this protection from our Government.

For more than 10 years now, we have lived with rising inflation. Now the program that we've set in force is begining to work, and if we all do our part, we can succeed in reducing inflation in our country step by step.

I'm determined to use the full authority of my office to make this effort succeed. And I believe the Congress and all Americans are ready to do their part.

VISIT TO MEXICO

The last comment I have is about my Mexico state visit. Two years ago, President José López Portillo of Mexico became the first head of state to visit me at the White House. This was no accident, but a carefully considered judgment, because I wanted to demonstrate the importance which I have placed from the very beginning on our relationships with our neighbor Mexico, the neighbor which shares the North American Continent with ourselves and with Canada.

About 40 hours from now, I will depart for Mexico City to return President López Portillo's visit and to renew our own personal dialog as part of the consultations and negotiations which have continued, since his visit, among our Ministers and top Government officials.

We will be discussing some very important and very difficult problems, including trade, energy, and border issues. I'm looking forward to extensive discussions of global and regional problems, as well. As you know, Mexico plays a vital role in the entire world on a number of crucial issues, such as economic development, arms restraint, and nonproliferation. These issues are very important, both to President López Portillo and to me.

Inevitably, there are differences in outlook between two such diverse and important neighbors as Mexico and the United States. But these differences are dwarfed by our common concerns, our common values, and our areas of cooperation.

I view this trip above all as an opportunity to listen and to learn. I want to hear President López Portillo's views, and I want to relay my own views to him. We will be working together toward an even better future relationship between our two countries.

Thank you very much.

Frank [Frank Cormier, Associated Press].

QUESTIONS

U.S. RELATIONS WITH IRAN

Q. Mr. President, do you see much realistic hope of entering into a mutually productive relationship with the new Government of Iran?

THE PRESIDENT. Yes, I see continued hope for very productive and peaceful cooperation with the Government of Iran. This has been our posture in the past, and it will continue to be our posture in the future.

In the last few hours, our Embassy has reported that the followers of designated Prime Minister Bazargan have been very helpful in ensuring the safety of Americans, and we've been consulting with them very closely. So, I believe that the people of Iran and their government will continue to be our friends and that the relationship will be helpful to us.

U.S. RELATIONS WITH TAIWAN

Q. Mr. President, you said in an interview over the weekend that a future President has the option of going to war and protecting Taiwan. Senator Jackson says you should be more restrained. My question is, would you go to war to protect Taiwan?

THE PRESIDENT. I have no intention of going to war. The relationship that we have with Taiwan is one based on mutual interest, and I wanted to point out that no future decision by myself or my successor is prevented. But our country is one that believes in peace, and I have no anticipation that there will be any requirement for war in the Western Pacific.

Q. Mr. President, on the same subject of Taiwan, two related questions. You had earlier said that no resolution by Congress was necessary and suggested that almost any resolution that might come out of Congress which would give any kind of reassurance to Taiwan might not meet with your approval. I wanted to ask you, in the first place, whether you've changed your mind in any way about that, whether there is any kind of resolution from Congress which might be accepted by you? I have in mind particularly the approach of Senators Kennedy and Cranston.

And secondly, there remains confusion resulting from your January statement that you had pursued the goal of getting from the Chinese Government a commitment for peaceful solution of the problem of Taiwan. And, as you know, that resulted in some misunderstanding, which you might like to clarify.

THE PRESIDENT. Well, to repeat what I said in the last press conference, I think we pursued the goal of getting a maximum commitment possible from China about the peaceful resolution of their differences with Taiwan successfully. We did get the maximum, in my opinion, that was possible.

I have never said that I would not accept any resolution from the Congress. I have said that I don't think a resolution is necessary, because the legislation we proposed to the Congress, in my opinion, is adequate.

I could not accept any resolution or amendment to the legislation that would contradict the commitments that we have made to the Government of China, on which is predicated our new, normal relationships. And I think that any resolution or amendment that would go as far or further with the defense commitments to Taiwan would be unacceptable.

ENERGY CONSERVATION

Q. Mr. President, you had a relatively optimistic statement about the energy shortfall a couple of minutes ago, I

257

thought. But isn't it more likely that in fact you're going to have to go to such measures as Sunday closing of gasoline stations? And as Senator Jackson said, the price of gasoline may go up to a dollar a gallon and we'll have long lines. Wouldn't it be better to sort of warn the American people about that?

THE PRESIDENT. Well, the situation is not crucial now; it's not a crisis. But it certainly could get worse. For instance, if we experience a worldwide shortage to the extent that our sharing commitment would be triggered, this would mean an additional shortage in our country that would go from 2½ percent up to 4 percent. And if the Iranian production is not restored in the next number of months, our shortage in this country could go as high as 5, 6, or 7 percent, under which circumstances we would have to take more strenuous action.

But I believe the first step is to implement fully the new legislation that we now have on the books and to encourage the American people, as we have been for the last 2 years, strictly to enforce voluntary conservation measures. One thing that's concerned me recently is the move on the part of some ill-advised State legislatures to raise the speed limit above 55, up to 65 or more. This would result in a termination of Federal funds allocated to them for highway purposes.

But I think there has to be built in the American consciousness a realization that we can accommodate these potential shortages in oil production on a worldwide basis if we carry out a shifting from oil to coal or natural gas, under some circumstances, or to solar power, other sources, and if we restrain our wastefulness in the consumption of oil as much as possible.

WELFARE SPENDING

Q. Mr. President, in your 1976 campaign, you pledged a program that would relieve the heavy burden of welfare costs on a number of States and communities.

THE PRESIDENT. Yes.

Q. Your new welfare program apparently will take effect in fiscal 1982. And yet, last year in communications with Congress—and I believe it's the administration's stand now—you still oppose emergency fiscal relief that would bridge the gap between the situation that occurred in '76 in your comprehensive program. Why is that?

THE PRESIDENT. That's not an accurate assessment. Last year, we did propose to the Congress substantial relief to major local areas, cities and counties, through our countercyclical aid proposal, which was focused on those communities that need the aid most. This proposal passed the Senate, but we were not able to get it out of the House Rules Committee, nor voted for favorably in the House in time to pass it.

We have resubmitted legislation for countercyclical aid which is now pending in the Congress, which I hope will pass. It's included within a very tight and restrained budget.

I think it's accurate to say, also, that some of the cities that were being burdened excessively by welfare costs, under the new administration—mine, working with the State and local governments—have severely, substantially reduced their welfare expenditures. And, of course, a part of this is because the unemployment rate has dropped substantially. But if you check the amount of money now being spent by New York City on welfare with what it was 2 years ago, you'll find substantial improvements there, substantial reductions in tax burdens for local people in paying for welfare, in addition to the countercyclical and other aid we've allocated already to local governments.

Judy [Judy Woodruff, NBC News].

U.S. RELATIONS WITH IRAN

Q. Mr. President, do you think that this Government should have been better prepared for the takeover by the Khomeini forces in Iran? And, also, in retrospect, do you think it was a mistake for you to embrace the Bakhtiar government as you did?

THE PRESIDENT. Well, obviously, had we had an exact prediction of what was going to happen. It's not the policy of our Government to go into the internal affairs of another people or country and try to determine who should be their leaders. This is contrary to the philosophy of our people. I think we've tried it once in the past in Vietnam and failed abominably. I think no one in this country of any responsibility wants to do that to a country, including Iran.

We have worked with the existing government. We worked closely with the Shah when he was in his office. We have worked with Bakhtiar, who was chosen, as you know, by the Iranian Parliament in accordance with constitutional provisions. Now Mr. Bakhtiar has resigned, and Mr. Bazargan is their Prime Minister. And the Majles, the parliament, has also resigned.

We will attempt to work closely with the existing government. But we have never tried to decide or to determine for the Iranian people or any other people on Earth who their leaders ought to be or what form of government they should have since I've been in office.

Q. But why did we have to make any statements of support for the Bakhtiar government? Why couldn't we just say nothing?

THE PRESIDENT. Well, we have statements of support and recognition for 150 nations on Earth. When we establish relationships with a government or a people, this is part of the diplomatic process. And when the governments change, quite often without delay, sometimes with a few days delay until the situation is clarified, we very quickly establish relations with the new government. But this is something that's historically been the case, and it's what we have pursued in Iran and what we will pursue in the future.

U.S.-SOVIET RELATIONS

Q. Mr. President, when Vice Premier Deng of China was in the United States, he made a number of anti-Soviet statements. In particular, on several occasions he said that the Soviets are seeking world domination. I wonder if you agree with that statement, and if you don't, I wonder what is your view of the Soviets' global intentions?

THE PRESIDENT. I have never tried to exercise censorship on a head of state or major official who came to our country. I didn't try to tell Mr. Deng what to say when he had press conferences. I didn't try to tell him what to say when he was meeting with the Members of Congress. I did not try to write his banquet toasts for him. And I think it's accurate to say that Mr. Deng's statements in our country are certainly no more noteworthy than the statements that he's made within his own country and that he's made in other nations. The position and attitude of the Chinese towards the Soviet Union have been very apparent to all of us for many years.

We have some areas where we disagree with the assessment of the Soviet Union as expressed by Mr. Deng. Our purpose, our goal, I would say, perhaps the most important responsibility I have on my shoulders as President is to preserve peace in the world, and especially to have good, sound relationships with the Soviet Union, based on a common desire for peace, which I am sure they share. We are working now every day to try to hammer out a SALT agreement with the Soviet Union. They have negotiated in good faith. So have we. This does not mean, however, that there are not areas of contention and areas where we have peaceful competition with the Soviet Union. This is expectable, and I think it will continue for many years in the future.

I don't have any inclination to condemn the Soviets as a people or even as a government. We'll explore in every way we can a way to carry out the purposes and honor the principles of our own Nation, to compete with the Soviet Union's people and government leaders peaceably when necessary, but to seek with them as much friendship, cooperation, trade as possible under those circumstances.

VISIT TO MEXICO

Q. Mr. President, in that you're going to Mexico, I'd like to ask a question on that subject. Given their new-found oil reserves and given the fact that you want to discuss such things as illegal aliens and trade, don't they have you pretty much over a barrel—pardon the bad pun—*[laughter]*—on the matter of illegal aliens, which they don't consider illegal, and on their protective trade rules, if we want any of their energy?

THE PRESIDENT. That's one of the reasons for going to Mexico is to explore the possibilities for resolving these acknowledged differences of opinion between our people and theirs. My goal will be to protect the interests of my Nation and the people whom I represent, and at the same time, obviously, to deal with the Mexicans openly and fairly and to understand and to honor the sensitivities that exist within that great country.

I'm sworn by oath to enforce the laws of our Nation, including immigration laws, to stop smuggling at the border, and in many areas those goals are compatible with the desires of the Mexican people and the Mexican Government. They've cooperated with us superbly, for instance, in stopping the illicit traffic in heroin. And I believe that this is one indication of how we can cooperate.

We are very proud of the recent discoveries of oil and natural gas in Mexico. Obviously, a burgeoning, improving economic situation in Mexico will provide hundreds of thousands of new jobs that will lessen the pressure on some of them to seek employment in our country. And I want to make sure that we minimize any illegalities relating to the border, and I want to make sure that when people are in our country, whether they are here as citizens or not, that we protect their basic human rights.

Another question about energy that you asked—a decision on how much to explore, produce, and sell oil and natural gas is a decision to be made exclusively by the Mexican people. We are interested in purchasing now and perhaps in the future even more oil and natural gas from Mexico. We'll negotiate with them in good faith. We'll pay them a fair price. We'd like to have those policies be predictable on delivery dates and also on price schedules. And we'll try to be a good customer. But we have no inclination to force them to give us a special privilege nor to do anything that would be damaging to the well-being of the Mexican people.

I don't see that these statements that I've made are incompatible with going to Mexico to meet with López Portillo, to talk to his Congress, to talk to his people. I think the best way to resolve differences which do exist is in a framework as I have just described to you.

POLICYMAKING PROCEDURES

Q. Mr. President, you campaigned on a platform of sunshine in government. And in the last few weeks you've been telling your advisers not to reveal what goes on in the decisionmaking process—some of the confusion and some of the disagreement.

THE PRESIDENT. I've never told them that.

Q. Can you enlighten us as to what you *have* told them? Are the reports in the paper wrong about you telling them to sort of cool it on that?

THE PRESIDENT. As has always been the case with Presidents and, I guess, other executive leaders, I have to have two basic relationships with my advisers and my subordinates that sometimes are incompatible. One is, I have to have the widest possible range of advice and counsel, tough debate, sometimes even open criticism as I evolve in my own mind a basic decision to be made on an important subject for the well-being of the people of this country. Then once I make that decision—and most of the controversial decisions are very difficult ones—once I make a decision, I expect my policy to be carried out with loyalty and with enthusiasm. When I make a policy decision that might be contrary to the advice received by some subordinate, if that particular subordinate cannot carry out my policy, then the only option for them is to resign.

There have been very few instances where I have permitted a deviation from that policy. I have never told my people who work under me in the State Department, NSC, Defense, Treasury, Housing, or anything else, not to have contact with the press. I do, however, have to insist upon a degree of teamwork, once a decision is made that relates to a sensitive issue like the Middle East or like SALT negotiations or like the relationships with Iran in recent months.

That's what I have admonished them to do, to have a free expression of opinion and to let me have their individual opinions up until the time I make a decision; once I make a decision, to comply with it.

Q. So, you do not object if members of your administration talk to reporters and tell them about the differences within the administration on a policy as it is moving up towards a final decision?

THE PRESIDENT. I don't think that's always appropriate. I wouldn't want to stand here and tell you that everybody that works in the Government is free to go and express their own personal opinions through the press as a policy is being evolved. Some of these decisions are based on highly secret information, either the attitudes of a foreign leader which cannot be revealed without embarrassment or based on security matters which, if revealed, might work contrary to the best interests of our country. So, I'm not going to issue a blanket permission for anybody in government to have a free access and to express their own views to the press.

I think that the policy that I have laid out is well understood by my people who work with me, both before and during and after a decision is made. And I think that I've described it about as thoroughly as I can this morning.

ENERGY CONSERVATION

Q. Mr. President, do you think that—well, you've spoken a lot about the energy legislation that has been passed by Congress and you also talk about enforcing wage and price guidelines, as well as implementing people's own voluntary efforts to reduce energy usage in the country. But my question is, most of the people, from our standpoint here, seem to feel that we are definitely not in an energy crisis per se. They still haven't been quite convinced. And then, when you say——

THE PRESIDENT. You mean the White House Press Corps or the—*[laughter]*——

Q. No, no, I'm talking about the average American citizen.

THE PRESIDENT. Okay. You said the people here——

Q. And then you talk about—well, you asked the poor people in the country about the energy crisis, and you asked whether or not they would be inclined to reduce, cut down on their usage of lights——

THE PRESIDENT. What's your question?

Q. ——or adhere to the 55-minute—power—my question essentially is, how are you going to enforce implementation of voluntary understanding of the energy crisis, the situation that we are in? And how are you really going to impress upon the people to voluntarily hold back, cut back on their energy?

THE PRESIDENT. Well, one obviously persuasive factor is the rapidly increasing prices of energy, which exercises economic restraint on people's wastefulness. When a person's electric power bill or heating bill goes up in a home, they are naturally more inclined to insulate their home, to cut down the thermostat, and so forth. When the price of gasoline goes up here and in other countries, people are naturally inclined to move toward more efficient automobiles or to reduce the unnecessary use of automobiles.

In addition to that, there's a patriotic element involved. When a President or other leaders call on the American people voluntarily to join together to enhance the economic well-being of the entire Nation, that has a good receptivity among the people of our country, now and in the past.

We have passed about 90—I'd say, 65 percent of the comprehensive energy proposals that I made to the Congress. Some of those are mandated by law, that there have to be shifts away from oil to coal, to solar power, and to natural gas, and to nuclear power, in some instances. Also, there are encouragements built into the law that now give people tax reductions if they shift toward a better insulation for their homes, for instance.

And the last thing is that we have mandated more efficient automobiles, that each year, step by step, the entire automobile production industry, here and abroad, have to comply with much more strict standards on automobile efficiency.

So, a combination of all those things, voluntary, patriotism, and mandated constraints, are the sum total of our energy policy.

THE FEDERAL DEBT

Q. Mr. President, your budget advisers are projecting sizable and rapidly growing budget surpluses after fiscal '81. This is sort of an old-fashioned idea, but I'd like to ask you, have you given any thought to using some of this money to reducing the Federal debt, which is now at $800 billion?

THE PRESIDENT. Well, obviously, when you have a budget surplus, that in itself reduces the Federal debt. The surplus is used to pay off existing debt. Those projections, however, many years in the future, 4 or 5 years in the future in some instances, are predicated on a fairly stable number of Federal programs. They do include basic welfare reform and an evolution into a comprehensive health program.

But what the security needs of our country might be in the future or what other social programs might be, implemented by myself or my successor as President and by the Congress, are hard to predict.

But when we do build toward a balanced budget and then a surplus, those surplus funds would inevitably go into reducing the Federal debt.

EGYPTIAN-ISRAELI PEACE NEGOTIATIONS

Q. Mr. President, do you anticipate that at some point in time you're going to have to call a three-way meeting between yourself, President Sadat, and Prime Minister Begin to get this Middle East peace process locked up and that that might be a natural outcome of the Foreign Ministers' meeting that's coming up?

THE PRESIDENT. I would say that the reality of having a Mideast peace settlement is one of my fondest hopes and dreams and my greatest commitment. I have probably spent more of my personal time on trying to have peace in the Middle East than any other single issue.

We made tremendous strides forward at Camp David, as you know, and we expected at that time to rapidly conclude the remaining 5 percent of the issues that had not then been resolved. That has not proven to be as easy as we thought. I think an inevitable next step is to have the Foreign Ministers of Israel and Egypt come here to meet with Secretary Vance—I might visit with them briefly—in an attitude of mutual commitment and flexibility and in a maximum state of isolation from public statements or commitments, which quite often form a very serious obstacle to progress.

If that hope is realized, there would be no need for any further summit conference. But I would guess that in this case that Mr. Khalil and Dayan would go back to Egypt and to Israel to report progress and to seek confirmation of their negotiated positions from their own government leaders, including President Sadat and Prime Minister Begin.

If that effort is not completely successful and the final peace treaty terms are not concluded, then if there's adequate evidence of flexibility and desire on the part of President Sadat and Prime Minister Begin, then I would certainly consider favorably having them here for a summit meeting.

But our hope is that the Foreign Ministers can be successful, provided they take advantage of our recommendation and routinely go back to Israel and to Egypt to seek further guidance during the negotiations themselves.

OIL PRICES

Q. Mr. President, remembering the revelations that followed the 1973 oil crisis about how the major oil companies ganged up on the American people to reap huge profits, I'd like to know what assurances can you give us in light of what's happening with the cutoff of oil from Iran and the recent announcements of curtailed deliveries by domestic companies that such is not being practiced on the American people again?

THE PRESIDENT. Well, as you know, we have very strict laws concerning the pricing and delivery of oil, both that that's imported and that that's produced and sold within our own country. The laws will change the circumstance in May, and the control of oil prices will be terminated, I think, in September of 1980 [1981] [1]. What will happen then, I don't know, but I don't have any evidence now that there is a violation of either the law

---

[1] Printed in the transcript.

or proprieties in the pricing or distribution of energy products.

MR. CORMIER. Thank you, Mr. President.

THE PRESIDENT. Thank you.

NOTE: President Carter's forty-fourth news conference began at 11:30 a.m. in Room 450 of the Old Executive Office Building. It was broadcast live on radio and television.

Department of Education

Message to the Congress Transmitting Proposed Legislation.   *February 13, 1979*

To the Congress of the United States:

I am sending to the Congress today my proposal to establish a Department of Education.

There is a compelling need for the increased national attention a separate Cabinet department will bring to education issues. Our Nation's pluralistic education system, considered the most competent and open in the world, faces many problems and challenges: a decline in public confidence in the quality of education; unacceptably high rates of high school dropouts and of young people who lack basic educational tools and specific skills for productive employment; and increasing demands for retraining and learning opportunities.

The primary responsibility for education in our Nation lies with State and local government. The Federal government has a limited, but critical responsibility to help public and private institutions meet these challenges: to ensure equal educational opportunities; to increase access to postsecondary education by low and middle income students; to generate research and provide information to help our educational systems meet

special needs; prepare students for employment; and encourage improvements in the quality of our education. The achievement of each of these goals will be enhanced by a new Department of Education.

Through our legislative and budget initiatives of the past two years, this Administration has given high priority to meeting these educational commitments. My budget for FY 1980 provides for $13.3 billion in education outlays, about a 45 percent increase above the level when I came into office. Last year, we established a legislative framework, the Middle Income Student Assistance program, to help solve one of our major education problems—the growing cost of a college education. The establishment of a Cabinet Department of Education will reflect the continued high priority my Administration places on education.

A Department of Education will bring our Nation's educational challenges and the Federal government's role in meeting them to the forefront of domestic policy discussion. Such discussion is vital to an activity that directly affects 60 million students, teachers and educational employees and constitutes a $120 billion public and private enterprise.

Establishing a separate Department will create, for the first time, a Cabinet-level advocate for education with direct access to the President, the Congress, and the public.

Second, it will give Federal education programs the full-time, high-level leadership and management that they cannot receive in a structure so large and complex as the Department of Health, Education, and Welfare. This will allow the Federal government to fulfill its responsibilities in education more effectively. It will eliminate duplication in the administrative and staff support activities within the Office of the HEW Secretary and the Education Division. It will allow improved financial management and more efficient administration of education programs. Separation of the education functions from HEW will also promote improved management of its closely-related health and welfare responsibilities.

Third, it will provide greater accountability. Submerged beneath HEW's dominant functions of health and welfare, Federal education programs lack full-time accountability at the Cabinet level. With a separate Department of Education, one Cabinet member will report directly to the President and be accountable to the Congress and the American people for the conduct of Federal education policies.

Fourth, it will provide simpler, more reliable, and more responsive support to states, localities, public and private institutions, giving them a direct line of Cabinet-level contact with the Federal government.

Fifth, the new Department will allow better coordination of education programs with related Federal activities, such as employment programs and research. It will also allow high-level consideration of the impact of other Federal policies, such as tax and energy, on education institutions and students.

Under the proposal I am submitting today, the Department of Education will include more than 150 programs and 16,-200 employees. With a budget of more than $13 billion, this Department will be larger than five other Departments including Energy, Commerce, Justice, Interior and State.

In addition to the 140 programs in the Education Division of the Department of Health, Education, and Welfare, the new Department of Education will handle ed-

ucational activities now carried out by several other departments. These include: the U.S. Department of Agriculture School, certain science education programs of the National Science Foundation, the overseas dependents' schools of the Department of Defense, the college housing loan program of the Department of Housing and Urban Development, the Law Enforcement Education and the Law Enforcement Internship Program of the Department of Justice, and the Migrant Education programs of the Department of Labor.

The proposed legislation establishes within the Department of Education separate Offices for Civil Rights, Elementary and Secondary Education, Postsecondary Education and Educational Research and Improvement, each headed by an Assistant Secretary. It establishes an office to administer functions related to the education of overseas dependents of Department of Defense personnel, an Inspector General, and a 20-member Intergovernmental Advisory Council on Education, appointed by the President, to promote better relations with the various levels of government and private institutions.

I urge the Senate and the House of Representatives to act promptly on this important proposal.

JIMMY CARTER

The White House,
    February 13, 1979.

International Whaling Commission

Message to the Congress Transmitting a Report.   February 13, 1979

To the Congress of the United States:

On December 14, 1978, Secretary of Commerce Kreps certified to me, pursuant to the Pelly Amendment to the Fishermen's Protective Act of 1967, that nationals of Peru, Chile and the Republic of Korea were conducting whaling operations in a manner that diminishes the effectiveness of the International Whaling Commission conservation programs.

Under the Pelly Amendment, such a certification must be followed by a report to the Congress. I am pleased to transmit the attached report which indicates that all three of these nations are becoming members of the International Whaling Commission and will therefore voluntarily become subject to its conservation programs. Thus, I am not at this time imposing sanctions against these nations.

JIMMY CARTER

The White House,
    February 13, 1979.

REPORT TO CONGRESS

The Pelly Amendment to the Fishermen's Protective Act of 1967, 22 U.S.C. § 1978 (1971), as amended, provides that when the Secretary of Commerce determines that nationals of a foreign country, directly or indirectly, are conducting fishing operations in a manner or under circumstances which diminish the effectiveness of an international fishery conservation program, the Secretary shall certify such determination to the President. Upon receipt of such certification, the President may direct the Secretary of the Treasury to prohibit the importation into the United States of fishery products of the offending country for such duration as the President determines appropriate to the extent that such prohibition is sanctioned by the General Agreement on Tariffs and Trade. Within sixty days following any such certification, the President is required to notify the Congress of any action taken pursuant to such certification.

On December 14, 1978, Secretary of Commerce Kreps certified to me, pursuant to the Pelly Amendment, that nationals of Peru, Chile and the Republic of Korea were conducting whaling operations in a manner and under circumstances that diminish the effectiveness of International Whaling Commission (IWC) conservation programs.

Peruvian vessels caught 592 Bryde's and sei whales in the waters off the western coast of South America during the 1975–1976 season, all of which were in excess of the IWC conservation quota of 198. Peruvian vessels also caught 1,261 sperm whales during the 1975–1976 season, which exceeded the IWC conservation quota for such whales by 396. During the 1976–1977 season, Peruvian vessels caught 1,140 sperm whales, despite the IWC prohibition of such catches. Peruvian vessels also caught 368 Bryde's and sei whales during the 1976–1977 season, despite the IWC prohibition of Bryde's whale catches and despite the catch by other countries of 298 of the 388 sei whales permitted by the IWC. Although precise information by species taken is not available for the 1977–1978 season, the Government of Peru established a unilateral quota of 300 sei and Bryde's whales and 900 sperm whales for that season, despite the IWC prohibition of Bryde's and sperm whale catches. Peruvian vessels continued to hunt in the waters off Peru and Chile during the 1977–1978 season, and at least 1,085 Bryde's and sperm whales were taken by Peruvian vessels during that season, despite the IWC prohibition of such catches.

Although precise information is not available for the 1975–1976 season, Chilean vessels caught at least 23 sei whales in the waters off the west coast of South America during that season, all of which were in excess of the IWC conservation quota of 198. During the 1976–1977 season, Chilean vessels caught 76 sperm whales despite the IWC prohibition of sperm whale catches. During the 1977–1978 season the Government of Chile established unilateral quotas allowing further catches of sperm whales despite the continuing IWC prohibition, and Chilean nationals acquired additional whaling equipment and continued to hunt in the area. It is therefore likely that Chilean vessels continued to exceed the IWC conservation quota for sperm whales during that season.

Vessels of the Republic of Korea caught 43 fin whales in the waters of the western North Pacific during the 1976 season according to information received from the Government of the Republic of Korea, despite the IWC prohibition of commercial catches of such whales. Information subsequently received from the Government of the Republic of Korea indicated that such whales were not fin whales but were Bryde's whales. However, since the IWC quota for Bryde's whales was almost entirely taken by Japanese and Soviet vessels during the season, the Korean catch of 43 whales, whether Bryde's whales or fin whales, exceeded the applicable IWC conservation quotas during 1976. During the 1977 season vessels of the Republic of Korea caught 1,033 minke whales despite the catch by other countries of 248 of the 541 minke whales permitted by the IWC, thereby exceeding the IWC conservation quota for such whales.

I have favored a ten-year moratorium on all commercial whaling since I was a member of the United States Delegation to the United Nations Conference on the Human Environment in Stockholm in 1972. Although we have not yet been able to achieve such a moratorium, in recent years we have made substantial progress in establishing selective moratoria for species of whales that need protection. For example, in 1973 the IWC quota for sei whales was more than 7,500 per year. Since 1975, the IWC has maintained a moratorium on the taking of sei whales in the North Pacific Ocean. At the 1978 IWC meeting in London, the sei whale quota was reduced to zero in the Southern Ocean, leaving a total allowable catch of only 84 sei whales per year in the North Atlantic. At the recent special IWC meeting in Tokyo, sperm whale quotas for the North Pacific were reduced by 41%. In addition, the IWC has become increasingly responsive to scientific information about the world's whales. As a result, since 1972 the annual allowable take of whales from populations now subject to IWC quotas has been reduced by nearly 60%, from 46,000 to less than 20,000.

This progress had been threatened by the continued failure of the Governments of Peru, Chile and the Republic of Korea to adhere to internationally accepted measures for the conservation of whales.

During the past year the Department of State has contacted the Governments of Peru, Chile and the Republic of Korea about this matter on a number of occasions, stressing United States concern about their whaling operations, urging that they join the IWC or otherwise adhere to IWC quotas, and informing them of possible application of the provisions of the Pelly Amendment. At the June 1978 meeting of the IWC, the Government of the Republic of Korea indicated its intention to join the IWC by its July 1979 meeting. The Governments of Peru and Chile also indicated their intention to join the IWC by that meeting, but stressed their concern about minimizing the impact on their fishing industries that would result from immediate adherence to IWC quotas.

I am pleased to report that substantial progress has been made since the June 1978 IWC meeting.

The Government of the Republic of Korea became a member of the IWC on December 29, 1978, and the whaling activities of its nationals are now subject to IWC conservation measures.

The Government of Peru has ratified the International Convention for the Regulation of Whaling and will shortly deposit its instrument of ratification with our Department of State effective as of the next IWC meeting in July 1979 or earlier. The Government of Peru will thus be a member of the IWC in time to participate in its next meeting, and the whaling activities of Peruvian nationals will be subject to IWC conservation measures by that time. In the interim, the Government of Peru has indicated that Peruvian nationals will not take any sei whales during the current season. I have also asked the State Department to work with the Peruvian Government in an effort to achieve interim reductions in sperm and Bryde's whale quotas.

The Government of Chile is now completing final arrangements for ratification of the Convention. The Government of Chile has indicated that the process will be completed, and that the instrument of ratification will be deposited with our Department of State, by the next IWC meeting in July 1979 or earlier, thereby subjecting the whaling activities of Chilean nationals to the conservation measures of the IWC as of that time.

In light of these developments, I believe trade sanctions should not now be imposed. In the event the Government of Chile has not completed its arrangements to join the IWC or otherwise adhere to IWC quotas before the next IWC meeting, I intend to reassess this position and take such additional actions as may be warranted. I will send to you a supplemental report at that time.

Law Enforcement Assistance Administration

Nomination of Henry S. Dogin To Be Administrator.   February 13, 1979

The President today announced that he will nominate Henry S. Dogin, of Armonk, N.Y., to be Administrator of Law Enforcement Assistance. He would replace Richard W. Velde, who has resigned.

Dogin was born December 26, 1934, in Brooklyn, N.Y. He received a B.A. from Cornell University in 1956 and an LL.B. from Columbia School of Law in 1961. He served in the U.S. Navy from 1956 to 1958.

From 1961 to 1967, Dogin was assistant district attorney for the county of New York. From 1967 to 1971, he was assistant counsel to the Waterfront Commission of New York Harbor. He served as Deputy Regional Administrator of the New York regional office of LEAA from 1971 to 1973.

Dogin was Deputy Assistant Attorney General for the Criminal Division from 1973 to 1975, and Acting Administrator of the Drug Enforcement Agency from 1975 to 1976. From 1976 to 1978, he was deputy commissioner of the New York State Division of Criminal Justice Services.

Since 1978 Dogin has been Deputy Administrator of LEAA for Policy Development and has served as Acting Administrator.

National Museum Services Board

Nomination of Two Members.
February 13, 1979

The President today announced that he will nominate for reappointment two current members of the National Museum Services Board for terms expiring December 6, 1983. They are:

DOUGLAS DILLON, president of the Metropolitan Museum of Art in New York City, and
NEIL HARRIS, a professor of history at the University of Chicago, specializing in art and cultural history.

Adolph Dubs

Statement on the Death of the U.S. Ambassador to Afghanistan.
February 14, 1979

I am shocked and saddened by the murder of Ambassador Adolph Dubs in Kabul this morning. The act of brutality which took his life has deprived our Nation of one of its most able public servants.

Throughout his distinguished career in the Foreign Service, Ambassador Dubs took on difficult and challenging jobs, performing them with exemplary dedication and skill. He died as he lived—in the service of his country—and the manner of his death redoubles our dedication to the struggle against the kind of senseless violence which took his life. My thoughts and prayers are with the family of Ambassador Dubs.

NOTE: Ambassador Dubs was kidnaped in Kabul by terrorists on the morning of February 14, and was subsequently killed during an attempt by Afghan police to free him from his captors.

Department of Defense

Nomination of Robert B. Pirie, Jr., To Be an Assistant Secretary.   February 14, 1979

The President today announced that he will nominate Robert B. Pirie, Jr., as Assistant Secretary of Defense for Manpower, Reserve Affairs and Logistics. He would replace John P. White, whom the President has nominated as Deputy Director of the Office of Management and Budget.

Pirie, of Bethesda, Md., was born September 10, 1933, in San Diego, Calif. He received a B.S. from the U.S. Naval Academy in 1955 and an M.A. from Oxford University in 1963.

Pirie served in the U.S. Navy from 1955 to 1975, where he served on several nuclear submarines, as a staff analyst in the Naval Forces Division of the Office of the Secretary of Defense, as commanding officer of the U.S.S. *Skipjack,* as senior staff assistant to the Director of the National Security Council's Net Assessment Group, and as Deputy Director of Net Assessment in the Office of the Secretary of Defense.

From 1975 to 1977, Pirie was deputy assistant director for national security of the Congressional Budget Office. Since 1977 he has been Deputy Assistant Secretary of Defense for Manpower, Reserve Affairs and Logistics.

Federal Regional Councils

Designation of Chairpersons for the 10 Federal Regions.   February 14, 1979

The President has designated 10 persons to serve as Chairpersons of the Federal Regional Councils in 10 Federal regions. The Chairpersons are selected from among the regional directors of the major domestic agencies and serve for 1 year.

Federal Regional Councils work with the Office of Management and Budget and the Interagency Coordinating Council to implement intergovernmental programs and resolve State and local issues at the regional level.

The 10 persons are:

Region I (Boston)—Joe Grandmaison, Federal Cochairman of the New England Regional Development Commission;
Region II (New York City)—Tom Appleby, Regional Director of HUD;
Region III (Philadelphia)—Tom Maloney, Regional Director of HUD;
Region IV (Atlanta)—Sara Craig, Principal Regional Official of HEW;
Region V (Chicago)—Doug Kelm, Regional Representative of DOT;
Region VI (Dallas)—Ed Coker, Secretary's Representative of Commerce;
Region VII (Kansas City)—John Kemp, Regional Representative of DOT;
Region VIII (Denver)—Betty Miller, Regional Director of HUD;
Region IX (San Francisco)—Bill Arntz, Regional Representative of Energy;
Region X (Seattle)—Bernard Kelly, Principal Regional Official of HEW.

Executive Schedule

Executive Order 12119.   February 14, 1979

LEVELS IV AND V OF THE EXECUTIVE SCHEDULE

By the authority vested in me as President of the United States of America by Section 5317 of Title 5 of the United States Code, and in order to place the position of Counselor on Legislative and Intergovernmental Policy, Department of the Treasury in level IV of the Executive Schedule, Executive Order No. 12076, as amended, is further amended by deleting "Assistant Attorney General, United States Attorneys and Trial Advocacy, Department of Justice." from Section 1–101

(f) and by inserting in lieu thereof "Counselor on Legislative and Intergovernmental Policy, Department of the Treasury.".

JIMMY CARTER

The White House,
    February 14, 1979.

[Filed with the Office of the Federal Register,
    2:37 p.m., February 14, 1979]

Communications Systems for Rural Areas

Announcement of New Measures Under the Rural Development Initiatives Program. February 14, 1979

The President today announced initiatives designed to overcome isolation in rural areas through modern communications technology.

The communications initiatives include FCC regulatory changes, a loan program to encourage telephone companies to provide television and associated broadband services to rural residents, and a number of demonstration grants. They are intended to encourage the use of modern communications systems in bringing health, education, information, and entertainment services to small towns and rural areas.

The communications initiatives are the latest to be announced in conjunction with the White House Rural Development Initiatives program. Along with recently announced measures dealing with health care and water and sewer programs, today's announcement is part of the administration's effort, articulated in the State of the Union message sent to Congress last month, to address the problems to rural America.

Coordination of the communications initiatives will be carried out by the Interagency Committee on Telecommunications.

Communications Satellite Corporation

Nomination of Jesse Hill, Jr., To Be a Member of the Board of Directors. February 14, 1979

The President today nominated Jesse Hill, Jr., of Atlanta, Ga., to be a member of the Board of Directors of the Communications Satellite Corporation until the date of the annual meeting of the Corporation in 1982.

He was initially nominated on January 18, 1979, for the remainder of a term which will expire in May of 1979.

Hill, 52, is president and chief executive officer of the Atlanta Life Insurance Co., the largest stockholder life insurance company or financial institution controlled and managed by black Americans. He is also president of the Atlanta Chamber of Commerce.

President's Commission on Pension Policy

Appointment of 10 Members. February 14, 1979

The President today announced the appointment of 10 persons as members of the President's Commission on Pension Policy. They are:

HENRY L. BOWDEN, an Atlanta attorney, chairman of the board of trustees of Emory University, and director of the First National Bank of Atlanta;

JOHN T. BRAGG, of Murfreesboro, Tenn., a Tennessee State representative, member of the Tennessee House council on pensions and retirement, and former chairman of the Southern Legislative Conference;

LISLE C. CARTER, JR., president of the University of the District of Columbia, formerly chancellor of the Atlanta University Center and a professor of public policy;

JAMES CLARK, JR., a Maryland State senator, chairman of the senate finance committee and the pension study committee, and a member of the National Conference of State Legislatures' public pensions task force;

PAUL R. DEAN, of Falls Church, Va., a neutral trustee of the United Mine Workers of America health and retirement funds, and a professor of law at Georgetown University;

WILLIAM C. GREENOUGH, of New York City, chairman and chief executive officer of the TIAA-CREF pension plan, an expert and author of numerous books on pension plans and social security;

MARTHA W. GRIFFITHS, of Romeo, Mich., a former Member of Congress, now an attorney with the firm of Griffiths & Griffiths;

HARVEY KAPNICK, of Winnetka, Ill., chairman of Arthur Anderson & Co.;

JOHN H. LYONS, of Potomac, Md., general president of the International Association of Bridge, Structural and Ornamental Iron Workers, and a member of the National Commission for Manpower Policy;

DOROTHY W. NELSON, of Pasadena, Calif., dean of the University of Southern California Law Center.

The Honorable Adolph Dubs

Executive Order 12120. February 14, 1979

As a special mark of respect to the memory of the Honorable Adolph Dubs, Ambassador of the United States of America to Afghanistan, killed while in the performance of his duty, it is hereby ordered, pursuant to the provisions of 36 U.S.C. 175(m), that on the day of interment, the flag of the United States shall be flown at half-staff on all buildings, grounds, and naval vessels of the Federal government in the District of Columbia and throughout the United States and its territories and possessions. I also direct that the flag shall be flown at half-staff on the same day at all United States em-

271

bassies, consular offices, and other facilities abroad, including all military facilities and naval vessels and stations.

JIMMY CARTER

The White House,
February 14, 1979.

[Filed with the Office of the Federal Register, 2:27 p.m., February 21, 1979]

Budget Deferrals

Message to the Congress.   February 14, 1979

To the Congress of the United States:

In accordance with the Impoundment Control Act of 1974, I herewith report revisions to three previously transmitted deferrals increasing the amount deferred by $33.8 million. These revisions to existing deferrals involve programs in the Departments of Transportation and the Treasury and the International Communication Agency.

The details of the deferrals are contained in the attached reports.

JIMMY CARTER

The White House,
February 14, 1979.

NOTE: The attachments detailing the deferrals are printed in the FEDERAL REGISTER of February 21, 1979.

Mexico City, Mexico

Remarks of President José López Portillo and President Carter at the Welcoming Ceremony.   February 14, 1979

PRESIDENT LÓPEZ PORTILLO. Mr. President of the United States of America, Mrs. Carter, upon your arrival to Mexico in the name of the people of Mexico, in the name of the country, in the name of the govern-

ment, in the name of my family, I cordially welcome you.

Two years ago it was my pleasure to be the first foreign head of state to visit your country during your administration. Now you are reciprocating this visit. Thus we continue with the possibility of the dialog that was started at that time.

At that time we said, and we say so once again now, that it is good for neighbors to be friends. It is my conviction, sir, that from our personal contact, a good friendship was started. This friendship is now being renewed.

Very objectively, Mr. President, that few countries in the world have so much to talk about, so many matters as we do.

In Mexico you will find that there is enormous interest in this visit and results that it will bring with it. For us, among all of our relations with the rest of the nations of the world, the ones that have more importance are those that we have with the United States. Expectation you will find in accordance with our pluralism and our freedom. You will find this expectation in all mass communication media—press, radio, television—in the streets and also on signs on the walls.

As regards all the subjects that we are going to deal with, I believe that we have already set up the system for such dealings with the system that we set up during my visit to Washington.

This system was established on the principles that are common to us both, and on mechanisms that we agreed to set up. However, I am completely certain that the most important thing of all is good will and a good disposition in order to take care of our problems; a will to agree, a will for peace, a will to establish our decisions on the mandates of the law; and perhaps the most important will of all, the will to be friends, which means reciprocal respect and dignity in our dealings.

Mr. President, we receive you within the framework of this spirit. We hope that in our future and, for us, very important talks, it is this spirit that will prevail.

This is what our people expect from us in fulfilling our responsibility. We welcome you, sir, and we hope your sojourn in Mexico will be a happy one.

[*At this point, President Carter responded to President López Portillo's remarks in Spanish. He then translated his remarks into English as follows.*]

PRESIDENT CARTER. And now I would like to say in my own language, for the benefit of the people of my country, that we are very delighted and honored to come again to the great country of Mexico, to increase my own understanding of the Mexican people and to enjoy an official visit with my friend, President López Portillo.

My wife Rosalynn and I have come to Mexico many times—first when I was a young naval officer, and later on a 3-week visit when we traveled through this great country trying to make ourselves understood in Spanish and to learn more about the impressive culture and history of Mexico. Also, I came here to visit for a promotion of trade when I was Governor of Georgia. But I've never had a welcome like this.

I come here now to reunite with my friend President López Portillo to discuss very important issues between Mexico and the United States. It's very important to strengthen the fundamental relationships between our two countries.

The basis for our discussions, of course, is a sincere recognition of some very important problems that require solutions, and also an appreciation of the common objectives and purposes and the great opportunities that we have between our two countries, in a spirit of peace, friendship, and mutual respect.

We live in a time of great change, dramatic and emotional change in Mexico, in the United States, and in the problems and opportunities we face together. We have a great deal to accomplish.

My wife and I, the entire party from the United States come here very pleased at a new opportunity to turn to your beautiful country to reinspire ourselves, to strengthen even further the friendship that binds us together with you, Mr. President, your wonderful family, and the people of this great country.

I cannot imagine a more appropriate day for our own reunion and to express the feelings that the people of my country have toward yours.

Happy St. Valentine's Day! Long live Mexico!

Thank you very much.

NOTE: The exchange began at 11:20 a.m. at Licenciado Benito Juarez International Airport. President López Portillo spoke in Spanish, and his remarks were translated by an interpreter.

Following the ceremony, President Carter proceeded to the Palacio Nacional for a meeting with President López Portillo.

Mexico City, Mexico

Toasts at the Luncheon Honoring President Carter. February 14, 1979

PRESIDENT LÓPEZ PORTILLO. *Mr. President of the United States of America, James Carter, Mrs. Carter, ladies and gentlemen:*

It has been 2 years now since we met for the first time. Since then, a great deal of water has flowed under the bridges of the Rio Grande. A great deal has also happened within our countries and between our countries, as it has in the world and to the world.

United by geography and the borders that scar it, and immersed in the conflicts of a sometimes bitter and invariably complex history, we have set out to order our conduct as neighbors according to the precepts of law and, even more important, on the favorable basis of mutual friendship. This implies good will, expressed in terms of respectful, fair, and worthy treatment.

Today, 2 years later, it is only fitting that we evaluate our objectives and face the facts that confront us. We know better now what each expects of the other, but I believe we also know that we have not yet put our friendship to the test, since we have not yet decided what we are willing to make of our relationship. We can view it as a problem, or we can think of it as a conflict. In the first case, there are solutions, which would be welcomed by our friends; in the second, confrontation, which would give joy to our enemies.

We know that in a world characterized by extraordinary and difficult changes and by the readjustment of forces, interests, resources, and positions, your great country is still in the process of redefining its policies and that this makes your decisions all the more difficult.

Nevertheless, we see in you a leader who has sought to revive the moral foundations of the political institutions of the United States. With great personal integrity, you have sought to replace provisional arrangements with lasting agreements.

That is what we are hoping for. That is what we are determined to do. Our peoples want definitive agreements, not circumstantial concessions.

Among permanent, not casual, neighbors, surprise moves and sudden deceit or abuse are poisonous fruits that sooner or later have a reverse effect.

Consequently, we must take a long-range view of ourselves. No injustice can prevail without affronting decency and dignity.

It is difficult, particularly among neighbors, to maintain cordial and mutually advantageous relations in an atmosphere of mistrust or open hostility.

We do not wish to view our history as one that uselessly anchors us, like so many pillars of salt, to a burden of resentment, just as we would not like you to contemplate your future in terms of the risks of silent migration. Neither anchors nor silence must impede our dealings with one another.

A good-neighbor policy presupposes a general climate of opinion in which respect prevails over prejudice and intelligence over sectarianism.

Over our 3,000 kilometers of common border, we are the most representative example of North-South relations—the confluence of two expanding civilizations, formerly separated by the desert, but now closely linked by a complex series of conurbations and exchanges.

But no matter how greatly our relations may have been intensified, they are neither exclusive nor excluding. As a world power, the United States is increasing its presence and its commitments on all continents. Mexico, as an independent country, recognizes no limitations on the diversification of its exchanges, other than its principles and its development requirements.

It is in that light that we must view the complex phenomenon of our interrelationship, which should never be confused with dependence, integration, or the blurring of borders. The two countries complement and need each other, but neither would want to depend on the other to the point of nullifying its own sovereign will, reducing the scope of its international activities, or losing its self-respect.

All this requires thoroughgoing analysis; we must not sacrifice what is important for the sake of what is urgent nor neglect international and continuing needs in favor of local and transitory interests. Thus, we must keep a firm grasp on matters of basic importance in devising solutions to our immediate problems.

Today, the United States is readjusting its power and influence in an irrational world that refuses to take rights and obligations into account in its pursuit of its interests and outbreaks of violence, a world in which Manichaean political structures impede development and make underdevelopment even more distressing. Meanwhile, supranational economic hegemonies—devoid of any sense of social responsibility and recognizing no country as their own—are dividing up the world among themselves and winning out over sovereign nations.

And today, in this same world and for the first time in its history, Mexico, because of a nonrenewable resource and the financial self-determination it provides, has been given the opportunity of becoming the free, secure, and just nation envisaged by its great leaders of the past, a nation ruled by the principles of a revolution that has evolved into a government and determined to live in peace nurtured by respect for the rights of others—a simple maxim, perhaps, but a valid one.

Mexico has thus suddenly found itself the center of American attention—attention that is a surprising mixture of interest, disdain, and fear, much like the recurring vague fears you yourselves inspire in certain areas of our national subconscious.

You and I, Mr. President, have the task of dealing with the problem, of rationalizing realities and prejudices, and fulfilling our responsibility to our nations by keeping insensitivity, ambition, fear, or self-seeking manipulation of illusions from casting a shadow on a relationship founded on friendship or eliminating any possibility of understanding.

Let us seek only lasting solutions—good faith and fair play—nothing that would make us lose the respect of our children.

Multilateral relations, economic order, trade and prices, demography, finance, currency, drugs, energy sources—land, sea, air, or gas—migratory labor, or human rights and all their associated questions constitute agendas that call for varying degrees of attention. What must not vary are the principles on which our relations are based, and the most fundamental of these is treating others as we ourselves would like to be treated. That is a canon that holds true for both men and nations, the test of our good will and the measure of our deeds.

It is with such good will that, within the context of that relationship, I want to assume my temporary responsibility for the permanent destiny of my people, which, like you, I have sworn to serve and have no right to endanger. I am certain that you feel the same way, and in token of this, let us join in a toast as we hope to join our wills.

I thank you.

PRESIDENT CARTER. *Mr. President, Mrs. López Portillo, distinguished guests who've come here both from the great nation of Mexico and from the United States:*

President López Portillo and I have, in the short time together on this visit, found that we have many things in common. We both represent great nations; we both have found an interest in archeology; we both must deal with difficult questions like energy and the control of inflation. We both look across the flowing waters of the Rio Grande with interest, expressions of friendship, concern, sometimes a lack of understanding, but a determination to make the future brighter.

We both have beautiful and interesting wives, and we both run several kilometers every day. [*Laughter*] As a matter of fact, I told President López Portillo that I first acquired my habit of running here in Mexico City. My first running course was from the Palace of Fine Arts to the Majestic Hotel, where me and my family were staying. In the midst of the Folklorico performance, I discovered that I was afflicted with Montezuma's revenge. [*Laughter*]

We have also noticed some remarkable changes at that time. My wife and I and my three sons stayed at the Majestic Hotel on the Zocalo for about a week, and we paid each day, $5.50. The view itself was worth that price.

At the end of my visit, I will have the honor of speaking to the Congress of Mexico. In your address to the United States Congress 2 years ago, Mr. President, you said, and I quote, "Mexico has never been, nor is it now, the leader of any continent or group of countries." I respect this modest view of your nation's role. Yet our world is changing very rapidly. It is no longer divided into monolithic ideological nor military blocs. The southern tier of our planet, the so-called developing world, is asserting its rights and the responsibilities that go with those rights. And no one can deny that Mexico's new strength, Mexico's new confidence, and Mexico's new importance in the world economy are casting your country in a new world role.

We seek to appreciate the individuality of each independent nation and to guide our own policies accordingly. My administration and the people of our country recognize the uniqueness of Mexico. By your own choice, as you have said, Mr. President, Mexico is not the leader of any bloc, but on many global issues the independent voice of Mexico is heard with increasing strength and persuasiveness.

Mexico's voice is heard, for example, on the crucial issue of the world's economic system—to make it more just, more equitable, and how to increase the participation of the people of the developing world. Because of the different levels of development, economically speaking, of our two countries, our respective visions of the pace and the kind of change are somewhat different. But our dialog is a creative one, beneficial to all countries of the world, regardless of the degree of their industrialization.

Mexico's voice is heard as an advocate of a truly international approach to human rights. The Mexican people have a history of long and successful struggle, not only for national independence but for social justice and the dignity of the individual.

Mexico has used its influence on behalf of internationally recognized standards of human rights, both political and economic. This has been one of my own most deeply felt concerns.

Our policies, both foreign and domestic, must reflect our values as a people. Those of us who are national leaders have a responsibility to speak out when human rights are violated abroad, and we also have a responsibility to protect human rights at home. That extends to the basic human rights of all those who, for whatever reason, are within the borders of our countries.

The struggle for human rights is not a static thing. It offers new challenges to every generation. During the 1960's in the United States, we enacted new laws to protect the civil and voting rights of all citizens regardless of language, race, or color. Here in Mexico, Mr. President, you've initiated an important political reform and an amnesty law, evidence of your belief in open debate and in the accommodation of opposing views.

Finally, and most important, the voice of Mexico is heard in the service of world peace. Your government has worked long and hard to control weapons and armaments, both nuclear and conventional, both in this hemisphere and throughout the world. It would not be going too far to say that of all the major countries on Earth, there is none more dedicated to arms control and more opposed to militarism than Mexico.

The leaders of this great country have taken an extremely important initiative in the Treaty of Tlatelolco, a treaty that was signed here at this place. This effort to make this region of the entire world into a nuclear weapons-free zone is one of the most creative steps that any country has taken since the invention of these terrible weapons of nuclear destruction.

Your approach is both visionary and practical, a difficult combination to achieve. I hope and I trust that it will serve as a model for other regions on Earth. And in the United Nations and elsewhere, you have [been][1] similarly creative in trying to stanch the spread of conventional arms.

We welcome Mexico's advocacy of these issues. Though our two countries may not agree with each other in every particular, there is a sense of shared concern and shared values which underline our relationships.

In the spirit of mutual respect and mutual regard and with great admiration, Mr. President, I look forward to continuing to work with you toward a

---

[1] Printed in the transcript.

world community of justice, diversity, and peace.

And now, I would like to propose a toast, Mr. President: First, to the health of the President of Mexico and to Mrs. López Portillo, to the continuing friendship and cooperation of the peoples of Mexico and the peoples of the United States of America, and to what we most desire, peace throughout the world.

Thank you.

NOTE: The exchange began at 4:25 p.m. in the Banquet Room at the Foreign Ministry Building. President López Portillo spoke in Spanish, and his remarks were translated by an interpreter.

Prior to the luncheon, President Carter had toured the Palacio Nacional and the Templo Mayor, an Aztec archeological site.

Mexico City, Mexico

Remarks at the United States Embassy. February 14, 1979

THE PRESIDENT. *Fellow employees of the United States Government:*

You and I are indeed fortunate to be partners in the service of a great nation, with the task of improving relationships among people who are bound together by intense and ancient ties of friendship, kinship, mutual problems, mutual opportunities, and a greater future.

It's no accident that this embassy here in the capital of Mexico is the largest United States embassy on Earth. This is because the relationships between the United States of America and the Republic of Mexico are so important to Americans, important not just to our own two countries and our two peoples but important indeed throughout this entire hemisphere.

You have a special challenge here. There are 20 million Americans who speak Spanish, most of them having come from Mexico or having their parents or ancestors having come from this great land. Your responsibility is to tie our two countries together economically, politically, and in matters of mutual interest and mutual security. But because of the unique relationship, because we share so much, your official duties, as I've just outlined so briefly, have important human concerns. Yours is not a sterile responsibility, and it's almost impossible in an embassy in this country, representing the United States, to separate matters of foreign policy from matters of domestic policy.

You, perhaps more than any other embassy representatives of our country, must be both diplomats and politicians—politicians in the finest sense of the word; understanding human needs, understanding the diversity that exists within this country and within our own Nation, understanding differences, and, more importantly, understanding similarities.

This special requirement for you is the reason that I was personally interested in asking my friend, former Governor Pat Lucey, to take on this important responsibility, because I knew that he and his wife, Jean, were fully capable of combining the finest in diplomacy with the finest in politics in human terms. I'm indeed proud of Ambassador Pat Lucey, and I'm indeed proud of every one of you.

I know that the visit of a President burdens you with greatly expanded duties, assignments, and responsibilities. It's a challenge when there are so many highly publicized issues which need to be resolved for you to make adequate preparations for a visit so important as this one.

I thank you for it, and I would also like to thank the members of the families of those who work here, because I know that you've been deprived of your wives or husbands, your fathers or your mothers, in preparing for my visit. And I'm sure that after I leave, having made my welcoming address at the airport and planning to address the Mexican Congress in Spanish, it'll take you 2 or 3 weeks to repair the damage that I will have done. [*Laughter*]

I would like to express special thanks to the employees here who are Mexican citizens. You understand much better than could a citizen of the United States the special needs and interests of the people of Mexico. Your closeness here within the embassy helps to ensure the closeness of the 220 million people who live in our country and the many millions of people who live here. In microcosm, you represent in the finest way the interrelationship between our two countries.

I want to say a word, too, to the young Americans who attend school here, and I'll combine them with all Americans who work here. I hope that you will take every possible advantage of this rare opportunity to learn what you can about an exciting, interesting, intriguing country and people. The culture, the history, the language, if learned about by you, will be an added value for the rest of your lives.

I hope that whenever your own duties permit, or consonant with your duties, that you will travel throughout this land, study its history, learn its people and places, and absorb the consciousness of the people who live in Mexico.

Yours is most important work, and I'm very grateful that our country has dedicated people like you, competent and professional, to represent our great Nation in this great nation.

Thank you very much.

And now, I would like to introduce to you my favorite First Lady, Rosalynn.

Mrs. Carter. I just wanted to add a word of thanks to you too for all you do for us. You are so important to us, you represent us so well. And sometimes I think in Washington we don't take time to adequately thank you for all you mean to us, or to adequately recognize how important you are and what you do to keep the relationship between our two countries stable and good.

And so, I'm just thankful that we could be here personally to say to you how much we do care for you and how much we do thank you for all you do for our country.

Thank you.

NOTE: The President spoke at 5:30 p.m. in the courtyard of the embassy building.

Earlier in the afternoon, the President participated in a wreathlaying ceremony at the Independence Monument.

That evening, President Carter and President López Portillo attended a performance of the Ballet Folklorico at the Palacio de Bellas Artes.

Reorganization of Foreign Assistance Programs

Announcement of the Administration Proposal. February 15, 1979

The White House announced today that President Carter will propose to the Congress a far-reaching reorganization of U.S. foreign assistance programs, the first such restructuring since AID was established in 1961. It is designed to improve the cost-effectiveness of U.S. assistance to developing nations.

The reorganization would consolidate policy direction of development agencies and responsibilities in a new International Development Cooperation Administration (IDCA). The IDCA Administrator would report both to the President and the Secretary of State, and would serve as the principal development adviser to each. The new Administration would be a small agency charged with coordinating,

providing policy guidance, and evaluating the development activities of:

—The Agency for International Development, which administers the U.S. bilateral foreign assistance program;

—The Overseas Private Investment Corporation, which insures and guarantees U.S. private investments in developing countries;

—The proposed new Institute For Technological Cooperation, which will support research and technological innovation to reduce obstacles to economic development.

The agency will also have the following responsibilities:

—To ensure that development goals are considered in executive branch decisionmaking on trade, technology, and other economic policy issues affecting the less developed nations.

—To participate in the selection of U.S. Executive Directors of Multilateral Development Banks (World Bank, Inter-American Development Bank, Asian Development Bank, and African Development Fund) and advise these Executive Directors on proposed projects and programs.

—To assume lead responsibility for U.S. budget support for policy advice to those international organizations and programs whose purpose is primarily developmental (U.N. Development Program; UNICEF; Organization of American States Technical Assistance Funds; U.N. Capital Development Fund; U.N. Educational and Training Program for Southern Africa; U.N./Food and Agriculture Organization (FAO) World Food Program; FAO Post Harvest Funds; and U.N. Disaster Relief Organization).

PURPOSE OF REORGANIZATION

The purpose of this reorganization is to manage more effectively U.S. development activities by making a single U.S. official responsible for formulating overall development policy, and for overseeing the numerous programs intended to implement that policy.

BACKGROUND

The reorganization was decided upon by the President after considerable consultation with interested members of Congress, and is consistent with the objectives of a bill submitted last year by the late Senator Hubert H. Humphrey.

METHOD OF REORGANIZATION

The reorganization will be implemented through a combination of reorganization plan (to be submitted to Congress in accordance with the reorganization authority enacted in 1977), legislation, Executive order, and administrative action. These steps will begin during the next several weeks.

Ixtlilco el Grande, Mexico

*Text of Remarks at the Town Square.
February 15, 1979*

Governor and Mrs. Bejarano, Secretary Roel, Secretary Merino, Mayor Flores, and all my new friends of Ixtlilco el Grande:

Rosalynn and I are very happy to be here with all of you today. You have been so kind and warm and considerate that we do not feel like strangers at all, but as if we were at home in our own village.

I know that during the past week it has been difficult for you to prepare for our visit. You have welcomed the people from my staff who came here to work with you in making preparations. I thank you.

I have had a busy and interesting visit here today. You showed me some of the finest tomatoes and onions and corn and cantaloupes and watermelons and rice that I have ever seen. And you showed me your peanuts. As you know, I have been a peanut farmer for much longer than I have been a President—and the peanuts of Ixtlilco el Grande look just as good as the ones on my own farm.

Cuco Sanchez and his family demonstrated the irrigation pump and explained to us how it benefits everyone in the village. At the school, we met Professor Sanchez and Maestra Vergara and some of the boys and girls who are so important to the future of Ixtlilco el Grande and to Mexico.

And what a delicious meal. We love the cooks.

Rosalynn and I are very fond of Mexican food. At the White House, in Washington, we have a Mexican meal every week, but the dishes you have served us today are the best I have ever had. I hope you will give Rosalynn the recipes.

Everything I have seen here has impressed me very deeply. Through the Program for Integrated Rural Economic Development, you are building a better life for yourselves and your children.

I know how much progress like this can mean. Rosalynn and I come from the small farming community of Plains, in the State of Georgia, which is not even half as big as Ixtlilco el Grande. When I was a boy our village had no electricity and no irrigation, and our facilities for education and health care and for marketing our crops were very poor. It made a great difference in our lives when we began to have these things, and I can see that it has also made a great difference here in Ixtlilco el Grande. Your government has helped, but it is really the great efforts of the people of Ixtlilco el Grande that have made this program a success.

What you are doing here meets basic human needs, and my country admires that achievement.

Again, I want to thank you—our new friends—for your hospitality and your kindness and your consideration. I will never forget this day. *¡Viva Mexico! ¡Viva Ixtlilco el Grande!*

NOTE: The President spoke at approximately 3:30 p.m. to Mexican dignitaries and town residents gathered for the luncheon. He spoke in Spanish, and the translation of his remarks, as printed above, was prepared in advance of delivery.

In his opening remarks, the President referred to Dr. Armando Leon Bejarano, Governor of Morelos, Secretary of Foreign Relations Santiago Roel, Secretary of Agriculture Francisco Merino Rabago, and Mayor Batuel Flores of Ixtlilco el Grande.

Following his tour of the town, the President returned to Mexico City.

Earlier in the day, President Carter met with President López Portillo at his residence, Los Pinos.

Mexico City, Mexico

Toasts at the Dinner Honoring President López Portillo. February 16, 1979

PRESIDENT CARTER. *President López Portillo, my good friend Carmen,*[1] *on my left, friends from North America and also from Mexico:*

We are very delighted to have you here with us as our guests tonight.

You have been blessed this evening with two beautiful concerts, the one that just concluded, and the remarkable performance by Leonard Bernstein and the beautiful musicians from Mexico City.

_____
[1] Mrs. López Portillo.

We have been blessed by three concerts, those two, plus the 2-hour contest between Bernstein and López Portillo— [*laughter*]—as to who could remember— and I don't know a different word for "sing"—the songs from Latin America in Spanish. [*Laughter*]

I would like to say just a very few words, because Leonard Bernstein has asked me to keep my toasts brief. [*Laughter*]

Mr. President, the relationship between our two countries is one of the most complex and one of the most intimate in all the world.

The border between our two countries is 2,000 miles long—3,000 kilometers— one of the longest undefended borders on Earth.

I'm committed to working with you, Mr. President, to create a framework of a relationship between our two peoples that's based on the principles of understanding, balance, and mutual cooperation.

We have much work to do in resolving specific interrelationships between our countries. But perhaps the greatest challenge that we face is to adopt attitudes toward each other that are based not on the past, but on the realities of the present and the needs of the future.

Mr. President, I've thought carefully about your remarks yesterday, and I would like to respond with the same degree of frankness and of friendship.

The people of the United States are fair and decent people in their relationships with each other and in dealing with people of other nations. We always try to negotiate with others in a spirit of candor and friendship.

We always believe it's best to recognize honest differences, to assess problems realistically and without fear or suspicion, and to work in harmony with our friends to solve those problems and to take advantage of common opportunities.

Each of us, as leaders, has a primary responsibility to represent the interests of our own people. Naturally, this leads to differences in perspective and differences of opinion as we do discuss complicated issues. Our discussions on this visit have been very productive. And we now have an even better prospect of resolving those inevitable differences which have sometimes been obstacles to further progress for many generations. We know that questions involving energy, trade, immigration, transportation, and fisheries are not easy to answer. But we are determined, working together, to succeed.

Mr. President, in your memorable speech to the Congress of the United States 2 years ago, you said something that bears repeating tonight. You said, and I would like to read your words, "It is difficult to be the neighbor of a nation as powerful as yours. We run two grave risks: arrogance, which is easy but sterile, and submission, which is easy but abject. We have chosen instead the difficult path of dignity, based on the liberty we want to maintain and the responsibility which we wish to assume."

That was a perceptive statement, Mr. President. And I would say in reply that it is sometimes difficult to be the neighbor of a nation such as yours—*[laughter]*—a nation of rapid change and development, a nation whose new economic power obliges its leaders to make difficult choices and to accept greatly expanded responsibilities.

To conclude, Mr. President, let me say that I agree that we must not go down the path of arrogance or the path of submission. Instead, I'm confident that we will walk with you on the path of dignity, toward a future of independence, sover-eignty, cooperation, mutual respect, and peace.

And now I would like to propose a toast: First, to the health of President López Portillo and Mrs. López Portillo; second, to the friendship of two great nations, the Republic of Mexico and the United States of America; and to a better life for all people in our two nations and throughout the world. *Salud.*

Thank you very much.

PRESIDENT LÓPEZ PORTILLO. *Mr. President of the United States, Mrs. Carter, my friends:*

Similarly to what was done by Mr. Carter, I wish to begin to speak by paying homage to genius. I wish to say that many, many years ago, I was present at the first performance when the musical selection "Salón México," by Copland, was played many years ago. Since then, I have heard it many times. But I want to say that it was tonight that I really discovered this piece. It was due to the genius of this man,[2] who made me discover the message that has been sent to us by the author, all the tenderness, all the violence, all the strength, all the graciousness, and all the intent of what used to happen in the Salón México, the Salón México to which I went sometimes as a youth. *[Laughter]*

All of this was what I discovered this evening in this extraordinary interpretation. I am not speaking about the other musical selections, because—and what I'm going to say now will only be understood by the people that are sitting around this table—I do not want to extend a—*[inaudible].* *[Laughter]*

Mr. President, for us, your visit has been extremely important. You and your associates have been very friendly and very patient. Our friendship has made it possible for us to be frank. And it is a beau-

---

[2] President López Portillo was referring to Mr. Bernstein.

tiful thing when human beings can communicate among themselves with frankness and openly, even if they have differences as the differences that exist between our two peoples.

You are very right; it is difficult for us to live next to the most powerful country in the world. It must be very difficult for you also to live next to a poor country and a developing one.

Things happen, and at times such as this one, it would be well to remember what was said by the classics in order to make an effort to bring harmony to the world in accordance with the principles that they advocated. Aristotle said that after the ideal state of Plato, very objectively and very realistically, he conceived of a society in which there would be no men that would be rich enough to buy other men and men so poor that they would have to sell themselves.

This, Mr. President, I believe, is the most serious matter of our times—the fact that there are men that can buy men and that there are men that have to sell themselves. And this is what happens very frequently with our poor people that go to the United States.

I confess, Mr. President, that I am deeply moved, and I shall try to be more stable.

But I must reflect upon the fact that we are living in a world of inequalities— that almost all political systems have been capable of denouncing these evils, but we have not had the capability of taking to practice the solutions that we have proposed.

And I wish to bring up a matter which I confess concerns me deeply. What is happening to the free world? Where has freedom led us?

And this is a matter that I wish to bring up and to state as one of the most serious questions that can be asked of the Mexi-

can revolution. We belong to the world of free democracies. It is a political system that would want to bring together liberty and justice. But, ladies and gentlemen, many times when we wished to uphold freedom, we had to sacrifice justice. And we must ask ourselves, "What have we done with our freedom?" Other countries, in order to obtain justice, in turn sacrificed freedom. No doubt they will have to ask themselves, "What have we done with justice?"

We would want to believe that there would be some kind of an order that could be established in the world in which it would be possible to have both values. And that is why we want to state this, for me, very serious question: Is it possible for the human being to be free and at the same time to be just? Is it possible to conceive of an international order that can avoid the state of affairs in which a man would sell himself and another one would buy another human being? When the question is asked by a theoretician, it is a good statement. But when it is asked by a statesman that has specific functions to perform, it becomes a tremendous responsibility.

I feel this responsibility. Convinced as I am of the great values of Western culture, certain as I am that it is impossible to live without freedom, there is no other alternative left but to make an effort to find the roads that will lead to justice. And this can only be found if we conceive of life among nations as a series of rights and duties, to find the people responsible without pointing a finger of guilt.

And I believe, Mr. President, that during the talks that we had yesterday and today, I believe that we have made statements and posed questions in such a manner as to feel satisfied. We have simply proposed those matters. We have simply brought them up. We have not opened up the road to their solution. But this does point a finger in the right direction.

From you and your associates, Mr. President, we have received great understanding as regards what troubles us. We have agreed that human rights are of fundamental importance. And we have expressed our will to decide all the matters that were included in our very broad agenda. And I believe that a very good way to begin is to express our will to do so, to commit our intelligence and our good faith. And I believe that this is what we have been able to do during our meetings, commit our intelligence and our good faith.

This is what I have understood this fruitful dialog to mean, a dialog which we have agreed to continue within a very short time.

Until that time comes, Mr. President, until our associates are able to clear the way, let us, Mr. President, keep alive our willingness to live in freedom and, without losing this freedom, resolve the very serious problems of international coexistence.

There is no other way but to respect values. For that great purpose, Mr. President, for the effort that you are making in your willingness to have human rights prevail in the world, for your expressed will to decide problems which are so difficult between two countries such as ours, for the merit it means to be fair when you are strong, I wish to raise my glass and offer a toast to your health, to the health of your wife, and to the great people of the United States.

Thank you.

NOTE: President Carter spoke at 12 midnight at the U.S. Ambassador's residence. President López Portillo spoke in Spanish, and his remarks were translated by an interpreter.

Earlier in the evening, President Carter and President López Portillo attended a performance of the Philharmonic Orchestra of Mexico City at the Teatro de la Ciudad.

Mexico City, Mexico

Remarks Before the Mexican Congress. February 16, 1979

Mr. President and distinguished Members of the Congress of Mexico:

As President of the fourth largest Spanish-speaking nation, I speak to you—as best I can—in the language of Mexico, the largest Spanish-speaking nation on Earth.

Nearly a decade ago, the great Mexican poet Octavio Paz wrote these words about the United States, and I quote:

"For more than a century that country has appeared to our eyes as a gigantic but scarcely human reality. Smiling or angry, its hand clenched or open, the United States neither sees nor hears us, but keeps striding on, and as it does so, enters our land and crushes us. It is impossible to hold back a giant. It is possible, though far from easy, to make him listen to others. If he listens, this opens the possibility of coexistence."

My friends, I have come to Mexico to listen.

This is a time to appreciate the mutual benefits of our historical friendship as neighbors. But it is also a time of exciting changes within our two countries and in our relationship with each other.

I have come here better to comprehend these changes and to gain a greater understanding of your views.

In the last 3 days, I have spent many hours with your President, José López Portillo. Together, we are working to shape a lasting relationship that is based on balance and equality, based on mutual respect for sovereignty and independence, and a mutual recognition of our shared destinies.

The relations between our two countries are extremely complex. To quote Octavio Paz once more: "What separates us is the very thing that unites us. We are two distinct versions of Western civilization."

Yet it is undeniable that our cultures and our civilizations are more and more related. After all, I am speaking to you in the language not only of Mexico but of 20 million of my fellow citizens in the United States of America.

This mutual interest we feel in our respective music, art, drama, and sports, and in the looks and sounds of our own landscape and our cities as well.

But it goes deeper than that. If the cultural reality of the present is a product of the past, it is also a map of the future. And on that map, the paths to progress for both our peoples increasingly converge. I strongly believe that the intermingling of our two cultures should be welcomed, for it will be a source of strength and vitality for both peoples.

For all the cherished differences between the customs and histories of our two countries, we are alike in another very important way: We are both pluralistic societies.

Mexico is the product of many cultural influences—influences which have shaped a distinctive whole society, while retaining, at the same time, much of its original character. The same can be said of the United States. It is natural for us to learn, and adopt from one another, ideas.

From our perspective, the 2,000-year history of Mexican civilization is impressive, even awesome. When the first English settlers came to the United States, the University of Mexico and Spanish settlements near my present home State were already 100 years old.

Mexico has produced a great and unique culture—one that today finds beautiful expression in art, literature, music, dance, and in architecture of extraordinary vitality.

We respect your culture, which enriches our own. But we also respect Mexico as a great and growing modern nation in constant growth.

President López Portillo has adopted many important steps to strengthen political participation, and he has set forth goals of wider economic participation and social justice as well. We admire and applaud these actions.

I have tried to develop a better approach to Latin America and the Caribbean also—one that emphasizes the uniqueness of each country. The United States views Latin American countries not just as regional actors but as important leaders in a wider system of global cooperation. This commitment is more than just words.

During my first year in office, the United States signed a new treaty with Panama on the Panama Canal, which recognizes the national pride and legitimate rights between people of Panama, and at the same time, it is consistent with the ideals and best interests of the people of the United States.

We particularly value the role that Mexico plays in international affairs in a world that is more and more varied and less and less dominated by super powers or by ideological blocs.

The influence and leadership of Mexico have been increased. You are a recognized force for international economic justice, for the principle of national sovereignty and nonintervention, for arms control and peace.

It has been said that war is too important to be left to the generals. It is equally true that peace is too important to be left solely to the super powers. Mexico's policy affirms that every country has a stake in control of nuclear arms. Through the Treaty of Tlatelolco, you have taken a unique and important initiative in inspiring Latin America to be permanently free of nuclear weapons.

In a world that can be traversed in an hour by satellite, and in an instant by radio, every country is, in a certain sense, the neighbor of every other country. Yet the closeness of Mexico and the United States is no abstraction. We share an open border more than 3,000 kilometers long. We are neighbors in every sense of the word—and, as President López Portillo said in his speech to our Congress 2 years ago, "We shall go on being neighbors as long as the Earth circles the Sun."

Our friendship has at times been marred by mistakes, and even by abuses of power. Our perceptions of each other have sometimes been distorted. But we have made progress, and I believe that in the coming years, we will make greater progress toward fuller cooperation, understanding, and mutual respect.

This will be so if the relations between us are the product of an honest dialog such as President López Portillo and I have had during the last few days.

In the 2 years since President López Portillo became the first head of state to visit me at the White House, we have recorded many accomplishments together. We have signed a civil aviation agreement that will bring the largest expansion of air service between two countries in a full generation. We have signed and ratified treaties on prisoner exchange, on maritime boundaries, and on fisheries, and on extradition.

We have worked together effectively to combat the heroin trade—and we know that the task is far from complete. We have cooperated and sought each other's counsel on international issues. We have strengthened the continuing consultative links between our two governments.

Yesterday we signed agreements to expand scientific cooperation in the areas of housing and in arid crop development. These accomplishments are important, not only for themselves but because they demonstrate our willingness and our ability to work together.

Difficult problems remain—especially in the areas of trade, energy, and migration. Each of these issues defies easy solution. Now and for years to come, each will require our best efforts to narrow our differences and find common ground.

As a result of the productive consultations of this visit, working groups will continue to study the problem. But they will make frequent reports to President López Portillo and to me. We have agreed to meet soon, preferably this summer, to assess progress and to resolve remaining problems.

This is important, and I want to repeat it in my language: [*In English*] Because of the great progress that has been made in this visit, we have assigned to working groups matters of negotiation and consultation. These groups will make frequent reports to President López Portillo and to me, and your President and mine [I] have agreed to meet very early again to assess the progress that has been made, and to add our personal influence in resolving remaining problems. Our hope and our expectation is that President López Portillo and I will meet again as early as this summer.

[*In Spanish*] Trade between our two countries, which already reaches an annual level of about $10 billion, is certain to grow even more rapidly in the future. We must work together as neighbors and as associates within the system of international trade in order to reduce the barriers to trade between our countries and to manage presently our commercial relations effectively.

For many reasons—some of them historical—the issue of energy has aroused strong emotion. You are justifiably proud of the great natural resources of Mexico. That is why I want to repeat today what I have emphasized in talking to the people of my own country: We understand clearly that the Mexican oil resources are the national patrimony of the Mexican people, to be developed and used and sold as Mexico sees fit.

We respect the decision that Mexico will produce at a rate suited to its development objectives. As a good customer, we are prepared to pay a fair and just price for the gas and oil that you may wish to sell.

Mexico's rapidly growing economic strength will help to provide many thousands of new jobs, a long-term answer to the difficult problem of unlawful migration.

As President, I am responsible for upholding the laws of my country, including its immigration laws. I will meet that responsibility as fairly and as humanely as I can. My consultations held here will help me to make the right decisions. I am deeply and personally determined to protect the basic human rights of all people within the borders of my country whether or not they are citizens of the United States.

You can be sure that I will meet that commitment. My country welcomes the growing strength of its great southern neighbor. We will not always agree, just as we do not always agree with other close friends and allies. But we are convinced that our own strength is enhanced by having strong and independent friends.

Our common problems will not be resolved without patient work over many years. But in our conversations, President López Portillo and I have begun to define a common vision of a better future.

It will be a future in which more trade flows freely between our countries, greater legal migration in both directions, greater cooperation between our economists, planners, and scientists, and a future in which we shall preserve and

enrich the cultures of both our countries as our peoples become increasingly bilingual.

Let us set the basis for our relations upon the words of one of the greatest figures in the history of human liberty, Benito Juarez. These words are emblazoned above, on the walls of this chamber:

"Among its individuals, as among its nations, the respect of the rights of others is peace."

These words are so important that I wish to repeat them in my own language:

[*In English*] "Between individuals, as between nations, respect for the rights of others is peace."

[*In Spanish*] Thank you all very much.

NOTE: The President spoke at 10:25 a.m. in the Chamber of Deputies of the Congress. He spoke in Spanish, except where noted above, and the translation follows the White House press release.

Earlier in the day, President Carter met at Los Pinos with President López Portillo.

Following his address, the President left the Chamber of Deputies for departure ceremonies at Licenciado Benito Juarez International Airport.

Mexico City, Mexico

Joint Communique Issued at the Conclusion of Meetings Between President Carter and President López Portillo.   February 16, 1979

At the invitation of the President of the United Mexican States, Licenciado José López Portillo, the President of the United States of America, Jimmy Carter, made a visit to Mexico from the fourteenth to the sixteenth of February, 1979.

Both Presidents held extensive discussions in an atmosphere of sincerity, friendship, and mutual understanding. They reviewed international issues, hemispheric problems and bilateral matters, from the time when President López

Portillo made a State visit to Washington, D.C.—the first visit by a foreign Head of State to the United States after the inauguration of President Carter.

Both Presidents reviewed the operation of the U.S.-Mexican Consultative Mechanism, which was established during that visit to examine issues facing the two countries within the context of an overall bilateral relationship. In this regard, they decided to strengthen the mechanism and provide it with more dynamism, cohesion and flexibility for its more effective operation. To this end, they agreed that, in the light of the guidelines spelled out in this Joint Communique, concrete recommendations would be made within a period of four months on ways the mechanism can more effectively solve problems, taking into consideration the close relationship among these problems.

Upon reviewing the international scene and the grave problems that affect world peace, both Presidents reiterated their confidence in the United Nations, convinced that this institution is the best alternative to achieve a peaceful world with equity and justice. They also agreed that all possible efforts should be made so that the United Nations can achieve new dynamism. They expressed their willingness to cooperate to this end within the Special Committee on the Charter of the United Nations and on the Strengthening of the Role of the Organization. They also expressed support for the important work of the Organization of American States and the need to strengthen and modernize this regional organization.

They emphasized that a new international system should be guided by accepted principles of international conduct, particularly the following: non-intervention of the internal affairs of other States, the prohibition of the use of threat or force, respect for the self-determination of peoples, the peaceful solution of conflicts, and the sovereign right of each nation to take full advantage of its natural resources for the economic and social development of its people.

Both Presidents expressed their agreement that peace is more than just the absence of hostilities; peace also includes the elimination of hunger, disease, illiteracy, poverty, ignorance and injustice—tasks in which all countries of the international community share responsibility.

The Presidents examined the development of their economies within a global context. They agreed that major efforts should be made to adjust and improve the international economic system to take into account the interests and concerns of developing countries. They expressed their concern over the world-wide problems of inflation, unemployment, protectionism and monetary and financial difficulties. They recognized that it is important to assure the adequate transfer of real resources to developing countries and to promote stable economic and social development throughout the world.

The Heads of State committed themselves to use their best efforts toward the execution of the goals set by the Tenth U.N. Special Session on Disarmament, and, within this context, they also recognized the importance of the Treaty for the Prohibition of Nuclear Weapons in Latin America (the Treaty of Tlatelolco). President López Portillo expressed his appreciation to President Carter for having signed Protocol I of the Treaty of Tlatelolco, and he also expressed his firm hopes that it will be ratified soon. President López Portillo recognized the importance of reaching an agreement on strategic arms limitations as a solid base for further agreements in this field.

The Presidents exchanged opinions on the possible measures to limit the transfer of conventional weapons, both at a world-wide and regional level, and, in this context, President Carter reiterated the support of his Administration for self-restraint in the transfer of conventional weapons—efforts initiated by the nations of Latin America and the Caribbean during a meeting held in Mexico, in August of 1978. He also reiterated his Administration's policy to respect the decisions undertaken by the countries interested in this matter. The Presidents also recognized the importance of the U.N. Conference on Conventional Weapons to be held later this year.

The Presidents expressed their particular interest in strengthening international organizations engaged in the protection of guarantees of individual rights. They especially commended the work of the Inter-American Commission on Human Rights and urged other nations in the hemisphere to give it their full support.

Both leaders expressed their deep concern over the crisis that continues to affect the people of Nicaragua, violating their most fundamental human rights, reaffirming their decision to continue working through the United Nations and the Organization of American States, in the search for a democratic and fair solution to the conflict.

Upon reviewing trade relations between their countries, both Presidents expressed their satisfaction with the continuous growth of this exchange. President López Portillo noted the historic trade deficit of Mexico with the United States, particularly if recent sales of Mexican oil are excluded, making known the convenience of taking all measures necessary to reduce it, permitting an increase in the export of Mexican merchandise, particularly those of higher value-added which would benefit both countries. President Carter emphasized the need to reduce trade barriers on a broad basis. In this connection, he called attention to the trade conces-

sions offered by the United States which would be of significant benefit to Mexico.

President López Portillo noted that the eventual membership of Mexico in GATT would depend, as it was stated in September, 1973, in Tokyo, on the consideration of special treatment to developing countries which should be measured in terms of equal treatment for equal countries and unequal treatment for unequal countries; on the final results of the multilateral trade negotiations; and on the terms of its negotiation on adherence to GATT, which it initiated on January 16 of this year. Mexico will make a decision which will depend on the compatibility of the liberalization of trade and with the stage and condition of Mexico's economic development.

President Carter expressed his strong support for expanding world trade and reducing trade barriers, and expressed his hope that Mexico would play a greater role in the shaping and the management of an improved world trading system.

The two Presidents agreed that the rapid and satisfactory conclusion of the Multilateral Trade Negotiations will represent an important step toward the improvement of the world's economy. They felt, however, that these negotiations could only end successfully if developing countries, such as Mexico, have an equitable participation in its results. In order to achieve this, it is necessary to fully implement the Tokyo Declaration, particularly with regard to differential treatment for developing countries.

They also agreed to try to conclude successfully and within the shortest period of time, their bilateral trade negotiations with the framework of the Multilateral Trade Negotiations. The Presidents reaffirmed the Tokyo Declaration to the effect that Mexico would make a contribution to the Multilateral Trade Negotiations only to the extent of its trade, finance and development possibilities. President Carter favorably recognized Mexico's effort in gradually eliminating non-tariff barriers and considered this effort as a potential contribution to the goals of the aforementioned negotiations.

The Presidents also agreed that the future expansion of trade between the two countries will require a continuous liberalization of both countries' trade policies, in accordance with the trade, financial and development needs of each nation. They also committed themselves to renew their efforts to this end and to carry out close consultations on trade and financial matters. President López Portillo reasserted the Mexican Government's decision to continue the process of gradually eliminating non-tariff barriers, and to do so with prudence, caution and according to international economic conditions. President Carter noted that his Administration had given special attention to Mexico's export needs in the implementation of U.S. trade laws and committed himself to continue to oppose protectionism and to resist attempts to reduce the security of access to U.S. markets for Mexican products.

Both Presidents recognized the mutual benefits deriving from the U.S. Generalized System of Preferences. However, President López Portillo pointed out that the system contains serious limitations for its full utilization and that measures should be taken to improve the system, particularly with regard to the liberalization of the application of the so-called "competitive need clause". President Carter noted that Mexico's exports that entered under GSP have doubled in the last two years and that Mexico is the leading beneficiary of trade preferences in Latin America.

President López Portillo expressed hope that the new rules of international trade would give due consideration to the interests of developing countries, and would not institutionalize the increasing protectionist actions by developed nations. President Carter noted that protectionism is a contagious condition which threatens all countries and pointed to his own record of opposition to protectionism which should be resisted in all countries.

The Presidents emphasized the importance of cooperation in the field of science and technology as a means for dealing with many economic and social problems. They also agree on the mutual advantages of intensifying this cooperation.

The Presidents expressed their satisfaction with regard to plans to reinforce the present mechanisms for scientific and technological cooperation between both nations, and asked the authorities in these fields of their respective nations to expedite the execution of these plans, within the framework of the mixed Scientific and Technological Cooperation Commission and the Consultative Mechanism.

To signal their commitment, the two Presidents took note of the two agreements signed during the visit, on Arid Lands Management and Urban Planning, and a Memorandum of Understanding on Scientific and Technical Cooperation, also signed during the visit. They also discussed plans for the Institute for Technological Cooperation, which they agreed would facilitate cooperative research and development between the two countries.

Both Presidents exchanged views on fishery matters because they considered this a priority interest for both nations, and agreed to carry on discussions in this important field.

The leaders had a wide-ranging discussion on energy, which included both its bilateral and global aspects. They agreed that it is not possible to separate energy resources from economic development, not only for countries who have them, but for countries that do not have them, and because of this, an economic order should be sensitive to the necessity to provide for the needs of the poor, and investment should be directed so as to encourage their industrialization.

Taking into consideration Mexico's potential as an energy-producing country, President López Portillo reiterated that energy resources must be considered as the patrimony of mankind, so that the production, distribution and consumption of these resources be made in an orderly and rational fashion, and so that all alternative sources of energy be developed, including the financing and transfer of technologies that are accessible to all developing countries. President Carter expressed interest in this idea and willingness to explore these subjects further.

The two Presidents decided to start immediately the design of plans to collaborate in the field of energy, with a strict observance of their respective national policies, and to initiate or expand, whatever might be the case, trade in hydrocarbon products, electricity and other energy resources.

Both Presidents agreed to plan a joint Mexican-U.S. study on the possibilities of exchange of electric energy on a rational basis along their common border.

With regard to nuclear energy, President Carter noted the need to speed up the export of enriched uranium to Mexico to put in operation the electric-generating plants that the Mexican Government is planning.

Both Presidents also agreed to support and promote scientific and technological cooperation in the field of energy, including solar and geothermal energy. President Carter said that his government would be helpful in cooperating to enhance the technological capabilities in Mexico.

The results of these agreements, studies and talks would be included in the report of the Consultative Mechanism.

With regard to the eventual sale of surpluses of Mexican natural gas to the United States, the Presidents discussed the future possibility of such transactions.

On the part of the United States, President Carter pledged to develop means for expediting sales by Petroleos Méxicanos to purchasing companies.

On the part of Mexico, the government will re-evaluate the amount of the possible surpluses, taking into consideration the needs to be generated with the establishment of the National Gas Pipeline Network.

On this basis the two Presidents agreed to have their governmental representatives meet as soon as possible and begin discussing the best means to facilitate decisions on these matters.

The two Presidents agreed to examine jointly the prospects of future sales of crude oil and petroleum products from Mexico to the United States.

The phenomenon of the Mexican migrant workers was discussed within the overall context of social and economic relations between both countries. The two Presidents committed themselves to carry out a close bilateral cooperation in order to find an integral, realistic and long-term solution which would respect the dignity and the human rights of these workers, and which would also respect the many social, economic and development problems that are involved in this matter.

In this context, they agreed that their governments would continue to consult closely on all aspects of the migration question, including its economic and social implications in both countries, and agreed that the Joint Consultative Mechanism should meet promptly to share fully and jointly the results of their respective research and studies on this issue.

President López Portillo reiterated that Mexico does not wish to export workers but goods, and also noted that the phenomenon of migrant workers is part of the employment problem whose solution is a priority concern of the Mexican State in a constitutional category and which is looked upon in Mexico's development programs. He added, however, that it is necessary to take into consideration that this is a matter of bilateral nature, of long history, that it is stimulated by a real demand, and that, in any event, it deserves respect with regard to its human aspect and requires a clear and objective analysis, taking into consideration that restrictive measures in other areas slow down the solution that both countries wish for this problem.

President Carter expressed concern about the problem of unlawful immigration into the United States and its impact on the United States. He took note of the responsibility of the United States Government to enforce the laws respecting immigration and the need to bring to justice those who traffic in undocumented migrants.

The Presidents discussed the status of border relations, reaffirming their goals to promote an adequate flow of goods and people, to fight all kinds of contraband which adversely affect the economies of both countries, and to strengthen cooperation between the authorities of both countries.

They noted with satisfaction the success of current programs in sharply reducing the traffic in dangerous drugs and pledged to continue to strengthen and expand their efforts to suppress the production and trafficking of illicit narcotics. President Carter took special note of the effective record of Mexican authorities in suppressing the traffic in narcotics. The two Presidents agreed to explore with neighboring countries the possibility of multilateral programs assisting them in strengthening narcotics control arrangements.

Both leaders reaffirmed the importance of having good quality and abundant water for the health and well-being of citizens on both sides of the border. They instructed the International Boundary and Water Commission, in the context of existing agreements, to make immediate recommendations for further progress towards a permanent solution to the sanitation of waters along the border.

The Presidents agreed to continue their consultations over a wide range of international political and economic matters, and reaffirmed their intention to maintain close contact and to give their personal and continuous attention to the reinforcement and broadening of the numerous areas of cooperation existing between their nations.

President Carter suggested that both Presidents meet again in the summer to examine the report of the Consultative Mechanism and to assess progress on the issues discussed in Mexico City. President López Portillo gladly accepted this suggestion.

Digest of Other White House Announcements

The following listing includes the President's public schedule and other items of general interest announced by the White House Press Office and not included elsewhere in this issue.

February 11

The President returned to the White House from Camp David, Md.

February 12

The President met at the White House with:

—Zbigniew Brzezinski, Assistant to the President for National Security Affairs;

—Frank B. Moore, Assistant to the President for Congressional Liaison;

—a group of civic and community leaders, to discuss his trip to Mexico.

The White House announced that the President received, on Friday evening, February 9, the report of the Emergency Board to investigate the dispute between Wien Air Alaska and the Air Line Pilots Association.

The President announced the persons who will represent the United States at the independence celebrations of Saint Lucia on February 22. The Honorable Frank V. Ortiz, Jr., U.S. Ambassador to Barbados, will head the U.S. Delegation, attending as personal representative of the President with the rank of Special Ambassador. Mrs. Ortiz will accompany the Ambassador. The representatives of the President, also with the rank of Special Ambassador, will be:

JASON BERMAN of Washington, D.C.;
CHARLES LOMAX of Chicago, Ill.;
I. I. OZAR of Kansas City, Mo.;
GERALD M. TABENKEN of Veazie, Maine;
RUTH K. WATANABE of Los Angeles, Calif.

The President will be represented at the funeral services for the late Edvard Kardelj in Ljubljana, Yugoslavia, by W. Averell Harriman, who will head the U.S. Delegation. Other members of the delegation are:

MRS. W. AVERELL HARRIMAN;
SENATOR JOSEPH R. BIDEN of Delaware;
REPRESENTATIVE JAMES L. OBERSTAR of Minnesota;
JOHN BLATNIK, former U.S. Representative from Minnesota;

DR. MICHAEL MUFTIC, national committeeman from Colorado, Democratic National Committee;
ANDREW VALUCHEK, special assistant to the chairman of the Democratic National Committee.

The President declared a major disaster for the Marshall Islands District as a result of Typhoon Alice, beginning about January 3, which caused extensive public and private property damage.

February 13

The President met at the White House with:

—Dr. Brzezinski;

—Mr. Moore;

—Senators Jennings Randolph and Robert C. Byrd and Representative Harley O. Staggers of West Virginia;

—Representatives Charles B. Rangel of New York and Henry A. Waxman of California;

—Stansfield Turner, Director of Central Intelligence, Hamilton Jordan, Assistant to the President, and Dr. Brzezinski;

—Elie Wiesel, Chairman of the President's Commission on the Holocaust.

February 14

The President met at the White House with Dr. Brzezinski.

The President left the White House for a visit to Mexico.

February 16

Following his return to the White House from Mexico, the President met with Vice President Walter F. Mondale, Secretary of State Cyrus R. Vance, Dr. Brzezinski, Mr. Turner, and other administration officials to discuss developments in the Middle East and Asia. He then left for a weekend stay at Camp David, Md.

NOMINATIONS SUBMITTED TO THE SENATE

The following list does not include promotions of members of the Uniformed Services, nominations to the Service Academies, or nominations of Foreign Service officers.

Submitted February 13, 1979

HENRY S. DOGIN, of New York, to be Administrator of Law Enforcement Assistance, vice Richard W. Velde, resigned.

GEORGE E. CIRE, of Texas, to be United States District Judge for the Southern District of Texas, vice a new position created by P.L. 95–486, approved October 20, 1978.

JAMES DEANDA, of Texas, to be United States District Judge for the Southern District of Texas, vice a new position created by P.L. 95–486, approved October 20, 1978.

The following-named persons to be members of the National Museum Services Board for terms expiring December 6, 1983:

DOUGLAS DILLON, of New York (reappointment).

NEIL HARRIS, of Illinois (reappointment).

Submitted February 14, 1979

ROBERT BURNS PIRIE, JR., of Maryland, to be an Assistant Secretary of Defense, vice John Patrick White, resigned.

JESSE HILL, JR., of Georgia, to be a member of the Board of Directors of the Communications Satellite Corporation until the date of the annual meeting of the Corporation in 1982 (reappointment).

CHECKLIST OF WHITE HOUSE PRESS RELEASES

The following listing contains releases of the White House Press Office which are not included in this issue.

Released February 13, 1979

Announcement: nomination of George E. Cire to be a United States District Judge for the Southern District of Texas

Announcement: nomination of James DeAnda to be a United States District Judge for the Southern District of Texas

Released February 15, 1979

News conference: on reorganization of U.S. foreign assistance programs—by Ambassador at Large Henry D. Owen, Special Representative of the President for International Economic Summits, John J. Gilligan, Administrator, Agency for International Development, and John P. White, Deputy Director, and Peter L. Szanton, Associate Director for Organization Studies, Office of Management and Budget

Advance text: remarks of President Carter at a dinner honoring President José López Portillo of Mexico

Released February 16, 1979

Advance text: remarks before the Mexican Congress (two releases)

ACTS APPROVED BY THE PRESIDENT

NOTE: No acts approved by the President were received by the Office of the Federal Register during the period covered by this issue.

Ambassador Adolph Dubs

*Remarks at Ceremonies Honoring the Late
U.S. Ambassador to Afghanistan.
February 18, 1979*

THE PRESIDENT. This morning I would like to say to Mary Ann Dubs and to Lindsey, to the members of Spike Dubs' family and his many friends that this is indeed a sad and painful moment for the United States of America. We've come here on this occasion to pay tribute to a good man, a courageous man, who served his country well and who gave his life for it.

We've come here to express our outrage at the senseless terrorism among those who pay inadequate value to human life. And we condemn those who perpetrated and who participated in such a despicable act of violence.

As President, I would like to pay honor, also, to the other men and women in the Foreign Service of our country, who serve with dedication and often great risk to their own lives so that all of us might enjoy a more peaceful existence in a world with better understanding, one for another.

Mary Ann, Lindsey, we share with you your great loss. The grief of our Nation can be expressed by me as President. And we also share with you a great pride in what your husband, what your father, did for our country. We are ready to help you in every way possible to share your loss. And I want you to know that our Nation, in every sense of the word, shares this loss with you and your family.

SECRETARY OF STATE VANCE. Mary Ann, Lindsey, your loss and ours is a profound one. Spike deeply loved this country, his family, and his friends. He was one of our very best, a fine officer and a fine person. It is tragic that a man, whose whole life and career was dedicated to the cause of peace, was killed as a result of terrorism and violence.

Events in Kabul and Tehran this week are terrible reminders that the diplomatic profession is dangerous as well as demanding. Courageous and selfless men of the Foreign Service like Spike Dubs have all too often in recent years sacrificed their lives for their country. We owe them a debt beyond price.

I pledge to you that we will spare no effort to protect our diplomats overseas, and we will fight terrorism with all of our resolve and our resources.

As a symbol of my respect and regard for Ambassador Dubs and tribute to him from the Foreign Service, to which he devoted his life, I have the sad honor to present to you, Mary Ann, in Spike's memory, the Secretary's Award, the highest award the State Department can give.

As I present this award, I note with regret that for health reasons Spike's parents could not be here as we honor him.

The citation reads: "To Adolph Dubs, for inspiring leadership, outstanding courage and devotion to duty for which he gave his life. Kabul. February 14, 1979."

NOTE: The President spoke at approximately 12:30 p.m. at Andrews Air Force Base, Md., where the Ambassador's body was returned from Afghanistan.

Atlanta, Georgia

Remarks at the Unveiling of the Official State Portrait Commemorating the President's Term as Governor. February 20, 1979

You don't know how nice it is to see a picture of yourself that's not 80 percent teeth. [*Laughter*]

It would be impossible for any of you to know the deep feelings of sentiment and emotion that I feel standing here at this podium. I'll never forget the first day I came to the senate, with five or six of you still members, and with many of those who stand on my left—Peter Zack Geer was Lieutenant Governor; Carl Sanders was Governor; Garland Byrd sat next to me. I was eager to learn about the duties of my first elected public office, and I made friends then that have stood me in good stead ever since.

Many of you helped me a great deal in those early days as a senator, as a candidate, as Governor, candidate again, and now as President. I know it has been somewhat of a surprise to many of you that I was successful in the elections. And as I look around, I have to admit that it's a surprise to me that some of you were re-elected so many times yourselves. [*Laughter*]

But I feel a sense of common purpose with you. As President of the greatest nation on Earth, I bear on my shoulders great and sobering responsibilities. But you, as Georgia senators, bear great and sobering responsibilities as well. And what makes it easier for us successfully to carry out our duties is the knowledge that we are not alone, that in a democracy built on freedom, on the worth of every individual human being, there's a sharing of difficulties, purpose, ideals, and hopes for an even greater future. And this sense of community that binds our Nation together has been most reassuring to me in recent years.

I'd like to thank you for honoring me in this way. I think this is a moment that I will never forget, with all its pleasant flood of memories and friendships.

I look forward to shaking hands with everyone who's a member of the senate or who has been a member in the past, and to pledge to you that the lessons that I learned here—of the importance of public service, of patriotism and dedication, of the ability and willingness to face difficult times with enthusiasm and confidence and purpose—will stay with me forever.

We live in the greatest nation on Earth, and the foundation of our Nation's greatness is its system of federalism, for the States were the original repository of responsibility and authority, and where the cities, counties, and even the Federal Government only have that authority and responsibility dedicated to us by the States.

Thank you again for honoring me. Thank you for your friendship. And I look forward to an even greater future for our State, which is still so dear to my heart and our great Nation.

I might say that Rosalynn was planning to be with us this morning. At this moment, they are having the funeral of Ambassador Dubs, who was killed in Afghanistan. But she wanted to send her personal love to every one of you, and in addition to my friendship, I extend my love to you also.

Thank you.

NOTE: The President spoke at 10:15 a.m. in the Senate Chamber of the State Capitol following the unveiling of his portrait which was painted by Robert Templeton.

Atlanta, Georgia

Remarks Before a Joint Session of the Georgia General Assembly.   February 20, 1979

Governor Busbee, Lieutenant Governor Miller, Speaker Tom Murphy, distinguished members of the Georgia House and the Georgia Senate, and my friends throughout my beloved State of Georgia:

I'm honored to come back to you.

I wish my wife was here with me. She was planning to come. But at this very moment, there are being conducted funeral services for a brave and distinguished American diplomat, Adolph Dubs, who gave his life in Afghanistan in the service of our country.

It's a sobering thing to realize that in a time of peace and prosperity, that the toughness of our Nation still is exhibited almost on a daily basis by the patriotism and the dedication of those who give their lives to public service. And I think it's well for us to remember that our own freedom has been dearly purchased even by the lives of some who have helped to serve for us and with us.

This capitol is where I have spent some of the most challenging and exciting and enjoyable days of my life—rewarding

times. And I can say from the bottom of my heart that it's good to be home.

I have to admit that as President, at times in Washington, this seems to be a haven of rest and companionship as I look back on my time as Governor of Georgia. On the way down here, though, I was looking at the list of committee chairmen who serve in the house and senate. And at moments like those, I'm glad I'm President, dealing with the Congress. [*Laughter*]

I have very closely read the newspapers from Georgia, and I notice with gratification that the same degree of cooperation, mutual support, harmony, and friendship exists among the Governor, Lieutenant Governor, and the speaker of the house as existed among the speaker, Lieutenant Governor Lester Maddox, and myself. [*Laughter*]

It's also pleasant for me to see the ease with which difficult problems, difficult questions have been dealt since I left the Governor's office. You've answered questions that I couldn't answer. For example, I was never able to deal successfully with the problem of the local option sales tax. [*Laughter*]

Progress is gratifying to see, and I want to say that because of the great progress of this General Assembly and the State of Georgia, that daily you bring a sense of gratitude and appreciation and pride to the heart of the President of the United States.

Many of the problems and the challenges of National Government are different from those of State government, yet the experience that I gained here and the lessons that I learned here have proven very valuable to me during the last 2 years of my life.

I learned here, for example, that the legislative process is sometimes slow, sometimes difficult, sometimes frustrating.

But I also know from experience as a State senator, as a Governor, as a candidate, and as President, that the needs and the problems of our age, our era, are too challenging and too complex to permit simple answers.

The same is obviously true at the national level, as at the State level. When the Founders wrote our Constitution, they didn't promise us that governing ourselves would be easy or that freedom would provide an automatic answer to every problem. They didn't promise us that democracy would be stagnant or easy or convenient. They talked instead about eternal vigilance, about duty, about sacrifice, and they made provisions in the Constitution for beneficial change.

Most of the amendments to our Constitution over the generations have been designed to extend and perfect rights and liberties for individual citizens of this Nation.

The Bill of Rights was the first major change setting forth our most basic safeguards for personal liberty. Later, former slaves were liberated, and they were granted their full rights as citizens. The people were allowed to vote directly for United States Senators, and later, women were brought into the electorate.

Continuing this trend, there are now two constitutional amendments which I hope you will ratify. They are politically controversial and difficult.

One of them will grant voting rights to almost a million people who live in the District of Columbia. This is a proposed amendment which I take to be appealing both to liberals and conservatives, one which received broad support from the Georgia delegation. It was supported by Senator Talmadge, Senator Nunn, and all but two of the members of the Georgia congressional delegation. This granting of fundamental rights was also supported by conservative Republicans like Strom Thurmond, Barry Goldwater.

And I would like to also remind you that half our people are still not guaranteed their full rights in the Constitution. We owe the women of Georgia and the people of the United States no less than the ratification of the equal rights amendment.

I've been told that you will not consider either one of these amendments this year. But I hope you will consider the passage of those amendments in the same spirit that the trend and the evolution of the United States Constitution has exhibited under even more difficult times in years gone by.

These decisions and many others are challenges for you. And there are challenges also for the President and the Congress. Let me just mention one of those major difficult issues that face me as President, which you share with me in a special way.

Because of problems that have developed over a long period of time, both at home and abroad, our Nation now faces increasingly complex and challenging tasks in the area of economics. The time ahead will be difficult, requiring us to draw out the best that's within us—our idealism, our willingness to face unpleasant realities, our readiness to put the long-term interest of all above the short-term interest of a few, sometimes above the interest of our own selves.

Later on today, at Georgia Tech, I'll discuss our responsibilities as a world power in the international—military, diplomatic, and political—arena. But we face equally grave tasks here at home. And the most difficult of these responsibilities is to control the persistent high inflation which threatens the health of our economy and the economic well-being of our people. And as President I pledge to you that I am determined to bring inflation under control.

The importance of this task is hard to overemphasize. We must grapple with inflation in a context that is far different from the expansive, free-spending days of the 1960's.

When I became President, I inherited both a huge budget deficit and an economy wracked by stagflation. We had the worst unemployment rate since the Great Depression. And at the same time, inflation for the 3 years before I became President had averaged over 8 percent.

We've moved forward firmly and strongly to tackle these problems. We have created in less than 2 years more than 7 million net new jobs, and we have cut the unemployment rate down already by more than 25 percent. We've set forth now an anti-inflation program that recognizes the basic causes of inflation and attacks this problem on a broad front.

Some of the causes of inflation, frankly, are beyond the control of the Federal Government. I'm determined to carry out the lessons that I learned here to keep our free enterprise system free.

I'm trying to reduce the amount of unwarranted intrusion of the Federal Government in personal lives, in the life of business—employers and employees. Also, of course, we cannot control the weather, which is demonstrated amply in Washington this week. And weather, of course, has an important impact on food prices. We cannot determine the nations' actions throughout the world which affect the prices of energy and other commodities, although we use our influence to some degree in a beneficial way. Nor can we erase the fiscal excesses of the 1960's and the early 1970's. But we can act ourselves, and by planning wisely, we can mitigate the adverse effect of these uncontrollable factors.

Because inflation is our most serious domestic problem, I have really taken it seriously in preparing my budget. The budget I proposed to the Congress cuts the Federal deficit. In fiscal year 1980, if my budget is adopted—and I expect it will be, in its overall commitment—the deficit will be $36 billion lower than it was when I was running for President; we have already cut the deficit more than 55 percent.

My budget also reduces the proportion of the total Nation's income that's collected and spent by the Federal Government to the lowest level it's been in over 7 years. And although in the past that trend was upward, we've turned that around, and the trend is now in the right direction. It's falling.

I set forth a goal in my campaign, and I'm using the powers of my office to move our Nation toward it, the goal of a balanced Federal budget. We can achieve this goal by sensible, sensitive, and well-considered public policy which will at the same time protect the strength of the American economy.

I've proposed a substantial increase for national defense. This afternoon, I'll analyze our international commitments in Europe, in the Middle East, and other parts of the world. We must have the muscle to meet these commitments.

The President of the United States has no greater responsibility and the Congress of the United States has no greater responsibility than to provide for the assurance of the defense of this Nation. Together, the Congress and I will meet this responsibility, and we will keep a strong America.

We must, of course, also meet the other needs of our Nation, such as those of the poor and the elderly. But there's a clear limit on the ability of the American people to pay higher and higher taxes to finance more and more new programs. That's why our efforts to cut waste, to eliminate fraud, and to end mismanagement of public funds is so important.

We've reformed the civil service system so that Government will deliver more and better services for every dollar spent and every employee hired.

I've now appointed Inspectors General in every major Federal agency to root out fraud and to bring to justice those who are responsible for it. We are already uncovering abuses in agencies like the General Services Administration. And I intend to see these investigations of fraud and abuse pursued aggressively, wherever they lead—let the chips fall where they may.

The Federal Government has neither the resources nor the wisdom to solve every problem by itself. The States and the localities and, most important, the people must do their part.

This is the time for restraint. Expenditures must be controlled. The deficit must be reduced. The Federal Government must set an example. But this kind of restraint is difficult. It asks each of us to serve the general good by accepting less than we want in our own specific area.

I have sent to the Congress a budget that's tight and fair. But as in every other year, the inevitable pressures to spend just a little more here or just a little more there, for someone's pet project or for someone's favorite interest group, have already begun.

I'm determined to fight these pressures. I'm determined to stand firm. I'm determined to use the full powers and resources of my office to hold the line on the Federal budget.

I was taught that as a senator and as Governor by a great leader in this chamber, former Chairman Sloppy Floyd.

In closing, let me say that to hold the line, I need and I ask for the help of every elected official and every American taxpayer who shares my concern about waste and inflation. I believe the people of this country are ready to build a new foundation for the 1980's, to regain control of our economy and our destiny as a nation.

From our earliest days, students of American democracy have warned that our freedom and our prosperity might tempt our citizens to get so caught up in their own personal pursuit of happiness and wealth that they would neglect the public business.

The challenge for us today is to put aside temporary gratifications for the sake of the long-term public good. The job will not be glamorous, and results will not come quickly or easily and may not always even be detectable. But I believe that we will succeed. And when we have, the monuments to our efforts will be a vital, healthy economy—sustaining the needs and hopes and dreams of all people. And we will have, you and I, working together, an even greater United States of America.

Thank you very much.

NOTE: The President spoke at 10:48 a.m. in the House Chamber of the State Capitol.

Atlanta, Georgia

Remarks at a Special Convocation of the Georgia Institute of Technology.
February 20, 1979

Chairman Milton Jones, Chancellor George Simpson, Dr. Joe Pettit, Mr. Kroll, honored guests, fellow Tech students and alumni, ladies and gentlemen:

I have always been proud that I attended Georgia Tech, and I've always been grateful for what I learned here.

I have attended as a full-time student four different colleges in my life. Georgia Tech is by far the most difficult—

[*laughter*]—and a number of years ago I decided that my being elected President was the only way that I would ever have a chance to get a degree from Georgia Tech. [*Laughter*] This has made it worthwhile. [*Laughter*]

I remember when I first came to Tech, the entire world was at war. Our Nation was under attack on two fronts and was desperately gearing up for a total war effort that we had not known since we fought each other in the 1860's.

In 1942, 1943, it was not yet a time for victories for the United States nor for our allies, and many people feared that Western democracies might be overwhelmed. We now face a very different world from the world in which I came of age. The old empires are gone, and the maps are covered with new and developing nations with names that we had then never heard.

But one thing has not changed as much as I had hoped. It's still a world of danger, a world in which democracy and freedom are still challenged, a world in which peace must be rewon day by day. Too many people still lack the simplest necessities of life, and too many are deprived of the most basic human rights. As the events of recent days have shown, peace remains a fragile thing, vulnerable to assaults from all sides.

Disturbances in Iran, the Western Indian Ocean, and Southeast Asia, are a challenge to our determination and our leadership. They underscore the importance of strength in our national defenses, wisdom in our diplomacy, and steadfastness in the pursuit of arms control and peace.

I want to speak to you today about America's role and America's purpose in this world of change and turbulence.

Ever since the end of the Second World War, the United States has been the leader in moving our world closer to a stable peace and genuine security. We have the world's strongest economy; we have the world's strongest military forces; and we share burdens of mutual defense with friends abroad whose security and prosperity are as vital to us as to themselves.

With our strong allies, we have succeeded in preventing a global war for more than one-third of a century—the longest period of general peace in modern times. And as President of the United States, I am determined to keep our Nation at peace.

We help to sustain a world trading and monetary system that has brought greater prosperity to more of the world's people than ever before in history. We are working to resolve conflicts among other nations so that each can develop its own future in independence and peace. And we've helped to maintain the conditions in which more than 100 new nations have come into being, and in which human hope—and its fulfillment—has taken a revolutionary leap forward.

In short, we in the United States provide the bedrock of global security and economic advance in a world of unprecedented change and conflict.

In such a world America has four fundamental security responsibilities: to provide for our own Nation's strength and safety; to stand by our allies and our friends; to support national independence and integrity of other nations; and to work diligently for peace.

We do not oppose change. Many of the political currents sweeping the world express a desire that we share—the desire for a world in which the legitimate aspirations of nations and individuals have a greater chance for fulfillment.

The United States cannot control events within other nations. A few years ago, we tried this and we failed. But we recognized as inevitable that the uncertainty and the turmoil that come with change can have its darker side as well. We saw this in a senseless act of violence last week in Afghanistan, when a brave and good man—Ambassador Adolph Dubs—gave his life in the performance of his duty as a representative of the United States.

As we meet here today at Georgia Tech—enjoying the blessings of freedom and peace—we must remember that we are indebted for those blessings to the sacrifice of men and women like Spike Dubs.

We also see the darker side of change when countries in turbulence provide opportunities for exploitation by outsiders who seek not to advance human aims, but rather to extend their own power and their own position at the expense of others.

As I speak to you today, the country of Iran—with which we have had close relations for the last 30 years—is in revolution. It's been our hope that Iran could modernize without deep internal conflicts, and we sought to encourage that effort by supporting its government, by urging internal change toward progress and democracy, and by helping to provide a background of regional stability.

The revolution in Iran is a product of deep social, political, religious, and economic factors growing out of the history of Iran itself. Those who argue that the United States should or could intervene directly to thwart these events are wrong about the realities of Iran. So, too, are those who spout propaganda that protecting our own citizens is tantamount to direct intervention.

We have not and we will not intervene in Iran, yet the future of Iran continues to be of deep concern to us and to our friends and allies. It's an important nation in a critical part of the world, an immediate neighbor of the Soviet Union, a major oil producer that also sits beside the principal artery for most of the world's trade in oil. And it is still a significant potential force for stability and progress in the region.

Iran is a proud nation with a long history—more than 2,000 years—of struggle to establish and to guarantee its own freedom. The independence of Iran is also in our own vital interest and in the interest of our closest allies—and we will support the independence of Iran.

Out of today's turmoil, it is our hope that these troubled people will create a stable government which can meet the needs of the Iranian people and which can enable that great nation not only to remain independent but to regain its internal strength and balance.

We are prepared to support that effort as appropriate and to work with the Iranian Government and the people as a nation which shares common interests and common aspirations with us.

But just as we respect Iran's independence and integrity, other nations must do so as well. If others interfere, directly or indirectly, they are on notice that this will have serious consequences and will affect our broader relationships with them.

At the same time, we are intensifying our efforts to promote stability throughout the Middle East so that the security and the independence of the nations of that part of the world will be maintained.

At my direction, the Secretary of Defense recently carried out comprehensive consultations in Israel, Egypt, Jordan, and Saudi Arabia, concerning the security of that region. We are determined to work with these nations and with others to put the peaceful development of the region on a sound and a lasting foundation.

Recent disturbances in the region have underlined the need to work even more urgently towards peace between Israel and its Arab neighbors. To this end, Israeli and Egyptian negotiators, the Foreign Ministers of both countries, will return to Camp David tonight at the invitation of the United States.

They will be meeting with Secretary of State Cyrus Vance. And I myself will do whatever I can to promote the success of the Camp David negotiations. And if it should be necessary, and the parties show adequate flexibility, I will call another summit conference to work for peace.

I urge all leaders throughout the Middle East to recognize the vital importance for their region for these talks to succeed.

For us in the United States, any crisis in the Middle East has the most immediate and serious consequences. But we are also deeply concerned by what is happening now in Southeast Asia. The same principles of American policy apply: We support the independence and integrity of the regional nations; we will stand by our friends; and we will continue as a nation to work for peace.

Just in the last few weeks we've seen a Vietnamese invasion of Cambodia and, as a result, a Chinese frontier penetration into Vietnam. Both actions threaten the stability of one of the world's most important and promising regions—Southeast Asia.

We have opposed both military actions. Let me outline very briefly the principles that govern our conduct.

First, we will not get involved in conflict between Asian Communist nations. Our national interests are not directly threatened, although we are concerned, of course, at the wider implications of what might happen in the future and what has been happening in the past.

We are using whatever diplomatic and political means are available to encourage restraint on all parties and to seek to prevent a wider war. While our influence is limited, because our involvement is limited, we remain the one great power in all the world which can have direct and frank discussions with all the parties concerned. For this reason, we have a useful and important role to play in the restoration of stability. We will continue our efforts, both directly with the countries involved and through the United Nations, to secure an end to the fighting in the region, to bring about a withdrawal of Vietnam forces from Cambodia and of Chinese forces from Vietnam, and to gain the restoration of the independence and integrity of all nations involved.

At the same time, we are continuing to express our deep concern that this conflict may widen still further—with unforeseen and grave consequences for nations in the region and also beyond.

In any event, the United States is fully prepared to protect the vital interests of our people wherever they may be challenged. We are in close consultation with our friends and allies in the region, especially the members of the Association of Southeast Asian Nations, the ASEAN nations. Their continued stability and prosperity are of great importance to us.

The normalization of relations between the United States and the People's Republic of China is already an accomplished fact and will not be reversed. This was the simple, long overdue recognition of the reality of the government in Peking.

In the last few days, we've consulted directly with leaders around the world— and with our own congressional leaders, as well—about events both in the Middle

East and Southeast Asia. The responsibilities that we face are serious, and they are shared by the administration and the Congress, by our Nation, and our allies—and our common understanding and our adherence to a common cause are vital.

All of us know that the internal affairs of Iran or combat even among Communist nations are of concern to us. Many nations are troubled, even threatened by the turmoil in Southeast Asia and in the Middle East. To stand by our friends and to help meet their security needs in these difficult times, I will consult with the Congress to determine what additional military assistance will be required. This added measure of support is crucial for stability throughout the Indian Ocean area.

And let me repeat, in the Middle East, in Southeast Asia, and elsewhere in the world, we will stand by our friends. We will honor our commitments. And we will protect the vital interests of the United States, and you can depend on it.

As we face this immediate series of crises, we also look constantly to the broader needs of security. If we are to meet our responsibilities, we must continue to maintain the military forces we need for our defense and to contribute to the defense of our allies.

This year, I have proposed a substantial real increase in the defense budget. The events of recent weeks underscore the responsibility of the Congress to appropriate these funds in full. There must be no doubt that the people of the United States are fully prepared to meet our commitments and to back up those commitments with military strength.

Turmoil and crisis also underscore the vital needs to work wherever possible to stabilize and to reduce competition in strategic nuclear weapons. This effort has the same ultimate goals as does our strong defense—the goals of security, stability, and peace. In pursuit of these goals, our Nation faces no more important task this year than the successful conclusion of a strategic arms limitation agreement.

Just as we work to support national independence and to aid our friends and allies in times of trial, we must work to regulate nuclear arms capable of threatening life throughout this planet. For a SALT agreement is a fundamental element of strategic and political stability in a turbulent world—stability which can provide the necessary political basis for us to contain the kinds of crises that we face today, and to prevent their growing into a terrible nuclear confrontation.

After more than 6 years of negotiations—conducted by three different Presidents—agreement has now been reached on most of the major components of a sound and verifiable SALT II treaty.

The emerging agreement will establish for the first time equal numbers of strategic arms for both sides. It will thus reverse the Soviet's numerical advantage which was temporarily established in the SALT I treaty of 1972, when they had about a 40-percent built-in negotiated advantage.

To reach these new levels, the Soviets will be required to reduce their overall number of strategic arms. Over 250 Soviet missiles or bombers—about 10 percent of their strategic forces—will have to be destroyed or dismantled. At the same time, because we are now well below the agreed ceiling, we could substantially increase our own operational strategic forces.

The SALT II agreement will also provide negotiated limits on building new types of weapons and limits on the improvement of existing ones—the so-called qualitative arms race can be controlled.

SALT II will limit the size of land-based missiles and the number of warheads that can be placed on them. Without these limits, the Soviets could vastly increase the number of warheads on their large land-based missiles—with grave implications to the strategic balance. SALT II will therefore contribute to our ability to deal with the growing vulnerability of our land-based missiles. Without it, the Soviet Union could continue to increase the number of their warheads, tending to nullify our effort to protect our missiles.

The agreement will also permit us and our allies to pursue all the defense programs that we believe might eventually be needed—the MX missile; the Trident submarine and its missiles; air, ground, and sea-launched cruise missiles; cruise missile carrier aircraft; and a new penetrating bomber. These would be permitted.

Thus SALT II would allow our own prudent programs to move ahead and also will place important limits on what the Soviets might otherwise do. And this SALT II agreement will be a basis for further negotiations for additional substantial cuts in the level of nuclear armaments.

Without the SALT II agreement, the Soviet Union could have nearly one-third more strategic forces by 1985 than with SALT II. We would, of necessity, as a nation, match such a buildup. The costs would be enormous, the risks self-evident. And both nations would wind up less secure.

The stakes in SALT are too high to rely on trust. Any SALT II treaty that I sign will be adequately verifiable, using our own independent means of guaranteeing Soviet compliance with terms of the agreement.

SALT II will specifically forbid any interference that would impede our ability to verify compliance with the treaty. Any effort on the part of the Soviet Union to interfere with our verification activities would be a detectable violation of the agreement itself, and an early signal of any possible cheating.

Finally, let me put this agreement in the context of our overall relations with the Soviet Union and the turbulence that exists in many parts of the world. The question is not whether SALT can be divorced from this complicated context. It cannot. As I have often said, our relationship with the Soviet Union is a mixture of cooperation and competition. And as President of the United States, I have no more difficult and delicate task than to balance these two. I cannot and I will not let the pressures of inevitable competition overwhelm possibilities for cooperation, any more than I will let cooperation blind us to the realities of competition, which we are fully prepared to meet.

Because this carefully negotiated and responsible arms control agreement will make the world safer and more secure, it is in our national interest to pursue it, even as we continue competition with the Soviet Union elsewhere in the world. Therefore, I will seek both to conclude this new SALT agreement and to respond to any Soviet behavior which adversely affects our interests.

To reject SALT II would mean that the inevitable competition in strategic nuclear arms would grow even more dangerous. Each crisis, each confrontation, each point of friction—as serious as it may be in its own right—would take on an added measure of significance and an added dimension of danger, for it would occur in an atmosphere of unbridled strategic competition and deteriorating strategic stability. It is precisely because we have fundamental differences with the Soviet Union that we are determined to bring this dangerous dimension of our military competition under control.

In today's world, it is vital to match the pursuit of ideals with the responsible use of force and of power. The United States is a source of both, ideals and power. Our ideals have inspired the world for more than two centuries; and for three generations, since World War II, our power has helped other nations to realize their own ideals.

The determination and strength of purpose of the American people are crucial for stability in a turbulent world. If we stand together in maintaining a steady course, America can protect its principles and interests and also be a force for peace.

Americans have always accepted the challenge of leadership. And I am confident that we will do so now.

Thank you very much.

NOTE: The President spoke at 12:30 p.m. in Alexander Memorial Coliseum. In his opening remarks, he referred to Milton Jones, chairman of the Board of Regents of the University System of Georgia, George L. Simpson, Jr., Chancellor of the University System, Joseph M. Pettit, president of the Georgia Institute of Technology, and Bernard Kroll, president of the institute's National Alumni Association.

Prior to the President's remarks, Mr. Simpson conferred upon him the honorary degree of doctor of engineering, and at the conclusion of his remarks, Mr. Kroll presented him with the Alumni Distinguished Service Award.

Anti-Inflation Program

Remarks at a White House Briefing for State and Local Officials.   February 21, 1979

I'm glad to notice that in spite of the weather, the room is packed with people who are intensely interested in one of the most significant subjects for our country that I have to face.

Obviously, you as State officials and local officials bear on your own shoulders tremendous responsibilities for serving the public, and so do I. And in this modern, fast-moving, technological age, the issues that in the past were adequately difficult are now much more complex, much more confused, and much more challenging. But when our country was founded, we never anticipated that in a democracy with freedom for everyone, with shared responsibilities—local, State, Federal, President, Congress, the court system—that our task would be easy.

I think the most serious problem that I face as President on the domestic scene is to control inflation and to ensure for our country in the future a sound, stable, strong economy. This will tax the courage of the American people. It will tax the vision and sound judgment of the American people, and it will even tax the idealism of the American people, because in controlling inflation, there is no clear, identifiable victory when an achievement is realized. And in almost every event or decision when progress is made, it's almost always made for the general good at the expense of some individual benefit.

There's an element of unselfishness in it that's not present in all the subjects that we, you and I together, have to address. I'm absolutely determined to bring inflation under control in our country. It's a commitment that I've made on my personal convictions. It's a commitment that I've made jointly with congressional leaders here in our Nation's capital city. It's a conviction and a commitment that I've made in harmony with many of you who helped me evolve the programs that we are now attempting to carry out together.

I presented my 1980 fiscal year budget to the Congress. It's lean and tough. It's not going to be easy to protect the principles described in that budget. But I don't intend to yield its general thrust.

When I was running for President, our Federal deficit was $66 billion. If the budget I presented to the Congress is approved—and I expect it will be in its totality; with some deviations, of course, but its general total thrust will be approved—we will have cut the deficit more than $36 billion, about a 55-percent reduction.

In addition to that, we will have reduced the amount of the American gross national product that is collected and spent by the Federal Government down to about 21 percent, the lowest percentage in more than 7 years. And we've now got the trend going downward instead of upward.

I think it's important to point out that we've had a broad approach to this very difficult question. We've established voluntary wage and price standards. The response from business has been overwhelmingly good. The response from labor is increasingly favorable and supportive. I think it's understandable and predictable that labor support is going to come after an identifiable success in establishing prices and in establishing government policy. But together we have been and are making progress.

There are some limits to what the Federal Government can do. As a businessman myself, as an engineer, in my general philosophy I'm inclined to let the free enterprise system stay free. I don't think the Federal Government ought to try to go in and control business—employers and employees. And that's a self-imposed limit that I don't think is counterproductive.

In addition, obviously, we cannot control the weather. And when there is a difficult crop season, food prices are going to go up. And that's what's occurred in the past. I hope we have a good crop this year. We are trying to stabilize farm income, make it more predictable, put more control of their own future in the hands of farmers, increase exports. But we can't control the weather, and food prices and many others in our domestic scene are not controllable by the Federal Government.

We have no control over the policies of other nations, who quite often determine or affect the price of energy or the price of other commodities. We can use our influence in a beneficial way, in a proper way, and we do so. But we have no control over them.

We do, however, have control over our own actions and our own decisions, and that's where you can be of great help to me. I think it's important to point out that the Congress has some decisions to make.

Real wage insurance is a simple concept, a new concept, an innovative concept that would help make it easier for workers to restrain their wage demands in the face of past history and present experience with very rapid, inflationary increases. But if they agree to comply with our wage guidelines or standards, then if, because of the actions of other employees or other factors, the inflation rate should go up more, then their income tax payments would be lowered to make sure they don't suffer because they are unselfish and others are selfish.

We hope to have this legislation clear the Ways and Means Committee in the near future, and I believe it's accurate to say that the more the Members of Congress have studied the basic principle and the details of our proposal, the more progress has been made and the more support evolves. Many of our key labor unions who were originally cool toward the idea or in opposition have now expressed their support for it.

We are establishing at the Federal Government level prudent purchasing procedures. We intend to make the best and most efficient purchases we can. And one obvious measure of a good place to buy is among those companies that are prudent in establishing price policies. And I would hope that this would be one example that you might emulate at the local and State level.

Waste, fraud, corruption is being rooted out with the utmost of my own personal ability and those who work with me. There's no place for it in government. We have been guilty in the past of some betrayals of public trust. We are now establishing Inspectors General offices in the major agencies of the Federal Government, and they will be dedicated to constantly exhibiting any betrayal of the public trust and setting an example so this might be prevented, not just detected after it happens.

In addition to that, we are trying to reduce the adverse effect of Federal regulations, paperwork, both on local and State governments, and also in the private sector. And over a longer period of time, we are exploring every possibility to increase the productivity of the American working men and women.

Well, I think you can see that none of these efforts that I've described to you will be simple or easy to achieve, and no single one of them, even if successful, could guarantee that we could control inflation. If there was ever an issue on which our system of federalism will be tested and in which our system of federalism can be productive if welded together, this is it.

Everything I've described to you at the Federal level can be almost directly used as a pattern for local and State government decisions. And in addition to that,

because of the wide diversity of circumstances that prevail in your own community or State, you can be much more innovative even than we can here in Washington. And I would hope that through your own insight and your probing minds and the special local circumstances, that you might uncover other ways in which we can help to control rampant inflation.

I might say that there have been some allegations made that controlling inflation works against the interests of the poor, the unemployed, the elderly, who are most dependent on government services. This is exactly contrary to the facts. The people who are the worst sufferers when inflation is uncontrolled are those who live on a fixed income or on a very low income or who are not well educated or who can't provide their families with mobility to move from one community to another or shift from one job to another to find better opportunities.

Those very people who are most vulnerable and who need government services are the ones who suffer most when inflation is not controlled. Quite often, they are not organized, they are not articulate, they are not politically influential, and they need to be protected.

Let me say in closing that there are going to be a lot of pressures on you and on me from different special interest groups, some benevolent in nature, some selfish in nature. "Take action to control inflation among others. Don't touch us." Those pressures are already building up on the Congress. And it would be much easier for us here in Washington to act forcefully and aggressively and consistently if we felt sure that we were acting in harmony with you, in partnership with you, and that there was a constant support from officials and others at the local and State level for what we are attempting to do here in Washington.

I'm sure there will be temptations for you to take the same position I've just described in critical terms. "Take out the inflationary action on others. Don't touch us." But I think your coming here is indicative of your willingness to join in this worthwhile fight.

We've had excellent relationships with you ever since I've been in the White House. When we evolved our energy policy, most of it was done in concert with you. Our urban policy, the same; civil service reform, the same; the evolution of hospital cost containment legislation, the same; the evolution of our overall approach to controlling inflation, the same. We've consulted closely with municipal, county, State officials from the very beginning. And that's been the basis on which we've enjoyed successes in many of these areas.

I think that it's obvious to you I consider this to be a very important task, a very difficult task. But it's one where I do not intend to fail. And with your help, I feel secure that we will be successful. I'll try to be answerable to you in setting a good example here in Washington.

I'm not going to back down. I'm not going to yield to pressure. I'm willing to fight openly and aggressively and consistently to control inflation in our country. And with your help and support and partnership, I believe we'll be successful in having an even greater United States of America in the future.

Thank you very much.

I want to thank all of you for coming today. It means an awful lot to us. We're glad you're here. I think you have already gotten a taste of the suggestions we're about to hand out to you. They're just examples of what you can do. And if you've got other suggestions or ways that we can improve on these, I know you well enough to realize that you won't be reticent about giving us your opinion.

Thank you very much.

NOTE: The President spoke at approximately 1:30 p.m. at the briefing conducted by administration officials in Room 450 of the Old Executive Office Building.

As printed above, this item does not include the remarks of Alfred E. Kahn, Advisor to the President on Inflation, which were included in the press release.

United States Savings Bonds Program

Memorandum From the President.
February 22, 1979

Memorandum for the Heads of Executive Departments and Agencies

In 1978, I appointed Ray Marshall, Secretary of Labor, to serve a two-year term as Chairman of the Interagency Savings Bonds Committee. I am confident that with your help he will be able to ensure that the 1979 Federal Savings Bonds Campaign is a most successful one.

Participants in the Payroll Savings Program choose this method of saving for a wide variety of excellent reasons. Whether their goals revolve around providing higher education for their children, a more comfortable retirement, or a ready reserve in the event of personal emergency, they all recognize this program as a safe and convenient means by which to save.

It is also important to understand the degree to which our government and our country benefit from the sale of U.S. Savings Bonds. Today Americans own over $80 billion worth of these securities. These holdings constitute nearly one-fifth of the publicly-held portion of the Federal debt, helping to protect the value of the dollar and stabilize our nation's economy.

As the heads of Departments and Agencies who make up the Interagency Savings Bonds Committee, you have the special responsibility of offering and promoting the Payroll Savings Plan to each and every Federal employee. I know you will carry out this responsibility with your usual diligence and attention.

JIMMY CARTER

Development and Military Assistance Programs in Afghanistan

Statement by the White House Press Secretary. February 22, 1979

The President has decided to severely reduce our development assistance program in Afghanistan below levels projected for the fiscal years 1979 and 1980. The President has also decided to terminate a military training program that was in the planning stages. These decisions have been taken in the light of an ongoing review of our relations with Afghanistan and the policies with that government. Only small developmental assistance programs that are already under way and that address the needs of the least privileged sectors of Afghan society will continue.

NOTE: Press Secretary Jody Powell read the statement at 11:40 a.m. to reporters assembled in the Briefing Room at the White House.

Foreign Policy Conference for Editors and Broadcasters

Remarks and a Question-and-Answer Session. February 22, 1979

U.S. FOREIGN POLICY

THE PRESIDENT. Before I take your questions this afternoon, I'd like to give you some of my own thoughts about the uses of American power in a changing and sometimes turbulent world. Recent events, particularly in Iran and Southeast Asia, have touched off a national debate about what America's role should be in dealing with turbulence, and in trying to guide inevitable change.

We've been going through debates like this ever since our first President served, George Washington, whose birthday this happens to be.

Looking back over the last several years, particularly the last 2 years, I've been struck by the increasing complexity, however, of international affairs. I'm encouraged by what I judge to be a willingness on behalf of the American people to attempt to understand complex issues, not to oversimplify them, and to support policies and decisions that basically and openly address these complex issues responsibly and realistically.

Of course, there has never been any change in America's determination or our willingness to maintain a strong military capability, or to promote the economic health and vitality of our country, or to deal with and enhance the political and moral strength of our Nation. Those commitments have always been constant and unswerving. But we must also see issues that are complex very clearly. And we must devise intelligent and thoughtful responses to them.

Neither of the two events that have been so newsworthy the last few weeks—

turmoil in Iran, the conflict in Southeast Asia—were of our own making. But both events place great demands on me as President and on our ability to define and to act upon the true interests of the American people. And there are likely to be many more events like this in the future.

As the world becomes more complex, it's more important than ever before that we do not oversimplify events abroad. Bad analysis inevitably leads to bad policy. Instead, we need to be aware of the deep historical forces at work in other countries. We need to be well informed. The revolution in Iran, for example, is a product of Iranian social, political, economic, religious factors, all intertwined. To ignore these realities or fail to understand them would lead us into taking actions that might be ineffective or irrelevant or even dangerous.

But in addition to understanding the complexity of individual nations, we must also understand how changes taking place in those nations can affect the future, both of that particular region, the entire world, and especially my responsibility, the United States of America.

We need to resist two temptations: to see all change as inevitably against the interests of the United States, as kind of a loss for us or a victory for them; or to imagine that what happens in a country like Iran will not have consequences for us and for other regions as well. We need to see what is happening not in terms of simplistic colors, black and white, but in more subtle shades; not as isolated events, but often as part of sweeping currents that have broad significance.

At this moment there is turmoil or change in various countries from one end of the Indian Ocean to the other; some turmoil as in Indochina is the product of age-old enmities, inflamed by rivalries for influence by conflicting forces. Stability in some other countries is being shaken by the processes of modernization, the search for national significance, or the desire to fulfill legitimate human hopes and human aspirations.

For us in the United States, change itself is not the enemy. Our concern is twofold. We must work to dampen conflict, to maintain peace, and we must make clear that it's dangerous for outside powers to try to exploit for their own selfish benefits this inevitable turmoil. That kind of exploitation can damage not only the integrity and independence of the nations that happen to be in a transition phase, but also can damage the effort to build a more secure and a more peaceful world for us all.

Let me repeat what I said at Georgia Tech earlier this week: In the Middle East, in Southeast Asia, and elsewhere in the world, we will stand by our friends. We will honor our commitments, and we will protect the vital interests of the United States.

The United States continues to be the most powerful nation on Earth—militarily, economically, and politically. And I'm committed to preserving and even enhancing that power, not for its own sake, but for the sake of the values and the ideals of our Nation. We will make responsible use of that power where our interests are directly involved or where we can help to create conditions for peace and for the independent development of other nations and for the realization of the hopes of human beings who live there.

We have forces in readiness, as you well know, which we will use if necessary. I hope that that need will never rise. I am proud that no member of the Armed Forces of our country has had to give his life in combat during my administration. And I'm determined to do all in my power to keep this precious peace. But let there be no mistake, our will and our determination are firm; our commitment to protecting our vital interest is unshakable. We must, therefore, be very clear about where our true interests lie.

In Iran, our interest is to see its people independent, able to develop, according to their own design, free from outside interference either by us or from any other power. In Southeast Asia, our interest is to promote peace and the withdrawal of outside forces and not to become embroiled in conflict among Asian Communist nations. And, in general, our interest is to promote the health and the development of individual societies, not to a pattern cut exactly like ours in the United States, but tailored rather to the hopes and the needs and the desires of the peoples involved.

To these ends we will broaden our cooperation with our friends in the Middle East and Southeast Asia, supporting their efforts to maintain national stability and independence. We'll consult closely with Congress to determine the need for additional military aid in this troubled region of the Middle East, to be used where it can be most effective. And we have called and will call on our allies to help whenever they can or will, working in partnership with us.

We are working hard for peace between Israel and her neighbors and also in other troubled areas of the world. In the future, I feel sure we will find demands on the United States to be increasing and not diminishing. We continue to bear the burdens of maintaining a strong defense, of supporting traditional allies who depend upon us, and working to reduce the spread of conventional and nuclear weapons.

But we also face a twilight world of change and sometimes of turmoil. We will increasingly be called upon to deal with events that do not represent basic challenges to our security, but still which require the responsible use of American influence and American power.

We have the strength and the will to act where need be, and I'm confident that as a nation we have the wisdom to act wisely.

That's my responsibility in brief terms, a responsibility which you share with me.

Now, I'd like to answer any questions that you might have for a few minutes.

QUESTIONS

THE MIDDLE EAST

Q. Mr. President, my name is Croskery, from Cincinnati. I'd like to know what we're going to do to ensure the stability of small oil-producing states in the Middle East during this time of instability in that part of the world?

THE PRESIDENT. I've just sent Secretary of Defense Brown into that region, as you know, to meet with the leaders of four nations: Saudi Arabia, Jordan, Egypt, and Israel. We have the top officials of Oman here consulting this last few days with Secretary Vance. And in the Emirates, in Bahrain, and other small countries we've assured them that our influence, our power as a nation will be used to preserve the basic security of that region free from any outside political or military power.

We are trying to bring them together in a spirit of peace and harmony and a recognition that their own national independence ought to be preserved by them and also preserved by us.

As I said in my brief remarks earlier, I am consulting with the Congress now, based on the reports that Harold Brown brought back, about how we might increase to some degree our military assistance efforts for those small countries that feel insecure, so that through their own strength they might feel better able to withstand any internal and outside disturbances that are unwarranted.

There are some nations that provide major stabilizing efforts. Egypt is a strong, powerful nation in the Arab world; Israel's strength is part of our own security. Iran, we hope and pray, in the future will still be a factor for stability in their region—in a different character, obviously, than it was under the Shah, but we hope will be independent and determined to maintain kind of a rock of stability in that region, impervious to outside influence and attack.

So, I'd say, working with individual nations, working collectively to reduce tensions among them and making sure they have adequate military capabilities and using our own influence to prevent some major outside power from having an inordinate influence—those are some of the things that we can do.

The last one, obviously, is to try to bring some peace between Israel and her own neighbors. I think if the Arab world, in a united way, working with us, perhaps with Israel in a peaceful pursuit, could face any outside disturbance rather than to focus their animosity, as it has been in the past, on Israel, it would certainly be a very stabilizing factor.

We derive great benefit from free access to oil from that region. Some of our allies and friends in Europe and Japan rely much more heavily, and we are trying to get them to use their own influence to parallel ours in maintaining the independence of individual nations and the stability therein.

There are a few instances in that region where economic aid, either through direct grants, which are fairly rare, or through guaranteed loans on a multilateral basis or through international lending institutions can also help. That's kind of a gamut of things that we explore and use with varying degrees of priority and emphasis.

EGYPTIAN-ISRAELI PEACE NEGOTIATIONS

Q. Mr. President, many observers of the Middle Eastern situation believe that the failure of Egypt and Israel to sign the Camp David agreements as originally conceived this fall, and, in fact, the subsequent delays in signing any agreement, are directly related to the lack of pressure by the United States not on Israel and Egypt, but on Jordan and Saudi Arabia to join the talks or at least to lend support to the negotiating process. Would you please comment on this?

THE PRESIDENT. Well, I think in a spirit of complete candor we have approached our limit on legitimate influence, perhaps even pressure in a proper way, on the countries in that entire region to support the Camp David accords and to participate in future discussions.

We have sent delegations to Jordan, to Saudi Arabia, even this past week, to encourage their tacit or public or active support of these accords. And I've used my own personal influence to a maximum degree within the bounds of propriety in the same pursuit.

As you know, my own involvement in the Camp David negotiations has been substantial. There is no other single item that has addressed my attention as President, on which I've spent more time, more effort, more study, more prayer, than to bring peace between Israel and her neighbors. We believe the Camp David accords are a very firm and well-advised foundation on which to predicate, first of all, an agreement between Israel and Egypt, combined with a comprehensive settlement as part of the same procedure that relates to Israel and her neighbors. And whatever we can do—to use the word again—within the bounds of propriety, recognizing the independence of other nations, we have done, are doing, and will do to bring about peace between Israel and her neighbors.

PEOPLE'S REPUBLIC OF CHINA

Q. Mr. President, if the Soviet troops decide to help Vietnam in their struggle, how will this affect normalization and the Taiwan question, which is also being questioned as to its defenses?

THE PRESIDENT. The normalization of relations between our country and the People's Republic of China is an accomplished fact. It will not be affected one way or the other by combat among the Asian Communist countries. We have used every bit of influence that we could with Vietnam, with China, with the Soviet Union to bring about a withdrawal of attacking forces whenever they've crossed an international border, and to bring about an end to combat there.

My hope is that this combat will rapidly be concluded. And even today we introduced to the United Nations a request for a complete analysis or debate of this question, calling upon Vietnam to withdraw their troops after they have invaded Kampuchea, and also calling upon China to withdraw her troops from Vietnam.

But I would say that the recognition of the Beijing government as the Government of China is already an accomplished fact and will not be abrogated, nor will there be any interference with it.

U.S. FOREIGN POLICY

Q. Mr. President, some columnists and commentators have come to regard the implementation of your foreign policy as a failure. They point specifically to the lack of a clear direction, a steady course. Aside from those areas covered in your opening remarks, what do you think has created that perception? Do you think it's possible that you yourself may have contributed to that problem? [*Laughter*]

THE PRESIDENT. I think that this allegation is to be anticipated. It's not unexpected for us.

There is a marshaling of public support in almost every instance when a President takes forceful action at a time when our Nation's security itself is endangered—obviously, in time of a war. When people feel that our Nation's security is challenged, there's a patriotic response to a President in a time of forceful action. It's not quite so easy to marshal overwhelming, enthusiastic, dedicated support in a time when a President's been able to search out a path and maintain peace. But I hope that that will be my achievement throughout the rest of my term.

In retrospect, I can't see that we should have done anything differently in the basic questions from what we have done. We have had some notable challenges.

I think that on a worldwide basis we've increased our friendships substantially with nations that are emerging as leaders. We have greatly repaired the dispirited nature and the relative weakness of NATO. I think there's now a renewed commitment to the strength of our alliance there.

Our relationships with Australia, New Zealand in the ANZUS agreement are very strong. For the first time in my lifetime, as a matter of fact, we now have better relationships with the three leading Asian countries than do the Soviet Union leaders, that is, India, Japan, and the People's Republic of China.

We've injected ourselves, I think, in a well-advised way in trying to resolve disputes among nations that might erupt into a broader conflict. I have just covered the part of my effort in the Mideast. We've tried to bring peace to Cyprus. We've worked with the British, trying to resolve the problems in Rhodesia, to give majority rule, a democratic government there, to end the racial discrimination that has existed.

We've worked very closely with four other major allies—Canada, France, West Germany, Britain—to bring about majority rule and independence of Namibia. And in other areas of the world we've tried to add our influence whenever we could in a constructive way to ensure stability, peace, and the realization of legitimate aspirations of people who are involved.

And the fact that we haven't a crisis, that we haven't had to go to war, that we have been successful in maintaining peace, I think, is an achievement.

But it hasn't required yet, and I hope never, a demonstration of courage on my part to call out the Armed Forces or to participate in an armed attack against other people.

THE MIDDLE EAST

Q. Mr. President, Secretary of Defense Brown has just returned from the Middle East, and it's reported that Egyptian President Anwar Sadat, concerned about the role of the Palestinians in Iran, is interested in becoming the region's policeman—which is how some newspapers are describing it—in return for heavy infusions of U.S. weapons. What's the likelihood for this?

And, also, Sadat has said that he would not use the equipment in conflict with Israel, but how can we be sure that if he's called upon by his Arab brothers to fight Israel that he wouldn't use it?

THE PRESIDENT. I think Sadat has demonstrated in a very dramatic way, and also a consistent way in the last few years, his peaceful intentions toward Israel. His trip to Jerusalem, his participation, successfully, in the Camp David negotiations, I think, is proof of his good intentions toward having peaceful relations with Israel.

As you probably know, Israel* is a very powerful element in the Arab world, economically; their population is very great; their military strength is great, compared to many other countries. And I think they can be a legitimate stabilizing force. They now have five divisions or more on the eastern side of the Suez confronting Israel. Part of the Camp David accords, part of the negotiated points that have already been concluded on the Sinai agreement would call for the withdrawal of these forces. They would perhaps never be used. But at least any entity that threatened to attack another country in the Mideast would be faced with the prospect that those Egyptian forces might very well be used to preserve the peace. I'm not predicting that this would happen, but the potential would be there for Egypt to help to protect relatively defenseless other Arab countries or to preserve peace in the Mideast.

I don't want to try to comment on any nation being a policeman for the region nor for the world. I think that's a very serious mistake.

There obviously have been requests made by many nations around the world for military or economic assistance that is in excess of what our Nation could provide. That situation might apply to the

---

*The President meant to say Egypt. [Printed in the transcript.]

request that President Sadat has recently made. But he certainly wouldn't be unique in that respect.

As you know, the two nations that receive the most aid from our country at this time, and for many years in the past, has been Israel and Egypt. And I think that the greatest single step we could take to preserving stability and peace in the Mideast, although it might be unpopular with some other Arab countries, would be a peace treaty between Israel and Egypt. That's our top priority, and we'll continue with that pursuit.

U.S.-SOVIET RELATIONS

Q. Mr. President, Gary Schuster from the Detroit News. How strained is the relationship now between the United States and Russia because of the recent events in Afghanistan, Iran, Rhodesia, and Vietnam? And, two, how does that strain, if there is any, translate into how easily the Senate might accept a SALT agreement, if and when it gets there?

THE PRESIDENT. I think it's inevitable for the foreseeable future that we will have competition with the Soviet Union for influence in nations who are either unaligned or who don't want to be completely under the domination of any other country. We have no desire to dominate another nation. But we would like to see each nation be independent, to be at peace, and to see the legitimate aspirations of those people be realized.

There have been changes made in the last 15 years or less that affect both our countries. I think it is true that in Afghanistan, a Communist nation* was re-

---

*What the President meant to say was that the regime in Afghanistan, a nation under Soviet influence, was replaced by a regime more closely aligned with the Soviet Union. [White House Press Office correction.]

placed by another Communist regime more closely aligned with the Soviet Union. Angola, it was completely under the domination and influence of the Soviet Union. And perhaps Cuba is now reaching out feelers or a hand of friendship to some of the Western nations. I think the same thing might apply to Mozambique, Tanzania.

This, I think, is a normal, evolutionary process. In the past under Mrs. Gandhi, India was very closely aligned with the Soviet Union. Their relationships with our country were strained. I would say that under Prime Minister Desai this has changed considerably. It wasn't too long ago that China and the Soviet Union were the closest of political and military allies. Now China has normal relationships with us and are very sharply estranged from the Soviet Union.

In the past, Egypt, the most powerful Arab nation, was an ally almost exclusively with the Soviet Union. Now they have an equally close friendship with us and are estranged from the Soviet Union. I think NATO in the past, immediately following the Vietnam war, was weakened. I know that some of our great Members of Congress, Mike Mansfield was calling for the withdrawal of all U.S. troops from Europe. Now I think there's been a revitalization of NATO, a strengthening of our alliance there which is very crucial to our own security.

I think, in balance, the trends in the last number of years have not been adverse to our country. But it's easy to single out one or two individual places like Afghanistan where those trends have been against our best interests. The point I'm trying to make is that the fluidity of this situation over a period of years is inevitable, and we can't freeze the world situation at any particular time or any particular region or country where it might be temporarily or historically to our advantage.

And we cannot say to the Soviet Union, "Unless all Cuban troops are removed from Angola we will never sign a SALT agreement with you."

Our negotiating of the SALT treaty has been in the best interest of the United States. It's in our best security interests. It lays a basis for enhanced prospects for peace. It gives us greater flexibility to use our conventional forces to carry out the purposes of our Nation that I recently, last few minutes ago, described to you.

I think every potential altercation or difference or competition with the Soviet Union in a troubled region of the world— and, as I say, these are inevitable—would be greatly exacerbated if we fail to conclude a SALT agreement or if we, on our own, refuse to negotiate with the Soviet Union to bring about a lessening of dependence upon nuclear weapons.

I consider the SALT treaty to be well negotiated in its present form, approaching a conclusion, I hope, in the best interests of our country standing on its own. And we could not permit the Soviet Union to say to us, "Unless you withdraw all your troops from South Korea, unless you reduce your military strength in NATO, unless you sever your relationships with Egypt, unless you permit us to come into the Mideast situation as a full negotiating partner, we will not sign a SALT agreement." We would consider that to be an absolutely unwarranted intrusion on the freedom of our country to make our own decisions based on what's best for our people.

And I think for us to claim that we can demand the same sort of restraint on the part of the Soviets as a prerequisite to the conclusion of a SALT agreement, that we consider it to be in our own best interest, is unwarranted and ill-advised

and, obviously, unacceptable to them or in our own best interests.

So, obviously, we will have to cooperate with the Soviets whenever we can, to lessen tensions, to cooperate on trade, to try to detect common purpose where we can cooperate, to conclude agreements that might lessen tension and improve the possibility for peace. At the same time, we will compete with the Soviet Union when we have differences with the fullest confidence that we will continue to be successful.

And I think those two ideas are not incompatible for a strong, secure, able, confident, enlightened nation like the United States.

Thank you very much.

NOTE: The President spoke at 2:10 p.m. in the Loy Henderson Conference Room at the Department of State.

National Caucus on the Black Aged

Remarks at a White House Luncheon Honoring Recipients of the Organization's Living Legacy Awards.   February 23, 1979

Well, I've had the privilege, which has not been the good fortune of many Americans, to be introduced twice in the same day by Aaron Henry, and I appreciate that.

Mr. Chairman and members of the National Caucus on Black Aged, it's really an honor for me as President of our Nation to participate in a ceremony, a social event, a gathering which indeed is unprecedented in the history of the White House.

I've looked with great care at the name of this organization—Aaron Henry has not let me forget it—since I've been President. And we're delighted to have a chance to be the hosts for an inspiring occasion like this one.

I notice there are a couple of words that I would change if I were naming the organization again. I think "national" is really a little too narrow in scope. If there ever was an event that has international overtones, I would say it is this one, because distinguished black Americans have not only been an inspiration to the people of the United States of America, they have set an example of leadership, dedication, courage, and achievement that's an inspiration throughout the world.

And the word "aged" to me seems a little inappropriate as I look around at the list of the honorees today. Maybe if it has to start with "a," maybe "ambitious"—[*laughter*]—or maybe "aspiring" or at least "ageless," because I can't imagine anyone looking on Dr. Martin Luther King, Sr., or Jesse Owens or Roy Wilkins or Gus Hawkins and thinking about the word "aged," because they have shown us that there is no age limit on achievement and inspiration and dedication. And every person who's being honored here today is indeed a notable citizen of our country whose own life's events and accomplishments far exceed their own circle of friends and personal acquaintances.

I would like to introduce each person individually who's being honored here today. As you well know, each one is worthy of a very extensive biographical description. But I'll just say a very few words about each one, not doing anyone justice, but letting them bask in the glory of the fellowship which they enjoy, because as they look around and see the others who are being honored, that in itself is a great honor indeed.

I'd like to begin my presentation with a man who has joined me in the last 2 years, since I've been President, as a great

and distinguished leader of the Congress, a man who's being honored today because of his accomplishments in one of the most aged professions, and that is politics, a man who is a Democratic Congressman from Los Angeles whose name has been associated with notable achievements in congressional history, who's been active in California politics up until the time he was elected to the Congress in 1962. He's an original native of Louisiana, and I would like to introduce to you one of our distinguished honorees, Augustus Hawkins.

Another very famous person who can't be with us today, who is ill, has been known by Americans of every race and creed because of her achievements in the field of literature. Ms. Margaret Walker Alexander, prominent poet, novelist, native of Birmingham, Alabama, her poetry includes: "Prophets for a New Day," "October Journey," and her very famous novel, "Jubilee."

And I'd like to recognize her in her absence and ask you to give her a round of applause, even though she isn't here.

The next person I'd like to recognize is Ms. Septima Poinsettia Clark, in the field of human services. She's a prominent educator.

Ms. Clark, just stay standing for a few minutes. I just want to say a few more words while you're standing. Let everybody look at you. [*Laughter*]

She did her graduate work at Hampton University. She taught in the Charleston, South Carolina, schools, and she exemplifies, as do many of those who are being honored today, a special courage that was required when she spoke out so courageously for the impetus in the early years of the civil rights movement. Because she was active in demanding civil rights for her people, she lost her job and she also lost her retirement pay. She's been active in the Southern Christian Leadership Conference, and I think she exemplifies not only notable achievement but superb courage in public service.

Thank you very much.

Mr. Malvin Goode, in the field of communications. Would you please stand?

Nowadays we see many black commentators on television, many black performers in the public arts. We hear many black voices on the radio, giving a balanced tone to the report of public events in our country. But this' honoree has served superbly for a long period of years.

He was a pioneer in news broadcasting, prominent news broadcaster for ABC, and also a United Nations correspondent for ABC, originally a native of Virginia. And he's brought a balanced analysis and accurate reporting of the news, the understanding of human events, not only in our country but internationally.

And I want to express my deep thanks to you for what you've meant for our country, Mr. Goode.

Dr. Montague Cobb. I think everyone knows the importance, not only in the present time but especially in past years, to have superb professional training in the service of black people when adequate education opportunities, adequate social services, adequate medical care was not available, when it required a special degree of dedication because of the extremely burdensome responsibilities, because of the small number of highly professional trained Americans to serve so many people for each one of those professionals.

We also know how difficult it must have been at the time, when one was a student, to get a doctorate in medicine. In the field of science and health, Dr. Cobb, a medical doctor, a medical educator, an editor, a professor of anatomy at one of our great medical schools, Howard University, a native of Washington, D.C.

On behalf of the people of the United States, Dr. Cobb, I thank you.

Reverend Dr. Gloster Current, a man who, when he stands, brings a lot of smiles on the faces of people who know him. A bright, invigorating personality, a great sense of humor, a natural leader, active in the NAACP since its early days, a native of Indianapolis, he has been a religious leader througout his adult life, has never even known the definition of the word "retirement," Bishop, New York Conference of the United Methodist Church.

Reverend Dr. Current, congratulations to you and my best wishes and thanks.

It would be difficult for me to single out any special person in this group, but if I had to single someone out, I think most of you could guess who it would be. And I would like to ask Dr. Martin Luther King, Sr., to stand. And remain standing, please. [*Laughter*]

I look on Dr. King not only from the perspective of a distinguished American honored by a President, but I look on him in many ways as a son would look on a father. He's a native of my State, and I have observed him and his most distinguished family being a beaconlight of truth and integrity, of distinguished service, of inspiration to me, to many others in this country, and indeed throughout the world.

I believe that in honoring a Methodist bishop, a Baptist preacher, that almost everyone, whether black or white, sees very clearly that the proper melding of deep religious conviction and leadership combined with the service of the downtrodden, sometimes the despised, the poor, the suffering, has been melded never so adequately in history, with the exception of the life of Christ, than it has in the black civil rights movement of recent years.

When it was impossible for a black voice to be heard clearly in the South, in a courtroom or a courthouse or even a public school, the black churches were a haven for liberty. The black colleges supported by churches were the origin of the development of high intelligence and dedication. And the organizational structure that resulted in this dramatic change in our Nation for all citizens originated in the deep, dedicated, unselfish service of the religious leaders.

Dr. King, as you know, is the pastor of Ebenezer Baptist Church in Atlanta, where I have been many times. His family has suffered more than it should, but in the suffering has produced martyrs whose influence has been explosive in affecting the lives of other people. He is one of the founders of the NAACP; his son, the leader of the Southern Christian Leadership Conference.

And I'm honored and our Nation is honored by the family of Dr. Martin Luther King, Sr., and by his own personal achievements, which have been an inspiration to his wife, his children, his many blood relatives, and those of us, like myself, who consider ourselves also to be part of his family.

In the performing arts, I'd like to recognize Ms. Dorothy Maynor.

The South is well represented here today. Ms. Maynor is a concert singer from Norfolk, Virginia, world famous, discovered by Mr. Koussevitsky in 1939. She sang in concerts more than 25 years all over the world. Sometimes she was permitted to sing in foreign countries when it was very difficult for her to find a stage or an audience where she could demonstrate her superb ability here in her own country. This took a special dedication and an extraordinary talent to overcome the obstacles that were placed in her path. When she retired from her full-time service to humanity as a superb performer, she founded the Harlem School of Arts to aid young Americans, and in every aspect of life, hers has been admirable.

And I express to you, Ms. Maynor, my congratulations, my thanks, and my love.

I guess it's impossible for a son to have two fathers, but I'd like to ask Dr. Benjamin Mays to stand.

One of the greatest educators this Nation ever produced. He didn't have to be a full-time preacher to preach. [*Laughter*] And he produced, through his inspirational leadership, wisdom, confidence in struggling young black Americans, leaders that indeed have inspired us and have been a great satisfaction to him as well; still very active in his commitment to the preservation of the character and the quality and the service of the predominantly black colleges, the historical black colleges and universities of our country.

The Atlanta University complex was the center for wisdom, judgment, and influence in the times when those attributes were difficult to find for a black American. And Dr. Mays represents these high ideals as well as anyone I have ever known. He's a past president of Morehouse College. I'm one of the distinguished honorary alumni of Morehouse. And as I always say, I may be the first alumni of Morehouse to be President, but I'm sure I won't be the last one.

As you know, he's presently the president emeritus of Morehouse and also is the president of the United Negro College Fund. This fund itself has not only kept the great black colleges alive, but through its own fundraising efforts and educational programs, it has acquainted many distinguished white American leaders with the superb accomplishments of black students, black educators, and other black Americans who have performed in their own lives so well.

He's a native of South Carolina, but we claim him from Georgia. And, Dr. Mays, I thank you on behalf of the 220 million Americans who've benefited from your life's service. And I urge you, as President, not to ever let that service terminate nor be lessened in any degree, and I'm sure you will answer my request. Congratulations to you.

I don't believe that Mrs. Rosa Parks has arrived yet. She was trying to get here. I presume that she's traveling this time by airplane. [*Laughter*]

Recently at the Black Caucus banquet I had the honor and pleasure of calling her up to the stage to put my arms around her and to let her know in front of several thousand people the debt that our Nation owes to her.

Most of the people that I've mentioned this afternoon have been highly trained. They were college graduates with masters or doctors degrees, highly specializing in education or the arts or religion. Rosa Parks was apparently an average citizen. I doubt if she could have expressed in as eloquent terms the aspirations of black Americans nearly so well as Dr. Benjamin Mays, nor Dr. Martin Luther King, Sr., or many of you, but in a quiet way, she let her own influence be felt in a far greater degree than many who had opportunities far exceeding her own.

She had a certain degree of intelligence and integrity, yes. But she had a superb degree of courage. And knowing the Deep South as I do—Americus, Georgia; Albany, Georgia; Montgomery, Alabama; Birmingham, Alabama; parts of South Carolina, Mississippi—and looking back 20, 25 years, the courage that she showed is truly overwhelming. And I know that all of you realize that it was her insistence that she would show the rights of black

Americans in an understandable way, a simple way, that aroused a nation eventually to accept those rights as a part of American life, and to correct ancient discriminatory actions even under the guise of American law. And I wish she was here, but in 1955, she took one small step that led to a revolution in our country.

She's a native of Alabama, the former State secretary of the Alabama NAACP, and a woman who's an inspiration to us all. And I would like again to express my thanks to her, my congratulations to her, and a recognition, as President, of what she's achieved for our country. She's indeed in her own way a great stateswoman of the United States. Thank you very much.

Another honoree who couldn't be here today is A. Phillip Randolph, representing the labor movement. But Bayard Rustin is here to represent Mr. Randolph.

I think that throughout the earliest days, even before the time when Rosa Parks or Martin Luther King, Jr., were famous, there was a sense throughout our Nation that A. Phillip Randolph stood for higher aspirations and equality of black Americans. He organized the Brotherhood of Sleeping Car Porters in 1925. He was the vice president of the AFL–CIO, organized the first March on Washington For Civil Rights in 1941.

He's a native of Florida. This year he's 90 years old. And I think that those who came later obviously saw him as having set a courageous example to be emulated. And Bayard, I hope that you will extend to Mr. Randolph my appreciation, recognition, and my friendship for the superb leadership that he gave many of those others who are being honored here in the White House this afternoon.

In Government, it's been indeed rare when a black American could become a member of the Cabinet of a President of the United States. And I'd like to ask Dr. Robert Weaver to stand, if you will.

Dr. Weaver has been an innovator. He's been a credit to our country in every sense of the word, in every job that's been assigned to him. He's an economist, an educator, and a superb public administrator. He's professor of urban affairs at Hunter College, a native of Washington, D.C., former Secretary of the Housing and Urban Development Department, and an inspiration to many of us, Dr. Weaver, who presently serve in the Federal Government. Thank you very much for your notable achievements.

Did Mr. Asa Spaulding arrive? Asa, you had me concerned.

He's being recognized for his achievements in business. He's a native of North Carolina. He's president of the North Carolina Mutual Life Insurance Company, and his extensive public service is exemplified by his willingness to perform superbly on the board of trustees of Howard University. And as all of you know, in his position of leadership in his own State and throughout the South, he's been a strong, active supporter and has added the financial strength and the prominence of his own achievements to the success of many of those who struggled to give black Americans their long overdue civil rights.

And I want to thank Mr. Spaulding and congratulate you, Mr. Spaulding, this afternoon.

Dr. Charles Wesley. Again, a man who combines the great achievements of a wonderful intellect in several realms of life, as an author, historian, educator, as a presiding elder in the AME Church, Dr. Wesley has indeed shaped the realization of Americans of the wonderful achievement of black citizens whose own lives' meaning might very well have been overlooked or ignored. He's a retired president of Central State University, Wilberforce, Ohio; he's pastor and presiding elder of the AME Church, and the author of books on black history; native of Louisville, Kentucky.

And I thank you, express my admiration and my congratulations to you, Dr. Charles Wesley.

Mr. James Van Derzee? Just hold your hand up and we'll applaud.

Mr. Van Derzee represents the fine arts category. He's the dean emeritus of black photographers in America. He's a person who shaped the attitudes and opinions and aroused the support of deprived, needy black Americans who lived in Harlem. He recorded on film in the most superlative way the lives of Afro-Americans who lived in urban centers, where life's deprivations are sometimes overlooked.

He received the American Society of Magazine Photographers Award for an exhibit called "Harlem On My Mind" at the Metropolitan Museum of Art in 1969. I don't think that Mr. Van Derzee would object to my saying that he's this year 93 years old. He's a native of Massachusetts and has honored us by his presence. Congratulations to you.

How many of you remember 1936? [*Laughter*] I've already been told that some of you were married in 1936, and if anyone asked me before this day, "What do you remember about 1936?", I would have said that the achievements of a black American athlete inspired the world. And I would like to ask Jesse Owens to stand.

Nineteen hundred and thirty-six was the year when Hitler was spouting the philosophy of racial superiority. The Olympics were being held in Germany, and it was a time in our own country when it was difficult for black athletic ability to be adequately recognized. There were no professional black baseball players in the American and National Leagues; professional teams excluded our own citizens. But a young man who possibly didn't even realize the superb nature of his own capabilities went to the Olympics and performed in a way that I don't believe has ever been equaled since.

Jesse Owens is a collegiate track star. He was the first athlete to win four gold medals in one Olympiad. He's a native of Alabama. And since this superb achievement, he has continued in his own dedicated but modest way to inspire others to reach for greatness.

And I thank you for what you did for us in 1936, and what you've done for us every year since, and what you will do for us in the future, Jesse Owens. Thank you very much.

Now I'd like to ask Mr. Roy Wilkins to stand, please. If you feel like it, Roy, please stay standing.

I've been really pleased today at how strong and vigorous and healthy he looks—much better than the last time I saw him, so he's being well taken care of.

On occasion in our country there lives a person whose life is one of decency, dedication, honesty, modesty, and superb achievement, who, because of his own inner convictions, in a quiet fashion, can organize, inspire, and lead others. Roy Wilkins, as you know, is a long-time executive secretary of the NAACP. He's been prominent in civil rights activities since the earliest days of a viable movement.

In times of discouragement and despair, he never lost his commitment nor his dedication nor his confidence that the right could ultimately prevail in a society of free men and women. And it's an honor for me, as President, to recognize again a man who's being honored by you in the field of civil rights, which has touched the life of every person here.

Roy Wilkins, on behalf of the people of our country, I thank you and I congratulate you.

Let me say in closing I know it's an honor to come to the White House. It's certainly an honor for a President to serve here. But in my opinion, today in a special way the White House has been honored.

Many thousands of people throughout our country have performed great service as black Americans to those who've looked to you for leadership and to others who share with you the privileges of citizenship in the greatest nation on Earth. You have helped to write history, and you've proven that the strength of the human spirit can achieve excellence, even in the face of extraordinary obstacles. You have a living legacy that exists in your own physical lifetime, and you have a legacy that will succeed all of us who are here today. And I want you to know that your lives have been a model already to many others.

This is a day of privilege for us to share with you this occasion. And it's a day of inspiration to have these potentially unsung heroes recognized, in many instances perhaps a little bit late, but the correction of this mistake by the action of the National Caucus on Black Aged has been a very well chosen decision. And my wife, Rosalynn, and I, all those who serve in our Government are pleased that we could be a part of such a wonderful and inspirational occasion.

Thank you very much.

NOTE: The President spoke at 12:45 p.m. on the State Floor of the White House. In his opening remarks, he referred to Aaron Henry, chairman of the National Caucus on the Black Aged.

International Exchange-of-Persons Program

Message to the Congress Transmitting a Report.   February 23, 1979

To the Congress of the United States:

In response to Section 203 of the Foreign Relations Authorization Act (P.L. 95–426), I take this opportunity to inform you of the Administration's current plans to increase exchange-of-persons activities administered by the International Communications Agency (USICA). A significant expansion of financial support for these activities is contained in the FY 1980 budget submission for USICA. The Administration's review of the USICA-administered cultural and educational exchange programs has also produced an agenda of important questions to be addressed in the year ahead. I enclose a detailed report on these matters provided to me by the Director of USICA.

As I stated in my message transmitting Reorganization Plan No. 2 of 1977: "Only by knowing and understanding each other's experiences can we find common ground on which we can examine and resolve our differences . . . As the world becomes more and more interdependent, such mutual understanding becomes increasingly vital." Because direct personal contact is such an effective and lasting form of communication, exchange-of-persons activities are fundamental to the achievement of these objectives.

Unfortunately, the vital long-term role played by these programs in our international affairs is too often obscured by more visible, more immediate, but frequently less fundamental matters. The recent administrative reorganization which established USICA affords an excellent opportunity to reexamine this important dimension of our international relations.

The reassessment is complex and difficult, but nonetheless essential to the development of a sound program. Because some critical data will require more time to collect, our reassessment will require a good deal of work beyond that already accomplished. However, some preliminary conclusions are reflected, already, in USICA's plans for FY 1979, its proposed budget for FY 1980, and planning levels for subsequent years.

Including domestic and overseas staff costs, the USICA FY 1979 budget for exchange programs is approximately $75 million. The FY 1979 allocation represents a program increase of $4,350,000 over FY 1978. Over sixty percent of the increase is allocated to already established programs with particular emphasis on projects involving African and Middle Eastern Countries. Initiatives being financed from increased funds include new projects with the People's Republic of China, the Hubert H. Humphrey Fellowship program, and additional counseling services for foreign students seeking admission to, or already attending, U.S. universities.

For FY 1980, an additional $4,450,000 is being proposed for the first full year of the Humphrey Fellowship program; an increase of $800,000 is being requested to extend and improve student counseling services; and an additional $350,000 is planned for exchanges with China.

For the period FY 1981–83, annual program increases of $5 million are currently being projected. The plan, thus, calls for a total increase in exchange programs of approximately $25 million over the period FY 1979–83. For this same period, further increases of over $30 million are projected to cover overseas costs increases.

This plan will, of course, be reevaluated on an annual basis. Final budget proposals and areas of priority emphasis will be subject to our continuing assessment of these programs, as well as to international developments and the Administration's over-all budgetary goals.

Finally, I should like to emphasize the Administration's readiness to work with the Congress on strengthening these programs. We need your counsel; we welcome your advice; we look forward to your support.

JIMMY CARTER

The White House,
    February 23, 1979.

NOTE: The report, entitled "Report of the Director of the International Communication Agency to the President on Plans for Expansion of the International Exchange-of-Persons Program," is included in the press release.

Clothespin Imports

Proclamation 4640.   February 23, 1979

TEMPORARY QUANTITATIVE LIMITATION ON THE IMPORTATION INTO THE UNITED STATES OF CERTAIN CLOTHESPINS

By the President of the United States

A Proclamation

1. Pursuant to section 201(d)(1) of the Trade Act of 1974 (the Trade Act) (19 U.S.C. 2251(d)(1)), the United States International Trade Commission (USITC) on December 12, 1978, reported to the President (USITC Report 201–36) the results of its investigation under section 201(b) of the Trade Act (19 U.S.C. 2251(b)). The USITC determined that clothespins provided for in items 790.05, 790.07, and 790.08 of the Tariff Schedules of the United States (TSUS) (19 U.S.C. 1202) are being im-

ported into the United States in such increased quantities as to be a substantial cause of serious injury to the domestic industry producing articles like or directly competitive with the imported articles. In order to remedy the serious injury to the domestic industry that it has found to exist, the USITC recommended the imposition of a 5-year quota on U.S. imports of wood and plastic spring-type clothespins with a dutiable value not over $2.10 per gross provided for under TSUS item 790.05.

2. On February 8, 1979, pursuant to section 202(b)(1) of the Trade Act (19 U.S.C. 2252(b)(1)), and after taking into account the considerations specified in section 202(c) of the Trade Act (19 U.S.C. 2252(c)), I determined to remedy the injury found to exist by the USITC through the proclamation of a 3-year quota on U.S. imports of wood and plastic spring-type clothespins with a dutiable value not over $1.70 per gross provided for under TSUS item 790.05. On February 8, 1979, in accordance with section 203(b)(1) of the Trade Act (19 U.S.C. 2253(b)(1)), I transmitted a report to the Congress setting forth my determination and intention to proclaim a quota and stating the reasons why my decision differed from the action recommended by the USITC.

3. Section 203(e)(1) of the Trade Act (19 U.S.C. 2253(e)(1)) requires that import relief be proclaimed and take effect within 15 days after the import relief determination date.

4. Pursuant to sections 203(a)(3) and 203(e)(1) of the Trade Act (19 U.S.C. 2253(a)(3) and 2253(e)(1)), I am providing import relief through the temporary imposition of a quota on U.S. imports of wood and plastic spring-type clothespins with a dutiable value not over $1.70

per gross provided for under TSUS item 790.05.

5. In accordance with section 203(d)(2) of the Trade Act (19 U.S.C. 2253(d)(2)), I have determined that the level of import relief hereinafter proclaimed pursuant to section 203(a)(3) of the Trade Act (19 U.S.C. 2253(a)(3)), permits the importation into the United States of a quantity or value of articles which is not less than the average annual quantity or value of such articles imported into the United States in the 73/78 period, which I have determined to be the most recent representative period for imports of such articles.

Now, THEREFORE, I, JIMMY CARTER, President of the United States of America, acting under the authority vested in me by the Constitution and the statutes of the United States, including sections 203 and 604 of the Trade Act (19 U.S.C. 2253 and 2483), and in accordance with Article XIX of the General Agreement on Tariffs and Trade (GATT) (61 Stat. (pt. 5) A58; 8 UST (pt. 2) 1786), do proclaim that—

(1) Part 1 of Schedule XX to the GATT is modified to conform with the actions taken in the Annex to this proclamation.

(2) Subpart A, part 2 of the Appendix to the TSUS is modified as set forth in the Annex to this proclamation.

(3) This proclamation shall be effective as to articles entered, or withdrawn from warehouse, for consumption on or after February 23, 1979, and before the close of February 22, 1982, unless the period of its effectiveness is earlier expressly modified or terminated.

IN WITNESS WHEREOF, I have hereunto set my hand this twenty-third day of February, in the year of our Lord nineteen hundred and seventy-nine, and of the Independence of the United States of America the two hundred-third.

JIMMY CARTER

[Filed with the Office of the Federal Register, 11:37 a.m., February 23, 1979]

NOTE: The annex is printed in the FEDERAL REGISTER of February 26, 1979.

Initial Fuel Assurances

Message to the Congress Transmitting a Report. February 23, 1979

To the Congress of the United States:

Pursuant to Section 104(b) of the Nuclear Nonproliferation Act of 1978, enclosed is a report on Preliminary Proposals on Initial Fuel Assurances.

As indicated in the report, we are continuing our assessment of alternative fuel assurances schemes and will inform you of any proposals as these assessments are concluded. The current alternatives envision uranium stockpiles with size ranges between 2 million and 10 million separative work units. Present estimates of the cost for these program alternatives, based on the current market value of the uranium fuel and the enrichment services, are approximately a half billion to more than 2 billion dollars.

JIMMY CARTER

The White House,
    February 23, 1979.

NOTE: The report is entitled "Preliminary Proposals for Initial Fuel Assurances—A Report by the President" (13 pages plus appendices).

Digest of Other White House Announcements

The following listing includes the President's public schedule and other items of general interest announced by the White House Press Office and not included elsewhere in this issue.

February 19

The President returned to the White House from Camp David, Md.

February 21

The President met at the White House with:

—Zbigniew Brzezinski, Assistant to the President for National Security Affairs;

—Frank B. Moore, Assistant to the President for Congressional Liaison;

—the Democratic congressional leadership;

—Vice President Walter F. Mondale, Stansfield Turner, Director of Central Intelligence, Hamilton Jordan, Assistant to the President, and Dr. Brzezinski;

—Vice President Mondale;

—James T. McIntyre, Jr., Director of the Office of Management and Budget.

The President has accepted the invitation of Prime Minister Pierre Eliott Trudeau of Canada to attend the 15th anniversary concert for the Symphonicum Europae Fund, Inc., in New York City on March 3. He will have a private dinner with the Prime Minister for an informal discussion of Canadian-American and world affairs. They will attend the concert at Carnegie Hall following the dinner.

February 22

The President met at the White House with:

—Secretary of the Treasury W. Michael Blumenthal, Stuart E. Eizenstat, Assistant to the President for Domestic Affairs and Policy, Charles L. Schultze, Chairman of the Council of Economic Advisers, Alfred E. Kahn, Advisor to the President on Inflation and Chairman of the Council on Wage and Price Stability, Barry P. Bosworth, Director of the Council on Wage and Price Stability, and Mr. McIntyre;

—David L. Aaron, Deputy Assistant for National Security Affairs;

—Mr. Moore;

—Douglas M. Costle, Administrator of the Environmental Protection Agency, and Mr. Eizenstat;

—Mrs. Carter, for lunch;

—Secretary Blumenthal, to discuss Mr. Blumenthal's forthcoming trip to the People's Republic of China.

February 23

The President met at the White House with:

—Vice President Mondale, Secretary of State Cyrus R. Vance, Secretary of Defense Harold Brown, Dr. Brzezinski, and Mr. Jordan;

—Dr. Brzezinski;

—Mr. Moore;

—representatives of solar groups.

NOMINATIONS SUBMITTED TO THE SENATE

The following list does not include promotions of members of the Uniformed Services, nominations to the Service Academies, or nominations of Foreign Service officers.

Submitted February 23, 1979

MARY LOU ROBINSON, of Texas, to be United States District Judge for the Northern District of Texas, vice a new position created by P.L. 95–486, approved October 20, 1978.

NORMAN W. BLACK, of Texas, to be United States District Judge for the Southern District of Texas, vice a new position created by P.L. 95–486, approved October 20, 1978.

CHECKLIST OF WHITE HOUSE PRESS RELEASES

The following listing contains releases of the White House Press Office which are not included in this issue.

Released February 20, 1979

Advance text: remarks before a joint session of the Georgia General Assembly

Advance text: remarks at a special convocation of the Georgia Institute of Technology

Released February 21, 1979

Announcement: nomination of Mary Lou Robinson to be United States District Judge for the Northern District of Texas

News conference: on the White House briefing for State and local officials on the antiinflation program—by Gov. Robert Graham of Florida, Mayor William H. McNichols of

CHECKLIST—Continued

Denver, Colo., and Alfred E. Kahn, Advisor to the President on Inflation

Announcement: visit of the President to New York City on March 3

Released February 23, 1979

Announcement: nomination of Norman W. Black to be United States District Judge for the Southern District of Texas

ACTS APPROVED BY THE PRESIDENT

NOTE: No acts approved by the President were received by the Office of the Federal Register during the period covered by this issue

Strategic Arms Limitation

White House Statement.   *February 24, 1979*

The President expects that a verifiable agreement on strategic arms limitations which protects American strategic interests can be negotiated and will be ratified.

The President's position is that this agreement will be submitted for Senate ratification as a treaty. If the Soviet Union, in the absence of a SALT treaty, were to engage in a significant arms build-up, the President would, of course, match it appropriately. By the same token, it is the President's intention not to escalate the arms race unilaterally in the absence of a treaty if comparable and verifiable restraint is shown by the Soviet Union.

Egyptian-Israeli Peace Negotiations

Remarks Following a Meeting With Egyptian Prime Minister Mustafa Khalil and Israeli Foreign Minister Moshe Dayan.
February 25, 1979

I have a statement to read, which has been drafted jointly by the Prime Minis-ter of Egypt and the Foreign Minister of Israel, and it is expressed from my own point of view.

During the past week, I, as President, have kept in close touch with the negotiations at Camp David, and Secretary Vance, Prime Minister Khalil, and Foreign Minister Dayan have now given me a firsthand report on their talks.

In light of the developments in the talks at Camp David this past week, we are discussing with the two governments the possibility of moving these negotiations to the head-of-government level later this week. Prime Minister Begin would then represent Israel, and Prime Minister Khalil, who has been authorized by President Sadat to conclude the negotiations on behalf of Egypt, would represent Egypt.

I would be going to Camp David with Prime Minister Begin and Prime Minister Khalil, accompanied by Secretary Vance. Prime Minister Khalil is leaving this afternoon for Cairo for consultations. Foreign Minister Dayan is returning to Israel this evening to report to the Prime Minister and to the Cabinet.

I am prepared to spare no effort in achieving the peace settlement foreseen in the Camp David accords reached last year. The other two partners in these negotiations share this determination.

Thank you very much.

NOTE: The President spoke at 2:45 p.m. to reporters assembled on the South Lawn of the White House.

Prior to his meeting with Prime Minister Khalil and Foreign Minister Dayan, the President met at the White House with Secretary of State Cyrus R. Vance and Zbigniew Brzezinski, Assistant to the President for National Security Affairs.

National Governors' Association

Remarks and a Question-and-Answer Session With Members of the Committee on International Trade and Foreign Relations. February 25, 1979

THE PRESIDENT. Last September, in a meeting of a few Governors, including the chairman, Julian Carroll, at the White House, we discussed very briefly the possibility of having a new National Governors' Association committee established to promote international trade.

As a former Governor of a Southeastern State, I probably devoted 25 percent of my time to either recruiting investments in Georgia from other States in the Nation and also from overseas, or trying to sell Georgia products to foreign countries. I visited, I think, 10 different nations when I was Governor to promote international trade. And we established trade offices in different places around the world in a very aggressive fashion.

After I became President, I could see with much more clarity not only the economic advantages of this effort but the political advantages as well, because a basis of friendship, commerce, common visitors, negotiations among even nongovernmental leaders is one of the soundest possible bases on which permanent political alliances can be maintained and

peace and harmony can be enhanced throughout the world.

Typically, my own expectations as they related to the National Governors' Association have been far exceeded by accomplishments. I had no idea a few months ago that we would be sitting in a room like this, with a packed audience, 30 or 35 Governors intensely studying the possibilities for the enhancement of international trade. I want to congratulate the chairman of the National Governors' Association, also my good friend, George Busbee, the chairman of this new committee. I think its potential is almost unlimited.

There's no question in my mind that relatively speaking, as a percentage of budget allocations, as a percentage of time invested, many States, perhaps almost all the States, do a far better job of promoting international trade than does the Federal Government. I think this is to be expected, because I cannot possibly devote 25 percent of my total time as President just to promoting international commerce itself. But there's no doubt in my mind either that working as new partners now, we can greatly enhance the ability of both Governors and a President to lead our respective Governments toward reaching a common goal.

There is a great advantage, in my opinion, in having 50 Governors directly involved through this committee and individually in this effort. Because of the diversity of interests of the States themselves, each one of the States is so different—different employment needs, different products evolved, different investment potential, different environment, different attitude—that you all can be, in effect, 50 experiment stations for determining how the Nation's thrust can be oriented to help in this very important realm of national interest.

We have a difficult assignment in controlling inflation in our Nation, in trying to have prosperity, providing jobs for our people, and in cementing, as I said earlier, closer relations with our natural friends and allies throughout the world. And the enhancement of international trade is a partial, sometimes almost a complete answer to some of those specific problems. We have a very high adverse trade balance, as you well know, primarily resulting from our extraordinary and excessive imports of oil from overseas. And the redressing of this trade balance by improved sale of American products overseas with which you can help is very beneficial indeed.

There's another element that ought to be mentioned. When I correspond directly and privately with President Brezhnev of the Soviet Union, I don't believe I've ever received a secret message from him that did not include an emphasis on his desire to improve trade relationships with our country. In my recent visit to Mexico, at the root of all our difficulties and potential successes in the future—the alleviation of tension, misunderstanding, the repairing of historical mistakes—the word "trade" can almost be considered a magic key to open up doors of progress in every one of those areas of question.

Mike Blumenthal is now in the People's Republic of China, a billion people now hoping for and expecting better relationships with our country, a wonderful opportunity if it's handled well. Secretary Kreps will be following his trip with her own. In our dealings with other countries who have historically been our friends, the same thing applies.

I've just left the White House a few minutes ago, having met with the Prime Minister of Egypt, the Foreign Minister of Israel to receive a report from them on progress made at Camp David this week and, hopefully, to prepare for a head-of-state meeting later on this coming week to proceed with these peace negotiations.

And again, at the root of basic problems, and as an incentive to further progress, is the question of trade, economic stability, economic prosperity, improving the quality of life of people in those countries.

We are now facing a difficult decision in Congress about how to handle the Taiwan question, to honor our commitments to those good friends. And as you well know, one of the things that I insisted upon in normalizing relations with the People's Republic of China was the continued trade and commerce and cultural exchange with the people of Taiwan.

So, in every one of these areas, the importance of trade cannot be overemphasized. Ambassador Bob Strauss has been negotiating day and night for months to bring about an international alleviation of obstacles to trade through the Multilateral Trade Negotiations, to reduce existing protectionism and to prevent the selfish protectionist tendencies that always exist in every country, including our own, from prevailing in the future. This is not going to be an easy agreement to have ratified or approved by the Congress. And speaking frankly, I hope that all of you will study the details of these agreements and the benefits that we can derive from them, and use your own influence, speaking constructively and soundly and from a basis of knowledge and intelligence, to encourage the Congress to approve these agreements once they have been reached.

I've recognized the limitations on what the Federal Government can do. And your chairman and I use that primarily as the reason for making this move among the Governors. I have tried to improve the quality of service by the Eximbank, for instance. I think in the 1977 budget, the total amount of money available to the Eximbank was about $700 million. In the budget that I've just presented to Congress, it's $4.1 billion, about six times as much. And we would like to make sure that this still limited amount of money is expended in the most efficacious way for our country.

When I made my own trade missions as a Governor, I almost invariably took a representative of the Eximbank along with me, because that is an avenue by which very good, sound investments of taxpayers' money in our own country can be greatly magnified in benefits. And I think your own private study or concerted study of trade opportunities using governmental entities like the Eximbank or OPIC or the Small Business Administration can be very helpful to you and to the people who look to you for leadership in your own States.

I'd like to just say two other things: There has been a study made by Juanita Kreps, under her, Secretary of Commerce, and your role in this expansion of trade will be significant, and she is working closely with you, as you well know.

There will be an analysis given to me in April of the regulatory obstacles to international trade so that we can see clearly what well-meaning regulations in the past established for international trade now have served their purposes or are ill-advised and ought to be removed because they are an obstruction to increased trade. And in these studies, working closely with Secretary Kreps and in concluding the recommendations on regulatory obstacles and other areas of the Federal Government's functions, I would like for the Governors to be a full partner with me.

Obviously, we can't have 50 new Secretaries of State. We've got at least enough Secretaries of State already. [*Laughter*] But I think that as you want to expand your own contacts with foreign countries, you need to have an intimate knowledge of the political circumstances or military circumstances or economic circumstances in the nations with which you are trying to enhance business. And we have now appointed, as you know, a very highly qualified Ambassador to work directly with you. And Secretary of State Vance, whom I left just 5 minutes before I arrived here, is very eager to participate in giving you detailed briefings and including, of course, you, in the knowledge that we share of other countries who look to us as a stabilizing factor in the world and admire our strength and who know that our own strength can be enhanced, our thrust for peace can be enhanced if your own efforts are successful.

Governor Busbee, I want to congratulate you for your new leadership role here and pledge, again, as I have in the past, my full support as an equal partner with you in this important element of American life.

Thank you very much.

GOVERNOR BUSBEE. We're going to continue with the questions and answers of the other panel members in just a few minutes, but the President says that he has time for two or three questions before he has to leave again for a meeting. So, I'll entertain the first question.

THE PRESIDENT. Or comment. If you all have——

GOVERNOR BUSBEE. Or comment. This is Governor Thompson.

QUESTIONS

GOVERNOR THOMPSON. Mr. President, has your administration yet concluded, following Vice Premier Deng's visit to the United States, to what extent substantially increased trade with the People's Republic of China will depend upon expansion of credit available, and if it will depend substantially on that, what plans the administration, perhaps Congress as well, has to expand credit relationships with China?

THE PRESIDENT. We, obviously, have done preliminary assessments of Chinese credit. My own guess is that other than extending most-favored-nation status to the People's Republic of China, that it would not involve any credit directly from our Government. The credit status of the PRC is very good, primarily because of the enormous resources of that country and also because they've been so reticent in the past in accepting any credits whatsoever. And now a multibillion dollar expansion program in their own trade and also a multibillion dollar expansion program in investments, commercial investments in China, could very easily be financed through normal or private business loans because of China's very excellent credit rating.

GOVERNOR BUSBEE. Next question? Representative Conable.

REPRESENTATIVE CONABLE. Mr. President, you announced an export policy last September, and you're going to have a review, apparently, this coming spring. To what extent will there be new legislation suggested, do you think, or are you going to be relying primarily on administrative changes? We've heard a lot here today about the extent to which the Government stands in the way of exports. Of course, if we're going to get through the MTN, we've got to be persuaded that Americans will benefit from an increased export trade.

THE PRESIDENT. I think the Export Administration Act is up for renewal in September.

REPRESENTATIVE CONABLE. It is, yes.

THE PRESIDENT. It will be completely reassessed, and I think in the renewal process, amendments will undoubtedly be proposed and considered. I've not gone into that in any detail yet. I would like to see as much as possible the obstacles removed from international trade and the emphasis be placed on the promotion or the enhancement of international trade.

I would like to express one caution, however. One of the prerogatives of a President is to have authority enough to carry out a major responsibility that the Constitution gives me, and that is to protect the security of our country. There must be times, inevitably, in the life of any President, when some trade restraints can be used effectively to prevail in an altercation or to protect American interests or the interests of our friends as an alternative to possible military or much more serious action. And with that one exception, and the protection of the American free enterprise system, I would like to see all the unwarranted obstacles, regulations to trade removed. And I think there's a lot of area of improvement there to be tapped when the studies are completed.

Secretary Kreps feels that this is so. My own White House staff members believe this is the case, and Secretary Vance feels the same. So, with the exception of protecting our own free enterprise system—and I'm a strong supporter of antitrust laws and deregulation and the protection of the President's prerogative to ensure that our Nation is protected itself—within those very tight bounds, I think everything that can be done ought to be done this year to remove any further obstacles to trade.

GOVERNOR BUSBEE. Governor Link had a question; North Dakota.

GOVERNOR LINK. Thank you, Mr. Chairman.

Mr. President, prior to recognition of mainland China, trade teams have visited and had been visiting individual States, making some purchases of commodities and goods and agricultural products that they wanted and needed.

What is the recommendation and the attitude of the administration regarding

333

continuation of negotiations between the individual States in response to the visits and the trade that had been already established?

THE PRESIDENT. I would like to see those efforts escalated. I might say that I believe that in this particular realm of trade, we are benefiting in both ways. I don't see any deleterious effect on our trade with Taiwan from our new normal relations with the People's Republic of China. And it opens up enormous new possibilities, as you well know, Art, for new trade and enhanced trade with China, mainland, itself.

As a matter of fact, after Japan normalized relations with the People's Republic of China several years ago, their trade with that great country exploded into tens of billions of dollars of presently existing contracts, more than $10 billion. At the same time, they established the same relationship with Taiwan that we have now proposed the Congress approve. And under those circumstances, their trade with Taiwan has more than tripled, almost quadrupled just in the last few years. So, I think we'll have a continuation or even an expansion of our trade with Taiwan and a greatly magnified, new opportunity for trade with the People's Republic of China.

I would hope that when Secretary Kreps returns from her trip to the People's Republic of China, that she could relay, through George Busbee, to all of you her assessment of the advisability of your making individual trips with trade missions to the People's Republic. I think this would be very good for your State. It would certainly be very good for our country, and it would, in addition, let the Chinese people understand us better and vice versa. I think through your own initiative and exploration of possibilities you can uncover opportunities that we could never hope to uncover, even with the best

organized and most enthusiastic effort from the Federal Government itself.

GOVERNOR LINK. You see, we've had a standing invitation even prior to the recognition of mainland China, and they indicated they hoped it would continue. And I was interested in knowing what the attitude——

THE PRESIDENT. I think you ought to accept the invitation.

Maybe one more question.

GOVERNOR BUSBEE. Mr. President, before you depart, the chairman of the National Governors' Association, Governor Carroll of Kentucky, wanted to make a statement.

GOVERNOR CARROLL. Mr. President, on behalf of the Governors, I want to say thank you for your suggestion. This committee would not be sitting here today were it not for this personal suggestion of the President of the United States, and I think the Governors should be grateful to him for his suggestion.

It was made at the White House while we were having lunch one day. And I said to him, "Well, Mr. President, if you're serious, would you mind writing a letter and asking us to do it." And he was that serious. He wrote the letter and suggested that it be done, and indeed the National Governors' Association executive committee then created this standing committee. And you see how enthusiastic the Governors are responding to it.

And indeed, we believe that it's going to create improved international relations from a resource that has never been utilized before by the Federal Government, and that's the resource of its own States. And we compliment you for it; we thank you for it and look forward to helping you. And as a Governor who's got all kinds of coal, I'm looking for some of those countries that are now burning oil that could burn coal and let us have their oil. [*Laughter*]

THE PRESIDENT. Well, let me say in closing—I've got to go back to another meeting at the White House—but let me say in closing that I'm very proud of what's been done already. I think this has tremendous, exciting potential.

One of the most delightful and fruitful efforts that I ever made as Governor—and sometimes I was disappointed in my projects—was in international trade. And I've seen a remarkable change take place in Georgia because we've had people come there from foreign countries, and now we understand people much better that were formerly quite alien to us. And the foreigner tag which used to be a source of vituperation has now become a matter of an avenue for new friendships. And nothing could help our Nation more.

I think had this committee been formed maybe back in 1936 or '38, we might very well have avoided the war with Japan—if there were constant, multiple avenues of commerce and trade and trade missions and Governors' exchange and the Congresses working closely, we might very well have avoided our breakdown in relationships with Japan. Nobody knows that. But there's no doubt in my mind that we can alleviate tensions and search out new avenues, not only of commercial benefit, but also new avenues of peace and excitement and an expanded quality of life for all our people by closer relationships between the States and foreign countries.

There are exceptional responsibilities on those State Governors who live on the border, in the south with Mexico and in the north with Canada. I know that historically those interrelationships have been very closely woven, and you can help me in dealing with the problems with Mexico if you give me advice and work closely with me in making sure that I can benefit from the knowledge and the historical interrelationships that have been enjoyed by the Southwestern States. The

same thing, obviously, applies to Canada.

So, I just can see many, many opportunities here for this meeting to go down in history as one of the great steps forward for our own great Nation and to let us become even greater in the future.

Thank you again.

NOTE: The President spoke at 3 p.m. in the Yorktown and Valley Forge Rooms at the Hyatt Regency Hotel.

Small Business Week, 1979

Proclamation 4641.   February 23, 1979

By the President of the United States of America

A Proclamation

Small business has been the economic backbone of American life since the earliest colonial days. Traders, craftsmen and merchants spurred the economy and played a vital role in the Nation's westward movement and growth. They helped create the multitude of opportunities which have become the hallmark of our free enterprise system—a system which has made American progress the envy of the world.

There are 13.9 million businesses in the United States today, and 13.4 million are small, including nearly three million farms. Together, they provide employment for over half the business labor force and account for more than 48 percent of the gross business product. They are an important source of the major innovations that create new markets and improve our quality of life. America's prestige in the world today could never have been achieved without this outstanding productivity by small business.

Meetings are currently being held in every State of the Union in preparation for the first White House Conference on

335

Small Business which I have called for in January of 1980. This year, every small business man and woman and indeed, every American, should be giving serious thought to how we may best secure and expand the small business sector of our economy in the years ahead.

Now, THEREFORE, I, JIMMY CARTER, President of the United States of America, do hereby proclaim the week beginning May 13, 1979, as Small Business Week, and I call on every American to join me in this very special tribute.

IN WITNESS WHEREOF, I have hereunto set my hand this twenty-third day of February, in the year of our Lord nineteen hundred seventy-nine, and of the Independence of the United States of America the two hundred and third.

JIMMY CARTER

[Filed with the Office of the Federal Register, 1:55 p.m., February 23, 1979]

NOTE: The text of the proclamation was released on February 26.

Meat Imports

Proclamation 4642.   February 26, 1979

QUANTITATIVE LIMITATION ON THE IMPORTATION OF CERTAIN MEAT

By the President of the United States of America

A Proclamation

The Act of August 22, 1964 (78 Stat. 594; 19 U.S.C. 1202 note), provides for the limitation of certain meat imports if import estimates exceed 110 percent of an adjusted base quantity for that year. The limitation applies to fresh, chilled, or frozen cattle meat and fresh, chilled, or frozen meat of goats and sheep, except lamb.

The Secretary of Agriculture has determined in accordance with Section 2(b)(1) of the Act that the adjusted base quantity of meat for the calendar year 1979 is 1131.6 million pounds. The Secretary has estimated (in the 1979 first quarterly estimate, 44 FR 1202) that the aggregate imports of meat for 1979 will be 1570.0 million pounds. This estimate exceeds 110 percent of the adjusted base quantity for 1979.

In accordance with Section 2(c) of the Act, the President must limit the import of meat to the adjusted base quantity for 1979 of 1131.6 million pounds, unless he increases or suspends that limitation pursuant to Section 2(d) of the Act.

Now, THEREFORE, I, JIMMY CARTER, President of the United States of America, by the authority vested in me by Section 2 of the Act, do hereby proclaim as follows:

1. The total quantity of the articles specified in item 106.10 (relating to fresh, chilled, or frozen meat) and item 106.20 (relating to fresh, chilled, or frozen meat of goats and sheep (except lamb)) of part 2B, schedule 1 of the Tariff Schedules of the United States, which may be entered, or withdrawn from warehouse, for consumption during the calendar year 1979, is limited to 1131.6 million pounds.

2. In accordance with Section 2(d) of the Act, I determine that the supply of meat described in Paragraph 1 hereof will be inadequate to meet domestic demand at reasonable prices.

3. The limitation proclaimed in Paragraph 1 hereof is suspended during calendar year 1979, which suspension shall remain in effect unless because of changed circumstances it becomes necessary to take further action under the Act, and I hereby determine that the suspension for such

period is necessary in order to carry out the purposes of Section 2(d) of the Act.

IN WITNESS WHEREOF, I have hereunto set my hand this twenty-sixth day of February, in the year of our Lord nineteen hundred seventy-nine, and of the Independence of the United States of America the two hundred and third.

JIMMY CARTER

[Filed with the Office of the Federal Register, 5:06 p.m., February 26, 1979]

Energy Coordinating Committee

Executive Order 12121.　February 26, 1979

By the authority vested in me as President by the Constitution of the United States of America, and in order to enlarge the membership of the Energy Coordinating Committee, Section 1–102 of Executive Order No. 12083 of September 27, 1978, is hereby amended by adding in alphabetical order the following:

"(x) The Director of the Community Services Administration.

"(y) The Chairman of the Council on Wage and Price Stability.".

JIMMY CARTER

The White House,
　February 26, 1979.

[Filed with the Office of the Federal Register, 5:07 p.m., February 26, 1979]

Office of Administration

Executive Order 12122.　February 26, 1979

By the authority vested in me as President by the Constitution and statutes of the United States of America, including Section 107(b) of Title 3 of the United States Code, in order to provide limited employment authority for the Office of Administration, it is hereby ordered that Section 4 of Executive Order No. 12028 of December 12, 1977, is amended to read as follows:

"Sec. 4. (a) Subject to such direction or approval as the President may provide or require, the Director shall organize the Office of Administration, contract for supplies and services, and do all other things that the President, as head of the Office of Administration, might do.

"(b) The Director is designated to perform the functions of the President under Section 107(b) of Title 3 of the United States Code.

"(c) The Director may appoint and fix the pay of employees pursuant to the provisions of Section 107(b)(1)(A) of Title 3 of the United States Code without regard to any other provision of law regulating the employment or compensation of persons in the Government service. Under that section the Director may also fix the pay of an employee serving in a competitive position or in the career service in order to avoid the pay limitation imposed by Section 114 of Title 3 of the United States Code. The provisions of other laws regulating the employment or compensation of persons in the Government service shall continue to apply to such employee.

"(d) The Director shall not be accountable for the program and management responsibilities of units within the Executive Office of the President; the head of each unit shall remain responsible for those functions.".

JIMMY CARTER

The White House,
　February 26, 1979.

[Filed with the Office of the Federal Register, 5:09 p.m., February 26, 1979]

Offshore Oil Spill Pollution

Executive Order 12123. February 26, 1979

By the authority vested in me as President of the United States of America by Section 303(b)(3), 305, and 312(a) of Title III of the Outer Continental Shelf Lands Act Amendments of 1978 (92 Stat. 674, 677, and 684, 43 U.S.C. 1813(b)(3), 1815, and 1822), relating to the Offshore Oil Spill Pollution Fund, and by Section 301 of Title 3 of the United States Code, and in order to assign certain management responsibilities related to protecting the environment from offshore oil spill damage, it is hereby ordered as follows:

1–1. *Assertion of Oil Pollution Claims.*

1–101. The authority vested in the President by Section 303(b)(3) of Title III of the Outer Continental Shelf Lands Act Amendments of 1978, hereinafter referred to as the Act (92 Stat. 674, 43 U.S.C. 1813(b)(3)), is delegated to the Secretary of Commerce with respect to those natural resources which are subject to his management or control.

1–102. The authority vested in the President by Section 303(b)(3) of the Act (92 Stat. 674, 43 U.S.C. 1813(b)(3)) is delegated to the Secretary of the Interior with respect to those natural resources which are subject to his management or control.

1–2. *Determination of Financial Responsibility and the Assessment and Compromise of Penalties.*

1–201. The authority vested in the President by Section 305(a)(1) of the Act (92 Stat. 677, 43 U.S.C. 1815(a)(1)), relating to vessels, is delegated to the Federal Maritime Commission.

1–202. The authority vested in the President by Section 305(b) of the Act (92 Stat. 678, 43 U.S.C. 1815(b)), relating to offshore facilities, is delegated to the Secretary of Transportation.

1–203. The authority vested in the President by Section 312(a)(2) of the Act (92 Stat. 684, 43 U.S.C. 1822(a)(2)), relating to the assessment and compromise of penalties concerning vessels, is delegated to the Federal Maritime Commission.

JIMMY CARTER

The White House,
    February 26, 1979.

[Filed with the Office of the Federal Register,
    5:10 p.m., February 26, 1979]

Offshore Oil Spill Pollution

*Memorandum From the President.
February 26, 1979*

Memorandum for the Secretary of Commerce, the Secretary of Transportation, the Attorney General, the Chairman, Federal Maritime Commission, the Chairman, Federal Trade Commission, the Chairman, Securities and Exchange Commission

Subject: Study of Oil Pollution Insurance

The Secretary of Commerce shall conduct the study required by Section 305(d) of Title III of the Outer Continental Shelf Lands Act Amendments of 1978 (92 Stat. 678, 43 U.S.C. 1815(d)), relating to the availability of, and competition in the market for, adequate private insurance against oil pollution. The Secretary shall perform all the functions vested in the President by that Section, except the submission of the final report to the Congress.

In conducting this study and in preparing the final report and recommendations for submission to the President the Secretary shall consult with the Secretary of Transportation, the Attorney General, the Federal Maritime Commission, the Federal Trade Commission, and the Securities and Exchange Commission. The advice of the full Interagency Council on Accident Compensation and Insurance Issues shall also be sought in preparing the final report and recommendations.

JIMMY CARTER

Department of Health, Education, and Welfare

Nomination of Benjamin W. Heineman, Jr., To Be an Assistant Secretary. February 26, 1979

The President today announced that he will nominate Benjamin W. Heineman, Jr., of Chicago, Ill., to be an Assistant Secretary of Health, Education, and Welfare for Planning and Evaluation. He would replace Henry J. Aaron resigned.

Heineman was born January 25, 1944, in Chicago. He received a B.A. from Harvard University in 1965, a B. Litt. from Oxford University in 1967, and a J.D. from Yale University Law School in 1971.

From 1971 to 1972, Heineman was law clerk to Associate Justice Potter Stewart. From 1973 to 1975, he was a lawyer for the Center for Law and Social Policy. From 1975 to 1977, he practiced law with the firm of Williams, Connolly and Califano.

From 1977 to 1978, Heineman was Executive Assistant to the Secretary of Health, Education, and Welfare. Since 1978 he has been Deputy Assistant Secretary of Health, Education, and Welfare for Planning and Evaluation.

Department of Labor

Nomination of Dennis R. Wyant To Be Deputy Assistant Secretary for Veterans' Employment. February 26, 1979

The President today announced that he will nominate Dennis R. Wyant, of Bethesda, Md., to be Deputy Assistant Secretary of Labor for Veterans' Employment. He would replace Roland Mora, resigned.

Wyant was born October 27, 1943, in Parsons, Kans. He received a B.S. from Southwest Missouri State University in 1965, an M.B.A. from Wright State University in 1971, and an Ed. D. from the University of Cincinnati in 1974.

From 1973 to 1975, Wyant was national field director for the Blinded Veterans Association. From 1975 to 1976, he was staff coordinator of the Committee on Disabled Veterans of the President's Committee on Employment of the Handicapped, and from 1976 to 1977, he was chief of economic concerns and disabled veterans.

Since 1977 Wyant has been Special Assistant to Administrator of Veterans Affairs Max Cleland.

Wyant is a consultant to the American Foundation for the Blind and the President's Committee on Employment of the Handicapped.

National Advisory Council on Women's Educational Programs

Nomination of Three Members. February 26, 1979

The President today announced three persons whom he will nominate as members of the National Advisory Council on

Women's Educational Programs for terms expiring May 8, 1981. They are:

SISTER M. ISOLINA FERRE, of Ponce, Puerto Rico, executive director of the Dispensario San Antonio, Inc., a program providing health care and counseling to women and children;

ANNA DOYLE LEVESQUE, of Portsmouth, R.I., a classroom teacher in Barrington, R.I., active in local and national teachers organizations;

SUSAN MARGARET VANCE, of Chicago, an attorney specializing in labor law, civil rights law, and family law, a consultant on compliance with equal employment opportunity laws, and former chairperson of the Illinois Fair Employment Practices Commission.

Federal Civil Justice System

Remarks to Reporters on Proposed Legislation. February 27, 1979

THE PRESIDENT. First of all, I want to express my thanks to the Attorney General, to Assistant Dan Meador,[1] and to the chairmen and members of the House and Senate Judiciary Committees for making this meeting and announcement possible.

Today, I'm sending a message to the Congress setting out the reforms proposed for the Federal civil justice system.

There's a general, worldwide recognition that the judicial system of the United States is admirable and worthy of emulation and has great strength, integrity, and competence. But there has been long recognition of problems that do exist. Sometimes, litigation is unnecessary and is required to take place in our courts; sometimes, necessary litigation is unnecessarily delayed and, when it does take place, is extremely costly.

Working with Chairman Rodino and Chairman Kennedy and the members of

---

[1] Assistant Attorney General, Office for Improvements in the Administration of Justice.

their committees, we have now developed a proposal, under the Attorney General, that will, I think, help to remove these obstacles from the judicial system in civil cases. This is not just a problem for judges and lawyers or Congress Members and Attorneys General and Presidents. It's a problem for all Americans and particularly those who are not wealthy and who have to deal with a court which is quite often a mystery to them and where delays are so costly that justice cannot be realized.

We will include in this recommendation a court-supervised arbitration as one of the major proposals, whereby without litigation, court-appointed arbitrators can resolve civil differences.

Secondly, there will be expanded the jurisdictional capability of Federal magistrates.

Third, there will be an opportunity now for removal from the Federal court system of strictly State cases when the litigants happen to come from two different States.

Fourth is, the Supreme Court will be given increased authority over its own docket. And there will be both resources and money made available for the development of procedures to resolve minor disputes.

In addition to these five points which will be proposed to the Congress, I've also sent the Federal Courts Improvement Act of 1979 to the Congress, which will combine the Court of Claims and the Court of Customs and Patents Appeals into the U.S. Court of Appeals. This will have a major beneficial effect when adopted, and I'm sure that with the leadership of those Members of the Congress assembled around me this morning that the Congress will take rapid action and let these benefits be realized by the American people.

I would now like to call upon the noted chairman of the House Judiciary Committee to make some comments, if he will. Chairman Rodino.

REPRESENTATIVE RODINO. Thank you very much, Mr. President.

Mr. President and colleagues, first of all, I'd like to applaud you, Mr. President, for taking this step. I believe that we, as Members of the Congress entrusted with a special responsibility in the area of dispensing justice, recognize the need for our improvement in the machinery of justice so that the quality of justice that is dispensed is such that we can be proud. And I believe that central to our responsibility in the House Judiciary Committee is our concern for how the citizens of this country view the system of justice. And I think very frankly, there has been some question.

And I believe that these proposals that have been advanced by Judge Bell and Dan Meador, which have been worked over for a period of time by the chairman of the Subcommittee on Courts and Civil Liberties and the Administration of Justice, Mr. Kastenmeier, along with Mr. Railsback and the ranking minority member of our Judiciary Committee, Mr. Mc-Clory—I think all of this indicates the great concern we have and the trust that we feel that we have, especially as members of the Judiciary Committee, in assuring that the system of justice is one that reflects the highest ideals of this country.

I believe that most important is whether or not we, as a society, can dispense justice in a manner to show that we are a just society and how just is our system of justice and whether or not the Federal court machinery, which is there as the administrator of the system, whether or not that Federal court machinery does treat the individual, with his certain basic belief in that this system is one that protects funda-mental liberties and rights, whether or not that Federal court machinery does reflect this. And I believe that this inures to the respect of our Nation when we do this.

I believe that all of these proposals, Mr. President, go generally toward these objectives and the strengthening of our system of justice. And I pledge you, as the chairman of that committee who takes a great deal of pride in what we have done and, along with Senator Kennedy as chairman of the Senate committee, that we will work toward that end and realize these objectives.

Thank you very much, Mr. President.

THE PRESIDENT. Well, with that pledge from the great committee chairman, I'm sure that the House will favorably consider these proposals without delay. And I'm very grateful to hear that.

And now, Chairman Kennedy.

SENATOR KENNEDY. We have a similar pledge, Mr. President.

THE PRESIDENT. Very good.

SENATOR KENNEDY. I, too, want to commend President Carter for this very extraordinary effort in trying to make our system of justice both more available and more efficient. I think it's completely consistent with the President's strong desire for efficiency in government and as well as for the protection of human rights, the millions of Americans who do not participate in our judicial system.

Mr. President, it's been some 50 years since the time that Charles Evans Hughes made a recommendation to President Roosevelt that we have had the kind of comprehensive recommendation that we have in this particular package which you and General Bell and, most singularly, Senator DeConcini and Howard Metzenbaum have worked out so effectively for the American people.

And I just want to join in commending you, to indicate we have already had 2 days of hearings already in this session on these general subject matters, and we would hope to handle this legislation as a very high priority in our Senate Judiciary Committee.

THE PRESIDENT. How would you assess the chances of passage?

SENATOR KENNEDY. I think they're good. [*Laughter*]

THE PRESIDENT. Very fine.

Before I introduce the Attorney General to answer your questions, I would like particularly to commend Dan Meador, who has been instrumental in the evolution of these proposals, which are historic in nature and very far-reaching and beneficial to all the American people.

I might say that we have stayed in close contact with the Supreme Court Justices and other advisers. This morning, the Attorney General talked to the Chief Justice. He fully supports these proposals. And I think they will be noted in every magistrate's court, district court, circuit court, all the way up to the court of appeals and to the Supreme Court of our country as a major step forward in the proper administration of justice. But I particularly want to thank Dan Meador.

And now I'd like to turn over the meeting to the Attorney General, who will add some further remarks and answer your specific questions.

Mr. Attorney General.

NOTE: The President spoke at 12:16 p.m. to reporters assembled in the Briefing Room at the White House.

Federal Civil Justice System

Message to the Congress on Proposed Legislation. February 27, 1979

To the Congress of the United States:

Today I am announcing my program to reform the Federal civil justice system.

My proposals are intended to increase the efficiency, cut the cost, and maintain the integrity of our Federal courts. I hope that the same spirit of cooperation which led to the 95th Congress' passage of historic civil service reform legislation, which had similar goals for the Executive Branch, will mark Congressional-Administration efforts in reforming the Judicial Branch.

The American system of justice—and the part our Federal courts play in it—has long been the envy of people throughout the world. An impartial and talented judiciary protects the rights of all Americans, ensuring due process guarantees and fair adjudication of disputes. But the courts cannot perform their traditional and essential function if they are required to operate with inadequate resources, saddled with outmoded procedures, and burdened with more business than they can fairly dispose of within a reasonable time. Nor can our citizens avail themselves of their "day in court" if, as is too often true in these days of rising litigation expenses, the price of participation in litigation is beyond their means.

Delay and expense play a part in our civil justice system. We have long recognized that justice delayed is justice denied. For many injured parties, having to wait a year or two to obtain legal relief in the courts is extremely harmful. The benefits of a legal victory are sometimes outweighed by the costs of achieving it. As litigation expenses and the size of court dockets increase, this seems to be happening with increasing frequency. Legal redress should not consume years of time and thousands of dollars.

These problems are not merely the special concern of a particular economic class or racial group, nor are they limited to certain geographic regions; they affect all segments of American society, in all areas of the country.

I am committed to improving access to justice by ensuring that every person involved in a legal controversy has a readily available forum in which that controversy can be resolved speedily, fairly, and at reasonable cost. To achieve this goal, we must do two things. First, we must develop new means for handling disputes that do not necessarily require full court resolution. Second, we must provide the courts with sufficient resources and improved procedures so that they can function fairly and effectively in those cases that must be brought before them.

I know that the Congress shares my concerns and is equally committed to taking effective remedial action. Last year the Congress made an excellent beginning when it created 152 new Federal judgeships and carefully reviewed a number of other legislative proposals designed to improve the administration of justice. But unless we improve the system of justice itself, we may find that the additional judges have been swallowed up by outmoded procedures and by an ever-rising volume of cases. We must take prompt and effective steps to eliminate the remaining obstacles to efficiency in the justice system, and to increase access to Federal courts by those with Federal claims.

Five of the specific measures by which we hope to accomplish these ends have previously been proposed, in whole or part, by my Administration, in the 95th Congress, dealing with arbitration, United States magistrates, the diversity of citizenship jurisdiction of the Federal courts, the Supreme Court's obligatory jurisdiction, and minor dispute resolution. Both before and during the last legislative session, each of these proposals received a great deal of careful Congressional thought and attention. They are introduced again, some

with modifications discussed in the last Congress. Each is now ripe for favorable action.

The arbitration proposal would provide an innovative means for resolving speedily, fairly, and at reduced cost certain types of civil cases in which the main dispute is over the amount of money that one person owes to another. This legislation is modeled on court-annexed arbitration plans that have proved successful in several States, including Ohio, Pennsylvania, and New York. It would allow Federal district courts to adopt a procedure requiring that tort and contract cases involving less than $100,000 be submitted to arbitration. This approach has been tested since early last year in three Federal courts and the experiences so far have been quite promising. Both litigants and the courts are benefiting from the procedure. Cases going to arbitration are being resolved faster than they otherwise could be and at significantly less expense to the parties. It is time that these benefits were extended to litigants in all Federal trial courts.

The second major element of our comprehensive civil justice program is a bill to enlarge the civil and criminal jurisdiction of Federal magistrates. These judicial officers, who are appointed by the district courts, constitute a potential resource of great value. If magistrates were given broader authority to decide civil cases and to handle less serious criminal matters, as we have proposed, the capacity of the Federal courts would be substantially increased. The result, especially in districts which currently have large case backlogs, would be speedier and less costly dispositions for the litigants.

The third measure that we regard as essential to improving the civil justice system would curtail the exercise of diversity of citizenship jurisdiction in the

Federal courts. Too many cases now jamming the dockets in Federal courts involve solely issues of State law that would be more properly and more efficiently disposed of in State courts. The historical basis for permitting these claims to be heard in Federal court—presumed prejudice towards citizens of one State in the courts of another—no longer appears valid. Moving these State law cases to the State courts where they belong would not create an undue burden on any State, but would enable the Federal courts to concentrate on serving the needs of those whose disputes involve questions of Federal law. Under my proposal, diversity jurisdiction would be abolished totally and cases could be brought in Federal court only where Federal law is involved.

The next component of our judicial reform package is a bill that would permit the Supreme Court to exercise greater control over its own docket. By eliminating the Supreme Court's mandatory jurisdiction, except for appeals in three-judge cases, this proposal would do away with the artificial and out-dated distinction between discretionary review and review of right. The change would enable the Court to focus its limited resources on the cases and issues truly deserving of its attention. This, in turn, would permit speedier clarification of the law, to the benefit not only of litigants in the lower courts but also persons wishing to avoid legal controversies.

The last of the proposals carried over from the previous Congress is a bill to improve the means available to the people of the United States for resolving everyday disputes, such as complaints by neighbors, customers, tenants, and family members. Everyday problems, small or large, if left unsettled, can fester and grow. They can lead to breakdowns in otherwise harmonious neighborhood relationships. They can even lead to crime. This legislation, entitled the Dispute Resolution Act, would provide Federal assistance to the States to improve the institutions that deal with these programs. The programs established by this bill would promote improvements in small claims courts and more widespread use of Neighborhood Justice Centers, a new concept that the Department of Justice is presently testing in Los Angeles, Kansas City, and Atlanta. This legislation would enable the Federal and State governments to work in partnership to improve the delivery of justice to all the people of the United States. No additional funding is being sought; existing funds in the Law Enforcement Assistance Administration will be used to finance these programs.

Passage of these five bills would be a major step in eliminating excessive delays, red tape, and exorbitant costs within the civil justice system. These bills have been discussed in the 95th Congress, and I hope that after further careful examination these bills will be enacted during the 96th Congress. These measures are necessary if we are to derive maximum benefit from the newly authorized judgeships. We will work for their enactment.

In addition to these bills, the Attorney General will transmit to Congress additional proposals to improve the courts which have been developed in consultation with Congressional leaders in this area. These new measures would solve a variety of problems relating to administration of the Federal judiciary, as well as practice and procedure in the courts in the following ways:

—Create a new intermediate Federal appellate court on the same tier as the existing courts of appeals. The new court, which would be known as the "United States Court of Appeals for the Federal Circuit", would be formed by merging the

Court of Claims and the Court of Customs and Patent Appeals into a single appellate tribunal with expanded, nationwide jurisdiction for appeals in patent and trademark cases as well as other matters. This new forum would induce economies from the combination of the two existing courts. Most import, however, it would expand the Federal judicial system's capacity for definitive adjudication of national law and thereby contribute to the uniformity and predictability of legal doctrine in these areas, which have long been marked by inconsistent appellate decisions, encourage industrial innovation, and in the long run reduce patent and trademark litigation. I further note that a similar need exists for uniformity and predictability of the law in the tax area, where conflicting appellate decisions encourage litigation and uncertainty. The Justice and Treasury Departments will work with Congress to develop an appropriate solution.

—Permit more effective means of rulemaking and administration within the Federal judiciary through the implementation of two proposals. One proposal requires each court of appeals to appoint an advisory committee composed of persons outside the court to make recommendations on the rules of practice and operating procedure within that court. These committees should do much to assist the courts in formulating sounder rules. The other proposal would restructure the membership of the circuit judicial councils, the governing administrative bodies in the eleven judicial circuits. The councils will be made smaller and more efficient and will include district judges in their membersip for the first time. If enacted, these proposals will help assure that the Federal courts conduct their business so as to serve the public more effectively.

—Allowing equitable interest on claims and judgments. There is a serious backlog in civil litigation. Sometimes years pass between the time of an injury and the granting of a judgment. More years may pass while that judgment is appealed. Current Federal law is ambiguous about whether and under what circumstances interest may be paid for the period prior to judgment, and permits unrealistically low as well as conflicting rates of interest while the decision is under appeal. Yet such interest may be essential in order to truly compensate the plaintiff or to avoid the unjust enrichment of the defendant. For instance, a plaintiff who is unlawfully deprived of the use of $20,000 in 1976 and who does not receive a judgment until 1979, could have obtained $4,500 in those three years by investing the money at 7% compounded interest. If a judgment on appeal is entered at a rate well below the prime interest rate, the losing party may well profit from the appeal. The bill proposes that where a defendant knew of his potential liability, interest be awarded for the pre-judgment period where necessary to compensate the plaintiff for his losses or to avoid the unjust enrichment of the defendant. Post-judgment interest rates would no longer be left to inconsistent State laws, but along with the new pre-judgment interest standard, would be based on a nationally uniform rate. Litigants would be encouraged to settle cases, and not drag them out needlessly causing additional expense.

—Other measures relating to the sound administration of the Federal judiciary are proposals providing more reasonable terms for chief judges, enhanced integrity for appellate panels, and easier transfer for any case inadvertently started in the wrong Federal court to the proper court without loss of litigants' rights and with savings of time and money.

345

Finally, I urge the Congress to give serious consideration to improving procedures for litigating class actions, especially for those cases where the alleged economic injury is widespread and large in the aggregate, yet small in its impact on each individual. The Justice Department will continue to have my support in working with Congress to devise class action procedures which will develop methods for courts to handle these complex cases more effectively and at less cost to the taxpayers and the parties involved.

The members of the Judiciary Committees of both houses have shown outstanding leadership in developing answers to the problems facing the justice system. It is now time for Congress as a whole to take action so that the American people will benefit from a more effective civil justice system.

JIMMY CARTER

The White House,
   February 27, 1979.

THE PRESIDENT'S NEWS CONFERENCE OF FEBRUARY 27, 1979

EGYPTIAN-ISRAELI PEACE NEGOTIATIONS

THE PRESIDENT. In my 2 years as President, I've spent more time and invested more of my own personal effort in the search for peace in the Middle East than on any other international problem. That investment of time and effort was and is appropriate because of the great importance of peace in that region to our own country and the vital importance of a peace agreement between Israel and Egypt to those two countries.

Some progress was made in the talks at Camp David last week, 4½ days of talks. I do not share the opinion that the proposals that we put forward were contrary to the Camp David agreements of last September or that they would make an Egyptian-Israeli peace treaty meaningless.

Based upon the developments of last week and the recommendations of all the parties involved, I had hoped to be able to convene without delay negotiations at a level which would permit the early conclusion of a peace treaty between Israel and Egypt, as a first step toward a wider settlement for the entire Middle East.

I regret that such direct negotiations are not possible at this time. I'm concerned about the impact of this development upon the prospects for peace. However, it was the belief of all those at Camp David—Secretary Vance and all the negotiators from Israel and Egypt—that the conclusion of an Egyptian-Israeli peace treaty is an urgent necessity. I share that view completely.

If we allow the prospects for peace that seemed so bright last September when we came back from Camp David to continue to dim and perhaps even to die, the future, at best, is unpredictable. If we allow that hope to vanish, then the judgment of history and of our own children will of necessity, and rightly, condemn us for an absence of concerted effort.

For that reason, I spoke personally this afternoon with Prime Minister Begin and with President Sadat. I've invited Prime Minister Begin to join me as soon as possible for a frank discussion of all the issues involved. I'm hopeful that these talks will lead to an early resumption of direct negotiations.

Prime Minister Begin has accepted my invitation. He will be arriving here Thursday evening for discussions with me.

I will then consider asking either Prime Minister Khalil or President Sadat to join in further discussions. I recognize that the public interest in this matter is intense. However, I have made it clear in the past that any premature public discussions of these very sensitive issues serve no useful purpose. For that reason, I will have no further comments to make on the Mideast peace negotiations this afternoon, but I will be happy to answer any further questions on other matters of interest to the American public.

QUESTIONS

EGYPTIAN-ISRAELI PEACE NEGOTIATIONS

Q. Well, Mr. President, I really think you should answer a couple of questions. One, are you saying that Camp David is back on track or you are trying to get it on? And also, were you led to believe by your own advisers or by the Israeli officials that Begin would come, or did you labor under some false assumption on your part?

THE PRESIDENT. I won't have any other questions to answer on that subject. I think I've covered it adequately. And Prime Minister Begin is making a simultaneous announcement in Israel, and I don't think it would be constructive for me to answer any questions further.

INFLATION AND ENERGY PRICES

Q. Mr. President, does the escalating price of oil and gasoline, which is continuing—does that cause you to have any second thoughts now about your prediction of inflation for the year?

THE PRESIDENT. Obviously, the unpredictable shortage of oil on the international market, caused by the Iranian disruption of supply and other factors, have caused the price of energy

to go up faster than we had anticipated. This adds inflationary pressures. The situation with supplies and prices is serious; it's not critical.

I have made proposals to the Congress for standby authority to take action, when necessary in the future, on a mandatory basis. Early next month we will present to the Congress, also for their approval, matters that I can take—action that I can take to deal with the temporary Iranian disruption.

As you know, we had in 1973 about a 2½ million barrel-a-day shortage brought about by the embargo. We now have a shortage of about 2 million barrels per day. But I think it's accurate to say that our own country and the international consuming nations, including us, are much better organized to take care of these changes that have been taking place. So, inflationary pressures do exceed what we had anticipated. I think we are much better prepared to deal with them.

CONDUCT OF FOREIGN POLICY

Q. Mr. President, some of your critics are saying that you are exhibiting weakness and impotency in your conduct of foreign affairs, that is, in your reaction to crises around the world. And although you argue that your policy is one of prudent restraint, is there not something to the idea that the perception itself adds to the problem of this country's interests? And, if so, is there anything you can do about it?

THE PRESIDENT. Obviously, perceptions have some importance in political terms and also in diplomatic terms. There is no doubt in my mind that the United States is adequately protecting its own interests, that we are adequately protecting the interests of our allies and friends as commitments bind us to do. We've had no complaints about them in this respect. And I think that an exercise of prudence in trying to contain our regional disputes and combat among other nations is in the best interest of our own country.

We are a strong nation, the strongest on Earth—militarily, politically, economically. I'm committed to preserving that strength of our Nation, even enhancing it. And I think it would be completely improper for us, for instance, to inject ourselves in any active way into the combat that's presently taking place among Communist Asian nations, or to try to intrude in a completely unwarranted fashion into the internal affairs, political affairs, of other nations. And I have no intention of making these foolish decisions and taking foolish action to the detriment of our Nation's interest, just to assuage some who criticize me because we have not become actively involved in these kinds of circumstances.

SECRETARY BLUMENTHAL'S TRIP TO CHINA

Q. Mr. President, given all of that, when the United States was displeased with the action that the Soviets had taken in the Shcharanskiy case, we held up the sale of some oil-drilling equipment to the Soviets. Given the fact that we have condemned the Chinese attack into Vietnam, why is it that Treasury Secretary Blumenthal is now in China negotiating new trade agreements with the Chinese?

THE PRESIDENT. Well, that's a completely different circumstance. We've not had any bilateral disharmony between ourselves and the Chinese. We are changing our interest offices into embassies on the 1st of March, and I need a major representative of our country to be there when that change is made. Our new Ambassador, Leonard Woodcock, has just recently been approved by the Senate yes-

terday and will not be able to arrive on time.

We do not agree with many of the actions that the Soviets take in dealing with other countries. We've not let that disrupt our bilateral relationships with the Soviets. Our SALT talks, for instance, have never been interrupted nor delayed. And we have expressed our very firm disapproval to the Chinese about their crossing the Vietnamese border, and we have expressed our strong disapproval to the Soviets and to the Vietnamese for the Vietnamese crossing of the Cambodian border.

But for us to terminate bilateral relationships because a major country, the Soviets or the Chinese, do something contrary to our desires would certainly be counterproductive. And I think the trip to China to establish relationships with the Chinese for the future by Secretary Blumenthal is proper and was well-advised.

BILLY CARTER

Q. Mr. President, your brother, Billy, has made some remarks concerning Jews, and I wonder, sir, if you deplore or condemn those remarks. I also have a followup.

THE PRESIDENT. I might say, first of all, I don't have any control over what my brother says or what he does, and he has no control over what I say or do.

I know Billy and have known him since he was born, and I know for a fact that he is not anti-Semitic and has never made a serious, critical remark against Jews or other people in our country. To the extent that any of his remarks might be interpreted as such, I certainly do not agree and do not associate myself with them.

Billy is my brother. He's seriously ill at this point. I love him. I have no intention of alleging to him any condemnation that I don't think is warranted, and I would say that I disassociate myself and my brother, Billy, from any allegations of remarks that might be anti-Semitic in nature.

ENERGY CONSERVATION

Q. Mr. President, you have outlined now the authority you'd like Congress to give you for mandatory conservation of fuel, but could you outline for us which steps you would take first and just how serious you regard the situation right now?

THE PRESIDENT. Well, the Congress has 60 days during which time they can decide whether or not to approve the standby authority that I have requested. What might be done first would remain to be seen. We don't have any present intentions of implementing any of those measures. We are asking for a complete rationing system on gasoline as a standby measure—which I think is a substantial improvement over the ones previously proposed—the right to prohibit the sale of gasoline on weekends, the right to control public advertising, and so forth. But I can't say at this point, not knowing the degree of shortage in the future of energy, and particularly gasoline, what I would do. But I think those standby rights that I could exercise if necessary are important, and I'll just have to make a judgment when the time comes.

PUBLIC BROADCASTING

Q. Mr. President, you were generally complimentary in your reaction to the Carnegie II report, which was released on public broadcasting recently. Specifically, I'd like to know, do you support the concept of a spectrum fee, of asking broadcasters to pay for their fair share of the use of the public's airwaves?

THE PRESIDENT. I don't know. I've not studied the issue well enough to answer the question.

AIR AND WATER POLLUTION STANDARDS

Q. Mr. President, Mr. Schultze was testifying before Congress today about proposals to change pending regulations. I'm wondering, have you decided to delay or postpone major air and water pollution regulations?

THE PRESIDENT. The answer is no. We have an excellent record on the enforcement of the air and water pollution standards and, also, on the strengthening of those standards. It's important, however, that the regulations be administered in the most effective way and that economic considerations be taken into account when necessary. The regulators, Doug Costle and others, know that they have authority to consider that item and then to make their judgments accordingly.

I have not interfered in that process. I have a statutory responsibility and right to do so, but I think it would be a very rare occasion whenever I would want to do so. But we are certainly not going to abrogate nor to cancel the enforcement of the air and water pollution standards.

THE MIDDLE EAST

Q. Mr. President, recently Secretary Brown was in the Middle East and met with the leaders of those countries, particularly Saudi Arabia. And you have expressed the need and the desire for the United States to strengthen the defensive perimeter of that part of the world to safeguard the flow of oil. There have been public reports that the Saudi Arabian Government has refused an offer by the United States for the stationing of U.S. troops. I can't vouch for that report, but could you tell us what your plans are for

349

that area and what we would be willing to do to safeguard the world's oil supply?

THE PRESIDENT. We have no desire to open military bases in that area or to station American troops in Saudi Arabia. And this proposal has not been made. That part of the report was erroneous. However, we do want to strengthen the combined responsibility and capability of our friends and allies who seek moderation and peace and stability to preserve the integrity of that region. Secretary Brown visited Saudi Arabia, Jordan, Egypt, and Israel for this purpose, and his trip was very successful.

It's important also for those nations and for others in that region to know that we have a real interest, a real national interest in the stability and peace of that region and, particularly, for the supply of oil, the routes through which the oil is delivered to ourselves and to our allies and friends throughout the world.

But any sort of action that we take would be contributory to peace, would not encroach on the prerogatives of individual nations. And we do not intend to become involved in the internal affairs of another country. We have no plans to establish military bases in that region.

PROPOSED CONSTITUTIONAL CONVENTION

Q. Mr. President, is Governor Brown talking sense or is he talking nonsense when he advocates his constitutional amendment to require a balanced Federal budget?

THE PRESIDENT. I think the convening of a constitutional convention to pass such an amendment would be very ill-advised, contrary to the best interests of our country. It would be a radical departure from the historic procedures that we have always used to amend our Constitution and might result in unlimited amendments which would change the basic thrust, the philosophy, and the structure of our Government itself. So, I would oppose very strongly any call of a constitutional amendment [convention] for that purpose.

I might say that there are other ways to do this. I have been a strong advocate for a balanced budget, and I'm doing all I can this year and will do it in subsequent years to reach a balanced budget. In my opinion, that's a subject that ought to be addressed through this kind of action and not through a very restrictive constitutional amendment.

Another thing that I would like to point out is that there would be a necessity for the careful drafting in such a constitutional amendment for exceptions. We would, obviously, have to deal with very serious economic circumstances if they did prevail, extremely high unemployment rate, or an extremely deep depression. In addition to that, we would have to meet the needs for national security if our Nation was threatened.

So, I consider the balancing of the budget to be best addressed by those of us who are working for it, within statutory limits that presently exist. If a constitutional amendment should take place, the constitutional convention process would be the worst imaginable route to that goal.

GOVERNOR JERRY BROWN

Q. If I may follow, do you think that Governor Brown would be a worthy adversary for you next year?

THE PRESIDENT. If I were looking for an adversary—[laughter]—then I would say that he or many others would be worthy.

OIL PRICES

Q. Mr. President, half a dozen OPEC countries have announced, or are threatening to do so, some kind of oil price hike in the last couple of weeks. It gives the impression that the United States is at their mercy and that we are helpless. Are we?

THE PRESIDENT. We have no control over prices that other nations establish for their products, including oil. This is a subject that I have addressed as forcefully as possible, since April of 1977, when we presented to the Congress a comprehensive energy proposal. Our best approach is to reduce exorbitant waste of oil and other energy products that presently exists in our country, to increase the production of oil and gas and other energy products within our Nation, and to use our legitimate influence when it can be exerted to minimize any increase in prices. But we cannot control other nations in this respect.

I might say that we are much better able now, as a world consuming community, to deal with these increases than we were back in 1973 and '4, when the price was quadrupled overnight without any warning, and before the consuming nations were working in harmony to provide reserves on hand, to increase exploration and production, which has since then occurred in the North Sea, in Mexico, obviously, in Alaska, and other places.

But we have no control over it. We deplore it. We would like for them to hold down the prices as much as possible. Our best response is to use energy in our own Nation efficiently, to cut out waste, and to increase our own production.

ENERGY CONSERVATION

Q. Mr. President, in view of what you've just said about the energy situation, why are you uncertain about whether you will impose the new conservation measures as soon as Congress gives you the authorization? It would seem that the country might be waiting for some sort of signal that things are really serious and that consumers must cut back.

THE PRESIDENT. If the Iranian production is not restored, then we would face a half-million-barrel-a-day shortage, more or less, possibly increasing later on to 700,-000 barrels a day. By the first of next month, in addition to the request to Congress that I've just put forward, we will have measures outlined for taking this action when it is necessary. As a matter of fact, we don't want to have stringent restraints placed on our economy that might cause very severe disruptions, high unemployment, and very adverse reactions not only in our country but throughout the world.

But with the standby authority, then I would have the responsibility, as authorized by Congress, to take action based upon the severity of the need.

We have, I think, a matter of judgment to be made in that respect. But to commit myself ahead of time to greatly constrain the American economy when it's not necessary would not be in the best interest of our country.

IRAN

Q. Mr. President, what is our Government doing, if anything, to try and influence the new Iranian Government to increase production, keep prices down, and, generally, how would you describe the relationship between our Government and the Khomeini government?

THE PRESIDENT. The Khomeini government has made it clear ever since it came into power, through our direct negotiations with Prime Minister Bazargan and our Ambassador and through their emissaries, who have even today talked to Secretary Vance, that they desire a close-working and friendly relationships with the United States.

They have also announced that oil production in Iran will be increased and that, very shortly, exports will be recommenced. And my own assessment is that they have strong intentions to carry out both these goals and that they are capable of doing so.

Q. Mr. President, there is, or there appears to be starting a public debate on the question, "Who lost Iran?" I noticed that former Secretary Kissinger was suggesting that your administration should bear some responsibility; former Under Secretary of State George Ball suggested that the Nixon-Kissinger administration did much to destabilize Iran with their billions in sophisticated military hardware. My question was, I suppose, do you agree with Ball? Who lost Iran, or was Iran ours to lose in the first place?

THE PRESIDENT. Well, it's obvious that Iran was not ours to lose in the first place. We don't own Iran, and we have never had any intention nor ability to control the internal affairs of Iran. For more than 2,000 years, the people in the Iran area, the Persians and others, have established their own government. They've had ups and downs, as have we. I think it's obvious that the present government in Iran, as I just answered, would like to have good relationships with us. I don't know of anything we could have done to prevent the very complicated social and religious and political interrelationships from

occurring in Iran in the change of government. And we'll just have to make the best of the change.

But, as I say, we cannot freeze the status quo in a country when it's very friendly to us. When the change is made by the people who live there, we do the best we can to protect American interests by forming new alliances, new friendships, new interrelationships, new trade relationships, new security relationships, perhaps, in the future, with the new government, and that's the best we can do.

But to try to lay blame on someone in the United States for a new government having been established in Iran, I think, is just a waste of time and avoids a basic issue that this was a decision to be made and which was made by the Iranian people themselves.

ISRAELI ACCESS TO OIL

Q. Mr. President, in view of the fact that we have some arrangement to support Israel in the event that they have oil shortages, do you view Iran's lack of desire to supply oil to Israel as creating problems for us in terms of our support for Israel in securing secondary sources?

THE PRESIDENT. When the supply of Iranian oil to Israel was interrupted, I immediately notified Prime Minister Begin and the Israeli Government that we would honor our commitment to them. So far, the Israelis have been able to acquire oil from other sources in the Sinai, and also on the world markets from different countries.

We will honor that commitment. I think that the total Israeli oil consumption is only about 1 percent of the consumption in the United States. So, even if Israel should have to depend upon us for a substantial portion of their oil, we would supply that oil from our country or from sources in other nations without disruption of the American economy.

PRESIDENT'S WEEKEND SCHEDULE

Q. Mr. President, in view of the decision for Prime Minister Begin to come here Thursday evening, do you still intend to go to Los Angeles on the weekend? [*Laughter*]

THE PRESIDENT. I don't think it will be possible for me to go to Los Angeles if Prime Minister Begin comes, as presently planned, and if he and I are off, for instance, at Camp David negotiating.

FARMERS' DEMONSTRATION

Q. Mr. President, a number of the Nation's farmers have been here for the past few weeks now——

THE PRESIDENT. Yes. I've heard that. [*Laughter*]

Q. —— protesting prices. And apparently they don't seem to feel that they're getting much sympathy from the administration. The demonstrations have continued tying up traffic. The other day, a goat was tossed over the White House fence and some farm equipment, and damage has been done to the Mall. How do you feel about the farmers' presence here, and do you agree with the suggestion that they perhaps should go home now?

THE PRESIDENT. You know, people have to stand in line to demonstrate in front of the White House. There are several demonstrations every day. And this is part of a free society, that this is permitted.

I think the farmers have a legitimate right to demonstrate their views or even their displeasure against the Congress action or against the action of this administration, as long as they do it within the

bounds of the law. And I think that in some instances, the farmers' demonstrations have caused unwarranted hardship or interference in the right of working people here in Washington to go to and from their homes. When this does occur, in my opinion, the farmers' demonstrations are counterproductive.

We have tried to provide the farmers with a forum here and to honor their desires as much as possible. I deplore, and many farmers throughout the country deplore, the damage that has been done to Washington—the chopping down of trees for firewood, the breaking of the bottom of the Reflecting Pool, the turning over of some of the shelters for people using rapid transit systems. Those things are deplorable. And I'm sure that almost all of the farmers who are actually here with their tractors did not want to see those things happen, either.

Secretary Bergland has made a policy of meeting not only with the farmers from a particular community or State but also with the congressional delegation who represented those particular farmers. And I think there's been a good exchange of ideas. I think we understand the farmers' desires and their complaints. There is no possibility, in my opinion, that the Congress would increase on a flat basis the parity support prices to 90 percent, which is a basic demand of the farmers here.

But they are welcome to stay as long as they demonstrate peacefully and legally. And I honor that right and indeed would cherish it.

FRANK CORMIER [Associated Press]. Thank you, Mr. President.

THE PRESIDENT. Thank you.

NOTE: President Carter's forty-fifth news conference began at 4 p.m. in Room 450 of the Old Executive Office Building. It was broadcast live on radio and television.

National Governors' Association

Toasts at a White House Dinner Honoring Governors Attending the Association's Winter Session. February 27, 1979

THE PRESIDENT. First of all, let me say that it's a great delight for Rosalynn and me to have you here in the White House. A few weeks ago, Rosalynn helped to pot these lilies of the valley, and they're for you to take home with you as a memento of tonight. When you leave through the Diplomatic Room, they'll be there, so each couple can pick one up and take it with you.

I was sitting here computing the time since I left the Governor's office in Georgia. It's exactly 49 years—[laughter]—49 months. I guess I spent 2 years campaigning and 47 years as President. [Laughter] But I don't think I've ever spent a more exciting and challenging and delightful 4 years than I did as Governor of Georgia.

And as the different Governors went by in the receiving line and I shook hands with you, I had a recurring sense that was hard for me at first to describe in one word. But I finally realized it was jealousy. [Laughter] Cecil Andrus had the same feeling. [Laughter]

There is a deep emotional sense that I have, as President, when I have the Governors of our Nation come to visit me here. Thinking back on the history of this house, it's almost overwhelming. Every President who served our Nation has lived in this house, except George Washington. And to see the furnishings in the rooms, to recall some of the history of this place is a sobering experience, but also a very challenging and inspirational experience. To see the room where Lincoln signed the Emancipation Proclamation, wrote the Gettysburg Address; to see a little, small writing desk, about this large,

that Thomas Jefferson made with his own hands, designed and carried around on the back of his horse when he was President, on the back of a buggy; to see the desk that belonged to Daniel Webster; and to see the sculpture here—it's really overwhelming.

But I think the basic strength of our country, that tides us over in times of trial and stress and tribulation and challenge, is our system of federalism. As you know, the local governments and the Federal Government only have the authority and the power that was delegated to those two governments by the States. And the depository of the remaining authority, power, initiative, opportunity for innovation, experiment, the consummation of ideals, the administration of laws that direct dealings with people remain in the hands of Governors and the governments of the States.

This is reassuring to me as President. We share a lot of responsibility, obviously, in the realm of domestic affairs—to control inflation, to decide how to amend the Constitution—[laughter]—to deal with the problems of energy, transportation, air pollution, water pollution, the aged, education—these kinds of things affect you and me both as equal partners. And if there is any inequality of it, the biggest responsibility is on your shoulders.

I think there's a new developing sense, however, among the Governors, partially initiated by me, of a sharing of a responsibility for foreign affairs as well. The new formation of a committee to enhance international trade may be one of the most historic developments in the history of the National Governors' Conference, now Association.

And I think it opens up not only an opportunity for us to learn about how to enhance job opportunities, to market American products, to extend hands of friendship and cooperation to foreign nations, but it also gives you an opportunity and a renewed responsibility to deal with foreign affairs as such.

Obviously, you can't negotiate for our Nation, you can't take the place of a President's constitutional responsibilities, but I thought tonight, in about 5 minutes, I would like to outline for you some of the foreign affairs considerations that affect me as a President. And I thought I'd go back to my early notes when I first was elected President. And the 10 goals that I set for myself then are still kind of guiding lights for me in these deliberations.

Obviously, this is an oversimplistic version, but I thought, following that, I would take about 10 minutes more time—and I'll time us so we won't go over—to answer a few questions that you might have on foreign policy. This has never been done before at a Governors conference, and I thought it might be a little bit different, since your own concepts and your own responsibilities and interests have been expanded in that direction.

The first thing that I wanted to do, of course, was to maintain the strength of our own Nation around the world, and particularly to align toward mutual concepts our European allies and Japan.

We've had a very good evolutionary process going on now, which is still continuing, and I think the basic Western democracies, including Japan in that stretched definition, is kind of core of the sense of democracy, commitment, freedom, idealism, and a beneficent influence that needs to be both strengthened and expanded.

We have a very good, personal friendship extant among those of us who are responsible for leadership in those countries, and I think that's one of the elements of our foreign policy that has, in the past, sometimes been overlooked.

The second thing, obviously, that is important for us is to deal with changing times. We can't control change. We don't want to prevent change. But we have to understand it and accommodate it and try to use it in an evolutionary way toward the goals and the ideals, the aspirations, the principles of our own country.

We also have to identify newly emerging leaders and try to make sure that our own relationships with them in key parts of the world are sound and strong and that there's a mutual benefit to be derived. Countries like Indonesia or Brazil or Venezuela, Nigeria, or India, obviously, are strong, vibrant nations, some of them very firmly committed to democracy. In the past, many of those have not been friends of ours at all, and we've tried to change that circumstance. And we've deliberately visited those countries—either I or the Secretary of State or Vice President Mondale or my wife, Rosalynn—to try to get firm relationships built with those newly emerging regional leaders.

Four or 5 years ago, for instance, when the Secretary of State wanted to visit Nigeria, he was not permitted to come into the country. Now Nigeria, which is the strongest, most vigorous, most populous, wealthiest black nation in Africa, is one of our soundest and most valued friends.

Another thing that we tried to do in this first few months is to strengthen our ties and our understanding with the developing nations of the world. There are people who have an average per capita income of only $90 or $95 or $100 a year. And the burgeoning sense of realization and aspirations on their part is and can be an overwhelming worldwide trend. Just in the last—in our generation, we've had a hundred new nations formed. And they go through a traumatic experience when they shake off colonialism or establish their own government.

Quite often they turn to the Soviet Union or some other ready suppliers of weapons in the revolutionary times, but eventually they turn to a more stable interrelationship and they become more nationalistic in spirit. But they still have enormous, almost indecipherable problems in the low quality of life of people. And they are reaching out to us for technology, for trade, and, quite often, we overlook them. We try to treat them as a homogeneous mass of people: We say "the people of South America," when the countries of South America are just as individualistic, perhaps even more so, obviously, than the countries, say, in Europe or in Asia. We've tried to treat those countries with respect, with decency, as equals, which they are, and as individuals.

I think this is a very important concept for us. In dealing with trade problems we quite often forget the fact that a small country has only one major export item. And the price of coffee or the price of tin or zinc or bauxite or sugar is life or death to them. And I have a responsibility, as do you, to learn about those nations and perhaps to visit them. You might be wanting to go to a small country in the Caribbean on vacation. It would really pay rich dividends for you to understand what their lifestyle is, what their needs are, what their yearnings are, what their frustrations are, what their political alignments are, what their challenges are. And just a small gesture of friendship is reciprocated in an overwhelming degree.

One of the major goals that I espoused when I was running for Governor [President] was eventually to have normal relations with the People's Republic of China and to deal fairly and simultaneously with the people of Taiwan. I think we've taken a major step in that direction, successfully. This is a quarter of the world's population. Coming from the South, being a Baptist, I grew up as a kid who used to give a nickel or a dime for missionaries to go to China. I've always had a warm feeling in my heart for the Chinese people. And I think they respond. I think the recent visit by Vice Premier Deng showed that there's an instant response when finally those barriers are broken and you can actually reach across and shake hands.

And we've been very careful in establishing this new relationship not to sever our good relationships with the people of Taiwan. I think we'll benefit in both those ways.

I would say the most important single responsibility on my shoulders is to have peace, an improved understanding, consultation, communication with the Soviet Union, because on the super powers' shoulders rests the responsibility for peace throughout the world.

We've spent 2 years now negotiating a SALT treaty. I spent an hour this afternoon with the Ambassador of the Soviet Union, talking about all the differences that we have between us, all the possibilities for improving our relations, and this preys very heavily on my shoulders. And I mentioned Sunday afternoon that I have never gotten a private letter from President Brezhnev that in the heart of his letter he didn't mention their intense desire to improve trade relationships with our country.

And I hope that over a period of years that all of you will take an opportunity to travel to China, to travel to the Soviet Union, and to help me engender peace, friendship with both those nations and, of course, with others as well.

Another thing, obviously, that we try to do is to stamp out disharmony, combat, confrontation in troubled areas of the world. In Namibia, Rhodesia, Cyprus, the Mideast, we have sometimes gratuitously injected ourselves into those disharmonies. And it's very difficult, because you quite often are castigated by both sides.

One of the most difficult and frustrating and discouraging experiences I've ever had in my life is dealing with the Mideast settlement between Israel and Egypt. Both peoples yearn so deeply for peace. We've come so close to the consummation of a peace agreement, and we still have some absolutely insignificant differences that are now creating apparently insurmountable obstacles. But we've been careful and tenacious and, I think, fair.

But both sides feel that we've not been fair. The Arab world thinks that we've been overly committed to the protection and the strengthening of Israel, and quite often the Israeli people feel that we've been at first evenhanded, since we were fair. They thought we ought to be biased toward Israel. But I think in the process we've not benefited politically, and we may fail. But that is a major challenge for us that we have not successfully resolved.

In southern Africa, our country had never been involved directly in Africa before; we were not a colonial power there, as you know. But we've tried to join forces with the Canadians, with the French, the British, the Germans, under auspices of the United Nations, to bring about the development of a new democratic nation in Namibia, formerly South West Africa, and to break that portion of southern Africa away from South African domination. And the South African Government has cooperated with the United Nations and with us and the other countries. And we're on the verge now of having free elections there and the establishment of a democratic government based on one-person-one-vote, majority rule,

which would be a very great step forward if it can be concluded.

Rhodesia—much more difficult. But there, Great Britain has legal ties to Rhodesia. We've worked in harmony with the British, and we hope to bring some peace, some resolution, some end of racism in that part of the world.

Just two other things I'd like to mention: We have strengthened NATO, and we've had a nationwide commitment to reducing armaments, not only with the SALT negotiations but also in other ways—the sale of conventional armaments, the promotion of the Treaty of Tlatelolco, which was evolved in Mexico before I became President, which absolutely bans any placement or transportation of or development of nuclear explosives in this Southern Hemisphere. And this is the kind of thing that we're trying to do. Test ban treaties are being negotiated, and I hope that this will be an effort that will be successful in the future.

And, of course, we've tried to raise the banner of human rights throughout the world. But we've been sometimes criticized for this, because the very concept of human rights, which seems to us kind of a hazy but admirable concept, in some countries is like a razor. It slashes through the obfuscation and the confusion to the very bone of people's sensitivities and yearnings and aspirations, and has caused governments to change. It's caused attitudes to change. It's created differences, sometimes, between us and our potential adversaries or our friends, but I feel that our Nation ought to stand firmly for the protection of the individual human being and basic concepts of human rights as was espoused and promulgated when our own Nation was founded.

This is kind of a conglomeration of concepts and thoughts and problems and opportunities that we face on a daily basis, and it's one of the things that makes being President both different from a Governor, in some respects, but also exceptionally challenging. And I really welcome the opportunity for you now to be an enhanced, much more important partner with me in pursuing these goals—and others that I don't have a chance to mention tonight—in months ahead.

I hope that as you plan trips on your own to promote trade or the sale of your own products overseas, that you won't hesitate to come to Washington to meet with Secretary Vance or myself or Dr. Brzezinski or Fritz Mondale or others that we would get to help you, working with Ambassador Carter, who's been designated to be your liaison, and prepare yourselves very thoroughly. And if you have questions, don't restrict them just to trade matters, but try to learn about the military interrelationships, political interrelationships, the human interrelationships, social interrelationships, religious interrelationships that might deal with the particular country you visit. I think, in that way, our country can be even stronger and more beneficially influential than it has been in the past. You'll certainly help to make my job easier, and that's the reason I invited you here tonight.

Before I give a very brief toast, I'll answer maybe two questions if anybody has them, and just on any of the foreign affairs matters that I described.

Yes, Jim?

GOVERNOR THOMPSON. Mr. President, on Sunday you talked about developing trade with the People's Republic of China, and I asked about the possibility of credit relationships. And you mentioned the possibility of most-favored-nation status as one of the ways by which the Government would extend credit.

THE PRESIDENT. Yes.

Q. It struck me afterwards, when I was thinking about it, that perhaps the extension of most-favored-nation status to China occurs—poses a political problem with regards to the Soviet Union——

THE PRESIDENT. Yes. You're very discerning.

GOVERNOR THOMPSON. ——their attitudes toward human rights. Am I making too much of the necessity for governmental credit relationships with China, or are you going to run into that problem? And, if so, how are you going to resolve it, given their current attitude towards human rights?

THE PRESIDENT. Well, I think the extension of credit is one thing that can be handled on a strictly private lending basis. We don't need to grant credits to China or to the Soviet Union directly, although that is done. But the most-favored-nations legislation would permit the reduction of trade barriers and the charging of tariffs. It means that whatever trade relationships we have with Great Britain, for instance, or Germany or France or Japan, we would also have to grant that same trade relationship with the Soviet Union or China.

The Jackson-Vanik amendment to the trade bill that was passed 2 or 3 years ago prevented our granting most-favored-nations treatment to a nation like the Soviet Union, for instance, or Romania or, perhaps, Hungary or others in the Eastern bloc if they had restrictions on the outmigration of citizens. This was designed primarily because of the restraints that the Soviet Union had on the outmigration of Jewish citizens who wanted to come here or to Israel or to some other place. In the last 6 months, the Soviet Union has permitted an outmigration of Jews in excess of 40,000 per year, which is right at the highest rate of outmigration, I think, in history, certainly in recent history.

So, I would guess that the Soviet Union is now approaching the point where they would comply with the most-favored-nations as interpreted by the Congress. And I would hope that we could have a removal of that restraint if the Soviets meet that standard, and increase our trade with the Soviet Union. There are legal restrictions on what we can sell to the Soviets. We cannot sell them anything under the law that would contribute directly to the enhancement of their military capability that might be used against us.

China is a different proposition altogether. They don't have the outmigration problem. As a matter of fact, when I mentioned the most-favored-nations restraints and the Jackson-Vanik amendment to Deng Xiaoping, he immediately said, "We'll qualify right now. If you want us to send you 10 million Chinese tomorrow"—*[laughter]*—"we'll be glad to do it." I said, "I'll reciprocate by sending you 10,000 news correspondents." He said, "No"—*[laughter]*—he said, "No, this might prevent normalization from going forward."

But I would hope, Jim, in the next few months, that we might find it possible to have most-favored-nations status granted both to China and to the Soviet Union. That's my hope, and that's my expectation. But the Congress, obviously, is involved in that decision.

Maybe one more question.

GOVERNOR BYRNE. Mr. President, in the wake of the upheaval in Iran there are renewed threats to "destroy Israel." Does the United States have a response to that, and is that response in any way dependent on the outcome of the continued Camp David discussions?

THE PRESIDENT. I think almost every responsible or significant element in Iran is strongly anti-Communist. The Shah's followers, those who challenged the Shah in the secular world, and the religious leaders all are intensely anti-Communist, although there is a small group, the Tudeh party there, who comprise maybe three or four thousand total—nobody knows exactly—who have relationships with the Soviets indirectly through East Germany.

Iran was supplying a large part of Israel's oil, and among the countries of that region, they were the only ones who had fairly advanced trade relationships with Israel. That has been terminated now. And they've severed relations with Israel, and the Israeli Ambassador has left, as you know.

Iran does not border on Israel, and I would guess that the Iranian Government, any time in the foreseeable future, would not find an opportunity to attack Israel directly.

This does create a change in attitude in the Mideast, and it cuts both ways. And I'll be very frank with you: I think it increases the importance of Egypt as a stabilizing factor in the Arab world, since Iran cannot be considered any more, if it ever was, the policeman of that region. I think Egypt, with their very large population, their very large armed forces, will be looked upon much more in the future as a possible stabilizing factor. I won't go into too much detail.

Another problem, though, that has arisen, demonstrated in Iran, has been the ability of the relatively few militants, who had deep and fervent commitments, to succeed against an all-powerful military force and an entrenched government. I think the success exceeded even the ones who were among the revolutionaries, the speed of it, the completeness of their victory. And I think this would tend to inspire or to instigate uprisings among the Palestinians, for instance, or other militant groups, in the future, to assert their own authority.

I don't have any doubt that in the West Bank, Gaza Strip area that the Israelis are strong enough to put down dissident groups who might arise. But the shedding of blood in a situation like that, even if it only involved a dozen people or a hundred people or maybe a thousand people, might very well escalate rapidly. It would certainly make it more difficult for Sadat to continue to negotiate with Israel under those circumstances, even though it was something that Israel couldn't prevent—they certainly would like to prevent any such thing—and something that Sadat couldn't directly become involved in.

The other factor, too, and this is typical of the confusion in the Mideast negotiations, is that Israel might—seeing Iran shaken so deeply—might be reluctant to withdraw from the Sinai, for instance, thinking that their own security would be best enhanced if they maintained the status quo for a while.

However, if the negotiations are delayed, my guess is that it will become increasingly difficult for Sadat to stand in limbo, where he's not part of a cohesive Arab world and he's apparently not making any progress in finding peace with Israel. He might be inclined to withdraw from the negotiations and go back and reestablish himself as part of the Arab world in a cohesive sense of brotherhood.

So, that's why we've been so insistent on trying to bring the talks to a conclusion. I think Israel is strong enough any time in the near future—4, 5, 10 years—adequately to protect themselves. And the overwhelming responsibility that I feel as President is to help guarantee the security of Israel, the permanence of

their government, and their ultimate peace. And I'm dedicated to it.

As I said before, we get criticized from both sides because we try to negotiate in good faith. I guess that's a role of a mediator, but I think it is accurate to say that both the Israelis and the Egyptians trust us and both desire us to continue in that role.

I don't have any idea what's going to happen when Begin comes over here Thursday night. We'll be negotiating all day Friday. We'll probably stop for the Sabbath on Saturday, and then negotiate some more. And if those talks open up an opportunity for improvement in the negotiation directly with Egypt, I have no doubt that Sadat and/or his Prime Minister would be here immediately to resume the negotiations.

But I think that Israel is secure. Obviously, they would be better off with peace. Egypt is the main military threat that could possibly attack Israel successfully, even in combination with all the other Arabs, and even then I don't think they could be successful. They've never insinuated privately or publicly that they want American military forces to be involved. They don't want American fighting men to be involved in Israel. They feel like if we give them economic and military aid, as we have in the past, that they are fully capable of protecting themselves. What the long-range trend might be 10, 15, 20, 50 years in the future, I don't know. But I don't have any doubt that whatever you project for the future, peace with Egypt is an integral requisite for the permanence of good relationships within Israel.

They have economic problems, as do many other countries, including our own. I think the inflation rate in Israel last year was in excess of 50 percent, for instance, and of course, they don't have the ability to trade with their normal neighbors. And I would hope that if we could ever get a peace treaty signed and open the borders and have diplomatic relations and exchange of ambassadors and student exchange and tourism and mutual trade and us and other nations help them develop water resources, mine different minerals like potash and so forth, the common use of the Suez Canal, common defense exchanges, that this would make it permanent. And we are that close to it.

The remaining differences on the peace treaty are absolutely insignificant. It's just disgusting, almost, to feel that we're that close and can't quite get it, but the feelings are deep and the sense of doubt and trust, on occasions, are just missing.

I've overanswered your question. I don't want to answer any more questions. It's an intriguing sort of thing, and I hope that over a period of months that you will become more and more involved in sharing with me some of the things that I described so briefly tonight.

In closing, I would like to propose a toast to the Governors of the States, to our great Nation, and to the people that you and I both represent, and to the United States of America.

Thank you.

GOVERNOR CARROLL. Mr. President, Mrs. Carter, again the Governors of America have come for your hospitality, and we particularly appreciate your intimate knowledge of the foreign affairs of the world.

One must be impressed by a President that can stand and speak so intimately about the problems of foreign affairs around the world. And I know that I speak for all of the Governors tonight, as well as your fellow Americans, that give

you our prayers and our blessings as you begin to further negotiate the differences between Egypt and Israel. And we will leave Washington tomorrow with a deep prayer on our hearts that your efforts will be successful.

We commend you for your excellent leadership. And you, probably, in being so candid as you are, are correct. I'm not sure that all the American people fully appreciate the difficulty of your task, one that you can really not be a winner in, because no negotiator is ever a winner. But no matter whether or not the effort is finally totally successful, your leadership has contributed substantially to world peace. And the Governors are pleased to be your partner in that effort.

As we said on Sunday afternoon, because of your leadership we have initiated a committee on international trade and foreign affairs. And it was our pleasure recently to host Vice Premier Deng, when he and other members of his delegation from the People's Republic of China were here. And our hearts were warmed like yours in finding that the people of China and the people of the United States had so much in common, knowing their interest in exchanging technology, in education, and certainly, in goods and services.

The Governors of America appreciate the partnership which we enjoy with the executive branch. Obviously, we have some differences. But no Governor, regardless of his particular political persuasion, would deny that we continue to negotiate to find common ground. And through our communication we have found common ground, because we begin to understand the burdens and responsibilities of each other.

We feel that our meeting, concluded this afternoon, has probably been one of the most successful in the history of our association. I believe most of the Governors would tell you they're somewhat exhausted tonight, because if words were a premium, we would have balanced your budget. [*Laughter*]

Indeed, as Governors, we come to support you totally in your effort to balance your budget. And Dr. Kahn was with us today. Indeed, Jim McIntyre was with us. And we understand the problems of inflation, and we are trying diligently to assist you, and we support you totally in that regard. And the other Secretaries and the directors of your various agencies and departments, along with the Members of the Congress, have certainly enlightened all of the Governors and, I'm sure, our 21 new Governors that have joined us in this conference.

And now, to the President and Mrs. Carter, particularly our prayers and our blessings as we toast the President and his First Lady, and to the United States of America, and to continued world peace. God bless you.

NOTE: The President spoke at 9:45 p.m. in the State Dining Room at the White House. Governor Julian Carroll of Kentucky is chairman of the National Governors' Association.

United States-Federal Republic of Germany Agreements on Social Security

Message to the Congress Transmitting the Agreements. February 28, 1979

To the Congress of the United States:

Pursuant to section 233(e)(1) of the Social Security Act as amended by the Social Security Amendments of 1977 (P.L. 95–216; 42 U.S.C. 1305 note), I am transmitting the Agreement between the United States of America and the Federal Republic of Germany (F.R.G.), signed on January 7, 1976, the Final Protocol to the 1976 Agreement, also signed on January 7, 1976, and the Administrative Agreement to implement the 1976 Agreement, signed on June 21, 1978.

These U.S.–F.R.G. agreements are similar in objective to the U.S.-Italian social security agreements which I submitted to the Congress on February 28, 1978. Such bilateral agreements, which are generally known as totalization agreements, provide for limited coordination between the United States and foreign social security systems to overcome the problems of gaps in protection and of dual coverage and taxation. In addition to remedying these problems, the 1976 U.S.–F.R.G. Agreement and Administrative Agreement would extend under specified conditions voluntary coverage rights under the F.R.G. system to U.S. citizens who have a prior connection with the F.R.G. system or who reside in the United States and were victims of persecution.

I also transmit for the information of the Congress a comprehensive report prepared by the Department of Health, Education, and Welfare, which explains the provisions of the Agreement and provides data on the number of persons affected by the agreements and the effect on social security financing as required by the same provision of the Social Security Amendments of 1977.

The Department of State and the Department of Health, Education, and Welfare join in commending this Agreement, Protocol, and Administrative Agreement.

JIMMY CARTER

The White House,
February 28, 1979.

Military Awards Program of the Departments of Defense and Transportation

Message to the Congress Transmitting Two Reports. February 28, 1979

To the Congress of the United States:

In accordance with the provisions of 10 U.S.C. 1124, I am forwarding reports of the Secretary of Defense and the Secretary of Transportation on awards made during Fiscal Year 1978 to members of the Armed Forces for suggestions, inventions and scientific achievements.

The participation of military personnel in the cash awards program was authorized by the Congress in 1965. More than two million submissions since that time attest to the program's success in motivating military personnel to find ways of reducing costs and improving efficiency. Of the suggestions submitted, more than 325,000 have been adopted, with tangible first-year benefits of more than a billion dollars.

Of the 98,011 suggestions submitted by military (including Coast Guard) personnel during Fiscal Year 1978, 14,830 were adopted. Cash awards totalling $1,001,257 were paid for adopted suggestions during Fiscal Year 1978. These awards were based not only on the tangible first-year benefits of $37,263,734 realized from adopted suggestions during Fiscal Year 1978, but also on many additional benefits and improvements of an intangible nature.

Enlisted people received $820,006 in awards during Fiscal Year 1978, representing 81 percent of the total cash awards paid during the periods. Officers received $181,251 during Fiscal Year 1978.

The attached reports of the Secretaries of Defense and Transportation contain statistical information on the military awards program and brief descriptions of some of the more noteworthy contributions of military personnel during Fiscal Year 1978.

JIMMY CARTER

The White House,
February 28, 1979.

North Atlantic Treaty Organization

Statement on the Appointment of Gen. Bernard W. Rogers as Supreme Allied Commander, Europe, and Commander in Chief of U.S. Forces in Europe. February 28, 1979

I am pleased today to announce that the Defense Planning Committee of the North Atlantic Council has appointed Gen. Bernard W. Rogers to be the Supreme Allied Commander, Europe, succeeding Gen. Alexander Haig, who has served with great distinction in that important post for the past 4½ years. In addition, I am appointing General Rogers to be Commander in Chief of United States forces in Europe, a position also being vacated by General Haig this June 30. General Rogers is currently serving as Chief of Staff of the U.S. Army.

The change of military command in NATO is an appropriate time to reflect upon the importance of the Alliance to the United States, to the West as a whole, and to the cause of world peace.

Thirty years ago, we joined European and Canadian friends in creating the North Atlantic Alliance. Since that time, NATO has been the cornerstone of U.S. security policy, reflecting the vital importance of the security and well-being of Western Europe to the security of North America. NATO has served us well: It has helped keep the peace in an area historically burdened by war, and it has brought the peoples of Europe and North America even closer together. To these ends, the Alliance has maintained strong military forces, and it has developed unique practices of political consultation. General Rogers will make important contributions to both of these efforts, drawing on his long and distinguished career as a soldier-statesman.

In recent years, the Alliance has faced difficult challenges. Most important is the steady growth and modernization of Warsaw Pact—and especially Soviet—forces. We are now moving together to meet that challenge. We will succeed. I have been deeply gratified by our Allies' response, through the NATO Long-Term Defense Program—adopted at the NATO Summit here last May—and through efforts to increase cooperation in defense procurement. It is vital to Allied security that the members of NATO fulfill these new commitments.

In the United States, we are making greatly needed increases in our defense capabilities. Much of this added strength will apply directly to NATO defense. We remain the world's most powerful country—militarily, politically, and economically—and I am determined that this position not be eroded. This strength, coupled with that of our NATO Allies, is the best hope for peace in Europe, and the best prospect for limiting and reducing the weapons of war.

In times of change and often turmoil in other parts of the world, the strength of NATO takes on an added dimension. It becomes even more important to guarantee security and stability in Europe, to give us added confidence in our ability to prevent the growth and spread of conflict, and to enable us to work effectively for peace in the world beyond the NATO area.

Because of the continuing importance of NATO, I am pleased that General Rogers will undertake these new and demanding responsibilities. He will play a key role in the revitalization of Alliance defenses, and in the strengthening of the political bonds of our relations with Canada and the European members of NATO. His distinguished career demonstrates his fitness to undertake these burdens—and he will have my full support and, I am sure, that of the Nation, as well.

Ambassador at Large and United States Coordinator for Refugee Affairs

Nomination of Dick Clark.
February 28, 1979

The President today announced that he will nominate Dick Clark, of Lamont, Iowa, to be Ambassador at Large and United States Coordinator for Refugee Affairs.

Clark was born September 14, 1928, in Central City, Iowa. He received a B.A. from Upper Iowa University in 1953 and an M.A. from the State University of Iowa in 1956. He served in the U.S. Army from 1950 to 1952.

From 1956 to 1959, Clark was a teaching assistant at the State University of Iowa, and from 1959 to 1965, he was an assistant professor of history at Upper Iowa University.

From 1965 to 1972, Clark was administrative assistant to Congressman John Culver. From 1973 to January 1979, he was U.S. Senator from the State of Iowa. He was a member of the Senate Foreign Relations Committee, and chairman of its Subcommittee on African Affairs.

Department of the Interior

Nomination of June Gibbs Brown To Be Inspector General.   February 28, 1979

The President today announced that he will nominate June Gibbs Brown, of Denver, Colo., to be Inspector General of the Interior Department.

Brown was born October 5, 1933, in Cleveland, Ohio. She received a B.B.A. (1971) and an M.B.A. (1972) from Cleveland State University, and a J.D. from the University of Denver in 1978.

From 1972 to 1975, Brown was director of internal audit for the Navy Finance Center in Cleveland, an office which produced auditing subsystems to deal with automated decision functions. From 1975 to 1976, Brown was Chief of Financial Systems Design for the Bureau of Land Management in Denver.

Since 1976 Brown has been project manager for the Bureau of Reclamation's Denver Pay-Personnel System Design, directing the development and implementation of a new integrated pay-personnel system for use throughout the Interior Department.

Department of Housing and Urban Development

Nomination of Charles L. Dempsey To Be Inspector General.   February 28, 1979

The President today announced that he will nominate Charles L. Dempsey, of Arlington, Va., to be Inspector General of the Department of Housing and Urban Development.

Dempsey was born June 7, 1928, in Morristown, N.J. He received a B.S. from Georgetown University in 1960. He served in the U.S. Army in 1952 and 1953.

Dempsey worked for the B. S. Saul & Company mortgage firm in Washington from 1954 to 1957, and for the Housing and Home Finance Agency from 1957 to 1968.

He joined the Department of Housing and Urban Development in 1968, where he served as Acting Director of Investigation (1970–1972); Assistant Inspector General for Administration (1972–1975); Acting Inspector General (1975); and Assistant Inspector General for Investigation (1975–1977). Since 1977 he has been Inspector General of the Department, serving on a nonstatutory basis.

Department of Labor

Nomination of Marjorie Fine Knowles To Be Inspector General.   February 28, 1979

The President today announced that he will nominate Marjorie Fine Knowles, of Tuscaloosa, Ala., to be Inspector General of the Department of Labor.

Knowles was born July 4, 1939, in Brooklyn, N.Y. She received an A.B. from Smith College in 1960 and an LL.B. from Harvard Law School in 1965.

In 1965 and 1966, Knowles was law clerk for U.S. District Judge Edward C. McLean of the Southern District of New York. From 1966 to 1967, she was assistant U.S. attorney for the Southern District of New York, and from 1967 to 1970, she was assistant district attorney for New York County.

From 1970 to 1972, Knowles was executive director of Joint Foundation Support, Inc., in New York City, a firm providing professional and administrative staff for a group of foundations focusing on projects to foster equal opportunity for poor people.

From 1972 to 1978, Knowles was on the faculty of the University of Alabama School of Law, as an associate professor, then a professor. In 1976–77 she was an American Council on Education fellow in academic administration, serving as a program associate in the office of the president.

Since 1978 Knowles has been Assistant General Counsel in the Inspector General Division at the Department of Health, Education, and Welfare.

Knowles is a member of the National Women's Political Caucus Advisory Board and of the Women's Action Alliance Board of Directors. She has served as chairperson of the advisory committee to the ACLU's Women's Rights Project, and as a member of the steering committee of the National Conference on Women and the Law. She has also served on the executive committee of the Southern Regional Council. She is the author of several articles in legal journals and has served as a consultant to a number of foundations.

Department of Agriculture

Nomination of Thomas F. McBride To Be Inspector General.   February 28, 1979

The President today announced that he will nominate Thomas F. McBride, of Washington, D.C., to be Inspector General of the Department of Agriculture.

McBride was born February 8, 1929, in Elgin, Ill. He received a B.A. from New York University in 1952 and an LL.B. from Columbia Law School in 1956. He served in the U.S. Army from 1946 to 1947.

From 1956 to 1959, McBride was assistant district attorney of New York County, and from 1959 to 1960, he was assistant counsel to the New York State Commission on Government Operations of the City of New York. In 1960 and 1961, he was an attorney and supervisory investigator for the Labor Department, and from 1961 to 1965, he was a trial attorney for the Justice Department.

From 1965 to 1968, McBride was Deputy Director of the Peace Corps for the Latin America Region. From 1968 to 1969, he was associate director of the Urban Coalition.

In 1969 McBride was deputy chief counsel to the U.S. House of Representatives Select Committee on Crime. In 1970 he was chief of the Center for Demonstrations and Professional Services of the National Institute of Law Enforcement and Criminal Justice, where he designed and carried out programs of criminal justice innovation in selected cities and counties. From 1970 to 1973, he was associate director and staff director of the Police Foundation, a Ford Foundation-funded program to support innovation and experimentation in police and criminal justice services.

From 1973 to 1975, McBride was associate special prosecutor with the Watergate Special Prosecution Force. He was head of the Campaign Contributions Task Force, the largest of the Office's task forces. He supervised more than 200 investigations and personally directed investigation and prosecution of over 30 individuals and 20 major corporations. He was responsible for liaison between the Special Prosecutor's Office and the IRS, the SEC, and other Federal agencies.

From 1975 to 1977, McBride was Director of the Bureau of Enforcement at the Civil Aeronautics Board, directing all economic enforcement activities in the field of U.S. air transport. Since 1977 he has served as Inspector General of the Agriculture Department on a nonstatutory basis.

Veterans Administration

Nomination of Allan L. Reynolds To Be Inspector General.   February 28, 1979

The President today announced that he will nominate Allan L. Reynolds, of Vienna, Va., to be Inspector General of the Veterans Administration.

Reynolds was born February 19, 1932, in San Rafael, Calif. He received a B.A. from San Jose State University in 1954.

Reynolds served with the Army Audit Agency from 1954 to 1967 and, during that time, participated in special reviews of the Civil Defense program, the Comptroller of the Army, and the internal operations of Army Audit itself. From 1967 to 1973, Reynolds was Kansas City regional audit manager for the Department of Health, Education, and Welfare Audit Agency and served as Deputy Director of the DHEW Audit Agency.

From 1973 to 1978, Reynolds was Director of the Interior Department's Office of Audit and Investigation. Since 1978 he has served as Inspector General of the Veterans Administration on a nonstatutory basis.

Reynolds is a member of the American Institute of Certified Public Accountants and serves on that organization's national advisory committee of members in industry and government. He is also a member of the Association of Government Accountants. He is the author of a number of articles in technical journals on audit subjects.

Generalized System of Preferences

Executive Order 12124.   February 28, 1979

AMENDING THE GENERALIZED SYSTEM OF PREFERENCES

By virtue of the authority vested in me by the Constitution and statutes of the United States of America, including Title V and Section 604 of the Trade Act of 1974 (88 Stat. 2066, 19 U.S.C. 2461 *et seq.*; 88 Stat. 2073, 19 U.S.C. 2483), and as President of the United States of America, in order to modify, as provided by Section 504(c) of the Trade Act of 1974 (88 Stat. 2070, 19 U.S.C. 2464(c)), the limitations on preferential treatment for eligible articles from countries designated as beneficiary developing countries, and to adjust the original designation of eligible articles taking into account information and advice received in fulfillment of Sections 503(a) and 131–134 of the Trade Act of 1974 (88 Stat. 2069, 19 U.S.C. 2463(a); 88 Stat. 1994, 19 U.S.C. 2151–2154), it is hereby ordered as follows:

SECTION 1. In order to subdivide existing items for purposes of the Generalized System of Preferences (GSP), the Tariff Schedules of the United States (TSUS) (19 U.S.C. 1202) are modified as provided in Annex I, attached hereto and made a part hereof.

SEC. 2. Annex II of Executive Order No. 11888 of November 24, 1975, as amended, listing articles that are eligible for benefits of the GSP when imported from any designated beneficiary developing country, is further amended as provided in Annex II, attached hereto and made a part hereof.

SEC. 3. Annex III of Executive Order No. 11888, as amended, listing articles that are eligible for benefits of the GSP when imported from all designated beneficiary countries except those specified in General Headnote 3(c)(iii) of the TSUS, is amended by substituting therefor the new Annex III, attached hereto and made a part hereof.

SEC. 4. General Headnote 3(c)(iii) of the TSUS, listing articles that are eligible for benefits of the GSP except when imported from the beneficiary countries listed opposite those articles, is amended by substituting therefor the new Annex IV, attached hereto and made a part hereof.

SEC. 5. General Headnote 3(c)(i) of the TSUS is modified—

(i) by adding, in alphabetical order, to the list of independent designated beneficiary developing countries for the purposes of the Generalized System of Preferences "Comoros", "Djibouti", and "Seychelles"; and by deleting from the list of non-independent designated beneficiary developing countries and territories "Comoro Islands", "French Territory of the Afars and Issas", and "Seychelles."

(ii) by deleting from the list of independent designated beneficiary developing countries "Central African Republic", "Congo (Brazzaville)", "Maldive Islands", and "Republic of China", and by substituting therefor, in alphabetical order, "Central African Empire", "Congo", "Maldives", and "Taiwan", respectively.

(iii) by deleting from the list of non-independent designated beneficiary developing countries "Falkland Islands (Malvinas) and Dependencies", "Pitcairn Island", and "Spanish Sahara", and by substituting therefor, in alphabetical order, "Falkland Islands (Islas Malvinas)", "Pitcairn Islands", and "Western Sahara", respectively.

(iv) by deleting from the list of non-independent designated beneficiary developing countries "Portuguese Timor."

SEC. 6. The amendments made by this Order shall be effective with respect to articles that are both: (1) imported on or after January 1, 1976, and (2) entered, or withdrawn from warehouse, for consumption on or after March 1, 1979.

SEC. 7. Effective March 1, 1980, Annex II to Executive Order 11888, as amended, is further amended by deleting item 652.97, TSUS.

JIMMY CARTER

The White House,
February 28, 1979.

[Filed with the Office of the Federal Register, 4:30 p.m., February 28, 1979]

NOTE: The annexes are printed in the FEDERAL REGISTER of March 2, 1979.

Small Business Conference Commission

Remarks at the Swearing In of the Commission's Membership.
February 28, 1979

This is, by far, the best organized group of small business leaders I've ever seen. [*Laughter*] And my guess is that after this, they won't be nearly so cooperative with each other, or orderly— I'm sure much more lively and committed to seeing beneficial change.

If there's one element of my own background as a human being that I value and have observed carefully to be beneficial to me as President, it has been my career as a small businessman. When I campaigned for President for 2 years, on every possible occasion when I had the opportunity to shake hands with employees in small and large plants, I always made a point to go in and have a private conversation with the owners, managers, operators of the business, and also with the representatives of labor groups, to try to discern at first hand not only the tremendous accomplishments of our free enterprise system in this country but also the problems, the needs, the concerns, the advice, and the opportunities for enhancing it even in the future.

When I became President one of my own initiatives was to pursue the idea with Congressman Smith, with Senator Nelson, later with Vernon Weaver, for a White House conference for small business leaders and for small business as an entity in our economic system.

This will be, by far, the largest White House conference ever held. It will also be the first, so far as I am able to determine, where the delegates will be chosen from the individual States. And, of course, it will also be preceded by regional meetings wherein there can be a great magnification of the knowledge, experience, influence, and information brought here by delegates who actually attend the conference at the White House.

We have a lot to learn from one another—I, as President, the members of my own administration, the Members of the Congress, and the general public from the small business community. And, of course, it will be mutually instructive for small business leaders of all kinds to learn from one another.

Quite often, a superb accomplishment in a certain field of effort economically, of necessity, narrows the focus even of the most broadminded and enlightened leader, to concentrate on particular day-by-day problems of organization, management, financing, production, delivery of the goods that make our Nation so great.

Obviously, you will be interested in seeing a reduction in unnecessary paperwork, an enlightenment of the Federal Government's attitude toward basic regulations, the enforcement of those regulations in an effective and nonburdensome way, an enhancement of the word "free" in our free enterprise system, the proper relationship between the business community and the Government itself.

Your voice will be listened to very carefully during the preparatory days and also the days of the White House conference as such.

In addition, I think foreign exports and the influence of small business spokesmen and spokeswomen on a broad gamut of decisions made here in Washington will be very beneficial. It would be impossible for me to say, "These are the areas where small business influence will be beneficial, but these other areas will not be beneficial." Obviously, in basic employment schemes, financing, Government loans, community development, almost every realm of American life can benefit from the sound advice and experience and enlightenment and proven success of leaders of the small business community.

Vernon Weaver is obviously one of you. He's a man who is a strong and able leader. He's made great progress in the Small Business Administration. But even there, that agency of Government has a very limited realm of influence and responsibility by law that will be far exceeded by the gamut of issues that you will discuss and assess as the White House conference is concluded.

As you know, Mr. Levitt will be the Chairman of this advisory group, responsible, with these fine other leaders behind me, for the evolution of the basic premises on which the Small Business Conference will be concluded and arranged for here at the White House.

I would like to say in closing that you are welcome here. We'll learn in our daily contacts with you, and I hope that you will feel, following this meeting, that a new avenue has been opened for consultation, advice, criticisms, and the mutual sharing of the opportunity to make our great Nation even greater in the future.

Together I believe we will succeed in opening up new vistas, new realms of success in your own business commitments, your own life interests, and also to make government in our country more enlightened, more wise, more influenced directly from those who benefit from its proper decisions.

Sometimes they've suffered in the past from its improper decisions. But in my judgment, this ease of communication and sharing of experiences and hopes can be a powerful force in strengthening our country in many different ways.

I can tell you accurately that the longer I'm here in the White House as President, the more I cherish my years as a small businessman. [*Laughter*] One of the main reasons I'm interested in the White House conference is that it'll give you an opportunity to help me do a better job for you as President.

Thank you very much for your friendship and coming here.

NOTE: The President spoke at 3:45 p.m. at the ceremony in the East Room at the White House. Prior to his remarks, Vice President Walter F. Mondale administered the oath of office to the 11 members of the Commission.

Energy Conservation Contingency Plans

Message to the Congress Transmitting Three Plans.   March 1, 1979

To the Congress of the United States:

As required by Section 201 of the Energy Policy and Conservation Act (EPCA), 42 U.S.C. 6261, I am hereby transmitting to the Congress for its approval the following three energy conservation contingency plans: Emergency Weekend Gasoline Sales Restrictions, Emergency Building Temperature Restrictions and Advertising Lighting Restrictions. I have also today directed the Secretary of Energy to publish these conservation plans in the FEDERAL REGISTER, as the final step in my prescribing these plans as required by Sections 202 and 523 of the EPCA.

The plans which I am transmitting are the product of extensive plan development and refinement. They can be effective tools in reducing consumption of energy in the event of a severe energy supply emergency. Work on the development of contingency plans is continuing and any additional measures will be transmitted for approval pursuant to Section 201 of the EPCA upon their completion.

Together with the Standby Gasoline Rationing Plan which I am also transmitting to the Congress today under separate letter, these energy conservation contingency plans could help mitigate the effects upon the United States of a severe energy supply interruption. These measures, along with voluntary conservation efforts and other measures contained in existing legislation and the Department of Energy's present contingency programs, will provide the government with several options to deal with energy emergencies of varying types and degrees of severity. Such flexibility is essential if we are to prevent unnecessary hardship to our citizens and harm to our economy in the event of future curtailments of our energy supplies.

As required by Section 201(f) of the EPCA, each energy conservation contingency plan is accompanied by an analysis which assesses the economic impacts of the plan.

The procedures for approval by Congress of a contingency plan are detailed in Section 552 of the EPCA, and require among other things that a resolution of approval be passed by each House of Congress within 60 days of submittal of the plan. The EPCA does not specify the form which the resolution of approval is to take. It is my view and that of the Attorney General that actions of the Congress purporting to have binding legal effect must be presented to the President for his approval under Article I, Section 7 of the Constitution. Therefore, I strongly recommend that Congressional approval of these plans be in the form of a joint resolution. If this procedure is followed, the plans themselves, agreed to by Congress and the President, will not later be subject to possible judicial invalidation on the ground that the President did not approve the resolution.

I urge the prompt and favorable consideration by the Congress of these plans.

JIMMY CARTER

The White House,
   March 1, 1979.

NOTE: The plans and accompanying analyses are printed in the FEDERAL REGISTER of March 8, 1979.

Standby Gasoline Rationing Plan

Message to the Congress Transmitting the Plan. March 1, 1979

To the Congress of the United States:

As required by Section 201 of the Energy Policy and Conservation Act (EPCA), 42 U.S.C. 6261, I am hereby transmitting to the Congress for its approval a Standby Gasoline Rationing Plan. I have also today directed the Secretary of Energy to publish the Plan in the FEDERAL REGISTER, as the final step in my prescribing a gasoline rationing plan by rule, as required by Sections 203 and 523 of the EPCA.

The Standby Gasoline Rationing Plan which I am transmitting today is the result of an extensive rulemaking proceeding in which over 1,100 comments from citizens throughout the United States were received and considered. I believe this plan, which would be implemented only in a severe energy supply emergency, would equitably allocate gasoline supplies and minimize economic hardships to the maximum extent possible without undue administrative costs and complexity.

Together with the energy conservation contingency plans which I am also transmitting to the Congress today under separate letter, the Standby Gasoline Rationing Plan would help mitigate the impact of a severe energy supply interruption. These measures, along with voluntary conservation efforts and other measures contained in existing legislation and the Department of Energy's present contingency programs, will provide the government with several options to deal with energy emergencies of varying types and degrees of severity. Such flexibility is essential if we are to prevent unnecessary hardship to our citizens and harm to our economy in the event of future curtailments of our energy supplies.

As required by Section 201(f) of the EPCA, the Standby Gasoline Rationing Plan is accompanied by an analysis which assesses the economic impacts of the Plan.

The procedures for approval by Congress of a contingency plan are detailed in Section 552 of the EPCA, and require among other things that a resolution of approval be passed by each House of Congress within 60 days of submittal of the plan. The EPCA does not specify the form which the resolution of approval is to take. It is my view and that of the Attorney General that actions of the Congress purporting to have binding legal effect must be presented to the President for his approval under Article I, Section 7 of the Constitution. Therefore, I strongly urge that Congressional approval of this plan be in the form of a joint resolution. If this procedure is followed, the plan itself, agreed to by Congress and the President, will not later be subject to possible judicial invalidation on the ground that the President did not approve the resolution.

I urge the prompt and favorable consideration by the Congress of this plan.

JIMMY CARTER

The White House,
    March 1, 1979.

NOTE: The plan and accompanying analysis are printed in the FEDERAL REGISTER of March 14, 1979.

Meeting With Prime Minister Menahem Begin of Israel

White House Statement.   March 1, 1979

The President and the Prime Minister met in the President's office from 6:30 to 8:30 p.m.

The President and Prime Minister agreed that their meeting this evening, which was conducted in a most friendly atmosphere, was a useful prelude to the extensive talks they will be having over the next days. The President and Prime Minister will be having extensive exchanges on a whole range of issues of key importance to Israel and the United States, to the peace process in the Middle East, and to the stability of that troubled region.

Democratic Fundraising Dinner

Remarks by Videotape to the Dinner in Los Angeles, California.   February 28, 1979

Good evening.

I'm very sorry that I can't be with you tonight. Nothing would have kept me away but the most urgent concerns of our country. And there is no concern more important to our Nation and, I know, to you and to me than our search for a lasting peace in the Middle East.

It was a Democratic President, Harry Truman, who first recognized the newly created State of Israel in the first minutes of its birth. Today, we carry on that legacy as we seek a secure and a peaceful future for Israel.

In my 2 years as President, I've devoted more time and invested more personal effort in the Middle East peace negotiations than in any other international problem. During the last 6 months, we have bridged chasms of suspicion and mistrust that have built for generations.

We've now come within inches of reaching a final agreement between Israel and Egypt. I'm determined to carry on this effort.

Prime Minister Begin and I are meeting now to discuss our goal of a lasting peace agreement. I need your prayers and your support. Throughout the peace process, one constant remains—America's unshakable commitment to the security of Israel will always be assured.

For 30 years, the people of Israel and Egypt have known suffering and war.

Now the time has come for peace. As President, I will spare no effort and will continue to pursue every possible avenue to bring peace in the Middle East.

The problems of the Middle East are a symbol of our times—difficult, deep-rooted, and complex. Around the world and here at home, we face new and unprecedented challenges as we begin our third century as a nation. We face a challenge of controlling inflation, of resolving an energy crisis, of revitalizing our Government, and restoring the public's trust. And we face the daily, awesome challenge of ensuring peace for future generations in a dangerous nuclear age.

The challenges of our times cannot be solved overnight by quick fixes or miracle cures. They demand from each of us our perseverance, our commitment, and our sense of common purpose.

We have no illusions that the world has become a safe or easy or manageable place to live. But today, after years of drift, we see an America standing up to face the difficult domestic challenges. And around the world we see an America not at war, but using its vast influence and strength for arms control and for peace. And we see a nation that has regained its special place of leadership in the struggle for basic human rights.

Together we are meeting the challenges of our time. For more than 2 years, you've given me and our party your encouragement, your counsel, and your support. I'm grateful for the support you've shown tonight. And I especially want to thank my good friend Lew Wasserman and all those who worked so hard to make this dinner a success.

I envy you all tonight. You get to hear two great American voices—Diana Ross and Fritz Mondale. My warmest, best wishes are with you all.

Good night, and enjoy your evening.

NOTE: The President's remarks were videotaped in the Map Room at the White House for use at the dinner on March 2.

In his remarks, the President referred to Lew R. Wasserman, president of Music Corporation of America, Inc., and entertainer Diana Ross.

The transcript of the remarks was released on March 2.

Postal Rate Commission

Nomination of James H. Duffy To Be a Commissioner. March 2, 1979

The President today announced that he will nominate James H. Duffy, of Bethesda, Md., to be a Commissioner of the Postal Rate Commission for a term expiring November 22, 1984. He would replace Carlos Villarreal, whose term has expired.

Duffy was born April 6, 1918, in Cranston, R.I. He received a Ph. B. from Providence College, an Ed. B. from Rhode Island College, and an LL.B. from Boston University Law School. He served in the U.S. Army from 1943 to 1946.

From 1948 to 1955, Duffy practiced law in Providence, R.I. From 1955 to 1975, he was chief counsel to the U.S. Senate Subcommittee on Privileges and Elections, where he participated in the drafting of Federal election laws and conducted investigations on contested elections and confirmations. From 1975 to 1977, Duffy was legislative assistant to Senator Robert C. Byrd. Since 1977 he has been secretary for the majority in the Senate.

Dewey Bartlett

*Statement on the Death of the Former
Senator From Oklahoma. March 2, 1979*

Rosalynn and I extend our deepest sympathy to the family of Dewey Bartlett.

He was the second Republican Governor in Oklahoma history, and although his Senate career was cut short by his illness, he had already established himself as a strong conservative voice in the Senate with an abiding concern for solving our Nation's energy problems.

We were often on opposite sides on issues, but I found him a worthy opponent and shared his colleagues' respect for Senator Bartlett's abilities and dedication, and join them in mourning his loss.

Geological Survey

*Statement on the 100th Anniversary of the
Founding of the Survey. March 2, 1979*

March 3, 1979, marks the 100th anniversary of the founding of the U.S. Geological Survey. On this day in 1879, President Rutherford B. Hayes approved legislation authorizing "the classification of the public lands and examination of the geological structure, mineral resources, and products of the national domain."

The Geological Survey has had a rich history. It grew from the necessity of our forebears to explore this vast and bountiful continent, to understand its geographical features, and to evaluate its natural resources. It also grew from a pioneering legacy—from heroic achievements ranging from the Lewis and Clark Expedition to the exploration of the Colorado River by John Wesley Powell.

The Geological Survey has served the Nation well, providing vital information upon which we make critical decisions and important national policy. That policy involves our mineral resources, our land, and our water. It helps us avoid the risks of natural disasters and provides knowledge useful for our urban planning, for sound construction practices, and for resolving many environmental and health problems.

While focusing mainly on the United States, the Survey's programs are also international in scope and make it possible for us to share geological knowledge and its benefits with other countries of the world.

Finally, the Survey is keeping pace with space-age science and technology. It is working on the geology of the Moon and the planets. It is involved in the remote sensing of the Earth's features and natural resources from our satellites and high altitude aircraft.

I am proud to recognize the Survey's century of valuable service to our Nation. I wholeheartedly applaud its high standards of excellence in past accomplishments and reaffirm the emphasis that this administration places upon the continuing importance of its scientific work.

My best wishes go out to those whose talents and dedication have made the U.S. Geological Survey such a vital part of our government.

Meeting With Prime Minister Begin of Israel

White House Statement. March 2, 1979

President Carter and Prime Minister Begin met for 2½ hours this morning in the Cabinet Room, accompanied by their advisers.

Cyrus Vance, Secretary of State; Zbigniew Brzezinski, Assistant to the President for National Security Affairs; Jody Powell, Press Secretary to the President; Alfred L. Atherton, Jr., Ambassador at Large; Samuel Lewis, U.S Ambassador to Israel; Harold H. Saunders, Assistant Secretary of State, Bureau of Near Eastern and South Asian Affairs; Edward Sanders, Advisor to the Secretary of State; Herbert J. Hansell, Legal Advisor, Department of State; and William B. Quandt, Jr., National Security Council staff member, were present on the American side.

Ephraim Evron, Israeli Ambassador to the United States; Yehuda Blum, Ambassador to the United Nations; Meir Rosenne, Legal Advisor, Ministry of Foreign Affairs; Yehuda Avner, Special Assistant to the Prime Minister; Yehiel Kadishai, Director of the Prime Minister's Bureau; Dan Patir, Official Spokesman; and Dr. Marum Gottesman, Prime Minister Begin's personal physician, were present on the Israeli side.

The meeting today was a serious, wide-ranging, and useful discussion of the situation in the region and the problems of building peace there. The talks included a detailed and comprehensive discussion of the unresolved issues in the implementation of the Camp David accords. The talks were conducted in an atmosphere of friendship and candor.

The two delegations will confer among themselves this afternoon following the working lunch which the Secretary of State is hosting at the State Department for the Prime Minister. At 7 p.m. today, the Prime Minister and Mrs. Begin have invited the President and Mrs. Carter for traditional Friday evening Sabbath dinner at the Blair House. The two leaders will be meeting again at the White House tomorrow evening.

Renegotiation Board

Nomination of William M. Burkhalter To Be a Member. March 2, 1979

The President today announced that he will nominate William M. Burkhalter, of Bethesda, Md., to be a member of the Renegotiation Board. He would replace Rex Mattingly, who has resigned.

Burkhalter was born November 21, 1914, in McKenzie, Tenn. He received a B.S. (1939) and a J.D. (1939) from the University of Tennessee. He served in the U.S. Navy from 1942 to 1946.

Burkhalter was assistant chief title officer for TVA's Land Acquisition Department from 1939 to 1942. He practiced law with the firm of Brown, Lund & Fitzgerald from 1946 to 1961, specializing in government contract law and securities law.

From 1961 to 1962, Burkhalter was temporarily assigned to the Office of Emergency Planning, Executive Office of the President, working on defense and economic mobilization problems. In 1962 he was appointed a member of the Renegotiation Board. He served as a member until 1969. Since then he has been Deputy General Counsel of the Renegotiation Board.

Digest of Other White House Announcements

The following listing includes the President's public schedule and other items of general interest announced by the White House Press Office and not included elsewhere in this issue.

February 24

The President met at the White House with Zbigniew Brzezinski, Assistant to the President for National Security Affairs.

February 25

The President attended a concert by Mikhail Baryshnikov and members of the New York City Ballet Company in the East Room at the White House.

February 26

The President met at the White House with:

—Dr. Brzezinski;

—Frank B. Moore, Assistant to the President for Congressional Liaison;

—the Cabinet;

—Vice President Walter F. Mondale;

—James T. McIntyre, Jr., Director of the Office of Management and Budget.

In a ceremony in the Oval Office, the President received diplomatic credentials from Ambassadors Felipe Doroteo Monterroso Miranda of Guatemala, Sidi Bouna Ould Sidi of Mauritania, and Sultan Muhammad Khan of Pakistan.

The President has appointed John E. Menario, executive vice president of the Greater Portland (Maine) Chamber of Commerce, as a member of the Endangered Species Committee, representing the State of Maine, to consider the exemption application of the Pittston Company, and as a member of the Review Board of that Committee.

The President announced the appointment of John P. White, Deputy Director of the Office of Management and Budget, as a member of the Board of Governors of the American Red Cross.

The President has named Ambassador Andrew J. Young to be his Special Representative at the Australian-American Week celebrations in Australia in early May. Ambassador Young was invited to be the guest of honor at these annual celebrations by the Australian-American Association. While there, Ambassador Young will consult with the Government of Australia on international issues of importance to Australia and the United States. Ambassador Young will be accompanied by Mrs. Young. During his trip, he will visit Canberra, Sydney, Melbourne, and Perth. After these annual celebrations by the Australian-American Association, he will be a joint guest of the Association and of the Australian Government.

February 27

The President met at the White House with:

—Dr. Brzezinski;

—Mr. Moore.

February 28

The President met at the White House with:

—newly elected Democratic Governors and their spouses;

—Dr. Brzezinski;

—Mr. Moore and members of the Budget Task Force;

—Vice President Mondale and members of the Congressional Black Caucus;

—Representative and Mrs. Harold T. Johnson of California;

—John C. White, chairman of the Democratic National Committee;

—a group of Senators and Congressmen, to discuss his recent trip to Mexico;

—Senator Lloyd M. Bentsen of Texas.

Prime Minister Pierre Elliott Trudeau of Canada has accepted the President's invitation to come to Washington on Saturday, March 3. The two leaders plan to have a working luncheon in the Oval Office. The Prime Minister is expected to arrive in Washington on Saturday and travel to New York City following the luncheon. The President had been scheduled to go to New York City on Saturday, but will be unable to do so because of his planned talks with Prime Minister Begin of Israel.

March 1

The President met at the White House with:

—Dr. Brzezinski;

—Mr. Moore;

—Clarence M. Mitchell, Jr., who is retiring as director of the Washington office of the National Association for the Advancement of Colored People;

—Mrs. Carter, for lunch.

In a ceremony in the Oval Office, the President received diplomatic credentials from Ambassadors Knut Hedemann of Norway, Carlos Alfredo Lopez Guevara of Panama, and Chai Zemin of the People's Republic of China.

In a ceremony in the Oval Office, the President received the first sheet of Easter Seals, which marked the start of the 1979 Easter Seal Campaign, from Claire Huckel, 7, of Philadelphia, Pa., the National Easter Seal Poster Child.

March 2

The President met at the White House with:

—Vice President Mondale, Secretary of State Cyrus R. Vance, Secretary of Defense Harold Brown, and Dr. Brzezinski;

—Dr. Brzezinski.

The President announced that he will nominate Richard E. Benedick, of Santa Monica, Calif., for the rank of Ambassador during the periods when he represents the United States at international conferences. Benedick is Coordinator for Population Affairs at the State Department.

The President announced that Robert W. Maher has been named to the White House Congressional Liaison Office. Maher will be working with the House Liaison staff.

NOMINATIONS SUBMITTED TO THE SENATE

The following list does not include promotions of members of the Uniformed Services, nominations to the Service Academies, or nominations of Foreign Service officers.

Submitted February 27, 1979

GABRIELLE ANNE KIRK McDONALD, of Texas, to be United States District Judge for the Southern District of Texas, vice a new position created by P.L. 95–486, approved October 20, 1978.

DENNIS R. WYANT, of Maryland, to be Deputy Assistant Secretary of Labor for Veterans' Employment, vice Roland Ray Mora, resigned.

BENJAMIN W. HEINEMAN, JR., of Illinois, to be an Assistant Secretary of Health, Education, and Welfare, vice Henry Jacob Aaron, resigned.

The following-named persons to be members of the National Advisory Council on Women's Educational Programs for terms expiring May 8, 1981:

SISTER M. ISOLINA FERRE, of Puerto Rico, vice Agnes M. Dill, term expired.

ANNA DOYLE LEVESQUE, of Rhode Island, vice Katherine K. Burgum, term expired.

SUSAN MARGARET VANCE, of Illinois, vice Theresa Aragon de Shepro, term expired.

Submitted February 28, 1979

DICK CLARK, of Iowa, to be an Ambassador at Large and United States Coordinator for Refugee Affairs.

JUNE GIBBS BROWN, of Colorado, to be Inspector General, Department of the Interior (new position).

THOMAS F. McBRIDE, of the District of Columbia, to be Inspector General, Department of Agriculture (new position).

MARJORIE FINE KNOWLES, of Alabama, to be Inspector General, Department of Labor (new position).

CHARLES L. DEMPSEY, of Virginia, to be Inspector General, Department of Housing and Urban Development (new position).

ALLAN L. REYNOLDS, of Virginia, to be Inspector General, Veterans' Administration (new position).

NOMINATIONS—Continued

Submitted March 1, 1979

KURT W. MUELLENBERG, of Maryland, to be Inspector General, General Services Administration (new position).

Submitted March 2, 1979

RICHARD ELLIOT BENEDICK, of California, Coordinator for Population Affairs, for the rank of Ambassador.

JOYCE HENS GREEN, of Virginia, to be United States District Judge for the District of Columbia, vice a new position created by P.L. 95–486, approved October 20, 1978.

JAMES H. DUFFY, of Maryland, to be a Commissioner of the Postal Rate Commission for the term expiring November 22, 1984, vice Carlos C. Villarreal, term expired.

CHECKLIST OF WHITE HOUSE PRESS RELEASES

The following listing contains releases of the White House Press Office which are not included in this issue.

Released February 26, 1979

Announcement: nomination of Gabrielle Kirk McDonald to be United States District Judge for the Southern District of Texas

Released February 27, 1979

News conference: on proposed reform of the Federal civil justice system—by Attorney General Griffin B. Bell

Fact sheet: proposed reform of the Federal civil justice system

Released February 28, 1979

Biographical data: Gen. Bernard W. Rogers

CHECKLIST—Continued

Released March 1, 1979

News conference: on reorganization proposals to consolidate major Federal natural resources programs into a department of natural resources, and to consolidate the Federal economic development programs and job creation efforts—by Vice President Walter F. Mondale, James T. McIntyre, Jr., Director, and W. Harrison Wellford, Executive Associate Director for Reorganization and Management, Office of Management and Budget, Stuart E. Eizenstat, Assistant to the President for Domestic Affairs and Policy, and Richard A. Pettigrew, Assistant to the President for Reorganization

Fact sheet: reorganization proposals to consolidate major Federal natural resources programs into a department of natural resources, and to consolidate the Federal economic development programs and job creation efforts

Released March 2, 1979

Announcement: nomination of Joyce H. Green to be United States District Judge for the District of Columbia

Announcement: naming of Robert W. Maher to the White House Congressional Liaison Office

---

ACTS APPROVED BY THE PRESIDENT

NOTE: No acts approved by the President were received by the Office of the Federal Register during the period covered by this issue.

Meeting With Prime Minister Pierre Elliott Trudeau of Canada

Remarks on the Departure of the Prime Minister.   March 3, 1979

THE PRESIDENT. Good afternoon, everybody.

Recently, Prime Minister Trudeau and I were scheduled to meet this evening in New York to attend the performance of the Winnipeg Symphony Orchestra. We were not able to do so, but we had a delightful lunch today and maybe made some good music together.

We were able to discuss international and bilateral issues concerning the economy. We spent a considerable portion of our time talking about energy matters. We both are resolved to work much more closely in the future even than we have in the past. We discussed the possibility of establishing a consultative mechanism so that we might exchange ideas on energy on a continuing basis.

We had a general review of world political problems, some of the fast-changing developments that are of interest both to us and to Canada and others who want peace and stability and a better quality of life throughout the world. We share with Canada, as you know, the longest open border in the world. We benefit from the stable and reliable and very valuable friendship that we have with the Canadian people. And I think it's accurate to say that the relationship that we have with the great Prime Minister of Canada, Pierre Trudeau, is accurately mirrored in this same context.

We've been successful in recent months in resolving some potentially very difficult issues concerning the exact border between our two countries and the open seas and also resolving fisheries agreements. These kinds of issues are ones that we discussed and resolved successfully as a matter of routine.

And I'm very grateful and honored and pleased to have Prime Minister Trudeau come and visit us for this substantive discussion. I think it is an indication of our past excellent relationships and, I think, an accurate precursor or prediction that our relationships will be equally favorable in the future for both countries.

Pierre, we're glad to have you again in our home.

THE PRIME MINISTER. Thank you. Well, I feel fortunate to have been able to meet with President Carter at this time. Naturally, there will be a lot of disappointed Canadians in New York who were hoping to see the President and myself hearing these great Canadian and international artists. But from the point of view of the timing and the substance, I feel it fortunate that it worked out this way, because I am meeting President Carter at a very important time in the development of international relations—in the midst of his meetings with the Prime Minister of Israel, following shortly after his meeting with the Vice Premier of China and on the eve, I hope, of the successful conclusion of SALT II, to which Canada and, I'm sure, all peace-loving peoples attach very, very great importance. And we're very supportive of the initiatives taken by the President and by Mr. Brezhnev in bringing the SALT II treaty, hopefully, close to a successful conclusion.

As the President said, apart from these international problems—in which I was mainly the listener and a willing listener—we did discuss a number of bilateral issues which are of great importance to both countries.

I feel that those discussions were well in the direction that we had set together a couple of years ago at our first meeting, in ensuring the political will of solving many of these issues. And we talked about the very ones which are coming now to a successful conclusion—the MTN negotiations, many of the environmental border issues, the fisheries dispute, which then seemed almost unsoluble and which we have solved in a successful way, at least on the east coast; and the fact that the areas which remain unsolved, particularly the border areas, have been referred or will be referred to arbitration as an indication of the confidence that exists between our two countries and administrations, that we trust each other enough to sort of say, "Well, if we can't agree, let's get a third party to agree for us." There's no browbeating and pushing around. It's a fair bargain between friends.

So, on all these issues, we have seen progress between our countries in the past few years.

I'm very grateful for the understanding of the Canadian points of view. We feel in some cases they got a better deal, but the President was telling me that he thought it was the contrary. So, it means both sides are pretty happy, I think, with the way in which we've settled the disputes in the MTN and the fisheries areas, in particular.

On energy, there is the major question of the Foothills Pipeline. And I was reassured that President Carter insisted that there was a desire on the part of the U.S. Government that it be proceeded with and that no one, certainly in his administration, had any doubts about that.

But there are a lot of secondary but important issues which have to be solved, having to do with our excess capacity in the east coast of refining capacity, having to do with what we do with the surplus of gas which was found in the West and Canada, the eventual disposition of the liquefied natural gas that we are planning for the Arctic, and so on.

And these issues do call for a much more direct and ongoing consultation between the two administrations. And I think the proposition was made to have an ongoing group of officials monitor it and report to us on a more frequent basis. It's a very good one, and I think in the short time ahead, it will prove of significant benefit to both our countries.

So, everything that I had hoped to talk about, including the Auto Pact, was covered in our talks. And I think it's fair to say that the lunch was pleasant, not only for the food but for the friendship between us and the results which were achieved, hopefully, to the benefit of our two countries.

And I'm very grateful to you, President Carter, for having received me at this very busy time.

THE PRESIDENT. Thank you, Pierre. Good luck to you.

THE PRIME MINISTER. Thank you.

NOTE: The President spoke at 1:32 p.m. to reporters assembled on the South Lawn of the White House.

Meeting With Prime Minister Trudeau of Canada

Joint Communique.   March 3, 1979

ENERGY

During their discussion today over lunch at the White House, the Prime Minister and the President discussed the world energy situation and noted that increased energy self-reliance is a major objective of both their governments. They reaffirmed that enhanced bilateral cooperation in the field of energy will serve the interests of both countries. They also agreed that maximizing the supplies of domestic energy available to each country was a common and shared objective.

Recent international events have served to underline the vulnerability of the USA and Canada and other oil-consuming countries to oil supply and pricing disruptions. The President and the Prime Minister endorsed the coordinated undertaking of March 2 by the member countries of the International Energy Agency to reduce demand for oil on the world market on an urgent basis in response to the current global supply situation. The Prime Minister noted that Canada is raising its oil production and that production in the first quarter of 1979 will be some 13 percent above the previous year, a portion of it being used to offset domestic shortfalls resulting from the Iranian situation. The United States plans to take appropriate action to increase its oil production to offset the world supply shortfall.

The Prime Minister outlined to the President the progress already achieved in Canada toward construction of the Northern Gas Pipeline. The President affirmed his government's strong commitment to the completion of the line, which will bring Alaskan gas to the lower 48 states and eventually Mackenzie Delta gas to Canadian markets. He noted that he is sending a reorganization plan to the Congress no later than April 1, establishing the Office of the Federal Pipeline Inspector. He also stated his determination to ensure that the U.S. regulatory process on all aspects of the Northern Gas Pipeline proceeds as quickly as possible.

The two leaders agreed to seek ways whereby any additional Canadian gas exports, should they be authorized, could facilitate timely construction of the entire Northern Gas Pipeline.

In order to enhance the already close and timely cooperation in other bilateral energy areas, the two leaders agreed to establish a consultative mechanism at the sub-cabinet level which would function at least to the end of 1979. This consultative mechanism is charged with:

—ensuring that decision-making processes in each country on the matter of a delivery system to transport Alaskan crude oil to the northern tier and other inland states proceed in a parallel and timely manner;

—developing options for decision by each government on a number of operational issues in bilateral energy relations, including oil supplies and oil exchanges, strategic petroleum storage, the utilization of surplus Canadian refinery capacity, electricity exchanges, possibilities for liquefied and synthetic natural gas exports to the U.S., and other energy-related tasks as may be appropriate.

The President and the Prime Minister will designate promptly senior officials from their respective governments to serve on this consultative mechanism.

MTN

The Prime Minister and the President expressed satisfaction over progress achieved between them in the Multilateral Trade Negotiations. They agreed that timely completion of a balanced MTN agreement involving all the participants would make a notable contribution to reducing inflation and improving the prospects for sustained and balanced growth in the world economy.

SALT

The President and the Prime Minister discussed prospects for the conclusion of a SALT II treaty with the Soviet Union and agreed that such a treaty would be a significant step forward in the important task of restraining the nuclear arms race and of developing a more stable basis for maintaining world peace and security. The President acknowledged the Prime Minister's contribution to the nuclear arms control debate and expressed his appreciation for Canada's support for the U.S. pursuit of SALT II negotiations.

Meeting With Prime Minister Menahem Begin of Israel

White House Statement. March 4, 1979

Over the past 4 days, the President and the Prime Minister, together with their advisers, have had 8 hours of intensive conversations. In a friendly, straightforward manner the two sides discussed the strategic situation in the Middle East and, in great depth, all the unresolved issues in the negotiations.

During the course of today's meetings, President Carter put forward suggestions designed to help resolve some of the outstanding differences between Egypt and Israel. Prime Minister Begin stated that he would seriously study these suggestions and consult with his colleagues.

In the meantime, President Carter will be in touch with President Sadat to review the situation in light of the American-Israeli discussions over the past few days.

———

The meeting today lasted 1 hour, 30 minutes. Those participating on the American side were: the President, the Vice President, Secretary of State Cyrus Vance, Secretary of Defense Harold Brown, the President's Assistant for National Security Affairs Zbigniew Brzezinski, White House Press Secretary Jody Powell, Ambassador Alfred Atherton, Assistant Secretary of State Harold Saunders, U.S. Ambassador to Israel Samuel Lewis, NSC staff member William Quandt, State Department Legal Adviser Herbert Hansell, and Adviser to the Secretary Edward Sanders.

Those participating on the Israeli side were: the Prime Minister, Israeli Ambassador to the United States Ephraim Evron, Director of the Prime Minister's Bureau Yehiel Kadishai, Military Secretary to the Prime Minister Brig. Gen. Ephraim Poran, Israeli Ambassador to the United Nations Yehuda Blum, Legal Advisor, Ministry of Foreign Affairs Meir Rosenne, Special Assistant to the Prime Minister Yehuda Avner, Press Secretary for the Prime Minister Dan Patir, and Minister of the Israeli Embassy Hanan Bar-On.

The President's Trip to Egypt and Israel

Announcement of the Trip.   March 5, 1979

President Carter has accepted invitations from Prime Minister Begin and President Sadat and will depart Washington on Wednesday afternoon for Egypt and Israel.

The President will arrive in Egypt on Thursday afternoon for talks with President Sadat. He will then fly to Israel on Saturday evening for talks with Prime Minister Begin.

The talks will focus on the peace process, regional security, and bilateral issues.

As he stated last Tuesday, the President believes that we must not allow the prospects for peace which seemed so bright last September to continue to dim and perhaps to vanish. If we do, the judgment of history and of our children will rightly condemn us.

NOTE: Press Secretary Jody Powell read the announcement at 12 noon to reporters assembled in the Briefing Room at the White House.

United States Ambassador to Czechoslovakia

*Nomination of Francis J. Meehan.
March 5, 1979*

The President today announced that he will nominate Francis J. Meehan, of Washington, D.C., to be Ambassador Extraordinary and Plenipotentiary of the United States to the Czechoslovak Socialist Republic. He would replace Thomas R. Byrne, resigned.

Meehan was born February 14, 1924, in East Orange, N.J. He received an M.A. from the University of Glasgow in 1945

and an M.P.A. from Harvard University in 1957. He served in the U.S. Army from 1945 to 1947.

Meehan was an administrative assistant at the Economic Cooperation Administration from 1948 to 1951, and served in Frankfurt, Hamburg, and at NATO between 1951 and 1956. From 1957 to 1959, he was an intelligence research specialist at the State Department, and from 1959 to 1961, he was a political officer in Moscow.

From 1961 to 1966, Meehan served in Berlin as economic officer, then political officer. From 1966 to 1967, he was Director of the State Department Operations Center, and from 1967 to 1968, he was Deputy Executive Secretary of the State Department.

From 1968 to 1972, Meehan was Deputy Chief of Mission in Budapest. From 1972 to 1975, he was counselor for political affairs in Bonn. He served as Deputy Chief of Mission in Vienna from 1975 to 1977, and since 1977 has been Deputy Chief of Mission in Bonn.

Hospital Cost Containment

*Remarks Announcing Proposed Legislation.
March 6, 1979*

THE PRESIDENT. Today I am submitting to the Congress one of the most critical anti-inflation legislative proposals that the Congress will ever consider, the Hospital Cost Containment Act of 1979.

Inflation remains our most serious domestic problem. It affects every person and every institution in this country. Inflation threatens the health not only of our domestic economy but of the basic structure of our own society.

The American people want me, and they want the other elected representatives, to take action, action that is strong, prompt, and effective. Ten years ago, the average cost of a stay of a patient in a hospital was $533. In just the past 2 years alone, this has increased by $317. It's a total now, for the average stay in the hospital of a patient, of $1,634.

These uncontrolled hospital costs are now doubling every 5 years.

When hospital costs go up, so do health insurance premiums. That pushes up consumer prices. It pushes up the budgets. It pushes up taxes at all levels of government. The only thing that goes down is the real income and the purchasing power of the American family.

Hospital cost containment is unique in two ways: It's uniquely severe in that it has been going up about twice the rate of other inflation in this country, and it is uniquely controllable if I and the Congress will act expeditiously and effectively.

We can eliminate thousands of unfilled, expensive hospital beds. We can stop subjecting people to unnecessary surgery and useless and unnecessary, very expensive medical tests. We can cut out pointless duplication of exceedingly expensive medical facilities.

Over the next 5 years, if this bill is passed, the American people will save some $53 billion. The American people will save $53 billion, of which $22 billion would be reduced Federal taxes and reduced Federal spending, without cutting back the quality of medical care at all.

Hospital cost containment will not be achieved without a difficult fight. Together with the Senators and the Members of Congress who are here with me today, I will lead the fight on behalf of the American people.

The hospital lobby defeated hospital cost containment legislation last year, although the Senate did pass an adminis-

tration-sponsored cost contained bill. That lobby opposing this legislation is even more determined this year, and it's equally well financed. But this year, we have a new Congress and a new opportunity to bring the outrageous increases in hospital costs under control.

The patience of the American people is wearing thin, and rightly so. It's time for the public interest to prevail. It's time for the Congress to demonstrate its commitment to the battle against inflation by promptly enacting the hospital cost containment of 1979.

We have with us today several congressional leaders who proved their commitment to this problem—the solution of it—last year. Senator Nelson is the sponsor this year of this legislation. Senator Talmadge, Senator Kennedy worked effectively last year to get the legislation through the Senate. Congressman Waxman, Congressman Rangel are two key subcommittee chairmen who will be responsible this year for action in the House in the commerce committee and, also, of course, in the Ways and Means Committee.

And others assembled behind me are equally determined that we shall control inflation by this very specific act that only the Congress can take this year to control inflation and to show our effectiveness and our determination to remove this blight from the American economic and societal scene.

Thank you very much.

I'd like to ask now if Senator Talmadge would like to make a comment, and then I'll call on others who have been so determined over many years to bring this very serious problem under control.

SENATOR TALMADGE. Thank you, Mr. President. I think you covered the issue very well. I have nothing to add to what you had to say, sir.

THE PRESIDENT. Thank you very much.

REPRESENTATIVE RANGEL. Mr. President, I'd just like to say that I support your efforts. I think that this time the patients, the consumers, who don't have trustees, will have the President of the United States and the Congress behind them.

And while I haven't studied your legislation, I am assured that it would make certain that the underserved communities are not adversely affected by the shrinkage in hospital services. And I thank you for that commitment.

THE PRESIDENT. Thank you very much, Congressman Rangel.

Congressman Rangel is chairman of the subcommittee in the Ways and Means Committee of the House. Congressman Waxman is chairman of the equivalent subcommittee in the commerce committee of the House.

REPRESENTATIVE WAXMAN. Well, Mr. President, I want to work with you to get this bill passed. It's an important measure for us to handle the inflation in health care costs. It's something that we need very badly. And it's going to be a tough fight, but I think we're going to win it, because I think the American people want it.

THE PRESIDENT. Very good.

SENATOR KENNEDY. Mr. President, I think we've seen or heard a great deal of rhetoric about dealing with the problems of inflation up on the Hill over the period of the last few weeks. I think this will be a key opportunity for the Members of Congress to do something about it, in supporting your efforts.

As you pointed out, this legislation was killed by special interests in the last Congress. And the American people will have a full opportunity to see who really is interested in dealing with the problems of inflation. And we're going to report that

legislation out very expeditiously and look forward to working with you and the administration in getting it achieved.

THE PRESIDENT. Last year, the floor leader, and this year's sponsor of the legislation, was Senator Gaylord Nelson. I wish you'd make a comment, Senator Nelson.

SENATOR NELSON. Mr. President, I want to commend you and the Secretary of HEW for designing what I think is a very creative piece of legislation, in the sense that it allows the hospitals to meet a standard rate of increase comparable to about the national rate, voluntarily, with no imposition of any controls whatsoever, as has been demonstrated by a number of States already can be done. Therefore, it's a voluntary effort, without any Federal interference, if the hospitals bring their own costs under control. I think it's a very good and creative approach.

And I would agree with Senator Kennedy that those who've been talking so much about economy will now have a chance to help balance the budget and reduce inflation.

THE PRESIDENT. Thank you very much.

We have many other very distinguished Members of the Congress here with us— Jack Javits, chairmen of several of the committees, Pete Williams. Does anyone else care to comment?

Congressman Staggers?

REPRESENTATIVE STAGGERS. I'll just say that last year we failed in our committee, but we did the best we could. And we certainly had an advocate in [Representative] Paul Rogers, very vociferous, who did everything in his power. And I tried to help him get it by the full committee. The subcommittee passed it and brought it before the full committee, but we could not get it by the full committee. We need your help, and we need Joe's [1] help, and we need anyone else that you can bring— *[laughter]*——

I would like to say in conclusion, good luck on your trip abroad. I wish you success.

THE PRESIDENT. Thank you very much.

SENATOR JAVITS. Mr. President, I probably interject a note of bipartisanship, which I think is urgently needed. It's everybody's fight. And secondly, I would hope very much that we will show the American people that quality care is not dependent upon waste. Squeezing out the waste and making the facilities over, rather than underutilized, dispensing with extra beds which aren't needed and other things which cost great sums of money will give the people a higher quality of care at prices they can more nearly afford.

THE PRESIDENT. Thank you.

Pete?

SENATOR WILLIAMS. Well, I just want to say this subject will have the highest priority in the Human Resources Committee, as I'm sure it will in the Finance Committee, our committee, and Senator Kennedy's subcommittee will start hearings immediately, Friday of this week; the highest priority, we'll stay on track.

THE PRESIDENT. Thank you.

REPRESENTATIVE RANGEL. I'd like to add, Mr. President, that the chairman of the full Committee of Ways and Means is prepared to schedule hearings on March 12, and I've checked with Chairman Waxman and understand there's been clearance there, so we'll start immediately.

THE PRESIDENT. Thank you. I might say that I appreciate the good wishes of Congressman Staggers on my trip to try to get a peace treaty in the Middle East.

––––––––––
[1] Secretary of Health, Education, and Welfare Joseph A. Califano, Jr.

But I would say within the most careful terms that successfully dealing with inflation in our country and around the world is of equal importance.

And this is a very profound subject with which we are dealing. I was not exaggerating when I said that continued inflation, if uncontrolled, will be a threat not only to our own American economy but to the basic societal structure of our country. So, domestic affairs and foreign affairs are intimately interrelated. And how forcefully and effectively the Congress deals with this issue will be a vivid demonstration of the will that our American people have to face difficult problems under trying circumstances.

And I feel reassured, as I always have since I've been in this office, in having the support and the confidence and a sense of partnership with the distinguished leaders of the Congress of the United States.

Thank you very much.

NOTE: The President spoke at 11:06 a.m. to reporters assembled in the Cabinet Room at the White House.

Hospital Cost Containment

Message to the Congress Transmitting Proposed Legislation.   March 6, 1979

To the Congress of the United States:

Inflation is America's most serious domestic problem. It affects every individual and every institution in the country, and it damages the health not only of our economy but of our society. The American people are demanding prompt action against inflation from their elected representatives—action that is strong, prompt, and effective.

One of the most important components of inflation is the soaring cost of hospital care, which continues to outpace inflation in the rest of the economy. A decade ago, the average cost of a hospital stay was $533. In just the past two years, the average cost of a hospital stay has increased by $317 to $1634 a day [1]—an increase of almost 24 percent.

Hospital cost inflation is uniquely severe. It is also uniquely controllable. It offers us one of our best opportunities to bring down the rate of overall inflation. This year, once again, I ask the Congress to join me in grasping that opportunity by enacting a tough program of hospital cost containment.

The Senate passed a Hospital Cost Containment bill last year, but the House did not complete action on it. The legislation I am transmitting to the Congress today is similar to the bill that passed the Senate last year. It responds to Congressional concerns that were raised during consideration of last year's bill, and it is strong enough to do the job.

The Hospital Cost Containment Act of 1979 will be one of the clearest tests of Congress' seriousness in dealing with the problem of inflation. Through this one piece of legislation, we can, at a stroke, reduce inflation, cut the Federal budget, and save billions of dollars of unnecessary public and private spending.

The legislation I am transmitting today will save $3.7 billion in fiscal year 1980. It will save $1.4 billion in the Federal budget, over $420 million in state and local budgets, and almost $1.9 billion in private health insurance and payments by individuals. Altogether, the potential savings that could result from this measure amount to some $53 billion over the next five years.

Because most hospital bills are paid by public or private insurance programs, the impact of hospital inflation is sometimes disguised. But that impact is painfully real for every American.

---

[1] EDITOR'S NOTE: The correct word is "stay," not "day."

When hospital costs rise, so do health insurance premiums. This means that workers take home smaller paychecks. It means that businesses are forced to charge higher prices. For example, over $140 of the cost of every automobile manufactured in this country goes to pay for health insurance premiums.

When hospital costs rise, so do health budgets of Federal, state and local governments. From 1969 to 1979, Federal government expenditures for hospital care rose by 330 percent. State and local government expenditures for hospital care rose by 140 percent. Sooner or later every taxpayer pays more to finance these increases.

When hospital costs rise, the elderly—who need more hospital services—are particularly hard hit. The Medicare hospital deductible paid by the elderly has almost quadrupled—from $44 in 1969 to $160 in 1979. If hospital cost inflation is not restrained, the deductible will reach $260 in 1984.

The inflationary rise in hospital costs is not inevitable. While there have been dramatic and desirable improvements in the quality of hospital services, much of the increase in hospital expenses has been unnecessary. No one's health is improved by the existence of thousands of unfilled hospital beds, by hospital stays that are unnecessarily long, by surgery and x-ray tests that are unneeded and sometimes harmful, by wasteful supply purchasing practices, by inefficient energy use, or by pointless duplication of expensive facilities and equipment. But these wasteful practices cost billions.

In the past, hospitals have had little incentive to be efficient. The hospital sector is fundamentally different from any other sector in our economy. Normal buyer-seller relationships and normal market forces do not exist. The consumer of

387

services—the patient—rarely pays the bill directly. Nor does the patient decide what services he or she will receive in the hospital. The person who makes those decisions—the physician—does not pay the bill either, and therefore has little or no incentive to see that services are provided in an efficient manner. Often, doctors do not even know the costs of the tests and x-rays they order.

There is a growing determination throughout the country to make hospitals efficient. Nine states—Colorado, Connecticut, Maryland, Massachusetts, New Jersey, New York, Rhode Island, Washington, and Wisconsin—have enacted mandatory cost containment programs. Hospitals in these states, which include many of the most renowned medical institutions in the world, have reduced cost increases substantially while continuing to provide care of high quality.

The legislation I am transmitting today would ensure that every hospital in this country has the incentive to be efficient. It establishes a reasonable goal for hospital cost inflation. It sets mandatory limits only for hospital cost inflation. It sets mandatory limits only for those hospitals which have been unable to meet this goal. Specifically, the Hospital Cost Containment Act of 1979 will:

—Establish an annual goal for the rate of hospital cost increases. This goal would reflect actual increases in the price of goods and services hospitals use, changes in population, and improvements in hospital services. In the event that the hospital industry does not, as a whole, meet the national goal, mandatory reimbursement limits on individual hospitals, also based in part upon the actual costs of goods and services, would go into effect on January 1, 1980.

—Exempt hospitals which individually meet the voluntary goal, have fewer than 4,000 admissions annually, are less than 3 years old, or have 75 percent of their patients enrolled in federally qualified health maintenance organizations.

—Exempt all hospitals in a state if the state on average met the voluntary goal or had an approved mandatory cost containment program.

—Provide for a system of bonuses and penalties to hospitals, depending on their efficiency relative to other hospitals of similar type and location.

—Include an adjustment for wage increases provided to nonsupervisory personnel in hospitals.

The Hospital Cost Containment Act of 1979 is reasonable and realistic. It permits a period of time for voluntary action, with mandatory limits only if voluntary action fails to meet the reasonable goals established in the bill. Under current assumptions the national goal will be 9.7 percent in 1979; it will be adjusted to reflect the actual increases in the price of goods and services hospitals use. In 1977, one-third of the Nation's hospitals—from all regions and of all types—had cost increases of 9.7 percent or less.

Even if triggered, the stand-by mandatory program holds regulation to a minimum. It does not interfere with the day-to-day management decisions of hospital administrators and physicians. Rather, the program establishes an overall limit on the rate of increase in reimbursements, permitting doctors and hospital administrators to allocate their own resources efficiently, responding to local needs and patient care concerns. The program changes the incentives under which hospitals have functioned, from a system in which hospitals receive guaranteed reimbursement for their services, whether efficiently provided or not, to one in which hospitals are rewarded or penalized for their actual efficiency and productivity.

Congress has debated hospital cost containment for almost two years. There is now no reason for delay. I call upon the Congress to demonstrate its commitment to the fight against inflation by promptly enacting the Hospital Cost Containment Act of 1979.

JIMMY CARTER

The White House,
    March 6, 1979.

Cancer Control Month, 1979

Proclamation 4643.   March 6, 1979

By the President of the United States of America

A Proclamation

Cancer strikes more than three-quarters of a million Americans a year.

Experts no longer believe that the disease occurs spontaneously, but suspect that it is largely a response to environmental factors. If these factors can be eliminated, substantially reduced, or counteracted, then some cancers may be prevented. Therefore, the trend toward increased emphasis in cancer prevention has accelerated during the past year.

Cause and prevention is not the entire story, however. Most cancers have a lengthy latent period. Over the next 20 or more years, the disease will manifest itself in millions of people who already have been exposed to cancer-causing agents. To overcome this serious threat, we must continue to seek effective methods of early detection and treatment.

The National Cancer Program, established in 1971, is being conducted devotedly and on a massive scale by both Federal agencies and non-Federal organizations under the aegis of the National Cancer Institute. A substantial portion of the Institute's research is in such areas as cell and molecular biology, virology, immunology and tumor biology. There is also growing attention and progress in continuing care activities, such as hospices and rehabilitation programs.

Despite our aggressive attack on cancer, current statistics reveal that about 395,-000 Americans will die of the disease in 1979. Only through unbending support of cancer research and control can we reverse this trend, and eventually reduce this figure to a minimum.

As a means of giving continued emphasis to the cancer problem, the Congress, by a joint resolution of March 28, 1938 (52 Stat. 148), requested the President to issue annually a proclamation setting aside the month of April as Cancer Control Month.

Now, THEREFORE, I, JIMMY CARTER, President of the United States of America, do hereby proclaim the month of April, 1979, as Cancer Control Month. I encourage the determination of the American people to meet the challenge of this critical health problem. And I ask the medical and health professions, the communications industries, and all other interested citizens to unite in public reaffirmation of our Nation's abiding commitment to control cancer.

IN WITNESS WHEREOF, I have hereunto set my hand this sixth day of March, in the year of our Lord nineteen hundred and seventy-nine, and of the Independence of the United States of America the two hundred and third.

JIMMY CARTER

[Filed with the Office of the Federal Register, 3:12 p.m., March 6, 1979]

Pan American Day and Pan American Week, 1979

Proclamation 4644.   March 6, 1979

By the President of the United States of America

A Proclamation

Each year the peoples of the Americas celebrate our common origins and continuing mutual ties. To the people of the United States Pan American Day commemorates the importance of mutual respect and cooperation which characterize the Inter-American system and its central institution, the Organization of American States.

No region of the world can boast a greater tradition of peace and tranquility among nations. No nations of the world have worked more consistently or harder to find solutions to the political and economic problems which they face in the world today. Our Organization of American States, the birth of which we will celebrate on April 14, has been and continues to be vital to this continuing effort.

In the past year alone, the Organization of American States has made important contributions to the welfare of the people of the hemisphere. It has helped to promote the cause of human rights and dignity in the Americas and to diffuse tensions in Central and South America.

The United States, on Pan American Day 1979, salutes the other nations of this hemisphere, and pledges its solidarity with them, and with the Organization of American States, in the continuing efforts to achieve the visionary democratic ideals of the founding heroes of our hemisphere. It is from these ideals that we derive our desire and our ability to cooperate for a common good and for the benefit of all our people.

Now, THEREFORE, I, JIMMY CARTER, President of the United States of America, do hereby proclaim Saturday, April 14, 1979 as Pan American Day and the week beginning April 15, 1979 as Pan American Week, and I call upon the Governors of the fifty States, the Governor of the Commonwealth of Puerto Rico, and appropriate officials of all other areas under the flag of the United States to issue similar Proclamations.

IN WITNESS WHEREOF, I have hereunto set my hand this sixth day of March, in the year of our Lord nineteen hundred seventy-nine, and of the Independence of the United States of America the two hundred and third.

JIMMY CARTER

[Filed with the Office of the Federal Register, 3:13 p.m., March 6, 1979]

The Albert Einstein Centennial

Message of the President.   March 6, 1979

March 14, 1979, marks the one hundredth anniversary of the birth of Albert Einstein—a man who profoundly influenced the shape of science and the course of history.

Albert Einstein set the tone for nearly a century of physics. He took a science that could no longer explain phenomena through the concepts of Newton and greatly expanded its viewpoint. His insights form the basis of much of our Twentieth Century comprehension and control of matter and energy. We are still following the path he outlined, and his genius remains a powerful stimulus and guide for future scientific discovery.

But Albert Einstein left his mark on humanity by more than just his brilliant scientific achievements. He will be remembered by all of us for the simplicity of his life, the humility and willingness with which he shared his talents and the dedication with which he pursued the greatest good of all mankind.

He believed that it was the nature of man to inquire thoroughly and endlessly. In a lecture at Oxford he stated: "The deeper we search, the more we find there is to know, and as long as human life exists, I believe it will always be so." And he believed such search was worthwhile. "The most incomprehensible thing about the world is that it is comprehensible," he said.

Einstein abhorred oppression. He fled from it in his native land and found freedom and friendship in the United States. His gentle nature led him toward pacifism, but he was at the same time deeply committed to the defense of freedom and rights of free people everywhere.

He sought and found order, understanding and beauty in the universe. He gave his findings freely to all the world. Our tallest tribute to him in this centennial year of his birth is to reaffirm our commitment to build vigorously on his enduring legacy of scientific discovery and social progress.

JIMMY CARTER

Intergovernmental Fiscal Assistance

Message to the Congress Transmitting Proposed Legislation. March 6, 1979

To the Congress of the United States:

Three years ago, at the lowest point of our Nation's deepest recession since the 1930's, many urban and rural communities were experiencing severe fiscal distress. The recession had weakened their revenue bases at the same time that their unemployment and service costs rose sharply.

In 1976, Congress enacted the Antirecession Fiscal Assistance program to provide emergency fiscal assistance to these distressed States and localities. When I came into office, I strengthened this program as part of my Economic Stimulus Package. Since 1976, approximately $3 billion has been spent under this program, which was effective in avoiding excessive layoffs of essential employees, service reductions and counterproductive tax increases in many areas.

Fortunately, nearly four years of national economic recovery have produced great progress in restoring the fiscal health of most of these communities. However, a number of communities still are experiencing severe fiscal problems and need more time to recover. The unexpected and abrupt termination of this program last fall has threatened many of these localities with painful reductions in vital services and with costly layoffs.

To assist these communities in regaining their financial stability and to protect State and local governments against unexpected future downturns in the economy, I am hereby transmitting to Congress the Intergovernmental Fiscal Assistance Amendments of 1979. These amendments outline a two-tier program, which meets the fiscal needs of our Nation's communities and which is consistent with the overall austerity of my budget.

The targeted fiscal assistance portion of this legislation (Title I), is designed only for those local governments with significant fiscal need—those urban and rural communities with unemployment rates of 6.5 percent or more. I am requesting that $250 million be spent in FY 1979 and $150 million in FY 1980 for this program. These funds would be distributed only to those local governments that face the most serious economic and fiscal problems—1231 local governments in FY

1979. No community will receive less than $20,000 annually or will be eligible if its per capita income exceeds 150 percent of the national average.

The legislation also provides a standby program of Federal fiscal assistance (Title II), to State and local governments through 1980. This assistance would be provided if national economic conditions deteriorate sharply, as evidenced by a national unemployment rate of 6.5 percent or higher in any quarter. In that event, governments with quarterly unemployment rates of 5 percent or more would receive aid. This program should not involve any budget outlays in the next two years. The Administration does not expect the national unemployment rate to rise above 6.5 percent. But, I urge the Congress to authorize this standby economic insurance program for State and local governments as a hedge against economic adversity and as an insurance policy in the event of an unexpectedly large downturn in the economy.

Our ability to act quickly to prevent the problems resulting from an economic downturn can reduce both the severity and duration of any downturn. Help that is delayed too long often takes effect after the crisis, and contributes to inflationary pressures during the economic recovery.

Together, this two-tier program addresses both immediate and prospective needs: a carefully targeted program for a limited number of fiscally strained communities and a more comprehensive standby program for State and local governments to protect them against an unexpectedly severe economic downturn. This proposal meets a pressing and immediate need and allows our Nation's communities to plan sensibly for the future. I urge Congress to enact this important legislation.

JIMMY CARTER

The White House,
    March 6, 1979.

Senior Executive Service Conversion Rights

*Memorandum From the President.
March 6, 1979*

Memorandum for the Heads of Executive Departments and Agencies

Subject: Senior Executive Service Conversion Rights of Career Appointees to Presidential Appointments

In my memorandum to you of November 8, 1978, I requested that you forward to me names of candidates for Inspector General positions who possess exceptional integrity and ability. This request reflected my desire to fill these Presidential appointments strictly on the basis of merit.

Some candidates for these positions, and for other Presidential appointments, come from the career service and are now occupying positions which will be placed in the Senior Executive Service. If they were to remain in their present assignment, they would be entitled to convert to the Senior Executive Service, but if they should accept Presidential appointment prior to the effective date of the SES, their entitlement to conversion is less clear.

It is unmistakably the intent of Congress that Inspector General positions will be filled on a merit basis. It is equally clear that the Congress intended to permit career members of the Senior Executive Service to accept Presidential appointments while retaining full SES career status and SES benefits (PL 95–454 § 3392(c) and 3393(b)).

To carry out the intent of Congress and to facilitate the merit appointment of able career executives to Presidential appointments during the few months before the Senior Executive Service goes into effect, I am hereby directing the heads of Departments and Agencies to take the following actions:

1. If a career executive in your agency has been nominated by me for a Presidential appointment and that executive is serving in a position which will be in the SES, the executive's *present* position should be officially designated SES immediately. (Such designation is authorized by Section 413 of PL 95–454, which became effective on October 13, 1978.)

2. The agency designation should be forwarded to the Office of Personnel Management for review and publication in the FEDERAL REGISTER.

3. On official designation by the agency, the career incumbent of this SES position should be given the option to convert to SES or to decline such conversion (PL 95–454 permits the incumbent up to 90 days to make a conversion decision, but the decision may be made at any time during that period. In this instance, the incumbent would need to make the decision before his/her Presidential appointment is confirmed by the Senate.)

4. If the career incumbent chooses to convert to SES, he/she may then elect to retain SES compensation and benefits as provided under PL 95–454 3392(c). Since SES compensation and benefits do not become effective before July 13, 1979, until that date the incumbent will serve under the Executive Level pay and benefit provisions.

If you need further guidance in carrying out this directive, the Office of Personnel Management will assist you.

JIMMY CARTER

Council on Wage and Price Stability

Message to the Congress Transmitting a Report.   March 7, 1979

To the Congress of the United States:

In accordance with Section 5 of the Council on Wage and Price Stability Act, as amended, I hereby transmit to the Congress the sixteenth quarterly report of the Council on Wage and Price Stability. This report contains a description of the Council's activities during the third quarter of 1978 in monitoring both prices and wages in the private sector and various Federal Government activities that may lead to higher costs and prices without creating commensurate benefits. It discusses Council reports, analyses, and filings before Federal regulatory agencies.

The Council on Wage and Price Stability will continue to play an important role in supplementing fiscal and monetary policies by calling public attention to wage and price developments or actions by the Government that could be of concern to American consumers.

JIMMY CARTER

The White House,
    March 7, 1979.

Senior Executive Service Pay Schedule

*Memorandum From the President.
March 7, 1979*

Memorandum for the Heads of Departments and Agencies

Subject: SES Pay Schedule

The Senior Executive Service (SES) will go into effect on July 13, 1979. The Civil Service Reform Act of 1978 provides for SES pay to range between the minimum rate for GS–16 of the General Schedule and EL–IV of the Executive Schedule. After consulting with the Director of the Office of Personnel Management I have determined that there shall be six salary rates for SES. Agency heads will, subject to the requirements of law, set the rate to be paid to each individual. In doing so agencies should be aware that the amounts payable to an individual before October 1, 1979, may be limited to the pay cap contained in Public Law 95–391. I am establishing the following as the initial SES Schedule:

ES–1 = $44,756
ES–2 = $46,470
ES–3 = $48,250
ES–4 = $50,100
ES–5 = $51,450
ES–6 = $52,800

The Director of the Office of Personnel Management will issue guidance and prescribe regulations for the administration of SES pay.

JIMMY CARTER

The President's Trip to Egypt and Israel

Remarks on Departure From the White House. March 7, 1979

THE VICE PRESIDENT. *Mr. President, Rosalynn, and friends:*

You leave tonight, Mr. President, on perhaps the most important and difficult mission of your Presidency. You seek a peace vital not only to the people of the Middle East but to the people of our own Nation and to all mankind.

There is no challenge more urgent than seeking that peace, for as the Bible tells us, it is the peacemakers who are blessed. And you, Mr. President, Prime Minister Begin, and President Sadat are three such peacemakers.

Your efforts are even more than a pivotal moment in the history of the Middle East, for as a poet once put it, "Peace hath her victories no less renowned than war."

Each generation bears two fundamental responsibilities to the next: One is to lay down our lives, if need be, for the things that we treasure; the other is to work ceaselessly so that our children will not be asked to make that sacrifice. Both duties are sacred. Both require courage. Both are filled with grave risks.

There are statesmen whose tasks it is to go to the brink of war. For others, their courage is tested by the challenge to go to the brink for peace. In the end, the truest measure of our humanity is how we rise to the second challenge.

Mr. President, tonight, as 6 months ago, you meet that demanding measure. Please know that you have our love, our prayers. The prayers of all humanity are with you this evening as you search for that nobler victory, the victory of peace.

THE PRESIDENT. Nothing could give me more encouragement and a more gratifying sense than to have surround me here not only the Vice President but the distinguished Members of Congress.

I leave tonight on a new mission in the service of the oldest of human dreams— the dream of peace. And nowhere is this hope for peace more fervent, more alive than in the Middle East; nowhere is the path to its realization more difficult; nowhere might the price of failure be more terrible.

Peace remains the goal of President Sadat and Prime Minister Begin and of the great peoples of Egypt and of Israel. I know that they share my determination that these long negotiations will bring fruit.

The Middle East has suffered too much and too long from war and from the fear of war. Arabs and Israelis alike must now understand that bloodshed and deprivation and death can never settle their differences, can never be the path toward renewal and hope.

For the first time in a generation, peace in the Middle East has come within reach. President Sadat's visit to Jerusalem, his great and courageous reception by Prime Minister Begin, the reciprocal visit by the Prime Minister to Egypt—all opened the way toward possible progress. At Camp David, we then worked together for 13 days to forge a political framework within which their differences might be resolved.

Our negotiations have been and are based on the idea that peace can only be achieved when we meet the legitimate needs of all those who are affected by the conflict.

Real peace will not come with a single treaty, important as it would be. But a treaty between Egypt and Israel is an indispensable step toward the broader comprehensive peace that we all seek.

Negotiation is a long and tedious process—I know from personal experience. But there are times when making peace demands more courage than making war. I believe that President Sadat and Prime Minister Begin possess that special kind of courage and that they possess, as well, the vision and the statesmanship to redeem the great hope which they themselves have helped to create.

So, it is with hope that I depart, hope tempered by sober realism. As a friend of Egypt and a friend of Israel, we will do our best to help them achieve the peace that they have paid for in blood many times over.

In doing this, in seeking to lay the basis for a stable and a peaceful Middle East, we will also be serving our own deepest national interests and the interests of all the people of the world.

I know that in this endeavor, I take with me the prayers and the good wishes of the American people. In the difficult work that lies ahead, I will draw strength and sustenance from those worldwide prayers and from your support.

Thank you very much. Goodbye, everybody, I'm on my way.

NOTE: The exchange of remarks began at 6:10 p.m. on the South Lawn of the White House.

International Development Cooperation Administration

Message to the Congress on the Proposed Agency. March 7, 1979

To the Congress of the United States:

As required by Title III of the International Development and Food Assistance Act of 1978, I am writing to inform you of the steps I have taken and propose to take to strengthen the coordination of U.S. economic policies affecting developing countries.

I propose to create an International Development Cooperation Administration (IDCA) as an independent agency within the executive branch. The IDCA Director would report both to me and to the Secretary of State, and would serve as our principal international development advisor. The Director would receive guidance concerning the foreign policy of the U.S. from the Secretary of State. He would submit his budget to the Office of Management and Budget after consulting with the Secretary.

The principal responsibilities of the IDCA Director would be to ensure that the varied instruments by which the U.S. contributes to development abroad are utilized effectively and in concert, and that the efforts of U.S. bilateral programs and those of the multilateral development institutions are complementary. To carry out those responsibilities, the IDCA Director would establish and control the budgets and policies of IDCA's several component agencies, and make recommendations to me concerning the appointment and removal of senior officials of each component. IDCA would contain:

• The Agency for International Development.

• The Overseas Private Investment Corporation, of whose Board of Directors the IDCA Director would become Chairman.

• A new Institute for Technological Cooperation designed to promote scientific and technological research in the developing countries, which I have proposed through legislative amendment.

In addition:

• Lead responsibility for policy and budget for our voluntary contributions to the following international organizations will be transferred to IDCA: UN Development Program; UNICEF; OAS Technical Assistance Funds; UN Capital Development Fund; UN Educational and Training Program for Southern Africa; UN/FAO World Food Program; FAO Post Harvest Losses Fund; and UN Disaster Relief Organization.

• Existing arrangements with regard to the multilateral development banks (MDBs) would be modified so that the Secretary of the Treasury will consult with the IDCA Director in the selection of candidates for the U.S. Executive Director and Deputy Executive Director positions in the MDBs, and the IDCA Director will advise U.S. Executive Directors on MDB projects and program proposals.

• The IDCA Director would take part in executive branch decisionmaking concerning such matters affecting international development as trade and monetary issues; he would speak to the relative priority of development and other U.S. objectives in respect of these and other issues. He would replace the AID Administrator as Chair of the Development Coordination Committee.

• I have directed OMB to review alternative organizational arrangements respecting all ACTION programs, and will consider the possible relation of Peace Corps to IDCA in light of the conclusions of that review.

I intend to propose the creation of IDCA under the reorganization authority renewed by Congress in 1977. In addition, various administrative and program adjustments will be made by Executive order and agency delegation.

I believe these steps will substantially strengthen the coordination of U.S. policies affecting the developing world, and will lead to a more coherent strategy of development and the more effective use of the various bilateral and multilateral instruments by which the U.S. can encourage the growth of developing economies. I am pleased that these actions and proposals are similar to those proposed last year by the late Senator Hubert H. Humphrey. I look forward to joining with you to put them into operation.

JIMMY CARTER

The White House,
    March 7, 1979.

NOTE: The text of the message was released on March 8.

National Credit Union Administration Board

Nomination of Lawrence Connell, Jr., To Be a Member. March 8, 1979

The President today announced that he will nominate Lawrence Connell, Jr., of Washington, D.C., to be a member of the National Credit Union Administration Board for a 6-year term. The President also announced that on confirmation, Connell will be designated Chairman of this Board.

Connell was born September 30, 1936, in New York City. He received an A.B. in economics from Harvard College in 1958, a J.D. from Georgetown University in 1966, and an M.A. in economics from Trinity College in 1973.

Connell worked in the Office of the Comptroller of the Currency from 1958 to 1968, beginning as a field examiner and ending as Deputy Regional Administrator of National Banks in New England. In 1962–63 he participated in the reorganization of the internal operations of the Washington office of the Comptroller of the Currency. He also participated in the first study of competition and branch banking by that office in 1963.

In 1968 he joined Hartford National Bank and Trust Co. as vice president and counsel, was promoted to cashier, and then became secretary of Hartford National Corp. He also served as an officer and director of a number of its subsidiaries.

From 1975 to 1977, Connell was bank commissioner of the State of Connecticut, and served on the Governor's Commission to Study Uniform Consumer Credit Code. In 1977 he was appointed Administrator of the National Credit Union Administration by President Carter.

National Railroad Passenger Corporation

Nomination of M. Athalie Range To Be a Member of the Board of Directors. March 8, 1979

The President today announced that he will nominate M. Athalie Range, of Miami, Fla., to be a member of the Board of Directors of the National Railroad Passenger Corporation for a term expiring July 18, 1981. Range was nominated for this position last session, but was not confirmed before the Senate adjourned.

She was born November 7, 1918, in Key West, Fla. She attended Booker T. Washington High School in Miami.

Range became involved in public service as president of the Liberty City PTA, where she led a building drive for schools in black areas. She served as a local and county PTA president for 16 years.

In 1965 Range was elected to the Miami City Commission. She was the first black and the second woman elected to that commission. She introduced ordinances including more stringent handgun controls and updating housing and fire codes.

In 1971 Range was appointed secretary of the Florida Department of Community Affairs. She resigned in 1973 to return to private business as owner and funeral director of the Range Funeral Home in Miami.

Range is a member of the board of directors of the Florida Legal Aid Commission and a member of the Southern Growth Conference Committee Policy Board. She is president of the Martin Luther King Boulevard Development Corp. and the Sixty-second Street Development Corp.

Department of Commerce

Nomination of Mary P. Bass To Be Inspector General.   March 8, 1979

The President today announced that he will nominate Mary P. Bass, of New York City, to be Inspector General of the Department of Commerce.

Bass was born July 10, 1935, in Detroit, Mich. She received a B.A. from the University of Chicago in 1954 and a J.D. from the University of Chicago Law School in 1957.

From 1957 to 1959, Bass was an attorney with the legal aid department of the Jewish Family and Community Service in Chicago. From 1966 to 1968, she was with the opinions and legislation division of the New York City Law Department. From 1969 to 1970, she was executive assistant to the director of the Office of Collective Bargaining.

From 1970 to 1972, Bass was with the appeals division of the Law Department, and from 1972 to 1973, she was head of the education section of the general litigation division. In 1973 she was assistant-in-charge of the family court division.

Since 1973 Bass has been general counsel and vice chancellor for legal affairs for the New York City Board of Higher Education. In this capacity, she is the chief legal officer of the board and of City University of New York.

Department of Transportation

Nomination of Frank S. Sato To Be Inspector General.   March 8, 1979

The President today announced that he will nominate Frank S. Sato, of Annandale, Va., to be Inspector General of the Department of Transportation.

Sato was born in March 16, 1929, in Puyallup, Wash. He received a B.A. in accounting from the University of Washington in 1953.

From 1953 to 1965, Sato was with the U.S. Air Force Auditor General's Office, serving in various positions, finally as Chief of the Logistics Audits Division. Since 1965 he has been with the Office of the Assistant Secretary of Defense (Comptroller), serving as Director for Special Activities Audits, Director for Audit Operations, Director for Defense Agencies Audits, and Deputy Comptroller for Audit Operations. Since 1974 he has been Deputy Assistant Secretary of Defense for Audit. He also serves as Director of the Defense Audit Service.

Sato is national president-elect of the Association of Government Accountants and is active in accounting and auditing associations.

National Aeronautics and Space Administration

Nomination of Eldon D. Taylor To Be Inspector General.   March 8, 1979

The President today announced that he will nominate Eldon D. Taylor, of Annandale, Va., to be Inspector General of the National Aeronautics and Space Administration.

Taylor was born July 29, 1929, in Holdenville, Okla. He received a B.A. and M.A. in public administration from American University. He served in the U.S. Air Force from 1951 to 1954.

From 1955 to 1959, Taylor was with the Navy's Bureau of Ordnance and

Bureau of Naval Weapons in a variety of assignments related to budgeting. He joined NASA in 1960 and worked on the initial planning and budgeting for space flight.

From 1962 to 1970, Taylor was with NASA's Office of Space Sciences and Applications as Director of the program review and resources management organization. From 1970 to 1973, he was a member of an OMB task force established to organize the Environmental Protection Agency, and served as EPA Deputy Assistant Administrator for Resources Management, where he was responsible for budgeting and accounting.

In 1973 Taylor joined the National Science Foundation as Deputy Assistant Director for Administration, and since 1974 he has been Assistant Director for Administration. He is responsible for management functions, including personnel, accounting, management analysis, and administrative budget.

Small Business Administration

Nomination of Paul R. Boucher To Be Inspector General. March 8, 1979

The President today announced that he will nominate Paul R. Boucher, of Vienna, Va., to be Inspector General of the Small Business Administration.

Boucher was born April 13, 1942, in Cambridge, Mass. He received a B.S. from Merrimack College in 1963 and a J.D. from Suffolk University Law School in 1969.

From 1964 to 1970, Boucher was a special agent and assistant senior resident agent for U.S. Naval Intelligence in Bos-

ton. From 1970 to 1972, he was staff assistant for legal matters at Naval Investigative Service Headquarters in Alexandria, Va. From 1972 to 1974, he was a trial attorney with the Criminal Division of the Justice Department.

From 1974 to 1975, Boucher was Assistant General Counsel of the U.S. Government Printing Office. Since 1975 he has been Deputy Section Chief of the General Crimes Section at the Justice Department's Criminal Division. In that capacity, he was selected to organize and direct task forces created by the Attorney General to investigate allegations of violations of Federal criminal law by United States intelligence agencies.

Interstate Commission on the Potomac River Basin

Appointment of Lois K. Sharpe as a Member. March 8, 1979

The President today announced the appointment of Lois K. Sharpe, of Falls Church, Va., as a member of the Interstate Commission on the Potomac River Basin. She replaces Loretta Nimmerrichter, resigned.

Sharpe, 72, holds a Ph. D. in geology from Northwestern University. She is a member of the Fairfax County Water Authority and a consultant to the National Science Foundation and the Office of Technology Assessment. She is a member of the U.S. Geological Survey's Advisory Committee on Water Data for Public Use.

Sharpe was with the League of Women Voters for 16 years, serving as a staff specialist on water resources and as environmental department coordinator.

White House Conference on Library and Information Services

Appointment of 12 Members of the Advisory Committee. March 8, 1979

The President today announced the appointment of 12 persons as members of the Advisory Committee of the White House Conference on Library and Information Services. They are:

REBECCA T. BINGHAM, director of media services for the Jefferson County (Kentucky) Public Schools;

C. E. CAMPBELL BEALL, of Martinsburg, W. Va., chairman of the West Virginia Library Commission;

ROBERT LEE CHARTRAND, of Chevy Chase, Md., senior specialist in information sciences for the Congressional Research Service of the Library of Congress;

SHIRLEY ECHELMAN, of Chicago, executive director of the Medical Library Association;

ROBERT M. HAYES, of Sherman Oaks, Calif., dean of the Graduate School of Library and Information Science at UCLA;

WARREN G. HILL, of Denver, Colo., executive director of the Education Commission of the States;

NICHOLAS JOHNSON, of Iowa City, chairman of the National Citizens Committee for Broadcasting and a former Commissioner of the Federal Communications Commission;

ROSE MARIE LOPEZ, of Phoenix, a teacher in the bilingual transitional program of Phoenix Elementary School District No. 1;

JUSTIN H. McDEVITT, of Richmond, Va., rehabilitation counselor at the Virginia Commission for the Visually Handicapped;

MARGARET C. McNAMARA, a founder and now national chairman of the Reading is Fundamental (RIF) program;

EDWARD J. MEADE, JR., deputy to the vice president and program officer in the Ford Foundation's division of education and research;

CARLTON J. THAXTON, director of the division of public library services of the Georgia State Department of Education.

Digest of Other White House Announcements

The following listing includes the President's public schedule and other items of general interest announced by the White House Press Office and not included elsewhere in this issue.

March 3

The President met at the White House with Zbigniew Brzezinski, Assistant to the President for National Security Affairs.

Prime Minister Menahem Begin of Israel and Mrs. Begin had dinner in the Residence with the President and Mrs. Carter. Following the dinner, the President and the Prime Minister met privately.

March 4

Prior to meeting with Prime Minister Begin and members of the Israeli delegation, the President met at the White House with Vice President Walter F. Mondale, Secretary of State Cyrus R. Vance, Secretary of Defense Harold Brown, and Dr. Brzezinski. After meeting with the Prime Minister, the President spoke by telephone with President Anwar al-Sadat of Egypt, and then met with a group of Members of Congress.

March 5

The President met at the White House with:

—Dr. Brzezinski;

—Prime Minister Begin;

—a group of officials of environmental organizations;

—Vice President Mondale.

The President spoke by telephone with President Sadat of Egypt and Prime Minister Begin of Israel.

March 6

The President met at the White House with:

—David L. Aaron, Deputy Assistant for National Security Affairs;

—Frank B. Moore, Assistant to the President for Congressional Liaison;

—the Democratic congressional leadership;

—Dr. Kenneth B. Clark, psychologist, author, and educator;

—James T. McIntyre, Jr., Director of the Office of Management and Budget;

—a group of State and local officials to discuss the proposed intergovernmental fiscal assistance legislation;

—Secretary of the Treasury W. Michael Blumenthal.

The President has asked Joan Mondale and Secretary of Labor Ray Marshall to head the U.S. Delegation to the inaugurations of Presidents-elect in Venezuela, on March 11 and 12, and in Brazil, on March 14 and 15. Vice President Mondale, who was scheduled to head the delegation, will remain in Washington while the President travels to the Middle East. The White House also announced that the President called Venezuelan President-elect Luís Herrera Campins and Brazilian President-elect João Baptista de Oliveira Figueiredo this afternoon to express his regrets that Vice President Mondale would be unable to attend their inaugurations. He wished them and their new administrations success, and he conveyed his personal wish that our Governments will continue to work closely together on issues of common concern. The Vice President looks forward to making an official visit to Venezuela and Brazil at a mutually convenient time.

March 7

The President met at the White House with:

—Mr. Aaron;

—Mr. Moore and members of the Budget Task Force;

—Vice President Mondale, Stansfield Turner, Director of Central Intelligence, Hamilton Jordan, Assistant to the President, and Mr. Aaron;

—Vice President Mondale, Secretary Blumenthal, G. William Miller, Chairman of the Board of Governors of the Federal Reserve System, Charles L. Schultze, Chairman of the Council of Economic Advisers, and Mr. McIntyre;

—a group of Members of Congress prior to his departure for Egypt.

In addition to Joan Mondale and Secretary of Labor Ray Marshall, who will head the U.S. Delegation to the inaugurations of Presidents-elect Herrera Campins of Venezuela and Figueiredo of Brazil, the President has asked the following people to serve as members of the delegation:

REUBIN ASKEW, of Key Biscayne, Fla., former Governor of Florida;

MAURICE FERRE, of Miami, Fla., mayor of Miami;

DR. ARNOLD GONZALES, of Corpus Christi, Tex., member, Texas State Legislature;

NEIL HARTIGAN, of Chicago, Ill., senior vice president, First National Bank of Chicago and former Lieutenant Governor of Illinois;

ROBERT KEEFE, of Washington, D.C., president, the Keefe Co.;

LUIS LAUREDO, of Coral Gables, Fla., president, Lauredo and Associates of Miami and president, National Coalition of Cuban-Americans;

DAVID LIZARRAGA, of Los Angeles, Calif., president, the East Los Angeles Community Union (TELACU);

FRANKLIN DELANO LOPEZ, of San Juan, Puerto Rico, chairman, Puerto Rico Democratic Party;

LIBBY MAYNARD, of Flint, Mich., vice chairperson, Michigan Democratic Party.

March 8

The President has declared a major disaster for the State of Hawaii as a result of severe storms and flooding, beginning about February 15, which caused extensive public and private property damage.

NOMINATIONS SUBMITTED TO THE SENATE

The following list does not include promotions of members of the Uniformed Services, nominations to the Service Academies, or nominations of Foreign Service officers.

Submitted March 5, 1979

FRANCIS J. MEEHAN, of the District of Columbia, a Foreign Service officer of Class one, to be Ambassador Extraordinary and Plenipotentiary of the United States of America to the Czechoslovak Socialist Republic.

WILLIAM MAYS BURKHALTER, of Maryland, to be a member of the Renegotiation Board, vice Rex M. Mattingly, resigned.

Submitted March 6, 1979

JOYCE HENS GREEN, of Virginia, to be United States District Judge for the District of Columbia, vice Howard F. Corcoran, retired.

Withdrawn March 6, 1979

JOYCE HENS GREEN, of Virginia, to be United States District Judge for the District of Columbia, vice a new position created by P.L. 95–486, approved October 20, 1978, which was sent to the Senate on March 2, 1979.

Submitted March 7, 1979

GEORGE P. KAZEN, of Texas, to be United States District Judge for the Southern District of Texas, vice a new position created by P.L. 95–486, approved October 20, 1978.

WILLIAM RAY OVERTON, of Arkansas, to be United States District Judge for the Eastern District of Arkansas, vice a new position created by P.L. 95–486, approved October 20, 1978.

LAWRENCE CONNELL, JR., of the District of Columbia, to be a member of the National Credit Union Administration Board for the term of 6 years (new position).

NOMINATIONS—Continued

Submitted March 7—Continued

M. ATHALIE RANGE, of Florida, to be a member of the Board of Directors of the National Railroad Passenger Corporation for a term expiring July 18, 1981, vice Mary J. Head, term expired.

MARY P. BASS, of New York, to be Inspector General, Department of Commerce (new position).

FRANK SABURO SATO, of Virginia, to be Inspector General, Department of Transportation (new position).

ELDON D. TAYLOR, of Virginia, to be Inspector General, National Aeronautics and Space Administration (new position).

PAUL ROBERT BOUCHER, of Virginia, to be Inspector General, Small Business Administration (new position).

CHECKLIST OF WHITE HOUSE PRESS RELEASES

The following listing contains releases of the White House Press Office which are not included in this issue.

Released March 6, 1979

News conference: on proposed hospital cost containment legislation—by Alfred E. Kahn, Advisor to the President on Inflation, and Secretary of Health, Education, and Welfare Joseph A. Califano, Jr.

News conference: on their meeting with the President to discuss proposed intergovernmental fiscal assistance legislation—by Stuart E. Eizenstat, Assistant to the President for Domestic Affairs and Policy, Gov. Brendan Byrne of New Jersey, Mayors Richard Hatcher of Gary, Ind., Henry Maier of Milwaukee, Wis., Lee Alexander of Syracuse, N.Y., John Rousakis of Savannah, Ga., Kenneth Gibson of Newark, N.J., and Joseph Toner, president of the Democratic County Officials

Fact sheet: proposed intergovernmental fiscal assistance legislation

Released March 7, 1979

Comments: support for the proposed hospital cost containment legislation, received by the White House from citizens and organizations

Advance text: remarks on departure from the White House for the trip to Egypt and Israel

CHECKLIST—Continued

Released March 8, 1979

Announcement: nomination of George P. Kazen to be United States District Judge for the Southern District of Texas

Announcement: nomination of William Ray Overton to be United States District Judge for the Eastern District of Arkansas

ACTS APPROVED BY THE PRESIDENT

Approved March 7, 1979

H.R. 1902_____ Public Law 96-2
An act to amend the Bank Holding Company Act Amendments of 1970.

S. 37_____ Public Law 96-3
An act to repeal a section of Public Law 95-630.

Editor's Note

The President's Trip to Egypt and Israel

On Friday, March 9, the President was in Alexandria, Egypt. Releases and announcements issued on the trip will be printed next week.

Cairo, Egypt

Remarks of President Anwar al-Sadat and President Carter at the Welcoming Ceremony. March 8, 1979

PRESIDENT SADAT. *My dear friend and brother, President Carter:*

On behalf of 40 million Egyptians, I welcome you in the cradle of civilization. You are held here with the highest esteem, as one of the greatest statesmen of our time. Your courage and wisdom are paralleled only by the strength of your commitment to morality and justice.

Never before has an American President been so firm in his devotion to the cause of world peace and the universal brotherhood of man. Never before has a statesman with your awesome responsibility devoted so much of his time and effort to the noble task of promoting peace and cooperation among nations.

This is a historic and courageous mission. On your departure yesterday, you said that you were undertaking it with hope and sober realism. We share your hope and pray for the success of your endeavor. You will find the Egyptian people firm in their dedication to a just and comprehensive peace in the area. We are determined to enable our Palestinian brothers to realize their national rights and regain their freedom.

In the days ahead, we will be working together to make these cherished hopes a living reality. We want to build a viable structure for peace that's based on the rule of law and legitimacy.

The reception you were accorded today by our masses is a testimony of the affection they have for you and for every American. Let us vow to cement the bonds of friendship and cooperation between our nations.

May God Almighty guide our steps and lighten our way and, God willing, we shall overcome.

Thank you.

PRESIDENT CARTER. *Salaam alaikum.* [Peace be upon you.]

Hundreds of thousands of Egyptians lined the streets this afternoon to express their deepest feelings—feelings not of personal friendship or admiration for me, or even for their noble and beloved leader, President Sadat, but their deepest feeling expressed hundreds of times over was a genuine desire for peace.

The greeting of peace has a special and urgent meaning for all of us today. I come to you, Mr. President, in the service of peace. You receive me in a spirit of peace.

We meet to resume together the sacred work of building peace.

It's an honor for me and my wife to be reunited with you, Mr. President, and your wife, and with our many other friends with whom we've worked so diligently in recent months.

It's a pleasure to be with you this time in Cairo. We bring with us the respect and the good wishes for President Sadat and for the people of Egypt from the tens of millions of people who live in the United States of America.

I've come to the Middle East to advance the cause of peace between Egypt and Israel. A treaty between these two great nations would be a beginning, not an end. It would bring us much closer to the broader goal we seek—a real peace, a comprehensive peace, a peace that would reflect the legitimate needs of all those who have suffered so deeply during the last 30 years of conflict, enmity, and war.

It would also be the beginning of a new chapter in the long history of Egypt, one in which the energies of all Egyptians can at last be turned in full force to the human task of building a future of dignity and hope.

I know from experience how deeply President Sadat wants that kind of future. In my many hours of conversation with him, I've learned to respect him as a man of great courage with a passion for peace. He has spoken eloquently, but more importantly, he has acted boldly and decisively.

In his electrifying trip to Jerusalem in November of 1977, President Sadat fully committed himself to the goal of a just and lasting peace. That was also our goal at Camp David, where President Sadat, Prime Minister Begin, and I agreed on a framework for a comprehensive peace and on the outlines of a treaty between Egypt and Israel. And that remains the goal of the talks that will continue today.

Our hope is to achieve an agreement which is honorable, just, and which provides security for each of the negotiating parties. But above all, our purpose is to achieve a peace that will last.

If the promise of peace is to be fully realized for the people of Israel and Egypt, then others must be encouraged to join the process of resolving differences through negotiations and accommodations.

The United States will work with any and all parties who are committed to these principles of genuine peace and security. As the relations among us grow stronger, we can all work more effectively to bring stability to the Middle East region as a whole.

President Sadat has written, and I quote, "No problem should ever be regarded as insuperable." In recent months, we've overcome many problems that once seemed insurmountable. I pray that, with God's help, we may remove the remaining obstacles to the conclusion of a peace treaty between Egypt and Israel and continue the negotiations with great determination on other issues, in accordance with the Camp David agreements.

The most important condition for success has already been met—the sincere conviction on both sides that peace is preferable to war, that differences can better be settled by the exercise of reason than by the spilling of blood.

The people of Egypt have spilled much blood. And in the eyes of the women, in particular, on the streets and in the balconies in the last few minutes, we've seen a desire and a hunger and a prayer that their sons and their husbands would never again have to suffer in a cause of combat and war.

President Sadat and I, in the car together, repledged ourselves not to disappoint those here, in Israel, among the Palestinians, among the countries also presently in a state of war, who depend on us and others to bring the long unrealized but deeply desired state of peace to this region.

Like you, Mr. President, I am dedicated to the cause of peace. Like you, Mr. President, I'm determined to persevere. Our common dedication, our common determination is rooted in the soil of common religious truth. Many signs said, "We believe in God." You and I, Mr. President, believe in God. We believe in truth, that truth takes different forms. But its underlying message is the same—it's a message of love, of faith, and of peace.

As we work together in the crucial discussions that are about to begin, let us pray God, in the words of the Christian Gospel, "to guide our feet into the way of peace."

Thank you very much.

NOTE: The exchange began at 3:30 p.m. on the terrace of Qubba Palace, where the President stayed during his visit to Cairo.

Earlier in the day, President Sadat met the President at Cairo International Airport, and the two Presidents traveled by motorcade to the palace for the ceremony.

Cairo, Egypt

White House Statement Following a Meeting Between President Carter and President Sadat.   March 8, 1979

The discussions tonight began at 6:40 p.m. between President Carter and President Sadat. At about 7:10 p.m., the two Presidents were joined by Vice President Mubarak and Prime Minister Khalil on the Egyptian side and Secretary of State Cyrus Vance and Assistant to the Presi-

dent for National Security Affairs, Dr. Zbigniew Brzezinski, on the American side. These discussions concluded at 9:05 p.m.

The talks this evening focused almost entirely upon the unresolved issues and the negotiation of a treaty of peace between Egypt and Israel.

NOTE: The meeting was held at Tahra Palace. Following the meeting, the President returned to Qubba Palace.

Train Trip From Cairo to Alexandria, Egypt

Informal Exchange With American Television Correspondents.   March 9, 1979

PRESIDENT SADAT. This is my Georgia.

Q. It is what?

PRESIDENT SADAT. My Georgia.

PRESIDENT CARTER. This is President Sadat's home province.

Q. He says it is his Georgia.

PRESIDENT CARTER. That is right. He lives about a half hour from here.

I think it's obvious that these people want peace.

Q. How are the talks going, sir?

PRESIDENT CARTER. I think very well. We still have some problems, obviously. But President Sadat genuinely wants peace. So do I. So does Prime Minister Begin. We don't know yet what will happen until we get through with the talks.

Q. Do you have a feeling that you can wrap up this end of it on the scheduled trip?

Q. Will you be able to leave on schedule, sir?

PRESIDENT CARTER. I don't know.

Q. Maybe stay another day?

PRESIDENT CARTER. I don't know. I really don't know.

407

Q. Mr. President, at where you are at the moment, would you think that you and Sadat will have an agreement by the time you leave?

PRESIDENT CARTER. That's hard to predict. Prime Minister Khalil and Secretary Vance are talking about language and specifics. President Sadat and I have always been basically in agreement on strategic matters. And that's the situation now. We'll get together in Alexandria with the whole group to see what differences still remain.

Q. You said, sir, before you came out, that you didn't think it would be easy. Is it any less difficult now that you're here?

PRESIDENT CARTER. That's hard to judge. We obviously came on this trip without any assurance of success. But I know two things: One is that the people of Israel and Egypt want peace. That's obvious. And I believe that the leaders of Israel and Egypt want peace.

Q. Mr. President, if it's possible that you may have to stay 1 more day, can we conclude that the talks are not going as you thought they might?

PRESIDENT CARTER. I don't think that's easy to predict, because if they should go well or shouldn't go well, 1 day in my life wouldn't be very significant, compared to the prospect of improving chances for peace. So, I don't believe that that would be a good measurement.

Q. If you went 1 day later, would that foul things up on the Israeli side, with the arrangements that they've made, sir?

PRESIDENT CARTER. No. I don't think there's any likelihood at all that I would get to Israel a day later. I think what it will do is to take to Israel either an encouraging prospect or one that would require some substantial modifications. And we really wouldn't know what the chances were until we got through with our discussions in Israel.

Q. Are you in communication with the Israelis while you are here?

PRESIDENT CARTER. Only through the Ambassadors. But there's really nothing to report to the Israelis yet, because we're in the process of discussing the specific terms on which there is a disagreement still. And I think it'll be after our meetings in Alexandria this evening and tomorrow that we'll know how close we are together. Obviously, we'll go to Israel with some differences still remaining. And I'll do the best I can to resolve those differences.

Q. Were you surprised by the Egyptian counterproposal?

PRESIDENT CARTER. No. We've had a very clear picture of the Egyptian position, both from the statements and attitudes of Prime Minister Khalil in Camp David and, also, my own private conversations and communications with President Sadat. So, there have not been any surprises.

Q. President Carter, how far apart do you presently regard the Israelis and Egyptians to be on the question of Palestinian autonomy?

PRESIDENT CARTER. Well, the question of Palestinian autonomy will have to be resolved in the talks that would commence 1 month after the Israeli-Egyptian peace treaty. The Palestinian autonomy description is best summarized in the Camp David agreements, and both President Sadat and Prime Minister Begin have reconfirmed their commitment to me that all of the Camp David agreements will be carried out. And the details, obviously, will have to be worked out over a period of a year after the peace treaty is signed.

Q. Mr. President, just to clear up one thing.

PRESIDENT CARTER. Yes.

Q. You expect it's possible that you may arrive in Israel 24 hours late?

PRESIDENT CARTER. No. I think we'll get to Israel on time.

Q. Even though you are having more difficulties here than perhaps you'd imagined?

PRESIDENT CARTER. Well, as I said, I have not been surprised after I got here. I've not been disappointed nor pleasantly surprised. It's about what we anticipated. But my expectation is that we'll get to Israel on time.

Q. Thank you very much, Mr. President.

PRESIDENT CARTER. Thank you.

Q. President Sadat, could we just ask you a question, sir? Could you characterize the talks for us so far? How do you think they've been doing, sir?

PRESIDENT SADAT. Well, let me say this: We had a 3-hours' talk yesterday, very intensive talks. I think there are progress, for sure there are progress. And I think it is time now that we can say that the signing of the agreement is not so far at all. From my side, as you know, I'm doing my best, and I shall be doing my best. But in all candor, without the intensive effort by President Carter and the American people and the Congress behind him, we would have never reached this. Let me hope that everything will be clear in this visit.

Q. What is the greatest problem, sir? What is the biggest difficulty?

PRESIDENT SADAT. Well, you know, I commented last night after the 3-hours' talk with President Carter, Vance, and Brzezinski, and the Vice President and the Prime Minister was with me. Let me tell you this: We must get rid of the distrust, because, unfortunately, there are still some shades of distrust until this moment, and it is not from the Egyptian side. We have dropped all complexes and

everything through my visit to Jerusalem. It is a word here, a word, but I don't see any difficulty in reaching an agreement upon the main principal issues.

And, as I told you, if it was not the effort and the perseverance of President Carter, we couldn't have achieved this. And it is needed now in this precise moment to reach the final result.

Q. President Sadat, on the basis of your discussions with President Sadat [Carter] and what you know from him of the Israeli position, are you now ready to sign an agreement?

PRESIDENT SADAT. I am ready to sign the agreement, yes.

Q. There will be nothing more required for Egypt to do or for Israel to do before an agreement can be consummated?

PRESIDENT SADAT. I can speak for myself, not for the Israelis. For myself, I am ready.

Q. Without making any significant changes in your basic position?

PRESIDENT SADAT. I beg your pardon?

Q. Without making any changes in the positions you held before President Carter came here?

PRESIDENT SADAT. Well, let me tell you this: In the very frank discussions we had last night, I found, really, that there is no obstacles in the way, because there is only a misunderstanding about the main issues. But apart from this—and this will be President Carter's, I mean, goal to do—yes, I think we are on the verge of an agreement.

Q. For example, sir, are you now satisfied with the question of full Palestinian autonomy in the occupied territories?

PRESIDENT SADAT. Well, let me tell you this: Let us always put emphasis on the Camp David documents. This is a great achievement, and maybe you heard me before saying that let us try and defuse the explosive situation. Camp David documents didn't defuse only the explosive situation but has opened the way to a comprehensive settlement. So, adhering to the Camp David two documents, for sure we shall be reaching an agreement.

Q. What is the main obstacle now, President Sadat? What is the main problem you still must solve?

PRESIDENT SADAT. I think—and it may appear, I mean, ridiculous—some words here or there, only some words here or there.

Q. Can that be resolved by tomorrow night, by Saturday night?

PRESIDENT SADAT. Between me and President Carter, be sure of one thing: Whatever arises between me and President Carter, we are identical, and we shall continue to be identical.

CORRESPONDENT. Thank you very much, Mr. President.

NOTE: The exchange began at 11:05 a.m. on board the train. Participants included Walter Cronkite of CBS News, John Chancellor of NBC News, and Peter Jennings of ABC News.

Following the trip, the President went to Ras-al-Tin Palace, where he stayed during his visit to Alexandria.

Alexandria, Egypt

White House Statement Following a Meeting Between President Carter and President Sadat. March 9, 1979

President Sadat and President Carter continued their discussions of the peace process and other matters of mutual interest. The discussions lasted from about 7:05 p.m. until 8 p.m. and were conducted in the atmosphere of friendship and candor.

Participants in the meeting were:

On the American side:

President Carter

Secretary of State Cyrus Vance

Secretary of Defense Harold Brown

Zbigniew Brzezinski, Assistant to the President for National Security Affairs

Harold Saunders, Assistant Secretary of State for Near Eastern and South Asian Affairs

Ambassador Herman Eilts

Ambassador at Large Roy Atherton

Bill Quandt, NSC staff

On the Egyptian side:

President Sadat

Prime Minister Mustafa Khalil

Vice President Husni Mubarak

General Hassan Ali, Defense Minister

Ahmed al-Sayegh, Economics Minister

Ambassador Ashraf Ghorbal

Hassan Kamel, Chief of Protocol

Butrus Ghali, Minister of State for Foreign Affairs

Secretary Vance and Prime Minister Khalil met this afternoon from 3:30 until 5 p.m. at the Palestine Hotel. Their discussions focused on the unresolved issues in the peace treaty negotiations.

The two Presidents will attend a working luncheon tomorrow at Mena House, near Cairo, to be followed by additional discussions.

President Carter will depart Egypt for Israel tomorrow evening.

NOTE: The meeting was held at Mamoura Palace.

Alexandria, Egypt

Toasts at a Dinner Honoring President Carter. March 9, 1979

PRESIDENT SADAT. . . . for the very noble cause of peace. My people have welcomed President Carter yesterday and today. For me, I want to tell you how happy I am and how proud I am to have our dear friend and brother among us on Egyptian soil. All I can say is this: Let us raise our glass for a great President of a great nation, and to Mrs. Carter.

PRESIDENT CARTER. On a rare occasion in a person's life and on extremely rare occasions in the history of all humankind, there comes along a man or person with extremely great courage, a man who has the sensitivity to understand a complicated issue, who recognizes the deep feelings that exist because of historical animosities and hatreds, who has himself suffered through tortuous political evolutionary times, even revolutionary times, and one who's seen his own people suffer on many occasions from combat and war. And when all others are too timid, too fearful—or whose horizons are too narrow, fear to act—that great leader acts and, therefore, inspires others to join with him in a common, noble effort.

President Anwar al-Sadat is such a man. He has aroused the admiration of the entire world. He has become a hero in many. nations, and he deserves this esteem and admiration completely.

I have never seen so many people as were along our route today from Cairo to Alexandria. And it was the most impressive political event that I have ever witnessed—hundreds of thousands of Egyptian citizens, millions of Egyptian citizens. The number itself was impressive, but the most impressive aspect of this tremendous outpouring of emotion was their love and respect for their President and their obvious appreciation for our common search for peace.

I look upon President Sadat as a partner, sharing with him a common past, a common present, and a common future. But I also look upon him as a brother. The closeness with which he and I work

and communicate, consult and plan and act, is reassuring to me. And I can well understand, now that I know him better, how he could have made such a momentous decision to slice through generations of hatred and, through a great expression of generosity, attempt to heal wounds.

I also have a great admiration for the Egyptian people. Tomorrow I will speak to your parliamentary leaders and make a more substantive description of my hopes for the future. But tonight I would say that I bring from 200 million Americans to 40 million Egyptians a heartfelt expression of the same kind of friendship and the same kind of mutual purpose that binds me with your President. I said today, as we watched the adoring crowds shouting out their slogan of a pledge of their heart and soul for President Sadat, that I would certainly hate to run against him for a public office in Egypt. But I would add very quickly, that I would also hate to run against him for a public office in the United States of America. [*Laughter*] I think it's accurate to say that he's, perhaps, the most popular person in our own country.

Tonight he and I share great hopes for the future. We recognize the difficulties that we face. Some of the distrust, some of the difficulties in communication, some of the ancient animosities still exist. But we share common faith in two things: One is that the people of Israel and Egypt pray for peace, and the other one is that the leaders of Israel and Egypt pray for peace.

This will be a first step only to a common peace for all the citizens of the Middle East and for the redressing of wrongs, for the realization of dreams and hopes. And I would like to offer a toast tonight to my friend, to a great and courageous leader who, himself, with the strength of his character, the nobility of his ideals and the purpose—which I share—is responsible above all others for this kindling of new hope in the hearts of those that join with us in this common effort.

To President Anwar al-Sadat, to the people of Egypt, to his lovely wife, and to peace.

NOTE: President Carter spoke at approximately 9:45 p.m. at Ras-al-Tin Palace. Because of technical difficulties, the White House Press Office was unable to provide a complete transcript of President Sadat's toast. The press release contains only the concluding portion, as printed above.

Prior to the dinner, the President received the Nile Collar award from President Sadat.

Cairo, Egypt

Address Before the People's Assembly.
March 10, 1979

I also come before you in the name of God, as a partner with my great and good friend, your President, Anwar al-Sadat, to address the Egyptian people through the Members of this People's Assembly of Egypt.

My heart is full as I stand before you today. I feel admiration for the land of Egypt, and I feel a profound respect for the people of Egypt and for your leader, President Sadat, a man who has reached out his strong hand to alter the very course of history.

And I also feel a deep sense of hope as I consider the future that will unfold before us if we have the will and the faith to bring peace. And we have that will and faith, and we will bring peace.

As a boy, like other schoolchildren all over the world, I studied the civilization of Egypt. In the last few days, I have at last seen the legacy of that great civilization with my own eyes. As a citizen of a very young country, I can only marvel at

the 7,000-year heritage of the Egyptian people, whom you represent.

For most of the last 500 years, Egypt suffered under foreign domination. But Egypt has again taken her place among the world's independent countries and has led the resurgence among the Arab people to a prominent place among the nations of the world. I'm very proud of that great achievement on your part.

Tragically, this generation of progress has also been a generation of suffering. Again and again, the energies of the peoples of the Middle East have been drained by the conflicts among you—and especially by the violent confrontations between Arabs and Israelis. Four wars have taken their toll in blood and treasure, in uprooted families, and young lives cut short by death.

Then, 16 months ago, one man, Anwar al-Sadat, rose up and said, "Enough of war." He rose up and said, "Enough of war. It is time for peace."

This extraordinary journey of President Sadat to Jerusalem began the process which has brought me here today. Your President has demonstrated the power of human courage and human vision to create hope where there had been only despair.

The negotiations begun by President Sadat's initiative have been long and arduous. It could not have been otherwise. The issues involved are complex, and they are tangled in a web of strong emotion. But among the people of Egypt and the people of Israel alike, the most powerful emotion is not hostility. It is not hatred. It is a will to peace. And more has been accomplished in 1 year of talking than in 30 years of fighting.

As the peace process has moved forward—sometimes smoothly, more often with pain and difficulty—the Government of Egypt has been represented by able diplomats, fully attuned to Egypt's national interests and continually mindful of Egypt's responsibilities to the rest of the Arab world.

Last September, the course of neogtiations took the President of Egypt and the Prime Minister of Israel to Camp David, in the wooded mountains near the Capital of the United States of America.

Out of our discussion there came two agreements: A framework within which peace between Israel and all her neighbors might be achieved, and the legitimate rights of the Palestinian people realized—and also an outline for a peace treaty between Egypt and Israel, in the context of a comprehensive peace for the Middle East.

Those agreements were rooted in United Nations Security Council Resolution 242, which established the basic equation between an Arab commitment to peace and Israeli withdrawal in the context of security. The treaty which is now being negotiated between Egypt and Israel reflects those principles.

Since the two agreements were signed, we have been working to bring both of them to fruition. The United States has served as a mediator, working to solve problems—not to press either party to accept provisions that are inconsistent with its basic interests.

In these negotiations, a crucial question has involved the relationship between an Egyptian-Israeli treaty and the broader peace envisioned and committed at Camp David. I believe that this body and the people of Egypt deserve to know my thinking on this subject.

When two nations conclude a treaty with one another, they have every right to expect that the terms of that treaty will be carried out faithfully and steadfastly. At the same time, there can be little doubt that the two agreements reached at

Camp David—negotiated together and signed together—are related, and that a comprehensive peace remains a common objective.

Just in recent days, both Prime Minister Begin in Washington and President Sadat here in Egypt have again pledged to carry out every commitment made at Camp David.

Both leaders have reaffirmed that they do not want a separate peace between their two nations. Therefore, our current efforts to complete the treaty negotiations represent not the end of a process, but the beginning of one, for a treaty between Egypt and Israel is an indispensable part of a comprehensive peace.

I pledge to you today that I also remain personally committed to move on to negotiations concerning the West Bank and the Gaza Strip and other issues of concern to the Palestinians and also to future negotiations between Israel and all her neighbors. I feel a personal obligation in this regard.

Only the path of negotiation and accommodation can lead to the fulfillment of the hopes of the Palestinian people for peaceful self-expression. The negotiations proposed in the Camp David agreements will provide them with an opportunity to participate in the determination of their own future. We urge representative Palestinians to take part in these negotiations.

We are ready to work with any who are willing to talk peace. Those who attack these efforts are opposing the only realistic prospect that can bring real peace to the Middle East.

Let no one be deceived. The effect of their warlike slogans and their rhetoric is to make them in reality advocates of the status quo, not change; advocates of war, not peace; advocates of further suffering, not of achieving the human dignity

413

to which long-suffering people of this region are entitled.

There is simply no workable alternative to the course that your nation and my nation are now following together. The conclusion of a treaty between Israel and Egypt will enable your government to mobilize its resources not for war, but for the provision of a better life for every Egyptian.

I know how deeply President Sadat is committed to that quest. And I believe its achievement will ultimately be his greatest legacy to the people he serves so well.

My government, for its part, the full power and influence of the United States of America, is ready to share that burden of that commitment with you. These gains which we envision will not come quickly or easily, but they will come.

The conclusion of the peace treaty that we are discussing will strengthen cooperation between Egypt and the United States in other ways. I fully share and will support President Sadat's belief that stability must be maintained in this part of the world, even while constructive change is actively encouraged. He and I recognize that the security of this vital region is being challenged. I applaud his determination to meet that challenge, and my government will stand with him.

Our policy is that each nation should have the ability to defend itself, so that it does not have to depend on external alliances for its own security. The United States does not seek a special position for itself.

If we are successful in our efforts to conclude a comprehensive peace, it will be presented, obviously, each element of it, to this body for ratification.

It is in the nature of negotiation that no treaty can be ideal or perfect from ei-ther the Egyptian or the Israeli point of view. The question we've faced all along, however, is not whether the treaty we negotiate will meet all the immediate desires of each of the two parties, but whether it will protect the vital interests of both and further the cause of peace for all the states and all the peoples of this region. That is the basic purpose and the most difficult question which we are resolved to answer.

Such a treaty, such an agreement, is within our grasp. Let us seize this opportunity while we have it.

We who are engaged in this great work, the work of peace, are of varied religious faiths. Some of us are Moslems; some are Jews; some are Christians. The forms of our faith are different. We worship the same God. And the message of Providence has always been the same.

I would like to quote the words of the Holy Koran: "If thine adversary incline towards peace, do thou also incline towards peace and trust in God, for he is the one that heareth and knoweth all things."

Now I would like to quote from the words of the Old Testament: "Depart from evil and do good; seek peace, and pursue it."

And now I would like to quote from the words of Jesus in the Sermon on the Mount: "Blessed are the peacemakers, for they shall be called the children of God."

My friends, my brothers, let us complete the work before us. Let us find peace together.

Thank you very much.

NOTE: The President spoke at 1 p.m.

Following his address, the President hosted a luncheon for President Sadat at the Mena House in Giza.

Giza, Egypt

**Remarks of President Carter and President
Sadat Following a Meeting. March 10, 1979**

PRESIDENT CARTER. President Sadat and
I have a few words to say about this visit.
First of all, on behalf of the American people and myself personally, I want to express my deep thanks to President Sadat
and to the people of Egypt for a welcome
that has been exhilarating to me and
which I will never forget.

We have had hours of discussion about
the issue of peace. It's obvious to me that
the Egyptian people, from their tremendous outpouring of welcome to me and to
President Sadat, genuinely want peace.

It's equally obvious to me that President Sadat and the people of Egypt and
Israel are determined to carry out all the
provisions, all the agreements made at
Camp David, not only for peace between
Israel and Egypt but for a full and comprehensive peace involving the realization of the rights of those who have suffered so long, and a step-by-step progres-
sion toward peace between Israel and all
her neighbors.

We have resolved some difficult issues
here. Difficult issues still remain to be resolved.

I will leave here this afternoon, going to
Israel to meet with Prime Minister Begin
and the officials of the Israeli Government.
I'm hopeful that the differences which
still remain can be resolved.

Thank you very much.

PRESIDENT SADAT. Let me seize this opportunity to express really how happy
my people and me were to receive
President Carter, for whom we hold great
esteem and great love, the man who has
really, through his patience, perseverance,
morale, and principles, has already
achieved more than 59 percent of the
whole problem, one of the most complicated problems in the whole world.

We are happy to receive President
Carter and Mrs. Carter, and we are
happy also to ask them to convey to our
friends, the American people, who supported my initiative wholeheartedly—we
ask him to convey to them our gratitude.
And in this precise moment, I prefer to
say only that we had a very fruitful talk.
Exactly as President Carter stated, we
have overcome some of the difficulties.
Some other issues are to be settled.

And in the name of the Egyptian people, my name, and my wife's name, we
wish to President Carter and Mrs. Carter
all the best wishes and fulfillment and
achievement in his visit to Israel.

Thank you.

NOTE: The President spoke to reporters at 4:35
p.m. on the terrace at Mena House, the hotel
where he and President Sadat held their meeting.

Following the exchange, the two Presidents
toured the Pyramids and the Sphinx and then
went to Cairo International Airport for the
departure ceremony.

Tel Aviv, Israel

**Remarks of President Yitzhak Navon and
President Carter at the Welcoming Ceremony.
March 10, 1979**

PRESIDENT NAVON. Mr. President and
Mrs. Carter, *shalom* and welcome to
Israel.

In the name of the people of Israel, it
is a great pleasure and privilege, together
with my wife, to greet you and the distinguished officials who have come with
you, with all our hearts in sincere friendship and profound appreciation.

We cherish these feelings towards you
personally and also as a representative of

the leading nation in the free world, the great and noble democracy of the United States, which has done so much to deserve our admiration and gratitude.

You come to us, Mr. President, on a unique mission for a goal which is dear to all of us and for which you have mustered all your energy, your dedication, and your leadership, to put an end to hatred and hostility and to open a new page of peace in the troubled annals of the peoples of this area.

At this moment we do not know as yet what tidings you carry with you from your visit to our great neighbor, Egypt. Does the dove of peace, which has emerged from the ark, carry an olive branch in its beak, or will it have to wait some time longer until the waters of the flood are abated from off the Earth, so that it can at last find a resting place for its feet?

Mr. President, you are not unaware, I'm sure, of the differences of opinion in our country in the sphere of foreign policy and national security. Two sentiments, however, are shared by all sections of our people: a sincere and ardent desire for true peace, and the profound conviction that in order to achieve that peace, Israel has made enormous sacrifices above and beyond what might have been expected or demanded of her.

These sacrifices, as you well know, take the form of very tangible things—withdrawal of our forces from strategic territories three times as large as the area of Israel, the evacuation of vitally important airfields and oil resources, the evacuation of flourishing villages. These concessions, once made, are irrevocable. In this situation, it is easy to understand our desire to ensure that the peace treaty we sign shall guarantee a true and permanent peace

and shall not contain elements liable to endanger the peace and our security.

During your visit here, you will meet the people which feel at one and the same time deep concern and a great hope. It is our prayer that your visit will remove that concern and justify that hope.

My dear President and Mrs. Carter, 5 years ago you toured our country as private citizens. Today Divine Providence has brought you here on an historic mission. I hope it will not be long before you can come to Israel again and see that the seedlings of peace which you planted will have grown into sturdy trees bearing plentiful fruit on every hill and valley in Israel, in Egypt, and the entire area.

Once again, a most hearty welcome.

PRESIDENT CARTER. *Mr. President, Mr. Prime Minister, and the people of Israel:*

As the elected leader and the representative of the people of the United States of America, I am indeed honored and pleased to set my foot on the soil of the free nation of Israel.

I come to you as a fellow worker in the cause of peace. I know how much this cause means to the people of this land. No people in all history have suffered more from violence than the Jewish people. The State of Israel was born as a refuge from that violence. You, after four wars in three decades, every Israeli citizen still knows at first hand what it is to grieve for a fallen loved one or a friend.

As I walked down the ranks of representatives of your military forces, certainly among the finest fightingmen on Earth, I said a silent prayer to God that none of these men nor their compatriots would ever again have to give their lives in war.

As Prime Minister Begin has said many times, Israel truly wants peace. Of that there can be no doubt. And I feel absolutely certain, after my experience of the past 3 days, that the people of Egypt fully share that desire for peace.

During the last 3 days I have spent many hours discussing with President Sadat what could be the final details of a treaty of peace in the context of comprehensive peace for the whole region. Prime Minister Begin and I will soon begin discussing the same details with the same end in mind—to seek in the present situation the means and the will to take this next crucial step toward a just and lasting peace for the Middle East.

We have come a great distance together—perhaps a greater distance than many would have dreamed of. Under the strong and courageous leadership of Prime Minister Begin, the Government of Israel has been willing to make difficult decisions, as your President has just said, all along the way. I need not add that it would be a tragedy to turn away from the path of peace after having come so far.

I have good reason to hope that the goal can now be reached. But, of course, the ultimate choice lies where those choices have always lain—with the chosen representatives of the people who have suffered directly from so many years of destruction and bloodshed. I look forward to completing the urgent business at hand on this brief visit.

I bring with me the best wishes of the American people and also the greetings of President Sadat, whom I left no longer than 1 hour ago, and the hopes for peace of the entire world.

The task we are striving to accomplish together demands more than reason, more, even, than will. It demands faith. For in a very real sense, the task of building peace is a sacred task. In the words of the Midrash, "Peace is important, for God's name is Shalom." Let us have *shalom.* Let us make peace together.

NOTE: The exchange began at 8:15 p.m. at Ben Gurion International Airport.

Following his remarks, the President went by motorcade with Prime Minister Menahem Begin to the entrance to the city of Jerusalem, where he participated in a welcoming ceremony at the site of a monument to those who died in the 1948 Israeli war for independence. He was greeted by Mayor Teddy Kollek at the ceremony.

Later in the evening, the President and Mrs. Carter had dinner with Prime Minister and Mrs. Begin at the Begin residence. Following the dinner, the President and the Prime Minister met privately, and then the President went to the King David Hotel, where he stayed during his visit to Israel.

Jerusalem, Israel

Remarks of the President and Prime Minister Menahem Begin Following a Meeting. March 11, 1979

THE PRESIDENT. This morning and this afternoon I, the Secretary of State, Secretary of Defense, National Security Adviser, and others have met with the Defense Council of the Government of Israel and with the Prime Minister to discuss the issues that still remain to be resolved between Israel and Egypt.

It was a friendly meeting, a frank meeting, a thorough meeting. We have not yet reached a final agreement. Important issues still remain to be resolved. All of us are dedicated to continue with our best efforts to reach success.

THE PRIME MINISTER. Thank you, Mr. President.

Ladies and gentlemen of the press, I subscribe to the statement made by the President. We had a long meeting with a break for luncheon. I can assure you, and my colleagues in the Cabinet say, it is one of the best they have ever eaten. And we are grateful to the President and his advisers that they honored not only our meeting but also our luncheon downstairs. And then after the luncheon we continued our talks, which were very serious; I suppose also very friendly, as the President said.

Now, we decided to call a Cabinet of the full—excuse me, we decided to call a session of the full Cabinet for tonight at 10 o'clock. And tomorrow the President will meet with our full Cabinet at 8 o'clock in the morning. So, certain issues concerning the peace treaty between us and Egypt will be clarified and decided upon by the Cabinet during the nocturnal session, so that we will be able tomorrow to give replies on those certain issues to the President.

These are the latest developments. Now we have to go to change and be prepared for the dinner in honor of our dear guest, the President of the United States.

THE PRESIDENT. Thank you, Mr. Prime Minister. That was a good statement.

[At this point, the Prime Minister addressed the press in Hebrew and then answered the following questions.]

THE PRIME MINISTER. I have to shave and change and prepare my speeches. You know, I make my speeches from memory. I don't write my speeches, and I have to decide not only what to say but what not to say. And if I ignore the second problem, then I have no time for the first.

REPORTER. Are we any closer to a peace treaty after these meetings?

THE PRIME MINISTER. I cannot answer that question. I would like to say in truthfulness and give this information to your audiences respectively in the States and in Europe: We are dealing with very serious issues concerning the peace treaty, and of course we look for a solution. But the issues are very serious, and therefore we decided to convene a nocturnal session of the Cabinet, to start at 10 o'clock.

If you consider the possibility that the session of the Cabinet lasts between 3 and 4 hours—and maybe it will even be longer—then you can understand that we shall sit until the small hours of the morning. And then at 8 o'clock, the Cabinet, the whole Cabinet, will meet with the President, and then we shall be able—I will be in a position on behalf of the Cabinet to tell the President about our decisions.

I do assume that after that, Secretary Vance will go to Cairo. I am not sure and it is not for us to decide, but it is my assumption, only an assumption.

Q. Did President Sadat request any changes to the American proposals?

THE PRIME MINISTER. I cannot speak on behalf of President Sadat. Now you will understand the delicacy of the situation. I cannot divulge anything as far as the contents of our talks are concerned. What I can say to you is the President and the Secretary of State and all their advisers, the American delegation, brought to us certain proposals from Cairo. And there are other issues on which, for the time being, there are no proposals but only ideas, and we shall deal tonight with all of them. And tomorrow we shall inform the Knesset about our decisions.

Q. Is there any likelihood that President Carter will prolong his stay here?

THE PRIME MINISTER. This question you must put to the President.

NOTE: The President spoke at approximately 5:40 p.m. to reporters assembled outside the Prime Minister's office, where the meetings were held. As printed above, the Prime Minister's exchange with the reporters follows the White House press release.

Earlier in the day, the President met with President Navon at the Israeli President's residence. Following the meeting, President Carter was met by Prime Minister Begin, and they went to Yad Vashem, the memorial to Jews killed during World War II. At Yad Vashem, the President visited the Hall of Names, which contains books listing the names of known victims of the Holocaust, and then went to the Hall of Remembrance for a wreathlaying ceremony.

The President and the Prime Minister then visited Mount Herzl, site of the cemetery where many Israeli war heroes and national leaders are buried.

Jerusalem, Israel

Toasts at a Dinner Honoring President Carter. March 11, 1979

PRESIDENT NAVON. *Mr. President and Mrs. Carter, Prime Minister and Mrs. Begin, very distinguished guests from near and far:*

It is my privilege to greet you in Jerusalem, the Eternal City of David.

We have met here this evening to honor an illustrious statesman, his distinguished and devoted wife, and his great country.

The United States of America is great, not only because of its scientific, technological, and military strength but also because of the profound human values that are deeply implanted in the hearts of its people. It is a beacon of hope for all those who walk in darkness.

Greatness in a man or a nation is no easy thing. It takes supreme wisdom to

refrain from exerting all the power at the disposal of the strong. To be leader of a nation which is responsible in large measure for the destiny of the entire world, a man needs profound faith and constant prayer. It is our profound conviction, Mr. President, that you have within you that fountain of living waters from which you can draw a never-failing source of inner faith.

By your side is your devoted helpmate, a loyal partner in your joys and sorrow. In voting for her forever, if you will permit me a personal note, you have realized one of your favorite watchwords, "Why Not the Best?". [*Laughter*]

In your life, my dear Rosalynn, you have also known the dark side of the Moon; hence your particular sensitivity towards those to whom fate has not been kind. Your heartfelt involvement in the welfare of the individual does not distract your attention from the problems of the great world, which is, in fact, composed of individuals. The Talmud has forbidden us to pronounce all the praises of any person in his presence. I will be content, therefore, to say no more than this: that all those who have met you have surrendered unconditionally to your sincerity, nobility, and warm personality.

Mr. President, one thread runs through the entire history of our people. It is a long and epic story of the few against the many, a prolonged struggle to preserve our spiritual character and identity against powerful forces that threaten to destroy us.

If it is not easy to be great, it is even harder to be small. We strive for two aims which, on the face of it, appear to be contradictory—to be equal, but different. We continue to cherish our national aims, to gather in our scattered people from the four corners of the Earth, to solve our social and economic problems, to make the desert bloom, and, above all, to build a society founded on the spiritual heritage of our fathers and universal human values.

We have worked hard to achieve these aims, even in times of stress and war. But we are profoundly convinced that only true peace will enable us to achieve these ideals. It is my sincere and earnest prayer, Mr. President, that the efforts you have devoted here towards that end and the efforts devoted by the Prime Minister, Mr. Begin, and the Government, will be crowned with success.

Mr. President and Mrs. Carter, while it is irrelevant now, I read that both of you shook hands, while running for the governorship of Atlanta, you shook, in 4 years, 600,000 hands. Yesterday we added a few more. Today we wanted to save you some, but the President went down and shook a few hands more, so I lost count of it. [*Laughter*] Anyhow, I can tell you those hands stretched to you and those whom you did not shake are very friendly hands.

Ladies and gentlemen, I will ask you all, please, to join me, to stand up and join with me in drinking a toast to our illustrious guests, the President of the United States and his honored lady, to the success of his noble mission, to the family, to Miss Lillian, to the friendship between our peoples, and to the progress and prosperity of the United States of America.

Lechayim.

PRIME MINISTER BEGIN. *Mr. President of the United States; Mrs. Carter; Mr. President of the Republic of Israel; Mrs. Navon; Mr. Speaker; Mr. President of the Supreme Court and Justices of the Supreme Court; our masters and teachers,* *the chief rabbis; members of the Cabinets of the United States and of Israel; members of the Knesset; the leader of our loyal opposition; the Chief of Staff of our Army; and Mr. Mayor of our capital city; ladies and gentleman; honorable guests:*

Mr. President, on behalf of the Government and the people of Israel, I welcome you to the eternal capital of the land of Israel, the indivisible Jerusalem.

The saga of America is living in our hearts. What is the saga of America? Thirteen colonies, ruled by a great nation, but by a foreign power, rising in revolt against a regular army, including mercenary troops, going through a horrible winter of suffering and deprivation, fighting on, ultimately winning the day and receiving the surrender of General Cornwallis, proclaiming its independence, explaining to the world why that separation took place.

That Declaration of Independence, written 13 years before the Declaration of Rights of Man and Citizen during the French Revolution, and—I, a Jew, dare say—which reads as a chapter of the Bible; proclaiming those self-evident truths for which man, almost in every generation, has to rise and fight; giving a constitution which is working for 200 years, and working well, which helps overcome every crisis in democracy; and then three times in 60 years saving all mankind from the dangers of militarism, from the peril of the most horrible tyranny ever known in the annals of mankind, and from Communist domination over the world—indeed saving thrice all mankind in a short period of 60 years.

The saga of America, to which in 25 years 2½ million Jews emigrated, one of the greatest phenomenon of people's wanderings; 100,000 per year, from the *shtetl*, bringing with them and transferring with them all the traditions of the *shtetl*, knowing no word of English, speaking their old language; and then giving birth to a new generation, to another generation; and then turning into the mightiest Jewish community in the history of our people since the days of Alexandria during the Second Temple, and contributing so much to the civilization and culture and development of the United States, and helping so much the State of Israel.

Since the famous words were written to America and about it, "Give us the poor," well if not for that miracle of those 25 years, millions more of Jews would go the way you and I, Mr. President, saw today when we visited Yad Vashem.

May I say, although it's a festive dinner, that when we both heard the children singing, [*in Hebrew*] "I believe with a perfect faith in the coming of the Messiah, and though He tarry, I shall wait daily for His coming," [*in English*] and knowing that with this prayer, our fathers and mothers went into the gas chambers, I couldn't help all the time thinking these children and smaller ones were dragged to a wanton death. If I said this, I said everything.

And this is the reason, Mr. President, why we, remembering the saga of America, who helped to save a whole section of our people, is living in our hearts; why we love and respect your country, not because of any interest, but from the heart; why we are your friend and your faithful ally; why we are grateful for your help; and why we help as much as we can your country.

And this is also the reason why we want, so much, peace with all our hearts, with all our souls; why we pray for it, why we yearn for it; why we made so great sacrifices for its sake; why this parliament gave an overwhelming support, with the sacrifices, to the completion of our labors to achieve peace.

Mr. President, we have to care for the security and the future of our people. This is our responsibility. We shall carry it out under any circumstances. Never again should a foe, a bloodthirsty enemy, be capable of killing Jewish children. And we shall do whatever is humanly possible to make their life secure, not only in this generation but for all generations to come, in this land of our forefathers, to which, as of right, we came back.

Therefore, we want a real peace treaty. It must be real. It cannot last a few months, or even a few years. It must last for generations, actually forever. Therefore, we must care of its wording, because it has to be clear that this is going to be a real peace, and with the peace must come security.

Therefore, we cannot and we shall not put under jeopardy and danger our civilian population. We shall defend it under any circumstances, even with our lives if necessary, as we have done. This is the problem. Some say to us, "What do you care? Even peace treaties are broken, can be broken." Respectfully, I would like to explain to the learned men who teach us this chapter in history that we, too, read some pages of history.

For instance, I always remember since my boyhood the famous saying made by the German Ambassador to Edward Grey, the Foreign Minister of Great Britain, on behalf of the German Chancellor, Bethmann Hollweg, when the German army swept through neutral Belgium, and so an international agreement which lasted for 84 years was trampled underfoot. And when Grey said, "If you don't evacuate Belgium, we shall go to war against you," that Ambassador, on behalf of his Chancellor, Bethmann Hollweg, said, "But, Mr. Minister, are we going to go to war for a scrap of paper?"

421

Those who say so pay a price for it. A peace treaty is not a scrap of paper. A peace treaty is, as it must be, a serious document. It should be carried out.

It can be broken by cynics, by enemies of peace, by enemies of mankind. But, of course, our nation, with our experience, cannot be asked to sign any document which would make legitimate a breach of the peace treaty. Therefore, we have problems.

Yes, Mr. President, you, and may I say respectfully, I will tell our peoples the truth. And therefore, here and now, it's my duty to say that we have serious problems to solve until we can sign the peace treaty with Egypt—and we want so much to have this serious document signed.

And today we dealt with the serious problems. We all work quite hard—you perhaps harder than anybody else—for the sake of peace. But we do work hard, and we shall go on during the night to deal with these difficult problems. We only hope we shall be able to solve them.

But there are serious issues and difficult problems. This is what it is my duty to say at this juncture, at this moment. Hopefully, we shall overcome the difficulties and be able to sign a peace treaty, a real peace treaty between Egypt and Israel, as a first step towards a comprehensive settlement in the Middle East.

We wouldn't like to have a separate peace treaty with Egypt and have an eastern-northern front, a combination of 6,500 tanks—excuse me, 5,600 tanks, more than 6,000 heavy guns, more than a thousand fighting, firstline planes, et cetera; it's a great danger to us. But, of course, we cannot compel anybody to come to the table.

We invited them. We are prepared at any moment to resume negotiations with them—with Syria, with Jordan, with Lebanon, with all our neighbors, with all Arab states—if they wish. Of course, nobody can force them to come. In God's good time, they will, I believe with all my heart, in God's good time. Until then, of course, the peace treaty with Egypt is the first step, and it must be a real document.

Mr. President, we are proud to have you with us, you and your gracious lady. We met many times in your great country, built on the saga of America, which is so dear to all of us. We meet here tonight in Jerusalem, in the Knesset, in the center of our democracy, this democracy which gives Israel the inherent stability which gives you a reliable and stable ally in the Middle East—and may I say the only democracy in the Middle East—and, therefore, *the* ally, *the* stable and reliable ally of the free world and of its leading power, the United States.

Mr. President, you hold the greatest office in the world, the most difficult office. But I believe that you will go down in history with a higher title than even that of President of the United States. And this higher title is "servant of peace."

In this spirit, ladies and gentlemen, may I raise my glass to our honored and dear guest, the President of the United States, and to Mrs. Carter, to the President of our Republic, Israel, and to Mrs. Navon, to peace and to the everlasting friendship between the United States of America and the State of Israel.

Lechayim.

PRESIDENT CARTER. *Mr. President, Mr. Prime Minister, distinguished officials of the great republic of Israel—legislative, judicial, executive officials of this great nation—friends of the United States here in Israel and friends of Israel from the United States who are also here—many visitors have come here to express their support for this momentous effort for peace:*

I thank you, Mr. President, and Mr. Prime Minister, for your gracious and your kind and your wise words. For both Rosalynn and for me, I want to express to President Navon and Mrs. Navon appreciation for the personal hospitality they've shown us.

We know that we are among friends within this room. Indeed, I have a sense that in many ways we are all one family. As in a family, the relationships between us are frank and sometimes very lively. But also like family members, we recognize that the bonds between our nations and our people are more than just strong for now. They are both strong and permanent.

We in the United States will stand by Israel, and we will never waver in our admiration for you or in our support for you for a strong and secure and a free State of Israel.

We realize that our own security is intimately tied with yours. There are bonds of blood between us, bonds of history, bonds of culture, bonds of religious belief. Perhaps most important of all are the enduring values which we share, the values for which my Nation was formed and exists, the values for which your nation was formed and exists—a belief in individual liberty, a common commitment to representative democracy, a common vision of human brotherhood, the conviction that there is no higher pursuit than that of peace with justice, not only among our own kin and our own kind, but we share this commitment with like men and women throughout the world.

We are now engaged together in a common effort, to achieve a real peace, a comprehensive peace in the Middle East, a peace that would enable the people of Israel and all Middle Eastern people to live in security, to live in prosperity, and to develop to their full potential.

We are now in sight of an important initial phase of that great objective. The events of the past 16 months, beginning with President Sadat's visit to Jerusalem and Prime Minister Begin's immediate response, have engendered that great hope. More progress has been made in the last 16 months than in all the previous three decades of bloodshed.

I myself, as President of the United States of America, have spent literally hundreds of hours in detailed negotiations trying to realize the peace which I have just described briefly.

We are not looking for just a peace document signed by two nations grudgingly. We are looking for a document of peace signed in a spirit of mutual trust, mutual friendship, mutual commitment, mutual understanding, mutual realization of common purpose, that will open the avenue in the future to an easy interrelationship between neighbors who are going to be permanent neighbors, either in a spirit of animosity and hatred and bloodshed, or in a spirit of cooperation and good will and progress.

We love Israel, but we are not jealous. We want you to have many other friends. That's our common hope and our common prayer. There have been disappointments and frustrations, some still remain. But the progress that has been made would not have been possible without Israel's great leader, Prime Minister Menahem Begin.

He's a man of courage, of integrity, of utter and selfless dedication. He and his colleagues have been tough negotiators. They know what is at stake for Israel. And I know they want the best agreement for Israel.

This concern is based on horrible historical fact, actions which we saw memorialized this morning, that brought horror to a world and which must not ever be forgotten. But in guiding the negotiations, the Prime Minister has never lost sight of his original vision, a strong, free, vibrant Jewish people, living in Israel—which you are now—but also living in peace. And we've all seen abundant evidence that he possesses the political skills to translate this vision into reality.

I am absolutely confident from my conversations within the last 3 or 4 days with President Sadat and from my conversations with Prime Minister Begin that both are determined not to let this great opportunity for peace slip from our grasp.

If we can resolve the few remaining differences—and I am still hopeful that we can—our meeting tonight will be just a prelude for an occasion of joyous celebration, the signing of the first peace treaty between Israel and an Arab nation.

I ask all of you to join me in a toast to our gracious hosts, President and Mrs. Navon, to Israel's courageous leader and his wife, Prime Minister and Mrs. Begin, and to our common goal: the transformation of the Middle East into a land of peace.

Lechayim.

NOTE: The exchange began at 10:05 p.m. in Chagall Hall at the Knesset.

Jerusalem, Israel

Address Before the Knesset.   March 12, 1979

Mr. President, Mr. Prime Minister, Mr. Speaker, distinguished members of the Knesset, and friends:

For the last 24 hours, I have been writing different versions of this speech. I have discarded the speech of despair; I have discarded the speech of glad tidings and celebration. I have decided to deliver the speech of concern and caution and hope.

I'm honored to stand in this assembly of free men and women, which represents a great and an ancient people, a young and a courageous nation.

I bring with me the best wishes and the greetings of the people of the United States of America, who share with the people of Israel the love of liberty, of justice, and of peace. And I'm honored to be in Jerusalem, this holy city described by Isaiah as a quiet habitation in which for so many of the human race the cause of brotherhood and peace are enshrined.

I am here in a cause of brotherhood and of peace. I've come to Cairo and also here to Jerusalem to try to enhance the bold, brave, and historic efforts of President Sadat and Prime Minister Begin and to demonstrate that the United States of America is as determined as these two leaders are to create lasting peace and friendship between Egypt and Israel and to put an end to war and the threat of war throughout the Middle East.

No people desire or deserve peace more than the Jewish people. None have wanted it so long. None have spoken of it more eloquently. None have suffered so much from the absence of peace. Pogrom after pogrom, war after war, Israel has buried its sons and its daughters.

Yesterday morning, at Yad Vashem, I grieved in the presence of terrible reminders of the agony and the horror of the Holocaust.

Modern Israel came into being in the wake of that historic crime, the enormity of which is almost beyond human comprehension. I know that Israel is committed and determined, above all, that nothing like it must ever, ever be permitted to happen again on Earth.

Americans respect that determination, and we fully share that determination with you. And Americans recognize that for Jews over the centuries, as for Israel since its independence, caution and wariness have been a practical and a moral necessity for survival. And yet, in these past months, you've made enormous sacrifices and you've taken great risks for peace.

This sacred dedication to peace, born and fostered in Jerusalem and in Cairo, has given to men and women everywhere renewed sense of hope that human reason, good will, and faith can succeed, can break down barriers between peoples who, in our lifetimes, have only known war.

As Prime Minister Begin said after the Camp David summit, the agreements reached there proved that any problem can be solved if there is some—and he repeated, just some wisdom. Those are truthful and also reassuring words. I know from my intense, personal involvement in these negotiations that President Sadat and Prime Minister Begin have not wavered from their often-expressed commitment to peace.

President Sadat told me in Cairo that he will let nothing stand in the way of our shared goal of finishing the treaty of peace between Israel and Egypt and of making it a living testament of friendship between the two neighboring peoples. I believe him, and I know in my heart that Prime Minister Begin and the Government of Israel are no less fervently committed to the same noble objective.

But we've not yet fully met our challenge. Despite our unflagging determination, despite the extraordinary progress of the past 6 months, we still fall short. It's now the somber responsibility of us all to exert our energies and our imaginations once again to contemplate the tragedy of failure and the legitimate exultation if we bring peace.

In this effort, the support of the members of the Knesset will obviously be crucial. Our vision must be as great as our

goal. Wisdom and courage are required of us all, and so, too, are practicality and realism. We must not lose this moment. We must pray as if everything depended on God, and we must act as if everything depends on ourselves.

What kind of peace do we seek? Spinoza said that peace is not an absence of war; it is a virtue, a state of mind, a disposition for benevolence, for confidence, for justice. Americans share that vision and will stand beside Israel to be sure that that vision is fulfilled.

In Egypt, I saw vivid evidence of this deep longing for peace among the Egyptian people, millions of them. But like you, they worry about the uncertainties of that first crucial stage in the broad task of pounding Middle East swords into plowshares. Like you, they hope to banish forever the enmity that has existed between the neighbors, the permanent neighbors of Egypt and of Israel. Like you, they want this peace, and like you, they want it to be real and not just a sham peace.

My friends, from my own experience as President of the United States, I understand all too well that historic decisions are seldom easy, seldom without pain. Benjamin Franklin, who negotiated the treaty of peace between England and America after our own War of Independence, once said that he had never seen a peace made, even the most advantageous, that was not censured as inadequate.

Throughout the peace process, both Israel and Egypt have understood that no treaty can embody every aim of both nations. What a treaty can do, what it can do far better than the fragile status quo, and infinitely better than the insidious tensions that will build if our efforts are further stalled or fail, is to protect the vital interests of both Israel and Egypt and open up the possibility of peace for all the states and all the peoples of this troubled region.

Doubts are the stuff of great decisions, but so are dreams. We are now at the very edge of turning Israel's eternal dream of peace into reality. I will not pretend that this reality will be free from further challenges. It will not. And better than most, the Jewish people know that life is seldom easy. But we must make this beginning. We must seize this precious opportunity.

Fifty-seven years ago, the Congress of the United States of America committed itself to a Jewish homeland. Twenty-six years later, President Harry Truman recognized the new State of Israel 11 minutes after your nation was born. Seven Presidents have believed and demonstrated that America's relationship with Israel is more than just a special relationship. It has been and it is a unique relationship. And it's a relationship which is indestructible, because it is rooted in the consciousness and the morals and the religion and the beliefs of the American people themselves.

Let me repeat what I said to Prime Minister Begin last year on the lawn of the White House, on the anniversary of the founding of the modern State of Israel, and I quote: "For 30 years we have stood at the side of the proud and independent nation of Israel. I can say without reservation, as President of the United States, that we will continue to do so, not just for another 30 years but forever."

We recognize the advantages to the United States of this partnership. You know that America deeply desires peace between Israel and Egypt, and that we will do everything we can to make peace possible.

The people of the two nations are ready now for peace. The *people* of the two nations are ready now for peace. The leaders have not yet proven that we are also ready

for peace, enough to take a chance. We must persevere. But with or without a peace treaty, the United States will always be at Israel's side.

Meeting in this hall of liberty reminds us that we are bound more than in any other way by instinctive, common ideals and common commitments and beliefs. This Knesset itself is a temple to the principle and the practice of open debate. Democracy is an essential element to the very nationhood of Israel, as it is to the United States.

You've proven that democracy can be a stable form of government in a nation of great diversity and in a time and a place of danger and instability. But Israel and the United States were shaped by pioneers—my nation is also a nation of immigrants and refugees—by peoples gathered in both nations from many lands, by dreamers who, and I quote, "by the work of their hands and the sweat of their brows" transformed their dreams into the reality of nationhood.

We share the heritage of the Bible, the worship of God, of individual freedom, and we share a belief in cooperative endeavor, even in the face of apparently insurmountable obstacles.

In nations around the world where governments deny these values, millions look to us to uphold the right to freedom of speech, freedom of the press, the right to emigrate, the right to express one's political views, the right to move from one place to another, the right for families to be reunited, the right to a decent standard of material life.

These are the kinds of unbreakable ties that bind Israel and the United States together. These are the values that we offer to the whole world. Our mutual dedication to these ideals is an indispensable resource in our search for peace.

The treaty between Egypt and Israel that we hope may be placed before you for approval promises to be the cornerstone of a comprehensive structure of peace for this entire region.

We all recognize that this structure will be incomplete until the peace can be extended to include all the people who have been involved in the conflict. I know and I understand the concerns you feel as you consider the magnitude of the choices that will remain to be faced even after a peace treaty is concluded between Israel and Egypt. And as the time for these choices approaches, remember this pledge that I make to you again today: The United States will never support any agreement or any action that places Israel's security in jeopardy.

We must proceed with due caution. I understand that. But we must proceed.

As recently as 2 years ago, after all, these present steps that have already been taken seemed absolutely unthinkable. We know that confrontation magnifies differences. But the process of negotiation circumscribes differences, defines the differences, isolates them from the larger regions of common interests, and so makes the gaps which do exist more bridgeable. We've seen the proof of that in the last 16 months.

At Camp David, Prime Minister Begin and President Sadat forged two frameworks for the building of that comprehensive peace. The genius of that accomplishment is that negotiations under these frameworks can go forward independently of each other, without destroying the obvious relationship between them.

They are designed to be mutually reinforcing, with the intrinsic flexibility necessary to promote the comprehensive peace that we all desire. Both will be fulfilled only when others of your Arab neighbors follow the visionary example of President Sadat, when they put ancient animosities behind them and agree to negotiate, as you desire, as you've already done with President Sadat, an honorable solution to the differences between you.

It's important that the door be kept open to all the parties to the conflict, including the Palestinians, with whom, above all, Israel shares a common interest in living in peace and living with mutual respect.

Peace in the Middle East, always important to the security of the entire region, in recent weeks has become an even more urgent concern.

Israel's security will rest not only on how the negotiations affect the situation on your own borders but also on how it affects the forces of stability and moderation beyond your borders.

I'm convinced that nothing can do more to create a hospitable atmosphere for those more distant forces in the long run than an equitable peace treaty between Israel and Egypt.

The risks of peace between you and your Egyptian neighbors are real. But America is ready to reduce any risks and to balance them within the bounds of our strength and our influence.

I came to Israel representing the most powerful country on Earth. And I can assure you that the United States intends to use that power in the pursuit of a stable and a peaceful Middle East.

We've been centrally involved in this region, and we will stay involved politically, economically, and militarily. We will stand by our friends. We are ready to place our strength at Israel's side when you want it to ensure Israel's security and well-being.

We know Israel's concern about many issues. We know your concern for an adequate oil supply. In the context of peace, we are ready to guarantee that supply.

427

I've recommitted our Nation publicly to this commitment, as you know, only in recent days in my own country.

We know Israel's concern that the price of peace with Egypt will exacerbate an already difficult economic situation and make it more difficult to meet your country's essential security requirements. In the context of peace, we are prepared to see Israel's economic and military relationship with the United States take on new and strong and more meaningful dimensions, even than already exist.

We will work not only to attain peace but to maintain peace, recognizing that it's a permanent challenge of our time.

We will rededicate ourselves to the ideals that our peoples share. These ideals are the course not only of our strength but of our self-respect as nations, as leaders, and as individuals.

I'm here today to reaffirm that the United States will always recognize, appreciate, and honor the mutual advantages of the strength and security of Israel. And I'm here to express my most heartfelt and passionate hope that we may work together successfully to make this peace.

The Midrash tells us that, and I quote, "Peace is the wisp of straw that binds together the sheaf of blessings." But the wisp of straw, we know, is fragile and easily broken.

Let us pray God to guide our hand. Millions of men, women, and children, in Israel and Egypt and beyond, in this generation and in generations to come, are relying on our skill and relying on our faith.

In the words of a Sabbath prayer, "May He who causes peace to reign in the high heavens let peace descend on us, on all Israel, and on all the world."

NOTE: The President spoke at 12:16 p.m. in the Knesset Chamber. In his opening remarks, he referred to Yitzhak Shamir, speaker of the Knesset.

Prior to his address, the President placed a wreath at the Knesset Memorial, a sculpture with an eternal flame dedicated to soldiers and civilians who gave their lives for Israel.

Following his address, the President attended a luncheon with members of the foreign affairs committee of the Knesset, and then returned to the King David Hotel.

In the evening, the President and Mrs. Carter, accompanied by Deputy Prime Minister Yigael Yidan, went to the Shrine of the Book, a part of the Israel Museum, to view the Dead Sea Scrolls.

Earlier in the day, the President had attended a breakfast meeting with Prime Minister Begin and members of the Israeli Cabinet at the Prime Minister's residence.

Tel Aviv, Israel

Remarks of the President and Prime Minister Begin at the Departure Ceremony.
March 13, 1979

THE PRESIDENT. *Mr. President, Mr. Prime Minister, and friends:*

As we depart for Cairo, and then for my own country, I want to express on behalf of Rosalynn, my wife, myself, and all the American party, our gratitude on the Government and to the people of Israel for your hospitality and for your kindness.

I came here in the service of a cause which binds together, which unites Israel, Egypt, and the United States of America—the sacred cause of peace. We have talked and reasoned together in that cause for many hours during the past 3 days. We've talked as friends, and our conversations have been characterized by the frankness, the honesty, the mutual respect and concern that true friendship demands.

In our discussions we've concentrated on the differences that still exist between Egypt and Israel in the peace process, differences that are now very small, compared to the much larger areas of agreement.

Good progress has been made. There are fewer differences than when I first arrived, and those few differences which still remain have been substantially narrowed.

Last night, there were further intensive discussions among members of the Israeli Cabinet and the United States delegation on the two or three most difficult issues. And this morning, building on those discussions, Prime Minister Begin and I were able to make substantial additional progress.

I will now fly to Cairo to review with President Sadat the discussions that we have had here and the progress which we have made together.

As I depart, I want to repeat once again what I said in the Knesset yesterday. The friendship between America and Israel is more than strong. It is indestructible.

In the past 3 days I have been impressed deeply by the extraordinary story of faith and perseverance in the face of adversity which is Israel.

President Sadat, Prime Minister Begin, and I remain determined to exert every ounce of effort at our command to bring the peace negotiations to a successful conclusion. We will not fail.

Thank you very much.

[*At this point, Prime Minister Begin responded to the President's remarks in Hebrew. He then translated his remarks into English as follows.*]

THE PRIME MINISTER. *Mr. President of the United States, Mr. President of the State of Israel, ladies and gentlemen:*

We take leave of you, Mr. President, on behalf of the Government and the people of Israel. On behalf of them, I wish to express our gratitude, my wife and myself, and all my colleagues in the Cabinet, that you honored us with your visit, you and your gracious lady, the Secretary of State and Secretary of Defense and your other advisers.

Undoubtedly, those 3 days of your visit to Israel were 3 hectic days, and there were also 3 white nights, but they are memorable days. I believe they will be unforgettable.

Mr. President, you came on the highest mission in humanity—for peace—and you have succeeded. We made real progress in the peacemaking process. Now, of course, it's the turn of Egypt to give its reply.

Nobody can deny that we worked as expeditiously as humanly possible and, therefore, we worked day and night. And we are not tired, because of the elation in our hearts that we did a good job in the service of peace.

Mr. President, may I say respectfully that you can leave this country with satisfaction, and we are happy that we could have helped you to the best of our ability. And when you embark on your journey and mission to Egypt, we wish you Godspeed.

And when you come back home, may I again ask you, tell the great American people that here is a free nation which loves and respects your great country, your people, and is grateful for their friendship and cherishes your personal friendship for Israel, which is a treasure in our time.

So, Mr. President, now we shall wish you all the success in Egypt, and we shall guard our friendship between America and Israel forever.

THE PRESIDENT. Thank you very much.

NOTE: The President spoke at 12:15 p.m. at Ben Gurion International Airport.

In the morning, Prime Minister and Mrs. Begin had breakfast with the President and Mrs. Carter in the Presidential Suite at the King David Hotel. Following breakfast, the President and the Prime Minister met privately and were then joined by their advisers.

Cairo, Egypt

Remarks Following a Meeting With President Sadat. March 13, 1979

I have a statement to make which I consider to be extremely important.

I have just given to President Sadat a full report on my discussions in Israel. During that visit the United States made proposals for resolving a number of outstanding issues, proposals which were accepted by Prime Minister Begin and his Cabinet.

President Sadat has now accepted these proposals. Based on discussions in Egypt and Israel, I have also presented United States proposals to President Sadat and to Prime Minister Begin for resolving the few remaining issues.

Earlier today, Prime Minister Begin agreed to present these proposals to his Cabinet for consideration. This will be done at the earliest opportunity.

President Sadat has carefully reviewed all these remaining issues and has accepted these same proposals. I have just informed Prime Minister Begin by telephone of President Sadat's acceptance.

I am convinced that now we have defined all of the main ingredients of a peace treaty between Egypt and Israel, which will be the cornerstone of a comprehensive peace settlement for the Middle East.

Thank you.

NOTE: The President spoke to reporters at 5:05 p.m. at Cairo International Airport following the meeting in the VIP Pavilion.

Following a departure ceremony at the airport, the President boarded Air Force One for the return flight to Washington.

The President's Trip to Egypt and Israel

Remarks on Arrival at Andrews Air Force Base, Md.   March 14, 1979

THE VICE PRESIDENT. Mr. President, 6 days ago you left for the Middle East in search of peace. You and Rosalynn took with you our love, our prayers, and the hopes of all humanity. You return tonight to a happy and a grateful nation, for you have drawn two ancient enemies to the brink of peace.

We thank you tonight, not only for the breakthrough in the Middle East, but we thank you also for renewing our confidence in the deepest of American values.

Where there were risks, you stood for hope. And where there were obstacles, you followed conscience. Where there were suspicions, you sought to build a lasting foundation of trust. It is the trust that you won from President Sadat and Prime Minister Begin that made these historic discussions possible. And it is that same trust that made these talks a success.

Mr. President, Rosalynn, welcome home to a proud and a hopeful nation.

THE PRESIDENT. Thank you. I'd like to ask Secretary Vance to come up here and stand.

Vice President Mondale, Speaker O'Neill, Senator Byrd, Members of the Congress—the tremendous group of the

Members of the Congress—members of my Cabinet, friends, and fellow citizens:

You are looking at a tired but a grateful man. [*Laughter*]

All of us who made this journey appreciate the opportunity that we have had to render some service in the cause of peace. Now the journey is done and we are glad to be home, back in our own country, our beloved United States of America.

It's good to see so many familiar and welcome faces, and I want to thank you for being out here in the middle of the night to greet us and to give us one of the best welcomes I have ever known. Thank you from the bottom of my heart.

As you know, we did not go to Egypt and to Israel in order to confirm what was already a guaranteed result. We went there to use our influence and our good offices to help the leaders of those two great nations move decisively toward that peace that is so ardently desired by the people whom they serve.

There were risks involved. They were pointed out to me by many people, political risks to me as President, therefore perhaps a risk even to the prestige of the United States.

Fortunately, our work has had a happy result. But I want to stress that the effort would have been worth making regardless of the outcome of this trip. Risk of failure should never deter us from a worthy goal. And no goal is higher than that of genuine peace.

In war, we offer our very lives as a matter of routine. And we must be no less daring, no less steadfast in the pursuit of peace.

For more than 30 years, the nations of Egypt and Israel, who have been and who will be perpetual neighbors, have existed in a continual state of hostility. That hostility has exploded into combat four times.

And each war has brought with it suffering and pain and the loss of life, renewed fear and hatred and great danger for that entire region and for the world far beyond. But in the last 16 months the way has finally been opened to peace.

When I decided to make this trip, the peace negotiations, as you know, seemed to have reached a stalemate. After long hours of discussion in both Egypt and in Israel, proposals were made for resolving all the outstanding issues. All but two of these issues have been resolved with Prime Minister Begin and the Israeli Cabinet.

Less than 3 hours from now the Prime Minister will present the remaining proposals to the Israeli Cabinet for consideration. I have even left instructions to wake me up if the news is good—[*laughter*]—and I believe it will be. As you also know, President Sadat has already accepted all of the proposals.

Therefore, we have now defined the major components of a peace treaty between the largest and most powerful Arab country, Egypt, and her neighbor and former enemy, Israel. There may be sharp internal debates before this process is complete. But the treaty that emerges can be the cornerstone of a comprehensive settlement, one that can bless with peace all the people who have suffered from the long, enduring conflict in the Middle East.

The leaders of Egypt and Israel are now daring to break the pattern of bitterness and war. They are following the advice of the Biblical proverb, "When a man's way please the Lord, he maketh even his enemies to be at peace with Him."

In choosing peace, President Sadat and the Prime Minister of Israel, Prime Minister Begin, are venturing into the unknown. But they know that the United States of America will be with them as

431

they begin to make peace a living reality for their own people.

I'm thankful that the friendships between their countries, both countries, and the United States will now grow even stronger when our own two friends are friends with one another.

Through private messages and public statements, many messages sent from Air Force One on the trip back here from Egypt, I am urging all other world leaders to support what Egypt and Israel have done, for it offers hope to all who love peace everywhere in the world.

My friends, let me thank you again for coming out to greet us. I believe that God has answered our prayers.

NOTE: The exchange began at 12:32 a.m.

Egyptian-Israeli Peace Negotiations

Statement on Action by the Israeli Cabinet Approving Proposals.   March 14, 1979

I am extremely pleased that the Israeli Cabinet has approved the two remaining proposals that I discussed with Prime Minister Begin on Monday in Jerusalem. Prime Minister Begin has just called me with this good news. This means that all of the outstanding issues in the negotiations between Egypt and Israel have now been successfully resolved.

At this historic moment, I want to congratulate the great leaders of both countries, President Sadat and Prime Minister Begin, for their leadership and the courage that they have consistently demonstrated. The peace which their peoples so clearly need and want is close to reality. I am proud that our country has been able to assist these two long-time adversaries

along the path of reconciliation and toward future cooperation. We stand ready to help in the implementation of the peace treaty, in the negotiations that lie ahead on other issues of concern, and in working with these two friends to build a stable and peaceful Middle East.

Secretary of Energy

Letter to Senator Dennis DeConcini of Arizona.   March 14, 1979

To Senator Dennis DeConcini

This is a response to your letter of March 12. While I welcome your views and recognize that the administration of the Department of Energy can always be improved, I continue to have full trust and confidence in Secretary James Schlesinger.

Sincerely,

JIMMY CARTER

[The Honorable Dennis DeConcini, United States Senate, Washington, D.C. 20510]

He has a very difficult job, and needs all the help and support he can get— He's got mine—

JC

NOTE: The text of the letter was released on March 15.

St. Patrick's Day, 1979

Message of the President.   March 15, 1979

St. Patrick's Day brings out all of the innate warmth, goodness and joy of living that Irish people have brought to this land. It joins us all in celebration of a legacy that is a vital part of our national character and way of life.

Rosalynn and I welcome this annual opportunity to greet our fellow citizens of Irish ancestry and to share in the sentiments of countless others who become Irish on this special day.

JIMMY CARTER

National Farm Safety Week, 1979

Proclamation 4645.   March 15, 1979

By the President of the United States of America

A Proclamation

America is blessed with an efficient and productive agriculture. As a result, we enjoy an abundance of high-quality food products at a lower cost relative to personal income than in most other countries. This abundance permits a strong flow of food exports, contributing many billions of dollars to our trade balance and enabling us to help relieve hunger in many parts of the world.

One of the most persistent barriers to agricultural well-being has been farm accidents. Last year, there were more than a half-million farm and ranch residents who suffered disabling injuries, many of which were handicapping or fatal. The cost of those accidents approached $5 billion. The pain and personal loss to the injured and to their families and friends cannot be measured.

It has been proven that most accidents on farms and ranches can be prevented by controlling hazards, ending unsafe practices and by the use of protective equipment. The effects of many injuries can be lessened if prompt and correct actions are taken subsequent to the accidents and disasters. The time and effort invested in these activities is relatively small compared to the losses America sustains every year through farm accidents.

Now, THEREFORE, I, JIMMY CARTER, President of the United States of America, do hereby designate the week of July 25 through July 31, 1979, as National Farm Safety Week. I urge all who live and work on the Nation's farms and ranches to employ every needed safety precaution and practice, at work and in recreation, at home and on the highway. I also ask those who serve agricultural producers to support their accident-reducing efforts by providing encouragement and educational aids. We must succeed in this important task, as no Nation with concern for the well-being of its people can afford to lose such vital human and productive resources. A safer agriculture will be economically stronger and more productive, thereby benefitting us all.

IN WITNESS WHEREOF, I have hereunto set my hand this fifteenth day of March, in the year of our Lord nineteen hundred seventy-nine, and of the Independence of the United States of America the two hundred and third.

JIMMY CARTER

[Filed with the Office of the Federal Register, 2:23 p.m., March 15, 1979]

Budget Rescission

Message to the Congress.   March 15, 1979

To the Congress of the United States:

In accordance with the Impoundment Control Act of 1974, I herewith report a revision to a previously transmitted rescission proposal for the Small Business Administration. This revision decreases the amount previously proposed by $6.0 million. The details of this revised rescission proposal are contained in the attached report.

JIMMY CARTER

The White House,
March 15, 1979.

NOTE: The attachment detailing the revised rescission is printed in the FEDERAL REGISTER of March 20, 1979.

Competitive Status for Handicapped Federal Employees

Executive Order 12125. March 15, 1979

By the authority vested in me as President of the United States of America by Sections 3301 and 3302 of Title 5 of the United States Code, and in order to permit severely physically handicapped and mentally retarded individuals to obtain civil service competitive status, Civil Service Rule 3.1 (5 CFR 3.1) is hereby amended by adding the following new subsection:

"(b) Upon recommendation by the employing agency, and subject to such requirements as the Office of Personnel Management may prescribe, the following classes of handicapped employees may acquire competitive status without competitive examination:

"(1) A severely physically handicapped employee who completes at least two years of satisfactory service in a position excepted from the competitive service.

"(2) A mentally retarded employee who completes at least two years of satisfactory service in a position excepted from the competitive service."

JIMMY CARTER

The White House,
March 15, 1979.

[Filed with the Office of the Federal Register, 2:23 p.m., March 16, 1979]

International Wheat Agreement, 1971

Message to the Senate Transmitting Protocols to the Wheat Trade Convention and the Food Aid Convention. March 15, 1979

To the Senate of the United States:

With a view to receiving the advice and consent of the Senate to ratification, I transmit herewith the Protocols for the Fourth Extension of the Wheat Trade Convention and Food Aid Convention constituting the International Wheat Agreement, 1971, open for signature in Washington from April 26 through May 17, 1978. The Protocols were established by a Conference which met in London on March 23, 1978.

I transmit also, for the information of the Senate, the report of the Department of State with respect to the Protocols.

The Protocol for the Fourth Extension of the Wheat Trade Convention, 1971, extends the Convention until June 30, 1979, and maintains the framework for international cooperation in wheat trade matters. It also continues the existence of the International Wheat Council.

The Protocol for the Fourth Extension of the Food Aid Convention, 1971, extends until June 30, 1979, commitments of donor member states to provide minimum annual quantities of food aid to developing countries.

Declarations of Provisional Application of both Protocols were signed and deposited for the United States on May 17, 1978, allowing our country to continue full and active participation in the International Wheat Council and Food Aid Committee. The Council and the Committee have granted the United States an extension through June 30, 1979, to deposit instruments of ratification.

It is my hope that the Senate will give early and favorable consideration to the two Protocols so that ratification by the United States can be effected and instruments of ratification deposited no later than June 30, 1979.

                                   JIMMY CARTER

The White House,
    March 15, 1979.

Corporation for Public Broadcasting

Nomination of Two Members of the Board of Directors.   March 15, 1979

The President today announced two persons whom he will nominate to be members of the Board of Directors of the Corporation for Public Broadcasting for terms expiring March 26, 1984. They are:

Michael A. Gammino, Jr., of Providence, R.I. Gammino, 56, is president and chief executive officer of the Columbus National Bank and chairman of the board of National Columbus Bancorp. He was originally appointed to this Board by President Johnson. He is active in civic affairs in Providence and is a member of the advisory committee for educational television channel 36.

José A. Rivera, of Brooklyn, N.Y. Rivera, 31, is an attorney specializing in equal opportunity matters and a consultant on equal employment opportunity. He has designed and conducted training programs in the field of equal opportunity for State and local agencies. Rivera has also been an assistant professor of law at the Rutgers University School of Law.

National Council on the Arts

Nomination of Two Members.
March 15, 1979

The President today announced two persons whom he will nominate to be members of the National Council on the Arts for terms expiring September 3, 1984. They are:

Thomas P. Bergin, of South Bend, Ind., dean of continuing education at the University of Notre Dame. Bergin, 55, is a member of the Indiana Governor's Commission on the Arts and serves on the board of directors of the South Bend Art Center and the Michiana Public Broadcasting Corp.

James A. Rosenquist, of Arepika, Fla., an artist whose paintings have been exhibited in the United States, Canada, and Europe. Rosenquist, 45, is a former artist in residence at the Aspen, Colo., Institute of Humanist Studies.

United States Air Force Academy Board of Visitors

Appointment of Two Members.
March 15, 1979

The President today announced the appointment of two persons as members of the Board of Visitors of the United States Air Force Academy. They are:

JOHN G. KESTER, of Alexandria, Va., a Washington attorney and former Deputy Assistant Secretary of the Army for Manpower and Reserve Affairs;

MICHAEL O'CALLAGHAN, who was Governor of Nevada from 1971 to 1978.

International Commission for the Conservation of Atlantic Tunas

Appointment of Harold F. Cary as a U.S. Commissioner.   March 15, 1979

The President today announced the appointment of Harold F. Cary, of San Diego, Calif., as a U.S. Commissioner on the International Commission for the Conservation of Atlantic Tunas.

Cary is executive director of the U.S. Tuna Foundation and a former vice president and general manager of Ocean Fisheries, Inc.

Egyptian-Israeli Peace Negotiations

Statement on Action by the Egyptian Cabinet Approving a Peace Treaty and Related Documents.   March 15, 1979

I am pleased that the Egyptian Cabinet now has approved the peace treaty between Egypt and Israel and the related documents. The Cabinet has now given its support to President Sadat's imaginative leadership and decisive action in moving to end more than three decades of conflict with Israel.

We look forward now to formal action on Sunday by the Israeli Cabinet, to be followed by the debate in the Knesset next week.

The Egyptian action today, along with the preliminary action of the Israeli Cabinet yesterday on the outstanding issues, continues the momentum toward a quick conclusion of a peace treaty between Egypt and Israel.

President Sadat and Prime Minister Begin continue to demonstrate their leadership and courage in building the cornerstone of peace in the Middle East. We will continue to assist Egypt and Israel to move their countries from war to peace, thereby releasing the resources that can bring a better life for their people.

United States Delegation to Discussions in the Middle East and Europe

Announcements of the Trip and Members of the Delegation.   March 16, 1979

At President Carter's direction, a delegation consisting of Dr. Zbigniew Brzezinski, the President's Assistant for National Security Affairs, Warren Christopher, the Deputy Secretary of State, Gen. David Jones, Chairman of the Joint Chiefs of Staff, and Chip Carter, the President's son, will visit Saudi Arabia and Jordan this weekend. They will consult on regional security issues and the recent agreement between Egypt and Israel. They will also continue the ongoing discussions on matters of bilateral concern. The discussions will be held in the spirit of friendship that has long characterized our relations with these two countries.

Also in the delegation will be Col. William Odom, Jerrold Schecter, and Gary Sick of the NSC staff, Michael Sterner, Deputy Assistant Secretary for Near Eastern and South Asian Affairs, Stephen Oxman of the Department of State, and Brig. Gen. Harold Todd of the Department of Defense (JCS).

———

The American delegation to the Middle East, consisting of Dr. Zbigniew Brzezinski, Assistant to the President for National Security Affairs, Warren Christopher, Deputy Secretary of State, Gen. David Jones, Chairman, Joint Chiefs of Staff, and Chip Carter, the President's son, will stop in Cairo on their return from the Middle East to review with President Anwar Sadat their talks in Saudi Arabia and Jordan.

The delegation will arrive in Cairo from Amman Sunday evening and is expected to depart Monday morning.

Deputy Secretary Christopher will proceed to Europe from Cairo where he will brief European allies. The remainder of the group will return to the United States. Details of Deputy Secretary Christopher's schedule will be announced later.

National Transportation Safety Board

Nomination of Patricia A. Goldman To Be a Member. March 16, 1979

The President today announced that he has nominated Patricia A. Goldman, of Washington, D.C., to be a member of the National Transportation Safety Board for a term expiring December 31, 1983.

Goldman was born March 22, 1924, in Newton, N.J. She received a B.A. in economics from Goucher College in 1964.

From 1964 to 1965, Goldman was a research assistant to the Joint Economic Committee. She was legislative assistant to the Ad Hoc Subcommittee on the War on Poverty of the House Education and Labor Committee in 1965 and 1966.

In 1966 Goldman was a research consultant to the U.S. Chamber of Commerce, and from 1967 to 1971, she was director of their manpower and poverty programs. In 1971 and 1972 she was legislative counsel to the National League of Cities and the U.S. Conference of Mayors. Since 1972 she has been executive director of the Wednesday Group of the U.S. House of Representatives.

Goldman is a lecturer at the Brookings Institution for senior government executives and a visiting professor with the Woodrow Wilson National Fellowship Program. She is chair of the Republican Women's Task Force of the National Women's Political Caucus.

Board for International Food and Agricultural Development

Appointment of Rebecca R. Polland as a Member. March 16, 1979

The President today announced the appointment of Rebecca R. Polland, of Philadelphia, Pa., as a member of the Board for International Food and Agricultural Development for a term of 3 years.

Polland, 57, is an assistant professor of political science at Rutgers University's Camden College of Arts and Sciences. She has served as a consultant to the Administrator of USDA's Food and Nutrition Service, and has been a delegate to the World Food Conference in Rome and the White House Conference on Food, Nutrition, and Health.

Committee for Purchase From the Blind and Other Severely Handicapped

Appointment of Dale R. Babione as a Member. March 16, 1979

The President today announced the appointment of Dale R. Babione as a member of the Committee for Purchase from the Blind and Other Severely Handicapped. Babione is Assistant Administrator for Acquisition Policy at the General Services Administration.

Mother's Day, 1979

Proclamation 4646.   March 16, 1979

By the President of the United States of America

A Proclamation

For 65 years we have set aside a special day to honor all American mothers and acknowledge the important contribution of mothers to the future of their children and of our Nation.

The activities and aspirations of many American women have changed dramatically in recent years. Whether or not they combine employment outside the home with their other responsibilities, the fundamental commitment of mothers to the welfare, development and future opportunities of their children remains as strong as that of mothers in past generations.

In this time when the family is subjected to many new pressures, the job of nurturing future generations is often both more difficult and more important than ever. Our children remain our major resource, and preserving the valuable aspects of our heritage while working to build a better world for the future is the duty of all Americans.

Our Nation has made great progress in providing educational opportunities, health care and adequate nutrition for our children, but we still have much to do to make sure all our children are able to develop their full potential. In addition to these basic necessities, parents must provide the love and training that produces the critical spiritual and social values as well as the motivation and self-discipline their children will need to live fruitful lives.

Mother's Day affords us an opportunity to express our thanks to our own mothers, and to honor the devotion, dedication and service of all mothers.

Now, THEREFORE, I, JIMMY CARTER, President of the United States of America, do hereby request that Sunday, May 13, 1979, be observed as Mother's Day. I direct Government officials to display the flag of the United States on all Government buildings. I urge all citizens to display the flag in appropriate ways as a sign of their gratitude to the mothers of America, and to seek ways to aid and support the important efforts of American mothers to provide the kind of influences and resources their children need to develop into strong, honest, capable and happy adults.

IN WITNESS WHEREOF, I have hereunto set my hand this sixteenth day of March, in the year of our Lord nineteen hundred seventy-nine, and of the Independence of the United States of America the two hundred and third.

JIMMY CARTER

[Filed with the Office of the Federal Register, 2:24 p.m., March 16, 1979]

International Export Credit Negotiations

Message to the Congress Reporting on the Negotiations.   March 16, 1979

To the Congress of the United States:

The Export-Import Bank Act of 1945 as amended in November 1978 (Sec. 1908(a) of Public Law 95–630) requested me "to begin negotiations at the ministerial level with other major exporting countries to end predatory export financing programs and other forms of export subsidies, including mixed credits, in third country markets as well as within the United States." The legislation called for a report to the Congress on progress toward meeting these goals.

As I indicated on September 26, 1978, in my Statement on Export Policy, this Administration attaches high priority to increasing American exports. The Export-Import Bank plays a very significant role in that effort. Accordingly, this Administration has sought to make the Bank's financing more competitive with the official export financing provided by other governments and, at the same time, to improve the International Arrangement on Export Credits so as to avoid costly and self-defeating export credit competition between sovereign governments.

I directed the Secretary of the Treasury to undertake the appropriate negotiations. In fact, Secretary Blumenthal had already alerted foreign governments to the need for a broadened and strengthened International Arrangement at the OECD Ministerial Meeting in June 1978 and the issue was again raised at the meeting which prepared the agenda for the Bonn Summit. In September 1978, Secretary Blumenthal emphasized to the Finance Ministers of our major trading partners the importance of substantive improvements in the International Arrangement on Export Credits. He presented detailed proposals designed to bring the financing terms set forth in the Arrangement closer to worldwide commercial practices and to broaden the Arrangement to cover sectors presently excluded from coverage.

Briefly, these proposals called for increases ranging from 1/2 to 3/4 of one percent in the minimum interest rates called for by the Arrangement, the elimination of local cost support by export credit agencies, and greater restraint in the use of highly concessional mixed credits. In addition, maximum repayment terms and minimum interest rates were proposed for aircraft, nuclear power plants and liquified natural gas (LNG) tankers, sectors presently excluded from the Arrangement. Similarly, a proposal was made to have the Arrangement cover credits for agricultural commodities in excess of three years but not more than ten years. Additional possibilities for improving the Arrangement emerged during the subsequent discussions.

These proposals were presented to the twenty-two countries participating in the International Arrangement on Export Credits for consideration at their October 1978 meeting. At our urging, these countries agreed to establish a working group to consider improvements in the Arrangement. The working group met in December 1978 and in January 1979. In addition, representatives of the U.S. Government discussed these proposals at length in bilateral meetings with other governments.

Although the substance of our proposals appeared to constitute a basis for negotiation, the required unanimity for the changes we sought in the Arrangement was lacking. As a result, no agreement regarding modifications in the Arrangement acceptable to the U.S. Government could be reached.

I have therefore reluctantly concluded that further negotiations would not be productive at this time. If the countries which have opposed the improvements we have suggested evidence their willingness to be more forthcoming, I would be prepared to resume negotiations at any time.

For the present, however, the lack of progress requires us to reexamine our own efforts to assure that we remain competitive in the export credit field. Our examination may well indicate that we should modify some of our own programs and policies until such time as there is more willingness among our trading partners to impose the needed self-discipline on export credit practices.

Meanwhile, the United States will continue to adhere to the International Arrangement on Export Credits because it remains a useful, if limited, instrument of international discipline in the provision of officially supported export credits. Within this framework, the Export-Import Bank, operating in consultation with the National Advisory Council on International Monetary and Financial Policy (NAC), will provide the necessary export financing support to allow American exporters to meet foreign official export credit competition. For example, Eximbank will continue its recently adopted policy of matching mixed credits on a selective basis, a policy which proved effective recently when an American exporter was awarded a contract based on an Eximbank financing package that matched the mixed credit offer of a foreign government.

Finally, in my FY 1980 budget, I have asked the Congress for $4.1 billion in direct lending authority for Eximbank, an increase of $500 million from the FY 1979 budget. I have asked for this increase, together with $6.8 billion in insurance and loan guarantee authority, in a year in which I am determined to cut the Federal budget deficit to below $30 billion. I expect the Bank to husband these new resources carefully, but I also expect the Bank aggressively to meet official export credit competition.

The attached annex details the discussions and the actions taken to improve the International Arrangement and provide competitive official export credit financing.

JIMMY CARTER

The White House,
March 16, 1979.

NOTE: The annex is included in the press release.

Digest of Other White House Announcements

The following listing includes the President's public schedule and other items of general interest announced by the White House Press Office and not included elsewhere in this issue.

March 12

The President declared an emergency for the State of Missouri because of the impact of an icejam and flooding in Andrew County on March 3 and 4.

The President declared an emergency for the State of Washington because of the impact of flooding in Franklin County from February 9 to 11.

March 13

The President declared an emergency for the State of Georgia because of the impact of flooding in the counties of Polk, Floyd, and Gilmer, from March 3 to 6.

March 14

The President participated in a briefing on his trip to Egypt and Israel, given at the White House for Members of Congress.

March 15

The President met at the White House with:

—Zbigniew Brzezinski, Assistant to the President for National Security Affairs;

—Frank B. Moore, Assistant to the President for Congressional Liaison;

—members of the executive board of the National Newspaper Publishers Association, on the occasion of Black Press Week.

The President left the White House for a stay at Camp David, Md.

The President declared an emergency for the State of New Hampshire as a result of flooding, beginning about March 5, for the purpose of implementing those programs which provide assistance to individuals only.

March 16

The President transmitted to the Congress the annual report of the Administration on Aging for fiscal year 1977.

NOMINATIONS SUBMITTED TO THE SENATE

The following list does not include promotions of members of the Uniformed Services, nominations to the Service Academies, or nominations of Foreign Service officers.

Submitted March 15, 1979

BAILEY BROWN, of Tennessee, to be a United States Circuit Judge for the Sixth Circuit, vice Harry Phillips, retired.

HAROLD DUANE VIETOR, of Iowa, to be United States District Judge for the Southern District of Iowa, vice a new position created by P.L. 95–486, approved October 20, 1978.

PAUL G. HATFIELD, of Montana, to be United States District Judge for the District of Montana, vice Russell E. Smith, retired.

DONALD JAMES PORTER, of South Dakota, to be United States District Judge for the District of South Dakota, vice a new position created by P.L. 95–486, approved October 20, 1978.

The following-named persons to be members of the Board of Directors of the Corporation for Public Broadcasting for terms expiring March 26, 1984:

MICHAEL A. GAMMINO, JR., of Rhode Island (reappointment).

JOSÉ A. RIVERA, of New York, vice Louis P. Terrazas, term expired.

The following-named persons to be members of the National Council on the Arts for terms expiring September 3, 1984:

THOMAS PATRICK BERGIN, of Indiana, vice James Wyeth, term expired.

JAMES ROSENQUIST, of Florida, vice Billy Taylor, term expired.

NOMINATIONS—Continued

Submitted March 15—Continued

PATRICIA A. GOLDMAN, of the District of Columbia, to be a member of the National Transportation Safety Board for the term expiring December 31, 1983, vice Philip Allison Hogue, term expired.

CHECKLIST OF WHITE HOUSE PRESS RELEASES

The following listing contains releases of the White House Press Office which are not included in this issue.

Released March 8, 1979

Advance text: remarks on arrival in Cairo, Egypt

Released March 10, 1979

Advance text: address before the People's Assembly in Cairo, Egypt

Advance text: remarks on arrival in Tel Aviv, Israel

Released March 14, 1979

Announcement: nomination of Bailey Brown to be a United States Circuit Judge for the Sixth Circuit

Announcement: nomination of Harold Duane Vietor to be United States District Judge for the Southern District of Iowa

Released March 15, 1979

Announcement: nomination of Paul G. Hatfield to be United States District Judge for the District of Montana

Announcement: nomination of Donald J. Porter to be United States District Judge for the District of South Dakota

Comments: support for the proposed hospital cost containment legislation, received by the White House from national organizations

Announcement: signing of Executive Order 12125, Competitive Status for Handicapped Federal Employees

ACTS APPROVED BY THE PRESIDENT

NOTE: No acts approved by the President were received by the Office of the Federal Register during the period covered by this issue.

Conservationist of the Year Award

Remarks on Accepting the Award From the National Wildlife Federation.
March 20, 1979

Mr. Scroggin. Good morning, Mr. President.

Four years ago, you spoke to our annual meeting in Pittsburgh, Pennsylvania, and if I remember correctly, your airplane ran into a bank of snow out at the airport that morning; also encountered a St. Patrick's Day parade on the way to the hotel. But nevertheless, he made it on time, and he made one whale of a good speech.

In fact, the reason we had invited him to that particular program was that he had demonstrated that he was a conservationist Governor. And little did we realize that we'd be here, some 4 years later, presenting an award to a conservationist President.

Mr. President, I'd like to read the citation.

[At this point, Dr. Fred Scroggin, president of the National Wildlife Federation, read the citation, the text of which follows:

CONSERVATIONIST OF THE YEAR

National Wildlife Federation is pleased to present its 1978 Conservationist of the Year

Award to President Jimmy Carter in recognition of the noteworthy environmental record he has compiled during the first two years of his term in office. This record includes his appointment of outstanding persons to positions of authority in the protection of the environment and management of natural resources, his efforts to stop wasteful and destructive pork barrel water projects spending, his selection of the least environmentally objectionable route for the transmission of Alaskan gas, his strong support of endangered species and solar energy, and his initiative to establish a major urban recreation program. In December, 1978, his record was crowned by forceful, courageous, and imaginative action taken to protect large portions of the fragile ecosystem of Alaska, following failure of the 95th Congress to protect this magnificent national heritage from reckless development. By invoking the 1906 Antiquities Act and various sections of the Federal Land Policy Management Act to withdraw 110 million acres and to create national parks and monuments, wildlife refuges, wild and scenic rivers, forests and wildernesses, President Carter personally, and through the Interior Department, has assured that the unmatched wealth of natural resources they contain can be preserved for future generations of Americans.]

President Carter, on behalf of the officers, board of directors, staff, and National Wildlife Federation, it is my pleasure to present to you this statuette of a whooping crane, recognized as our top conservationist award for 1978.

Congratulations, Mr. President.

THE PRESIDENT. *President Fred Scrog-*

gin and my other friends in the National Wildlife Federation:

I don't know of any award that I could get that would mean more to me or be more in keeping with my lifetime love of the out-of-doors and the quality of our environment.

As you know, I grew up as a farmboy in the woods and fields and swamps of Georgia, and an important element of my life then, in the Navy, as Governor, as President, has been my love of the out-of-doors and the quality of life of American people.

As a hunter and a fisherman, as a canoeist, as a hiker, camper, lately as a cross-country skier, and in my other moments of diversion and enjoyment, there's no place that I would rather be than in the beautiful out-of-doors of our country.

I want to thank you for this award. For a long time in Government, the quality of our environment was either ignored or taken for granted. But in recent years, all of us have become increasingly concerned about how Americans will live now and in future generations, with the pressure of industrial development a major element in Americans lives.

The Wildlife Federation is a group of practical, dedicated, courageous, knowledgeable men and women who are committed to ensuring that the environment will stay in a high or improved quality and that Americans can continue to live a life of high quality.

We have had some accomplishments in the last 2 years, with your help, some notable accomplishments. But we have a long way to go. We cannot afford to take for granted any element of threat to America's out-of-doors or to the environment in which we live.

We still have not permanently resolved the question of the Alaska lands. My administrative action will stand until the Congress passes superior legislation. And if a threat is made to the standard that we have already established for the Alaskan lands, then I intend to use the full resources and authority of me, as President, to protect that beautiful country. We want to be fair to the people who live in Alaska. We want to develop our energy resources. But at the same time, these two desires to protect the quality of Alaska and to see it grow appropriately are not incompatible, in my opinion.

I have proposed to the Congress, or will shortly, the establishment of a department of natural resources, to bring into one coherent form an effort to use and to preserve the quality of our country. And this is not going to be an easy legislative effort. I need the help and support of the National Wildlife Federation as we embark on this new, major step toward realizing the goals that have held together your own federation.

I meet with Tom Kimball, representing your group, and with another very good group of environmentalists at least every 6 months. We sit around this table in the Cabinet Room, and we discuss the far-reaching aspects of the many decisions that a President has to make. These decisions that affect your and my goals are not just restrained to so-called environmental law; they affect almost every decision made here in Washington. And I know that with your continued support and interest and advice and counsel and, sometimes, criticisms when I don't meet your very high standards in every respect, that we can continue to make our partnership effective in preserving the beauty and quality of the life of people who live in the greatest nation on Earth.

Thank you very much.

NOTE: The presentation ceremony began at 9:30 a.m. in the Cabinet Room at the White House.

Vietnam Veterans Week, 1979

Proclamation 4647.   March 20, 1979

By the President of the United States of America

A Proclamation

We are a peace-seeking Nation and we are at peace, but we must not forget the lessons war has taught us, nor the brave men and women who have sacrificed so much for us in all our wars.

The decade now drawing to a close began in the midst of a war that was the longest and most expensive in our history, and the most costly in human lives and suffering.[1] Because it was a divisive and painful period for all Americans, we are tempted to want to put the Vietnam war out of our minds. But it is important that we remember—honestly, realistically, with humility.

It is important, too, that we remember those who answered their Nation's call in that war with the full measure of their valor and loyalty, that we pay full tribute at last to all Americans who served in our Armed Forces in Southeast Asia. Their courage and sacrifices in that tragic conflict were made doubly difficult by the Nation's lack of agreement as to what constituted the highest duty. Instead of glory,

---

[1] The White House Press Office later issued a corrected release in which the phrase reads ". . . and most costly in human lives and suffering."

they were too often met with our embarrassment or ignored when they returned.

The honor of those who died there is not tarnished by our uncertainty at the moment of their sacrifice. To them we offer our respect and gratitude. To the loved ones they left behind, we offer our concern and understanding and our help to build new lives. To those who still bear the wounds, both physical and psychic, from all our wars, we acknowledge our continuing responsibility.

Of all the millions of Americans who served in Southeast Asia, the majority have successfully rejoined the mainstream of American life.

To them, and to all who served or suffered in that war, we give our solemn pledge to pursue all honorable means to establish a just and lasting peace in the world, that no future generation need suffer in this way again.

Now, THEREFORE, I, JIMMY CARTER, President of the United States of America, call upon all Americans to observe May 28 through June 3, 1979, the week of our traditional Memorial Day, as Vietnam Veterans Week. On this occasion, let us as a Nation express our sincere thanks for the service of all Vietnam era veterans.

I urge my fellow citizens and my fellow veterans, and their groups and organizations, to honor the patriotism of these veterans, and to recognize their civilian contributions to their communities in America today.

I call upon the state and local governments to join with me in proclaiming Vietnam Veterans Week, and to publicly recognize with appropriate ceremonies and activities yesterday's service and today's contributions of Vietnam era veterans.

IN WITNESS WHEREOF, I have hereunto set my hand this twentieth day of March, in the year of our Lord nineteen

445

hundred and seventy-nine, and of the Independence of the United States of America the two hundred and third.

JIMMY CARTER

[Filed with the Office of the Federal Register, 11:43 a.m., March 20, 1979]

International Monetary Fund

Nomination of Donald E. Syvrud To Be U. S. Alternate Executive Director.
March 20, 1979

The President today announced that he will nominate Donald E. Syvrud, of McLean, Va., to be U.S. Alternate Executive Director of the International Monetary Fund. He would replace Thomas Leddy, resigned.

Syvrud, 54, is Director of the Office of International Monetary Affairs at the Treasury Department. He has been with the Treasury Department since 1971, and has also been a Federal executive fellow at the Brookings Institution and an international economist with the Office of Developing Nations. He was an international economist with the State Department from 1954 to 1963.

National Advisory Council on Indian Education

Appointment of Five Members.
March 20, 1979

The President today announced the appointment of five persons as members of the National Advisory Council on Indian Education. They are:

JOY J. HANLEY, of Window Rock, Ariz., vice president for academic and student affairs at Navajo Community College in Tsaile, Ariz.;

RUBY B. LUDWIG, of Grove, Okla., an elementary schoolteacher and learning disability laboratory instructor;

WAYNE A. NEWELL, of Princeton, Maine, director of the Wabnaki bilingual education program at the Indian Township School;

VIOLET E. RAU, of Toppenish, Wash., director of the Yakima Indian Nation early childhood education programs and a child development associate specialist for the University Research Corporation Indian Migrant Programs Division;

ROBERT J. SWAN, of Havre, Mont., education director of the Fort Belknap Community Council, recently named National Indian Educator of the Year by the National Indian Education Association.

Recording Industry Association of America

Remarks at a White House Reception.
March 20, 1979

It's nice to meet personally with a group with whom I spend about 10 hours a day. The music that you make not only pleases the President of the United States, but I think it extends the beneficial impact of American life throughout the world. As you well know, because you've achieved this high standard of accomplishment, the American sound recording industry has indeed been innovative, dynamic, pleasant, profitable, and— [*laughter*]—I was just trying to see which one of those adjectives appealed to you most. [*Laughter*]

But for people who have the talent to both create and produce sound recordings, I want to express my thanks to you as President. I've got a lot of friends in this room. You've been my friends when the Jimmy Carter performance was on the top of the chart and also when it was on the bottom. [*Laughter*] And I thank you for it very much.

I understand that my dancing partner, Beverly Sills, is here. Is she? Is Beverly here?

Hi, beautiful. Good to see you.

I understand that she's going to be honored tonight with your top award for cultural music performer. In this very room, not too long ago, she not only thrilled a very wonderful audience but she gave me a good dancing lesson, and I enjoyed being with her.

And I've just walked over here with Chet Atkins. I have been a fan of his for 20 years or more, and I still listen to his music often. Last night he was in Ohio with my wife, and she called about 9:30 to say that his performance there not only was an inspiration to her personally, and his friendship was very important to her, but the whole audience that heard him play his guitar were electrified, as usual. You're not surprised at that. I might say this is not the first time he has had an interrelationship with the Carter family. He started out with them, or they with him, a long time ago in Nashville,

I do want to say that Chet Atkins, who's practically a classical performer— we had Andrés Segovia play in this room a couple of Sundays ago—and Chet, also represent the highest kind of personal artistic achievement—Beverly Sills, who has made opera come to life for many people with her personal beauty and her acting talent as well as her lovely voice— represent the gamut of offerings that you have made available to us in this great country and also throughout the world. And I am deeply indebted to you personally and want to express, on behalf of more than 200 million Americans, our thanks for what you mean to us.

I believe that you know how close I feel to many of you personally. Phil

Walden,[1] a good Georgian, informed me when I was Governor about some of the problems with the pirating of recordings and soundtapes. We passed an excellent bill in Georgia to correct that deficiency, and I began to understand a little more about your industry from his instruction and his concern. And, of course, as you also know, I have been to your conventions and have met many of you in very favorable circumstances.

This is your home. We have a very good partnership throughout our country. Many things divide Americans, one from another—differences of perspective, background, interests. And, of course, many more things divide Americans from other people throughout the world. International borders are very difficult to bridge. Tedious, long negotiations are sometimes necessary to tear down hatreds, misunderstandings, animosities. But I think if there's one industry that I can imagine that has been successful in bridging these gaps and bringing an alleviation of tension and a better understanding of one another not only in our own country but throughout the world, across the most impenetrable political borders, it has been the sound recording industry.

And I don't know if you think about your achievement in this way, but as President, it's a very sobering and a very gratifying thought for me. And I want to congratulate you, welcome you here to the White House, thank you for your tremendous achievements in the past. And I believe that the future will see an even brighter future for you and for your industry and for peace and harmony, understanding, good will, even love throughout the world.

Thank you very much.

NOTE: The President spoke at 3:42 p.m. in the East Room at the White House.

---

[1] Member of the board of directors, Recording Industry Association of America.

Administrator of General Services

Exchange of Letters on the Resignation of Joel W. (Jay) Solomon.   March 21, 1979

March 21, 1979

To Jay Solomon

I accept your resignation with regret and with gratitude for the services you have rendered to this Administration and to the American taxpaper.

Because of your leadership and integrity, decades of waste and corruption at the GSA are now being exposed, and those who have betrayed the public trust are being identified and punished. That process will be continued and expanded.

Your willingness to be available to assist your successor after March 31st will help me to insure that the investigations, reorganization and administrative improvements you began will be pursued aggressively.

You take with you my warmest personal affection and best wishes.

Sincerely,

JIMMY CARTER

[The Honorable Joel W. Solomon, Administrator, General Services Administration, Washington, D.C. 20405]

___

March 14, 1979

Dear Mr. President:

In accordance with understandings reached in previous conversations, I hereby tender my resignation as Administrator of The General Services Administration, effective March 31, 1979.

It has been a high privilege and honor to serve my country in the Carter Administration, and I am deeply grateful to you for having made that possible.

Best wishes for your Administration's continued success.

Respectfully,

JAY SOLOMON
Joel W. Solomon

[The President, The White House, Washington, D.C. 20500]

President's Committee on the National Medal of Science

Appointment of Nine Members. March 21, 1979

The President today announced the appointment of nine persons as members of the President's Committee on the National Medal of Science. They are:

W. DALE COMPTON, of Birmingham, Mich., director of chemical and physical sciences, executive director of the science research staff, and vice president of research for the Ford Motor Co.;

CARL DJERASSI, professor of chemistry at Stanford University;

MARY LOWE GOOD, the Boyd professor of chemistry at the University of New Orleans;

LEON M. LEDERMAN, the Eugene Higgins professor of physics at Columbia University;

CALVIN C. MOORE, dean of physical sciences at the University of California at Berkeley;

DOROTHY M. SIMON, of Greenwich, Conn., vice president and director of research for AVCO Corp.;

JOHN B. SLAUGHTER, of Chevy Chase, Md., Assistant Director for Astronomical, Atmospheric, Earth and Ocean Sciences at the National Science Foundation;

STEVEN WEINBERG, Higgins professor of physics at Harvard University;

JOHN R. WHINNERY, professor of electrical engineering and former dean of the College of Engineering at the University of California at Berkeley.

Egyptian-Israeli Peace Negotiations

Statement on Action by the Israeli Knesset Approving a Peace Treaty.   March 21, 1979

The Israeli Knesset spoke with a voice heard around the world today—a voice for peace. We welcome this historic decision. The overwhelming vote in favor of the peace treaty between Israel and Egypt affirms the deep and long-felt desire of the people of Israel for peace with their neighbors. In taking this action, Israel's democracy has lived up to its promise, providing a free and open discussion of all the issues, and then deciding in favor of peace.

The bonds of shared values and common purpose between the United States and Israel are strong and enduring. The achievement of peace between Israel and Egypt will strengthen even more our relations with these two partners in peace and help move toward a stable, cooperative, and peaceful future for all the peoples of the Middle East.

Convention on International Civil Aviation

Message to the Senate Transmitting Protocols to the Convention.   March 22, 1979

To the Senate of the United States:

I transmit herewith, for advice and consent of the Senate to ratification and acceptance, respectively, the following two related Protocols:

—The Protocol Relating to an Amendment to the Convention on International Civil Aviation (Chicago, 1944), done at Montreal September 30, 1977.

—The Protocol on the Authentic Quadrilingual Text of the Convention on International Civil Aviation (Chicago, 1944), with annex, done at Montreal September 30, 1977.

I also transmit, for the information of the Senate, the Report of the Department of State with regard to these Protocols.

The 1944 Chicago Convention establishes the International Civil Aviation Organization (ICAO) and a framework for the safe and reasonable conduct of international civil aviation. The 1977 Protocols are designed to permit the establishment of an authentic Russian language text of the Chicago Convention on an equal footing with the English, French and Spanish texts, which are currently the only existing authentic texts. The U.S.S.R. has been a Party to the Chicago Convention since November 14, 1970, and Russian has been an official working language at ICAO since early 1972.

Additionally, several other Eastern European States use Russian in ICAO. While these Protocols impose no new substantive obligations on the United States, they would appear to be quite important in facilitating the complete integration of the Russian language speaking States, or States which use Russian for aviation purposes, into the international civil aviation community. I therefore recommend that the Senate give early and favorable consideration to these Protocols and advice and consent to their respective ratification and acceptance.

JIMMY CARTER

The White House,
     March 22, 1979.

449

United States-Mexico Treaty on Extradition

Message to the Senate Transmitting the Treaty.   March 22, 1979

To the Senate of the United States:

With a view to receiving the advice and consent of the Senate to ratification, I transmit herewith the Treaty of Extradition Between the United States of America and the United Mexican States, signed at Mexico City on May 4, 1978.

I transmit also, for the information of the Senate, the report of the Department of State with respect to the Treaty.

The Treaty is one of a series of modern extradition treaties being negotiated by the United States. It expands the list of extraditable offenses to include narcotics offenses, aircraft hijacking, bribery, and obstruction of justice, as well as many other offenses not now covered by our existing Extradition Treaty with Mexico. Upon entry into force, it will terminate and supersede the existing Extradition Treaty and Additional Conventions between the United States and Mexico.

This Treaty will make a significant contribution to international cooperation in law enforcement. I recommend that the Senate give early and favorable considerations to the Treaty and give its advice and consent to ratification.

JIMMY CARTER

The White House,
    March 22, 1979.

Select Commission on Immigration and Refugee Policy

*Appointment of the Four Public Members.
March 22, 1979*

The President today announced the appointment of the four public members of the Select Commission on Immigration and Refugee Policy. They are:

Reubin Askew, who was Governor of Florida from 1971 to 1979, and is now practicing law in Miami. Askew was a Florida State representative and State senator prior to his election as Governor. He has also been designated Chairman of this Commission.

Rose Matsui Ochi, executive assistant to Los Angeles Mayor Tom Bradley and director of criminal justice planning for the city of Los Angeles. Ochi was previously a staff attorney for the Western Center on Law and Poverty.

Joaquin Francisco Otero, international vice president of the Brotherhood of Railway and Airline Clerks. Otero, of Springfield, Va., was born in Cuba in 1934 and emigrated to the United States in 1954. He became a naturalized citizen in 1960. Otero has worked actively with the AFL-CIO/COPE in creation of a Labor Council for Latin American Advancement.

Cruz Reynoso, associate justice of the Third Appellate District in Sacramento, Calif. Reynoso has taught law at the University of California and the University of New Mexico and has served as director of California Rural Legal Assistance.

The Commission also includes:

—the Secretary of State, the Attorney General, the Secretary of Labor, and the Secretary of Health, Education, and Welfare, ex officio;

—four members of the Senate Judiciary Committee, appointed by the President pro tem of the Senate. Those appointed, who were announced in the Senate on March 19, are Senators Kennedy, DeConcini, Mathias, and Simpson;

—four members of the House Judiciary Committee, appointed by the Speaker of the House. Those appointed, who were announced in the House on March 19, are Representatives Rodino, Holtzman, McClory, and Fish.

30th Anniversary of NATO

Proclamation 4648.   March 22, 1979

By the President of the United States of America

A Proclamation

Thirty years ago in Washington on April 4, 1949 the North Atlantic Treaty was signed. From that act grew the North Atlantic Treaty Organization, or NATO, an alliance welded together by a common dedication to perpetuating democracy, individual liberty and the rule of law.

For three decades, NATO has successfully deterred war and maintained stability in Western Europe and North America, thus securing the well-being and prosperity of its fifteen member states: Belgium, Canada, Denmark, France, the Federal Republic of Germany, Greece, Iceland, Italy, Luxembourg, the Netherlands, Norway, Portugal, Turkey, the United Kingdom, and the United States of America.

Though collective defense against possible aggression was the most urgent requirement at its founding, NATO has always been much more than just a military pact. The spontaneous political development of the Alliance demonstrates that true security is far more than a matter of weaponry and armed battalions. In the final analysis, true security flows from the freely-given support of the people and their willingness to participate in the defense of common ideals.

Since NATO's inception, the interna-

tional situation has evolved in many respects and NATO has adapted to these changes—militarily, politically and economically. Today the Alliance remains as relevant and centrally important to our security and way of life and to the independence of the United States as it was in 1949. Then as now, the firm support of Congress and the American people for NATO reflects their deep conviction that NATO is the cornerstone of United States foreign policy.

As NATO moves forward into another decade of achievement, we look toward the future with confidence, aware that continuing Allied cooperation will provide the international stability and security upon which our ideals, our civilization, and our well-being depend. As NATO begins this new chapter in its distinguished history, I am proud to rededicate the United States to the NATO objectives which have served the cause of peace so well.

Now, THEREFORE, I, JIMMY CARTER, President of the United States of America, do hereby direct the attention of the Nation to this thirtieth anniversary of the signing of the North Atlantic Treaty; and I call upon the Governors of the States, and upon the officers of local governments, to facilitate the suitable observance of this notable event throughout this anniversary year with particular attention to April, the month which marks the historic signing ceremony.

IN WITNESS WHEREOF, I have hereunto set my hand this twenty-second day of March, in the year of our Lord nineteen hundred seventy-nine, and of the Independence of the United States of America the two hundred and third.

JIMMY CARTER

[Filed with the Office of the Federal Register, 11:18 a.m., March 23, 1979]

Nuclear Non-Proliferation Act of 1978

Message to the Congress Transmitting a Report. March 22, 1979

To the Congress of the United States:

I am pleased to submit the first report, as called for by Sections 601 and 602 of the Nuclear Non-Proliferation Act of 1978 (Public Law 95–242), on the activities of the Government Departments and Agencies to prevent proliferation.

The report, consisting of four volumes, is enclosed. The first volume contains a summary and chapters detailing the progress made in the following areas:

—The International Nuclear Fuel Cycle Evaluation (INFCE)

—An international nuclear fuel regime

—Development of common export and domestic policies

—Encouraging adherences to the Treaty on the Non-Proliferation of Nuclear Weapons (NPT)

—Strengthening IAEA safeguards

—Negotiating agreements for cooperation

—Cooperation in energy with developing countries

—Cooperation in protection of the environment

—Procedures for processing export-related matters

In discussing the Government's activities in these areas, the report notes that considerable progress has been made in increasing international appreciation of the importance of minimizing risks of proliferation inherent in future fuel cycle developments. It points out that, through INFCE, the United States has stimulated a general reexamination of long-held technical assumptions concerning fuel cycle activities and awareness of the need to consider proliferation concerns. Progress is also reported in obtaining wider adherence to the NPT, in strengthening IAEA safeguards, and in continued consultations among nuclear suppliers.

The report notes that a number of problems have been encountered, particularly the perception by other countries that the United States is attempting to impose its own standards unilaterally on peaceful nuclear cooperation and that those standards are unnecessarily strict or impracticable. Doubts about the reliability of the United States as a nuclear supplier persist, as well as differences of views between ourselves and others concerning the proliferation risks and economic benefits of reprocessing and the recycling of plutonium in light water reactors. These problems and others noted in the report will continue to be addressed in our efforts to achieve international support for and consensus on our nonproliferation objectives.

Chapter XI of the report contains the analyses of the agreements for cooperation. It consists of two unclassified volumes, which are enclosed, and a classified volume which is being submitted to the Senate Foreign Relations Committee and the House International Affairs Committee, in accordance with Section 602(d) of Public Law 95–242.

JIMMY CARTER

The White House,
   March 22, 1979.

NOTE: The report is entitled "Report of the President to the Congress, Pursuant to Section 601 of the Nuclear Non-Proliferation Act of 1978—January 1979."

Interview With the President

Question-and-Answer Session With Dan Shilon of Israeli Television.   March 22, 1979

MR. SHILON. Mr. President, less than 2 weeks ago, when you addressed the Israeli Knesset, you said, and I quote, "The people of the two nations are ready now for peace. The leaders have not yet proven that we are also ready for peace, enough to take the chance."

Now, after the leaders approved the peace treaty, it seems that the leaders are celebrating. The peoples are still a bit cautious about it. How can you explain it?

THE PRESIDENT. Well, let me correct you, first of all. I didn't say the leaders of the two nations; I said we leaders. And I was referring also to the adjacent countries, Syria and Jordan, where I believe a substantial portion of the population are intensely desirous of peace and an end to hatred and terrorism and destruction and death. So, that's what I meant when I talked to the Knesset.

I don't believe that the peace treaties can have their full, permanent, beneficial impact if they are just based on a relationship between or among leaders or documents, because Sadat, Begin, Carter will not be in office many years under the best of circumstances. And until we have a genuine interrelationship among the people of, say, Egypt and Israel, we can't have the full connotation of the meaning of peace. We need students to move freely back and forth between the two countries, tourists, open borders, free use of the Suez Canal, the Straits of Tiran. We need increased trade, mutual investment, exchange of employees back and forth between the two countries, an opening up of trade between Israel and the United States, Egypt and the United States and Western Europe, that hasn't been there before.

As soon as the people of the two countries get to know each other, to trust each other, to like each other, to become mutually dependent on each other, to recognize their common future, common problems, common opportunities, at that point, peace will be permanent and will be full.

And I think that's the best way to demonstrate to the Palestinians, to the Jordanians, to the Syrians, and others, the full advantages to them of emulating what Egypt and Israel have already done.

MR. SHILON. But on the other hand, what are the risks to Israel and to Egypt, if there are any, by signing the peace treaty?

THE PRESIDENT. Well, I think the risks of not signing it are much greater than the risks of signing it. Obviously, there is going to be a period of time within which the PLO and some of the Arab countries will threaten increased violence or economic punishment, terrorism, instability. I really believe that that period is going to be relatively brief.

So, to compare the risks with the advantages of signing the peace treaty, obviously, the advantages far outweigh the risks.

There are some doubts about the future. This is kind of a new life, and both countries are going into the unknown with great predictions of problems. I think the problems have been grossly exaggerated from the very beginning. And, of course, to the extent that we can use our influence in a beneficial way, the United States is not only willing but eager to guarantee that the outcome of the peace negotiations will be fulfilled to their complete degree.

And we can help to alleviate some of these concerns. And if problems do arise that we cannot presently anticipate, we'll be full partners in trying to address those problems when they become evident.

Mr. Shilon. Can you foresee realistically that Syria, Jordan, and the Palestinians, encouraged by Saudi Arabia, will cooperate with the continuation of the peace process?

The President. I think this is a very good possibility in the future. But there's going to be a transition period when they try to posture and threaten and see if they can weaken the ties of friendship and peace between Israel and Egypt.

I think they'll be unsuccessful in trying to destroy the peace process when it becomes evident that the advantages of peace directly improve the quality of life of the Israelis and the Egyptians. In my opinion, the large number of Jordanians who also presently want peace will become much more vocal, and perhaps King Hussein and the other Arab leaders will say, "Well, this is a good thing for me and my people as well." I think that could very well happen in the future.

Mr. Shilon. Mr. President, during the past year, you mentioned several times the right of the Palestinians to participate in their own determination of their own future.

The President. Yes.

Mr. Shilon. This participation is now defined as self-rule or autonomy. Could the following steps, after establishing the self-rule, lead to an independent Palestinian state?

The President. Well, we drafted this language, the Palestinians' right to participate in the determination of their own future, very carefully. It's been adopted by both Israel and Egypt as a basis for the Camp David agreements. And, of course, that's incorporated within the peace treaties themselves. Also, the principles expressed in United Nations Resolutions 242 and 338 are part of the Camp David agreements, and also this treaty.

It's not up to the United States to decide the ultimate status of the West Bank or the Gaza area. This is the reason for the future negotiations, in which not only the Palestinians but also the Jordanians and the Egyptians will negotiate.

So, I don't want to say what the ultimate status or who has sovereignty might be. The first step, to define what is—to use Prime Minister Begin's word—full autonomy, will be difficult enough without my trying to decide here what decision might be reached 5 years in the future on the permanent status.

Mr. Shilon. Can you define the exact American attitude these days towards the PLO?

The President. Our attitude these days is the same as it has been for a long time. The PLO have not been willing to recognize the applicability of United Nations Resolution 242, and the PLO have not been willing to accept the right of Israel to exist. Until the PLO is willing to do these things, we will not deal with the PLO.

Mr. Shilon. Mr. President, are you actually suggesting a defense treaty between Israel and the United States?

The President. No. We've never suggested this. But there will be a memorandum of understanding that will exist between Israel and the United States for the first time. It will be fairly far-reaching, and it's exactly what we want and exactly what Israel wants as well.

We've never had any sort of proposals on either side that there be an actual defense treaty between our two countries. I think Israel has always cherished the concept that they are perfectly able to defend themselves. And I think that's an accurate assessment.

MR. SHILON. It seems that accomplishing this goal was important to you personally, at least as important as to the parties involved.

THE PRESIDENT. Yes.

MR. SHILON. Why was that?

THE PRESIDENT. It's important to my country. We have a political, a philosophical, and a moral commitment to Israel—Israel's right to exist, to exist permanently, to exist securely, to exist in prosperity, and to exist in peace. And this is not a personal—this is not *merely* a personal belief of mine, but it's a belief that accurately represents the overwhelming portion of the American people.

Additionally, we have a strong friendship with Egypt. And obviously, it's to our own Nation's advantage to have our two friends, who are permanent neighbors, be friends with each other.

So, in addition to the personal commitment that I've had, I think I accurately represent what's best for my country and the aspirations which the people of my country have cherished for many years.

MR. SHILON. Mr. President, finally, during the ups and downs of the negotiations, was there any moment in which you felt despair or thought of giving up your efforts?

THE PRESIDENT. I despaired many times, but I never reached such a state of discouragement that I thought about giving up. I was always determined to continue the peace process as long as I hold the office of President of the United States. And if there should evolve, in the future, problems, I'll be just as determined to work for peace as I have been in the past.

MR. SHILON. Mr. President, thank you so much for spending your time with us.

THE PRESIDENT. It's been a pleasure for me. Thank you.

NOTE: The interview began at 3 p.m. in the Map Room at the White House. It was taped for later broadcast in Israel.

The transcript of the interview was released on March 23.

Interview With the President

Question-and-Answer Session With Adib Andrawes of Egyptian Television. March 22, 1979

MR. ANDRAWES. Mr. President, you have committed the United States to be a full partner in the peace process until the Palestinian problem is settled, which is the core of the Middle East conflict. Would you care, Mr. President, to tell us what are your immediate plans for the Palestinian people?

THE PRESIDENT. The immediate plans are specified in the Camp David agreements and also in the terms of the peace treaty. They involve, to use part of the language, the right of the Palestinians to have a voice in the determination of their own future and to recognize the legitimate rights of the Palestinians. This is encompassed in the mutual agreement, signed by Prime Minister Begin, President Sadat, and myself: first of all—to use Prime Minister Begin's words—full autonomy for the Palestinians who live in the West Bank and Gaza areas; secondly, the termination of the Israeli military government; third, the withdrawal of Israeli troops into specified security locations.

I think the success of this effort will depend to a substantial degree on the willingness of the Palestinians and others to participate in the negotiations themselves.

Obviously, President Sadat and I and Prime Minister Begin and our representatives can do a substantial amount for the Palestinians, even in their absence. But the full realization of their expectations under these terms would obviously be dependent on how willing they are to participate themselves.

MR. ANDRAWES. Mr. President, the Palestinian people feel they have been victims and evicted from their homes; the United States, as a super power, should take the lead in inviting them and asking them to come and talk with the administration on their needs and their problems and so on. Could this be envisaged in the very near future?

THE PRESIDENT. Yes. We would like to have direct relations with the Palestinians, and we will, as part of the negotiating process in the future. The Palestinians who live in Gaza and the West Bank will be invited and encouraged to participate in these discussions, the mayors of the cities and other representatives to be chosen by the Palestinians themselves.

We have a problem with the PLO. The PLO has never yet been willing to accept the applicability of United Nations Resolution 242, the basis for the Camp David agreements and, I think, a document that's been adopted by all of the Arab nations as a foundation for future progress. The PLO has never been willing to accept this document. Also, the PLO has never recognized Israel's right to exist. And as soon as the PLO itself, as an organization, is willing to accept these bases, then we'll immediately start working directly with that organization as such.

But in the meantime, the Palestinians who reside in the West Bank, Gaza area, the Palestinians who reside in Egypt and Jordan, and even others who don't reside in either of these countries, if they're mu-

tually acceptable, will participate in the negotiations.

MR. ANDRAWES. But wouldn't it be useful, Mr. President, if you, as a super power, took the first step and explained to the Palestinian people the necessity of accepting Resolution 242 and getting into the peace process? You have actually said before and invited them to participate in the process, even accepting 242 with reservations.

THE PRESIDENT. Yes, and I hope they will do that.

We have not only sent representatives to meet with Palestinian leaders in the West Bank and Gaza areas—both from the administration, the State Department, and also, for instance, the majority leader of the Democratic Party in the U.S. Senate met with a representative group—but when I've met with President Asad of Syria and King Hussein of Jordan and with King Khalid and Crown Prince Fahd in Saudi Arabia, I have encouraged them to do everything they could, possibly, to involve the Palestinians in the peace process.

As you know, there are threats made and there are demonstrations of terrorism which tend to prevent the Palestinians who want to have peace and who want to have full autonomy from participating in these processes. And I think the threats of terrorism and the hatred that presently exists, the threat of war, the threat of economic boycotts and punishment against Egypt, are certainly not conducive to realizing the hopes of the Palestinian people.

There is no leader in the Mideast who has done more to open up an opportunity for progress and the restoration of the rights of the Palestinians than President Sadat. If the other leaders in Jordan and Syria and Saudi Arabia would do half as much as President Sadat has done, then these hopes that have been described in the agreements reached could be realized very quickly.

MR. ANDRAWES. Mr. President, how do you see Prime Minister Begin's recent statements in the Knesset that Israel will not allow a Palestinian state or will not go back to the borders of '67? Are these useful at that time?

THE PRESIDENT. I don't want to characterize either the statements made by Prime Minister Begin nor Prime Minister Khalil, and so forth. You know, we're in the process now of completing the first step in a long process that will lead to a comprehensive peace. These treaties, which have now been concluded after laborious negotiation, will just be a cornerstone, as President Sadat and I have said, for that comprehensive peace that we desire.

We've specified a negotiating process. And the differences that presently exist between, say, Egypt and Israel on the definition of full autonomy are substantial, substantial differences. But they're not nearly as wide as the differences that existed before the Camp David agreements.

So, you know, it's inevitable that both nations, both negotiating parties, will express their own point of view in the strongest possible terms originally. But after a while, as they get to understand one another and see the mutual advantages of agreement, I hope and expect that both positions will be moderated to some degree and an agreement can be reached. And we'll add our good offices as a negotiating partner. But I can't approve specifically what one leader or another says at the beginning. We'll be there to try to help them reach agreement.

MR. ANDRAWES. Are you prepared, Mr. President, to invest as much time and labor as you have with the Egyptian-Israeli peace treaty on the second phase?

THE PRESIDENT. I would hope that my personal involvement would be much less and that the negotiating teams could make substantial progress.

MR. ANDRAWES. Do you think they can, without your personal intervention from time to time as you've——

THE PRESIDENT. I believe so, because the terms of the agreement and the ultimate goal of the agreement have now been spelled out between myself, Prime Minister Begin, and President Sadat. And this gives kind of a framework or a guideline for the negotiators in the future. We didn't have any such document, we didn't have any agreements to start with less than a year ago when we went to Camp David. And I think the results of what we've done now will make it much easier in the future for subordinates to negotiate than has been the case in the past.

MR. ANDRAWES. Are the talks going to be in Washington?

THE PRESIDENT. I would presume that the talks would be in the Middle East. I hope that 3 months from now, that Egypt will be the sovereign power over El Arish and will have control of this region. And it could be that that beautiful seacoast town, as a part of Egypt, with no Israeli occupying forces, somewhere like that might be a good place to negotiate.

I never had a chance to visit El Arish or Mount Sinai and so forth, but I've told President Sadat that when it's under Egyptian control, I'd like to come back sometime.

MR. ANDRAWES. Very good. Mr. President, you visited Egypt and you've seen the Egyptian people.

THE PRESIDENT. Yes.

MR. ANDRAWES. What impression did you leave with?

THE PRESIDENT. Perfect. I saw people who were friendly toward me, who supported their wonderful leader, President Sadat, and who demonstrated to the world that they genuinely want peace and an end to hatred and war and death and destruction; a people who want a better life in the future and who now have opened up an opportunity to benefit from a new relationship not only with Israel but with other nations in the world.

So, I could not have been more pleased or favorably impressed than I was in my visit to Egypt. It was a great visit.

MR. ANDRAWES. Thank you very much, Mr. President.

THE PRESIDENT. Thank you.

NOTE: The interview began at 3:15 p.m. in the Diplomatic Reception Room at the White House. It was taped for later broadcast in Egypt.

The transcript of the interview was released on March 23.

Administrator of General Services

Nomination of Rear Adm. Rowland G. Freeman III.   March 23, 1979

The President today announced that he will nominate Rear Adm. Rowland G. Freeman III of Fort Belvoir, Va., to be Administrator of the General Services Administration. He would replace Jay Solomon, who has resigned effective March 31.

Freeman is currently the Commandant of the Defense Systems Management College at Fort Belvoir. He has served in that position since June 30, 1977.

Freeman was born February 11, 1922, in New York City. He attended the University of Massachusetts from 1940 to 1942, when he enlisted in the Naval Reserve. He served as a naval aviator from 1943 to 1947, participating in most of the major engagements in the Southwest Pacific during World War II. From 1947 to 1950, he held several assignments involving test pilot flying duties.

From 1950 to 1953, he attended Harvard University, graduating with an MBA degree. Freeman served as Head of the Workload and Components Purchase Section of the Bureau of Aeronautics from 1954 to 1957, and from 1957 to 1960, he headed the Astronautics and Missile Departments of the Naval Missile Center at Port Mugu, Calif.

Freeman served as a squadron commanding officer from 1960 to 1961, and as air officer and navigator of the U.S.S. *Oriskany* in 1962 and 1963. From 1963 to 1964, he was Bureau of Naval Weapons representative in St. Louis, with collateral duties as production test pilot for the Navy F–4 Phantom II fighter. In 1965 and 1966, he commanded the U.S.S. *Procyon,* a refrigerator supply ship serving bases in Southeast Asia.

From 1966 to 1968, he served as project manager of the Navy F–111B program, and from 1968 to 1973, Freeman was Deputy Chief of Naval Material Procurement and Production. From 1974 until 1977, he was Commander of the Naval Weapons Center at China Lake. The center is the Navy's single largest laboratory complex, with 4,000 employees, 1,000 military personnel, and an annual budget of $200 million. In 1977 Freeman became Commandant of the Defense Systems Management College.

He is a fellow and member of the board of advisors of the National Contract Management Association, a fellow and member of the board of advisors of the

Society of Logistic Engineers, a member
of the American Institute of Aeronautics
and Astronautics, and a member of the
American Society of Naval Engineers.

Freight Rail Industry Deregulation

*Message to the Congress Transmitting
Proposed Legislation.   March 23, 1979*

To the Congress of the United States:

Today I am submitting my proposals to
deregulate the nation's freight rail industry. This legislation is part of a continuing effort to promote more competition in America's transportation system,
and to reduce the burden of federal regulation on the nation's economy. It follows
last year's successful laws deregulating air
freight and passenger service. Later this
spring I will submit proposals addressing
motor carriers and intercity passenger
buses.

The private freight railroads are the
backbone of our industrial and agricultural production. But today the private
freight railroad industry faces a crisis,
which could have grave consequences for
our nation's economy.

Though the railroads still carry more
than a third of the nation's freight and
most of its bulk commodities such as coal,
grain, and chemicals, the industry is in a
deep and dangerous decline. Year by year,
the percentage of freight carried by the
railroads has shrunk, while profits have
fallen and costs have soared.

Many factors contribute to these problems:

• Government regulation of virtually
every aspect of rail operations has restrained innovative management and efficient pricing.

• Increasing competition from unregulated trucks and barges has eroded rail
markets.

• The industry has been slow to adapt
to changing freight patterns and unable
to rationalize its system.

• Improvements in labor productivity
have not kept pace with the rest of the
economy.

A recent study by the Department of
Transportation develops the grim consequences of these trends. The study, *A Prospectus for Change in the Freight Railroad Industry* shows that without major
changes in structure and operation, the
railroads will be unable to generate the
funds needed to sustain themselves. Within a few years, this shortfall of funds could
become so severe that it will paralyze the
private railroad system and jeopardize its
existence.

The facts pointing to these sobering
conclusions are overwhelming. Railroad
revenues have not met railroad costs, and
to survive in a tightly regulated environment railroads have been forced to consume their assets. Deferred maintenance
on branch and main lines now totals $5.4
billion, while total industry profits for the
year ending September 30, 1978, were
only $50.2 million. A sixth of all track in
the nation can only be served at restricted
speeds, yet even with these restrictions
accidents due to track defects have quadrupled in the past ten years. The DOT
Prospectus estimates that the capital
needed to sustain the freight rail system
between now and 1985 will total $42.5
billion; it estimates that the industry itself
is capable of generating or borrowing less
than $30 billion. These figures do not in-
clude the federally-aided Conrail system
in the Northeast which is losing $300–$400
million per year. All railroads are caught
in the squeeze between tight regulation on

459

the one hand, and increased competition on the other. If the situation is not changed, even some healthy railroads of the South and West will face grave difficulties within a few years.

The solution to the railroads' difficulties is not massive government subsidies or new government intervention. Simply to maintain the current rail system would require $2.5 billion of federal funds each year between now and 1985 with the totals likely to grow larger after that. Investing such large sums of tax dollars to preserve an outmoded system would be highly inflationary and ultimately fruitless.

Deregulation presents the only viable option to either massive increases in federal subsidies to the railroads or increased government intervention in their operation—both of which are highly undesirable. Instead of relying on huge federal subsidies we must seek to create an environment in which the railroads themselves can regain their economic health by aggressively improving their operations and profitability. We must eliminate the outmoded rules that have prevented railroads from managing their operation efficiently, responding to competitive opportunities and utilizing equipment profitably. We must allow the industry the flexibility to set rates at levels that generate a fair return on the investment and that attract traffic lost to unregulated modes. Where continued regulation of market abuse is still necessary, we must insure that ICC decisions are rendered promptly, fairly and consistently.

The legislation that we are proposing results from a full examination of the existing regulatory system for railroads. The legislation would create a far more limited regulatory scheme—one that reflects the railroads' current competitive and financial status, and one that provides incentives for the railroads to cut costs, improve service and productivity, and price services competitively.

Specifically these proposals would:

• Allow railroads to set prices for their services without interference from the government. To prevent sudden dislocations, this rate freedom would be phased in gradually over five years with real rate ceilings allowed to increase by 7 percent per year. At the same time, inflationary general rate increases should be gradually phased out in favor of company-by-company pricing of services.

• Transfer jurisdiction over rail mergers from the ICC to the Justice Department under standard anti-trust laws. There is no reason why railroads that do not compete with each other should be treated differently from other businesses seeking to merge.

• Set new guidelines for ICC approval of rail abandonments. These tests would insure that railroads are not forced to continue to serve money losing lines, but would allow shippers, states or communities to provide subsidies to maintain service.

• Clarify provisions preventing discrimination among shipping communities, ports or connecting carriers. The new rules would continue to prevent abuses without tying railroads to rigid price structures.

• Establish new rules to protect railway employees who may be affected by rail mergers or abandonments.

• Eliminate ICC jurisdiction over many day-to-day aspects of managing the rail system.

The transition period to the new regulatory environment may involve some dislocations and may lead to temporary uncertainty for some shippers, railroads and communities. To the extent possible we shall continue to use existing federal programs enacted by previous Congresses to meet these needs as they arise. In addition, new federal resources will be available to compensate, retrain, and relocate workers who are affected by the restructuring of the system.

These regulatory changes alone will not be enough to fully solve problems of the rail industry. Revitalizing the railroads will take a concerted effort by railroad management and labor, working with shippers and communities. Only a complete overhaul of the nation's rail system leading to higher labor productivity and more efficient use of plant and equipment may be able to reverse current unfavorable trends. The government can assist in that effort but the most important contribution must be made by the industry itself.

Without regulatory changes, however, it is certain that the industry will not be able to pull out of its long decline. Without the changes I am recommending, we will face a catastrophic series of rail bankruptcies, sharply declining service and massive federal expenditures.

Unless we act expeditiously the unfortunate pattern we have seen among eastern railroads will be repeated on a national scale. Bankruptcies, followed by huge federal bailouts will spread to the Midwest and ultimately throughout the country. We can act now, while there is still time to address the crisis in an orderly way; or we can wait and have events dictate drastic solutions.

All of us—railroads, shippers, communities, workers and the public—have a vital interest in solving this rail crisis. I am confident that we can work together to solve it. I urge the Congress to act promptly on this important legislation.

JIMMY CARTER

The White House,
   March 23, 1979.

The Cyprus Conflict

Letter to the Speaker of the House and the Chairman of the Senate Foreign Relations Committee.   March 23, 1979

To Speaker Tip O'Neill: (To Senator Frank Church:)

In accordance with the provisions of Public Law 95–384, I am submitting the following report on the progress made during the past sixty days toward the conclusion of a negotiated solution of the Cyprus problem.

During the past two months, as I outlined in my report of January 29, the United Nations has persisted in its active efforts, to bring about a resumption of the Cyprus intercommunal negotiations on a sound and effective basis. The focus of this effort is to develop a meaningful agenda acceptable to both Cypriot parties. The Secretary General's Special Representative in Cyprus has held frequent consultations with both sides in Nicosia, eliciting their reactions to each other's comments on the present draft agenda and seeking their acceptance of compromise suggestions. These consultations are continuing on an intensive basis. Meanwhile, some consideration has also been given to the possibility of direct consultations involving representatives of the two Cypriot communities and the Secretary General this spring.

While we believe that both sides would welcome meaningful talks, we should not underestimate the magnitude of the differences between them on matters of substance. The compromises that must be made if an enduring settlement is to be achieved will be politically difficult for both sides.

The Department of State has remained in close and frequent contact with the United Nations Secretariat and with the parties concerned. We have urged both parties to show flexibility and to respond constructively and imaginatively to the ongoing United Nations initiative. We will continue to make every effort to help bring about a productive resumption of negotiations.

Sincerely,

JIMMY CARTER

NOTE: This is the text of identical letters addressed to Thomas P. O'Neill, Jr., Speaker of the House of Representatives, and Frank Church, chairman of the Senate Foreign Relations Committee.

Joint Financial Management Improvement Program

Memorandum From the President.
March 23, 1979

Memorandum for the Heads of Executive Departments and Agencies

Subject: 30th Anniversary of the Joint Financial Management Improvement Program

Thirty years ago the Executive and Legislative Branches saw the need for a closer working relationship to improve financial management in Government. The advances that have been made since the establishment of the Joint Financial Management Improvement Program and the passage of the Budget and Accounting Procedures Act reflect the efforts of many dedicated individuals. The 30th anniversary of the Joint Program is a timely reminder that significant accomplishments are possible through cooperative efforts without creating new and bigger bureaucracies.

One of my goals as President is to have an efficient and effective Government responsive to the needs of the American people. With the passage of the Civil Service Reform Act, Federal managers now have new incentives to eliminate waste and inefficiency, to develop innovative solutions to complex problems, and to build a new foundation for more effective Government. I am confident that Federal managers will respond to this challenge with efforts that will have a lasting impact on the public service.

We need to re-establish public confidence in Government, and we are making progress. We are placing Inspectors General in each Cabinet-level Department to detect and eliminate fraud and abuses. They have broad powers and a substantial degree of independence. The significant features of this program must be extended throughout the Federal Government. The Office of Management and Budget will make sure that the auditing and investigative functions are meshed in a smooth and effective way.

In November 1977, we started a comprehensive review of cash management policies, practices, and organizations throughout the Executive Branch. The Office of Management and Budget and the Department of the Treasury have been working with Federal agencies to accelerate Federal collections, to time disbursements properly and to develop incentives to make Federal employees better cash managers. I am pleased that the review has identified $400 million in interest cost savings during its first year alone.

A Government-wide effort led by the Office of Management and Budget and the General Accounting Office has now resulted in a breakthrough in auditing Federally assisted programs—a single guide to replace the almost one hundred guides now in use. We need to bring the same kind of simplicity to other Government programs without sacrificing effectiveness.

The spirit of cooperation exemplified by these efforts is an essential ingredient in establishing a new foundation for responsible and responsive Government. JFMIP has pioneered the cooperative approach and produced major improvements in Federal financial management during the past 30 years.

Every anniversary is a time to look back and a time to look ahead. This anniversary reminds us not only of progress made, but also that improved financial management must be a continuous effort, and one that involves every agency of government. I look to the future with great confidence as we put in place many new innovative techniques to make better use of our resources—everything from our cash to our human resources. The objectives of the Joint Program are clearly compatible with and reinforce those of my Administration to attain greater efficiency and effectiveness in Government operations. Therefore, I urge all of you to renew your commitment to the Joint Program and to better financial management in Government.

JIMMY CARTER

Federal Advisory Committees

Message to the Congress Transmitting a Report.   March 23, 1979

To the Congress of the United States:

In accordance with the provisions of Section 6(c) of the Federal Advisory Committee Act (Public Law 92–463), I am transmitting the seventh annual report on the status of Federal advisory committees.

This report reflects further progress toward accomplishing the objectives I set in 1977: to assure that unnecessary committees are terminated, and new committees are established only when they are essential to meet the responsibilities of the government. At the end of 1978:

—The total number of committees was 816, 59 fewer than at the beginning of the year; and

—Since the beginning of 1977 the total number of committees has been reduced by 343 (from 1,159).

JIMMY CARTER

The White House,
   March 23, 1979.

NOTE: The report is entitled "Federal Advisory Committees, Seventh Annual Report of the President Covering the Calendar Year 1978—March 1979" (Government Printing Office, 154 pages).

Advisory Commission on Intergovernmental Relations

Appointment of Richard W. Riley as a Member.   March 23, 1979

The President today announced the appointment of Richard W. Riley, Governor of the State of South Carolina, as a member of the Advisory Commission on Intergovernmental Relations for a 2-year term. He replaces Reubin Askew, former Governor of Florida.

President's Committee on Employment of the Handicapped

Appointment of Three Members. March 23, 1979

The President today announced the appointment of three persons as members of the President's Committee on Employment of the Handicapped. They are:

Harold J. Russell, of Waltham, Mass., who is also designated Chairman of the Committee. Russell, who lost both hands in a wartime training accident in the Army, has been a member of the Committee since 1948 and Chairman since 1964. He is a past national commander of AMVETS, and is currently president of Harold Russell Associates, Inc.

Judith E. Heumann, of Berkeley, Calif., deputy director of the Center for Independent Living, cochairman of the advisory board of the Disabled Community Health Clinic at Herrick Hospital in Berkeley, a consultant on problems of the disabled, and former teacher of disabled students.

Robert G. Sampson, of Arlington Heights, Ill., vice president and special assistant to the president of United Airlines, Inc. Sampson, an attorney, is a member of People to People International Committee for the Handicapped and its affiliate, Disabled Professionals. He has been confined to a wheelchair since age 9 due to muscular dystrophy.

John F. Kennedy Center for the Performing Arts

Appointment of 89 Members of the Advisory Committee on the Arts.　March 23, 1979

The President today announced the appointment of 89 persons as members of the Advisory Committee on the Arts (John F. Kennedy Center for the Performing Arts). They are:

GARY JAY NORTHROP AAMODT, of Madison, Wis., founder and director of a firm which publishes modern editions of old music;

CLARK D. AHLBERG, president of Wichita (Kansas) State University;

ARTHUR D. AMIOTTE, of McLaughlin, S. Dak., a Native American arist;

MARLIN ARKY, of Miami, Fla., a public affairs specialist working with the internship program at Florida International University and Plays for Living;

ELIZABETH W. BLASS, of Little Rock, Ark., a professional photographer and member of the board of the Arkansas Museum of Science and History;

WILLIAM L. BONYUN, of Wiscasset, Maine, a consultant who conducts teachers workshops on American folk music;

FRANCIS T. BORKOWSKI, of Columbia, S.C., provost of the University of South Carolina;

ANN MARIE BOYDEN, of Salt Lake City, a soloist, actress, and producer, and owner of an advertising firm;

MARY LOUISE CHANEY, of Bellevue, Wash., on the acoustics technology staff of the Boeing Co. and a patron of the Seattle Repertory Theater;

CAROLYN G. CLARK, of Long Valley, N.J., executive vice president of the New Jersey Ballet Company;

MAURICE C. CLIFFORD, a Philadelphia physician active in community affairs;

KELLY COHEN, of Savannah, Ga., a fundraiser for the Savannah Symphony and active in community affairs;

PAUL COLLINS, of Grand Rapids, Mich., a portrait artist;

ESTHER LIPSEN COOPERSMITH, of Potomac, Md., former chair of the Civic Opera Association of Washington, D.C.;

SUSANNE SHUTZ CURRY, a director of children's plays in Kansas City, Mo., and member of the Missouri Repertory Theater Guild;

HENRY CUTLER, of Waterloo, Iowa, member and legal adviser of the Black Hawk Children's Theatre Board and a charter member of the Metro Dance Theatre Board, Cedar Arts Forum;

MITCHELL S. CUTLER, a Washington attorney and former Special Assistant to President Kennedy;

GEORGE F. DAVIGLUS, a Miami surgeon, president of Ballet Concerto and member of the Miami Ballet Association;

CLARENCE C. DAY, a Memphis, Tenn., businessman and president of the Memphis Academy of Arts;

PATRICIA O'REILLY DIAZ, a professor at Puerto Rico Junior College and member of Friends of the Casals Festival, Inc.;

JENNIE TABER CLARKSON DREHER, of Columbia, S.C., patron of the Town Theatre, the Columbia Museum of Art, and the Columbia Ballet Company;

WALTER J. DUNFEY, of Portsmouth, N.H., president of Dunfey Hotels and a member of the Capital Funds Committee for Theatre by the Sea;

EARL EUGENE DYSON, president of the Georgia Business and Industry Association;

PATRICIA G. EDINGTON, of Mobile, Ala., president of Historic Mobile Homes Tours;

PAULA H. ELKINS, of Cape Elizabeth, Maine, an attorney and member of the Portland Committee on the Humanities;

FRANK E. FOWLER, of Chattanooga, an adviser on American art to major museums and collectors;

CHRISTINE MILES GITLIN, of Berea, Ohio, a music therapist and organizer and trustee of the Ohio Chamber Orchestra;

ROBERT F. GOLDHAMMER, of Winchester, Mass., vice president of Kidder, Peabody & Co.;

SHARON KAYE GOWDY, of Texhoma, Okla., a member of the Oklahoma Humanities Committee;

CAROLYN B. HAFFENREFFER, president of the Rhode Island Federation of Garden Clubs;

PAUL HALPERN, of Eugene, Oreg., a songwriter and instructor at Lane Community College;

EDYTHE C. HARRISON, of Norfolk, Va., founding president and manager of the Virginia Opera Association;

HERMENE D. HARTMAN, of Chicago, a social science professor at Chicago City Colleges and producer of a public affairs television show;

RON HULL, of Lincoln, Nebr., programing manager for the Nebraska Educational Television Network;

LELA G. JACOBSON, of Miami Shores, Fla., member of the Chamber Music Society and Opera Society;

LINDA J. JADWIN, of Minneapolis, a member of the Women's Art Registry, a fundraising group to assist artists;

JAMES F. KELLEY, of Indianapolis, chairman of the membership campaign of the Indianapolis Museum of Art;

HENRY L. KIMELMAN, of St. Thomas, V.I., chairman of the board of the West Indies Corp.;

ELISE KUHL KIRK, of Dallas, Tex., a concert pianist and Ph. D. in musicology;

IRA MCKISSICK KOGER, of Jacksonville, Fla., director of the executive committee, Public Broadcasting Service;

RONALD S. LAUDER, of New York City, corporate vice president of Estee Lauder, Inc., and member of the visiting committee of the department of drawings at the Metropolitan Museum of Art;

DANIEL LECHT, of East Greenwich, R.I., president and chairman of the Rhode Island Lithograph Corp., and a member of the board of Artist Internationale;

RUTH MCWILLIAMS LEFFALL, of Washington, D.C., a member of the board of directors of the Shakespeare Summer Festival and the National Symphony Orchestra;

RON M. LINTON, of Washington, D.C., chairman of Linton and Co., who was a press aide and advance man on John F. Kennedy's Presidential campaign;

ROBERT F. LUSK, president of the Lusk Corp., New Canaan, Conn., active in civic affairs;

ALYNE QUEENER MASSEY, of Nashville, Tenn., a member of the board of the Nashville Symphony and Vanderbilt University;

DOROTHY WATSON MCCLURE, of Columbus, Ga., president of the Springer Opera House and a member of the Georgia Council for the Arts;

ALICE GREENE MCKINNEY, of Indianapolis, a member of the board of the Indianapolis Opera Company, and the Metropolitan Arts Council;

DOROTHY PIERCE MCSWEENY, of Washington, D.C., oral historian for the Presidential papers of President Johnson;

JOSE F. MENDEZ, of Puerto Rico, president of the Ana G. Mendez Educational Foundation;

LUIS E. MESTRE, of New York City, founder of Luis Mestre Fine Arts;

ROBERT I. MILLONZI, a New York attorney and former trustee of the Kennedy Center; Millonzi has also been appointed Cochair of this Advisory Committee;

CHASE MITCHELL MISHKIN, active in civic affairs in Los Angeles;

ARLENE MONTGOMERY MMAHAT, of New Orleans, a member of the New Orleans Symphony Society Junior Committee, the New Orleans Opera Junior Committee, and the Women's Committee for the Museum of Art;

JOAN REED MOMJIAN, of Huntingdon Valley, Pa., an art teacher and collector;

Ana Marta Morales, of New York, executive director of the Puerto Rican Center for the Arts, and a lecturer at Hunter College on Puerto Rican history and culture;

Christopher Jay Murphy III, a South Bend, Ind., banker and director of the Midwest Chamber Orchestra;

Elizabeth R. Ochenrider, of Arlington, Va., active in volunteer work and other civic affairs;

Patrick J. O'Connor, a Minnesota attorney and sponsor of the Guthrie International Theatre, Minnesota Opera, Children's Theatre Company, and the Minnesota Society of Fine Arts;

Jacqueline D. O'Reilly, of Foxboro, Mass., a founding trustee of the Boston Ballet Company;

Eduardo J. Padron, of Miami, Fla., president of Eduardo J. Padron & Associates, and former director of the Institute of Culture and Language Training;

Jographia Pappas, of Altoona, Pa., an operatic singer and doctoral student in education, and member of the Pennsylvania Council on the Arts;

Elizabeth Petrie, of New York City, vice president of the Philadelphia Museum of Art, member of the International Exhibitions Committee and the University of Pennsylvania Museum, and a trustee of the Corcoran Gallery; she has also been appointed Cochair of this Committee;

Paul C. Porter, of Boston, Mass., owner of a management consulting firm;

Sumner Murray Redstone, of Newton Centre, Mass., president of Northeast Theatre Corp.;

Barbara B. Rogers, of Hillsborough, Calif., board member of the San Francisco Symphony and San Francisco Opera Guild;

Marina Rubal, a Chicago physician and member of the Cuban American Coalition and the Museum of Modern Art;

Marjorie B. Runnion, publicity director of the Brattleboro (Vermont) Music Center;

Fred Rzepka, a Cleveland businessman active in civic affairs;

Manuel Sanchez, a Los Angeles attorney, general counsel to Blue Cross of Southern California, and a former consultant to KCET educational television on the "Cancion de la Raza" program;

Milton T. Schaeffer, of Germantown, Tenn., member and past president of the Memphis Arts Council;

Kerin Rodgers Scianna, of Las Vegas, Nev., founder and organizer of the Los Angeles County Senior Citizens Art Festival;

Carole J. Shorenstein, of San Francisco, a producer at the Curran Theatre;

Ted Simon, chairman of the board of commissioners of Westmoreland County, Pa.;

Judy Glissen Snowden, of Little Rock, Ark., founder and president of the Guild of Arkansas Orchestra Society;

Betty J. Stephens, of Santa Barbara, Calif., member of the Los Angeles Music Center, the Santa Barbara Symphony, and the Santa Barbara Ballet Theater;

Patsy S. Stone, of Florence, S.C., a member of the board of the Florence Little Theater and director;

Herman Sulsona, a professor and special adviser to the chancellor of the Regional Colleges in Puerto Rico;

Gerald M. Tabenken, of Bangor, Maine, past commissioner of the Maine State Commission on the Arts and Humanities;

Suzanne Dabney Taylor, a member of the board of the Boise (Idaho) Philharmonic Association and the Idaho Alliance for Arts and Education;

Julio Torres, of New York City, founder and director of the Puerto Rican Dance Theater, Inc.;

Benjamin M. Tucker, of Savannah, Ga., general manager of WSOK radio station, and producer of jazz concerts;

Marta Moreno Vega, of the Bronx, project director of the Visual Arts Research and Resource Center Relating to the Caribbean;

Constance Wahl, of Wilmington, Del., a member of the Council of Delaware Artists, the Philadelphia Art Museum, and the Chester County Art Association;

Marcia Webb, of Cookeville, Tenn., a member of the board of Theater Cookeville and the Association of Tennessee Symphony Orchestras;

Marcia Simon Weisman, of Beverly Hills, a member of the board of trustees of the San Francisco Art Institute;

Rosine McFaddin Wilson, of Beaumont, Tex., a member of the board of directors of the Southeast Texas Arts Council;

Connie Wimer, of Des Moines, Iowa, a member of the Des Moines Art Center and the Des Moines Ballet Association;

Martha Sinnard Wright, of Annapolis, Md., an actress and director of musicals, operas, and children's theater.

Digest of Other
White House Announcements

The following listing includes the President's public schedule and other items of general interest announced by the White House Press Office and not included elsewhere in this issue.

March 19

The President returned to the White House from Camp David, Md., where he had met during the day with his economic and energy advisers.

March 20

The President met at the White House with:

—David L. Aaron, Deputy Assistant for National Security Affairs;

—Danny C. Tate, Deputy Assistant for Congressional Liaison (Senate), and William H. Cable, Deputy Assistant for Congressional Liaison (House);

—the Democratic congressional leadership;

—James T. McIntyre, Jr., Director of the Office of Management and Budget;

—Vice President Walter F. Mondale.

The President transmitted to the Congress the initial "Report to the Congress on the Status of Health Information and Health Promotion," prepared by the Secretary of Health, Education, and Welfare.

March 21

The President met at the White House with:

—Zbigniew Brzezinski, Assistant to the President for National Security Affairs;

—Frank B. Moore, Assistant to the President for Congressional Liaison, Robert Thomson, Special Assistant for Congressional Liaison (Senate), Mr. Tate, and Mr. Cable;

—Joel W. (Jay) Solomon, Administrator of the General Services Administration;

—Stansfield Turner, Director of Central Intelligence, Hamilton Jordan, Assistant to the President, and Dr. Brzezinski.

March 22

The President met at the White House with:

—Secretary of the Treasury W. Michael Blumenthal, Lyle E. Gramley, member of the Council of Economic Advisers, Alfred E. Kahn, Advisor to the President on Inflation and Chairman of the Council on Wage and Price Stability, Barry P. Bosworth, Director of the Council on Wage and Price Stability, Stuart E. Eizenstat, Assistant to the President for Domestic Affairs and Policy, John N. Gentry, Deputy Adviser on Inflation and Counselor on Labor-Management Relations, and Mr. McIntyre;

—Dr. Brzezinski;

—Mr. Moore;

—Hilmar L. Solberg, president of Kiwanis International;

—Mrs. Carter, for lunch;

—Secretary of Labor Ray Marshall, Secretary of Commerce Juanita M. Kreps, Ambassador Robert S. Strauss, Special Representative for Trade Negotiations, a group of Senators and Congressmen, and representatives of the textile industry, to discuss the administration's textile program.

President Anwar al-Sadat of Egypt and Prime Minister Menahem Begin of Israel have accepted President Carter's invitation to sign the peace treaty between Egypt and Israel at the White House on March 26.

March 23

The President met at the White House with:

—Secretary of State Cyrus R. Vance, Secretary of Defense Harold Brown, Dr. Brzezinski, and Mr. Jordan;

—Dr. Brzezinski;

—Mr. Moore.

The President participated in a briefing on the administration's programs and policies given for civic and community leaders from Massachusetts in Room 450 of the Old Executive Office Building.

The President has extended an invitation to Prime Minister Masayoshi Ohira of Japan for an official visit to the United States on May 2 to discuss bilateral and multilateral policies and economic issues of mutual concern.

NOMINATIONS SUBMITTED TO THE SENATE

The following list does not include promotions of members of the Uniformed Services, nominations to the Service Academies, or nominations of Foreign Service officers.

Submitted March 20, 1979

DONALD EUGENE SYVRUD, of Virginia, to be United States Alternate Executive Director of the International Monetary Fund for a term of 2 years, vice Thomas Byron Crawford Leddy, resigned.

D. CLIVE SHORT, of Nebraska, to be United States Marshal for the District of Nebraska for the term of 4 years, vice Ronald C. Romans, term expired.

CHECKLIST OF WHITE HOUSE PRESS RELEASES

The following listing contains releases of the White House Press Office which are not included in this issue.

Released March 19, 1979

Statement: U.S. delegation's visit to Saudi Arabia, Jordan, and Egypt—by Zbigniew Brzezinski, Assistant to the President for National Security Affairs

Released March 20, 1979

Announcement: nomination of D. Clive Short to be United States Marshal for the District of Nebraska

Released March 22, 1979

Announcement: signing ceremony for the peace treaty between Egypt and Israel and the schedule of additional events related to the visit of President Anwar al-Sadat of Egypt and Prime Minister Menahem Begin of Israel

Released March 23, 1979

Announcement: status report to the Congress on Federal advisory committees

News conference: on proposed freight rail industry deregulation legislation—by Secretary of Transportation Brock Adams, Stuart E. Eizenstat, Assistant to the President for Domestic Affairs and Policy, and Representative James J. Florio of New Jersey

---

ACTS APPROVED BY THE PRESIDENT

NOTE: No acts approved by the President were received by the Office of the Federal Register during the period covered by this issue.

PRESIDENTIAL DOCUMENTS

Week Ending Friday, March 30, 1979

Elk City, Oklahoma

Remarks and a Question-and-Answer Session at a Town Meeting.   March 24, 1979

THE PRESIDENT. None of you could know how good it felt for me to come back to Elk City this evening to be with all of you.

I would guess that during the campaign in 1975–1976, that I visited more than a thousand cities and towns in the United States of America. I never visited a single place that gave me as warm and as open-hearted and as exciting a welcome as you did then, and you have equaled your-selves this evening. And I thank you for it.

I'm particularly glad that Senator Boren is here; Governor Nigh is here; Lieutenant Governor; Congressman English; your fine mayor, who was in the fore-front of the welcoming committee when I was here before.

As you know, I'm going to spend the night with Larry and Mary Jane this evening. I believe in open government. I know Larry does, too. He tells me that every time he has a meeting of the city government, that it's open to the press.

I'm also going to be attending Sunday school and church in the morning, and

I hope that all of you Baptists will be there with me.

As a Baptist, as you know, I'm not very enthusiastic about gambling. But I modi-fied my views somewhat when I heard they had a lottery tonight—[*laughter*]—to decide who was coming to the meeting. The only problem is that nobody told me whether I was speaking to the winners or to the losers. [*Laughter*]

One of the nice things about being President is you get to go to a lot of very important places. Just recently, I've been in Mexico City; I've been in Jerusalem; I've been in Cairo, Egypt; and now, to Elk City.

Three and a half years ago, Novem-ber 11, 1975, I promised to come back as President. You helped me become Presi-dent, and here I am.

ADMINISTRATION POLICIES

I want to say just a few words before I start taking questions. I'm here because of your friendship and because of a promise, but I'm here for another reason as well.

I and all Presidents make decisions every day that affect the lives of everyone who lives in our great country. We make speeches quite often, trying to explain

469

what we do, why we make certain decisions, take certain actions. But it's important that Presidents listen to people also, not just the ones that are able to come to Washington to express their concerns but also to the farmers and the housewives, the storeclerks, the schoolteachers who never have a chance to get to Washington.

Sometimes, the very size of our country and the complexity of the issues makes people feel that just one person doesn't make a difference. I think that those who live in relatively small cities like Elk City can clearly see how your own attitudes, how your own lives do affect those who live around you. You can see at first hand that unselfish participation and cooperation are essential to the success of your schools and your churches and your town.

We need the same sort of cooperation, the same recognition that every person matters if we're going to solve the difficult problems which our Nation faces today.

We've always been able, in a time of crisis, to muster that sense of common purpose, particularly in wartime, but it's just as crucial in times of peace. President Franklin Roosevelt said in 1933, and I'd like to quote, "It is a mistake to assume that the virtues of war differ essentially from the virtues of peace. All life is a battle against the mistakes and the human limitations of man, against the forces of selfishness and inertia, and laziness and fear."

We especially need that spirit that Franklin Roosevelt called upon us to assume in 1933 in our current battle against inflation. The decisions and actions of all of us—government, business, labor, consumers—contribute to inflation. It's not a problem that government can solve alone while everyone else continues business as usual. All Americans will either win the battle against inflation, or we will

all lose the battle against inflation together.

I believe that in a few weeks, we will begin to see the results of this common battle. I need your total support in this fight.

I was deeply disturbed yesterday at the Consumer Price Index figures. A large part of that increase was obviously due to international commodity items, to world oil prices, to severe late winter weather, and other factors which were beyond our control. But those factors do not account for the sharp increase in prices for many goods and services. That inflation level is unacceptable. And those figures are a warning and a message to government, business, labor, and consumers: This must be a time of restraint.

I've been very encouraged by the willingness of working people to join in this battle, but we still face a series of crucial labor negotiations. It's vitally important that those who are responsible for the outcome of those negotiations recognize their obligation to show moderation and concern for the economic well-being of our country. I expect restraint, and the American people expect restraint. Fueling inflation is not in the long-term interest of any American.

On the price side, many of our very largest corporations, whom we monitor every day, seem to be complying with the program. But I'm very disappointed that many medium-sized and smaller businesses are not showing the same sort of restraint. Too many business leaders seem to feel that the anti-inflation program just doesn't apply to them. And the result is higher prices for everybody.

I will take very firm steps to deal with this problem in the immediate days ahead. I intend to substantially increase the staff responsible for monitoring these prices, and we will also be working with labor and consumer groups and with you in a national price-monitoring effort.

I've instructed the Council on Wage and Price Stability to use its legal authority to get regular reports on price increases, all price increases, from firms in problem industries where prices are going up too high.

We've already identified several companies which appear to have broken the guidelines that we've established. We'll be identifying others in the days ahead. They'll be given a chance to explain the purpose or the reason for their high prices. But I will not hesitate to identify those companies that violate the price guidelines, so that the people of this Nation can take appropriate action.

An absolutely vital element in the fight against inflation is to restrain Federal spending. We cannot tolerate ever-increasing Federal spending. I am committed to a balanced budget, and that's a goal I intend to achieve. And I need for you to help me with it.

In the past 2 years, we've cut the $66 billion deficit that I inherited by more than half. This year, I've sent the Congress a tight, responsible budget that cuts the deficit even further. I'm determined to hold the line on Federal spending this year, and I hope you'll give me your support.

And finally, let me say that the problem of inflation is difficult, frustrating, terribly complex. It's been with us now for more than 10 years. But it is not beyond our power to control.

For 30 years, many believed that the chance for peace between Israel and Egypt was beyond our grasp. But on Monday, our Nation will welcome Prime Minister Begin of Israel and President Anwar Sadat of Egypt to the White House to sign a treaty of peace. We never thought it would be possible.

We never thought it would be possible just a few months ago, but with courage and determination and cooperation, success is now within our grasp. We need that same kind of daily commitment, determination, courage, and cooperation to lick the problems that face our own country— the problem of inflation. These qualities have always been part of American life. And I know the same spirit exists among you and among other Americans throughout this great country. I know that we have the will and the ability to win this fight together.

And now, I would like to have your questions, and I'll start with the first microphone on my left.

QUESTIONS

EGYPTIAN-ISRAELI PEACE TREATY

Q. Mr. President, I'm Jimmy Dillard, and I'd like to know, how sound is the peace treaty, whose foundation is built with 5 billion inflated American tax dollars?

THE PRESIDENT. This peace treaty is a result of 30 years of war and the lessons which our Nation has learned from it. We have two notable friends in the Middle East, among others—Israel and Egypt. At this moment, they are in a state of declared war against each other. Thousands of people in each country have lost their lives. Our own interests are directly involved. We will provide part of the cost of removing the armed forces from the Sinai Desert. This is a very expensive proposition.

The Egyptians have five divisions on the Israeli side of the Suez Canal. The Israelis have two divisions, two large airfields built on Egyptian territory. Israel is very much in need of economic stability. Their inflation rate last year, for instance, was more than 50 percent. We will help them bear the costs for these peacetime changes. The cost will run a little more than a billion dollars a year for 3 or 4 years for both nations combined. Our Nation can well afford it. It's an excellent investment, and I believe the American people are strongly in support of this very modest cost for peace, when the cost of war, even to our own Nation, to our own taxpayers, would be much, much greater.

I believe it's a very good investment.

REINSTATEMENT OF THE DRAFT

Q. Mr. President, my name is Danny Vinyard, and I'm a senior at Oklahoma State University. I have a lot of questions I'd like to ask you, but what I'd really like to know is whether or not you think it's fair to reinstate the draft and randomly make young males sacrifice for the whole society, or would you be in favor of increasing salaries so that the military could be remanned on a voluntary basis?

THE PRESIDENT. As you know, I have the authority at this moment to require registration for the draft. But to induct young people into the Armed Forces would have to require an act of Congress. I don't see any present need to do it, but it is being considered, and we'll make a final decision later on.

If we ever find this to be necessary, I would certainly want to institute some different draft procedures. I don't think in the future, for instance, that just because a young person is in college and probably comes from a more wealthy family, that they ought to be excluded from the same treatment as the poorer young men who have to struggle.

We have now provided, with the help of the Congress and my own predecessors

in the White House, I think very reasonable salary levels and very high training and good career opportunities for those who volunteer.

We are meeting the needs of our Armed Forces with the present volunteer arrangement. Some of our Reserve units are short of volunteers, and I would like to appeal tonight to all those who listen to my voice to consider the Armed Forces as a career and, certainly, to volunteer to help with the Reserve forces. But at the present time, we don't need to reinstitute the draft.

PRESIDENT'S RELIGIOUS BELIEFS; EQUAL RIGHTS AMENDMENT

Q. Mr. President, my name is Jim Fowler, and I feel it's an honor to be here this evening, and I welcome you to Elk City.

My question is a three-point question, if I may ask one. First, I know that you're a man of religious principles and endeavors, and I've seen much written in the papers and such. And I know that you're attending church tomorrow. But I'd like to hear you state with your own mouth that you are a believer of Jesus Christ and you accept him as your Lord and Savior. And the second point is, I'd like to know, as leader of this country, how much time that you spend in prayer and study as far as the direction of this country. And the third point, Mr. President, I ask in all due respect: I would like to know by what scriptural basis you and Mrs. Carter support the ERA by scripture?

THE PRESIDENT. All right.

I am a believer in Jesus Christ and a born-again Christian. I do worship regularly. I spend a lot of my own time in prayer. Every evening, my wife and I have religious services together, one of the last things we do each day. And we never miss under any circumstances. Since I was going to be gone tonight, we had our worship service before I left the White House today about 3 o'clock. So, I do perform my partial duties as a Christian. I still fall far short of what God expects of me.

I don't predicate my support of the ERA on scriptural references. I think if one reads different parts of the Bible, you can find a good argument either way. I know that Paul felt very strongly that there ought to be a sharp distinction between men and women, and women's role ought to be minimal. But I have a feeling that Christ meant for all of us to be treated equally, and He demonstrated this in many ways.

But I really don't think that it would be possible for me to prove all the arguments for or against ERA by reference to the Bible. I look to the Bible as a source for guidance and pray for God's guidance. But that's about the best answer I can give you on the ERA.

MEETING WITH ELK CITY FARMERS

Q. Good evening, Mr. President. I'm Pat Walker. And since this is an agricultural area to which you have returned, and we are primarily a farming community here, would it be possible for you to meet with our Elk City farmers—not a radical agriculture committee from out of State, but with our hard-working young farmers in this area?

THE PRESIDENT. I'll try to. I don't know when I'll have time to do it, but I would like very much to. Do you think that a group of them could come to Washington to see me?

Q. I think so, sir. If they had a special invitation, I'm sure they would. [*Laughter*]

THE PRESIDENT. I extend to a group of Elk City young farmers an invitation to come and visit me at the White House. I will be glad to listen to them. And I also would not object at all to their bringing along some of the so-called radical farmers. [*Laughter*]

I have no objection to their expressing their beliefs and their desires. I have recognized many years of my own life, when I was a full-time farmer, the need for the farmers' voice to be heard. And I look forward to having them come, and you can contact me directly at the White House for arranging the time for the visit.

Q. Thank you, Mr. President.

THE PRESIDENT. I'd like to ask one of my staff members to—it might be better for us to contact you, because I get about an average of more than 50,000 [5,000] [1] letters every week, and I would certainly hate to see your letter, Ms. Walker, get lost. So, Keech,[2] if one of you would contact Ms. Walker and get the address. We'll contact you, okay?

CORPORATE PROFITS

Q. Noel Patten from Viola, Kansas. It is indeed a pleasure to be here tonight. I would like to extend to you a personal greeting from the Wheat State.

THE PRESIDENT. Very good.

Q. Mr. President, recently it was announced that there was a 26.4-percent increase in corporate profits over last year. Is the Government really going to be able to control business in its fight against inflation?

THE PRESIDENT. It's hard to say. As you know, the profits fluctuate so wildly from one quarter to another or one month

---

[1] Printed in the transcript.
[2] Keech LeGrand, White House staff advance person.

to another, that it would be a mistake to judge the entire business community's actions on the basis of that one statistic. I think the trend over the last 10 years—I was examining this today, as a matter of fact—show that business profits have been well in line with the average income increases of American families. This is a wheat State; Oklahoma is very heavily dependent on energy and on agriculture.

Last year, the average net income for farm families in this country went up 30 percent, and I don't hear many of the farmers who were sitting on their tractors complaining about their income going up too rapidly. So, I think those statistics that come out, although they are very shocking when one first hears them, have to be taken in the context of the entire Nation's economic structure.

There's no doubt in my mind that some business firms have cheated on the wage and price guidelines by increasing their prices more than was warranted. But I think you have to remember that all over the world at this point, there are inflationary pressures that neither I nor anyone else can control.

Let me just give you a few quick examples. There's a beef shortage worldwide. We have an import quota at this point, and as you know, we are having a difficult time having that quota itself filled, because there's a shortage in other countries at the present that in the past have been eager to sell their beef; now they have a very ready market for it.

International commodities, including food, feed grains, soybeans, aluminum, bauxite, copper, silver, gold—these kinds of things are going up quite rapidly in price. Oil prices are going up as well.

So, on an international basis, prices are going up, and you couldn't blame them on a President or the consumers or any one entity or person.

You have other things that are produced in our Nation, where no company can control them. For instance, we've been building about 2.2 million home units per year for the last 2 or 3 years, a very high rate of production of homes for American families. This has created a shortage in some building materials—plywood, lumber, insulation materials, and so forth. And no one company, obviously, controls the price of timber being sold by landowners, nor the price of lumber products coming from that timber.

So, a lot of the causes for inflation are almost uncontrollable, and they're because people around the world are getting more affluent. They can buy more beef, they can buy more wheat than they could in the past.

So, I don't believe it would be fair, even though it would be easy, for me to blame business for inflation just because their profits seemed to be high last quarter. They were very high. I was surprised. But it would be easy for me to say, "Well, the working people and the farmers are great, the consumers are great, I'm a great President, let's blame American business." That's not fair, and not exactly accurate. We're all in it together. Unless we do cooperate and not try to find a scapegoat or someone to blame, we won't be successful. I think we ought to form a partnership and all of us see what we ourselves can do. I believe that if we work together, we can control inflation in harmony, not by blaming one another.

FEDERAL REGULATION

Q. Mr. President, I'm Darlene James. Our doctors, pharmacists, and hospitals spend so much of their time filling out Federal forms, even here in Elk City. Do you foresee any possibility of less Federal control in our medical system, or are we destined for socialized medicine?

THE PRESIDENT. I don't think we're going towards socialized medicine. But I think that the Federal Government is going to continue to play a major role in medical care for our people. We have reduced substantially the number of forms and reports and requests that have been required, in the last 12 months.

I was looking at some statistics on the way here, because I'm going to talk about that tomorrow when I get to Dallas. HEW has eliminated 300 different forms that are used in medical care alone. That's dealing with Medicaid and Medicare. But quite often the different Federal agencies, each one individually in the past, have required a separate form to be filled out.

We are making some progress with it. I'm going to submit legislation to Congress this coming week on deregulation that will restrict substantially the number of new regulations, forms, and reports that can be required in the future and put the responsibility on each one of the agencies in Government to mandate a benefit-cost analysis before a new form can be instituted or a new regulation can be promulgated.

I might add that it's not all the Federal Government. We've just had an instance with Sohio Company. We were very hopeful, for instance, that the Sohio Company would build an oil pipeline across our country to bring Alaskan oil to the central part of the Nation and to the northern tier of States.

When we investigated the reason why they withdrew from this project, we found they had to fill 715 permits. Only 12 of those were Federal permits; the other 700 were required by the different States through which that pipeline had to come.

And for that reason, Sohio withdrew from the project. We are now working to try to get Sohio, you know, to go back and build a pipeline to bring oil from the west coast.

I might say that they completed all the Federal forms more than a year ago. So, the States and the Federal Governments are both at fault. And I would hope that we can make some continued improvement in the future.

One of the most heavily criticized agencies in Government, before I became President and shortly afterwards, was OSHA. And in 1 day last year, OSHA eliminated a thousand of their regulations, I think without any adverse effect on the health or safety of American workers.

We are making some progress, but it is a very difficult thing to do.

PRICE CONTROLS ON BEEF

Q. Mr. President, welcome to the short-grass country. The cattlemen in this country can now look back on 5 bad years. During those years, their land was mortgaged and debts increased. Now that cattle prices are high enough to reduce some of the loans, do you expect to put controls on cattle prices?

THE PRESIDENT. As long as I'm in the White House serving as your President, there will never be price controls on beef, and you can depend on it.

VIEWS ON THE PRESIDENCY

Q. Mr. President, my name is Danny George, and I'm originally from Butler, Oklahoma. Before I could get out of the house today, my little daughter ran over to me and asked me, "Daddy, where are you going tonight?" And I said, "Well, dear, I'm going to see the President of the United States." And she said, "Oh, goody, can I go and play with Amy?" [*Laughter*] And I told her, I said, "No, dear, not

tonight, but maybe some other time."
[*Laughter*]

My question falls around a picture I saw the other day. And in this picture was Atlas holding the world, and Atlas was a little bit different than usual. He was gray-haired. And in 1975, Mr. President, when you were running for the Presidency, your hair seemed to be a little darker. [*Laughter*] And I was wondering, now that it seems to be a little lighter, if you would attribute that towards holding the highest position in the United States?

THE PRESIDENT. Well, tell your daughter I hope she can come and see Amy, first of all. Secondly, I can't deny that the Presidency of our country is a tremendous responsibility. A lot of things fall on my shoulders that no one else can answer. If a question is easy to answer, it's ordinarily resolved in a person's life or within a family. If the family can't resolve it, maybe at the city hall. And if he can't do it in the county or city, it goes to the State legislature. And then if it's so complicated or so difficult or so far-reaching that it can't be resolved at the State level, it comes to Washington. And then, of course, it's the responsibility of the Congress and the President.

In addition to the legislation that we have to deal with, which is very controversial and quite often there's no way to win, politically speaking, there are responsibilities of international peace, the defense and security of our own country, dealing with foreign nations, trying to raise the banner of human rights, trying to repair some damage that was done to our Government by Vietnam and Watergate and the CIA revelations. So, it is a very heavy responsibility.

I might say that it's a voluntary job. Nobody made me run for it. And I enjoy it. I have never yet gotten up in the morning—and I get up quite early—that I haven't looked forward to the day, be-

cause I recognize that in spite of the gray hairs that come along with the job, it's one of the most exciting and gratifying jobs on Earth, because I represent the greatest country on Earth.

Q. Thank you very much, Mr. President.

THE PRESIDENT. Hello.

REQUEST FOR A KISS

Q. Mr. President, my name is Karen Ensey, and I'm from Dill City, Oklahoma, and I'd like to know if I can have a kiss. [*Laughter*]

[*At this point, the President kissed Ms. Ensey.*]

THE PRESIDENT. I might say that I don't have any rule against the same question being asked more than once. [*Laughter*]

[*At this point, the President kissed several women in the audience.*]

I didn't blush the first time, but I blushed that time.

PRESIDENT'S ROLE OF PEACEMAKER

Q. Now I have double butterflies. My name is Lorene Mikles, and I'm from Sayre, Oklahoma, and we do welcome you to Elk City, Mr. President.

And instead of a question, I have a comment. As a citizen of the United States of America, of western Oklahoma, and of the rural community and, more particularly, as mother of three teenage sons, I want to express to you my personal prayers and gratitude for your role as peacemaker in the world today.

THE PRESIDENT. Thank you, Mrs. Mikles, very much. I don't think the program could get any better from here on. Thank you so much.

VOLUNTARY WAGE GUIDELINES

Q. Mr. President, my name is Gene Johnson, and I promise I'm not going to ask the same question they did. [*Laughter*]

THE PRESIDENT. Thank you.

Q. Mr. President, I have a two-pronged question. First of all, I left a wife and three kids at home that didn't get to see your motorcade, and I promised them that if I was lucky enough to get to ask you a question, I'd ask you to tell them hello. So, it's Stef and Jeff and Kevin and——

THE PRESIDENT. If your father thinks of your name, I'll—[*laughter*]—Stef and Jeff—I tell them hello.

Q. Thank you, Mr. President. Mr. President, my main question—you alluded to it a little bit in your opening remarks concerning inflation, which definitely, to the middle-income and lower income people, it is the number one problem.

THE PRESIDENT. Yes, it is.

Q. And our increased labor costs seem to snowball this thing. And other than voluntary restraint, what can be done to, in your opinion, to keep these labor demands from being quite so inflationary?

THE PRESIDENT. Well, I might say that so far, since we promulgated the voluntary guidelines or restraints, labor has complied almost completely with the hundreds of labor settlements throughout the country that take place every week. Some of them are very small groups of working people; some of them are larger. And the ones that have tried to violate the guidelines so far have been very highly publicized.

It's always important for a labor union or a worker who's not a member of a union to take a lower wage increase than the rate of inflation. And I have realized from the very beginning that in order to make the wage and price guidelines work on a voluntary basis that I would have to do my share, as President, in the budget and so

forth, and also encourage price restraint in order to have a permanent compliance by labor. But I think it's accurate to say, looking at all the statistics, that so far, labor has complied.

We now face two or three very large wage negotiation problems. The first will be the Teamsters. The next will be the rubber workers; later on in the fall, the UAW, the United Auto Workers. I hope that we can demonstrate to these three groups that we are sincere enough and determined enough and successful enough in holding down the general inflationary trends to make it advisable for them to hold down wage demands.

Most wage earners, judging by a Gallup poll recently, said they would rather take a lower wage increase if inflation was being controlled than to take a higher wage increase with uncertain inflation. And I think everyone who thinks about it knows that you cannot start inflation being controlled in just 1 or 2 months. It's got to take 3 or 4 months, at least, before you can see the first indications of these restraints being felt.

I believe that we can be successful, and I believe that we can continue the good cooperation that we've already received from labor if we do our part together.

Thank you.

TWO-INCOME FAMILIES

Q. Mr. President, with inflation increasing every month, can you foresee a time when the average American family will be able to live on one salary again? Or are we doomed to be working housewives?

THE PRESIDENT. I would guess that the trend for more than one person working in a family would continue. Now the two people working make a much higher income, much more than twice as much income, as a single person working in a family did 10, 15, 20 years ago. We have a much higher standard of living.

I remember when I was a boy, for a family to have an automobile made them one of the richest families in the community. And I grew up without electricity or running water in my home. And many things now that are taken for granted, even by supposedly poor families, would have been considered extremely wealthy, you know, back just when I was a child.

So, I would guess that because people do want to live a better life, to have more leisure time, to learn more about the world, to do more study, to have more recreation, that they will continue to want to have a higher wage income even than one person can provide.

I know many people—I know you do as well—where a husband might make a fairly high income, $50,000 or $100,000 or more, where the wife decides to work because she wants to express herself or because she has some special talent or wants to expand her life beyond the family itself, certainly after the children are grown or able to take care of themselves.

So, I would guess the trend would continue. It's not all because the families would starve without the wives' help. But I know that in this time of inflation that two incomes can give a family that standard of living which they want and deserve.

I don't think I've answered your question very well, but to say that I think it's a permanent fixture on the American scene to have many double wage earners or even more, with children counted, in a family, I think that's a time that's come. I think it's going to stay with us. I don't see anything wrong with it.

ABORTION

Q. Mr. President, my name is Sonja Merz, and my question is dealing with the subject abortion. And I'm very against the subject, and I was just wondering what your feelings are on it.

THE PRESIDENT. Yes. As President, I have a feeling that I should do everything possible to hold down abortion in this country. I am not in favor of Government funds, for instance, being spent for abortions. I would like to see a time in our Nation come when every child is a wanted child.

This is a very sensitive issue. It's one that's very divisive. And as I watched the 1978 election returns coming in in November, I saw many of the Members of the Congress, particularly who had favored encouragement of abortions, lose their seats because of the strong feelings against it.

I want to be fair with you: I'm not in favor of a constitutional amendment to prohibit abortions, but I think that within the realm of legislation and the action that can be taken by Government and by private organizations and by individual Americans, we should do everything we can to minimize any need for abortions.

Q. Thank you.

REQUEST FOR A KISS

Q. My name is Joanne Savage Mefford, and this is my daughter, Kelly. And through Community Action, I work with children at Head Start that have special needs.

Mine is not a question, really, but a welcome to you to my hometown and a request for you to fulfill. I am a farmer's wife, and I have mixed feelings towards you. But I respect you and like to believe that more can be attained through love than through violence.

This is where my request comes in. Some people save many different things for memories. My mementos fall in a little different category. The last person to fulfill my request was Governor Nigh. I don't believe he quite remembers. But I don't want it to get old, but I'll be darned if I'm going to miss out on the kisses. Okay?

THE PRESIDENT. Very fine. [*Laughter*]

[*At this point, the President kissed Ms. Mefford.*]

This is my favorite place. I'm just on the verge of promising to come back to Elk City again.

TAXATION OF MILITARY PERSONNEL

Q. My name is Myra Crawford, and I'm from Lawton, Oklahoma. And if I had known all this was going on, I would have asked you 2 years ago to kiss me in the back seat of the car when we were riding together. [*Laughter*] I got to tell you just a bit of trivia. I guess my car has—I rode with the President before he was President, and then his lovely wife after. And I didn't even ask for a kiss from either one of them. My goodness, what did I miss? [*Laughter*]

Anyway, the one thing I want to ask, and as I asked you the evening I was riding with you, about military subsistence and Category B. I don't know if a lot of people know what Category B is here. You do, don't you?

THE PRESIDENT. I'm not sure.

Q. Okay. Category B is where people live off the base and they work on base and don't pay taxes.

THE PRESIDENT. I understand.

Q. You understand?

THE PRESIDENT. Yes, ma'am.

Q. You know, then?

THE PRESIDENT. Yes.

Q. This is in dire need. Lawton, Oklahoma, will lose $1.6 million for the school system, and we cannot survive if we don't get that money. I wish you would please look at it again before you turn your head against it. That's all I ask. Thank you.

THE PRESIDENT. I understand. Thank you, ma'am.

UTILITY BILLS

Q. Mr. President, I'm Willie Rogers. I'm the State representative for the area where you're standing.

THE PRESIDENT. Very good.

Q. I would like to know what you plan to do in order to help the elderly, retired, disabled, and lower income people with their utility bills.

THE PRESIDENT. Well, as you know, it's very difficult to answer that question successfully, because one of the major component parts of the utility bill charges is the price of energy that goes to generate electricity, primarily.

We have passed legislation that supplements the ability of a family to insulate homes and to cut down on the waste of heat and electricity. Also, we have new legislation just passed last fall that gives us the right to change the rate structure for electrical charges, so that if a person is poor and can use electricity at a time during the day when it's most efficient to produce or when the demand is low, that they could again have a lower charge for their utilities.

The other thing that I would add is that the general allocation of Federal funds for the poor people has been substantially improved.

Last year I submitted a budget that's now in effect during 1979 that increased total allocation of Federal funds for the poor by $4.5 billion. And next year, even though it's a very tight budget for fiscal

479

year 1980, beginning this October, we again increased the allocation of funds for the poor $4 billion more. So, with the change in aid for the elderly who are genuinely poor and for the changes in the rate structure of electricity and the help for insulating homes, that's what the Federal Government can do.

There are many things, of course, that State governments can do, as Governor Nigh well knows, with circuit breaker-type charges for, say, property taxes, where, if a person is both old and poor, they might be forgiven part of their property taxes.

And of course, there are some States that provide special, low-cost electrical services from the utility companies and the State makes up the difference. But I think for the Federal Government to take additional action on a nationwide basis would be very difficult. And I think what I've described is at least some help—maybe not enough.

FOOD STAMP PROGRAM

Q. Good evening, Mr. President, and welcome to Elk City. My name is Glorya Wilmoth, and what I'd like to ask you is why does the Government, every time you turn around, take food stamps and welfare away from the elderly to give to the dependent children for the mothers that are able to work, that won't work, when the elderly really do need the money, especially when they're in their seventies and are unable to work?

THE PRESIDENT. Well, I don't deny that we give help to mothers with dependent children. But I don't think it's accurate to say that we take money away from the elderly in order to do so.

We have made a very substantial change in the food stamp laws since I've

been in office by not requiring that they pay a certain amount for the food stamps themselves. Quite often, particularly elderly people living on a fixed income were not able to raise enough cash money to pay the cash portion of the food stamps themselves. So, we have removed that requirement from the law now. I think we are increasing the ability of the elderly to get food stamps in that respect.

We've also tried to channel food stamp use more accurately to people who need it most. In the past it was abused, because the original law, as it was written, let people get food stamps who didn't really need or deserve those stamps. So, I think we are focusing in much more accurately now on the people that you described who do really need help in acquiring food, but I don't agree with your premise that we have robbed the elderly in order to benefit another group of poor people. I think we are treating them relatively fair.

Q. Okay, and I would also like to have a kiss or a handshake.

THE PRESIDENT. Okay. That will be fine.

[*At this point, the President kissed Ms. Wilmoth.*]

55-MILE-PER-HOUR SPEED LIMIT

Q. Mr. President, I'm Abbie Tillman from Elk City. And I had three questions in mind. Two of them have been touched on, so I'll just forget them. But, first of all, my boys said to tell Amy Happy Birthday.

THE PRESIDENT. Very good.

Q. Okay. What I wanted to know is why does the Government threaten to stop the Federal money that we pay in taxes if the State of Oklahoma raises the speed limit to 65? Because as many or more accidents are caused from faulty vehicles that—Oklahoma has the safety inspection law. And there's a bill in the House to cancel it. And I also wondered why the Federal Government doesn't do something about the safety inspection laws.

THE PRESIDENT. The safety inspection laws are left up to the States to administer. And the inspection procedure is completely handled by the States, and I think that's the way it ought to be.

The Federal Government, in 1973 or 1974, when we had another energy shortage, passed laws through the Congress, signed by the President, which I am sworn to carry out on my oath.

One provision of that law is that if any State does not comply with the nationwide requirement on the 55-mile-per-hour speed limit, that all transportation funds will be withheld from that State. If any State should change its speed limit from 55 up to 65, those funds will be lost.

That's a State option to take. One of the houses in your legislature has already done so. I realize that. But if the other house should change the speed limit upward and the Governor should sign the law and make it effective, then I think Oklahoma should realize that under the United States law, that I'm required to uphold, those funds will be withheld.

I think that the law should be enforced. I think the speed limit of 55 should be maintained. I don't want to mislead you about it. I know you apparently disagree. But if the speed limit is changed, Oklahoma is going to lose the money. I hope they don't change the law.

Q. Do we really save that much in energy?

THE PRESIDENT. I think it saves a considerable amount in energy, and I also

think it saves a considerable number of lives to have the 55-mile-per-hour speed limit. That's my own opinion.

Q. Thank you.

THE PRESIDENT. I'm sorry, but our time has run out. Let me say this in closing: I think all of you see the breadth of interest of the people of Elk City in international affairs, nationwide problems, and local matters of interest. This is part of our American system.

I've had townhall meetings now in many places, in Pennsylvania, Massachusetts, in Oregon, in Mississippi, in Poland—Warsaw, Poland, in West Berlin in Germany, in São Paulo, Brazil.* And I think it's one of the best ways possible for me to learn what your interests and your concerns are.

I feel close to you. You've made me feel that I have come home. And you'll never know how much it means to me to have a sense that, occupying the highest political office, perhaps, in the world, I'm still an average American, part of your family, living in the greatest nation on Earth, standing before the flag which still inspires me every time I see it. You've inspired me, and I thank you from the bottom of my heart.

NOTE: The President spoke at 7:32 p.m. in the Elk City High School gymnasium.

Following the town meeting, the President met with members of the executive committee of the Oklahoma Democratic Party in a room at the high school. He then spent the night at the home of Mrs. Paul R. Wade, mother of Elk City Mayor Larry Wade.

---

*NOTE: The President has held townhall meetings in the following locations: Clinton, Mass., Yazoo City, Miss., Bangor, Maine, Nashua, N.H., Spokane, Wash., West Berlin, Federal Republic of Germany, and Aliquippa, Pa. [Printed in the transcript.]

THE PRESIDENT'S NEWS CONFERENCE OF MARCH 25, 1979

Held in Dallas, Texas

THE PRESIDENT. *Thank you, President Wasilewski. Dr. Stevens, Mayor Folsom, officers and members of the National Association of Broadcasters, friends:*

This afternoon, instead of giving a long speech, I thought I would make just a few brief remarks and then turn the rest of the time over to you for questions.

I think it's only fair for a change that an elected official offer the broadcasting industry equal time. [*Laughter*]

It's hard for me to believe that less than 60 years ago, our country was served by only three full-time radio stations, or that only 30 years ago, television was a fledgling pioneer which most people expected to fail.

Today, you bind America together with instant communications. You shape our culture, our language, our perception of ourselves, and our understanding of the entire world.

What you see and say and show is reality for millions of Americans. They may never visit Jerusalem in Israel, or Cairo in Egypt, never set foot on the Moon, never even go to Washington, D.C., or come here to Texas. But the people of our country know what these places look like, and they participate in important events because of the communications you provide.

When I grew up, we had no electricity on our farm or in our home. And I remember vividly sitting outdoors at night with my family gathered around a battery-powered radio, hooked to the battery in my father's car, listening to the news or Glenn Miller or a political convention in some distant city. Broadcasting in those days opened up new worlds to us, just as it has done for millions of other people.

All over the world, broadcasting is helping to break down barriers of time and distance, of misunderstanding and mistrust, of hatred, that have separated and divided the world's people one from another. I wonder whether the people of Israel and Egypt would have taken that final step towards peace and reconciliation had they not been able to see the faces of each other on television or heard the voices of each other on radio, when there was a prospect for peace and they saw within their own hearts, through the broadcast medium, that others in a country that was completely distant and alien also were willing to take a chance on peace and an end to war.

And tomorrow, broadcasting will bring to the entire world a truly historic sight: Prime Minister Menahem Begin and President Anwar Sadat signing a treaty of peace.

REGULATORY REFORM

I believe the public interest can best be served by a broadcasting industry which is healthy, independent, and diverse. And I will also continue to support vigorously opportunities for minority ownership and a strong public broadcasting system free from political control.

I applaud the hard work and the leadership of your chairman, Don Thurston, on behalf of the NAB minority ownership fund. My administration will continue to work with the FCC and the Congress to encourage diversity and independence in your industry, instead of Government paperwork and controls.

As broadcasters, you have a special sensitivity both to the benefits and to the burdens of Government regulation.

Tomorrow, I'm submitting to the Congress a comprehensive proposal to reduce, to rationalize, and to streamline the regulatory burden throughout American life. And I want to speak to you very briefly about that legislation today.

The call for regulatory reform is not a demand that all regulation be abolished; it's a call for common sense. And I believe that most Americans do support responsible regulation to provide equal opportunity for employment, a clean environment, safe drugs and food, a healthy workplace, and a competitive marketplace.

Because of responsible regulation, the air we breathe is cleaner today; our automobiles are safer and they burn less gasoline; millions of American workers have won new protections against injury and cancer. And I understand that for the first time in 20 years, fish are now swimming in places like the Connecticut River and the Houston Ship Channel. Both the American people and I, as President, are determined to continue the progress that we've made toward these social goals.

Our challenge is to pursue the legitimate goals of regulation in ways that are rational, predictable, and effective. For far too long, we have acted as if we could throw another law or another rule at every problem in our society without thinking seriously about the consequences of it.

When I came to Washington a little more than 2 years ago, I found a regulatory assembly line which churned out new rules, paperwork, regulations, and forms without plan, without direction and, seemingly, without supervision or control.

With the best of intentions, 90 separate regulatory agencies were issuing 7,000 new rules every single year. These rules affect teachers, truckdrivers, broadcasters, farmers, small business, and local government. But no one had stopped to say, "Does each of these rules make sense? Does it do the job? How much does it cost, and is there a cheaper way to achieve goals just as effectively?"

The FCC now requires 18 million manhours each year from broadcasters to fill out the paperwork imposed by its rules and regulations. Perhaps you've noticed this already. [*Laughter*] But Chairman Charlie Ferris is working to reduce that load through a zero-based review of every FCC rule and regulation.

I know that he will succeed in this effort to reduce paperwork. He has my full support. And he also, of course, needs your support.

For too many Americans, today's contact with government at every level means a bewildering mass of paperwork, bureaucracy, and delay. And the costs of compliance with government regulations has been steadily on the rise. It eats up productivity and capital for new investment. It adds to inflation, and the burdens often fall most heavily on those who are least able to bear those burdens—small businesses, local government, nonprofit organizations.

Our society's resources in this country are vast, but they are certainly not infinite. Americans are willing to spend a fair share of those resources to achieve social goals through regulation, but they want their money's worth. They will not support—and I will not permit—needless rules, excessive costs, duplication, overlap, and waste.

It's time that we take control of Federal regulations in America, instead of regulations continuing to control us. As

President, I take the management of the regulatory process as seriously as I do the goals it's intended to achieve.

The legislation which I will submit to Congress tomorrow will continue and streamline our own reform efforts and expand them to every independent regulatory agency. It will accomplish five major goals, which I will list very briefly in closing.

First, this legislation will make sure that the costs and benefits of all major regulations and rules are weighed before they are issued. From now on, regulators will have to get the job done at the least possible cost, and they will have to justify the bill to the American people.

Secondly, this legislation will help us to clean up the enormous backlog of rules and regulations that have accumulated over the years, but have long since outlived their usefulness.

By deregulating airlines last year, we saved consumers $2½ billion in reduced fares. We have brought record profits to the airline industry, and we have begun, for the first time in my memory, to dismantle a Federal bureaucracy.

Third, it'll put a brake on the regulatory assembly line. It will make sure that Government plans ahead, that the American people know what new rules are going to be proposed, and that regulations are developed not in the secret inner sanctums of the bureaucracy, but under the supervision of senior officials who are accountable to the people, to me as President, and to the Congress.

Fourth, this legislation will end needless delays and endless procedural nightmares which have plagued too many Americans for too long. It should not have taken 12 years and a hearing record of over 100,000 pages for the FDA to decide what percentage of peanuts there ought to be in peanut butter. [*Laughter*] I would

have used that example even if I had grown soybeans and wheat, by the way. [*Laughter*]

And finally, this legislation will open up the rulemaking process. It will ensure that all Americans have a voice—consumers and small business, local officials, State governments, certainly, you—not just the best financed and the best organized interest groups.

In regaining control of the regulations that govern our lives, we can also regain our faith in self-government. Together, we will reaffirm that our future depends not on fate or accident or impersonal forces beyond our control, but on our own decisions as a free people in the freest democracy on Earth, which I am determined to see become even more free.

Thank you very much. I'd now like to answer some questions.

QUESTIONS

RENEWABLE ENERGY SOURCES

Q. Mr. President, George Allen of KLGA, Algona, Iowa. Iowa is corn country, and Iowans are concerned about the lack of appropriations to test and develop gasohol as an energy source. Are you planning any actions from the White House?

THE PRESIDENT. Yes. The testing and the use of gasohol and other energy sources derived from replenishable materials is a very high priority for us. We are increasing every year the allocation of funds for that purpose. The Congress is now considering, as you know, some mandatory, step-by-step increment increase in the amount of gasohol that has to be mixed with gasoline. We are considering this proposal. It's being sponsored by, I think, Senator Church and others. The final decision is yet to be made.

Within the next week, I will make a decision about the regulatory process for the Government in energy prices, as you know. And by September of 1981, the present authority for regulation of oil prices expires. Any additional income that is derived from possible taxes in the future on which I've not yet decided would certainly be channeled into new energy sources, as well as conservation and the enhancement of our American domestic production. Gasohol and other similar replenishable sources of fuel will certainly be near the top of the list.

BROADCAST INDUSTRY DEREGULATION

Q. I'm Katherine Broman, president of Springfield Television in Springfield, Massachusetts. And you were up visiting us a few years ago.

THE PRESIDENT. Yes, and my wife was there last week.

Q. That's right. You have taken my question and practically answered it before, because I was going to ask you about deregulation of the broadcast industry. But let me ask you, can you give us a timetable as to when we are going to be free of some of the paperwork that you have discussed?

THE PRESIDENT. I think Charlie Ferris, who is here with me today and will stay until Wednesday to answer your questions specifically, can give you a better timeframe.

This legislation that will be proposed to the Congress tomorrow covers not only the FCC but all other independent regulatory agencies, and I've already covered the regulatory agencies under my control or influence already.

As you know, most of these agencies have to be under the control of laws themselves, because the President, of necessity, has no control over them.

We've already made a great deal of progress. In the health field, for instance, HEW has already eliminated more than 300 specific reports that have to be brought in in health. In 1 day last year, OSHA eliminated 1,000 regulations as a wonderful gift to the American public and to the President.

And Charlie Ferris flew from Washington to Oklahoma, now down here with me yesterday and this morning, and he is absolutely determined that the FCC will equal the achievements that I have just described. He's got my support and my help.

So, in a generic sense, because of legislation and in the FCC itself—which has an equal determination administratively—we will make that progress that I've described to you.

I might point out that many of the regulations that presently are burdensome have been proposed and supported and are still supported by the broadcasting industry itself. So, we've got to be very careful as we remove regulations not to interfere in the orderly processes of your industry. But I can assure you that my own direct Presidential influence and interest is in it for political benefits to myself, if I succeed, as well as what I detect to be in the best interests of our country.

FIRST AMENDMENT PRIVILEGES

Q. Mr. President, I'm Dick Chapin with KFOR in Lincoln, Nebraska, and I'd like to ask the question if you believe that broadcasters are entitled to the same first amendment privileges as are the newspapers?

THE PRESIDENT. That's a hard question for me to answer, because it has so many ramifications. [*Laughter*]

Q. It surely is.

THE PRESIDENT. As you know, the Federal Government doesn't license newspapers and assign a certain spectrum to them within which they can operate. And for me to say that I would want to remove all regulation of the Federal Government in assigning frequencies or issuing licenses to the broadcasting industry would not be—I mean, I would have to say no. But as far as interference in the content of news programs, as far as honoring the principles of the first amendment, obviously I would say yes. I can't answer your question any better than that, because it has such far-reaching ramifications.

But there are so many wide differences between the newspaper industry and the broadcasting industry—spectrum is just one example—that I can't say that I would give the same identical freedom to the broadcasting industry as newspapers. But I think we'll have less restraints on your industry when I go out of office by far than existed when I came into office.

INFLATION

Q. Mr. President, my name is Wade Hargrove. I'm general counsel for the North Carolina Association of Broadcasters. Despite your commendable efforts to control inflation and not unduly burden the country with wage and price controls, none of these efforts, or in fact the efforts of your recent predecessors, really seemed to have worked. Where do we go from here?

THE PRESIDENT. Well, it's too early to say that the efforts have not worked. I think it's going to take 3 months or so, still, before the full impact of what we have tried to do with voluntary wage and price guidelines can be accurately assessed.

I can tell you without any fear of contradiction, for instance, that in the last 2 or 3 months, wage settlements throughout this country have averaged well within the guidelines that we've established. Also, we have monitored very closely the Fortune 500 businesses, the 500 largest businesses in our country. As far as we know, there have been none of those large companies that have violated the price standards.

Now we're expanding the coverage to the medium-sized and smaller companies, many of whom have not even felt that the voluntary guidelines apply to them. We will identify in the very near future four or five companies which have indeed violated the guidelines. They have a 10-day appeal period during which they can prove that they have complied. If they don't prove that, then we'll identify them. Any company so identified will have their names made public, so that the general populace, the consumers, can take action accordingly.

In addition, because of prudent purchasing practices, we will terminate or sharply reduce any Federal purchases from those companies involved. In addition, we will greatly beef up, within the next few weeks, the number of personnel who are monitoring these companies to make sure we have a broader base on which to predicate our future decisions.

I might say that some of those larger companies, within the guidelines which were deliberately somewhat flexible, have utilized the guidelines to their own advantage. That was predictable. We were not surprised at that. They took advantage of every loophole in the guidelines themselves. Now, with 2 or 3 months' experience which we have, we will tighten up those original issued guidelines to make them conform more stringently.

I'd like to add one other thing: Many of the inflationary pressures that are now becoming obvious in our country exist worldwide. Neither I, as President, nor any other head of state nor any government has control over the price, for instance, that exists worldwide for things like copper, aluminum, oil.

Beef is in short supply throughout the world. Our present import quota, for instance—we are having a difficult time even meeting the quota, whereas, 8 or 9 months ago, every time I talked to anyone from Costa Rica or New Zealand or Australia, what they wanted was a higher beef quota. Now they can't even meet the quota that they have for us.

So, many food items, many commodity items, energy, are at a high price all over the world.

Domestically, it's very difficult to lay the blame on anyone for an increase in lumber prices. No single company arbitrarily says, "I'm going to increase my price for lumber or other building materials—wallboard, for instance, or insulation materials."

We have sustained in the last couple of years a very high level of home construction, about 2.2 million homes per year. And because of the demand for houses, we're just short on supply. I'm not particularly concerned about the high profit margins that were revealed last quarter, because we need to have a reinvestment of those profits back in higher productivity, increased jobs, to meet some of the short supply demands.

We're now very near maximum capacity in some of our industries. So, I think it's too early to say that we ought to abandon this program because we do have bad CPI index figures this week.

I am not considering—no one in my administration dares to propose to me and never has proposed that we have manda-

tory price and wage controls. But I am determined to do the best I can, within the broad guidelines established, to get industry and labor to comply with controlling wage and prices. And I'm going to do my part as President.

I'm working toward a balanced budget. We've already cut down the deficit that existed when I ran for President, which was $66 billion, to considerably less than $30 billion next year.

I'm working on a balanced budget. So, I'm going to do all I can to bring in the kind of demonstrated achievement that would inspire the American consumer, business, and labor to cooperate with me. And I'd like to remind all of you here that as you established your own prices for advertisement or for other things that you market, that you help to join in a partnership to bring control of inflation.

But I'm not about to abandon a very tough posture on controlling wages and prices on a voluntary basis, and I believe that we can and will succeed.

EGYPTIAN-ISRAELI PEACE TREATY

Q. Mr. President, Bill Sims, Wycom Corporation, Laramie, Wyoming. First of all, forgive me, sir, before my question, if you could leave a little piece of paper with your name on it at the podium, a big fan of yours would love to have it. [*Laughter*]

My question, sir: With sometimes conflicting reports coming from the Middle East almost daily, how can the American public be sure that the agreement you will sign this week is not just window dressing? Sir, does this agreement really have meaningful significance to the world?

THE PRESIDENT. I think perhaps a hundred years from now, 50 years from now, what occurs tomorrow may be the most significant occurrence during my own term of office as President. We are a nation at peace. It's a notable achievement for a country as large as ours to be at peace.

In the Mideast, war there not only afflicts the lives of everyone involved, but it's a constant constraint on the quality of life when the people in Egypt, people in Israel—who deeply desire to live in harmony with their neighbors—have never been able to do it since Israel was founded.

When I go back 8 or 9 months to assess what did exist then and see where we stand now, it's almost unbelievable. Sadat said when I was in Egypt recently that what we achieved at Camp David was a miracle, that he never expected either Egypt or Israel to reach an agreement when he went there.

I think that we now have a posture where our excellent friends, the Israelis, and our excellent friends, the Egyptians, can be friends with one another. We're going to have a short period of time—I believe it will be short—with threats and posturing and possibly some acts of terrorism mounted against [by] [1] those who oppose peace in the Middle East.

But my belief is that if we can open those borders and have thousands of students going back and forth between Cairo and Jerusalem, and Tel Aviv and Alexandria, and tourists going to visit the Pyramids and coming to see the Dead Sea Scrolls, and open trade and commerce, that the people themselves will so deeply appreciate the difference in their quality of life and their attitude toward life, that no matter who the leaders might be in the future, this peace will be permanent.

We're going to not stop here. We've

---

[1] Printed in the transcript.

got to address the very difficult question of the Palestinian problem.

The Israelis are committed to this proposition, the Egyptians are committed to this proposition, and so are we. But I think as we let the other Arab entities— the PLO, Jordanians, Syrians, Lebanese, Iraqis—see the tremendous benefits of the peace between Israel and Egypt, it's going to be much easier to bring them in the process and therefore achieve what I dream about—which may not come during my own term of office, but I'll continue to work for—and that is a comprehensive peace throughout the Middle East.

So, I think it is very significant, it is permanent, it's a first step. But as Sadat says, it's a foundation for what we all dream for—that comprehensive peace in the Middle East. I think it's a very good step.

TAXATION OF COMMERCIAL BROADCASTERS

Q. Mr. President, I'm Forrest Amsden, King Broadcasting Company, Seattle, Washington. There are a number of proposals in Congress and emanating from some members of the regulatory commissions for a high spectrum tax on commercial television and radio stations, as high as perhaps half or three-quarters of a million dollars a year for a television station in, let's say, Dallas. These funds would be used for a number of social purposes not really affecting broadcasting, and also for public broadcasting. Have you a position on this?

THE PRESIDENT. My administration has no intention of introducing legislation like that. As you know, Senator Fritz Hollings and Barry Goldwater and others in the Senate, Congressman Van Deerlin in the House, have introduced legislation similar to what you've described. I have not interpreted that legislation to want to channel those funds into social programs, however.

We've not yet taken a position on it. I've not seen a detailed analysis of what they have proposed. So, I really can't answer your question any better than that. We will monitor it. I'll listen to my advisers. I'll certainly hear from you, I'm sure, and we want to make certain that the legislation is not onerous on you.

I believe that there are some tradeoffs that might have been proposed in the legislation, which you did not mention. There may be some fees assessed for the use of spectra, but on the other hand, there will be an additional freedom for your own industry to operate in. And I believe, in addition, there were some more extended times for the licenses to be prevailing, that sort of thing.

But I'm not trying to say what my position is. I've just read about it very briefly in preparation for this visit. We've not yet taken an administrative position, and I doubt if I will take one until the hearings have been completed and we see more clearly the attitude of the Congress and the attitude of this organization as well.

Maybe one more question, and then they tell me my time is up.

Q. Len Hensel, WSM in Nashville, Tennessee. Sir, Mr. Amsden stepped on my question. But while considering that same proposal, I would appreciate it, sir, if you would consider what we call the repugnance of commercial broadcasting financing public broadcasting from taxes as opposed to the general fund.

THE PRESIDENT. I will certainly consider that. [*Laughter*]

Q. Thank you.

INFLATION

Q. Mr. President, I'm Carol Rosenweig, and I'm here with my husband, Saul, who is also a president. He's president of ATO Communications, which owns WILX–TV in Lansing, Michigan. He also was in your Naval ROTC class at Georgia Tech.

My question deals also with inflation. Washington places much of the blame for inflation on business and labor. But since the Government controls the printing press and is by far the biggest spender in the Nation, I'd like to ask you, doesn't the primary responsibility for inflation really lie with the Federal Government and just filter down to the rest of us? [*Applause*]

THE PRESIDENT. That seems to be the most popular question so far. [*Laughter*]

Q. Thank you.

THE PRESIDENT. I would say the answer is no. [*Laughter*] But let me explain.

One of the causes for continued inflationary pressures, which have existed at an extraordinary level for the last 10 years or more, is a natural inclination on the part of Americans to find a scapegoat.

I felt, when I ran for President in 1975 and 1976, that the Federal deficit was entirely too high. I established then as one of my major goals the balancing of the Federal budget. We've made a great deal of progress. By the 1980 fiscal year budget, if it's adopted the way I presented it— and it may be even better when the Congress and I get through with it—we will have cut the deficit by over 55 percent. This is major progress in times of heavy demand for governmental services.

And, as you know, I have taken the step of strengthening our own Nation's security commitment and defense commitment in NATO and other places.

It's obvious to me that industry, all employers, labor, the government at all levels, and consumers are in this together. And until each one of us does our part, we'll never find a resolution of the problem.

Last night I was in Elk City, Oklahoma. A farmer stood up and asked me if I didn't think that business was responsible for inflation because last quarter profits were 26 percent higher than they had been a year before. And then I asked him what his profession was. He said he was a farmer. I said, "Do you realize that in 1978 net farm income was up 30 percent? Would you say that the farmers were responsible for inflation?" And he very quickly said no.

The point is I'm doing all I can as head of our Government to control inflation. You need to do all you can within the area of your own influence. But if your own prices and charges go up more than our guidelines, you will have directly contributed to inflation and have hurt your own country.

And it's a responsibility that each of us ought to accept. I certainly accept my share of the responsibility as President. I hope you will do the same. I hope all business and labor will also take responsibility, and the consumers as well. Only by assessing it as a partnership and not trying to find a scapegoat can we possibly succeed. But I am absolutely determined and I am absolutely convinced that if we work together we can bring inflation under control.

Let me say in closing that I have thoroughly enjoyed being with you. I hope that you listened very carefully to my opening remarks, because I recognize that perhaps there is no other industry on Earth that has a greater impact on the consciousness of people and, therefore, a greater impact on the evolution of our Nation in a positive direction.

What the rest of the world thinks about America is primarily determined by you. And I think the honesty, the integrity, the accuracy, the freedom of the American broadcasting industry is absolutely crucial to making our Nation, which is the greatest nation on Earth, even freer and greater in the future. In that respect, you and I are also partners.

Thank you very much.

NOTE: President Carter's forty-sixth news conference began at 3:30 p.m. at the Dallas Convention Center, on the occasion of the opening session of the 57th annual convention of the National Association of Broadcasters. Vincent T. Wasilewski is president of NAB, and Paul Stevens is president of radio and television communications of the Southern Baptist Convention, Ft. Worth, Tex.

Prior to the news conference, the President attended a luncheon for members and elected officials of the Democratic Party at the home of Ambassador Robert S. Strauss, Special Representative for Trade Negotiations, in Dallas.

Egyptian-Israeli Peace Treaty

Joint Statement Issued by President Carter, President Anwar al-Sadat of Egypt, and Prime Minister Menahem Begin of Israel. March 25, 1979

At the convening of the Camp David summit meeting we issued a communication which stated in part—"Conscious of the grave issues which face us, we place our trust in the God of our fathers from whom we seek wisdom and guidance. We request people of all faiths to pray with us that peace and justice will result from these deliberations."

Our trust in God was well-placed. On Monday, a treaty of peace will be signed between Egypt and Israel within the framework of a comprehensive peace settlement in the area. We are grateful to the people around the world who joined us in prayer. We now ask people of all faiths to join again in a day of prayer and thanksgiving for what has been accomplished, and then ask God to guide our nations in the days ahead as we continue to work for a comprehensive, just and lasting peace. With God's help, we and generations to come will know peace between our peoples. To this end, we ask that Monday, March 26, be a day of prayer around the world.

Regulatory Reform

Message to the Congress on a Program of Legislative and Executive Actions. March 26, 1979

To the Congress of the United States:

I am today announcing a program of major reforms in the regulatory process, including both legislative and executive action. This program will make new regulations more efficient and effective; ensure reviews of existing regulatory laws and individual rules to eliminate or revise those that are outmoded; and reduce the burden of regulation and paperwork without jeopardizing our progress toward vital regulatory goals.

Since the first Federal regulatory agency was established nearly a century ago, regulatory programs have grown steadily in number, scope, and impact. During that time, however, little attention has been paid to the management of the regulatory process. There was little effort to re-examine rules which no longer served the public or to ensure that needed programs are run on a common sense basis, so that missions are accomplished with maximum results and minimum burdens.

The time has come to stop this neglect. Just as we have injected a new sense of discipline into the management of Federal budgetary and personnel resources, we must reform the government's regulation of others' resources.

Much of Federal regulation is vitally important to modern society. Goals such as equal opportunity, a healthy environment, a safe workplace, and a competitive and truthful marketplace cannot be achieved through market forces alone. In the last decade, the regulatory programs created to achieve these goals have produced a wide range of benefits, such as:

• Workplace health standards have been established which are protecting more than two and one-half million workers exposed to cancer causing substances, such as asbestos, arsenic, and vinyl chloride.

• Automobile safety devices such as seat belts, collapsible steering wheels, interior padding, and side door strength are saving an estimated 9,000 lives per year.

• Fuel economy standards are reducing automobile gasoline consumption by about 1.5 billion gallons this year.

• Populated areas have more protection against fires, explosion and the spilling of hazardous materials transported by rail because of new rules on tank cars.

• We are making real progress on water pollution. Salmon are swimming in the Connecticut River for the first time in almost two centuries.

• Regulations requiring child-proof containers for such products as household cleaners and drugs have prevented as many as 200,000 accidental poisonings of young children.

• Emission controls for automobiles helped reduce carbon monoxide air pollution by 20% between 1972 and 1977.

The regulatory programs that produced these benefits are essential to the Nation's well-being. I am committed to continuing this progress.

The overall regulatory system, however, has become burdensome and unwieldy. We now have 90 regulatory agencies issuing some 7,000 rules each year. When Congress established these programs, it usually focused on isolated objectives. There was little effort to coordinate overlapping agency mandates or to assess cumulative impact. Little attention was given to analyzing the benefits and costs of proposed rules or to using regulatory approaches which could reduce the cost of achieving the goals. Many regulatory programs were allowed to continue unreviewed for decades, in spite of changing conditions. Some rules, such as certain rules affecting transportation rates and routes, came to do more harm than good by crippling competition. The last comprehensive legislation to improve regulatory procedures was passed more than 30 years ago.

We can no longer afford this neglect. Regulation has a large and increasing impact on the economy. Uncertainty about upcoming rules can reduce investment and productivity. Compliance with regulations absorbs large amounts of the capital investments of some industries, further restricting productivity. Inflexible rules and massive paperwork generate extra costs that are especially burdensome for small businesses, state and local governments, and non-profit groups. Regulations that impose needless costs add to inflation.

Our society's resources are vast, but they are not infinite. Americans are willing to spend a fair share of those resources to achieve social goals through regulation. Their support falls away, however, when they see needless rules, excessive costs, and duplicative paperwork. If we are to continue our progress, we must ensure that regulation gives Americans their money's worth.

During the past two years, I have used my authority as President to improve regulatory management.

• After extensive public comment, I issued Executive Order 12044, establishing far-reaching new procedures for development of regulations by Executive agencies. Under that Order, agencies are now analyzing the costs of all major new regulations to seek out the most cost-effective approach; they are expanding opportunities for public participation; and they are starting to identify and eliminate outdated rules.

• To assist individual agencies in meeting the goals of Executive Order 12044, I established the Regulatory Analysis Review Group, which prepares reports on particularly important proposed rules.

• Until this year, there was no way to get a picture of upcoming regulations. Now, each agency is publishing agendas of the rules it is developing. To provide a government-wide picture of major rules, I have established a Regulatory Calendar to be published twice a year. The first Calendar, issued last month, listed 109 rules being developed this year.

• I created the Regulatory Council to prepare the Calendar and use it to identify and deal with areas of overlapping and conflicting regulations. The Council is composed of Executive regulatory agencies plus those independent commissions that agreed to join.

The men and women I appointed to head the regulatory agencies are working to implement these steps and improve regulatory management. They are achieving results. HEW has eliminated 300 pages of rules. OSHA voided nearly 1,000 nitpicking rules, and the Federal Trade Commission cancelled 145 more. The FCC rewrote its rules on citizens band broadcasting into plain English. The FAA reduced the hours small airlines have to spend filling out their forms by more than two-thirds. EPA designed creative procedures that allow companies flexibility in meeting pollution standards, leading to potential savings of millions of dollars without sacrificing clean air goals. We reorganized regulation of pension programs to eliminate duplication and reduce paperwork.

These efforts will continue in 1979. We have important non-legislative initiatives underway, including: a wide-ranging review of rules affecting technological innovation; revisions of all OSHA safety standards to make them simpler and more flexible; overhauls of the regulations imposing costs on hospitals; streamlining EPA permit procedures; review of restrictions on banking; development of a coordinated policy on identification and regulation of cancer-causing substances; and increased research to improve the factual basis for regulatory decisions on toxic chemicals, air pollutants and radiation. We will continue to scrutinize major new rules to ensure that they accomplish their statutory mandates without imposing needless burdens.

These steps are having an impact. Regulatory programs were created by legislation, however, and we need legislation to achieve comprehensive reform. Last year we and Congress made an important beginning. The Airline Deregulation Act substantially deregulated a major industry and enabled more people to fly while saving passengers $2.5 billion in air fares.

My regulatory reform program has two elements:

• We must work together to review the laws that established the regulatory programs. Those that needlessly restrict competition, impose rigidity, or are otherwise out of date must be revised or eliminated.

• For the programs that are needed, we must assure that the statutory mandates are executed sensibly. We must identify alternative means of achieving goals, choose efficient and effective approaches, and improve planning and coordination. We must make it easier for the public and those affected by regulations to anticipate them, participate in developing them, comply with them, and benefit from them. We must provide common sense management for the regulatory process.

This year I am proposing that Congress act in three areas:

I. REGULATION REFORM ACT OF 1979

Once a statute creating a regulatory program is passed, the quality of the program depends mainly on the men and women who are running it. We have a competent and dedicated group of regulators in government now, and they are producing real advances in regulatory reform.

We need legislation to set uniform standards for the work they do and give them the tools to continue their progress. I am submitting, with this Message, a bill to revamp regulatory procedures. This bill strengthens the reforms introduced by E.O. 12044, makes them permanent, and applies them to the independent regulatory commissions. It also overhauls key parts of the Administrative Procedure Act, for the first time since 1946. It sets vital new rules for the regulators:

• *Cost-Effectiveness:* The bill requires that when an agency develops a major rule, it lists the alternative means of accomplishing the objective and the costs and benefits of each alternative. The public will be asked to comment on that analysis and to suggest any additional options that should be considered. The agency must select the least costly way to achieve the rule's objective, or—if another is needed—explain the reasons.

• *Review of Old Rules:* Each agency will establish a schedule to review its major rules and smaller rules which may be outmoded or ineffective. The reviews, to be conducted over a 10-year period, will be used to ensure that rules are kept up-to-date or eliminated.

• *Planning and Management:* The bill requires agencies to publish semi-annual agendas of upcoming rules; ensures that senior officials are fully involved in developing rules; and strengthens selection and oversight for the Administrative Law Judges who make many key regulatory decisions.

• *Delay:* To eliminate needless legal formality and delay, the bill revamps the procedures for agency hearings. It also requires that agencies set deadlines on most proceedings.

• *Public Participation:* The bill helps those affected by regulation participate in the regulatory process, through more notice to the public, a longer comment period, and consultation with affected state and local governments. It also authorizes limited funding for groups that would present important information and could not otherwise afford to participate.

The Office of Management and Budget will oversee the key management reforms. The Administrative Conference of the U.S. will oversee administrative law judges and use of the participation funds. I will soon submit a reorganization plan to enable the Conference to carry out these missions.

II.   PAPERWORK REDUCTION

The Federal Government must collect information from the public to enforce the laws, analyze the economy and estab-lish sound public policy. But too many paperwork requirements are duplicative, unnecessary, or place an unreasonable burden upon small organizations. Over the past two years, we have cut the time the public spends filling out Federal forms by about 15%. But we must do more.

The job of reviewing Federal paperwork requirements should be performed in one place—not divided as it is now, among OMB, GAO and other agencies. I shall submit legislation to the Congress to centralize this mission in the Office of Management and Budget.

In addition, I will soon issue an Executive Order to further reduce the paperwork burden. The Order will require agencies to consider the special problems that small businesses and organizations face in filling out Federal forms and will authorize simpler forms and requirements for such groups. It will establish a "paperwork budget" for Executive agencies and create an information locator system to help agencies determine whether the information they need is already available elsewhere. No report should be approved if the information can be obtained, within privacy and confidentiality protections, elsewhere in the government.

III.   REFORM OF INDIVIDUAL STATUTES

All regulatory programs were created by legislation and many of their problems can be solved only by amending individual statutes. Much of the trouble with regulation built up because laws have gone unchanged in spite of changing needs.

This problem applies to many Federal programs in addition to regulation. One answer is to pass a sunset bill. This legislation would set a schedule for Congressional review of each program, once every 10 years. The reviews would be timed so that related programs are considered simultaneously. To ensure that the reviews are serious, spending authority would terminate unless Congress acts to renew or revise the program.

Sunset will make a crucial contribution to the effort to cut the waste from government regulation and government spending. An excellent sunset bill passed the Senate last year. With the addition of sunset reviews for Federal tax expenditures, this legislation will make a great contribution to effective management. I urge Congress to put it into law.

In addition, my Administration will work with Congress this year to reform several individual regulatory statutes. We just submitted the first of our proposals to reduce economic regulation of surface transportation. We will submit legislation on drugs, nuclear plant siting, meat and poultry inspection and other areas. And we will work with Congress on bills already introduced to revamp regulation of communications.

To reform regulation, we and Congress must act in partnership, within our respective spheres of responsibility under the Constitution. The program I have stated follows that principle. From Congress, it asks reform of underlying statutes and modernization of the ground rules for administering them. From me, and from the agency heads I have appointed to help me execute the laws, it demands competent management and coordination.

I ask Congress to join me in this effort and to refrain from seeking authority to veto individual regulatory decisions and thereby to administer the laws itself. The legislative veto is an illusory solution to the problems of regulation. In some cases it would make rules weaker; in others it would make them stricter. But in all cases, it would increase delay, undermine fair procedures, and fragment responsibilities.

It would disrupt our effort to manage the regulatory process, and it would distract Congress from the fundamental job of reforming underlying statutes. Any serious effort to administer the legislative veto would require a major increase in congressional staff and threaten the Constitutional division of power.

The program I am proposing will not solve all the problems overnight. But these steps will make regulation a more effective tool to improve our lives. They will help get needless rules and paperwork off our backs, and they will help marshal our resources to attack the real problems with maximum efficiency. By doing so, they will help us advance our national commitment to the regulatory goals we all believe in—a healthier, safer and fairer America.

JIMMY CARTER

The White House,
    March 26, 1979.

NOTE: The text of the message was released on March 25.

Egyptian-Israeli Peace Treaty

*Treaty and Related Documents.
March 26, 1979*

TREATY OF PEACE BETWEEN THE ARAB REPUBLIC OF EGYPT AND THE STATE OF ISRAEL

The Government of the Arab Republic of Egypt and the Government of the State of Israel;

PREAMBLE

Convinced of the urgent necessity of the establishment of a just, comprehensive and lasting peace in the Middle East in accordance with Security Council Resolutions 242 and 338;

Reaffirming their adherence to the "Framework for Peace in the Middle East Agreed at Camp David," dated September 17, 1978;

Noting that the aforementioned Framework as appropriate is intended to constitute a basis for peace not only between Egypt and Israel but also between Israel and each of its other Arab neighbors which is prepared to negotiate peace with it on this basis;

Desiring to bring to an end the state of war between them and to establish a peace in which every state in the area can live in security;

Convinced that the conclusion of a Treaty of Peace between Egypt and Israel is an important step in the search for comprehensive peace in the area and for the attainment of the settlement of the Arab-Israeli conflict in all its aspects;

Inviting the other Arab parties to this dispute to join the peace process with Israel guided by and based on the principles of the aforementioned Framework;

Desiring as well to develop friendly relations and cooperation between themselves in accordance with the United Nations Charter and the principles of international law governing international relations in times of peace;

Agree to the following provisions in the free exercise of their sovereignty, in order to implement the "Framework for the Conclusion of a Peace Treaty Between Egypt and Israel":

ARTICLE I

1. The state of war between the Parties will be terminated and peace will be established between them upon the exchange of instruments of ratification of this Treaty.

2. Israel will withdraw all its armed forces and civilians from the Sinai behind the international boundary between Egypt and mandated Palestine, as provided in the annexed protocol (Annex I), and Egypt will resume the exercise of its full sovereignty over the Sinai.

3. Upon completion of the interim withdrawal provided for in Annex I, the Parties will establish normal and friendly relations, in accordance with Article III(3).

ARTICLE II

The permanent boundary between Egypt and Israel is the recognized international boundary between Egypt and the former mandated territory of Palestine, as shown on the map at Annex II, without prejudice to the issue of the status of the Gaza Strip. The Parties recognize this boundary as inviolable. Each will respect the territorial integrity of the other, including their territorial waters and airspace.

ARTICLE III

1. The Parties will apply between them the provisions of the Charter of the United Nations and the principles of international law governing relations among states in times of peace. In particular:

a. They recognize and will respect each other's sovereignty, territorial integrity and political independence;

b. They recognize and will respect each other's right to live in peace within their secure and recognized boundaries;

c. They will refrain from the threat or use of force, directly or indirectly, against each other and will settle all disputes between them by peaceful means.

2. Each Party undertakes to ensure that acts or threats of belligerency, hostility, or violence do not originate from and are not committed from within its territory, or by any forces subject to its control or by

any other forces stationed on its territory, against the population, citizens or property of the other Party. Each Party also undertakes to refrain from organizing, instigating, inciting, assisting or participating in acts or threats of belligerency, hostility, subversion or violence against the other Party, anywhere, and undertakes to ensure that perpetrators of such acts are brought to justice.

3. The Parties agree that the normal relationship established between them will include full recognition, diplomatic, economic and cultural relations, termination of economic boycotts and discriminatory barriers to the free movement of people and goods, and will guarantee the mutual enjoyment by citizens of the due process of law. The process by which they undertake to achieve such a relationship parallel to the implementation of other provisions of this Treaty is set out in the annexed protocol (Annex III).

ARTICLE IV

1. In order to provide maximum security for both Parties on the basis of reciprocity, agreed security arrangements will be established including limited force zones in Egyptian and Israeli territory, and United Nations forces and observers, described in detail as to nature and timing in Annex I, and other security arrangements the Parties may agree upon.

2. The Parties agree to the stationing of United Nations personnel in areas described in Annex I. The Parties agree not to request withdrawal of the United Nations personnel and that these personnel will not be removed unless such removal is approved by the Security Council of the United Nations, with the affirmative vote of the five Permanent Members, unless the Parties otherwise agree.

3. A Joint Commission will be estab-

lished to facilitate the implementation of the Treaty, as provided for in Annex I.

4. The security arrangements provided for in paragraphs 1 and 2 of this Article may at the request of either party be reviewed and amended by mutual agreement of the Parties.

ARTICLE V

1. Ships of Israel, and cargoes destined for or coming from Israel, shall enjoy the right of free passage through the Suez Canal and its approaches through the Gulf of Suez and the Mediterranean Sea on the basis of the Constantinople Convention of 1888, applying to all nations. Israeli nationals, vessels and cargoes, as well as persons, vessels and cargoes destined for or coming from Israel, shall be accorded non-discriminatory treatment in all matters connected with usage of the canal.

2. The Parties consider the Strait of Tiran and the Gulf of Aqaba to be international waterways open to all nations for unimpeded and non-suspendable freedom of navigation and overflight. The Parties will respect each other's right to navigation and overflight for access to either country through the Strait of Tiran and the Gulf of Aqaba.

ARTICLE VI

1. This Treaty does not affect and shall not be interpreted as affecting in any way the rights and obligations of the Parties under the Charter of the United Nations.

2. The Parties undertake to fulfill in good faith their obligations under this Treaty, without regard to action or inaction of any other party and independently of any instrument external to this Treaty.

3. They further undertake to take all the necessary measures for the applica-

tion in their relations of the provisions of the multilateral conventions to which they are parties, including the submission of appropriate notification to the Secretary General of the United Nations and other depositaries of such conventions.

4. The parties undertake not to enter into any obligation in conflict with this Treaty.

5. Subject to Article 103 of the United Nations Charter, in the event of a conflict between the obligations of the Parties under the present Treaty and any of their other obligations, the obligations under this Treaty will be binding and implemented.

ARTICLE VII

1. Disputes arising out of the application or interpretation of this Treaty shall be resolved by negotiations.

2. Any such disputes which cannot be settled by negotiations shall be resolved by conciliation or submitted to arbitration.

ARTICLE VIII

The Parties agree to establish a claims commission for the mutual settlement of all financial claims.

ARTICLE IX

1. This Treaty shall enter into force upon exchange of instruments of ratification.

2. This Treaty supersedes the Agreement between Egypt and Israel of September, 1975.

3. All protocols, annexes, and maps attached to this Treaty shall be regarded as an integral part hereof.

4. The Treaty shall be communicated to the Secretary General of the United Nations for registration in accordance with the provisions of Article 102 of the Charter of the United Nations.

DONE at Washington, D.C. this 26th day of March, 1979, in triplicate in the English, Arabic, and Hebrew languages, each text being equally authentic. In case of any divergence of interpretation, the English text shall prevail.

For the Government of the Arab Republic of Egypt:

A. SADAT

For the Government of Israel:

M. BEGIN

Witnessed by:

JIMMY CARTER
Jimmy Carter, President of the United States of America

ANNEX I

PROTOCOL CONCERNING ISRAELI WITHDRAWAL AND SECURITY ARRANGEMENTS

ARTICLE I

Concept of Withdrawal

1. Israel will complete withdrawal of all its armed forces and civilians from the Sinai not later than three years from the date of exchange of instruments of ratification of this Treaty.

2. To ensure the mutual security of the Parties, the implementation of phased withdrawal will be accompanied by the military measures and establishment of zones set out in this Annex and in Map 1, hereinafter referred to as "the Zones."

3. The withdrawal from the Sinai will be accomplished in two phases:

a. The interim withdrawal behind the line from east of El Arish to Ras Muhammed as delineated on Map 2 within nine months from the date of exchange of instruments of ratification of this Treaty.

b. The final withdrawal from the Sinai behind the international boundary not later than three years from the date of exchange of instruments of ratification of this Treaty.

4. A Joint Commission will be formed immediately after the exchange of instruments of ratification of this Treaty in order to supervise and coordinate movements and schedules during the withdrawal, and to adjust plans and timetables as necessary within the limits established by paragraph 3, above. Details relating to the Joint Commission are set out in Article IV of the attached Appendix. The Joint Commission will be dissolved upon completion of final Israeli withdrawal from the Sinai.

ARTICLE II

Determination of Final Lines and Zones

1. In order to provide maximum security for both Parties after the final withdrawal, the lines and the Zones delineated on Map 1 are to be established and organized as follows:

a. Zone A

(1) Zone A is bounded on the east by line A (red line) and on the west by the Suez Canal and the east coast of the Gulf of Suez, as shown on Map 1.

(2) An Egyptian armed force of one mechanized infantry division and its military installations, and field fortifications, will be in this Zone.

(3) The main elements of that division will consist of:

(a) Three mechanized infantry brigades.

(b) One armored brigade.

(c) Seven field artillery battalions including up to 126 artillery pieces.

(d) Seven anti-aircraft artillery battalions including individual surface-to-air missiles and up to 126 anti-aircraft guns of 37 mm and above.

(e) Up to 230 tanks.

(f) Up to 480 armored personnel vehicles of all types.

(g) Up to a total of twenty-two thousand personnel.

b. Zone B

(1) Zone B is bounded by line B (green line) on the east and by line A (red line) on the west, as shown on Map 1.

(2) Egyptian border units of four battalions equipped with light weapons and wheeled vehicles will provide security and supplement the civil police in maintaining order in Zone B. The main elements of the four border battalions will consist of up to a total of four thousand personnel.

(3) Land based, short range, low power, coastal warning points of the border patrol units may be established on the coast of this Zone.

(4) There will be in Zone B field fortifications and military installations for the four border battalions.

c. Zone C

(1) Zone C is bounded by line B (green line) on the west and the international boundary and the Gulf of Aqaba on the east, as shown on Map 1.

(2) Only United Nations forces and Egyptian civil police will be stationed in Zone C.

(3) The Egyptian civil police armed with light weapons will perform normal police functions within this Zone.

(4) The United Nations Force will be deployed within Zone C and perform its functions as defined in Article VI of this Annex.

(5) The United Nations Force will be stationed mainly in camps located within the following stationing areas shown on

Map 1, and will establish its precise locations after consultations with Egypt:

(a) In that part of the area in the Sinai lying within about 20 Km. of the Mediterranean Sea and adjacent to the International boundary.

(b) In the Sharm el Sheikh area.

d. Zone D

(1) Zone D is bounded by line D (blue line) on the east and the international boundary on the west, as shown on Map 1.

(2) In this Zone there will be an Israeli limited force of four infantry battalions, their military installations, and field fortifications, and United Nations observers.

(3) The Israeli forces in Zone D will not include tanks, artillery and anti-aircraft missiles except individual surface-to-air missiles.

(4) The main elements of the four Israeli infantry battalions will consist of up to 180 armored personnel vehicles of all types and up to a total of four thousand personnel.

2. Access across the international boundary shall only be permitted through entry check points designated by each Party and under its control. Such access shall be in accordance with laws and regulations of each country.

3. Only those field fortifications, military installations, forces, and weapons specifically permitted by this Annex shall be in the Zones.

ARTICLE III

Aerial Military Regime

1. Flights of combat aircraft and reconnaissance flights of Egypt and Israel shall take place only over Zones A and D, respectively.

2. Only unarmed, non-combat aircraft of Egypt and Israel will be stationed in Zones A and D, respectively.

3. Only Egyptian unarmed transport aircraft will take off and land in Zone B and up to eight such aircraft may be maintained in Zone B. The Egyptian border units may be equipped with unarmed helicopters to perform their functions in Zone B.

4. The Egyptian civil police may be equipped with unarmed police helicopters to perform normal police functions in Zone C.

5. Only civilian airfields may be built in the Zones.

6. Without prejudice to the provisions of this Treaty, only those military aerial activities specifically permitted by this Annex shall be allowed in the Zones and the airspace above their territorial waters.

ARTICLE IV

Naval Regime

1. Egypt and Israel may base and operate naval vessels along the coasts of Zones A and D, respectively.

2. Egyptian coast guard boats, lightly armed, may be stationed and operate in in the territorial waters of Zone B to assist the border units in performing their functions in this Zone.

3. Egyptian civil police equipped with light boats, lightly armed, shall perform normal police functions within the territorial waters of Zone C.

4. Nothing in this Annex shall be considered as derogating from the right of innocent passage of the naval vessels of either Party.

5. Only civilian maritime ports and installations may be built in the Zones.

6. Without prejudice to the provisions of this Treaty, only those naval activities specifically permitted by this Annex shall

be allowed in the Zones and in their territorial waters.

ARTICLE V

Early Warning Systems

Egypt and Israel may establish and operate early warning systems only in Zones A and D, respectively.

ARTICLE VI

United Nations Operations

1. The Parties will request the United Nations to provide forces and observers to supervise the implementation of this Annex and employ their best efforts to prevent any violation of its terms.

2. With respect to these United Nations forces and observers, as appropriate, the Parties agree to request the following arrangements:

a. Operation of check points, reconnaissance patrols, and observation posts along the international boundary and line B, and within Zone C.

b. Periodic verification of the implementation of the provisions of this Annex will be carried out not less than twice a month unless otherwise agreed by the Parties.

c. Additional verifications within 48 hours after the receipt of a request from either Party.

d. Ensuring the freedom of navigation through the Strait of Tiran in accordance with Article V of the Treaty of Peace.

3. The arrangements described in this article for each zone will be implemented in Zones A, B, and C by the United Nations Force and in Zone D by the United Nations Observers.

4. United Nations verification teams shall be accompanied by liaison officers of the respective Party.

5. The United Nations Force and Observers will report their findings to both Parties.

6. The United Nations Force and Observers operating in the Zones will enjoy freedom of movement and other facilities necessary for the performance of their tasks.

7. The United Nations Force and Observers are not empowered to authorize the crossing of the international boundary.

8. The Parties shall agree on the nations from which the United Nations Force and Observers will be drawn. They will be drawn from nations other than those which are Permanent Members of the United Nations Security Council.

9. The Parties agree that the United Nations should make those command arrangements that will best assure the effective implementation of its responsibilities.

ARTICLE VII

Liaison System

1. Upon dissolution of the Joint Commission, a liaison system between the Parties will be established. This liaison system is intended to provide an effective method to assess progress in the implementation of obligations under the present Annex and to resolve any problem that may arise in the course of implementation, and refer other unresolved matters to the higher military authorities of the two countries respectively for consideration. It is also intended to prevent situations resulting from errors or misinterpretation on the part of either Party.

2. An Egyptian liaison office will be established in the city of El Arish and an Israeli liaison office will be established in the city of Beer-Sheba. Each office will be headed by an officer of the respective

country, and assisted by a number of officers.

3. A direct telephone link between the two offices will be set up and also direct telephone lines with the United Nations command will be maintained by both offices.

ARTICLE VIII

Respect for War Memorials

Each Party undertakes to preserve in good condition the War Memorials erected in the memory of soldiers of the other Party, namely those erected by Israel in the Sinai and those to be erected by Egypt in Israel, and shall permit access to such monuments.

ARTICLE IX

Interim Arrangements

The withdrawal of Israeli armed forces and civilians behind the interim withdrawal line, and the conduct of the forces of the Parties and the United Nations prior to the final withdrawal, will be governed by the attached Appendix and Maps 2 and 3.

APPENDIX to ANNEX I

ORGANIZATION OF MOVEMENTS IN THE SINAI

ARTICLE I

Principles of Withdrawal

1. The withdrawal of Israeli armed forces and civilians from the Sinai will be accomplished in two phases as described in Article I of Annex I. The description and timing of the withdrawal are included in this Appendix. The Joint Commission will develop and present to the Chief Coordinator of the United Nations forces in the Middle East the details of these phases not later than one month before the initiation of each phase of withdrawal.

2. Both Parties agree on the following principles for the sequence of military movements.

a. Notwithstanding the provisions of Article IX, paragraph 2, of this Treaty, until Israeli armed forces complete withdrawal from the current J and M Lines established by the Egyptian-Israeli Agreement of September 1975, hereinafter referred to as the 1975 Agreement, up to the interim withdrawal line, all military arrangements existing under that Agreement will remain in effect, except those military arrangements otherwise provided for in this Appendix.

b. As Israeli armed forces withdraw, United Nations forces will immediately enter the evacuated areas to establish interim and temporary buffer zones as shown on Maps 2 and 3, respectively, for the purpose of maintaining a separation of forces. United Nations forces' deployment will precede the movement of any other personnel into these areas.

c. Within a period of seven days after Israeli armed forces have evacuated any area located in Zone A, units of Egyptian armed forces shall deploy in accordance with the provisions of Article II of this Appendix.

d. Within a period of seven days after Israeli armed forces have evacuated any area located in Zones A or B, Egyptian border units shall deploy in accordance with the provisions of Article II of this Appendix, and will function in accordance with the provisions of Article II of Annex I.

e. Egyptian civil police will enter evacuated areas immediately after the United Nations forces to perform normal police functions.

f. Egyptian naval units shall deploy in the Gulf of Suez in accordance with the provisions of Article II of this Appendix.

g. Except those movements mentioned above, deployments of Egyptian armed forces and the activities covered in Annex I will be effected in the evacuated areas when Israeli armed forces have completed their withdrawal behind the interim withdrawal line.

ARTICLE II

Subphases of the Withdrawal to the Interim Withdrawal Line

1. The withdrawal to the interim withdrawal line will be accomplished in subphases as described in this Article and as shown on Map 3. Each subphase will be completed within the indicated number of months from the date of the exchange of instruments of ratification of this Treaty.

a. First subphase: within two months, Israeli armed forces will withdraw from the area of El Arish, including the town of El Arish and its airfield, shown as Area I on Map 3.

b. Second subphase: within three months, Israeli armed forces will withdraw from the area between line M of the 1975 Agreement and line A, shown as Area II on Map 3.

c. Third subphase: within five months, Israeli armed forces will withdraw from the areas east and south of Area II, shown as Area III on Map 3.

d. Fourth subphase: within seven months, Israeli armed forces will withdraw from the area of El Tor—Ras El Kenisa, shown as Area IV on Map 3.

e. Fifth subphase: Within nine months, Israeli armed forces will withdraw from the remaining areas west of the interim withdrawal line, including the areas of Santa Katrina and the areas east of the Giddi and Mitla passes, shown as Area V on Map 3, thereby completing Israeli withdrawal behind the interim withdrawal line.

2. Egyptian forces will deploy in the areas evacuated by Israeli armed forces as follows:

a. Up to one-third of the Egyptian armed forces in the Sinai in accordance with the 1975 Agreement will deploy in the portions of Zone A lying within Area I, until the completion of interim withdrawal. Thereafter, Egyptian armed forces as described in Article II of Annex I will be deployed in Zone A up to the limits of the interim buffer zone.

b. The Egyptian naval activity in accordance with Article IV of Annex I will commence along the coasts of Areas II, III, and IV, upon completion of the second, third, and fourth subphases, respectively.

c. Of the Egyptian border units described in Article II of Annex I, upon completion of the first subphase one battalion will be deployed in Area I. A second battalion will be deployed in Area II upon completion of the second subphase. A third battalion will be deployed in Area III upon completion of the third subphase. The second and third battalions mentioned above may also be deployed in any of the subsequently evacuated areas of the southern Sinai.

3. United Nations forces in Buffer Zone I of the 1975 Agreement will redeploy to enable the deployment of Egyptian forces described above upon the completion of the first subphase, but will otherwise continue to function in accordance with the provisions of that Agreement in the remainder of that zone until the completion of interim withdrawal, as indicated in Article I of this Appendix.

4. Israeli convoys may use the roads south and east of the main road junction east of El Arish to evacuate Israeli forces and equipment up to the completion of interim withdrawal. These convoys will proceed in daylight upon four hours notice to the Egyptian liaison group and

United Nations forces, will be escorted by United Nations forces, and will be in accordance with schedules coordinated by the Joint Commission. An Egyptian liaison officer will accompany convoys to assure uninterrupted movement. The Joint Commission may approve other arrangements for convoys.

ARTICLE III

United Nations Forces

1. The Parties shall request that United Nations forces be deployed as necessary to perform the functions described in this Appendix up to the time of completion of final Israeli withdrawal. For that purpose, the Parties agree to the redeployment of the United Nations Emergency Force.

2. United Nations forces will supervise the implementation of this Appendix and will employ their best efforts to prevent any violation of its terms.

3. When United Nations forces deploy in accordance with the provisions of Articles I and II of this Appendix, they will perform the functions of verification in limited force zones in accordance with Article VI of Annex I, and will establish check points, reconnaissance patrols, and observation posts in the temporary buffer zones described in Article II above. Other functions of the United Nations forces which concern the interim buffer zone are described in Article V of this Appendix.

ARTICLE IV

Joint Commission and Liaison

1. The Joint Commission referred to in Article IV of this Treaty will function from the date of exchange of instruments of ratification of this Treaty up to the date of completion of final Israeli withdrawal from the Sinai.

2. The Joint Commission will be composed of representatives of each Party headed by senior officers. This Commission shall invite a representative of the United Nations when discussing subjects concerning the United Nations, or when either Party requests United Nations presence. Decisions of the Joint Commission will be reached by agreement of Egypt and Israel.

3. The Joint Commission will supervise the implementation of the arrangements described in Annex I and this Appendix. To this end, and by agreement of both Parties, it will:

a. coordinate military movements described in this Appendix and supervise their implementation;

b. address and seek to resolve any problem arising out of the implementation of Annex I and this Appendix, and discuss any violations reported by the United Nations Force and Observers and refer to the Governments of Egypt and Israel any unresolved problems;

c. assist the United Nations Force and Observers in the execution of their mandates, and deal with the timetables of the periodic verifications when referred to it by the Parties as provided for in Annex I and in this Appendix;

d. organize the demarcation of the international boundary and all lines and zones described in Annex I and this Appendix;

e. supervise the handing over of the main installations in the Sinai from Israel to Egypt;

f. agree on necessary arrangements for finding and returning missing bodies of Egyptian and Israeli soldiers;

g. organize the setting up and operation of entry check points along the El Arish-Ras Muhammed line in accordance with the provisions of Article 4 of Annex III;

h. conduct its operations through the use of joint liaison teams consisting of one Israeli representative and one Egyptian representative, provided from a standing

Liaison Group, which will conduct activities as directed by the Joint Commission;

i. provide liaison and coordination to the United Nations command implementing provisions of the Treaty, and, through the joint liaison teams, maintain local coordination and cooperation with the United Nations Force stationed in specific areas or United Nations Observers monitoring specific areas for any assistance as needed;

j. discuss any other matters which the Parties by agreement may place before it.

4. Meetings of the Joint Commission shall be held at least once a month. In the event that either Party or the Command of the United Nations Force requests a special meeting, it will be convened within 24 hours.

5. The Joint Commission will meet in the buffer zone until the completion of the interim withdrawal and in El Arish and Beer-Sheba alternately afterwards. The first meeting will be held not later than two weeks after the entry into force of this Treaty.

ARTICLE V

Definition of the Interim Buffer Zone and Its Activities

1. An interim buffer zone, by which the United Nations Force will effect a separation of Egyptian and Israeli elements, will be established west of and adjacent to the interim withdrawal line as shown on Map 2 after implementation of Israeli withdrawal and deployment behind the interim withdrawal line. Egyptian civil police equipped with light weapons will perform normal police functions within this zone.

2. The United Nations Force will operate check points, reconnaissance patrols, and observation posts within the interim buffer zone in order to ensure compliance with the terms of this Article.

3. In accordance with arrangements agreed upon by both Parties and to be coordinated by the Joint Commission, Israeli personnel will operate military technical installations at four specific locations shown on Map 2 and designated as T1 (map central coordinate 57163940), T2 (map central coordinate 59351541), T3 (map central coordinate 59331527), and T4 (map central coordinate 61130979) under the following principles:

a. The technical installations shall be manned by technical and administrative personnel equipped with small arms required for their protection (revolvers, rifles, sub-machine guns, light machine guns, hand grenades, and ammunition), as follows:

T1—up to 150 personnel
T2 and T3—up to 350 personnel
T4—up to 200 personnel.

b. Israeli personnel will not carry weapons outside the sites, except officers who may carry personal weapons.

c. Only a third party agreed to by Egypt and Israel will enter and conduct inspections within the perimeters of technical installations in the buffer zone. The third party will conduct inspections in a random manner at least once a month. The inspections will verify the nature of the operation of the installations and the weapons and personnel therein. The third party will immediately report to the Parties any divergence from an installation's visual and electronic surveillance or communications role.

d. Supply of the installations, visits for technical and administrative purposes, and replacement of personnel and equipment situated in the sites, may occur uninterruptedly from the United Nations check points to the perimeter of the technical installations, after checking and being escorted by only the United Nations forces.

e. Israel will be permitted to introduce

505

into its technical installations items required for the proper functioning of the installations and personnel.

f. As determined by the Joint Commission, Israel will be permitted to:

(1) Maintain in its installations firefighting and general maintenance equipment as well as wheeled administrative vehicles and mobile engineering equipment necessary for the maintenance of the sites. All vehicles shall be unarmed.

(2) Within the sites and in the buffer zone, maintain roads, water lines and communications cables which serve the sites. At each of the three installation locations (T1, T2, and T3, and T4), this maintenance may be performed with up to two unarmed wheeled vehicles and by up to twelve unarmed personnel with only necessary equipment, including heavy engineering equipment if needed. This maintenance may be performed three times a week, except for special problems, and only after giving the United Nations four hours notice. The teams will be escorted by the United Nations.

g. Movement to and from the technical installations will take place only during daylight hours. Access to, and exit from, the technical intallations shall be as follows:

(1) T1: through a United Nations check point, and via the road between Abu Aweigila and the intersection of the Abu Aweigila road and the Gebel Libni road (at Km. 161), as shown on Map 2.

(2) T2 and T3: through a United Nations checkpoint and via the road constructed across the buffer zone to Gebel Katrina, as shown on Map 2.

(3) T2, T3, and T4: via helicopters flying within a corridor at the times, and according to a flight profile, agreed to by the Joint Commission. The helicopters will be checked by the United Nations

Force at landing sites outside the perimeter of the installations.

h. Israel will inform the United Nations Force at least one hour in advance of each intended movement to and from the installations.

i. Israel shall be entitled to evacuate sick and wounded and summon medical experts and medical teams at any time after giving immediate notice to the United Nations Force.

4. The details of the above principles and all other matters in this Article requiring coordination by the Parties will be handled by the Joint Commission.

5. These technical installations will be withdrawn when Israeli forces withdraw from the interim withdrawal line, or at a time agreed by the parties.

ARTICLE VI

Disposition of Installations and Military Barriers

Disposition of installations and military barriers will be determined by the Parties in accordance with the following guidelines:

1. Up to three weeks before Israeli withdrawal from any area, the Joint Commission will arrange for Israeli and Egyptian liaison and technical teams to conduct a joint inspection of all appropriate installations to agree upon condition of structures and articles which will be transferred to Egyptian control and to arrange for such transfer. Israel will declare, at that time, its plans for disposition of installations and articles within the installations.

2. Israel undertakes to transfer to Egypt all agreed infrastructure, utilities, and installations intact, inter alia, airfields, roads, pumping stations, and ports. Israel will present to Egypt the information necessary for the maintenance and opera-

tion of these facilities. Egyptian technical teams will be permitted to observe and familiarize themselves with the operation of these facilities for a period of up to two weeks prior to transfer.

3. When Israel relinquishes Israeli military water points near El Arish and El Tor, Egyptian technical teams will assume control of those installations and ancillary equipment in accordance with an orderly transfer process arranged beforehand by the Joint Commission. Egypt undertakes to continue to make available at all water supply points the normal quantity of currently available water up to the time Israel withdraws behind the international boundary, unless otherwise agreed in the Joint Commission.

4. Israel will make its best effort to remove or destroy all military barriers, including obstacles and minefields, in the areas and adjacent waters from which it withdraws, according to the following concept:

a. Military barriers will be cleared first from areas near populations, roads, and major installations and utilities.

b. For those obstacles and minefields which cannot be removed or destroyed prior to Israeli withdrawal, Israel will provide detailed maps to Egypt and the United Nations through the Joint Commission not later than 15 days before entry of United Nations forces into the affected areas.

c. Egyptian military engineers will enter those areas after United Nations forces enter to conduct barrier clearance operations in accordance with Egyptian plans to be submitted prior to implementation.

ARTICLE VII

Surveillance Activities

1. Aerial surveillance activities during the withdrawal will be carried out as follows:

a. Both Parties request the United States to continue airborne surveillance flights in accordance with previous agreements until the completion of final Israeli withdrawal.

b. Flight profiles will cover the Limited Forces Zones to monitor the limitations on forces and armaments, and to determine that Israeli armed forces have withdrawn from the areas described in Article II of Annex I, Article II of this Appendix, and Maps 2 and 3, and that these forces thereafter remain behind their lines. Special inspection flights may be flown at the request of either Party or of the United Nations.

c. Only the main elements in the military organizations of each Party, as described in Annex I and in this Appendix, will be reported.

2. Both Parties request the United States operated Sinai Field Mission to continue its operations in accordance with previous agreements until completion of the Israeli withdrawal from the area east of the Giddi and Mitla Passes. Thereafter, the Mission will be terminated.

ARTICLE VIII

Exercise of Egyptian Sovereignty

Egypt will resume the exercise of its full sovereignty over evacuated parts of the Sinai upon Israeli withdrawal as provided for in Article I of this Treaty.

MAP 1 – International Boundary and the Lines of the Zones

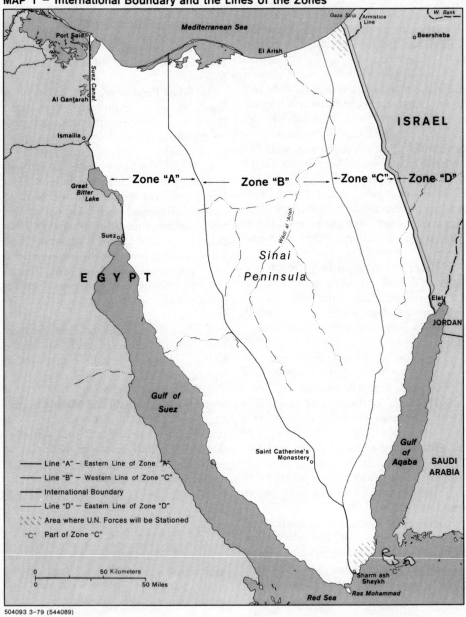

504093 3-79 (544089)

MAP 2 – Lines and Zones Effective when Israeli Forces are on the El Arish - Ras Mohammad Line

504094 3-79 (544089)

MAP 3 – Sub-Phases of Withdrawal to the El Arish-Ras Mohammad Line

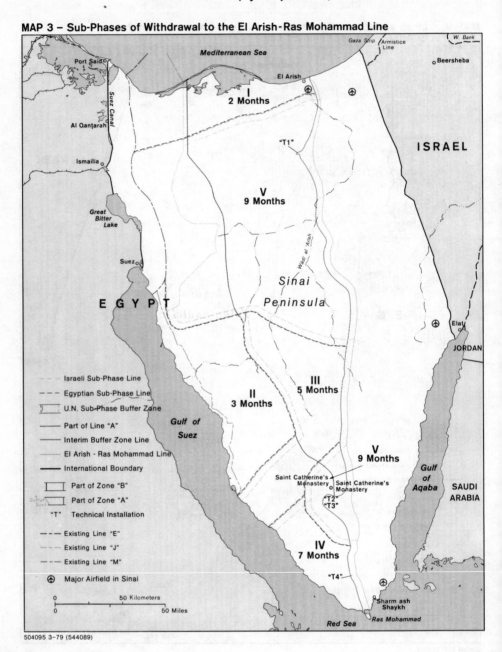

504095 3-79 (544089)

ANNEX II – International Boundary

504096 3-79 (544089)

ANNEX III

PROTOCOL CONCERNING RELATIONS OF
THE PARTIES

ARTICLE 1

Diplomatic and Consular Relations

The Parties agree to establish diplomatic and consular relations and to exchange ambassadors upon completion of the interim withdrawal.

ARTICLE 2

Economic and Trade Relations

1. The Parties agree to remove all discriminatory barriers to normal economic relations and to terminate economic boycotts of each other upon completion of the interim withdrawal.

2. As soon as possible, and not later than six months after the completion of the interim withdrawal, the Parties will enter negotiations with a view to concluding an agreement on trade and commerce for the purpose of promoting beneficial economic relations.

ARTICLE 3

Cultural Relations

1. The Parties agree to establish normal cultural relations following completion of the interim withdrawal.

2. They agree on the desirability of cultural exchanges in all fields, and shall, as soon as possible and not later than six months after completion of the interim withdrawal, enter into negotiations with a view to concluding a cultural agreement for this purpose.

ARTICLE 4

Freedom of Movement

1. Upon completion of the interim withdrawal, each Party will permit the free movement of the nationals and vehicles of the other into and within its territory according to the general rules applicable to nationals and vehicles of other states. Neither Party will impose discriminatory restrictions on the free movement of persons and vehicles from its territory to the territory of the other.

2. Mutual unimpeded access to places of religious and historical significance will be provided on a nondiscriminatory basis.

ARTICLE 5

Cooperation for Development and Good Neighborly Relations

1. The Parties recognize a mutuality of interest in good neighborly relations and agree to consider means to promote such relations.

2. The Parties will cooperate in promoting peace, stability and development in their region. Each agrees to consider proposals the other may wish to make to this end.

3. The Parties shall seek to foster mutual understanding and tolerance and will, accordingly, abstain from hostile propaganda against each other.

ARTICLE 6

Transportation and Telecommunications

1. The Parties recognize as applicable to each other the rights, privileges and obligations provided for by the aviation agreements to which they are both party,

particularly by the Convention on International Civil Aviation, 1944 ("The Chicago Convention") and the International Air Services Transit Agreement, 1944.

2. Upon completion of the interim withdrawal any declaration of national emergency by a party under Article 89 of the Chicago Convention will not be applied to the other party on a discriminatory basis.

3. Egypt agrees that the use of airfields left by Israel near El Arish, Rafah, Ras El Nagb and Sharm el Sheikh shall be for civilian purposes only, including possible commercial use by all nations.

4. As soon as possible and not later than six months after the completion of the interim withdrawal, the Parties shall enter into negotiations for the purpose of concluding a civil aviation agreement.

5. The Parties will reopen and maintain roads and railways between their countries and will consider further road and rail links. The Parties further agree that a highway will be constructed and maintained between Egypt, Israel and Jordan near Eilat with guaranteed free and peaceful passage of persons, vehicles and goods between Egypt and Jordan, without prejudice to their sovereignty over that part of the highway which falls within their respective territory.

6. Upon completion of the interim withdrawal, normal postal, telephone, telex, data facsimile, wireless and cable communications and television relay services by cable, radio and satellite shall be established between the two Parties in accordance with all relevant international conventions and regulations.

7. Upon completion of the interim withdrawal, each Party shall grant normal access to its ports for vessels and cargoes of the other, as well as vessels and cargoes destined for or coming from the other. Such access shall be granted on the same conditions generally applicable to vessels and cargoes of other nations. Article 5 of the Treaty of Peace will be implemented upon the exchange of instruments of ratification of the aforementioned Treaty.

ARTICLE 7

Enjoyment of Human Rights

The Parties affirm their commitment to respect and observe human rights and fundamental freedoms for all, and they will promote these rights and freedoms in accordance with the United Nations Charter.

ARTICLE 8

Territorial Seas

Without prejudice to the provisions of Article 5 of the Treaty of Peace each Party recognizes the right of the vessels of the other Party to innocent passage through its territorial sea in accordance with the rules of international law.

AGREED MINUTES TO ARTICLES I, IV, V AND VI AND ANNEXES I AND III OF TREATY OF PEACE

ARTICLE I

Egypt's resumption of the exercise of full sovereignty over the Sinai provided for in paragraph 2 of Article I shall occur with regard to each area upon Israel's withdrawal from that area.

ARTICLE IV

It is agreed between the parties that the review provided for in Article IV(4) will be undertaken when requested by either party, commencing within three months of such a request, but that any amendment can be made only with the mutual agreement of both parties.

ARTICLE V

The second sentence of paragraph 2 of Article V shall not be construed as limiting the first sentence of that paragraph. The foregoing is not to be construed as contravening the second sentence of paragraph 2 of Article V, which reads as follows:

"The Parties will respect each other's right to navigation and overflight for access to either country through the Strait of Tiran and the Gulf of Aqaba."

ARTICLE VI(2)

The provisions of Article VI shall not be construed in contradiction to the provisions of the framework for peace in the Middle East agreed at Camp David. The foregoing is not to be construed as contravening the provisions of Article VI (2) of the Treaty, which reads as follows:

"The Parties undertake to fulfill in good faith their obligations under this Treaty, without regard to action or inaction of any other Party and independently of any instrument external to this Treaty."

ARTICLE VI(5)

It is agreed by the Parties that there is no assertion that this Treaty prevails over other Treaties or agreements or that other Treaties or agreements prevail over this Treaty. The foregoing is not to be construed as contravening the provisions of Article VI(5) of the Treaty, which reads as follows:

"Subject to Article 103 of the United Nations Charter, in the event of a conflict between the obligations of the Parties

under the present Treaty and any of their other obligations, the obligations under this Treaty will be binding and implemented."

ANNEX I

Article VI, Paragraph 8, of Annex I provides as follows:

"The Parties shall agree on the nations from which the United Nations force and observers will be drawn. They will be drawn from nations other than those which are permanent members of the United Nations Security Council."

The Parties have agreed as follows:

"With respect to the provisions of paragraph 8, Article VI, of Annex I, if no agreement is reached between the Parties, they will accept or support a U.S. proposal concerning the composition of the United Nations force and observers."

ANNEX III

The Treaty of Peace and Annex III thereto provide for establishing normal economic relations between the Parties. In accordance therewith, it is agreed that such relations will include normal commercial sales of oil by Egypt to Israel, and that Israel shall be fully entitled to make bids for Egyptian-origin oil not needed for Egyptian domestic oil consumption, and Egypt and its oil concessionaires will entertain bids made by Israel, on the same basis and terms as apply to other bidders for such oil.

For the Government of Israel:

M. BEGIN

For the Government of the Arab Republic of Egypt:

A. SADAT

Witnessed by:

JIMMY CARTER
Jimmy Carter, President of the United States of America

March 26, 1979

Dear Mr. President:

This letter confirms that Israel and Egypt have agreed as follows:

The Governments of Israel and Egypt recall that they concluded at Camp David and signed at the White House on September 17, 1978, the annexed documents entitled "A Framework for Peace in the Middle East Agreed at Camp David" and "Framework for the conclusion of a Peace Treaty between Israel and Egypt."

For the purpose of achieving a comprehensive peace settlement in accordance with the above-mentioned Frameworks, Israel and Egypt will proceed with the implementation of those provisions relating to the West Bank and the Gaza Strip. They have agreed to start negotiations within a month after the exchange of the instruments of ratification of the Peace Treaty. In accordance with the "Framework for Peace in the Middle East," the Hashemite Kingdom of Jordan is invited to join the negotiations. The Delegations of Egypt and Jordan may include Palestinians from the West Bank and Gaza Strip or other Palestinians as mutually agreed. The purpose of the negotiations shall be to agree, prior to the elections, on the modalities for establishing the elected self-governing authority (administrative council), define its powers and responsibilities, and agree upon other related issues. In the event Jordan decides not to take part in the negotiations, the negotiations will be held by Israel and Egypt.

The two Governments agree to negotiate continuously and in good faith to conclude these negotiations at the earliest possible date. They also agree that the objective of the negotiations is the establishment of the self-governing authority in the West Bank and Gaza in order to provide full autonomy to the inhabitants.

Israel and Egypt set for themselves the goal of completing the negotiations within one year so that elections will be held as expeditiously as possible after agreement has been reached between the parties. The self-governing authority referred to in the "Framework for Peace in the Middle East" will be established and inaugurated within one month after it has been elected, at which time the transitional period of five years will begin. The Israeli military government and its civilian administration will be withdrawn, to be replaced by the self-governing authority, as specified in the "Framework for Peace in the Middle East." A withdrawal of Israeli armed forces will then take place and there will be a redeployment of the remaining Israeli forces into specified security locations.

This letter also confirms our understanding that the United States Government will participate fully in all stages of negotiations.

Sincerely yours,

For the Government of Israel:

M. BEGIN

For the Government of the Arab Republic of Egypt:

A. SADAT

[The President, The White House.]

EXPLANATORY NOTE

President Carter, upon receipt of the joint letter to him from President Sadat and Prime Minister Begin, has added to the American and Israeli copies the notation:

"I have been informed that the expression 'West Bank' is understood by the Government of Israel to mean 'Judea and Samaria.' "

This notation is in accordance with similar procedures established at Camp David.

March 26, 1979

Dear Mr. President:

In response to your request, I can confirm that, within one month after the completion of Israel's withdrawal to the interim line as provided for in the Treaty of Peace between Egypt and Israel, Egypt will send a resident ambassador to Israel and will receive a resident Israeli ambassador in Egypt.

Sincerely,

A. SADAT

[The President, The White House.]

March 26, 1979

Dear Mr. Prime Minister:

I have received a letter from President Sadat that, within one month after Israel completes its withdrawal to the interim line in Sinai, as provided for in the Treaty of Peace between Egypt and Israel, Egypt will send a resident ambassador to Israel and will receive in Egypt a resident Israeli ambassador.

I would be grateful if you will confirm that this procedure will be agreeable to the Government of Israel.

Sincerely,

JIMMY CARTER

[His Excellency Menachem Begin, Prime Minister of the State of Israel.]

March 26, 1979

Dear Mr. President:

I am pleased to be able to confirm that the Government of Israel is agreeable to the procedure set out in your letter of March 26, 1979 in which you state:

"I have received a letter from President Sadat that, within one month after Israel completes its withdrawal to the interim line in Sinai, as provided for in the Treaty of Peace between Egypt and Israel, Egypt will send a resident ambassador to Israel and will receive in Egypt a resident Israeli ambassador."

Sincerely,

M. BEGIN

[The President, The White House.]

March 26, 1979

Dear Mr. President:

I wish to confirm to you that subject to United States Constitutional processes:

In the event of an actual or threatened violation of the Treaty of Peace between Egypt and Israel, the United States will, on request of one or both of the Parties, consult with the Parties with respect thereto and will take such other action as it may deem appropriate and helpful to achieve compliance with the Treaty.

The United States will conduct aerial monitoring as requested by the Parties pursuant to Annex I of the Treaty.

The United States believes the Treaty provision for permanent stationing of United Nations personnel in the designated limited force zone can and should be implemented by the United Nations Security Council. The United States will exert its utmost efforts to obtain the requisite action by the Security Council. If the Security Council fails to establish and maintain the arrangements called for in the Treaty, the President will be prepared to take those steps necessary to ensure the establishment and maintenance of an acceptable alternative multinational force.

Sincerely,

JIMMY CARTER

[His Excellency Mohamed Anwar El-Sadat, President of the Arab Republic of Egypt.]

March 26, 1979

Dear Mr. Prime Minister:

I wish to confirm to you that subject to United States Constitutional processes:

In the event of an actual or threatened violation of the Treaty of Peace between Israel and Egypt, the United States will, on request of one or both of the Parties, consult with the Parties with respect thereto and will take such other action as it may deem appropriate and helpful to achieve compliance with the Treaty.

The United States will conduct aerial monitoring as requested by the Parties pursuant to Annex I of the Treaty.

The United States believes the Treaty provision for permanent stationing of United Nations personnel in the designated limited force zone can and should be implemented by the United Nations Security Council. The United States will exert its utmost efforts to obtain the requisite action by the Security Council. If the Security Council fails to establish and maintain the arrangements called for in the Treaty, the President will be prepared to take those steps necessary to ensure the establishment and maintenance of an acceptable alternative multinational force.

Sincerely,

JIMMY CARTER

[His Excellency Menachem Begin, Prime Minister of the State of Israel.]

Egyptian-Israeli Peace Treaty

Remarks of President Carter, President Anwar al-Sadat of Egypt, and Prime Minister Menahem Begin of Israel at the Signing Ceremony.   March 26, 1979

PRESIDENT CARTER. During the past 30 years, Israel and Egypt have waged war. But for the past 16 months, these same two great nations have waged peace. Today we celebrate a victory—not of a bloody military campaign, but of an inspiring peace campaign. Two leaders who will loom large in the history of nations, President Anwar al-Sadat and Prime Minister Menahem Begin, have conducted this campaign with all the courage, tenacity, brilliance, and inspiration of any generals who have ever led men and machines onto the field of battle.

At the end of this campaign, the soil of the two lands is not drenched with young blood. The countrysides of both lands are free from the litter and the carnage of a wasteful war. Mothers in Egypt and Israel are not weeping today for their children fallen in senseless battle. The dedication and determination of these two world statesmen have borne fruit. Peace has come to Israel and to Egypt.

I honor these two leaders and their government officials who have hammered out this peace treaty which we have just signed. But most of all, I honor the people of these two lands whose yearning for peace kept alive the negotiations which today culminate in this glorious event.

We have won at last the first step of peace, a first step on a long and difficult road. We must not minimize the obstacles which still lie ahead. Differences still separate the signatories to this treaty from

517

one another, and also from some of their neighbors who fear what they have just done. To overcome these differences, to dispel these fears, we must rededicate ourselves to the goal of a broader peace with justice for all who have lived in a state of conflict in the Middle East.

We have no illusions—we have hopes, dreams, and prayers, yes, but no illusions.

There now remains the rest of the Arab world, whose support and whose cooperation in the peace process is needed and honestly sought. I am convinced that other Arab people need and want peace. But some of their leaders are not yet willing to honor these needs and desires for peace. We must now demonstrate the advantages of peace and expand its benefits to encompass all those who have suffered so much in the Middle East.

Obviously, time and understanding will be necessary for people, hitherto enemies, to become neighbors in the best sense of the word.

Just because a paper is signed, all the problems will not automatically go away. Future days will require the best from us to give reality to these lofty aspirations.

Let those who would shatter peace, who would callously spill more blood, be aware that we three and all others who may join us will vigorously wage peace.

So let history record that deep and ancient antagonism can be settled without bloodshed and without staggering waste of precious lives, without rapacious destruction of the land.

It has been said, and I quote, "Peace has one thing in common with its enemy, with the fiend it battles, with war; peace is active, not passive; peace is doing, not waiting; peace is aggressive—attacking; peace plans its strategy and encircles the enemy; peace marshals its forces and storms the gates; peace gathers its weapons and pierces the defense; peace, like war, is waged."

It is true that we cannot enforce trust and cooperation between nations, but we can use all our strength to see that nations do not again go to war.

All our religious doctrines give us hope. In the Koran, we read: "But if the enemy incline towards peace, do thou also incline towards peace, and trust in God; for He is the One that heareth and knoweth all things."

And the prophet Isaiah said: "Nations shall beat their swords into plowshares and their spears into pruninghooks: nation shall not lift up sword against nation, neither shall they learn war any more."

So let us now lay aside war. Let us now reward all the children of Abraham who hunger for a comprehensive peace in the Middle East. Let us now enjoy the adventure of becoming fully human, fully neighbors, even brothers and sisters. We pray God, we pray God together, that these dreams will come true. I believe they will.

Thank you very much.

PRESIDENT SADAT. *President Carter, dear friends:*

This is certainly one of the happiest moments in my life. It is a historic turning point of great significance for all peace-loving nations. Those among us who are endowed with vision cannot fail to comprehend the dimensions of our sacred mission. The Egyptian people, with their heritage and unique awareness of history, have realized from the very beginning the meaning and value of this endeavor.

In all the steps I took, I was not performing a personal mission. I was merely expressing the will of a nation. I'm proud of my people and of belonging to them.

Today, a new dawn is emerging out of the darkness of the past. A new chapter is being opened in the history of coexistence among nations, one that's worthy of our spiritual values and civilization. Never before had men encountered such a complex dispute, which is highly charged with emotions. Never before did men need that much courage and imagination to confront a single challenge. Never before had any cause generated that much interest in all four corners of the globe.

Men and women of good will have labored day and night to bring about this happy moment. Egyptians and Israelis alike pursued their sacred goal, undeterred by difficulties and complications. Hundreds of dedicated individuals on both sides have given generously of their thought and effort to translate the cherished dream into a living reality.

But the man who performed the miracle was President Carter. Without any exaggeration, what he did constitutes one of the greatest achievements of our time. He devoted his skill, hard work and, above all, his firm belief in the ultimate triumph of good against evil to ensure the success of our mission.

To me he has been the best companion and partner along the road to peace. With his deep sense of justice and genuine commitment to human rights, we were able to surmount the most difficult obstacles.

There came certain moments when hope was eroding and retreating in the face of crisis. However, President Carter remained unshaken in his confidence and determination. He is a man of faith and compassion. Before anything else, the signing of the peace treaty and the exchanged letter is a tribute to the spirit and ability of Jimmy Carter.

Happily, he was armed with the blessing of God and the support of his people. For that we are grateful to each and every American who contributed in his own way to the success of our endeavor.

We are also heartened by the understanding of hundreds of thousands of Israelis who remained unwavering in their commitment to peace. The continuation of this spirit is vital to the coronation of our effort.

We realize that difficult times lay ahead. The signing of these documents marks only the beginning of peace. But it is an indispensable start. Other steps remain to be taken without delay or procrastination. Much will depend on the success of these steps. We are all committed to pursue our efforts until the fruits of the comprehensive settlement we agreed upon are shared by all parties to the conflict.

President Carter once said that the United States is committed without reservation to seeing the peace process through until all parties to the Arab-Israeli conflict are at peace. We value such a pledge from a leader who raised the banners of morality and ethics as a substitute for power politics and opportunism.

The steps we took in the recent past will serve Arab vital interests. The liberation of Arab land and the reinstitution of Arab authority in the West Bank and Gaza would certainly enhance our common strategic interests.

While we take the initiative to protect these interests, we remain faithful to our Arab commitment. To us, this is a matter of destiny. Pursuing peace is the only avenue which is compatible with our culture and creed.

Let there be no more wars or bloodshed between Arabs and Israelis—let there be no more wars or bloodshed between Arabs and Israelis. Let there be no more suffering or denial of rights. Let there be no more despair or loss of faith. Let no mother lament the loss of her child. Let no young man waste his life on a conflict from which no one benefits. Let us work together until the day comes when they beat their swords into plowshares and their spears into pruninghooks. And God does call to the abode of peace. He does guide whom He pleases to His way.

[At this point, President Sadat repeated the last two sentences in Arabic.]

Thank you.

PRIME MINISTER BEGIN. *Mr. President of the United States of America; Mr. President of the Arab Republic of Egypt; Mr. Vice President; Mr. Speaker of the House of Representatives; Mr. Speaker of the Knesset; Members of the Cabinets of the United States, of Egypt, and Israel; Members of the Congress and the Knesset; Your Excellencies; chairman of the board of governors of the Jewish Agency; chairman of the executive of the Zionist Organization; Mrs. Gruber, the mother of the sons;* [1]*distinguished guests; ladies and gentlemen:*

I have come from the land of Israel, the land of Zion and Jerusalem, and here I am in humility and with pride as a son of the Jewish people, as one of the generation of the Holocaust and redemption.

The ancient Jewish people gave the world a vision of eternal peace, of universal disarmament, of abolishing the teaching and the learning of war.

Two prophets, Yishayahu Ben Amotz and Micah Hamorashti, having foreseen the spiritual unity of man under God,

---

[1] Rivka Gruber, an Israeli public figure since her loss of two sons in the 1948 war of independence, and author of the book "The Mother of the Sons."

with these words coming forth from Jerusalem, gave the nations of the world the following vision—expressed in identical terms—"And they shall beat their swords into plowshares and their spears into pruninghooks: nation shall not lift up sword against nation, neither shall they learn war any more."

Despite the tragedies and disappointments of the past, we must never forsake that vision, that human dream, that unshakable faith.

Peace is the beauty of life. It is sunshine. It is the smile of a child, the love of a mother, the joy of a father, the togetherness of a family. It is the advancement of man, the victory of a just cause, the triumph of truth. Peace is all of these and more, and more.

These are words I uttered in Oslo, on December 10, 1978, while receiving the second half of the Nobel Peace Prize. The first half went, rightly so, to President Sadat. And I took the liberty to repeat them here on this momentous, historic occasion.

It is a great day in the annals of two ancient nations, Egypt and Israel, whose sons met in battle five times in one generation, fighting and falling.

Let us turn our hearts to our heroes and pay tribute to their eternal memory. It is thanks to them, to our fallen heroes, that we could have reached this day.

However, let us not forget that in ancient times, our two nations met also in alliance. Now we make peace, the cornerstone of cooperation and friendship.

It is a great day in your life, Mr. President of the United States. You have worked so hard, so insistently, so consistently to achieve this goal. And your labors and your devotion bore God-blessed fruit.

Our friend, President Sadat, said that you are the unknown soldier of the peace-making effort. I agree, but as usual, with an amendment. [*Laughter*] A soldier in the service of peace, you are. You are, Mr. President, even, *mirabile dictu,* an intransigent fighter for peace. But Jimmy Carter, the President of the United States, is not completely unknown. [*Laughter*] And so it is his efforts which will be remembered and recorded by generations to come.

It is, of course, a great day in your life, Mr. President of the Arab Republic of Egypt. In the face of adversity and hostility, you have demonstrated the human value that can change history—civil courage.

A great field commander once said, "Civil courage is sometimes more difficult to show than military courage." You showed both, Mr. President. But now it is time for all of us to show civil courage in order to proclaim to our peoples and to others: No more war, no more bloodshed, no more bereavement. Peace unto you, *shalom, salaam*—forever.

And it is, ladies and gentlemen, the third greatest day in my life. The first was May 14, 1948, when our flag was hoisted. Our independence in our ancestors' land was proclaimed after 1,878 years of dispersion, persecution, humiliation and, ultimately, physical destruction.

We fought for our liberation alone, and with God's help, we won the day. That was spring. Such a spring we can never have again.

The second day was when Jerusalem became one city and our brave, perhaps most hardened soldiers, the parachutists, embraced with tears and kissed the ancient stones of the remnants of the wall

destined to protect the chosen place of God's glory. Our hearts wept with them in remembrance.

[*In Hebrew*] "Our feet shall stand within thy gates, O Jerusalem. Jerusalem is builded as a city that is compact together."

[*In English*] This is the third day in my life. I have signed a treaty of peace with our great neighbor, with Egypt. The heart is full and overflowing. God gave me the strength to persevere, to survive the horrors of Nazism and of the Stalinite concentration camp and some other dangers, to endure, not to waver in nor flinch from my duty, to accept abuse from foreigners and, what is more painful, from my own people, and even from my close friends. This effort, too, bore some fruit.

Therefore, it is the proper place and the appropriate time to bring back to memory the song and prayer of thanksgiving I learned as a child, in the home of father and mother that doesn't exist anymore, because they were among the 6 million people—men, women, and children—who sanctified the Lord's name with the sacred blood which reddened the rivers of Europe from the Rhine to the Danube, from the Bug to the Volga, because, only because they were born Jews, and because they didn't have a country of their own, and neither a valiant Jewish army to defend them, and because nobody, nobody came to their rescue, although they cried out, "Save us, save us"—*de profundis*—"from the depths of the pits and agony." That is the Song of Degrees, written 2 millennia and 500 years ago, when our forefathers returned from their first exile to Jerusalem and Zion.

[*At this point, Prime Minister Begin spoke in Hebrew.*]

I will not translate. Every man, whether Jew or Christian or Moslem, can read it in his own language in the Book of the Books. It is just Psalm 126.

NOTE: The President spoke at 2:12 p.m. on the North Lawn of the White House. Prior to their remarks, President Sadat and Prime Minister Begin signed, and President Carter witnessed, the treaty and related documents.

The ceremony was attended by officials of the three Governments and invited guests. It was broadcast live on radio and television.

Earlier in the day the President held separate meetings with President Sadat and Prime Minister Begin and, prior to the ceremony, the President and Mrs. Carter hosted a private luncheon for President and Mrs. Sadat and Prime Minister and Mrs. Begin at the White House.

Following the ceremony, the President met at the White House with Members of Congress to discuss U.S. assistance to Egypt and Israel.

Egyptian-Israeli Peace Treaty

Toasts at a State Dinner Honoring President Sadat and Prime Minister Begin.
March 26, 1979

PRESIDENT CARTER. *President Sadat, Prime Minister Begin, Egyptian friends, Israeli friends, American friends:*

This is one of those evenings that it's been hard for me to stay seated also, I've been so excited.

Most of the times in history when a peace treaty was signed, one nation has been a victor and the other nation has been vanquished. One nation has won; the other nation has lost. Today we've signed a peace treaty when both nations have won.

This is indeed a joyous occasion. We've prayed for peace, and we have worked for peace. And now we humbly give thanks to God that we can celebrate the beginnings of peace in the Middle East.

I've gotten to know these two men on my right in the last 18 months—sometimes too well. [*Laughter*] We have spent days and days together, hours and hours together, planning, arguing, debating, negotiating. And I have come to know them and to respect them, to form a friendship, a sense of brotherhood and even love with both of them. They are men of great courage, great sensitivity, great patriotism and statemanship; men who never feared to face difficult questions and seek persistently for the answers. They've been men who have inspired me and who have been inspired by the people in their own great nations whom they represent.

The peace that was born today has a meaning that comes down to us through many years or generations, even centuries. In ancient days, God promised Abraham that from his seed would come many nations. And as you know, that promise has been fulfilled. Yet for much too long, the people of Israel and the people of Egypt—two of the nations of the children of Abraham, trusting in the same God, hoping for the same peace—knew only enmity between them. That time, thank God, is now at an end.

Now, after 30 years, four wars, countless deaths, terrible anguish, we can see a new era ahead, an era, we hope, in which violence no longer dominates the Middle East. And the just concerns of all of us can find a peaceful solution to the problems that we share and a peaceful expression of the hopes and dreams of people who look to us for leadership.

The path for peace has brought us a long way in a short time. It was only 16 months ago that President Sadat made his extraordinary and historic journey to Jerusalem. He was received there by Prime

Minister Begin and was followed by Prime Minister Begin's equally historic trip to Ismailia.

Their vision and their courage stirred hopes in the hearts of people throughout the world.

The distance we've come since then is little short of miraculous. There were difficult moments, many difficult moments; times when the differences seemed impossible to overcome. But at each of those times, just a few simple realities summoned us to renewed effort: first of all, the knowledge that the people—the people of Egypt and the people of Israel—no matter what the leaders might have done, deeply and passionately desired peace; second, the awareness that the process which we had initiated was the only practical route to progress; third, the obligation that was felt to those who have suffered so much—to the young, to the old, and to future generations; and I think above all, the depth of our common faith in a just and a merciful God.

These things sustained us, and they've brought us here tonight.

I would like to note here a simple fact: that when others could not or would not move to end the seemingly endless tragedy of the Middle East, two men—President Anwar Sadat and Prime Minister Menahem Begin—dared to think the unthinkable, dared to do what others feared could not be done, dared to seize history in their hands and to turn history toward peace. And I am thankful to them both.

Theirs is the vision of the psalmist who said: "Behold, how good and how pleasant it is for brethren to dwell together in unity!"

But this is an achievement not just of leaders but of peoples, strong and creative peoples, proud of past heritage and present achievements, and wise enough to know that future well-being can be assured only through cooperation and a very difficult element of mutual trust.

Tonight we commemorate not an end, but a beginning, for a treaty between Egypt and Israel is but the first step along a long and a rough and a narrow and a very difficult road.

We hope that the Palestinians and others will soon join us in our efforts to make this treaty the cornerstone of a comprehensive peace, a true and a lasting peace, a just peace for the entire Middle East. I welcome and invite those who have so far held back—for whatever motive they might honor—to join us in the future. The way is long and the way is hard, but peace is the way.

We share a vision of a time when all the people of the Middle East may turn their energies back to the works of life, when young people can marry and start families and have a hope of seeing and knowing their own children's children, when the old can end their lives quietly after witnessing many a gentle spring. We pray for that time, and we shall continue to work for that time.

This is a season of renewal, when the Earth brings forth life. The Koran tells us of a prophet and a king of Israel for whom God's power "made the violent wind blow tamely." The Old Testament tells us the words of that same king, the words of King Solomon, David's son: For every thing there is a season, and a time to every purpose under the heaven.

For centuries the people of Israel were dispersed around the world, often despised and persecuted. For centuries the people of Egypt suffered under foreign domination. Only in the past generation

523

have these two proud and ancient peoples again become independent nations.

But that generation, to use the words of King Solomon, has also been a time to die, to pluck up that which was planted, a time to kill, a time of breaking down, a time to mourn, a time of weeping, a time to lose, a time to hate, and a time for war. We pray that the season of weeping is past. And to continue the words of that same king, that now will come a time to heal, a time to plant, a time to build up, a time to laugh, a time to dance, a time to embrace, a time to love.

We pray to God that at last the children of Abraham have come to a time of peace.

And now, I would like to propose a toast: To the President of the Arab Republic of Egypt, Anwar al-Sadat, and to the Prime Minister of the State of Israel, Menahem Begin; to the great peoples they serve, the people of Egypt and the people of Israel, now joined together in hope; and to the cause we all serve: *salaam, shalom,* and to peace.

PRESIDENT SADAT. *President Carter, Prime Minister Begin, dear friends:*

Only a few hours ago we laid down a solid foundation for a lasting peace in the Middle East. We did so in a determined effort to heal the wounds of the past and usher in a new era of love and fraternity. At long last cousins will be able to revive the traditions of the glorious past when they lived side by side in peace and harmony.

Our great friend, President Carter, who was the architect of the entire process, spoke of the new reality which is dawning. We all share his hopes and aspirations. We want to see a steady progress on the road to peace. This will require a positive movement on all fronts.

Within a few weeks, we will be entering into negotiations with the goal of establishing a self-governing authority with full autonomy on the West Bank and Gaza. The success of these negotiations will depend largely on the ability of all parties to rise to the level of events and demonstrate their good faith. Above all, it depends upon an active American role. President Carter has promised me to spare no effort to ensure the coronation of our efforts.

I have full confidence in him. He has been a wonderful partner and a courageous statesman. He has shown an unparalleled understanding of the plight of the Palestinian people. He is sensitive to their legitimate call for the eradication of the injustice that was inflicted upon them in the unhappy past.

We all realize their need to be reassured that they will be able soon to take the first step on the road to self-determination and statehood. A dialog with their representatives will be very helpful. It would also be consistent with American tradition.

It is with this in mind that we proceed towards the completion of this sacred mission. None of us can bear the responsibility of defeating the expectations of millions across the borders. None of us can interfere with the course of history or turn the clock back.

We should seize this opportunity. We should seize this opportunity, this historic opportunity in this historic gathering, which is hosted by the American people, to pledge ourselves to the continuation of the process. We should vow to employ all the moral strength we muster, to ensure the ultimate success of our endeavor.

Dear friends, I ask you to rise in a tribute to President Carter, his spouse, the American people, and to the millions of people of good will everywhere, Mr. Begin and Mrs. Begin.

PRIME MINISTER BEGIN. *President Carter, Mrs. Carter, President Sadat, Mrs. Sadat, ladies and gentlemen:*

Amongst the many guests assembled here, there is a lady from Norway. Her name is Mrs. Lionaes. She was, until recently, the chairman of the committee of the Norwegian Parliament for the Nobel Peace Prize. I invited her to come today and to be with us, because when the award was granted by that committee to two men, she was under certain criticism from some circles. And I asked her, after the ceremony of signing, whether now she can say that she and her colleagues did not make a mistake. And she said, with very characteristic bravery, "I never had any doubts." [*Laughter*]

Now, my dear friend, Mrs. Lionaes, when you come back home, I have a request to you, respectfully, to get in touch with your former colleagues, the members of the Nobel Prize committee of the democratic parliament of your country. I suggest, ladies and gentlemen, that all of us—President Sadat and myself, members of the three Cabinets of the United States, of Egypt, and Israel, Members of Congress of both Houses, Members of the Knesset, writers, singers, all of us assembled here—do decide to nominate President Jimmy Carter as a candidate— [*applause*]—I didn't yet say a candidate for what—[*laughter*]—as a candidate to receive the Nobel Peace Prize of 1979. And please, no sharing of the award. [*Laughter*] All the prize is due to the President of the United States. And, Mr. President, if on the 10th of December, this year, you go to Oslo, and you invite President Sadat and me to be witnesses for that ceremony, I am positive that both of us will be in Oslo. It is due to you, my dear friend, Mr. President. You deserve it amply. And I am sure on the 10th

of December you will be crowned with the great, international, famous award, the Nobel Peace Prize.

Now, ladies and gentlemen, I would like to pay tribute to a man who is the main adviser of the President of this great country, and his friend and my friend. And as I know all the goings and comings and all the legal formulations about every word or letter, or even comma, I can say to you tonight that a great service was rendered to the United States, to Egypt, to Israel, and to the cause of peace by a gentleman who did so much day and night with his inventive mind, with his great learning and knowledge, and who bears another title. He is also the husband of the perfect lady whom my wife and I love dearly and respect highly. I refer to the Secretary of State, Cyrus Vance.

And the last remark, ladies and gentlemen, will be absolutely personal. And I will apologize for making it, but I have to. In the afternoon, I spoke about survival and perseverence. Tonight, in your presence, I would like to thank for that ability to persevere one human being who is here, whom I met when she was 17 years old, my own wife.

And again, I will quote a prophet, Yirmeyahu. This time I will translate.

[*At this point, the Prime Minister spoke in Hebrew.*]

"And I will remember the grace of your youth, the love of your nuptials following me into the desert, into a land sown with mines."

Now we arrived to be here on this day. Let us thank God Almighty that he gave us, together, and our children and our grandchildren the strength to withstand all the tests, which sometimes were quite difficult, until I could, on behalf of our people, to do the greatest human act, sign a peace treaty. In the circle of friendship of President Carter, President Sadat, and

525

myself, we stand together. And we vow to continue to be always together and work for peace.

And therefore, I raise my glass. I raise my glass to President Carter, President of the United States of America, the mighty democracy which saved the world twice from the danger of tyranny, militarism, and totalitarianism, and which is still the guarantee for human liberty; and to President Sadat, whom I met for the first time in Jerusalem. And since then—as it is true, it comes from my heart—I have a deep sentiment for him. And under any circumstances, I will guard it in the depths of my heart.

And let us raise a toast to friendship between America, Egypt, and Israel, forever. Thank you.

PRESIDENT SADAT. Ladies and gentlemen, until last night, whenever I meet with Premier Begin, we seldom come in conformity. [*Laughter*] The miracle was achieved today. And let me say this in all candor: I am in full conformity with Premier Begin, and let us hope that we shall continue. I support his proposal that our dear friend, President Carter, be elected as the man of peace of '79. Thank you.

PRESIDENT CARTER. Thank you.

I might point out to President Sadat and to Prime Minister Begin that if the next 9 months of negotiations are completely harmonious, constructive, cooperative, and in a spirit of friendship, and if we meet all the requirements of the Camp David agreements and the peace treaty we signed today, then I might consider accepting their nomination. Otherwise, they have made their toasts in vain.

I think we've proven today, and in the last 18 months or so, that there can be peace between our three nations and an

inspiration for the whole world. I can feel a certain sense of satisfaction and gratitude, of harmony, friendship, inspiration, kind of an electrical current of common purpose in this group tonight. And I think it extends to Egypt and to Israel and, indeed, throughout the world.

Political achievement has been wonderful. But now I think it's time for us to shift our attention to another sense of harmony, to show that superb talent can indeed transcend national boundaries. Each of our nations, through the leaders, have suggested for tonight's program superb performers. President Sadat has requested Omar Khorshed to come to represent Egypt; a superb musician, a superb composer, and a superb actor. Prime Minister Begin, to represent Israel, has asked Itzhak Perlman, a very well-known and beloved performer, and Pinchas Zukerman, who will accompany him, two of the most talented men who have ever lived. And my wife and I have requested Leontyne Price to sing to represent the United States of America.

We will witness, without further introductions, a higher reality of human achievement, beauty, excellence, high ambition, reached by human beings.

Some of the performers had to overcome great handicaps, physical handicaps, racial handicaps. But they will all show tonight that what they are is the exemplification of humanity that can indeed be an inspiration to us all.

Now for a few minutes, I think we will enjoy some of the finest examples of achievement from our three countries.

I am indeed grateful that you've come tonight. It's a wonderful and historic evening. And I believe it will be an exciting and enjoyable evening as well. And you will certify that, I am sure, with your own applause after these performers give us the inspiration for which they are so greatly qualified.

Thank you again. Good evening.

NOTE: The President spoke at 10:30 p.m. in a tent which had been erected for the occasion on the South Grounds of the White House.

Law Day, U.S.A., 1979

Proclamation 4649. March 27, 1979

By the President of the United States of America

A Proclamation

The Congress of the United States has set aside the first day of May as Law Day, U.S.A.

This year will mark the Nation's twenty-second annual celebration of Law Day—a special day for reflection on our heritage of individual liberty and for re-dedication to the observance of the rule of law.

The rule of law is not automatic. Each citizen must accept a share of responsibility to administer and obey the law, if the rights and opportunities of all citizens are to be preserved.

Americans also have a responsibility and a constitutional right to change the law by orderly process, when such change is needed. Our forefathers gave us this birthright, so that the Nation and its people might remain free.

In the words of Thomas Jefferson, "Laws and institutions must go hand in hand with the progress of the human mind."

The theme selected in recognition of Law Day, 1979, therefore, is most appropriate: "Our Changing Rights."

In a rapidly changing world, it is vital that we preserve and strengthen our ability to respond to the needs for legitimate change while safeguarding the rights of all citizens.

Now, THEREFORE, I, JIMMY CARTER, President of the United States of America, invite the American people to observe Tuesday, May 1, 1979, as Law Day, U.S.A., and to reflect upon individual and collective responsibilities for the effective administration of the law.

I call upon the legal profession, the courts, educators, clergymen, and all interested individuals and organizations to mark the twenty-second nationwide observance of Law Day, U.S.A., with programs and events which underscore our Nation's devotion to the principle of equal justice for all. To that end, I call upon all public officials to display the flag of the United States on all government buildings on that day.

IN WITNESS WHEREOF, I have hereunto set my hand this twenty-seventh day of March, in the year of our Lord nineteen hundred seventy-nine, and of the Independence of the United States of America the two hundred and third.

JIMMY CARTER

[Filed with the Office of the Federal Register, 10:02 a.m., March 28, 1979]

Department of Labor

Nomination of Janet L. Norwood To Be Commissioner of Labor Statistics. March 27, 1979

The President today announced that he will nominate Janet L. Norwood, of Bethesda, Md., to be Commissioner of Labor Statistics at the Labor Department. She would replace the late Julius Shiskin.

Norwood has been serving as Acting Commissioner of Labor Statistics since April 1978.

She was born December 11, 1923, in Newark, N.J. She received a B.A. from Douglass College, Rutgers University, and an M.A. and Ph. D. from Tufts University.

Norwood has been with the Bureau of Labor Statistics since 1963, beginning as an economist in the Office of Foreign Labor and Trade. She has also served as chief of the Division of Consumer Prices and Price Indexes and as Deputy Commissioner for Data Analysis. She is the author of numerous articles in professional journals on statistics and labor law.

Federal Labor Relations Authority

Nomination of H. Stephan Gordon To Be
General Counsel.   March 27, 1979

The President today announced that he will nominate H. Stephan Gordon, of Kensington, Md., to be General Counsel of the Federal Labor Relations Authority for a 5-year term.

Gordon is Chief Administrative Law Judge at the Department of Labor and also serves as Chairman of the Labor Department's Board of Contract Appeals, Chairman of the National Review Panel, and a member of the Administrative Conference of the United States.

Gordon was born December 4, 1922, in Vienna, Austria. He received an A.B. from Indiana University in 1946 and a J.D. from the George Washington University in 1949. He served in the U.S. Army from 1942 to 1945.

From 1949 to 1958, Gordon was employed by the National Labor Relations Board in various capacities, including trial attorney, chief law officer in the Atlanta regional office, director of appeals, and special assistant to the General Counsel.

From 1959 to 1961, he served as Assistant General Counsel of the NLRB in charge of the General Counsel's Legal Policy Branch. From 1961 to 1971, he was Associate General Counsel in charge of the Board's field operation. He has been Chief Administrative Law Judge at the Labor Department since 1971.

National Science Board

Nomination of Lewis M. Branscomb To Be
a Member.   March 27, 1979

The President today announced the nomination of Lewis M. Branscomb, of Armonk, N.Y., to be a member of the National Science Board.

Branscomb, of Armonk, N.Y., is vice president and chief scientist for IBM Corp., former Director of the National Bureau of Standards, and an expert in atomic physics.

Science and Technology

Message to the Congress.   March 27, 1979

To the Congress of the United States:

This year the world marks centennials associated with two great men of science and technology. Albert Einstein, who was born March 14, 1879, enlarged our knowledge and understanding of the universe and changed the way we look at space and time. He was an early pathfinder in the remarkable era of scientific exploration in which we live. In that same year, Thomas Alva Edison invented the electric light. He was a great technologist who devoted his life to the creation of new products to meet human needs.

The world was changed by the work of these two men. The vast changes that have grown out of their work are part of the reason that the forces these two men represent, science and technology, have become increasingly important in our lives over the last century. We look to the fruits of science and technology to improve our health by curing illness and preventing disease and disability. We expect science and technology to find new sources of energy, to feed the world's growing population, to provide new tools for our national security, and to prevent unwise applications of science and technology. The health of our economy has been especially tied to science and technology; they have been key factors in generating growth, jobs, and productivity through innovation. Indeed, most of the great undertakings we face today as a Nation have a scientific or technological component.

Yet, despite the centrality of science and technology in our lives, the Federal government has rarely articulated a science and technology policy for the future. This Message sets forth that policy. The thesis is that new technologies can aid in the solution of many of our Nation's problems. These technologies in turn depend upon a fund of knowledge derived from basic research. The Federal government should therefore increase its support both for basic research and, where appropriate, for the application of new technologies. My Administration has done just that.

Within the coming months, the Congress and I must work together on strategic arms limitation, national health care, energy supply, industrial innovation, and economic growth—all of which have significant scientific and technological dimensions.

This message to the Congress:
—describes the Administration's policy perspective on science and technology and the roles of government, industry, universities, and the public in support of science and technology;
—highlights some of the most important science and technology initiatives undertaken in my Administration in domestic, national security, and international arenas;
—outlines the potential effects of science and technology on our Nation for the decade of the 1980s and beyond; and
—assists the Congress in its task of considering the research and development programs of our Departments and agencies as recommended in my 1980 budget.

In transmitting this message, I call on the Congress to join my Administration in its commitment to nonpartisan investment in science and technology for our future.

OVERVIEW OF RESEARCH AND
DEVELOPMENT

The Federal government's support of research and development is critical to the overall advance of science and technology. Federal responsibility lies in three major categories:

1. The largest fraction of the Federal investment serves the government's direct needs and responsibilities, such as defense, space, and air traffic control. Because of the technical challenges involved in meeting these national needs, there is a relatively large and broad Federal investment in research and development.

2. The Federal government undertakes research and development where there is a national need to accelerate the rate of development of new technologies in the private sector. This is especially true when

the risk is great or the costs inordinately high, such as with many aspects of energy and transportation. However, we look to private industry to finance research and development activities having near-term commercial payoff. Industry is most sensitive to the marketplace, to the benefits of competition, and to the commercialization of new technologies. This view is consistent with that of industrial leaders who ask the Federal government more for a climate that fosters innovation, rather than for direct support of research and development with commercial potential. My proposals for applied research and development in Fiscal Year 1980 reflect my overall view of the Federal responsibility.

3. The Federal government supports basic research to meet broad economic and social needs. Basic research is a quest for new knowledge. Research to advance scientific understanding—in astronomy, geology, chemistry, the behavioral and social sciences, and other areas—expresses our innate curiosity about ourselves and the universe. But basic research also is the forerunner of new inventions, advances in health care, nutrition and agricultural production, many new products of commerce, and new technologies for defense, space, energy, and environmental protection.

Although the Federal government has long accepted its dominant role in basic research, support declined seriously in the late 1960s and early 1970s, especially in mission agencies whose objectives are ultimately dependent on research. I have sought to reverse these trends, by urging the Congress to increase funds for basic research and by redirecting attention toward longer-range needs of the Nation. I have proposed a 26 percent increase in basic research in the two years of my Ad-

ministration. This policy is both feasible and necessary, even as we seek to reduce our Federal deficit and move towards a balanced budget. The $4.6 billion requested for basic research in Fiscal Year 1980 in various Departments' and agencies' budgets is essential, and deserves the full support of the Congress. Prudent planning for the future demands a deliberate and continued commitment to basic research.

The majority of Federal support for basic research is in the mission agencies, with the Departments of Health, Education, and Welfare (National Institutes of Health), Defense, Energy, and the National Aeronautics and Space Administration leading the way. Strengthening the commitment of these agencies to the support of basic research is a central element of our science and technology policy. The National Science Foundation is critical to balanced support for all scientific and engineering disciplines. My budget request this year for the Foundation exceeds $1 billion. In presenting this request, I urge that Congress consider the critical role played by the Foundation. I have instructed the Foundation to improve the instrumentation of our university research laboratories and to investigate the need for special programs to support young scientists.

With the budget for Fiscal Year 1979, and full approval of my Fiscal Year 1980 requests, we will have made major steps in restoring the necessary balance and commitment to our scientific future. I would ask the Congress, in acting on agency budgets, to be aware of the interrelationships and the importance of each agency's contribution to a comprehensive, national program in support of science and technology.

MEETING DOMESTIC NEEDS

The United States is acutely aware of its energy problems, its need for natural resources, the deleterious effects of inflation on all Americans, and suffering from disease. Our future as a democratic society depends on our ability to confront these challenges successfully.

While science and technology alone will not solve all our domestic problems, they hold the key to many aspects of the solutions. During this century, the United States has built a system of industrial, university, and government research laboratories that is unparalleled in the world. We have the national capacity to generate new basic knowledge, and to apply this knowledge to a broad range of problems. In this context I want to explain how my Administration is marshalling science and technology in terms of six domestic objectives:

—stimulating innovation in industry to sustain economic growth and improve productivity;

—meeting our energy, natural resource, and food needs;

—promoting better health for all;

—improving the regulatory process;

—expanding the beneficial use of space; and

—understanding the forces of nature, natural disasters, and changes induced by man.

STIMULATING INNOVATION IN INDUSTRY

As a Nation, we face problems of inflation, unemployment, foreign competition, and a decline in the growth of national productivity. Yet, traditionally we have been an innovative society. Our economic growth depends on an ability to produce and market new goods. Between 30 and 40 percent of the Nation's economic growth in the last three decades resulted from technological innovation. Innovative industries are our most productive, create more new jobs, and are the most competitive in world markets. When too few new industries are established, or older ones do not develop enough new products and more efficient operations, the stagnation is reflected in our economy. A lag in productivity worsens inflation. Innovation is essential to our battle against inflation.

More and more countries are industrializing, building industries in which this country once was preeminent. These are countries whose competition is healthy. We welcome their prosperity. We do not seek to limit their growth through tariffs and other trade barriers. Rather, we must seek to improve our own performance through renewed innovation in fields where we excel—such as agriculture, drugs, microelectronics, computers, aircraft, space satellite systems and many other technologies. We also need to make our lower-technology industries more competitive through innovation.

Americans have not lost their ability to innovate. But there are restrictive elements at work. I began a domestic policy review of the factors affecting industrial innovation. This study, which will be completed in the near future, is headed by the Secretary of Commerce. It involves thirty Federal agencies and many advisory groups from private industry, labor, universities, and public interest. I expect many practical recommendations to help make our industries more innovative.

I also have established a Productivity Council consisting of many of the senior members of my Administration. The Council is examining how science and technology can improve Federal, State and local government productivity, as well as the productivity of the private sector.

531

MEETING OUR ENERGY, NATURAL
RESOURCE, AND FOOD NEEDS

The United States is richly endowed
with natural resources, both renewable
ones such as fresh water, clean air, timber,
and agricultural land; and nonrenewable
resources such as fossil fuels and minerals.
These resources have been a key factor in
our prosperity as a Nation.

We are currently using the energy and
mineral resources that are the richest, the
easiest to find, and the cheapest to produce—with substantial depletion of some.
Growth in population, industrial activity,
and a new awareness of the need to protect our environment are straining even
our renewable resources in many regions.
We are being forced to make difficult decisions about allocating water and land
to one or another competing uses.

Energy

In energy, we have closely related
objectives:

- reducing dependence on foreign oil
  and minimizing the effects of supply
  disruptions, with conservation a key
  element;
- implementing programs and policies
  that encourage domestic energy production and efficient use, without
  serious inflationary impact;
- developing   inexhaustible   energy
  sources   for   sustained   economic
  growth through the next century;
- making the transition from primary
  reliance on depletable oil and gas to
  predominant use of more abundant
  energy sources;
- developing safe nuclear power systems which, while limiting the potential for international proliferation of
  nuclear weapons, will increase our
  energy supply; and

- using all energy sources in ways that
  do not endanger the environment
  and the health or safety of our
  citizens.

Today's scientific and technological investments can have only limited impact
on these objectives in the near term. It
takes time to bring new technologies to
the stage of economic competitiveness, to
develop industrial capacity, and to allow
energy users to adapt to change. My near-
term program thus emphasizes conservation, the reduced consumption of oil
where alternatives are available, and removal of obstacles to the use of currently
available energy sources, such as nuclear
power, coal, or solar water heating, and
providing adequate incentives for crude
oil and natural gas exploration.

In the mid- to longer-term, however,
science and technology will help resolve
our current dilemma. They will assist in
locating and developing new sources of
supply and in using those supplies more
efficiently with reduced damage to health
and environment. Recognizing this, the
government is engaged in an aggressive
research and development effort. In this
year of limited budget resources, difficult
judgments had to be made. Nevertheless,
my budget for Fiscal Year 1980 recommends an investment of nearly $3.5 billion
in civilian energy research and development.

This country is blessed with a uniquely
abundant supply of energy in the form
of coal and oil shale. Over one-third of
the known world reserves for coal belong
to the United States. A major challenge
is to demonstrate technologies that will
enable us to substitute these energy
sources for our ever increasing oil imports. My program provides for the government to work closely with American

industry to accelerate the demonstration of commercial-scale technologies that show promise of entering the commercial market. Such demonstrations will test technical feasibility and the economics of conversion processes. They will give us needed information on the environmental and institutional impact of the technologies involved.

For the longer-term, there are many options. Technologies such as solar energy and fusion, promise virtually inexhaustible supplies of electricity in the future. But if these technologies are to be a significant factor, we must invest now in developing them. And we are doing so, as illustrated in solar research and technology development. Our national investment in this field has grown from almost nothing five years ago to $850 million in FY 1980.

In working with the private sector, it is particularly important that the government does not displace the resources of industry devoted to new energy technology. We must be mindful that appreciable energy producing capacity will be developed only if the private sector is actively involved and committed to our research and development efforts. We must carefully structure the Federal programs in a way that will lead industry to invest in, and ultimately commercialize, new energy technologies.

Nonfuel Minerals

In the area of nonfuel minerals, we must recognize the importance of new technology and understanding of earth sciences and chemical processing to permit us to find, produce, and utilize scarce and lower grade ores without degrading the environment. A major study of non-fuel minerals is being conducted by the Secretary of the Interior under the Domestic Policy Review process managed by the Domestic Policy Staff. The adequacy and orientation of private sector and government investment in minerals research and development are being examined. I will report on the Secretary's recommendations later this year.

Agriculture

Our agricultural science and technology have made us preeminent in the world. Our ability to maximize yield from agricultural land, to develop pest-resistant, productive crop strains, and to improve animal husbandry is unsurpassed. We are able to produce sufficient quantities of agricultural products to meet the basic needs of Americans and simultaneously supply much of the rest of the world. Agricultural products form the largest category of our civil exports. A key element in our success is our traditional system of cooperation among all levels of government, universities, producers, and rural communities.

My Administration has strengthened agricultural research and development by focusing attention on basic plant and animal sciences; integrated pest management; human nutrition and food safety; land and water use and conservation; energy research, especially production of biomass for energy, and production of alcohols from agricultural residues. We also are working to strengthen Federal research, development, transfer, and assistance programs in freshwater and marine aquaculture. We have supplemented these activities with a competitive research grant program. This program will attract researchers from many branches of science to advance knowledge on which future gains in plant productivity, genetic breeding, and nutrition ultimately will depend. The competitive grant program—which will help us meet our future agricultural needs—merits strong Congressional support.

Water

Our understanding of the Nation's water supply and how to use it wisely has increased over the years, but many opportunities for improvement still remain. River basin assessments, ground water flow and recharge patterns, efficient irrigation methods, and pollution control techniques are receiving careful attention by the Departments of Agriculture and Interior, the Environmental Protection Agency, the Corps of Engineers, and others. As greater demands are placed on our water supply, particularly in the West, we must understand how best to use and conserve it. And we must assess the long-term implications of our actions. Protecting water quality is also important for agriculture and in our urban and rural communities. I am directing the Secretary of Interior and Director of the Office of Science and Technology Policy to set research priorities aimed at meeting our future water needs.

Ocean science and engineering have opened a new region of the globe for exploration and resource development. As we explore new areas of our continental shelf and deeper water for oil and gas, we must have the world's best technical capability to protect our ocean and coastal environment, to find new resources, and to tap them efficiently. Science and technology will continue to play a major role in these activities.

Department of Natural Resources

Developing and utilizing science and technology requires effective Federal organization. My proposal for creation of a Department of Natural Resources will permit better integration of research and development activities in the area of natural resources and the environment.

PROMOTING BETTER HEALTH FOR ALL AMERICANS

As I stated in my State of the Union Message, the opportunity to lead a healthier life is denied to many in our country because health care services are inaccessible or unaffordable or inefficient. My Administration is dedicated to correcting this situation through initiatives that will influence the structure, function, and economics of our health services systems.

The biomedical capability developed in this country since World War II is a magnificent demonstration of our scientific and technological prowess; it is the envy of the world. The biomedical, social, and behavioral sciences have made countless contributions to the health of our people in recent years. Over the past generation, we have seen polio vaccine and new drugs developed, the introduction of heart-lung machines, organ transplantation, and a new understanding of the chemistry of the brain. And we have made major gains against high blood pressure, heart attack, stroke, specific kinds of cancer, birth defects, infant and childhood disease, and mental retardation and mental illness.

Much remains to be done. The Department of Health, Education, and Welfare is developing a health research strategy with increased emphasis on promotion of good health and prevention of disease.

There are many elements to this strategy. We are emphasizing research on reproductive biology and the underlying mechanisms of normal development and of disease. This work exploits the modern techniques of molecular biology, the neurosciences, behavioral sciences, and genetics. We are increasing laboratory, clinical, and epidemiological research on the role of nutrition in normal development, good health, and disease. We are expanding research and services to reduce unwanted pregnancy, smoking, and alcohol and drug abuse among adolescents. We are placing more emphasis on the causes of common disabling conditions such as diabetes, arthritis, and neurological and digestive diseases. And we are stressing research on the biological and behavioral aspects of mental illness, drug abuse, and alcoholism to reflect the recommendations of the Commission on Mental Health.

In spite of our desire for better health, government spending alone will not ensure success. As we have learned from the emphasis on cancer over the last decade, advances depend on new discoveries whose rate cannot be predicted. Therefore, we must nurture a broadly-focused program of research, with a clear, long-term commitment. Accordingly, in view of the substantial increases provided by Congress last year above my requested increase, I believe an effective biomedical research effort can be maintained without any further increase in 1980. This pace for biomedical research is appropriate; over the period of fiscal years 1979 and 1980, funding will increase at an average of twelve percent per year, thus maintaining our vigorous national effort in biomedical research. We have every reason to be optimistic that health research in the years ahead will save lives and improve the quality of life for millions of people.

IMPROVING THE REGULATORY PROCESS

Over the past 15 years our Nation has established or improved programs dealing with air and water pollution, toxic substances, noise, radiation, automotive safety and fuel economy, worker health and safety, and numerous other hazards. My Administration will continue to enforce these important laws faithfully. But additional improvements are possible and desirable. I am convinced that continued investment in science and technology is required to improve our regulatory programs. Environmental, health and safety regulatory decisions must have a sound scientific basis. Consequently I am strengthening the research and development base in both regulatory and research agencies. I have proposed an increase in the Environmental Protection Agency's health effects research program for Fiscal Year 1980, with greater emphasis on long-term research.

In addition, we have begun three interagency activities that will improve regulatory decisions. The Regulatory Council, which I established last fall to ensure that regulations achieve their statutory goals in the most economic and balanced way, has prepared the Nation's first Regulatory Calendar—an outlook of proposed regulatory activity. During the coming year, I expect the Council to identify government-wide scientific needs—programs, resources, and policies—that will improve the regulatory process. Second, the Interagency Regulatory Liaison Group—comprised of the Environmental Protection Agency, the Food and Drug Administration, the Occupational Safety and Health Administration, and the Consumer Product Safety Commission and Agriculture's Food Safety and Quality Service—will coordinate the participants' regulatory activities and research programs. Third, the regulatory agencies and the environmental health research agencies have joined in the new National Toxicology Program to set priorities for the testing and evaluation of toxic chemicals.

To ensure that we make effective use of science and technology in the regulatory process, I am asking the Director of the Office of Science and Technology Policy to give this issue personal attention in the coming year. He is to work with the heads of agencies, the Chairman of the Regulatory Council, and others to identify gaps in research programs, seek ways for research and development agencies to work with regulatory agencies, and develop procedures for proper use of scientific and technological data.

EXPANDING THE BENEFICIAL USE OF SPACE

Two decades ago mankind entered the space age. In that short time we have witnessed remarkable accomplishments—evidence of this country's progress in science and technology. Americans have explored the moon. Space probes are examining the planets of our solar system, as recently highlighted by the historic encounter of the Voyager I spacecraft with Jupiter. Satellites are indispensable components of our communications networks, weather forecasts and international security systems.

With the advent of the Space Shuttle, we are entering a new era. The Space Shuttle—our national space transportation system for the coming decades—will increase the flexibility of space operations, reduce costs, improve national security, and make possible new cooperative activities with other nations. To meet the challenges ahead, I have established a Na-

tional Space Policy that sets the direction of our space activities over the coming years. We will emphasize applications not only by the National Aeronautics and Space Administration, but also by other Federal agencies, foreign governments, and the private sector. The policy stresses the use of space technologies to meet human needs here on earth. The new technologies of the space age can further revolutionize our communication and possibly can provide new energy supply. They can improve our ability to manage wisely our renewable and nonrenewable resources, and monitor our environment. Assessment and forecasting of crop conditions and yields, and extension of communications to remote areas are examples. I am committed to the continuity of remote sensing data over the coming decade and I expect to propose additional initiatives in remote sensing of the earth's ocean, land resources, and environment in future years.

My space policy also encourages continued scientific investigation of the universe. We will conduct a vigorous program of exploration to understand the origin and evolution of the solar system. The space telescope—to be launched and serviced by the Space Shuttle—and free-flying satellites will usher in a new era of astronomy. From the clear environment of space, these new eyes will allow us to explore the distant galaxies and other astronomical phenomena—quasars, pulsars, and black holes. They will vastly expand our knowledge and understanding of the universe.

It is important that we maintain our world leadership in space. My policy is designed to encourage further advances in our use and exploration of space. We will provide adequate resources to maintain that leadership.

UNDERSTANDING THE FORCES OF NATURE,
AND MAN-INDUCED ENVIRONMENTAL
CHANGES

Man exists on this planet only with the consent of Nature. Natural forces like earthquakes, floods, storms, tsunamis, and landslides, as well as changes in weather that bring drought or excess rainfall, cause untold tragedy in loss of life, destruction of property, and disruption of economic and social structure.

Scientific advances of the past twenty years in geophysics, meteorology, and climatology have improved our understanding of natural phenomena. However, our predictive capability is limited and needs to be improved. And our capability for influencing natural forces for human benefit is nonexistent. On the other hand, our engineering skills, our ability to plan, our early warning and communications systems, and our ability to react quickly to prevent a breakdown of social order help to reduce the toll when natural disaster does strike. We possess sophisticated technology for construction, communications, transportation, monitoring and interpretation of data on natural processes. My commitment to increase our progress is strong. The Congress recognizes that fundamental advances in understanding natural forces are important, and I welcome the partnership we have forged.

The National Earthquake Hazards Reduction Program established by the Earthquake Hazards Reduction Act of 1977 resulted in a national hazard mitigation plan that I transmitted to Congress in June, 1978. This effort will involve Federal agencies, experts in the universities and private sector, and the States and localities to improve our understanding of earthquakes and our reactions to earthquake warnings.

To improve our ability to react to natural disasters and assist those affected, the Congress approved my reorganization recommendation to create the Federal Emergency Management Agency. This new Agency will have oversight of Federal programs to assist the areas and individuals affected by such civil emergencies. It will give us the ability to focus science—and the insight of the social sciences—on the mitigation of natural hazards as well as on post-disaster relief. The Agency will work closely with State and local jurisdictions to apply the benefits of available technology.

We also have focused increased research on climate. Within the framework of the National Climate Program Act of 1978, a national program has been organized. This program emphasizes impact assessment, diagnosis and projection, climate dynamics, and data management. My budgets in this area have more than doubled in the last two years. Advances that can be made in understanding climate change, in predicting it—and perhaps in influencing it beneficially—will be of enormous help to us and the rest of the world.

Another problem we face is the risk that man's own activities—now significant on a global scale—might adversely affect the earth's environment and ecosystem. Destruction of the ozone layer, increase in atmospheric carbon dioxide, and alteration of oceanic flow patterns are examples of the problems we must understand before changes are irreversible or the consequences inevitable. Many Federally-sponsored research activities, including basic research in the atmospheric, oceanic and earth sciences, and space observations, contribute to better understanding of the natural processes affecting the earth. They should receive serious attention in the coming decades. The increases that I have requested for basic research support this objective.

SCIENCE, TECHNOLOGY AND INTERNATIONAL RELATIONS

Science and technology is increasingly international in its scope and significance. This international dimension affects the planning and conduct of our research and development activities. Such activities, whether carried out by us or by others, serve to increase the fundamental stock of human knowledge. They can also foster commercial relationships, impact on the quality of life in all countries, and affect the global environment. Both our domestic planning and our foreign policy must reflect an understanding of this wide-ranging impact of science and technology.

Much of the existing international cooperation in science and technology takes place in academic or commercial channels. There is, however, a growing role for governmental cooperation as other nations make new commitments to scientific and technological growth. If used wisely these future opportunities for scientific and technological cooperation can support our foreign policy objectives.

Several themes have shaped my Administration's policy in this area. We are:

—pursuing new international initiatives that advance our own research and development objectives;

—developing and strengthening scientific exchanges that bridge political, ideological, and cultural divisions between countries;

—formulating programs and institutions that help developing countries use science and technology; and

—cooperating with other nations to manage technologies with global impact.

PURSUING NEW INTERNATIONAL INITIATIVES

United States scientific and technological objectives are advanced by cooperating with other nations. For example, we work together with many nations on large scale scientific programs; joint funding of expensive research, development, and demonstration projects; and efforts to alleviate common problems.

Two decades ago, the International Geophysical Year set a pattern for international cooperation on large-scale scientific problems. This model has been extended to most fields of science. Today the world's weather is studied jointly by nations through the Global Atmospheric Research Project. With the European Space Organization we are planning a space mission to examine polar regions of the sun. These programs are yielding new knowledge about our solar system and our earth's natural processes. They are providing important practical dividends.

As the cost of large-scale research programs and research facilities rises, all countries find the financial support increasingly burdensome. We must join together to support the most expensive and significant projects. We are discussing with other nations a program to drill deeply into the offshore continental margins between the continental shelves and ocean basins. This program would provide new knowledge of the sea floor and help us assess the margins' potential for resources. Other large-scale scientific programs that could be pursued jointly include the next generation of high energy physics accelerators, telescopes, and fusion energy research facilities.

Through the International Energy Agency we are cooperating on energy-related research and development. At the economic summit in Bonn in 1978, and more recently in Washington, I discussed the importance of intensifying joint energy research and development with the President of the European Economic Community. Similarly, in my discussions with the Prime Minister of Japan we agreed to increase cooperation in large-scale projects, particularly nuclear fusion and synthetic fuel production from coal. These agreements will help both nations achieve new energy sources—faster and at lower cost than if the research were pursued independently.

Environmental problems caused by industrialization are another area appropriate for cooperation. During my Administration we have started efforts with other nations to deal with problems of transboundary air pollution. Canadian and American scientists, for example, are working jointly to alleviate damage from acid rain caused by the long-range pollutants across our common border.

During my visit this February with Mexico's President José López Portillo, we agreed to intensify scientific and technological cooperation to alleviate problems of mutual concern. We will explore ways to cooperate on research for developing the vast arid lands on both sides of our border. This will include research on new crops suitable for these lands and research on effective use of scarce water resources. We also will exchange information and begin joint work on housing and urban planning for cities close to our common border.

DEVELOPING SCIENTIFIC EXCHANGES THAT BRIDGE DIFFERENCES BETWEEN COUNTRIES

Most nations value scientific and technological cooperation with the United States. We can use this fact to build bridges with countries where official relationships have been absent or strained. Our scientific and health exchanges with the Soviet Union and Eastern European countries, beginning after World War II, can be viewed in this light. These exchanges are now mature and extensive.

Our scientific exchanges with the Soviet Union are of special significance. At the sixth meeting of the U.S.-Soviet Joint Commission on Science and Technology in Moscow in February 1979, we agreed to add new cooperative areas of interest to both sides. I expect to see continuing improvement in the quality of our exchanges with the Soviet Union. I also expect these programs to support and remain compatible with our overall political relationship.

The normalization of our relations with the Peoples Republic of China is a major event in American foreign policy. Since the signing of the Shanghai Communique of 1972, scientific and technological relationships have played a critical role in building the relationship. In order to accelerate this process, my Science and Technology Adviser led a delegation of senior government scientists to China in July of 1978. This delegation was followed by visits of the Secretaries of Energy and Agriculture. Chinese delegations subsequently visited the United States to discuss educational exchanges and space technology programs.

These missions led to the science and technology agreement that I signed with Vice Premier Deng Xiaoping during his recent visit to the United States. The agreement covers programs of interest to both countries, including development of a satellite communications system that will provide China with the means for nationwide television and telephone service. The agreement provides for exchange of scholars and students, exchange of plant materials for genetic research on crops, and cooperation in high-energy physics and other areas. The agreement enhances opportunities for U.S. industry participation in China's modernization efforts. Our new relationship provides a sound beginning for increased technical social ties between our countries.

HELPING DEVELOPING COUNTRIES USE
SCIENCE AND TECHNOLOGY

The United States has an opportunity and responsibility to share scientific knowledge and appropriate technological skills with the developing world. Our purpose is to assist other countries in developing technology for their own needs. We must accomplish this purpose both for humanitarian reasons and because overcoming the problems of poverty, overpopulation, and scarcity of food and natural resources, will promote a stable world, enhancing our own security and wellbeing.

Recognizing these facts, I have submitted legislation to create an Institute for Scientific and Technological Cooperation, which will be charged with helping developing countries improve their scientific and technological capacity. Working with the Agency for International Development, the Institute will expand the use of science and technology to overcome obstacles to development.

The Institute will help individual developing countries choose and develop technologies that suit their own needs. At the same time, it will enable them to contribute to the solution of problems that affect developed as well as developing nations. For example, the Institute will work with developing countries on multiple crop farming systems for areas not suited to continuous cropping of food grain, tech-

nologies for clean water and sewage in rural areas where most of the poor live, modern information systems, prevention and cure of tropical diseases, and appropriate energy systems. The Institute also will establish means for developing countries to draw on United States government agencies, universities and institutes, as well as private industry. In this way the Institute will enhance coordination of the international activities of our government agencies.

An important dimension of the Institute is its mandate to work with the more advanced countries of the developing world, the "middle tier" nations. These countries have the infrastructure and science and technology capacity to become true partners with us in addressing regional and international problems and needs of the poor majority.

The Institute will call on industry, labor, and private voluntary organizations for development and management skills and improvement of the health and safety levels of modernizing societies. Already twenty-five percent of our current exports go to non-OPEC third world nations. Our trade in manufactured goods will expand as developing countries become better able to purchase and use our products.

Finally, we plan to take an active role in the United Nations Conference on Science and Technology for Development next summer. Father Theodore Hesburgh, President of the University of Notre Dame, will lead our delegation to the Conference. I view this Conference as an opportunity for discussing technology-related issues of concern to developing countries and reaching agreement on common objectives.

COOPERATING WITH OTHER NATIONS TO
MANAGE TECHNOLOGIES WITH GLOBAL
IMPACT

Much of modern technology requires global cooperation and management. The telecommunications network and activities of international organizations like the World Meteorological Organization, the International Civilian Aviation Organization, and the World Health Organization are noteworthy examples. The monitoring activities organized through the United Nations Environmental Program is a more recent example. Among other activities, we are working with other nations to update electromagnetic spectrum allocation, strengthen international controls on nuclear materials, and develop a regime for rapidly expanding transnational data flows. International cooperation in the management of technology for the mutual benefit of all nations will become even more important in the coming decades.

I call the attention of Congress to two international discussions of great importance, one dealing with nuclear fuel cycle evaluation and the other with allocation of radio frequencies. The Congress knows of my concern over a spreading nuclear weapons capability as more countries meet their energy needs with nuclear power. Our own research and development programs have been reoriented toward developing technologies more resistant to misuse. At our suggestion, over forty countries have convened in the International Nuclear Fuel Cycle Evaluation to consider how we can minimize risks. I am hopeful that new institutional controls and technological approaches will emerge from these deliberations.

The electromagnetic spectrum—including the radio frequencies—is one of the reusable natural resources available to mankind. We are at a point in history where increasing worldwide demands for these frequencies are being made; demands that exceed the availability of the resource. All nations, large or small, have rights of equitable access as signatories to the International Telecommunications Convention. It is only through international cooperation and planning that these rights can be guaranteed. The 1979 Worldwide Administrative Radio Conference will review the allocation of radio frequencies for communications and other purposes. Results of this conference will guide the use of communications and electronic equipment and the pattern of domestic and international communications systems for the next several decades.

NATIONAL SECURITY

Our national security depends in large measure on our technological capability. Our future security will depend in part on our ability to deploy new weapons systems that embody more advanced technology. Our potential adversaries are investing heavily in military personnel, equipment, and technology. Accordingly, we must look to our research and development programs to enable us to maintain a modern and responsive defense capability.

In the context of this message on science and technology, I wish to emphasize several facets of their relationship to national security. We must ensure that we are:

—maintaining technological leadership in weapons systems;

—utilizing technology to reduce costs in an era of expensive defense systems;

—building our defense research base to provide for our national security in the future;

—preventing export of technological products and processes with military applications that would erode our security; and

—utilizing advanced technological capability in the pursuit of arms limitation agreements.

MAINTAINING TECHNOLOGICAL LEADERSHIP IN WEAPONS SYSTEMS

Our military investments in new technology over the years have contributed immeasurably to our security. Now, as other nations are becoming more proficient in science and technology, we must make certain that our own capabilities remain at the frontier of knowledge. We must be spared the shock of major technological surprises. It is absolutely essential for us to remain second to none in the development and production of new weapons.

We are moving ahead with major development programs to increase our military capabilities. In the strategic area, programs are underway to strengthen each element of the triad—air, land, and sea—in order to preserve our deterrent capabilities. Examples are the M–X intercontinental ballistic missile, cruise missiles, and the Trident submarine and missile system. We are also pursuing the development of more survivable and reliable strategic warning and command control systems.

In order to improve our capability to fight a conventional war, we are developing and procuring new generations of aircraft, ground vehicles and munitions. The F–15, F–16, F–18 and A–10 aircraft, the XM–1 tank and the Patriot air defense missile are examples.

UTILIZING TECHNOLOGY TO REDUCE COSTS

Science and technology—properly applied—can increase efficiency, thereby reducing acquisition costs and improving the effectiveness of weapons. Science and technology enable us to develop new materials and components at lower costs. They can give our weapons greater reliability and efficiency, thereby reducing personnel needs. And they improve our manufacturing productivity. Cooperation with our allies also will help reduce costs without sacrificing our modernization programs. Standardization and common operational capability among NATO allies are important objectives.

In the procurement of weapons, we are emphasizing competition between potential suppliers to help keep costs down. And we have adopted new management techniques to ensure that economies are not overlooked. We also are analyzing carefully the best mix of systems needed to meet anticipated contingencies. We have concluded that future shipbuilding efforts should concentrate on larger numbers of small ships, with enhanced mobility and firepower. Similarly, we are building a new, comparatively low-cost tactical airplane, the A–10, that emphasizes mobility and munitions designed for engagement of enemy tank forces. With imagination and effort, these various approaches will enable us to maintain technological superiority at acceptable cost.

BUILDING OUR DEFENSE RESEARCH BASE

The development cycle from proposal of a new concept to a deployed weapons system can take a decade or more. The length of time for dividends from investments in basic research is even longer. Moreover, research and development are inexpensive compared to the acquisition cost of weapons systems. The proper strategy, therefore, is to expand our options in the early stages of the acquisition process through research, and then be very selective at the costly engineering, development, and production stage.

For these reasons, our science and technology base related to national security must be the best in the world. Thus, I am deeply concerned over the declining support for research and technology in the defense budgets that occurred in the early part of this decade. My budgets for Fiscal Year 1979 and 1980 reverse that trend and strengthen our technology base. The two year average growth in the technology base will be about 14 percent, including an increase in basic research of about 20 percent.

The Department of Defense also is taking steps to strengthen its relationship with universities in order to use the research and development resources of the academic community more effectively. Defense support of university research will have increased more than 20 percent between Fiscal Years 1978 and 1980.

PREVENTING EXPORT THAT ERODES OUR TECHNOLOGICAL SUPERIORITY

Within the framework of national security, export controls on technology are important to ensure that our technological advantage is not compromised. A comprehensive study of the implications of international technology transfer was undertaken early in my Administration. I am persuaded that the export control process must seek to balance the conflicting goals of trade promotion, selected trade restriction based on national security considerations, and furthering our foreign policy objectives. Decisions in specific export licensing cases must be made on their merits by considering these three goals. In particular we are taking steps to refine and expedite the government's decision-making processes. I must emphasize, however, that while sound export controls are important, only a strong research and development program, as I have proposed, ensures our technological leadership in defense.

UTILIZING ADVANCED TECHNOLOGICAL CAPABILITY FOR ARMS CONTROL

National security is enhanced by prudent arms control, as well as new weapons systems. To this end I have pursued a new Strategic Arms Limitation Treaty with the Soviet Union, a comprehensive nuclear test ban treaty, and other arms control measures. As these agreements enter into force, our choices in weapons development must meet our own needs, while giving our adversaries the incentive to participate seriously in negotiations. Successful arms control depends on science and technology to provide adequate technical means of verification. Our current national capability to verify arms agreements is excellent. It includes observation satellites and extensive capabilities for seismographic detection and interpretation. We must continue to pursue scientific and technological advances to maintain these capabilities.

Harnessing the National Capability

Equally as important as the substance of our science and technology policies is our strategy for managing it and ensuring its vitality. This task is a challenging one because of the diversity of the participants—business and industry, universities, the Federal agencies, government at all levels, and the public. Each sector has distinct goals and objectives and special institutional qualities. Yet each can work with the others in a lively process of cooperation, so long as some independence is assured and our policies are adaptable to each.

The partnership between the Federal government and universities needs renewed attention. Many leaders of university research centers believe the government has intervened too deeply in university affairs to the point of affecting institutional independence and diversity. The problem stems from the need to ensure accountability of research funds. On the one hand accountability is important to me, to Congress, and to the taxpayers; we must improve the government's ability to manage and account for public funds. On the other hand it is equally important that the pendulum not swing so far that we stifle progress. We must allow flexibility both for the government agencies and for the research institutions. We should not confuse excess paperwork with proper accountability. Both the National Science Foundation and the National Institutes of Health have taken significant steps to reduce unnecessary demands on their grantees. These initiatives follow from my interest in reducing needless paperwork throughout the government. Moreover, in the recent development of the cost principles that govern the financial relations between the government and universities in research, we sought to the maximum extent possible to solicit and incorporate the views of the academic community. It is clear, however, that our partnership with universities needs further strengthening. We must continue to experiment with new approaches.

Another partnership in science and technology is with State and local governments. Throughout the Nation there is public resistance to the increasing costs of public services. If we are to avoid the reduction or elimination of such services, then we must develop better ways to reduce costs. The Federal government has a large stake in the effectiveness of State and local government: $80 billion are transferred annually to meet a range of national, State, and local needs.

Few State and local governments alone can support the research and development needed to mount a broad-scale effort at problem-solving. Within the budgets I have proposed for Federal research and development, I expect the needs of State and local governments to be addressed. Federal research and development programs should be formulated with participation by State and local governments. The Intergovernmental Science, Engineering, and Technology Advisory Panel, co-chaired by Dr. Frank Press and Governor James Hunt of North Carolina, is helping Federal agencies identify research and development to meet State and local needs. This intergovernmental group already has focused attention on satellite remote sensing data, US Fire Administration research, the National Technical Information Service, the problems of the elderly, and disposal of chemical wastes. I am directing the Panel to increase its efforts in planning technical assistance and research and development for problem-solving.

A better awareness of partnership also is needed among the Federal agencies. We must have coordinated policy and program planning, implementation, and evaluation. Through a variety of formal and *ad hoc* mechanisms, I have stimulated interagency cooperation in space application, earthquake hazard mitigation, dam safety, ocean pollutions research and monitoring, aquaculture, nutrition, management of radioactive wastes, and many others. Consistent with the wishes of Congress, I have asked the Office of Science and Technology Policy to coordinate programs involving many agencies using interagency coordination through the Federal Coordinating Council for Science, Engineering, and Technology.

A fourth partnership is between universities and industry. Universities are the chief performers of the fundamental research that underlies technological advance; industry puts this research to work and also identifies problems requiring new knowledge. The flow of people and information between the campus and industry is an important element in both scientific and technological advance. The National Science Foundation is beginning to experiment with projects that involve cooperative activities by people in industry and universities. Other efforts to strengthen the partnership are needed in the years ahead. I will give this issue attention as I review the recommendations coming from the study of industry innovation.

We must also strive to increase public understanding and participation in our scientific and technology activities. The changes induced by science and technology are infused in the fabric of society, profoundly altering the way we live. The understanding of those changes and their causes, as well as successful adaptation to them, requires an informed citizenry. I have supported measures, such as intervenor funding, that contribute to informed public participation in decisions where technology is important. Science education—preparing our children for tomorrow's technical society—will receive emphasis in the proposed Department of Education and programs of the National Science Foundation. In addition, the Federal Departments and Agencies conducting research and development will continue to support programs that train future generations of scientists and engineers. My Administration is committed to overcoming barriers that discourage career opportunities for minorities and women in science and technology.

Finally, if we are to make the best use of our scientific and technological progress, we must maintain continuity and consistency in our support and policies. This Nation's scientific capability is the greatest in the world, but it will not remain so in an environment of uncertainty and changing priorities and policies. We must recognize that it takes many years to train new scientists and to complete some research projects. Technology development projects and many research missions, such as our space probes, require sustained work over a decade. If research and development activities are started and stopped abruptly, the chance of their success is diminished and the probability of benefits to the Nation decreased. The Congress and the Administration must join in recognizing the long-term nature of many research and development activities. Together we must provide the necessary assurances and commitments. The policies of my Administration, as articulated in this message, are intended to serve that purpose.

CONCLUSION

In our lifetime the world has been reshaped by two prevailing forces of change: the desire of peoples everywhere for freedom from tyranny and the advance of science and technology.

Given the stunning achievements of science, it is natural to wonder whether we can expect similar accomplishments in the future. Or, are we in danger of running out of new ideas? The forecast today—and as far ahead as we can imagine—is the same as stated thirty years ago by Vannevar Bush: science is "the endless frontier." The opportunities inherent in today's scientific research are limitless in all fields—from new understanding of the evolution of the universe to the insights revealed by the genetic code. Indeed, we are in the midst of a remarkable era of explosive growth in knowledge and its use by society, unparalleled in any period of history.

It is not possible to predict the political or technological directions in the century ahead. I am certain, however, that strong support for science and technology by the Nation is one of the most important ways to prepare for the future.

Building on the strengths of our American system, I have developed policies that should serve as guidelines for Federal programs for science and technology for the years ahead. In this task, I have given attention to the balance of our Federal effort, directing it toward many issues that will in my judgment be the critical issues for the remainder of this century.

I seek to ensure that technology is used wisely for the benefit of all. With the support of our government and our people, and the skills from the scientific and technological community, science and technology can help us chart the way to a more meaningful and productive future for all mankind.

JIMMY CARTER

The White House,
    March 27, 1979.

Egypt-U.S. Business Council

Remarks at a Dinner Honoring President Sadat. March 27, 1979

Prime Minister Khalil, Chairman Considine, President Lesher, distinguished friends from the United States of America and the Arab Republic of Egypt:

I never thought I would speak to an American audience to introduce a foreign head of state and feel at least as much at home with the visitors as I do with my own people. But I've spent much more time recently with President Sadat and his Cabinet than I have with my own Cabinet. And I feel like I'm coming home when I sit next to my good friend. [*Laughter*]

My role is to introduce him. But I would like to say a few words at the beginning.

About a year ago, my wife and I and Amy got up early one Saturday morning to come to the museum of art to see a remarkable exhibit of King Tutankhamen, a very tiny portion of the ancient treasures of Egypt. We arrived early before the museum opened, and when we arrived the sidewalks for several blocks were covered with blankets and pallets and sleeping Americans who had spent all night waiting to get in to see the beauty of ancient Egypt.

I couldn't believe my eyes when I saw these treasures. I had never been to Egypt. And now I've come to realize that this is indeed just a tiny portion of the tangible demonstration of the craftsmanship, the sensitivity, the idealism, the competence, the dedication, the intelligence, the inspiration of the people of that great and ancient land.

Recently, I had a chance to visit the Pyramids and the Sphinx, to see a superb statue of Ramses in the heart of the great city of Cairo.

I was blessed to ride with President Sadat on a train, in an open railcar built in 1870, across the Nile Delta from Cairo to Alexandria. I saw there people who were industrious. I grew up on a farm when there were no machines—and still, in many parts of Egypt, with the extremely rich land, four crops per year, beautifully irrigated, superb variety of the produce of that country, people ·hard at work, still using in some instances oxen, camels, water buffalo, their hands, as well as the most modern tools of agriculture.

Forty million people, only recently an independent nation after almost 2,000 years of foreign domination, a country ready to expand rapidly economically; and now, because of the leadership of an inspired man, those 40 million people changing their whole attitude and commitment from war to peace.

I'm proud to have been part of it. But my thought, as I made my brief trip through that country, was how rich an opportunity existed there for the realization of the hopes and ambitions of many of my own fellow Americans.

As you know, my background is as an engineer and a businessman. And I could think of the immediate prospects for drastic and prosperous change when the Suez Canal is now opened to Israeli ships. In 2 months, we expect the borders to be open to unrestricted travel between Egypt and Israel, an end to the crippling and constraining embargo. Government-to-government interrelationships have already been established at almost every Cabinet level between the United States and Egypt.

But the most important interrelationship has not yet been adequately explored. I believe that the peace just confirmed will last, not because Carter, Sadat, Begin can be in office many more months or years, but because once those borders are open and thousands of students, tourists, mothers, fathers, tradesmen, merchants, scholars, archaeologists move back and forth across those borders, the benefits of peace will be so obvious and so tangible and so precious that a change in the leadership of those two countries in the future cannot possibly have a deleterious effect.

I want to see very rapidly the relationship between our country and Egypt change in the same way. Ours is a system of free enterprise, where our Government plays a minimal role compared to the thrust of our dynamic economic system, where the major progress and the quality of life of our people has been attributable to people, leaders like yourselves. And I sincerely hope that this dream that I have of Egypt and you joining together to realize a great, mutual advantage will be rapidly realized.

Today I had a private luncheon with Prime Minister Khalil, also an engineer, a businessman, a volunteer in government who was sought by President Sadat, a man who is Prime Minister, who manages the day-by-day affairs of the Government, a man of unimpeachable integrity, of quiet competence, who will in the future play an expanded role in guaranteeing that the routine and almost inevitable bureaucratic obstacles will be rapidly removed, a man who's approachable by those who see an opportunity to invest in Egypt for the benefit of the people whom he serves.

I want to see you and me and other Americans help to build an even greater Egypt.

What are their needs?—the same as ours a few years ago: more food, more food production, homes, roads, seaport facilities, airport facilities, telecommunications, power, water—the things that American genius and American business is so easily able to provide on a profitable basis.

I and all the members of my Cabinet, Secretary of Commerce Kreps here in front of me, will be eager to cooperate with you. The good will of the people of the United States now reaches out to encompass the people of Egypt in the most heartfelt, sincere, and intense way. And I want to be sure that that good will is exemplified in tangible benefits for the quality of life of the people of Egypt, whom I also have come to love.

It's a time for us to explore those new horizons. I wanted to come tonight to add my personal voice in this effort to realize the enormous, mutual benefits that can come from this new and increased interest and investment in a great and a rich and a growing and expanding, a dynamic land.

And now it is my good duty to introduce a man who has come to love me and whom I have come to love as a brother. I have the greatest possible personal affection and admiration for him. He's a man of unmatched political courage.

It certainly has required no courage on my part to participate as a mediator between Israel and Egypt, but President Sadat on a daily basis has shown not only great political courage but physical courage as well.

He's a man of great intelligence, instantly able to comprehend the most complicated diplomatic nuances and bring order out of them when that would serve his own people. He's a man who's sensi-

tive about the needs of those whom he serves. He's a man whose word is his bond. I have never once had him tell me that this is the position of Egypt and then subsequently, under the most intense pressure and when the temptations must have been real and genuine and strong, had him deviate one iota from what he pledged to do. And I would almost stake my own reputation in guaranteeing you that that would be the attitude of himself and Prime Minister Khalil as they work with you in the future.

He's a man who's convinced that the future will bring great spiritual, moral, political, and economic riches to his own people, and he's willing to give his life for those goals. He's a man worthy of admiration by all who know him and who know of him.

And now, I would like to introduce to you a friend of mine, a man whom I introduced almost a year ago and would like to introduce now as the world's foremost peacemaker, President Anwar al-Sadat.

NOTE: The President spoke at 9:21 p.m. in the Hall of Flags at the headquarters of the Chamber of Commerce of the United States. Frank W. Considine is chairman of the Egypt-U.S. Business Council, the unit of the Chamber of Commerce which hosted the dinner for President Sadat, and Dr. Richard L. Lesher is president of the Chamber of Commerce.

Following the remarks of President Carter and President Sadat, a panel discussion was held. Participants in the panel included President Sadat, Prime Minister Mustafa Khalil, Deputy Speaker of the People's Assembly Ali al-Sayed, Minister of Planning Abdel-Meguid, Minister of Finance Ali Loutfi, Mr. Considine, and Dr. Lesher.

On the same day, the White House announced that Vice President Walter F. Mondale would attend a luncheon hosted by the Israel-U.S. Business Council in honor of Prime Minister Menahem Begin at the Plaza Hotel in New York City on March 28.

Asian/Pacific American Heritage Week, 1979

Proclamation 4650.   March 28, 1979

By the President of the United States of America

A Proclamation

America's greatness—its ideals, its system of government, its economy, its people—derives from the contribution of peoples of many origins who come to our land seeking human liberties or economic opportunity. Asian-Americans have played a significant role in the creation of a dynamic and pluralistic America, with their enormous contributions to our science, arts, industry, government and commerce.

Unfortunately, we have not always fully appreciated the talents and the contributions which Asian-Americans have brought to the United States. Until recently, our immigration and naturalization laws discriminated against them. They were also subjected to discrimination in education, housing, and employment. And during World War II our Japanese-American citizens were treated with suspicion and fear.

Yet, Asians of diverse origins—from China, Japan, Korea, the Philippines, and Southeast Asia—continued to look to America as a land of hope, opportunity, and freedom.

At last their confidence in the United States has been justified. We have succeeded in removing the barriers to full participation in American life, and we welcome the newest Asian immigrants to our shores—refugees from Indochina displaced by political, and social upheavals. Their successful integration into American society and their positive and active participation in our national life demonstrates the soundness of America's policy of continued openness to peoples from Asia and the Pacific.

The Ninety-fifth Congress has requested the President by House Joint Resolution 1007, approved October 5, 1978, to designate the seven-day period beginning on May 4, 1979, as "Asian/Pacific American Heritage Week."

Now, THEREFORE, I, JIMMY CARTER, President of the United States of America, declare the week beginning on May 4, 1979, as Asian/Pacific American Heritage Week. I call upon the people of the United States, especially the educational community, to observe this week with appropriate ceremonies and activities.

IN WITNESS WHEREOF, I have hereunto set my hand this twenty-eighth day of March, in the year of our Lord nineteen hundred seventy-nine, and of the Independence of the United States of America the two hundred and third.

JIMMY CARTER

[Filed with the Office of the Federal Register, 11:47 a.m., March 28, 1979]

National Nursing Home Week, May 13–20, 1979

Message of the President.   March 28, 1979

The conscientious, considerate care provided in American nursing homes is essential to the well-being of a large number of our valued older citizens. Over the years we have come to realize more fully just how important the excellence of nursing home care is to us and to our families.

The state of nursing homes today is a far cry from the situation that existed in the early part of this century. Many health professionals in nursing homes today are educated in the theory and practice of geriatrics. They are better able to meet the medical, social and emotional needs of their patients. By their resourcefulness and dedication these individuals are helping to relieve the burdens of families across this land.

I therefore welcome this opportunity to pay tribute to the unselfish individuals who provide service for those in nursing homes. New research and technology have helped to improve the quality and longevity of life; and thanks to these devoted professionals, America's nursing homes are meeting the challenge of maintaining the highest standards of patient care. I ask all Americans to join in the spirit of this observance.

JIMMY CARTER

Tokyo Economic Summit Conference

Announcement of the Meeting.
March 29, 1979

The heads of state and government of Canada, France, Germany, Italy, Japan, the United Kingdom, and the United States have agreed to hold the next summit meeting in Tokyo on June 28 and 29, 1979, at the invitation of Prime Minister Ohira. The European Community will be represented by the President of the Council and the President of the Commission in sessions dealing with matters within the Community's competence.

The participants at the Tokyo Summit will discuss policies for the stable expansion of the world economy in the spirit of mutual cooperation that has been fostered by the previous summit meetings. Having reviewed progress on the five spe-

cific areas covered in their Declaration at the 1978 Bonn Summit, they will deal with current economic problems requiring immediate attention and will examine the basic issues that confront them in the longer term. Preparatory work is now going ahead on an agreed basis.

Federal Civil Service Reorganization

Executive Order 12126.   March 29, 1979

CORRECTION IN EXECUTIVE ORDER No. 12107

By the authority vested in me as President by the Constitution of the United States of America, and in order to delete an erroneous reference to a revoked Executive order in Executive Order No. 12107 of December 28, 1978, relating to the Civil Service Commission and Labor-Management in the Federal Service, the number "11512" is deleted from Section 2–101(b) of that Order.

JIMMY CARTER

The White House,
    March 29, 1979.

[Filed with the Office of the Federal Register, 12:33 p.m., March 29, 1979]

Prayer for Peace, Memorial Day, May 28, 1979

Proclamation 4651.   March 29, 1979

By the President of the United States of America

A Proclamation

This day was originally set aside to honor the dead in a conflict that divided our Nation more than a century ago. That wound has healed.

We come now also to honor the dead of many other wars. That we must do so is a tragic reminder that the freedoms we cherish are constantly under siege. Each generation is called upon to preserve and defend our liberties anew, often with their lives. The fact that their suffering has not yet bought a permanent peace does not make their sacrifice in vain. They preserved that which we hold most dear so that we might strive again for what they sought—a just and honorable peace in which all people settle their differences without bloodshed or oppression.

Today America celebrates peace. We gratefully remember those who gave up their hopes and lives that we might enjoy the liberties they loved—on this day and through all our tomorrows—in peace. We cannot call them back to give them our thanks, nor can we raise a monument to them any more meaningful than the one they have already left us, a free and peaceful America. They have given us a gift too valuable ever to repay, save by preserving that peace, that liberty, that America.

We have seen how easily the hopes of peace are dashed. Yet we must keep faith with those who have gone before, with those throughout the world who share our dream, and with the generations yet unborn whose very existence may depend upon the success of our efforts.

We earnestly pray that all the people of the world will join us in our struggle, so that one day all the earth may share the blessings of liberty, justice and peace.

Now, THEREFORE, I, JIMMY CARTER, President of the United States of America, do hereby designate Memorial Day, Monday, May 28, 1979, as a day of prayer for permanent peace, and I designate the hour beginning in each locality at 11 o'clock in the morning of that day as a time to unite in prayer.

I urge the press, radio, television, and all other information media to join in suitable observances of this day.

I also call upon the appropriate officials of all levels of government to fly the flag at half-staff until noon during Memorial Day on all buildings, grounds, and naval vessels throughout the United States and in all areas under its jurisdiction and control, and I request the people of the United States to display the flag at half-staff from their homes for the same customary forenoon period.

IN WITNESS WHEREOF, I have hereunto set my hand this twenty-ninth day of March, in the year of our Lord nineteen hundred seventy-nine, and of the Independence of the United States of America the two hundred and third.

JIMMY CARTER

[Filed with the Office of the Federal Register, 1:15 p.m., March 29, 1979]

ACTION

Nomination of Richard F. Celeste To Be Director of the Peace Corps.
March 29, 1979

The President today announced that he will nominate Richard F. Celeste, of Delaware, Ohio, to be Director of the Peace Corps. He would replace Carolyn Payton, resigned.

Celeste served as Lieutenant Governor of Ohio from 1975 until January 1979. He was the Democratic candidate for Governor of Ohio in November 1978.

Celeste was born November 11, 1937, in Lakewood, Ohio. He received a B.A. in African history from Yale University in 1959. The next year he taught at Yale as a Carnegie Teaching Fellow, and he then studied at Oxford University as a Rhodes Scholar, doing research on U.S.-African relations.

In 1963 Celeste accepted a 6-month assignment in Washington as staff liaison officer with the Peace Corps' Division of Volunteer Support for Latin America. From 1963 to 1967, he worked on a special agricultural development assignment in India, at the special request of U.S. Ambassador to India Chester Bowles. Based in New Delhi, he traveled throughout the country, taking a special interest in food production and community development efforts.

In 1967 Celeste returned to Cleveland and joined the National Housing Corp., a small firm specializing in the development of housing for senior citizens of moderate income. In 1972 he became president of the company.

From 1971 to 1975, Celeste was an Ohio State representative.

Celeste is a trustee of AFS International, formerly known as the American Field Service, and a board member of the Overseas Development Council. In 1977 he visited West Africa with a group sponsored by the Overseas Development Council to study food production problems. He also visited several European countries to study regional development strategies under a grant from the European Economic Community. He is a former president of the National Methodist Student Movement.

Occupational Safety and Health Review Commission

Nomination of Timothy F. Cleary To Be a Member and Designation as Chairman. March 30, 1979

The President today announced that he will nominate Timothy F. Cleary, of Bethesda, Md., for reappointment as a member

and Chairman of the Occupational Safety and Health Review Commission.

Cleary, 54, has been a member of the Commission since 1973 and Chairman since 1977. He served as Chief Counsel to former Commissioner Alan F. Burch from the Commission's inception in 1971 until 1973. He has also served as an attorney in the Office of the Solicitor at the Labor Department and in the New York City Police Department Legal Bureau.

American National Red Cross

Appointment of Jerome H. Holland as Chairman of the Board of Governors. March 30, 1979

The President today announced the appointment of Jerome H. Holland as Chairman of the Board of Governors of the American National Red Cross. He replaces Frank Stanton, who has retired from the post.

Holland is a former Ambassador to Sweden and former president of Hampton Institute. He has been serving as Vice Chairman of the Red Cross Board of Governors. He is vice chairman of the National Conference of Christians and Jews.

Presidential Advisory Board on Ambassadorial Appointments

Appointment of Seven Members. March 30, 1979

The President today announced the appointment of seven persons as members of the Presidential Advisory Board on Ambassadorial Appointments. They are:

DINA G. BEAUMONT, district vice president of the Communications Workers Association in Los Angeles;

CLARK M. CLIFFORD, former Secretary of Defense and now a partner in the Washington law firm of Clifford, Warnke, Glass, McIlwain & Finney;

HANNA HOLBORN GRAY, president of the University of Chicago;

BARBARA JORDAN, former U.S. Representative from Texas, now a lecturer at the Lyndon B. Johnson School of Public Affairs at the University of Texas;

ESTHER G. KEE, of New York, founder of the Council of Asian American Women, and active in community organizations;

CAROL C. LAISE, former Director General of the Foreign Service;

BENJAMIN E. MAYS, president emeritus of the Atlanta University Center.

Digest of Other White House Announcements

The following listing includes the President's public schedule and other items of general interest announced by the White House Press Office and not included elsewhere in this issue.

March 24

The President met at the White House with Zbigniew Brzezinski, Assistant to the President for National Security Affairs.

The President declared an emergency for the State of Florida because of the impact of severe storms and flooding in the counties of Escambia and Santa Rosa, beginning on March 3. The President's action will permit implementation of the Individual and Family Grant program for eligible flood victims along with Federal assistance in repairing uninsured damage to University Hospital in Escambia County.

March 26

The President met at the White House with:
—Dr. Brzezinski;

—Frank B. Moore, Assistant to the President for Congressional Liaison;

March 27

The President met at the White House with:

—Dr. Brzezinski;

—Vice President Walter F. Mondale, Secretary of Energy James R. Schlesinger, Charles L. Schultze, Chairman of the Council of Economic Advisers, Stuart E. Eizenstat, Assistant to the President for Domestic Affairs and Policy, James T. McIntyre, Jr., Director of the Office of Management and Budget, and Mr. Moore;

—Mr. Moore;

—Secretary Schlesinger and a group of Members of Congress, to discuss nuclear energy;

—Prime Minister Mustafa Khalil of Egypt;

—Mr. McIntyre.

March 28

The President met at the White House with:

—the Joint Chiefs of Staff;

—Dr. Brzezinski;

—Mr. Moore, Danny C. Tate, Deputy Assistant for Congressional Liaison (Senate), and William H. Cable, Deputy Assistant for Congressional Liaison (House);

—Frank C. Carlucci, Deputy Director of the Central Intelligence Agency, Hamilton Jordan, Assistant to the President, and Dr. Brzezinski;

—Mrs. Carter and Sarah Weddington, Special Assistant to the President, for lunch;

—a group of Members of Congress, to discuss solar energy.

In connection with the American Cancer Society's April Crusade, the President met in the Oval Office with representatives of the society and invited guests, and

553

presented the society's Cancer Courage Award to Tracy Andrus, daughter of Secretary of the Interior and Mrs. Cecil D. Andrus, who also attended the ceremony.

March 29

The President met at the White House with:

—Dr. Brzezinski;

—Vice President Mondale, Secretary of the Treasury W. Michael Blumenthal, Alfred E. Kahn, Advisor to the President on Inflation and Chairman of the Council on Wage and Price Stability, Barry P. Bosworth, Director of the Council on Wage and Price Stability, Mr. Schultze, Mr. Eizenstat, and Mr. McIntyre;

—Mr. Moore;

—Secretary Blumenthal, Mr. Schultze, Mr. Kahn, Mr. Bosworth, Anne Wexler, Assistant to the President, and a group of business leaders, to discuss the anti-inflation program;

—Secretary Schlesinger and the Democratic congressional leadership, to discuss energy.

March 30

The President met at the White House with:

—Vice President Mondale, Secretary of State Cyrus R. Vance, Secretary of Defense Harold Brown, and Dr. Brzezinski;

—Dr. Brzezinski;

—Mr. Moore;

—Mr. Schultze;

—members of the American Press Institute (transcript will be printed next week).

In a ceremony in the Oval Office, the President received diplomatic credentials from Ambassadors Francis Bugotu of the Solomon Islands, Roberto Arce Alvarez of Bolivia, Timothy Thahane of Lesotho,

Alfonso Arias-Schreiber of Peru, and 'Inoke Faletau of Tonga.

NOMINATIONS SUBMITTED TO THE SENATE

The following list does not include promotions of members of the Uniformed Services, nominations to the Service Academies, or nominations of Foreign Service officers.

Submitted March 28, 1979

JANET L. NORWOOD, of Maryland, to be Commissioner of Labor Statistics, United States Department of Labor, for a term of 4 years, vice Julius Shiskin, deceased.

H. STEPHAN GORDON, of Maryland, to be General Counsel of the Federal Labor Relations Authority for a term of 5 years (new position).

LEWIS M. BRANSCOMB, of New York, to be a member of the National Science Board, National Science Foundation, for a term expiring May 10, 1984, vice Russell D. O'Neal, term expired.

Submitted March 29, 1979

RICHARD FRANK CELESTE, of Ohio, to be Director of the Peace Corps, vice Carolyn R. Payton, resigned.

CHARLES B. WINBERRY, JR., of North Carolina, to be United States District Judge for the Eastern District of North Carolina, vice a new position created by P.L. 95–486, approved October 20, 1978.

CHECKLIST OF WHITE HOUSE PRESS RELEASES

The following listing contains releases of the White House Press Office which are not included in this issue.

Released March 24, 1979

Advance text: opening remarks at the town meeting in Elk City, Okla.

Released March 25, 1979

Advance text: opening remarks at the National Association of Broadcasters convention in Dallas, Tex.

Released March 26, 1979

Advance text: remarks at the signing ceremony for the Egyptian-Israeli peace treaty

Advance text: toasts at the State dinner honoring President Anwar al-Sadat of Egypt and Prime Minister Menahem Begin of Israel

CHECKLIST—Continued
Released March 29, 1979

Announcement: nomination of Charles B. Winberry, Jr., to be United States District Judge
for the Eastern District of North Carolina

Released March 30, 1979

Announcement: nomination of Frank M. Johnson, Jr., to be United States Circuit Judge
for the Fifth Circuit Court of Appeals

ACTS APPROVED BY
THE PRESIDENT

Approved March 30, 1979

H.R. 2301_____ Public Law 96–4
An act to amend the Federal District Court
Organization Act of 1978 with respect to
certain administrative matters arising from
the redrawing of the Federal judicial districts
in the State of Illinois.

PRESIDENTIAL DOCUMENTS

Week Ending Friday, April, 6, 1979

Interview With the President

Remarks and a Question-and-Answer Session With American Press Institute Editors. March 30, 1979

THE PRESIDENT. Good afternoon, everybody.

I would like to open by commenting on one very important issue, and that is the subject of energy, and then spend the rest of our time answering your questions about subjects that you choose.

ENERGY

Almost exactly 2 years ago, I presented to the Nation and to the Congress a description of the energy problems and a proposal for the evolution of a national energy policy that I thought would be adequate. After 18 months of debate, the Congress passed the national energy act, and it encompasses roughly 50 or 60 percent of what we did propose. It's a major and a very important beginning.

Since then, the energy problems that I described have gotten worse, not better. Recent interruption of the Iranian oil supply, the increases in OPEC oil prices—which I think are a prelude of what is going to be the case for the next number of years—have emphasized the extreme importance of our country taking firm action.

We must conserve all the energy that we can. We must shift toward a dependence on domestic production of petroleum products more than we have in the past and, of course, shift toward alternative fuel supplies on a more permanent basis.

I have a great confidence in American technology and American vision, American innovation, American courage, and the will of the American people to resolve this question ultimately in a satisfactory fashion.

But for the immediate future, we will continue to be dependent upon petroleum. And the prices and supplies of petroleum products are under the control of a cartel whose interests are not always compatible with our own. And, as you know, we now import about 50 percent of our total oil supplies.

Next week, I'll make a statement to the American people and to the Congress on this subject. And I hope and believe that the American consumers, the American energy industry, and the Congress will join in with me in a firm partnership to alleviate the threat to our Nation's economy and security and to resolve this issue as best we can.

I would be glad to answer your questions now on any matter.

QUESTIONS

SUBMARINES

Q. Mr. President, I am from New London, Connecticut, and that means nuclear accidents or whatever—I have to ask an ex-submariner about submarines.

THE PRESIDENT. Yes.

Q. As the cost overruns on the 688 class and Trident submarine amounted into the hundreds of millions of dollars, there have been voices in the Congress and in the Navy that have said that the submarines are overdesigned and that the Navy would be better off with a large number of smaller, less expensive boats. Do you think that the 688 and Tridents under their current dimensions are cost effective, or do you think the Navy would be better off spending the available dollars for more, smaller submarines?

THE PRESIDENT. Well, it costs so much to change designs, as you know, that I'm not sure that even a slightly smaller or different design would give us, in the long run, more submarines or more effective submarines.

As an ex-submariner one who was in the initial program, I think I'm personally biased. But I think that if there ever has been any one single weapons system that has ensured our Nation's integrity and security, it has been the nuclear submarines, with a strategic weapon capability.

It's a great insurer of the peace. And I think the Trident and the 688 combination, as far as the immediate future is concerned, are the best that we have to offer. And, of course, we are exploring new technologies, and they'll always be available for future designs. But to change from those two designs because there have been cost overruns, based primarily on natural inflation that has occurred and an improvement in design during construction phase, I think would be an error.

So, I don't think we'll terminate those programs, change the design. I think they are very adequate, and I'm very proud of what they've already done and will do in the future.

NUCLEAR POWERPLANTS

Q. Mr. President, I realize this is probably a little premature, but I can't think of any other more pertinent question at the time. Do you feel that the near disaster in Harrisburg will constitute a reevaluation of your policy toward nuclear power as it is a part of the overall energy mix in the country?

THE PRESIDENT. Well, I first went into the program, I think, in 1952, and almost a decade before that, we were involved in the production of nuclear materials. Until I became President, until just recent months, we've never had a proposal even to the Congress for the storage of spent fuel rods for possible later use, nor the disposal of waste.

We have had, and still have until this moment, a remarkable safety record in the production of nuclear power, both for our own defense systems, which we've just described, and also the production of electricity. My own experience has been that over the years, the safety standards have been greatly improved with much more stringent protection for the public.

Just this morning, I've talked to Governor Thornburgh and also to the Chairman of the Nuclear Regulatory Commission, Dr. Hendrie, about the situation that exists in the Three Mile Island plant. We are monitoring it very closely. I think the precautionary measures that have been taken and that will be taken in the future are adequate so far as we can foresee. Based on my own knowledge of the basic design of the plants, I think everything is being done at this point to ensure the safety of our people.

But I believe that this accident certainly will make all of us reassess our present safety regulations and precautions, limitations on radioactivity levels, and will probably lead inexorably toward even more stringent safety design mechanisms and also standards.

TRANSFER OF NUCLEAR FUELS TO OTHER COUNTRIES

Q. Mr. Carter, last year you broke a tie vote in the Nuclear Regulatory Commission by giving your approval to a shipment of nuclear fuel to India. Last week, another shipment of fuel for India was approved by the Commission. In the light of India's continuing refusal to abide by safeguard provisions of the Nuclear Non-Proliferation Treaty, do you think that the Nuclear Regulatory Commission took the right action last week in approving the shipment of fuel? And does the U.S. have any future plans to bring back from India used nuclear fuel for restorage and reprocessing in the United States?

THE PRESIDENT. I do think the NRC took the right action. We considered the assurances of the Indian Government at this point to be adequate. We would like for them and many other governments in the future to join in more and more stringent requirements for the handling of spent nuclear fuel and disposal of waste. We have no authority now and no plan for the shipment of those waste products back to our own country.

This is part of the legislation that Congress will consider this year, three major items. One is the expedition of deciding where a proper site exists for a nuclear powerplant and the decision on whether a license should be issued; secondly, how to dispose of spent fuel rods away from the site of power production; and, third, how to dispose ultimately of waste products.

I might add that more than 50 nations now are involved in an international nuclear fuel cycle evaluation study, wherein—we are a member of the Non-Proliferation Treaty signers, and others who are not—those who have nuclear weapon capability, as we do, and those who do not can approach this problem in a much more equitable and understandable fashion.

We are a supplier, as you know, of nuclear fuel products to our allies and friends around the world, provided they meet very rigid standards. And quite often, we have been embroiled in altercations with very friendly governments, because their concepts are different from our own.

I might say that—to abbreviate my answer—that there are two crucial issues that our country must pursue in order to encourage countries like India—and I won't name 11 or 12 others who have nuclear weapon capability—to refrain from developing those weapons; and that is how we act on the SALT treaty, whether we can consummate and ratify an agreement with the Soviet Union to restrain atomic weapons, and how we act on the control of nuclear explosive tests and our general attitude on nonproliferation issues.

If, for instance, our own Nation should reject a SALT treaty once it's signed, it would be extremely difficult for me, as President, or for some future President to restrain nations like India or Pakistan or South Africa or, perhaps, other countries that I won't name at this point from turning to the nuclear option.

So, this is a very complicated subject. I think our Nation has taken a leadership role in constraint of nuclear proliferation. But our own actions have not yet been adequate to encourage other countries like India to meet those very high standards that we hope to make more stringent in the future.

It's a little bit difficult for me to talk to Prime Minister Desai, who has publicly sworn that their government will never again turn to a nuclear explosive and never turn to nuclear weapons, when we ourselves have not yet restrained the spread of nuclear weapons.

So, it's difficult, sensitive, complicated, and there's an additional factor of nationalism and pride and self-autonomy. All these factors make it very difficult for us. But I think we've got to set a good example and deal in good faith with other countries and let them understand from a common perspective the dangers of unrestrained spread of nuclear production, of power, and how to handle the waste and prevent explosives from being developed.

WAGE AND PRICE GUIDELINES

Q. Mr. President, a question on the wage and price guidelines. How satisfied are you on how well they're working, particularly with regard to the fact that the Teamsters settlement appears to be shaping up somewhat in excess of what Mr. Kahn and the Council has sought?

THE PRESIDENT. I think, in general, the American working people, organized labor, organizations, and others have complied very well. I hope that their cooperation will continue. The Teamsters negotiation is a very important test case. So far, I think the truckers and the Team-

sters are negotiating in good faith, attempting to find a resolution that will meet our standards.

Secondly, the major corporations, which are the first ones that we have monitored because of a very limited staff—you might say the Fortune 500— so far as I know, have complied with our price guidelines. They have some flexibility built in. And I think it's accurate to say that predictably, the companies have interpreted those guidelines technically correctly, but to their advantage, when there was some flexibility.

We've asked them to be more stringent in setting prices. Some of the middle and smaller sized companies have not felt that the guidelines applied to them. Most of them have. We are now extending our monitoring capability to companies of the middle and smaller size. We have identified maybe 15 to 20 companies in the whole Nation that we think are not in compliance. We are now giving them a chance to justify price increases that they have already initiated. If they can't justify them adequately, then we will expose those companies' names, we will take what action is necessary to stop or to curtail procurement from them, and let the American consumer know if there are violations of the guidelines so that they can take voluntary action themselves.

In addition to that, in particular areas of supply where a particular product has gone up higher in price than we think is advisable, we are requiring companies to file with the Council on Wage and Price Stability now a record of their price increases to make it easier for us to monitor their compliance.

We have taken all these actions simultaneously in trying to set a good example in the Government itself, with control of hospital costs, with the substantial reduction in budget deficits, and other eliminations of, say, costly regulations when they're unwarranted.

So, it's a combination of business, labor, consumers, and government. We're trying to keep the partnership together and set an example in my own actions.

ADMINISTRATION'S ACHIEVEMENTS

Q. Mr. President, you've been criticized by the liberals——

THE PRESIDENT. For almost everything, haven't I? [*Laughter*]

Q. From a political point of view, the liberals are uncertain about supporting you, the conservatives won't support you, business has been critical, the minorities, labor. What do you think, going in the 1980 elections, are the elements of your political constituents?

THE PRESIDENT. Well, I'm not talking as a candidate. I'm not a candidate and won't make a decision on that or an announcement until later on. But I think in the assessment by the American people of my own administration's achievements, there are some encouraging factors. I think the general public opinion poll results show that people think I'm doing the best I can, that I'm honest and well-motivated. There have been some notable successes recognized at the time, but then forgotten.

In a period of a campaign, the achievements of the Democratic Party would be better publicized than they are at this point. Our Nation is at peace. We have strengthened our ties with our historical and very important alliances around the world. We have a very strong and adequate defense capability. Unemployment has been reduced drastically.

I think the equity of treatment in the government and in private society has been enhanced for minority groups. We've corrected some of the deficiencies that

exist in the system of federalism. I think there's a much more harmonious interrelationship, for instance, between local government, State government, and the Federal Government.

I think I've got a much better relationship now with the business community than I had when the election took place. I'll always remember a poll that I think *Business Week* conducted where, after I was elected, only 5 percent of the leading businessmen thought that I would be an adequate President and/or would support me.

So, I think we've made some progress. And I hope between now and election time—if I decide to be a candidate—that I'll have more achievements to point out to the American people in a beneficial way. But there's a great doubt among the American people about the adequacy of government, the integrity of government, and this, I think, is a remnant of the Vietnam war, Watergate, the CIA revelations, and so forth, when there was legitimate reason for cynicism or concern.

I've tried to alleviate that concern by restoring integrity to the Government and openess that, quite often, encourages debate and dissension and creates an image of confusion, which is sometimes exaggerated. There are good things and bad things that the public sees in our administration, but I think, on balance, we've done a good job.

ENERGY CONSERVATION

Q. Mr. President, your inflation chief, Mr. Kahn, just told us that the appeal for voluntary conservation of petroleum products is "for the birds" and that price is the only way to go, indicating that he's afraid that decontrol would aggravate inflation and that sometimes he'd like to have rationing, but he has to be honest with himself and say that price is the only way to go.

Does that reflect your feelings, that conservation appeals are for the birds? [*Laughter*]

THE PRESIDENT. I've had several conversations with Fred Kahn within the last week. He's not expressed his opinion to me in just those terms. [*Laughter*] It obviously requires a well-coordinated, broadly based, very complicated, interrelated approach. Voluntary restraint in the use of energy sources is an integral part of the overall process. Mandatory restraints are another part. We've asked Congress for authorization for that action, if necessary, in the future.

The increasing prices, which are inevitable, will certainly cause additional concern among the American people in how well they design their homes, how high they turn their thermostats, the degree of insulation, the size of their automobiles. All these things are interrelated.

Shifting away from petroleum products, whose supply is limited under the best circumstances, toward more plentiful energy sources—coal, nuclear power, ultimately, solar and other replaceable supplies—is an integral part. But I would say that voluntary compliance on the part of American people is one of the crucial elements.

If we relied on it exclusively, it would not be adequate.

CONSTITUTIONAL AMENDMENT TO
BALANCE THE BUDGET

Q. Mr. President, about this time a year ago, most of us on editorial pages in California were opposing Proposition 13 on the grounds that it was rash and risky and irresponsible. And you know how much the people followed our advice.

Now Governor Brown is talking about a constitutional amendment to force a balanced Federal budget, and most editorial writers are opposed to that as rash, risky, and irresponsible. But it obviously has wide popular appeal. As we move toward 1980, what will you do, as President and/or as a candidate, to take that issue away from Brown?

THE PRESIDENT. I was under the impression that 24 States had passed some sort of resolution before Governor Brown ever proposed it to the California Legislature. I'm not sure what the final action of the California Legislature will be. I have heard some preliminary reports on the subject already that were of interest to me.

I think the convening of a constitutional convention with the ostensible purpose of passing an amendment against any deficit spending would be one of the most ill-advised things that I can envision. This is a transient problem, and we've never cluttered up our Constitution with amendments of that kind before. And I hope we never will. The only time we tried to do it was with the 18th amendment, prohibiting the sale of alcoholic beverages.

My belief is that the best way to handle it is the way I've done it, to continue to cut down the deficit, to eliminate wasteful spending, to harmonize my own efforts with the inclinations of the American people and the Congress to bring about a balanced budget.

If you start writing the exemptions and the caveats to a balanced budget requirement in the Constitution, this particular amendment would of necessity be longer than all the Bill of Rights put together. And you would have to say that if an emergency existed under certain circumstances, on extremely high unemployment, or if the thirties depression times came back, or if our national security was endangered, and so forth, that you'd have to make an exception.

So, I don't think the right way to handle it is through a constitutional amendment at all, certainly not a constitutional convention, which is the original proposal of Governor Brown.

I don't think very many States have ratified—I mean have passed a resolution on this since Governor Brown came out in favor of it. Others may do so. But I have written a letter, I think, to one of the State legislators in Ohio, who asked for my opinion. And if you would ask Jody Powell later on, he can give you a copy of that letter that might explain in a little more voluminous way what my concerns would be about this.

The Congress is very interested in a balanced budget. This interest has been extant long before Governor Brown's second inauguration, and it's a concern that I shared throughout my own campaign. And I think because I pledged to reduce the deficit and work toward a balanced budget, this was a major factor in my own election.

1980 ELECTION

Q. Mr. President, how do things look for you in Alabama, with the second primary, and in the South as a whole?

THE PRESIDENT. I don't know. I really don't want to comment on 1980 from the perspective of a candidate. I have not crossed that bridge yet. I think the best thing for me to do is to stay out of the campaign arena until much later when I make a decision on it.

U.S.-MEXICAN BORDER FENCE

Q. Mr. President, in El Paso, Texas, we understand that the decision is now in the White House as to whether you're going to go ahead and replace the fence

that exists in various downtown areas along the border.

THE PRESIDENT. Yes.

Q. Is that decision to be made here and, if so, when?

THE PRESIDENT. A proposal reached me earlier—two proposals; one through the news media, when I discovered that people were considering a fence that might damage people who tried to cross it, and I immediately vetoed that crazy idea as soon as I heard about it.

Secondly, a proposal was made to me to extend the fence substantial numbers of miles beyond the present limits of it, and I have also disapproved that.

I do approve, however, the keeping in repair of the fence which presently exists.

FOREIGN ARMS SALES

Q. Mr. Carter, in May of 1977 you pledged to strictly limit U.S. arms sales abroad. But according to the Defense Department statistics released recently, government-to-government arms sales rose from $11.3 billion to $13.5 billion by the end of fiscal year 1978, and Defense Department figures project that fiscal 1979 arms sales will reach $14 billion. How does this increase square with your promise to reduce the U.S. role as an arms supplier overseas?

THE PRESIDENT. I have absolutely kept my promise. I'd like for you to read it. The promise that I made was, outside of our NATO commitments, where we have defense alliances, that we would cut down unilaterally, whether or not other nations did the same, our total defense sales at least 8 percent per year.

Last year, we cut back in excess of 8 percent—I think a reduction of about $700 million. And this year, we'll do the same. And we have also begun working with other countries, including the Soviet

Union and our own military allies who can produce weapons, to join us in this effort. But I have met my standard very accurately, even exceeded those reductions, and I'm very proud of that achievement.

UNDOCUMENTED ALIENS

Q. Mr. President, what's the administration's policy now on illegal immigration? Is amnesty still a proposal?

THE PRESIDENT. We are opposed to it, as you know. When I was inaugurated, I took an oath, as have all my predecessors, to uphold the laws and the Constitution of the United States. And I'm constrained to do the best I can to enforce the laws.

We have, obviously, been aware of the fact that there are hundreds of thousands of undocumented workers who crossed the border into our country and who live here at the present time. We worked a number of months on this particular problem, with all its ramifications of sensitivity and international relationships, and made a proposal to the Congress, I think, about 18 months ago on what should be done about it. The Congress has not yet acted.

When I was in Mexico recently, I discussed this matter with President López Portillo and other members of the Mexican Government and have now set up an immigration commission, which will be headed by Governor Reubin Askew from Florida. Governor Askew will add his own judgment and his results of consultations to my own and make a recommendation on a permanent solution, we hope, to this problem, that will be satisfactory.

But there has been no one who's discovered an adequate answer. My own belief is that ultimately the rapidly improving economic circumstances in Mexico will be the best answer. But when people can find a job—and I am very proud of the new potential prosperity for Mexico that seems to be in prospect because of discoveries, unanticipated discoveries of oil and natural gas. But we are working harmoniously within the Government itself, U.S. Government, working harmoniously with the Mexican Government now, and trying to enforce the boundary laws of all kinds.

I think we've had excellent success in dealing with the illegal or illicit drug traffic. The Mexicans point out that we have not had adequate success in controlling contraband from the United States going into Mexico on which duty is not paid.

And we are working together to resolve the problem of the undocumented workers. But it's something that no one has found an adequate answer to. But we're still trying.

MR. WURFEL. Thank you, sir.

THE PRESIDENT. I'll get one more question.

U.S. FOREIGN POLICY

Q. Mr. President, the new relationship that we have with Red China, our policy at the present, pursuit of the peace on the Mideast, and the deterioration of the situation in Iran suggest a major reshuffling of global foreign policy as far as the United States is concerned. And some of us feel that it's not going to stop here, that Turkey might be next for an enhancement of an alliance. May we ask, what next; in what general direction you intend to go?

THE PRESIDENT. My own feeling is that in the last 10, 15 years, even lesser period of time, that our influence around the world has been substantially enhanced. One of the things that I look at, for instance, is our relationship with countries that formerly were not friends of our Nation, vis-a-vis the Russians.

This is the first time in my memory, for instance, that we've had really a better relationship with India, Japan, and China than has the Soviet Union. Egypt is a major new friend and ally of ours, formerly completely in the Soviet camp. I think we've improved the relationship with the Eastern European nations—excellent relationships with countries like Romania, Yugoslavia, Poland, and others. The NATO Alliance has been substantially strengthened in the last couple of years.

For the first time in our Nation's history, we are now playing a viable role, an influential role in Africa in a very constructive way—not trying to dominate anyone. But in the past, the United States had practically no role to play among the black African nations.

Indonesia is now a very excellent friend of ours; in the past, this was not the case. I believe that our relationship with the Philippine Government has improved recently. The ASEAN nations look upon us as a major ally and friend. Last year I met around this same table with the foreign ministers of those countries.

The Soviets did have some success in Afghanistan, compared to what their previous relationship was with that government, although Afghanistan has always been very close to the Soviet Union. Now very serious problems have arisen in Afghanistan with their present government. We are concerned that the Soviets might play an excessive role there in trying to interfere in the internal affairs of Afghanistan.

We were disappointed, obviously, in the change in Iran. But this was a matter that concerned the people themselves. We had no desire nor capability of perpetuating the Shah's government against the will of the Iranian people. We tried this, as you know, a few years ago in Vietnam and were not successful in doing it. We do not intend to interfere in the internal affairs of another country unless our own direct security is threatened.

I think the recent achievement of a peace treaty between Israel and Egypt is a major step in the right direction.

So, in balance, I think, we've got a very good, well-rounded progress that's been proven in our relationship with other countries around the world.

We are treating all of the Latin American nations as individuals, as equals. I've traveled extensively in Latin America, so has my wife, other officials of our Government. For the first time, a Vice President or a Secretary of State or a President can go to almost any nation in Latin America now, and there are no demonstrations against us. There are expressions of friendship and good will and harmony.

The Caribbean—we have a new interest in the economic and social stability and prosperity in the Caribbean that was not there in the past.

We, obviously, see many countries as equals, whereas formerly we had a dominant position, and that dominance was overt. I look on Mexico, for instance, and Canada and many other countries around the world as our equals in every sense of the word.

So, I think that our competition with potential adversaries has been very well consummated. And I think that the good will that the American people have towards other peoples is very exemplary. Our absence of any desire to dominate other countries gives us an advantage. So, I think the future will be even better than it has in the past.

Thank you very much.

NOTE: The interview began at 1:15 p.m. in the Cabinet Room at the White House. Walter W. Wurfel is a Deputy Press Secretary.

The transcript of the interview was released on March 31.

Federal Emergency Management Agency

Executive Order 12127.   March 31, 1979

By the authority vested in me as President by the Constitution and laws of the United States of America, including Section 304 of Reorganization Plan No. 3 of 1978, and in order to provide for the orderly activation of the Federal Emergency Management Agency, it is hereby ordered as follows:

1–101. Reorganization Plan No. 3 of 1978 (43 FR 41943), which establishes the Federal Emergency Management Agency, provides for the transfer of functions, and the transfer and abolition of agencies and offices, is hereby effective.

1–102. The Director of the Office of Management and Budget shall, in accord with Section 302 of the Reorganization Plan, provide for all the appropriate transfers, including those transfers related to all the functions transferred from the Department of Commerce, the Department of Housing and Urban Development, and the President.

1–103. (a) The functions transferred from the Department of Commerce are those vested in the Secretary of Commerce, the Administrator and Deputy Administrator of the National Fire Prevention and Control Administration (now the United States Fire Administration (Sec. 2(a) of Public Law 95–422)), and the Superintendent of the National Academy for Fire Prevention and Control pursuant to the Federal Fire Prevention and Control Act of 1974, as amended (15 U.S.C. 2201 *et seq.*), but not including any functions vested by the amendments made to other acts by Sections 18 and 23 of that Act (15 U.S.C. 278f and 1511). The functions vested in the Administrator by Sections 24 and 25 of that Act, as added by Sections 3 and 4 of Public Law 95–422 (15 U.S.C. 2220 and 2221), are not transferred to the Director of the Federal Emergency Management Agency. Those functions are transferred with the Administrator and remain vested in him. (Section 201 of the Plan.)

(b) There was also transferred from the Department of Commerce any function concerning the Emergency Broadcast System which was transferred to the Secretary of Commerce by Section 5B of Reorganization Plan No. 1 of 1977 (42 FR 56101; implemented by Executive Order No. 12046 of March 27, 1978). (Section 203 of the Plan.)

1–104. The functions transferred from the Department of Housing and Urban Development are those vested in the Secretary of Housing and Urban Development pursuant to Section 15(e) of the Federal Flood Insurance Act of 1956, as amended (42 U.S.C. 2414(e)), and the National Flood Insurance Act of 1968, as amended, and the Flood Disaster Protection Act of 1973, as amended (42 U.S.C. 4001 *et seq.*), and Section 520(b) of the National Housing Act, as amended (12 U.S.C. 1735d(b)), to the extent necessary to borrow from the Treasury to make payments for reinsured and directly insured losses, and Title XII of the National

Housing Act, as amended (12 U.S.C. 1749bbb *et seq.*, and as explained in Section 1 of the National Insurance Development Act of 1975 (Section 1 of Public Law 94–13 at 12 U.S.C. 1749bbb note)). (Section 202 of the Plan.)

1–105. The functions transferred from the President are those concerning the Emergency Broadcast System which were transferred to the President by Section 5 of Reorganization Plan No. 1 of 1977 (42 FR 56101; implemented by Executive Order No. 12046 of March 27, 1978). (Section 203 of the Plan.)

1–106. This Order shall be effective Sunday, April 1, 1979.

JIMMY CARTER

The White House,
    March 31, 1979.

[Filed with the Office of the Federal Register, 10:46 a.m., April 2, 1979]

Federal Emergency Management Agency

Appointment of Gordon Vickery as Acting Director. March 31, 1979

The President has signed an Executive order which sets the effective date for the establishment of the Federal Emergency Management Agency as April 1, 1979.

The President today announced the appointment of Gordon Vickery as Acting Director of the Federal Emergency Management Agency, also effective April 1, 1979.

Vickery, 58, is Administrator of the United States Fire Administration. He is a former Seattle firechief. He received the Municipal League of Seattle Award for Outstanding Public Official of 1972.

Airey Neave

Message to Prime Minister James Callaghan of the United Kingdom on the Death of the Conservative Party Member of Parliament. March 31, 1979

I have been deeply shocked by the murder of Airey Neave. It is an outrage to civilized values. Such violence does not contribute in any way to the resolution of political problems and must be abhorred by all men of conscience everywhere. Please convey my deepest condolences and those of my fellow Americans to Mr. Neave's family and his parliamentary colleagues.

JIMMY CARTER

Wausau, Wisconsin

Remarks at a Fundraising Reception for Representative David R. Obey. March 31, 1979

Senator Nelson, Congressman Dave Obey, Congressman Reuss, Congressman Baldus, and Congressman McHugh from New York, Chairman White, and my good friend Ambassador Pat Lucey, friends of David Obey and, I hope, friends of mine:

There are 535 Members of the House and Senate. A President does not have time to visit many congressional districts in this Nation, personally, to support and to endorse a Member of the Congress. This allotment of the time and interest of the President has to be very carefully chosen and apportioned. But there was no doubt in my mind, when I had an opportunity to come here, that it was a sound investment, because it is so crucial to our Nation that David Obey stay in the Congress and continue to serve you, the President, and our country.

If you're going to work hard in the future elections to keep him in the Congress, would you just raise your hand so I can see how you feel? I'll join you. Thank you very much.

I want to express my thanks to you for the wonderful reception. At the airport, there were three or four thousand people who had come out and stood in the cold to wait for me, and alongside the highways there were large numbers of people who had American flags and signs of welcome. And this packed auditorium really makes me feel good. It wasn't that way the first time I came to Wisconsin. [*Laughter*]

I made the mistake of going to the university at Madison, a southerner, peanut farmer. I was bombarded with peanuts. [*Laughter*] I was thankful I didn't grow watermelons. [*Laughter*]

And then when I came back the night of the primary, you almost treated me the same way. Most of my people went to bed crying. I stayed up and eventually developed an enormous, grateful smile, when late in the evening, as you may or may not remember, the people in this area helped to put me over and gave me the delegate vote from Wisconsin. I want to thank you for it.

I've come here this afternoon to outline very briefly some of the thoughts that are on my heart. As Dave has pointed out to you, and to me on the way here, this group, the Better Way Club, is an extremely large and growing representation of America—farmers, working people, teachers; just average, sound, patriotic, dedicated, competent Americans who feel that the structure of government can best be served if government is removed from the unwarranted influence of the powerful and the selfish. That's what you've done for the last 10 years in this district to provide the right kind of influence.

The 10th anniversary of the special election which put Dave Obey in the Congress is an important event for you, for Dave, for Wisconsin, and for me, as President. Eight of those years that Dave has served were under Republican Presidents. And he pointed out the attitude and the problems of America when Hubert Humphrey came here to endorse him as a young man, about 30 years old, who was seeking his office for the first time in the Congress in 1969.

The Democratic Party at that time was at a low point. We had lost a heartbreaking election in 1968, when one of the finest men I've ever known, Hubert Humphrey, was narrowly defeated.

I came into office a little more than 2 years ago. The unemployment rate was 8 percent. There was a spirit of despair and discouragement throughout our country. Since then, we have had a net increase, with the help of Senator Nelson, Dave Obey, the other Members of Congress, of 7.6 million new jobs.

I was looking at the statistics for Milwaukee on the way up here. The unemployment rate in the last 2 years in Milwaukee has dropped from 9.4 percent to 4.1 percent. We have given America a chance to go back to work, a remarkable achievement, one of great and gratifying change.

We were afflicted then and we are afflicted now, for the last 8 years, by an inflation rate that's extremely high. The 3 years before I became President, the inflation rate was 8 percent, and there was talk again of restoring mandatory price and wage controls or having a deliberate recession to put people out of work again to hold down the inflation rate.

We are making much better progress than that. We still have a long way to go.

But I can tell you that you've got two men behind me on the stage, among others, who have done as much to control inflation as anyone I know.

Hospital costs are doubling every 5 years. The impact of hospital costs permeates every facet of our lives. The Congress is now struggling with a hospital cost containment bill. When you buy an automobile, $120 of the cost of that automobile is what the auto workers have to pay for hospital insurance.

The leading light in the Senate is Gaylord Nelson, and I believe that with his help this year, the Senate will pass again hospital cost containment. And with the help of the House Members on the stage with me, we will finally get hospital cost containment legislation passed in 1979, and I hope you'll help us with it.

I campaigned for 2 solid years and planned even before that. And I think it's accurate to say that there was a searching in our Nation to correct some basic defects that had preyed on the hearts and minds of the American people. There was a loss of confidence in our Government. The Vietnam war had been costly not only in the 50,000 lives lost, as Dave has pointed out, but the American people had lost confidence in the sound judgment, the integrity, the honesty, the commitment, the spirit, the ideals of our country. The Watergate scandals swept across us like a cold, damp fog. And, of course, the CIA revelations were equally bad in severing the trustful interrelationship that must exist in a democracy between the people and their government.

One of the prime needs in making those changes, obviously, was to maintain peace. And I'm very proud that in the last 26 months—and I hope as long as I'm in the White House—we have not had a young man's life endangered on a field of battle

anywhere on Earth. We're at peace, and we're going to stay there.

We have passed a sound ethics bill to bring to the Congress extremely high standards of performance and, also, to apply those same standards in the executive branch of government and in the judiciary.

The leading light in the House of Representatives is David Obey, and the leading light in the Senate is Senator Nelson. Many joined with them, of course, because the legislation has been passed and signed into law. It was not as rigid in its standards as I would have liked or as the Wisconsin delegation in its entirety would have liked. But for the first time now, we have a law to restrain the abuse of public office. And my guess is that in the future it will be constantly strengthened and appreciated by the American people.

If David Obey had not done anything else in the last 10 years, this would have been worth the investment of this district in the Congress. And I want to thank you for him and for that great achievement.

The social security system was bankrupt. It's now in a sound condition. Our foreign policy has been brought into the open. There was a time when the President and the Secretary of State and other leaders evolved foreign policy in secret and then sprung upon the Congress and the American people, as was the case in Angola, a proposal for involvement of our country in the internal affairs of foreign countries. That time is changed.

There was a time in the fall when the United Nations General Assembly met; every knowledgeable and thinking American would flinch, because we knew that two-thirds of the nations on Earth would use the United States of America as a target for attack as a butt for their jokes. Now we've changed that.

Our country has a reputation that's admirable. We've raised the standards of our foreign policy. We've brought it out in the open. We have tough, open debates in which you yourselves can participate. We have raised the flag of basic human rights, and as long as I'm in the White House, that flag will remain flying high and our country will be known as a protector for basic human rights throughout the world.

I just want to mention one other thing, and then I'd like to close by making a few, specific remarks about Congressman David Obey.

We've had problems with our Nation's economy. When I came to Wisconsin, I not only visited the urban centers of your State and the university campuses, but I went out on the farms, when I didn't have a large entourage of Secret Service agents or news people either, when I used to really brighten up if I saw one person with a tape recorder in his hand or a scratch pad. [*Laughter*] And I studied from data given to me by your own universities, the fact that the average dairy farmer in Wisconsin, the average family, had a net income per year of less than $7,000 and an average investment of over $150,000. Farm income was going down steadily. We were approaching a time of recession in the agricultural communities of our country. Those who grew grain were constantly flinching, because periodically the Republican administrations would declare embargoes and cut off farm exports.

Since then, the Congress has passed, in 1977, a new farm bill. It went into effect a little more than a year ago. Last year, net farm income went up 30 percent for the American farm family. Exports hit an alltime high. Wisconsin farm exports last year went up an unbelievable 35 percent in just 12 months. I think we are well on the way now to a renewed farm prosperity, and I hope to keep us on that road.

We have a need to strengthen the ties not only between the President and the Congress but between Washington, the State capitals, and the cities and towns and counties of our Nation. We've made good progress in this respect in restoring the basic system on which our Nation is founded, a system of federalism.

We've tried to shift responsibility closest to the people themselves. It's very difficult in a modern, fast-changing, technological world, with the confusion of conflicting ideas and conflicting demands, to have a proper balance in serving the people who send you to Washington. David Obey, as much as anyone whom I know, has that capability. He's a man who's not only honest and decent and competent, but he's also sensitive and compassionate. And he has common sense.

As you know, he's one of the leaders in working to correct the problems of the handicapped. He's one of the leaders in meeting the legitimate needs of the senior citizens of this country. He's worked hard for improvement in mental health. My wife admires and loves him for that.

He's worked to point out the dangers to the average working man and woman in this country because of chemicals in the air, in the environment where they work, to improve their health. He pointed out on the ride in from the airport with me that more than 20 percent of all cancer existing in our Nation is caused by environmental problems on the job.

These kinds of actions are those of a man whose heart is filled with understanding and love. But David Obey is not

an impractical dreamer. He's not someone with his head in the clouds, because
he knows that you have to pay the bill
when the Federal Government provides
services.

He has a remarkable, almost unique
honor of serving both on the Appropriations Committee and also on the Budget
Committee. He's a sound fiscal manager.
He's worked hard to make sure that unnecessary regulations and redtape are
eliminated from the Government process.
He's worked hard to reduce our deficits.

When I came here to campaign in 1976,
our Federal budget deficit was more than
$66 billion. We have slashed it more than
half. Next year, we'll cut it even more.
And we're working now to achieve a balanced Federal budget, without cutting
back on the beneficial services which go
to our people.

David Obey has a special leadership
role, however, that has endeared him to
me. I believe that the strength and power
and influence of the United States must
be maintained to exert our own American
ideals throughout the world in a beneficial and idealistic way, to make us proud.
But we need not do it by interfering militarily in the internal affairs of other countries.

We've tried that and we failed. What
David Obey has done that's so important
is to see that the tremendous strength of
our Nation must be maintained—moral
strength, economic strength, political
strength, and military strength—but that
our beneficial influence should be exerted
through peaceful means.

He's chairman of the subcommittee on
the Appropriations Committee which is
responsible for allocating very carefully,
very precisely, in a targeted way, American economic assistance to other countries
in such a fashion that they can be made

good customers of ours, can recognize the
advantages of our own free enterprise
system, and can eliminate rather than
cause conflict and war.

This is not an easy thing to do. You
will never know, not having served in
Congress, what a tremendous amount of
political courage it takes to play a leadership role in handling a foreign assistance
bill. But it's a matter of supreme statesmanship, and that's the kind of leadership that you have sent to Washington in
David Obey as a Congressman.

I could go on and on talking about
David Obey. I want to lead a nation that's
committed to some very simple
principles—to peace instead of war, to
exemplify in the highest sense equity, fairness, and justice for all, to keep high our
standard of civil rights or human rights,
and to give our own citizens a better
quality of life.

Those are notable goals. They are goals
which I think we are capable of achieving. We've got a strong nation, a competent nation, a bold nation. And I hope
that we can continue a superb partnership between the people of this country,
the President who serves in the White
House, and superb leaders in the Congress.

I hope you will continue to support our
Government in a constructive way, recognizing that partnership as the basis for a
democratic society, so that you and I,
Dave Obey, Senator Nelson, others,
can make the greatest nation on Earth
even greater in the future.

Thank you very much.

NOTE: The President spoke at 4:30 p.m. in
the Newman High School gymnasium. In
his opening remarks, he referred to John C.
White, chairman of the Democratic National
Committee.

Milwaukee, Wisconsin

Remarks at a Reception for Representative
Clement J. Zablocki.   March 31, 1979

THE PRESIDENT. *Father Raynor and Chairman Clem Zablocki, distinguished alumni and friends of Marquette University:*

It's a great honor for me to be here. The last time I was at Marquette, I had achieved some degree of fame or notoriety during the campaign. And I will always remember that a large group of students were banging on the walls and pounding on the door, demanding the right to come into the auditorium, which was already very crowded. This was quite a remarkable change from the earlier part of my campaign. [*Laughter*]

And because of the dramatic difference that occurred here at Marquette, I'll always remember with a great deal of gratification and friendship the attitude that your students expressed toward me.

You're honoring a very fine statesman, a man who is the chairman of one of the most important committees in the Congress.

When I was growing up as a Georgia young man, we almost took for granted that the chairmen of the important committees were southerners. [*Laughter*] But I noticed that the Banking Committee, which is one of the most important of all, is headed by Henry Reuss, and the committee that has control of all the foreign affairs, the House International Relations Committee, is headed by Clem Zablocki, both from this community.

I don't know what is the basis for this remarkable achievement. Obviously, sound judgment on the part of the voters, but maybe it's something in the Milwaukee beer that—[*laughter*]——

Clem and I have a good partnership when important matters arise. He's one of the very few leaders in Congress to whom I have to turn with increasing frequency, because his sound judgment and his awareness of not only parochial but national and international affairs is a great reservoir of advice and counsel and strength for me.

I've called on Clem also, because of his remarkable rapport with different people around the world, to represent me in important affairs. When Mrs. Meir died, I asked Clem to go to Israel to represent me. And with the investiture of Pope John Paul II, Clem, without too much urging on my part—[*laughter*]—agreed to go and make a great sacrifice to represent me there. It was a glorious event.

Clem has an achievement that I can't claim. He is the only person that I know personally who has played poker with my mother and won. [*Laughter*] Every time I see my mother, she says, "You have got to get that man Clem Zablocki back to play poker with me. I cannot stand to ruin my reputation by being a permanent loser."

REPRESENTATIVE ZABLOCKI. $2.65.

THE PRESIDENT. $2.65—Mother will never forget it. [*Laughter*]

But I might also say that when we have important international events that take place, Clem is there. He's one of the top congressional advisers to our own negotiating team trying to hammer out the terms of a strategic arms limitation agreement with the Soviet Union. And I think this is the kind of role that Clem Zablocki plays in a very quiet and modest and unpublicized way, that the people in this room, who love him and admire him, ought to know about.

When I had extreme difficulty the last 18 months in arranging the basis for negotiating the peace treaty between Egypt and Israel, Clem Zablocki could always give me a sense of the Congress. And immediately after the signing ceremony Monday, I met with a tiny group of key congressional advisers. Clem Zablocki was obviously at the top of the list, to tell him the terms of the treaty, the agreements that had been consummated, and to ask his counsel on how to proceed in the future. And now, of course, the honoring of American commitments in the House of Representatives is in the hands of Clem Zablocki, and I'm proud of it.

In many ways, a university is measured by the quality of its alumni. Marquette is a remarkable university because of many reasons. That's obviously one of them. I know that sometimes there are disappointments in things like the NCAA playoffs—[*laughter*]—which I will not mention tonight. But if the NCAA included as an athletic event the production of remarkable and distinguished alumni, Clem Zablocki alone would still have Marquette in the finals. And I want to thank you from the bottom of my heart for producing such a great statesman and a personal friend. And I want to express my admiration for your sound judgment in choosing him the Outstanding Alumnus of the Year.

Thank you very much for letting me be part of it.

NOTE: The President spoke at 7:16 p.m. at the Milwaukee Performing Arts Center. He was introduced by Father John P. Raynor, S.J., president of Marquette University, whose alumni association sponsored the event.

Milwaukee, Wisconsin

Remarks at the State Democratic Party's Jefferson-Jackson Day Dinner.
March 31, 1979

Secretary of State Vel Phillips, Chairman Bleicher, Senator Nelson, Senator Prox- *mire, Chairman Reuss, Congressman Aspin, Chairman Zablocki, Al Baldus, Mayor Maier, Ambassador Lucey, my good friends in Wisconsin:*

I'm glad to be back with you.

This is indeed a great week for me and for our Nation. I have personal gratitude for one single event that I'll never forget the rest of my life, and that is an opportunity to come here and join you at the Jefferson-Jackson Day banquet in Wisconsin.

Seriously, it's a gratifying experience indeed to work very closely with two men of wide ethnic background differences, different religion, who have to live and work closely in proximity to one another, sometimes divided by strife and differences in the past, and to see them come together in the spirit of harmony and cooperation. I believe this arrangement might be permanent. As a matter of fact, Dr. Brzezinski and Cy Vance have been friends ever since Monday, and I'm very grateful for it. [*Laughter*]

We have an opportunity to observe from the White House superb achievement. This Wisconsin congressional delegation is a source of great pride to me. You occupy, because of seniority and sound judgment and competence, chairmanships of some of the major committees, as you well know.

But in addition to the congressional delegation, this State, this city has a lot of which to be proud. Mayor Maier is one of the leaders among the leaders of the great metropolitan mayors and county officials of our country. And when I have a very serious problem to address that relates to improving the life of people in the cities throughout the country, Henry is one of those to whom I turn for advice and counsel and support. And I thank him for it.

One of my earliest friends in Wisconsin is your former Governor, Pat Lucey. I asked Pat to take a very major responsibility on his shoulders a few months ago, as you know.

I have visited a lot of foreign countries. I have been with a lot of our own diplomatic leaders. I've had assessments made by many heads of state, Presidents, Prime Ministers, Kings. I have never been to a country since I've been President and had more repetitive and enthusiastic congratulations on the superb service of an Ambassador, than I did when I went to Mexico City recently and talked to the Foreign Minister of Mexico, Roel, and the President of Mexico, López Portillo, when they told me that they had never had an Ambassador in Mexico as good as Pat Lucey, and they hoped that I would keep him there. And I will keep him there as long as he wants to stay, because I have the utmost confidence in him.

You know what he did for Wisconsin. I don't think any State has ever had a better Governor. He was an adviser for me, a partner with me, and a personal friend when we were Governors together.

And this afternoon as I flew up toward your State, I looked down the list of achievements in one area only, that of energy, and found that the programs that he initiated as Governor are now paying rich dividends not only for Wisconsin but for the rest of the Nation.

In spite of the fact that your State ranks 12th in industrial commitment, and in spite of the fact that Wisconsin has very severe climatic conditions that require extra heat during the winter, the average person in Wisconsin used 20 percent less energy than the rest of the Nation.

You have inventories and assessments made of homes to cut down on the waste of fuels, and the business community in Wisconsin, almost without exception, have committed themselves to a program which I hope the rest of the Nation will emulate, thanks to the superb leadership of Pat Lucey when he was your Governor. And I want to thank you, Pat, and the people of Wisconsin for setting an example for the rest of the people.

It's good to come and speak to a Democratic organization that also has set an example for the rest of the Nation for many years of openness, honesty, and a progressive commitment. I also have a personal appreciation for the superb, overwhelming victory you gave me in the Wisconsin primary. I'll never forget that evening—[laughter]—and I thank you again for your sound judgment then, and also in the general election.

Our country is comprised of people with widely divergent backgrounds. When I was in Israel recently and spoke to the Knesset there, I reminded those friends of ours that the United States of America is a country of immigrants. It's a country of refugees.

We will never be a homogeneous population. We pride ourselves on individuality. We pride ourselves on maintaining our ethnic ties. It gives us an opportunity to lead the rest of the world in many areas of life, because we can understand the special sensitivities of those who live in other regions of the world.

We are tied to them because of common commitments of philosophy. Our security is often interrelated with that of people of other countries, and we have a blood-kin relationship with the people of almost every nation on Earth.

We are a country which has never been afraid of challenge. We are still a country of pioneers. We have the strongest nation on Earth economically, militarily, politically, and, I believe, also ethically and morally.

We are a nation that has been able to struggle with diversity and even deep disappointment and embarrassment, without permanently damaging the fabric of our societal structure.

Often it's time for us to stop and take stock of where we are, what we are, where we might go in the future. We are a nation inclined toward open debate, and we're also a nation which has never been fearful of exposing our mistakes, our trials, our tribulations, and our problems.

I think the American press, the American people are inclined, as a matter of character, to emphasize the differences which divide us, the reasons for dispute and debate, to emphasize the problems that we've not yet solved, the questions that we have not yet answered.

And because of this, often Americans fail to remember the vast reservoir of common purpose, common belief, the superb achievements and the basic strength of our country. Often I meet with labor leaders, business leaders, political leaders, representatives of special interest groups—sometimes selfish, sometimes benevolent in nature—in the Oval Office, in the Cabinet Room, or in larger groups. And I remind them of all the things for which we can honestly give thanks in our country and ask them to recognize and to strive to overcome difficulties and obstacles, but to do it with a sense of realization, of innate strength worthy of our confidence, not to lose the boldness with which we face the future.

We are a nation that believes in justice, justice enshrined in an ever-improving United States Constitution, which started out as an example for the rest of the world almost 200 years ago, but which has constantly been improved because the people of our country demand more, not less freedom; more and not less equality of opportunity.

We're a nation which believes in strength. We're a nation which believes even in military strength, but we are also a nation which believes in investing that military strength for the cause of peace.

Sometimes we have departed from our basic principles in the past, and in the process, we have had a deterioration in the quality of our social life and our political life.

In recent years, because of the Vietnam war, Watergate, CIA revelations, we lost a great reservoir of trust and natural interrelationship between the people of our country and our own Government.

One of the major responsibilities of us Democrats, the last 2 years, has been to restore that element of trust, with openness of government, the passage of strict ethics legislation, more direct communication with the press, restoring the structural federal system, so that county, city, State, and Federal officials can work in harmony and not at odds.

We've been willing for a change to focus on crises and needs. And I can tell you that the Congress has had superb courage in the last 2 years to deal with inevitably divisive issues, within which there was no possibility of political gain, when courageous action was taken, when courageous votes were cast.

There was no way for a Member of the Congress to benefit politically by supporting the Panama Canal treaties. But the Senate, with superb courage, did so, and identified our Nation as having extra strength—strength not of a coward and a bully, but strength of quiet confidence, so that we can deal with a small nation equitably and fairly. And it gave our country a genuine reputation not only in this hemisphere but throughout the world as one that genuinely believed in human rights and didn't just preach human rights for others.

We're a nation which recently has been involved more and more deeply in trying to bring peace to southern Africa, based on one-person-one-vote, majority rule, an end to racism, an end to apartheid. We've suffered in the process, because a peacemaker often gets condemned from both sides. But our Nation has not been willing to shrink from this new involvement to ensure peace in a potentially troubled area of the world.

We've now opened our arms to embrace as friends, as new friends, a billion people who live in China and, in the process, to retain our commitment to the independence, the openness, the trade relationships, the cultural relationships, and the peaceful life of the people of Taiwan. These decisions have not been easy ones, but our country has not shrunk from this commitment.

In the past, our Government has been too close to every dictatorship that exists throughout the world if it might benefit us in a selfish and transient way. But we've changed all that. As I mentioned this afternoon in Wausau, I and many of you formerly shrank from the prospect of the United Nations General Assembly beginning its annual fall debates, because we knew that our Nation, which we loved, would inevitably be the target of every attack, the butt of every joke cast at us by more than a hundred small, new, weak, black, brown, or yellow nations on Earth.

I thank God that time has changed, and now those struggling nations look on us as a friend and not an enemy, as an equal and not a superior, as a nation to be trusted, as a nation to be sought out as a source of help.

We are now approaching the conclusion of negotiations on a SALT treaty and on a comprehensive test ban agreement. I hope that when I go out of office

that we will have taken a major stride toward the ultimate goal of our Nation which I espouse, and that is once and for all to eliminate the threat of nuclear weapons from the face of the Earth.

This is not going to be an easy action for the Senate to take, to ratify the SALT II treaty. But I think the consequences of a rejection of this treaty will be so profound and so damaging to our country, its reputation, that ultimately the sound judgment of the American people will prevail. And I would like to ask every one of you in this room to extend your influence even beyond Wisconsin, and wherever you have a friend or an acquaintance or a customer or a relative, to encourage upon them the importance of joining in the support of this major step toward a nuclear-free world.

We have in addition to that many serious problems domestically. Inflation has been with us now for 10 years. The 3 years before I became President, the average inflation rate was about 8 percent; 6 years ago, it was 15 percent.

The inflation rate is still creeping up. Every group tends to lay the blame on someone else—business on labor, labor on business, the average citizen on the Government, Americans on OPEC. But we're all in it together. It will require a partnership not only of analysis but also of commitment and action. And every family in our country can make a major step toward assuaging inflationary pressures if we adopt an unselfish and an incisive and a knowledgeable attitude toward controlling this blight on our country.

I particularly wanted to thank Senator Nelson, who has led the battle successfully in the Senate last year and who, I'm sure, will lead it again this year, to control hospital costs and to pass a hospital cost containment bill. At the present time, medical cost in hospitals is doubling every 5 years. The inflationary rate in hospital costs has been almost twice the already excessively high inflation rate throughout the rest of the country. It extends into ways that you'll never realize, not only your own family budget. If you've bought an average-priced car this past 12 months, $120 of the cost of that automobile had to go to pay hospital insurance for the workers who built it.

This is difficult to achieve. We were not able to pass hospital cost containment legislation last year, but I believe that we'll succeed this year with your help.

When I was running for President in 1976, we had a Federal deficit of more than $66 billion. I think in times of adequate prosperity, which we are enjoying now, that the Federal budget deficit should be balanced. We've already cut this deficit more than half, and I'll continue to work with the Congress with that goal in mind.

I might add that we also have a very serious problem that's not yet resolved, concerning energy supplies for our country in the future. I doubt that the Congress of the United States has ever tackled a more difficult, complicated, and politically divisive piece of legislation. In the final stages of this debate and congressional action, which unfortunately lasted almost 18 months, almost every key vote between the conference committees was decided with one Senator or one Member of the House of Representatives finally being persuaded to vote.

We achieved about 60 percent of what I originally proposed to the Congress almost exactly 2 years ago. We've got a long way to go. We do indeed have an energy crisis. Many Americans still believe that it does not exist, that they suffer from

higher fuel costs because there's some sort of collusion between the Federal Government and the oil companies designed to rip off the American family. This is not the case.

There is a dwindling supply of energy sources. The prices are going to rise in the future no matter who is President, no matter which party occupies the administration in Washington, no matter what we do. But Americans are going to have to conserve energy. We're going to have to shift toward more plentiful supplies of fossil fuels like coal, and we are also going to have to open up the tremendous reservoir of technical ability and innovation and commitment of the American public and the free enterprise system to find adequate sources of energy from replenishable supplies like solar energy.

As you know, we presently have a very serious problem with one of the atomic powerplants on Three Mile Island in Pennsylvania. I've just had word from that site that the situation is still stable and slowly improving. But many people in that region have been severely frightened, and the crisis is not yet over.

I think the result of this will be, perhaps, to remind the American people that energy sources are doubtful. In the near future, we will have to continue to rely not only on coal but on nuclear power. And we will also have a joint responsibility— the private enterprise system and government at all levels and private citizens—to ensure that atomic plants that are presently in existence or now being constructed will indeed be even safer than we have thought them in the past. And this particular incident, I believe, will give us a knowledge and a renewed concern that will lead to improved safety precautions.

In the near future, I will be going to Three Mile Island to learn personally about the situation there, so that I, as President, can better represent you when plans for the future use of this source of power is continued.

Let me say one other thing, and I'd like to close.

Our Nation is one that's been tested successfully. I think we have the admiration of many other people in the world.

The Democratic Party, to me, is a precious possession in my own political life. I've been inspired by its leaders. Our principles have never changed. We've always been in the forefront of exploring new ways to give people a freer life, a more independent life, a more democratic life, enhanced civil rights, increased prospects for peace, and to raise the standards of equity and fairness and basic human rights not only in our own country but throughout the world.

We have a lot to make us thankful. And I believe that if we harness our own efforts together in the future, we can be successful in resolving these very serious problems that still face our Nation—not with fear or timidity or trepidation or concern, not yielding to the temptations to be divisive, nor to try to cast blame on one another, but with a sure sense that with the confidence that our Nation gives us to deserve, and with the boldness that's always exemplified Americans' willingness or eagerness to meet difficult challenges, we together, as partners, can set an example for the rest of the world and make the greatest nation on Earth, the United States of America, even greater.

Thank you very much. God bless all of you.

NOTE: The President spoke at 8:25 p.m. in the East Hall of the Milwaukee Exposition Convention Center and Arena. In his opening remarks, he referred to Michael M. Bleicher, chairman of the Wisconsin Democratic Party.

Middletown, Pennsylvania

Remarks to Reporters Following a Visit to the Three Mile Island Nuclear Facility.
April 1, 1979

My primary concern in coming here this afternoon has been to learn as much as I possibly can, as President, about the problems at the Three Mile Island nuclear powerplant and to assure the people of this region that everything possible is being done and will be done to cope with these problems, both at the reactor and in the contingency planning for all eventualities that might occur in the future.

I want to commend Governor Thornburgh and other State and local officials for their leadership. And I would like to express my personal admiration and appreciation for the citizens of this area who, under the most difficult circumstances, have behaved in a calm and a responsible manner.

I would also like to express my thanks and admiration for the civilian and government personnel who continue to devote themselves without reservation to solving the problems at the reactor site.

The working relation among State, local, Federal, and private personnel has been excellent. And it's also been productive.

The primary and overriding concern for all of us is the health and the safety of the people of this entire area. As I've said before, if we make an error, all of us want to err on the side of extra precautions and extra safety.

I've learned that the radiation levels are being very carefully monitored throughout the area, and any trend toward higher levels would immediately be reported to me and to Governor Thornburgh and others. And every effort will be made to keep those radiation levels down to the present state, which is quite safe for all concerned.

The challenge in the future will be to cool down the reactor core itself to a safe level. And at the present time, all those who are involved here, who are highly qualified, tell me that the reactor core is indeed stable.

However, within the next few days, important decisions will be made on how to bring the reactor down to a cold and stable state. As always, in that transition period, careful preparations are being made, every eventuality is being assessed, and, above all, the health and safety of people involved will be paramount.

I would like to say to the people who live around the Three Mile Island plant that if it does become necessary, your Governor, Governor Thornburgh, will ask you and others in this area to take appropriate action to ensure your safety. If he does, I want to urge that these instructions be carried out calmly and exactly, as they have been in the past few days.

This will not indicate that danger is high. It will indicate that a change is being made in the operation of the cooling water system to permanently correct the present state of the reactor, and it's strictly a precautionary measure.

It's too early yet to make judgments about the lessons to be learned from this nuclear incident. Once the job of satisfactorily dealing with the present circumstances is completed, then there will be a thorough inquiry into the original causes and, obviously, into the events that have occurred since the incident, and additional safety precautions will undoubtedly be evolved. Perhaps some design changes will be implemented to make sure that there is no recurrence of this incident or one similar to it.

We will also do everything possible—

I will be personally responsible for thoroughly informing the American people about this particular incident and the status of nuclear safety in the future.

I intend to make sure that the investigation is conducted, is conducted thoroughly, and the results are made public.

And now, I would like to have the honor of introducing a man who has done a superlative job in coordinating this entire effort. And because of the trust of the American people in him, and particularly those who live in this region, potential panic and disturbance has been minimized.

And I again want to congratulate you, Governor Thornburgh, and thank you on behalf of our country for doing such a superb job.

Thank you very much.

NOTE: The President spoke at 3 p.m. at the Middletown Townhall.

Earlier in the day, the President left the White House and went by helicopter to the Air National Guard Facility in Middletown, where he was met by Gov. Richard Thornburgh, who accompanied the President throughout his visit. In the flight planning room at the facility, the President was briefed by Harold Denton, Director, Office of Nuclear Reactor Regulation, Nuclear Regulatory Commission.

Following the briefing, the President went to the Three Mile Island facility for an inspection tour of the control room. He then returned to the White House.

United States Ambassador to Liberia

Nomination of Robert P. Smith. April 2, 1979

The President today announced that he will nominate Robert P. Smith, of McLean, Va., to be Ambassador Extraordinary and Plenipotentiary of the United States to Liberia. He would replace W. Beverly Carter, Jr., who has been transferred to a new position as head of the State Department's Office of Liaison with State and Local Governments.

Smith was born March 5, 1929, in Joplin, Mo. He received a B.A. in 1954 and an M.A. in 1955 from Texas Christian University. He served in the U.S. Marine Corps from 1946 to 1949 and 1950 to 1952.

Smith joined the Foreign Service in 1955 and served as an information specialist in the News Division, consular officer in Lahore, and economic, then political officer in Beirut. In 1961–62 he took African area studies at Northwestern University under Foreign Service Institute auspices.

From 1962 to 1965, Smith was principal officer in Enugu. From 1965 to 1969, he was officer in charge of Ghanian affairs at the Bureau of African Affairs, and in 1969–70 he attended the National War College.

From 1970 to 1974, Smith was Deputy Chief of Mission in Pretoria. From 1974 to 1976, he was Ambassador to Malta. Since 1976 he has been Ambassador to Ghana.

Swing was born September 11, 1934, in Lexington, N.C. He received a B.A. from Catawba College in 1956 and an M.Div. from Yale University in 1960.

In 1961 Swing was a schoolteacher in Germany, and from 1961 to 1963, he was associate director of the Council on Religion in Independent Schools in New York. He joined the Foreign Service in 1963 and took consular and African area studies at the Foreign Service Institute.

From 1964 to 1966, Swing was vice consul in Port Elizabeth, and from 1966 to 1967, he was an international economist at the State Department. From 1968 to 1972, he was head of the visa section, then chief of the consular section, in Hamburg.

Swing was desk officer for the Federal Republic of Germany at the State Department from 1972 to 1974. From 1974 to 1976, he was Deputy Chief of Mission in Bangui.

In 1976–77 Swing was a fellow at the Harvard University Center for International Affairs. Since 1977 he has been Alternate Director of the Office of Central African Affairs at the State Department.

United States Ambassador to the People's Republic of the Congo

Nomination of William L. Swing.
April 2, 1979

The President today announced that he will nominate William L. Swing, of Lexington, N.C., to be Ambassador Extraordinary and Plenipotentiary of the United States to the People's Republic of the Congo. He would be the first Ambassador to the People's Republic of the Congo since our resumption of diplomatic relations in June 1977.

Days of Remembrance of Victims of the Holocaust, April 28 and 29, 1979

Proclamation 4652.   April 2, 1979

By the President of the United States of America

A Proclamation

Thirty-four years ago today the United States Armed Forces liberated the Dachau concentration camp during the closing days of World War II in Europe. Words alone cannot convey the shock and horror that accompanied this tangible evidence of the Nazi regime's systematic program of genocide.

Dachau and other death-centers like Buchenwald, Auschwitz and Treblinka were the means by which the Nazi regime murdered six million Jewish people and millions of other victims in a planned program of extermination. These crimes have few if any equals in history. Their legacy left deep moral scars on all humankind. No one who participated in the liberation of these camps or who has studied their history can ever forget—least of all the quarter-of-a-million survivors who found a home and built a new life in this country after the war.

During my recent trip to Israel, I visited Yad Vashem, the Israeli memorial to the victims of the Holocaust. I vowed then, and I repeat now, that the world must never permit such events ever to occur again.

We must never forget these crimes against humanity. We must study and understand the record of the Holocaust. From this, we must learn to remain eternally vigilant against all tyranny and oppression. We must rededicate ourselves to the principle of equality and justice for all peoples, remembering the terrible fruits of bigotry and hatred.

A joint resolution of the Congress (H.J. Res. 1014) approved September 18, 1978, authorized and requested the President to issue a proclamation designating April 28 and 29, 1979, as "Days of Remembrance of Victims of the Holocaust."

Now, THEREFORE, I, JIMMY CARTER, President of the United States of America, do hereby designate April 28 and April 29, 1979, as "Days of Remembrance of Victims of the Holocaust." I ask the people of the United States to observe this solemn anniversary of the liberation of Dachau

with appropriate study, prayers and commemoration as a tribute to the spirit of freedom, justice and compassion which Americans fought to preserve.

On the recommendation of the President's Commission on the Holocaust, I also ask the people of the United States to note International Holocaust Commemoration Day of April 24, 1979.

IN WITNESS WHEREOF, I have hereunto set my hand this second day of April, in the year of our Lord nineteen hundred seventy-nine, and of the Independence of the United States of America the two hundred and third.

JIMMY CARTER

[Filed with the Office of the Federal Register, 11:58 a.m., April 2, 1979]

National Privacy Policy

Message to the Congress on Proposals To Protect the Privacy of Individuals. April 2, 1979

To the Congress of the United States:

I am announcing today sweeping proposals to protect the privacy of individuals.

"The right to be let alone," Justice Brandeis wrote 60 years ago, "is the right most valued by civilized men." That right is built into our Constitution, which forbids unwarranted searches of citizens and their homes. At the time the Constitution was written—a time when private conversations were conducted face-to-face or through the mail and most private records were kept at home—those protections seemed adequate.

The growth of society and technology has changed all that. We confront threats to privacy undreamed of 200 years ago. Private conversations are often conducted by telephone. Many personal records are held by institutions, such as banks and government agencies, and the Supreme Court has held that the individual has no constitutional rights over such records. Important judgments about people— such as the decision to extend credit or write an insurance policy—are often made by strangers, on the basis of recorded data.

Whenever we take out a loan, apply for insurance, receive treatment at a hospital, obtain government assistance, or pay our taxes, we add to the store of recorded information about our lives. That store is growing exponentially: in 1940, for example, 1.2 billion checks were written—in 1970 it was 7.2 billion. Personal information on millions of Americans is being flashed across the nation from computer to computer.

These changes are not the product of any plan to invade our privacy. They have developed naturally with the growth of our economy, the expansion of public and private institutions, the mobility of our citizens and the invention of computers and telecommunications systems.

Modern information systems are essential to our economy. They contribute to the comfort and convenience of our lives. But they can be misused to create a dangerously intrusive society.

Our challenge is to provide privacy safeguards that respond to these social changes without disrupting the essential flow of information.

Much has already been done. Laws are in place to restrict wiretapping. Last year Congress strengthened those protections by legislating restrictions on national security wiretaps. The Privacy Act of 1974 set rules for Federal agencies' record keeping. The Fair Credit Reporting Act and related Acts gave consumers the right to know information about themselves contained in the records of credit-reporting bureaus. The Family Educational Rights and Privacy Act gave students the right to see personal records held by educational institutions. Last year, the Congress passed the Financial Privacy Act, placing controls on Federal agencies' access to bank records.

These protections are a good beginning, but they were adopted piecemeal and have limited scope. It is time to establish a broad, national privacy policy to protect individual rights in the information age, as recommended by the Privacy Protection Study Commission.

I propose a privacy policy based on two principles:

• *Fair Information Practices.* Standards must be provided for handling sensitive, personal records. Individuals should be told what kind of information is being collected about them, how it will be used, and to whom it will be disclosed. They should be able to see and obtain a copy of the records and correct any errors. They should be told the basis for an adverse decision that may be based on personal data. And they should be able to prevent improper access to the records.

• *Limits on the Government.* Government access to and use of personal information must be limited and supervised so that power over information cannot be used to threaten our liberties.

The policy I am proposing will not disrupt the flow of information needed for legitimate business operations. Businesses gain by establishing good record-keeping systems and by keeping the trust of their customers and employees.

Nor will this policy prevent government agencies from collecting the information they need to enforce the laws. It will strengthen, not impede, the ability of reporters to cover the news. It will not impose heavy costs, and it will not create any new regulatory structures. Instead, it will establish a framework for private and government activity to prevent privacy abuses.

The responsibility for implementing this policy should be shared by the Federal government, by state and local governments, and by private institutions. I propose that the Federal government concentrate on improving its own activities and on setting standards for non-Federal record systems that contain particularly sensitive data and either involve Federal funding or require nationwide, uniform rules. We are submitting three bills to Congress today to address these areas, and a fourth major proposal will follow soon.

State and local governments should build on this base to ensure that their own record systems are properly protected. In addition, a key element of the policy I am proposing is voluntary action by private businesses and organizations.

I. Fair Information Practices

To establish privacy safeguards for key record systems, I have these proposals:

MEDICAL RECORDS

The "Privacy of Medical Information Act" is being submitted to you today. It establishes privacy protections for information maintained by almost all medical institutions. The Act will give individuals the right to see their own medical records. If direct access may harm the patient, the Act provides that access may be provided through an intermediary. This legislation allows the individual to ensure that the information maintained as part of his medical care relationship is accurate, timely, and relevant to that care. Such accuracy is of increasing importance because medical information is used to af-

fect employment and collection of insurance and other social benefits.

The Act also limits the disclosure of medical information, and makes it illegal to collect medical information under false pretenses. The legislation allows disclosure when it is needed for medical care and other legitimate purposes, such as verifying insurance claims, and for research and epidemiological studies. In such cases, redisclosure is restricted.

FINANCIAL RECORDS

The Administration will soon submit the "Fair Financial Information Practices Act." This bill will expand the laws on consumer credit and banking records to provide full fair information protections. It will ensure that consumers are informed about firms' record keeping practices and thereby help them decide which firm to patronize. Specific requirements will be tailored to fit the varying information practices of the industries.

The bill will also provide, for the first time, national privacy standards for insurance records. This is a major step forward into an area where individuals have few such protections. The bill is not intended to change the existing pattern of regulating insurance at the state level, and it allows state regulators to oversee compliance. However, it will minimize the danger that a welter of differing state privacy standards will confuse the public and impose heavy costs on the insurance industry.

In addition, this bill will restrict disclosure of data from electronic funds transfer (EFT) systems. Although the emergence of EFT is relatively recent, its potential impact on our lives is enormous. Americans are benefitting from EFT in a variety of ways: automatic deposit of a paycheck in a bank account; automatic payment of a mortgage installment; cash dispensing machines; and so on. EFT terminals have the potential to supplant cash, checks and credit cards in a broad range of consumer transactions, from supermarket purchases to auto rentals. Such systems are efficient, but they pose major privacy problems. Not only do they contain extensive personal data on individuals, but they can be used to keep track of people's movements and activities. This legislation will erect safeguards against misuse of these systems while allowing flexibility for commercial and technological innovation.

RESEARCH RECORDS

Federally-supported research collection is vital for improved medical care, for cost-effective regulations, for economic analysis, and for many other purposes. In most cases, the information collected for these purposes is submitted voluntarily, is quite personal, and is collected on an express or implied pledge of confidentiality. That pledge is often essential to obtain individuals' cooperation in providing the information and ensuring its accuracy and completeness. However, in most cases there is no legal basis at present to guarantee the promise of confidentiality.

The "Privacy of Research Records Act" is being submitted today. This bill will ensure that personal information collected or maintained for a research purpose may not be used or disclosed in individually identifiable form for an action that adversely affects the individual.

We are also developing separate legislation to reduce the amount of information government collects in the first place through improved oversight and through carefully controlled sharing arrangements.

OTHER RECORD SYSTEMS

The Privacy Commission recommended against Federal legislation on employment records and proposed instead that employers be asked to establish voluntary policies to protect their employees' privacy. I agree.

Many employers are already adopting the standards established by the Commission. Business groups, including the Business Roundtable, the Chamber of Commerce, and the National Association of Manufacturers, are encouraging such voluntary action. I urge other employers to take similar action, and I have instructed the Secretary of Labor to work with employer and employee groups in the implementation of these standards.

The Commission did urge one piece of legislation in the employment area— limits on the use of lie detectors in private employment. Such legislation already has been introduced in this Congress, and I urge you to proceed favorably with it.

I also urge commercial credit grantors and reporting services to adopt voluntary fair information standards, to avoid any need for Federal legislation in this area.

It is critical that the privacy of those who receive public assistance and social services be adequately protected. I call upon the states to move forward with legislation to provide such protections, consistent with the Privacy Commission's recommendations and the need to prevent fraud in these programs. I have instructed the Secretary of Health, Education and Welfare to develop minimum privacy standards for these Federally funded programs.

I also urge the states to act on other state and local record systems, particularly those of criminal justice agencies.

II. FEDERAL GOVERNMENT ACTIVITIES

I am also announcing measures to strengthen safeguards on Federal investigations and record-keeping.

The bills on medical and financial records will ensure that the government obtains access to such records only for legitimate purposes. In most cases, the individual will be notified and given an opportunity to contest such access. I have these additional proposals:

GOVERNMENT ACCESS TO NEWS MEDIA
FILES

The Supreme Court's decision last year in *Zurcher* v. *Stanford Daily* poses dangers to the effective functioning of our free press. I announced in December that we would develop legislation to protect First Amendment activities from unnecessarily intrusive searches while preserving legitimate law enforcement interests. Although regulations already restrict Federal officers' investigation of the news media, the problems raised by the *Stanford Daily* case require new, stringent safeguards against Federal, state and local governmental intrusion into First Amendment activities.

I am submitting this legislation today. It will restrict police searches for documentary materials held by the press and by others involved in the dissemination of information to the public. With limited exceptions, the bill will prohibit a search for or seizure of "work product"—such as notes, interview files and film. For documents which do not constitute work product, the bill requires that the police first obtain a subpoena rather than a search warrant. This ensures that police will not rummage through files of people preparing materials for publication and that those subject to the subpoena have the opportunity to contest the government's need for the information.

WIRETAPPING

The privacy of personal communication is an important civil liberty. Americans are entitled to rely on that privacy, except where a legitimate and urgent law enforcement or national security purpose creates an overriding need. The fact that the person who is the target of surveillance is usually unaware of it argues for the tightest controls and for public accountability for the officials who authorize surveillance.

Title III of the Omnibus Crime Control and Safe Streets Act of 1968 governs the use of electronic surveillance of wire and oral communications except in matters involving foreign intelligence and counterintelligence. The National Commission for the Review of Federal and State Laws Relating to Wiretapping and Electronic Surveillance has studied the experience under Title III and has issued findings and recommendations.

I am transmitting to Congress today a letter which sets forth my detailed views concerning those recommendations. In general I endorse the recommended adjustments which would strengthen Title III's protections for individual privacy. I do not, however, support the recommendation to amend the law to allow Federal officials below the rank of Assistant Attorney General to apply to the courts for wiretaps. Such a change would diminish accountability and increase the danger of misuse. Also, I am not convinced that the list of criminal statutes for which electronic surveillance orders may be obtained should be expanded. I have asked the Attorney General to consult with the Secretary of the Treasury and with the Congress on those Commission recommendations.

The Federal Government holds almost four billion records on individuals, most of them stored in thousands of computers. Federally-funded projects have substantial additional files. This information is needed to run the social security system, collect taxes, conduct research, measure the economy, and for hundreds of other important purposes. Modern technology, however, makes it possible to turn this store into a dangerous surveillance system. Reasonable restrictions are needed on the collection and use of this information.

The Privacy Act of 1974 established privacy safeguards for Federal records. It prevents agencies from collecting certain kinds of information, such as information about political beliefs; requires public notice whenever a new data system is established; gives individuals the right to see and correct their records; and limits disclosure of personal information.

While the Privacy Act is working reasonably well and is too new to decide on major revisions, I have ordered a number of administrative actions to improve its operation.

We are issuing today final guidelines for Federal agencies on the use of "matching programs." These programs compare computerized lists of individuals to detect fraud or other abuses. Such programs are making an important contribution to reducing abuse of Federal programs and are thereby saving taxpayers' money. However, safeguards are needed to protect the privacy of the innocent and to ensure that the use of "matching" is properly limited. The guidelines, which were developed with public participation, will ensure that these programs are conducted:

- only after the public has been notified and given the opportunity to identify privacy problems;
- with tight safeguards on access to the data and on disclosure of the names of suspects identified by matching;
- only when there are no cost-effective, alternative means of identifying violators.

I have also directed that action be taken to:

- extend Privacy Act protections to certain data systems operated by recipients of Federal grants;
- strengthen administration of the "routine use" provision of the Privacy Act, which governs disclosures of personal information by Federal agencies;
- ensure that each Federal agency has an office responsible for privacy issues raised by the agency's activities;
- improve the selection and training of the system managers required by the Privacy Act;
- improve oversight of new Federal information systems at an early state in the planning process; and
- limit the amount of information the government requires private groups and individuals to report.

The Office of Management and Budget, as the unit responsible for overseeing Federal agency record-keeping, will implement these actions. I have assigned the Commerce Department's National Telecommunications and Information Administration to be the lead agency on other privacy matters and to work with Congress on the continuing development of privacy policy.

The enormous increase in personal data records in the U.S. has been matched in other advanced countries. Throughout Western Europe, as well as in Canada, Australia, and Japan, records of personal data have grown at explosive rates. Our concerns about privacy are shared by many other governments.

International information flows, however, are increasingly important to the world's economy. We are, therefore, working with other governments in several international organizations to develop principles to protect personal data crossing international borders and to harmonize each country's rules to avoid needless disruption of international communications. Enactment of the proposals I have outlined will help speed this process by assuring other countries that the U.S. is committed to the protection of personal data.

Privacy is a permanent public issue. Its preservation requires constant attention to social and technological changes, and those changes demand action now.

I ask the Congress and the public to join me in establishing a comprehensive framework of reasonable privacy protections. Together we can preserve the right to privacy in the information age.

JIMMY CARTER

The White House,
    April 2, 1979.

Wiretapping and Electronic Surveillance

Message to the Congress Reporting on Recommendations of the National Commission for the Review of Federal and State Laws. April 2, 1979

To the Congress of the United States:

In accordance with Section 6(b) of the Federal Advisory Committee Act (PL 92–463), I am pleased to report to the Congress my views concerning the recommendations contained in the "Report of the National Commission For The Review of Federal and State Laws Relating to Wiretapping and Electronic Surveillance."

The Commission was charged by the Congress to study and evaluate the effectiveness of Title III of the Omnibus Crime Control and Safe Streets Act of 1968 (PL 90–351; 18 U.S.C. Sec. 2510–2520) which governs the use of electronic surveillance of wire and oral communications, except in matters involving foreign intelligence and counterintelligence.

From my viewpoint, the most significant findings of the Commission in carrying out this Congressional mandate are that the provisions of Title III are an indispensable aid to law enforcement, particularly in obtaining evidence of offenses committed by organized criminals; that the procedural requirements of Title III have effectively minimized the invasion of individual privacy in electronic surveillance investigations by law enforcement officers; and that Title III has reduced the incidence of illegal interceptions through its controls on the manufacture, sale, and advertising of wiretapping devices and its criminal sanctions for their use.

It is particularly reassuring to note the Commission's finding that the carefully designed Title III controls and procedures have effectively minimized the invasion of individual privacy in electronic surveillance investigations by law enforcement officers, and that there were no cases among the many studied by the Commission in which law enforcement authorities sought a Title III court order for an apparently corrupt purpose. From the very inception of its use in criminal cases, the Department of Justice has developed a highly centralized review system for the approval of Title III authorization requests as well as detailed instructions governing execution of court orders designed to protect the substantive rights of both innocent persons and those under investigation. In this connection I am pleased to note the Commission's finding that Federal officials responsible for administering wiretap application review procedures have shown a commendable concern for adhering to the requirements of Title III.

We must always bear in mind that Title III both permits law enforcement officials to fight crime while it protects citizens against unjustified invasions of privacy. It is clearly a criminal statute designed both to prohibit private citizens from conducting illegal interceptions and to regulate governmental conduct by prohibiting law enforcement officials from violating or disregarding specific procedures for conducting wiretaps.

The Commission has made a number of findings and recommendations which it believes will both improve the effectiveness of the use of court-authorized electronic surveillance in criminal investigations and will also strengthen enforcement of Title III strictures against illegal electronic surveillance. In general, I support the objectives of most of these proposals. I am, however, strongly opposed to a few and believe others to be unnecessary.

I support the Commission's recommendation that misdemeanor and civil penalties should be included in Title III for the prosecution and punishment of nonprofessional electronic eavesdroppers. At present the only sanction applicable to the nonprofessional who engages in electronic surveillance is the felony provision of 18 U.S.C. Sec. 2511. In many instances it is simply too severe a sanction for the offense committed and has resulted in considerable judicial distaste for prosecutions brought under Section 2511

against nonprofessionals. Such persons frequently indicate a desire not to contest such charges, yet still proceed with a contested trial in the absence of the alternative of pleading guilty to a misdemeanor.

The Commission's recommendation that Title III should be amended to explicitly allow the disclosure of illegal interceptions when relevant in a prosecution for illegal interceptions is sound. I also agree with the Commission that judges should retain the discretion to deny admission of the evidence where relevance is outweighed by undue loss of privacy to the victim. While it is often possible to pursue such a prosecution without playing any of the illegal tapes, situations occasionally arise where a portion of such a tape is critical to the Government's case. A violator should not escape punishment by hiding behind the exclusionary rule embodied in 18 U.S.C. Sec. 2515, which appears on its face to allow him to move to have such evidence excluded from his trial.

In addition, I support those Commission proposals recommending that a court order for electronic surveillance expressly authorize entry upon a private place or premises to install an eavesdropping device if such entry is necessary to execute the warrant and that the Congress undertake studies of encroachments on individual privacy by new forms of the art, such as computer technology. Similarly, periodic comprehensive studies and reviews of the operations of Title III would help to determine their continuing effectiveness in law enforcement and in stemming illegal surveillance. Congressional studies also are needed to determine whether some form of notice should be required to assure that customers whose conversations and actions are monitored in the ordinary course of a business, have given their implied consent based upon some reasonable public understanding of the need for such monitoring.

On the other hand, I am strenuously opposed to those proposals of the Commission which recommend that Title III be amended to authorize the Attorney General to designate, by name, any United States Attorney or any Federal Strike Force Chief to authorize applications for court-ordered wiretapping, and that the Department of Justice consider some decentralization and streamlining of procedures for the review and approval of such applications by greater delegation of screening requests and decision-making responsibility to United States Attorneys or Federal Strike Force Chiefs.

The statute (18 U.S.C. Sec. 2516) permits the Attorney General to delegate application authorization to any Assistant Attorney General and the Attorney General has delegated this authority to specified Assistant Attorneys General. As the legislative history of this statute indicates, this provision centralizes in a publicly responsible official subject to the political process the formulation of law enforcement policy on the use of electronic surveillance techniques. It thus avoids the possibility that divergent practices might develop and insures that if abuses occur the lines of responsibility will lead to an identifiable person subject to the political process. Any further delegation of this authority would greatly attenuate this centralized control and responsibility which the Congress determined was essential to its use. Further delegation of such authority to the field level would also likely result in a greater number of application requests and court orders. While under existing procedures application requests are currently reviewed by United States Attorneys and Federal Strike Force Chiefs in the field, the final review and approval authority must re-

main the responsibility of the Assistant Attorneys General designated by the Attorney General to approve such applications.

The Commission has recommended that the Congress consider expanding the list of Federal crimes for which electronic surveillance orders may be obtained to include such crimes as customs offenses, manufacture, sale, and interstate shipment of illegal firearms, and fencing of stolen goods affecting interstate commerce. In view of the expression of Congressional concern respecting the limitation of Federal criminal jurisdiction which was demonstrated by the extensive debate during formulation of this provision (18 U.S.C. Sec. 2516) on the floor of the Congress, I believe that a more up-to-date examination of the experiences of the Treasury and Justice Departments in investigating these crimes should be made before the recommendation of the Commission is either endorsed or rejected. I have asked the Attorney General to consult with the Secretary of Treasury on this matter.

Finally, although I support the substance of certain other of the Commission's important proposals, I do not believe that any remedial legislation in this area is necessary since the essence of these recommendations has been implemented by administrative controls adopted by the Department of Justice as a result of its experience with Title III or in response to court decisions interpreting the statute. Recommendations in this area include amending Title III to require an additional showing of facts in order to obtain an extension of a Title III court order and that the explanation of exhaustion of alternative investigative techniques include consideration of the case under investigation insofar as practicable.

The Commission's final Report and its five volumes of supporting materials constitute the most exhaustive compilation of information on the subject of wiretapping and electronic surveillance ever assembled. The record of the Commission stands as an enduring monument to the difficult and conscientious work of its distinguished members and dedicated staff. While its conclusions may be subject to differing degrees of public acceptance, there can be no doubt that the Commission has rendered outstanding service to the American public by its thorough and sensitive exposition of the conflicting demands of law enforcement and individual privacy which inhere in the use of court-authorized electronic eavesdropping.

The Commission's Report has reaffirmed my belief that the Federal Government has used this extraordinarily effective investigative technique in the investigation of serious crimes in a highly responsible and circumscribed manner, and that so used, it has preserved and will continue to preserve the delicate balance that must be maintained between the needs of law enforcement and the demands of personal privacy.

JIMMY CARTER

The White House,
April 2, 1979.

Egyptian-Israeli Peace Treaty

Letter to Six Congressional Committee Chairmen on Legislation To Implement the Treaty.   April 2, 1979

I am writing to you to urge your immediate attention to the authorizing legislation and the 1979 supplemental appropriations request I will soon be transmitting to implement the Peace Treaty between Israel and Egypt. This supplemental request requires urgent enactment prior to the likely consideration of other pending supplementals in order to avoid delays which could threaten timely implementation of the Treaty.

The legislation to be transmitted will provide $4.8 billion in special financial aid to the two countries over the next three years. This will be in addition to ongoing regular programs of military and economic assistance. Because much of the military financing will take the form of guaranteed loans, requiring only fractional appropriations, budget authority for the assistance package will be $1.47 billion. Estimated budget outlays over the next four years will total $1.1 billion, with $350 million occurring in 1979 and $315 million in 1980.

Within the $4.8 billion total for special aid, I am proposing that $3 billion be made available to Israel in two components.

—The first provides $800 million in grants to cover the direct costs of relocating two Israeli airbases now located on territory to be returned to Egypt.

—The second provides $2.2 billion in foreign military sales credit financing to Israel. These funds will finance other Israeli relocation costs and some upgrading of force structure consistent with the new territorial arrangements.

For Egypt, I am also proposing a two part aid package totalling $1.8 billion.

—The larger component provides $1.5 billion in military sales credit financing on the same terms offered to Israel. It will help Egypt maintain a modern well-equipped military force, and play a responsible role in promoting stability and moderation in the region.

—In addition, I will propose to provide Egypt with $300 million of special economic aid loans under economic support fund authorities. These funds will help meet Egypt's large development needs and help satisfy the expectations of the Egyptian people for a better life.

As you begin your consideration of these proposals, I urge you to give particular attention to three elements which I can personally assure you are critical.

—First, the proposed assistance is evenhanded. The financing package I will request reflects a careful assessment of the near-term burdens of the treaty balanced against the military and economic circumstances of each country. Our future influence in the Middle East depends on the perception by all affected countries that we do not unfairly support any one country. Alteration of the proposed amounts or terms of assistance to either Israel or Egypt could impair this perception.

—Second, the amounts of aid proposed and the terms offered are the result of a careful balancing of foreign policy needs and fiscal policy constraints. Thus, while substantial U.S. assistance is required to assure successful implementation of the Treaty, I have made every effort to limit United States funding in light of our current budgetary constraints and my desire to avoid imposing any unnecessary burden on the U.S. taxpayer.

—Third, the proposed United States assistance is a coherent, interrelated package which requires urgent congressional action. Piecemeal treatment would threaten both evenhandedness and the careful balance between foreign policy and budget requirements. Delay in congressional action on the legislation could critically disrupt the carefully negotiated timing for Treaty implementation.

I regard this initiative as the most important foreign affairs proposal currently before the Congress. I am sure I can count

on your support for favorable and prompt congressional action.

Sincerely,

JIMMY CARTER

NOTE: This is the text of identical letters addressed to Frank Church, chairman of the Senate Foreign Relations Committee, Edmund S. Muskie, chairman of the Senate Budget Committee, Warren G. Magnuson, chairman of the Senate Appropriations Committee, Clement J. Zablocki, chairman of the House Foreign Affairs Committee, Robert N. Giaimo, chairman of the House Budget Committee, and Jamie L. Whitten, chairman of the House Appropriations Committee.

Alaska Natural Gas Transportation System

Message to the Congress Transmitting Reorganization Plan No. 1 of 1979.
April 2, 1979

To the Congress of the United States:

I am submitting to you today Reorganization Plan No. 1 of 1979 to create the Office of Federal Inspector for the Alaska Natural Gas Transportation System and establish the position of Federal Inspector. Creation of this Office and the transfer of appropriate Federal enforcement authority and responsibility is consistent with my September 1977 *Decision and Report to the Congress on the Alaska Natural Gas Transportation `System.* This decision was approved by the Congress November 2, 1977.

The Alaska Gas Transportation System is a 4,748-mile pipeline to be constructed in partnership with Canada. Canada completed legislation enacting a similar transfer last year and has already appointed an official to coordinate its activities prior to and during pipeline construction. The Northwest Alaska Pipeline Company has been selected to construct the pipeline, with completion scheduled in late 1984. Estimated construction costs are $10–$15 billion, to be financed by private investment.

Natural gas is among the Nation's most valuable fuels. It is in the national interest to bring Alaskan gas reserves to market at the lowest possible price for consumers. Construction of a gas pipeline from the Prudhoe Bay reserves in Alaska through Canada to points in the West and Midwest United States will provide a system which will deliver more Alaskan natural gas at less cost to a greater number of Americans than any alternative transportation system. Every effort must be made to ensure timely completion of the pipeline at the lowest possible cost consistent with Federal regulatory policies.

As a result of our experience in construction of the Trans-Alaska Oil Pipeline, we recognize the need for the Federal government to be in a strong position to manage its own role in this project through prompt, coordinated decision-making in pre-construction approval functions and in enforcing the terms and conditions of the permits, certificates, leases, and other authorizations to be issued by various Federal agencies. We must avoid duplicating the delays and cost escalations experienced in the construction of the Trans-Alaska Pipeline System. The Plan I am submitting would establish clear responsibility for the efficient functioning of Federal enforcement activities by assigning the Federal Inspector authority to carry out these responsibilities.

The Alaska Natural Gas Transportation Act of 1976 only provided for monitoring the construction of the pipeline. The Plan transfers to the Federal Inspector the authority to supervise the enforcement of terms and conditions of the permits and other authorizations, including those to be issued by the Departments of Agriculture, Interior, Transportation, and Treasury, and the Environmental Protection Agency, the Federal Energy Regulatory Commission, and the U.S. Army Corps of Engineers. The Plan provides for the Federal Inspector to coordinate other Federal activities directly related to the pipeline project. Federal agencies retain their authority to issue permits and related authorizations, but enforcement of the terms and conditions of these authorizations is transferred to the Federal Inspector. Transfer of enforcement authority from Federal agencies to the Federal Inspector is limited in scope to their participation in this project and in duration to the pre-construction, construction, and initial operation phases of the project.

The *Decision and Report* to the Congress recommended an Executive Policy Board with policy-making and supervisory authority over the Federal Inspector. I plan to sign an Executive Order upon approval of this Plan by the Congress which will create an Executive Policy Board which will be only advisory, but which will enhance communication and coordination among Federal agencies and with the Federal Inspector. The Plan modifies the *Decision and Report* in that regard. The Federal Inspector will use the policies and procedures of the agencies involved in exercising the transferred enforcement responsibilities to the maximum extent practicable. The Board provides the opportunity for agencies to contribute to the policy deliberations of the Inspector and exercises an oversight role to insure that pipeline activities are carried on within existing regulatory policy. The Board is required to review the budget of the Office of the Federal Inspector and periodically report to me on the progress of construction and on major problems encountered. I am convinced that the Federal Inspector must have authority commensurate with his responsibilities.

Each of the provisions of this proposed reorganization would accomplish one or more of the purposes set forth in Section 901(a) of Title 5 of the United States Code. The appointment and compensation of the Federal Inspector is in accordance with the provisions of the Alaska Natural Gas Transportation Act of 1976, and the Reorganization Act of 1977. The provisions for appointment and pay in this Plan are necessary by reason of a reorganization made by the Plan. The rate of compensation is comparable to rates for similar positions within the Executive Branch. This reorganization will result in a reduction in the cost of construction for the pipeline system and ultimately in savings to American consumers. A small increase in cost to the Federal government will result from the creation of the Office of the Federal Inspector. The Plan requires that the Office and the position of Federal Inspector will be abolished upon the first anniversary date after the pipeline becomes operational.

JIMMY CARTER

The White House,
    April 2, 1979.

REORGANIZATION PLAN NO. 1 OF 1979

Prepared by the President and transmitted to the Senate and House of Representatives in Congress assembled, April 2, 1979, pursuant to the provisions of Chapter 9 of Title 5 of the United States Code.

OFFICE OF THE FEDERAL INSPECTOR FOR CONSTRUCTION OF THE ALASKA NATURAL GAS TRANSPORTATION SYSTEM

PART I.   OFFICE OF THE FEDERAL INSPECTOR AND TRANSFER OF FUNCTIONS

SECTION 101. *Establishment of the Office of Federal Inspector for the Alaska Natural Gas Transportation System*

(a) There is hereby established as an independent establishment in the executive branch, the Office of the Federal Inspector for the Alaska Natural Gas Transportation System (the "Office").

(b) The Office shall be headed by a Federal Inspector for the Alaska Natural Gas Transportation System (the "Federal Inspector") who shall be appointed by the President, by and with the advice and consent of the Senate, and shall be compensated at the rate now or hereafter prescribed by law for Level III of the Executive Schedule, and who shall serve at the pleasure of the President.

(c) Each Federal agency having statutory responsibilities over any aspect of the Alaska Natural Gas Transportation System shall appoint an Agency Authorized Officer to represent that authority on all matters pertaining to pre-construction, construction, and initial operation of the system.

SEC. 102. *Transfer of Functions to the Federal Inspector*

Subject to the provisions of Section 201, 202, and 203 of this Plan, all functions insofar as they relate to enforcement of Federal statutes or regulations and to enforcement of terms, conditions, and stipulations of grants, certificates, permits and other authorizations issued by Federal agencies with respect to pre-construction, construction, and initial operation of an "approved transportation system" for transport of Canadian natural gas and "Alaskan natural gas," as such terms are defined in the Alaska Natural Gas Transportation Act of 1976 (15 U.S.C. 719 *et seq.*), hereinafter called the "Act", are hereby transferred to the Federal Inspector. This transfer shall vest in the Federal Inspector exclusive responsibility for enforcement of all Federal statutes relevant in any manner to pre-construction, construction, and initial operation. With respect to each of the statutory authorities cited below, the transferred functions include all enforcement functions of the given agencies or their officials under the statutes as may be related to the enforcement of such terms, conditions, and stipulations, including but not limited to the specific sections of the statute cited. "Enforcement", for purposes of this transfer of functions, includes monitoring and any other compliance or oversight activities reasonably related to the enforcement process. These transferred functions include:

(a) Such enforcement functions of the Administrator or other appropriate official or entity in the Environmental Protection Agency related to compliance with: national pollutant discharge elimination system permits provided for in Section 402 of the Federal Water Pollution Control Act (33 U.S.C. 1342); spill prevention, containment and countermeasure plans in Section 311 of the Federal Water Pollution Control Act (33 U.S.C. 1321); review of the Corps of Engineers' dredged and fill material permits issued under Section 404 of the Federal Water Pollution Control Act (33 U.S.C. 1344); new source performance standards in Section 111 of the Clean Air Act, as amended by the Clean Air Act Amendments of 1977 (42 U.S.C. 7411); prevention of significant deterioration review and approval in Sections 160–169 of the Clean Air Act, as amended by the Clean Air Amendments of 1977 (42 U.S.C. 7470 *et seq.*); and the resource conservation and recovery permits issued under the Resource Conservation and Recovery Act of 1976 (42 U.S.C. 6901 *et seq.*);

(b) Such enforcement functions of the Secretary of the Army, the Chief of Engineers, or other appropriate officer or entity in the Corps of Engineers of the United States Army related to compliance with: dredged and fill material permits issued under Section 404 of the Federal Water Pollution Control Act (33 U.S.C. 1344); and permits for structures in navigable waters, issued under Section 10 of the Rivers and Harbors Appropriation Act of 1899 (33 U.S.C. 403);

(c) Such enforcement functions of the Secretary or other appropriate officer or entity in the Department of Transportation related to compliance with: the Natural Gas Pipeline Safety Act of 1968, as amended (49 U.S.C. 1671, *et seq.*) and the gas pipeline safety regulations issued thereunder; the Federal Aviation Act of 1958, as amended (49 U.S.C. 1301, *et seq.*) and authorizations and regulations issued thereunder; and permits for bridges across navigable waters, issued under Section 9 of the Rivers and Harbors Appropriation Act of 1899 (33 U.S.C. 401);

(d) Such enforcement functions of the Secretary or other appropriate officer or entity in the Department of Energy and such enforcement functions of the Commission, Commissioners, or other appropriate officer or entity in the Federal Energy Regulatory Commission related to compliance with: the certificates of public convenience and necessity, issued under Section 7 of the Natural Gas Act, as amended (15 U.S.C. 717f); and authorizations for importation of natural gas from Alberta as predeliveries of Alaskan gas issued under Section 3 of the Natural Gas Act, as amended (15 U.S.C. 717b);

(e) Such enforcement functions of the Secretary or other appropriate officer or entity in the Department of the Interior related to compliance with: grants of rights-of-way and temporary use permits for Federal land, issued under Section 28 of the Mineral Leasing Act of 1920 (30 U.S.C. 185); land use permits for temporary use of public lands and other associated land uses, issued under Sections 302, 501, and 503–511 of the Federal Land Policy and Management Act of 1976 (43 U.S.C. 1732, 1761, and 1763–1771); materials sales contracts under the Materials Act of 1947 (30 U.S.C. 601–603); rights-of-way across Indian lands, issued under the Rights of Way Through Indian Lands Act (25 U.S.C. 321, *et seq.*); removal permits issued under the Materials Act of 1947 (30 U.S.C. 601–603); approval to cross national wildlife refuges, National Wildlife Refuge System Administration Act of 1966 (16 U.S.C. 668dd–668jj) and the Upper Mississippi River Wildlife and Fish Refuge Act (16 U.S.C. 721–731); wildlife consultation in the Fish and Wildlife Coordination Act (16 U.S.C. 661 *et seq.*); protection of certain birds in the Migratory Bird Treaty Act (16 U.S.C. 703 *et seq.*); Bald and Golden Eagles Protection Act (16 U.S.C. 668–668d); review of Corps of Engineers dredged and fill material permits issued under Section 404 of the Federal Water Pollution Control Act (33 U.S.C. 1344); rights-of-way across recreation lands issued under the Land and Water Conservation Fund Act of 1965, as amended (16 U.S.C. 4601–4–4601–11); historic preservation under the National Historic Preservation Act of 1966 as amended (16 U.S.C. 470–470f); permits issued under the Antiquities Act of 1906 (16 U.S.C. 432, 433); and system activities requiring coordination and approval under general authorities of the National Trails System Act, as amended (16 U.S.C. 1241–1249), the Wilderness Act, as amended (16 U.S.C. 1131–1136), the Wild and Scenic Rivers Act, as amended (16 U.S.C. 1271–1287), the National Environmental Policy Act of 1969 (42 U.S.C. 4321 *et seq.*), the Act of April 27, 1935 (prevention of soil erosion) (16 U.S.C. 590a–f), and an Act to Provide for

the Preservation of Historical and Archeological Data, as amended (16 U.S.C. 469–469c);

(f) Such enforcement functions of the Secretary or other appropriate officer or entity in the Department of Agriculture, insofar as they involve lands and programs under the jurisdiction of that Department, related to compliance with: associated land use permits authorized for and in conjunction with grants of rights-of-way across Federal lands issued under Section 28 of the Mineral Leasing Act of 1920 (30 U.S.C. 185); land use permits for other associated land uses issued under Sections 501 and 503–511 of the Federal Land Policy and Management Act of 1976 (43 U.S.C. 1761, 1763–1771), under the Organic Administration Act of June 4, 1897, as amended (16 U.S.C. 473, 474–482, 551), and under Title III of the Bankhead-Jones Farm Tenant Act of 1937, as amended (7 U.S.C. 1010–1012); removal of materials under the Materials Act of 1947 (30 U.S.C. 601–603) and objects of antiquity under the Antiquities Act of 1906 (16 U.S.C. 432, 433); construction and utilization of national forest roads under the Roads and Trails System Act of 1964 (16 U.S.C. 532–538); and system activities requiring coordination and approval under general authorities of the National Forest Management Act of 1976 (16 U.S.C. 1600 *et seq.*); the Multiple Use-Sustained-Yield Act of 1960 (16 U.S.C. 528–531); the Forest and Rangelands Renewable Resources Planning Act of 1974 (16 U.S.C. 1601–1610); the National Trails System Act, as amended (16 U.S.C. 1241–1249); the Wilderness Act, as amended (16 U.S.C. 1131–1136); the Wild and Scenic Rivers Act, as amended (16 U.S.C. 1271–1287); the Land and Water Conservation Fund Act of 1965, as amended (16 U.S.C. 460 *et seq.*); the Federal Water Pollution Control Act of 1972 (33 U.S.C. 1151 *et seq.*); the Fish and Wildlife Coordination Act and Fish and Game Sanctuaries Act (16 U.S.C. 661 *et seq.* and 694, 694a–b, respectively); the National Historic Preservation Act of 1966, as amended (16 U.S.C. 470–470f); an Act to Provide for the Preservation of Historical and Archeological Data, as amended (16 U.S.C. 469–469c); the National Environmental Policy Act of 1969 (42 U.S.C. 4321 *et seq.*); the Watershed Protection and Flood Prevention Act, as amended (16 U.S.C. 1001 *et seq.*); the Soil and Water Conservation Act of 1977 (16 U.S.C. 2001 *et seq.*); and the Act of April 27, 1965 (prevention of soil erosion) (16 U.S.C. 590a–f);

(g) Such enforcement functions of the Secretary or other appropriate officer or entity in the Department of the Treasury related to compliance with permits for interstate transport of explosives and compliance with regulations for the storage of explosives, Title XI of the Organized Crime Control Act of 1970 (18 U.S.C. 841–848);

(h)(1) The enforcement functions authorized by, and supplemental enforcement authority created by the Act (15 U.S.C. 719 *et seq.*);

(2) All functions assigned to the person or board to be appointed by the President under Section 7(a)(5) of the Act (15 U.S.C. 719e); and

(3) Pursuant to Section 7(a)(6) of the Act (15 U.S.C. 719e), enforcement of the terms and conditions described in Section 5 of the *Decision and Report to the Congress on the Alaska Natural Gas Transportation System,* as approved by the Congress pursuant to Public Law 95–158 (91 Stat. 1268), November 2, 1977, (hereinafter the *"Decision"*).

PART II. OTHER PROVISIONS

SEC. 201. *Executive Policy Board*

The Executive Policy Board for the Alaska Natural Gas Transportation System, hereinafter the "Executive Policy Board", which shall be established by executive order, shall advise the Federal Inspector on the performance of the Inspector's functions. All other functions assigned, or which could be assigned pursuant to the *Decision,* to the Executive Policy Board are hereby transferred to the Federal Inspector.

SEC. 202. *Federal Inspector and Agency Authorized Officers*

(a) The Agency Authorized Officers shall be detailed to and located within the Office. The Federal Inspector shall delegate to each Agency Authorized Officer the authority to enforce the terms, conditions, and stipulations of each grant, permit, or other authorization issued by the Federal agency which appointed the Agency Authorized Officer. In the exercise of these enforcement functions, the Agency Authorized Officers shall be subject to the supervision and direction of the Federal Inspector, whose decision on enforcement matters shall constitute "action" for purposes of Section 10 of the Act (15 U.S.C. 719h).

(b) The Federal Inspector shall be responsible for coordinating the expeditious discharge of nonenforcement activities by Federal agencies and coordinating the compliance by all the Federal agencies with Section 9 of the Act (15 U.S.C. 719g). Such coordination shall include requiring submission of scheduling plans for all permits, certificates, grants or other necessary authorizations, and coordinating scheduling of system-related agency activities. Such coordination may include serving as the "one window" point for filing for and issuance of all necessary permits, certificates, grants or other authorizations, and, consistent with law, Federal government requests for data or information related to any application for a permit, certificate, grant or other authorization. Upon agreement between the Federal Inspector and the head of any agency, that agency may delegate to the Federal Inspector any statutory function vested in such agency related to the functions of the Federal Inspector.

(c) The Federal Inspector and Agency Authorized Officers in implementing the enforcement authorities herein transferred shall carry out the enforcement policies and procedures established by the Federal agencies which nominally administer these authorities, except where the Federal Inspector determines that such policies and procedures would require action inconsistent with Section 9 of the Act (15 U.S.C. 719g).

(d) Under the authority of Section 15 of the Act (15 U.S.C. 719m), the Federal Inspector will undertake to obtain appropriations for all aspects of the Federal Inspector's operations. Such undertaking shall include appropriations for all of the functions specified in the Act and in the general terms and conditions of the *Decision* as well as for the enforcement activities of the Federal Inspector. The Federal Inspector will consult with the various Federal agencies as to resource requirements for enforcing their respective permits and other authorizations in preparing a unified budget for the Office. The budget shall be reviewed by the Executive Policy Board.

SEC. 203. *Subsequent Transfer Provision*

(a) Effective upon the first anniversary of the date of initial operation of the Alaska Natural Gas Transportation Sys-

tem, the functions transferred by Section 102 of this Plan shall be transferred to the agency which performed the functions on the date prior to date the provisions of Section 102 of this Plan were made effective pursuant to Section 205 of this Plan.

(b) Upon the issuance of the final determination order by the Director of the Office of Management and Budget for the transfers provided for by subsection (a) of this section, the Office and the position of Federal Inspector shall, effective on the date of that order, stand abolished.

SEC. 204. *Incidental Transfers*

So much of the personnel, property, records and unexpended balances of appropriations, allocations and other funds employed, used, held, available, or to be made available in connection with the functions transferred under this Plan, as the Director of the Office of Management and Budget shall determine, shall be transferred to the appropriate agency or component at such time or times as the Director of the Office of Management and Budget shall provide, except that no such unexpended balances transferred shall be used for purposes other than those for which the appropriation was originally made. The Director of the Office of Management and Budget shall provide for the terminating of the affairs of the Office and the Federal Inspector upon their abolition pursuant to this Plan and for such further measures and dispositions as such Director deems necessary to effectuate the purposes of this Plan.

SEC. 205. *Effective Date*

This Plan shall become effective at such time or times as the President shall specify, but not sooner than the earliest time allowable under Section 906 of Title

5 of the United States Code, except that the provisions of Section 203 shall occur as provided by the terms of that Section.

Commodity Futures Trading Commission

Nomination of Read P. Dunn, Jr., To Be a Commissioner. April 3, 1979

The President today announced that he will nominate Read P. Dunn, Jr., of Chevy Chase, Md., to be a Commissioner of the Commodity Futures Trading Commission for the remainder of the term expiring April 13, 1980, replacing William Bagley, who has resigned.

Dunn, 65, has been a Commissioner of this Commission since 1975.

He was born in Greenville, Miss., and received a B.S. from Millsaps College in 1936. He served in the U.S. Navy from 1942 to 1945.

From 1945 to 1966, Dunn was director of foreign trade for the National Cotton Council. From 1966 to 1975, he was executive director of the International Institute for Cotton.

Commission on Presidential Scholars

Appointment of Marilyn W. Black as a Member. April 4, 1979

The President today announced the appointment of Marilyn W. Black as a member of the Commission on Presidential Scholars.

Under the law governing this Commission, the person chosen each year as National Teacher of the Year shall serve on the Commission. Ms. Black has been chosen 1979 National Teacher of the

Year. She teaches art and kindergarten in Hanover, N.H.

NOTE: On the same day, the President presented the Teacher of the Year Award to Ms. Black in a ceremony in the Cabinet Room at the White House.

United States-Japan Treaty on Extradition

Message to the Senate Transmitting the Treaty. April 4, 1979

To the Senate of the United States:

With a view to receiving the advice and consent of the Senate to ratification, I transmit herewith the Treaty of Extradition Between the United States of America and Japan, together with a related exchange of notes, signed at Tokyo on March 3, 1978.

I transmit also, for the information of the Senate, the report of the Department of State with respect to the treaty.

The treaty is one of a series of modern extradition treaties being negotiated by the United States. It expands the list of extraditable offenses to include narcotics offenses, aircraft hijacking, bribery, and obstruction of justice, as well as many other offenses not now covered by our existing extradition treaty with Japan. Upon entry into force, it will terminate and supersede the existing Treaty of Extradition and the Supplementary Convention of Extradition between the United States and Japan.

This treaty will make a significant contribution to international cooperation in law enforcement. I recommend that the Senate give early and favorable consideration to the treaty and give its advice and consent to ratification.

JIMMY CARTER

The White House,
   April 4, 1979.

Federal Emergency Management Agency

Appointment of Gloria C. Jimenez as Acting Associate Director.   April 4, 1979

The President today announced the appointment of Gloria C. Jimenez as Acting Associate Director of the Federal Emergency Management Agency (FEMA).

The reorganization plan creating FEMA established four Associate Director positions, one of which was designated for insurance and hazard mitigation functions that will be transferred to FEMA from HUD's Federal Insurance Administration (FIA).

Jimenez has been Administrator of FIA since February 1978.

Jimenez, 46, is a former deputy commissioner and general counsel of the North Carolina Department of Insurance. She has also served as a housing consultant and assistant director of the Low Income Housing Development Corporation in Durham, N.C., and as director of housing and urban programs for the North Carolina Department of Local Affairs. She holds an LL.B. from Brooklyn Law School.

Council of Economic Advisers

Nomination of George C. Eads To Be a Member.   April 4, 1979

The President today announced that he will nominate George C. Eads, of Santa Monica, Calif., to be a member of the Council of Economic Advisers. He would replace William Nordhaus, resigned.

Eads has been a consultant to the Council since last March. He was previously with the Rand Corp. as director of the regulatory policies and institutions program.

Eads was born August 20, 1942, in Clarksville, Tex. He received a B.A. from the University of Colorado in 1964, and an M.A. in 1965 and a Ph. D. in 1968 from Yale University.

In 1968 and 1969, Eads was an assistant professor of economics at Harvard University, and from 1969 to 1972, he was an assistant professor at Harvard University. In 1971 and 1972, he was special economics assistant to the Assistant Attorney General for the Antitrust Division of the Justice Department.

From 1972 to 1975, Eads was associate professor of economics at George Washington University. In 1974 and 1975, he was Assistant Director for Government Operations and Research at the Council on Wage and Price Stability.

From 1975 to 1977, Eads was Executive Director of the National Commission on Supplies and Shortages, a temporary study commission which reported to the President and the Congress. In 1977 and 1978, he was senior economist at the Rand Corp.'s economics department. He was director of the regulatory policies and institutions program at the Rand Corp. from March 1978 until he joined the Council of Economic Advisers last month.

Public Works and Economic Development

Message to the Congress Transmitting Proposed Legislation.   April 4, 1979

To the Congress of the United States:

I am today transmitting to Congress the National Public Works and Economic Development Act of 1979. To millions of Americans in distressed urban and rural communities this legislation will mean new private sector jobs and economic progress, new income and new hope for the future.

This legislation will help strengthen the economic development of distressed urban and rural communities. It will provide new private sector jobs and badly-needed income to the citizens of these communities. It will strengthen their tax bases and attract new private investment. It will help these communities support essential public services without imposing high property taxes on their citizens. And it will help these communities and their citizens become more self-sufficient in the future.

This legislation is based on one overriding fact of our economic life today. Our Nation can no longer afford to rely only on government to provide jobs and income to our disadvantaged citizens and to our distressed communities. We must continue to harness the vast resources of the private sector to help us meet these important challenges. The legislation that I am sending to Congress today is another major step in this direction.

Two years ago when I took office, our economy was struggling to recover from the deepest recession since the great Depression. Unemployment was high, industrial capacity was idle and the incomes of American workers were well below expectations.

Today more than 7.5 million new jobs have been created in our economy and factories across the country have regained high levels of production. Family incomes, after adjustment for inflation, have risen substantially and so have business profits. Our economy is much stronger today than when I took office, just two years ago.

Despite this period of strong economic expansion, there are numerous rural and urban areas that have not participated fully in our Nation's economic health.

These areas still have very high unemployment, low average incomes, substantial poverty and loss of jobs. They do not have enough private investment to provide jobs to their residents, nor do they have the private sector tax base to support essential public services.

The problems of these rural and urban communities have not been solved fully by national economic policies. These communities require special targeted aid to bring in new private sector jobs and investment. Only with this targeted assistance can we be assured that all areas of our Nation, both rural and urban, will participate in the Nation's economic prosperity.

Since taking office, I have focused the resources of the Federal government on programs that will retain existing jobs, bring in new jobs and income, and expand the tax base of these economically troubled communities. I have expanded both the tax incentives and the Federal grant and loan programs available to businesses that remain or locate in these areas. With the help of the Congress we already have accomplished a great deal.

• I have proposed, and Congress has enacted, legislation establishing the Urban Development Action Grant (UDAG) program in the Department of Housing and Urban Development. This program, which I propose to fund at $675 million in my Fiscal Year 1980 budget, provides grants to economically distressed cities and urban counties for projects that create private sector jobs and new tax base in these communities. The first $599 million of UDAG grants have stimulated more than $3.6 billion of private investment in these communities. In addition, we have encouraged cities and counties to use more of their Community Development Block Grant funds for economic development projects.

• I have expanded funding for the economic development grant, loan and loan guarantee programs that are administered by the Economic Development Administration (EDA) in the Department of Commerce. EDA programs were funded at approximately $400 million in FY 1977 when I took office. If the legislation I am transmitting today is approved, our FY 1980 budget will contain approximately $1.3 billion in budget authority for EDA's economic development programs.

• With Congress' approval, I have greatly expanded the Farmer's Home Administration's business and industry loan program from approximately $350 million in loan guarantees in FY 1977 to $1 billion in FY 1980. This increase complements the substantial growth that I have proposed for FmHA's overall program.

• With Congress' approval, I expanded the existing Investment Tax Credit (ITC) to provide a ten percent tax credit for the rehabilitation of factories, warehouses, hotels, stores and other businesses. Previously, the ITC had applied only to new plant and equipment. My FY 1980 budget projects that $1.8 billion of private sector rehabilitation will be assisted by this tax credit.

• With the help of Congress, I have implemented a significant new tax credit to encourage private sector businesses to hire the economically disadvantaged. The targeted jobs tax credit will provide a tax credit of 50 percent of the wages, up to $3000, for any employee hired from one of seven target groups. My budget estimates that a tax expenditure of $500 million will be required to implement this program in FY 1980.

• I proposed and Congress enacted amendments to the Comprehensive Employment and Training Act (CETA) which include provisions to make CETA more responsive to the needs of private sector employers. CETA's new private sector jobs initiative will allow CETA to reimburse private employers for part of the wages and other expenses incurred as part of on-the-job training or job-upgrading programs. I have requested $400 million in a supplemental that is urgently needed this year to fund this program.

As a result of these actions and the legislation I am transmitting today, the Federal government will provide more than $3 billion of direct expenditures and tax expenditures and almost $3 billion of loan guarantees to stimulate private sector jobs and investment in economically troubled communities and to encourage private sector businesses to hire the economically disadvantaged. This amounts to a 700 percent increase in both the amount of budgetary assistance and the amount of loan guarantee aid provided for these purposes above Fiscal Year 1977 levels.

To assist these communities further in regaining their economic and fiscal stability, I am hereby transmitting to Congress the National Public Works and Economic Development Act of 1979. This legislation is part of my overall effort to strengthen the Federal government's economic development programs. That effort will include:

• the National Public Works and Economic Development Act of 1979;

• a $275 million increase in the authorization for the UDAG program submitted early in March;

• a reorganization plan to be submitted later this year that will transfer the Farmers' Home Administration's (FmHA) business and industrial loan program and the Small Business Administration's (SBA) State and local development corporation programs to EDA;

• separate legislation that will consolidate the programs currently managed by

SBA and FmHA into the consolidated economic development financing program in EDA. This legislation will be submitted after Congress has completed action on the reorganization plan; and

• legislation that will reauthorize and expand the work of the Multi-State Regional Action Planning Commissions.

The National Public Works and Economic Development Act of 1979 will strengthen and expand the Federal government's ability to bring private sector jobs and investment to economically troubled urban and rural areas. The bill provides various incentives—grants, direct loans to businesses, loan guarantees and interest subsidies—to encourage businesses to invest in areas with high unemployment, low average incomes, significant poverty and loss of jobs. The bill will help to rejuvenate economically troubled communities in both rural and urban areas.

There are three major elements to this legislation. The first is a consolidated and substantially expanded public works and economic development grant program. It consolidates into one grant program the authorities previously included in Titles I, IV and IX of the current EDA legislation. The public works and economic development grants will be available for the design, construction and rehabilitation 'of public facilities; the capitalization of State and local government revolving loan programs; the funding of State economic development projects; the provision of assistance to private sector businesses that expand or locate in economically troubled areas; and the financing of special projects that provide immediate jobs for the unemployed. I will request $575 million of budget authority in FY 1980 for this grant program.

A second part of this legislation authorizes a variety of financing incentives to encourage private sector businesses to re-

main, locate or expand in economically distressed urban and rural areas. The consolidated economic development financing program will make available direct loans, loan guarantees and interest subsidies to businesses that provide private sector jobs in economically distressed communities. It consolidates the loan and loan guarantee assistance currently available under EDA's Title II program with the financing incentives previously proposed for the National Development Bank. It will be the foundation for the consolidated economic development loan and loan guarantee program that I have proposed as part of my reorganization effort. My budget proposes that $570 million of budget authority and $1.8 billion of loan guarantee authority be available for this program in Fiscal Year 1980.

The third key part of this legislation will provide economic development planning assistance to urban and rural areas and technical assistance to both the public sector and the private sector. It will help State and local governments and the private sector strengthen their capacity to work together to rebuild the economic base of economically distressed urban and rural communities. I will request that approximately $90 million of budget authority be provided in Fiscal Year 1980 for this program.

The National Public Works and Economic Development Act will provide the foundation for the consolidated economic development loan and loan guarantee program that I announced as part of my reorganization proposals. Later this year, I will transmit to Congress a reorganization plan that transfers to EDA the business and industry loan program from FmHA and the State and local development company loan programs from SBA. This reorganization plan will bring the major economic development loan and loan guarantee programs together into one economic development financing program in EDA. It will make it possible for the Federal government to provide one-stop service to urban and rural communities and private businesses that are seeking economic development loan and loan guarantee assistance. It also will streamline Federal aid in this area, reduce Federal red tape and improve the management of the economic development financing programs. After Congress has acted upon the reorganization plan, I will submit legislation that consolidates the SBA and FmHA program requirements into EDA's economic development financing program.

The economic development legislation, reorganization plan and accompanying program consolidations will substantially expand the economic development aid available to rural and urban areas. I intend to ensure that both rural and urban areas are guaranteed a fair share of the new resources. In addition, I will take every step to preserve and strengthen our capacity to deliver this aid to rural and urban areas efficiently and promptly.

This package of economic development legislation and reorganization proposals represents an important departure from previous urban and rural assistance efforts. For the first time, the Federal government is committing substantial resources to attracting private sector jobs and investment to the lagging areas of our country. For the first time, we are asking the private sector to join us in our redevelopment efforts. I am hopeful that Congress will join me in this sensible approach to urban and rural problems and will enact this important legislation.

JIMMY CARTER

The White House,
April 4, 1979.

Budget Deferrals

Message to the Congress. April 4, 1979

To the Congress of the United States:

In accordance with the Impoundment Control Act of 1974, I herewith report two new deferrals of budget authority totalling $109.8 million. The deferrals involve aircraft research and development activities of the Department of Defense and the Interior Department's exploration program at the National Petroleum Reserve in Alaska.

The details of the deferrals are contained in the attached reports.

JIMMY CARTER

The White House,
April 4, 1979.

NOTE: The attachments detailing the deferrals are printed in the FEDERAL REGISTER of April 9, 1979.

Hospital Cost Containment

Remarks at a White House Briefing on the Proposed Legislation. April 4, 1979

How many of you think we need to pass hospital cost containment legislation? [*Laughter*] Would you raise your hand? How many of you will help us with it? Would you raise your hand? How many of you think we are going to win it? [*Laughter and applause*] You don't need me. [*Laughter*]

I think all of you know that one of the major responsibilities of a President is to detect problems that exist in our society and to try to marshal enough of an effort to correct those problems or to answer difficult questions that affect the well-being of our Nation. I don't know of any issue that is more important to me at this point than controlling inflation, because it not only impacts directly upon the quality of life of the people whom I represent and who also look to you for leadership, but growing inflation separates people, one from another. It drives wedges between us. And it arouses a distrust in the average American's mind about organized labor, about business, about the free enterprise system, about local, State, and Federal Government.

It's a very insidious thing. And as you know, for the last 10 years, inflation has been an ever-present problem for me and my predecessors, and for you and those who work with you.

It's hard to detect specific things that can be done. There's no way that I can affect the price of aluminum or wheat or lumber. It's almost impossible to have a direct impact on international markets. And quite often, or most often, I would say, the prices of commodities—barring some extreme shortage, or awareness of an existing shortage—the prices move up fairly well together.

Hospital treatment, medical treatment, is an exception to the rule. The laws of supply and demand, the free enterprise system principles don't work, because neither hospital owners or administrators or doctors or patients have a built-in incentive to try to control prices. Ninety percent of all the hospital bills are paid either by insurers or by the Government. And quite often, if a family has paid hospital insurance for 5 or 6 years and nobody gets sick, and someone does feel ill, their natural, human inclination is to go to the hospital and get part of their money back and, in the process, obviously be treated for a real or imagined illness.

It's much more easy for a medical doctor to put someone in the hospital for treatment and to keep them there, readily accessible, than it is to do otherwise. And quite often, the medical doctors are part owners of the hospitals themselves, and keeping extant beds occupied is one of the factors that go into the profit of the hospital operation itself.

The rate of increase of prices of hospital care has been extraordinarily high— in the last number of years, twice as great as the excessive inflation rate for society as a whole. And this indicates that something ought to be done.

As you well know, the hospital costs have been and are now doubling every 5 years. And quite often, the price of hospital care doesn't show up just because a family has someone go for medical care personally. When you buy an automobile, on the average, $120 of the price of that car that you pay goes to buy hospital insurance for the workers who made the car. So, it feeds back into society and shows up in the Consumer Price Index, and therefore is compounded in its adverse effect on us all.

I'm a product of the free enterprise system. I served for years on a hospital authority. My uncle, my mother, my brother—all of us have been an integral part of the Sumter County Hospital Authority.

And I have seen in retrospect, from a little different perspective, that we were naturally inclined to buy a new machine whenever it became available and then to mandate, to require that every person who came to the hospital had to submit a blood sample or some other aspect of their body to the machine for analysis, whether they needed it or not, in order rapidly to defray the cost of the purchase of the machine. And I didn't realize then that I was ripping off people; never thought about it too much. [*Laughter*] But it was a fact back in the late fifties and early sixties. It's even more an important element of hospital care now than it was then.

Many of the machines obviously play

a very real role in adequate health care. I don't want you to interpret my remarks as condemning hospital administrators or owners or doctors or patients or insurance companies. I think the fact is that we're all in it together. And many of the hospital administrators and medical doctors support this program enthusiastically. Many have already accomplished even more than the legislation envisions.

In New England, for instance, last year hospital costs went up about 8½ percent. We now have nine States, as you know, that have mandatory cost containment legislation on the books. It's being administered well; it's worked well. The hospitals still prosper, and, of course, the patients and the medical care system have not suffered at all.

We've received extraordinarily broad support for this legislation—business, labor, consumers, local officials, State officials, the elderly—but we have a formidable lobbying group marshaled against us. And their concentrated effort on individual Members of Congress, in the commerce committee and otherwise, who have a special interest and a long-time friendship and allegiance—at least a knowledge of the lobbyists—is a very difficult obstacle to overcome. We were successful last year in the Senate. We were almost successful in the House.

We have redoubled our efforts, but the opposition has also redoubled their efforts. And the outcome of the struggle is certainly still in doubt.

It would not be enough for you merely to come here, to go back home and say, "I spent the afternoon at the White House; I met with the President," and use that as a conversation piece. You're welcome to do it if you wish—[*laughter*]—but if you derive any gratification from it or any social escalation from it—[*laughter*]—I would like for you to compensate by actually personally and substantively helping to get this legislation passed.

Every one of you is a leader in your own right, and many people listen to your voice. You can help to shape public opinion at home. And more importantly, you can marshal, I'd say, benevolent influence on the Members of the Congress to let them know how much you care.

If you head up a business or a labor organization or a consumer organization, I hope that you will be personally responsible for marshaling the writing of a hundred or so letters or telegrams, or call every Member of the Congress with whom you are acquainted. I don't know of anything that you could do as an investment of time or effort that would pay richer dividends for you or for our country.

It's very difficult to get people to express themselves, because quite often it's a little embarrassing or it takes a little extra time. But I think if you would search in your own mind for the particular project that's of most interest to you—your own business or, perhaps, golf, or perhaps the collection of stamps, or whatever—and just see how much time you put in on it and then just allot a partial amount of time to this effort, I would be deeply grateful to you.

We have a partnership, whether we like it or not. I personally like it. I hope you do as well. We're partners in continuing an inflationary spiral that robs us all, or we can be partners in doing a tangible thing to help abbreviate the rate of increase of inflation and, perhaps, level it off and begin to bring it down.

I know you've received all the specific information about the legislation that you need—perhaps more than you want. But still I hope that you will carry from here not just the knowledge that you've derived but also a personal commitment to help by doing something about it.

I might close by saying this will save an awful lot of money—in the next 5 years, $53 billion; in the very stringent 1980 fiscal year budget, $1.4 billion.

And I might point out that this does not create any new agencies. It does not create any additional, costly reporting whatsoever. It's phased in in a very careful way by someone, your President, who is deeply committed to the principles of the American free enterprise system.

The first step is completely voluntary. Any hospital which voluntarily complies with the very moderate guidelines is not covered. Any hospital covered by a State program is not covered by any future Federal action. Only if both these steps are avoided does the Federal program come into effect.

So, I think you can see that it's carefully considered. It's been improved substantially over what we originally introduced last year, because we've learned a lot and we've not had a closed mind about it. We've listened to hospital owners, administrators, medical doctors, patient groups, and others.

I'm very proud that you would come here. It shows your interest. And I hope that your action after this meeting will make your trip here worthwhile. I believe we can win. And it'll be a great victory not only for you and for me but for our whole country.

Thank you very much.

NOTE: The President spoke at 3:03 p.m. to a group of civic and community leaders assembled in the East Room at the White House.

Employee-Management Relations in the Foreign Service

Executive Order 12128. April 4, 1979

By the authority vested in me as President by the Constitution and statutes of the United States of America, in order to permit a representative of the Federal Labor Relations Authority to participate in labor-relations decisions affecting Foreign Service employees, it is hereby ordered as follows:

1–101. Section 5(a) of Executive Order No. 11636 is amended to read as follows:

"(a) There is hereby established, as a Committee of the Board, an Employee-Management Relations Commission composed of three senior level representatives, one designated by each of the following: the Secretary of Labor, the Director of the Office of Management and Budget, and the Federal Labor Relations Authority. The representative designated by the Federal Labor Relations Authority shall be the Chairman of the Commission.".

1–102. In Section 2–101(b) of Executive Order No. 12107, the reference to Executive Order No. 11636 is deleted.

1–103. Section 2(a) of Executive Order No. 11636 is amended to read as follows:

"(b) "Foreign affairs agency" means the Department of State, the International Communication Agency, the Agency for International Development, and their successor agencies.".

JIMMY CARTER

The White House,
April 4, 1979.

[Filed with the Office of the Federal Register, 10:52 a.m., April 5, 1979]

National Maritime Day, 1979

Proclamation 4653. April 5, 1979

By the President of the United States of America

A Proclamation

The influence and the importance of the American Merchant Marine extend well beyond our thriving ports. It affects all Americans. Our Merchant Marine carries the products of our farms and factories to consumers in our domestic trades, among our fifty States and possessions, and links the U.S. industrial and agricultural heartland with our overseas trading partners. Most of the gross tonnage carried in U.S. foreign trade is waterborne.

In addition to their vital role in commerce and trade, America's shipping and shipbuilding industries have distinguished themselves in providing logistic and combat support to our armed forces in times of war.

The men and women of our Merchant Marine can be justly proud of their contributions to our Nation's economy and national defense. In these dual roles, American seafarers have carried out their responsibilities with great dedication and ability.

In recognition of the importance of the American Merchant Marine, the Congress, by joint resolution of May 20, 1933 (48 Stat. 73, 36 U.S.C. 145), designated May 22 of each year as National Maritime Day in commemoration of the departure from Savannah, Georgia, on that date in 1819 of the SS SAVANNAH on the first transatlantic voyage by any steamship and requested the President to issue annually a proclamation calling for its appropriate observance.

Now, THEREFORE, I, JIMMY CARTER, President of the United States of America, do hereby urge the people of the United States to honor our American Merchant Marine on May 22, 1979, by displaying the flag of the United States at their homes and other suitable places, and I request that all ships sailing under the American flag dress ship on that day.

IN WITNESS WHEREOF, I have hereunto set my hand this fifth day of April, in the year of our Lord nineteen hundred seventy-nine, and of the Independence of the United States of America the two hundred and third.

JIMMY CARTER

[Filed with the Office of the Federal Register, 3:38 p.m., April 5, 1979]

Ohio River Basin Commission

Appointment of Fred J. Krumholtz as Chairman. April 5, 1979

The President today announced the appointment of Fred J. Krumholtz, of Dayton, Ohio, as Chairman of the Ohio River Basin Commission.

Krumholtz, 65, is deputy treasurer of Montgomery County, Ohio. He has also served as a commissioner of the Ohio Liquor Control Commission and assistant director of the Montgomery County, Ohio Board of Elections.

National Institute of Building Sciences

Withdrawal of the Nomination of John P. Millhone To Be a Member of the Board of Directors. April 5, 1979

The President today announced that he is withdrawing the nomination of John P. Millhone as a member of the Board of Directors of the National Institute of Building Sciences.

Millhone requested that this nomination be withdrawn, because since he was nominated, he has accepted the position of Director of the Office of Buildings and Community Systems of the Conservation and Solar Applications Office at the Department of Energy.

607

Emergency Weekend Gasoline Sales Restrictions

Message to the Congress Transmitting an Amendment to Standby Conservation Plan No. 1. April 5, 1979

To the Congress of the United States:

Pursuant to Sections 201(d)(1) and 552 of the Energy Policy and Conservation Act (EPCA), 42 U.S.C. 6261(d)(1) and 6422, I am hereby transmitting to the Congress for its approval an amendment to Emergency Weekend Gasoline Sales Restrictions (Standby Conservation Plan No. 1) which I transmitted on March 1, 1979.

The purpose of the amendment is to expand the scope of "comparable programs" which a state may develop in order to qualify for an exemption from the Federal plan. The amendment will further encourage states, or political subdivisions thereof, to develop conservation programs which will qualify them for an exemption from the operation of Federal energy conservation contingency plans should those plans ever be put into effect. Such exemptions for "comparable programs" are authorized under Section 202(b) of the EPCA.

The amendment reflects my belief that states should be given the flexibility to meet their share of any energy shortfall prior to the adoption of nationwide measures. The amendment would expand the size of allowable comparable state programs in two ways. First, it would eliminate the requirement that any alternative state plan be a mandatory one. If a state is able to achieve comparable energy savings through a voluntary plan, this should be permissible. Second, the language in the plan requiring that state alternatives deal with "the same subject matter" as the Federal plan would be eliminated and a requirement that savings be of the same fuel would be substituted. This would allow states to propose any alternative approach so long as it achieved comparable savings of the same fuel.

The procedures for approval by Congress of an amendment to a contingency plan are detailed in Section 552 of the EPCA, and require among other things that a resolution of approval be passed by each House of Congress within 60 days of submittal of the amendment. Inasmuch as the subject of this amendment has been considered thoroughly by the Congress in its deliberations on the conservation contingency plans, I urge the Congress to give this amendment expedited consideration so that it may be approved together with the Emergency Weekend Sales Restrictions plan.

The EPCA does not specify in Section 552 the form which the resolution of approval is to take. As I noted in my submission of the conservation contingency plans on March 1, 1979, it is my view and that of the Attorney General that actions of the Congress purporting to have binding legal effect must be presented to the President for his approval under Article I, Section 7 of the Constitution. Therefore, I strongly recommend that Congressional approval of the amendment be in the form of a joint resolution. If this procedure is followed, the amendment itself, agreed to by the Congress and the President, will not later be subject to possible judicial invalidation on the ground that the President did not approve the resolution.

I urge the prompt and favorable consideration by the Congress of this amendment.

JIMMY CARTER

The White House,
　April 5, 1979.

NOTE: The text of the amendment is printed in the FEDERAL REGISTER of May 1, 1979.

Corporation for Public Broadcasting

Message to the Congress Transmitting a Report. April 5, 1979

To the Congress of the United States:

Enclosed is the "Annual Report of the Corporation for Public Broadcasting for FY 1978," prepared in accordance with the requirement of the Public Broadcasting Act of 1967 (Public Law 90–129) as amended.

The Corporation has again prepared a thoughtful report which highlights its efforts for the past fiscal year. The accomplishments of public broadcasting are well articulated with emphasis on television and radio programming, technological innovation, and human development services.

It should be noted that the projections of long range Federal financial contributions from the Federal Government exceed levels contained in the Administration's legislative proposal to reauthorize the Corporation for the period FY 1981–85.

The Annual Report is being forwarded so that it is available to the Congress for its deliberations.

JIMMY CARTER

The White House,
April 5, 1979.

Urban Aid Program Funds

Statement by the White House Press Secretary. April 5, 1979

I would like to express, on behalf of the President, his concern over the action of the House Budget Committee in eliminating funds for the Urban Aid program.

Those funds are desperately needed by our cities. They are highly targeted to bring relief to those areas of our country and to those segments of our society who have not profited from the overall improvement in employment and the economic situation in our country, as have the rest of us over the past few years.

We will be working to get these funds restored. We hope, as a matter of fact, that even some of those who were somewhat critical of the President in the past, because they thought and felt that he had not proposed enough in appropriations for these programs, will join with us and help to restore these funds.

As you know, some several weeks ago when the Black Caucus was here, as I told many of you, the President told them that while he understood the differences that we had—they feeling that we should be budgeting more money in these areas—he warned that he feared that the big fight would be to maintain in the Congress those funds and those programs which we had proposed.

I think this is an indication that his concern was correct at that time, and we will be making every effort to restore these badly needed funds for our urban areas.

NOTE: Press Secretary Jody Powell made the statement at approximately 12:10 p.m. during the regular news briefing held in the Briefing Room at the White House.

Energy

Address to the Nation. April 5, 1979

Good evening.

Our Nation's energy problem is very serious—and it's getting worse. We're wasting too much energy, we're buying far too much oil from foreign countries, and we are not producing enough oil, gas, or coal in the United States.

In order to control energy price, production, and distribution, the Federal bureaucracy and redtape have become so complicated, it is almost unbelievable. Energy prices are high, and they're going higher, no matter what we do.

The use of coal and solar energy, which are in plentiful supply, is lagging far behind our great potential. The recent accident at the Three Mile Island nuclear powerplant in Pennsylvania has demonstrated dramatically that we have other energy problems.

So, what can we do? We can solve these problems together.

Federal Government price controls now hold down our own production, and they encourage waste and increasing dependence on foreign oil. Present law requires that these Federal Government controls on oil be removed by September 1981, and the law gives me the authority at the end of next month to carry out this decontrol process.

In order to minimize sudden economic shock, I've decided that phased decontrol of oil prices will begin on June 1 and continue at a fairly uniform rate over the next 28 months. The immediate effect of this action will be to increase production of oil and gas in our own country.

As Government controls end, prices will go up on oil which has already been discovered, and unless we tax the oil companies, they will reap huge and undeserved windfall profits. We must, therefore, impose a windfall profits tax on the oil companies to capture part of this money for the American people. This tax money will go into an energy security fund and will be used to protect low-income families from energy price increases, to build a more efficient mass transportation system, and to put Ameri-

can genius to work solving our long-range energy problems.

Now, let me explain all of this in more detail. This is very important, and I hope all of you will listen carefully and then give me your cooperation and support.

The energy crisis is real. I said so in 1977, and I say it again tonight, almost exactly 2 years later. Time is running short.

While the situation at Three Mile Island is improving and we've taken every precaution to protect the people of the area, this nuclear accident obviously causes all of us concern. I've directed the establishment of an independent Presidential commission of experts to investigate the causes of this accident and to make recommendations on how we can improve the safety of nuclear powerplants. You deserve a full accounting, and you will get it.

Although this accident is of immediate concern, the fundamental cause of our Nation's energy crisis is petroleum—oil and gas.

We are dangerously dependent on uncertain and expensive sources of foreign oil. Since the 1973 embargo, oil production in the United States has actually dropped. Our imports have been growing. Just a few foreign countries control the amount of oil that's produced and the price that we must pay.

Just 10 years ago, we imported hardly any oil. Today, we buy about half the oil we use from foreign countries. We are by far the largest customer for OPEC oil, buying one-fourth of that foreign cartel's total production. This year, we Americans will pay out $50 billion for imported oil— about $650 for every household in the United States.

This growing dependence has left us dangerously exposed to sudden price rises and interruptions in supply. In 1973 and

1974, shipment of oil was embargoed, and the price quadrupled almost overnight. In the last few months, the upheaval in Iran again cut world supplies of oil, and the OPEC cartel prices leaped up again.

These shocks have sent us stern warnings about energy, but our Nation has not yet responded to these warnings. Our national strength is dangerously dependent on a thin line of oil tankers stretching half-way around the Earth, originating in the Middle East and around the Persian Gulf, one of the most unstable regions in the world.

The National Energy Plan, which I proposed in April 1977, was the first major effort to deal with all these problems. Then, for 18 long months, Congress debated, and special interests struggled for advantage. Some of my original proposals were enacted, and the benefits are already obvious. But proposals dealing with oil were not adopted, and we have now lost precious time that we could not afford.

With new legal authority, I am now able to act without delay.

There is no single answer. We must produce more. We must conserve more. And now we must join together in a great national effort to use American technology to give us energy security in the years ahead.

The most effective action we can take to encourage both conservation and production here at home is to stop rewarding those who import foreign oil and to stop encouraging waste by holding the price of American oil down far below its replacement or its true value.

This is a painful step, and I'll give it to you straight: Each of us will have to use less oil and pay more for it. But this is a necessary step, and I want you to understand it fully.

Excessive Federal Government controls must end. Phased decontrol will grad-ually increase the price of petroleum products. In the short run, it will add a small amount to our rate of inflation, but that is the cost we must pay to reduce our dependence on the foreign oil cartel.

In the longer run, the actions I'm announcing tonight will help us to fight inflation. Other nations will join and support us as we cut down our use of oil and increase our own production of energy. The foreign oil cartel will then find it harder to raise their prices. The dollar will grow stronger, and the prices we pay for many imported goods will be less. This will strengthen our economy and reduce inflation in future years.

But decontrol could also further inflate the already enormous profits of oil companies. As I've said, part of this excessive new profit will be totally unearned—what is called a "windfall" profit. That's why we must have a new windfall profits tax to recover the unearned billions of dollars and to ensure that you, the American people, are treated fairly.

I want to emphasize that this windfall profits tax is not a tax on the American people. It is purely and simply a tax on the new profits of the oil producers which they will receive but not earn.

Even with the windfall profits tax in place, our oil producers will get substantial new income—enough to provide plenty of incentive for increased domestic production. I will demand that they use their new income to develop energy for America, and not to buy such things as department stores and hotels, as some have done in the past.

Congressional leaders who share my belief that a windfall profits tax is necessary warn me that we face two very real threats to these proposals.

First, as surely as the Sun will rise tomorrow, the oil companies can be expected to fight to keep the profits which they have not earned. Unless you speak out, they will have more influence on the Congress than you do.

Second, the inevitable scrambling by interest groups for a larger share of these revenues can leave the Congress divided, bogged down, and, therefore, unable to act. Unless your voice is heard, once again the selfishness of a few will block action which is badly needed to help our entire Nation.

I will fight to get this tax passed, to establish the energy security fund, and to meet our future energy needs. And tonight I appeal to you for your support. Please let your Senators and Representatives in Congress know that you support the windfall profits tax and that you do not want to see the need to produce more energy be turned into an excuse to cheat the public and to damage our country.

We can meet our energy challenge, but I am not going to put an undue burden on people who can hardly make ends meet as it is. Part of the proceeds of the windfall profits tax will go to help those among us who will be hurt most by rising energy prices.

I will also ask every State to pass laws protecting Americans from arbitrary cutoffs of heat for their homes. We will also channel the tens of millions of dollars we are winning in lawsuits against oil companies for price-gouging into further energy assistance for lower income citizens. And for the sake of fairness, I will ask Congress to close foreign tax credit loopholes that now give unnecessary benefits to the major oil companies.

In order to ease short-run inflationary pressures for the time being, I will see that action is taken to lift existing fees and duties on imported crude oil and its products.

Besides removing Government controls on oil to encourage production, we must take other actions to increase supply and to make the most of our own domestic fuel reserves.

I have today signed an Executive order that will set strict deadlines for cutting through Federal redtape on important new energy projects, such as pipelines to serve the northern part of our country, seaports, and also refineries.

We will move to eliminate bureaucratic barriers to construction of the pending pipeline from California to Texas, which has been stuck in a quagmire of more than 700 State and local permit applications for the last 14 months.

We will step up exploration and production of oil and gas on Federal lands.

This week, my personal representatives began negotiations in Mexico City which we hope will lead to an agreement on sales of Mexican natural gas to the United States at a price that is fair to both countries.

The three Federal agencies which regulate the coal industry will report to me within 60 days on ways to encourage greater use of coal, our most abundant fuel resource. And I will soon announce significant measures to increase and to accelerate the use of solar energy.

In addition to producing more energy, we must conserve more energy. Conservation is our cheapest and cleanest energy source. It helps to control inflation, and every barrel of oil we save is a barrel we don't have to import.

We have recruited 19 other consuming nations to join us in pledging to reduce expected oil consumption by 5 percent. To help accomplish this conservation goal in our country, I've asked Congress to grant me standby authority in four areas, one of which, for example, is to require that thermostats in all commercial buildings be set no higher than 65 degrees in winter and no lower than 80 degrees in summer. As soon as I get that authority, I will use it.

Steps will be taken to eliminate free parking for Government employees in order to reduce the waste of energy, particularly gasoline, in commuting to and from work.

We will use tax credits to encourage the use of wood-burning stoves.

I'm asking all citizens to honor, and all States to enforce, the 55-mile-per-hour speed limit. This is one of the most effective ways to save fuel.

I will set targets for our 50 States to reduce gasoline consumption and ask each State to meet its target. The timetable will be strict. If States fail to meet their targets when gasoline shortages exist, then I will order mandatory steps to achieve the needed savings, including the weekend closing of service stations.

If these savings are not made, we will almost certainly have gasoline shortages as early as this summer.

In addition, I ask each of you to take an important action on behalf of our Nation. I ask you to drive 15 miles a week fewer than you do now. One way to do this is not to drive your own car to work every day. At least once a week take the bus, go by carpool or, if you work close enough to home, walk.

This action can make a significant difference for our country. For each day that we do this, we can save hundreds of thousands of barrels of oil. This will help to hold down the prices of fuel, and you obviously will save money you otherwise would have spent on gasoline.

As needed, on a temporary basis, I may extend certain environmental deadlines and make regulatory changes to help avoid serious shortages of gasoline.

Unless utilities do so voluntarily, they may be ordered to run non-oil-burning generating plants at full capacity and then to transmit the extra power to areas where oil burners can be phased out.

So far, I have spoken about producing more energy and conserving more energy. Now, in the next few minutes, I would like to talk about the third and the most promising part of our battle for energy security—shifting to more abundant sources of energy by the development and the use of American technology.

We're already investing some $3½ billion each year to develop the new energy supplies we will need for the future. But we must step up this effort. Just as we harnessed American dedication and brainpower to put men on the Moon, we will make the same kind of massive, purposeful effort to achieve the goal of national energy security through technology. We must begin now so that we can regain control over our energy future.

That's why the energy security fund—with the tax on windfall oil profits that will pay for it—is so vitally important.

That's why every vote in Congress for this tax and for this fund will be a vote for America's future, and every vote against it will be a vote for excessive oil company profits and for reliance on the whims of the foreign oil cartel.

The energy security fund will let us pursue a sound strategy of energy research and development.

In years to come, we can then design automobiles, buildings, appliances, and engines that serve us better and use less energy.

We can improve mass transit and make our entire transportation system cleaner, faster, and more efficient. We can broaden the use of our huge coal deposits by turning coal into clean gas, liquid, and solid fuels.

We can learn how to use our immense reserves of oil shale.

From the products of our forests and croplands, we can produce more gasohol, already being used to replace gasoline in several Midwestern States. We can promote the use of small-scale hydroelectric plants, powered by the flow of ordinary streams, without the need for big dams.

And we can turn increasingly toward the ultimate source of all our energy—the Sun.

There are, of course, already solar techniques that are economical right now. With existing tax credits and with our new energy security fund, we can encourage even more rapid development and more use of solar power.

In the future, we will use solar energy in many other ways, including the direct conversion of sunlight into electricity. We already use this method for limited purposes, such as in our space program, but scientific discoveries will be needed to make it more useful directly in our homes and factories.

The energy security fund, derived from the windfall profits tax, will pay for these exciting new energy programs.

All of these steps can be part of a wider international effort. Other nations are eager to cooperate.

The actions and plans that I have announced tonight will move us away from imported oil and toward a future of real energy security.

These actions will give us a better life. These are necessary steps, because our country faces a serious petroleum problem and a broader energy challenge.

The future of the country we love is at stake. We Americans have met equal challenges in the past. Our Nation has endured and prospered. Ours is a great country, and we have bountiful resources and technological genius.

We must recognize the urgency of this challenge—and we must work together

to meet it. Then we, too, will endure. We, too, will prosper. We, too, will triumph.

Thank you, and good night.

NOTE: The President spoke at 9 p.m. from the Oval Office at the White House. His remarks were broadcast live on radio and television.

Critical Energy Facility Program

Executive Order 12129.   April 5, 1979

By the authority vested in me as President by the Constitution and statutes of the United States of America, and in order to provide for timely coordinated Federal decisions on critical energy facility permit applications, it is hereby ordered as follows:

1-101. The Director of the Office of Management and Budget shall establish a Critical Energy Facility Program.

1-102. The Director of the Office of Management and Budget, after consulting with the Executive agencies listed in Section 1-103, shall make recommendations to the President as to which non-nuclear facilities should be included in the Program. The President shall identify non-nuclear energy facilities which he deems to be of critical national importance and which need Federal permits for siting, construction, or operation. Those facilities shall be included in the Program. The Director of the Office of Management and Budget shall establish a system through which deadlines will be established for final administrative decision-making by Executive agencies, consistent with statutory requirements.

1-103. The following Executive agencies shall participate in the Program and the Director of the Office of Management and Budget may invite others to participate where appropriate:

(a) Department of the Interior.

(b) Department of Agriculture.

(c) Department of Commerce.

(d) Department of Transportation.

(e) Department of Energy.

(f) Environmental Protection Agency.

(g) Council on Environmental Quality.

(h) Department of the Army.

1–104. Each Executive agency in the Program shall submit such data and information as the Director of the Office of Management and Budget may require with respect to a critical energy facility, including:

(a) Date a completed application is expected to be received from the sponsors of a critical energy facility project.

(b) Targeted final decision date for each significant permit or statutory review.

(c) Compilation of the actions required of other Executive agencies before a participating Executive agency may make a final decision.

(d) Compilation of the actions required of non-Federal authorities before a participating Executive agency may make a final decision.

(e) Compilation of significant actions required of the applicant before a final decision may be made.

(f) Progress reports, including reasons for any changes in any targeted final decision dates.

1–105. On the basis of information received pursuant to Section 1–104, the Director of the Office of Management and Budget will provide to the President, to the participating Executive agencies, to the Governor of any affected State, and to the applicant a schedule of deadlines for Federal actions concerning each critical energy facility.

1–106. The Director of the Office of Management and Budget shall provide for appropriate interagency mechanisms for the conduct of multiple agency reviews; but, only where such reviews are consistent with the statutory obligations of the agencies, and only when such reviews will assist in the expeditious processing of facility permits.

1–107. The Director of the Office of Management and Budget shall assist participating Executive agencies with the establishment of joint Federal and State and local agency reviews. Such assistance shall be limited to those circumstances which are consistent with the legal obligations of the reviewing Federal and State and local agencies, and which will result in the expeditious processing of facility permits.

1–108. The Director of the Office of Management and Budget shall keep the President informed on agency performance in meeting scheduled decision deadlines.

1–109. The Director of the Office of Management and Budget shall, where appropriate, coordinate the procedures established herein with those procedures adopted by the Council on Environmental Quality pursuant to Executive Order No. 11991 (40 CFR Parts 1500–1508).

1–110. Nothing in this Order is intended to modify in any way (a) the review and decision-making responsibilities imposed by Federal or State statutes, or (b) the opportunity for timely State and local government and public participation in agency decision-making.

JIMMY CARTER

The White House,
    April 5, 1979.

[Filed with the Office of the Federal Register,
        11:21 a.m., April 6, 1979]

NOTE: The text of the Executive order was released on April 6.

Department of Health, Education, and Welfare

Nomination of Richard B. Lowe III To Be Deputy Inspector General.　April 6, 1979

The President today announced that he will nominate Richard B. Lowe III, of New York City, to be Deputy Inspector General at the Department of Health, Education, and Welfare. He would replace Charles Ruff, resigned.

Lowe was born July 26, 1941, in New York City. He received a B.S. from the University of Wisconsin in 1964 and a J.D. from St. John's University in 1967.

Lowe has been with the New York County District Attorney's Office since 1967. He has served as a trial attorney and as chief of the major felony program, the Complaint Bureau, the Early Care Assessment Bureau, and the Trial Bureau. Since 1976 he has been chief of the Trials Division.

World Trade Week, 1979

Proclamation 4654.　April 6, 1979

By the President of the United States of America

A Proclamation

A strong position in world trade is one of the foundations of the American economy. By expanding our trade, we enlarge the opportunities for U.S. companies to prosper under our free enterprise system and for U.S. workers to find employment throughout the American industrial complex.

Trade also joins us with other nations of the world in a partnership of peace and trust that advances the well-being of people everywhere. It encourages the international exchange of ideas, knowledge and experience, and assists in developing fuller and more fruitful use of the world's resources.

We in the United States are dedicated to policies that promote freer, wider trade and that avoid the destructive consequences of protectionism. We believe our economy is best protected, and our citizens better served, when barriers to trade between nations are lowered rather than raised.

We are the world's largest trading nation. Yet compared to many of our trading partners, we export less of our rich and varied production than we should.

World Trade Week gives us the opportunity to pledge ourselves to exporting as a national priority and renew our determination to succeed in the world marketplace.

Now, Therefore, I, Jimmy Carter, President of the United States of America, do hereby proclaim the week beginning May 20, 1979, as World Trade Week, and I request all Federal, State and local officials to cooperate in the observance of that week.

I urge business, labor, agricultural, educational, professional and civic groups, and all the people of the United States to observe World Trade Week with gatherings, discussions, exhibits, ceremonies and other appropriate activities that promote awareness of the importance of world trade to our economy and our relations with other nations.

In Witness Whereof, I have hereunto set my hand this sixth day of April, in the year of our Lord nineteen hundred seventy-nine, and of the Independence of the United States of America the two hundred and third.

Jimmy Carter

[Filed with the Office of the Federal Register, 3:58 p.m., April 6, 1979]

Three Mile Island Nuclear Facility

White House Statement.   April 6, 1979

The President is concerned about reports that some members of the public fear the purity of food from the area surrounding the Three Mile Island nuclear plant.

These fears are not grounded in fact. Current readings show nothing to fear from food grown, harvested, or produced in that area. Both the Food and Drug Administration and the Food Safety and Quality Service of the USDA, on the Federal side, and State health officials are making exhaustive tests on foodstuffs in that area. They have found absolutely no danger to exist.

Tests of fish taken from the Susquehanna River downstream from the nuclear plant, of fish from a hatchery, of food in processing plants, of meat and poultry in packing houses, and of solid food taken from grocery store shelves in the immediate area have all been negative. No radioactivity above the ever-present background levels has been found in these foods—even within 3 miles of the nuclear plant.

USDA officials briefly closed six small packing plants near Three Mile Island on Friday until they had the results of their tests. That was out of an abundance of caution. When the tests came in negative, the plants were reopened on Monday.

Measurements of milk found—as has been fully reported—a barely discernible level of radiation that is only one quarter of 1 percent of what could be considered a potential health hazard. That tiny measurement in milk alone was much lower than the level of radioactivity found elsewhere in the United States following a Chinese nuclear test. And that milk was safe to drink.

As far as it is humanly possible to determine, the food from the Three Mile Island area is as safe to produce, buy, transport, prepare, and eat as the food available at any other place in the United States.

Digest of Other White House Announcements

The following listing includes the President's public schedule and other items of general interest announced by the White House Press Office and not included elsewhere in this issue.

March 31

The President met at the White House with:
—Zbigniew Brzezinski, Assistant to the President for National Security Affairs;
—a group of past district governors of the Georgia Lions International.

The President spoke with Harold R. Denton, who is in Pennsylvania, concerning the situation at the Three Mile Island nuclear facility. Mr. Denton is Director of the Office of Nuclear Reactor Regulation of the Nuclear Regulatory Commission.

April 2

The President met at the White House with:
—Dr. Brzezinski;
—Frank B. Moore, Assistant to the President for Congressional Liaison;
—the Cabinet;
—Vice President Walter F. Mondale;
—Senator John H. Glenn, Jr., of Ohio.

The President spoke with Mr. Denton concerning the situation at the Three Mile Island nuclear facility.

617

The President has received the 1979 Federal Strategy for Drug Abuse and Drug Traffic Prevention, prepared by the Strategy Council on Drug Abuse, and also has designated Lee I. Dogoloff, Associate Director of the Domestic Policy Staff, as Executive Director of the Council.

April 3

The President met at the White House with:

—Dr. Brzezinski;

—Mr. Moore;

—the Democratic congressional leadership;

—members of the National Association of State Attorneys General;

—James T. McIntyre, Jr., Director of the Office of Management and Budget.

President Anwar al-Sadat of Egypt and Prime Minister Menahem Begin of Israel called the President to report to him on the Prime Minister's trip to Egypt. The two leaders discussed with the President the status of their talks and the next steps in the continuing peace process. Both leaders thanked the President again for his efforts to bring about a lasting peace in the Middle East.

The President spoke with Mr. Denton concerning the situation at the Three Mile Island nuclear facility.

April 4

The President met at the White House with:

—Dr. Brzezinski;

—Vice President Mondale, Mr. Moore, Danny C. Tate, Deputy Assistant for Congressional Liaison (House), William H. Cable, Deputy Assistant for Congressional Liaison (Senate), and Robert G. Beckel, Special Assistant for Congressional Liaison (House);

—Vice President Mondale, Stansfield Turner, Director of Central Intelligence, Hamilton Jordan, Assistant to the President, and Dr. Brzezinski;

—Rev. Jesse Jackson, national president of Operation PUSH (People United to Save Humanity).

In a ceremony in the Cabinet Room, the President received the final report of the National Commission on Neighborhoods.

April 5

The President met at the White House with:

—Dr. Brzezinski;

—Mr. Moore;

—bishops of the African Methodist Episcopal Zion Church;

—members of the Supreme Lodge of the Order of AHEPA (American Hellenic Educational Progressive Association);

—the Cherry Blossom princesses for 1979.

In the evening, the President attended a reception for volunteers from the 1976 campaign headquarters in Georgia.

April 6

The President met at the White House with:

—Vice President Mondale, Secretary of State Cyrus R. Vance, Secretary of Defense Harold Brown, Dr. Brzezinski, and Mr. Jordan;

—Mr. Moore;

—Richard N. Gardner, U.S. Ambassador to Italy;

—a group of editors and news directors (transcript will be printed next week).

The White House announced that the President completed his annual physical examination on April 5. Rear Adm. William M. Lukash, USN, Physician to the President, reported that the President has achieved a high level of physical conditioning and is in excellent health.

The President declared an emergency for the State of Iowa because of the impact of severe storms and tornadoes on March 29 and 30. The President's action will permit the donation of Government-owned mobile homes to the State to provide temporary housing for those families who lost their homes as a result of the severe storms and tornadoes.

The President left the White House for a stay at Camp David, Md.

NOMINATIONS SUBMITTED TO THE SENATE

The following list does not include promotions of members of the Uniformed Services, nominations to the Service Academies, or nominations of Foreign Service officers.

Submitted April 2, 1979

ROBERT P. SMITH, of Virginia, a Foreign Service officer of Class one, to be Ambassador Extraordinary and Plenipotentiary of the United States of America to Liberia.

WILLIAM LACY SWING, of North Carolina, a Foreign Service officer of Class two, to be Ambassador Extraordinary and Plenipotentiary of the United States of America to the People's Republic of the Congo.

FRANK MINIS JOHNSON, JR., of Alabama, to be United States Circuit Judge for the Fifth Circuit Court of Appeals, vice a new position created by P.L. 95–486, approved October 20, 1978.

ROWLAND G. FREEMAN III, of California, to be Administrator of General Services, vice Jay Solomon, resigned.

TIMOTHY F. CLEARY, of Maryland, to be a member of the Occupational Safety and Health Review Commission for a term expiring April 27, 1985 (reappointment).

Submitted April 3, 1979

READ P. DUNN, JR., of Maryland, to be a Commissioner of the Commodity Futures Trading Commission for the remainder of the term expiring April 13, 1980, vice William T. Bagley, resigned.

NOMINATIONS—Continued

Submitted April 4, 1979

DOLORES KORMAN SLOVITER, of Pennsylvania, to be United States Circuit Judge for the Third Circuit, vice a new position created by P.L. 95–486, approved October 20, 1978.

GEORGE C. EADS, of California, to be a member of the Council of Economic Advisers, vice William D. Nordhaus, resigned.

Withdrawn April 5, 1979

JOHN P. MILLHONE, of Minnesota, to be a member of the Board of Directors of the National Institute of Building Sciences for a term expiring September 7, 1980, which was sent to the Senate on January 18, 1979.

CHECKLIST OF WHITE HOUSE PRESS RELEASES

The following listing contains releases of the White House Press Office which are not included in this issue.

Released April 2, 1979

News conference: on the President's message to Congress on national privacy policy—by Vice President Walter F. Mondale, David Linowes, Chairman, Privacy Protection Study Commission, Stuart E. Eizenstat, Assistant to the President for Domestic Affairs and Policy, Phil Heyman, Assistant Attorney General, Department of Justice, Henry Geller, Assistant Secretary of Commerce, and Richard Neustadt, Assistant Director, Domestic Policy Staff

Announcement: 1979 Strategy for Drug Abuse and Drug Traffic Prevention

Released April 4, 1979

Announcement: nomination of Dolores K. Sloviter to be United States Circuit Judge for the Third Circuit

Advance text: remarks at the annual members dinner of the Chicago Committee of the Chicago Council on Foreign Relations—by Zbigniew Brzezinski, Assistant to the President for National Security Affairs

Released April 5, 1979

Excerpts: address to the Nation on energy
Advance text: address to the Nation on energy
Fact sheet: the President's program on energy

CHECKLIST—Continued

Released April 6, 1979

Announcement: nomination of Cornelia G. Kennedy to be United States Circuit Judge for the Sixth Circuit

News conference: on consumer involvement in the anti-inflation program—by Alfred E. Kahn, Advisor to the President on Inflation, and Esther Peterson, Special Assistant to the President for Consumer Affairs

ACTS APPROVED BY THE PRESIDENT

Approved April 3, 1979

H.R. 2534_____ Public Law 96–5
An act to provide for a temporary increase in the public debt limit, and for other purposes.

H.R. 1147_____ Public Law 96–6
An act to extend temporarily the authority of the Secretary of the Treasury to waive the imposition of countervailing duties.

Interview With the President

Remarks and a Question-and-Answer Session With Editors and News Directors. April 6, 1979

THE PRESIDENT. I hate to interrupt Jody when he's in trouble—*[laughter]*—which is most of the time.

This part of the press will only be in here a few minutes.

ADMINISTRATION POLICIES

I did want to just outline in brief terms some of the issues that I am facing at this moment. I think you all know what they are. We are trying to carry out the momentum of the Mideast treaty. We are dealing with the energy question, I think, in a very responsible and bold and adequate way. Inflation is still a heavy problem on all of us, which has certainly not been resolved. We took action this morning, announced by Fred Kahn and Esther Peterson, to enhance the interrelationship between the Government and the consumer groups and also to inform the public about certain items which are heavily impacted by rapidly rising prices, so that there can be more cautious and prudent buying.

On the Hill, we have several reorganization proposals in the prospect of being passed: deregulation, reduction in paperwork, which is very important for us. The budget, I think, is in basically good condition—a very stringent 1980 fiscal year budget. I think the Congress has recognized and joined in the general philosophy about budgeting this year, which is compatible, I think, with the attitude of the American people.

We have, obviously, other international and domestic concerns. But I think at this moment it would be better for me to let you ask questions rather than to continue this dissertation. And I'm available to you for the next few minutes.

QUESTIONS

COAL

Q. Mr. President, I'm Walter Dear from Henderson, Kentucky. My wife joins me in thanking you for your personal leadership in resolving this problem between Israel and Egypt. God bless you. We really do appreciate that.

And now, with my other hat, because I'm from Kentucky, I urge you to come to Kentucky in 60 days, after you've got the results from the three agencies on the implementation of coal, and launch a Manhattan Project and do, likewise, to resolve the question of 10,000 miners being unemployed, hundreds of mines being shut down, and having this 400-year coal opportunity.

And, frankly, at the Hill and elsewhere, we feel that with all the 26 pages in the fact sheet last night, there are about three graphs on coal. How much is too much? This may not be enough. Can you help us in this area?

THE PRESIDENT. Yes. Obviously, we want to have more coal production, under the presently existing state of technology, and to expand sales not only within our own country but overseas.

Secondly, the new technology to give us clean burning gas, liquid, and solids from fuel—from coal, will depend heavily on whether or not we get passed the windfall profits tax. The oil companies are going to fight it, I'm sure, tooth and nail. But I'm determined to see this put on the books. And I'm willing to go to the wall and use my utmost influence among the public and in the Congress to get this tax passed. Otherwise, there will be tremendous, unwarranted profits going to the oil companies, and we won't have available the major coal solvent refining plants, one of which would be constructed, undoubtedly, in Kentucky.

We've got, as I said last night in my talk, tremendous reservoirs of coal. We're not going to back off on the safety and health standards for coal miners. But within those bounds, and also within the bound of not destroying the environment, I think that coal has a wonderful opportunity in the future for increased growth in production and increased prosperity for those regions that produce it.

WAGE AND PRICE GUIDELINES;
OIL PRICE DEREGULATION

Q. Mr. President, are the wage-price profit guidelines completely ineffective as applied to these windfall profits? Is there no way that it could be brought into play in some effective way?

THE PRESIDENT. Well, the wage-price guidelines, as you know, are voluntary. And I think, in general, wages have been within the guidelines—some few exceptions, but on the average, within. And as we've monitored the major corporations—the 500 top ones, the Fortune 500, so-called—they've complied fairly well.

The application of that to oil would be a difficult proposition. I think that we have assessed the inflationary impact of deregulation fairly carefully—and the statistics are available to you in the handout sheets—one- or two-tenths of a percentage point. This has been one of the reasons for the quandary that I've had to face—that any deregulation of any product that presently has its price constrained would be inflationary in nature.

But to artificially hold down the price of domestic oil and to, therefore, encourage the importation of expensive foreign oil and to have this vast Federal bureaucracy that's getting more and more complicated, I think, is a burden that we can no longer bear.

There's an additional factor, also, in that coal and oil and gas are not replenishable. And we have excessive consumption of these increasingly scarce materials, not only in our country but around the world, because of artificially low prices.

So, I think it's better to go ahead and let the prices go up on a carefully scaled basis, in accordance with the present law, and accept the temporary adverse effect on the inflation rate. And as I said last night in my speech, my belief is that the net result of this will be, in the long run, a natural reduction in inflation.

ENERGY CONSERVATION IN RURAL AREAS

Q. Mr. President, I'm Philip Williams from WBNZ in Frankfort, Michigan. What effect are the conservation measures that you've asked for going to have on rural areas, where we depend on the automobile for driving to work, to the store, to everywhere?

I'm sure you are aware of the problems in the rural part of the world. We also depend on it for harvesting our fruits and our vegetables in our area. We also depend upon it for our tourism. If we don't have the tourism that we expect every year, for the 3 months out of the year during the summer, we're going to be in a depression. It's simple as that. What can we do to——

THE PRESIDENT. I grew up in a rural area where every time we went a half-mile, we jumped in the automobile and went there and came back; did it frequently; went to Plains, 2½ miles away, shopping sometimes two or three times a day. And most often, you see on the highways or streets of our country now, automobiles with one passenger in them. In addition to that, Americans don't get enough exercise. [*Laughter*]

The average automobile now travels 10,000 miles a year. And to call on a family to cut down their automobile travel by 15 miles per week is not a very great sacrifice. I pointed out last night how this could be done—by using either a bus or some other form of rapid transit or a carpool, once a week, or perhaps by walking if you don't live too far from work, or cutting out an unnecessary shopping trip, and so forth. I don't think it will work a hardship.

As far as the areas that depend on tourism, we have carefully constructed and will carefully construct the directions of gasoline conservation to the States to give the State Governors and legislatures the option on how to reach those targets.

I was a Governor during the 1973–74 oil embargo, and we were allotted that responsibility by the Federal Government. At first, in order to accommodate States' needs, we were given a 5-percent allocation base. It worked so well that we cut that 5-percent allocation base down to only 3 percent of total consumption. And eventually, we came up here and advised the President and his subordinates to cut the amount of fuel that we had allocated down to only 1 percent of the total State's consumption because it worked so well.

But we depended on this reduction in oil and gas consumption by using State and local volunteers, some small administrative structure, and the regular distribution system. And there's no doubt in my mind that any State in the Nation can cut back its gasoline consumption, for instance, 5 percent, if given the flexibility to do so, which they will have, without wreaking any havoc in their tourism industry if that's their dependence. I don't think there's any doubt that we can do that.

U.S. PALESTINIAN POLICY

Q. Mr. President, I wondered if you could—I'm changing the subject, but if you could redefine your Palestinian policy. Exactly what is the current position?

THE PRESIDENT. Well, I wouldn't want to redefine it, because it's been very consistent from the beginning. [*Laughter*] And I wouldn't change one part of it.

As far as direct relations or consultations or negotiations with the PLO is concerned, we will not do this unless the PLO endorses the United Nations Resolution

242—the basis for all our discussions, and a resolution that's been endorsed by all of the Arab countries, as well as the Israelis—and also recognizes Israel's right to exist. As long as the PLO and its constitution and commitment is dedicated to the destruction of Israel, we will not negotiate with them.

As far as the Palestinian people themselves are concerned, we are eager to see them join in the discussions and negotiations to effectuate the agreements reached at Camp David and encompassed in the recent Mideast treaty and all its ancillary documents.

My hope is that in a couple of months, when El Arish is returned to Egypt and the borders between Israel and Egypt are open, that the free travel of Palestinians and Egyptians, for instance, back and forth between their homes, will alleviate the tension and let the Palestinians escape from the unwarranted constraint of the threat of terrorism against them if they negotiate to get full autonomy, to use Mr. Begin's expression—full autonomy.

I think Sadat has done more for the Palestinians and their cause than any other Arab leader. And now they are fearful of the carrying out of threats of death by some of the more radical Arab elements in the Mideast.

So, we're eager to see the Palestinian people participate, to have full autonomy. And we will not deal with the PLO unless they meet the requirements that I described.

ENERGY SECURITY FUND

Q. Mr. President, Bill Franklin from WNJR in Newark, New Jersey. I want to just extend the greetings of our staff. You were with us before you were elected. We'd like you to come back to the ghetto and visit your friends sometime. [*Laughter*]

My question is, last night, sir, in your message to the Nation, you asked the poor people of this Nation to pay more for gas, and you said you would give the money back to them. How do you propose to do that, sir? Would you define that, please?

THE PRESIDENT. It's defined, I think, in the handout sheet that you are all welcome to take.

I believe that we've set up for those poor families $100-per-family allocation that would cover for the poorer families the increase in the costs that would be attributable to the deregulation. It'll be a simple mechanism. Exactly how it comes back, we have not yet described. But in the reserve fund, there will be money set aside for that purpose.

THREE MILE ISLAND NUCLEAR FACILITY

Q. Mr. President, Don Mulford, Montclair, New Jersey, Times. Are you satisfied that the parameters of the peril in Pennsylvania have been adequately presented to the American people and that the radiation levels have been adequately monitored, so that you can go before the Nation and say with confidence that you have the information necessary to reassure the people who want to come back to their homes near Three Mile Island?

THE PRESIDENT. Yes. The answer is yes. I don't want to minimize the seriousness of the accident and the importance of the lessons that we will learn from it. I think the result of that unfortunate accident will be a much more careful assessment of nuclear power, and the product will be a much more stringent set of safety regulations and operating procedures than we have followed in the past.

But I felt perfectly safe last Sunday when I was in the control room, just a hundred feet away from the reactor core itself. The level of radiation was carefully monitored even before they found out the President was coming. [*Laughter*] And as I pointed out, I was getting about one-third the radiation in the control room that I would have been getting if I was in an airplane flying from Washington to Los Angeles at 35,000-foot altitude.

We have monitored very carefully the entire region, as you know, around Three Mile Island. And we've not found any evidence that there's an excessive level of radiation. It had been well within the safety precautions. And I think the same thing applies to the water in the Susquehanna River as well.

The entire government structure and the nuclear industry, I think the entire country—indeed, the whole world—is concerned about maintaining an even safer set of standards in the nuclear industry. But I can tell you that I felt perfectly safe when I was there with my wife. And I believe that they have done a good job in protecting the safety of the people who live in that area.

TUITION TAX CREDITS

Q. Mr. President, Gerard Sherry, the Voice, in Miami. Several private groups, school groups especially, have suggested you have reneged on your precampaign promise to support tax tuition credits. Can you give me some idea where you feel this might be in error, in relation to the charge that you have reneged on a campaign promise to support tax credits?

THE PRESIDENT. I don't think it's reneging at all. I've always been concerned about the constitutional prohibition against the mixing of church and state and pointed out frequently during the campaign what we had done in Georgia when I was Governor.

We authorized a direct allocation of State funds to the colleges of Georgia, both private and public, on a per capita basis, beginning, I think, with $400 per student, increasing it while I was Governor to $600 per student. So, there are some elements of aid to private colleges of which I strongly approve.

But to see a substantial amount of very limited funds for education going outside the public education system, I thought, and still believe, has been in error. And this would have been an extremely costly proposal to the Federal budget. And my objection was on that basis and not [just] [1] on constitutional grounds.

Q. Thank you.

PRAYER IN PUBLIC SCHOOLS

Q. Mr. President, the Helms amendment to the education bill calls for the opportunity for voluntary prayer in public schools and other public buildings. That's obviously going to be a constitutional issue. Do you see it as unconstitutional?

THE PRESIDENT. I won't try to judge. I'm not a lawyer, and I don't know. The Constitution, I think, has been interpreted by the Supreme Court in such a way that students should not feel a constraint to pray while they are in a public school. And as a Baptist, not particularly a President, I agree with that. I think that prayer should be a private matter between a person and God.

There are constraints that are placed on students other than ordering a child to pray. If everyone else in the classroom is engaged in public prayer and doing it voluntarily, for a young 7- or 8-year-old child to demand the right to leave the room is a difficult question to answer. But in general, I think the Government ought to stay out of the prayer business and let

[1] Printed in the transcript.

it be between a person and God and not let it be part of a school program under any tangible constraints, either a direct order to a child to pray or an embarrassing situation where the child would feel constrained to pray.

It's a difficult question to answer. And I don't know if I have given you an adequate answer.

U.S. RELATIONS WITH THE PHILIPPINES

Q. Mr. President, Joseph O'Hare from America Magazine in New York City. As you know, there have been some complaints by critics of the Marcos government in the Philippines of the recent pact that we have completed with the Philippine Government over the bases. Could you comment on the choices that we were confronted with in dealing with the question of the bases and how your emphasis—which I salute very strongly—on human rights seems to be somewhat compromised by the support that we're now giving the Marcos government as a result of the leasing agreement?

THE PRESIDENT. Before I became President, I think in the fall of 1976, Kissinger and, I think, Romulo, negotiated a base settlement. The one that we have recently negotiated is much more attractive to our own country. The Philippine Government rejected that agreement several years ago, I think early in 1977.

I have never been under any doubt, as a former Navy man nor as the present Commander in Chief of our military forces, that we genuinely need to maintain the right to base our naval forces in the Philippines.

We have made the human rights issue, arguments, as strongly as we could possibly make them with the Marcos government, to the extent of even straining our relationships with the Philippine Government. This has been done at the top level by me and also by others who worked within the State Department itself.

So, we are obviously not pleased with the human rights situation in the Philippines, as measured by our own standards here in our country nor in many other nations that I could name. But I don't have any apology to make about the agreement on the Philippine base rights.

I don't think that our displeasure with meeting American-type standards on human rights protection ought to interfere with our consummating this agreement.

HUMAN RIGHTS

Q. Now that human rights has been mentioned—I travel a great deal, and particularly with newspaper people on—[*inaudible*]—trips, and almost consistently during the last year and a half I've heard leaders of foreign countries complain about our talking about human rights on the ground that, number one, that we seem to be talking down to them; number two, that we don't seem to understand their backgrounds, their religions, their economic problems, and so forth.

For instance, the President of Bangladesh—the military governor, now President—said, "We have trouble even feeding the people. When your Government says, 'Look to human rights,' you're inciting to rebellion." Now, I've been bothered by those things.

I didn't want to mention human rights; I wanted to be a gentleman for once in my life—[*laughter*]—but somebody mentioned it. Now, would you mind addressing that, cause that's bothered me now for 2 years.

THE PRESIDENT. Well, there have been a number of occasions around the world where our human rights policy, which I espouse very strongly and think we ought to maintain, has been a diplomatic problem—in dealing with the People's Republic of China, the Soviet Union, South Korea, Argentina, Chile, Brazil, the Philippines—just been described—and other countries. I could name a lot of them.

Q. Afghanistan.

THE PRESIDENT. Afghanistan and others. I acknowledge that. I think, in balance, it's one of the best things that we have ever done since I've been President. I think for us to raise the banner of being deeply committed to human rights has been and has had an enlightening effect on the rest of the world.

Some of the administrations or the regimes in other nations have been embarrassed. But I can assure you—and I don't think I'm saying this in a gloating way— that in previous administrations, quite often—even in very popular administrations—when visits were made to countries, say, in Latin America just to use an example, there have been, sometimes, massive anti-American demonstrations against very popular leaders, like Eisenhower or Truman or Nixon or Rockefeller and others.

When we have visited those countries, the response has been overwhelmingly favorable and friendly among the people, even when I drove through the streets of Rio de Janeiro in the midst of an argument where human rights and nuclear power were raised.

I think the people have responded well, even though the leaders in some countries have been somewhat embarrassed.

I think it's also reminded the American people about our own Nation's principles. And sometimes the arguments with the totalitarian regime that has several thousands of people imprisoned without trial and without any charge, those arguments have made vivid in the minds of Ameri-

cans that we are indeed better, or different—I think better—in our basic philosophy than those philosophies espoused in some other countries.

There has been a substantial shift toward democratization in many of those nations, partially encouraged by our own standards on human rights. And there have been literally tens of thousands of political prisoners released from within those countries in the last year and a half or so because of our human rights position.

The last point that I would like to make in this answer is that it's raised the issue of human rights to a high degree of intensity. There are very few leaders in the world, in the 150 countries that now exist, who don't every day or every week have to remind ourselves—including me—"to what degree are we violating basic human rights? To what degree are we earning the condemnation of the rest of the world? To what degree are we arousing the animosity or distrust or displeasure or disappointment among our own people because we violate those rights?"

I'm very proud of what we've done. And I think in balance, this posture on human rights has helped us considerably.

If you would go back 3 years or so and look at the attitude, for instance, in the General Assembly of the United Nations every fall when it convened, where our Nation was the butt of every joke and the target of every attack mounted by almost 100 nations on Earth, and compare it with the difference now, the last 2 years, part of that improvement is because we have espoused basic human rights.

I think this is particularly true in Africa where black people now feel they've got a friend in the United States; they can depend on us.

So, to answer your question, I think we've got the right policy, and I intend not only to maintain it but to elevate our commitment to that principle.

MR. WURFEL. Thank you, sir.

OVERSEAS TRIPS BY JOURNALISTS

Q. Could I ask you one question, sir?

THE PRESIDENT. Just one quick one, then I've got to go.

Q. In the 1950's and the 1960's, the State Department encouraged journalists to make trips overseas, and we were briefed—for a day and a half, we came to Washington. Would you think of restoring a program like that to encourage more groups to go overseas?

THE PRESIDENT. I think it would be a good idea.

Q. Thank you very much, sir.

THE PRESIDENT. I wonder if I could do something. I've got another meeting, and I've only got 3 minutes left. Would you all mind if I have a photograph with each one of you individually?

Q. No. [*Laughter*]

THE PRESIDENT. Okay. Thank you.

NOTE: The interview began at 1:16 p.m. in the Cabinet Room at the White House. Walter W. Wurfel is a Deputy Press Secretary.

The transcript of the interview was released on April 7.

Imports of Petroleum and Petroleum Products

Proclamation 4655.   April 6, 1979

By the President of the United States of America

A Proclamation

The Secretary of Energy has advised me that the continuation of shortages in international petroleum and petroleum product supplies has resulted in escalating world oil prices which impact directly on the United States economy. This situation requires that imports of crude oil and petroleum products be adjusted by temporarily suspending tariffs and the system of license fees which have been imposed since 1973 under Proclamation No. 3279, as amended. In light of the current market shortages and price conditions the continued imposition of import fees and tariffs, at least for the near term, do not serve the purposes of the Mandatory Oil Import Program and are detrimental to the economy. As a consequence, for the period that the shortages persist, continued imposition of the tariffs and import fees has become unnecessary and burdensome to the American public.

Therefore, the Secretary of Energy has recommended that I temporarily suspend imposition of the import fees and tariffs. Suspension of the fees and tariffs will serve to alleviate some of the world oil price impacts on the American consumer and should also improve access to certain refined products which are threatened to be in short supply. I agree with the changes proposed by the Secretary and they are consistent with the purposes of Proclamation No. 3279, as amended. The temporary suspension of fees and tariffs does not alter the long term purposes or benefits of the import control program established pursuant to Proclamation No. 3279, as amended. This action will adjust the imports of petroleum and petroleum product supplies so that they are not imported in such quantities or under such circumstances as to threaten to impair the national security.

Now, THEREFORE, I, JIMMY CARTER, President of the United States of America, by the authority vested in me by the Constitution and the laws of the United States, including Section 232 of the Trade Expansion Act of 1962, as amended (19 U.S.C. 1862), do hereby proclaim that:

SECTION 1. Section 3(a)(1) of Proclamation No. 3279, as amended, is further amended in subparagraphs (i) and (ii), and by the addition of a subparagraph (viii), to read as follows:

"(i) with respect to imports of crude oil (other than that imported by the Department of Energy, or by another person or agency of the Federal Government acting on behalf of the Department, for the Strategic Petroleum Reserve Program) and natural gas products over and above the levels of imports established in Section 2 of the Proclamation, such fees shall be $0.00 per barrel for the period April 1, 1979 through June 30, 1979. Effective July 1, 1979 such fees shall be $0.21 per barrel unless the Secretary makes the finding prescribed in paragraph 3(a)(1)(viii) in which case the fees shall remain at the $0.00 level;

"(ii) with respect to imports of motor gasoline, unfinished oils, and all other finished products (except ethane, propane, butanes, asphalt and finished products imported by the Department of Energy, or another person or agency of the Federal Government acting on behalf of the Department of Energy, for the Strategic Petroleum Reserve Program), over and above the levels of imports established in Section 2 of this Proclamation, such fees shall be $0.00 per barrel for the period April 1, 1979 through June 30, 1979. Effective July 1, 1979, such fees shall be $0.63 per barrel unless the Secretary makes the finding prescribed in paragraph 3(a)(1)(viii) in which case the fees shall remain at the $0.00 level;

"(viii) with respect to the fees imposed pursuant to paragraphs 3(a)(1)(i)-(ii), the Secretary may defer the imposition of either the $0.21 or $0.63 fee for a period, not to exceed six months, with respect to any type of crude oil, unfinished oil, or finished product for which the Secretary finds that imposition of the fees would not be in accordance with the purposes of this Proclamation. Reimposition of the fees may be deferred for one additional period, not to exceed six months, upon a similar finding.".

SEC. 2. Section 4 of Proclamation No. 3279, as amended, is amended by the addition of subsections (d) and (e) to read as follows:

"(d) Such regulations may provide for allocation periods of other than one year's duration; *provided,* that the applicable average barrel per day level of imports not subject to the payment of fees provided in Section 2 of this Proclamation is not exceeded on the average in any such period established.

"(e) Notwithstanding the levels established in Section 2 of this Proclamation, such regulations may provide for the suspension of the issuance of licenses not subject to the payment of fees with respect to any type of crude oil, unfinished oil, or finished product for any period in which a fee of $0.00, as provided in Section 3 of this Proclamation, is in effect.".

SEC. 3. Effective as of April 1, 1979, tariffs upon imports of petroleum and petroleum products listed in Schedule 4, Part 10—"Petroleum, natural gas and products derived therefrom," and tariffs upon imports of hydrocarbons listed in Schedule 4, Part 2—"Chemical Elements, Inorganic and Organic Compounds, and Mixtures", of the Tariff Schedules of the United States shall be and are suspended until July 1, 1979, at which time the tariffs shall be reimposed except with respect to any item in Schedule 4, Part 2 or Part 10, for which the Secretary of Energy finds that the reimposition of a tariff would not be in accordance with the purposes of Proclamation No. 3279, as amended. Upon such a finding, the Secretary may defer imposition of the tariff for a period not to exceed six months and may defer imposition of the tariff for one additional period, not to exceed six months, upon a similar finding.

IN WITNESS WHEREOF, I have hereunto set my hand this sixth day of April, in the year of our Lord nineteen hundred seventy-nine, and of the Independence of the United States of America the two hundred and third.

JIMMY CARTER

[Filed with the Office of the Federal Register, 10:30 a.m., April 9, 1979]

NOTE: The text of the proclamation was released on April 7.

Richmond, Virginia

Remarks at the State Democratic Party's Jefferson-Jackson Day Dinner. April 7, 1979

In a few minutes, you will hear me make a speech from the other room, but I would like to say if I could choose one audience in the entire Nation that I would rather speak to tonight, it would be an overflow crowd at a Democratic fundraising event in Richmond, Virginia.

I won't have very much time in here. And since you won't be in the other room, you're very generous to let me come in ahead of time to speak to you.

I've only got about 7 minutes, so rather than making an extra speech, if you don't mind, I would kind of like to walk down this aisle and over and back, and maybe shake a few hands. I won't have a chance

to do that in the large room, but I particularly want to thank you especially.

[*The President spoke to dinner guests at 7:22 p.m. in the Marshall Room at the John Marshall Hotel. He then went to the Virginia Room at the hotel, where he delivered the following remarks at the main dinner.*]

Lieutenant Governor Robb, Congressman Satterfield, Congressman Daniel, Congressman Harris, Congressman Fisher, my good friend Andy Miller, my good friend Henry Howell, Chairman Dick Davis, Speaker Cooke, and future victorious Virginia Democrats:

I am very proud to be with you. I'm glad to be back in Richmond. The first time I ever spent a night with my wife in a hotel was in Richmond, Virginia, in the old Jefferson. [*Laughter*]

It was a month before we got married—[*laughter*]—the night of June Week at the Naval Academy, and my mother and father stayed in the room, unfortunately, between us. [*Laughter*]

But I've always had a special place in my heart for Richmond ever since that time. I have a lot of warm feelings about Virginia. My ancestors came from your State. My first son was born in Virginia, because my wife and I started our married life in this great State. This is the birthplace of the Nation that I love, and, as you know, it's the home of the father of the Democratic Party. So, I feel at home with you, and I'm very glad to be here.

I try, when I come, to think of some good things to say about the State, and it's not difficult in Virginia.

Last weekend I was in Wisconsin, in Milwaukee and in Wausau. I spoke to a group in Wausau—this is the fourth group I've met with since I've been in Richmond tonight—and they told me that in Wausau, I was the first President who had been there since Calvin Coolidge.

He was in Wausau on a fishing trip. And when he spent all weekend fishing north of Wausau, he came back and had a two-word press conference. They came up and asked him, "How do you like the fishing in Wisconsin?" And he thought for a while and he said, "Prefer Maine." [*Laughter*]

Well, my feelings toward Virginia are quite different from Calvin Coolidge's toward Wisconsin.

This last decade or more has been an era of dissension and disappointment for Democrats of Virginia. There have been too many agonizingly close defeats. In 1973, I came here to campaign twice— all one weekend, and another time while I was Governor of Georgia, for Henry Howell. And he lost by seven-tenths of one percentage point. In 1976, another campaign in which I participated, along with Fritz Mondale, we lost by about 20,000 votes out of 1.6 million cast. And, as you know, last year Andy Miller lost a heartbreaking election by only, I think, 4,800 votes out of 1.4 million.

So, we have had some serious setbacks, very close campaigns lost, and the candidates have obviously been disappointed. So have I. But Virginia has suffered in the past; in the future, it will be quite different. I think it's sobering to think that in a State which is the birthplace of the Democratic Party, this is the only State in the Nation which, since 1966, has not elected a Democratic Governor or a Democratic United States Senator and has not cast an electoral vote for a Democratic candidate for President. But that's all behind us now.

You won the Lieutenant Governor's race with Chuck Robb, and there is no one in this room who thinks that Chuck Robb's career in politics will stop with Lieutenant Governor. And other great

Virginia Democratic candidates will join him for future victories. I think the future of the Democratic Party in Virginia is bright indeed.

Tonight, all segments of the party are here. And when I looked down at the list of notable Democrats who are attending, my heart was warmed indeed. I wish I could claim credit for the great turnout, but I know the real drawing card is Speaker John Warren Cooke. It's an honor for me to be here with him. He is famous in Virginia, but he's famous all over the country as well. As you know, he was honored as the National Legislator of the Year in 1975 for his long and outstanding service, and he's honored again by you tonight, and I'm honored to be with him.

The next 2½ years will be a time of testing for the Virginia Democrats. You'll have the opportunity to elect Democrats to almost every State and local office. Today, you have the organization, the unity, the spirit, the finances, and the determination to regain the rightful place of leadership in the State where American democracy was born. Virginians can win, and the Democrats will win in Virginia. And I'll be there helping you to win those victories.

I feel a partnership with you, much closer, perhaps, than many of you would realize. It's of intense interest to me how Virginia goes in future elections. And I've been happy when you've won and heartbroken when you've lost, in the last few years, since I've gotten to know many of you. We've shared common problems, and we share a common future.

We have honored the ancient principles of our party in victory and defeat. And I think more and more, the Democratic Party on the national level and the Democratic Party on the State and local level has come with its modern programs to take its place in the broad and glorious and progressive mainstream of America and Virginia as well.

I inherited, along with you, a Republican mess in Washington a little more than 2 years ago. But we Democrats at that time formed a partnership. You've helped me since I've been there. And we have made a great deal of progress.

The 2 years since I became President have been a time for rebuilding. I'm proud of what we've accomplished, but our work, as you well know, is far from done.

When they write the history of these years, I hope they will say four things about what has been accomplished, what we've done together.

I want them to say that we were not afraid to tackle the difficult and sometimes unpopular problems, such as energy, and that we placed the long-term good of our country above petty political advantage.

I want them to say that we have restored what was lost, the trust and faith of American people in our own Government.

I want them to say that we have made America prosperous again and put our people back to work.

And, most of all, I want them to say that America has been at peace, and that we as a nation have contributed to a world without war.

If we can continue to build this New Foundation for peace, trust, and prosperity, we will have kept faith with our party and with our country.

Two nights ago, as you may have noticed, I spoke on television to the American people about our Nation's very serious energy problem. Our energy problem is, above all, an oil problem. We use too much oil; we waste too much oil. We

don't produce enough oil in our own country, and our progress in developing alternatives to oil are being pursued all too slowly. As a result, we are importing oil now to the tune of $50 billion this year—that's $225 spent for foreign oil by every man, woman, and child in the United States of America.

So, our economy and our security are dangerously subject to the whims of a foreign oil cartel.

Two years ago, almost exactly 2 years ago, I introduced a comprehensive plan to the Congress to deal with this problem. And then after more than a year and a half of debate and special pleading and struggling among the various interest groups, Congress finally passed a program that was a beginning, a good beginning. But that program which Congress did pass, because of the political difficulties involved, did not deal at all with the oil problem. So, we still face the basic reality about America's use of oil: We must use less, and we must pay more for what we use.

That's not a pleasant message for any of us, but it's the truth. And the American people have shown time and time again that when they get the truth, they will respond. I did not make the decision that I announced because I expected it to be pleasant or popular. I made it because it's right, and it's necessary, and it's in the best interest of our Nation. But, having made it, I will not allow this painful but necessary step to become an excuse for a massive ripoff of the American people by the American oil companies. That's why I will fight for a windfall profits tax just on the unearned, excess profits of the oil companies.

With the revenues from this tax, we will establish an energy security fund. We will ease the financial burden of higher oil prices on those who can least afford to pay it. And we will develop a better mass transit system. We will finance an all-out effort by American science and technology to meet our long-term energy needs—with everything from gasification and liquefaction of coal to harnessing the power of the Sun.

But we must face facts. The oil lobby does not like the idea of the American [energy] [1] security fund for the American people. The oil lobby is going to be all over Capitol Hill like a chicken on a june bug. [*Laughter*] It's certain, and you know it. And we are being told by them that we should just turn all the money over to them; they will wisely know how to spend it for the benefit of the American consumer. Now, I don't question their sincerity—[*laughter*]—and I certainly do not question their enormous political influence.

They've blocked the energy legislation in the Congress now for more than 2 years. But the American people know that they are wrong. And I refuse to believe that the Congress of the United States will vote to make a few, already rich companies billions of dollars richer off the necessary sacrifices of Americans who are struggling to make ends meet.

Some people are already urging and wringing their hands and saying that this windfall profits tax and the energy security fund will never pass. They say that the oil lobby has more influence on the Congress than the American people. Even some Members of Congress say so. I say to you, let's prove them wrong. I say, let's prove that the Government of the United States belongs to the people of the United States.

Now, I'm not looking for a fight; I've got enough to keep me busy. But I'll promise you this: I am prepared to fight,

---

[1] Printed in the transcript.

if that's what it takes. And with your help, I do not intend to lose this fight.

Coal. Coal, which is one of the Nation's—and Virginia's—most abundant resources, is a significant part of the plan that I outlined 2 nights ago. We are already in the first part of the program, passed by Congress, restoring the health and the vitality of the coal industry, and Virginia is sharing in this renewed prosperity.

The energy security fund, derived from the windfall profits tax, will allow us to develop more quickly new alternatives of energy at affordable prices. Then we can rely on coal liquefaction and coal gasification and the purification of coal in a solid form, to light the way toward a more self-reliant future. I know that you in Virginia will be especially eager to give me your help on this facet of the energy problem.

I'd like to cover now very briefly with you a basic question. What kind of government do we need in Washington? Thomas Jefferson declared in his first Inaugural Address, and I'd like to quote from him, "A wise and a frugal government, which shall restrain men from injuring one another, which shall leave them otherwise free to regulate their own pursuits of industry and improvement, and shall not take from the mouth of labor the bread it has earned. That," he said, "is the sum of government."

When I campaigned for the Presidency in all our States for more than 2 years, everywhere I went, I heard how sick and tired the American people were of bureaucracy, redtape, and government inefficiency. Since taking office, I have worked hard to do something about it.

We have restored our system of federalism, forming a new partnership, an eager productive partnership, between county governments, city governments,

State governments, and the Federal Government. I served for Governor for 4 years. I had absolutely no access, no cooperation, no communication, no consultation with the Federal Government in Washington, no matter how hard I tried. That's been changed. Any Governor in our Nation, any mayor in our Nation, Republican or Democrat, will tell you that what I say is true.

We have passed, for the first time in almost a hundred years, a landmark civil service reform bill that will now reward accomplishment, not mediocrity. It will give our thousands of excellent Federal employees a chance again to be proud of their own lives' work. And you'll see a difference when you call a Government agency or participate in a Federal program. We can make government work for you.

The American people complained about the regulatory nightmare, and we heard their voices. Our reforms in just a few areas have already saved consumers $2½ billion, for instance, in reduced airline fees. We've eliminated a thousand unnecessary OSHA rules that harassed employers without protecting our workers' health or safety. Our new regulatory reform bill, now in Congress, will bring much needed rationality to the entire regulatory process.

We can protect the health and the safety of our people—and the environment. And we can lift the unnecessary burden of meddlesome regulations that threaten to smother our people in a mountain of paperwork. And I'm determined to be successful in this effort.

I found, in Washington, good Federal employees at all levels of responsibility concerned about a bureaucracy where waste and fraud were so common that often investigators and auditors could not even estimate the extent of it. We've given

the people honest and competent government.

In cleaning up the GSA scandals, in cracking down on fraud in HEW and other departments, in appointing Inspectors General now in all major agencies, we've been following Andrew Jackson's credo, which he gave us in 1832. "There are no necessary evils," he said, "in government. Its evils exist only in its abuses."

It's not enough for our Government to work. Our economy must work also. The American people expect stable prices and jobs for all who seek them. As President, I intend to see that we have both.

We are in the midst of the longest economic boom in the history of our Nation. We have tended recently to become depressed over every individual item of the day's economic news. That kind of pessimism about our country and its strength is unwarranted, and it should not detract from what our Nation is nor should it detract from our accomplishments.

In 2 years, we have reduced unemployment by 25 percent in our Nation. Today, almost a hundred million Americans have jobs. We've created a net increase of more than 7½ million of those jobs since I took office. And every one of these jobs means that another American is contributing to our productive economy. We have put America back to work.

And I would like to say, as a former businessman, that business has shared in these good times. Profits have grown by more than 34 percent since January of 1977. And last year, net farm income increased 30 percent.

But our economy will not be truly healthy until we bring inflation under control. It's been a burden for our Nation for the last 10 solid years.

Five months ago, I announced a tough program of voluntary standards to slow the rate of inflation. I cautioned then that it was a long-term program which would not provide instant results or immediate gratification.

We have had some important successes. It's unfortunate that they've been obscured by inflationary forces, many beyond our own control, such as OPEC oil prices, the very small cattle herds which are now being rebuilt, and the severe winter weather that made fruit and produce so scarce.

Most of our Nation's largest corporations have promised to abide by our guidelines. They have let us monitor their performance, and I can tell you they are keeping their word.

We have had problems with some smaller companies that in the past didn't think the guidelines applied to them, but now they're beginning to understand what we are attempting to do. But we are greatly increasing our price-monitoring effort to make sure that every business in our country does its share.

And without fanfare or headlines, often without recognition, the working people of this country, both organized and unorganized, are sharing in the fight against higher prices. As of mid-March, contracts that meet the guidelines have been negotiated by unions covering 325,000 workers, hundreds of contracts.

Inflation, however, is still a very serious problem. Our guidelines are voluntary, and there are times when they will be violated. But in almost every case, wage or price increases that exceed the standards will still be significantly lower than if we had chosen to do nothing.

We'll fight to make the guidelines more and more effective, week by week. And as we get the first quarter's results and analyze them, any company which is exceeding the guidelines will have a very

difficult time selling their products to the Federal Government.

We must be prudent buyers. And I hope that you will also be prudent buyers. We will be sending out now, on a monthly basis, a report to you on those items which we believe have exceeded and are exceeding the prices that are most attractive for you and for your family. And I hope that you will purchase your supplies, your food, very carefully. And we've joined in with consumer groups and others to monitor the prices, still on a voluntary basis.

If we're going to curb inflation, however, the Federal budget must also set an example of restraint. And that's where my direct responsibility comes in.

Republicans talk about balanced budgets, but it takes Democrats to reduce the deficit. A recent poll, nationwide poll, showed that for the first time since the two parties have been formed, more people in this country now believe that Democrats are fiscally responsible than Republicans. We have always been more fiscally responsible; now people know it.

One reason is that in 1976, when I was running for President, the Federal budget deficit was over $66 billion. The budget that I've just submitted to Congress will realize a net reduction in our deficit of more than 55 percent, which will get us more than halfway toward our goal of what you want, and that's a balanced budget for the Government of the United States.

The important thing is that we have trimmed the fat in our budget without jeopardizing the programs that help the poor and the disadvantaged and the [un]employed and which give our Nation prosperity and give our Nation a strong defense, because we know that prosperity at home depends on our military strength and on our commitment to peace.

As Thomas Jefferson wrote to Andrew Jackson in 1806, Americans must convince the world that we are just friends and we are also brave enemies. This is still an excellent summary of the goals of American foreign policy.

The purpose of America's military forces is not to wage war but to preserve peace. And to do that, we must make sure that no nation seriously doubts our ability or our will to meet any challenge to the country which we love. We must continue to improve our ability to respond quickly and to respond effectively to military threats.

In 1818, looking back on his long years of service to our Nation, Thomas Jefferson noted with pride, and I quote, "During the period of my administration," he said, "not a drop of the blood of a single fellow citizen was shed by the sword of war."

I am also proud that no drop of American blood has been shed in war during my own administration. And I pray, literally, several times a day, that when my years as President are over, that I can still share Jefferson's achievement of peace for our people.

Jefferson predicted that we would one day have greater power than the European empires which were so powerful when he lived. But he also cautioned, and I quote again, "I hope our wisdom will grow with our power and teach us that the less we use our power, the greater it will be."

Our military strength and our national will are abundantly clear now to all nations. We do not need to prove our strength through rash and reckless military adventures. Rather, our military capacity gives us a rare opportunity to lead the world toward peace.

I promised, when I was campaigning among the American people, that when I took office, that I would make our foreign policy reflect our own highest ideals and standards.

Here in the home of George Washington and Patrick Henry, it's well to remember who we are. Here the age-old dreams of mankind grew into the ideas that have made our Declaration of Independence a statement—not just of the goals and beliefs of our Nation but of the hopes and dreams of all the world's people.

When I promised this country a government as good as our own people, some critics dismissed it as meaningless rhetoric. But they missed what I was really talking about. But I guess, looking at the results of the election, that a majority of the voters must have understood.

Our foreign policy is as good as our people when we speak out for human rights around the world, and we will. Our foreign policy is as good as the American people when we work to bring peace to ancient enemies, and we have done so.

A victory for this kind of foreign policy was won when the peace treaty was signed last week by Egypt and Israel, and now we must make the full hopes and dreams that went into the signing of that treaty be realized for the people of the Middle East who yearn for peace.

The United States was able to perform a crucial role at a critical point to help make that possible. But that treaty was not a personal accomplishment, though I was proud and grateful to be a part of it. The treaty was a tribute to two courageous men, and also it was a triumph of moral strength and leadership of our Nation.

Whatever I'm able to do in easing the tensions of our world is based on the strength of the American people and how much support I have from you and on the power of the principles on which our Nation was founded.

If we can help the nations of the Middle East eventually to work out a permanent peace, it will be because they trust the American people and our principles, and not because they trust any one particular American President.

This is true not just in this administration, but from the moment of our birth as a nation, through all times, as long as we call ourselves a free people. We must set an example for the rest of the world, who look to us with such eager, questioning, often admiring eyes.

Our next major goal, I would like to say in closing, is a SALT treaty, to curb the horrible threat of nuclear destruction. Our Nation was shaken within the last few days by a potential serious accident in Pennsylvania. I hope that one result of that fright will be to remind every American how vastly more destructive to a hundred million American people, almost half our population, if there should be a nuclear exchange of powerful and destructive weapons between us and the Soviet Union. It's the most serious threat we face.

Any treaty that I sign will be negotiated very carefully. I have already spent 2 years in these detailed negotiations. They've been going on now for more than 6 years, including my own predecessors in the White House. Any treaty that I sign will enhance the safety and security of our country. And any treaty I sign will be adequately verifiable so that we can know with our own means whether or not the Soviets are complying with its terms.

I will need your strong support in the ratification of this necessary step toward peace through strength. Peace and prosperity through strength—peace and prosperity through strength—this is the

source of our Nation's true power on which all else must rest. This is the foundation for good leadership at all levels of government. We Democrats offer this kind of leadership, and this is why the future of this party, the future of this State, and the future of this Nation is so bright.

Thank you very much.

NOTE: The President spoke at 7:35 p.m. in the Virginia Room. In his opening remarks, he referred to Richard J. Davis, chairman of the Virginia Democratic Party.

Energy Emergency in Florida
Presidential Determination. April 6, 1979

Based on a Petition submitted to me by the Governor of the State of Florida, pursuant to Section 110(f) of the Clean Air Act, I hereby determine that a regional energy emergency exists in the State of Florida of such severity that a temporary suspension of certain particulate and opacity control regulations which apply to fossil-fuel fired electric generating plants under the Florida Air Quality Implementation Plan may be necessary, and that other means of responding to the energy emergency may be inadequate. This determination shall be effective for not more than thirty (30) days. If, during the period of suspension, I find that a regional energy emergency no longer exists in Florida, I will direct that this determination of regional energy emergency be rescinded and that all suspension orders issued by the Governor be terminated effective on the day of that rescission. The Administrator of the Environmental Protection Agency retains full authority to disapprove temporary suspensions of regulations in Florida and to exercise his emergency powers authority under Section 303 of the Clean Air Act, when and if necessary.

I commend the Governor for his commitment to act with care if he suspends air pollution regulations under the authority provided by this determination, since such regulations are important to protect public health. I commend him for undertaking energy conservation measures and for his commitment that no suspension will be granted if the result would be a violation of any national ambient primary or secondary air quality standard.

This determination shall be published in the FEDERAL REGISTER.

JIMMY CARTER

Date: April 6, 1979.

[Filed with the Office of the Federal Register, 10:31 a.m., April 9, 1979]

NOTE: The text of the determination was released on April 9.

Egyptian-Israeli Peace Treaty

Letter to the Speaker of the House and the President of the Senate Transmitting Proposed Legislation To Implement the Treaty. April 9, 1979

Dear Mr. Speaker: (*Dear Mr. President:*)

I hereby transmit a bill "to authorize supplemental international security assistance for the fiscal year 1979 in support of the peace treaty between Egypt and Israel and related agreements, and for other purposes", and urge its prompt enactment. The bill authorizes appropriations of $1,470,000,000 to finance programs totalling $4,800,000,000.

The bill authorizes the President (1) to enter into contracts for the construction of air bases in Israel, as contemplated by the Treaty, to replace air bases on the Sinai peninsula, and (2) to furnish as a grant to the government of Israel $800,000,000 in defense articles and services for such construction. In addition, the bill authorizes appropriations of $220,000,000 to guarantee $2,200,000,000 in loans to Israel to finance procurement through fiscal year 1982 of defense articles and defense services.

For Egypt, the bill authorizes appropriations of $150,000,000 to guarantee $1,500,000,000 in loans to finance procurement through fiscal year 1982 of defense articles and defense services. In addition, the bill authorizes appropriations of $300,000,000 in economic assistance to Egypt.

The supplemental assistance to Egypt and Israel authorized in the attached bill will provide tangible evidence of U.S. dedication to the peace process. It will clearly demonstrate to the people of these two countries—more than words alone—that we will help them reap the advantages of peace. The costs set forth in the bill are directly related to implementation of the Peace Treaty. Swift Congressional action to enact the bill will demonstrate U.S. capacity to move quickly and decisively to support our friends in the Middle East.

Unless both Egypt and Israel are confident of their security, enduring peace can neither be solidified between them nor broadened to other parties. This legislation will demonstrate that while the United States continues as an active and responsive partner in the pursuit of a comprehensive Middle East peace we will continue to be sensitive to the security concerns of Egypt and Israel.

We believe the proposed security assistance legislation should be viewed as an integrated whole. All elements of the package—FMS financing, grant and economic assistance—complement one another in providing the type of comprehensive program called for under current circumstances.

Construction of air bases in Israel is not only a critical element in that country's security, but is essential in order for Israel to fulfill its undertaking to withdraw from the Sinai within the three-year period agreed in the Peace Treaty. This withdrawal is, of course, of vital importance to Egypt and to the continued momentum of the entire peace process.

The provision of direct assistance to Egypt will ensure that the Egyptians understand that our sensitivity to Israel's security requirements is paralleled by a concern for their security and national development. Provision of FMS financing to Egypt will enable the Egyptian government to begin modernization of its armed forces. In turn, this will enhance Egypt's capabilities to fulfill legitimate needs for self-defense to meet any threats which might arise.

Both Egypt and Israel face immediate economic problems as they enter the post-Treaty era. The financial cost to Israel of withdrawal from the Sinai will be substantial. For its part, the Egyptian government has an urgent and critical need to demonstrate to its people the economic benefits of peace. The proposed legislation will provide funds to move quickly to meet some new requirements; we likewise will work to accelerate implementation of our current programs.

Prompt and favorable action by the Congress on the attached legislation will provide the clearest possible signal of U.S. determination to support the results achieved thus far in the Middle East and will give impetus to the search for a comprehensive settlement. The peace process

must not be allowed to languish. We seek your support for a good beginning designed to sustain momentum towards a wider peace.

Sincerely,

JIMMY CARTER

NOTE: This is the text of identical letters addressed to Thomas P. O'Neill, Jr., Speaker of the House of Representatives, and Walter F. Mondale, President of the Senate.

Vice President Mondale's Visit to the Nordic Countries and the Netherlands

Remarks to Scandinavian and Dutch Journalists Concerning the Visit. April 10, 1979

THE VICE PRESIDENT. Mr. President, we gave a brief report on what this trip is about and the importance we place on our relations with these nations and the fact that right now, I think, in every case our relationships are just about as good as they could be. We have no serious or contentious issues.

THE PRESIDENT. I might say that the lights did not go out in the Oval Office. [*Laughter*]

Well, I don't think there's anything more important to us, to our country, than to have a good relationship and a strong alliance with those who share common principles and goals with our country. And this is obviously true with the nations that the Vice President will be visiting very shortly.

But it is equally important that we have a chance for quiet and comprehensive discussions between the heads of state and Vice President Mondale, who speaks directly and with authority for me. And I look forward to the report that Vice President Mondale will bring back to our country. I think it will make us much better able to prepare our own Nation's policies in consonance with our friends and allies who will be visited by the Vice President.

So, I want to thank all of you for being willing to come and meet with the Vice President this morning. I think his trip and the impact of it will be very beneficial for our own country, and I hope it will be equally pleasing and helpful to the nations that he will visit.

I think it will be good for you to either report from your own observations or, perhaps, after consultation with some of the American journalists who've covered the White House for many years, the degree of authority that Vice President Mondale enjoys as compared to his predecessors. He's a partner with me. He participates in all of the major decisions of our country—in defense and political affairs, economic and military affairs—and comes to the countries that you represent with absolute authority to speak for our country's Government.

REPORTER. Thank you, Mr. President.

NOTE: The President spoke at approximately 9:30 a.m. in the Roosevelt Room at the White House, following the Vice President's interview with the journalists. Vice President Mondale began his trip on April 11.

United States Trade Mission to Egypt and Israel

Announcement of the Mission.   April 10, 1979

The President has asked Special Trade Representative Robert Strauss to lead a U.S. trade mission to Egypt and Israel from April 16 to April 20.

In meetings with trade, business, and labor officials of both countries, the U.S. delegation will explore ways to carry out the President's commitment to increased U.S. trade and investment in both Egypt and Israel.

The group will include Members of Congress and representatives of U.S. agencies, as well as industry and labor leaders. They will leave Washington for Cairo on April 16 and will spend April 17 and 18 in Egypt and April 19 and 20 in Israel.

Taiwan Relations Act

Statement on Signing H.R. 2479 Into Law. April 10, 1979

I am today signing into law H.R. 2479, the Taiwan Relations Act. This legislation will enable the American people and the people on Taiwan to maintain commercial, cultural, and other relations without official Government representation and without diplomatic relations.

The act contains all of the authority that I requested in order to enable us to maintain such unofficial relations with the people on Taiwan. It authorizes the American Institute in Taiwan, a nongovernmental entity incorporated under the laws of the District of Columbia, to conduct these relations. Similarly, the people on Taiwan will conduct relations through a nongovernmental organization, the Coordination Council for North American Affairs.

The act is consistent with the understandings we reached in normalizing relations with the Government of the People's Republic of China. It reflects our recognition of that Government as the sole legal government of China. Having normalized relations with China in the spirit of the Shanghai communique, I look forward in the coming years to a deepening and broadening of U.S.-China relations which will contribute to the welfare of our two peoples and to peace in the world.

I wish to express my appreciation to the Congress for the speed and diligence with which it has acted. I believe a different treatment of the issue of diplomatic properties belonging to China would have been preferable, and my action today is without prejudice to any subsequent adjudication of the legal status of these properties. In most respects, however, the Congress and the executive branch have cooperated effectively in this matter.

In a number of sections of this legislation, the Congress has wisely granted discretion to the President. In all instances, I will exercise that discretion in a manner consistent with our interest, in the well-being of the people on Taiwan, and with the understandings we reached on the normalization of relations with the People's Republic of China, as expressed in our Joint Communique of January 1, 1979, on Establishment of Diplomatic Relations.

NOTE: As enacted, H.R. 2479 is Public Law 96-8, approved April 10.

National Architectural Barrier Awareness Week, 1979

Proclamation 4656. April 10, 1979

By the President of the United States of America

A Proclamation

Architectural and other barriers often keep millions of Americans from participating in and contributing to our society.

These barriers come in all shapes and sizes—from a six-inch curb and inaccessible bus to an unbrailled menu and uncaptioned news broadcast.

These physical and other kinds of barriers deny daily access for millions of America's elderly and handicapped citizens to jobs, transportation, recreation and public service. Attitudes and customs contribute to this problem.

Physical access often determines whether people can enjoy their rights and freedoms and exercise their responsibilities. Most of us take such access for granted. However, many disabled and disabled elderly cannot.

The first Federal legislation to eliminate barriers was the Architectural Barriers Act of 1968. To help implement that law, Congress created—within Section 502 of the Rehabilitation Act of 1973—the Architectural and Transportation Barriers Compliance Board.

The Board has worked to remove and prevent environmental barriers in this country. By doing so it helps ensure that disabled persons can enter and use facilities that their tax dollars support. And it helps inform Federal agencies that these facilities must be accessible from the time United States dollars are used to design, build, alter or lease them.

The Board has mounted a national media campaign about barriers under its slogan, "Access America." In May 1979 it will launch a series of national seminars on barriers for leaders in business, industry and education. The Board is also surveying more than 1,000 federally-owned and funded facilities in the ten federal regions to assess compliance with Federal law.

A number of agencies have already taken important steps to eliminate barriers. The Veterans Administration, for example, has surveyed all of its 172 hospitals and has earmarked $1.2 million for 86 barrier-removal projects in fiscal year 1979. The General Services Administration intends to obligate $26 million between now and 1982 to retrofit many of its properties. I will continue to support such efforts.

But many barriers that block people from opportunity and fulfillment need the attention of State and local governments and the private sector. I herewith call upon all State and local governments and the private sector to join with the Federal Government in a partnership to eliminate barriers which limit full social participation by our disabled citizens. Only by working together as a Nation can we promote and provide full access to all of our citizens.

To encourage this national commitment, the Ninety-fifth Congress adopted House Joint Resolution 578 authorizing the President to proclaim the third weeks of May of 1978 and 1979 as National Architectural Barrier Awareness Week and to call for its appropriate observance.

Now, THEREFORE, I, JIMMY CARTER, President of the United States of America, do hereby designate the third week of May 1979 as National Architectural Barrier Awareness Week and ask all Americans to do all that lies within their power to remove all barriers—architectural, social, and psychological. Together we can make access a reality for all Americans.

IN WITNESS WHEREOF, I have hereunto set my hand this tenth day of April, in the year of our Lord nineteen hundred seventy-nine, and of the Independence of the United States of America the two hundred and third.

JIMMY CARTER

[Filed with the Office of the Federal Register, 2:16 p.m., April 10, 1979]

United States International Development Cooperation Agency

Message to the Congress Transmitting Reorganization Plan No. 2 of 1979. April 10, 1979

To the Congress of the United States:

I transmit herewith Reorganization Plan No. 2 of 1979, to consolidate certain foreign assistance activities of the United States Government. I am acting under the authority vested in me by the Reorganization Act, chapter 9 of title 5 of the United States Code, and pursuant to title III of the International Development and Food Assistance Act of 1978, which requires that I report to the Congress my decisions on reorganization in this area. The purposes of this reorganization are to make more coherent our economic policies and programs affecting the developing nations and to improve the effectiveness of United States foreign development activities.

This Nation is committed—not only in the interest of the people of developing countries, but in our own interest as well—to help those countries in their efforts to achieve better lives for their citizens. To this end, we conduct a number of bilateral development assistance programs, participate in a number of multilateral development assistance programs, and engage in a variety of other economic activities that affect developing countries.

When this Administration took office, United States support of international development suffered from four major problems. First, no single U.S. official was charged with responsibility for establishing a comprehensive and coherent strategy for our Nation's efforts in this field. Second, no agency or official had the authority to ensure that the various U.S. programs affecting development were consistent with each other or complemented the programs of the multilateral organizations to which we contribute. Third, none of the agency heads testifying before the Congress about his particular portion of our foreign assistance efforts was able to speak authoritatively for the program as a whole or for the Administration's overall development policies and priorities. Finally, because there was no authoritative spokesperson, developmental concerns were at times accorded insufficient weight in executive branch decision-making on trade, monetary, and other non-aid economic issues that affect developing nations.

Just before his death a year ago, Senator Hubert H. Humphrey prepared a bill intended to solve these problems. Congressman Clement Zablocki introduced a similar measure in the House. Although the Congress took no action last year on the organizational provisions of the Humphrey-Zablocki bill, it directed me, in title III of the 1978 development assistance authorization act, to institute a strengthened system of coordination of U.S. economic policies affecting the developing countries, and urged me to create an agency with primary responsibility for coordination of international development-related activities.

In response to the Humphrey-Zablocki bill and the Administration's own analyses, I took a number of steps last year to strengthen aid coordination and improve the effectiveness of our development assistance programs. The Reorganization Plan transmitted with this message continues that process. It will provide stronger direction of U.S. policies toward the developing world, ensure a more coherent development strategy, promote the more effective use of the various U.S. bilateral instruments by which the U.S. can encourage economic and social progress in developing countries, and ensure that U.S. bilateral programs and the multilateral programs to which we contribute better complement each other.

This reorganization would create a new agency, to be known as the International Development Cooperation Agency (IDCA). IDCA would become a focal point within the U.S. Government for economic matters affecting U.S. relations with developing countries. Subject to guidance concerning the foreign policy of the United States from the Secretary of State, the IDCA Director would be the principal international development advisor to the President and to the Secretary of State. The Director would replace the AID Administrator in chairing the Development Coordination Committee. The IDCA Director would make recommendations to me concerning the appointment and tenure of senior officials of each component of IDCA, and would establish and control the budgets and policies of the Agency for International Development and the bilateral foreign assistance programs it administers, and of the Institute For Technological Cooperation, proposed in legislation transmitted to the Congress on February 26, 1979, which would support research and technological innovation to reduce obstacles to economic development.

The Overseas Private Investment Corporation, which insures and guarantees U.S. private investments in developing countries against certain hazards, would also be a component of IDCA, but OPIC's Board of Directors, which the IDCA Director would chair, would continue to set OPIC policy.

Each of these agencies would retain its individual identity and substantial day-to-day operating autonomy. A principal responsibility of the IDCA Director—who would be supported by a small staff—

would be the achievement of consistency and balance among the policies, major programs, and budgets of the component agencies.

To help ensure that U.S. bilateral efforts and the programs of major multilateral development institutions better complement each other, the IDCA Director would participate in the selection of U.S. Executive Directors of multilateral development banks (World Bank Group, Inter-American Development Bank, Asian Development Bank and African Development Fund), and would advise these Executive Directors on development policy and proposed projects and programs. Additionally, IDCA would assume lead responsibility for budget support and policy concerning United States participation in those organizations and programs of the United Nations and the Organization of American States whose purpose is primarily developmental. These are the UN Development Program, UNICEF, the Organization of American States Technical Assistance Funds, the UN Capital Development Fund, the UN Educational and Training Program for Southern Africa, the UN/Food and Agriculture Organization (FAO) World Food Program, the FAO Post-Harvest Losses Fund, and the UN Disaster Relief Organization.

The IDCA Director would be responsible for ensuring that development goals are taken fully into account in all executive branch decision-making on trade, technology, and other economic policy issues affecting the less developed nations, and would submit an annual development policy statement to the Congress. The Director would also prepare a comprehensive foreign assistance budget, which he would submit to the Office of Management and Budget after consulting with the Secretary of State, and would lead the Administration's presentation of that budget to the Congress.

When IDCA is established, I intend to delegate to it the principal authority for the bilateral development assistance program administered by AID (now vested in me by law, delegated to the Secretary of State, and redelegated to the Administrator of AID). Certain functions vested in me under the Foreign Assistance Act will continue to be delegated to the Secretary of State, Secretary of the Treasury, Secretary of Defense, or elsewhere; but most functions relating to the assistance program will be delegated directly to the IDCA Director, who will in turn redelegate these functions, as appropriate, to the Administrator of AID. I also intend to delegate to the Director of IDCA authority proposed to be vested in me to establish an Institute For Technological Cooperation; the IDCA Director would redelegate these functions, as appropriate, to IFTC.

The reorganization would increase program effectiveness through improved coordination, as requested in the 1978 authorization act. I estimate that it would achieve that goal with no increase in expenditures or personnel. After investigation, I have found that this reorganization is necessary to carry out the policy set forth in section 901(a) of title 5 of the United States Code. This plan abolishes one of the statutory officers that the President may appoint under section 624(a) of the Foreign Assistance Act of 1961 (22 U.S.C. 2384(a)). No statutory functions are abolished by the plan. The provisions in this plan for the appointment and pay of the Director, Deputy Director, and Associate Directors of IDCA have been found by me to be necessary by reason of the reorganization and are at rates applicable to comparable officers in the executive branch.

This proposal constitutes the first major restructuring of the U.S. foreign aid program since the creation of the Agency for International Development in 1961. It will provide the United States with governmental machinery far better able to fulfill our commitment to assist people in developing countries to eliminate hunger, poverty, illness and ignorance. It responds to the mandate of the Congress. Let us work together to ensure its successful and effective implementation.

JIMMY CARTER

The White House,
    April 10, 1979.

REORGANIZATION PLAN NO. 2 OF 1979

Prepared by the President and transmitted to the Senate and the House of Representatives in Congress assembled, April 10, 1979, pursuant to the provisions of chapter 9 of title 5 of the United States Code.

UNITED STATES INTERNATIONAL
DEVELOPMENT COOPERATION AGENCY

SECTION 1. *Establishment   of   the United States International Development Cooperation Agency*

There is hereby established in the executive branch an independent agency to be known as the United States International Development Cooperation Agency (hereinafter referred to as the "Agency").

SECTION 2. *Director*

The Agency shall be headed by the Director of the International Development Cooperation Agency (hereinafter referred to as the "Director"), who shall be appointed by the President, by and with the advice and consent of the Senate, and shall receive compensation at the rate prescribed by law for Level II of the Executive Schedule. Under the guidance of the President, the Director shall have primary responsibility for setting overall development assistance policy and coordinating international development activities supported by the United States. The Director shall serve as the principal advisor to the President and the Secretary of State on international development matters and shall report to the President and the Secretary of State. The responsibility of the Director for the exercise of the functions and authorities vested in or delegated to the Director or the Agency shall be subject to the guidance of the Secretary of State as to the foreign policy of the United States. The Director shall designate the order in which other officials shall act for and exercise the powers of the Director during the absence or disability of the Director and the Deputy Director or in the event of vacancies in both such offices.

SECTION 3. *Deputy Director*

The President, by and with the advice and consent of the Senate, may appoint a Deputy Director of the Agency, who shall receive compensation at the rate prescribed by law for Level III of the Executive Schedule. The Deputy Director shall perform such duties and exercise such powers as the Director may from time to time prescribe and, in addition, shall act for and exercise the powers of the Director during the absence or disability of the Director or during a vacancy in such office.

SECTION 4. *Associate Directors*

The President, by and with the advice and consent of the Senate, may appoint two Associate Directors of the Agency, who shall perform such duties and exercise such powers as the Director may from time to time prescribe and who shall receive compensation at the rate prescribed by law for Level IV of the Executive Schedule.

SECTION 5. *Performance of functions*

The Director may from time to time establish, alter, consolidate, or discontinue organizational units within the Agency, and delegate responsibility for carrying out any function or authority of the Director or the Agency to any officer, employee or unit of the Agency or any other officer or agency of the executive branch.

SECTION 6. *Transfers of functions*

(a) There are hereby transferred to the Director all functions and authorities vested in the Agency for International Development or in its Administrator pursuant to the following:

(1) sections 233(b), 296(e), 297(d), 298(c)(6), 299(d), 601 (a) through (d), and 624(f)(2)(C) of the Foreign Assistance Act of 1961 (22 U.S.C. 2193(b), 2220a(e), 2220b(d), 2220c(c)(6), 2220d (d), 2351 (a) through (d), and 2384(f) (2)(C));

(2) section 407 of the Agricultural Trade Development and Assistance Act of 1954 (7 U.S.C. 1736a); and

(3) section 706 of the Foreign Relations Authorization Act, Fiscal Year 1979 (49 U.S.C. 1518).

(b) There are hereby transferred to the Director all functions and authorities vested in the agency primarily responsible for administering part I of the Foreign Assistance Act of 1961 or in its Administrator pursuant to sections 101(b), 119, 125, 531(a)(2), 601(e)(2), and 640B of such Act (22 U.S.C. 2151(b), 2151q, 2151w, 2346(a)(2), 2351(e)(2), and 2399c).

(c) There are hereby transferred to the Director all functions and authorities vested in the Secretary of State pursuant to the following:

(1) section 622(c) of the Foreign Assistance Act of 1961, insofar as it relates to development assistance (22 U.S.C. 2382(c)); and

(2) section 901 of Public Law 95–118 (22 U.S.C. 262g).

SECTION 7. *Abolition*

One of the positions that the President may appoint under section 624(a) of the Foreign Assistance Act of 1961 (22 U.S.C. 2384(a), 5 U.S.C. 5315(5)) is hereby abolished.

SECTION 8. *Other transfers; interim officers*

(a) So much of the personnel, property, records, and unexpended balances of appropriations, allocations and other funds employed, used, held, available, or to be made available in connection with the functions and authorities affected by the establishment of the Agency, as the Director of the Office of Management and Budget shall determine, shall be transferred to the appropriate agency or component at such time or times as the Director of the Office of Management and Budget shall provide, except that no such unexpended balances transferred shall be used for purposes other than those for which the appropriation was originally made. The Director of the Office of Management and Budget shall provide for terminating the affairs of any agency abolished herein and for such further measures and dispositions as such Director deems necessary to effectuate the purposes of this reorganization plan.

(b) Pending the initial appointment of the Director, Deputy Director, and Associate Directors of the Agency, their functions and authorities may be performed, for up to 60 days after section 1 of this reorganization plan becomes effective, by such individuals as the President may designate. Any individual so designated shall be compensated at the rate provided herein for the position whose functions and authorities such individual performs.

SECTION 9. *Effective date*

This reorganization plan shall become effective on July 1, 1980, or at such earlier time or times as the President shall specify, but not sooner than the earliest time allowable under section 906 of title 5 of the United States Code.

Reduction in Energy Use by the Federal Government

Memorandum From the President.
April 10, 1979

Memorandum for the Heads of Executive Departments and Agencies

Subject: Required 5% Reduction in Agency Energy Use

The U.S. has taken the lead to get the member nations of the International Energy Agency to reduce petroleum consumption. Our goal, as part of this commitment, is to reduce oil imports by a level equal and up to 5% of projected domestic consumption. This goal must be met to help reduce the upward pressure on world oil prices.

The Federal Government will do its part. I am directing that Executive departments and agencies reduce energy consumption by 5% for the twelve-month period beginning April 1, 1979, as compared with the preceding twelve months.

In achieving this reduction, the following specific actions are to be taken:

• Set thermostats in all Federally-operated buildings, except where required for health and safety or special purposes, at not more than 65 degrees during working hours and 55 degrees during non-working hours for the heating season and at not lower than 80 degrees for the cooling season.

• Reduce use of all automotive fuels by 10%.

Each agency will have to take additional steps to achieve the full 5% reduction goal. These initiatives should be selected so as to avoid adverse programmatic impacts. As directed in my February 2, 1979 memorandum, for example, heads of agencies may reduce lighting and other electrical use throughout agency activities and reduce petroleum use by eliminating unnecessary activities and vehicle trips. Credit will be given for fuel switching from oil to gas or coal.

Within 30 days, please submit to the Secretary of Energy a plan for achieving the reduction in energy use. Each agency that now reports quarterly energy consumption to the Secretary of Energy should identify in the quarterly status reports the actual energy savings attributable to this effort.

I have directed the Secretary of Energy, in consultation with the Office of Management and Budget, to monitor compliance with the provisions of this directive. They will periodically report to me on accomplishments, problems with respect to adverse impacts on agency missions, and further actions which may be required.

JIMMY CARTER

NOTE: This is the text of identical memorandums addressed to the heads of executive departments and agencies. The memorandum to the Secretary of Defense concludes with an additional paragraph, which reads as follows: "Department of Defense operational readiness activities are exempt from this directive."

Economic Assistance to Turkey

Letter to the Speaker of the House and the President of the Senate Transmitting Proposed Legislation. April 10, 1979

Dear Mr. Speaker: (Dear Mr. President:)

I hereby transmit a bill "to authorize supplemental economic support for the fiscal year 1979 for Turkey, and for other purposes", and urge its prompt enactment. The bill authorizes appropriations of $100,000,000 in assistance for Turkey under the Economic Support Fund.

Turkey's economic situation continues to deteriorate, and its foreign exchange shortage is critical. The Government of Turkey has begun taking steps necessary to restore economic equilibrium, and is considering others. Even with a major stabilization effort, however, significant improvement in the Turkish balance of payments will take time. Without substantial official assistance in 1979, Turkey would be unable to obtain imports necessary to meet the basic needs of the Turkish economy. This in turn would aggravate serious domestic political and social problems and could ultimately affect Turkey's stability and its Western orientation.

In January, governments friendly to Turkey agreed to organize a multilateral emergency assistance effort, subject to satisfactory Turkish government measures of economic stabilization and reform. As that effort has taken shape, it has become clear that for it to succeed additional assistance will be required from the United States and other countries.

An additional contribution by the United States of $100 million from the Economic Support Fund and substantial increases from other major donors will give the multilateral effort the momentum necessary for success. We have been in touch with other governments to urge them to increase their contributions on the basis of equitable burdensharing.

In accordance with the requirements of section 620C(d) of the Foreign Assistance Act of 1961, as amended, I hereby certify that the furnishing of the security assistance for Turkey proposed in this bill will be consistent with the principles set forth in section 620C(b) of that Act.

In this regard, it remains the firm policy of the United States to support the resolution of all differences among countries in the region peacefully, to encourage all parties to avoid provocative actions, and to oppose any attempt to resolve disputes through force or threat of force. With regard to the Cyprus problem, the United States continues to support fully efforts, especially those of the United Nations, to bring about prompt, peaceful settlement on Cyprus, including the withdrawal of Turkish military forces from the island. The United States continues to support the maintenance of the ceasefire on Cyprus pending achievement of a negotiated solution. The assistance to be furnished to Turkey under this bill will help create the stability and security that are important underpinnings to progress toward these goals.

I strongly urge early passage of the enclosed legislation.

Sincerely,

JIMMY CARTER

NOTE: This is the text of identical letters addressed to Thomas P. O'Neill, Jr., Speaker of the House of Representatives, and Walter F. Mondale, President of the Senate.

THE PRESIDENT'S NEWS CONFERENCE OF APRIL 10, 1979

THE PRESIDENT. Good afternoon, everybody. One statement about energy, and then I'll answer questions.

ENERGY

First of all, we must move more aggressively to utilize the vast coal reserves in our country. In addition to the three agencies that regulate coal, which I mentioned in my speech to the Nation earlier this week, I've asked Governor Jay Rockefeller, who heads the President's Coal Commission as its Chairman, to hold public hearings within the next 60 days to identify acceptable ways to hasten the substitution of coal for oil.

The Nation's energy policy has been paralyzed for years over the question of controls over domestic energy prices. I have now cut the Gordian knot and put that decision behind us. The question is no longer whether or not we decontrol domestic oil prices; Congress mandated an end to controls effective September 1981. And they will be phased out to avoid a sudden inflationary shock in 1981, and also phased out to provide incentives in the immediate future for increased domestic production of oil and gas.

The issue now is to make sure that the necessary step is carried out in a way which is effective, fair, and equitable. What we must do now is to impose a windfall profits tax on the excess, unearned profits of the oil producers and to use these revenues to create an energy security fund to protect our Nation's energy future.

This tax proposal will be sent to Congress immediately after their return from their Easter recess. And this fund will be used for three critical needs: first, to help low-income Americans meet the increased cost of energy; second, to provide for a better transportation system, particularly mass transit; and third, greatly to expand research and development of alternative future sources of energy, with the same scientific effort that put a man on the Moon.

Even after all other taxes and royalties are taken into account, the windfall profits tax will still leave over $6 billion of new dollars, over the next 3 years, to plow back for domestic oil production and for domestic oil exploration. But I want to issue a warning. We have already begun to hear a good deal of talk from the oil companies about so-called plowbacks. But what this talk covers up is that this proposal, as it will be presented with the windfall profits tax, already provides $6 billion in increased revenue, after all taxes and royalties, to the oil companies over the next 3 years.

The Nation has a right to expect that all of this new income will be used for exploration for oil and gas and not to buy timberlands and department stores.

In addition to this built-in plowback for the oil companies to spend on domestic production, we must also have the windfall profits tax and the energy security fund it will finance. I'm committed to it; the country needs it; it's already clear that the people demand it. And I am also confident that we can get it.

The American people are willing to face the hard reality of the petroleum problem. And they are willing to see oil priced on a realistic basis. But they are not, and I am not, willing to see their sacrifices mocked by a wholly unjustified giveaway to the oil companies, particularly when the needs that would be met by the energy security fund are so urgent and pressing. That's why I am making the passage of this tax and the establishment of the security fund for energy one of my highest legislative priorities.

Thank you, and I would be glad to answer questions.

Mr. Cormier [Frank Cormier, Associated Press].

QUESTIONS

INFLATION

Q. Mr. President, you have already mentioned that you've reached some very difficult decisions on energy policy. Don't you at this point face, perhaps, equally painful decisions on inflation?

THE PRESIDENT. Yes. I don't think there's any doubt that the most urgent remaining issue for us to resolve on the domestic scene is the control of inflation. We have been very disappointed with recent statistics on inflationary pressures. They've been brought about to a great degree by oil prices and energy prices.

I think it's important that we adhere to the strict interpretation and the principle of the voluntary wage and price guidelines. Most of the wage settlements—and there have been hundreds of them in the last 6 months—have been within the wage guidelines. And most of the large corporations, the so-called Fortune 500, have adhered rigidly to the price guidelines.

But we are getting more and more effective in our ability to monitor and to encourage compliance with the guidelines, and I believe it's important that for the next few months we stick with them. I believe that we will see a turn very shortly in the inflationary trend downward, and we will continue to devote our utmost ability to this goal.

Q. Are you saying, Mr. President, that the guidelines should be enough?

THE PRESIDENT. Well, it's not just the guidelines, obviously. We are also working to cut down, for instance, the Federal deficit, to control inflation. We're also trying to remove redtape and Government regulation which adds to inflation. We're trying to encourage the American people, because of patriotic inclinations, to do everything they can within the family structure and within a business, individually, to cut down on inflation. And we're trying to reduce the importation of excessive amounts of goods from overseas compared to what we export. We're trying to strengthen the American dollar. We're doing everything we can to hold down OPEC oil price increases.

So, these things all go together. And I think there must be a recognition that no single scapegoat can be found and it's counterproductive for any American, including a President, to try to find someone else on whom to blame the cause of inflation. It requires a joint effort, a consistent effort, a persistent effort, and we shouldn't give up just because we have a few weeks of adverse statistics come forward.

NUCLEAR ENERGY

Q. Mr. President, in view of the Three Mile Island nuclear accident, and the dangers that it exposed to the public——

THE PRESIDENT. Yes.

Q. ——are you still as strong an advocate of nuclear power as you were, and are you going to still pursue this business of speeding up the licensing of nuclear plants?

THE PRESIDENT. The fact is that we now derive about 12 or 13 percent of our total energy supplies in the United States from nuclear power. I'll be establishing very quickly a Presidential commission to look into the causes of the accident at Three Mile Island. I've not yet decided on the chairman of that commission, nor the members. But it will be done expeditiously. They will present a report to me and, obviously, to the American people and to the Congress on the causes of the accident and how we can strengthen safety standards, better design techniques, and also operating procedures to make safety better in the future.

There is no way for us to abandon the nuclear supply of energy in our country in the foreseeable future. I think it does not contribute to safety to have a bureaucratic nightmare or maze of redtape as licensing and siting decisions are made. So, I think anything that we can do to clarify the procedure and to make it more open, more clear, more obvious to the American people what the issues are involved, would be a step in the right direction.

ALFRED KAHN

Q. Mr. President, Alfred Kahn, your inflation adviser, appears to be constantly making impressions, though not the impression that you want to make or, perhaps, the impression that he wants to make. He says things which in their own terms may seem logical but then produce headlines which indicate floating trial balloons about possible mandatory price controls or perhaps predicting a recession. Do you think there is anything more that you can do now to set straight what it is that Mr. Kahn does that produces so much confusion?

THE PRESIDENT. It's obvious that neither Alfred Kahn nor I have discovered an ability to control the headlines. [*Laughter*]

I think he does the best he can under very difficult circumstances in putting forward to the American people the options that we have to control inflation. The particular recent incident to which you may have referred said that there are two unacceptable alternatives. One is mandatory price and wage guidelines, and the other one is a deliberate recession that would cause very high unemployment. Those are unacceptable to me.

I might point out, as a matter of interest to the public, because this is quite often not recognized, the President of the United States does not have the authority to impose mandatory wage and price guidelines. In 1973 President Nixon did have that standby authority, and he used it. I do not want such standby authority, and there would be no way, in my opinion, for the Congress to pass such legislation. I think it would arouse tremendous opposition in the Congress, including filibuster, and so it's a prospect that I don't think will be materializing at all.

If the Congress should attempt to grant standby wage and price authority, mandatory wage and price authority, I would resist it.

Q. Is your confidence in Mr. Kahn as a spokesman diminished?

THE PRESIDENT. My confidence in Mr. Kahn as a spokesman is undiminished.

INCOME TAX SURCHARGE

Q. Mr. President, we've heard a lot of talk recently about balanced budgets, and you've stated that's your goal. I'm wondering if you'd consider asking Congress for an income tax surcharge similar to the one former President Johnson asked for in the mid-sixties. You have a similar economic situation, demand-oriented inflation. If you could get an income tax surcharge, you would automatically wipe out your budget deficit, and it would make all these folks who want the balanced budget, you know, put up or shut up, so to speak. Or is this sort of thing not politically possible?

THE PRESIDENT. Well, I don't think it's advisable. Because of inflationary pressures, the income revenues inevitably go up year by year. Even before I became President, there was a routine reduction of income tax rates from time to time. And for me to ask for an increase in the income tax rate would be both inadvisable for the well-being of the Nation and, also, I think, impossible. So, I would not consider doing that.

STRATEGIC ARMS LIMITATION

Q. Mr. President, a question on SALT. Secretary Vance and Ambassador Dobrynin have met several times in the last few days. Secretary Brown and Dr. Brzezinski made some major statements last week. Would you tell us now, or give us your assessment of the current state of play on SALT, any detail you could give us on the remaining issues and the prospects for a Soviet-American summit?

THE PRESIDENT. After many mistakes, I have promised the public that I would not predict a date for a summit or for the conclusion of the SALT negotiations. But I can tell you that persistently we have made progress. There has never been an interruption in the negotiating process, there's never been a setback nor a delay. Recently, there have been additional steps toward concluding a SALT agreement. There are still a few issues that remain to be resolved, clarifications in the stance of the United States negotiators and the Soviet negotiators.

My guess is that we will not approach the question of where or when a summit meeting between myself and President Brezhnev will be held until after we resolve these remaining SALT differences.

HANDGUN CONTROL

Q. Mr. President, during the campaign you supported tighter controls on handguns. The White House helped draw a gun control bill last year. Now there are reports that the White House has abandoned lobbying efforts for gun control on the Hill. Can you tell us whether you do still support stiffer gun controls and whether an administration bill will go to Congress this year?

THE PRESIDENT. Well, we'd be glad to cooperate with the Congress on this. Last year, the Treasury Department issued a routine requirement concerning the registration of the serial numbers, I think, on certain types of handguns. The Congress

not only rejected that idea, but they removed from the Treasury budget, I think, $4½ million that could have been used to administer that program. I think that indicates the attitude of the Congress.

So, although I do favor increased safety of the American people because of this step, I think to pursue it aggressively in the Congress would be a mistake. But we will cooperate with the Congress.

LOANS TO CARTER'S WAREHOUSE

Q. Mr. President, about the peanut warehouse business, you have said and your spokesmen have said that no money was diverted into your '76 Presidential campaign for those loans. My question is, did you know in 1976 or anytime thereafter that the terms of the loans might not have been complied with, that is, that the bank might not have been repaid on the schedule and according to the terms that the loans were set out in?

THE PRESIDENT. I have never known, nor do I now know, of any illegal action taken at Carter's Warehouse. There have been allegations widely discussed in the press and verbally by some people about the channeling of loan funds to Carter's Warehouse into the campaign itself. I don't know of any evidence that's ever been put forward to the public from any source that could form a basis for those allegations. Those allegations are absolutely and totally untrue.

A special investigator has been now appointed to look into allegations about which there are no bases, so far as I know. We will cooperate completely with the special investigator. And I hope that his work will be thorough, and I hope that he will expedite a conclusion.

There is nothing at Carter's Warehouse that I know of or have ever heard of that would arouse any conviction in the mind of the special investigator that illegalities were present.

Q. Mr. President, you brought up the matter of cutting Federal expenses as a means of controlling inflation.

THE PRESIDENT. Yes.

Q. This fits into quite a bit of activity in this area over quite a number of months, going back to Proposition 13 in California, efforts to amend the Constitution to get a balanced budget.

I wonder if I could ask you if, given your campaign pledge to balance the budget before your first term ends, whether you will, in fact, next January, submit a balanced budget?

THE PRESIDENT. My hope is to do so. Obviously, you can't predict what economic circumstances will be. We have cut down the budget deficit that I inherited by more than half, I think better than 55 percent. And there's a growing inclination, not only on the part of the American people but also the Congress, to cooperate in my efforts to balance the budget. So, that is my intention. But I can't predict all economic circumstances to guarantee it to the American people.

It would be a very attractive accomplishment politically. It would be completely compatible with my own economic and political philosophy. And it's a goal that I aspire to achieve.

ECONOMIC ASSISTANCE TO TURKEY

Q. Mr. President, 3 months have passed since the Guadeloupe summit, where you and the Western leaders made a pledge for an urgent economic aid to Turkey.

THE PRESIDENT. Yes.

Q. Where does the matter stand now, and what is the American Government doing on this subject? Would you give us some information?

THE PRESIDENT. Yes. At Guadeloupe, the decision was made by all four of the leaders there that Chancellor Helmut Schmidt and his government would take the leadership in trying to approach the Turkish economic problem from a multinational basis. We have cooperated with Chancellor Schmidt. We've also advocated to the Congress just recently that a total increase above and beyond our loans and grants of about $150 million would be added to our budget request.

We anticipate that Germany and, perhaps, other countries would more than match this allocation of our own aid to Turkey. We don't yet know what the outcome will be. We will certainly discuss this again at the Tokyo economic summit when we arrive there in June. And the Congress will make a decision on this matter unilaterally in our own country.

WINDFALL PROFITS TAX

Q. Mr. President, by decontrolling domestic oil prices without your hoped-for excess profits tax, and seemingly a lot of opposition to it in Congress and elsewhere, aren't you taking a heck of a chance on the good will of the oil companies and their desire to supply the Nation with oil, as opposed to making more and more money? And why should they be more inclined to do that now and to invest in exploration and development now than they were when they reaped their first windfall back in the early seventies?

THE PRESIDENT. I am not depending on the oil companies to get the windfall profits tax passed. My prediction is that they will not support this tax. [*Laughter*] But I believe that the tax will pass.

There's a different mood in the country now than there was when I proposed the crude oil equalization tax. There were several obstacles to the passage of that tax. One was that I had a multiplicity of responsibilities in energy, because it was a comprehensive package. I couldn't focus on one particular part of it. Secondly, if the Congress had passed the crude oil equalization tax that I proposed 2 years ago, they would at the same time have had to be responsible for decontrol. I have taken that responsibility on my own shoulders, as mandated by the Congress, to be accomplished by September of 1981.

I think the Congress is much more willing now to prevent the oil companies from reaping this great windfall from unearned profits. And I believe that the American people can focus much more accurately and intensely on this one basic issue.

One of the reasons that I decided to take the action which I announced on television the other night was to narrow down the focus of congressional debate, primarily on that one issue—should we or should we not let the oil companies capture about $15 billion which they have not earned, or should we retain a substantial portion of that to meet the needs of the American people?

That's the basic issue. And I think because the issue is so clearly defined and the mood of the country has changed and I can focus on that issue with the full resources of my own office, I believe that it will pass.

OIL COMPANY DIVESTITURE OR NATIONALIZATION

Q. By way of followup, Mr. President, are you any more in favor of divestiture or even nationalization now than when you were first asked about it?

THE PRESIDENT. No, I'm not in favor of nationalization. I think there is some exploration to be done on the subject of divestiture, particularly in horizontal divestiture, so-called, where there have been allegations made in the past, some of which I believe, that some of the major energy companies have invested—for instance, oil companies have invested in coal mining and then used their ownership of new coal mines to reduce production of those mines, therefore, to minimize competition and also to control prices.

I think the horizontal divestiture area should be explored thoroughly, but I am not in favor of nationalization of the energy industry in this country.

REINSTATEMENT OF THE DRAFT

Q. Mr. President, do you have a comment about the reinstatement of the draft? There are many young Americans that are worrying that the draft is going to be reinstated, sir. Do you have a comment on that, please?

THE PRESIDENT. I don't see any immediate prospect that we would want to reinstate the draft. We are meeting the needs of our regular Armed Forces adequately with the present voluntary recruitment program. There are some problems in the Reserve forces which we are trying now to address. We will continue to assess the needs. We do have the authority, as you know, to register persons for a draft in the future, if it's needed.

I would like to say that if we ever do institute a draft, I would like to make it universal in its scope. I don't think that just because someone is wealthy enough or influential enough to go to college that they ought to be excused from being susceptible to the draft. But at the present time, I see no immediate prospect of reinstitution of the draft.

PRAYER IN PUBLIC SCHOOLS

Q. As a born-again Christian, Mr. President, what is your position on prayers in public schools?

THE PRESIDENT. My preference is that the Congress not get involved in the question of mandating prayer in school. I am a Christian; I happen to be a Baptist. I believe that the subject of prayer in school ought to be decided between a person, individually and privately, and God.

And the Supreme Court has ruled on this issue. And I personally don't think that the Congress ought to pass any legislation requiring or permitting prayer being required or encouraged in school. Sometimes a student might object even to so-called voluntary prayer when it's public and coordinated. It might be very embarrassing to a young person to say, "I want to be excused from the room because I don't want to pray."

So, I don't know all of the constitutional aspects of this very difficult and sensitive of questions, but I think that it ought to be an individual matter between a person and God.

GASOLINE RATIONING

Q. Mr. President, we are still in a crisis that is, as you called it, a moral equivalent of war. Why not move to rationing? I mean, wouldn't that be the fair way of doing it? And isn't the American public now ready for that kind of a sacrifice?

THE PRESIDENT. I don't think the gasoline shortages are so severe that they warrant rationing. But we have asked the Congress for standby authority to impose rationing if and when it is needed in the future. Prior to then, though, we will pursue both voluntary and some mandatory conservative measures.

My own inclination is to let the States make the first effort to meet reduced gasoline consumption standards. If they don't, then we would turn to other measures, like the closing of service stations on weekends and so forth. But I would rather let the people do it voluntarily first, let the States do it secondly, and hold in reserve gas rationing for some time in the future.

I hope it would be a distant future, and I hope that we'll be so conscious of the need to produce gasoline in our own country, to have more efficient automobiles, to move toward carpooling and the use of mass transit, that we would not require gasoline rationing.

CONSTRAINTS ON OIL COMPANIES

Q. Mr. President, in your opening statement today, you said that the American people have the right to expect that the oil companies will use the profits they do receive to develop more oil.

THE PRESIDENT. Yes.

Q. Beyond the right to expect, is there or do you have in mind any way to compel the oil companies to do that, to use those profits for production and development and research?

THE PRESIDENT. The oil companies will get, after the windfall tax is levied, about $6 billion in increased revenue or income in the next 3 years. That money should be plowed back into increased production of oil and gas. And I would favor any constraints placed on the oil companies by the Congress or administratively, within my own sphere of influence, to encourage that use of increased revenues for oil and gas production.

Q. Would you require it?

THE PRESIDENT. Yes, I would be glad to put restraints on them. I don't know if you could require it in every instance, but I would certainly favor either laws or administrative actions to put constraints, so that they would plow back that oil into energy production.

As I said in my opening statement, for them to take that money and use it to buy circuses or to buy timberlands or to buy motels or department stores, I think contravenes the need of our country, and it contravenes the purpose that I and the Congress have in mind when we give them that additional income.

ITINERARY FOR EAST ASIAN TRIP

Q. Mr. President, you said that you're going to the economic summit conference in Tokyo in June, I believe.

THE PRESIDENT. Yes, in June.

Q. Will you also be going to South Korea? Will you also be going to any other countries?

THE PRESIDENT. I don't know yet.

Q. You are uncertain about South Korea?

THE PRESIDENT. That's right. We've not decided on the itinerary yet.

MIDDLE EAST

Q. Within the last few hours, Mr. President, a terrorist bomb was exploded in Tel Aviv, and Israel has bombed Lebanon. Isn't there likely to be even more violence in the Middle East than there was before the treaty, and what can you do about it? And would you be willing to stop arms sales, all arms sales to the Mideast?

THE PRESIDENT. First, I would not be willing to stop all arms sales to the Middle East, because I think the countries there must have an adequate means of defending themselves—Israel, Egypt, and others.

Secondly, I believe that the terrorist bombing is a longstanding problem. It's not something that just has arisen because the treaty has been signed. I think the terrorism threats are counterproductive. My own hope is that the best way to alleviate this constant dependence on death and hatred and destruction and terrorism is to prove the viability and the advantages of the peace process.

I would like to see, as early as possible, but by the end of next month, all the borders open between Israel and Egypt, a free passage of students and tradesmen, diplomats, tourists, and for the demonstrated advantages to Israel and Egypt to be very apparent to the citizens of Jordan and Syria and Lebanon and to the Palestinians, wherever they live, hoping to convince them that that's the best approach to achieve their own purposes and goals— that is, peace and a realization of the right to control their own future.

But I don't think there's any doubt that terrorism will continue in the coming months. I hope it will wane as it's proven that the peace treaty is permanent and that it is going to work.

An immediate step that will tend to convince everyone that it is permanent and cannot be disrupted by terrorist acts will be the quick ratification of the treaty by the Egyptian Parliament and the exchange of the documents themselves. And then the return of El Arish and the first part of the Sinai to Egypt—I think that will be a step in the right direction.

ENERGY CONSERVATION AT THE
WHITE HOUSE

Q. Mr. President, in your speech last week, you asked the American people to cut back on the use of energy. Do you and your family have any plans to do likewise? And if so, could you elaborate on that a little bit, please?

THE PRESIDENT. Well, we comply with the thermostat settings and have ever since the first time I began to work on that in 1977. We've shifted, as you know, the White House fleet of cars to smaller and more efficient automobiles. Our travel is pretty much official, except for rare vacations, which we hope to take on Easter.

I hope we can set an example for the rest of the Nation. We have just begun the construction of a solar heating unit on top of the West Wing, just behind the Oval Office, this month, which will be completed before the end of April.

So, we are trying to do a few personal things to demonstrate our belief in the principles that I described the other night.

MR. CORMIER. Thank you, Mr. President.

NOTE: President Carter's forty-seventh news conference began at 4 p.m. in Room 450 of the Old Executive Office Building. It was broadcast live on radio and television.

Labor Dispute in the Trucking Industry
Statement by the President. April 11, 1979

Last night, all the outstanding issues in the labor dispute between the Teamsters and the trucking industry were settled. I welcome this news for three important reasons. First, normal operations in the trucking industry will be resumed very quickly. Second, the settlement is within the administration's voluntary pay standard. Third, the increase in wages and cost of fringe benefits under the new contract will be substantially less than in the previous contract that was negotiated 3 years ago.

I commend the parties for the responsibility they have shown in making a very important contribution to controlling inflation.

NOTE: Alfred E. Kahn, Advisor to the President on Inflation, read the statement on the President's behalf at approximately 11:40 a.m. to reporters assembled in the Briefing Room at the White House.

President's Commission on the Accident at Three Mile Island
Remarks Announcing Establishment of the Commission. April 11, 1979

THE PRESIDENT. In my address to the Nation last week, I announced that I would appoint a Presidential commission to investigate the nuclear accident at Three Mile Island. It's essential that we learn the causes of this accident and make sure that the safety of our own citizens is never again endangered in this way.

I'm pleased to announce today that I have signed the Executive order creating the Presidential commission, and I have appointed 11 distinguished Americans to serve on it.

I have just met with the Commission's Chairman, Dr. John Kemeny, who is president of Dartmouth College and who possesses one of the most brilliant and incisive minds in this country. He has devoted his life to analyzing and to solving some of the most difficult, technical problems of our generation.

His skills and his background, widely recognized, ideally qualify him for the complicated task of determining the truth behind the accident at Three Mile Island. I have no doubt that Dr. Kemeny will succeed completely in this effort.

The other 10 members of the Commission who have been chosen are also very talented and highly qualified. They provide the Commission with the knowledge and the diverse experience needed to complete its task successfully.

That task will be one of the most important ever undertaken by a Presidential commission. The Commission will find out what happened at Three Mile Island. It will assess how the accident could have been prevented. It will review how the Government and others responded, and it will make recommendations to enable us to prevent any future nuclear accidents.

There can be no doubt that the eyes of the Nation and, indeed, of the entire world will be on this Commission. Its judgments will have enormous impact. I am confident that during its 6 months of operation, this Commission will make the right judgments, and the Nation will long be in its debt.

I would now like to introduce to you Dr. John Kemeny.

DR. KEMENY. Thank you.

Mr. President, this is an awesome responsibility. Frankly, I have tried to think of every reason why I should not accept. But when the President of the United States asks one to perform a major service for the Nation, the only possible answer is yes.

I think the public should know something about me—that I hope to spend the rest of my life at Dartmouth College. There is no personal ambition served by accepting this assignment. I represent no special interest. My total commitment as Chairman of the Commission will be the discovery of truth and the formulation of recommendations in the national interest.

The Commission will make a full-scale investigation of the causes of and the responses to the accident at Three Mile Island. We will examine the actions of State and Federal Government agencies and of private industry as they reacted to the accident. We will be looking at questions of public access to information, as well as questions of technology. We will report what we find honestly, as required by the gravity of the event.

Mr. President, for this effort I pledge to you and to the citizens of our country the very best of which I am capable.

THE PRESIDENT. Good luck. I'm here to help you.

REPORTER. Dr. Kemeny, can we ask you a question? I just wondered if you had spoken out previously on nuclear power and, if so, what your views as expressed in the past have been on this subject.

MR. POWELL. I don't think we want to get into a Q&A at this point. Thank you.

Q. Just to see if you had a previous——

DR. KEMENY. Those are my instructions. You will find I've not spoken out widely on this issue.

Q. When do you start? When does this Commission start?

DR. KEMENY. As soon as possible.

Q. So, you haven't prejudged nuclear power per se?

DR. KEMENY. No, I think I can assure you I've not prejudged it.

MR. POWELL. Jack will be available to answer the questions on how the thing is going to get started, and so forth.

NOTE: The President spoke at 4:30 p.m. to reporters assembled in the Briefing Room at the White House. Following Dr. Kemeny's remarks, Press Secretary Jody Powell and Jack H. Watson, Jr., Assistant to the President for Intergovernmental Affairs, answered reporters' questions concerning the Commission.

President's Commission on the Accident at Three Mile Island

Executive Order 12130.   April 11, 1979

By the authority vested in me as President by the Constitution of the United States of America, and in order to provide, in accordance with the provisions of the Federal Advisory Committee Act (5 U.S.C. App. 1), an independent forum to investigate and explain the recent accident at the nuclear power facility at Three Mile Island in Pennsylvania, it is hereby ordered as follows:

1–1. *Establishment.*

1–101. There is established the President's Commission on the Accident at Three Mile Island.

1–102. The membership of the Commission shall be composed of not more than twelve persons appointed by the President from among citizens who are not full time officers or employees within the Executive Branch. The President shall designate a Chairman from among the members of the Commission.

1–2. *Functions.*

1–201. The Commission shall conduct a comprehensive study and investigation of the recent accident involving the nuclear power facility on Three Mile Island in Pennsylvania. The study and investigation shall include:

(a) a technical assessment of the events and their causes;

(b) an analysis of the role of the managing utility;

(c) an assessment of the emergency preparedness and response of the Nuclear Regulatory Commission and other Federal, state and local authorities;

(d) an evaluation of the Nuclear Regulatory Commission's licensing, inspec-

tion, operation and enforcement procedures as applied to this facility;

(e) an assessment of how the public's right to information concerning the events at Three Mile Island was served and of the steps which should be taken during similar emergencies to provide the public with accurate, comprehensible and timely information; and

(f) appropriate recommendations based upon the Commission's findings.

1–202. The Commission shall prepare and transmit to the President and to the Secretaries of Energy and Health, Education and Welfare a final report of its findings and recommendations.

1–3. *Administration.*

1–301. The Chairman of the Commission is authorized to appoint and fix the compensation of a staff of such persons as may be necessary to discharge the Commission's responsibilities, subject to the applicable provisions of the Federal Advisory Committee Act and Title 5 of the United States Code.

1–302. To the extent authorized by law and requested by the Chairman of the Commission, the General Services Administration shall provide the Commission with necessary administrative services, facilities, and support on a reimbursable basis.

1–303. The Department of Energy and the Department of Health, Education and Welfare shall, to the extent permitted by law and subject to the availability of funds, provide the Commission with such facilities, support, funds and services, including staff, as may be necessary for the effective performance of the Commission's functions.

1–304. The Commission may request any Executive agency to furnish such information, advice or assistance as it deems necessary to carry out its functions. Each such agency is directed, to the extent permitted by law, to furnish such information, advice or assistance upon request by the Chairman of the Commission.

1–305. Each member of the Commission may receive compensation at the maximum rate now or hereafter prescribed by law for each day such member is engaged in the work of the Commission. Each member may also receive travel expenses, including per diem in lieu of subsistence (5 U.S.C. 5702 and 5703).

1–306. The functions of the President under the Federal Advisory Committee Act which are applicable to the Commission, except that of reporting annually to the Congress, shall be performed by the Administrator of General Services.

1–4. *Final Report and Termination.*

1–401. The final report required by Section 1–202 of this Order shall be transmitted not later than six months from the date of the Commission's first meeting.

1–402. The Commission shall terminate two months after the transmittal of its final report.

JIMMY CARTER

The White House,
April 11, 1979.

[Filed with the Office of the Federal Register,
10:46 a.m., April 12, 1979]

President's Commission on the Accident at Three Mile Island

Appointment of 11 Members. April 11, 1979

The President today announced the appointment of 11 persons as members of the President's Commission on the Accident at Three Mile Island. They are:

John G. Kemeny, president of Dartmouth College, Hanover, N.H., who will serve as Chairman of the Commission. Kemeny, 52, is a mathematician and philosopher who has done extensive work in the analysis of complex systems. He is a pioneer in the fields of mathematical models and computer programing.

Kemeny is a native of Hungary who became a naturalized citizen in 1945. His early career included work as a researcher on the Manhattan Project at Los Alamos, N.M., teaching and research in mathematics and philosophy at Princeton University, and 2 years as a research assistant to Dr. Albert Einstein. He became a professor of mathematics at Dartmouth in 1954 and served as chairman of the mathematics department from 1955 to 1967. He has been president of the college since 1970.

Kemeny is the author of numerous books and articles on philosophy, mathematics, and computer science. He is the coinventor of the computer language "BASIC."

Bruce E. Babbitt, Governor of Arizona. Babbitt, 40, holds a master's degree in geophysics and a law degree. He was elected State attorney general of Arizona in 1974 and was sworn in as Governor on March 4, 1978, following the death of Gov. Wesley Bolin. He was elected Governor in November 1978.

Patrick E. Haggerty, of Dallas, Tex., who was president, chief executive officer, and chairman of the board of Texas Instruments, Inc., until his retirement in 1976. Haggerty, 65, has a B.S. in electrical engineering and a law degree. He is chairman of the board of trustees of Rockefeller University and a trustee and member of the executive committee of the University of Dallas.

Paul A. Marks, of New York City, vice president for health sciences at Columbia University. Marks, 52, is a physician (hematologist) and biochemist. He has

PHOTOGRAPHIC PORTFOLIO

President Jimmy Carter

rleaf: With President Sadat and
ne Minister Begin at the signing
mony for the Egyptian-Israeli
ce treaty on the North Lawn of
White House, March 26. *Above*
With President Giscard d'Es-
g, Prime Minister Callaghan, and
ncellor Schmidt during their
tings at Guadeloupe, January 5.
w left: Following acceptance of
Martin Luther King, Jr. Non-
ent Peace Prize in Atlanta,
rgia, January 14. *Above right:*
e of the Union address in the
se Chamber at the Capitol,
uary 23. *Below right:* Arrival
mony for Vice Premier Deng on
South Lawn of the White House,
uary 29.

Above: Visiting a school in Ixtlilco el Grande during the state visit to Mexico, February 15. *Left:* Participating in dedication ceremonies for La Placita de Dolores in Los Angeles, California, May 5. *Right:* Inspection tour of the Three Mile Island Nuclear Facility near Middletown, Pennsylvania, April 1.

Left: Meeting with Federal employees in the Cabinet Room at the White House, May 21. *Below:* Following a meeting with President Sadat at Mena House near Cairo, Egypt, March 10. *Right:* At the dinner honoring the President at the Knesset, in Jerusalem, Israel, March 11.

Left: During a performance hono[r]
the Black Music Association on t[he]
South Lawn of the White House,
June 7. **Below:** With President L[.]
Brezhnev at the signing ceremony [of]
the strategic arms limitation treat[y at]
the Hofburg, in Vienna, Austria,
June 18.

been associated with the College of Physicians and Surgeons at Columbia University throughout his career. He serves as professor of human genetics and director of the Cancer Center. He is a current member of the President's Cancer Panel and served on the President's Biomedical Research Panel in 1975–76. He is a founding member of the Radiation Effects Research Foundation of Japan and served on the science council advisory to the board of directors of that foundation.

Cora B. Marrett, associate professor of sociology at the University of Wisconsin in Madison. Marrett, 36, has served as a consultant to the Army Scientific Advisory Panel and chairs the Panel on Personnel Research in the Navy as a member of the National Research Advisory Committee. Her research and publications are primarily in the areas of organizational structure and communication and of opportunities for women and minorities in science and engineering. She has served previously on the faculties of the University of North Carolina and Western Michigan University. She has served on numerous panels for the National Research Council and the National Science Foundation.

Lloyd McBride, international president of the United Steelworkers of America, and a vice president of the AFL–CIO. McBride, 63, has been active in labor affairs for more than four decades and has held a number of union positions nationally and in his home State of Missouri. He is a member of the National Commission on Air Quality and the President's Advisory Committee for Trade Negotiations.

Harry C. McPherson, Jr., a Washington, D.C., attorney. McPherson, 49, is a former Deputy Under Secretary of the Department of the Army and has also served as Assistant Secretary of State for Educational and Cultural Affairs. He was Special Counsel to President Johnson. He is presently a partner in the firm of Verner, Liipfert, Bernhard & McPherson.

Russell Peterson, former Governor of Delaware and Chairman of the President's Council on Environmental Quality, now president of the National Audubon Society. Peterson, 62, is a chemist by training and was associated with E. I. du Pont de Nemours & Co. from 1942 to 1969, when he became Governor of Delaware. He served as Chairman of the Council on Environmental Quality from 1973 until 1978, when he became Director of the Office of Technology Assessment of the United States Congress. He resigned in 1979 to become president of the National Audubon Society. He is the recipient of many civic and conservation awards.

Thomas Pigford, a professor and chairman of the department of nuclear engineering at the University of California at Berkeley. Pigford, 56, has also served on the faculty at Massachusetts Institute of Technology. Among his areas of special expertise are nuclear reactor design and reactor safety. He has received the Arthur H. Compton Award of the American Nuclear Society and served as a member and chairman of several Government review committees and advisory committees. He was a member of the American Physical Society's study group on nuclear fuel cycles and waste management. He received his training in nuclear and chemical engineering at the Georgia Institute of Technology and the Massachusetts Institute of Technology.

Theodore B. Taylor, professor of aerospace and mechanical science at Princeton University. Taylor, 53, is a physicist and reactor specialist. He designed the TRIGA nuclear research reactor, the design most in use around the world today.

He has been associated with Los Alamos Scientific Laboratory and has served as Deputy Director of the Defense Atomic Support Agency. He has received the Lawrence Memorial Award and the Secretary of Defense's Meritorious Civilian Service Medal.

Ann Trunk, a Middletown, Pa., housewife. Trunk, 44, is the mother of six children. She is the former president of the Middletown Civic Club and has been active in other local civic organizations. Her husband is a professor at Pennsylvania State University. He participated in the community effort after the nuclear powerplant accident in Middletown by taking radiation checks in the area.

Loyalty Day, 1979

Proclamation 4657.   April 11, 1979

By the President of the United States of America

A Proclamation

In our country, loyalty has a deep and complex meaning. It does not refer to allegiance to the tenets of an ideological doctrine nor does it convey a blind faith in a single leader or political party. A respect for our flag is part of what we mean by loyalty, but the concept goes well beyond a reverence for our national symbols.

To the citizens of our country, loyalty means a devotion and a dedication to our democratic traditions of liberty and justice. It is an acknowledgement of our responsibilities and duties as citizens to nurture and preserve those freedoms. It also conveys a respect for our fellow citizens who have fought, and sometimes died, to establish and protect our country and our ideals.

To encourage the people of the United States to reflect on our democratic heritage and institutions, the Congress, by a joint resolution approved July 18, 1958 (72 Stat. 369) has designated May 1 of every year as Loyalty Day, and has requested the President to issue a proclamation inviting the people of the United States to observe that day with appropriate observances.

Now, THEREFORE, I, JIMMY CARTER, President of the United States of America, call upon all Americans to observe Tuesday, May 1, 1979, as Loyalty Day. I also ask the appropriate officials of the Government and all citizens to display the flag of the United States on all Government buildings and other fitting places.

IN WITNESS WHEREOF, I have hereunto set my hand this eleventh day of April, in the year of our Lord nineteen hundred seventy-nine, and of the Independence of the United States of America the two hundred and third.

JIMMY CARTER

[Filed with the Office of the Federal Register, 10:45 a.m., April 12, 1979]

Multilateral Trade Negotiations Agreements

Statement by the President.   April 12, 1979

The United States today has entered into international agreements that will bring a new order to the world trading system.

Trade negotiators representing 41 nations, accounting for more than 90 percent of world trade, have agreed in Geneva on the final, substantive results of the Tokyo Round of international trade talks. These Multilateral Trade Negotiations (MTN), the seventh round since World War II, are the most comprehensive and far reaching since establishment of the General Agreements on Tariffs and Trade (GATT) in 1947. For the first time, agreements or "codes" have been concluded on a broad range of "nontariff" obstacles to trade. Phased tariff reductions averaging about 33 percent were also approved.

The agreements, when approved by Congress, will establish new trading rules that will increase the opportunities of all nations, rich and poor, to exchange their goods under equitable conditions. Through such fair and open trade, we strengthen peace and trust in the world and make more efficient use of the world's human and material resources.

The agreements steer us away from destructive protectionism and into a path of greater export opportunities, with the prospects of new jobs, improved productivity, and increased industrial and agricultural production. The new opportunities that are thus developed will be realized through vigorous efforts by government, industry, and agriculture to promote exports.

The trade agreements that we have signed are the product of years of work, during which time American negotiators have been advised and assisted by concerned Members of Congress and by hundreds of men and women from the private sector.

I wish to take this opportunity to reemphasize this administration's commitment to the national export policy that stimulates our export trade. I also wish to commend all those in the United States and abroad whose labors resulted in the new international trade agreements.

United States-United Kingdom Convention on Taxation and Fiscal Evasion

Message to the Senate Transmitting a Protocol to the Convention. April 12, 1979

To the Senate of the United States:

I transmit herewith, for Senate advice and consent to ratification, a Third Protocol further amending the Convention between the Government of the United States of America and the Government of the United Kingdom of Great Britain and Northern Ireland for the avoidance of double taxation and the prevention of fiscal evasion with respect to taxes on income and capital gains signed at London on December 31, 1975, as amended by an exchange of notes dated April 13, 1976, and by Protocols signed at London on August 26, 1976 and March 31, 1977. For the information of the Senate, I also transmit the report of the Department of State on the Third Protocol.

The Third Protocol will enter into force immediately after the expiration of 30 days following the date on which instruments of ratification are exchanged.

I recommend that the Senate give early and favorable consideration to the Third Protocol and give advice and consent to its ratification.

JIMMY CARTER

The White House,
April 12, 1979.

Federal Reserve System

Nomination of Emmett J. Rice To Be a Member of the Board of Governors. April 12, 1979

The President today announced that he will nominate Emmett J. Rice, of Washington, D.C., to be a member of the

Board of Governors of the Federal Reserve System. Mr. Rice replaces Stephen Gardner, who has died. This term expires in 1990.

Rice, 50, was born in Florence, S.C. He received a B.B.A. (1941) and an M.B.A. (1942) from City College of New York and a Ph. D. in economics from the University of California at Berkeley in 1955. He served in the U.S. Air Force from 1942 to 1946.

In 1950 and 1951, Rice was a research assistant in economics at Berkeley, and in 1952 he was a research associate at the Reserve Bank of India as a Fulbright Fellow. In 1953 and 1954, he was a teaching assistant at Berkeley.

From 1954 to 1960, Rice was an assistant professor of economics at Cornell University. From 1960 to 1962, he was on leave from Cornell to work as an economist at the Federal Reserve Bank of New York. From 1962 to 1964, he was an adviser to the Central Bank of Nigeria in Lagos.

From 1964 to 1966, Rice was Deputy Director, then Acting Director, of the Treasury Department's Office of Developing Nations. From 1966 to 1970, he was U.S. Alternate Executive Director for the International Bank for Reconstruction and Development (World Bank), the International Development Association, and the International Finance Corporation.

From 1970 to 1971, Rice was executive director of the Mayor's Economic Development Committee for Washington, D.C., on leave from the Treasury Department. Since 1972 he has been senior vice president of the National Bank of Washington.

Federal Reserve System

Nomination of Frederick H. Schultz To Be a Member of the Board of Governors.
April 12, 1979

The President today announced that he will nominate Frederick H. Schultz, of Jacksonville, Fla., to be a member of the Board of Governors of the Federal Reserve System. Mr. Schultz replaces Philip Jackson, resigned, whose term expires in 1982.

Schultz was born January 16, 1929, in Jacksonville. He received an A.B. from Princeton University in 1952. He served in the U.S. Army from 1952 to 1954 and attended the University of Florida Law School from 1954 to 1956.

Schultz was employed in the executive training program of the Barnett National Bank of Jacksonville in 1956 and 1957. In 1957 he opened his own office, concentrating his efforts in securities markets and in providing risk capital for new and expanding ventures.

Schultz is now chairman of the board of Barnett Investment Services, Inc., a subsidiary of Barnett Banks of Florida, and a director of Barnett Banks of Florida.

From 1963 to 1970, Schultz served as a member of the Florida House of Representatives, and in 1968 he was elected speaker of the Florida House. He was chairman of the Citizens' Committee on Education, a 2-year study of education in Florida. He served on the Jacksonville Expressway Authority from 1961 to 1963.

United States Ambassador to Barbados, Grenada, and Dominica, and Minister to Saint Lucia

Nomination of Sally Angela Shelton.
April 13, 1979

The President today announced that he will nominate Sally Angela Shelton, of Texas, as Ambassador to Barbados, Grenada, the Commonwealth of Dominica, and as Minister to Saint Lucia.

She would succeed Frank V. Ortiz, Jr.,

who is being transferred to another post, as Ambassador to Barbados and Grenada. She would be the first accredited American Ambassador to Dominica and our first accredited Minister to Saint Lucia.

Miss Shelton was born August 29, 1944, in San Antonio, Tex. She received her B.A. in 1966 from the University of Missouri and her M.A. in 1968 from Johns Hopkins School of Advanced International Studies. In 1968 she was a Fulbright Scholar at the Institute des Sciences Politiques in Paris, and in 1969 she was a Ph. D. candidate at Georgetown University.

In 1969 she was a research assistant at Brookings Institution, and from 1970 to 1971, she was professor of international relations at National Autonomous University of Mexico and Iberoamerican University in Mexico City.

From 1971 to 1977, she was legislative assistant to U.S. Senator Lloyd Bentsen. In 1977 she served as Deputy Assistant Secretary of State for Inter-American Affairs. From 1978 to 1979, she was Special Adviser to the United States Mission to the U.N. in New York.

Superior Court of the District of Columbia

Nomination of Two Associate Judges.
April 13, 1979

The President today announced that he will nominate Shellie F. Bowers and Harriett R. Taylor to fill two vacancies on the Superior Court of the District of Columbia.

Bowers, 42, received a B.A. from Lincoln University in Missouri in 1957 and LL.B. and LL.M. degrees from Georgetown Law Center in 1962 and 1963, respectively. He worked for the Justice

Department for 1 year and has since been in private practice in the District of Columbia.

Taylor is an administrative law judge in the District of Columbia's Office of Consumer Protection, a position she has held since 1976. She has practiced law in Washington since 1961. Taylor attended Brooklyn College and Columbia Law School, receiving an LL.B. in 1955. She is 46.

Tornado Disaster in Wichita Falls, Texas

Telegram to Mayor Kenneth Hill.
April 13, 1979

Jack Watson of my staff is en route to Wichita Falls as my personal representative to assure that all appropriate and necessary federal assistance is being made available.

Mr. Watson has the authority to ensure that the federal government's response to this tragedy is timely and of maximum assistance to the people of the area, and he will report to me upon his return to Washington.

My thoughts and prayers are with you and your fellow citizens.

JIMMY CARTER

Digest of Other White House Announcements

The following listing includes the President's public schedule and other items of general interest announced by the White House Press Office and not included elsewhere in this issue.

April 7

Following his visit to Richmond, Va., the President returned to Camp David, Md.

April 8

The President returned to the White House from Camp David, Md.

April 9

The President met at the White House with:

—Zbigniew Brzezinski, Assistant to the President for National Security Affairs;

—Frank B. Moore, Assistant to the President for Congressional Liaison;

—freshman Members of the House of Representatives;

—Charles L. Schultze, Chairman of the Council of Economic Advisers;

—James T. McIntyre, Jr., Director of the Office of Management and Budget.

The President announced that he will nominate Richard F. Celeste to be an Associate Director of ACTION. Mr. Celeste was nominated last month to be Director of the Peace Corps.

April 10

The President met at the White House with:

—Dr. Brzezinski;

—Mr. Moore;

—a group of newly elected Democratic State chairmen;

—Vice President Mondale.

The President has invited Chancellor Helmut Schmidt of the Federal Republic of Germany to meet with him at the White House on the morning of Wednesday, June 6. The Chancellor will be in the United States from June 5 to 8. During that time, he will receive an honorary degree from Harvard University and will attend the convocation of the University of South Carolina at Columbia. He will also be the guest of the American Council on Germany, in New York.

April 11

The President met at the White House with:

—Dr. Brzezinski;

—Secretary of Commerce Juanita M. Kreps;

—Mr. Moore, Danny C. Tate, Deputy Assistant for Congressional Liaison (House), and Robert G. Beckel, Special Assistant for Congressional Liaison (House);

—Secretary of Health, Education, and Welfare Joseph A. Califano, Jr., Stuart E. Eizenstat, Assistant to the President for Domestic Affairs and Policy, Anne Wexler, Assistant to the President, Dr. Schultze, and a group of insurance company executives;

—Stansfield Turner, Director of Central Intelligence, Hamilton Jordan, Assistant to the President, and Dr. Brzezinski;

—Representative Lee H. Hamilton of Indiana.

The Chinese People's Institute of Foreign Affairs of the People's Republic of China has invited a bipartisan congressional delegation to visit China during April. The delegation will depart April 11 and return April 22. The group will be led by Representative Jack Brooks. While in China, the delegation will meet with high-level Chinese officials to discuss U.S. and Chinese foreign policies and Sino-Soviet relations. Other members of the group include Representatives Dante B. Fascell (D-Fla.), James C. Corman (D-Calif.), Benjamin Rosenthal (D-L-N.Y.), James J. Howard (D-N.J.), David R. Obey (D-Wis.), Robert A. Roe (D-N.J.), Robert F. Drinan (D-Mass.), William R. Archer (R-Tex.), Cardiss Collins

(D-Ill.), Robert E. Bauman (R-Md.), John Burton (D-Calif.), Martin A. Russo (D-Ill.), Allen E. Ertel (D-Pa.), and Dan Mica (D-Fla.). The mutual exchange relationship fulfills that part of the Shanghai communique in which both sides pledged to foster broader under-standing and engage in cultural and scientific exchanges. This group is the last of the White House-facilitated congressional delegations to China as part of the normalization process.

The President declared a major disaster for the State of Arkansas as a result of a tornado on April 8, which caused extensive public and private property damage.

April 12

The President met at the White House with Dr. Brzezinski.

The President left the White House for an Easter vacation at Sapelo Island, Plains, and Calhoun, Ga.

The President has declared a major disaster for the State of Texas as a result of severe storms and tornadoes on April 10 and 11, which caused extensive public and private property damage.

The President announced that Secretary Califano has appointed James (Jim) Guy Tucker as the Chairperson of the White House Conference on Families.

NOMINATIONS SUBMITTED TO THE SENATE

The following list does not include promotions of members of the Uniformed Services, nominations to the Service Academies, or nominations of Foreign Service officers.

Submitted April 9, 1979

CORNELIA G. KENNEDY, of Michigan, to be United States Circuit Judge for the Sixth Circuit, vice a new position created by P.L. 95–486, approved October 20, 1978.

NOMINATIONS—Continued

Submitted April 9—Continued

RICHARD BRYANT LOWE III, of New York, to be Deputy Inspector General, Department of Health, Education, and Welfare, vice Charles F. C. Ruff, resigned.

RICHARD L. WILLIAMS, of Virginia, to be United States District Judge for the Eastern District of Virginia, vice a new position created by P.L. 95–486, approved October 20, 1978.

RICHARD FRANK CELESTE, of Ohio, to be an Associate Director of the ACTION Agency, vice Carolyn R. Payton, resigned.

Submitted April 12, 1979

EDWARD C. REED, JR., of Nevada, to be United States District Judge for the District of Nevada, vice a new position created by P.L. 95–486, approved October 20, 1978.

JOSEPH RANSDELL KEENE, of Louisiana, to be United States Attorney for the Western District of Louisiana for the term of 4 years, vice Edward L. Shaheen, resigned.

Submitted April 13, 1979

SALLY ANGELA SHELTON, of Texas, to be Ambassador Extraordinary and Plenipotentiary of the United States of America to Barbados, and to serve concurrently and without additional compensation as Ambassador Extraordinary and Plenipotentiary of the United States of America to Grenada and the Commonwealth of Dominica, and as Envoy Extraordinary and Minister Plenipotentiary of the United States of America to Saint Lucia.

SHELLIE FOUNTAIN BOWERS, of the District of Columbia, to be an Associate Judge of the Superior Court of the District of Columbia for a term of 15 years, vice DeWitt S. Hyde, retired.

HARRIETT ROSEN TAYLOR, of the District of Columbia, to be an Associate Judge of the Superior Court of the District of Columbia for a term of 15 years, vice Robert H. Campbell.

CHECKLIST OF WHITE HOUSE PRESS RELEASES

The following listing contains releases of the White House Press Office which are not included in this issue.

CHECKLIST—Continued

Released April 7, 1979

Advance text: remarks at the Jefferson-Jackson Day dinner in Richmond, Va.

Released April 9, 1979

Announcement: nomination of Richard L. Williams to be United States District Judge for the Eastern District of Virginia

News conference: on the implementation of the President's urban policy—by Jack H. Watson, Jr., Assistant to the President for Intergovernmental Affairs

Fact sheet: on the Interagency Coordinating Council's report describing the administration's progress in implementing the President's urban policy

Released April 11, 1979

Press announcement: concerning the labor dispute in the trucking industry—by Alfred E. Kahn, Advisor to the President on Inflation

Announcement: nomination of Edward C. Reed, Jr., to be United States District Judge for the District of Nevada

Announcement: nomination of Joseph Ransdell Keene to be United States Attorney for the Western District of Louisiana

CHECKLIST—Continued

Released April 12, 1979

Announcement: appointment of James (Jim) Guy Tucker as Chairperson of the White House Conference on Families by Secretary of Health, Education, and Welfare Joseph A. Califano, Jr., and biographical information on Mr. Tucker

Released April 13, 1979

Announcement: trip by Jack H. Watson, Jr., Assistant to the President for Intergovernmental Affairs, to Wichita Falls, Tex., as the personal representative of the President

---

ACTS APPROVED BY THE PRESIDENT

Approved April 9, 1979

H.R. 2439_____ Public Law 96-7
An act to rescind certain budget authority contained in the message of the President of January 31, 1979 (H. Doc. 96-46), transmitted pursuant to the Impoundment Control Act of 1974.

Approved April 10, 1979

H.R. 2479_____ Public Law 96-8
Taiwan Relations Act.

Editor's Note

The President's Trip to Georgia

On Friday, April 13, the President was at Sapelo Island, Ga., as part of an Easter vacation in Georgia to last until April 22. Releases and announcements issued on the trip will be printed in following issues.

PRESIDENTIAL DOCUMENTS

Week Ending Friday, April 20, 1979

Sapelo Island, Georgia

Informal Exchanges With Reporters.
April 15, 1979

THE PRESIDENT. Good morning everybody. Happy Easter.

Q. Thank you. Tell us about your vacation.

THE PRESIDENT. Well, I'd rather talk about the vacation than the fishing. [*Laughter*] We've had a good vacation so far.

Q. What about the fishing? Have you caught anything?

THE PRESIDENT. We caught a few.

Q. Numbers? Size?

THE PRESIDENT. No numbers and sizes. [*Laughter*]

Q. Are you going to name a Middle East negotiator like Scranton to take over for Atherton?

THE PRESIDENT. Not any time soon.

I think they're ready to start. I hope you all can hear the singing and all. It's really good.

REPORTER. Thank you.

[*The exchange began at approximately 11 a.m. as the President was entering the First African Baptist Church for Easter services. Following the services, at approximately 1:15 p.m., the President spoke with reporters as follows.*]

Q. Perfect day, isn't it?

THE PRESIDENT. Yes, it is.

Q. The sun is beautiful.

Q. Mr. President, have you been driving all week? I thought it had been a long time since you'd driven a car.

THE PRESIDENT. Well, I drive when I go down to the farm in Plains.

Q. So you don't forget how.

THE PRESIDENT. No, I think they gave me a sacrificial jeep. So far I haven't sacrificed it. [*Laughter*]

Q. Is this your first time driving a jeep?

THE PRESIDENT. Well, when I hunt quail at home, on my farm, I drive a jeep some.

Q. Have you seen any alligators or snakes?

THE PRESIDENT. A couple of alligators.

Q. Any deer?

Q. Did you stop?

THE PRESIDENT. The boat that we used to fish, when they turned it over yesterday, it had a big rattlesnake under it. I've only seen one snake myself. That's all.

Well, we've seen a lot of deer, and just saw two turkeys on the way over here to the church. A lot of wild turkey on this island, and also a lot of deer, a few alligators.

Q. Mr. President, anything you'd like to say to the American people on Easter?

THE PRESIDENT. No. I think you might quote what I said—you know, it's just a wonderful place to be on Easter, you know, see the sunrise and know what Christ's life meant and to be with other Christians.

Q. Are you coming back next year?

THE PRESIDENT. Well, I'd like to. Somebody suggested I move down here. [*Laughter*]

We used to come down here before I was Governor and stay with Fred Marlin, Dr. Marlin, that they had stand up. We used to kind of camp in his house, he and his wife and, I think, two children. When I was Governor, I came back.

It's a beautiful island. I've been to almost all the Georgia islands.

Q. What have you been doing since you got to Sapelo Island? We haven't gotten much information about that.

THE PRESIDENT. Well, I always jog every day. I've read four or five books. Every morning I have a good bit of paperwork to do, the daily briefing from the State Department, from Secretary Vance, and the daily briefing on intelligence. That comes in early every morning. And I get a memorandum from the National Security Council as well, almost every day. And then documents to sign, appointments of people to positions in government. And we've had several emergency declarations to complete in the areas where the tornadoes have done damage.

Q. Are you worried about the Rhodesian situation?

THE PRESIDENT. Well, I've been keeping up with it, both through the news media and also through the daily briefings we get.

Q. Anything to say about the spy plane in South Africa?

THE PRESIDENT. No, I think not. I don't want to make any international news. [*Laughter*]

Q. You're going to enhance the tourist trade, but they can't come here, can they? [*Laughter*]

THE PRESIDENT. No. I hope you all have a chance to drive around and take a look at the island.

Q. They won't let us. You won't let us. [*Laughter*]

THE PRESIDENT. Right. Right.

Q. You nod, huh?

THE PRESIDENT. Very good.

Q. How do you like your house that you're staying in?

THE PRESIDENT. Well, it's beautiful.

Q. Is it as elaborate as it once was?

THE PRESIDENT. I guess so.

Q. What were the books, sir, that you said you read?

THE PRESIDENT. Well, I have no comment. [*Laughter*] There's an extensive library in the mansion there, I guess a couple thousand books. I read one of a, kind of a collection of Hemingway's stories, "Death in the Afternoon."

Earthquake in Yugoslavia
Message to President Josip Broz Tito. April 15, 1979

Dear Mr. President:

I was distressed to learn of the violent earthquake which struck the southern coast of Yugoslavia earlier today. Please accept my deepest sympathy and that of my family in the face of this tragic event. I have asked Ambassador Eagleburger to convey to Mr. Veljko Milativic, President of the Presidency of the Socialist Republic of Montenegro, and through him to the families of the victims, my personal condolences and those of the American people.

The United States stands ready to assist in efforts to relieve the suffering. I have instructed Ambassador Eagleburger to remain in close touch with the appropriate authorities to determine how we may best be of assistance.

Again, Mr. President, please accept my deepest sympathy and condolences.

JIMMY CARTER

NOTE: The text of the message was released on April 16.

National Forest System Lands

*Statement Announcing Decisions on
Wilderness Designations. April 16, 1979*

We have reached a decision on the future of 62 million acres of roadless and undeveloped National Forest System lands.

Through the Department of Agriculture's Roadless Area Review and Evaluation—known as RARE II—we sought public assistance in establishing the best future uses of these lands. We struck a reasonable balance between accommodating the Nation's needs for wilderness and for the other goods and services produced from these lands.

I am recommending to Congress wilderness designations for about 15.4 million acres of RARE II lands. I already have sent to Congress wilderness recommendations for lands in the two National Forests in Alaska, including about 5.5 million acres identified in RARE II. I will now recommend wilderness designation for about 9.9 million additional acres on 118 National Forest System units in 35 other States and the Commonwealth of Puerto Rico.

These recommendations from RARE II will more than double the present size of the National Forest System segment of the National Wilderness Preservation System and will more than quadruple the number of National Forest wildernesses in the highly populated States east of the Mississippi.

The balance of the 62 million acres falls into two categories. The first is "further planning." We need more information to determine the best uses for about 10.6 million acres in this category. Decisions on these areas will be made as soon as possible. In the second category are about 36 million acres which will be managed for multiple uses other than wilder-

ness. I am asking Secretary Bergland to proceed immediately with the planning and management of these areas under existing law.

For many years, the process of determining the best uses of National Forest has been a slow, piecemeal effort. This process has been the source of frustration and controversy for all interest groups— recreational, environmental, and industrial. RARE II provided a comprehensive, nationwide review and evaluation of these important public lands. It is my hope that the decision being announced today will help resolve the longstanding controversy over their case.

This decision will assure the American people that high-quality areas will be protected for wilderness consideration by the Congress and for enjoyment by future generations. It also will assure a continuing, sustained yield of goods and services from those lands not recommended as wilderness. This will help our national economy, as well as the growth and stability of many local communities, by providing additional oil and gas, minerals, and timber products, which are essential to restraining inflation and increasing productivity.

This decision also meets two major administration goals. First, the recommendations fulfill the pledge in my May 23, 1977, environmental message to enlarge the Nation's treasury of wilderness resources. And second, by releasing some of the land for uses other than wilderness, we respond to our urgent need for energy, wood products, livestock forage, minerals, and a broad array of recreational opportunities. In sum, our recommendations are vital to the effort to reduce inflation, control unemployment, and encourage energy development.

All the nonwilderness lands in the National Forest System will be managed to reflect environmental concerns while sustaining their multiple resource values.

I have asked Secretary Bergland to provide Congress with maps and resource data to accompany my recommendations for wilderness designations. Since some of the areas involved are contiguous to areas previously recommended for wilderness as a result of the earlier review of National Forest Primitive Areas, the Secretary will also include updated information on these areas.

Included in my fact sheet is a State-by-State listing of the acreage in wilderness, in the further planning and nonwilderness categories, and a listing of changes made in the Secretary's January 4 proposal. The changes are based on comments received from Governors, Members of Congress, and Federal agencies during the interagency review process.

NOTE: The fact sheet is included in the press release.

Disaster Emergency in Mississippi

Telegram to Governor Cliff Finch and Mayor Dale Danks of Jackson. April 17, 1979

I am sending Bill Simpson of my staff to Mississippi as my personal representative to assure that all appropriate and necessary federal assistance is being made available. He is due to arrive in Jackson at approximately 9:15 a.m. Tuesday, April 17.

As you know, Bill is a native of Mississippi and served until recently as administrative assistant to former Senator Eastland. He has the authority to insure that the federal government's response to this disaster situation is timely and of maximum assistance to the people of the affected areas, and he will report to me on his return to Washington.

My thoughts and prayers are with you and your fellow citizens.

JIMMY CARTER

Commandant of the Marine Corps

Nomination of Gen. Robert H. Barrow. April 18, 1979

The President today announced he will nominate Gen. Robert H. Barrow, USMC, to be Commandant of the Marine Corps. He would replace Gen. Louis H. Wilson, who is retiring on June 30, 1979.

General Barrow is currently Assistant Commandant of the Marine Corps, a post he has held since July 1, 1978.

He was born February 5, 1922, in Baton Rouge, La. He attended Louisiana State University and the University of Maryland, where he received a B.S. degree in 1956. He has done graduate work at Tulane University.

He was commissioned in May 1943, and served during the latter part of World War II with a Chinese guerrilla force which operated in enemy-occupied territory in central China. During the Korean conflict, he participated in the Inchon-Seoul operation and the Chosin Reservoir campaign as a rifle company commander.

From 1964 to 1967, Barrow served as the plans officer, Fleet Marine Force, Pacific, and as an infantry regiment commander whose regiment participated in numerous combat actions in the vicinity of the DMZ, Khe Sanh, and A Shau Valley.

He was Commanding General for 3 years at the Marine Corps Base, Okinawa, and then served as Commanding General, Marine Corps Recruit Depot, Parris Island, S.C., for 32 months.

In 1975 he was appointed Lieutenant General and assigned as Deputy Chief of Staff for Manpower at Marine Corps Headquarters. From October 1976 until assuming his present duties, he served as Commanding General, Fleet Marine Force, Atlantic, in Norfolk, Va.

Barrow's personal U.S. decorations include the Navy Cross, the Army Distinguished Service Cross, the Silver Star, three Legions of Merit, two Bronze Stars, and the Joint Service Commendation Medal.

Older Americans Month, 1979

Proclamation 4658.   April 18, 1979

By the President of the United States of America

A Proclamation

The older American embodies not only a lifetime of experience and accomplishment, but also invaluable and often unrecognized resources of talent, energy and wisdom. Our country's awareness of the contributions and potential of our older people has steadily grown in recent years, as an increasing number of Americans have shown that their later years can indeed be rewarding ones for themselves and their communities.

Yet for too many of our people, the later years are often wasted and miserable because of health problems. This year's theme for the May observance of Older Americans Month is "Better Health Through Better Care."

Health is defined by the World Health Organization as a "state of complete physical, mental and social well-being, not merely the absence of disease and infirmity." Good adequate health requires more than just the treatment of sickness and injury, though providing treatment is vital. Good health care must also include proper nutrition, preventive and health maintenance services, as well as provision for long-term care.

In older persons the interrelationship between physical and mental health is especially important. Mental health services for the elderly have been sadly lacking in this country. Active and satisfying lives are both dependent upon and necessary to maintaining the health of older Americans.

The accessibility of all types of health services is critically important to the elderly, and holding down the costs of both crisis-oriented and preventive services is essential if the real needs are to be met.

As we make greater use of the abilities of older Americans, and find ways to better meet their special needs, particularly in relation to health services, all of our people will benefit.

Now, THEREFORE, I, JIMMY CARTER, President of the United States of America, do hereby designate the month of May 1979 as Older Americans Month. I ask public officials at all levels, doctors, nurses, and other health professionals, and people of all ages, to promote better health care and social services for older people, and to undertake appropriate projects both on a public and on a personal level to ensure the best possible health for older people.

IN WITNESS WHEREOF, I have hereunto set my hand this eighteenth day of April, in the year of our Lord nineteen hundred seventy-nine, and of the Independence of the United States of America the two hundred and third.

JIMMY CARTER

[Filed with the Office of the Federal Register, 3:40 p.m., April 18, 1979]

Disaster Emergency in Mississippi

Telegram to Governor Cliff Finch.
April 19, 1979

Bill Simpson of my staff is finalizing a report on the flood conditions in Mississippi following his visit to Jackson.

The people of Mississippi have met this disaster—and the tragedy it has wrought—with strength, resolve and faith. My prayers are with them, and I am confident that their spirit will prevail over this unprecedented flood as it has over previous natural disasters.

While I am concerned about the scope of the flooding and the suffering inflicted on our citizens, I am heartened to know that an effective working partnership has already been achieved among all levels of government and the private sector to relieve the situation.

This partnership, which reaches from the White House through the Governor's office into every county and community involved in this catastrophe, insures we will succeed in our efforts to rebuild homes, businesses and livelihoods in every afflicted area of the state.

JIMMY CARTER

NOTE: The text of the telegram was released on April 20.

Death of Rogers C. B. Morton

Statement by the President.   April 20, 1979

Americans who care about conservation and the environment have lost a champion with the death of Rogers C. B. Morton. He fought gallantly for the outdoors he cherished. In Congress, in the Cabinet, and in politics he was both an ardent partisan and a perfect gentleman.

His spirit, courage, and humor enhanced our public life and will be greatly missed.

NOTE: Mr. Morton served as Secretary of the Interior during the Nixon administration and as Secretary of Commerce during the Ford administration. He had also been chairman of the Republican National Committee and a U. S. Representative from Maryland.

Digest of Other White House Announcements

The following listing includes the President's public schedule and other items of general interest announced by the White House Press Office and not included elsewhere in this issue.

April 14

The White House announced that the President yesterday declared a major disaster for the State of Oklahoma as a result of severe storms and tornadoes, beginning on April 10, which caused extensive public and private property damage.

The White House announced that the President yesterday amended his April 11 declaration of a major disaster for the State of Arkansas to provide Federal assistance also for damage inflicted by severe storms and tornadoes occurring after April 8, but a part of the same weather system.

The President declared an emergency for the State of Mississippi because of the impact of severe storms, tornadoes, and flooding, beginning on or about April 11. The President's action will permit the donation of Government-owned mobile homes to the State to provide temporary housing for those families who lost their homes.

April 16

The President declared a major disaster for the State of Mississippi as a result of severe storms, tornadoes, and flooding, beginning on or about April 8, which caused extensive public and private property damage.

April 18

The President transmitted to the Congress the 1977 reports of the National Cancer Advisory Board and the Director on the National Cancer Program.

April 19

The White House announced that the President yesterday declared a major disaster for the State of Alabama as a result of severe storms, high wind, and flooding, beginning on or about April 11, which caused extensive public and private property damage.

The President has accepted the invitation of President Park Chung Hee to visit the Republic of Korea immediately following the conclusion of the economic summit conference in Tokyo. The details of the visit are being worked out by the two governments.

April 20

The President left Sapelo Island and went to Plains, Ga.

NOMINATIONS SUBMITTED TO THE SENATE

The following list does not include promotions of members of the Uniformed Services, nominations to the Service Academies, or nominations of Foreign Service officers.

NOMINATIONS—Continued

Submitted April 18, 1979

R. LANIER ANDERSON III, of Georgia, to be United States Circuit Judge for the Fifth Circuit, vice a new position created by P.L. 95–486, approved October 20, 1978.

ALBERT J. HENDERSON, of Georgia, to be United States Circuit Judge for the Fifth Circuit, vice a new position created by P.L. 95–486, approved October 20, 1978.

CHECKLIST OF WHITE HOUSE PRESS RELEASES

The following listing contains releases of the White House Press Office which are not included in this issue.

Released April 17, 1979

Announcement: trip by Bill Simpson, Deputy Assistant to the President, to Jackson, Miss., as the personal representative of the President

Released April 18, 1979

Announcement: nomination of R. Lanier Anderson III to be United States Circuit Judge for the Fifth Circuit

Announcement: nomination of Albert J. Henderson to be United States Circuit Judge for the Fifth Circuit

Released April 20, 1979

Announcement: water and sewer services program for low-income rural areas

---

ACTS APPROVED BY THE PRESIDENT

Approved April 19, 1979

H.J. Res. 283_____ Public Law 96–9
A joint resolution reaffirming the United States commitment to the North Atlantic Alliance.

PRESIDENTIAL DOCUMENTS

Week Ending Friday, April 27, 1979

National Academy of Sciences

Remarks at the Academy's Annual Meeting.   April 23, 1979

President Handler, distinguished members of the National Academy of Sciences, guests who are equally distinguished in your own field of work:

I'm indeed pleased to be here. I know that election to the National Academy is the highest honor that can be paid to a scientist or an engineer in the United States, and I again congratulate all of you.

I understand that in the Soviet Union, when someone is chosen to their National Academy of Sciences, his or her salary immediately doubles—[*laughter*]—and a chauffeured car is made available for use. I understand there's a slight difference in our own country. [*Laughter*] You immediately get a bill for membership dues, and you are pledged voluntarily to give advice to your Government free of charge. [*Laughter*] And I thank you for that.

I am honored to address this distinguished convocation and to join with you in commemorating the 100th anniversary year of the birth of Albert Einstein.

The National Academy of Sciences was already a thriving institution when Albert Einstein was born. In 1942, soon after taking out American citizenship, Dr. Einstein was elected to this Academy, becoming at once its newest and, perhaps, its most eminent member. His coming to our country was a matter of carefully considered choice. In this respect, he was like many thousands of scientists from all over the world—drawn to this country by an atmosphere of intellectual freedom, adventure, and hospitality for the pursuit of scientific truth.

That atmosphere has invigorated American life from our Nation's beginnings. Scientists-statesmen such as Benjamin Franklin and Thomas Jefferson were among the authors of our own national independence. Their influence helped to establish the young American republic as a place where scientific endeavor was not only encouraged but was honored.

We've never deviated from that commitment. And it's significant, I believe, that the Congress and President Lincoln chartered this National Academy of Sciences at the height of our gravest national crisis. In so doing, they demonstrated a deep understanding of the importance of science to the very survival of our Nation.

There is little that we can predict with certainty. But we can be very sure that whatever the future holds, we will be better prepared for it if we pursue a strong national program of support for science and technology. That's why even in this time of budgetary restraint, I have remained firmly committed to such a program.

Scientific enterprise will be a key to our future strength, but we in this room cannot take this for granted. In this centennial year, it's well to remember that faith in the future was a notable quality of Albert Einstein. Only an optimist could have undertaken the incredibly ambitious task that Dr. Einstein set for himself— the discovery and the explication of the underlying order of our universe.

Throughout his life, Dr. Einstein sought not only to discover order in the natural world, but also to promote order in the human world.

Einstein the humanitarian has much to teach us, as does Einstein the physicist. He saw the pursuit of science as good in itself, but he also saw that the uses of science are only as good—or as bad—as the moral and political choices that determine those uses. In his own words, and I quote, "Concern for man himself and his fate must always form the chief interest of all technical endeavors—in order that the creation of our minds shall be a blessing and not a curse."

The tree of science is always beautiful, but its fruits can be bitter as well as sweet. Our task is to nourish the tree of science and to attempt as best we can to harvest the fruits that are sweet. And that task must be shared by all of us—scientists, engineers, industrial leaders, educators, and public officials alike.

I hope that science and technology in the United States will continue to be shaped by Einstein's vision of knowledge that keeps the good of human beings always at the forefront.

It's in that context that I want to share with you briefly some ideas and observations about basic research, about a strategy for energy technology, about industrial innovation, about scientific cooperation among nations, and about the role of science in helping to control its own most fearsome offspring—nuclear weapons. I'll be very brief.

The last President to address a con-

vocation of the National Academy of Sciences, John F. Kennedy, spoke of basic research in these words: "We realize now," he said, "that progress in technology depends on progress in theory; that the most abstract investigations can lead to the most concrete results; and that the vitality of a scientific community springs from its passion to answer science's most fundamental questions."

One month to the day after President Kennedy spoke those words, he was stricken down by an assassin's bullet. And then began a long period of political trauma in our country. But in many ways, those following years were exciting ones in science and technology—years of breakthrough discoveries in molecular biology, particle physics, and many other fields, and of technological progress epitomized by the triumphant landing of men on the Moon. Yet for scientists, as for so many of the rest of us in politics and other fields, they were also difficult years. American science found itself beleaguered by two very different kinds of anti-intellectualism: on the one hand, by the romantic antirationalism of the counterculture and, on the other, by the veiled hostility of a national administration that distrusted the academic and the scientific community.

The latter presented the most serious threat. Federal policy toward science became infected with a simplistic search for a simple fix. Research that seemed to promise a quick payoff was more amply funded, while support of basic research was allowed to decline. The future of our scientific and technological primacy was put at risk.

I came to office determined to reverse that dangerous, shortsighted trend. And today I reaffirm to you my commitment to basic research, the bedrock of our scientific and technological future.

During the 2 years of my own administration, I've proposed increases already of more than 25 percent in Federal funding of basic research. I've asked the Congress to support this increased funding in order to meet the long-term needs of our Nation.

I've also sought to strengthen basic research in the individual Federal agencies. Each agency has been asked to reexamine its own budget request to see how basic research commitments could be strengthened. And we've tried to resolve nonbudgetary problems that have inhibited research in our universities—problems of unnecessary Government regulation and excessive bureaucratic papershuffling.

Economists estimate that advances in knowledge have accounted for three quarters of our own country's economic growth in this century. By itself, that is a decisive reason for us to support the basic research that undergirds our technological might. But the value of basic research is even higher and deeper than meeting payrolls and spawning new industries; the fundamental concern of basic research is the discovery of truth about the natural universe. The search for truth is a central part of what it means to be human.

No issue illuminates our Nation's practical need for science and technology more than the energy problem.

Oil remains by far the most important energy source, and we are in the painful situation of relying on a greedy and unreliable foreign cartel for nearly half the oil we use in this country. As that onrushing river of foreign oil flows into our country, a river of American money flows out, threatening the health of our economy, the stability of our currency, and even the security of our Nation.

Science and technology can change that, but only if we commit ourselves to a national strategy of developing energy alternatives. We have such a strategy—one that will enable us to move away from imported oil and increasingly move toward nonfossil fuels—and I'm determined that we will pursue it.

Over the next decade or so, we must rely mostly on existing technologies, but we will pave the way for future progress by fostering conservation, domestic production of oil and gas, greater use of coal, the safety of nuclear plants, and the use of solar power.

From about 1990 through the second decade of the next century, we will pass through a dramatic and sometimes bumpy period of transition. Conservation will be forced upon us, and the mix of our energy resources will change as we turn increasingly toward unconventional sources of fuel.

By the second quarter of the 21st century, we will have learned to rely on cleaner, essentially inexhaustible sources of energy. The principal candidates include, of course, fusion and such solar technologies as photovoltaics.

We are preparing right now for these stages of our energy future. Our energy research and development is already larger in its program size than those of all our allies combined. But we must do more. That's why I have proposed the creation of an energy security fund to supplement our normal budget mechanisms. The revenues for this fund will come from a windfall tax on the unearned, excess profits that would otherwise go to the oil companies because of the decontrol of oil prices—over and above needed incentives for exploration and production within our country.

The energy security fund will provide relief to those least able to pay for more costly energy, and large sums will go to finance projects that are important to our energy future, including a regional petroleum reserve, better mass transit, coal and oil shale development, new incentives for solar techniques, and other basic and applied research projects with which many of you are already intimately acquainted.

The energy security fund faces a difficult passage through Congress, but we are making progress because the public supports our proposals. Many of those who only a few weeks ago were dedicated to killing outright the windfall profits tax have now given up on that fight. But the battle is far from over. New strategy seems to be to try to hoodwink the American people by passing a windfall profits tax that is in fact a charade—a tax designed primarily to provide loopholes to the oil companies so that they will get another $4 or $5 billion, in addition to the $6 billion in increased revenue that they would get under decontrol with an honest windfall profits tax proposal passed.

They will try to pass this charade off on the American people as a so-called plowback provision. But it isn't a plowback; it is a plowunder and a kickback, and what is going to be plowed under is the energy security fund with its aid to research and its aid to the poor. And what's going to be kicked back to the oil companies is the money that would go to finance these absolutely necessary programs for the well-being of the future of our country.

I ask for your support in the battle to pass an honest windfall profits tax to finance a real energy security fund for our Nation, in consonance with the program that will give greatly increased incentive and greatly increased profits for the oil companies to explore and to discover and to produce additional sources of domestic oil and natural gas.

And I also call on all of you in the scientific and engineering communities to fulfill the trust of the American people by creating the new energy technologies that are so vital to the future well-being of our country.

We need innovation on a broader scale as well, for new ideas in America are central not only to reducing our dependence on foreign oil but also on our efforts to control inflation, to improve productivity of our workers, to protect the environment, and to ensure the prosperity of the American people.

We tend to think of the inventiveness of American industry as a kind of inevitable birthright, but complacency is the last thing we can afford. Too many of our industries in this country have gone stale. Innovative industries in countries like Japan and West Germany put too many of ours to shame. Our competitiveness has begun to slip.

The American free enterprise system has always been vigorous enough and able enough and dedicated enough and well-supported enough to prevail. I have no doubt that it still retains those capabilities.

We must nurture an environment in which the new idea and the fresh approach are put to use. The Federal Government bears a large share of this responsibility. We must change government practices that thwart innovation, while enhancing government policies which encourage the development of new products and new processes.

Last year, I directed the Secretary of Commerce to begin a major study of industrial innovation. That study, involving some 30 Federal departments and agencies and consultations with industry, labor, and the universities and the public, will soon be completed. I look forward to reviewing the recommendations and to acting on them, hopefully with your help.

Many of you in this room today are leaders of American business and industry, and I call on you to emphasize innovation in the companies which you serve. Like Federal support of basic research, industrial development and investment in research, both basic and applied, in new products and new processes, is a practical testament of faith in our own future.

Since Kepler's day and before, scientists have been perhaps the most international of all professions in their outlook. In our own time, the explosion of communications and technology has made international scientific communication both easier and more urgent than ever before.

Albert Einstein himself operated on what even then was a very modest budget. He needed little more than a few sharpened pencils and a quiet place to think. But as you know, the task of building upon his work can be much more expensive. Many of the key experiments yet to be done—in both basic and applied technology—are on a monumental scale.

Our choice in the years ahead will be between carrying out the few large projects we can afford on our own, as Americans—or by doing many more projects, perhaps even more effectively, in cooperation with other nations. We must continue to choose cooperation—for reasons that go beyond the considerable benefits of sharing the costs and sharing ideas.

With our traditional friends, scientific and technological cooperation can strengthen existing bonds. With others, who may not be quite so friendly, it can help to bridge political and ideological and cultural divisions.

One of the most important purposes of international cooperation in technology and science is to meet the developing needs of the poorer countries of the world.

The future of the advanced countries is increasingly tied up with that of the developing world. Yet, only about 1 percent of the world's civilian research and development is devoted directly to the problems of the poorer half of humanity—problems such as poverty, disease, hunger, education, and resource development. We should be doing more.

A year ago, I proposed the creation of a new Institute for Scientific and Technological Cooperation to mobilize the talents of scientists and engineers in this country and in the developing world to address these critical problems. Instead of providing relief, we would aid the Third World in building its own corps of development scientists and decisionmakers. And we would join them in mutually beneficial projects in agriculture, medicine, industrialization, and appropriate energy systems.

The Institute for Scientific and Technological Cooperation has been approved already by the House of Representatives and is now before the Senate for consideration. It needs your full support.

Let me turn now to the use and exploration in space where, as on Earth, our purpose is human betterment—material, intellectual, and spiritual.

In the coming era, we will reap a good return on the more than $100 billion the United States has invested in space. From platforms in space, we can indeed continue to improve our world. Every year, satellites make new contributions in such areas as agriculture, environmental monitoring, land use, resource discovery, climatology, and communications.

With the advent of the space shuttle, we will have an unmatchable ability to work in space. We will see a flowering of research and industrial activities in space, and we will make quantum jumps in international cooperation, advancing the causes of peace and human development.

Mankind's leap into space has changed human consciousness forever. The era of manned exploration of deep space is still well in the future, but our senses are already penetrating the outer reaches of the solar system and beyond. No one who has seen those breathtaking pictures of Jupiter and its moons sent back from Voyager I could fail to have been surprised and delighted by them. We can expect many more such surprises, many more such delights, as we probe further into the universe and its mysteries.

And finally, let me say that of all the fruits of science, none is more bitter than nuclear weapons. And of all the responsibilities of nations, none is more urgent than the control of this most terrible menace to our lives and to our civilization.

All of us are thankful that the recent accident at Three Mile Island in Pennsylvania ended without harm to the public. That accident may even have served some positive purpose. It has, of course, led us to redouble our determination to improve the safety of nuclear power. Even more importantly, however, it has reminded us vividly of the dreadful consequences of nuclear war.

We have lived too long with nuclear weapons. We've grown too accustomed to their shadowy presence in our lives. We are too apt to forget what the ultimate horror would be: the instant death of millions and the slow and agonizing death of many millions more; the destruction of the cultural legacy of all mankind; the poisoning of air and soil and water for many dark generations to come. In an all-out nuclear exchange, the victim would be nothing less than the past, present, and future of our own human species.

When President Kennedy addressed this body 16 years ago, the Senate had just ratified the most significant step in nuclear arms control until that time—the atmospheric test ban treaty. The SALT II treaty, now nearing completion, is part of the same process—a long, slow

progress of gradual steps toward sanity, based on mutual self-interest. And after SALT II, that process will continue with a comprehensive nuclear test ban and then with SALT III.

SALT II will reduce the risk of nuclear war by lowering levels of strategic arms, by containing development of new weapons systems, and by contributing to a more stable political interrelationship between ourselves and the people of the Soviet Union.

Many of the issues involved in assessing the treaty are very complex technically, and the American people will look to the scientific community to help shape an educated public debate. Many of you devoted much effort to the debate over SALT I, and you played a major role in forming the consensus that developed to support that treaty. Today, I ask for a renewal of that commitment.

If science gave us nuclear weapons, it's no less true that science has given us the extraordinary means of verifying compliance with treaties to control those weapons. In the great SALT II debate, which has already begun, the participation of scientists will indeed be crucial.

Albert Einstein also said these words, "The importance of securing international peace was recognized by the really great men of former generations. But the technical advances of our times have turned this ethical postulate into a matter of life and death for civilized mankind today, and made it a moral duty to take an active part in the solution of the problems of peace, a duty which no conscientious law [man] can shirk."

These words were more prophetic than anyone could know, for they were spoken more than a decade before the explosion of the first atomic bomb. Those words are important. I urge you to heed them as we conclude SALT II, the next step towards nuclear arms control and a stronger and more sure worldwide peace.

Americans once had an unquestioned faith in science as a savior. We've grown more skeptical of science, as of so much else in our lives. But we still look to our scientists and to our engineers, our medical researchers and to our doctors, to our inventors and to our thinkers, to improve our lives and to improve the lives of our children.

My concern for the state of American science and technology has made our present efforts a keystone in building a new and a more solid foundation for our common future. I look to the members of this Academy, to the entire scientific and engineering community, to the Members of the Congress, and to the people of our country, to join these efforts through science for a greater America.

Thank you very much.

NOTE: The President spoke at 2:32 p.m. in the auditorium of the National Academy of Sciences building. Philip Handler is president of the Academy.

United States Arms Control and Disarmament Agency

Message to the Congress Transmitting a Report. April 23, 1979

To the Congress of the United States:

There is no more important responsibility for me as President than ensuring the safety and security of our nation. Like Presidents before me, I am meeting this responsibility: (1) by maintaining sufficient military forces to protect ourselves and our Allies; and (2) by seeking equitable and verifiable arms control measures to reduce the risk of war. The attached report is a summary of the actions taken through the U.S. Arms Control and Dis-

armament Agency in 1978 toward this latter goal.

The SALT process, which has been carried forward by four Administrations since 1967, is the most fundamental of our arms control efforts. A SALT II agreement to limit strategic offensive weapons will serve as the linchpin of all of our other arms control efforts, including: SALT III, where we hope to achieve further strategic arms limitations; a ban on tests of nuclear explosives; mutual and balanced force reductions in Europe; limitations on antisatellite capabilities, chemical weaponry, and conventional arms transfers; and prevention of nuclear weapons proliferation.

To prevent war—and to redirect the resources of nations from arsenals of war to human needs—will be a formidable challenge to all mankind in this last quarter of the 20th Century. It is a challenge that I am determined to meet.

JIMMY CARTER

The White House,
   April 23, 1979.

NOTE: The 151-page report is entitled "Annual Report 1978, U.S. Arms Control and Disarmament Agency."

The text of the message was released on April 24.

Meeting With President Aristides Royo of Panama

Announcement of President Royo's Forthcoming Visit. April 24, 1979

President Carter will meet with the President of the Republic of Panama, Dr. Aristides Royo, in Washington on May 10.

The President extended an invitation to President Royo on April 9 to meet in an informal working session to discuss the progress both countries have made in planning for implementation of the Panama Canal treaties, which go into effect October 1, 1979, as well as other bilateral and multilateral issues. President Royo will arrive in Washington after completing state visits to the United Kingdom, France, Spain, and Italy.

Dr. Royo, who was Panama's chief treaty negotiator, will be in the United States for the first time since his inauguration last October 11. The two heads of state are expected to talk about measures designed to assure a smooth transition period when the treaties take effect and will discuss generally the efforts of both countries to assure the fulfillment of both the letter and the spirit of the accords.

With less than 6 months to go before treaty day, cooperation between the representatives of the United States and Panama has been excellent, although much work remains to be done, including passage of implementing legislation by the United States Congress.

Days of Remembrance of Victims of the Holocaust

Remarks at a Commemorative Ceremony. April 24, 1979

I am honored and also grave and solemn as I participate in this ceremony during Days of Remembrance for Victims of the Holocaust.

Just 5 weeks ago, during my trip to Israel, I visited again Yad Vashem—the Memorial to the Six Million. I walked slowly through the Hall of Names. And like literally millions before me, I grieved as I looked at book after book, row after row, each recording the name of a man or woman, a little boy or a little girl, each one a victim of the Holocaust. I vowed then—as people all over the world are doing this week—to reaffirm our un-

shakable commitment that such an event will never recur on this Earth again.

A philosopher has written that language itself breaks down when one tries to speak about the Holocaust and its meaning. Our words pale before the frightening spectacle of human evil which was unleashed on the world and before the awesomeness of the suffering involved; the sheer weight of its numbers: 11 million innocent victims exterminated, 6 million of them Jews.

Although words do pale, yet we must speak. We must strive to understand. We must teach the lessons of the Holocaust. And most of all, we ourselves must remember. We must learn not only about the vulnerability of life but of the value of human life. We must remember the terrible price paid for bigotry and hatred and also the terrible price paid for indifference and for silence.

It's fitting also that we recall today the persecution, the suffering, and the destruction which has befallen so many other people in this century, in many nations, people whose representatives have joined us for this observance. For the central lesson of the Holocaust must be that, in the words of the poet, "Each man's death diminishes me."

To truly commemorate the victims of the Holocaust, we must harness the outrage of our memories to banish all human oppression from the world. We must recognize that when any fellow human being is stripped of humanity, when any person is turned into an object of repression, tortured or defiled or victimized by terrorism or prejudice or racism, then all human beings are victims, too.

The world's failure to recognize the moral truth 40 years ago permitted the Holocaust to proceed. Our generation—the generation of survivors—will never permit the lesson to be forgotten. Human rights and human dignity are indivisible.

America must and always will speak out in the defense of human rights, not only in our own country but around the world.

That commitment imposes special responsibilities on us to uphold the highest possible standards of human justice and human rights here at home. I applaud the Congress in calling for this day of remembrance of the Holocaust. And I renew my call to the Senate to take a long overdue step this year by ratifying the International Treaty on the Prevention and the Punishment of Genocide. Without concrete action, our words are hollow. Let us signify by deed as well as by word that the American people will never forget.

It is, perhaps, ironic that we meet today in a season of rebirth and renewal to recall a time of darkness and destruction that has no parallel in human history. And yet it's also fitting that we do so in this Rotunda, along with actual survivors of the Holocaust itself. For the Holocaust is also a story of renewal and a testament to the power of the human spirit to prevail.

People who saw their homes destroyed helped build a new homeland in the State of Israel. People like Elie Wiesel, the Chairman of my Holocaust Commission, who witnessed the collapse of all vision, created and shared with us a new vision. It's an incredible story of a people who refused to allow despair to triumph, who, after having lost their children, brought new families into the world.

It is our collective task as well to learn from this process of renewal the roots of hope—a hope not based on illusion or ignorance, but hope grounded in the rebirth of the human spirit and a reaffirmation of the sacredness of life.

With that hope, we will strive to build out of our memories of the Holocaust a world joined by a true fellowship of human understanding, a world of tolerance and diversity in which all peoples can live in dignity and in peace.

NOTE: The President spoke at 12:43 p.m. in the Rotunda of the Capitol.

Non-Proliferation Treaty Review Conference

Accordance of Rank of Ambassador to Charles N. Van Doren While Serving as Head of the U.S. Delegation to the Preparatory Committee Meetings. April 24, 1979

The President today announced that he has accorded Charles N. Van Doren, the Assistant Director of the United States Arms Control and Disarmament Agency, the rank of Ambassador while serving as Head of the United States Delegation to the Preparatory Committee meetings of the second Non-Proliferation Treaty Review Conference.

United States Ambassador to Iran

Nomination of Walter L. Cutler. April 24, 1979

The President today announced that he will nominate Walter L. Cutler, of Alexandria, Va., to be Ambassador Extraordinary and Plenipotentiary of the United States to Iran. He would replace William H. Sullivan, who has resigned.

Cutler has been a Foreign Service officer since 1956 and has served as Ambassador to the Republic of Zaire since 1975.

He was born November 25, 1931, in Boston, Mass. He received an A.B. from Wesleyan University in 1953 and an M.A. from the Fletcher School of Law and Diplomacy in 1954. He served in the U.S. Army from 1954 to 1956.

Cutler served as consular officer in Yaounde from 1957 to 1959, and as a foreign affairs officer at the State Department from 1959 to 1961. From 1961 to 1962, he was staff assistant to the Secretary of State.

Cutler was political officer in Algiers from 1962 to 1965, principal officer in Tabriz from 1965 to 1967, and political officer in Seoul from 1967 to 1969. He was political officer in Saigon from 1969 to 1971. From 1971 to 1973, he was international relations officer at the State Department, and in 1973–74 he was in the Senior Seminar at the Foreign Service Institute.

From 1974 to 1975, Cutler was Country Director of Central African Affairs at the State Department. Since 1975 he has been Ambassador to Zaire.

United States Ambassador to Nicaragua

Nomination of Lawrence A. Pezzullo.
April 24, 1979

The President today announced that he will nominate Lawrence A. Pezzullo, of Bethesda, Md., to be Ambassador Extraordinary and Plenipotentiary of the United States to Nicaragua. He would replace Maurice Solaun, who is being assigned to the State Department.

Pezzullo is currently Ambassador to Uruguay.

He was born May 3, 1926, in New York City. He received a B.A. from Columbia University in 1951. He served in the U.S. Army from 1944 to 1946.

Pezzullo was a public schoolteacher in Levittown, Long Island, from 1951 to 1957. He joined the Foreign Service in 1957, and from 1958 to 1960 served as consular officer in Ciudad Juarez. He was

a foreign affairs officer at the State Department from 1960 to 1962.

From 1962 to 1965, Pezzullo was general services officer in Saigon. He was a political officer in La Paz from 1965 to 1967, in Bogotá from 1967 to 1969, and in Guatemala from 1969 to 1971. He attended the National War College in 1971–72.

From 1972 to 1974, Pezzullo was at the Office of Central American Affairs at the State Department, as international relations officer, then Deputy Director. In 1974 and 1975, he was special assistant to the Ambassador at Large.

From 1975 to 1977, Pezzullo was Deputy Assistant Secretary of State for Congressional Relations. Since 1977 he has been Ambassador to Uruguay.

National Cancer Advisory Board

Appointment of Six Members and
Designation of Chairman.   April 24, 1979

The President today announced the appointment of six persons as members of the National Cancer Advisory Board for terms expiring March 9, 1984. They are:

Maureen M. Henderson, of Seattle, Wash., assistant vice president for health affairs at the University of Washington's Health Sciences Center. She was previously chairman of the department of preventive medicine of the University of Maryland and is an internationally known epidemiologist.

Janet D. Rowley, of Chicago, professor of medicine at the University of Chicago, a geneticist known for her work in cytogenetics (chromosomal abnormalities) and credited with major advances in the identification of chronic myelogenous leukemia.

Sheldon W. Samuels, of Alexandria, Va., director of health, safety, and environment for the AFL–CIO's Industrial Union Department. Samuels was trained as a theoretical biologist and has worked extensively in environmental health regulation. He has frequently been the labor participant in OSHA and congressional hearings on environmental regulation.

Morris M. Schrier, of Scarsdale, N.Y., vice president and secretary of MCA, Inc. (for reappointment).

Irving J. Selikoff, of Ridgewood, N.J., professor of community medicine and director of the division of environmental medicine at Mount Sinai Hospital in New York. Selikoff is also program director of the Environmental Health Sciences Research Center at Mount Sinai. He is an expert on the health effects of environmental factors, especially in airborne pollutants, and is an environmental epidemiologist.

Gerald N. Wogan, of Bedford, Mass., professor of toxicology in the department of nutrition and food science at Massachusetts Institute of Technology, a recognized authority in nutritional carcinogenesis (reappointment).

The President also announced the designation of Henry C. Pitot as Chairman of this Advisory Board. Pitot, of Madison, Wis., has been a member of the Board since 1976. He is director of the McArdle Laboratory for Cancer Research and chairman of the department of oncology at the University of Wisconsin Medical School.

United States Military Academy Board of Visitors

Appointment of Two Members.
April 24, 1979

The President today announced the appointment of two persons as members of the Board of Visitors of the United States Military Academy. They are:

SYLVIO L. DUPUIS, president of Catholic Medical Center in Manchester, N.H., and a former mayor of Manchester;

JAMES R. KILLEEN, court clerk of Wayne County, Mich.

National Capital Planning Commission

Appointment of Helen M. Scharf as a Member. April 24, 1979

The President today announced the appointment of Helen M. Scharf, of Bethesda, Md., as a member of the National Capital Planning Commission for a term expiring January 1, 1985.

Scharf, 78, has been vice chairman of the Montgomery County (Maryland) Planning Board since 1973, and has participated in the development of sector plans for a number of areas in the county. She is a commissioner of the Maryland National Capital Park and Planning Commission.

She has been a member of the League of Women Voters since 1941 and chaired two of their publications on the metropolitan Washington area.

Personal Representative of the President to the Middle East Peace Negotiations

Remarks Announcing Ambassador Robert S. Strauss' Role in the Negotiations. April 24, 1979

THE PRESIDENT. There are too few times in life when one not only enjoys the company and friendship of another man but also admires and appreciates his abilities and his talents as a working partner.

687

That's the feeling that I have about Bob Strauss.

Bob agreed reluctantly to come into government and to serve in my administration, in the Cabinet as a Special Trade Representative. He's done a magnificent job negotiating on behalf of our country. And we hope to have action on the Multilateral Trade Negotiations before the summer congressional recess.

After congressional action on MTN is completed, Bob had planned to leave government and to return to private life. However, I am proud to announce today that Secretary Vance and I have prevailed on Bob Strauss to remain in government in the special and unique role as Ambassador at Large, responsible for our country's participation in the crucial, upcoming Middle East peace talks.

By accepting this difficult but very important challenge, Bob Strauss will be relieving Secretary Vance and me of our time-consuming and heavy personal role in the peace talks, which we have experienced over the past 2 years.

Although the Egypt-Israeli peace treaty stands as a demonstration of the ability of leaders and people to rise above the conflicts and hostility of the past, it is more than a monument to past efforts; it's a promise for a comprehensive peace in the Middle East in the future. That promise must be kept.

Next month, negotiations will begin on the complex issues involving the West Bank and the Gaza Strip. I have personally promised President Sadat and Prime Minister Begin that the United States will contribute our good offices to see that those negotiations are as successful as those which resulted in the treaty which was signed between Israel and Egypt last month.

No one believes that the road to peace in the future will be any less arduous than the path which we have already followed. But we've learned that perseverance, patience, faith, and trust can overcome what appear to be impossible obstacles. Those are the objectives which guided me and the Secretary of State in choosing a distinguished American to be the personal representative of our Nation during the next phase of negotiations.

Secretary Vance and I welcome Bob Strauss in this effort as a partner, as do President Sadat and Prime Minister Begin, with whom I spoke today. Their response was positive and enthusiastic. I'm sure that Bob Strauss' special friendship and relationship with me and Secretary Vance and his close relationship with the Members of the Congress, his knowledge of our Nation, his close relationship with leaders in both parties will give him the support and strength that he will need to undertake and to successfully complete this very important assignment on behalf of our country and on behalf of world peace.

SECRETARY OF STATE VANCE. Our country and all of us are fortunate indeed that Bob Strauss has agreed to take on this new and terribly important responsibility. There is nobody that I know of who is better qualified than Bob Strauss to take on the complex and difficult negotiations that lie before us. And all of us know that he will handle his new responsibilities in this area with the distinction that Bob has always shown in every job that he's taken on.

So, I personally want to say from the bottom of my heart how thankful I am to Bob for what he is doing and how grateful all of our country is to him for being willing to do this.

Thank you, Bob.

AMBASSADOR STRAUSS. Thank you, Mr. Secretary.

I usually have something glib to say

when I come before this group, but I don't today.

I suspect that of all the tasks I've undertaken since I became an adult, this is far the most complex and certainly the most difficult and the one that offers the greatest rewards. I told Helen last evening that from time to time I wonder why I had done this or that or the other in business or in law or in banking or in politics and in government, but I'm reasonably well convinced that it was all just in training for this assignment, an assignment that's been carried so far by President Carter, Secretary Vance, two courageous leaders in the Middle East, President Sadat and Prime Minister Begin.

And I want to assure each of you, assure the President and the Secretary of State, and assure those of the American public who hear and see this broadcast, that whatever energies, whatever talent, and whatever background and experience I have, I shall apply with all the vigor and all the dedication that you would want.

Thank you very much.

THE PRESIDENT. Thank you very much.

REPORTER. Could you take a question?

AMBASSADOR STRAUSS. Jody, any questions? I'll take a few questions, yes.

Q. Could I ask you whether you had to consider your own religious origin as a possible obstacle?

AMBASSADOR STRAUSS. I never considered my own religious origin as an obstacle to anything, not in this or anything else I've ever done.

Next question?

Q. Mr. Ambassador, knowing your desire to get out of government and back to Dallas, are we to take this appointment as an indication that you are going to expeditiously finish this new job?

AMBASSADOR STRAUSS. Now we can begin to be smart with each other again. [*Laughter*]

Of course I'm not going to expeditiously finish this new job. And it's with considerable hesitation and reluctance that I undertook the job. I must say that as much concern as I had about undertaking the job, Helen had even more concern about my having more leisure time to spend at home.

Q. When do you expect to go out to the Middle East and to get started on this?

AMBASSADOR STRAUSS. I just returned from the Middle East on Saturday night. We spent several days out there on an economic mission.

I would hope that we will complete the trade legislation before the summer recess, and I think we will, with the cooperation of Congress. We've had great bipartisan support there, Republicans and Democrats alike. If that continues, we'll complete that legislation, that legislative process, and shortly thereafter, I'll be thinking about going to the Middle East.

In the meantime, I've got a great deal to learn and a good deal of intensive briefing to go through.

Q. Does that mean, sir, that you will not get directly involved in the negotiations when they begin within the next few weeks, because you'll be busy with the trade, still?

AMBASSADOR STRAUSS. It's my understanding that the parties themselves feel that the negotiations will commence at a deputies level, if you will, and proceed at that level for a period of months, or "a period of time" might be better.

So, it fits in rather well with my schedule. And I would expect to be following them carefully, to be, as I say, informing myself. I have a lot of learning to do. But the time schedule works out rather well if I can complete my trade negotiations. I've got a lot to do, yes.

Q. You don't see a dual role, though, for the time being? You will finish one and then start the other?

AMBASSADOR STRAUSS. I do not see a dual role, no.

Yes, final question.

Q. When did you first get word or an idea that the President had you in mind for this?

AMBASSADOR STRAUSS. Oh, I think it was about 2 weeks ago the President asked me to the office. And we spent about an hour going over it, and my initial reaction, of course, negative. But he explained it very carefully as we spent that hour, and I left with more positive thrust.

Thank you very much. I look forward to discussing this with each of you in the future on a personal basis.

NOTE: The President spoke at 5:03 p.m. to reporters assembled in the Briefing Room at the White House.

Standby Gasoline Rationing and Energy Conservation Contingency Plans

Statement Urging Congressional Approval of the Plans.   *April 25, 1979*

On March 1, 1979, I forwarded to the Congress the Standby Gasoline Rationing Plan and three mandatory Conservation Contingency Plans. Submission of these plans had been urged by both Houses of Congress as necessary if the United States is to be prepared for supply interruptions. Now congressional approval of these plans is crucial if the Nation is to have the standby capability to respond to energy shortfalls. That essential congressional approval is in doubt.

Should serious supply interruptions occur, America's arsenal of available measures must include contingency plans to ration gasoline and to mandate conservation by the American public. If these standby plans are not passed by the Congress, the public could rightly ask why their Government was not prepared for an emergency, particularly after the warning given by the Iranian supply curtailment.

Yesterday, the House Interstate and Foreign Commerce Committee voted to forward the Emergency Building Temperature Restrictions Conservation Plan to the House of Representatives with a favorable recommendation. However, the committee voted not to forward the Emergency Gasoline Sales Restrictions Plan, even though this plan would only be implemented if a State failed to develop its own plan for conserving gasoline. There is, however, still the opportunity for Congress to approve the latter plan. Failure to pass this plan would raise serious questions about the seriousness of Congress in dealing with our energy problem.

In the Senate, the Energy Committee has already voted against a plan to restrict unnecessary outdoor lighting in a time of severe energy shortages. The House Committee on Interstate and Foreign Commerce will vote today on the Standby Gasoline Rationing Plan.

My authority to put this plan into a state of readiness is essential to the energy security of our Nation. Although the petroleum shortfall we are now experiencing does not warrant implementation of a rationing plan, prudence and common sense demand that we must be prepared should other disruptions seriously deepen current shortfalls and create a situation of true national crisis.

We must demonstrate to the American public and the world that this country can be prepared and ready for emergencies rising from oil supply interruptions.

Failure to do so will demonstrate a weakness of resolve that is simply unacceptable in current circumstances. I hope that the Congress will live up to its responsibility to the American people.

Death of Marvella Bayh

Statement by the President.   April 25, 1979

Rosalynn and I were deeply saddened by the death of Marvella Bayh, whose courage and candor in her 8-year battle against cancer served as an inspiration for all Americans. Marvella Bayh worked tirelessly to spread understanding of this dread disease and the importance of early detection of its warning signs. At this sad moment, our hearts go out to Senator Bayh and their son, Evan Bayh.

NOTE: On April 27, the President attended memorial services for Mrs. Bayh held at the National Cathedral in Washington, D.C.

President's Commission on the Accident at Three Mile Island

Remarks at a Meeting With the Commission.   April 25, 1979

THE PRESIDENT. I would like to say, first of all, that my selection of this group to serve on the Commission to investigate the events at the Three Mile Island nuclear powerplant has been one of the most important responsibilities of my Presidency. This Commission will be scrutinized very carefully not only throughout our own Nation but, indeed, throughout the world.

The Vice President has just returned from a visit to six countries, most of them in Scandinavia, and there was a deep and intense interest in the ultimate report that

will be forthcoming from this Commission.

We've had similar inquiries, as you well know, from major countries—Germany, France, Great Britain, and others around the world—who want to know the facts about the Three Mile Island incident—what occurred there; what were the causes of the accident; what mistakes were made; the roles that were played by the power company managing the plant, the Nuclear Regulatory Commission, the local, State, and Federal Government agencies, and others who were directly charged with certain responsibilities; how those responsibilities were handled; how well they were interrelated in sharing roles of responsibility; how well prepared all of those entities were for an accident of this kind?

Obviously, the most important aspect is how can a future accident of this sort be prevented; what authority needs to be assigned specifically, for instance, to the Nuclear Regulatory Commission that it doesn't presently have; how are its procedures deficient; what can be done in the future to have a better and immediate coordination of effort among the different government and private agencies responsible for the protection of the health and safety of the American people?

One item of particular interest is what were the facts as they occurred and how closely did those facts relate to the information given to the public, because public impressions are very important, and it's extremely important that they be based on accurate reporting. Was the information given to the news media accurate as best could be determined? If there were errors, what were the cause of those errors? How well did the public understand what was going on?

These questions are in the Executive order that I signed establishing this Commission. Your report will be made to me, to the Secretary of Energy, and to the Secretary of Health, Education, and Welfare, and, obviously, to the public at large.

I am here to help you. This is a diverse group. Each one of you brings to the Commission a special insight, a special background, special area of knowledge or interest. And I think as you get to know one another, you will mutually assess the superb quality of the Commission in its entirety. I have complete confidence in Chairman Kemeny. He knows that I am available to help him personally. Every agency of the Government is eager and willing to help this Commission do a good job. So, my confidence in you is complete.

I would say that overriding all of your responsibilities, the most important is that when your report is made, that it be of such quality and of such accuracy, and this Commission have such a high degree of integrity that the American people will trust what you say. If there's any doubt about the quality of your work, then the entire report will be of very little value to me or to the public. I really believe that it's important that all of you guard very carefully your own personal, perhaps, even, offhand remarks, because if you inadvertently made an error in a public statement and it was attributed to a member of this Commission and later it was found to be erroneous, then the integrity of the whole Commission would be questionable.

And so, I think it's very important that you let the deliberations be made public, but until the final determinations are made and you know what you're saying, that you restrain yourself in any sort of ad lib, individual remarks that might be interpreted by the press as your speaking for the Commission.

I might say in closing that when you make your recommendations to me and to the public, I intend to carry them out within the bounds of my authority and responsibility as President. And I intend to share your recommendations and your findings with the leaders of other nations around the world. Your deliberations will have to be expedited. You have adequate resources, financial and staff, on which you can depend. And I need to have your recommendations within 6 months. I know this is a very tight schedule, but I think to delay the report in order to have it a little more comprehensive or a little more complete would be a mistake. The public is eager to hear from you and, of course, so am I.

If, in the interim period, there is a particular fact evolved or a particular recommendation that you discern which ought to be implemented more expeditiously, I hereby ask the Chairman to come to me directly and say, "Mr. President, although we are not ready for our final report, this is something that we believe should be done immediately in order to ensure enhanced safety for the nuclear powerplants now in existence or those presently being constructed." You need not wait for the full 6 months before you make a specific recommendation to me if you think it is propitious to do it earlier.

So, to summarize, I've got confidence in you and so does the public. And your report will be extremely important throughout the world, and I know that you will do a superb job. Your acceptance of this assignment indicates to me that you're willing to devote the time and effort required to carry out the responsibilities that you have assumed.

I'm grateful to you, and you've got a partner here in the Oval Office who will be available to help you if any unforeseen obstacle should arise. I'll help you overcome that obstacle, and I'll help you make your working status and environment within which you perform your duties as pleasant and as productive as possible.

Mr. Chairman, I thank you very much.

DR. KEMENY. Mr. President, may I tell you something, that I'm very proud of the fact that although you appointed this Commission 2 weeks ago today, all 11 commissioners are present here. And we have a nuclear staff of three senior appointees whom I will be introducing to the press.

The one thing I wasn't able to tell you 2 weeks ago, with the permission of my board of trustees. I'm available for half time for the entire lifetime of this Commission. And I made it clear to my board of trustees that this will be my highest priority during this period.

THE PRESIDENT. Very fine.

DR. KEMENY. We will do everything we can to carry out the charge, Mr. President, as you instructed us.

THE PRESIDENT. Thank you. Thank you all very much.

NOTE: The President spoke at 9:40 a.m. in the Cabinet Room at the White House.

New York City, New York

Remarks at the Annual Convention of the American Newspaper Publishers Association. April 25, 1979

President Al Neuharth, distinguished members of the American Newspaper Publishers Association, other guests and friends:

I want, first of all, to commend and to endorse the theme of this convention: the defense of the first amendment of our Constitution and the freedom of the press.

Liberty of expression is our most important civil right, and freedom of the press is its most important bulwark. We can never afford to grow complacent about the first amendment; on the contrary, you and I and others must actively protect it always.

The American press has grown enormously since the Nation's early days—not only in its size and breadth but in its concepts of its own duties and its own responsibilities. The highest of these duties is to inform the public on the important issues of the day. And no issue is more important than the one I want to discuss with you today in a solemn and somber and sincere way—the control of nuclear arms.

Each generation of Americans faces a choice that defines our national character, a choice that is also important for what it says about our own Nation's outlook toward the world.

In the coming months, we will almost certainly be faced with such a choice—whether to accept or to reject a new strategic arms limitation treaty. The decision we make will profoundly affect our lives and the lives of people all over the world for years to come. We face this choice from a position of strength, as the strongest nation on Earth economically, militarily, and politically.

Our alliances are firm and reliable. Our military forces are strong and ready. Our economic power is unmatched. Along with other industrial democracies who are our friends, we lead the way in technological innovation. Our combined economies are more than three times as productive as those of the Soviet Union and all its allies. Our political institutions are based on human freedom. Our open system encourages individual initiative and creativity, and that, in turn, strengthens our entire society. Our values and our democratic way of life have a magnetic appeal for people all over the world which a materialistic and a totalitarian philosophy can never hope to challenge or to rival.

For all these reasons, we have a capacity for leadership in the world that surpasses that of any other nation. That leadership imposes many responsibilities on us, on me as President, and on you, other leaders who shape opinion and the character of our country.

But our noblest duty is to use our strength to serve our highest interest— the building of a secure, stable, and a peaceful world. We perform that duty in the spirit proclaimed by John F. Kennedy in 1963, the year he died. "Confident and unafraid," he said, "we labor on—not toward a strategy of annihilation, but toward a strategy of peace."

In our relations with the Soviet Union, the possibility of mutual annihilation makes a strategy of peace the only rational choice for both sides.

Because our values are so different, it is clear that the United States of America and the Soviet Union will be in competition as far ahead as we can imagine or see. Yet we have a common interest in survival, and we share a common recognition that our survival depends, in a real sense, on each other. The very competition between us makes it imperative that we bring under control its most dangerous aspect—the nuclear arms race. That's why the strategic arms limitation talks are so very important. This effort by two great nations to limit vital security forces is unique in human history; none have ever done this before.

As the Congress and the American people consider the SALT treaty, which is now nearly complete, the debate will center around four basic questions: Why do we need SALT? How is the treaty related to our overall defense strategy? Can Soviet compliance be verified? How does the treaty relate to Soviet activities which challenge us and challenge our interests?

Let me address each question in turn.

First, why do we need a strategic arms limitation treaty? We need it because it will contribute to a more peaceful world— and to our own national security.

Today, we and the Soviet Union, with sharply different world outlooks and interests, both have the ominous destructive power literally to destroy each other as a functioning society, killing tens of millions of people in the process. And common sense tells us—as it tells the Soviet Union—that we must work to make our competition less dangerous, less burdensome, and less likely to bring the ultimate horror of nuclear war.

Indeed, the entire world has a vital interest in whether or not we control the strategic arms race. We have consulted closely with our allies, who count on us not only to maintain strong military forces to offset Soviet military power but also, and equally important, to manage successfully a stable East-West relationship. SALT is at the heart of both these crucial efforts. That's why the leaders of France and Great Britain, Germany, England, Canada, and other nations have voiced their full support for the emerging treaty.

Some nations which have so far held back from building their own nuclear weapons—and at least a dozen other nations on Earth now have that capability— will be strongly influenced in their decision by whether the two nuclear super powers will restrain our weapons. Rejection of the new strategic arms limitation treaty would seriously undermine the effort to control proliferation of these deadly weapons. And nothing—nothing—would more surely damage our other critical efforts in arms control—from a ban on all nuclear testing to the prevention of dangerous satellite warfare in space; from equalizing NATO and Warsaw Pact forces to restraining the spread of sophisticated conventional weapons on Earth.

Every President since the dawn of the nuclear age has pursued the effort to bring nuclear arms under control. And this must be a continuing process.

President Kennedy, building on the efforts of Presidents Truman and Eisenhower, signed the first agreement with the Soviet Union in 1963 to stop the poisonous testing of nuclear explosives in the atmosphere.

In 1968, 5 years later, under President Johnson, the United States and the Soviet Union joined other nations throughout the world in signing the Non-Proliferation Treaty, an important step in preventing the spread of nuclear explosives to other nations.

In 1972, under President Nixon, the SALT I agreement placed the first agreed limits on the number of offensive weapons, and the antiballistic missile treaty, the ABM treaty, made an enduring contribution to our own security. President Ford continued in negotiations at Helsinki and at Vladivostok.

Each negotiation builds on the accomplishments of the last. Each agreement provides a foundation for further progress toward a more stable nuclear relationship.

Three Presidents have now spent more than 6 years negotiating the next step in this process—SALT II. We have all negotiated carefully and deliberately. Every step of the way, we've worked with our military leaders and other experts, and we've sought the advice and counsel of the Members of Congress.

An overwhelming majority of the American people recognize the need for SALT II. Our people want and our people expect continued, step-by-step progress toward bringing nuclear weapons under control.

Americans will support a reasoned increase in our defense effort, but we do not want a wholly unnecessary return to the cold war and an all-out arms race, with its vastly greater risks and costs. Through strength, we want world peace.

Let me turn to the second question—how is SALT II related to our overall defense strategy?

The strategic forces of the United States and the Soviet Union today are essentially equivalent. They have larger and more numerous land-based missiles. We have a larger number of warheads and, as you know, significant technological and geographical advantages.

Each side has the will and the means to prevent the other from achieving superiority. Neither side is in a position to exploit its nuclear weapons for political purposes, nor to use strategic weapons without facing almost certain suicide.

What causes us concern is not the current balance but the momentum of the Soviet strategic buildup. Over the past decade, the Soviets have steadily increased their real defense spending, year by year, while our own defense spending over that decade has had a net decrease.

In areas not limited by SALT I, they have launched ambitious programs to strengthen their strategic forces. At some future point, the Soviet Union could achieve a strategic advantage unless we alter these trends. That is exactly what I want to do—with the support of the American people and the bipartisan support of Congress.

We must move on two fronts at the same time. First, within mutually accepted limits, we must modernize our own strategic forces. Along with the strengthening of NATO, that is a central purpose of the increased defense budget that I've submitted to Congress—improvements which are necessary even in a time of fiscal restraint. And second, we must place more stringent limits on the arms race than are presently imposed by SALT I. That is the purpose of the SALT II treaty.

The defense budget I've submitted will ensure that our nuclear force continues to be essentially equivalent to that of the Soviet Union.

This year, we've begun to equip our submarines with new, more powerful, and longer range Trident I missiles. Next year, the first of our new, even more secure Trident submarines will be going to sea, and we are working on a more powerful and accurate Trident II missile for these submarines.

Our cruise missile program will greatly enhance the effectiveness of our long-range bomber force. These missiles will be able to penetrate any air defense system which the Soviet Union could build in the foreseeable future.

We are substantially improving the accuracy and the power of our land-based Minuteman missiles. But in the coming decade, missiles of this type, based in fixed silos, will become increasingly vulnerable to surprise attack. The Soviets have three-quarters of their warheads in such fixed-based missiles, compared to only one-quarter of ours. Nevertheless, this is a very serious problem, and we must deal with it effectively and sensibly.

The Defense Department now has under consideration a number of options for responding to this problem, including making some of our own ICBM's mobile. I might add—and this is very important—that the options which we are evaluating would be far more costly—and we would have far less confidence of their effectiveness—in the absence of SALT II limits, for without these limits on the number of Soviet warheads, the Soviet Union could counter any effort we made simply by greatly increasing the number of warheads on their missiles.

Let me emphasize that the SALT II agreement preserves adequate flexibility for the United States in this important area.

Our strategic forces must be able to survive any attack and to counterattack military and civilian targets in the aggressor nation. And the aggressor nation must

know that we have the ability and the will to exercise this option if they should attack us. We have had this capacity—which is the essence of deterrence—in the past; we have it today; and SALT II, plus the defense programs that I've described, will ensure that we have it for the future.

The SALT II agreement will slow the growth of Soviet arms and limit the strategic competition, and by helping to define future threats that we might face, SALT II will make our defense planning much more effective.

Under the agreement, the two sides will be limited to equal numbers of strategic launchers for the first time, ending the substantial Soviet numerical advantage which was permitted in the currently effective SALT I treaty.

To reach these new and lower levels, the Soviets will have to reduce their overall number of strategic delivery systems by 10 percent—more than 250 Soviet missile launchers or bombers will have to be dismantled. Naturally, the Soviets will choose to phase out their older systems, but these systems are still formidable.

The missiles, for instance, to be torn down are comparable in age and payload to our Minuteman II missiles and to our Polaris missiles, presently deployed. Under the agreement, they will not be permitted to replace these dismantled systems with modern ones. Our own operational forces have been kept somewhat below the permitted ceiling. Thus, under the agreement, we could increase our force level, if necessary.

SALT II will also impose the first limited but important restraints on the race to build new systems and to improve existing ones—the so-called qualitative arms race.

In short, SALT II places serious limits on what the Soviets might do in the absence of such an agreement. For example, without SALT II, the Soviet Union could build up to some 3,000 strategic systems by 1985. With SALT II, we will both be limited to 2,250 such weapons.

This new arms control agreement will, obviously, serve our national interests. It will reduce the dangerous levels of strategic arms and restrain the development of future weapons. It will help to maintain our relative strength compared to the Soviets. It will avert a costly, risky, and pointless buildup of missile launchers and bombers—at the end of which both sides would be even less secure.

Let me turn now to the third of the four questions—how can we know whether the Soviets are living up to their obligations under this SALT agreement?

No objective—no objective—has commanded more energy and attention in our negotiations. We have insisted that the SALT II agreement be made verifiable. We are confident that no significant violation of the treaty could take place without the United States detecting it.

Our confidence in the verifiability of their agreement derives from the size and the nature of activities we must monitor and the many effective and sophisticated intelligence collection systems which we in America possess.

For example, nuclear submarines take several years to construct and assemble. Missile silos and their supporting equipment are large and quite visible. Intercontinental bombers are built at a few plants, and they need major airfields. Our photo-reconnaissance satellites survey the entire Soviet Union on a regular basis, and they give us high confidence that we will be able to count accurately the numbers of all these systems.

But our independent verification capabilities are not limited only to observing these large-scale activities. We can determine not only how many systems there are, but what they can do. Our photographic satellites and other systems enable us to follow technological developments in Soviet strategic forces with great accuracy. There is no question that any cheating which might affect our national security would be discovered in time for us to respond fully.

For many years, we have monitored Soviet strategic forces and Soviet compliance with the SALT agreements with a high degree of confidence. The overall capability remains. It was certainly not lost with our observation stations in Iran, which was only one of many intelligence sources that we use to follow Soviet strategic activities. We are concerned with that loss, but we must keep it in perspective.

This monitoring capability relates principally to the portion of the new agreement dealing with the modernization limits on ICBM's and to only a portion of such modernization restraints.

The sensitive intelligence techniques obviously cannot be disclosed in public, but the bottom line is that if there is an effort to cheat on the SALT agreement, including the limits on modernizing ICBM's, we will detect it, and we will do so in time fully to protect our security.

And we must also keep in mind that quite apart from SALT limits, our security is affected by the extent of our information about Soviet strategic forces. With this SALT II treaty, that vital information will be much more accessible to us.

The agreement specifically forbids, for the first time, interference with the systems used for monitoring compliance and prohibits any deliberate concealment that would impede verification. Any such concealment activity would itself be detectable, and a violation of this part of the agreement would be so serious as to give us grounds to cancel the treaty itself.

As I have said many times, the stakes are too high to rely on trust, or even on the Soviets' rational inclination to act in their own best interest. The treaty must—and the treaty will be—verifiable from the first day it is signed.

And finally, how does SALT II fit into the context of our overall relations with the Soviet Union?

Because SALT II will make the world safer and our own Nation more secure, it is in our national interest to control nuclear weapons even as we compete with the Soviets elsewhere in the world.

A SALT II agreement in no way limits our ability to promote our interests or to answer Soviet threats to those interests. We will continue to support the independence of Third World nations who struggle to stay free. We will continue to promote the peaceful resolution of local and regional disputes and to oppose efforts by any others to inflame these disputes with outside force. And we will continue to work for human rights.

It's a delusion to believe that rejection of a SALT treaty would somehow induce the Soviet Union to exercise new restraints in troubled areas. The actual effect of rejecting such a treaty might be precisely the opposite. The most intransigent and hostile elements of a Soviet political power structure would certainly be encouraged and strengthened by our rejection of a SALT agreement. The Soviets might very well feel that they then have little to lose by creating new international tensions.

A rejection of SALT II would have significance far beyond the fate of a single treaty. It would mean a radical turning away from America's long-time policy of seeking world peace. We would no longer be identified as the peaceloving nation. It would turn us away from the control of nuclear weapons and from the easing of tensions between Americans and the Soviet people under the system of international law based on mutual interests.

The rejection of SALT II would result in a more perilous world. As I said at Georgia Tech on February 20, each crisis, each confrontation, each point of friction—as serious as it may be in its own right—would take on an added measure of significance and an added dimension of danger, for it would occur in an atmosphere of unbridled strategic competition and deteriorating strategic stability. It is precisely because we have fundamental differences with the Soviet Union that we are determined to bring this most dangerous element of our military competition under control.

For these reasons, we will not try to impose binding linkage between Soviet behavior and SALT, and we will not accept any Soviet attempts to link SALT with aspects of our own foreign policy of which they may disapprove.

Again, SALT II is not a favor we are doing for the Soviet Union; it's an agreement carefully negotiated in the national security interests of the United States of America.

I put these issues to you today, because they need discussion and debate and because the voices of the American people must be heard.

In the months ahead, we will do all in our power to explain the treaty clearly and fully to the American people. I know that Members of Congress from both parties will join in this effort to ensure an informed public debate. And you, more than any other group I can imagine in the United States, share this responsibility with me and with the Congress.

During this debate, it's important that we exercise care. We will be sharing with the Congress some of our most sensitive defense and intelligence secrets. And the leaders in Congress must ensure that these secrets will be guarded so that the debate itself will not undermine our own security.

As the national discussion takes place, let us be clear about what the issues are—and are not.

Americans are committed to maintaining a strong defense. That is not the issue.

We will continue to compete, and compete effectively, with the Soviet Union. That is not the issue.

The issue is whether we will move ahead with strategic arms control or resume a relentless nuclear weapons competition. That's the choice we face—between an imperfect world with a SALT agreement, or an imperfect and more dangerous world without a SALT agreement.

With SALT II, we will have significant reductions in Soviet strategic forces; far greater certainty in our defense planning and in the knowledge of the threats that we might face; flexibility to meet our own defense needs; the foundation for further controls on nuclear and conventional arms; and our own self-respect and the earned respect of the world for a United States demonstrably committed to the works of peace.

Without SALT, the Soviets will be unconstrained and capable, and probably committed to an enormous, further buildup.

Without SALT, there would have to be a much sharper rise in our own defense spending, at the expense of other necessary programs for our people.

Without SALT, we would end up with thousands more strategic nuclear warheads on both sides, with far greater costs—and far less security—for our citizens.

Without SALT, we would see improved relations with the Soviet Union replaced by heightened tensions.

Without SALT, the long, slow process of arms control, so central to building a safer world, would be dealt a crippling and, perhaps, a fatal blow.

Without SALT, the world would be forced to conclude that America had chosen confrontation rather than cooperation and peace.

This is an inescapable choice we face, for the fact is that the alternative to this treaty is not some perfect agreement drafted unilaterally by the United States in which we gain everything and the Soviets gain nothing; the alternative now, and in the foreseeable future, is no agreement at all.

I am convinced that the United States has a moral and a political will to control the relentless technology which could constantly devise new and more destructive weapons to kill human beings. We need not drift into a dark nightmare of unrestrained arms competition. We Americans have the wisdom to know that our security depends on more than just maintaining our unsurpassed defense forces. Our security and that of our allies also depends on the strength of ideas and ideals and on arms control measures that can stabilize and finally reverse a dangerous and a wasteful arms race which neither side can win. This is a path of wisdom. This is a path of peace.

NOTE: The President spoke at 12:35 p.m. in the Grand Ballroom at the Waldorf Astoria Hotel. Allen H. Neuharth is president of the association.

Portsmouth, New Hampshire

Remarks and a Question-and-Answer Session at a Town Meeting. April 25, 1979

THE PRESIDENT. It's good to be back in New Hampshire. And it's also good to be back in Portsmouth. One of the most exciting events of my campaign in 1976 took place when I was spending the night with Senator Preston. The news media came out the next morning and said that I had been chosen one of the 10 best dressed men in the world. [*Laughter*]

From January 1975, when I began my campaign, until the convention took place, in the summer of 1976, I had three blue suits, they cost $42 each. [*Laughter*] And that's all the clothes I had. [*Laughter*] So, perhaps three blue suits in a political campaign can get you to be one of the 10 best dressed men in the world.

It's good to be here with Governor Hugh Gallen. And I'm very proud that Senator Tom McIntyre came down with me on the plane today—came up. And Senator John Durkin, thank you for coming with me, too. And Congressman Norm D'Amours, thank you. And I would like to say also how thankful I am for the large welcoming crowd who were out at the airport to meet me and the members of the Governor's Council, Dudley Dudley, and thank you for coming out. And also, Chris Spirou, a great leader in the legislature, and other members of the legislature, the mayors of this region and, particularly, you.

The people of New Hampshire, public officials or otherwise, are very important to me and very special in my life. Portsmouth, Berlin, Nashua, Keene, Claremont, Charlestown, Meredith, many other towns are not just names on a map, but they are reminders of the faces and the voices of friends like you who told me about your concerns and about your hopes for the country when I was in the early stages of learning about the job of President. One of the advantages of being an unknown candidate, when I came to New Hampshire for the first time to campaign in 1975, was that my family and I could talk to you individually or in groups of five or six, in living rooms and in kitchens, across the counter at the drug store, or on the street, in the beano halls. [*Laughter*]

I don't get a chance to do that very much any more. And I miss it. But the best way to regain that personal contact, I found, is to come and answer questions in a town meeting like this.

ADMINISTRATION POLICIES

Recently, I talked to you and the other people of our country on television about our serious energy problems. Energy is still very much on my mind. And I know it's on your minds, too. We are using too much foreign oil. And this threatens our future as Americans.

We've learned one simple, painful fact: We must use less oil, and we must pay more for what we use. A phased-in decontrol of domestic oil prices will commence June 1, and I have proposed to Congress that we use income from a windfall profits tax on the oil companies to finance an energy security fund. Some of this money will go to help those who are least able to pay the increasing energy costs. The rest will go to tap one of America's greatest strengths, our scientific and technological ability to develop new resources to fuel our economy in the future.

I'm not going to try to sugar-coat it for you. The energy future will not be pleasant for you or for me or for other Americans. You will pay more for oil. But the gap between what you pay here in New England and New Hampshire and what other Americans pay, which is much lower now—this gap will narrow, and that smaller difference in price will lessen the incentive for industry and jobs to move out of New England.

I know how important it is to have oil to heat your homes. As a result of a cold winter and the crude oil shortages brought about by the prices in Iran, light fuel stocks used for home heating are now at historical lows. I have therefore directed the Secretary of Energy to see to it that inventories of fuel which supply home heating oil are built up to approximately 240 million barrels by October of this year, so there will be adequate supplies, no shortages of heating oil in New England as we head into the next winter.

Here in New England, because of the superb work of your Members of Congress, we will now be able to turn to the two oldest sources of power—your rushing streams and your abundant forests.

New Hampshire's industrial revolution was powered by its streams. Many of those generating plants were dismantled or abandoned, because the law allowed electric power companies to insist that they supply all the power of a town or an industry needed or the power companies would supply none.

Last year we changed that law. Now New England's towns and industries will be able to develop small-scale hydroelectric power to help you meet your energy needs. We've already chosen one site in New Hampshire, I believe in Berlin, to demonstrate the potential of these small-scale hydroelectric plants. And we are studying three other sites in New Hampshire.

Forests have been a major factor in New Hampshire's economy since the first boatload of settlers arrived on your shore. But now we are not using forests enough to produce energy. Our studies indicate that we could meet one-third of New England's residential and commercial space heating needs with the wood which we now leave wasting on the ground. And as you can well see, the use of this wasted wood would create many new jobs in New Hampshire. There will be tax credit given in the future for those who use wood-burning stoves, and this will be of great help to you.

After the accident at Three Mile Island, we must take some hard decisions on nuclear energy. To get to the bottom of what happened there, I turned to a New Hampshire man—I met with him and the Commission this morning—the president of Dartmouth College, John Kemeny, to head a Presidential Commission which will study this accident and make a report to us and to the entire world. There's nothing more important than the safety and the security of American people. Every nuclear plant must be made safer than we once thought either possible or necessary.

We must also recognize the dangers in mining and burning coal, in piping and shipping oil, just as we recognize dangers in producing nuclear power. And we must remember that every bit of energy we waste unnecessarily multiplies all these problems. That is why energy conservation is the cornerstone of my and your energy policy.

In closing my remarks, let me add just a word about inflation before I take your questions. All of you know how bad inflation is. And it will not get much better in the near future. I'm not going to kid you about this either. We're going to see high inflation figures coming out week after week for the next few months.

The inflation that we have today has been gaining momentum for more than 10 years. It cannot be halted overnight, because it has seeped into the very fabric of our economy. There is no easy solution to it. And, frankly, anyone who says that there is an easy solution is either a liar or a fool. But with enough commitment and firmness, the problem can be solved. And in my judgment, the anti-inflation program that we have now is the best and perhaps the only way to solve it.

That program has four main parts: a tight budget and fiscal policy, leading to a balanced budget for our Nation; a tight monetary policy; reforms to attack unneeded regulation; and standards to help slow down the spiral of wages and prices chasing each other ever higher.

Too often in the past, for political reasons, Presidents and other public officials have given in to the temptation just before election time to try sudden gimmicks that lead to temporary paper improvements in the economic figures. But that has cost this country severely in the long-term economic damage. And I refuse to do it. We have begun a long-term effort to conquer inflation. For my part, I intend to stick with it. I need your understanding about the deep-rooted nature of this problem. And above all, I need your support and your determination to stay with this fight as long as it takes us to win it together.

And now I'd like to answer your questions.

QUESTIONS

CLEAN WATER ACT APPROPRIATIONS

Q. Mr. President, Robert Nixon, a selectman from Newfields, New Hampshire. It is my understanding that only three States, including New Hampshire, have qualified for full amounts allowed under the 1977 Clean Waters Act, amending the 1972 Federal Water Pollution Control, and that the Congress is considering reducing appropriations.

Would you approve the reapportionment of unused funds to States that have endeavored to carry out the purpose and spirit of the law?

THE PRESIDENT. My desire is to use the full amount of funds appropriated by Congress for the Clean Water Act implementation. Within the bounds of the law, I will certainly do what I can to reallocate any funds left over and unused at the end of the time period.

Q. Thank you, Mr. President.

THE PRESIDENT. And I hope New Hampshire is one that will qualify.

NUCLEAR POWERPLANT SAFETY

Q. Welcome, Mr. President. My name is Barbara Hayes. I live here in Portsmouth, and I'm also a transplanted southerner. [*Laughter*]

I'd like to preface my question with this statement: I will say I am pro nuclear power. I think it's a valid source of energy. However, I'm not insensitive to the needs of further safety study. My question is this, and it's probably from a simplistic viewpoint: I would like to see the Federal Government really focus in on the safety study not unlike the Manhattan Project or the space program to really bring in an answer of safety in nuclear power. You sort of touched on this, but maybe you would like to elaborate on it.

Thank you.

THE PRESIDENT. This morning I met with Chairman Kemeny and the other members of the President's Commission to study the Three Mile Island incident to determine accurately what caused the accident; what might have been done to prevent it; how well the Nuclear Regulatory Commission, the power company, the Federal, State, and local officials and others worked together in that incident; how they might work together better in the future to assess design mistakes or areas where, in the design of nuclear powerplants or the modification of those already there, they might be improved; to increase the authority, if necessary, for the Nuclear Regulatory Commission to deal more effectively with such an accident and to prevent, above all, and also to change their policies, if necessary.

We also will assess within the next 6 months the facts as they occurred, and as they were understood by the people in that area, particularly, to make sure that there was no lies told and no errors made in reporting to the people the facts.

This report will be observed and read by people throughout the world. Leaders, already, of the Scandinavian countries, Germany, France, Great Britain, England, have asked for full access to this report once it's conducted. This report will not only apply to the Three Mile Island plant; it will assess all the interrelationships that go among nongovernment or government entities in design, building, operating, supervising nuclear powerplants to enhance safety to the utmost. And they will make this report to the public at the end of 6 months.

I might add one other thing: Their deliberations, their hearings will also be conducted in public so that they can be reported accurately to the American people as the talks go on.

I instructed John Kemeny this morning that if in this 6-month period they detect any change that might be implemented immediately that would enhance the safety of the existing or being-designed nuclear plants, to let me and the public know it without delay so they wouldn't wait 6 months to make a beneficial suggestion.

I believe this is something that's long overdue. Although the Three Mile Island incident was a very serious threat and it caused us great consternation and concern, there may be a gold or silver lining to this cloud, because we may learn from it the limits of nuclear power and how to enhance the safety of nuclear power in the future.

That's a good question, and I thank you for it.

MIDDLE EAST PEACE NEGOTIATIONS

Q. Hello, Mr. President. My name is Vickie Hinesly, and I'm from York, Maine. And I'd like to welcome you from the people of Maine.

First, I'd like to congratulate you on your peace treaty with the Middle East. First, I'd like to ask you, now that we have a partial peace with the Middle East, what are your plans to secure peace in the rest of the Middle East and to secure the flow of oil through the U.S.?

THE PRESIDENT. Good. Yesterday, as you may have noticed in the news, I appointed Robert Strauss to be our new negotiator and talked to both Prime Minister Begin and to President Sadat on the phone yesterday afternoon. Their new relationship has been very exciting to me since the peace treaty was signed. And I can tell you in complete confidence if you won't relay it to anyone else—*[laughter]*— that sometimes those two men were not completely compatible with one another. *[Laughter]*

Q. I'll bet.

THE PRESIDENT. Since the peace treaty was signed, I honestly believe that they have learned to know and to like and to respect one another. President Sadat yesterday said, "Prime Minister Begin," he said, "that man has really changed," he said, "changed for the better." And he said, "We are now talking to each other on the phone, not just when a crisis develops but on a routine basis whenever a question arises that concerns our two countries."

Next month, almost exactly a month from now, the first part of the Sinai will be returned fom Israel to Egypt—El Arish. They will met there together. They will fly together to Beersheba and will appear before the student body at the Ben Gurion University and then will open direct flights between Israel and Egypt for the first time in anyone's memory. I'm very thankful for that.

At this time, however, the other neighbors of Israel are trying to create every possible obstacle to the carrying out of the peace treaty terms. I don't want to criticize them, although I wish they would eliminate terrorism and murder as an element of their effort. The best way to change their attitude—that is, Jordan, Iraq, Syria, Lebanon, and others—is to demonstrate in the coming negotiations that the legitimate rights of the Palestinian people will be honored and that the terms of the Camp David agreement will indeed be carried out.

We have a good relationship with almost all the countries that produce and sell us oil. We have maintained that firm relationship. One thing that I would like to do, however, in addition to keeping that friendship with them, is to develop more independence by increasing the production of American oil and by shifting to things like I've already described: increased use of coal, increased use of small dams, increased use of wood, and also conservation.

So, I would say the Mideast peace negotiation is on track. I've been very pleased since the treaty was signed. We have a good relationship with the oil-supplying nations, but we want to become less and less dependent on them in the future.

INFLATION

Q. Mr. President, I'm Mary Keenan, a city councilman in the city of Portsmouth. I ask my question for the mothers of America. I want you to know how concerned we are with inflation. It's attacking the American family. Young people are no longer able to buy homes of their own. They are no longer able to choose to stay home and raise the next generation. Can you tell me what your administration is doing to reverse this situation?

THE PRESIDENT. I'll do the best I can.

I can say that I'm at least as concerned about it as you are. It's ever-present on my mind. It's one of the biggest responsibilities on my shoulders and one of the most difficult questions to answer.

The first thing that we can do, I as a President, is to set an example with the Federal Government policies.

When I was running for President and was in New Hampshire and Portsmouth last, our Federal deficit was $66 billion. The Federal deficit that I have proposed to the Congress is much less than $30 billion for next time. We've cut it more than half. We have tried to maintain, through available money supplies, an adequate ability for people to buy homes, in spite of the high inflation.

In 1977 and 1978, we have averaged more than 2 million new homes being built in our country. And the level of home building is being maintained fairly high. I know that part of this is that young people see future prices of homes even higher. And if they can borrow the money, even at a high interest rate, they think, perhaps correctly, that it's a good investment.

Inflation also must be controlled by voluntary work of consumers by careful shopping, by voluntary aid of our economy by business and labor leaders, and also in many instances by local and State government officials. We are trying to cut down waste in government. And sometimes when we try to tighten up on the budget to some degree, there are outcries from very dedicated, very fine special interest groups.

We've asked that every price increase established by business be lower than the average of the previous 2 years and that the wage settlements also be restrained. So far, we've had excellent response. I think the early indications now are that these policies are working. But a lot of momentum was built in that's now showing up.

We had two things over which—three things that I'll mention, over which we had no control, that we could not predict.

One was a very severe winter, which cut down on the production of things like fresh vegetables and fruits and which made it very difficult to produce poultry and pork and also which made energy very scarce. The other thing that we didn't anticipate was the crisis in Iran, which caused a shortage of oil and OPEC prices to go very high. And the other thing is the result of previous mandatory price controls, and that is very small beef herds. So, these things—I'm not trying to make any excuses—but these are some of the causes over which we did not have control.

But with tight government constraint on spending, tight monetary constraint to prevent unnecessary demand for goods, increased productivity, increased soundness of the dollar, increased export of American goods, and voluntary price and wage constraints, I believe that all of us together can turn this inflation spiral around. If we can level it off in the next 3 or 4 months and start it downhill, you and I can celebrate together.

GASOLINE AND OIL SUPPLIES

Q. Welcome, Mr. President.

THE PRESIDENT. Thank you.

Q. I'm Susan Hedman from Hampton. And my question is, I would like to know if the situation with the shortage of gas is really true, or is it being built out of proportion? And also, would you ever consider rationing gas?

THE PRESIDENT. When you said shortage of gas, you meant gasoline for the cars, right?

Q. Yes.

THE PRESIDENT. We anticipate a shortage of gasoline in the summer and an even greater shortage of gasoline next year. Although we have held down and even reduced in the last 3 months our total consumption of oil, the American motorists have continued to increase the amount of gasoline they are burning. I would ask any of you as you go to and from work in the morning or to and from the shopping center, to see how many automobiles only have one person in them. And there has never yet been embedded in the consciousness of America the fact that we might actually have permanent shortages of gasoline.

I have had to mandate to the Secretary of Energy that a certain amount of oil products be set aside to heat your homes next winter. That's going to mean that not quite so much gasoline is going to be produced, because you either produce heating oil or you produce gasoline.

In 1975, the Congress required the President and the executive branch of Government to come forward with a standby rationing program. It would not go into effect unless the President and the Congress later approved it, but to give the President authority to initiate rationing after a program was developed.

Today, in a very sad mistake, the commerce committee of the House of Representatives, after we developed the proposal and presented it to the Congress, recommended that it not be approved. This means that if we do have a shortage in the future, rather than having a standby rationing plan that could be implemented only if the President and the Congress approve it, we would have to wait 6 or 7 additional months even before a rationing plan could be evolved.

So, we're trying to take precautionary measures now so that if we do have a shortage in the future, because of an absence of conservation or an interruption in our supplies, we can move immediately to minimize any disruption in the lives of the American people. The shortage is real. It's not going to leave. But if we can work together to prepare for it, we can prevail and minimize any damage to us. I'm willing to take the political consequences and the political criticism by proposing a gasoline rationing plan if it is needed. I hope it won't be needed. But I need for the Congress to be courageous enough to give me the authority simply to develop the plan. And this morning the House commerce committee did not do that.

So, to summarize, I don't believe we're going to need rationing any time in the future. We are going to have gasoline shortages. The American people are going to have to help by reducing waste of gasoline.

NUCLEAR POWERPLANT SAFETY

Q. Mr. President, my name is Dennis Lapoint. I'm from Somersworth, New Hampshire. And if you bear with me a second, I have to modify my question some, because you have touched on it.

THE PRESIDENT. Fine.

Q. As a result of the recent accident in Pennsylvania—and I believe a Wiscasset, Maine, plant had a 4,000-gallon radioactive water leak recently—as I see it, there are three major areas of concern, as I would look at it. One would be in the area of training and operations. It appears that, as I look at it, both plants fell on their face. The other one would be in the area of safety and preventive maintenance. The two go hand in hand. And apparently, from what happened in Wiscasset, I assume that there was no preventive maintenance or inadequate preventive maintenance to lose 4,000 gallons through a gasket.

The other would be in the area of waste disposal. As you well know, the work in the nuclear industry requires not only doing the operations as well as maintenance field, a lot of generated contaminated waste has to be disposed of, low-level radiation waste. Now, that is costly, and in my opinion, the overall cost of all this

would be something that's already shown up in the waste as a result of shielding problems that have occurred in Pennsylvania. The private industry cannot support this type of cost.

What is the government going to do in order to upgrade these safety, training, operations standards, the preventive maintenance standards of these companies, and what is the government doing relative to waste disposal?

THE PRESIDENT. Thank you, Dennis. Those are thought-provoking questions.

In 1952 and 1953, I was a senior officer of the crew that was building the second atomic submarine, the U.S.S. *Seawolf,* and had advanced training in reactor technology in a very fine college in Schenectady, New York. I'm familiar with basic design problems and also waste disposal problems and have operated several atomic powerplants myself.

I believe that we will benefit tremendously from the aroused American interest in the subject. You probably see the public opinion polls, a very substantial majority of American people still think that we should depend, to some degree, on atomic powerplants for energy. Many other countries are having to depend much more heavily than are we. About 12 percent now of our electricity in this country comes from the nuclear powerplants. I believe that what we learn with this new study under Dr. Kemeny will be very beneficial to us and to others as well, not just in analyzing the mistakes that were made, but also how training, operation, maintenance can be improved.

We have proposed to the Congress legislation for the first time in 35 years concerning waste disposal, and it's before the Congress now for consideration. We've also proposed to the Congress a kind of partner legislation, parallel legislation for the storage of spent fuel rods—two separate pieces of legislation—which can be stored, of course, and must be stored in a safe condition.

But those questions that you raised have been with us for three decades at least, and they've become much more acute. I think the aroused public opinion about nuclear power is beneficial, because it has caused scientists, engineers, operators, and politicians to pay much closer attention to questions that in the past were not addressed adequately or were addressed in private. In 1976, during the Presidential campaign, I think there were 22 States that had nuclear power referenda on the ballot when I was running for office. And I think that intense interest is going to continue.

My guess is that we'll have a much more accurate assessment of a need for nuclear power and how it can be made more safe because of this incident and because of interest of people like you.

INTEREST RATES

Q. I am Leon Gaidmore from Dover, a retired toolmaker from the naval yard. Mr. President, why have interest rates been allowed to climb to the present record high level? Isn't this high interest most unfair to our young people? They haven't lived long enough to accumulate money, so they must borrow to buy homes and raise their kids. Older people have money to lend but need it the least. Their lives are behind them. Isn't this all wrong?

THE PRESIDENT. That is a good question—[*laughter*]—and my answer to you is, yes, it is all wrong. I think we ought——

Q. It is.

THE PRESIDENT. I remember when I was Governor of Georgia back in '73 and '74, interest rates got up to 18 or 20 percent on short-term borrowings. And

Georgia had surplus money under my superb administration—[*laughter*]—and we were investing our money at that high interest rate. And now they've crept up again.

Interest rates are determined, as you know, directly by the inflation rate. When the inflation rate is, say, 8 percent and someone lends money at 8 percent, they merely break even. In order to make a profit on their money above and beyond inflation, they have to get more than 8 percent. So, the best way to control interest rates in the long run is to bring the inflation rate down.

In our country more than 100 years ago, the Congress decided that interest rates would basically be controlled by the Federal Reserve Board. And the Federal Reserve does modify the tightness of money by various means to control the interest rates. But I have to say in complete frankness that the President and the Congress also have a role to play in interest rates.

The President has a direct role by proposing budget deficits. If the President can cut the budget deficit down, then, of course, the interest rates and inflation rate ultimately will go down. If the Congress is extremely liberal on cutting taxes, then, of course, that creates more money in the economy and money becomes much more available, and of course, that affects the interest rates as well.

So, the Federal Reserve is directly responsible. The President and the Congress are also responsible. But basically the interest rates are determined by the inflation rate. We are doing all we can to hold down Federal deficits and to control spending and to eliminate unnecessary regulations. But we've got a long way to go.

The only thing I can add is what I said earlier to Mary with the question about the homes. An investment in a home, even at a high interest rate, is a good investment if there's a surety that the interest rates will be maintained high or if property values will go up. But I don't know how to answer your question any better except to say that I agree with you; we'd be much better to have low inflation, low interest rates, and I'm doing the best I can as President to bring them both down.

IMPACT AID FUNDING

Q. Mr. President, my name is John Sullivan, and I'm a member of the board of education here in Portsmouth. Mr. President, one of the most serious problems facing the city of Portsmouth today is the lack of equitable funding for the education of military students. This year alone here in Portsmouth, the average tuition rate for Portsmouth students averages $1,545, while under HEW public law 874 they have authorized us $1,260. This falls $285 short for a student, or in our school system it means that the taxpayers of the city of Portsmouth must pick up an extra $315,000.

Now, I was just wondering if this is a reasonable solution to our educational program and the process between the city, the State, and the Nation, sir.

THE PRESIDENT. It does not sound like a reasonable solution to me. [*Laughter*] I presume you're talking about impact aid funds.

Q. Yes, I am, sir.

THE PRESIDENT. We are trying to reform the impact aid law, with very little success. But perhaps you could join me in this battle.

What's happening now is that the impact aid formulae are so constructed that some communities that have absolutely no justifiable claim on these funds are getting greatly enriched, whereas communi-

nities like your own, where you actually do care for the dependent children of service families, get underpaid.

And I would like for you to contact, if you would write the name down, Stu Eizenstat in my office in the White House and call him and talk to him about how you can let your voice be heard in the Congress. This is very important, because as long as extremely wealthy counties— some of which are right around Washington, D.C.—who don't actually educate the children get enormous payments of impact aid funds, it means that that much money which you deserve cannot come to you. And we really need to modify and to reform the impact aid formula. It's not right for you to have to pay an excessive amount of money to educate a military child. Obviously the full amount should be allotted to you, and I believe we could do this if the law was reformed.

Q. Thank you, Mr. President. Thank you for coming to Portsmouth.

THE PRESIDENT. I'm glad I came.

EDUCATION PROGRAMS

Q. Mr. President, excuse me if I'm nervous, but the last time I won anything in a government raffle, I was drafted. [*Laughter*]

I find that my question is similar to Mr. Sullivan's and it was an observation more than a statement. My name is Joe Arnstein, and I teach in this high school.

That is, we receive our tax dollars back towards education in two ways in this town and in this community, this area. The one way is through the impact aid, in which our schools receive dollars that can be spent as local people see that they need to be spent, whether that's for books or salaries or if the roof is leaking. The other way we receive money back is through HEW. And from HEW we receive programs, forms to be filled out, title this, title that, and we have to tie up some of our own competent people to shuffle papers back and forth between Portsmouth and Washington.

As a teacher and as a person that believes in teaching by example, along with many in my profession, I would suggest that before we have a department of education, you consider whether this is going to add to the shuffling back and forth of paper, or whether this is going to furnish money to students who need it, to teachers, to administrations that need it.

THE PRESIDENT. Thank you, Joe. Let me respond very briefly.

My first public office was a member of the Sumter County School Board, where I live. And I became familiar then with some of the elements that you've just described.

One of my first meetings as President was with the 50 State school superintendents. I asked them to go back to their own States, including the superintendent of New Hampshire, and to give me a list, my Office of Management and Budget, of all those forms and reports and requests that they considered to be unnecessary. This has been done. And a great number of those forms and reports have been eliminated. Some are required by Congress, and we've not yet been able to get the laws changed. But I know that this is an onerous burden that separates the local community from the Federal Government rather than binding the two together, with the local government controlling, to let Federal Government help with education.

In the last 2 years, we've just about doubled the allocation of Federal funds for education. We are trying to help. At the same time, we are trying to prevent any encroachment of the Federal Government into decisions being made at the local government on how the schools should be operated.

I would like for you to send to me, through your Congressman or through your Senator, a list of specific forms that you think are unnecessary or that can be consolidated or eliminated or abbreviated or made more infrequent in their required sending to Washington. And I will personally look into this that you send me, as President of the United States, if you as a teacher will do your share of this bargain. Would you mind doing that for me?

Q. No, I wouldn't. Thank you, Mr. President.

THE PRESIDENT. And I'll carry out my part of the deal, too. Thank you, Joe.

THE PRESIDENT. John, you and Norm, when Mr. Arnstein sends you this list of forms, you come to the Oval Office, if you don't mind, and bring them to me. And I'll try to do something about it, because probably what applies to him in his classroom applies to people all over the United States, and I'd really like to do something about it.

Yes, ma'am?

FEDERAL MORTGAGE PROGRAMS

Q. Mr. President, my name is Pamela Foster. I am very proud to be an American, and I'm even more proud that you are my President.

THE PRESIDENT. Thank you very much.

Q. But I'm also especially proud that I, too, am from the South—[*laughter*]— Woodruff, South Carolina. I am associated with a real estate firm here in Portsmouth.

And my question, sir, is, do you see, in the near future, any Federal mortgage money coming to the seacoast area? Seacoast area.

THE PRESIDENT. I heard what you said. [*Laughter*] I heard your question. I was trying to think of the answer. [*Laughter*]

Well, the reason I hesitate is because, as you know, there is a tremendous amount of varying kinds of Federal mortgage money that does, indeed, come through the Farm Home Administration, the veterans programs, the FHA, through HUD. And also, as you know, with the new money certificates, we have stabilized the available supply of money for home construction even in spite of the very high interest rates which would formerly have put the housing construction industry almost in a recession.

I don't know of any additional new programs that are in prospect of being evolved. I have not proposed any to the Congress. Can you ask me one followup question about the specific kind of mortgage money to which you refer?

Q. We'll take any kind, anything. [*Laughter*]

THE PRESIDENT. That's a good answer. Well, I thank you. But those home programs are being maintained. And as I said earlier, because of various factors, we have sustained, for this past 2 years, since I have been in office, I think the highest level of home construction in history, in spite of the very high interest rates. This has been one of the causes of inflation, by the way, because so many homes have been built, I think an average of 2.2 million homes each of the 2 years.

We have cut the unemployment rate in the construction trade down 35 percent, because people have gone back to work building homes. And, of course, the lumber industry, the timber industry, the sheetrock industry, the insulation industry has done extremely well. In some cases a demand for these building supplies has been greater than the supply. And that's one of the industries where prices have gone up very high.

But we'll try to do all we can to channel more mortgage money to the seacoast area.

Thank you very much.

Q. Thank you, Mr. President.

THE PRESIDENT. Yes, ma'am?

AMY CARTER

Q. Hello, Mr. President. I was wondering, does Amy boast or brag because you're the President of the United States? [*Laughter*]

THE PRESIDENT. I was trying to remember a time when she's ever boasted or bragged. [*Laughter*]

No, I don't believe so. I think the only time in the last 2 years that I can recall is the morning after I got back from the Middle East, Amy got up early and came in where I was—we had got in long after midnight—and she crawled up on the bed with me and said, "Daddy, I'm proud that you are my father, and I'm proud that you're President." But ordinarily, Amy, being the daughter of a President, probably does more apologizing than she does bragging. [*Laughter*]

You didn't tell me what your name was.

Q. Paloma Kressmann.

THE PRESIDENT. Paloma?

Q. Yes, sir.

THE PRESIDENT. Crestman—that's a pretty name. Do you ever come to Washington, Paloma?

Q. No. [*Laughter*]

THE PRESIDENT. Perhaps you could come sometime and see both me and Amy. Would you like to do that?

Q. Yes.

THE PRESIDENT. Okay. Well, I'd like you to come. Is your last name Crestman, C-r-e-s-t-m-a-n?

Q. What do you want me to do? [*Laughter*]

THE PRESIDENT. I want you to come to see me. But I asked how do you spell your last name. Is it——

Q. K-r-e-s-s-m-a-n-n.

THE PRESIDENT. I got it. [*Laughter*] And where do you live?

Q. I live in Portsmouth. 228 Highland Street.

THE PRESIDENT. 228. I'll write you an invitation—I'll let Amy write you an invitation.

Q. Thanks. [*Laughter*]

PROPOSED DEPARTMENT OF EDUCATION

Q. Welcome to Portsmouth, Mr. President.

THE PRESIDENT. Thank you.

Q. My name is Vernis Jackson. I'm an elementary schoolteacher here in Portsmouth. My question is, during your campaign for the Presidency, you promised to work for the establishment of a Cabinet-level department of education, separate from HEW. Can you tell me whether your endeavors toward this goal have been fruitful, and do you have a timetable as to when it should be achieved?

THE PRESIDENT. Yes. We've made good progress on that. Last year the Senate approved the legislation. This year we resubmitted the legislation, and I think it's in excellent shape in both the House and Senate. I predict that we will have established a separate department of education this year. And I will be very eager to sign the legislation when the Congress passes it.

Q. Thank you.

FEDERAL AID TO COLLEGE STUDENTS

Q. Hello, Mr. President.

THE PRESIDENT. Good afternoon.

Q. My name is Forrest Snowden, and I'm a freshman at Winikana High School in Hampton. What I would like to know is what have you done to cut down the financial costs for high school students going to college?

THE PRESIDENT. Good. Last year the

Congress passed the finest package of aid programs for college students that this country's ever seen. The only other year when the Congress took equally effective action was back in 1965 when the Higher Education Act was first passed.

I think the total benefits that were allotted to college students amounted to maybe six or eight billion dollars. They consisted of direct grants to college students who are poor, but who are capable of doing college work.

They consisted of increased loans to college students whose parents have some income but who can't afford the high cost of college; the banks in the local region lend the students money. They pay it back after they finish college and get a job, and the Federal Government supplements the interest rates to keep the interest rates down low. And they also provided a special allocation of money for college work programs, whereby a student can go to college and, at the same time he or she gets an education, can get a job, financed partially by the Federal Government—kind of a work-study program.

So, I think these new programs, when they are known throughout the country—and the legislation just passed last year—will be one of the finest opportunities ever. And I hope that you will have a chance before long to take advantage of these programs.

Q. Okay. Thank you.

THE PRESIDENT. Thank you. Yes, sir?

SPACE TECHNOLOGY

Q. My name is John Williamson from Rye. I want to thank you for not quitting. It's a very unruly country we have.[1]

---

[1] The questioner was referring to several incidents of heckling which had taken place earlier during the town meeting.

I think we need alternatives to nuclear power, and I'm very excited by developments in solar power and electrical generating stations in Earth orbit. It sounds a little off-the-wall, I know.

The more I read though, the more possible I think it has become. Yet I heard nothing out of Washington on the subject. What is the administration's approach to aerospace industry?

THE PRESIDENT. I spoke earlier this week to the National Academy of Sciences. Two of the four things that I discussed with them were energy and space. The next step for us in space is the space shuttle, where we will begin to capitalize on more than $100 billion of investment, primarily in space exploration. These shuttle vehicles will begin to fly shortly, and we will lease space on them, first of all, to agencies of the Federal Government for defense, intelligence, and for research and for other means, astronomy and so forth.

We'll also lease space to private industry for the evolution of new kinds of technologies such as you've described, and we will also make some space on our space shuttles available to foreign countries.

As you know, these vehicles, like airplanes, will be launched into space, will fly around the Earth as long as they desire, and then will come back into the atmosphere and land like an airplane. It will be a very efficient way to make space use routine, rather than a great adventure every time one is launched.

I think following that period of research and development of the science of collecting energy and its transmission would come a move toward the kind of energy evolution that you've described.

The photovoltaic cell technique has been that which made possible the space flights already. And this so far is very expensive for the actual production of power. And I would say a major opportunity for us in the next 10 or 20 years would be to make the production of power directly from the sunlight through the photovoltaic cells feasible. I think that would be a prerequisite for us to do that on Earth before we could do it effectively in space.

So, I'd say the space shuttle advanced research in space, by private, U.S. Government, foreign government entities, and the development of the photovoltaic cells would be the precursors to the accumulation of Sun's rays in space, their transmission to Earth as energy.

Not even one more? One more quick question, and then our time's up.

NUCLEAR POWERPLANTS

Q. Good afternoon, President Carter. I'm Scott Nason from Portsmouth, New Hampshire. I worked on the Seabrook nuclear power construction project. I was wondering if you've ever had the opportunity to actually see a project of this magnitude while in its construction stage? Also, due to the recent unfortunate events, morale throughout this industry is low. What do you feel should be done about it?

THE PRESIDENT. To answer your first question, yes, I have seen a major atomic powerplant in the construction phase. While I was Governor, one was completed there in the southwestern part of the State, and I was there, more than once, while it was being constructed. Also, I was involved in the early stages of the development of atomic power for propulsion of submarines, as I described earlier.

I think the low morale that exists not only in the designers, builders, operators of atomic powerplants, but those who live around them and who fear for their own safety, will all be aided by a frank, honest, competent report to the American people about the status of nuclear power, and its degree of safety and what can be done to make nuclear powerplants safer in the future. And that's why I believe that the Kemeny Commission will play a very constructive role. I think it would help to assuage the concern of people like yourself. I think it would help to assuage the concern of environmentalists who are deeply concerned about all atomic power. I think it would help to assuage the concern of people who live around powerplants and who still believe that they ought to be there. So, in my opinion, this will kind of clear the air and give us a great degree of guidance for the future.

Let me say this in closing. I've made notes of each person's name and the type of question here on a piece of scratch paper, and the interest that you've shown in such a wide diversity of subjects is really overwhelming. I don't claim to know the answer to all questions. I have an excellent opportunity to learn. And coming here, hearing of your interests and getting your own, sometimes criticisms, sometimes congratulations, sometimes advice, is very beneficial to me.

We've got such a wonderful and such a great country. And if I can just leave one thought with you before I depart: I hold perhaps the most important political office in the world, certainly the most important elective political office in the world. And I represent a nation made up of people who are absolutely free to express yourselves, to agree, to disagree, to debate, to criticize a President, to criticize the Members of Congress, to criticize a mayor, to make constructive suggestions, to ask questions, even though they might be embarrassing. And this gives us strength.

And most of the time when we read the newspapers or see the evening television or listen to the radio, what we hear about is the current problems, and what we hear

about are the current arguments, and what we hear about are the current disappointments. But what we don't hear enough about is the solid, stable, superb strength of a great nation.

And I hope that in the future when you are concerned about schools, taxes, energy, inflation, nuclear power, that you will remember that in some countries your concern could not be expressed. And in some countries these kinds of problems would not even be noticed by you, because you would be deprived of freedom and your children would be starving and your voice would never be heard, and the independence to make your own decisions would be absolutely missing.

So, as we face the future, let's remember our blessings. And one of the greatest blessings of all is a free American people like you who have never been afraid to speak your mind and to let public officials have an opportunity to listen.

Thank you very much.

NOTE: The President spoke at 3:30 p.m. in the Portsmouth Senior High School auditorium.

Manchester, New Hampshire

Remarks at a Reception for Governor Hugh Gallen. April 25, 1979

Governor Gallen, distinguished officials on the stage with us, young Democrats, volunteers, friends of mine from throughout the State of New Hampshire:

This State has a special place in my own heart and also, whether or not you realize it, a special place in the political life of our country. There is no other State like it which has the opportunity to shape the political policies and the political consciousness of America.

My own first visit here came in 1974, when I first met Norm D'Amours, a young, not very well known candidate for Congress, and I walked the streets and stood in the factory lines with him and got to have experience at first hand about what true democracy means. There is no way to slip into office in New Hampshire if you are a national candidate or a candidate for Governor or Congress, because you require, the people of New Hampshire require political candidates to express themselves frankly to you and to listen to you in the process.

I came here many times in 1975, 1976. My wife came here many times. My mother Lillian came here many times. My Aunt Sissy came here many times. My son Jack and his wife, Judy, my son Chip and his wife, Caron, Amy came here. We all came to New Hampshire to learn, to let you know us, and to listen.

And many of the policies that I took to Washington and proposed to the Congress that are now being put into effect to give our people better housing, better education, finally, an energy policy, to deal with the problems of the environment, to improve the relationship between the local, State, and Federal Government, to work toward a balanced budget, to let people have a direct voice in their own affairs, to have more morality in foreign policy, have all come from ideas given to me by you in your homes, on the streets, in the drugstores, where I had a chance to know what your concepts are of what our country ought to be. I'm thankful to you for that.

I even was accused one time of shaking hands with a mannequin in a store because I was moving so fast and because I was so tired. I don't think I got that vote—[*laughter*]—but I got enough votes to win the primary here, and I thank you for it.

You've got wonderful opportunities here in New Hampshire, and I would say that there has been a tremendous change for the better in New Hampshire now

that Hugh Gallen and Irene represent you as the first family of your State.

In addition to Norm D'Amours in Congress, you have a fighting Senator, John Durkin, who knows you, listens to you, serves you well, and also represents the entire United States.

And you've got a senior statesman who also still represents New Hampshire in the finest possible way to set an example for many of us to follow, and that is Tom McIntyre, whom I admire and love.

Tom McIntyre has just written a book that will be published the 1st of May. I promised him I would put in a plug for his book—[*laughter*]—and he's the kind of person that all of us can learn from.

And I would like to say in closing, thank you for being the kinds of volunteers who are not afraid to invest your own lives in a better life for our country. There are many things that can be improved in our Nation. But let's not ever forget that we live in the greatest nation on Earth, and you and I together, working in a free and democratic society, can make it even greater in the future.

Thank you and God bless all of you.

NOTE: The President spoke at 6:25 p.m. in the Memorial High School gymnasium.

Bedford, New Hampshire

Remarks at a State Democratic Party Fundraising Dinner.   April 25, 1979

Governor Hugh Gallen—Governor Hugh Gallen—doesn't that sound great?—[applause]—it just makes all the difference in the world; I thought that Meldrim Thomson was already working full-time for the John Birch Society—[laughter]—Senator Durkin, Senator Tom McIntyre, Congressman D'Amours, House Leader Spirou, Senate Leader Preston, chairman of our National Democratic Party, John White, Chairman Dorval, Councilor Dudley, friends of mine in New Hampshire, and visitors from adjacent States:

I'm indeed proud to be here. This has been a typical, very busy day in the life of a President. This afternoon, earlier, I gave a speech too, in New York at the Waldorf Astoria, praising America's newspaper publishers for their responsible and objective journalism. [*Laughter*] Here in Manchester, that speech would not be appropriate—[*laughter*]—so, I think I'll choose another subject for this evening. [*Laughter*]

When I first began to come here in 1975, I was not accustomed to your winters, you were not accustomed to the way I talked—[*laughter*]—and almost nobody was accustomed to the idea that I might someday be President. [*Laughter*] But we got to know each other, and we also listened to each other. You gave me support when I had very few friends in this country, and I will never forget it. And I thank you for it.

One thing that Georgia and New Hampshire formerly had in common is that we were formerly one-party States. For generations, Georgia voted right—always Democratic—[*laughter*]—but New Hampshire, unfortunately, chose another path. Some would say you went astray, and for a long time you stayed that way.

But then things began to change. Some Georgia voters sadly fell from grace, and here in New Hampshire, a great revival began to take place. [*Laughter*]

You elected a courageous Democratic Senator, an inspiration to me and to you, Tom McIntyre.

In 1974, you elected Norm D'Amours to Congress, and you elected another great Democratic Senator, John Durkin, even though it took you two elections to do it. [*Laughter*]

And last November, you took State government out of the hands of the special interests and brought it back to the people by electing Hugh Gallen as Governor of New Hampshire, and I thank you for it.

The last 2 years for the United States of America have been a time of rebuilding. We've accomplished a great deal, and there is much more to be done.

When they write the history of these years, I hope that they will say four things about what you and I have done together.

I want them to say that we've made America prosperous again and that we believe, as Democrats, in hard work and that we have put our people back to work.

I want them to say that we have never been afraid to tackle tough and controversial problems, and that we placed the long-term good of our beloved country always above the short-term political advantages which we might have gotten.

And I want them to say that we have restored the trust and the confidence of the American people in our own Government.

It's sobering to think back 3 years, 4 years, 5 years, and to remember the interrelationship between the people of this country and our Government in Washington. It's a sobering thought, and great changes have taken place.

But most of all, I want them to say that America has been at peace and that we have helped to lead the world away from war.

If we can continue to build a new foundation of peace, trust, and prosperity, we will have kept the faith with our party and with the American people. We will enter the 1980's as a proud, confident, strong, and a unified nation. We'll bring our Nation and the world closer to a time when war, hunger, and poverty and hatred will be no more. This is what you and I can do, and this is what you and I are doing, and this is what you and I will do together.

In early 1976, I told you here in Manchester that, and I quote, "our country's single most important priority must be a job for every American who wants to work." If you think back 3 years, that was the crucial issue. I said this at a time when in New Hampshire almost 1 out of every 10 people was without a job, when thousands more were working short hours or were threatened every payday with a layoff.

That was Republican economics at work. That was the doctrine of fighting inflation with the jobs and the lives and the living incomes of hard-working Americans. They called it "tightening our belts," but you know whose belt got tightened. That kind of policy might not sound so bad in some Washington bureaucracy or board room, but on the streets of Manchester, I tell you from experience that people were hurting.

I walked these streets, and I saw what kind of economics was doing to you and to your neighbors and to your children. We both knew then, in 1976, that it was time for a change. And we have brought that change.

I like Democratic economics much better. I'm proud that we have been able, working together, to put the people of New Hampshire and the entire country back to work. In 2 years, we have created more than 7½ million net new jobs—50,-000 or more of those new jobs right here in New Hampshire.

Your State, which bore the brunt of a planned Republican recession, now has one of the lowest unemployment rates in our country. Today, the jobless rate in New Hampshire is less than half what it was when I took office. In fact, in January of this year, the unemployment rate in New Hampshire was only 3.2 percent. Just seeing a Democratic Governor on the way did wonders for your State.

That's why I like Democratic economics better. Not that we've solved all our problems in economics—for 10 years now, rising prices have been casting a long shadow over our economy and over our very lives. We all know what inflation can do to our paychecks. We know what it does to the poor, the elderly, to those who worked and saved and now watch the value of their savings disappear as each day passes. I am fighting with the best of my ability to bring inflation under control, and I am determined to win this fight. But I will not do it through a planned recession that will take jobs away from millions of Americans who want to work.

And I also will not tie our economy in knots by trying to impose mandatory Federal Government controls which may sound like a solution, but which only treat the symptoms and not the disease. The historical record is clear on this. Such controls do not solve the problem; they just create another cumbersome, meddlesome Federal bureaucracy and often make the problem worse.

Everyone must help to control inflation. I know that Government cannot control inflation by itself, but there are important things that Government can do. For instance, I believe in a balanced Federal budget. And I am proud that the 1980 budget will have reduced the Republican deficit by more than 55 percent since I ran for office. We've done that by cutting wasteful, inefficient, and unnecessary programs and—listen to this—while increasing substantially our commitment to the elderly, the poor, to education, to housing, to transportation, and to the unemployed.

Down through history, we've learned the hard way that there is no easy or painless cure for inflation. Six months ago, I announced a program of wage and price standards to slow the rate of inflation. This program is voluntary. But it also has teeth, and we are already having some very important successes. Most businesses, most working people, and most consumers are cooperating. But their efforts have been obscured by inflationary forces beyond our control, such as OPEC oil prices, which have risen much higher than anybody could have anticipated or influenced, and by severe winter weather 2 years in a row.

In the past few months though, the rate of inflation in the parts of the economy that we can control has slowed significantly. The producer price index, a very good indicator, shows these changes. It has dropped by more than 40 percent already this year—from 13 percent in January to 7½ percent in March. This is an important sign that we are beginning to get a grip on inflation.

Other evidence which we can already detect very clearly suggests that food prices will stop going through the roof as well. But I'm not going to kid you about this: Our number one domestic problem, inflation, is bad, and it will be months, at the very least, before it gets substantially better. Frankly, we will continue to see discouraging price figures coming out for some time to come.

Too often in the past, Presidents have tried to improve their political fortunes by coming up with sudden gimmicks that produce misleading, temporary paper gains in the inflation figures. The trouble is that this just led to bigger spurts of inflation down the road, and it ended up doing long-term economic damage to our country. It's a temptation, but I refuse to play politics with the economic health of the United States of America.

That's why I am calling on every one of you and on all Americans throughout our country to cooperate with a steady, solid anti-inflation effort. Only a tenacious, long-term approach can solve the tenacious, long-term problem of inflation.

But I will persevere. And I ask for your understanding about the deep-rooted nature of the problem, and I ask for your patience to give our efforts time to succeed. And most of all, I ask for your determination and your dedication to the common good in sticking to this fight until it is won.

Again, in New Hampshire, in Concord, more than 4 years ago, as a candidate during one of my first visits to New Hampshire, I told you the truth about our energy problems. I said then, and I repeat today, and I quote, "There is no workable plan that does not require sacrifice and self-restraint from the American people."

New Hampshire, like the rest of New England, knows that it is not a good situation to be dependent on a long, thin line of oil tankers stretched all the way from the Middle East to these shores. Foreign oil is expensive and getting more so. And we cannot control it. In an uncertain world, our growing appetite for foreign oil makes us dependent on the whims of foreign powers.

The days of cheap energy are over. Only demagogs deny the unpleasant truth: We must pay more and we must use less.

In order to increase production of American oil, we will soon begin to decontrol slowly, predictably, in a phased way, domestic oil prices. It's a step that has to be taken if we are ever going to conserve energy and have a rational energy policy.

The choice is not between cheap or expensive domestic oil. It's between some inconvenience now that's controllable, and some far greater hardship later on, which we may not be able to control.

The great difference between the price of energy in New England and the rest of the Nation will be reduced, helping to keep industry and jobs here at home where they belong.

I know better than many Americans what a New Hampshire winter is like. I spent two winters outside in the street. I know that families in New Hampshire, in their homes, living on less than $5,000 a year, have to pay 24 percent of their inadequate income for fuel.

That's why the oil companies must not be allowed to keep the excess and unearned profits from the rising price of oil. This is very important. There is no excuse for permitting any such massive ripoff. We must, and we will, have a good windfall profits tax.

Now, you know, as Tom and John and others have already said, that the oil lobby is one of the most powerful special interests in Washington. They feel about the windfall profits tax about the same way that Daniel Webster felt about the devil. The oil lobby already is and will be all over the tax bill like—as we say in Georgia—like a chicken on a june bug.

But I refuse to believe that the Congress of the United States will permit these oil companies, already reaping huge profits, to become billions of dollars richer at the expense of the American people.

The money from higher oil prices must go to solve our serious energy problems. That is what the fight over windfall profits is all about.

The oil companies want all the money for themselves. I want it to go for exploration for new oil, yes, but also to create the energy security fund.

With this fund, we will give direct financial aid to families who are least able to afford the growing energy costs, and

we will harness American know-how to do what we should have done years ago—to develop economical alternatives to oil.

This will finally let us develop power from the Sun, from the wind, from geothermal energy. Here in New Hampshire, this means that we will be looking at the State's oldest sources of power, your streams and your forests, for energy.

We can develop the energy potential of New England. New Hampshire will no longer have to mortgage its future in exchange for foreign oil. Small streams and forests will again help to power New Hampshire. We'll have a pilot project in Berlin very soon, using small hydroelectric powerplants to provide power for the community. We have three more projects that we are presently considering just within New Hampshire.

These are some of the benefits of a rational, Democratic energy policy. But I need you to help me with it.

On that night, on that great night in 1976 when I won the New Hampshire primary, I told you then that as President, if I was elected, I would repair the damage that has been done to the relationship between our people and our Government.

I have been proud to keep that pact with the people of New Hampshire. There are no more government lies, there are no more enemies lists, there are no more sellouts to the special interests. Working together, we have restored integrity and trust to the American Government.

I used to hear how sick and tired the people of New Hampshire were of bureaucracy, redtape, and government inefficiency. These complaints had been building up for a long time, and it took Democrats to do something about them. With the help of Senator John Durkin and Congressman Norm D'Amours, we have passed a landmark civil service reform bill.

Now the Government will encourage and reward good performance—which is what the Federal employees want, almost to a person—not mediocrity and laziness. We can make government work better and we can make it work for you.

We've put Inspectors General in every major Federal agency to root out fraud and dishonesty. We are cleaning up the GSA scandals, which have festered for years. We will stop those who dare to steal the taxpayers' money.

We've shut off the regulatory assembly line. Government regulations will be fewer, more sensible, fair, and written in plain English, so even a peanut farmer can understand them.

Just one quick example. By lifting the heavy hand of Government regulation from the airline industry, we have saved American consumers $2½ billion in reduced airfares. We have made some progress, but we still have a lot of improvement still waiting to be done.

And finally, I recall in Antrim, New Hampshire, I stated that the Soviet Union, and I quote, "is just as frightened of nuclear proliferation as we are." And I promised "never to get this country into a position that would make us subject to nuclear blackmail."

For more than 30 years, we have lived with the horror of nuclear weapons. We live with a nightmare that we and the Soviet Union have the capacity to destroy all life on this bountiful planet.

Peace will never be fully secure as long as the shadow of nuclear war hangs over the world. A SALT treaty will lessen the danger of nuclear destruction, while safeguarding our military strength.

For more than 6 years, under three Presidents, we have been very carefully negotiating the SALT II treaty. As President, I assure you that it will enhance our Nation's security, and we can make certain that the Soviet Union is living up to every single one of the treaty's provisions.

Neither our Nation nor the Soviet Union would benefit from an uncontrolled race to build ever more deadly, more devastating nuclear weapons. A SALT treaty will give us more military security in a more stable and predictable and peaceful world. Failure to ratify this treaty will cause us all to pay a horrible price, both in terms of unnecessary military spending and also in terms of increased global instability and the threat of a devastating war.

I am confident that when the American people and the American Congress weigh the merits of the SALT II treaty, they will conclude that it is an important step both toward peace and toward military security. I need you, as individual Americans, to help me take this important step in our eventual goal, the goal that I set for you and for me in my speech the day of inauguration—to eliminate nuclear weapons from the face of the Earth once and for all.

In 1818, the founder of our party, Thomas Jefferson, looked back on his long years of service to the Nation, and he noted with pride—I quote from him, "During the period of my administration, not a drop of the blood of a single fellow citizen was shed by the sword of war."

I am also proud that not a single drop of American blood has been shed in war during my own administration. And I pray to God every day that when my years as President are over that I can still share Thomas Jefferson's achievement.

The purpose of America's military forces is not to wage war, but to preserve peace. That's why I believe in military strength as strongly as I believe in peace.

Tom McIntyre shares these beliefs. For 16 years in the Senate, he worked to make sure this country had the most modern weapons systems in the world. We miss his leadership in Washington. But John Durkin and Norm D'Amours carry on this same great Democratic, New Hampshire tradition.

Our military strength and our national will are clear, and they are well known to all nations. We do not need to prove our strength or our will through rash or reckless military adventures; rather, our military capacity gives us a rare opportunity to lead the world toward peace.

Here in New Hampshire, I promised you a government as good as the people. Some critics dismissed that statement as meaningless campaign rhetoric: How could a government try to be as good as the people? But you understood what I was talking about. Our foreign policy is as good as our people when we speak out for human rights around the world. We have and we will continue to protect human rights as long as I am President.

Our foreign policy is as good as the American people when we fight for freedom and for justice, and we have and we will continue to preserve these ancient American principles.

Our foreign policy is as good as the American people when we work to bring peace not only to ourselves but to ancient enemies. We have and we will continue to work for peace around the world.

We won a victory of this kind when a peace treaty was signed last month between Egypt and Israel. The United States was able to play a crucial role at the critical time to make that possible.

That treaty was not a personal accomplishment, though I was proud and grateful to be part of it. That treaty was a tribute to two courageous leaders, President Sadat and Prime Minister Begin. But it

was also a triumph for the moral strength and the leadership of our Nation.

If we can help the nations of the Middle East eventually to work out a lasting peace, it will not be because they trust any particular American President; it will be because they recognize that the American people will always support those who seek freedom and justice and peace.

This is not just for one administration, but from the moment of our birth as a nation, through all times, as long as we call ourselves a free people.

Freedom, peace, and justice are the sources of our true power on which all else must rest. This is what makes America so great.

Thank you very much.

NOTE: The President spoke at 9:05 p.m. in the Sheraton Wayfarer Hotel Convention Center. In his opening remarks, he referred to former New Hampshire Governor Meldrim Thomson, Christos C. Spirou, house minority leader, Robert F. Preston, senate Democratic leader, Romeo Dorval, New Hampshire Democratic Party chairman, and Dudley Dudley, member of the Governor's Council.

Budget Deferrals

Message to the Congress.   April 26, 1979

To the Congress of the United States:

In accordance with the Impoundment Control Act of 1974, I herewith report three new deferrals of budget authority totalling $164.1 million and a revision to a previously transmitted deferral increasing the amount deferred by $1.0 million. The items involve the fossil energy construction and Strategic Petroleum Reserve programs in the Department of Energy and the payment of Vietnam prisoner of war claims in the Foreign Claims Settlement Commission.

The details of the deferrals are contained in the attached reports.

JIMMY CARTER

The White House,
   April 26, 1979.

NOTE: The attachments detailing the deferrals are printed in the FEDERAL REGISTER of May 1, 1979.

Windfall Profits Tax and Energy Security Trust Fund

Message to the Congress.   April 26, 1979

To the Congress of the United States:

On April 5, I announced the phased decontrol of oil prices beginning on June 1 of this year, and ending with the expiration of price control authority on October 1, 1981. The decontrol program I have established will increase domestic oil production, encourage conservation of existing energy supplies, and make it possible to accelerate development of alternative energy supplies and thereby lessen our dangerously heavy reliance on imported foreign oil.

To prevent unearned, excessive profits which the oil companies would receive as a result of decontrol and possible future OPEC price increases, I proposed a windfall profits tax. I further proposed that the revenues generated by that tax be used to establish an Energy Security Trust Fund which will have three major purposes:

• to provide assistance to low-income households who can least afford energy price increases;

• to increase funding for mass transit; and

• to undertake a major program of new energy initiatives and investments which will permit us to develop critically needed alternatives to imported oil.

This Message sets out the detailed specifications of the windfall profits tax and the Energy Security Trust Fund. I look forward to working closely with you to act on this proposal as quickly as possible.

THE WINDFALL PROFITS TAX

SUMMARY OF THE WINDFALL PROFITS TAX

Under the Energy Policy and Conservation Act of 1975 (EPCA), which amends the Emergency Petroleum Allocation Act (EPAA), all authority to control the price of domestically-produced crude oil expires on September 30, 1981. However, as of June 1, 1979, the amount by which oil prices may increase becomes discretionary with the President.

The Department of Energy has been directed to undertake administrative actions designed to phase out controls on all domestic crude oil by September 30, 1981. Department of Energy regulations implementing some of these changes were published in the FEDERAL REGISTER on April 12, 1979 (44 FR 22012). The phased decontrol program will begin as of June 1, 1979 and will extend through September 30, 1981.

In order to prevent oil producers from reaping excessive profits from decontrol a windfall profits tax is proposed. This tax would apply to windfall revenues from sales of lower and upper tier oil which are attributable to decontrol and to revenues from the sales of domestic crude oil which are attributable to any future OPEC price increases in excess of adjustments for inflation.

The gradual deregulation of domestic oil prices will bring the price of oil to world oil price levels, with the following benefits: First, it will eliminate the current subsidy provided to imported oil, which has increased consumption and dependence on foreign supplies. Second, it will encourage producers of oil to seek out additional supplies and to continue production from marginally economic operations. Third, decontrol will phase out the complex system of controls which presently produces inequities and inefficiencies. Fourth, through replacement cost pricing, new sources of energy will come into commercial use, further reducing U.S. dependence on foreign oil. Fifth, it will strengthen the stability of the dollar and reduce balance of payment flows, both directly through reduced oil payments abroad and indirectly through confidence that the U.S. is attacking its energy problem.

However, deregulation of domestic oil prices will also provide enormous windfall gains for domestic producers of oil. These windfall gains will be generated by two aspects of deregulation: First, there are those gains which will result from the lifting of price controls on lower and upper tier oil. Producers of lower tier oil (controlled at an average price of $5.75 per barrel in January of 1979) will be able to sell increasing volumes of their oil at upper tier prices (controlled at an average price of $12.66 per barrel in January of 1979). At the same time, the controlled price of upper tier oil will be allowed to rise gradually to the world price.

Second, there are those gains that may result from the future actions of the OPEC cartel.

It is estimated that deregulation will increase domestic oil producer income before tax by $1.0 billion in 1979, $5.0 billion in 1980 and $9.3 billion in 1981. In order to capture the windfall portion of these increased revenues, a windfall profits tax of 50 percent is proposed. The proceeds of the tax and of increased income tax revenues attributable to higher producer profits during the deregulation period will be allocated to an Energy Security Trust Fund, described later in this Message.

The tax is designed to reduce to the greatest possible extent the complexity and excessive regulation associated with the existing price control mechanism. The entitlements program will be phased out. For purposes of administering the tax it will no longer be necessary to police the price at which oil and oil products are sold. The records that are to be kept will, in large part, be the same records that taxpayers are required to retain for income tax purposes. Finally, because the volume of oil at the lower tier and the upper tier base price will both phase out, only a simple tax will remain in place permanently.

THE DECONTROL SCHEDULE

The phased decontrol schedule is as follows:

• As of June 1, 1979, newly discovered oil will be permitted to receive the world market price.

• The Department of Energy has promulgated a rule under which, as of June 1, 1979, a substantial percentage of production from marginal properties may be sold at the upper tier price. The base production control level against which current production volumes are measured to determine upper tier volumes each month for marginal properties are set at 20 percent of the average monthly production and sale of lower tier crude oil from marginal properties. Marginal properties are those properties which produced below a certain volume of oil per well per day depending upon the average completion depth of all crude oil producing wells on such properties. The schedule of average well depths and average daily production volumes used to determine a marginal property are:

Under 20 barrels/day between 2,000 and 4,000 feet

Under 25 barrels/day between 4,000 and 6,000 feet

Under 30 barrels/day between 6,000 and 8,000 feet

Under 35 barrels/day below 8,000 feet.

• On January 1, 1980, the base production control levels for marginal properties will be reduced to zero and all current production will be eligible for the upper tier price.

• Effective June 1, any incremental new production from wells employing specified enhanced recovery techniques (e.g., tertiary recovery), may receive the world price. Beginning on January 1, 1980, producers who invest in enhanced recovery projects after June 1 may release specified volumes of lower tier oil to the upper tier price in order to finance that investment.

• Beginning on January 1, 1980, the upper tier oil price will increase in equal monthly increments until it reaches the world price on October 1, 1981.

• The Department of Energy has promulgated a rule under which base production control levels for all properties other than marginal properties will be permitted to decline lower tier oil at a rate of 1½ percent per month from January 1, 1979 through December 31, 1979. Between January 1, 1980 and October 1, 1981, the decline rate will equal 3 percent per month.

TECHNICAL EXPLANATION OF THE
WINDFALL PROFITS TAX

1. *Imposition of Tax*

An excise tax will be imposed at the wellhead on the owners of property interests in domestic crude oil (i.e., producers and royalty owners). The tax will not be imposed upon royalties paid to the Fed-

eral government. The tax will be withheld and paid over by the person having responsibility for settling with the various property interest owners under a division order. This is generally the first purchaser.

The person having responsibility for withholding and paying over the tax will deposit the tax semi-monthly with authorized depositories. That person will be required to file quarterly returns setting forth the amount collected and deposited for the return period.

Production from the Alaska North Slope (and any other oil transported through the TAPS line) is excluded entirely from the tax. This is because the transportation costs of bringing this oil to market are high, and the actual price received at the wellhead by producers of such oil is significantly below the upper tier price level.

Since the windfall profits tax is an excise tax, it is deductible for income tax purposes.

2. *Amount of Tax*

One tax is to be imposed at a rate of 50 percent. The tax is to be imposed on the difference between the price at which each taxable barrel of oil is sold and its base price, multiplied by the volume of oil subject to tax. There are three base prices: the controlled price of lower tier oil; the controlled base price of upper tier oil; and, for the production of unregulated oil, the market incentive price.

3. *Oil Subject to Tax*

(a) *Definitions*

The windfall profits tax applies only to crude oil produced in the United States. For this purpose, the United States includes Puerto Rico, all United States possessions and the Continental Shelf.

The terms "crude oil", "lower tier oil", "upper tier oil", "stripper well", and "marginal well" will be defined in the same manner as those terms are defined by current Department of Energy regulations.

(b) *Effective date*

The tax is to be effective on January 1, 1980. It is a permanent tax.

(c) *Tax bases*

Lower tier. Under the President's decontrol schedule, lower tier oil will be released to the upper tier price in accordance with a decline rate applied to the producer's base period control level (BPCL). The BPCL is determined as of January 1, 1979 under recently issued Department of Energy regulations. For decontrol purposes, the decline rate is 1½ percent per month during 1979, and 3 percent per month thereafter.

The taxable volume of lower tier oil will be the volume of lower tier oil freed to the upper tier under decontrol which exceeds the volume of oil which would be freed by reducing the January 1, 1980 volume of lower tier oil by 2 percent of the BPCL per month.

For purposes of computing taxable volume, the 2 percent reduction continues even after price controls expire on September 30, 1981. Consequently, the taxable volume of lower tier oil equals zero at the end of May, 1983.

For purposes of computing the tax on lower tier oil, the base price is the controlled price of lower tier oil. Thus, oil which is now selling below its controlled price will be taxed only on the difference between the former controlled price and the price at which it is sold when freed to the upper tier.

For the period following the termination of controls, a constructive lower tier controlled price, generally based upon the present Department of Energy regulations, will be used in computing the lower

tier base price. The constructive lower tier base price will be adjusted for inflation (as measured by the GNP deflator) by the Secretary of the Treasury in the same manner as the controlled price is currently adjusted for inflation under Department of Energy regulations.

Any lower tier oil released to the upper tier under decontrol and not includible in the lower tier taxable volume will be included in the upper tier taxable volume and will be taxed at that level.

The computation of the windfall profits tax at the lower tier level is illustrated by the following example:

Producer A's BPCL for lower tier oil as of January 1, 1979 is $100X$ barrels per day. Under the Department of Energy decontrol schedule the volume of oil subject to lower tier prices on December 31, 1979 will be $82X$ barrels per day ($100X$ barrels per day less $18X$ barrels per day representing a 1½ percent decline for the 12 months of 1979). During January, 1980 A produces $83X$ barrels per day. Of that production, $4X$ barrels can be sold as upper tier oil, since the lower tier volume for January 1980 is $79X$ barrels per day. One X barrels per day, the difference between the application of the 3 percent decline permitted under the Department of Energy decontrol schedule and the 2 percent decline permitted for purposes of computing the lower tier taxable volume, is the taxable volume of oil. Thus, if the controlled price of lower tier oil in January 1980 is $6 per barrel and the $1X$ taxable barrels per day are sold at the wellhead for $13 per barrel, the amount of tax would be equal to: 50 percent $\times$ ($1X$ barrels per day $\times$ 31 days) $\times$ ($13 per barrel $- $6 per barrel) $=$ $108.50X$. The other decontrolled oil produced in January 1980 (31 days $\times$ $3X$ barrels per day) will be included in the upper tier taxable volume.

The lower tier taxable volume will not include marginal well production nor production that is released beginning on January 1, 1980 in order to finance investment in tertiary recovery. However, this production is included in the upper tier taxable volume. The lower tier taxable volume also will not include production from wells that would be considered to be stripper wells had controls continued beyond October 1981. However, this production is included in the market incentive tier taxable volume.

Upper tier. The windfall profits tax will apply to all upper tier oil beginning on January 1, 1980. The taxable volume of upper tier oil includes *all* upper tier oil except oil subject to tax at the lower tier level. Under the Department of Energy decontrol schedule, beginning on January 1, 1980, the upper tier oil price reaches the world price on October 1, 1981. For purposes of the tax, the controlled base price of upper tier oil is the price at which upper tier oil would be controlled if the Department of Energy decontrol schedule had not been implemented. This constructive upper tier controlled base price will be adjusted for inflation (as measured by the GNP deflator) by the Secretary of the Treasury in the same manner as the controlled price is currently adjusted for inflation under Department of Energy regulations.

The tax at the upper tier level is computed by applying the 50 percent rate to the upper tier taxable volume, multiplied by the difference between the price at which upper tier oil is sold and its controlled base price.

As in the case of lower tier oil which is now selling below its controlled price, upper tier oil will be taxed only on the difference between its controlled base price and the price at which it is sold.

The constructive upper tier base price will increase in monthly increments beginning in November 1986 so that over a 50-month period the difference between the upper tier controlled base price and the market incentive price (see below) will disappear. Consequently, at the end of the 50-month period, the upper tier tax base will be phased out. The Secretary of the Treasury will prescribe by regulations the applicable monthly increments.

The upper tier tax base will not include new production or incremental tertiary production.

Market incentive tier. The market incentive tier tax will be based on the difference between the price at which the uncontrolled oil is sold and the market incentive base price. The market incentive base price for the fourth quarter of 1979 is $16.00 per barrel. This base price will be adjusted for domestic inflation (as measured by the GNP deflator) and determined by the Secretary of the Treasury on a quarterly basis.

The taxable volume of the market incentive tier includes all uncontrolled oil except any oil subject to tax in the lower or upper tier taxable volume and Alaska North Slope oil. The tax at the market incentive tier is computed by applying the 50 percent rate to the taxable volume, multiplied by the difference between the price at which the oil is sold and the market incentive base price.

4. *Application of Other Tax Provisions*

For purposes of computing percentage depletion, gross income is reduced by the amount subject to the 50 percent windfall profits tax.

5. *Revenue Effect*

The gross windfall profits tax will equal $0.4 billion in fiscal year 1980, $1.8 billion in fiscal year 1981, and $3.0 billion in fiscal year 1982. The net windfall profits tax (after reduction for income tax deductions of the excise tax and gain from disallowance of percentage depletion) will equal $0.2 billion in fiscal year 1980, $1.3 billion in fiscal year 1981, and $2.0 billion in fiscal year 1982.

THE ENERGY SECURITY TRUST FUND

SUMMARY OF THE ENERGY SECURITY TRUST FUND

The Energy Security Trust Fund is proposed to be established by statute in the Treasury of the United States to receive on a regular basis the revenues from the windfall profits tax and to receive for fiscal years 1980, 81, and 82, an additional amount to be appropriated from general revenues which will be based on an estimate of additional income taxes paid in 1980, 81, and 82 resulting from decontrol. The Administration will request an appropriation as soon as the windfall profits tax is enacted. The revenues in the Trust Fund will be used for three basic purposes:

• not to exceed $800 million annually for assistance to low-income households;

• not to exceed $350 million annually for additional funds for energy efficient mass transit purposes; and

• a range of energy program initiatives, including those set forth in the White House Fact Sheet issued on April 5, 1979, and additional initiatives, for long-term energy R&D, conservation, and energy-related environmental R&D, which Trust Fund revenues will support.

The Energy Security Trust Fund programs will be undertaken only if the windfall profits tax is enacted and provides (along with the additional corporate income taxes for fiscal years 1980, 81, and 82) revenues adequate to cover full costs. The Trust Fund is being proposed to insure that all revenues resulting from decontrol are used for the specified purposes.

TRUST FUND STRUCTURE AND OPERATION

The Energy Security Trust Fund will be established by statute and will be credited with revenue from two sources:

• all revenues actually received from the windfall profits tax on domestic crude petroleum less tax credit reimbursement; and

• additional income taxes that are estimated by Treasury to be collected as a result of phased decontrol during fiscal years 1980, 81, and 82.

The assistance to low-income households will be given priority on Trust Fund resources.

The total estimated costs for approved Trust Fund initiatives will not be permitted to exceed available resources within the Trust Fund. Total cost estimates by fiscal year will be developed for the expected life of each proposed initiative. The total for all proposed uses of the Trust Fund shall not exceed expected revenue estimates under constant world oil price assumptions.

The estimated out-year costs of approved initiatives will be calculated by year from the first year of the Trust Fund's operation to insure that revenues are adequate to meet commitments. This is necessary because of the substantial out-year costs of certain initiatives such as the shale oil tax credit and the uncertainty about revenues beyond 1985. To the extent that projected resources are in excess of projected commitments, additional energy initiatives which contribute to reducing United States dependence on imported oil may be undertaken. Purposes may include: energy research, development, demonstration, energy related environmental R&D, conservation, etc. All spending from the Trust Fund will be subject to authorization and appropriation in the annual budget process.

The Treasury Department will be responsible for holding the Trust Fund and for current year and long range revenue estimates and for tax expenditure estimates. The extent of resources in the Trust Fund which shall be available for new initiatives shall be determined on the basis of estimates, by fiscal year, of receipts and revenue foregone made by the Secretary of the Treasury, and the total costs of all other demands upon the Trust Fund as determined by the Office of Management and Budget.

Office of Management and Budget responsibilities will include:

• completing reviews of proposed new initiatives and determining whether adequate revenues exist for new initiatives to be undertaken and making recommendations to the President;

• providing annual projections of budget authority and outlays for the life of each approved spending initiative; and

• providing an annual report to the President and Congress describing the operation of the Trust Fund and the projections of future balance.

The Department of the Treasury will be responsible for:

• an estimate for the FY 80–FY 82 period of the amounts of added income taxes paid in consequence of the President's decontrol decision;

• annual estimates of the tax expenditures and foregone excise tax revenues (if any);

• long range revenue estimates updated annually, based on constant real world oil prices; and

• Trust Fund accounting.

Line agencies will be responsible for developing annual budget estimates for approved initiatives, proposing new initiatives for energy purposes if adequate Trust Fund balances are estimated to exist by OMB, justifying Presidentially approved requests before Congress and implementation of appropriated programs. The Department of Transportation will be responsible for developing and implementing the additional mass transit assistance program. The Department of Energy will be responsible for developing and implementing through the normal budget process the energy initiatives specified by the President and other initiatives to the extent permitted by Trust Fund balances estimated by the Office of Management and Budget.

REPORT TO CONGRESS

Each year a full report on Trust Fund projections and activities, will be transmitted to Congress along with any required specific authorization and appropriation requests for approved spending initiatives.

CONCLUSION

Prompt enactment of legislation built on these specifications is essential to a sound energy policy for the future of our country. This initiative is one of the most important of my Presidency.

Taken together, the windfall profits tax and the Energy Security Trust Fund will provide us with the means to move ahead to maximize domestic energy production, to establish stronger conservation habits, and to build toward the day when our reliance on imported oil no longer threatens the very security of this Nation. It will do so in a way which is fair and equitable and which protects the neediest in our society.

The Members of my Cabinet and Senior Staff and I look forward to working with each of you in the Congress to ensure that these vital proposals are quickly and fully enacted.

JIMMY CARTER

The White House,
April 26, 1979.

Windfall Profits Tax and Energy Security Trust Fund

Remarks on Signing the Message to the Congress.   April 26, 1979

THE PRESIDENT. I have just signed a message to Congress asking for the passage of a windfall profits tax and the establishment of an energy security trust fund. This is one of the most important legislative proposals of my administration.

A windfall profits tax is the only thing that stands between the oil companies and a huge bonanza of unearned, unnecessary, and unjustified profits. The energy security trust fund is a bridge between the America of today, dependent on foreign oil and shot through with wasteful patterns of consumption, and the America of tomorrow, in which our technology can make us far less dependent on foreign oil.

Under this proposal, the oil industry will get $6 billion, which should be used for additional exploration for domestic oil and gas. This is a net increase, after all Federal and State taxes are paid. Oil company profits are already high, and, as you well know, they're growing rapidly.

The windfall tax revenue must go to create the energy security trust fund for the American people. This fund will help low-income Americans pay the higher energy costs that will come from decontrol. While decontrol will lessen our reliance on the foreign oil cartel, we cannot, in good conscience, place a new and a harsh burden on those who are fighting to escape poverty.

This fund will also help us to improve our mass transportation and will stimulate development of new and unconventional energy sources. We can make it economical to harness the energy of the Sun, the wind, the tides, and the geothermal power of the Earth.

Increased energy can also come, and will come, from better uses of oil shale, coal, our forests, and our streams. American innovation has given us the greatest industrial capacity on Earth. We must use our technology and our technological daring to solve our present energy problems.

The windfall profits tax will be levied not on American families, but on the oil companies, who are already awash with their greatest profits since the OPEC oil embargo.

The congressional battle over the windfall profits tax and the energy security trust fund will be a classic confrontation pitting the common and public good against the enormous power of a well-organized special interest.

If the oil companies cannot defeat these proposals outright, they will try to gut them so they will have no meaning. This will be an excellent opportunity for the Congress to prove to a sometimes doubtful public that in such a test of political strength, the people's interests can prevail.

Abraham Lincoln once asked his Cabinet, "If you call a dog's tail a leg, how many legs will a dog have?" The Cabinet all responded, "Five." Abraham Lincoln said, "This is wrong. Calling a dog's tail a leg doesn't make it a leg." Calling something a windfall profits tax doesn't make it one if it has the kind of loopholes that you can sail an oil tanker through.

Calling something an energy security trust fund doesn't make it one if it's just an accounting device to pump additional billions of dollars to the oil companies. The American people will not stand for that, and neither will I. That's why I intend to give the Congress my full support as it considers the details of the windfall profits tax and the energy security trust fund.

Equality and fairness demand an honest windfall profits tax. Our country needs an effective energy security trust fund. And I intend to see that we get both.

Thank you very much.

REPORTER. Mr. President, if they pass a bill with some significant plowback in it, would you veto that?

THE PRESIDENT. I will do everything I can to oppose any additional plowback, which is an allocation of money to the oil companies above what they will get, as I said just then. Under this proposal which I have submitted to Congress, the oil companies will already get, in effect, a $6 billion plowback after they pay all their Federal and State income taxes.

So, any further plowback would be a travesty, and I would oppose it to the utmost of my ability.

NOTE: The President spoke at 1 p.m. to reporters assembled in the Oval Office at the White House.

injured. This Administration is committed ultimately to the cessation of such violence and immediately to the relief of those who suffer its consequences.

To address this growing crisis I am asking the Secretary of Health, Education, and Welfare to chair an Interdepartmental Committee on Domestic Violence to coordinate a review of federal programs which currently provide or could provide assistance to victims of domestic violence, and to formulate a work plan by June 15 to guide our future actions. Please designate a policy-level member of your department or agency to serve as a member of this committee with Secretary Califano.

This directive manifests my personal concern that the tragedy of domestic violence be eliminated and its victims be comforted and assisted wherever possible.

JIMMY CARTER

Interdepartmental Committee on Domestic Violence

Memorandum From the President.
April 27, 1979

Memorandum for the Secretary of Defense, the Attorney General, the Secretary of the Interior, the Secretary of Agriculture, the Secretary of Labor, the Secretary of Health, Education, and Welfare, the Secretary of Housing and Urban Development, the Director of the ACTION Agency, the Chairman of the Commission on Civil Rights, the Director of the Community Services Administration

Each year three to six million acts of severe violence occur in American homes. Victims, who represent every race and socio-economic status, are often seriously

United States Advisory Commission on International Communication, Cultural and Educational Affairs

Nomination of Six Members and Designation of Chairman.   April 27, 1979

The President today announced six persons whom he will nominate to be members of the United States Advisory Commission on International Communication, Cultural and Educational Affairs. They are:

JOHN HOPE FRANKLIN, the John Matthews Manly Distinguished Service professor of history at the University of Chicago, author of numerous books, and an expert on the history of black Americans;

LEWIS MANILOW, a Chicago attorney and president of the Museum of Contemporary Art of Chicago;

OLIN C. ROBISON, president of Middlebury College, Middlebury, Vt., and a former Regional Director for the Peace Corps (on confirmation, he would be designated Chairman of the Commission);

NEIL C. SHERBURNE, secretary-treasurer of the AFL–CIO Minnesota Federation of Labor until his retirement in 1978, a member of the board of regents of the University of Minnesota, and active in civic affairs;

LEONARD L. SILVERSTEIN, a Washington attorney, vice president and director of the National Symphony, and a trustee of the Corcoran Gallery of Art;

MAE SUE TALLEY, of Scottsdale, Ariz., former president of the Castle Hot Springs Corp., former publisher and editor of the Arizonian newspaper, and active in civic affairs and support of the arts.

United States Naval Academy Board of Visitors

*Appointment of Two Members.
April 27, 1979*

The President today announced the appointment of two persons as members of the Board of Visitors to the United States Naval Academy for terms expiring December 30, 1981. They are:

PASTORA SAN JUAN CAFFERTY, of Chicago, an associate professor in the School of Social Service Administration and the Committee on Public Policy Studies at the University of Chicago;

WALTER J. LEONARD, of Nashville, Tenn., president of Fisk University.

Clinch River Breeder Reactor

Statement on Action by the House Science and Technology Committee. April 27, 1979

Thursday's House Science and Technology Committee's vote to proceed with construction of the liquid metal fast breeder nuclear reactor at Clinch River was a significant setback to a rational and responsible nuclear energy policy. In spite of forceful leadership by the committee's chairman, Don Fuqua, the members of the committee voted to force continuation of spending at a rate of $15 million per month, or more, for this unneeded project.

The Clinch River breeder reactor is technically unsound. It is a waste of more than 1½ billion of our taxpayers' dollars. It is inconsistent with our nonproliferation policy.

During a time when our attention should be riveted on improving the safety and operation procedures of the light water reactor technology which we now use, the debate over the Clinch River breeder reactor spurred on by special interests has diverted our time and resources toward a new and unnecessary plutonium technology. I have proposed an orderly and scientifically sound breeder research and development program which will make this technology available to us if and when it is needed.

Now we do not need the Clinch River breeder reactor, which was originally undertaken as a crash program to commercialize plutonium breeder reactors. Corners were cut, and designs have been locked into place without the benefit of the scientific improvements which research continues to make available.

We have plenty of time to develop a safe, efficient, technically sound, and proliferation-resistant breeder design. We have an immediate need to make needed assessments of and improve the safety of our current nuclear technology, which the Three Mile Island accident shows are so vitally needed. We do not need to decide now to build a plant based on a wholly new technology about which far less is known than the nuclear reactors we now use.

I want to repeat my longstanding and consistent request to the Congress to deny the strong efforts of the big utilities and energy companies and to terminate the Clinch River breeder reactor. We have a far more immediate task at hand—putting our existing nuclear power policies in order.

I will continue to oppose the construction of this unnecessary, wasteful, and unsound project on the House floor and in the Senate. I urge all those who share my concerns to make their voices heard.

United States-Soviet Union Exchange of Prisoners

White House Statement. April 27, 1979

In accordance with arrangements worked out by the United States Government and the Government of the Soviet Union, the President today commuted the sentences imposed on Valdik Enger and Rudolf Chernyayev, and they are in the process of leaving the country.

At the same time, the Soviet Government has released the following individuals: Mark Dymshits, Alexander Ginzburg, Edward Kuznetsov, Valentyn Moroz, and Georgi Vins, who have now arrived in the United States. The immediate families of the five will join them very shortly.

NOTE: Press Secretary Jody Powell read the statement at 3:50 p.m. to reporters assembled in the Briefing Room at the White House.

Digest of Other White House Announcements

The following listing includes the President's public schedule and other items of general interest announced by the White House Press Office and not included elsewhere in this issue.

April 21

The President went from Plains to Calhoun, Ga.

April 22

While in Calhoun, the President attended the dedication service at the First Baptist Church for his granddaughter, Sarah Rosemary Carter, daughter of Jack and Judy Carter. He returned to the White House in the afternoon.

April 23

The President met at the White House with:

—Zbigniew Brzezinski, Assistant to the President for National Security Affairs;
—Frank B. Moore, Assistant to the President for Congressional Liaison;
—the Cabinet;
—Vice President Walter F. Mondale.

April 24

The President met at the White House with:

—Dr. Brzezinski;
—Mr. Moore, Robert G. Beckel, Special Assistant for Congressional Liaison (House), and William H. Cable, Deputy Assistant for Congressional Liaison (House);
—Representative Martin A. Russo of Illinois;
—Gov. Cliff Finch and Lt. Gov. Evelyn Gandy of Mississippi.

The President met in the Oval Office with Atal Bihari Vajpayee, Minister of External Affairs of India, who was in the United States in connection with the annual meeting of the Indo-U.S. Joint Commission, which he cochairs with Secretary of State Cyrus R. Vance. The President invited Mr. Vajpayee to the White House

731

to exchange views on topics of mutual interest. Mr. Vajpayee brought greetings from President N. S. Reddy and Prime Minister Morarji Desai, and he delivered a letter to the President from the Prime Minister.

The President transmitted to the Congress the annual report for 1978 of the United States-Japan Cooperative Medical Science Program.

April 25

The President met at the White House with:

—Dr. Brzezinski;
—leaders of the Building and Construction Trades Department of the AFL-CIO;
—Mr. Moore, Danny C. Tate, Deputy Assistant for Congressional Liaison (Senate), James C. Free, Special Assistant for Congressional Liaison (House), and Mr. Cable.

April 26

The President met at the White House with:

—Vice President Mondale, Secretary of the Treasury W. Michael Blumenthal, Charles L. Schultze, Chairman of the Council of Economic Advisers, James T. McIntyre, Jr., Director of the Office of Management and Budget, Alfred E. Kahn, Advisor to the President on Inflation and Chairman of the Council on Wage and Price Stability, Barry P. Bosworth, Director of the Council on Wage and Price Stability, and Stuart E. Eizenstat, Assistant to the President for Domestic Affairs and Policy;
—Dr. Brzezinski;
—Mr. Moore, Robert Thomson, Special Assistant for Congressional Liaison (Senate), Mr. Tate, and Mr. Cable;

—a group of Congressmen, to discuss the windfall profits tax proposal;
—Stansfield Turner, Director of Central Intelligence, Hamilton Jordan, Assistant to the President, and Dr. Brzezinski.

The President declared a major disaster for the State of Texas as a result of severe storms, tornadoes, and flooding, beginning on or about April 18, which caused extensive damage to private property.

The President declared a major disaster for the State of North Dakota as a result of severe storms, snowmelt, and flooding, beginning on or about April 11, which caused extensive public and private property damage.

April 27

The President met at the White House with:

—Secretary of State Cyrus R. Vance, Secretary of Defense Harold Brown, Mr. Jordan, and Dr. Brzezinski;
—Dr. Brzezinski;
—Mr. Moore;
—Mr. Schultze;
—members of the United Press International Newspaper Advisory Board (transcript will be printed next week);
—officers of the National Association of Home Builders.

NOMINATIONS SUBMITTED TO THE SENATE

The following list does not include promotions of members of the Uniformed Services, nominations to the Service Academies, or nominations of Foreign Service officers.

Submitted April 25, 1979

WALTER LEON CUTLER, of Virginia, a Foreign Service officer of Class one, to be Ambassador Extraordinary and Plenipotentiary of the United States of America to Iran.

NOMINATIONS—Continued

Submitted April 25—Continued

LAWRENCE A. PEZZULLO, of Maryland, a Foreign Service officer of Class one, to be Ambassador Extraordinary and Plenipotentiary of the United States of America to Nicaragua.

CHECKLIST OF WHITE HOUSE PRESS RELEASES

The following listing contains releases of the White House Press Office which are not included in the issue.

Released April 23, 1979

Advance text: remarks at the annual meeting of the National Academy of Sciences

Released April 24, 1979

Advance text: remarks at a commemorative ceremony for Days of Remembrance of Victims of the Holocaust

Released April 25, 1979

Advance text: remarks at the annual convention of the American Newspaper Publishers Association

Advance text: remarks at a town meeting in Portsmouth, N.H.

Advance text: remarks at a New Hampshire State Democratic Party fundraising dinner in Bedford

Released April 26, 1979

News conference: on the proposed windfall profits tax and energy security trust fund—by Stuart E. Eizenstat, Assistant to the President for Domestic Affairs and Policy, Elliot R. Cutler, Associate Director for

CHECKLIST—Continued

Released April 26—Continued

Natural Resources, Energy and Science, Office of Mangement and Budget, Donald C. Lubick, Assistant Secretary of the Treasury (Tax Policy), and Alvin L. Alm, Assistant Secretary of Energy for Policy and Evaluation

Fact sheet: proposed windfall profits tax and energy security trust fund

Released April 27, 1979

Announcement: nomination of Reynaldo G. Garza to be United States Circuit Judge for the Fifth Circuit

Announcement: nomination of Jon O. Newman to be United States Circuit Judge for the Second Circuit

Announcement: nomination of Patricia M. Wald to be United States Circuit Judge for the District of Columbia Circuit

Announcement: nomination of Marvin E. Aspen to be United States District Judge for the Northern District of Illinois

Announcement: nomination of Valdemar A. Cordova to be United States District Judge for the District of Arizona

Announcement: nomination of Curtis W. Guyette to be United States Marshal for the Middle District of Pennsylvania

Announcement: nomination of Carolyn D. Randall to be United States Circuit Judge for the Fifth Circuit

---

ACTS APPROVED BY THE PRESIDENT

NOTE: No acts approved by the President were received by the Office of the Federal Register during the period covered by this issue.

PRESIDENTIAL DOCUMENTS

Week Ending Friday, May 4, 1979

Interview With the President

Remarks and a Question-and-Answer Session With Members of the United Press International Newspaper Advisory Board. April 27, 1979

THE PRESIDENT. I would like to say, first of all, that I'm grateful that you would come here. You represent an organization that's extremely important to our country.

Many of you—I think some of you, at least—were in New York when I made an address earlier this week on SALT. It was a very fine occasion for me to relate to the American people just one of the many issues that I, as President, have to face almost on a daily basis. This is one of the most important, but a typical foreign affairs issue. We've got others of a domestic nature, which take up by far most of my time.

ADMINISTRATION POLICIES

Right now we're dealing with the energy question, trying to evolve, hammer out over a long period of time a comprehensive energy policy for our country, which has been hotly debated, perhaps one of the most controversial issues that Congress has ever faced, and one of extreme complexity.

I think with the decontrol mechanism, which will be implemented beginning the 1st of June, and with the passage of the windfall profits tax, with the creation of an energy security trust fund, we will make another major stride forward in having a policy that will restrain waste of energy, shift away from heavy dependence—even growing dependence on foreign oil—escalate the production of oil and gas in our own country, shift to more common supplies of energy already known about, existing in our country, and also let us open up an avenue of increased use of energy sources with which we're not presently fully acquainted or which are economically not feasible.

In the process, we can provide aid for the poor people who will be particularly hurt in the next number of months by the decontrol of oil itself. The estimate that I made in April of the revenues for the Federal Government from the windfall profits tax was slightly below what we will realize from the message that I sent to Congress yesterday. We'll get about a hundred million dollars per year more than we had anticipated with the fact sheets that we used to brief the press back in April.

In general, for the oil that is decontrolled, the increase in price—for each

735

dollar, the Federal Government will get about 55 cents. The industry will realize about 25 cents, roughly. We can't tell exactly, because part of the tax, as you know, is predicated on how much OPEC prices go up above and beyond the inflation rate. If they continue to rise relative to the inflation rate, the tax levies would be proportionately higher.

This leaves the oil industry, as a result of decontrol, after they pay Federal and State taxes, about $6 billion, which should and I hope will be used to invest in increased production of oil and gas in our country.

Another major problem that I face at this point is the economy. We had very good news today on our balance of trade position. We've been heavily emphasizing increased exports, and we've been encouraged by the trends. We've also been very encouraged by the stabilization of the value of the dollar since we took strong action last November. And as you know, the gross national product of our country is sound and, we think, is increasing at approximately the proper rate, one that we would choose if we could arbitrarily select one.

The inflation rate is very high. Most of the inflation does come from the items over which we have and can have no control—commodity prices traded on the international markets, oil prices, the price of food products that are heavily affected by adverse weather conditions, like the extremely severe winter weather, and low beef herds that are a result of the price controls that were imposed 5 or 6 years ago.

But we have been very encouraged with the response, both of the working people of our country and also of management, in trying to hold down wages and prices under the voluntary system. It does have teeth. It is effective. And I think we have

been blessed by having it. It's not always perfect; we've had to evolve it in a hurry. But the response from the business community and the labor community has been encouraging to us.

I think the best thing for me to do now is to respond to any questions that you might have. I'll try to be brief and to the point, and I'll recognize you arbitrarily.

QUESTIONS

U.S.-MEXICAN RELATIONS

Q. Mr. President, the relations with Mexico are very important in our energy program. We heard there for quite a while that Portillo was making statements, and we were countering. I haven't heard, really, lately, where that situation stands. Have we improved our relations? Have there been any new negotiations with Mexico on their oil exports?

THE PRESIDENT. Compared to the reports in the press, the situation was already improved. [*Laughter*] It never has been nearly so bad as it was projected immediately prior to my visit there. But there seemed to be a wave of reporting that swept the country, almost in an uncontrollable fashion. And when I was there, meeting for literally hours in a harmonious relationship with López Portillo, he and I were both deeply concerned about the exaggeration of differences between us.

Obviously, Mexico has a rapidly increasing prospect for development—domestic consumption and also the exporting of oil and gas. What they do about these factors—exploration, production, and distribution—is entirely and completely a decision for them to make. They guard this prerogative very jealously. And I agree completely. We do not want to get involved in that.

Whatever gas and oil they desire to sell, we are ready to be good customers. We already buy about 85 percent of all the oil that Mexico exports. And we have an advantage as a customer because of the proximity of our country to Mexico.

As they produce oil, because of the configuration of their oil and gas deposits, they inevitably produce more gas. They need a market for this gas. And we want to treat Mexico fairly in the price. The original proposal by Mexico on how to price gas, I did not think was the best for American consumers. As a result of deregulation of natural gas, brought about by the energy legislation last year, we now have a very good supply of natural gas in our own country. We did not need to buy Mexican gas on a crash basis at a price that would have greatly escalated not only [the price of] [1] the gas from Mexico but all the gas produced in our country.

So, we are now negotiating on a daily basis in a spirit of harmony and cooperation with Mexico for contracts to buy increasing supplies of Mexican gas in the future. So far as I know, and I've had reports almost every day, these negotiations are on track. We want to buy their gas in a way that protects the interests of American consumers; Mexico certainly wants to get as high a price as they can for it.

But I've got a problem in that the price we pay for Mexican gas will heavily influence the price demanded for domestically produced gas and, also, the price for natural gas that we buy from Canada, and the price for gas that we will ultimately bring down through Canada into our country from Alaska.

So, it's a complicated problem, and the fact that we didn't yield and immediately accept the highly favorable price

---

[1] Printed in the transcript.

of natural gas, looking at it from a Mexican perspective, was strongly condemned in our own country. I was protecting the American consumers, and I think our judgment was right. And now we have a very good, continuing relationship with Mexico on this and many other issues.

RHODESIAN ELECTIONS

Q. Mr. President, on the recent Rhodesian elections, do you consider that they were a step in the right direction? And do you see any possible recommendation on your part if there's a change in what you have not recommended?

THE PRESIDENT. Let me say that I think it was a step in the right direction, yes. I would rather not comment on the elections yet, because we are still assessing how they were conducted and whether or not the extant legislation, primarily the Case-Javits amendment, has been honored or not.

The law requires me to wait until the new government is installed before I make a judgment to the Congress and to the American people on whether the new election results were adequate. So, let me defer that question, because the law requires me to do so. But it was certainly a step in the right direction.

PRESIDENT'S HEALTH AND EXERCISE

Q. Sir, with all these problems, I am curious to know how you find time to go jogging—*[laughter]*—what time of day you do it, and how often, and how far have you gotten up to now?

THE PRESIDENT. Well, I'll be brief. The most I jog in one day is 10 miles. Ordinarily, I jog 4 miles. When I'm on vacation—down in Georgia, I averaged about 6 miles.

When I'm in Jerusalem, or Cairo, or Mexico City, or Alexandria, or Guadeloupe, or wherever, we generally jog about 35 or 40 minutes, early in the mornings. When I'm around the White House here, it's more convenient for me to jog later on in the afternoon, 4:30, 5 o'clock. I enjoy it. And I don't have any present intention of going above 10 miles, because of the time constraints; that takes me about an hour and a half.

I might say that I called Bill Rogers the other day after he won his magnificent, third Boston Marathon, and congratulated him. And he said he was still sore.

Sometimes I get sore as well. But I'm in good shape. I've deliberately dropped my weight down to about 148, which is what the doctors say I ought to do, and my pulse rate has dropped about half—well, from 60 down to 40. So, I feel better; enjoy it.

My wife jogs an average of about 2 miles a day. Her longest distance is 4 miles, but that was in the mountains, and it's pretty hard to jog in the mountains.

It's been a good sport for me. It has a minimum requirement for time, compared to almost any other sport of that much exercise.

PRESIDENT'S CAMPAIGN ACTIVITIES

Q. Mr. President, this week you had one or two political appearances in the Northeast. I come from California, where we have an evolving foreign policy on Africa. [*Laughter*] I'm wondering if you intend to step up your campaign activities and appearances in California in the months ahead?

THE PRESIDENT. No. I don't intend to make any campaign appearances in the foreseeable future. But I am going to be out in Los Angeles before too long, as President. We've had this trip planned for

a good while. I'll be stopping in Iowa on the way for some events there.

I have habitually taken advantage of an opportunity as President to have things like townhall meetings not only in our own country—in Mississippi, in Massachusetts, in New Hampshire, in Oregon, and so forth—but also in other countries, places like West Berlin, where I had just an open, free-style townhall meeting. And I might possibly have one in Japan when I go over there later on in June. But I'm going to stay out of the campaigning business for a while.

PRESIDENTIAL TERM OF OFFICE

Q. Mr. President, in light of an upcoming campaign, do you feel that Presidents of the future should have their terms limited to one, maybe 6-year term, so that you wouldn't have the possibility of——

THE PRESIDENT. I didn't use to think so, even after I became President. But I've begun to realize lately that if I could just, by the stroke of a pen, change the Constitution, I think one 6-year term would be preferable. The reason is that no matter what I do as President now, where I am really trying to ignore politics and stay away from any sort of campaign plans and so forth, a lot of the things I do are colored through the news media and in the minds of the American people by, "Is this a campaign ploy or is it genuinely done by an incumbent President in the best interests of our country without any sort of personal advantage involved?"

I think that if I had a 6-year term, without any prospect of reelection, it would be an improvement. This is the case in some countries, as you know. And I've come to that conclusion reluctantly, not that I have any inclination to avoid a campaign if I decide to run in the future, but because of that reason that I've described to you.

And there are some others as well. I think it would strengthen my hand with the Congress. The lameduck aspect doesn't concern me at all. And I think there could be some appropriate constitutional prohibitions against trying to be a kingmaker and being involved in choosing one's own successor.

This, for instance, applies in Venezuela, where there is a prohibition against involvement in a succeeding campaign. So, 6 years would be better, I think.

CONGRESSIONAL TERMS OF OFFICE

Q. Do you feel that should go for the Hill, too?

THE PRESIDENT. I'm sorry?

Q. For Congress?

THE PRESIDENT. No, I think not. I would personally not want to. The Senate, obviously, has 6 years. I think it's good for the House to be constantly campaigning. I think one branch of the Congress ought to be constantly under the political pressure of maintaining contact with the people back home. It's onerous for incumbents, but I think it's good.

NEW ENGLAND ENERGY PRICES

Q. Mr. President, in New Hampshire the other day, you said that the disparity of energy prices in New England and the rest of the country would decrease in the future. That led to some speculation that the prices themselves would be less in New England than they are now. Is that the impression you intended to leave?

THE PRESIDENT. No, I didn't. I think if you read what I said, I was very careful to say that prices would increase in the future and we had to use less oil. I eliminated all special taxes on imported oil. We had already eliminated part of it; fees, they're called. And I think with a more ready distribution of oil throughout our country, that the difference in prices will be lessened.

We have now a situation where New England imports about, I think, 80 percent of all the oil they use. And they are heavily dependent on oil for major power production, as contrasted with other parts of the country where they use more coal and natural gas. I think New England now uses about 2 percent natural gas. Georgia, just as a contrasting interest, gets 85 percent of its electricity from coal. Not only does New England use 80 percent oil, but they also import 80 percent of all the oil they use.

So, I think the new energy program, with increasing supplies coming in from Canada, with the pipelines that we can evolve, with increased uses of alternate energy sources, improved quantities of domestic oil and natural gas, decreased dependence upon imported oil, the use of forest wood, low-height dams—all this will help to reduce the wide disparity in prices of energy paid by New England. But in general, all of the prices for energy in our country have gone up and will go up.

I might point out that all increases that have taken place now that cause consternation among our people have taken place under control legislation. And I think that our new opportunity to create the energy security fund will let us help to alleviate these disparities.

WAGE AND PRICE GUIDELINES

Q. Mr. President, the economy, as you have mentioned, is a serious problem. And by some, the voluntary wage and price mechanism is seen as less than a complete success, with the Teamsters contract and with others pending. Is there a next step in this battle, or what is your plan to attempt to combat rising inflation?

THE PRESIDENT. Well, we've only had 6 months, I think roughly 6 months, since the day I announced the voluntary price and wage standards. I have been very pleased at the results. We called originally for the corporations to have a deceleration program, to cut back on the increase in prices a half a percentage point below what they did the previous 2 years. The present standards are more stringent than that. We have monitored all of the Fortune 500 corporations, and now, an increasing number of the medium-sized and smaller corporations in our country.

We have found remarkable compliance. I think we are now looking at about 13 of those corporations about which there is some doubt. Three or four, we believe, have been out of compliance. One or two of those three or four have, in the last 2 days, agreed to modify their price structure and to comply. In a few instances, they have made rebates to their customers when they overcharged.

I called a major company in the United States yesterday to tell them that we thought they were out of compliance and that we were going to announce this fact in the near future. The executives of that company asked me for one more chance to come and meet with our wage and price people to see if they couldn't work out a way to get in compliance.

The Teamsters settlement is one that also caused us a great deal of concern. I don't want to get involved in exactly whether they did or did not specifically comply with the guidelines. The guidelines, in my opinion, without a doubt at all, have drastically reduced, substantially reduced the settlements, compared to what they would have been without the guidelines.

We are going to fight in every instance, to the limit of my ability, to keep prices and wages within the guidelines. And I think there's been a general tone of support. General Motors, for instance, sent out, early this month, letters to 22,000 of their suppliers, stating that they themselves, General Motors, were going to comply completely with the guidelines, and they encouraged all their suppliers to do so. And in the process of that, I think their attitude will have a beneficial effect on the United Automobile Workers union, later, when the negotiations take place.

I'm not trying to predict what's going to happen. But a common commitment to holding down inflation, I think, is a patriotic gesture, and I've been pleased so far.

Let me say that there's no way that I can control or would want to control prices that are traded internationally, like lead, zinc, molybdenum, silver, gold. I can't control oil prices. Most of our products that are produced in our country of a same nature, like beef, where there's a worldwide shortage of beef herds, or soybeans, corn, wheat, or timber products—these are the kind of things that you cannot control, no matter how much you try, even if you had legislation.

So, I think among those items that we have an ability to control, through voluntary standards, we have been remarkably successful. And I'm very proud of that program. I think we'll begin to see results. But it's going to be a few more months before tangible results can be ascertained.

One other point I'd like to make is that we gave the companies some flexibility. For instance, in mail-order catalog companies—and there are literally hundreds or maybe thousands of those around the country—as you know, they print up the catalogs 6 months ahead of time. You can't expect them to abolish all of those price systems. And also, we let the companies, in order to get compliance agreements from them, have the option, over a period of time, to initiate the price increases at the beginning, first of all, of a year; then we cut it down to the beginning of a 6-month period; and lately, we've modified that, that they agreed to have the price increases only in 3-month increments, which holds down the impact.

So, I've been pleased so far. Inflation is my biggest domestic problem. I don't know an answer to it that's easy. And I think that we will have a growing realization that our wage and price standards are working. I think they're working.

NUCLEAR ENERGY

Q. Mr. President, 15 or 20 years from now, when we're looking back on the Three Mile Island accident, what do you think the significance of that episode will have proved to have been in terms of the role of nuclear power in this country?

THE PRESIDENT. I think you realize that the number of new nuclear plants purchased in our country in the last few years has been almost nonexistent. I think in 1 year, the year I became President, there were no orders placed domestically for new powerplants. We now have, I think, 70, 72, that are operable, and others being constructed.

When I ran for President in '76, on the same ballot with me there were 22 States that had referenda where the people themselves were trying to consider, "Should we authorize any nuclear plants in our State, or should we prohibit them, or under what circumstances should they be authorized?" I think the Three Mile Island accident will help to clear the air.

I think this report—which will not have to wait 20 years, but will be coming to me within 6 months—will accurately determine the cause of the accident; the defects in administration immediately following the accident by the Nuclear Regulatory Commission, the Federal, State and local government agencies, the power company; the way that facts were revealed by those officials to the press, and the way the press related them to the public; whether there was an excessive amount of concealment of the facts, whether that concealment was deliberate or not; I think, the design criteria, the operation criteria; whether or not the NRC has adequate authority, whether they exercised that authority properly. I think all these questions that had been festering for literally years, maybe even more than a decade, will now be resolved to a substantial degree.

The American people still believe, by a substantial majority, even immediately following the Three Mile Island incident, that there is a place for nuclear power in the production of energy in our country. And I think that following this incident, many of those questions—I'll use the word "festering" again—will be answered.

The Congress is about to make a serious mistake, in my opinion, in launching us into a plutonium society. The Clinch River breeder reactor is a proposal which was well under way before I became President. I have tried to stop it because of the reason I've just described to you. It's a brand new technology that advances far beyond the light water uranium reactor into a very complicated new technology—liquid metal, a coolant with plutonium, which in my opinion wastes over $1½ billion of American taxpayers' money. And I hope that the new sense of concern will help to stop that wasteful project. In the meantime, we will continue to promote safety of the light water plants, and we'll continue our research and development program for the breeder reactor, which is a plutonium reactor, so that it can be built in our Nation if and when in the future we need it. We do not need it now.

So, I think the answers will come quickly, they're long overdue.

Ms. PEEK. Thank you, Mr. President.

THE PRESIDENT. Thank you.

NOTE: The interview began at 1:20 p.m. in the Cabinet Room at the White House. Linda K. Peek is Special Assistant in the Office of Media Liaison.

The transcript of the interview was released on April 28.

National Association for Equal Opportunity in Higher Education

Remarks at the Association's Annual Dinner. April 28, 1979

If I could think of one group which is most responsible for the transformation of the United States of America from a racist and segregation society to a free and integrated society, I would say it's this group whom I'm addressing right now.

The black colleges of our country and the black churches of our country several years ago, several decades ago, several generations ago, stood firmly and courageously and innovatively for what was right and decent. It was not an easy thing for you to do nor for your predecessors to do. But you have indeed transformed our country, and I thank you for it, because one of the consequences of these changes that I have just described is that I, as a southerner and an ex-Governor of Georgia, was made a viable candidate. And I would not be here as President tonight if it had not been for you.

As you know, I have been on many of your campuses as a candidate and since I've been President. And when I couldn't come, I sent some of my best representatives—recently, for instance, to Tuskegee; my mother has been there as a visitor, the Vice President's been there as a visitor. And as Wade Wilson[1] knows, I'll be speaking at Cheyney State for graduation exercises shortly if the invitation is still good. [*Laughter*] I will try to behave myself the next 30 days, Wade, so I can— [*laughter*]——

I know you've been here almost 3 days, and I know how important your visit to Washington is to you and to me and to the people of our country. My own commitment is not just to make the President and the Vice President and the special members of the White House staff available to you to help when you are in trouble, nor to provide a constant, easy avenue of communication and consultation, advice, counsel, and criticism even when you're not in trouble, in time when crises do not exist, but I want to be sure that every single agency of the Federal Government is tuned to your needs and to your hopes and aspirations and desires and to the dreams of your students and the parents who love them.

I pledge to you that whenever there is a problem which I myself can address or the leaders in my Cabinet who have met with you can address, that I'm available to you personally, and so is Vice President Mondale, and so are all the members of my staff.

My major disappointment is that I will not be here to hear Judge Higginbotham's address. And I know how he is admired by all of you. We have made every effort, through his leadership and others like him, through your honoree tonight, Mary Berry,[2] and others like her, to open up the councils of government in posi-

---

[1] President, Cheyney State College.

[2] Assistant Secretary for Education, Department of Health, Education, and Welfare.

tions of top leadership, where policy is made to the black citizens of our country, who have too long been excluded. When those private groups met, policy was decided before the public was aware of the questions even being discussed. And in the regulatory agencies of our Government—some of which I have no control except to appoint the members; the FCC, the CAB, and others—I'm trying to open up those to the voice of the minority groups of our country.

I can't always meet your demands. If I could, then I would say that your demands were not quite stringent enough. [*Laughter*] I know that you have never been timid in letting me or my predecessors know what you expected. [*Laughter*] But that's part of the American life, and that's why so much progress has been possible.

I'm eager to serve you well. I pray to God, my brothers and sisters in this room, that I will never be a disappointment to you nor to those whom you serve so well and who look to you not only for present leadership and guidance but for future leadership and for an even greater United States of America in the years to come.

Thank you very much.

NOTE: The President spoke at 9:25 p.m. in the Crystal Ballroom at the Washington Hilton Hotel.

White House Correspondents Association

Remarks at the Association's Annual Dinner. April 28, 1979

President Aldo, incoming President Ralph:

Very few people can comprehend the awesome responsibilities which must be borne by a President of the United States.

My duties in an average day indeed vary from the sublime to the ridiculous. [*Laughter*]

I have just come, a few minutes ago, from addressing the distinguished black education leaders of our Nation. As you know, the predominantly black colleges literally transformed the United States, our societal structure, from one of hatred and division and segregation, into one of progress and hope, freedom and peace. I would say that the motivations of these men and women and their achievement, their purpose in life, literally approached the sublime. And now I have come to address—the White House correspondents. [*Laughter*]

Members of the Cabinet, Congress, other distinguished American citizens, and also the remaining survivors of last year's White House correspondents dinner— [*laughter*]—I understand this is the 65th White House correspondents banquet, and it's obvious that many of the founding fathers are here tonight. [*Laughter*]

I'm honored to be here to substitute for Jody Powell. [*Laughter*] I notice a few chuckles. I am sure that you may remember Jody—Jody Powell. He's the one who filled in for me last year, and I hope you don't mind my substituting for him this year. [*Laughter*]

The quality of his performance will never be forgotten. And I must say with regret that it has had an obvious impact on your treatment of my administration during the last 12 months. [*Laughter*] I want to thank you very much. Yeah, thanks a lot! [*Laughter*]

As a matter of fact, Jody picked up most of his best lines from some of the most emotional moments in the Oval Office as we discussed the performance of the press. It became obvious to me last year in reading the reports of the previous White House dinner that some people

743

simply cannot recognize a joke. Other people can. We are, therefore, after contemplation, considering some substantial changes in the makeup of the White House senior staff. [*Laughter*]

Although I prefer not to call any names, in order to hold down the enthusiasm of the group, I can say that in the foreseeable future, the population of Vienna, Georgia, will grow by about 2 percent. [*Laughter*] I understand that Atlantic Monthly has already made him an offer. [*Laughter*]

Seriously, I have to admit that Jody does have some good ideas. For instance, he has literally been encouraging me to reopen the indoor White House swimming pool—[*laughter*]—suddenly, as a matter of fact—[*laughter*]—during one of his briefings. Any survivors, of course, would be permitted to have permanent swimming privileges. I would have to personally arrange to put you on the swimming schedule. [*Laughter*] Come to think of it, I probably should not have kicked Jim Fallows [1] off the tennis court. [*Laughter*]

A lot of people genuinely just do not understand the awesome responsibility of the President of the United States. As you know, I'm really very busy. But only some great world crisis could have kept me from coming here this evening. As a matter of fact, Dr. Brzezinski almost got fired this afternoon because he couldn't find one. [*Laughter*]

Of course, I also hated to meet [miss] [2] the Los Angeles fundraising banquet last month. Competent investigative reporting may some day reveal the real reason that we presently have a Mideast peace treaty. After all, I guess if I could go to Jerusalem and Cairo to make peace, that I could come to the Washington Hilton for the same purpose. [*Laughter*] But you're a tougher group than the Knesset. I just

---

[1] Former White House Chief Speechwriter.
[2] Printed in the transcript.

thank God that they don't drink so much. [*Laughter*] As a matter of fact, you're more like my own Knabinet—[*laughter*]—I mean, Cabinet.

But I've noticed that alcohol, even a lot of alcohol, doesn't seem to affect your judgment very much. You're still able, under conditions of either sobriety or otherwise, to concentrate about with the same facility on the important issues of the day. [*Laughter*] You are always trying to root out that genuine insider's background story. And tonight to show my good will, I'm going to give you such an inside story—off the record, of course, so put away your crayons. [*Laughter*]

In 1980, as you may have heard, the most important position of public leadership in America will once again be open, and we must continue to have strong leadership. However, image is obviously just beginning to be a factor. Now, that John Connally is a master. But on my own, without using my staff, I have discovered his secret. I noticed a few months ago that he parts his hair on the left side. [*Laughter*] And I decided, again on my own—I must take full credit for this—to eliminate this insidious Republican advantage by a bold stroke of the comb. [*Laughter*] The result has been truly remarkable. For 2 weeks after I took this action, neither my wife nor my barber noticed the change. But the best result was that Sam Donaldson no longer recognized me at all. [*Laughter*]

In spite of this episode, which is interesting, I think you will admit the better members of the press seldom miss a trick. You probably already have surmised that this change from right to left is only for the primaries—[*laughter*]—and then for the general election, right down the middle. [*Laughter*]

With responsibilities of statecraft constantly on my shoulders, I really get annoyed, though, with this kind of political discussion or political problem. Even Amy, my little daughter, has been asking me why everyone talks about John Connally or Ronald Reagan or Jerry Brown instead of about me. And I've explained to her very carefully, "I'm only the President, they're candidates." But then she just looks at me, and she says, "Yes, but, Daddy, Teddy Kennedy is not a candidate." [*Laughter*]

I wish you wouldn't laugh at her. She's only a little child. [*Laughter*] She's really not old enough to understand the awesome responsibilities that fall on the shoulders of a President of the United States.

For instance, I get a lot of calls from world leaders. Just last night, Jim Callaghan wanted me to get Tip O'Neill to endorse Mrs. Thatcher. [*Laughter*] And this morning, as soon as I got up, Prime Minister Ohira was on the phone calling to be sure that when I go to Japan in June, that Linda Ronstadt will be with me. [*Laughter*] I've not yet gotten the answer from Rosalynn.

But I have found a way through experience and through long discussions to explain to these foreign leaders why we have such colorful opposition within my own party. This is California's way of celebrating the Year of the Child. [*Laughter*]

A lot of people keep asking me if I'm running. And I keep asking them, "Running what?" [*Laughter*]

You understand better than most the awesome responsibility that falls on the shoulders of a President of the United States. And that's why your understanding and our closeness is the reason that I'm becoming increasingly interested, personally, in our Nation's news media—the television, radio, newspapers. As a matter of fact, to illustrate my own interest, I've recently asked Fred Kahn to take a care-ful look at your advertising rates and at your first quarter's profits. And I can assure you that you will be hearing from us very shortly. [*Laughter*]

Inflation is really tough. It's just one of my many problems. A lot of people just don't understand this awesome responsibility of being a President. But at least I'm living proof that the President, even in this modern, turbulent, confused America, still has tremendous powers of influence and persuasion. Just take, for instance, the most recent wage guideline dispute. I can tell you in complete candor, and I hope some degree of confidence, that I had no trouble at all in persuading the Teamsters to consider my position before they put their guidelines into effect. [*Laughter*]

I'm not the only one, by the way, who's interested in the news media. A lot of people were puzzled that the Supreme Court would suddenly permit prosecutors to peer into the contents of reporters' minds, and frankly, so was I. I didn't even know the Court had a sense of humor. [*Laughter*]

My most conservative friends were really shocked at the ultimate consequences of this action. And I agreed with them, that, of course, you couldn't just let anyone know what was found. They are already demanding a law, for instance, to protect children under 18. For my part, I promise never to ask what you have in your mind when you write about one of my programs if you won't ask what was in my mind when I thought it up. [*Laughter*]

Well, you're certainly not the only one in trouble with the law. They're looking into my peanut business, just like they're looking into editors' minds. But you and I know we have nothing to fear. We both know they won't find anything. [*Laughter*]

Which reminds me of Bob Strauss. [*Laughter*] Many of you know him, and you'll have to admit that he is an ideal man, under the circumstances, to inject into the problems of the Middle East. He got stuck with this position when he sold the fewest number of tickets to the big state dinner in the circus tent. [*Laughter*] And that was not the only disappointment for me. This event actually delayed our "energy plan of the month." [*Laughter*] We had to wait until after this fundraiser—and you can well understand this—before announcing the windfall profits tax. They thought it was "You scratch my back, I'll scratch yours." [*Laughter*]

This careful scheduling arrangement does show that I've learned a lot about the oil companies. And I may have made some unfair accusations against them. Of course, I wouldn't admit this in public. I have learned, for instance, that they really never wanted to buy a circus; they were really after the Congress and just got confused. [*Laughter*]

And speaking of confusion, I would like to say in all sincerity that you, the White House correspondents, are some of my best and closest friends. We have a wonderful, almost unprecedented personal relationship. "I'm proud of you." [*Laughter*] As a group, I consider you one of our Nation's treasures. And I'm working on plans to develop for you a permanent and a suitable homeland. [*Laughter*]

It's been a pleasure being with you tonight and to have shared a few quiet moments on this solemn occasion. In our day-to-day dealings with each other, we occasionally—in our day-to-day dealings with each other, we often—in our day-to-day dealings with each other, we almost always aggravate the hell out of each other. [*Laughter*]

And sometimes we do engage in what Washington semanticists call an adversary

relationship. But as President of one of the greatest nations on Earth, I hope that we never forget that the people who founded this country planned it that way. This Nation of ours would be unimaginable without a free and a vigorous press. That's why, when the Founders wrote the Bill of Rights, they made the first amendment the lead. And may that never change.

We have a lid until 9 o'clock Monday morning. [*Laughter*]

Thank you very much.

NOTE: The President spoke at 11 p.m. in the International Ballroom at the Washington Hilton Hotel. In his opening remarks, he referred to Aldo B. Beckman, president, and Ralph Harris, incoming president of the White House Correspondents Association.

White House Conference on Library and Information Services

Appointment of Helen Meyer as a Member of the Advisory Committee. April 30, 1979

The President today announced the appointment of Helen Meyer, of South Orange, N.J., as a member of the Advisory Committee of the White House Conference on Library and Information Services.

Meyer is editorial consultant to Doubleday & Co., and former chairman of the board of Dell Publishing Co.

Permanent Committee for the Oliver Wendell Holmes Devise

Appointment of Paul J. Mishkin as a Member. April 30, 1979

The President today announced the appointment of Paul J. Mishkin as a member of the Permanent Committee for the

Oliver Wendell Holmes Devise for an 8-year term.

Mishkin, 52, of Oakland, Calif., is the Emanuel S. Heller professor of constitutional law at the University of California at Berkeley. He is a member of the Supreme Court Historical Society.

The Committee was established by Public Law 84–246, of August 5, 1955, to administer the fund bequeathed to the Treasury by Justice Holmes. The fund is to be used for the preparation of a history of the Supreme Court by distinguished scholars and financing annual Oliver Wendell Holmes Lectures.

Father's Day, 1979

Proclamation 4659.   April 30, 1979

By the President of the United States of America

A Proclamation

We live in a time of transition for the American family, but the strength and stability of a healthy, loving family life continues to remain the bedrock on which our society is organized.

The evolving roles of men and women in our society have posed new challenges and opened new opportunities, for fathers as well as mothers. To the degree that mothers are assuming a more active role in the nation's workforce, fathers are being asked to play an even greater role in the upbringing of their children. At the same time, they continue to carry out their traditional duties of helping to support their families financially, emotionally and spiritually.

Traditionally, our nation each year sets aside Father's Day as a special time to honor America's fathers.

The character of each of us has been molded and shaped in part by our own fathers. Father's Day is a time for all of us to reflect on the sacrifices our fathers have made on our behalf. It also is a time for fathers to receive that most precious gift, the love and gratitude of those they have nurtured and protected for so many years.

Now, THEREFORE, I, JIMMY CARTER, President of the United States of America, do hereby request that Sunday, June 17, 1979, be observed as Father's Day. I direct Government officials to display the flag of the United States on all Government buildings on this day and I urge all citizens to display the flag at their homes and other suitable places.

IN WITNESS WHEREOF, I have hereunto set my hand this thirtieth day of April, in the year of our Lord, nineteen hundred and seventy-nine, and of the Independence of the United States of America the two hundred and third.

JIMMY CARTER

[Filed with the Office of the Federal Register, 2:30 p.m., April 30, 1979]

THE PRESIDENT'S NEWS CONFERENCE OF APRIL 30, 1979

ENERGY CONSERVATION

THE PRESIDENT. Good afternoon, everybody. I have a brief opening statement concerning one of our most important domestic issues, and that is energy.

Last month, I sent to the Congress, as requested by the Congress, a standby gasoline rationing plan. This plan would give us the opportunity to anticipate and to plan for possible gasoline shortages in the future. Without the plan, it would take us 6 or 7 months to prepare such a plan if we were faced with a severe shortage of gasoline brought about by an interruption in supplies.

Tomorrow, the House commerce committee will have another very important vote to determine whether or not we will even have a standby plan to deal with such an emergency. It's imperative for our Nation's energy preparedness that the committee approve this standby gasoline rationing plan.

If, after the plan is evolved, it needs to be implemented, both the Congress and the President would have to approve before it goes into effect. It's a simple matter of common sense for us to do everything we possibly can to reduce our vulnerability to another oil embargo or a Middle East crisis or an interruption in our own domestic supplies. We do not face any of these contingencies now, but we must be prepared for the worst. We must make certain that gasoline can be distributed promptly and fairly in case of an emergency.

No one likes gasoline rationing, and we will avoid it if it is possible. But I will not hide from my responsibility to the Nation, and Congress likewise needs to shoulder its share of the responsibility.

It's not easy to vote for a rationing plan. I understand this. But the tough votes are never easy. The Nation's attention will properly be focused on the House commerce committee tomorrow, and I urge the members of that committee to place responsibility for the Nation's well-being above all other concerns and to vote to approve the standby rationing plan.

I also urge the Congress to pass the three other standby energy conservation plans that I submitted last month. I'm particularly concerned about the possibility that the standby plan for gasoline conservation might be killed. This plan would be implemented only in the States

that fail to develop their own plans for conserving gasoline, and then only in case there are severe shortages.

But we face the possibility of gasoline shortages even as early as this summer, and common sense tells us both that my administration and the Congress must do our part if we are to be ready.

Now, Mr. Pippert [Wes Pippert, United Press International], I'd like to answer your questions.

QUESTIONS

OIL PRICE DECONTROL

Q. Mr. President, I'd like to ask you further about the fairness, the simple justice of your gasoline decontrol proposals.

THE PRESIDENT. Good.

Q. First, gasoline already is nearing a dollar a gallon at the pumps. And this will not keep the wealthy from driving, because they can and probably would pay $2 or $3 a gallon. But these prices put a tremendous burden on the ordinary person. Is this fair?

And secondly, you've used strong language in talking about oil companies and the excess profits that they stand to gain from decontrol. Yet an analysis by the Treasury Department shows that when its application on all categories of domestic oil are considered and an adjustment is made for using some of this tax to offset Federal income taxes, the net effect is that the new tax would recapture only about 10 percent of the windfall profits. Is this fair?

THE PRESIDENT. I think in both instances the answer is yes, it is fair, as well as we can devise an equitable plan to deal with an unfortunate subject.

The allocation of scarce supplies of energy must be done in the light of intense public scrutiny and after close consultation between myself and the public, and myself and the Congress. Any action that the Congress can take to make the rationing plans or the allocation plans or the conservation plans more fair, I would obviously be glad to accommodate these improvements.

Now, as far as the net effect of the windfall profits tax is concerned, we decided to decontrol in a phased way the prices of gasoline and other energy supplies based on oil in accordance with the congressional mandate, the congressional law that was passed and approved in a previous administration. I think this is necessary action to be taken. We also recognize that one of the purposes of such action is to increase domestic production. There cannot be a confiscatory tax to take away all the proceeds that would go to the oil producers as the decontrol takes place.

We tried to balance it as best we could, and I believe we've done an excellent job. Whenever a dollar is realized in increased revenue, resulting from decontrol of oil prices, under our proposal, the windfall profits tax proposal, the oil companies would retain 29 cents. That 29 cents out of each dollar is designed to be invested back into increased production of domestic oil and gas. The other part of the dollar would go for Federal taxes, local taxes, and the payment of royalties.

I might say this in closing: I don't claim that this is a perfect proposal. If, during the hearing process and during the passage of legislation, the Congress is able to make the tax more stringent, I would look with favor if the proposals are fair. If the Congress has an inclination to make the tax less stringent—in other words, to let the oil companies keep more of the profits—I would strongly disapprove.

TRADE WITH SOVIET UNION AND CHINA

Q. Mr. President, what are the prospects right now for an early extension of most-favored-nation trading status to the Soviet Union and China?

THE PRESIDENT. I personally favor the extension of the most-favored-nations treatment to both the Soviet Union and China if it can be done in compliance with existing law.

I think it's good for us, for our country, to be able to export more goods, to provide more jobs for our own people, and to improve the relationships between ourselves and foreign countries, including the Soviet Union and China, brought about by increased economic interchange or trade.

So, when the time comes that I think these requirements can be met, I would personally favor the extension of most-favored-nations to these two countries.

Q. Might that time come soon?

THE PRESIDENT. I hope so, yes.

STRATEGIC ARMS LIMITATION

Q. Mr. President, can you provide any more enlightenment on our ability to verify SALT; and are those within the administration who say this ability is, say, from 1 to 4 years away, are they wrong?

THE PRESIDENT. Well, the Secretary of Defense made a statement concerning 1 year. That was applying to specifically how rapidly we could overcome the setback resulting from the loss of our Iranian monitoring stations. But in the same brief statement, he replied to a news question that as soon as the SALT treaty is effective, when it's signed and ratified, we would be able to verify the treaty adequately.

There is no doubt in my mind that this is the case. I would not sign nor present to the Congress or to the American people any treaty which in my opinion could not be adequately verified from the first day it's effective. Many of the concerns that we have relate to very complicated questions. For instance, we can't guarantee that every time a test missile is launched by the Soviet Union, that every aspect of that flight can be completely comprehended by us.

There are limits on what we can do. But as the Secretary of Defense has testified publicly, in order for the Soviets to develop any kind of significant new missile, they would have to have like 20 to 50 test launchings. And during that process, it is a very high likelihood that we ourselves would be able to detect any violation of the SALT treaty.

There's another factor that must be considered. If the only purpose of the Soviet Union in the long, tedious negotiations of a SALT treaty is to have a document that they can violate and that's their only purpose in existence, is to violate the SALT treaty, it would make our problem much worse. But there is an element of rationality and stability, because the Soviets know that if we ever detect any violation of the SALT agreement, that that would be a basis on which to reject the treaty in its entirety; there would be a possible termination of the good relationships between our country and the Soviet Union on which détente is based; and it might very well escalate into a nuclear confrontation.

So, the consequences would be very severe, and that is an additional constraint imposed upon the Soviet Union and on us that strengthens my statement that we can verify. But absent that very important factor, we can still verify to our complete satisfaction the SALT agreement through various means that we have available to us.

Q. Mr. President, you've been quoted by historian James MacGregor Burns as saying that even if the SALT treaty is rejected by the Senate, that you would abide by its terms. I would like to know how far you would go in this. Would you, for instance, abide by the limitations on the range of land- and sea-based cruise missiles? And more generally, don't you think abiding by a treaty that's been rejected by the Senate would amount to thwarting the will of the public?

THE PRESIDENT. I have no inclination to minimize the importance of the constitutional processes whereby treaties are negotiated by the Executive and ratified or rejected by the Senate.

My belief is that the treaty will be sound enough when it's completely scrutinized by the public and the Senate, that it will be ratified. If, because of some factor that I cannot anticipate, the treaty is not ratified, then I would do all I could, monitoring very closely Soviet activities, to comply with the basic agreements reached.

It would certainly not be proper for me, if the treaty were not ratified, to immediately launch our country into a massive nuclear arms race. And the constraints placed on me and the Soviet Union, monitored very carefully by each other, would be a basis on which to constrain ourselves and to avoid such a nuclear confrontation in the absence of a treaty. But I still believe that we will have the treaty.

SOVIET DISSIDENTS

Q. Mr. President, can you tell us, sir, how the list was arrived at concerning which Soviet dissidents would be released in exchange for the two Soviet spies? And in view of this exchange, you're now hopeful of gaining the release of other Soviet religious and political dissidents such as Mr. Shcharanskiy?

THE PRESIDENT. We've not forgotten any human rights activist in the Soviet Union who is being punished or imprisoned.

The recent exchange was the result of long and tedious and detailed negotiations extending, I would say, at least over a 6-month period. The final agreement was approved personally by me and, I presume, by President Brezhnev. The identity of the human rights activists who came here from the Soviet Union was one that was the subject of detailed negotiation, where the Soviets would put forward names and we would assess those names and repeatedly reject them because we did not think they were adequate.

In my final judgment, reached just a week or so ago, I felt that the list of names was a fair exchange and, therefore, approved them. And I cannot tell you any more detail than that about the negotiations.

STRATEGIC ARMS LIMITATION

Q. Have you considered taking your SALT case to the public next year to try to get a Senate that would approve the treaty?

THE PRESIDENT. No. I have every intention to conclude the SALT negotiations at the earliest possible moment. No one has ever seriously considered, in my administration, to my knowledge, any slightest delay in concluding the SALT treaty for political purposes or for any other purpose. And my understanding is that if the SALT treaty can be concluded fairly early, that it will be considered as a very top priority by the Senate, and the action by the Senate will be concluded this year.

JAMES FALLOWS

Q. Mr. President, how do you respond to the statements by Jim Fallows, who was your chief speechwriter for more than 2 years, on a number of things, but specifically that while you hold specific positions on a number of individual issues, that you have no broad, overall philosophy about where you'd like to see the country go? And on another point, Fallows says that you signed off personally on the use of the White House tennis courts, but you told Bill Moyers that you didn't. What's the truth about that?

THE PRESIDENT. Let me say, first of all, that I think Jim Fallows is a fine young man. And he didn't express these concerns to me while he was employed by us. This is the kind of question that has to be faced by any President when someone leaves the White House. It's happened many times in the past.

Jim Fallows and I agree on most things. His assessment of my character and performance is one of those things on which we don't agree—[*laughter*]—and this is unfortunate, but understandable. He left the White House employment with a very good spirit of friendship between me and him, and with no insinuation that there were things about which he was disappointed.

The White House tennis court: I have never personally monitored who used or did not use the White House tennis court. I have let my secretary, Susan Clough, receive requests from members of the White House staff who wanted to use the tennis court at certain times, so that more than one person would not want to use the same tennis court simultaneously, unless they were either on opposite sides of the net or engaged in a doubles contest.

PRICE AND WAGE GUIDELINES

Q. Mr. President, you have said frequently in the past that you wouldn't hesitate to point out people, organizations that are not complying with your wage and price voluntary guidelines and that you think are helping to add to inflation.

THE PRESIDENT. That's right.

Q. Yet, if I'm not mistaken, I have not heard you do so yet. Can you today tell us any organization, any labor union, any company that you think is letting the American people down in this regard?

THE PRESIDENT. Every week since we have had our voluntary wage and price standards in place, I have had a meeting with my top economic advisers—an early morning breakfast meeting once a week— at which time we discuss in some detail the degree of compliance both of the top businesses of our Nation and also the important unions of our Nation.

I think the last report that we had was that there were 13 companies who may or may not be out of compliance. We have inquired to the executives of those companies, telling them about our concern. This is done through the Council on Wage and Price Stability.

We then give them a chance to respond either to justify their price, which we think might be too high, or to change their prices if we can demonstrate to them that their prices are indeed too high.

Last week when we had this meeting that I'm describing now, there were four companies that we thought were out of compliance. The only one that we were sure had not at that time achieved compliance was Sears. I called executives of Sears and pointed this out to them, told them that I had seen the data and in my opinion they were not in compliance.

They asked for a chance to meet again with the Council on Wage and Price Sta-

bility personnel, and they modified their prices to come into compliance. I do not know at this point of any company where we can prove that they are out of compliance because they modify their prices, or either convince us that they indeed are meeting the guidelines.

Wages—this is a voluntary program, and I do not want to get involved in wage negotiations. Only Wayne Horvitz, who is the Federal mediator, is authorized by me to do so. But we make our position very clear when a major wage negotiation is approaching that we consider this or that demand to be either within or not within the guidelines, and we let this position be known publicly.

I think that this is the proper procedure, and we will continue to do so. It has applied in the case of the Teamsters. It's now applying in the case of the rubber workers. It will apply in the future in the case of the United Automobile Workers. And when they are doubtful about whether a particular proposal does come within the guidelines, they make an inquiry. But neither I nor the Secretary of Labor nor Alfred Kahn nor Barry Bosworth gets involved in the actual negotiations themselves.

We're doing the best we can. It's not perfect, but I think we've made a great deal of progress.

WINDFALL PROFITS TAX

Q. Mr. President, Senator Kennedy, in his speech this afternoon before the American Society of Newspaper Editors, says that you have been intimidated by the oil lobby into throwing in the towel on price decontrol without a fight and that your proposed windfall profits tax is but a token that is no more than a transparent figleaf over vast profits by the oil industry.

Do you think that's unfair, that criticism is unfair?

THE PRESIDENT. That's just a lot of baloney. [*Laughter*]

I really can't believe that Senator Kennedy said this unless the phrases were taken out of context, because everyone knows who's in the Congress that decontrol is mandated in the present law, controls to be terminated in October of 1981. This is not a decision that I made. I am complying with an existing law. And in order to minimize the impact of decontrol, we are carefully and slowly phasing out controls over roughly a 28-month period.

I have made a proposal to the Congress which, in my judgment, is eminently fair. It lets the oil companies keep 29 cents out of every dollar of increased revenue which they derive from decontrol. As I said earlier in this news conference, if the Congress, including Senator Kennedy, wants to tighten up on that windfall profits tax with their proposals that I consider to be fair, I will gladly support such more stringent windfall tax proposals. I will not support any move in the Congress to make the windfall tax more lenient on the oil companies.

But I have a responsibility as President to make the best judgment on what needs to be done in the future and to comply with the Federal laws when I make decisions for the present. And I'm always amenable to proposals made by Senator Kennedy or anyone else to make the laws fairer or more stringent if the Congress thinks they should be made more stringent.

STRATEGIC ARMS LIMITATION

Q. Mr. President, on Capitol Hill today, a number of Republican Senators who say that they are uncommitted on SALT II were critical of Admiral Turner, the director of intelligence. They claim that he has been making speeches around the country in support of the treaty, and they feel that he should not get involved in what may become a partisan issue.

What is your understanding of Admiral Turner's role? Is he an advocate of SALT II? And if so, is this at your direction?

THE PRESIDENT. No. I've never asked him to make any such speech. I think, as is the case with almost every major official in the Federal Government—in the executive branch, at least—they are called upon to make speeches on matters of great moment and importance to the people. Even in the case of the CIA Director, responsible for intelligence, he's not confined just to expressing an opinion on collection techniques, most of which are highly secret in any case.

I don't know what comments Admiral Turner has made. I happen to know that he's basically in favor of the SALT treaty.

WINDFALL PROFITS TAX

I might say, to get back to the previous question about the Congress attitude toward the windfall profits tax, this is not an easy question to address, but we've made a lot of progress in the last 2 weeks.

When the windfall profits tax was first mentioned, when I started talking about it back in April, there was an almost unanimous opinion expressed on Capitol Hill that no windfall profits tax could be passed, and those of you in the media reported these comments, and now some of those very same people who said that it was not possible for a windfall profits tax to be passed at all are now quarreling about whether we should take from the oil companies 29 cents out of each dollar, or 25 cents or 24 cents or whatever.

But I think we've made great progress in the last 2 weeks in selling to the American public, and therefore to the Congress, the need for the windfall profits tax just because I have spoken out strongly and fervently and with deep feeling on the subject.

So, we're making good progress. And I'm eager to work with the Congress on how to make my proposals even better.

ENERGY, FOOD, AND HOUSING PRICES

Q. Mr. President, among the inflation figures, the most stubborn seems to be those of food, fuel, and housing, and those also seem to be the least susceptible to controls of any kind. Is there no hope for progress in this area until those prices become so high that people can't afford the things they really need?

THE PRESIDENT. There is some hope in the area.

Fuel, to a major degree, is affected by oil prices established by an international cartel over which we have very little control. However, we can reduce our dependence on foreign imported oil by the implementation of a sound national energy policy. I've worked on that for 2 years.

In food, I would say one of the major leading items in food price increases has been beef. And every agricultural economist, every farmer knows that the main cause for high beef prices is sustained high demand and very low sizes of American beef herds. It takes 5 or 6 years to slowly build up your breed cows, and then to have an increased herd to produce more beef.

One of the causes of the present shortage was the price controls imposed upon beef under the Nixon administration, and at the time, the farmers sold their brood cows and heifers instead of keeping them for future beef production.

Pork, because of the short gestation period of swine, and poultry, with an even shorter period of increase in production, can be increased fairly rapidly, and I've been very pleased at how fast those two items particularly are being increased. The production of fish for American consumption is a slower process, because it depends upon the habits and the number of fishing boats and fishermen available in that industry.

So, I think we've got a good prospect in the future for food prices to drop somewhat, or at least the price levels not to rise so rapidly.

This past winter and the previous winter, coincidentally, were two very severe periods of adverse weather, and this additionally affected food in the case of perishable vegetables and fruits.

Housing—we have had in the last 2 years a rate of housing construction of over 2 million per year in spite of high interest rates and high prices. And this has provided an increased demand for lumber, for plywood, for insulation materials, and for all other building materials that go into home construction. Recent statistics, unfortunately, show that the rate of construction of housing is dropping off. This will decrease demand if the trend continues to be less than, say, 2 million per year. And we are trying within the Federal Government to increase the rate of production of timber.

So, although we don't control these three items that you mentioned, there are elements that we can now detect that indicate some hope for the future after several months go by.

ISRAELI SETTLEMENT POLICY

Q. Mr. President, the Israeli Cabinet has recently approved two new settlements on the West Bank. In light of the enormous cost to the United States of implementing the Egyptian-Israeli peace treaty, isn't it reasonable to expect the Israelis to cease from settlement policy which violates international law? And secondly, why should the American people pay for policies of the Israelis that undermine the peace process and run counter to American foreign policy?

THE PRESIDENT. Well, the position of the United States historically has been consistent, and my own position on settlements in the West Bank, Gaza area and on the Golan Heights, and in the Sinai have—my position has been consistent. The Israeli Government knows perfectly well, after hours of discussion on this issue, what my position is.

We do consider the creation of Israeli settlements in these areas as being inconsistent with international law, and, as I've said many times, they are an obstacle to peace. Knowing that, the Israeli Government still on occasion authorizes new settlements. They interpret the law differently from myself.

I hope that the Israeli Government will severely restrain any inclination, either approved by the Knesset or done without legal sanction, in establishing new settlements. But there is a limit to what we can do to impose our will on a sovereign nation.

RHODESIA

Q. Mr. President, the administration position on the Rhodesian election has been, until now, that you are assessing the situation. Can you tell us, though, however, whether you personally are inclined to lifting sanctions against Rhodesia, recognizing the new government there, and if you do do that, what impact do you think that will have on your Africa policy? Won't it cause you severe troubles for what you've been trying to do on that continent?

THE PRESIDENT. I am constrained by the law to wait until after the new government is established before I make a decision on whether or not the recent elections have been adequate in my judgment to lift the sanctions. And we are now going through a very careful process of assessing the conduct of the elections themselves and also the consequences of the election.

I'm not going to comment any further on it than that, but I will say that we have not varied our position that the Government of Rhodesia ought to be established through democratic principles, the election should be held with all parties willing to vote or run for office being permitted to do so, and that this should be based on the one-person-one-vote principle.

We have worked in consonance with most other Western nations—all, so far as I know—and closely with the British, who have a legal responsibility for Rhodesia. We have kept the United Nations informed, and I think that our position is a proper one. But after the new government is installed in office, at that time I will make a judgment under the Case-Javits amendment and decide whether or not I think the elections were enough progress toward those principles that I've just described to warrant the lifting of sanctions. I cannot make that judgment at this time.

FRANK CORMIER [Associated Press]. Thank you, Mr. President.

NOTE: President Carter's forty-eighth news conference began at 4 p.m. in Room 450 of the Old Executive Office Building. It was broadcast live on radio and television.

Department of Education

Statement on Senate Action on the Legislation. April 30, 1979

I applaud the Senate's vote in support of a separate department of education. This department will bring tighter management to more than 150 Federal programs. It will eliminate the bureaucratic duplication necessitated by the current organizational structure. It will cut redtape for States, local governments, and others who deal with Federal education programs. It will make one Cabinet official responsible full-time for the effective, economical management of programs which cost the American taxpayer $13 billion annually.

Today's Senate vote confirms the inadequacy of the existing administrative structure. I would like to thank Senators Ribicoff and Byrd for giving this very important legislation the priority it deserves. I hope the House will move quickly to ensure that Federal education programs receive the full-time management attention and accountability that they clearly require.

United States Sinai Support Mission

Message to the Congress Transmitting a Report. May 1, 1979

To the Congress of the United States:

I am pleased to transmit herewith the Seventh Report of the United States Sinai Support Mission. It covers the Mission's activities during the sixth-month period ending April 1, 1979 in fulfillment of obligations assumed by the United States under the Basic Agreement signed by Egypt and Israel on September 4, 1975. This Report is provided to the Congress in conformity with Section 4 of Public Law 94–110 of October 13, 1975.

The Egyptian-Israeli Peace Treaty signed in Washington on March 26, 1979, which supersedes the 1975 Basic Agreement, calls for the United States to continue its monitoring responsibilities in the Sinai until Israeli armed forces withdraw from areas east of the Giddi and Mitla Passes. This withdrawal is to be completed within nine months from the date of the exchange of instruments of ratification. In the meantime, the United States will continue to discharge its responsibilities in the Sinai in the same objective and balanced manner that has characterized the operations of the Mission since its inception in early 1976.

This year, funding of the Sinai Support Mission is authorized under Chapter 6, Part II of the Foreign Assistance Act, "Peacekeeping Operations". Careful control over program costs is expected to reduce expenditures by at least $500,000 below the amount appropriated for Fiscal Year 1979.

The Mission will be closed sometime next year, thus completing a successful U.S. initiative begun over three years ago. All Americans may be justly proud of the U.S. contribution to peacekeeping in the Sinai, and I know the Congress will continue its support of the Mission until the end of this important phase in the search for peace in the Middle East.

JIMMY CARTER

The White House,
    May 1, 1979.

NOTE: The report is entitled "Report to the Congress—SSM: United States Sinai Support Mission" (20 pages plus annexes).

Federal Election Commission

Nomination of Two Members.   May 1, 1979

The President today announced two persons whom he will nominate to be members of the Federal Election Commission (FEC). They are:

Thomas E. Harris, of Alexandria, Va., for reappointment to a term expiring April 30, 1985. Harris, 66, has been a member of the FEC since 1975. From 1948 to 1975, he was associate general counsel with the CIO, then the AFL-CIO.

Harris received an LL.B. from Columbia Law School in 1935. He practiced law with several firms and also worked for the Justice Department, the Federal Communications Commission, and the Office of Price Administration before joining the CIO.

Frank P. Reiche, of Princeton, N.J., for a term expiring April 30, 1985. He would replace Vernon W. Thomson, whose term is expiring.

Reiche, 49, is an attorney specializing in taxation and estate planning, and chairman of the New Jersey Election Law Enforcement Commission.

He received an LL.B. from Columbia Law School in 1959, and also holds a master's degree in foreign affairs from George Washington University and a master of laws degree in taxation from New York University Law School. He has been with the Princeton firm of Smith, Stratton & Wise since 1962.

Reiche was a member of New Jersey Governor William T. Cahill's Tax Policy Committee from 1970 to 1972. He was a Republican county committeeman for 8 years.

Law Day, U.S.A., 1979

Remarks at a White House Reception. May 1, 1979

My instructions were to be here at 3 o'clock, and I think I'm right on time. But I think you all know that I've been providing employment for the Attorney General for the last 2 years or so as a favor to the people of Georgia—*[laughter]*—and the country, and I think to keep him busy for a few minutes is not out of keeping with our relationship in the last few months.

Mr. Chief Justice and Attorney General Bell, President Tate, distinguished members of the United States Supreme Court, Senator Kennedy and other Members of Congress, distinguished attorneys from around our country, and other guests who are interested in the functions of our system of justice in this Nation:

I'm indeed pleased to have you here.

This is not my first Law Day speech. *[Laughter]* And this is always a moving experience for me to meet with professional members of our community who are responsible for our system of justice, as someone who is not an attorney, but who is intensely interested as a life's commitment to realizing the benefits of and enhancing the quality of the legal system.

Today all elements of the legal system are present, from the most distinguished and famous judges, perhaps, in the world, the enforcers of the law, the writers of new law, those who interpret the law through administrative action, private attorneys who are interested in the protection of the rights of corporations and the protection of the rights of indigents, those who are concerned about the elimination of racial or other discrimination, those who are concerned about the quality of our environment, those of you who in a voluntary way are committed to the improvement of the system of justice itself. All of us together share a great responsibility.

Sunday I went to church with a man who 48 hours before was in the Soviet Union as a prisoner.[1] He was in a cattle-car being moved from one part of Siberia to another. And Sunday morning he was worshipping with us.

On occasion, I teach a Sunday school lesson, and it just happened that for many weeks, I had planned to teach this lesson. I described to the class, him included, that the highest purpose of a government, the highest goal that a government or societal structure could hope to achieve is justice. It's an end in itself; it's a means to an end; and it's a pursuit which is never completely realized. There are always challenges to it brought about by the fallibilities of human beings, the intense pressure of competition in a free society, the constraint of liberty where freedom does not exist. It's a responsibility on us, as it is on the shoulders of the leaders of every nation on Earth.

The deprivation of justice is a serious matter. It can be observed, if we are sensitive, by those of us who don't suffer much from it, who quite often, perhaps inadvertently, benefit from a deprivation of justice, because those who are with power or with wealth or with social prominence are very likely to benefit when an advantage is meted out in a competitive society by the perhaps less reputable influence of our peers who, in representing themselves for some advantage, cause those advantages to accrue to us.

And if we stand silent and reap the benefits of injustice, then we ourselves are equally culpable with those who initiated the injustice for their own direct benefit and with deliberation. And those who suf-

---

[1] Ukrainian Baptist leader Georgi Vins.

fer from it are the poor and the black and those who can't speak English well, those who are timid or inarticulate, perhaps even illiterate.

We tend to have an attitude in our own country to take great pride in what we are, and that pride is justified. But we also tend to think that in each millennium, each generation has reached a pinnacle of achievement and all the discriminations that in the past afflicted our society have in general been removed. That's obviously not the case. But when women were given the right to vote, there was a general sense in our Nation that we had indeed eliminated the last vestige of discrimination, not recognizing the facts that black people in many parts of our country couldn't even register to vote or, if registered, couldn't vote without an overt display of personal courage on Election Day. And many of us were part of that system that approved or condoned deprivation of rights in perhaps the freest society on Earth.

Today there are still deprivations of justice brought about by confusion, by delay, by complexity, by design, by a demand for personal wealth in order to obtain adequate legal counsel, the remnants of racial or sex discrimination, the dominance of the powerful over the weak—those elements of concern still exist in the United States. And a Congressman or a Governor or a President sees examples of that quite often, and when someone like myself raises the question, quite often the final answer is, "Well, that's the law. That's legal." It concerns me. And I know it concerns you as well.

But with that concern should come action and determination and sacrifice and commitment and a proper degree of courage to challenge the existing system, sometimes when it arouses the displeasure of one's own immediate peer group; because it's not a matter of mutual condemnation when we strive for a higher standard of justice, because a human being has a higher standard that might be reached than justice. A human being can reach a degree of commitment and equality and friendship and ultimately justice, but a human being can also reach love, a genuine desire to sacrifice for others, and to represent in the purest possible form God's ultimate law on which secular law is almost always based.

We are all striving together to contribute as best we can to improve our system, because we love our country and we've seen the results of challenge in the past, even challenge to the law as it existed, to change it for the better.

I have a unique responsibility, almost in the history of our country, with the exception, perhaps, of the first Presidents, to choose and to nominate to the Senate about one-third of the total Federal judges in our country. The Attorney General, I, Members of the Senate, advisory commissions, many of you in the ABA are trying to perform this duty well, because it can shape the quality of justice in our country for many years to come.

First of all, I'm concerned about the quality, the wisdom, the knowledge, the training, the experience, the sensitivity of people whom I nominate. And with that commitment unshaken, I am also concerned about equity of opportunity and a representative group of Federal judges. It's time for women to be adequately represented, those who speak Spanish, and the black. And for a Senator or for a selection committee of the most distinguished citizens to choose district judges to say, "Well, I cannot find a qualified black, because there are none who serve in the State court system, or there are none who have had 20 years' experience

in a distinguished law firm," this in itself is a reason to perpetuate a travesty of justice, because basing present discrimination on past discrimination is obviously not right.

I might err on a few occasions in appointing a woman or a black to the Federal court who doesn't prove to be as efficient or as effective as they might have been, because they've not been given the opportunity in the past to prove themselves or to get experience as a white Caucasian has. But I'll do the best I can to avoid that mistake, because my own experience in politics—and I know yours in the judicial system, the justice system—has been that when a person is finally given an opportunity, he or she ordinarily performs very well.

Well, in closing, let me say this: There's no way to prevent change in the law. There's no way to prevent changes in a societal structure, in economics. There's no way to prevent change in politics. But change can be for the better if there's a determination to realize that goal.

James Madison wrote, as he was explaining to the American people the essence of our Constitution, that either justice had to be enthusiastically pursued or our liberty would be lost. And Thomas Jefferson said that law, in order to be effective in its administration, had to be simple, so that it could be understood by, as he said, the common man, and it had to be based not on technicalities, but on common sense.

We've reaped great benefit from the wisdom of our Founding Fathers, and I hope we won't forget the simple lessons which they taught us, because a modern, fast-growing, ever-changing, technological world is naturally inclined to be extremely complex. And the deciphering of the complexities among those who are privileged can accrue to them great benefits at the expense of others unless our system of justice performs well.

I'm very proud that I am able to share these responsibilities with you. I'm in good company, and I thank God that we live in a nation where individual concern, individual aspiration, individual ideals, individual ideas and initiative can be harnessed in the most heterogeneous society that the world has ever known in a nation of refugees toward the common good.

We've got a lot to be thankful for, and I hope, working together, we can give an even greater basis for thanks for those whom we serve and those who follow us in service in the greatest nation on Earth.

Thank you very much.

NOTE: The President spoke at 3:02 p.m. in the East Room at the White House. In his opening remarks, he referred to Chief Justice of the United States Warren E. Burger, Attorney General Griffin B. Bell, and S. Shepherd Tate, president of the American Bar Association.

Agency for International Development Personnel System

Message to the Congress Transmitting Proposed Regulations. May 1, 1979

To the Congress of the United States:

Pursuant to Title IV of the International Development and Food Assistance Act of 1978, I transmit herewith regulations affecting the personnel system of the Agency for International Development, together with explanatory information. The purpose of these regulations is to extend the Foreign Service personnel system to all employees of AID in the United States and abroad who are responsible for planning and implementing AID's overseas development program and activities.

These regulations provide that by October 1, 1979, all positions in AID shall be designated as to the personnel service in which the incumbent should serve. Positions will be designated as Foreign Service unless the position is in the United States and unless it is determined that the functions of the position are primarily of a support character and can be performed without significant overseas experience or understanding of the overseas development process, or that the position requires continuity of incumbency and specialized knowledge and skill so that it is impractical to assign the incumbent abroad. The regulations provide that, when positions so designated for Foreign Service incumbency become vacant, appointments to them will be made under the Foreign Service Act. In this manner, the Administrator will be able progressively to bring to bear important field experience in the development process to key policy positions in Washington, thereby strengthening policy development and management and providing more interesting and challenging careers. These regulations, which have been prepared after extensive consultations with the appropriate committees of the Congress, are designed to have no adverse effects upon the existing rights of employees of the Agency.

The personnel regulations I am presenting today are an important step in strengthening the administration of our foreign assistance programs. As you know, I am also proposing, under the Reorganization Act of 1977, an improved organizational structure for those programs. I urge the Congress to consider favorably both of these measures to enhance the efficiency and effectiveness of our economic assistance to developing countries.

JIMMY CARTER

The White House,
   May 1, 1979.

NOTE: The proposed personnel regulations are printed in the FEDERAL REGISTER of May 4, 1979.

Visit of Prime Minister Masayoshi Ohira of Japan

Remarks at the Welcoming Ceremony.
May 2, 1979

THE PRESIDENT. This morning it's a wonderful pleasure for me, on behalf of the people of our Nation, to welcome to our country, to our Capital City, the distinguished Prime Minister of Japan, Mr. Ohira, and his wife; and also members of his government who've come to consult with us on matters of great import to the people of both countries.

This welcome is extended to you, Mr. Prime Minister, with our deepest feelings of a common purpose and a realization of the importance of the friendship which binds us together. We are especially honored because this is your first trip abroad after assuming your new responsibilities.

The United States and its people have a great admiration for the people of Japan. We recognize your deep commitment to the principles of democracy. We trust the basic motivations and ideals of your country. We are proud of the close cooperation which we have seen exhibited in times of testing and trial, and I believe that this cooperation bodes good for the other people of the world.

Our people are naturally friends. There is an innate appreciation of one another,

from the highest levels of government and business to the average tourist who always comes back from a visit to the other country with a sense of hospitality and welcome having been extended.

Our own Nation's security and yours are both enhanced by this close relationship. And, of course, in international political affairs, in economics and trade, we share common problems and we share common opportunities.

We had a large group of Asian Americans who came to visit me a few minutes ago before this ceremony. And I pointed out to them that our Nation is blessed by approximately 4 million Asian Americans, who have enriched our country. And I also pointed out to them that our Nation is a country of refugees. We look upon the Pacific Ocean not as an obstacle to be overcome, but as a broad highway which we can use with freedom and with ease to bind our countries even closer together in the future.

We are dependent on trade. As you know, I, as you, have been a farmer during most of my life. There are more acres of food being produced for Japan in the United States than there are acres of food being produced in Japan for Japan.

We value the wonderful market which you extend for agricultural products. There are more exchanges between the members of the American Congress and the Diet of your country than between. any other two legislative bodies on Earth. We consider the relationship with Japan to be the cornerstone of the implementation of American policy throughout Asia. And as you may know, these interrelationships extend on a personal basis. My daughter, Amy, studies violin as a beginning student under the direction of the great Japanese teacher Suzuki.

We have some economic problems between us. They are being thoroughly discussed. They are important. They are being addressed without timidity and without concealment. But I have no doubt that the bases which I've already described as a foundation for our interrelationship will serve with certainty as a basis for resolving our present economic differences.

I'll be going to Japan in June for an official visit at your invitation, which I certainly appreciate. I hope to have a chance personally to prove to the Japanese people the importance that we attach to their own personal friendship toward us.

And you and I will be meeting with five other leaders of great nations at an economic summit further to pursue some of the ideas that I've outlined so briefly.

The Japanese people are almost uniquely vigorous and disciplined and productive. And they combine these overt characteristics of strength with a certain grace and quietness and a degree of personal humility and an appreciation for beauty and art and culture that has aroused the legitimate admiration of the people of our country.

Above all, we appreciate the Japanese influence for peace, your commitment to peace which serves as a standard for other nations to emulate.

We have in the past, we do now, and we will in the future strengthen one another because of shared ideals, and I'm sure that we will continue in the most profound way to help one another. We're glad to have you here.

In Japan, this is Golden Week, a week dedicated to holidays and joy. And we hope that in addition to your visit being fruitful in the diplomatic and economic and security area, that it will also be a visit of joy for you personally.

Welcome, Mr. Prime Minister, to our country.

THE PRIME MINISTER. Mr. President, thank you for your warm welcome. I have looked forward to this opportunity for us to become better acquainted and explore together the ways in which Japan and the United States may join in even closer partnership than ever before to realize the aspirations of both our peoples for peace and a stable expansion of the world economy.

Recently, economic frictions have surfaced between Japan and the United States. The economic problems between our two countries are serious, and we both are endeavoring to resolve these problems through mutual cooperation. I am determined to continue to do my utmost to that end.

In resolving our economic frictions, we should never forget that the Japanese-American relationship today in all its aspects is absolutely sound and secure, bound by mutual confidence and trust.

As we look to the 1980's, we cannot see any quick or easy solutions to the complex political, economic, and social challenges facing mankind. Under these circumstances, the constructive roles to be played by the industrial democracies of the world, especially Japan and the United States, are of crucial importance.

I am convinced that Japan and the United States can overcome a variety of challenges to fulfill their constructive roles. I believe this because we have among us the spiritual resources as well as abundant material and technical resources to see these tasks through to a successful conclusion.

Japan, I assure you, Mr. President, is fully cognizant of its responsibilities in all these areas. In close and productive partnership with the United States, our irreplaceable friend and ally, we have great tasks to perform. That is why I have come.

Thank you.

NOTE: The President spoke at 10:10 a.m. on the South Lawn of the White House. Prime Minister Ohira spoke in Japanese, and his remarks were translated by an interpreter.

Following the ceremony, the President and the Prime Minister held a meeting. They met again in the afternoon.

United States Army Chief of Staff

Nomination of Lt. Gen. Edward C. Meyer. May 2, 1979

The President today announced that he will nominate Lt. Gen. Edward C. Meyer for assignment as Chief of Staff, United States Army, and for appointment to the grade of general.

Meyer is presently serving as Deputy Chief of Staff for Operations and Plans, U.S. Army. He would succeed Gen. Bernard W. Rogers, who has been named Supreme Allied Commander, Europe.

Meyer was born December 11, 1928, in St. Mary's, Pa. He holds a B.S. in military engineering from the United States Military Academy and an M.S. in international affairs from George Washington University.

Meyer has served in the Army since 1951. In 1970 he was Chief of Staff of the 1st Calvary Division in Vietnam, and in 1970–71 he was a Federal executive fellow at the Brookings Institution. In 1971 and 1972, he was Assistant Division Commander of the 82d Airborne Division at Fort Bragg, N.C., and in 1972 and 1973, he was Deputy Commandant of the U.S. Army War College at Carlisle Barracks, Pa.

In 1973 and 1974, Meyer was Deputy Chief of Staff for Operations for U.S. Army, Europe, and the Seventh Army. From 1974 to 1975, he was Commanding General of the 3d Infantry Division (Mechanized); U.S. Army, Europe. He was Assistant Deputy Chief of Staff for Operations and Plans from 1975 until he assumed his current duties as Deputy Chief of Staff in 1976.

Visit of Prime Minister Ohira of Japan

Joint Communique. May 2, 1979

PRODUCTIVE PARTNERSHIP FOR
THE 1980's

MAY 2, 1979

1. At the invitation of the Government of the United States, Prime Minister Ohira paid an official visit to the United States between April 30 and May 6, 1979. President Carter and Prime Minister Ohira met on May 2 in Washington to review the current state of U.S.-Japan relations and discuss regional and global cooperation, with a view to laying a foundation for productive partnership between the two countries for the 1980's based on their shared political and economic ideals and reflecting their responsibilities in world affairs. The discussions were held in an informal and cordial atmosphere consistent with the close friendship between the two countries. The President and the Prime Minister deepened their relationship of mutual trust and agreed to maintain close contact. The Prime Minister reconfirmed the standing invitation by the Government of Japan to President and Mrs. Carter to pay a state visit to Japan and invited them to

visit in late June just before the Tokyo Summit. President and Mrs. Carter accepted with pleasure.

SECURITY RELATIONS

2. The President and the Prime Minister reaffirmed that the friendly and cooperative relationship between the United States and Japan, including the Treaty of Mutual Cooperation and Security between Japan and the United States of America, has been and will remain the cornerstone of peace and stability in Asia. The security relationship between the two countries has never been so strong and mutually advantageous as at present. This is exemplified by such significant recent developments as the adoption last year of the Guidelines for Japan-U.S. Defense Cooperation under the Security Treaty, increased procurement by Japan of defense equipment from the United States which will contribute to the increase of Japan's self-defense capability, and Japanese initiatives to increase financial support for the stationing of United States forces in Japan. The President stated that in coming years the United States will maintain and improve the quality of its present military capabilities in East Asia. The Prime Minister stated that Japan will continue its efforts to improve the quality of its self-defense capabilities, while maintaining effective working security arrangements with the United States as the foundation of its defense policy.

INTERNATIONAL RELATIONS

3. The President and the Prime Minister agreed that the United States and Japan share many political, economic and other interests in Asia and other parts of the world. Cooperation and consultation between the two countries concerning issues in these areas have grown over the years, become closer than ever in recent months, and will deepen further in the 1980's.

4. The President and the Prime Minister agreed that the recent developments in relations between Japan and the People's Republic of China and the establishment of U.S.–PRC diplomatic relations are major contributions to long-term stability in Asia. Both the United States and Japan seek a constructive relationship with China and will pursue this course in harmony with one another. The growth of such relations with China will hamper neither the United States nor Japan from continuing to develop good relations with other countries.

5. The President and the Prime Minister noted that the maintenance of balanced, cooperative relations with the Soviet Union will continue to be important to both the United States and Japan. The President stated that the United States is working to complete a SALT II agreement with a view to increasing strategic stability and security, and the Prime Minister stated that Japan supports this effort. Each side stated that it will continue to seek development of friendly and mutually beneficial relations with the Soviet Union.

6. The President and the Prime Minister reaffirmed that the maintenance of peace and stability on the Korean Peninsula is important for peace and security in East Asia, including Japan. The United States is firmly committed to the security of the Republic of Korea. Its policy toward future ground force withdrawals from Korea will be developed in a manner consistent with the maintenance of peace and stability on the Peninsula. The United States and Japan will cooperate to reduce tension on the Peninsula and will continue efforts to foster an international environment conducive to this purpose.

Progress in the dialogue between the South and the North is indispensable to this process. The United States and Japan welcome the recent efforts to resume the dialogue and hope that these efforts will be fruitful.

7. The President and the Prime Minister noted that the United States and Japan have a profound interest in the peace and stability of Southeast Asia and are impressed by the vitality of ASEAN and its commitment to economic and social development. Both governments will continue cooperation and assistance in support of the efforts of the ASEAN countries toward regional solidarity and development.

8. The President and the Prime Minister expressed their concern about the recent increased tension in Indochina brought about in particular by the continued armed conflicts in Cambodia involving foreign troops and the recent fighting between China and Vietnam. The United States and Japan will make utmost efforts to reduce tension in this area and seek establishment of a durable peace based on the principles of respect for the sovereignty, territorial integrity and independence of all nations. The President and the Prime Minister expressed their concern over use of facilities in Vietnam by foreign forces.

9. The President and the Prime Minister noted that the outflow of Indochinese refugees is a cause of instability and a source of great humanitarian concern in the Asian-Pacific region that must be dealt with urgently. The President stated that the United States is accepting 7,000 refugees per month from Indochina for permanent resettlement in the United States and will continue its other major efforts to deal with this tragic problem. The Prime Minister stated that Japan has set a target number for the resettle-ment of displaced persons and eased conditions for permanent resettlement. The Prime Minister further stated that Japan will continue to expand its cooperation and financial support for the United Nations High Commissioner for Refugees (UNHCR). The United States and Japan welcome the ASEAN initiative to create a refugee processing center, and both governments will make substantial contributions to that project, together with other countries, as it materializes.

10. The President and the Prime Minister agreed that peace and stability in the Middle East and the Gulf area are very important to the well-being of the peoples of the region as well as the world as a whole. The Prime Minister stated that Japan will actively continue and expand its cooperation with the peoples of the area in their endeavors toward a better future. The President and the Prime Minister agreed that a comprehensive Middle East peace should be brought about in full accordance with all the principles of United Nations Security Council Resolution 242 and through the recognition of and respect for the legitimate rights of the Palestinian people. To this end, utmost efforts should be made to promote the peace process subsequent to the signature of the Peace Treaty between Egypt and Israel.

ECONOMIC RELATIONS

11. The President and the Prime Minister agreed that the time has come for a more constructive approach to U.S.-Japan economic relations. They reached a clear understanding about the basic policies that each will follow over the next several years to produce a more harmonious pattern of international trade and payments. They agreed on a framework and procedure for continuing bilateral

discussions. They recognized that such discussions will focus more on overall trade and current account trends than on specific actions to shape these trends; these actions are the national responsibility of each government.

12. The President and the Prime Minister stressed the very strong economic interests which link the United States and Japan. More than ever before, the two countries' welfare and futures are intertwined. Joint action to establish a new and stronger basis for economic cooperation will enhance the well-being of their peoples and promote widening trade. It will make it possible to remove contentious bilateral economic issues from the forefront of their relations and to mount cooperative efforts to resolve problems common to their societies, while ensuring a sustained, mutually productive relationship among their peoples.

13. For these reasons, the President and the Prime Minister agreed on a common approach, which will contribute to a stable pattern of international payments. They recognized that the 1978 current account surplus of Japan and the 1978 current account deficit of the United States were not appropriate in existing international circumstances. Recent actions by both governments, together with earlier changes in exchange rates, have led to a significant reduction in their payments imbalances during the last few months. They agreed that appropriate action should be taken to ensure progress, and to sustain it.

14. To this end, the Prime Minister affirmed that it is the policy of Japan to continue:

—to encourage a shift to greater reliance on rising domestic demand to sustain Japan's economic growth, and

—to open Japan's markets to foreign goods, particularly manufactured goods.

15. In following these policies, it is the objective of Japan to promote a continued reduction in its current account surplus, until a position consistent with a balanced and sustainable pattern of international trade and payments has been achieved.

16. The United States will pursue a broad range of policies to reduce the U.S. rate of inflation, to restrain oil imports, and to promote U.S. exports. In following these policies, it is the objective of the United States to promote a continued reduction in its current account deficit, until a position consistent with a balanced and sustainable pattern of international trade and payments has been achieved.

17. Accomplishment of these goals will require several years. The present U.S.-Japan subcabinet group, composed of officials from both governments, will examine developments and results at periodic intervals.

18. A small group of distinguished persons drawn from private life will also be established, and will submit to the President and the Prime Minister recommendations concerning actions that the group considers would help to maintain a healthy bilateral economic relationship between the United States and Japan.

19. In reaching this understanding about economic relations between the United States and Japan, the President and the Prime Minister further noted that:

—Free and expanding trade is necessary for the development of the world economy; successful conclusion of the Tokyo Round of Multilateral Trade Negotiations is a significant step forward. It is essential to continue to reject protectionism, and to proceed with domestic measures to implement the results of the Tokyo Round negotiations as quickly as possible.

—The two countries will work with others at the Summit meeting scheduled for Tokyo in June to ensure that this meeting makes a substantial contribution to a healthier world economy.

—Bilateral and multilateral cooperation among industrial nations to improve the world energy outlook has become even more important in recent years. It is imperative that the industrial nations, including the United States and Japan, increase energy production, enhance the development of alternative energy sources, and implement fully the agreement on energy conservation reached by the International Energy Agency on March 2. The signing of the bilateral U.S.-Japan Agreement on Cooperation in Research and Development in Energy and Related Fields represents a major contribution to these objectives. The two governments will study seriously the prospects for cooperative efforts in other areas of basic and applied research.

—To meet the increasing demand for energy, there is an urgent need to promote further peaceful use of nuclear energy, consistent with non-proliferation and the requirements of safety and environmental protection. They agreed to expand joint research to enhance nuclear reactor safety and reliability. The Prime Minister stressed that, while sharing fully with the President a common concern over the danger of nuclear proliferation, for Japan nuclear energy is the most reliable alternative to oil in the short and medium term. The President and the Prime Minister agreed that the United States and Japan, in full cooperation, should continue to pursue the policies of nuclear non-proliferation, while avoiding undue restrictions on necessary and economically

justified nuclear development programs. The President and the Prime Minister took special notice of the technical studies in progress in the International Nuclear Fuel Cycle Evaluation (INFCE) and expressed their strong hope that these technical studies will lead to satisfactory results.

—The United States and Japan should improve their official development assistance to developing countries. It is particularly important for them to strengthen aid in the field of human resource development and to strengthen support of research and development in such areas as health, food, and energy. The two countries will explore, through bilateral discussions and consultation with developing countries, how to promote cooperation in technical assistance and in research and development in these areas.

—Japan, which has been the most important single customer for American agricultural exports, and the United States, which has been Japan's most important single supplier, will cooperate closely to ensure that their mutually beneficial agricultural trade meets Japan's import needs. Relevant authorities of the Governments of the United States and Japan will periodically exchange information and meet to consult, as appropriate, on the supply and demand situation of agricultural products that figure in trade between the United States and Japan.

CULTURAL AND EDUCATION EXCHANGE

20. The President and the Prime Minister noted with satisfaction that cooperation and exchanges in the fields of culture and education are flourishing and are of major importance in deepening mutual understanding and friendship between the peoples of the United States and Japan. Both governments will seek to

enhance these activities and will jointly fund an expanded Fulbright Program of educational exchange. The Prime Minister stated that the Government of Japan will make a donation to help pay the cost of construction of new headquarters for the Asia Society in New York, and that it intends to make financial contributions for the construction of a new Oriental art gallery of the Smithsonian Institution and a Japanese gallery of the New York Metropolitan Museum of Art and for the establishment of a fund for international energy policy research at the Massachusetts Institute of Technology. The President expressed his appreciation.

NOTE: On the same day, Associate Press Secretary Jerrold Schecter read the following announcement at 3:45 p.m. to reporters assembled in the Briefing Room at the White House:

The President and the Prime Minister have instructed their negotiators to continue discussions diligently about the few remaining unresolved trade issues and to settle them in mutually acceptable fashion.

Visit of Prime Minister Ohira of Japan

Toasts at the State Dinner.   May 2, 1979

THE PRESIDENT. A poem written by the Emperor Meiji says, "All the seas everywhere are brothers to one another. Why, then, do the winds and the waves of strife rage so violently to the world?"

I think that there are two countries on Earth which have seen the winds and the waves rage violently between them, and then to realize that all the oceans on Earth are brothers—it would be our country and Japan.

We are honored tonight to have you here as guests. And we are also honored, of course, to have our friends from Japan,

a delegation come to visit us, headed by Prime Minister Ohira, accompanied by his lovely wife.

Prime Minister Ohira has been a Finance Minister. He's been Foreign Minister, I think, twice. He's been the Minister of Trade and Development, and now he has been elected in the most popular type of election in the history of Japan, to hold the highest office, the highest elective office in his country.

Recently I have read his autobiography, and I have noticed with great attention that he comes from one of the southernmost islands of Japan. [*Laughter*] I'm not surprised. [*Laughter*] I have always had a conviction, never yet contravened, that statemanship is not incompatible with residence in the South. [*Laughter*]

I met Prime Minister Ohira in 1975. And in a very concise, but interesting, even an exciting interview—I did not hold public office; I was a relatively unknown candidate, in May of 1975, while Bob Strauss was supporting two other candidates—[*laughter*]—and I could not get an appointment with him— [*laughter*]—Mr. Ohira was kind enough to give me his ear and to give me his advice. And when I got through talking to him, he said, "Well, what do you think your chances are?" And I said, "My friend, Mr. Ohira, the next time I see you we'll be in the White House." [*Laughter*]

And I never thought he would be Prime Minister. [*Laughter*] So, I was really much more frank with him than he was with me. [*Laughter*]

But I can say for the benefit of this audience and for the benefit of the press, after my own experiences today, consulting with Bob Strauss, our trade representative, consulting with Secretary Vance, that this has been one of the most productive days in my own diplomatic life.

The economic problems are well on the way to being resolved. And I believe that I can state without concern to the American people that we have made tremendous progress and that the hopes for success are very good, thanks to the statesmanship of Prime Minister Ohira and thanks to the common purpose that binds our nations so tightly together, that I can't think of any predictable problem that could possibly separate us for more than a few months.

This is a powerful nation. Japan is emerging, as you well know, as one of those countries on Earth bound most closely to us because of their commitment to democratic principles; because of their deep commitment to peace; because of their concern, based on experience, about the proliferation of nuclear explosives; a nation of great economic achievement, based on the dedication, the hard work, the innovation, the scientific knowledge, the cohesiveness of their society, the individual workers; intense competitors who keep us all on our toes; but still a nation comprised of people who are gentle and who are polite and modest, who are cultural in their inclinations, dedicated to the finest, most sensitive exhibitions of artistic achievement.

I have never talked to a diplomat, a public official, or an average American tourist who came back from Japan disappointed. But there's always been a sense of compatibility and a realization of hospitality and of a mutual destiny. This is important to us, as you well know.

I will be going to Japan next month, at the end of the month, for an official state visit to return this one. My wife and Amy will go with us. And I look forward to that opportunity.

And Japan, for the first time in its history, will be the host for a multinational summit meeting, where the leaders of several of the great democratic nations will meet to discuss mutual problems and mutual opportunities.

My prediction is that this will be one of the most exciting visits that I myself have ever made to a foreign country. And I look forward to it with a great deal of anticipation and pleasure.

Japan is a nation, too, that's been able to accommodate extremely rapid change, which has aroused the legitimate admiration of the world. But at the same time, the Japanese people have been able to preserve the cohesiveness and the unity of their society, their nation, and the cohesiveness and unity of communities, and I think perhaps even more importantly, the cohesiveness and unity of the Japanese family.

We have a great future together, and I think all of you realize that with the explosion of technology and communications and population, the shortage of food, the intense competition in trade, the potential divisiveness between developed nations and nations still struggling for the basic elements of life, the vast advancement in the quality of weapons, the contentiousness of regional arguments spreading instantaneously throughout the world—it's become increasingly difficult for nations to live in harmony, but it's become increasingly imperative for nations to live in harmony.

And I believe that our own experience with Japan is a very good pattern or model for other nations to emulate in the future, not only distant nations but our Nation in its relationship with other countries. When we have differences which are profound and of great importance, we are absolutely dedicated to resolving those differences without delay. And the negotiators, the Presidents, the Prime

Ministers have no doubt that that inclination to restore friendship and to restore understanding and to eliminate disagreements is an imperative forced on us by the deep feelings of the citizens whom we represent.

Well, in closing, I would like to say that I'm very proud of the productive partnership that we enjoy now with Japan and which will be a foundation for our Nation's foreign policy in Asia and one of the foundations for our worldwide foreign policy throughout the 1980's. And a great deal of the credit for this achievement can rest upon the superb leadership which has represented the people of Japan so well.

Trees in America are kind of a precious thing, and I know that the first assignment that Prime Minister Ohira had to a foreign nation was to Inner Mongolia. He accepted the assignment with a great deal of anticipation. When he arrived there—I won't go into detail—but one of the disappointments was that there was not a tree in the city where he had to live for 18 months.

But when the people of this Capital City think of Japan, or when the people of Georgia think of Japan, the first thought is the beauty of a cherry tree in April. And the Japanese, recognizing this characteristic of Americans, on our 200th birthday for a gift gave us a superb collection of bonsai trees, which we enjoy frequently in the White House and which visitors also enjoy.

I would like to say, in closing, that I have learned a lot from Prime Minister Ohira. I'm a little too impulsive, perhaps, as a politician, and maybe this is a characteristic of Americans—we don't have the patience to deal with intransigent problems in a careful, considered, often a productive way.

And in his book, in one of the latter chapters, when a young politician asked him for his best advice, he said something that's caused me to think a great deal today. He said, "It's better to correct a wrong than it is to initiate many rights."

We had quite a discussion here at the table between Bill Rogers, our finest athlete, who's won the Boston Marathon three times, and Joan Benoit, who is one of the most superb women athletes in the world, and Peter Falk, who's a great actor and who has one of his finest fans sitting across the table from him—two of his finest fans. But we discussed what the Prime Minister meant about that. And we decided that to correct wrongs was a great attribute of a political leader.

I would like to propose a toast: To the Prime Minister of Japan, Mr. Ohira, to his wife, to the wonderful people of Japan, to peace, to prosperity, to progress, and through the political system, to the correction of wrongs.

Mr. Prime Minister, we are proud to have you here, sir.

THE PRIME MINISTER. *President and Mrs. Carter, excellencies, ladies and gentlemen:*

I appreciate your kind words, Mr. President, for my countrymen and for me.

When we last met in 1975—you, as the former Governor of Georgia, and I, as Japan's Minister of Finance—I recall that you said, "Next time, let us meet in the White House." And here we are. [*Laughter*]

Mr. President, I also recall one piece of my personal history. Some 30 years ago, I was a guest of your Government's National Leaders program, under the auspices of the Department of Army, for a 3-month orientation visit to this country. It was a deeply rewarding experience.

On my return to Japan, I visited towns

and villages of my constituency to make speeches on contemporary American affairs by making good use of my American experiences. It was my first campaign for a seat in the Diet. In a sense, therefore, the political career that has brought me to the White House this evening began three decades ago, in my first exposure to your great country.

Both of us, Mr. President, have been given by our fellow citizens the highest trust they can bestow—to lead them, as best we can, and with faith, through the difficult choices, domestic and foreign, which our two democracies now face in the world.

The responsibilities of the President of the United States are indeed awesome, because of America's unique power and mission in the maintenance of global peace, and because of your wide commitments in leadership of the free world.

Japan's responsibilities are also great and growing, and I am determined that we shall play an increasingly creative and effective role in world economic and political affairs, in closest partnership with our trusted friend and ally, the United States.

One of the great satisfactions of my present post as the Prime Minister of Japan is the opportunity to work with you, Mr. President, and your Government and people. I am eager to work to make the Japanese-American partnership a more powerful and productive force for the progress of the world community toward a more stable peace and a more widely shared prosperity.

I welcome this opportunity, because I know you share the deep conviction that there is spiritual meaning to man's being. I also believe that the eternal now is the only time we have to act on our convictions, and that you and I will, therefore, always be ready to make the

difficult decisions which cross our desks each day.

I look forward to our collaboration.

Ladies and gentlemen, will you join me in toasting the health of the President of the United States, and the well-being and success of the American people.

Thank you.

THE PRESIDENT. Thank you very much. That's beautiful English—beautiful.

NOTE: The President spoke at 10 p.m. on the West Terrace of the White House.

League of Women Voters of the United States

Remarks to Members of the National Council. May 3, 1979

The first school I went to when I assumed my initial political office was the League of Women Voters. [*Laughter*] I was interested in being on the education committee and involved in higher education when the South was going through the integration phase of its development back in 1962. And when I arrived in Atlanta as a new legislator, the most knowledgeable and dedicated and courageous people there in this very sensitive area of changing southern life were the members of the League of Women Voters.

I worked closely with them then and have found throughout my own political career that this is a stabilizing influence when stability is important and a dynamic and courageous and innovative influence when change is necessary.

I'm very proud that you've come to Washington to become more thoroughly briefed on some of the issues that face me and face the Congress, face our Nation during the coming months. You received an intense briefing on SALT, and I would hope that this would be escalated to a very high degree of priority in your own hearts and minds and that your influence might be felt strongly as the debate begins in the next few weeks.

I don't know if you've had an opportunity to get my own personal beliefs, but I hope that, Sarah,[1] perhaps you can get a copy of the speech that I made to the National Newspaper Publishers convention in New York recently, which encapsulates in a fairly brief form the need for strategic arms limitation, the elimination of nuclear weapons as a threat to our lives in the finest and clearest way that I can express it at this moment.

We are at the final stages of negotiating the terms of a SALT agreement. And my guess is that following that agreement, I would meet with President Brezhnev and discuss a broad range of issues that are important to all of us, because the future peace and stability of the world might very well depend upon this relationship.

You've been supportive, and I thank you for it. And I believe that one of the basic reasons for the tremendous influence of the League is that Americans have a sure sense that before you take a stand on a controversial issue, that you do your homework. It's not just an emotional, instantaneous, aroused group which can be effective. But I think there's a stability there and a soundness there and a caution there that provides integrity and belief and confidence and trust in you.

I'm also grateful that you've been willing to help with the problem of inflation and also the problem of energy. We have finally come to the point of realizing, I

---

[1] Sarah C. Weddington, Special Assistant to the President.

think, to an increasing degree, that we do indeed have an energy crisis, that it's not something that's going to pass away. If anything, it's going to get worse. And unless the American people are prepared for it psychologically, and unless the bureaucracy is prepared to deal with an impending deterioration in the energy part of Americans' life, then whatever eventuality does materialize, it's going to have a much more severe adverse impact on the American family, which is least able to deal with it and most vulnerable to rapid changes in prices or perhaps even shortages.

No matter how well intentioned Americans are, when a crisis does occur, the powerful and the influential always suffer least, and the weak and dependent and the inarticulate always suffer most. And to the extent that we can make careful preparations ahead of time for as many possibilities as possible in the energy field, we can have fairness and justice and equity in dealing with inevitable shortages and inevitable increases in price.

I'm doing the best I can to work with you also in the selection and appointment of women to positions as U.S. attorneys and judges. We are starting from scratch. As you know, I think, when I took over as President, there were, I think, zero U.S. attorneys in the United States, and we are trying now to find and to put them into office.

We've had good luck on circuit judgeships, a little more difficulty in dealing with district judgeships, because, in effect, both the Senator involved and I have to be unanimous in our support. And we've had a problem with getting minorities and women recommended to us by Senators.

I think in this area, you can work with

Sarah and with Ruth [2] and with your other leaders to identify those States where we do have a problem and let you help us find and recruit women to serve.

One of the things that I mentioned to the most distinguished group of jurists, I guess, who's ever assembled at the White House this week on Law Day, was that it's not fair to expect people who have been deprived of an opportunity in the past to meet experience standards. If women have consistently been excluded from State judgeships or district judgeships for generations, then you can't have as a criterion that they must have 15 or 20 years experience in State court judgeships before they go on to district courts and so forth.

My remarks were completely extemporaneous that day. I only had about 10 minutes before I even knew I was going. But I think what I said is significant, and I think you can use it as a good argument.

I would like to have as complete a partnership with you as possible. It would be helpful to me and our country, and I have no aversion to your very stringent criticisms when you feel that we don't measure up to the standards which you maintain, which are extremely high.

So, to summarize, I'm grateful to you. I have to depend upon you, as President of the United States, in a nonpartisan way to help with the issues that are important to our country, and I'm very grateful that you would take this time to come meet with me. And if you will pardon perhaps the chauvinistic expression, I love every one of you and what you stand for. [*Laughter*]

Thank you very much.

NOTE: The President spoke at 10:05 a.m. in the Rose Garden at the White House.

---

[2] Ruth Hinerfeld, national president of the League of Women Voters.

Alaska Public Lands

Remarks at a White House Briefing.
May 3, 1979

SECRETARY OF THE INTERIOR ANDRUS. Thank you very much for joining us, Mr. President.

There are some people here today that would like to make a presentation to you, two separate groups. But I would ask them to come up at this time, if they would, please. If you'd, please, just come right on up to make the presentation. And, Mr. President, I'll introduce to you a person that is no stranger to you, but Cathy Douglas, who will introduce the balance of the group.

Cathy.

Ms. DOUGLAS. Thank you, Mr. Secretary.

Mr. President, for our first presentation, three native chiefs from the Admiralty Island would like to present you with a beaded vest and make you an honorary member of their tribe. The chiefs are Chief Matthew Fred, Chief of all the tribes on the Admiralty; Chief Daniel Johnson, Chief of the Bear Tribe; Chief William Nelson, Chief of the Dog Salmon Tribe.

CHIEF FRED. President Carter, my people join me in thanking you for making Admiralty Island a National Monument. Such a noble decision in our Tlinget culture does not go unrecognized. My people have preserved this island, its natural resources, its wildlife, from time immemorial. My brother-in-law, Daniel Johnson, Sr., will place the vest upon you. Would our Eagle Ladies please take his jacket off.

The people of Angoon have sent you this vest, and my clan of the Raven Beaver have sent you a noble name, *Nahoo-woo,* meaning "a great nation in migration."

This name was given birth when my nation was coming back to their beloved coastal home after the ice had receded from the land, and that is a long time ago. We are now going to warm the name upon your forehead as a stamp of our legal adoption.

Nahoo-woo ah', Nahoo-woo ah,' Nahoo-woo ah'.

You are now my brother of the Raven Beaver Clan and an honorary chief of Angoon and of all Admiralty Island.

We have one more presentation.

CHIEF JOHNSON. There is a saying that behind every great man stands a woman. And we can't leave Mrs. Carter out. So, we are presenting the President—hopefully, he will present it to Mrs. Carter—a little token that was made by my brother-in-law, the Chief of the Raven Tribe. It's an eagle. You can't be married to your own side, so we'll make Mrs. Carter the Eagle Clan.

THE PRESIDENT. Very fine.

With my new name, *Nahoo-woo,* I think it's appropriate for me to say *Goonalth-cheesh,* which means, for those of you who are not Native Americans—[*laughter*]—"Thank you very much."

This is indeed an honor for me. I feel more at ease in the woods or in a field or in a swamp or on a mountain or underneath a kayak on a beautiful mountain stream than I do encapsulated in an urban society. And for me to meet these distinguished Tlinget leaders and to have them express to me their deep feelings, historic feelings, paramount feelings about the importance of the preservation of the quality of life and the quality of the land in the Alaska region is indeed an honor for me.

As symbols of the Raven and the Eagle, they've honored me and my wife by letting us be part of their heritage. This symbol of freedom of the spirit is indeed also important to recognize.

We have many difficult decisions to make in a modern, fast-changing, technological society, where quite often the small and the isolated, the quiet person or group is never heard, or heard too late, after their own lives are destroyed—sometimes by well-meaning leaders who don't have a comprehension of the significance of preserving God's earth and God's oceans the way they were created.

I'm deeply grateful for this honor, and I want to express to the Tlinget tribe and to others who are deeply committed to the outdoors, to the heritage of our Nation, my permanent commitment never to betray their trust.

Thank you.

Ms. DOUGLAS. Thank you, Mr. President.

Mr. President, there are two more groups represented on the platform. First is the Alaska Coalition, under the leadership of Mr. Clusen, who has worked so hard in the vineyard out on the Hill to get the legislation the way it is; and, secondly, Americans for Alaska, which is represented, in addition by me, to Ambassador Lodge, Larry Rockefeller, and our person who will present you with an award.

So, on behalf of these organizations, and on behalf of the millions of people that love our land, we would like to honor you for your leadership in preserving the great natural heritage of Alaska. Conservationists feel that you have done more than any President since President Teddy Roosevelt to preserve our natural heritage, so we thought it very appropriate today that Teddy Roosevelt give the Americans for Alaska Award to you, Mr. President.

Teddy Roosevelt IV.

MR. ROOSEVELT. Mr. President, no cause was closer to the heart of my great-grandfather than the conservation of our natural resources. When he tripled the size of our Nation's forests, he was acting on behalf of all Americans, for he believed firmly that we must act as stewards for our children's children. Were he here today, I think he'd be amongst the first to applaud your efforts to preserve our priceless jewels in Alaska for future Americans, and he'd probably use his favorite adjective, "bully," to describe your efforts.

THE PRESIDENT. It would be hard to choose between the Tlinget tribe and Theodore Roosevelt as to which was the best exemplification of what America has to preserve. Of all the people who've ever lived here, there's no question that Theodore Roosevelt was the preeminent conservationist. And no matter how many Presidents might come after me, there's no doubt in my mind that Theodore Roosevelt will always be the preeminent conservationist.

He was attacked by many special interest groups, and the American people realized, a vast majority of them realized that he was right. And as each decade has gone by since the National Forest Service was established under his administration, the appreciation of what he did has grown.

It was probably a close call when he first made it. And I have no doubt that there were well-meaning and dedicated and honest and competent Members of the Congress and members of the public who sharply disagreed that a very large acreage should be set aside for future generations. But he was the kind of man who could balance properly immediate benefits, from which our Nation has never suffered, and the long-range benefits, which we are now beginning to realize in their fullest sense.

He believed in systematic protection, carefully considered, broad in scope, well-defined, and ultimately endorsed overwhelmingly by the American people.

That's what we have tried to do, to have our decisions be both wise and balanced. And I'm thankful for this photograph with the inscription on it, which will always remind me of my obligations to you and to the people of our Nation.

Thank you very much.

I would just like to say a word in closing.

The top environmental priority of my administration, perhaps my entire life, has been a carefully considered, proper protection of the wild and precious lands of Alaska. This is not a decision that relates only to Washington, D.C., and Capitol Hill and the White House on the one hand, and Alaska itself on the other; it's a decision that affects the life of every single American now living and who might live in the future.

This legislation was as carefully drafted and as thoroughly discussed and debated as any which has ever passed the Congress, over a number of years, out of an abundance of caution, with an almost unique sharing of responsibility between the legislative and executive branches of Congress [Government],[1] both of us recognizing that undoubtedly the judicial branch would also ultimately become involved. We've prepared our case accordingly.

And the House last year with a substantial margin passed legislation which I consider to be well-advised and adequate. Because of reasons which I need not discuss now, it was not possible to get the legislation passed through the Senate and approved before the Congress adjourned. Now we've started the process again.

I'm afraid that those who were so intensely involved in previous years have not adequately marshaled our strength for this present contest in the legislative branch. We must be almost sacrificial in

---

[1] Printed in the transcript.

our commitment to the passage of this legislation. It is not a partisan issue. Mo Udall, John Anderson, and the other Members of Congress here, almost equally divided—I just looked at the list—between Republicans and Democrats, have prepared a proposal to go to the House floor when the vote comes up within the next few days.

I will do my utmost to support this legislation in the House and Senate, and I hope that you will greatly magnify your own influence throughout the Nation and let individual Members of the House and Senate know how American people truly feel.

This legislation encourages the economic development of Alaska. There is no constraint at all that would interfere with the proper growth of Alaska in population and material wealth.

Last year, as you know, I took executive action, which is not the easiest course to follow, to establish 17 permanent National Monuments, including, I think, 56 million acres. I will not hesitate to use administrative action in the future, if necessary, to protect the Alaskan lands from abuse. But a far better approach is to pass permanent legislation, approved by a majority of the Congress and signed by me into law.

And to summarize, you have my commitment, and I need your help—not just quiescent personal endorsements, which might salve a troubled conscience, but an absolute, coherent, sharply focused, sacrificial commitment the next few days to do everything you can to overcome any obstacle and to have this legislation passed into law.

There's nothing you could do for future generations in the environmental field that would pay richer dividends. And when this task is accomplished—and I

believe it will be—we can all be legitimately proud.

Thank you very much.

NOTE: The President spoke at approximately 3 p.m. in the East Room at the White House.

United States–Canada Maritime Boundary and Fishery Treaties

Message to the Senate Transmitting the Treaties.   May 3, 1979

To the Senate of the United States:

I transmit herewith, for the advice and consent of the Senate to ratification, two separate but closely related treaties with Canada: the Treaty between the Government of the United States of America and the Government of Canada to Submit to Binding Dispute Settlement the Delimitation of the Maritime Boundary in the Gulf of Maine Area, and the Agreement between the Government of the United States of America and the Government of Canada on East Coast Fishery Resources. Both Treaties were signed at Washington on March 29, 1979, and they will enter into force together upon exchange of instruments of ratification.

I also transmit for the information of the Senate the report of the Secretary of State with respect to these Treaties.

These Treaties will make an important contribution to good relations between the United States and Canada by resolving, in a way that is fair to both Parties, a vexing dispute over fisheries and the maritime boundary in the Atlantic which was brought to the fore when both countries extended fisheries jurisdiction to 200 nautical miles in 1977.

The maritime boundary settlement treaty provides for the delimitation of the maritime boundary in the Gulf of Maine Area by a Chamber of the International Court of Justice or, if such a Chamber cannot be constituted in accordance with the wishes of the Parties, by an *ad hoc* Court of Arbitration. Resolution of the maritime boundary by impartial dispute settlement has proved necessary because the two countries have not been able to agree upon the location of the maritime boundary in the Gulf of Maine Area.

The fisheries treaty contains provisions for the conservation, management and utilization of fish stocks of mutual interest off the east coast of both countries. Detailed entitlement shares for various fish stocks are set forth in the agreement, with the shares subject to review every ten years. A joint fisheries commission will be established to implement the agreement, and dispute settlement mechanisms will be included as part of the institutional framework to resolve differences that might arise in the interpretation or implementation of the agreement.

I believe that these treaties are in the best interests of the United States. The fisheries treaty protects United States interests in the important fisheries on Georges Bank; and settlement of the boundary will facilitate development of the non-living resources of the continental shelf. Further delay in resolution of these issues would be detrimental to conservation of the fishery resources and could lead to serious irritants in United States relations with Canada.

I recommend that the Senate give early and favorable consideration to these treaties and give its advice and consent to their ratification.

JIMMY CARTER

The White House,
May 3, 1979.

Northwest Atlantic Fisheries Convention

Message to the Senate Transmitting the Convention. May 3, 1979

To the Senate of the United States:

I am pleased to transmit the Convention on Future Multilateral Cooperation in the Northwest Atlantic Fisheries for advice and consent to accession. The Convention was signed in Ottawa on October 24, 1978, by nine parties, not including the United States, and subsequently entered into force on January 1, 1979.

The Convention creates a successor organization to the International Commission for the Northwest Atlantic Fisheries (ICNAF) established by the International Convention for the Northwest Atlantic Fisheries, done at Washington, February 8, 1949 (the ICNAF Convention). The United States withdrew from the ICNAF Convention effective December 31, 1976, because it was inconsistent in several ways with the establishment of the extended fishery management authority of the United States under the Fishery Conservation and Management Act of 1976. The United States subsequently participated in the negotiation of the successor Convention. Its provisions are completely consistent with the provisions of the Act.

Under this Convention, the United States will receive and provide scientific data, participate in the planning and coordination of research activities, and have available a multilateral scientific council to review scientific studies and hypotheses pertaining to fish stocks in the Convention Area. United States adherence to the Convention will facilitate continuity of the data base established and accumulated over a period of 27 years under the ICNAF Convention. In addition, the

United States will be able, if desirable, to request and receive scientific advice related to fisheries subject to its exclusive management jurisdiction. Finally, the United States will have an opportunity for membership in the Fisheries Commission, the body responsible for conservation and management of fisheries in the Regulatory Area, defined as the part of the convention area beyond the fishery conservation zones of the Contracting Parties, should its vessels wish to participate in such fisheries.

I transmit also for the information of the Senate the report of the Secretary of State with respect to the Convention.

I urge the Senate to act favorably at an early date on this Convention.

JIMMY CARTER

The White House,
   May 3, 1979.

Convention on the Intergovernmental Maritime Consultative Organization

Message to the Senate Transmitting Amendments to the Convention.
May 3, 1979

To the Senate of the United States:

I transmit herewith, for the advice and consent of the Senate to acceptance, amendments to the Convention on the Intergovernmental Maritime Consultative Organization, signed at Geneva on March 6, 1948, which were adopted on November 14, 1975 and November 17, 1977, by the Assembly of the Intergovernmental Maritime Consultative Organization (IMCO) at its ninth and tenth sessions. I transmit also, for the information of the Senate, the report of the Department of State describing the amendments, their purpose, and effect.

Support for these amendments will contribute to the demonstrated interest of the United States in facilitating cooperation among maritime nations. To that end, I urge that the Senate give early and favorable consideration to these amendments and give its advice and consent to their acceptance.

JIMMY CARTER

The White House,
   May 3, 1979.

United States-United Kingdom Convention on Taxation and Fiscal Evasion

Message to the Senate Transmitting the Convention. May 3, 1979

To the Senate of the United States:

I transmit herewith, for Senate advice and consent to ratification, the Convention between the Government of the United States of America and the Government of the United Kingdom of Great Britain and Northern Ireland for the Avoidance of Double Taxation and the Prevention of Fiscal Evasion with Respect to Taxes on Estates of Deceased Persons and on Gifts, signed at London on October 19, 1978. For the information of the Senate, I also transmit the report of the Department of State with respect to the Convention.

The Convention would replace the estate tax convention with the United Kingdom which was signed at Washington on April 16, 1945, and has been in force since 1946. It would apply in the United States to the federal gift tax, the federal estate tax, and the federal tax on generation-skipping transfers. In the United Kingdom it would apply to the capital transfer tax. The Convention is similar in principle to the United States estate tax convention with the Netherlands, which was signed at Washington on July 15, 1969, and entered into force in 1971, and to the United States model estate and gift tax convention published by the Department of the Treasury in 1977.

The general principle underlying the Convention is to grant to the country of domicile the right to tax estates and transfers on a worldwide basis. The Convention also permits a credit for tax paid to the other country in which certain property was taxed on the basis of its location. The Convention would provide rules for resolving the issue of domicile.

The Convention would enter into force on the thirty-first day after instruments of ratification are exchanged and would have effect in the United States with respect to estates of individuals dying and transfers taking effect after that date.

I recommend that the Senate give early and favorable consideration to the Convention and give advice and consent to its ratification.

JIMMY CARTER

The White House,
May 3, 1979.

Federal Programs To Improve Management and Combat Waste and Fraud

Memorandum From the President.
May 3, 1979

Memorandum for the Attorney General, the Director, Office of Management and Budget, the Director, Office of Personnel Management
Subject: Improving Management and

Combating Fraud and Waste in Federal Programs

Since the beginning of my Administration I have emphasized the high priority I place on improving the operations of Federal agencies. Implementation of the Civil Service Reform Act and the Inspector General Act provides an opportunity to strengthen our efforts to improve agency management practices and manage the resources of the government well, free of waste, fraud, and inefficiency. I want to seize this opportunity.

In recent months I have asked each of you to assume specific responsibilities which include:

- the Director of OMB providing direction and assistance in implementing the Inspector General legislation and overseeing government-wide efforts to combat fraud, waste, and mismanagement in program operations;
- the Attorney General assuring that the activities of Inspectors General and similar officers are coordinated with other investigative and prosecutorial activities; and
- the Director of OPM working with the Attorney General and the Secretary of the Treasury to improve the training of investigative and audit staffs throughout the Executive Branch.

I believe we should now launch a management improvement program that builds on Civil Service reform and on our other ongoing efforts to improve both management practices and program performance across the entire government. At the same time we should pursue a coordinated anti-fraud and waste campaign that focuses on implementing the Inspector General program. While these two efforts should be organizationally separate, each of you should assure that they complement each other.

EXECUTIVE GROUP TO COMBAT FRAUD AND WASTE IN GOVERNMENT

I am establishing an Executive Group to Combat Fraud and Waste in Government to assure effective implementation of the Inspector General Act of 1978 and other efforts to combat fraud and waste in programs of the Federal Government. The Deputy Attorney General shall serve as Chairman and the Deputy Director of the Office of Management and Budget shall serve as Vice Chairman of the Executive Group. Its membership will consist of the statutory Inspectors General, the Deputy Director of the Office of Personnel Management, and the Special Counsel of the Merit Systems Protection Board, and representatives of the Federal Bureau of Investigation, Internal Revenue Service, and Postal Inspection Service. Other officials should be brought in to work with the Executive Group as appropriate. The Department of Justice and the Office of Management and Budget should provide the necessary staff support.

The responsibilities and functions of the Executive Group include:

• Providing leadership, and formulating policy and operational guidance, to the Inspectors General and other officers of the Executive Branch in combating fraud and waste in government programs, including the development and promotion of:

—programs that prevent and detect fraud and waste in Federal programs;
—procedures to assure that investigations by the Inspectors General and similar officials are coordinated with investigative and prosecutorial activities by law enforcement agencies; and

—improvements in training for audit and investigative personnel.

• Promoting coordinated allocation and direction of audit and investigative resources.

• Studying and seeking to resolve extraordinary problems or issues relating to fraud and waste which are beyond the capacity or authority of the individual executive departments or agencies.

• Developing recommendations for needed legislation and other actions that can be taken to reduce fraud and waste in the Federal Government.

PRESIDENTIAL MANAGEMENT IMPROVEMENT COUNCIL

I am establishing a Presidential Management Improvement Council to support efforts to improve Federal management and program performance and to further the government-wide management improvements envisioned in the Civil Service Reform Act of 1978. The Council shall be co-chaired by the Directors of the Office of Management and Budget and the Office of Personnel Management. Its membership will consist of representatives from Federal agencies, as appropriate, and the private sector, including corporate executive officers and foundation and academic leaders. The Office of Management and Budget and the Office of Personnel Management should provide the necessary staff support for the Council.

The identification of critical management problems for consideration by the Council shall be the joint responsibility of the Office of Management and Budget and the Office of Personnel Management, in consultation with departments and agencies. In addition, I will ask the Council to undertake specific management improvement projects from time to time.

I expect the Council to work cooperatively with the Comptroller General, agency Inspectors General, and senior program management and administrative officials in the departments and agencies. The Council should keep me informed of its activities and bring significant problem areas to my attention.

JIMMY CARTER

Federal Emergency Management Agency

Nomination of John W. Macy, Jr., To Be Director.　May 3, 1979

The President today announced that he will nominate John W. Macy, Jr., of McLean, Va., to be Director of the Federal Emergency Management Agency (FEMA). He would be the first Director of FEMA, the agency created last year to combine disaster planning and response and civil defense programs previously located in five departments and agencies.

Macy is currently president of the Development and Resources Corp. He is a former Chairman of the Civil Service Commission and was the first President of the Corporation for Public Broadcasting.

Macy was born April 6, 1917, in Chicago. He received a B.A. from Wesleyan University in 1938. He was with the War Department in Washington and Chicago as a personnel specialist from 1940 to 1942, and as assistant director of civilian personnel from 1942 to 1943, and 1946 to 1947. From 1943 to 1946, he served in the U.S. Army Air Force.

From 1947 to 1951, Macy was director of personnel and organization of the Atomic Energy Commission's Los Alamos Project. He was assistant for management improvement to the Secretary of the Army from 1951 to 1953. From 1953 to 1958, he was Executive Director of the Civil Service Commission. From 1958 to 1961, he was executive vice president of Wesleyan University.

In 1961 Macy returned to the Civil Service Commission as Chairman, a post he held until 1969. From 1969 to 1972, he was President of the Corporation for Public Broadcasting. From 1973 to 1975, he was president of the Council of Better Business Bureaus. He has been president of the Development and Resources Corp. since 1975.

Macy is a member and former national president of the American Society for Public Administration. He served on the International Civil Service Advisory Board from 1964 to 1970. He was a public member of the American Stock Exchange's board of governors from 1972 to 1977.

Pension Benefit Guaranty Corporation

Appointment of Phyllis R. Spielman as a Member of the Advisory Committee. May 3, 1979

The President today announced the appointment of Phyllis R. Spielman, of White Bear Lake, Minn., as a member of the Advisory Committee to the Pension Benefit Guaranty Corporation for a term expiring February 19, 1982.

Spielman, 70, is administrator of the pension protection division of the Minnesota Department of Labor and Industry.

From 1947 to 1972, she was coowner and copublisher of the Trimont Progress and Ceylon Herald in Martin County, Minn. In 1973 she was legislative aide for the Minnesota House of Representatives majority caucus, and in 1973 and 1974, she was administrative assistant for the labor-management and transportation committees of the Minnesota House. She has been administrator of the pension protection division since it was established in 1974 by the Minnesota Pension Protection Law, which she helped draft.

Committee for the Preservation of the White House

Appointment of Jay P. Altmayer as a Member. May 3, 1979

The President today announced the appointment of Jay P. Altmayer, of Mobile, Ala., as a member of the Committee for the Preservation of the White House.

Altmayer, 64, is an attorney, real estate developer, and director of the First National Bank of Mobile. He is active in civic affairs and is a collector of art, 18th century furniture, and presentation swords. He has given the White House a gold sword presented to Zachary Taylor by the Commonwealth of Virginia, and has a painting on loan to the White House ("North Shore of Lake Pontchartrain" by Richard Clague).

Senator Abraham Ribicoff

Statement on the Connecticut Senator's Decision Not To Seek Reelection. May 3, 1979

Over the past two generations, Senator Abraham Ribicoff has compiled a distinguished career of public service that can serve as a model of decency, compassion, and ability. As a Senator, he has had the vision to take unpopular stands that are vindicated by subsequent events. His courage, leadership, and counsel have helped to pave the way for peace between Israel and Egypt.

Senator Ribicoff and I both share a deep concern about government efficiency. As chairman of the Senate Governmental Affairs Committee, he has shepherded through the Senate a series of proposals to reorganize and streamline the Federal Government. On the Senate Finance Committee, he has been one of the architects of our tax laws and has fought to see that the elderly and the disadvantaged receive the benefits they need and deserve.

Rosalynn and I wish Senator Ribicoff and his wife, Casey, health and happiness in the years ahead.

Department of Commerce

Nomination of Luther H. Hodges, Jr., To Be Under Secretary.   May 4, 1979

The President today announced that he will nominate Luther H. Hodges, Jr., of Charlotte, N.C., to be Under Secretary of Commerce. He would replace Sidney Harman, resigned.

Hodges is a professor of management at the Graduate School of Business Administration of Duke University.

He was born November 19, 1936, in Eden, N.C. He received an A.B. in economics from the University of North Carolina at Chapel Hill in 1957, and an M.B.A. from the Harvard Graduate School of Business Administration in 1961.

From 1961 to 1962, Hodges was a research associate and instructor of corporate finance at the School of Business Administration of the University of North Carolina at Chapel Hill. From 1962 to 1977, he was with the North Carolina National Bank, serving as chairman of the board and member of the executive committee from 1974 to 1977. In 1977 and 1978, he was the Democratic candidate for the U.S. Senate. Since 1978 he has been at Duke University.

Hodges is a director of the Research Triangle Foundation of North Carolina and a former director of the Business Foundation of North Carolina. He is former chairman of the North Carolina Manpower Council.

United States Ambassador to Guatemala

Nomination of Frank V. Ortiz, Jr.
May 4, 1979

The President today announced that he will nominate Frank V. Ortiz, Jr., of Santa Fe, N. Mex., to be Ambassador Extraordinary and Plenipotentiary of the United States to Guatemala. He would replace Davis Eugene Boster, who has retired from the Foreign Service.

Ortiz is currently Ambassador to Barbados and the State of Grenada and Special Representative to Dominica and Saint Lucia, and to the Associated States.

He was born March 14, 1926, in Santa Fe, N. Mex. He received a B.S. from Georgetown University in 1950 and an M.S. from George Washington University in 1967. He served in the U.S. Army from 1944 to 1946.

From 1951 to 1953, Ortiz was international relations officer at the State Department, and from 1953 to 1956, he was economic officer in Addis Ababa. He was political officer in Mexico from 1956 to 1958, and a foreign affairs officer at the State Department from 1958 to 1961.

From 1961 to 1963, Ortiz was special assistant to the Ambassador in Mexico City. He was country desk officer for Spain from 1963 to 1966, and attended the National War College in 1966–67.

From 1967 to 1970, he was counselor for political affairs in Lima.

From 1970 to 1973, Ortiz was Deputy Chief of Mission in Montevideo. He served as Country Director for Argentina, Uruguay, and Paraguay from 1973 to 1975. He was Deputy Executive Secretary at the State Department from 1975 until 1977, when he assumed his present post.

Overseas Private Investment Corporation

Nomination of William M. Landau To Be a
Member of the Board of Directors.
May 4, 1979

The President today announced that he will nominate William M. Landau, of Scarsdale, N.Y., to be a member of the Board of Directors of the Overseas Private Investment Corporation. He will replace Wallace Bennett, who has retired.

Landau is currently a managing partner in the firm of Mann Judd Landau Certified Public Accountants.

He was born September 10, 1926, in New York City. He received a B.S. degree from Lehigh University and an LL.B. degree from New York Law School. He served 2 years in the U.S. Army Infantry, and he joined the firm of Mann Judd Landau Certified Public Accountants (formerly Fred Landau & Co.) in 1951.

Landus is a certified public accountant in the States of New York, Illinois, and California, a member of the American Institute of CPA's, and a member of the New York Bar Association. He is a past member of the committee on cooperation with bankers and the professional ethics committee of the New York State Society of CPA's.

Federal Labor Relations Authority

Nomination of Leon B. Applewhaite To Be a Member.   May 4, 1979

The President today announced that he will nominate Leon B. Applewhaite, of New York City, to be a member of the Federal Labor Relations Authority. This is a new position.

Applewhaite is currently an assistant professor at the State University of New York.

He was born September 4, 1927, in Brooklyn, N.Y. He received a B.A. degree from New York University, a J.D. degree from Brooklyn Law School, and an LL.M. degree from Brooklyn Graduate Law School. He served in the U.S. Army from 1952 to 1954.

From 1955 to 1959, he served as a claims authorizer for the U.S. Social Security Administration, and from 1959 to 1963, he was legal secretary to Justice Francis E. Rivers. He served as a member of the New York State Commission for Human Rights in 1963 and 1964, and from 1964 to 1967, he was a labor arbitrator and mediator for the New York State Board of Mediation.

From 1968 to 1979, he served as chief regional mediator for the New York State Public Employment Relations Board. During that time he also served as an arbitrator for the public and private sectors in a number of national labor cases.

From 1971 to the present, he has served as a part-time adjunct professor at Cornell University I.L.R. School and Labor College of the State University of New York, Hofstra University, and Pace University. He became assistant professor of the State University of New York at Farmingdale earlier this year.

Applewhaite is a member of the American Arbitration Association, the New Jersey State Board of Mediation, the New York County Lawyers Association, the Harlem Lawyers Association, and the Industrial Relations Research Association.

The President's Export Council

Executive Order 12131.   May 4, 1979

By the authority vested in me as President by the Constitution and statutes of the United States of America, and in order to expand the membership of the President's Export Council, in accord with the provisions of the Federal Advisory Committee Act (5 U.S.C. App. I), it is hereby ordered as follows:

1-1. *Establishment and Membership.*

1-101. There is established the President's Export Council.

1-102. The membership of the Council shall be as follows:

(a) The heads of the following Executive agencies or their representatives:

(1) Department of State.

(2) Department of the Treasury.

(3) Department of Agriculture.

(4) Department of Commerce.

(5) Department of Labor.

(6) Office of the Special Representative for Trade Negotiations.

(7) Export-Import Bank of the United States.

(b) Three members of the United States Senate, designated by the President of the Senate, and three members of the United States House of Representatives designated by the Speaker of the House.

(c) Not to exceed 28 citizens appointed by the President. These individuals shall be selected from those who are not full-time Federal officers or employees. They shall include representatives of business and industry, agriculture, and labor.

1–103. The President shall designate a Chairman and a Vice Chairman from among the members appointed by the President.

1–104. The Secretary of Commerce, with the concurrence of the Chairman, shall appoint an Executive Director.

1–2. *Functions.*

1–201. The Council shall serve as a national advisory body on matters relating to United States export trade, including advice on the implementation of the President's National Export Policy, which was announced on September 26, 1978. It shall, through the Secretary of Commerce, report to the President on its activities and on its recommendations for expanding United States exports.

1–202. The Council should survey and evaluate the export expansion activities of the communities represented by the membership. It should identify and examine specific problems which business, industrial, and agricultural practices may cause for export trade, and examine the needs of business, industry, and agriculture to expand their efforts. The Council should recommend specific solutions to these problems and needs.

1–203. The Council may act as liaison among the communities represented by the membership; and, may provide a forum for those communities on current and emerging problems and issues in the field of export expansion. The Council should encourage the business, industrial, and agricultural communities to enter new foreign markets and to expand existing export programs.

1–204. The Council shall provide advice on Federal plans and actions that affect export expansion policies which have an impact on those communities represented by the membership.

1–205. The Council may establish, with the concurrence of the Secretary of Commerce, an executive committee and such other subordinate committees it considers necessary for the performance of its functions. The Chairman of a subordinate committee shall be designated, with the concurrence of the Secretary of Commerce, by the Chairman of the Council from among the membership of the Council. Members of subordinate committees shall be appointed by the Secretary of Commerce.

1–3. *Administrative Provisions.*

1–301. The Secretary of Commerce shall, to the extent permitted by law, provide the Council, including its executive and subordinate committees, with administrative and staff services, support and facilities as may be necessary for the effective performance of its functions.

1–302. Each member of the Council, including its executive and subordinate committees, who is not otherwise paid a salary by the Federal Government, shall receive no compensation from the United States by virtue of their service on the Council, but all members may receive the transportation and travel expenses, including per diem in lieu of subsistence, authorized by law (5 U.S.C. 5702 and 5703).

1–4. *General Provisions.*

1–401. Notwithstanding the provisions of any other Executive order, the functions of the President under the Federal Advisory Committee Act (5 U.S.C. App. I), except that of reporting annually to the Congress, which are applicable to the Council, shall be performed by the Secretary of Commerce in accordance with guidelines and procedures established by the Administrator of General Services.

1-402. Executive Order No. 11753 is revoked; however, nothing in this Order shall be deemed to require new charters for the Council, including its executive and subordinate committees, which were current immediately prior to the issuance of this Order.

1-403. The Council shall terminate on December 31, 1980, unless sooner extended.

JIMMY CARTER

The White House,
May 4, 1979.

[Filed with the Office of the Federal Register 5:03 p.m., May 4, 1979]

Digest of Other
White House Announcements

The following listing includes the President's public schedule and other items of general interest announced by the White House Press Office and not included elsewhere in this issue.

April 30

The President met at the White House with:

—Zbigniew Brzezinski, Assistant to the President for National Security Affairs;
—Frank B. Moore, Assistant to the President for Congressional Liaison;
—Secretary of Transportation Brock Adams;
—Vice President Walter F. Mondale;
—former President Gerald R. Ford.

The President transmitted to the Congress the 1977 annual report of the Upland Cotton program.

The President declared a major disaster for the State of Minnesota as a result of severe storms and flooding, beginning on or about April 14, which caused extensive public and private property damage.

The President declared a major disaster for the State of Illinois as a result of severe storms and flooding, beginning on or about March 1, which caused extensive public and private property damage.

May 1

The President met at the White House with:

—Dr. Brzezinski;
—Mr. Moore;
—the Democratic congressional leadership;
—a group of Congressmen to discuss the department of education legislation;
—Senator John C. Stennis of Mississippi;
—James T. McIntyre, Jr., Director of the Office of Management and Budget.

The President attended a portion of the briefing by administration officials for members of the Advertising Council held in Room 450 of the Old Executive Office Building.

The President transmitted to the Congress the 1977 annual report of the Department of Transportation.

May 2

The President met at the White House with:

—Dr. Brzezinski;
—Mr. Moore, Danny C. Tate, Deputy Assistant for Congressional Liaison (Senate), and William H. Cable, Deputy Assistant for Congressional Liaison;
—Thomas Murphy, chairman of General Motors Corp., and winners of the General Motors Cancer Research Foundation Awards;
—members of the Japanese Diet.

The President hosted a reception for Asian/Pacific Americans on the State Floor at the White House.

The President declared a major disaster for the State of Louisiana as a result of severe storms and flooding, beginning on or about April 20, which caused extensive public and private property damage.

May 3

The President met at the White House with:

—Dr. Brzezinski;

—Mr. Moore;

—Vice President Mondale, Stansfield Turner, Director of Central Intelligence, Hamilton Jordan, Assistant to the President, and Dr. Brzezinski;

—Representative William H. Gray III of Pennsylvania and the National Championship Chess Team from Vaux Junior High School, Philadelphia;

—Mrs. Carter, for lunch;

—Emile Van Lennep, Secretary General of the Organization for Economic Cooperation and Development;

—Ambassador Chai Zemin of the People's Republic of China, Secretary of State Cyrus R. Vance, and Dr. Brzezinski.

May 4

The President met at the White House with Vice President Mondale, Secretary Vance, Secretary of Defense Harold Brown, and Dr. Brzezinski.

The President left the White House for a trip to Iowa and California.

NOMINATIONS SUBMITTED TO THE SENATE

The following list does not include promotions of members of the Uniformed Services, nominations to the Service Academies, or nominations of Foreign Service officers.

NOMINATIONS—Continued

Submitted April 30, 1979

REYNALDO G. GARZA, of Texas, to be United States Circuit Judge for the Fifth Circuit, vice Homer Thornberry, retired.

JON O. NEWMAN, of Connecticut, to be United States Circuit Judge for the Second Circuit, vice a new position created by P.L. 95–486, approved October 20, 1978.

CAROLYN D. RANDALL, of Texas, to be United States Circuit Judge for the Fifth Circuit, vice a new position created by P.L. 95–486, approved October 20, 1978.

PATRICIA M. WALD, of Maryland, to be United States Circuit Judge for the District of Columbia Circuit, vice a new position created by P.L. 95–486, approved October 20, 1978.

MARVIN E. ASPEN, of Illinois, to be United States District Judge for the Northern District of Illinois, vice a new position created by P.L. 95–486, approved October 20, 1978.

VALDEMAR A. CORDOVA, of Arizona, to be United States District Judge for the District of Arizona, vice a new position created by P.L. 95–486, approved October 20, 1978.

CURTIS W. GUYETTE, of Pennsylvania, to be United States Marshal for the Middle District of Pennsylvania for the term of 4 years, vice John L. Buck, term expired.

The following-named persons to be members of the United States Advisory Commission on International Communication, Cultural and Educational Affairs for the terms indicated:

For a term of 1 year

LEONARD L. SILVERSTEIN, of Maryland (new position).

For a term of 2 years

JOHN HOPE FRANKLIN, of Illinois (new position).

NEIL C. SHERBURNE, of Minnesota (new position).

For a term of 3 years

LEWIS MANILOW, of Illinois (new position).

MAE SUE TALLEY, of Arizona (new position).

For the term expiring April 6, 1982

OLIN C. ROBISON, of Vermont (reappointment).

787

NOMINATIONS—Continued

Submitted May 1, 1979

THOMAS EVERETT HARRIS, of Virginia, to be a member of the Federal Election Commission for a term expiring April 30, 1985 (reappointment).

FRANK P. REICHE, of New Jersey, to be a member of the Federal Election Commission for a term expiring April 30, 1985, vice Vernon W. Thomson, term expiring.

Submitted May 3, 1979

AMALYA L. KEARSE, of New York, to be United States Circuit Judge for the Second Circuit, vice a new position created by P.L. 95–486, approved October 20, 1978.

HENRY A. POLITZ, of Louisiana, to be United States Circuit Judge for the Fifth Circuit, vice a new position created by P.L. 95–486, approved October 20, 1978.

MARY M. SCHROEDER, of Arizona, to be United States Circuit Judge for the Ninth Circuit, vice a new position created by P.L. 95–486, approved October 20, 1978.

PETER J. WILKES, of Illinois, to be United States Marshal for the Northern District of Illinois for the term of 4 years, vice Harvey N. Johnson, Jr., deceased.

CHECKLIST OF WHITE HOUSE PRESS RELEASES

The following listing contains releases of the White House Press Office which are not included in this issue.

CHECKLIST—Continued

Released May 1, 1979

Advance text: remarks at the annual convention of the American Society of Newspaper Editors in New York City, N.Y.—by Zbigniew Brzezinski, Assistant to the President for National Security Affairs

Released May 2, 1979

Announcement: list of participants in the U.S.-Japanese meetings

Announcement: nomination of Amalya L. Kearse to be United States Circuit Judge for the Second Circuit

Announcement: nomination of Henry A. Politz to be United States Circuit Judge for the Fifth Circuit

Announcement: nomination of Mary M. Schroeder to be United States Circuit Judge for the Ninth Circuit

Announcement: nomination of Peter J. Wilkes to be United States Marshal for the Northern District of Illinois

ACTS APPROVED BY THE PRESIDENT

NOTE: No acts approved by the President were received by the Office of the Federal Register during the period coverd by this issue.

Editor's Note

Note Concerning the Closing Time of This Issue

The President was in California at the closing time of this issue. Releases and announcements issued on the trip will be printed in next week's issue.

PRESIDENTIAL DOCUMENTS

Week Ending Friday, May 11, 1979

Des Moines, Iowa

Remarks to the Iowa State Association of Counties. May 4, 1979

President Al Ohrt; distinguished members of the Iowa State Association of Counties; my friend Lynn Cutler, who brings to the deliberations of our National Government a constant, forceful, experienced, and effective voice for Iowa. No matter what the subject may be—taxation, welfare, agriculture, education, local development—Lynn Cutler has been one of the very few, but leading county officials who has been involved in every decision made which impacts on municipal and county government. You are fortunate to have her and so am I. Congressman Smith, a strong, forceful voice for this district and for the State; Tom Harkin, an outstanding man who has his feet firmly planted in the soil of Iowa, but whose effective and practical representation of American ideals has given him a nationwide reputation; and Ambassador Dick Clark, who is one of the finest men I have ever known; guests, friends:

I'm very glad to be back here in Iowa. My political life began in county government. And I and my father before me, my father's only brother have all served for many years in local county government. I feel a kinship with you.

There are many difficulties involved in public administration, particularly in these last few years. Sometimes the controversial issues are such that there's no way to win, no matter how hard you try. When food prices go up, the city dwellers are raising Cain; if food prices go down, the farmers are extremely unhappy. Sometimes I don't know whether it's harder for a President to try to establish peace in the Middle East or peace in the Middle West. [*Laughter*]

But I think there is an interesting, I think encouraging sign that among the farm families of this State, the Secretary of Agriculture is more popular than the President. [*Laughter*] So this, I think, bodes well for the status of the Iowa farm family and for those you represent in the cities as well.

Today I want to discuss two very important and major issues from a perspective which I think would suit you. There's no doubt that Americans are afraid that we're going to wind up with worthless money and no gas. And as these fears grow, based on daily headlines and based on daily experiences, so do the demands grow for some quick, simple, and painless solution. So, now Washington is full of people selling snake-oil cures for inflation, or telling science fiction stories about how the energy crisis might be resolved overnight.

You know, there are times when I wish that Washington was Iowa's 100th county. [*Laughter*] But I'm sure that you don't want it. [*Laughter*] So, I will continue to assume that responsibility for you.

But county officials and other local officials, so close to the people, daily accountable, have to tell the truth to people about whether a road can or cannot be resurfaced, about whether a water or sewage line can or cannot be extended, and about where the money to pay for those things is going to come from. That's exactly the kind of directness I have tried to bring to the Federal Government to practice, and that's why I'm here today.

Let's start with the truth about 10 years of inflation. It's a sickness born originally from overindulgence, too much spending with tax reductions combined, and sustained by years of neglect. It's been a long time developing. In the short run, inflation may even get worse. There is no miracle cure, and the measures that will work are going to hurt.

Inflation cannot be fought by the way people usually expect the Federal Government to address a problem—by appropriating vast sums of money for it. That approach had a lot to do with our present problem in the first place, and it's also one reason that I'm very proud that, working closely with your own congressional delegation, in less than 2½ years, we will have cut the Federal deficit in half. And I am absolutely determined to balance the Federal Government [budget].[1]

---

[1] Printed in the transcript.

But as you well know, also, the Federal Government cannot fight inflation alone. Either we do it together or it will not be done. And we need to learn some of these same tough lessons about energy.

The Federal Government has no secret, scientific miracle tucked away that will suddenly produce a cure for our long-standing overdependence on foreign oil. That's why we must use less and we will pay more for what we use, and that is why we must have passed by the Congress this year, without delay, a windfall profits tax and let the oil companies help us pay for the future.

This is important not just because it's not fair for the oil companies to profit from our pain, but because we must have the energy security fund established to develop long-term ways to ease the pain.

You may remember that a few weeks ago all the political experts were saying that we had no chance in Congress to pass a windfall profits tax. Now, the very same people have decided that a windfall tax is an accomplished fact and we can quit worrying about it. They were wrong then, and they are wrong now. Because the people have spoken on this subject, we do have a much better chance than the prophets and commentators thought we had just a few weeks ago.

The windfall tax that we proposed to the Congress will let the oil industry keep, to use for new production of domestic oil, about 29 cents out of every dollar they get because of decontrol. It may even be possible—and I would favor this—to get a stronger bill out of the House. But I warn you that the battle to get a windfall profits tax at all, and to get it under the terms that I have recommended to the Congress, is a battle which is not yet won. And I need your continued support to make sure that a real tax is passed and the important programs in the energy security fund will be financed.

On energy, just as inflation, we have to help ourselves more directly, more individually and, particularly, I'd like to discuss today, more locally.

One of the most frequent questions that I hear people ask is, "If we can put men on the Moon, why can't we figure out a way to furnish cheap energy?"

Well, that is just a dream if it means there is some dramatic, single solution to energy shortages. But it's a good thought if it means that thousands of smaller steps by individual people, by scientists, by researchers, by local officials, business, can lead to an eventual goal of energy self-sufficiency for our country.

Now, I know that small towns and rural counties and farms have a special series of problems that the rest of the country does not always understand. It's hard for many Americans to understand, for instance— but I know, as a farmer—that the production of corn crops in Iowa is greatly affected by the demands of distant Arab nations and giant oil companies for excessive profits on the very energy that you must have for crop-drying and for fertilizer and, also, for transportation and cultivation.

Last year, for example, Iowa agriculture consumed 360 million gallons of gasoline and an additional 200 million gallons of diesel fuel. But I also know that American agriculture provides for export revenues to pay for 18 times as much energy as the farmers use. Our Nation can indeed be thankful for Iowa farmers.

Shortly before we landed, a few minutes ago, Neal Smith proposed that we arrange with our friends in Mexico an exchange of corn for oil. It sounds like a darned good idea to me.

Tomorrow, coincidentally, I'll be meeting with the Foreign Minister of Mexico,

Mr. Roel. I'll discuss this with him, Neal, and if we can't get an exact swap, which is what you proposed, then we will take action and are negotiating very enthusiastically to get an energy agreement with Mexico.

We already buy about 85 percent of all the oil that Mexico exports, and now, as you know, we are working out an agreement on natural gas. But I intend to take other firm steps to guarantee that you will have adequate supplies of gasoline and other fuel during this very difficult farm season. And you can depend on that.

Let me explain these steps very quickly.

First, I want to announce today that Secretary Bergland has determined, under the Natural Gas Policy Act of 1978, that 100 percent of current requirements for natural gas in Iowa agriculture will be maintained.

Second, we will have given authority to State energy offices to set aside 4 percent of the total diesel fuel supplies in every State to alleviate possible hardship cases in agriculture. And we've asked suppliers of diesel fuel to give first priority to agriculture.

And third, we are now reallocating proportionately larger amounts of oil to suppliers who serve rural and agricultural markets. This obviously applies to small towns. I will not allow agricultural production to be disrupted by a shortage of petroleum. And I will not allow rural America to run dry.

We will also authorize users and local suppliers to borrow temporarily during the planting and cultivating season against future allocations of oil and diesel fuel and, if necessary, I will use my standby authority to provide 100 percent not only of the natural gas requirements but also of other fuel requirements for farmers.

Now, rural areas have special needs, but they also have special opportunities, being the best places to apply the virtues of practical thought and local initiative, sometimes on a small-scale, experimental basis. You understand the values of individual effort and small-scale cooperative projects. I've seen this in the so-called hollers of West Virginia, the hamlets of south Georgia, the villages of New England, the pueblos of New Mexico, and the coastal towns of the Pacific Northwest. And I've seen these rural values all over Iowa, perhaps, as Lynn pointed out, in more cities and towns than you yourselves have visited in your own State. I've seen it in your communities, in your schools, in your churches—an attitude.

Some American communities can regain their self-sufficiency by doing things that we have almost forgotten, like burning wood and using small dams that were abandoned in the era of cheap oil. That doesn't apply to Iowa. But there are also new technologies like solar energy, that are a long way from being practical everywhere, but can help your communities toward energy security right now. And there are products like gasohol, methanol, and others that we've known about for years without ever tapping their full potential.

Let me tell you briefly what we are doing to encourage use of these kinds of energy supplies.

Gasohol is a classic example of American ingenuity. Fifty years ago, many Americans were manufacturing gasohol on their own farms or in their own homes and filling up their Model-T Fords with it. Gasohol was simple and practical, since it put our agricultural abundance to work in a new and exciting and different way for those times. But in the era of cheap oil, at a time when we never thought the wells would ever run dry, we stopped trying to harness or test its potential.

The Government forgot about gasohol, and so did the experts. But here and there, an individual American remembered the stories or rediscovered old books in the library, and with a little knowledge and encouragement from Washington or without, the idea has recently been spreading.

I'm today announcing that between now and 1981, we will assist farmers and farm co-ops to build as many as 100 plants to produce gasohol in varying sizes of plants. And I believe this will set an example for the rest of our country.

In the last year, we've already guaranteed loans of about $30 million to construct large gasohol plants in Florida and Texas. And this year, the Agriculture Department will be spending an additional $4 million on gasohol research at some of our leading land-grant universities, obviously including Iowa.

We're also creating economic initiatives for the private development of gasohol. Producers are now eligible for a special 10-percent investment tax credit that has been extended through 1983. And I've recommended that gasohol be permanently exempted from the Federal excise tax on gasoline, once Congress approves the energy security fund.

Everything from wood products to sugar beets to corn, wheat, food processing wastes, animal wastes can be used to make gasohol. The potential is great. Our best calculations are that our Nation can produce 300 million gallons of gasohol annually by 1982—and double that again by 1985.

Equally promising is our rediscovery of the potential of small-scale hydroelectric power. New England used to harness its streams to produce electricity, and it can do so again. We did the same thing in Georgia—so can the Pacific Northwest.

Here in Iowa, rushing, wild rivers may be as scarce as oil wells, but you should search even for those relatively rare opportunities to use water to drive small turbines.

I'm announcing today a reprograming of $300 million of existing funds to rehabilitate 100 rural hydroelectric turbines. The Army Corps of Engineers has identified nearly 2,000 places where we can build or restore this type of hydroelectric plant. Eventually, we should be able to produce enough electricity to save almost 140 million barrels of oil each year— enough to meet the energy needs of 8½ million people.

Again, extracting natural gas from coal mines and from shale reserves is something else we need to do. Over 6,500 rural communities are located near coal or shale reserves, and many have existing gas distribution systems already in place. These communities could use these reserves to produce a steady, dependable supply of natural gas with a slightly lower Btu content, without damaging the environment.

Let me explain how this works. A portable drilling rig can tap the natural gas that exists around deposits of coal and shale. All you then need to do is to cap this well with a device about the size of a fire hydrant. With minimum processing, out comes gas of sufficient pressure and quality to heat the homes, light stoves, and power factories.

The Energy Department has already awarded $3.8 million in grant money to the American Public Gas Association to demonstrate that natural gas can be recovered from coal and shale *and* at competitive prices. If this experiment is a success—and I believe it will be—we will reprogram another $300 million in existing Federal funds to finance development of these new supplies of natural gas between now and 1981.

Last week I was in New Hampshire, and they were very excited to know that last year alone, 750,000 Americans bought wood-burning stoves to heat their homes. Right now, the energy equivalent of more than 500,000 barrels of oil is being produced by wood. We should be able again to double that figure by 1985.

I grew up with wood-burning stoves and open fireplaces, but the new designs of stoves are absolutely remarkable. They burn not only the wood, but the gases from the wood. They are highly efficient, have automatic thermostats, and two or three oak logs or hardwood logs will last for as long as 8 or 10 hours. By the way, I intend to install one quite soon, before next winter, in the White House, and I'll be using it next winter.

But in order to encourage this trend, which is very, very good, I will seek a tax credit for the purchase of wood-burning stoves to be funded out of the revenues from the windfall profits tax. Throughout the Government, we are now working on projects like this to enable us to improve the use of our forests for energy, and particularly the wood we now waste.

Two-thirds of all the home heating, for instance, in some New England States— the same would apply to Georgia and, obviously, to places in the Northwest— can be derived from the wood in our forests that's now left on the ground and completely wasted. This would provide enormous opportunities, as you can see, for additional employment.

The point I'm trying to make is this: Rural America is the best place to experiment with solar energy or with renewable products that come from the Sun. In my 1980 budget, I've proposed that we establish two research centers to work on applying alternative energy sources, including solar energy, to agriculture.

Already the Federal Government is supporting 50 separate experiments in this area. Iowa State University is one of the leaders in this field, a statement which I'm sure does not surprise this audience at all. And they are particularly working on the projects that relate to the better use of solar power to dry crops. It may even be possible to store energy that's received from the Sun during the summer months, and then use that same energy in the winter months. We are planning 91 additional projects, with particular emphasis on using solar energy to heat swine and poultry houses.

We all recognize how important a stable, secure supply of energy is for the economic development of rural areas and small towns. The first question anyone asks before building a plant in a rural community or small town is this: "Can you meet my energy needs?" The answer can be "yes" if rural America applies the same ingenuity and determination to energy that it has to agriculture.

Moving towards energy self-sufficiency in rural America has a very personal meaning to me. I remember how excited my family was by the arrival of the first electricity on our farm when I was 14 years old. It was the biggest single event of my childhood. It had the greatest impact on the way my family lived. It let us stretch our lives and our horizons and gave us the first glimpse of leisure time during the average day.

But I also remember how farms had windmills to pump water. The Sun dried our crops, our meal and our flour were water-ground, and we burned wood for fuel, and there was never a tractor on our farm until after I was old enough to go off to college. We hadn't thought about energy shortages then, or minimum tillage, or gasohol, but I'm sure we would have considered new energy ideas to be not farfetched, but farsighted.

And they now represent a return to our old principle: that government should encourage but never dictate the decisions made by American people or by local initiative. That's a philosophy of government that it's time to resurrect, in my opinion.

Since October of 1978, we've extended this good old principle to four other areas of rural life—health, the housing and social services for elderly citizens, water and sewage systems, and communications. And we're now working on transportation. The overall idea—which has been missing a long time with Federal programs, as you well know—is that by the time we are ready to announce the Nation's first comprehensive rural development policy this summer, many of these initiatives and programs will already have been tested and will already be in existence, here and now.

For example, on January 31, here in Des Moines, Jack Watson,[2] whom Lynn Cutler mentioned, announced a demonstration project to integrate social services with housing for old people. The response since then has been very successful. As a result, this concept will now be incorporated in all such housing throughout the country, and the demonstration has been expanded from 6 to 10 sites. I'm very pleased to announce today that one of the first sites to be chosen will be here in Iowa, in Decatur County.

The rural health initiative is resulting in the construction or the renovation of 300 primary health care clinics over the next 3 years. These clinics will provide accessible, low-cost care to more than 1,250,000 people who previously lacked any access to such primary health care.

On December 1, in the White House, I announced a fundamental reform of the way the Federal Government administers,

[2] Assistant to the President for Intergovernmental Affairs.

each year, over $2½ billion worth of rural water and sewage programs. Instead of 6 sets of 16 different Federal requirements, we've reduced it down to 1. And as a result of these cost-cutting reforms, I'm able to announce water and sewage grant awards of $6½ million across the State of Iowa. And I might add that we're getting OSHA under control for the first time, and letting it serve its proper role of protecting the safety and health of American workers.

Well, to conclude, let me say that all of these initiatives directly address problems which are all too prevalent today in our country. But the knowledge that we can deal with these special problems, using proven, sometimes ancient principles which our ancestors would understand very well, gives me confidence that we can control the enormous, overall problems of energy and inflation.

Together we can overcome real obstacles—instead of just promising simple answers.

Together we can meet challenges—not by pretending that a cry of pain is a cure for a problem, but by drawing once again on the strength that we Americans have within us.

We've done it in our space programs. We've done it in our search for world peace. And we can do it in the toughest fight of all—finding new energy for ourselves here at home, because the greatest energy sources in the world are right here—in our country, in our towns, on our farms, in ourselves.

Thank you very much.

NOTE: The President spoke at 11:35 a.m. in the Grand Ballroom at the Airport Hilton Inn.

In his opening remarks, the President referred to Alvin Ohrt, president, and Lynn Cutler, board member, Iowa State Association of Counties; Representatives Neal Smith and Thomas R. Harkin of Iowa; and former Iowa Senator Dick Clark, Ambassador at Large and U.S. Coordinator for Refugee Affairs.

THE PRESIDENT'S NEWS CONFERENCE OF MAY 4, 1979

Held in Des Moines, Iowa

THE PRESIDENT. Good afternoon. It's good to be back in Iowa. I have one brief statement to make before I answer questions.

CLINCH RIVER BREEDER REACTOR

Today, I spoke to the Iowa county officials about the need to develop new and innovative approaches to our serious energy problem. No one feels more strongly than I do about the need to harness cost-effective technology to solve our energy problems, but we must never allow ourselves to become the victim of our own technology.

If we've learned anything about the recent accident at Three Mile Island, it should be this: As we develop our Nation's energy policy, the safety of every American must be uppermost in our minds.

More than 2 years before the accident in Pennsylvania, I began an effort to kill the Clinch River breeder reactor, so that this country could have a rational, safe, and responsible nuclear energy policy. This is no time to change America into a plutonium society.

The recent vote by the House Science and Technology Committee to proceed with the Clinch River fast breeder reactor over my consistent opposition is a major, potential setback to this effort. The Clinch River breeder reactor is a technological dinosaur. It's a waste of more than $1½ billion of taxpayers' money. It's an assault on our attempts to control the

795

spread of dangerous nuclear materials. It marches our nuclear policy in exactly the wrong direction.

As nuclear power plays a part in our overall energy policy for the foreseeable future, we must proceed cautiously. We must minimize the risks to our society, and above all, we must not plunge into potentially dangerous, unproven, and unnecessary new technologies which may never produce benefits to offset their costs and risks.

We can avoid that mistake by proceeding with an orderly and scientifically sound breeder research and development program, but our immediate attention must be focused on improving the safety of our current nuclear technology to ensure that a Three Mile Island accident never happens again.

We do not need to build a plant based on a wholly new technology about which far less is known than the nuclear reactors that we currently use.

I want to repeat today my longstanding and consistent request to the Congress to deny the well-financed efforts of the big utilities and the energy companies. We must terminate the Clinch River breeder reactor. We have a far more immediate task at hand—putting our existing nuclear power into order and ensuring safety.

I will continue to oppose the construction of this unnecessary, wasteful, and unsound project, and I urge the advocates of the Clinch River project to reconsider their efforts to salvage this ill-conceived idea.

I also urge all those who share my concern about controlling, and the safety of nuclear power to let your voices be heard in the Congress before it's too late.

And now, I would like to recognize Mr. Bill Baker for the first question.

QUESTIONS

INFLATION

Q. Mr. President, I'm from the Clinton, Iowa, Herald. I'd like to ask you what counsel and advice you can offer to those on fixed incomes, particularly the elderly, and all sorts of those workers employed by firms that are conscientiously attempting to follow your 7-percent wage-price guidelines, especially in view of the fact that the inflation rate is now approaching 13 percent.

THE PRESIDENT. I think the inflation rate is going to turn and go down in the foreseeable future, after a few months. We have early indications of that. Also, as you know, built into the social security system, for instance, is an automatic escalator clause to protect our old people from the devastating effects of inflation. Only this week we increased social security payments, I believe, about 9 percent, based on history, recent history, in the inflationary trend.

We are doing everything we can to encourage the anti-inflation fight to be a nationwide fight—not trying to find scapegoats, not believing that the Government itself can do it all.

In spite of the fact that we have cut the budget deficit more than half, we have a very tight budget proposal. We have a sound dollar now. We are increasing exports considerably. Our balance of trade overseas has become very favorable, compared to what it was previously.

We still have some uncontrollable factors. One of those is the price of foreign oil. We're trying to reduce our dependence upon it. Another, obviously, is the high cost of food items which are in scarce supply—fresh fruits and vegetables—caused by a very severe winter in the growing States; very short beef herds, brought about by beef price controls put on by the previous Republican administration; and other factors over which the Government nor private industry nor labor have any control.

But I can say that out of the last 90 wage settlements, 80 of them have been fully within the wage and price standards. And we have carefully monitored the 500 largest corporations, all of them and most of the middle-sized and smaller corporations, and they are substantially within the guidelines in establishing their specific prices. When we identify one that we believe to be out of compliance, we contact them directly. And in almost every case so far, they have voluntarily changed their prices downward and, in one or two cases, have even refunded to their customers overcharges that they had initiated before we caught them in their violations.

So, I think the essence of it is, things look better in the future if we are patient. This is a 10-year inflationary burden. We're trying to turn it downward, but everybody is going to have to cooperate.

And now, I understand that Michael Holmes [Associated Press] has the next question.

ENERGY CONSERVATION

Q. Mr. President, noting Governor Brown's plan for limited gas rationing in California and the ever-increasing demand for energy supplies, is there any way to convince people to voluntarily conserve, or are mandatory controls inevitable?

THE PRESIDENT. I think there is a way to convince people voluntarily to control the waste of energy. I think, first of all, the Congress is going to have to be convinced.

A few years ago, I was mandated by the Congress, for instance, to develop a standby gasoline rationing plan—not to be put into effect instantly, but to be developed very carefully and to make sure that it's equitable and fair—just to have it on the shelf if we do have a nationwide shortage of gasoline. It could then only be implemented if both the President and the Congress thought it was necessary. I think we're going to have to have, perhaps, a few demonstrable shortages, as is now being faced in California, to show that this is necessary.

Another thing that we need to do is to have mandatory savings programs like the setting of thermostats in public buildings, to hold the temperature no lower than 80 degrees in the summer and no higher than 65 degrees in the winter. This saves a lot of energy.

And I believe there's a tremendous desire on the part of American people to go back to those simple forms of energy that I described to the county officials this morning. For instance, 750,000 Americans bought wood stoves last year, a very good move in the right direction.

And we're doing all we can within the Government to encourage Americans voluntarily to restrain themselves. We also have some mandatory laws. I don't have time to go into all of them. One of them is a very stringent law that, year-by-year, will require Detroit and other cities where automobiles are manufactured to give us more efficient automobiles. And we are exploring technology, in cooperation with them and other manufacturers, to make the items that use energy, necessary for us, to be more efficient.

It's a long, tedious process. We've never had a national energy policy before. The Congress has courageously addressed this very difficult issue, and I believe that the benefits will be obvious in the future. But it's going to have to be a combination of mandatory controls and voluntary, with the heavy emphasis on voluntary.

Ms. Thomas [Helen Thomas, United Press International].

AMERICAN PRISONER IN ISRAEL

Q. Mr. President, you were recently instrumental in securing the release of several Russian dissidents. In similar terms of humanity, would you be willing to exert influence on the Israeli Government to secure the release of a young American woman? Her name is Terre Fleener of San Antonio, and she is wasting away in Israeli jails.[1]

THE PRESIDENT. I'm not familiar with the case, but before this day is over, I will contact the Secretary of State and ask him to initiate an investigation and seek her release, if it's considered to be advisable.

PRESIDENT'S CANDIDACY FOR REELECTION

Q. Mr. President, Mark Braun, with KCCI–TV in Des Moines. Since Iowa was the State that changed "Jimmy Who?" to "Jimmy Carter" 3 years ago——

THE PRESIDENT. Thank you.

Q. ——don't you think it would be appropriate to make your formal announcement right here that you're going to run for reelection? [*Laughter*]

THE PRESIDENT. No. [*Laughter*]

Q. Any indication one way or the other?

THE PRESIDENT. No. I think it's best for me, in this time of some excitement about progress and some concern about problems, to remain a full-time President.

---

[1] Terre Fleener was convicted of giving information on Israeli security arrangements to members of the Palestine Liberation Organization. She was released from prison on June 30, 1979, after serving 20 months of a 5-year sentence.

It's too early for me to get involved in any discussion about an upcoming election.

But I will always remember that my visit—as someone pointed out this morning—to, I think, 119 Iowa cities, and my going on farms at the time land was being broken, corn was being planted, fertilizer applied, cultivation, harvest season, when pigs were being farrowed—I think I got a picture of our Nation, particularly the farm community, that stands me in good stead now. And I also learned about the plight of American farmers under the previous administration that has stood me in good stead in choosing Secretary Bergland and qualified farmers to run the department. But I benefited greatly from my visits to Iowa as a President. But I'll remain a President for the foreseeable future and devote my full time to that job.

Judy [Judy Woodruff, NBC News].

NUCLEAR POWER

Q. Mr. President, we know your position on the breeder, the nuclear breeder reactor.

THE PRESIDENT. Yes.

Q. But in light of the information that Secretary Califano presented yesterday on Capitol Hill, that as many as 10 people could die of cancer directly because of the accident at Three Mile Island, have you begun to rethink your attitude about the light water reactor? After all, it was that kind of reactor where this accident happened.

THE PRESIDENT. I'm deeply concerned about it and, as you know, have appointed a special Presidential commission to look into the causes of the accident, to see what mistakes may have been made in the design or operation of the plant, to make more effective the Nuclear Regulatory Commission and, also, to make sure that if we have a repetition at any time of a similar accident, that there be a better coordination between private, local, State, Federal officials.

Obviously, nuclear reactor safety is the preeminent concern, and I believe that this is an opinion shared by Americans throughout our Nation. It's not a new concern for me. I've been involved in nuclear power in one form or another since 1952, and I'm familiar with the limitations of it, and I'm familiar with the concerns about it.

It's hard to estimate accurately how many people's lives may have been affected by very low levels of additional radiation. It's hard to quantify them. But if any single person either dies prematurely or has any sort of injury or aberration, it would be of deep concern to me.

But I think we have a proper degree, now, of commitment, through this Commission—which will report very expeditiously, commensurate with a broad range of their discussions and investigations in 6 months—to prevent any further accidents of this kind.

Q. Do you still consider yourself a strong supporter of the concept of nuclear power?

THE PRESIDENT. I have always thought that nuclear power should be used as a last resort in the evolution of energy. But I also recognize that when you use what oil is available, and what natural gas is available, and what coal is available, and what solar energy is available, up until now we have seen a need to use nuclear power.

We now get about 12 percent, I think, of our electricity from nuclear power. Some States, like Illinois, for instance, get a great deal more of their power from nuclear powerplants. And it would not be advisable to terminate this use peremptorily. The thing to do is—those that have to continue to provide needed power—to make sure they are safe and, in the future, to try to have conservation, which we've never emphasized in our country ade-

quately, and to shift to alternative means of power to reduce the necessary dependence upon atomic power which we have experienced in recent years.

GASOHOL

Q. Mr. President, Mike Waring, from the Blackhawk Stations. In your speech this morning, you mentioned the increased spending for gasohol development by the Federal Government. So far, the Department of Energy has downplayed the importance of gasohol. Why do you think gasohol should be developed, and how much can we count on it in the future for downplaying our gasoline usage?

THE PRESIDENT. It's one of those incremental approaches to energy that will be of aid. To decrease the gasoline consumption of automobiles to get 1/2 mile more per gallon has a tremendous benefit over our country. Other nations, like Brazil in some regions, have at least 10 percent of all their automobile fuel consisting of gasohol or similar materials.

I think gasohol has a possibility beyond its actual cost and use, because gasohol can be evolved from waste products that are presently very costly. It's extremely costly, for instance, in the making of, say, paper, where you take the entire tree, minus its bark, and through chemical processes, extract paper. Formerly those gases were sometimes dispensed into the atmosphere. It was a very costly process. The heat had to be generated anyhow, and you were fouling the atmosphere with very precious gases. Now those same companies, through new techniques that they've just learned in the last few years, are condensing those gases and using them in a form similar to gasohol or methanol.

Additionally, animal wastes, food wastes that are resulting from the processing of all kinds of foods, including animals, city garbage, these kinds of things can be used for fuel and to produce gasohol.

I was in India last year and went to a very small town in a poverty-stricken region. One of the most interesting things that the very poor people had there was a small tank, three or four hundred gallons, where they dumped their human and animal wastes, extracted from it gas, through a pipe, to use in several homes for both heating and cooking, and then after this process was over, they drained the remaining sediment off and used it for fertilizing the fields.

So, on a very tiny basis of that kind, with a very small plant, all the way up to a large production plant, I think we have a good possibility in the future.

And we don't know what the future might bring. At even existing levels of price, gasohol may not be economically advisable. But as the price of oil, for instance, in the future goes up—in a very slow process, I hope—then gasohol will become ever more competitive. I think it has a good possibility. It's one of those things that we cannot ignore.

GASOLINE SHORTAGES

Q. Mr. President, do you think Governor Brown was warranted to today authorize the counties of California and the local subdivisions to put in this odd-even gas allocation plan? And is there anything the Federal Government could do to help California out of this sort of abnormal shortage because of the glut of high-sulfur oil, but the lack of the type of oil it needs?

THE PRESIDENT. Yes, he was warranted. I'll be meeting with Governor Brown this afternoon when I arrive in California. The proposal that we have made to the Congress for standby author-ity to implement limited days for purchase can only go into effect after the Governor of a particular State goes through this process presently being experienced in California.

In other words, the first thing is a voluntary conservation measure to cut back on, say, gasoline, 2 or 3 percent, whatever is required. Secondly, the Governor proposes either odd-even days or weekend purchases or some other means to save gasoline. Only after that process takes place does the Federal Government institute a possible weekend closing. We've not yet been able to get the Congress to approve that. But I do think that he has acted properly and I do think he's acted responsibly.

I would do anything within my power to aid Governor Brown in this particular time, with a gasoline shortage. And I would say that this is not the first, it's certainly not the last gasoline shortage that our country will experience.

And we've almost forgotten now what we did see in 1973 and 1974. And this is an early indication of a repetition of gasoline shortages. As I said a couple of weeks ago and again in my energy speech a little bit longer ago, we anticipate gasoline shortages this summer. The California experience is a few months before I thought it would be.

Next summer, we think the shortages are going to be even greater. And one reason is that we have got to have an adequate supply of home heating oil, for instance, in New England, and we have got to have an adequate supply of gasoline and distillate for farm tractors and other equipment to use to produce food.

So, the average motorist is going to be faced with more shortages of gasoline in the future than we have experienced today. And we ought to be ready for it. And we're not yet ready for it.

WOOD-BURNING STOVE FOR THE WHITE HOUSE

Q. Dave Beeder, from the Omaha World-Herald. You said today you were planning to buy a stove for the White House. What room are you going to heat with that stove?

THE PRESIDENT. I didn't say I was going to buy it. [*Laughter*] One of the stove manufacturers—[*laughter*]—sent a letter to one of the United States Senators and said they had a stove that they would like to contribute to the American people to be used in the White House or at Camp David. And I have asked for further information about it. And I intend to install it, depending on its configuration and so forth, either in one of the rooms where we live or, perhaps, in my private office in the West Wing. But this is a contribution to the American people, and I might hasten to add that when I leave the White House, the stove will stay there. [*Laughter*]

OIL PRICE CONTROLS

Q. Mr. President, the other day in a news conference when talking about deregulation, you said it wasn't your idea, and you indicated that the reason you hadn't pushed it was because chances in Congress were very unlikely for passage. My question now is, would you support deregulation or an extension of price controls on gasoline if it passes both the House and Senate this year?

THE PRESIDENT. This question concerns me because it has a very complex effect, perhaps, on what Congress does. I don't think there's a chance in the world that the Senate, with a potential filibuster, will possibly pass legislation to extend price controls on oil. If the House and Senate pass this legislation and send it to me, I

will certainly not veto it. We will live with it. The thing that concerns me is that there are many people, because of varying motivations, who want to stop the passage of a windfall profits tax. And as long as they can hold out a glimmer of hope that we won't have either—we won't have decontrol, so therefore we need not have a windfall profits tax—I'm afraid that the oil companies might escape the sure implication of a windfall profits tax.

So, to summarize, if the Congress should pass extended controls, I would not veto it, but I believe we need to concentrate our efforts on passage of a real, strong windfall profits tax.

Q. A brief followup. Will you continue to fight it in the House as you did the other day—the extension of controls?

THE PRESIDENT. Well, we didn't make an all-out effort to stop it. What we did do was to point out to the Members of the House the argument that I've just described to you, that it's almost impossible to conceive of extended controls passing the entire Congress and, therefore, let's don't sidetrack the congressional effort and let the oil companies escape the imposition of the windfall profits tax.

My judgment is that no matter what the House does, the Senate will never pass an extension of oil price controls. And so, we have got to focus our attention not on a fruitless effort with that legislation, but on a real, genuine test of strength between the American people and the oil companies and get a windfall profits tax passed.

EXCHANGES OF AGRICULTURAL PRODUCTS FOR OIL

Q. Mr. President, this morning you mentioned that you're going to be talking with Mexican officials this weekend about possibly swapping American grain for Mexican oil.

THE PRESIDENT. Yes.

Q. I was wondering at this time, would you be willing to take that one step further and speak to the OPEC countries about that kind of a swap?

THE PRESIDENT. Well, I think you know that corn, for instance, or soybeans or wheat is sold to the OPEC countries on a worldwide marketing system. There's a plentiful supply at this time. We have desperately been trying to avoid the kind of confusion that existed when I first came to Iowa. We have increased exports every year to set record levels—last year $27 billion worth of American farm products were sold overseas. This year we hope to reach $30 billion worth. So, I don't think it would be feasible to try to work out any sort of swap deal with the OPEC nations.

But with Foreign Minister Roel, tomorrow at the Cinco de Mayo celebrations in Los Angeles, I will discuss this proposal made by Congressman Neal Smith. That may be a sound basis on which to reach an agreement, because the proximity to Mexico means that we can have special delivery both of oil from them to us, including natural gas in the future, and also grain. But to have a similar swap deal, I think, would probably be infeasible for the OPEC countries as a whole.

OIL COMPANY PROFITS

Q. Mr. President, in the first 3 months of this year, the American oil companies had profits that were twice the average profits for all American corporations. Your Secretary of Energy, Mr. Schlesinger, in a television appearance last month, said that the profits of oil companies are not too high, they're perfectly in line with everyone else. Now, implicit in your windfall tax proposal is the assumption that if it isn't passed, and you have decontrol, that the oil companies will reap very, very high profits. My question to you is, leaving aside the windfall profits tax and the question of decontrol, do you think oil profits are too high now?

THE PRESIDENT. Compared to other corporations, the oil companies' profits are at a high level, not higher than any other corporations. On a comparison between capital investment and return on investment, I think they're running 12 or 13 percent, which is a bountiful return on investment.

If those returns are invested back into increasing American production of natural gas, oil, and other related materials, I think it's a very sound thing for our country. But the decontrol process will give them additional income above and beyond what I've described.

Under the windfall profits tax, of every dollar in increased income from that source, they would only be permitted to keep 29 cents. My hope, again, is that they would take that 29 cents and reinvest it back into the further production of oil and gas.

So, this is what I'm concerned about, and the reason that I think in some instances the profits have been excessive in the past, above what they needed for production, is that some of the oil companies have gone far outside their field, even completely beyond the realm of energy, and bought fast food market chains, or motels and hotels and things of that kind, that have no relation to energy. I want to see them invest their profits back into energy production.

FUEL SUPPLIES FOR AGRICULTURE

Q. Mr. President, in your speech this morning you indicated, or tried to reassure this State they would have the diesel fuel supplies that they need.

THE PRESIDENT. That's correct.

Q. Now, the State Energy Policy Council here doesn't feel that way. They feel that there are going to be some severe shortages in the State as far as diesel fuel goes. And what I'm asking you is, what do you feel that the proposals that you offered this morning to the State association are going to do to alleviate any of these predicted shortages that the State here feels are definitely going to happen?

THE PRESIDENT. Well, I would be glad to repeat the things that I said this morning.

First of all, when any shortage occurs on a nationwide basis, I have the authority to establish priorities and to make a limited degree of allocation. And along with hospitals, ambulances, police protection, and fire protection, in the top priority comes food production, agriculture. And if all the items that I described this morning should prove to be inadequate, then I would use that authority of mine to make an emergency allocation of additional fuel oil, distillate, and gasoline to the farmers to get their crops planted, cultivated and, ultimately, harvested.

Secretary Bergland has already determined that under the natural gas legislation passed in 1978, that he will make available to farmers 100 percent of their needs for natural gas, primarily used in the crop-drying season. So, I can assure you that this will be adequate.

If local imbalances occur, then we will give the Governors the authority to take 4 percent of all of the fuel oil and gasoline that comes into the State and allocate it themselves at the State level, where there's more sensitivity about local need, directly to those areas that might have a temporary imbalance.

And the other thing that we will do is to permit suppliers of fuel oil and gasoline to borrow on their future allocations if there is a shortage.

Now, I'm familiar with the fact that the groundbreaking season and the planting season in Iowa has been delayed. There's going to be a rush among the farmers to catch up with lost time. And we have already assimilated this. Secretary Bergland, Secretary Schlesinger, and I have made as careful preparations as possible to assure that there is no shortage of fuel in Iowa during this year.

And I've given you the best answer I can, and within the bounds of my authority and human competence and my complete dedication, what I said this morning will be carried out.

Ms. THOMAS. Thank you, Mr. President.

THE PRESIDENT. Thank you.

[President Carter's forty-ninth news conference began at 2 p.m. in the Lower Monterey Room at the Des Moines Hyatt House. As he was leaving the room, the President answered an additional question from a reporter as follows.]

BRITISH ELECTIONS

Q. Sir, if you'd been asked about the change in the British Government, what would you have said?

THE PRESIDENT. I talked with Mrs. Thatcher within the last hour and pledged her my support and cooperation, congratulated her on her victory. We made arrangements to consult very quickly through the Foreign Secretary of Great Britain, who will be named tomorrow, and the Secretary of State, Secretary Vance.

I've already talked to Secretary Vance as a followup, and told him to be prepared for this consultation. She and I will be exchanging messages and letters. We will be meeting with each other next month, at the latest, in Tokyo. And we've made arrangements to have a private meeting so that we can compare the policies of our two nations at that time. In the meantime, our Cabinet members will be consulting even more closely and perhaps more personally.

But I'm obviously convinced that the outcome of the election will not in any way interfere in the superb relationships that have always existed between our countries since I've been in office and for many years before that.

Des Moines, Iowa

Remarks at a State Democratic Party Reception. May 4, 1979

My son Chip loves you—[*laughter*]—my mother loves you and I love you. I think my mother considers Des Moines a second home and particularly the Dixieland band who went to Ireland with her. Thank you very much.

I'm really proud to be back. None of you could ever know the feelings, even, of emotion that sweep over me when I walk into the room and I see Iowa people who, when no one else in our Nation knew or cared who I was, took me into your homes and considered me to be a friend—I'm sure, privately figured that I had no chance ever to become President, but didn't let that doubt stand in your way—and who've now become almost like a member of our own family.

I can tell you that there's not much difference between Iowa people and those where I live. In fact, throughout the country, folks are interested in the control of inflation, better life for our people, control of nuclear weapons, peace, the way the President parts his hair. [*Laughter*] So, I feel like I'm part of you, and I am glad to be back.

It is a superb development, I think, in Iowa to see how you've continued one of the most dynamic and dedicated and competent Democratic Party organizations in our country. This has been an opportunity to show the leadership of Ed Campbell,[1] and I want to express my personal thanks to him as President of our country and as the titular head of the Democratic Party for the great job he's doing here in Iowa.

I want to say also that above every other political consideration, no matter what it might be, the number one priority for me in 1980 in Iowa is the reelection of a superb Senator, John Culver.

And I want to thank you for the great support you gave Dick Clark when he ran both times. This was a tragic loss for the United States Senate, when Iowa abandoned its usual sound judgment and did not send him back to Washington. But I brought him back, and I am grateful and I would like to say to you that he's one of the finest men I've ever met. And he has not only the competence and the dedication, the knowledge of human affairs, but also the sensitivity and idealism to finally make a success out of our own policy toward refugees. And I'm glad that he was able to ride with me from Washington back to Iowa. And I want to personally thank Dick Clark for what he means now, what he will mean in the future, and what he's always meant to you. Dick Clark, thank you.

I knew that if I mentioned Dick Clark the applause would take up all my time. [*Laughter*] But I certainly have time to express my thanks also for two superb Congress Members who came to Iowa with me today and who gave me a new and up-to-date briefing on the concerns

---

[1] Chairman of the Iowa State Democratic Party.

and the challenges and the future of your State. Congressman Neal Smith and Congressman Tom Harkin, who are personal friends of mine and superb Representatives of a great State, thank you for being with us.

I don't want to make a long speech. I've already spoken to the county officials, and I just had a 30-minute press conference. I think I've covered most of the points. But I would like to ask you as Americans and as Democrats to help me in the upcoming crucial battles that will face the United States Congress.

First of all, there's the ratification of SALT. When we do conclude the negotiations, which will be very shortly now, I will then meet with President Brezhnev, if no unforeseen developments should occur, and then present to the Senate later on this year the SALT II treaty for ratification. The issue is in doubt, but in my opinion, there could not possibly be a more important challenge to the American people than the continuation of control of nuclear weapons.

My goal, as you well know, is to eliminate nuclear weapons completely from the face of the Earth. And I need your help and your support, and if you let your voice be heard and let all the voices of your neighbors be heard throughout Iowa, both Democrat and particularly Republican, I believe we'll have an excellent chance to get this treaty ratified. I'm committed to it. I'm dedicated to it. I don't know of anything more important to my own administration or to the future of our country than to continue this progress toward controlling nuclear weapons.

The second thing I want you to help me with is the consummation of an adequate national energy policy for our country. We must save energy. We must be innovative in evolving new domestic supplies of all kinds. And we need to impose a windfall profits tax on the oil companies to give us the funds necessary for the further development of solar power and other advanced technologies that might let us be energy-independent in the future.

We've had good luck so far in letting the spirit of America be felt throughout the world. I think we've reestablished in other nations the sure knowledge that our Nation has not abandoned the principles on which it was founded 200 years ago— faith in God, freedom, independence, peace, equality of opportunity, individual initiative, and a commitment to basic human rights. These will be the policies of our Government as long as I'm in the White House. And we have seen one implementation already, in the signing of the Mideast peace treaty. It's a first step. We've got a long way to go. But I hope you will help me in this respect as well.

And the last thing I want to mention to you is this: I don't know exactly why, but I have read the public opinion polls taken among farmers in Iowa that show a belief that I and, to a lesser degree, the Secretary of Agriculture are not sensitive to the needs of farm families of our country. This is not the case. Anyone with any memory at all, or any sound judgment at all, would recall the situation among farm families of our Nation when I first began to come to Iowa and to walk from door to door and to drive or fly from one town to another. I witnessed the life of the farm families then. I learned elements of agriculture that wasn't a part of my past existence.

But at that time, as you know, grain embargoes were a normal part of the farm community's life. In 1973, 1975, all exports were terminated. When we finally made a sale, like to the Soviet Union, we were embarrassed because the farmers got cheated and grain dealers got rewarded. And Dick Clark and John Culver and the

Members of the House, as you well know, finally put some integrity in the quality of farm products, particularly grain we sell overseas.

Net farm income in the short 2 years— *net* farm income has gone up 40 percent, and exports every year hit a new record. We've now provided an opportunity for farmers to control their own harvest until it's ultimately sold with increased farm storage.

These are the kinds of things that I could spend a long time talking about that ought to be emphasized. And if anybody criticizes the Democratic Party, the Members of Congress, my administration, for the courageous action that we've tried to take, just ask them to think back 3 years and compare their life then and their life now. We obviously still have problems in our country but we are not afraid to face them.

I'd like to say this in closing: I've got a little time set aside, and I've already expressed my thanks to you for what you mean to me personally, and to our country, from this podium. But I don't like to approach Iowa people on opposite sides of a velvet rope. So, I would like to ask you, if you don't mind, to come by one at a time and let me shake your hand and thank you personally and pledge my complete, dedicated service to make you proud of our Nation. And if you don't mind, I'd like to get an individual photograph with you as well. Okay?

Thank you.

NOTE: The President spoke at 2:35 p.m. in Monterey Rooms 3 and 4 at the Des Moines Hyatt House.

Undocumented Aliens

Letter to State Governors. May 4, 1979

During my visit to Mexico City in mid-February, I had a frank and useful dis-
cussion with President López Portillo on the complex issue of border law violations and particularly the problem of undocumented workers. We agreed to cooperate closely to explore the question in the context of the social and economic problems involved—a solution that also respects the dignity and human rights of those concerned. One aspect of this question, the treatment of undocumented workers in the United States, has been of particular concern to me and to President López Portillo.

As I stated in Mexico, it is my responsibility to enforce our immigration laws. Those individuals who violate the law will be dealt with as the law prescribes. But it is also our responsibility to deal fairly and humanely with any persons accused of being undocumented workers.

For some time we have been making a special effort at the Federal level to ensure their fair treatment under the law. The Immigration and Naturalization Service has steadily improved the conditions under which undocumented workers are temporarily confined and has adopted a number of measures to prevent mistreatment and to allow apprehended aliens time to settle their affairs before departure. The Department of Labor is making a special effort in those areas believed to have a sizeable presence of undocumented workers to enforce wage, hour, safety and health standards and to assure that workers who are apprehended and removed from the country receive all wages due them.

Since many of the problems that undocumented aliens experience are under state and local jurisdiction, I ask that you give these concerns your close personal interest. I, in turn, would welcome your suggestions of areas you might suggest in which further Federal action would be useful.

The Department of Justice is giving special attention to investigating and, where warranted, prosecuting, possible civil rights violations against any persons of Hispanic origin.

Our country's deep commitment to standards of justice and humaneness requires us to protect the basic rights of all people who find themselves in this nation.

JIMMY CARTER

San Francisco, California

Remarks at a Memorial Tribute for Former Mayor George Moscone. May 4, 1979

If I had only attended Lowell High School—[*laughter*]—perhaps I would have been part of the program instead of in the intermission. [*Laughter*]

I want to say a few words as President, because the death of George Moscone was a national tragedy. And I want to say a few words as President, because you've come here not for oratory, but to pay tribute to a fallen leader and to enjoy the performance of superb artists. I know that George Moscone, had he been able to choose a program this evening, would have called on Maestro Adler [1] to present to us what we have been honored and privileged to enjoy.

George Moscone was a lover of music and a lover of people and a lover of this city. He was always gracious to me and to Rosalynn when we came to visit San Francisco, far beyond what his duties as mayor would have required. And I knew him, as President, as a superb mayor, a leader throughout America who had a special vision of what urban America ought to be. He helped me when we be-

---

[1] Kurt Adler, general director of the San Francisco Opera.

gan to draft a plan for the entire Nation, and he showed a special compassion for a city and also a special compassion and concern for the rights of others, particularly when they were a minority or poor or timid or quiet or inarticulate or abused.

Gina, you know that we extend to you our sympathy, but we also express our pride in what George was and what he helped to create here.

For Americans in the last 16 years, assassination has partially blighted our lives, because those who have been killed have been America's finest. Assassination of a public official robs us all, in a way. It takes away our freedom. It takes away our rights to enjoy the blessings of democracy, to be able to choose our own leaders and then to have those leaders govern us throughout their entire term of office. That's why it's such a shattering blow and always again so unexpected when a tragedy of this kind occurs.

George Moscone spent most of his adult life, as you know, serving the people of this city and this county in a financially sacrificial way. That's one of the results of personal integrity and honesty. And he was not able to live to leave a large financial estate for his family, as you know. But he left them a personal heritage that's even more precious and which is dramatically proven tonight and in previous efforts by those who loved him and appreciate him and Gina and the children and Lee, his mother, who have established this foundation to provide for security and a greater life for them.

San Francisco has shown its ability to survive shocks, and this event tonight, your participation in it, what's gone on before, has helped us all to realize that San Francisco is still strong enough and united enough to survive this second major shock that came during the end of 1978.

I appreciate Dianne Feinstein,[2] who, with her calm and compassionate leadership, preserved the precious attributes of this city during those trying days. It's a magical city on the bay, which has the admiration and appreciation and love of the entire country. And you demonstrated again a special spirit by being able, during this event, to change grief and loss into love and hope.

NOTE: The President spoke at 7:05 p.m. at the War Memorial Opera House.

Following the performance, the President left for Los Angeles, where he spent the night at the home of Mr. and Mrs. Stephen Rodriguez.

Gasoline Shortages in California

Statement by the President. **May 5, 1979**

Although this particular crisis came on suddenly, we have known since 1973–74 that something like this was bound to happen.

The reason for the gas lines and terrible inconvenience here—and the rest of the Nation faces similar problems later this summer and maybe worse next year—is that we have failed to be prepared.

I sent up proposals in 1977 as part of the National Energy Plan to increase production, reduce consumption, and cut back on our reliance on imported oil— COET, industrial users tax, etc.—none of these proposals were passed into law.

A few weeks ago, I announced phased decontrol and asked Congress to pass a windfall tax, a standby rationing plan, a gasoline conservation plan, and two other conservation measures. We have a decent chance on the windfall tax—three of the other four are doubtful.

***

[2] Ms. Feinstein succeeded Mr. Moscone as mayor of San Francisco.

Too many people are afraid to vote for steps that may be a little unpopular. As a result, we continue to dream while our problems grow worse and worse.

The fact of the matter is that once a shortage is on us, there is no way to create more gas out of thin air. By then, it is too late for immediate relief.

Immediate causes of the problem seem to be:

(1) Less oil than expected coming in because of Iran—which underscores our dependence on imports and thus our vulnerability.

(2) Increased consumption here and nationwide.

(3) My decision that priority in a time of shortage must be given to heat for homes, hospitals, etc., and to food production.

I have taken these steps:

(1) Directed Secretary Schlesinger to immediately determine the facts of this situation, in consultation with State and local government and private leaders— why it developed as it did; what steps can be taken, if any, beyond those I have already recommended to Congress, to alleviate the situation now and in the future. He is to report his findings to me by the end of next week.

(2) Directed the Department of Energy to move immediately to ensure that recent changes in the allocation program to provide additional gasoline to high-use areas, such as southern California, are strictly enforced.

(3) I want to ask drivers in this area to resist the urge to try to keep their tanks full at all times. This only exacerbates the problem, and obviously there is a great need to avoid all nonessential use of gasoline.

But let me repeat, the only way we can avoid increasingly frequent and more severe repetitions of this type of problem is for Congress to forget about the idea that there is some way around the hard fact that we must use less energy and pay more for it—and pass the proposals now before them.

It is time for responsible national leaders in the Congress and elsewhere to forget about extending controls or taking away my power to begin phased decontrol. Those proposals will never pass. They offer no solution to the problems faced by people here in southern California, and they are a waste of time and a distraction from the real task we face.

There are simply no easy answers—no answers that do not involve higher costs for energy and using less energy. That is the truth. To imply otherwise, to waste more valuable time looking for a painless way out can have only one result: more weekends like this here in southern California—and all over the country.

NOTE: The statement was released in Los Angeles, Calif.

Los Angeles, California

Remarks at Dedication Ceremonies for La Placita de Dolores de Los Angeles. May 5, 1979

Thank you, Mayor Tom Bradley. Distinguished guests and friends, distinguished Foreign Minister of the Republic of Mexico, Mr. Roel:

I would like to say a few words in Spanish, if you will bend your ear very closely to understand my southern accent.

[*At this point, the President spoke in Spanish. He then translated his remarks as follows.*]

I can also speak some English.

And I'm very proud to be here to dedicate this Placita de Dolores in Los Angeles. This is the birthplace of this great city, which has the largest Spanish-speaking population in the United States. This plaza will provide a permanent resting place for the replica of the Bell of Dolores, the original of which hangs in the Capitol Building in Mexico City. As you know, this replica was presented to this city, Los Angeles, by President Gustavo Diaz Ordaz of Mexico 11 years ago.

This plaza will also give the Hispanic community—indeed all the people of Los Angeles—a gathering place, a place for exhibits by artists and craftsmen, a place for celebrations, and a place for festivals. And I'm delighted that this project, funded partially by a Federal grant, will also provide employment within the community.

Projects such as this—which meet public needs, enhance historic places, and create needed jobs—and they show what the Federal Government can do to help revitalize our cities, working in harmony with local officials and private citizens.

As we dedicate this plaza, it's good to remember the village priest, Father Miguel Hidalgo y Castilla, who rang the parish church bell, the original Bell of Dolores, to summon patriots to fight for independence. The freedom and independence that Mexico and the United States now enjoy are ours because millions of our people throughout the years have had the courage to do what was necessary, no matter what the odds might have been against their sometimes lonely efforts.

Freedom is never permanently ours, despite the noble sacrifices of past generations. We must daily rewin the fight against injustice and prejudice and ignorance, and against those in power who believe that they know better than the people what is best.

Many have died heroically that we may stand here on this beautiful day and celebrate human freedom which we enjoy. And many more have lived quietly, defending day by day against the cynical, the selfish, and the unconcerned, the principles that we hold dear—often they have done this in their homes or in their small communities, often at great cost and without any praise, without any recognition, without any glory.

I pray that we will never again have to defend our freedoms in battle with the shedding of blood, and that the love of peace which fills our hearts will at last prevail. But to survive, our system must not only beat back the sword of aggression; it must also beat back the silent hand of injustice that's armed only with our own apathy and our own timidity.

I'm committed to making sure that all the people—all the people—within our borders, no matter how they may have gotten here, are treated always with dignity and with justice. And I am also committed to protecting the basic human rights of every person in this country, whatever their legal status might be.

I will make sure, within the bounds of my authority and capability as President of the United States of America, that no one is exploited or abused, either by unscrupulous employers, unprincipled gang bosses or smugglers, who prey on poverty, ignorance, and human misery, and who sometimes even hold little children as hostages to wring a few extra dollars from empty pockets and work-worn hands.

[At this point, the President again spoke in Spanish. He then translated his remarks as follows.]

Justice and respect for each individual's rights—wherever that individual might come from—must be practiced every day by every one of us. It's not enough to be fair to most of the people most of the time. We must be fair to all, all of the time. Our own independence in the United States is meaningless without this unless it means the guaranteeing of rights of all those who dwell within our borders. It's meaningless if it does not mean freeing the human spirit in our midst, whatever the language in which its voice, its dreams.

Thank you very much.

NOTE: The President spoke at 11:30 a.m. at the plaza, located in El Pueblo de Los Angeles State Historical Park.

Earlier in the day, the President attended separate meetings with Los Angeles community leaders, black leaders, and members of the California Chicano Caucus.

Los Angeles, California

Remarks at a Cinco de Mayo Celebration.
May 5, 1979

¡Buenos tardes a todos! [Good afternoon, everybody!]

Thank you for the "Viva Carter" signs. Now put them down so the folks can see, please.

Senator Cranston; Governor Brown; Mayor Bradley; distinguished Members of the Congress; President Hahn; my good friend Ed Edelman, who sponsored this celebration; Senator Montoya; Assemblyman Alatorre and Art Torres; other friends who've come here together today:

As President of a nation which has a great number of citizens who speak Spanish, I would like to say a few words, first of all, in Spanish.

[At this point, the President spoke in Spanish. He then translated his remarks as follows.]

To demonstate that I can speak two languages, I will now use English.

As you know, we are here to celebrate the spirit of liberty and independence that Mexican Americans have symbolized by Cinco de Mayo. That day in Puebla in

1862 when the battle was finally won, freedom from foreign domination had not been achieved. It was 5 years more before Mexicans had control of their own land.

The shots that were fired in our country in Lexington and Concord, shots heard around the world, not because the American colonists at that time achieved their independence, but because they had made clear their irrevocable determination to be free.

The victory at Puebla proved the Mexican people's staying power and love of freedom and their irrevocable will and determination to be free.

The United States of America is a nation of immigrants. We're a nation of refugees. We've always been a people of many backgrounds, with a varied cultural heritage. We've come together from all parts of the world, speaking many languages of the Earth, drawn by a common belief in human freedom, human justice and opportunity.

Spanish settlements not far from my own hometown in Georgia were already 100 years old when the first English settlers arrived on this continent at Plymouth Rock. Spanish roots are an important part of our diverse heritage. But quite often this fact is obscured, because the history books were written by the English.

Spanish-speaking people in this modern day must share more of the responsibilities of government. I have not accomplished all I hope to do; neither has any other public official in our land. And I have not accomplished all I plan to do. But I have increased the participation in the Federal Government by Spanish-speaking Americans.

I've appointed more than 150 Hispanics to high levels of position in my administration—in positions where their sensitivity to the needs of Chicanos and others who speak Spanish can be brought to my

attention on a daily basis—in my own staff in the White House, Rick Hernandez. Ernie Camacho heads the White House Conference on Small Business, to bring together businessmen from all over the nation, no matter what their nationality. Ernie Camacho will coordinate this effort. Lou Moret has served as Deputy to SBA, Small Business Administration, Office of Minority Economic Impact, to be sure that minority-owned businesses have their just rights fulfilled.

I'm happy to announce my intention to appoint Lou Moret as an Assistant Secretary of Energy. And he will help to answer some of the signs I see, as the energy shortages, which are inevitable, might impact on the minority community in our country. As you know, he was formerly executive director of the Chicano caucus in the legislature here.

I want job opportunities for Hispanics at all levels of government. Unfortunately, the Congress did not fully go along with my recommendations in civil service reform, which would have opened up many other opportunities. But we are not yet through. They have helped tremendously, and we are making all the people in Government service sensitive to the needs of a people who have long been deprived of their just rights, the people of the United States who speak Spanish, or whose parents or ancestors did speak Spanish.

The situation for many Mexican immigrants is somewhat different, as you know, from immigrants from other lands, either in the early days of our Nation or in modern times. Those from Mexico do not come here fleeing for their lives or because their basic liberties are being denied in Mexico. Immigrants from Mexico do not have to cross any formidable ocean, but they walk here across a 2,000-mile open border between friendly nations. They do not come seeking escape, but seeking opportunity; they do not come seeking asylum, but seeking employment, jobs.

For those who enter legally, things are not easy, but they at least have all the protections of everyone else who live in this country. The undocumented workers, however, sometimes living in fear, exploited by those who mistreat them and take advantage of the most vulnerable among us, exist outside our legal system. They are hunted not for crimes—because they've committed no crimes—but because they are here without permission. They are people who seek only a better life for their children and a better opportunity for themselves. This is exactly what my own ancestors sought when they first came to this country.

Leonel Castillo, a Mexican American, as you know, who's director of the Immigration and Naturalization Service, is trying to bring an incredibly antiquated immigration service into modern times. When we came into office, he found a situation where it was impossible to call the Los Angeles service of the immigration, because all the lines were always busy. Letters were lost in rooms piled high with unopened mail. The only hope of communicating with the immigration office 2 years ago was to come in person and to stand in line. He found people getting in line at midnight just to make an appointment to stand in line at a later time. Often that next appointment was months away.

He found people waiting 4 years to get a petition acted on—petitions to bring in a wife or a husband or a child, particularly legally, to reunite families, to apply for citizenship, or to visit a dying mother in Mexico—things they were entitled to do under the law.

He has cut that time lag dramatically to 90 days or less for most applications, and he's desperately trying to have a more efficient service as every week goes by. He understands, and so do I, that these were not merely paperwork problems or traffic problems, but human problems, involving the rights and the hopes of suffering men, women, and children who could not wait 4 years for an answer.

I'm committed to bringing [making] [1] our Government work so that no one has to wait for an answer, but Leonel Castillo and I have never pretended that there was no problem. I am committed to finding a humane solution to the problem of undocumented workers now in this country.

I cannot promise you any simple solutions. We cannot solve the immigration problems on this side of the border alone. Mexico is fully aware that the solution to this problem is to continue the good progress now being made in Mexico in economic development and jobs.

I have told President López Portillo that we are ready to cooperate in every way with the Mexican Government in furthering this goal which he and I share together.

In the short term, there are disagreements on the best solutions, even within the Chicano community, as you know. But there can be no disagreement over the need to deal humanely and fairly with this problem. Overall, there is no nation with whom our relationship is more important than Mexico. And you've heard Foreign Minister Roel say the same thing a few minutes ago.

I have also appointed a special commission on immigration that includes Judge Cruz Reynoso and Joaquin Otero. The Chairman of this commission, Reubin Askew, former Governor of Florida, met with President López Portillo, Foreign Minister Roel, and other senior Mexican officials in Mexico April the 18th

---

[1] Printed in the transcript.

to the 20th on the question of undocumented workers. This commission will also be listening to the ideas of Mexican Americans in this country so that it can recommend a fair, realistic, and effective solution.

When I was in Mexico in February, we made significant progress in every important area. We have been buying, as willing customers, about 85 percent of all the oil exported from Mexico. And the government-to-government negotiations on natural gas are going well. The negotiating team met first in Mexico and just yesterday completed a second round of negotiations in Washington. Negotiations are under way on programs in agriculture, energy research, scientific and technical cooperation, and increasing trade.

Our concern does not end the question of citizenship. No matter how concerned we are, we still have the problem. Unemployment among Hispanic young people is unacceptably high. The Hispanic worker, whether part-time or full-time, is twice as likely as other workers to earn an income below the poverty line. This is a problem of opportunity—of education and training, of bilingual programs that must meet the real needs of young people who will have to cope in a society where the majority speaks a different language.

But this is not a problem of preparation alone. Education and training, even when they are equal, traditionally have opened fewer doors for Hispanics. There's also a problem of equity, fairness, justice, and affirmative action, to which I am fully committed.

I'm committed to breaking down the discrimination against Hispanic Americans wherever it remains in this country.

The record increase in Federal funding for education, particularly programs for disadvantaged youngsters to help them master basic skills, will help to guarantee that the young people who will enter the workforce of the future will not be considering inadequate preparation as a barrier as often as they do today. Our young people are our most valuable resource. They cannot wait a generation for slow change. They need their chance now.

I would like to close by saying a few more words in Spanish.

[*At this point, the President again spoke in Spanish. He then translated his remarks as follows.*]

President López Portillo told me that Mexico is still struggling for its independence. In the 19th century, Mexico won its political independence. In this century, Mexico is winning its economic independence. The freedom and independence of Mexico is tied to a continuing struggle for freedom and independence of individual citizens in the United States, and to quote the historic words of Benito Juarez, "Among nations as among men, respecting the rights of others is the way to peace."

Thank you very much.

NOTE: The President spoke at 12:15 p.m. at the Los Angeles County Hall of Administration. In his opening remarks, he referred to Kenneth Hahn, chairman, and Edmund Edelman, supervisor, Los Angeles Board of Supervisors.

Following his remarks, the President went to the Biltmore Hotel for a luncheon with the editorial board of the Los Angeles Times. He then visited actor John Wayne at the UCLA Medical Center before returning to Washington, D.C.

Standby Gasoline Rationing Plan

Message to the Congress Transmitting Contingency Plan No. 5. May 7, 1979

To the Congress of the United States:

Pursuant to Sections 201(d)(1) and 552 of the Energy Policy and Conservation Act (EPCA), 42 U.S.C. 6261(d)(1) and 6422, I am hereby transmitting to the Congress for its approval an amendment to the Standby Gasoline Rationing Plan (Standby Gasoline Rationing Plan No. 1) which I transmitted on March 1, 1979.

During the consideration of the Standby Gasoline Rationing Plan, concerns were raised by both Houses of Congress that the Plan did not treat states and the citizens within states equitably. The purpose of this amendment is to add new provisions to the rationing plan to eliminate the potential for disparities during plan operation. The first provision alters the procedure for determining allotments of ration rights by including a historical gasoline use factor in each state, and expands the State Ration Reserve, thereby compensating for disparities both within and among states. The second change limits the number of vehicle allotments each household could receive, reflecting my belief that households with over three vehicles should not receive excessive benefits at the expense of other households.

Under this amendment, each state will be provided with an expanded State Ration Reserve of eight percent not only to provide for the needs of the handicapped and hardship applicants as already provided in the plan, but to provide additional flexibility to the states in dispensing supplemental ration allotments to citizens with special needs. The National Ration Reserve is anticipated to remain at approximately two percent of the available gasoline supply.

The amendment also provides a new method for calculating the ration rights to be alloted to each registered vehicle. Instead of allocating the net total available gasoline supply equally to vehicles in all states, the amendment provides for half the available gasoline supply to be

distributed equally to vehicles and half to be allotted on the basis of historical gasoline use in the respective states.

Another provision limits the number of ration rights received by each household to three vehicle allotments. Ration rights not distributed to members of a household pursuant to the limitation of this amendment will be distributed to the State Ration Reserve in the state in which such household is located. This amendment would not preclude members of a household from obtaining additional ration rights from the State Ration Reserve on the basis of hardship or other factors.

The procedures for approval by Congress of an amendment to a contingency plan are detailed in Section 552 of the EPCA, and require among other things that a resolution of approval be passed by each House of Congress within 60 days of submittal of the amendment. I urge the Congress to give this amendment expedited consideration so that it may be approved promptly with the Standby Gasoline Rationing Plan.

The EPCA does not specify in Section 552 the form which the resolution of approval is to take. As I noted in my submission of the Standby Gasoline Rationing Plan on March 1, 1979, it is my view and that of the Attorney General that actions of the Congress purporting to have binding legal effect must be presented to the President for his approval under Article I, Section 7 of the Constitution. Therefore, I strongly recommend that Congressional approval of the amendment be in the form of a joint resolution. If this procedure is followed, the amendment itself, agreed to by the Congress and the President, will not later be subject to possible judicial invalidation on the ground that the President did not approve the resolution.

Prompt Congressional approval of the Standby Gasoline Rationing Plan is essential. Failure of the Congress to act will leave the Nation vulnerable to economic disruption and long gasoline station lines. It is obviously impossible to develop a plan which will be perceived to be fair by each person. The proposed plan, as amended, is designed to be broadly equitable, practical and administrable. If we fail to approve a standby rationing system, the Nation's resolve to deal with a serious supply interruption will be called into question. The resulting damage to the economy and personal hardships to our citizens could be substantial.

I urge the prompt and favorable consideration by the Congress of the Standby Gasoline Rationing Plan and this amendment.

JIMMY CARTER

The White House,
May 7, 1979.

NOTE: The text of the amendment is included in the press release.

Council on Wage and Price Stability

Message to the Congress Transmitting a Report.   May 7, 1979

To the Congress of the United States:
In accordance with Section 5 of the Council on Wage and Price Stability Act, as amended, I hereby transmit to the Congress the seventeenth quarterly report of the Council on Wage and Price Stability. This report contains a description of the Council's activities during the fourth quarter of 1978 in monitoring both prices and wages in the private sector and various Federal Government activities that may lead to higher costs and prices with-

out creating commensurate benefits. It discusses Council reports, analyses, and filings before Federal regulatory agencies and the Council's role in the anti-inflation program.

The Council on Wage and Price Stability will continue to play an important role in supplementing fiscal and monetary policies by calling public attention to wage and price developments and Government actions that could be of concern to American consumers.

JIMMY CARTER

The White House,
May 7, 1979.

World Health Organization

Announcement of the U.S. Delegation to the 32d World Health Assembly.   May 7, 1979

The President today announced the members of the U.S. delegation to the 32d World Health Assembly of the World Health Organization, to be held in Geneva from May 7 to 25. They are:

Chief Delegate:
JOSEPH A. CALIFANO, JR., Secretary of Health, Education, and Welfare

Delegates:
JULIUS B. RICHMOND, Assistant Secretary of HEW
JOHN H. BRYANT, Deputy Assistant Secretary of HEW for International Health

Alternate Delegates:
NEIL A. BOYER, Director of the Agency Directorate for Health and Narcotics Programs, Bureau of International Organizations, Department of State
LEE M. HOWARD, Director of Health Services for AID
WILLIAM J. VANDEN HEUVEL, Representative of the United States to the European Office of the U.N. in Geneva

National Energy Plan

Message to the Congress Transmitting the Second Plan. May 7, 1979

To the Congress of the United States:

I am pleased to transmit to the Congress the second National Energy Plan as required by Section 801 of the Department of Energy Organization Act (Public Law 95–91).

The First National Energy Plan, which I sent to the Congress two years ago, was the first comprehensive effort to deal with the broad scope of the Nation's energy problems. The resulting National Energy Act, passed last autumn, acted on a number of my proposals, and will have an important and lasting role in preparing for the Nation's energy future.

But much remains to be done. And we must now deal jointly with a number of issues which have matured since April 1977.

As I said in my April 5th energy message, our Nation's energy problems are real. They are serious. And they are getting worse. Every American will have to help solve those problems. But it is up to us—the Congress and the Executive Branch—to provide the leadership.

We must now build on the foundation of the National Energy Act. In my April 5th energy address, I laid out a program for action in five areas.

First, in accordance with the Energy Policy and Conservation Act of 1975, I have announced a program to phase out controls on domestic crude oil prices by September 30, 1981. Oil should be priced at its true replacement value if we are to stop subsidizing imports, increase U.S. oil production, reduce demand, and encourage the development and use of new energy sources.

Second, the increased revenues from decontrol must not unduly or unjustly enrich oil producers at the expense of consumers. For this reason, I have proposed a tax on the windfall profits due to decontrol. Proceeds from the tax would be used to establish an Energy Security Trust Fund, which would be available, in part, to assist those low-income Americans who can least afford higher energy prices.

Third, we must provide additional emphasis on conservation and on the development of new domestic energy sources and technologies. The Energy Security Trust Fund will also provide funds for energy saving mass transit and for tax incentives and accelerated research and demonstration of new energy technologies.

Fourth, we must find ways to expeditiously develop and use our energy resources, while protecting and enhancing the quality of the environment. The length and complexity of many Federal, State, and local permitting procedures, however, has created needless complexity and increased time and cost, without improving the protection to the public or the environment. We must remove the needless red tape which is tying up many needed energy projects. I have signed an Executive Order to expedite Federal decision-making for certain energy projects, which are deemed to be in the National interest.

Fifth, we must provide international leadership to deal with the crisis before us today. The members of the International Energy Agency have joined in a common commitment to reduce energy consumption in response to current shortages. The United States has provided leadership in gaining this commitment. I will assure the United States does its part to meet that commitment.

The energy program I announced on April 5th puts the country in a strong position to achieve these goals. The Plan I am forwarding today shows how these programs relate to our overall energy problem, and to the other policies and programs which we must carry forward.

This National Energy Plan explicitly recognizes the uncertainties—geologic, technological, economic, political, and environmental—which confront us. It presents a strategy for dealing forthrightly with the uncertainties, with the threats and promises of our energy future.

The analysis in the Plan shows the need to move aggressively to meet the grave energy challenges to our Nation's vitality. My April 5th proposals confront those challenges squarely. Together with the National Energy Plan, we are providing a firm foundation for dealing with these challenges today and for decades to come.

JIMMY CARTER

The White House,
May 7, 1979.

Energy Emergency in Florida

Memorandum From the President.
May 7, 1979

Memorandum for the Administrator, Environmental Protection Agency

Based on a request submitted to me by the Governor of the State of Florida to extend my April 6, 1979 determination that a regional energy emergency exists in the State of Florida of such severity that a temporary suspension of certain particulate and opacity control regulations which apply to fossil-fuel fired electric generating plants under the Florida Air Quality Implementation Plan be necessary, and that other means of responding to the energy emergency may be inadequate, I hereby extend that deter-

mination from May 5 to June 4, 1979. This extension shall be effective for not more than thirty (30) days and is limited by the same conditions as my original determination. If, during the extension, I find that a regional energy emergency no longer exists in Florida, I will direct that this extension be rescinded and that all suspension orders issued by the Governor be terminated on the day of that rescission. You will continue to retain full authority to disapprove temporary suspension of regulations in Florida and to exercise your emergency powers authority under Section 303 of the Clean Air Act, when and if necessary.

It is important to keep suspensions to an absolute minimum since Section 110(f) of the Clean Air Act limits each suspension to a maximum duration of 120 days.

This determination shall be published in the FEDERAL REGISTER.

JIMMY CARTER

[Filed with the Office of the Federal Register, 11:04 a.m., May 8, 1979]

NOTE: The memorandum was announced on May 8.

Flag Day and National Flag Week, 1979

Proclamation 4660.   May 8, 1979

By the President of the United States of America

A Proclamation

Two years after the Battle of Bunker Hill, on June 14, 1777, the Continental Congress chose a flag which tellingly expressed the unity and resolve of Colonials who had banded together to seek independence. The delegates voted "that the flag of the thirteen United States be thirteen stripes, alternate red and white; that the union be thirteen stars, white in a blue field representing a new constellation."

With the addition of thirty-seven stars, and after more than two centuries of history, the flag chosen by the Continental Congress in Philadelphia is our flag today, symbolizing a shared commitment to freedom and equality.

To commemorate the adoption of our flag, the Congress, by a joint resolution of August 3, 1949 (63 Stat. 492), designated June 14 of each year as Flag Day and requested the President to issue annually a proclamation calling for its observance. The Congress also requested the President, by joint resolution of June 9, 1966 (80 Stat. 194), to issue annually a proclamation designating the week in which June 14 occurs as National Flag Week and to call upon all citizens of the United States to display the flag of the United States on those days.

To focus the attention of the American people on their country's character, heritage and future well-being, the Congress has also, by joint resolution of June 13, 1975, set aside the 21 days from Flag Day through Independence Day as a period to honor America (89 Stat. 211).

Now, THEREFORE, I, JIMMY CARTER, President of the United States of America, do hereby designate the week beginning June 10, 1979, as National Flag Week, and I direct the appropriate officials of the Government to display the flag on all Government buildings during the week. I urge all Americans to observe Flag Day, June 14, and Flag Week by flying the Stars and Stripes from their homes and other suitable places.

IN WITNESS WHEREOF, I have hereunto set my hand this eighth day of May, in the year of our Lord nineteen hundred seventy-nine, and of the Independence of the United States of America the two hundred and third.

JIMMY CARTER

[Filed with the Office of the Federal Register, 11:05 a.m., May 8, 1979]

Emergency Board To Investigate a Railway Labor Dispute

Executive Order 12132.   May 8, 1979

CREATING AN EMERGENCY BOARD TO INVESTIGATE A DISPUTE BETWEEN THE NATIONAL RAILWAY LABOR CONFERENCE AND CERTAIN OF ITS EMPLOYEES

A dispute exists between the National Railway Labor Conference and certain of its employees represented by the American Train Dispatchers Association, a labor organization;

This dispute has not heretofore been adjusted under the provisions of the Railway Labor Act, as amended; and

This dispute, in the judgment of the National Mediation Board, threatens substantially to interrupt interstate commerce to a degree such as to deprive a section of the country of essential transportation service:

Now, THEREFORE, by the authority vested in me by Section 10 of the Railway Labor Act, as amended (45 U.S.C. 160), it is hereby ordered as follows:

1-101. *Establishment of Board.* There is established a board of three members to be appointed by the President to investigate this dispute. No member of the board shall be pecuniarily or otherwise interested in any organization of railroad employees or any carrier.

1-102. *Report.* The board shall report its finding to the President with respect to the dispute within 30 days from the date of this Order.

1–103. Maintaining Conditions. As provided by Section 10 of the Railway Labor Act, as amended, from this date and for 30 days after the board has made its report to the President, no change, except by agreement, shall be made by the National Railway Labor Conference, or by its employees, in the conditions out of which the dispute arose.

JIMMY CARTER

The White House,
May 8, 1979.

[Filed with the Office of the Federal Register, 2:40 p.m., May 8, 1979]

Emergency Board To Investigate a Railway Labor Dispute

Announcement Concerning Executive Order 12132 and Appointment of the Membership of the Board. May 8, 1979

The President has signed an Executive order creating an emergency board to investigate the dispute between the National Railway Labor Conference and certain of their employees represented by the American Train Dispatchers Association.

He also appointed three persons as members of the Emergency Board. They are:

James J. Reynolds, a former Assistant Secretary of Labor and Under Secretary of Labor in the Kennedy and Johnson administrations. Reynolds was a member of the National Labor Relations Board in the Truman administration, and was president of the American Institute of Merchant Shipping from 1969 until his retirement in 1978. He will serve as Chairman of this Emergency Board.

Ida Klaus, of New York City, an arbitrator and mediator with more than 40 years' experience in the labor relations field. She has served as special arbitrator under the U.S. Steel agreement since 1975. She has also served as solicitor for the National Labor Relations Board and labor counsel for New York City. From 1962 to 1975, she was executive director of the Office of Labor Relations and Collective Bargaining of the New York City Board of Education.

Nicholas H. Zumas, a Washington, D.C., attorney and arbitrator. Zumas, currently in private practice, is a member of the District of Columbia Board of Labor Relations and has also served as assistant to the Under Secretary of HEW and counsel for the House Special Subcommittee on Education of the Education and Labor Committee.

This Emergency Board is created under the procedures of the Railway Labor Act. It will report its findings and recommendations to the President within 30 days, and the parties must then consider the Board's recommendations and try to resolve their differences within the next 30-day period. Without the creation of this Board, the dispute would threaten a shutdown on May 10 of 52 of the Nation's railroads, the number represented by the National Railway Labor Conference.

United States Ambassador to Egypt

Nomination of Alfred L. Atherton, Jr. May 8, 1979

The President today announced that he will nominate Alfred L. Atherton, Jr., of Palm Beach Gardens, Fla., to be Ambassador Extraordinary and Plenipotentiary of the United States to the Arab Republic of Egypt. He would succeed Hermann F. Eilts, who is retiring from the Foreign Service.

Atherton is currently Ambassador at Large at the State Department.

He was born November 22, 1921, in Pittsburgh, Pa. He received a B.S. in 1944 and an M.A. in 1947 from Harvard University. He served in the U.S. Army from 1943 to 1945.

Atherton joined the Foreign Service in 1947, and served in Stuttgart, Bonn, Damascus, and Aleppo. From 1959 to 1961, he was Iraq-Jordan desk officer, then Officer in Charge for Cyprus, in the Bureau of Near Eastern and South Asian Affairs at the State Department.

In 1961–62 Atherton took advanced economic studies at the University of California at Berkeley. From 1962 to 1965, he was economic officer in Calcutta, and from 1965 to 1966, he was Deputy Director of the Office of Near Eastern Affairs at the State Department.

In 1966 and 1967, Atherton was Country Director for Iraq, Jordan, Lebanon, and Syria. From 1967 to 1970, he was Country Director for Israel and Arab-Israel Affairs.

From 1970 to 1974, Atherton was Deputy Assistant Secretary of State for the Bureau of Near Eastern and South Asian Affairs. From 1974 to 1978, he was Assistant Secretary for Near Eastern and South Asian Affairs. Since 1978 he has been Ambassador at Large.

United States Tax Court

Nomination of Arthur L. Nims III To Be a Judge.   May 8, 1979

The President today announced that he will nominate Arthur L. Nims III, of Madison, N.J., to be a Judge of the U.S.

Tax Court. He would replace Arnold Raum, who has retired.

Nims was born January 3, 1923, in Oklahoma City. He received a B.A. from Williams College in 1947, an LL.B. from the University of Georgia Law School in 1949, and an LL.M. (Tax) degree from New York University in 1954. He practiced law in Macon, Ga., from 1949 to 1951.

Nims was a trial attorney before the Tax Court in the Office of the Regional Counsel of the Internal Revenue Service (IRS) in New York City from 1951 to 1954. He was an attorney in the Legislation and Regulations Division, Chief Counsel's Office, IRS, from 1954 to 1955. In 1955 Nims became an associate with the Newark firm of McCarter & English. Since 1961 he has been a partner with that firm.

During the past year Nims has served as secretary of the section of taxation of the American Bar Association. From 1974 to 1976, he was chairman of the partnership committee. He served as chairman of the New Jersey Bar Association's section of taxation from 1961 to 1971.

Standby Gasoline Rationing Plan

Message to the Congress Transmitting Contingency Plan No. 6.   May 8, 1979

To the Congress of the United States:

Pursuant to Sections 201(d)(1) and 552 of the Energy Policy and Conservation Act (EPCA), 42 U.S.C. 6261(d)(1) and 6422, I am hereby transmitting to the Congress for its approval an amendment to the Standby Gasoline Rationing Plan (Standby Gasoline Rationing Plan No. 1) which I transmitted on March 1, 1979. This amendment is a substitute for Contingency Plan No. 5 which I transmitted on May 7, 1979.

During the consideration of the Standby Gasoline Rationing Plan, concerns were raised by both Houses of Congress that the Plan did not treat states and the citizens within states equitably. The purpose of this amendment is to add new provisions to the rationing plan to eliminate the potential for disparities during plan operation. The first provision alters the procedure for determining allotments of ration rights by basing allotments on a historical gasoline use factor in each state, and expands the State Ration Reserve, thereby compensating for disparities both within and among states. The second change limits the number of vehicle allotments each household could receive, reflecting my belief that households with over three vehicles should not receive excessive benefits at the expense of other households.

Under this amendment, each state will be provided with an expanded State Ration Reserve of eight percent not only to provide for the needs of the handicapped and hardship applicants as already provided in the plan, but to provide additional flexibility to the states in dispensing supplemental ration allotments to citizens with special needs. The National Ration Reserve is anticipated to remain at approximately two percent of the available gasoline supply.

The amendment also provides a new method for calculating the ration rights to be allotted to each registered vehicle. Instead of allocating the net total available gasoline supply equally to vehicles in all states, the amendment provides for the available gasoline supply to be allotted on the basis of historical gasoline use in the respective states.

Another provision limits the number of ration rights received by each household to three vehicle allotments. Ration rights not distributed to members of a household pursuant to the limitation of this amendment will be distributed to the State Ration Reserve in the state in which such household is located. This amendment would not preclude members of a household from obtaining additional ration rights from the State Ration Reserve on the basis of hardship or other factors.

The procedures for approval by Congress of an amendment to a contingency plan are detailed in Section 552 of the EPCA, and require among other things that a resolution of approval be passed by each House of Congress within 60 days of submittal of the amendment. I urge the Congress to give this amendment expedited consideration so that it may be approved promptly with the Standby Gasoline Rationing Plan.

The EPCA does not specify in Section 552 the form which the resolution of approval is to take. As I noted in my submission of the Standby Gasoline Rationing Plan on March 1, 1979, it is my view and that of the Attorney General that actions of the Congress purporting to have binding legal effect must be presented to the President for his approval under Article I, Section 7 of the Constitution. Therefore, I strongly recommend that Congressional approval of the amendment be in the form of a joint resolution. If this procedure is followed, the amendment itself, agreed to by the Congress and the President, will not later be subject to possible judicial invalidation on the ground that the President did not approve the resolution.

Prompt Congressional approval of the Standby Gasoline Rationing Plan is essential. Failure of the Congress to act will leave the Nation vulnerable to economic disruption and long gasoline station lines. It is obviously impossible to develop a plan which will be perceived to be fair by each person. The proposed plan, as amended, is designed to be broadly equitable, practical and administrable. If we fail to approve a standby rationing system, the Nation's resolve to deal with a serious supply interruption will be called into question. The resulting damage to the economy and personal hardships to our citizens could be substantial.

I urge the prompt and favorable consideration by the Congress of the Standby Gasoline Rationing Plan and this amendment.

JIMMY CARTER

The White House,
May 8, 1979.

NOTE: The text of the amendment is included in the press release.

United States-Hungary Convention on Taxation and Fiscal Evasion

Message to the Senate Transmitting the Convention. May 9, 1979

To the Senate of the United States:

I transmit, herewith, for Senate advice and consent to ratification, the Convention between the Government of the United States of America and the Government of the Hungarian People's Republic for the Avoidance of Double Taxation and the Prevention of Fiscal Evasion with Respect to Taxes on Income, signed at Washington February 12, 1979. For the information of the Senate, I also transmit the report of the Department of State with respect to the Convention.

This Convention is the first income tax convention to be negotiated between the United States and the Hungarian People's

Republic. It is intended to facilitate economic relations and the exchange of scholars between the two countries by removing tax obstacles to the flow of investment and the travel of persons.

The Convention follows closely the United States model income tax convention and the 1977 model convention of the Organization for Economic Cooperation and Development (OECD). It clarifies taxing rules, reduces or waives the tax at source on investment income and income from limited business or employment activities, ensures nondiscriminatory taxation and provides for administrative cooperation between the tax authorities of the two countries to avoid double taxation and to prevent fiscal evasion with respect to taxes on income. An accompanying exchange of notes clarifies some technical points and includes some administrative provisions.

I recommend that the Senate give early and favorable consideration to the Convention and give advice and consent to its ratification.

JIMMY CARTER

The White House,
May 9, 1979.

United States-Tuvalu Treaty of Friendship

Message to the Senate Transmitting the Treaty. May 9, 1979

To the Senate of the United States:

I transmit herewith, for the advice and consent of the Senate, the Treaty of Friendship between the United States of America and Tuvalu. The report of the Department of State is enclosed for the information of the Senate.

The Treaty meets the practical interests of both countries. It will satisfy the desire of the Tuvaluan people that their claim to sovereignty over half of the inhabited islands in their country, including their capital, will not be encumbered by a conflicting claim by the United States. It will protect United States interest in assuring nondiscriminatory future access to the fishing grounds of Tuvalu which supply fish to the canneries on American Samoa. United States security interests in a peaceful, secure, and stable South Pacific are served by the consultation clauses in times of international crisis.

The Treaty will further United States foreign policy interest in promoting peace, security and development of the region and assure nondiscriminatory access to the region by the United States fishing fleet and other vessels contributing to the American Samoan economy. I recommend that the Senate give early consideration to the Treaty and give its advice and consent to ratification.

JIMMY CARTER

The White House,
    May 9, 1979.

Standby Gasoline Rationing Plan

Statement on Senate Approval of the Plan.
May 9, 1979

I applaud the Senate for showing the Nation and the world that this country is ready to deal with an unexpected future energy shortage, through its strong endorsement of the Standby Gasoline Rationing Plan.

I call upon the House of Representatives to place the national interest above narrower interests, as the Senate has done.

Congress required the executive branch to submit a standby rationing plan in the Energy Policy and Conservation Act of 1975. The plan which the Senate passed was submitted pursuant to that requirement. This is not a plan to achieve mandatory conservation, but is simply a standby measure to permit an orderly distribution of gasoline in the event of a significant shortage. Congress will have the opportunity to pass upon the plan again before it can be implemented.

The plan passed by the Senate creates a national ration reserve to deal with critical national emergencies; a significant State ration reserve of 8 percent to be allocated within States at the discretion of the Governors to deal with special State problems which may occur as a result of severe gasoline shortages; provides for priority allocation of gasoline to critical sectors of the economy, such as farmers; and distributes the balance to owners of registered vehicles based upon historic use of gasoline within the States. This is an efficient and equitable way to distribute gasoline allotments.

State consumption figures would be regularly updated so that in the unexpected event that the standby plan had to be implemented, the latest data would be available.

For reasons of equity, we have limited the gasoline allotments to no more than three vehicles per household.

We do not expect that we will ever need to use this plan, but, as with our military forces, we would be foolhardy not to be prepared should such a need ever arise.

Defeat of this plan would leave this country vulnerable and defenseless against a supply interruption. The Government would require 6 to 8 months to develop, pass, and implement a new plan—time we could ill-afford during an energy crisis.

I urge the Members of the House of Representatives to recognize the national

823

interest and to send a message to the country and the rest of the world that this country will not be helpless if an unexpected shortage develops.

Drug Policy Functions

Executive Order 12133.   May 9, 1979

By the authority vested in me as President by the Constitution and laws of the United States of America, including Section 5C of Reorganization Plan No. 1 of 1977 (42 FR 56101), and in order to clarify the performance of drug policy responsibilities within the Domestic Policy Staff, it is hereby ordered as follows:

1-101. The Domestic Policy Staff has been assigned to assist the President in the performance of the drug policy functions transferred by Section 5C of Reorganization Plan No. 1 of 1977 (42 FR 56101). (Section 2(c) of Executive Order No. 12045.)

1-102. Within the Domestic Policy Staff, the Associate Director for Drug Policy shall be primarily responsible for assisting the President in the performance of all those functions transferred from the Office of Drug Abuse Policy and its Director. In particular, the Associate Director for Drug Policy shall be primarily responsible for assisting the President in formulating policy for, and in coordinating and overseeing, international as well as domestic drug abuse functions by all Executive agencies.

1-103. The Associate Director for Drug Policy shall be directly responsible for the activities of a drug policy staff within the Domestic Policy Staff.

JIMMY CARTER

The White House,
May 9, 1979.

[Filed with the Office of the Federal Register, 10:18 a.m., May 10, 1979]

Printing Services Within the Executive Office

Executive Order 12134.   May 9, 1979

By the authority vested in me as President by the Constitution and laws of the United States of America, including Reorganization Plan No. 2 of 1970 (5 U.S.C. App. II), Section 202 of the Budget and Accounting Procedures Act of 1950 (31 U.S.C. 581c), and Reorganization Plan No. 1 of 1977 (42 FR 56101; 5 U.S.C. App. II), and in order to provide for the transfer of the printing and duplicating service activity from the Office of Administration in the Executive Office of the President to the Department of the Navy, it is hereby ordered as follows:

1-101. (a) The primary responsibility for performing the common and usual administrative support and services that are related to printing and duplication and that are assigned to the Office of Administration in the Executive Office of the President by Section 3(b)(5) of Executive Order No. 12028, as amended, is transferred and reassigned to the Department of the Navy.

(b) The Department of the Navy shall be primarily responsible for providing to the Office of Administration, both onsite and offsite, that common and usual administrative support and service related to printing and duplication. It shall be provided in a manner consistent with available funds and other resources, or in accord with Section 7 of the Act of May 21, 1920 (41 Stat. 613), as amended (31 U.S.C. 686, referred to as the Economy Act).

1-102. The records, property, personnel, and unexpended balances of appropriations, available or to be made available, which relate to the functions transferred or reassigned by this Order, shall be transferred to the Department of the Navy.

1–103. The Director of the Office of Management and Budget shall make such determinations, issue such orders, and take all actions necessary or appropriate to effectuate the transfers or reassignments provided by this Order, including the transfer of funds, records, property, and personnel.

1–104. Such transfers shall be effective on May 6, 1979.

JIMMY CARTER

The White House,
May 9, 1979.

[Filed with the Office of the Federal Register, 10:19 a.m., May 10, 1979]

President's Advisory Committee for Women

Executive Order 12135. May 9, 1979

By the authority vested in me as President by the Constitution and statutes of the United States of America, in accordance with the provisions of the Federal Advisory Committee Act (5 U.S.C. App. I), and in order to amend the organization and responsibilities of the National Advisory Committee for Women, it is hereby ordered as follows:

1–1. *Establishment of the Committee.*

1–101. The National Advisory Committee for Women is continued and redesignated the President's Advisory Committee for Women.

1–102. The President shall appoint not more than thirty individuals to serve on the Committee. The President shall designate one member to chair the Committee and may designate two members as vice-chairs.

1–2. *Functions of the Committee.*

1–201. The Committee shall advise the President on a regular basis of initiatives needed to promote full equality for American women.

1–202. The Committee shall assist in reviewing the applicability of such initiatives, including recommendations of the 1977 National Women's Conference, to particular programs and policies.

1–203. The Committee shall provide advice on appropriate ways to promote the national observance of the United Nations Decade for Women, Equality, Development and Peace (1975–1985).

1–204. The Committee shall gather information relating to its responsibilities and shall disseminate such information, through newsletters or other appropriate means, to the Executive Branch and to interested members of the public.

1–205. The Committee shall consult regularly with the Interdepartmental Task Force, whose existence is continued by Section 1–402.

1–206. The Committee shall establish such procedural regulations as are necessary to carry out its responsibilities.

1–3. *Administrative Provisions.*

1–301. The Committee may request any agency of the Executive Branch of the government to furnish it with such information, advice, funds and services as may be useful for the fulfillment of the Committee's functions under this Order. Such agencies are authorized, to the extent permitted by law, to honor the Committee's requests.

1–302. Each member of the Committee may receive compensation at the maximum rate now or hereafter prescribed by law for each day such member is attending a regularly scheduled meeting of the Committee or a subcommittee thereof. Each member may receive travel expenses,

825

including per diem in lieu of subsistence (5 U.S.C. 5702 and 5703).

1–4. *General Provisions.*

1–401. Notwithstanding the provisions of any other Executive Order, the functions of the President under the Federal Advisory Committee Act which are applicable to the Committee, except that of reporting annually to the Congress, shall be performed by the Secretary of Labor in accordance with guidelines and procedures established by the Administrator of General Services.

1–402. The Interdepartmental Task Force (created by Section 6 of Executive Order No. 12050) is continued.

1–403. The Committee shall conclude its work and shall make a final report to the President by December 31, 1980, at which time it shall terminate.

1–404. Executive Order No. 12050, except for Section 6, and Executive Order No. 12057, are revoked.

JIMMY CARTER

The White House,
    May 9, 1979.

[Filed with the Office of the Federal Register,
    10:20 a.m., May 10, 1979]

President's Advisory Committee for Women

Appointment of Chair, Vice-Chairs, and Four Members. May 9, 1979

The President today announced that Lynda Johnson Robb will chair the President's Advisory Committee for Women, and he announced that he will appoint four new members, who will join members who previously served on the National Advisory Committee for Women. Marjorie Bell Chambers and Elizabeth Koontz will serve as Vice-Chairs of the Committee.

The President today signed an Executive order which reestablishes the National Advisory Committee for Women as the President's Advisory Committee for Women. The order also limits the number of members on the Committee to 30, and extends its work to December 31, 1980.

The President's Advisory Committee for Women will work to carry out the President's mandate to promote equality for women in the cultural, social, economic, and political life of this country.

The President's choice of Lynda Johnson Robb to chair the Committee emphasizes the importance he places on women's right to choose freely among playing the role of wife and mother, combining work in the home with work outside, and pursuing a career outside the home.

Robb is a homemaker with three children, who is also actively involved in civic affairs and her business interests. The President feels that she can bring to the Committee greater understanding of the concerns of women who have chosen the role of homemaker, and that she can provide these women with greater perspective on the effects of women's issues on their lives.

Robb, 35, is a homemaker in McLean, Va., and the mother of three daughters aged 10, 8, and 10 months. She is a contributing editor to Ladies Home Journal, and was on the staff of McCall's magazine from 1966 to 1968. She is vice president of the L.B.J. Co. and of Northern Virginia Broadcasting, and is on the board of directors of station KLBJ in Texas. She is a director of the L.B.J. Family Foundation and serves on the National Advisory Board of Reading is Fundamental. She has worked actively for passage of the equal rights amendment in Virginia and attended the National Women's Conference in Houston. A 1966 graduate of the University of Texas, Robb is the daughter of former President Lyndon Baines Johnson, and the wife of Virginia Lieutenant Governor Charles S. Robb.

The four new members announced today, in addition to Robb, are:

LINDA J. LEE, an assistant on human resources issues to New York City Council President Carol Bellamy and president of the Council of Asian American Women;

ALICE McDONALD, executive assistant to the mayor of Louisville, Ky., and former director of the Neighborhood Development Office there;

ANN S. RAMSAY, director of the office of budgets of Harvard University, previously first deputy secretary of the Commonwealth of Massachusetts;

JILL L. SCHROPP, a Seattle real estate investor and former journalist who was campaign manager for Citizens to Retain Fair Employment in Seattle.

Marjorie Bell Chambers, newly named Vice-Chair of the Committee, has served as Acting Chair since January. The President expressed his thanks to her for her outstanding work as Acting Chair. She is president of the American Association of University Women.

The other Vice-Chair, Libby Koontz, is assistant State superintendent of education for North Carolina and chair of the National Commission on Working Women.

Democratic Congressional Campaign Dinner

Remarks at the Dinner.   May 9, 1979

After that introduction, I'll have to quit thinking about Fritz Mondale as a lame-duck Vice President. [*Laughter*] I would have been here earlier tonight to enjoy the first part of the program with you, but I heard it was going to be a partisan affair. [*Laughter*] Some joker told me you had baloney for supper. [*Laughter*]

As a matter of fact, the last few months, I have been looking for invitations to

speak. [*Laughter*] On a strictly nonpolitical basis, of course. I even visited one State that does not have an early primary next year. The darned scheduler resigned before I could fire him. [*Laughter*]

I've traveled a lot around the country. I know some of you have, too. And I have noticed a few people quite upset about inflation. Maybe you've noticed this. [*Laughter*] It's hard for me to understand. I've watched this trend very carefully from the perspective of Washington. You can still get a wonderful meal, good entertainment, pleasant company, beautiful surroundings, same price as last year, $1,000 a plate. [*Laughter*]

I think we owe our tremendous victories over inflation to one man. And I hope you'll join in with me in giving a wonderful round of applause to the number one inflation fighter, proven by his record in our country, the honorable Bob Strauss. [*Applause*] Our hats are off to you Bob—those of us who still have a hat. [*Laughter*]

I called Bob in not too long ago and said, "Because of your superb work in fighting inflation, I'm going to give you a new job." He smiled with great anticipation, looking forward to rushing out and holding another press conference. [*Laughter*] And I said, "Bob, it's not an easy job. It's one of the most difficult jobs on Earth." I said, "I want you to be responsible for establishing peace between people who have been at war since ancient times, filled with hatred, combat." And he interrupted, "Mr. President," he said, "I have already been chairman of the Democratic Party once." [*Laughter*]

But I think you know he's helped these fine fund raisers on my left, using his new job as the Mideast negotiator as kind of an unofficial lever in his inimitable style. I understand that he's even sold five tables' worth of tickets, jointly, to the Egyptian and the Israeli Embassies—[*laughter*]—

827

and got the Saudis to pay for it. [*Laughter*] He told them that Arafat was the main speaker, unfortunately. [*Laughter*]

And this afternoon they tried to stop payment on the check but were unsuccessful. I know from experience how fast they can move down at the National Bank of Georgia in Atlanta. [*Laughter*]

The problem in the Middle East, as it is in our own country, is the difficulty of people just to get to know each other. I guess it's a problem everywhere. I've been President now for 2½ years, almost, and some of the columnists, my dear friends and yours—[*laughter*]—say that even some people in the country still don't know me.

Well, I don't put much faith in that kind of talk, but I was in Iowa last Friday morning. I was talking to a small group of men and women about my plans for the Nation, what I thought we could do as a combined partnership of all kinds of people. And one fellow came up after the little meeting, and he said, "Mr. Carter, you make a lot of sense to me." He said, "Have you ever considered running for public office?" [*Laughter*] And I said, "Well, as a matter of fact, I've even thought about the Presidency." And he said, "Well, would you mind if I organize kind of a 'Draft Carter' movement?" He said, "We have to get that dope out of the Oval Office that's there now." [*Laughter*]

I didn't mind that much, but he said, "I understand he's just a wishy-washy hairdresser." [*Laughter*]

This is a serious thing tonight. I have tried to keep my speech on that plane. [*Laughter*] The main thing I want to do is to recognize the great work of Congress. And I have to admit, as a newcomer to Washington, I think about the achievements of Congress every time Rosalynn and I drive by the National Visitors

Center. [*Laughter*] And it's not just brick and mortar that has made you great. It's not just accurate assessment of budget costs for prospective projects. I think you've helped to deal inflation a death blow by providing free parking for congressional employees. That's helped a great deal. [*Laughter*]

And the Senate, as you know, has shown superb personal courage. I remember last year I read about the sacrifice that the Senators have been willing to implement by putting a real limit on their own personal income. And I want to congratulate them on that great move. [*Laughter*]

And then, of course, as I said earlier, there's the National Visitors Center. I can't give you all the credit for it. I know almost all of you are Democrats, or either Republican contributors who think the Democrats are going to be here for a long time—which I think we will. [*Laughter*] So, it's more or less a bipartisan achievement, those I've outlined for you.

Today, the Senate even gave me, in a very gracious manner, I thought, the full responsibility for implementing in the future gas rationing when it's needed. [*Laughter*]

I've wondered ever since the vote why the Republicans voted unanimously for the proposal. But I think the analysis of past achievements and past glory has been adequately covered, and I'd like to take the time to look to the future.

We're here tonight to lay the groundwork, the financial groundwork, for next year's congressional elections, 1980, a year of victory for Democrats.

For 24 years, Democrats have controlled the House and the Senate of the United States Congress. Each Democratic President—John Kennedy, Lyndon Johnson and myself—have depended upon and have never been disappointed with the cooperation and the support of these strong Democratic majorities.

I may be biased or I may be prejudiced, but I firmly believe that there have never been two finer congressional leaders than Speaker Tip O'Neill and Majority Leader Robert Byrd.

There is a responsibility on all of us to preserve that team as our leaders. We must preserve those Democratic majorities in the House and Senate. We must not return to the dark days of divided government. We must not afflict this country with Republican victories in 1980. And we'll work together to achieve those goals, and you can depend on it.

But we will win if we give the American people what they want—strong, competent, and compassionate Democratic leadership.

Above all, we will win if we tell the American people the truth, and if you and I, under some of the most difficult possible political circumstances, have the courage to make the tough decisions when they are necessary.

The last 2 years have been years of rebuilding in our country. Often in small groups I ask a particular crowd to think back 3 years or 4 years or 5 years. There's no need to enumerate the discouragement and the despair, the embarrassment, the failure that we were experiencing in those days. But working together, we have accomplished a great deal. We obviously have a long way to go. A great deal more remains to be done. But when they write the history of these years, I want them to say four things about what you and I've done together.

I want them to say that you and I have made America prosperous and that we have put Americans back to work. And we've done that.

And I want them to say that you and I have never lacked the courage to tackle controversial problems and that we placed the long-term good of our beloved Nation above any short-term political benefit for ourselves. And we have done that.

And I want them to say that we have restored the trust and the confidence of the American people in our own Government. And, most of all, I want them to say that America, under our leadership, has been at peace and that we have led the rest of the world away from war. And we've done that.

This is the record that we will take to the American people next year, and it's a record that makes me confident that we will reelect Democrats here tonight who are in the House and Senate.

In the last 2 years we've taught the country the difference, for instance, between Republican and Democratic economics. You remember Republican economics—continued high inflation being fought with the jobs and the livelihood of working Americans. You and I know the high cost, human cost, of a planned recession combined with high prices.

The Democratic economic policies are built around jobs. We believe in hard work. And we believe that those who want to work can find a job. In 2 years, as you know, we have created more than 7½ million jobs. We have cut the unemployment rate more than 25 percent. And in spite of the high inflation, we've kept the unemployment rate at that low level.

We're working to improve it even more. We have leveled with the American people. We've never tried to mislead them. We've not gone in for political gimmicks. We have told them that there is no instant or quick solution for chronic problems like inflation.

The Federal Government is now setting an example though, in its battle against inflation. We've restored sanity to the Federal budget. And I'm proud that with the 1980 fiscal year budget, the Democratic Congress will have reduced the Republican deficit by more than 55 percent just since I ran for office in 1976. And what is more important, we have done this while increasing substantially, often in an unprecedented way, our commitment to the elderly, the poor, the unemployed, to education, to housing, to transportation, and to better cities and towns and stronger farm families.

That's the record of Democratic economics—and it's a winning record.

As Democrats, we've also faced the hard truth about energy—perhaps the most complex issue ever faced by the United States Congress in the history of our Nation.

Last year, Congress passed the first comprehensive energy program in our Nation's history. It was not easy. It did not yet deal with oil, but it was a major achievement.

Now the challenge ahead of us is to pass the windfall profits tax and create the energy security fund. You remember when the armchair experts just a few weeks ago said that the Congress would never seriously consider passing a windfall profits tax, that it was a hopeless gesture. We've heard from the American people, though, and in a few short weeks this tune has changed. We know the fight is still to come, but they've learned something important about the strength and the courage and the responsibility of a Democratic Congress. We will have the energy security fund, financed by a real, genuine windfall profits tax, to protect the American people. And you can depend on that.

When I ran for President, I promised a government as good as the American people. Some critics said this was corny, some said it was just political rhetoric in an election year. But working together, we've proven them wrong. We have restored integrity and honesty to the American Government. There are no more official Government lies, no more enemies lists prepared in the Oval Office, and we are eliminating sellouts to special interests.

The American people were sick and tired of waste, redtape, and Government over-regulation. We heard their voices and we responded.

We've passed a landmark civil service reform bill. We've placed Inspectors General in every major Federal agency to root out fraud and dishonesty. We've shut off the regulatory assemblyline. We've eliminated hundreds and hundreds of useless OSHA regulations and let that agency function as it should. And we've decontrolled airline rates and saved the consumers over $2.5 billion.

But no accomplishment is more important than our commitment to peace.

A foreign policy should be built upon the best instincts of the American people. It should not ever be based on cynicism or deceit.

We've worked hard to construct a foreign policy that is worthy of our Nation's noble heritage. We've spoken out for human rights around the world with a strong voice, and we will continue to promote and to protect basic human rights as long as I'm President and as long as you serve in the Congress. And that's an important, unswerving commitment of the United States of America.

We must be committed to peace, but we must also be militarily strong. We do not need to prove our strength through rash or reckless military adventures. But our military forces must be adequate to deter any others who may be tempted toward adventurism. We Democrats will keep the United States of America strong. Peace will never be fully secure as long as the shadow of nuclear war hangs over the world. A SALT treaty will lessen the danger of nuclear destruction, while safeguarding our military security in a more stable, predictable, and a more peaceful world.

After more than 6 years of negotiations under three different administrations, we've essentially completed our work on a new SALT agreement. President Brezhnev and I will schedule a summit meeting as soon as it can be arranged, after which the treaty will be submitted to the Senate for ratification this year. We will announce a time and a place for the summit meeting this week.

During these long and tedious months, no President could possibly have a better Secretary of State or a better Secretary of Defense than Cyrus Vance and Harold Brown. And we can all be thankful for them.

SALT II continues and strengthens the process of controlling the nuclear arms race. It establishes for the first time the principle of equal numbers of strategic missile systems, both overall limits and limits on individual types of missiles, which will result in the first negotiated decrease in operational Soviet nuclear systems. It will also impose the first important restraints on the race to build new systems or to improve existing ones— the so-called qualitative nuclear arms race. This is the first time it's ever been done.

The SALT II treaty is not a substitute for a strong defense. We'll continue to maintain an effective and flexible strategic capability. The SALT II treaty and the protocol preserve our right to pursue all of the defense programs we've planned or which we may need, in my judgment or in the judgment of the Joint Chiefs of Staff. But SALT II also helps to limit and define the threats that we must face. Thus, it will make our defense efforts more certain and less costly with this treaty.

This issue must be fully aired in open debate before the American people. I know that you will contribute to that discussion. And I look forward to working closely with you individually on this vital issue and to your support on this important step toward greater American security and world peace.

I've only got one life to live and one opportunity to serve in the highest elected office in our land. I will never have a chance so momentous to contribute to world peace as to negotiate and to see ratified this SALT treaty. And I don't believe that any Member of the Senate will ever cast a more important vote than when a final judgment is made to confirm and ratify this negotiated treaty.

A peaceful world is perhaps the most precious gift that we can pass on to our children. We won a victory for that kind of world when the peace treaty was signed between Egypt and Israel, as the Vice President mentioned. The United States was able to play a crucial role in that crucial time to make it possible.

But although I was proud to be a part, that treaty was not a personal accomplishment for us. The treaty was a tribute to two courageous leaders, President Sadat and Prime Minister Begin. But it was also a tribute to the moral strength and to the leadership of this Nation. It was possible only because the people of Israel and the people of Egypt recognized that the American people will always support those who seek freedom and justice and peace.

That was the foundation on which the mutual trust was based that led to this achievement.

In 1818 the founder of our party, Thomas Jefferson, looked back on his long years of service to our Nation, and he noted with pride—and I quote in closing—"During the period of my Administration, not a drop of blood of a single fellow citizen was shed by the sword of war."

I'm also proud that during this administration, not a single drop of American blood has been shed in war. And I pray to God each day that when my years as President are over, that I can still share Thomas Jefferson's achievement.

Woodrow Wilson said, "A political party exists to serve a great and urgent purpose." In the last 2 years, our party has lived up to those high standards set by a Democratic President, Woodrow Wilson—by restoring prosperity, by displaying political courage, by demonstrating integrity in government, and by working for world peace.

There's one thought that I would like to leave with you tonight.

I hold, as you know, one of the most important political offices in the world. And I represent a nation made up of people who are absolutely free to express themselves—to agree, to disagree, to debate, to criticize the Members of Congress, as you well know, and also to criticize the President. This open debate, this freedom to criticize, is what makes our wonderful Nation so special among the 4 billion people who comprise the population of this Earth.

We set high standards for ourselves and for our Nation. That's why we sometimes become discouraged when the newspapers or the evening news broadcasts emphasize current problems or disagreements or failures or disappointments. But we don't hear enough, and perhaps we don't speak enough about the solid, stable, steady strength of a great nation.

So, as we face the future together, let us remember our blessings. And one of the finest blessings of all is our freedom to speak our minds, to join in the debate, to analyze our problems, to criticize, and to strive to make a great country even greater.

Free people striving for excellence—free people striving for excellence—is the true strength of America on which all else must rest and on which must rest our own Democratic political contributions. Good work in 1979 will certainly bring us good luck and a victory in 1980. I'm convinced of that.

Thank you very much.

NOTE: The President spoke at 10:15 p.m. in the International Ballroom at the Washington Hilton Hotel.

American Retail Federation

Remarks at a White House Breakfast.
May 10, 1979

Let me say, first of all, how thankful I am that you are here. You are welcome to come to the White House. It's your home as well as it is mine.

As you know, every President since John Adams has lived here, all except Washington. And the historical nature of this home is truly impressive for me personally and, I think, for everyone who comes in here to conduct the business of our country.

It's important for me to be with the American Retail Federation. I doubt that any person in Washington has helped me more, outside Government employees and full-time workers, than has Lloyd Hackler. And I want to thank you personally, Lloyd, for this superb advice and counsel.

There have been several difficult issues that I've had to face since I've been President, and I've never hesitated to call Lloyd on how to deal with an important economic question, an important question involving foreign affairs. And he's been willing to come into the White House, sometimes late at night, quietly, to counsel with me, in a group of two or three or four, about how we ought to address these major problems for the benefit of our country.

You represent an industry which involves about, I think, 35 or 36 percent of our gross national product, encompassing 13 million American jobs. And not only that, but everyone in this room and those whom you represent occupy positions of leadership in your own local communities, through your own civic clubs, your church groups, your involvement in school affairs, public affairs, in the business and professional world. Your voice can have a profound impact on the consciousness of America—what our people believe, what they strive to achieve, how they overcome difficult challenges and problems, how much confidence they have in government, how much confidence they have in our free enterprise system, which is so important a basis on which we all predicate our lives and our future.

I think it's important for me to mention just two or three things. I'll be brief.

We are faced with 10 years of excessive inflation which impacts very heavily on you and on your customers. We've not been successful yet in solving this problem. We are taking strong action to do it.

I want to thank you for your cooperative spirit, sometimes under difficult circumstances, in complying with the voluntary wage and price standards that we have established. And even in very difficult cases involving some highly publicized differences of opinion, I might say that your members have been superb in cooperating with us.

Recently both Sears and Giant Foods, for instance, took action on their own initiative in order to comply with the voluntary wage and price standards, and I want to express my thanks to you.

As onerous as they might be on occasion, we have tried to minimize paperwork; we've minimized the intrusion of government into your own affairs. And I believe that almost all of you would agree they are much superior to mandatory wage and price controls, which I never intend to impose in this country short of a threat to our own national security. I hope you support me in that position.

We are working for a balanced budget. We've made a lot of progress. And I would say that compared to the time when I ran for President, we had about a $66 billion Federal deficit. We have cut down substantially on that deficit. By the time we implement the fiscal year 1980 budget, we will have cut down the deficit perhaps 60 percent or more.

The Congress has joined in that spirit, and I believe you would agree it's a step in the right direction. I'm determined to achieve a balanced budget. That's my goal, and I believe the American people have now joined in this goal. And, of course, the Congress are willing partners in that effort.

You can help a great deal. I might say we have done it in the spirit of my own political party. I know many of you are Republicans; many of you are Democrats. But we've never neglected the effort to put people back to work, to provide jobs, to encourage better education, better transportation, better health care, better attention given to the very poor, to the elderly. We've not neglected those things. Most of the achievements in reducing the deficit have been because of greater efficiency, establishment of proper priorities, zero-based budgeting, and the cooperative spirit both in the special interest groups, mostly highly benevolent, and the Congress working with us.

You've been a part of this.

We've tried to eliminate onerous regulation. We've not yet fully succeeded, of course. But I think we have made tremendous improvements, for instance, in OSHA. I remember one of the happiest days of my Presidency was when we eliminated 1,000 OSHA regulations in 1 day.

I would like to ask you, through Lloyd, if there are specific Government regulations or reports that you consider to be unnecesary and ill-advised, to document them specifically, do a little work on your own, or let Lloyd do it—[laughter]—he'll cooperate in this—[laughter]—see if the regulation or report is required by law or if it's an administrative decision and then let Lloyd bring that information to me.

If it's encompassed in law, I'll work with the Congress to get it changed. If it is an administrative decision, I'll immediately call the Cabinet officer involved and see if we can't remove the onerous part of it.

If it's a report required weekly and you think it could be done better monthly, or monthly and you think it could be done better semiannually, or eliminated altogether or made briefer or combined with another report that went to a separate agency—if you'll do the work to give me a specific example, not just generalities, then I'll do the work as President to try to accommodate your desires, because this is a major cause of inflation—excessive Government regulation.

We have been successful in working with the Congress, for instance, on airline deregulation. Everyone who flies—and I guess that's most of you who've come here—would agree that rates have dropped tremendously, not only in domestic circles but also in foreign air travel. We've already saved, we believe, about $2.5 billion in reduced fares for American tourists and American business leaders, and we really appreciate your help in getting this legislation passed.

We are now faced with some other very difficult decisions—hospital cost containment, we would like for you to help us.

The Multilateral Trade Negotiations have been worked out substantially with the cooperation and advice of your own people. And this is now facing approval in the Senate. It will greatly enhance the well-being of all of you and also greatly enhance the well-being of the consumers of our country. And I hope that you will exert every effort to work with Bob Strauss and with me to eliminate the obstacles to the ratification or approval of the Multilateral Trade Negotiation.

I'd like to close by saying this: I've only got one life to live on this Earth, as you have—I think the most important single achievement that could possibly take place for our Nation during my lifetime is the ratification of the SALT treaty that we have just negotiated with the Soviet Union. It's a fair treaty. I have to say in complete candor that the Soviets have been tough negotiators; so have we. They have been fair negotiators; so have we. It's a kind of treaty where both parties reap tremendous benefits.

It maintains strategic equivalency, which means that our atomic arsenals are roughly balanced. There is no advantage to either country that might precipitate an initial strike without the sure knowledge that a retaliatory strike would kill a hundred million people or more.

I won't go into the details. That's not necessary. The details are available to you, and I know that Lloyd will be forwarding to the key members of this organization, or those of you who volunteer to help with it, exact details to the limit of your desire.

Rejection of this treaty, now that it has been negotiated, would be a devastating blow to the United States of America and to the Soviet Union. It would harm our Nation's security, and it would be a massive destructive blow to world peace.

I won't go into any further detail, but I would like to say this: Ours is a nation that believes in peace. Ours is a nation that values human life. Ours is a nation that has taken the leadership, since the evolution of nuclear power itself, to put constraints on the evolution of nuclear weaponry, not only in our own country and the Soviet Union but among other nations who are not presently nuclear powers.

We are struggling to have the image in the nonaligned countries of a nation that's admirable and which has, as our present policy, the implementation of principles and ideals on which our country was founded in its initial days.

All of those efforts, which have been shared not only by me but by every President since President Eisenhower, would be endangered if we now reject this treaty. We would be looked upon as a warmonger, not as a peaceloving nation by many other people of the world. Our own NATO Allies would be severely shaken in their confidence in us as a nation determined to have détente with the Soviet Union and not to initiate a nuclear conflict whose effect might first fall on Europe and only later, perhaps, cause death and destruction in our own country.

We've been working—I have personally been working among 10 or 12 nations who have complete capability to develop nuclear weapons, but who have so far refrained. We have aired our voice and added our influence to continue their refraining from going into the development of nuclear weapons.

If we show now that we reject this mutually advantageous voluntary constraint on our own nuclear weaponry and initiate the prospect of a massive nuclear arms race, those countries—like Pakistan, India, Taiwan, South Korea, South Africa, and others that I won't name here—would feel that there was no longer any constraint on them—"Why should we listen to the voice of the United States encouraging us not to develop nuclear weapons when they themselves will not approve a treaty designed for the same purpose?"—still leaving the nation with massive and superior nuclear weapons ourselves.

In our own hemisphere, we've been working to have the complete ratification of the Treaty of Tlatelolco, which leaves the southern half of this hemisphere free of nuclear weapon development or deployment.

We are now down to the last two or three countries. We've been working very closely with Argentina and Brazil, two countries who have the capability, scientifically and technologically, to have nuclear explosives, and we are trying to set an example for them. But this example would be wiped out completely if we did not ratify the now negotiated SALT treaty.

I'd like to ask you to take this on as a project for yourselves, collectively and individually, to help me sell to the American people and directly to the U.S. Senate the advantages of ratification and the devastating disadvantage if the treaties are rejected.

The treaty's complicated; some Senators will study every word in it, as have I. Some will listen primarily to the voice of America, as represented by you and those

835

who look to you for leadership. And I have come here this morning to congratulate you on the fine working spirit that we've enjoyed so far, but to ask you from the bottom of my heart, as President of our great country, to help me with this most important issue which will ever address me while I occupy this home.

I think it's the best way to preserve our Nation's security. It's the best way to preserve world peace and give us better lives in the future as citizens of the greatest nation on Earth.

Thank you very much.

NOTE: The President spoke at 8:33 a.m. in the State Dining Room at the White House.

Federal Summer Employment Program for Youth

Memorandum From the President.
May 10, 1979

Memorandum for the Heads of Departments and Agencies

Within a few weeks, schools will close for the summer and many of our young people will be seeking summer jobs. To some the money earned from summer employment may affect whether they return to school in the fall or discontinue their education. For others, summer employment will enable them to help out at home or to gain experience which may assist them in making decisions regarding their future careers.

This year, we are again faced with a high rate of unemployment among our youth. Many of you are already participating in the task force reviewing youth employment and training programs under the Vice President's leadership. As one of several solutions to the problem of un-

employment, we as Federal managers along with managers within the private sector should increase our efforts to provide productive summer experiences for young men and women.

I am again asking all of you to continue your personal support for the Federal Summer Employment Program for Youth. Federal programs should be a balanced effort to employ those who qualify through successful competition in the Summer Employment Examination as well as through agency merit staffing procedures. Additionally, we must continue to support summer employment for needy youth. To accomplish this objective, I am again setting a general goal to employ one needy youth for every 40 regular employees. We exceeded this goal on a governmentwide basis last summer.

Director Alan K. Campbell and his staff at the Office of Personnel Management will continue to provide leadership to the Government's Summer Employment Program.

JIMMY CARTER

Meeting With President Aristides Royo of Panama

Joint Press Statement.   May 10, 1979

President Carter met this morning for about an hour with Aristides Royo, President of the Republic of Panama, in an atmosphere of sincere and cordial friendship.

The two Presidents discussed matters relating to the implementation of the Panama Canal Treaties which will enter into force on October 1, 1979. In the course of the discussion, they expressed their confidence that the new relationship established by the treaties would develop satisfactorily, to the benefit of both countries, and pledged their best efforts to ensure that both nations carry out the treaties, faithfully respecting both their letter and spirit.

The President took note of the historic significance of the treaties and their importance, not only for the signatories but also for the entire international community, as an example of how large and small nations can reconcile their interests, to their mutual benefit, through understanding, cooperation, and respect for the national identity and dignity of each.

President Carter expressed interest in the favorable prospects for the social and economic development of Panama and the increased private investment that will result from the implementation of the treaties.

The two Presidents also discussed various regional and international issues. They reviewed the situation of human rights in the hemisphere and deplored the continuing violence in Central America that causes unnecessary bloodshed and results in deprivation and suffering for the people of that region. President Royo expressed the satisfaction of his government with the conclusion of the peace treaty between Egypt and Israel.

The two Presidents agreed that democracy and human dignity are inseparable and that the possibilities for the balanced development of free peoples are infinite. Panama and the United States of America symbolize, in their new relationship established through the Canal Treaties, what free men, working together, can accomplish.

NOTE: On the same day, the White House released the following announcement.

The President met with President Aristides Royo today at 11 a.m. in the Cabinet Room. Those attending the meeting were:

United States participants
THE PRESIDENT
SECRETARY OF STATE CYRUS VANCE
DEPUTY SECRETARY OF STATE WARREN CHRISTOPHER
SECRETARY OF THE ARMY CLIFFORD ALEXANDER
ASSISTANT SECRETARY OF STATE VIRON P. VAKY
AMBASSADOR AMBLER MOSS, U.S. Ambassador to Panama
MR. ROBERT PASTOR, National Security Council staff member

Panama participants
PRESIDENT ARISTIDES ROYO
FOREIGN MINISTER CARLOS OZORES
AMBASSADOR GABRIEL LEWIS, Director, Panama Canal Authority
AMBASSADOR ALFREDO LOPEZ, Panama Ambassador to the United States

Death of Cyrus Eaton

Statement by the President.   May 10, 1979

With the death of Cyrus Eaton, America has lost both a leading industrialist and an enthusiastic advocate of world peace. As a businessman, Mr. Eaton helped make the Midwest a center of finance. As a private citizen, he helped begin the process of change that led to détente between the United States and the Soviet Union. The Nation honors his memory and the many contributions he made.

House-Senate Bipartisan Senior Citizen Intern Program

Remarks to Participants in the Program. May 11, 1979

I had a report this morning from the White House escort group, or the guides, that this was the most vigorous and dynamic group they've ever taken through the White House. I asked them if you were trying to take the paintings off the wall and so forth. They said, "No, they're just interested in everything, and they really are eager."

I'm very glad to welcome here the senior citizens who are participating in the seventh year of the legislative intern program. This is, I think, vivid proof that you don't have to have a massive Federal bureaucracy to have an excellent program. And I'm very proud that you would come and let me share in your experience here in learning about our Federal Government at first hand.

I know you've had thorough briefings on many of the things that apply directly to the retired people of our Nation concerning social security. I know you've learned that this Congress quite courageously in the last 2 years has protected the integrity of the social security system. When I was campaigning for President in 1976, I don't think I ever had a meeting with a group that I didn't get a question, "What are we going to do about social security, because it's facing bankruptcy?"

It's no longer facing bankruptcy. It's sound. And I hope that you'll express your appreciation to the Members of Congress who did take this politically courageous step. It's not always easy, as you know, to increase taxes on those who are working in our country. But we saw the necessity for bringing social security back to a sound financial condition.

I think it's important to point out, too, that although inflation is a problem for us all, we have, from the Government perspective, made that portion of your income, in effect, inflation-proof. And your July checks, as you well know, will encompass an increase that would accommodate inflation having been measured in the month of June.

I wish that all aspects of inflation could

be alleviated. You can help me a great deal when you go back to your home, when you have influence on the preparation of the policies of senior citizens groups. I hope that you'll remember that the most singly important step that the Congress can take this year on inflation is to pass hospital cost containment.

Many of you may feel that since Medicaid and Medicare takes care of many of the hospital bills, that this is all you need. But that's not true at all, because the extraordinary increase in hospital costs, about twice as rapid an increase as the general inflation rate, doubling every 5 years, not only prevents our moving into a more comprehensive health program, because of the extraordinary costs, we have got to control costs before we can have a full-time program.

But I'd like to point out to you that everything you buy in this Nation is affected by the impact of rapidly increasing health care costs. I won't take much time, but let me give you one example.

If any of you buy an automobile this year or next year, the cost of health care for automobile employees, those who make the automobiles, is greater in your automobile cost than the cost of all the steel that goes into the automobile. So, you are paying in everything you buy for these extraordinary increases in health care, much above what it ought to be.

In the States like Connecticut, for instance, and others that have imposed hospital cost containment, everyone has benefited. Those who go to the hospital as patients, the owners of hospitals, the general public has benefited, and, of course, your money goes in, if you pay taxes, to finance the unwarranted, excessively high cost of hospital care. I need your help on that.

You've gotten briefings on transportation; you've gotten briefings on consumer affairs from Esther Peterson. You've gotten briefings on other very important elements of government that apply directly to you. But I don't look on senior citizens as just being interested in things that apply to you personally.

In effect, you come here as students, and I know the tremendous benefit of continued education programs. I'm under the process of being educated every day myself as President. And I hope that you will set an example of how a senior citizen's mind and heart can continue to grow and to expand every day of life.

My mother is, obviously, that way. She'll be 81 this summer and she's growing every day, and I know all of you are. And I think this dynamic expression of the ability of senior citizens, not only to grow within yourself but to continue to contribute just as greatly, perhaps some of you contribute even more to a better America now than you did when you were full-time employees at a young, vigorous age.

Now, in your older, vigorous age, I want you to do the same thing. And I want our Government to force us to recognize that. But I also want you to be interested in other things as well. SALT is important. The security of our country, the contribution to world peace is just as great a responsibility on your shoulders as it is on the shoulders of your sons and daughters or your grandsons and granddaughters, and as it is on mine. And I know that your own concept of responsibilities of our Government has been greatly expanded by your presence here.

The last thing I'd like to say is that you will, in effect, be ambassadors in the coming months and years, because those around you in your own home communities and your own families will look upon you as having had a special privilege to come and meet with and serve with Members of the Congress, to be briefed by top

administration officials, to come to the White House to meet personally with the President. That's an experience and a privilege that many people don't have.

And so, you will be observed very carefully as you go back home, and as the months and years go by as a special ambassador for the Government of the United States of America. And so, in effect, you'll be partners with me and with the Congress. And I have great appreciation for your contribution so far and even greater appreciation for the tremendous increased contribution that you'll make in the future.

Thank you very much. God bless all of you.

NOTE: The President spoke at 9:38 a.m. in the Rose Garden at the White House.

Meeting With President L. I. Brezhnev of the Soviet Union

Announcement of the Forthcoming Meeting in Vienna, Austria.   May 11, 1979

By mutual agreement, the meeting of the President of the United States, Jimmy Carter, with the General Secretary of the Central Committee of the Communist Party of the Soviet Union and the President of the Presidium of the Supreme Soviet of the U.S.S.R., Leonid Brezhnev, will take place from June 15 to 18 in Vienna, Austria.

The two leaders will confirm and sign the treaty on the limitation of strategic offensive arms, the work on which is now being completed, and will discuss other issues of mutual interest to the United States and the Soviet Union.

NOTE: Zbigniew Brzezinski, Assistant to the President for National Security Affairs, read the announcement at 10:45 a.m. to reporters assembled in the Briefing Room at the White House.

Standby Gasoline Rationing Plan

*Remarks on the House of Representatives
Disapproval of the Plan.   May 11, 1979*

Two years ago, I presented to Congress a comprehensive energy plan for our Nation, and the Congress took some action on it. But they avoided taking action on the subject of oil, and this failure to take action to deal with the oil problem is part of the reason for our present gasoline shortage.

Yesterday, I was shocked and I was embarrassed for our Nation's Government when, after the Senate gave me authority to develop a Standby Gasoline Rationing Plan, that the House refused to take the responsibility for giving me this authority.

Ninety-five percent of the Republicans in the House of Representatives voted "no." Forty percent of the Democrats voted "no." The Nation owes a debt of gratitude for those Members of the House of Representatives who did have the courage to vote "yes."

The only conclusion that I can draw is that in spite of the strong leadership of Senator Byrd, Senator Jackson, and a majority of the Senate, Speaker O'Neill, Congressman Dingell, Congressman Bolling, and others in the House, that the majority of the House Members are unwilling to take the responsibility, the political responsibility for dealing with a potential, serious threat to our Nation.

If we should have a serious interruption of oil and gasoline supplies, our Nation would be unprepared to deal with it. We would be in a vulnerable position, and I would have no authority at all to meet what could be a national crisis.

If we had an interruption in gasoline supplies, we would have no plan to allot gasoline equitably among the States or to meet the needs of farmers and others who produce food, the handicapped, policemen, firemen, other major users of gasoline on a priority basis.

I'm not predicting that we will have a shortage—I hope that we will not have a shortage—but I'm not willing to accept the judgment of a majority of the House of Representatives, whose Members have apparently put their heads in the sand and refused to take action, refused to acknowledge the threat, and refused to deal with what is acknowledged to be a very difficult political issue.

There is nothing easy about energy. All of us have learned that from experience. But what can we do now? This is one of the most serious questions that I face. The House has not rejected the plans on their own merit. The House has refused to give me the authority to develop the standby rationing plan so that if and when it is needed, it could only be implemented, provided at that time the House and the Senate also agreed with the President that it ought to be implemented.

This question indicates—and I hate to say this—that a majority of the House of Representatives have been willing to put local or parochial interests and let political timidity prevent their taking action in the interest of our Nation.

I have a sure knowledge that anyone who wants to have gas rationing has taken leave of their senses, but anyone in a position of authority who is not willing to recognize the potential threat to our country and to be prepared to deal with the threat when and if it comes is irresponsible.

There is no need for me under the present circumstances to submit another plan for gas rationing in an emergency. The Congress has indicated that the merits of the plan is not the problem. The problem is the unwillingness of a majority of the House of Representatives to vote for any plan because it's politically difficult.

I challenge the Congress within this next 90 days to develop their own rationing plan—fair, equitable, and balanced. Obviously, I will give them every possible assistance if and when they are willing to exhibit the willingness to take this necessary action in the interest of our country.

Thank you very much.

NOTE: The President spoke at 12:05 p.m. to reporters assembled in the Oval Office at the White House.

Digest of Other White House Announcements

The following listing includes the President's public schedule and other items of general interest announced by the White House Press Office and not included elsewhere in this issue.

May 5

The President returned to the White House from a trip to Iowa and California.

May 7

The President met at the White House with:

—Zbigniew Brzezinski, Assistant to the President for National Security Affairs;
—Frank B. Moore, Assistant to the President for Congressional Liaison;
—Representative Ed Jenkins of Georgia;
—the Cabinet;
—administration officials and environmental and community leaders to discuss nuclear power;

—Vice President Walter F. Mondale;
—Oklahoma State officials and farmers from Elk City, Okla.

May 8

The President met at the White House with:

—David L. Aaron, Deputy Assistant for National Security Affairs;
—Mr. Moore;
—the Democratic congressional leadership;
—a group of Senators to discuss the Environmental Protection Agency's proposed emission standards for the coal industry;
—James T. McIntyre, Jr., Director of the Office of Management and Budget.

The President attended a portion of the briefing by administration officials given for black community and civic leaders from Texas, Oklahoma, and Louisiana in the State Dining Room at the White House.

The President participated in a briefing by administration officials on the Panama Canal treaty implementation legislation given for a group of Congressmen in the East Room at the White House.

The President last night declared a major disaster for the State of Tennessee as a result of severe storms, tornadoes, and flooding, beginning on or about May 3, which caused extensive private property damage.

The President transmitted to the Congress the 1975 annual report on occupational safety and health.

May 9

The President met at the White House with:

—Vice President Mondale, Secretary of the Treasury W. Michael Blumenthal, Charles L. Schultze, Chairman of the Council of Economic

Advisers, Alfred E. Kahn, Advisor to the President on Inflation and Chairman of the Council on Wage and Price Stability, Barry P. Bosworth, Director of the Council on Wage and Price Stability, Stuart E. Eizenstat, Assistant to the President for Domestic Affairs and Policy, and Mr. McIntyre;

—Mr. Moore, Danny C. Tate, Deputy Assistant for Congressional Liaison (Senate), Robert G. Beckel, Special Assistant for Congressional Liaison (House), and Robert W. Maher, Special Assistant for Congressional Liaison (House);

—Vice President Mondale, Stansfield Turner, Director of Central Intelligence, Hamilton Jordan, Assistant to the President, and Dr. Brzezinski;

—His Holiness Justin, Patriarch of the Romanian Orthodox Church;

—members of the national advisory board of the National Center of Economic Education for Children;

—Nancy Katz and Michael A. Allara, the Multiple Sclerosis Mother and Father of the Year, and officials of the National Multiple Sclerosis Society and its District of Columbia chapter.

May 10

The President met at the White House with:

—Dr. Brzezinski;
—Mr. Moore.

In a ceremony in the Oval Office, the President received diplomatic credentials from Ambassadors Ousman Ahmadou Sallah of the Republic of Gambia, Yao Grunitzky of the Republic of Togo, Mamady Lamine Conde of the People's Revolutionary Republic of Guinea, and Ionatana Ionatana of Tuvalu.

The President transmitted to the Congress the first annual report of the Department of Energy.

May 11

The President met at the White House with:

—Vice President Mondale, Secretary of State Cyrus R. Vance, Secretary of Defense Harold Brown, Dr. Brzezinski, and Mr. Jordan;

—Dr. Brzezinski;

—Mr. Moore;

—the Cabinet;

—a group of editors and news directors (transcript will be printed next week);

—Gov. Fob James of Alabama.

The President participated in a briefing on the administration's programs and policies given for civic and community leaders from Alabama in the East Room at the White House.

The President left the White House for Andrews Air Force Base, Md., where he met Mrs. Carter on her return from her overseas trip. They then went on to Camp Hoover, Va., for a weekend stay.

NOMINATIONS SUBMITTED TO THE SENATE

The following list does not include promotions of members of the Uniformed Services, nominations to the Service Academies, or nominations of Foreign Service officers.

Submitted May 7, 1979

LUTHER H. HODGES, JR., of North Carolina, to be Under Secretary of Commerce, vice Sidney Harman, resigned.

FRANK V. ORTIZ, JR., of New Mexico, a Foreign Service officer of Class one, to be Ambassador Extraordinary and Plenipotentiary of the United States of America to Guatemala.

WILLIAM M. LANDAU, of New York, to be a member of the Board of Directors of the Overseas Private Investment Corporation for a term expiring December 17, 1980, vice Wallace F. Bennett, term expired.

NOMINATIONS—Continued

Submitted May 7—Continued

LEON B. APPLEWHAITE, of New York, to be a member of the Federal Labor Relations Authority for a term of 3 years (new position).

Submitted May 8, 1979

ALFRED L. ATHERTON, JR., of Florida, a Foreign Service officer of the Class of Career Minister, to be Ambassador Extraordinary and Plenipotentiary of the United States of America to the Arab Republic of Egypt.

FRANCIS D. MURNAGHAN, JR., of Maryland, to be United States Circuit Judge for the Fourth Circuit, vice a new position created by P.L. 95–486, approved October 20, 1978.

ARTHUR L. NIMS III, of New Jersey, to be a Judge of the United States Tax Court for a term of 15 years after he takes office, vice Arnold Raum, retired.

CHECKLIST OF WHITE HOUSE PRESS RELEASES

The following listing contains releases of the White House Press Office which are not included in this issue.

Released May 4, 1979

Advance text: remarks to the Iowa State Association of Counties in Des Moines

Fact sheet: congregate rural elderly housing program

Fact sheet: rural energy development initiative

Advance text: opening statement at the President's news conference in Des Moines

Advance text: remarks at a memorial tribute for George Moscone in San Francisco, Calif.

CHECKLIST—Continued

Released May 5, 1979

Advance text: remarks at dedication ceremonies for La Placita de Dolores in Los Angeles, Calif.

Advance text: remarks at a Cinco de Mayo celebration in Los Angeles, Calif.

Released May 8, 1979

Announcement: nomination of Francis D. Murnaghan, Jr., to be United States Circuit Judge for the Fourth Circuit

Released May 9, 1979

Advance text: remarks on the strategic arms limitation negotiations—by Secretary of State Cyrus R. Vance and Secretary of Defense Harold Brown

Transcript: remarks on the strategic arms limitation negotiations—by Secretary Vance and Secretary Brown

Advance text: remarks at the Democratic Congressional Campaign Dinner

Released May 10, 1979

News conference: on the Civil Aeronautics Board—by Jody Powell, Press Secretary to the President, Alfred E. Kahn, Advisor to the President on Inflation, and Marvin S. Cohen, Chairman of the Civil Aeronautics Board

---

ACTS APPROVED BY THE PRESIDENT

Approved May 10, 1979

H.R. 2283_____ Public Law 96–10 An act to amend the Council on Wage and Price Stability Act to extend the authority granted by such Act to September 30, 1980, and for other purposes.

Interview With the President

Remarks and a Question-and-Answer Session With Editors and News Directors.
May 11, 1979

THE PRESIDENT. It's a pleasure to have you here. I understand this morning you've already been briefed, to some degree at least, on SALT and Multilateral Trade Negotiations and perhaps some other issues. And I want to welcome you here. This is somewhere between the 40th and 50th group that we've had come to the White House since I've been in office to give the editors around the Nation a briefing on matters that are of interest to you and your readers, or viewers or listeners.

I'd like just to make an opening statement, very brief.

ADMINISTRATION POLICIES

Our Nation is faced with several—both very important international issues and also very important domestic issues. I would say the most important of all is now the consummation, the signing, and the ratification of a SALT agreement.

Perhaps more important than anything that I will address while I'm President and perhaps the most important vote that

the incumbent Members of the Senate will ever cast is concerning the ratification of SALT II.

It's a fair treaty, enforceable treaty, verifiable treaty, and rejection of this treaty would have a devastating, adverse effect on our Nation's relationship with the Soviet Union, on our ability to deal effectively with our allies, with uncommitted nations, and with the control of nuclear weaponry or explosives in the future throughout the world. That's one issue.

Of course, the Middle East peace treaties now signed between Israel and Egypt are extremely important to us and to stability in the Middle East—I think perhaps even indirectly to the rest of the world. We stand staunchly behind our allies and friends, Israel and Egypt.

We hope that the other nations in that region will soon realize the importance of these treaties. We'll do all we can to implement them fully and to demonstrate to all those who are interested that we believe in and are committed to a comprehensive peace settlement.

We have some additional problems that face NATO, although it's been substantially strengthened. Turkey is obviously one problem. They have economic matters to address jointly with us, with the Germans, the French, and others who are interested in the stability and strength both politically and economically of Turkey. They are important along with Greece in dealing with the southern flank of NATO, and we have that as a partial responsibility of our own.

Domestic affairs: The control of inflation is important. I would say that the most important single action that the Congress can take this session is to pass the hospital cost containment legislation. So far, we've been disappointed in the response of the House of Representatives. We hope that they will see that this is something they can contribute to the control of inflation.

And the unfortunate vote of the House yesterday on the gasoline rationing standby plan, which I would have the authority to evolve—it will take 8 or 9 months—and which could be implemented only if there was a genuine emergency, as assessed by me and the Congress jointly, was a very severe setback—as I said earlier—in my opinion, an embarrassment, indeed, a shock to me.

Those are a few of the many issues that we face. I think as we go through the coming months and years, we're going to see that the energy shortage is not a transient thing. It's not something that somebody caused deliberately. It's something that's with us permanently. And we are dealing with a limited supply of energy of all kinds; we are trying to shift away from reliance on imported oil toward greater production in our own country, shifting to alternate supplies, strong conservation of energy in all its forms.

We have announced this morning a 100-percent allocation of diesel fuel for farmers and for fishermen. This is a hundred percent of their needs. And, of course, next winter we'll be faced with a requirement that home heating oil needs be met. This will be guaranteed also for those who live in the colder regions of our country.

This means that with a given, limited supply of oil, the motorists who have perhaps unnecessary transportation will have to conserve, which they have not yet shown a willingness to do.

None of these issues are simple; none of them are easy. And I hope that when I go out of office, that the American people can say that I and the Congress have dealt with these issues courageously and have put the long-range interest of our country ahead of any short-term political gains we might derive from avoiding these kinds of problems which have been with us, some of them, for a long time.

I'll be glad to answer any questions that you might have now on any issue.

QUESTIONS

RHODESIA; MINORITY ISSUES

Q. Yes, Mr. President, I'm the editor of the California Voice, which is the oldest black newspaper west of the Rockies. So, my question is going to be dealing with what our readers think is important for them.

THE PRESIDENT. Good.

Q. Can I have your personal opinion on the *Weber* case? And I'd also like to know what do you tell blacks who are saying that a wave of conservatism in this country, Proposition 13 and *Bakke,* is starting to erode many of the gains that blacks made in the late sixties? That's my second part of the question. And my third and final part is——

THE PRESIDENT. Well, I'm not—you know we've got 35 people in the room. [*Laughter*] I'm not sure that we can let one person have three questions. Can I take my choice among your questions? [*Laughter*]

Q. Well, okay, in that case——

THE PRESIDENT. Go ahead. I was just joking. Go ahead and ask the other question, and I will respond briefly.

Q. I guess I'll give you three short questions.

THE PRESIDENT. I noticed that.

Q. So, you can give me three short answers. [*Laughter*]

THE PRESIDENT. I'm not going to have time for an answer, though.

Q. Okay, and my third question is, is it true that within a month you are going to make a decision on whether to recognize the government in Rhodesia?

THE PRESIDENT. Well, the third one first. No, it's not a matter of recognition. The law requires me, at the end of the establishment of the government of Muzorewa and Smith and others, to make a determination of whether or not sanctions should be lifted, which means whether or not we should trade with them again. I will make that decision within 2 weeks after the newly elected government is installed.

On the trend in black and other minority rights, I think the trends are still in the right direction. I think we are now in a posture of consolidating the gains that have been made legally in guaranteeing equality of treatment, equality of rights of voting, employment, access to public funds. My own administration's been heavily committed to this proposition, to continue progress in a sustained fashion. I'll just give you a couple of quick examples.

One of the omissions has been that black-owned or minority-owned businesses didn't have access to Government contracts. In the local public works bill that we passed the first year I was in office, we built into the law a requirement that 10 percent of all the contracts would have to be allotted to businesses or contractors owned by minority stockholders. We have substantially increased our allocation of Federal funds to be deposited in minority-owned banks, and I have issued a directive for a substantial increase in purchasing from minority-owned businesses.

We set as a goal for ourselves when we first came in office a tripling of Federal purchases of supplies, file cabinets, and so forth, from minority-owned businesses by 1980. We will reach that goal. The sum total then will be at least $3 billion in purchases from minority-owned businesses.

We've reorganized the equal employment opportunity agencies of the Federal Government, and I think it's greatly strengthened them. And we have had an unrestrained buildup in Federal allocation of funds for the enforcement of and the enhancement of basic rights of equality of treatment for minority groups.

I'm particularly concerned about Spanish-speaking Americans having been abused in the South and Southwest, and the Attorney General, the Secretary of State, the Governors, and I have all started a new program to make sure that these abuses that have been extant in the past are removed.

The *Weber* case is one on which the Attorney General will take a stand, and has. We want to protect the right of people for employment, not only for equal employment but also for affirmative action. We took a stand, as you know, in the *Bakke* case, that has been already resolved. So, I would say that we've got, in general, a commitment that has not been attenuated.

I'm now in the process of appointing judges, a large number of them. We're trying to make sure that Spanish-speaking people, blacks, and women are adequately represented in the circuit courts and also in district courts, and to ensure employment in the policymaking positions, including the regulatory agencies, of minorities that have—in the past, have been excluded.

HEATING OIL RESERVES

Q. Mr. President, I'm Merrill Lockhard from Nashua, New Hampshire. This 100-percent allocation of diesel fuel for the fishing industry and farmers, is this going to have an adverse effect on the supplies of heating oil——

THE PRESIDENT. No.

Q. —— or is it going to have any effect at all?

THE PRESIDENT. No, the heating oil reserves by next October will be adequate to supply New Hampshire, New England, and the other colder regions of our country with their full needs throughout the winter of 1979, 1980.

ENERGY SECURITY TRUST FUND

Q. Mr. President, my name is Mick De Rienzo. I'm from New Jersey. And in the northwestern part of New Jersey, we have no mass transit. People depend on their car to get to and from work and do shopping and things of that type. Does the Government have to plan anything in the fields of mass transit?

THE PRESIDENT. Yes. In addition to substantial increases in the allocation of funds for rapid transit, mass transit, that's already been put into effect, under the windfall profits tax, which I now expect to pass through the Congress, we will establish an energy security fund designed to do three things. One is to meet the needs of very low income families who are adversely impacted by increases in oil price; secondly, to set up a research and development program for the development of alternate supplies of energy; and, thirdly, to improve rapid transit or mass transit.

So, those three basic functions of the reserve fund will be implemented in addition to the funds already allocated for that purpose.

SENATOR EDWARD M. KENNEDY

Q. Fremont Power, Indianapolis. Mr. President, I can imagine several quick answers you could give to this one. I wonder if you'd give us your candid opinion as to whether or not Ted Kennedy is going to go for the nomination in '80 or not?

THE PRESIDENT. I don't think so. Senator Kennedy has announced many times that he did not have any intention to run, that if I ran, that he would give me his support.

ASSISTANCE FOR PRIVATE SCHOOLS; DEPARTMENT OF EDUCATION

Q. Sir, Paul Wright from Greenville, South Carolina. Assuming we do have a Cabinet-level office for education, what will be your position on the private school movement on the secondary level in this country, sir?

THE PRESIDENT. Yes. Well, my position wouldn't change. I served as Governor of Georgia and, obviously, treated the private schools as a necessary part of the educational program. I have set aside, as Governor of Georgia, an allocation of financial resources for the private colleges of Georgia that began with $400 per student allocated out of State funds and then increased while I was Governor to $600 per student per year for tuition at the higher level.

I'm not in favor of the Federal Government helping to finance the routine operation of private schools. But I think there's a very strong role for them to play, and, of course, in some areas where the constitutional requirements permit it, we have participated in meeting the needs of private schools, partial needs in the field of health, food, some books and training supplies, and so forth, at the elementary and secondary level. I think there's a strong role to be played by private schools.

My own inclination is to keep the Federal Government out of the administration and the decisionmaking involving public education, and this is one of the guarantees that I would like to carry out when a new department is set up.

I started my public career as a member of the local county school board in Sumter County back in the early sixties, late fifties. In my judgment, the absence of an identifiable department of education in Washington is one of the reasons that we have had so many lawsuits and altercations which increasingly have involved the Federal Government into the affairs of a local school system.

I think, had I been able, as a member of the school board, or had I been able, as a chairman of a committee in the Georgia Senate or as a Governor of Georgia, to come to Washington and sit down with a person whose unique responsibility was to education as a Cabinet Secretary, we could have avoided some of the altercations that arose that couldn't be resolved and had to go into the Federal courts.

So, I believe that this is a very good move in the right direction.

Also, we have computed that the establishment of a department of education would result in the saving of about $100 million in administrative costs. And the elevation, I think, of education to a higher visibility by a Cabinet-level officer being around this table with me every 2 weeks would be a very healthy commitment of our Nation to better education.

We've got some problems in education. But all of these reasons—and I could name

others—speak well, I think, for a separate department. It would let the Secretary of Health and Welfare then concentrate much more on those two closely related issues. And I believe that that separation is logical and would work better.

I've served as Governor where they were separated. I've served as President where they were all together. And I'm basing my opinion partially on my own experience.

WAGE AND PRICE CONTROLS

Q. Mr. President, Paul Gruchow from Minnesota. On the matter of inflation, I wonder if you could say what convinces you that price controls will not work or are not a practical answer at the moment.

THE PRESIDENT. Well, they've never worked. We've tried them on many occasions. The only time they ever have worked is during an actual time of war, where you had to allocate not only prices and wages but also materials themselves, where the war effort got first priority and where many nonvolunteers were conscripted and sent overseas to endanger their own lives. And I think in that kind of an environment, you would not want to have anything other than minimum profit being derived from either employment or trade.

I'd like to point out something that's often overlooked. I do not have the authority to implement mandatory wage and price controls. When President Nixon did it shortly before, I think, the '68 election year, he did have the authority and this was—I think it was 1970, shortly before the '72 election. After that happened, the experiences with wage and price controls were so bad that the Congress did not see fit to renew the Presidential authority. And we still are suffering from the implementation, for instance, of price controls on beef. The farmers depleted their herds so severely that we still have a very serious beef shortage.

If any proposal was made in the Congress of a serious nature to pass wage and price controls, it could not possibly actually pass the Congress under any circumstances that I can envision. And merchants and others would automatically begin to raise their prices in an uncontrollable fashion to build a high price base on which to predicate future price increases.

So, under no circumstances would I ever approve the Congress passing that law, and I would be very reluctant to ever see it implemented unless our Nation is in a problem area that endangers our security.

Q. May I follow that up just briefly?

THE PRESIDENT. Yes, you can follow it up.

Q. How do you convince the public to agree to wage constraints in the face of news of record profits, which is how the price control question comes up for the public?

THE PRESIDENT. It's not easy. [*Laughter*] I don't claim it to be. But I can say that in those items where prices can be restrained voluntarily, under understood guidelines, we've been very successful.

We have carefully monitored, for instance, the Fortune 500, the 500 biggest corporations. We have found them to be in compliance. We are now with increasing experience able—and with an increasing capability in the Council on Wage and Price Stability—able to monitor the middle-sized and smaller companies.

We are increasing our publicity about it. And when we have found a few companies potentially out of compliance or actually out of compliance, when we've brought that to their attention in a forceful way, and they have reversed themselves.

One company in California actually refunded money. Sears, Roebuck, when I called the head of that company and said, "We believe you're out of compliance," not only reduced their prices in retail stores but actually have reduced their prices in the existent catalog, which couldn't be reprinted. We've just had a similar experience with Giant Foods, and Giant Foods has now agreed to comply.

So, on the price side, we've pretty well helped considerably already. If you would compare the wage settlements this year with what they were a year or 2 years ago, we've had a substantial deceleration in wage increases. Of 90 or so wage settlements—some very large, some relatively small—that I have monitored or that we have monitored, at least 80 of them are completely within the guidelines without any question whatsoever.

And I think even the Teamsters' settlement—you can argue whether it's round or flat—but even in the Teamsters' settlement, there was a substantial reduction in the size of the increase, compared to previous wage increases without constraints.

We have had excellent response. The things that have been going up so high in price are beef, which I've already covered, which kind of leads food; fresh fruit and vegetables, because we've had two succeeding, extraordinarily severe winter seasons that cut down production; and oil, which is controlled outside our own country. And these material prices and supply prices obviously have caused us great concern. But the present wage level, the present price level, and also the ones in the months ahead, are substantially lower than they would have been without the wage and price guidelines.

I think the response has been responsible. And I would like, obviously, for the wage settlements and price settlements to be even lower. We have tightened up as we've gone along with more experience, and we've found a ready compliance.

STRATEGIC ARMS LIMITATION

Q. Mr. President, could we have your assessment on SALT and whether you can get it through the Senate in much the same form in which you intend to sign it?

THE PRESIDENT. Well, you know, we've negotiated this SALT treaty now for going on 7 years, under three Presidents, and it's been negotiated in the most extreme specificity, much greater specific, detail negotiation than ever existed with the limited test ban or SALT I or the ABM treaty.

There's been a hard negotiation, a tough negotiation on both sides, and the Soviets, I think, as have we, have been not only tough but fair. We have gotten the best deal we can. It's not perfect. I could have written a unilateral treaty if I didn't have to consult with the Soviets, that it would have been more attractive to us and less attractive to them. But for the Senate to expect the Soviets substantially to change their posture just because we unilaterally want them to do so is fruitless and, I think, would cause a rejection of SALT treaty completely.

I think the treaty is to our great advantage and also to the Soviets' great advantage. And I need not go into all the details of SALT II, but I think that it's, at the least, very fair, well-balanced, stable, verifiable, adequate, and a move in the right direction. It leads to SALT III, which will be even better.

Rejection of the treaty, however, will have the most devastating consequences to our country and, I think, to world peace. It will sever, to a substantial degree, the workable relationship between ourselves and the Soviet. It will shake the confidence of our own NATO Allies in our ability to get along reasonably well with the Soviets and leave them in an increasingly vulnerable position. It would make it almost impossible for us to pursue successfully the control of nuclear weapon development in countries like India, Pakistan, Iraq, Argentina, Brazil, Taiwan, South Korea, and other nations who have the technical ability to produce nuclear weapons, but have refrained from doing so because they saw an overall, worldwide restraint.

If we show that we are not willing to restrain our own nuclear arsenal, when it's to our advantage and the Soviets' both to do it—we would already have several thousand nuclear weapons—there's no way that I could go to someone like Prime Minister Desai in India, with whom I have had long discussions on this, and say, "We have set a good example for you, now you restrain yourself and don't ever develop another explosion in India." It would be almost impossible for me to do it. So, it would wipe out any real good opportunity for us to constrain nuclear weaponry.

And as you know, there are three ways that we can compete with the Soviet Union. One is militarily through a prospective or actual war, which we both want to avoid. The other is what we are doing. We are meeting them competitively in the political realm and also in the philosophical and moral and ethnic realm. And that's where the competition goes on.

If the Soviets should sign SALT II and, in effect, ratify it—which is, I think, inevitable—and if we should sign it and then reject it, we would lose our competitive ability to reach effectively the hearts and minds of other people around the world who will be making a choice between us, on the one hand, and the Soviets, on the other, in the future for military, political, trade alliances; because the Soviets can put themselves through a massive propaganda effort, which would be inevitable, too, in their role of a powerful but fair and peace-loving nation.

We would be put in the role of a powerful nation that was, in effect, in their opinion, a warmonger who refused even to participate in an equitable restraint on the most destructive weapons on Earth. And how we could deal effectively as a nation in competition with the Soviets after we rejected the SALT treaty is something that I cannot understand and which I would hate to have to face as a President.

So, I am asking the Senators—the ones that were sitting around this table day before yesterday—"Before you vote on SALT, take yourselves out of the role of a Senator or out of the role of the chairman or a member of the Armed Services Committee or the Foreign Relations Committee, and put yourself in the position of the President, who would have to implement a national policy and an international policy after our Nation was crippled, in effect, by the consequences of a SALT II rejection."

This is undoubtedly the most important single issue that I will ever have to face as President, unless we are faced with actual war. And I hope that every American will join in with me, not in a quiescent way, just observing what's going on, but in an active way. And I particularly hope the news media will assess the details of the SALT agreement, the consequences of either passage or rejection, and let your voices be heard in the strongest possible way.

It transcends partisanship; it transcends the necessary objectivity of the news media toward politicians. And I hope that legitimately, within the bounds of the role of the news media, that you will actively support and promote the ratification of the SALT treaty.

Ms. Bario. Thank you, sir.

The President. Thank you.

NOTE: The interview began at 1:15 p.m. in the Cabinet Room at the White House. Patricia Y. Bario is an Associate Press Secretary.

The transcript of the interview was released on May 12.

Middle East Peace Negotiations

Appointment of James Leonard as Deputy to Ambassador Strauss.   May 12, 1979

The President has appointed Ambassador James Leonard as Deputy to Ambassador Robert Strauss for the negotiations on the West Bank and Gaza. Ambassador Leonard, who had planned to retire from his present position as Deputy U.S. Representative to the U.N. this summer, has agreed to defer his retirement. He will attend the opening of the negotiations with Secretary Vance and lead the U.S. delegation at the talks following the Secretary's departure. He will begin working immediately with Ambassador Strauss on all aspects of the American participation in the negotiations. The President, Secretary Vance, and Ambassador Strauss are delighted to have a man of Ambassador Leonard's experience and background undertake these negotiations.

Presidential Scholars

Announcement of the Selection of 121 Students as Presidential Scholars of 1979.
May 14, 1979

The President today announced the Presidential Scholars for 1979. They are

121 graduating high school seniors, chosen on the basis of academic excellence, leadership, and accomplishment in other areas such as the visual and performing arts. The scholars will visit Washington from June 17 to 20 as the guests of the White House and the U.S. Office of Education.

The Presidential Scholars program, established by Executive order in 1964, annually honors one boy and one girl from each State, the District of Columbia, Puerto Rico, Americans living abroad, and 15 students selected at large. The students, from both public and private schools, are initially identified through scores on precollege examinations nationally administered in secondary schools. The scholars are selected by the Commission on Presidential Scholars, a panel of private citizens from a variety of fields, who serve without compensation.

During their visit to Washington, the scholars will receive Presidential Scholars medallions in a White House ceremony. They will also attend seminars with authorities in many fields, meet with their elected officials, and visit historic sites. The scholars receive no financial award.

1979 PRESIDENTIAL SCHOLARS

Alabama

GORDON A. TURNBULL, Mobile
BRENDA J. SWAIN, Anniston

Alaska

PHILIP R. ROBISON, Anchorage
DOUGLAS R. FRANKLIN, Anchorage
CHARLOTTE A. HAMMOND, Eagle River

Arizona

BRIAN L. JARVIS, Phoenix
KAREN A. CUROSH, Phoenix

Arkansas

BRENT A. RICHERT, Texarkana
ELIZABETH A. THIELE, Fort Smith

California

JAMES S. MCGUIRE, Palo Alto
SCOTT A. LAPE, Chico
SARAH L. GIBBONS, Palo Alto

Colorado

WILLIAM P. MACKENDRICK, Hotchkiss
SUSAN P. MIZNER, Englewood

Connecticut

JAMES P. CRIMMINS, Wilton
FRANCESCA A. HAYSLETT, Woodbridge

Delaware

ANTHONY DEH-CHUEN SO, Wilmington
PHILIPPA J. WEBSTER, Wilmington

District of Columbia

JAMIN B. RASKIN
MARIA A. SULLIVAN
JACQUELINE A. BERRIEN

Florida

TODD G. KOCOUREK, Tampa
TERRI M. WILLIAMSON, Ft. Myers

Georgia

BROOKS R. BURDETTE, Hogansville
JAMES H. GILLAND, Atlanta
LLOYD S. HAWK, Atlanta
MARY W. MCCARTHY, Decatur

Hawaii

JONATHAN V. SELINGER, Honolulu
SHEILA LI TIEN LING, Honolulu

Idaho

KARY D. SMOUT, Pocatello
ANNA J. JOHNSON, Eden

Illinois

CARL A. HESS, Northfield
CRAIG F. PRESTON, E. St. Louis
SUSAN H. ROSENBERG, Evanston

Indiana

JOHN E. BERNERS, South Bend
LAURA J. RIGGS, Danville

Iowa

DUFFY CRAVEN, West Des Moines
LLOYD K. MITCHELL, Des Moines
BARBARA A. KNAPP, Council Bluffs

Kansas

DAVID S. CUNNINGHAM, Salina
LESLIE J. MAY, Oskaloosa

Kentucky

GAGE R. JOHNSON, Bowling Green
LISA C. CANNON, Eddyville

Louisiana
MICHAEL T. ANDERSON, New Orleans
LOULAN J. PITRE, JR., Galliano
DEBORAH L. THURBER, New Orleans
PHOEBE E. BRIAN, Alexandria

Maine
THOMAS E. MELENDY, Rockland
MYRNA L. KOONCE, Oakland

Maryland
DAVID F. INNIS, Hyattsville
SHARON L. GRAY, Rockville

Massachusetts
JEFFREY J. LOBO, Westford
LAWRENCE J. HOBBIE, Falmouth
CATHERINE DURSO, South Hadley

Michigan
RONALD E. ELLIS, Okemos
MARY G. ARMSTRONG, Grand Blanc

Minnesota
THOMAS J. LENK, Aurora
ARTURO C. MADRID, Minneapolis
JACQUELINE K. GIROUX, St. Cloud

Mississippi
GEORGE F. RICE, Vicksburg
LAURIE I. HAMILTON, Pascagoula

Missouri
STEVE S. GOLSTON, Camdenton
CORNELIA A. HECKER, St. Joseph

Montana
MICHAEL J. ROAM, Billings
ARDIS A. MOE, Billings

Nebraska
JOHN R. WILSON, Hastings
KRISTINE L. PETERSEN, Omaha

Nevada
ROGER V. VOGELER, Elko
REBECCA F. HAAG, Boulder City

New Hampshire
PANG-YEN FAN, Exeter
ANDREA FINK, Durham

New Jersey
STEVEN RAPKIN, Millburn
SIMINA M. FARCASIU, Princeton

New Mexico
CHRISTOPHER A. SHERA, Los Alamos
CAROL J. O'ROURKE, Los Alamos

New York
THEODORE E. SPERLING, Bronx
WILLIAM D. URQUHART, North Babylon
ARI M. LIEMAN, New York City
ANNALIESE S. KAMBOUR, Schenectady

North Carolina
JEEN KIM, Greenville
DAGMAR HERZOG, Durham

North Dakota
GARRETT J. STUCK, Minot
CHRISTINE M. EVANS, Grand Forks

Ohio
ROBERT E. WENZ, North Royalton
JULIE E. JACOBS, Columbus

Oklahoma
DWIGHT N. PETERSON, Edmond
CARY L. STANFORD, Tulsa

Oregon
PHILLIP D. BROWN, JR., Lake Oswego
MARION S. BRET-HARTE, Hillsboro

Pennsylvania
SCOTT B. SMITH, Fairless Hills
ANN F. MOHRBACHER, Flourtown

Puerto Rico
EDUARDO R. JUNCOSA, Rio Piedras
CARMEN M. ARIAS, Miramar

Rhode Island
MARK J. WEGNER, Providence
SHANNON L. REAGAN, Middletown

South Carolina
CHRISTOPHER J. FALTER, Columbia
MARGARET J. GREEN, Charleston

South Dakota
BRILSFORD B. FLINT, Rapid City
PAMELA R. RASMUSSON, Dell Rapids

Tennessee
ALAN L. HALBERT, Oak Ridge
ANNE-ALISON G. BURTON, Memphis

Texas
WILLIAM N. CREAGER, Midland
VICTORIA L. EASTUS, Dallas

Utah
DOUGLAS P. HANSEN, Provo
WENDY L. MATIS, Ogden

Vermont
JAMES C. LINDNER, Burlington
EILEEN A. McARDLE, Rutland

Virginia

MURRAY D. TANZER, Arlington
JAMES T. HAMILTON, Alexandria
ELIZABETH E. KISS, Alexandria
KAREN WHITING, Richmond

Washington

PAUL F. SJOHOLM, Everett
DEBORAH K. UNDERWOOD, Walla Walla

West Virginia

JEFFREY D. ADKINS, Beckley
MARY E. CONNELLY, Charleston

Wisconsin

MARTIN E. POITZSCH, Eau Claire
ANNE E. BECKER, Whitefish Bay

Wyoming

MIKE F. DUNLEAVY, Powell
PATRICIA S. HOLLAND, Worland

Virgin Islands

GREGORY V. SMITH, St. Thomas

Canal Zone

CATHERINE A. CIEPIELA, Balboa

Alaska Public Lands Legislation

Letter to the Members of the House of Representatives. May 14, 1979

You and your colleagues in the House of Representatives will soon cast the most important conservation vote of this century. Your vote on the Alaska lands bill is an opportunity to determine the protection and use of millions of acres of Federal land and resources in America's last frontier.

The Udall-Anderson substitute bill is balanced. It will allow development of nearly all of Alaska's oil and gas resources and most of its other minerals as well. It will allow timber production and related employment to increase. Valid mining claims will be honored. The fishing industry will be protected. Extensive sport hunting opportunities are preserved. And the Udall-Anderson bill protects what is essen-

tial to Alaska's native cultures, scenic wonders and abundant wildlife.

The other bills before the Congress are unacceptable. In these bills, the Arctic National Wildlife Range—the calving grounds and migratory route for the last great caribou herd—would be threatened by oil and gas exploration activities. Two of the most significant Alaska National Monuments—Admiralty Island and Misty Fiords—would be chopped in half. There are many other objectionable features of these bills which Administration officials have enumerated.

After the 95th Congress adjourned I took a number of steps to protect Alaska lands, including the establishment of 17 National Monuments covering 56 million acres. Legislative action offers Congress the opportunity not only to designate the Federal lands in Alaska but also to provide for tailor-made management schemes which in some cases are more lenient than the current situation. However, should legislation not strike an appropriate balance in Alaska, I will not hesitate to continue administrative protections.

This is an issue where the pressures of the moment must not be allowed to outweigh our responsibilities to future generations. I urge you to support the Udall-Anderson bill.

Sincerely,

JIMMY CARTER

NOTE: This is the text of identical letters addressed to each Member of the House of Representatives.

The text of the letter was released on May 15.

Nuclear Regulatory Commission

Nomination of Victor Gilinsky To Be a Member. May 15, 1979

The President today announced that he will nominate Victor Gilinsky, of

Bethesda, Md., for reappointment as a member of the Nuclear Regulatory Commission.

Gilinsky has been a member of the NRC since 1975.

He was born May 28, 1934, in Warsaw, Poland. He received a bachelor of engineering physics degree from Cornell University in 1956 and a Ph. D. in physics from California Institute of Technology in 1961.

From 1961 to 1970, Gilinsky was a physicist with the Rand Corp. From 1971 to 1972, he was special assistant to the Director of Regulation of the U.S. Atomic Energy Commission. From 1972 to 1973, he was Assistant Director for Policy and Program Review in the Office of Planning and Analysis at the AEC. From 1973 to 1975, he was head of the physical sciences department at the Rand Corp.

Postal Rate Commission

Nomination of A. Lee Fritschler To Be a Commissioner, and Designation as Chairman. May 15, 1979

The President today announced that he will nominate A. Lee Fritschler, of Washington, D.C., to be a Commissioner of the Postal Rate Commission for the term expiring October 14, 1982. He would succeed Frank Saponaro, whose term has expired.

The President also announced that on confirmation by the Senate, Fritschler would be designated Chairman of the Commission.

Fritschler is acting dean of the College of Public Affairs and professor of government at the American University.

He was born May 5, 1937, in Schenectady, N.Y. He received a B.A. from Union College, Schenectady, in 1959, and an M.P.A. (1960) and Ph. D. (1965) from Maxwell School of Citizenship and Public Affairs at Syracuse University.

From 1964 to 1967, Fritschler was an assistant professor at the American University and academic director of the Washington Semester Program. Between 1968 and 1971, he held numerous appointments as visiting lecturer and faculty fellow at institutions including the College of William and Mary, the National War College, the Washington Center for Metropolitan Studies, UNESCO's International Institute for Educational Planning, the Institute of Social Studies at The Hague, and the University of Cologne in the Federal Republic of Germany.

From 1969 to 1971, Fritschler was also director of the National Center for Education in Politics at the American University, and in 1971–72 he was director of the public administration program. From 1972 to 1977, he was dean of the school of government and public administration in the College of Public Affairs. Since 1977 he has been acting dean of the College of Public Affairs.

Fritschler has written extensively on bureaucratic policymaking, business participation in administration, and urban politics. He is the recipient of numerous research appointments and grants in the United States and abroad.

President's Commission on the Accident at Three Mile Island

Appointment of Carolyn Lewis as a Member. May 15, 1979

The President today announced the appointment of the 12th member of the President's Commission on the Accident at Three Mile Island.

She is Carolyn Lewis, an associate professor of journalism at Columbia Graduate School of Journalism.

Lewis, 47, was a reporter for United Press in Australia for 14 years. She was with the Washington Post from 1964 to 1968, and was the Capitol Hill correspondent for WTOP radio from 1968 to 1974. In 1974 and 1975, she was Capitol Hill correspondent for the National Public Affairs Center for Television (NPACT).

Lewis was an associate professor of journalism at Boston University from 1975 until 1978, when she joined the faculty at Columbia as associate professor and coordinator of the broadcast division.

Mental Health Systems Legislation

Remarks Announcing the Proposed Legislation. May 15, 1979

THE PRESIDENT. Just a few weeks after I became President, I appointed a Presidential Commission on mental health with Tom Bryant as its Chairman, and with my wife, Rosalynn, as the Honorary Chairperson. This was done because of my deep interest in mental health, the experience that Rosalynn and I had together in Georgia in trying to improve the mental health situation there, and also because, on a nationwide basis, this is a very serious problem.

Their report was made last year, and it was comprehensive and very specific and very helpful. Some of the recommendations have already been implemented through budget requests and through administrative action. And, for instance, we have increased substantially the requests for funds for basic research to deal with the mental health problem and have increased substantially the payment for outpatient services for those under Medicare who are chronically mentally ill.

We have still a very serious problem for those who are mentally or emotionally disabled. Some estimates indicate that between 10 and 15 percent of all the people in our country have a mental or emotional problem of some kind, and we have now more than 1½ million people who are institutionalized. Because of an absence of a cohesive program and an absence of close cooperation and a partnership between the local, State, and Federal officials and private agencies, many mentally ill people have to choose between unnecessary institutionalization, sometimes staying in a mental hospital for their entire lives, on the one hand, and inadequate community services on the other.

We also don't have enough help for the very poor, for minority groups, for young children, and for the elderly.

Today I have sent to the Congress a proposal, a message from me, to be followed up by legislation called the Mental Health Systems Act. This will be introduced jointly by Senator Kennedy and by Congressman Waxman, and I understand several other sponsors will attach their names to this very important legislation.

It will deal with some of the very serious problems that I have already outlined. One of the things that will be accomplished is to provide more flexible funding. Quite often we have seen that local communities with limited needs and also limited ability have been required in the past either to have a fully comprehensive and very costly mental health program or no program at all. Under the new legislation, specifically focused mental health care can be provided to meet the requirements of the community and also to be within the limits of the community resources.

We'll have an additional emphasis in the future on the prevention of mental illness. This is the most cost-effective means to approach mental illness. Research and common experience has shown that an early treatment, even beginning with prenatal care, in some instances, and with the early life of a child can prevent a very serious and perhaps permanent impairment of the mental capabilities of that person.

We'll shift toward more help for deprived areas, rural areas and the inner city areas, for instance. We've had a substantial increase in nurses, medical doctors, and also paraprofessionals in the last few years, but they are inadequately distributed throughout the country now.

And the last thing is that so many different people are interested in mental health from widely diverse points of view, that the bureaucratic confusion has been excessive. We hope to address that problem as well and to guarantee the basic human rights or civil rights of the mentally ill through advocacy programs. Quite often if a person is mentally ill, we assume that they are subhuman, and on many occasions their basic legal rights are not only taken away from them but are never explained to them. And this is the kind of comprehensive approach that Rosalynn, Tom Bryant, and Joe Califano have evolved.

I believe this legislation will have a far-reaching beneficial impact on our country and on the millions of people in our Nation who suffer at this time in an unwarranted and unnecessary fashion from the ills brought about by emotional or mental disturbance.

My wife will make a few comments, and then Joe Califano, following that, will explain to you the details of the legislation. Rosalynn.

MRS. CARTER. Well, I'm very pleased that this new Mental Health Systems Act is going to Congress today. I've tried to be an advocate for the mentally afflicted—within the White House, with Congress, and with the American people. And I've had many, many people who've joined with me in working to improve the lives of those persons who suffer from mental afflictions.

I have sometimes—I might even say often—been frustrated at how long it takes to move the bureaucracy and develop programs. But I'm very pleased today that we do have a good bill. It's sound, it's doable, and it is a very important first step in seeing that mental health services are accessible to all those people in our country who need the services.

It's going to be difficult at this time to pass this legislation through Congress this year. I feel an urgency to do this, and I'm going to be working very hard to see that we do get it passed. Tomorrow I'm going to Chicago to speak to the American Psychiatric Association. I'm going to ask their help in working with Congress to push the legislation through to take quick action this year.

I'm going to be working with the major organizations that are interested and concerned about mental health. And also there were literally hundreds of persons who worked with me on the President's Commission on Mental Health in developing that report. And this legislation is developed from that report. It was used as a blueprint for this legislation.

There are so many people in our country who are concerned about those with mental afflictions. There's been so much fragmentation in efforts. And I think that this is one time that we can join together in a coordinated way to do something really positive and help those people in our country who need help.

Joe Califano has worked closely with me. He's going to describe the legislation to you now, brief you on the legislation. I am going to meet with the Congressional Relations staff and start—work out a strategy for getting the legislation passed through Congress.

Thank you.

Joe, I leave you with it.

Joe just went with me to the World Health Organization. I spoke about mental health there, because I think it is a worldwide problem. And we had some long discussions on the airplane about the legislation and how we can get it passed. And he's going to brief you now on maybe what we talked about.

Thank you.

NOTE: The President spoke at 11:03 a.m. to reporters assembled in the Briefing Room at the White House.

Secretary of Health, Education, and Welfare Califano's remarks and a news conference on the proposed legislation are included in the press release.

Mental Health Systems Legislation

Message to the Congress Transmitting the Proposed Legislation.   May 15, 1979

To the Congress of the United States:

I am today submitting to Congress the Mental Health Systems Act. This proposed legislation establishes a new partnership between the federal government and the states in the planning and provision of mental health services. It seeks to assure that the chronically mentally ill no longer face the cruel alternative of unnecessary institutionalization or inadequate care in the community. It provides local communities with more flexible federal support for mental health services and places a new emphasis on the prevention of mental illness.

I am deeply committed to reducing the tragic toll which mental illness exacts from our citizens and our country. Less than one month after entering office I signed an Executive Order creating the President's Commission on Mental Health with Rosalynn Carter as Honorary Chairperson. I directed the Commission to undertake an intensive study of the mental health needs of our nation and to recommend appropriate ways of meeting these needs.

During our years in Georgia, both Rosalynn and I became keenly aware of the unmet needs of people in our state who suffered from mental and emotional disabilities. Those with chronic mental illness were too often locked away in isolated institutions far from family and friends. Children and adults with signs of developing mental and emotional problems did not have access to early detection and prevention programs. Community-based care was beginning to develop but was constantly stripped of its full potential by inflexible program models designed for the "average" community, rather than for the particular needs of a given locale or state. Special populations such as the elderly, children, and racial and ethnic minorities were not receiving care designed to meet their special needs. For those who required hospitalization there were almost no alternatives to large state mental hospitals. Aftercare was almost non-existent for patients released from those hospitals who returned to their home communities.

While I am proud of what we accomplished in Georgia to begin to solve these problems, my concern that similar problems exist throughout the nation prompted me to establish the Commission and to ask it to report back to me in one year with its findings and recommendations. The excellent final report of the Commission presented to me last April made clear that the past 30 years had seen tremendous achievement on behalf of our mentally ill population. Not only had there been a dramatic shift of emphasis from inpatient care to community-based care, but great strides had been made in mental health-related research, and thousands of mental health personnel had been trained. However, the report also contained unmistakable evidence that there are unmet needs in every region of our country.

Some of the key Commission findings dramatically illustrated the challenges this nation faces in meeting the needs of the mentally ill:

—According to the most recent estimates, between ten and fifteen percent of the population—20–32 million Americans—need some form of mental health services at any one time.

—Substantial numbers of Americans do not have access to mental health care of high quality and at reasonable cost. For many, this is because of where they live; for others, it is because of who they are— their race, age, or sex; for still others, it is because of their particular disability or economic circumstance.

—There are approximately 1.5 million chronically mentally disabled adults in mental hospitals, nursing homes and other residential facilities. Many of these individuals could lead better lives in less restrictive settings if mental health and supporting services were available in their communities. The problem is that for them—and for the hundreds of thousands of patients who have been returned to their communities from large institutions over the past few years—such support services are seldom readily available. As a result, evidence indicates that half the

people released from large state mental hospitals are readmitted within a year of discharge.

—There is insufficient emphasis at federal, state, and local levels on prevention and early detection of mental disorders. Infants and children would especially benefit from expanded prevention efforts, since early intervention with problems in physical, emotional and cognitive development can prevent more serious mental and emotional problems in the future.

—Conflicting policy objectives in various Federal health and mental health programs and between federal and state programs often lead to confusion, fragmentation of services, and a lack of continuity of care for those with mental and emotional problems. In addition, diverse federal planning requirements and poorly developed planning capabilities at the state and local levels have perpetuated the lack of integrated planning necessary to build a nationwide network of accessible public and private mental health services.

—The lack of flexibility in Federal funding of community-based services has prevented some communities from providing services to their underserved populations. Although over 700 Community Mental Health Centers provide services to almost 3 million patients annually, this model of organizing services cannot fit the needs of all people and all communities. Therefore, varying approaches to developing comprehensive community mental health services should be encouraged.

—About two-thirds of all mentally ill persons being treated in this country every year are receiving care in the general health care system. Nevertheless, cooperative working arrangements between general health care settings and community mental health programs are rare.

—Over the past several years, there has been a marked increase in the number of professional and paraprofessional mental health practitioners. However, rural areas, small towns, and poor urban areas still have only a fraction of the personnel they need. Many mental health facilities have a shortage of trained personnel. The mental health professions still have too few minority members, and there is a shortage of specialists trained to work with children, adolescents, and the elderly.

—Since 1969, our national mental health research capacity has undergone substantial erosion and our investment in mental health research is now so low that the development of new knowledge is jeopardized.

To deal with these and other problems in the mental health arena, the Commission developed a series of recommendations for bold new action to improve our nation's mental health. Many of these recommendations served as a blueprint for the proposed Mental Health Systems Act.

The proposed Act charts a new course for mental health care which promises comprehensiveness, flexibility and innovation. For the first time in the history of federal involvement with mental health care, a true, performance-based partnership would be created between the federal and state governments. Special emphasis is placed on the chronically mentally ill. Recognizing that this population has long been the most neglected of any mentally ill group, the proposed Act provides support to states which are phasing down large state hospitals, upgrading the quality of services in remaining institutions, and providing quality alternatives to institutionalization. I believe that these provisions of the Act will encourage the development of a comprehensive, integrated system of care designed to best serve the needs of chronically mentally ill adults and children.

Another innovation is the proposed Act's emphasis on prevention. States and localities are awarded grants to develop preventive and mental health promotion programs through public and professional education and demonstration projects. Such programs, I believe, will lay the foundation for the future in mental health care as we learn how to prevent mental illness before it occurs.

The proposed legislation gives a new and much needed flexibility to community mental health programs. It authorizes funds for one or more mental health services without requiring that a comprehensive package be developed as a prerequisite for financial assistance. This new flexibility will enable communities to provide services to their most underserved populations—whether the chronically mentally ill, children, the elderly, racial and ethnic minorities, the poor, rural residents, or other groups—and build toward a comprehensive system of care for the entire community over time. In addition, by providing financial incentives for closer coordination between ambulatory health care providers and mental health care providers, the Act takes an important step toward assuring that appropriate mental health care is available for all who need help.

The Act also guarantees increased availability of mental health personnel in underserved areas by requiring that mental health professionals who receive federal support for training work in an area with a shortage of mental health personnel for a period equal to the length of the support.

It is, of course, impossible for any one piece of legislation to meet all the mental health needs of the nation. The federal government has already sought to implement many of the recommendations of the Commission in other ways:

—To increase the development of new knowledge about mental illness, the 1980 budget provides additional funding for research into disabling mental illness, and for determining ways to improve the delivery of mental health care.

—To increase the availability of mental health services for the elderly, changes have been proposed increasing the Medicare reimbursement ceiling for outpatient mental health services and decreasing the beneficiary's co-payment requirement. Also, the Child Health Assurance Program will mandate that states provide mental health services for Medicaid-eligible children.

—To assist the chronically mentally ill to function effectively outside of institutions, the Departments of Health, Education, and Welfare and Housing and Urban Development have initiated a joint demonstration project which provides both housing and support services.

—To promote protection of the rights of the mentally ill, the Administration is funding demonstration projects which deliver advocacy services to the mentally ill and is studying existing advocacy programs to determine the appropriate role for the federal government in this area.

I am convinced that these actions and the passage of the Mental Health Systems Act will reduce the number of Americans robbed of vital and satisfying lives by mental illness. I ask the Congress to join with me in developing a new system of mental health care designed to deal more effectively with our nation's unmet mental health needs.

JIMMY CARTER

The White House,
    May 15, 1979.

Energy

Remarks at a White House Briefing for Community and Civic Leaders. May 15, 1979

A couple of weeks ago, I was in New Hampshire. And the primary concern of the people in that State, I believe, above every other issue, was the prospect of entering next winter without an adequate supply of home heating oil. Eighty percent of the homes in New England use oil for heating, and more than 80 percent of their oil comes from overseas.

Last weekend, I was in Iowa, and no matter what I wanted to talk about, the number one consideration of a county officials' convention and the press conference was what the farmers were going to do when they finally got in the fields to plant—they're about 3 weeks behind—without an adequate supply of tractor fuel, diesel fuel, and gasoline for tractors. And they were equally concerned that when their crops were harvested in the fall, that they may not have enough natural gas or propane to dry their crops.

And then I went to California directly. [Laughter] And there was a situation bordering on panic with just 2- or 3-percent shortage of gasoline. They had evolved panic buying—those with tanks three-quarters full were sitting in line for hours and hours to buy $2, $3 worth of gas. The average purchase of gasoline during the preceding week had been less than $3 per purchase.

This puts a very sobering responsibility on my shoulder and on yours. More than 2 years ago, I informed the American people, in a speech on television—the next night I spoke directly to the Congress, one of my few appearances before the Congress—that we faced an energy crisis with "the moral equivalent of war." There was a lot of frivolity about the alarmist approach. And the Congress considered this legislation for 18 months, finally passed about 60 to 65 percent of what I had advocated, did not pass anything concerning oil.

Many of the Members of Congress who've served 25 or 30 years told me that that was the worst session of Congress they had ever served in and that the energy legislation was the most complicated and difficult that they thought the Nation had ever addressed in its 200-year history.

The situation is not going to get any better. My guess is that it will get worse. We're going to have less oil in the future on a worldwide basis compared to demand, and the price is going to continue to increase. That means the American people are going to have to use less to meet a given need, and they're going to have to pay more for it.

This is not an attractive statement to make, because people ordinarily look to political leaders for the expression of words of a panacea, the resolution of a difficult problem with a simple or simplistic answers, and the alleviation of problems, at least a promise of alleviation of problems.

Those hopeful and pleasant political dreams are not going to come true. We've not had adequate support from Congress, and the American people still refuse to face the inevitable prospect of energy shortages, even the most well-meaning and patriotic Americans—still looking for a scapegoat.

Many believe that there is no energy shortage and there's not going to be an energy shortage, that the problem is that the Federal Government in some way is in collusion with the oil companies, that artificial shortages are being contrived in order to drive up prices and that if prices could get high enough, all of a sudden there would be enough energy for every-

one. That's obviously a false analysis or premise. So, what do we do about it?

The Congress in 1975 mandated that then-President Ford and his successors would evolve a gasoline rationing plan. Nobody but a political fool would advocate the implementation of gasoline rationing in this country on a voluntary basis. But I was mandated by law to present to the Congress a gasoline rationing plan as a standby. I don't have the authority to develop a gasoline rationing plan. It takes a lot of money. It would require some Federal employees to evolve a gasoline rationing plan with coupons, regulations, and all that go with it. But we presented to the Congress an outline of a plan to be developed, a process that would ordinarily require about 8 or 9 months.

After that time, if an emergency should arise, then the President and the Congress would both have to agree that the rationing plan would be put into effect. Even under those circumstances, the Congress refused to give me the authority to develop a standby gasoline rationing plan—I thought a remarkable demonstration of political timidity.

We have now tried to assess on a continuing basis what can be done. Obviously, the most inexpensive and effective means of dealing with the energy crisis is to eliminate waste of energy. For a given level of income, per capita income, the American public consumes about twice as much energy as, say, a resident of Germany, most European countries. We have an enormous amount of waste.

In the last 2 years, there has been a substantial improvement in the efficiency of energy consumption within the corporate world because of the pressures of savings and the profit motive which is an integral part of our Nation's societal structure based on the free enterprise system which I cherish.

Among the average American consumer, that has not been the case. In spite of the large amount of publicity that has swept the Nation, indeed the whole world, in the last 12 months about energy shortages, the consumption of gasoline, for instance, continues to rise quite rapidly. It's much higher now than it was in California a year ago. And I think there's a general sense among American people that the issue's going to go away.

But conservation is obviously the best approach, if we can ever induce the American people to recognize the need for conservation, to hold down thermostat settings, to obey the 55-mile-per-hour speed limit, to cut off unnecessary consumers of energy, equipment, to eliminate unnecessary trips; that's not yet been done. I see no indication of it being done so far in our country. The second thing that we can do, obviously, is to increase American production of oil, gas, and other energy sources. And, of course, the third thing is to shift toward more permanent types of energy, replenishable energy sources, and to increase the production and use of coal.

We have been addressing this issue in a fruitless way, almost, for the last 2 years. The Congress has a law on the books that gives me the authority as of June 1 to decontrol oil if I choose. I have announced that over a 28-month period, step by step, carefully phased, oil prices will be decontrolled. In October of 1971 [1981],[1] the control law expires. And rather than having a peremptory decontrol of all energy prices overnight, which would have an adverse impact and uncontrollable inflationary pressure on our economy, my judgment was to phase out

---

[1] Printed in the transcript.

controls carefully in a predictable and controllable fashion. And I do not want the increase in oil prices to go to enrich the oil companies.

I have no animosity against the oil companies, but I believe that their profits are adequate. And as these prices are decontrolled, the oil companies will reap an additional income, about 29 cents on each dollar of price increase, which amounts to about $6 billion over the period. And this can be used, in addition to the present oil company profits, for substantial increases in exploration and production of American oil and natural gas.

We need additional money in the Federal Treasury earmarked for the specific problem that I've described to you. There are some very poor families in our Nation who will have to suffer personally if the decontrol results in an increased price of energy when their budgets are severely limited. That's one need that I am determined to meet.

The second need that I am determined to meet is to provide some alternate transportation for people in urban areas other than automobiles. And so, an additional supply of money is needed to increase even beyond what we are presently doing for rapid transit.

And the third need, of course, is for the Government itself to embark upon a substantial research and development program that would build year by year, in addition to what we've already got going now. So, we've advocated to the Congress, that began hearings last week on the 9th of May, a windfall profits tax which would leave the oil companies about 29 cents out of every dollar. We would tax the increase in price above and beyond what it would have been, plus future increases on OPEC prices, and establish an energy security fund. And that fund would be used for the three purposes that I've described: to help the very poor families meet the increased price of energy; to improve our rapid transit system, mass transit systems; and then to allocate funds for research and development in the field of new energy sources.

At first, the following day after I made my announcement, Senator Jackson, Senator Kennedy, many others, said that it was absolutely impossible to have a windfall profits tax passed. Now some of the same voices say that it's an accomplished fact, that the windfall profits tax is not severe enough, and we don't have to worry about it getting passed in its present form. I can tell you that my own experience is, it is not going to be easy to get a windfall profits tax through the House and Senate with the degree of severity or stringency built into my own proposal. My guess is that the Congress and the House might pass a little bit more stringent tax bill. My guess is that when the House and Senate get through with the legislation, that we will be very fortunate indeed to get the windfall profits tax passed in the form that I advocated.

If the Congress wants to strengthen the bill, to have a heavier tax burden imposed on the increase in profits, I would favor it if I consider it to be fair and equitable. But it's going to require a lot of support throughout the Nation from leaders like you who've come here from all over the country, a few associated with the oil industry itself; others, distributors; others, consumers; others, civic leaders. I need to have you join in with me in addressing one of the most serious threats to our Nation in peacetime that I have seen in my life, because there is a destruction of the confidence of American people in our future.

I think just facts, demonstration of political will, and predictability about the future will go a long way toward alleviating this problem. And then we can get people to join in, in a self-sacrificial, patriotic way, so that the adverse impact of energy shortages will fall very lightly on the shoulder of any particular American, if we form a partnership based on mutual trust, not trying to blame one another, but to address an issue in a way that has been used historically in our country under times of difficulty and trial.

Our proposals are fair, equitable, simple, and workable. And I'll be doing the best I can under existing law to deal with the energy problem, but I do need, in order to address this on a permanent basis, to have the windfall profits tax passed and the energy security trust fund established.

I think this, combined with the legislation passed last year by Congress on natural gas and other elements of the energy problem, will give us a fairly good package for me as President, for Governors, local officials, private citizens, and leaders like you, to meet the future with confidence.

Our country is so strong and so able and so secure, that it's almost heartbreaking to see some issue like this, which festers like a cancer, carry on from one month to another, sapping away the basic strength of our Nation and the confidence that people ought to have in a governmental and a free enterprise system.

And I hope that every one of you will leave this room, having been thoroughly briefed by the Secretary of Treasury and by my own staff aide, Stu Eizenstat, and become not just a quiet supporter of these proposals if someone asks but to become a strong and fervently committed American, a leader who joins in with me to meet a challenge successfully, showing that the strength and the will of Americans is still adequate to meet a challenge as we have so frequently done in the past to make our Nation so great.

I need your help. I'm willing to do my part, and I believe that you will do yours. Together, we can solve this problem and have an even greater America in the future.

Thank you very much.

NOTE: The President spoke at 2:17 p.m. in the East Room at the White House.

President's Commission on Executive Exchange

Executive Order 12136. May 15, 1979

By the authority vested in me as President by the Constitution and statutes of the United States of America, and in order to amend the responsibilities of the President's Commission on Personnel Interchange and to continue its work of enriching both the Government and the private sectors by enabling the most promising executive to work in the other sector, it is hereby ordered as follows:

1-1. *Establishment of the Commission.*

1-101. The President's Commission on Personnel Interchange is continued and renamed the President's Commission on Executive Exchange.

1-102. The Commission shall be composed of such officials in the Executive agencies and such persons from the private sector as the President may from time to time appoint. The Chairman shall be designated by the President. The members of the commission and the Chairman shall serve two-year terms at the pleasure of the President.

1-103. Members of the Commission who are officers or employees of the Federal Government shall receive no additional compensation by reason of this Order, and members who are not such officers or employees shall serve without

compensation, but shall be provided with travel expenses, including per diem in lieu of subsistence, as authorized by law.

1-2. *Functions of the Commission.*

1-201. The Commission shall develop an Executive Exchange Program in which promising executives from the Executive agencies, and from the private sector, who have demonstrated the ability to rise to high management positions, will be selected as Exchange Executives and placed in positions in the other sector which offer significant challenge, responsibility, and regular and continuing contact with senior officials.

1-202. The Commission shall develop an education program which places the work experience of the Exchange Executive in the broader context of both the Federal Government and the private sector.

1-203. The Commission shall supervise and review the operation of the Program, and recommend to the President ways to promote and improve the exchange between the Government and the private sector.

1-204. The Commission shall ensure that the Program operates in compliance with the merit principles set forth in Section 2301 of Title 5 of the United States Code.

1-3. *Responsibilities of Executive Agencies.*

1-301. Each Executive agency shall, to the extent permitted by law, cooperate with the Commission and furnish it with such assistance as the Chairman may request in connection with the Program.

1-302. The head of each Executive agency shall designate a presidential appointee who is not a member of the Commission to serve as liaison to the Commission.

1-4. *Administrative Provisions.*

1-401. The Office of Personnel Management shall provide the Commission with administrative services, staff support, and travel expenses, as authorized by law.

1-402. Executive Order No. 11451 of January 19, 1969, is superseded.

JIMMY CARTER

The White House,
   May 15, 1979.

[Filed with the Office of the Federal Register, 3:02 p.m., May 15, 1979]

Human Rights in Uganda

Memorandum on the Normalization of U.S.- Ugandan Trade Relations.   May 15, 1979

Memorandum for the Secretary of State, the Secretary of the Treasury, the Secretary of Commerce

Subject: Trade with Uganda

Pursuant to the authority vested in me by Section 5 of Public Law 95–435, I hereby determine and certify that:

The Government of Uganda is no longer committing a consistent pattern of gross violations of human rights.

The Secretary of State is requested to report this determination to the Congress on my behalf, as required by law.

The Secretaries of Treasury and Commerce are requested to take the appropriate steps permitting the immediate resumption of imports from and exports to Uganda.

This determination shall be published in the FEDERAL REGISTER.

JIMMY CARTER

[Filed with the Office of the Federal Register, 3:03 p.m., May 15, 1979]

Human Rights in Uganda

Statement by the President.   May 15, 1979

All Americans were appalled by evidence of the truly deplorable human rights violations which occurred during the Amin regime. While my administration publicly condemned this situation, I would particularly like to commend Senators Hatfield and Weicker and Congressmen Pease and Bonker for the intense concern which they exhibited about the human rights situation in Uganda. The breaking of the pattern of gross violations of human rights heralds a brighter day for Ugandans and, indeed, for all in the world concerned with human rights.

Public Participation in Federal Agency Proceedings

*Memorandum From the President.
May 16, 1979*

Memorandum for the Heads of Executive Departments and Agencies

Executive Order 12044 of March 23, 1978, formalized the Administration's commitment to public participation in Federal agency proceedings. Widespread participation can improve the quality of agency decisions by assuring that they are made on the basis of more complete and balanced records.

Experience has shown, however, that citizen groups often find the cost of meaningful participation in agency proceedings to be prohibitive. Many citizen groups are unable to pay the costs of experts and attorneys' fees, clerical costs, and the costs of travel to agency proceedings. As a result, the views and interests of consumers, workers, small businesses, and others often go unrepresented, or underrepresented, in proceedings that may have substantial impacts on their health, safety, or economic well-being.

In recognition of the cost problems faced by many citizen groups, several agencies have established programs to provide financial assistance to persons (1) whose participation in a proceeding could reasonably be expected to contribute to a fair disposition of the issues and (2) who would be unable to participate effectively in the proceeding in the absence of such assistance. These programs have improved agency decisionmaking, and I believe they should be utilized in other agencies.

Accordingly, I direct each Executive Department and Agency to take the following steps:

1. Each department and agency that has not already established a public participation funding program should determine whether it has statutory authority to do so. I note in this regard that the Department of Justice has advised Federal agencies that they may determine for themselves whether they have explicit or implicit authority to fund such programs.

In the event that an agency concludes that it does not have this authority, it should immediately apprise my Special Assistant for Consumer Affairs of that conclusion and of the grounds upon which it is based.

2. Each department and agency that finds it has authority to establish a public participation funding program should assess the extent of its need for such a program. A preliminary evaluation, as well as a tentative timetable for the development of program regulations, should be forwarded to my Special Assistant for Consumer Affairs within 60 days of the issuance of this memorandum. After appropriate consultation with other White House and Executive Office of the Presi-

dent officials, my Special Assistant will report to me on these evaluations.

I have supported, and will continue to support, legislation to create, standardize, and adequately finance public participation funding programs government-wide. Independent of these legislative efforts, there is a current need for public participation funding and I strongly encourage each department and agency with the requisite authority to institute a public participation funding program. Until new legislation is enacted, however, additional programs of this sort will have to rely upon agency funds already allocated. My Special Assistant for Consumer Affairs and her staff will be available to provide technical assistance and advice regarding the structure and standards of such programs.

JIMMY CARTER

National Small Business Person of the Year

Remarks at the Presentation Ceremony for Gary L. McDaniel.   May 16, 1979

THE PRESIDENT. To Vernon Weaver, who manages very effectively the Small Business Administration, and to the distinguished honorees here this afternoon, to their wives or husbands, and to the guests who've come to represent the small business community, I want to say welcome.

I guess if there's one group in the Nation with whom I feel most closely associated because of my past experience, my trials and tribulations and worries and problems, it would be with the small business community of the Nation.

This is the third year that I have participated in the award for the outstanding small business person of our Nation. It's always been an exciting experience for me and one that brings honor to the person who's been chosen, and also to the small business community, to the White House, and, I think, to the entire country.

Two-thirds of all the new jobs in our country originate among small businesses—I think a remarkable tribute to the spirit and the innovation and the dynamic commitment to the free enterprise system exhibited by you and those in almost all the States, in Puerto Rico, Virgin Islands that are represented here.

This is a time, I think, for very careful assessment of what will happen in the future with the small businesses of our Nation. I brought here an almost abhorrence or horror of government intrusion and unjust, unnecessary paperwork, reports, and application forms, government inspectors, regulations. And since I've been in this office, I've tried as best I could to do something about it, all the way from HEW, which has eliminated more than 300 pages of fine print, regulations that applied to small businesses, down to OSHA, of which you may have heard—[*laughter*]—which eliminated a thousand regulations in 1 day. We've been pleased with the progress made.

And I have introduced this year into the Congress for their consideration a bill to deal in a more generic or broad-based sense to eliminate unnecessary regulations that are established in our Government by law.

There's a limit, as you know, to what can be done through administrative action. My business in the past was peanuts. I sold seed, I planted, harvested, cured, shelled, sold, and ate—[*laughter*]—peanuts. And it's almost inconceivable that to determine through the Food and Drug Administration what percentage of peanuts ought to be present in peanut butter

would take 12 years of hearings, and the report includes 100,000 pages of government documents. This is an actual fact. And it's such a ridiculous situation in government that it's indeed almost unbelievable.

One of the first things that I discussed with the congressional leaders involved, and also with Vernon Weaver when he came here to help me, was to have a small business conference at the White House. This is a rare occasion in my life, and indeed it's a rare occasion in the life of the White House, to have a carefully prepared, designated White House Conference. But I wanted it to be done.

We've already had 57 regional hearings around the Nation, and many more are scheduled. We've had more than 20,000 people who attended those hearings already. They've come to listen to one another, to compare notes, to give suggestions, and to give criticisms about how the small business community, individual businesses, could be made stronger, more effectively, how competition could be enhanced, how customers could be served better, how products could be evolved and produced and distributed faster, and how our free enterprise system could work in a more enhanced way.

Next January, 1980, we'll collect all of those data and suggestions and criticisms, comments, and come together here at the White House for a very in-depth analysis of the strengths and the weaknesses and the potential of the small businesses of our Nation.

I know that you're already involved in it—you couldn't be the outstanding small business person of your State if you were not—not just selfishly involved in a particular local business but involved in the free enterprise system and its improvement in general. And I hope all of you will participate in this preparation in a more aggressive way even when you go home than you have in the past.

Today, the purpose of this meeting is to recognize the outstanding small business people of our country, and particularly the outstanding small business person of the Nation. This is intense competition, and it takes a long and laborious analysis to determine who is the best among a lot of superior and outstanding people.

I'm very glad that we have a number of minority business leaders represented here, a number of businesswomen represented here. And I hope that this trend can continue, because these choices are not made just to honor a woman or just to honor someone who can speak Spanish or who happens to be black. The competition is among all. And I think the fairness of it has now been demonstrated most vividly this year than ever before.

Well, I'm very pleased to do this, and I'd like to ask Vernon to come forward now with the award and Gary McDaniel from Kansas to come, and I guess I'll participate in the delivery of the award.

This is Gary McDaniel and his senior partner, Virginia, who 10 years ago invested $23,000 of their own money into a new business to produce air filters. They also got a $25,000 loan from the Small Business Administration. And since that time, their sales volume has been, since that first year, has multiplied more than a hundred times. And now this originally tiny, new flower on the free enterprise garden of the United States has become a flourishing garden, and their air filters have not only brought profit and now fame—[*laughter*]—to the McDaniels but has also helped us to have a cleaner environment and Americans to have a better life.

And I want to congratulate Gary on this superb achievement and to read the award. "The United States of America, Small Business Administration, presents the National First Place Small Business Person of the Year Award to Gary L. Mc-Daniel, Kansas City, Kansas, for exemplifying the imagination, initiative, independence, and integrity by which the American small business person makes a vital contribution to the Nation, to the economy, and to the free enterprise system, Washington, D.C., May 16, 1979." Signed, Vernon Weaver.

I would like to say they are from Sabetha, Kansas, and not Kansas City. How far are you from Kansas City?

Mr. McDANIEL. A hundred miles.

The PRESIDENT. A hundred miles from Kansas City. Well, that's—congratulations to you.

Mr. McDANIEL. Thank you very much, Mr. President.

I really don't know what to say. I am quite honored. And I think the first thing I'd like to say is the honor has my name on it only, but it really should include Virginia's, because she works in the business as many hours as we do, and has from the day it started.

I wish to thank the National Advisory Council for selecting us. I wish to thank the SBA for the confidence they had in us in the beginning in providing us with the operating capital we needed to get started. As one person asked me one time, "Why do you keep going back to the SBA?" Well, if you find a well with good water, don't hesitate to go back and drink it. [*Laughter*]

We've gone to the SBA four times for loans to expand our business. The only other thing I can say is thank you, and we're very flattered and honored.

Mr. WEAVER. I'll just say a few words, because I never keep the President waiting.

I don't think those of you who paid your own way to come here today realize what it means to the agency, to me, its top officers. Running an agency like the SBA has its bad moments, and we don't always get good press. We're not always saluted; we're criticized. But during this week, when we have 50 of you come here and demonstrate your success, we meet your families, we know how you've prospered, it makes it all worthwhile for us.

And we are, all of us, from me down to the last SBA employee in Washington and all over the country, are gratified, and our faith is rekindled by having the chance to associate with all of you for a few days in Washington.

We thank you very much.

NOTE: The President spoke at 1:32 p.m. in the Rose Garden at the White House. Also attending the ceremony were the winners of the State and Territorial Small Business Awards for 1979.

Interstate Commerce Commission

Nomination of Two Members.
May 16, 1979

The President today announced two persons whom he will nominate to be Commissioners of the Interstate Commerce Commission. They are:

Darius W. Gaskins, Jr., of Washington, D.C., for a term expiring December 31, 1984. Gaskins is currently Deputy Assistant Secretary of Energy for Policy Analysis.

He was born September 16, 1939, in Washington, D.C. He received a B.S. from the U.S. Military Academy in 1961, M.S.E. degrees in astronautical engineering and instrumentation engineering from the University of Michigan in 1963, and a Ph. D. in economics from the University of Michigan in 1970.

From 1963 to 1967, Gaskins served as a captain in the Air Force as an instructor at the Aerospace Research Pilots School. From 1970 to 1973, he was an assistant professor of economics at the University of California at Berkeley. From 1973 to 1974, he was Assistant Director for Economics in the Interior Department's Office of Policy Analysis.

In 1974 Gaskins was Acting Director of Interior's Office of Minerals Policy Development, and in 1975 he was Director of the Office of Outer Continental Shelf Program Coordination. From 1975 to 1976, he was an assistant professor of economics at Berkeley, and from 1976 to 1977, he was Director of the Bureau of Economics of the Federal Trade Commission. Gaskins was Director of the Office of Economic Analysis of the Civil Aeronautics Board from 1977 until 1978, when he joined the Energy Department.

Thomas A. Trantum, of Ridgefield, Conn., for a term expiring December 31, 1985. Trantum is a financial analyst specializing in transportation with the New York City firm of L. F. Rothschild, Unterberg, Towbin.

He was born July 25, 1944, in Englewood, N.J. He received a B.A. from the College of Wooster in 1966 and an M.B.A. from New York University Graduate School of Business in 1968. He served in the U.S. Army from 1968 to 1971.

Trantum was with Wainwright Securities from 1971 to 1978 as a financial analyst with responsibility for the motor carrier, airline, and airfreight forwarding industries. He has been with L. F. Rothschild, Unterberg, Towbin since 1978. He has testified before the Senate as an expert witness on airline regulatory reform.

Gasoline Shortages in California

Remarks Announcing Measures To Improve the Situation. May 16, 1979

THE PRESIDENT. Last week when I was in California, I witnessed personally the deep distress of the people of that State because of the long gasoline lines and because of an obvious shortage in fuel necessary to get them to and from their jobs, to and from shopping, and to perform the necessities of life. This causes me great concern as President, and I have done what I could, since I returned from California, to prepare a series of steps that might help to alleviate the problem. I think we can accurately say that the State and local officials, the Congress, and my administration are all working in cooperation to alleviate this serious problem.

This morning I met with the Governor of California, with the mayor of Los Angeles, the speaker of the house in California, and the congressional delegation, to consult together on what additional steps might be taken.

This is a national problem, but it particularly affects adversely States like California and Nevada that are growing quite rapidly and have additional automobiles on the highways, additional population to consume gasoline, when in the past the base for allocation of gasoline supplies was many years old. Also, of course, as many of us know, in California there's a heavy dependence on individual automobiles and a very low dependence upon mass transit systems.

We have now changed the allocation system and moved its base up to a much more recent period. This was done the 1st of May. And I believe it will have a substantial beneficial effect when its full impact is felt in California.

In addition to that, we have evolved several steps to improve the situation today. These are being promulgated in written form by my staff this afternoon. This is a continuing problem, and I think it's obvious that in the future the primary thrust has got to be to improve production of oil in our own Nation and to have a heavy emphasis on conservation.

We have not found any evidence of collusion or illegalities among the oil companies, but I have directed the Department of Justice and the Department of Energy to launch an investigation to assure that there are no improprieties or any illegalities or evidences of collusion in the withholding of fuel supplies for California or any other State. In addition, we will be deriving better data in the future so that we can know more accurately than we have in the past how much fuel is available now and how much will be available in the future.

We've discussed with Governor Brown, other State and local officials of California and Nevada, today the steps that can be taken at the State level to encourage conservation—rigid enforcement of the speed limits and some modification in other rules for increased consumption of gasoline—if the State officials desire to take such action.

I have designated Charles Warren [1] on my staff, a high official in the White House, to be my personal representative to California and Nevada in the coming days, to work very closely with the officials in those States to make sure that the supplies of gasoline are improved with the most expediency possible. Charles Warren is a very competent person. He's familiar with the processes here in Washington. He happened to have been the former chairman of the committee in the

---

[1] Chairman of the Council on Environmental Quality.

California Legislature dealing with energy.

More than 2 years ago, I submitted to the Congress a comprehensive package to deal with the impending energy problem in our Nation. The Congress took some action, but they ignored completely the need to take action on oil. This is a politically difficult issue to address, but it's crucial that it be handled properly.

We will now begin to decontrol oil over the next 28 months in a very carefully phased manner. This will encourage domestic production. It will decrease our dependence upon imported foreign oil, and it will also help to encourage conservation.

I have also asked the Congress to pass a windfall profits tax to be sure that the people of our Nation are protected from unwarranted and unearned profits by the oil companies resulting from the decontrol of oil prices.

The last thing I'd like to say this afternoon is that it's very important that the consumers of our Nation, the producers and refiners of oil, the developers of other sources of energy, the President and my whole administration, the Congress, State and local officials, all work together to deal with the energy shortage in an effective and cooperative basis.

It's nonproductive to seek a scapegoat. It's a serious problem that's going to be with us for years in the future. We can resolve it if we take actions similar to those that we have taken in the last few days, which I am sure will improve the situation in California, Nevada, and other States that have been heavily and adversely impacted over the last few days because of gasoline shortages.

This is an important issue to our country, and I've been very encouraged the last few days at the close cooperative re-

lationship that exists among all those who are involved in seeking a solution.

Thank you very much.

REPORTER. Did you say that June would be better—did you tell the Governor that June would be better than May as far as gasoline supplies?

THE PRESIDENT. We think that these changes that were made the 1st of May in allocation formulas and the improvements now in supplies that are available to refiners and for distribution brought about by the restoration of Iranian production will have a beneficial effect in the future, yes.

NOTE: The President spoke at 4:34 p.m. to reporters assembled in the Briefing Room at the White House.

Gasoline Shortages in California
Statement by the President.   May 16, 1979

Over the last month, California has been plagued by gasoline shortages and long lines at service stations. With the actions which I am taking today and the cooperation of the elected officials and the citizens of California, from this point we should begin to overcome the severe difficulties we have encountered.

California and certain other Western States have been particularly hard hit by the nationwide tightness in gasoline supplies. When I was in California, I learned firsthand of the frustration and anger which the gasoline shortage has caused. For Californians trying to get to work, to meet emergencies, and to carry out the essential business of their daily lives, the shortage has caused acute and unacceptable problems, particularly where public transit is unavailable. I share the concerns of and sympathize with Californians who are stymied by long lines in trying to do their normal daily tasks.

California is a fast-growing State; jobs have increased, thereby contributing to the health of our economy. This growth naturally increases demand for gasoline. We must act to ensure that jobs and economic growth are not lost.

We are still feeling the effects of the Iranian cut-off. It takes 2 months to transport oil from Iran to the United States, and additional time to get that crude oil through the refining and distribution system. This has contributed to making late April and May the low point in gasoline availability.

The Department of Energy, to help alleviate the shortage in California, recently changed its allocation rules to bring the basis for allocating supplies among the States up to date and to include growth as a factor. This will help California since it is a fast-growing State, and old or out-of-date allocation bases hurt more there than in States with steady or declining populations. Once this new allocation formula is fully in place, California will begin to feel relief.

As I requested when I visited California on May 5, the Department of Energy has prepared a report on the underlying causes of the shortages and long lines in California. This report is now complete, and it is being released at the same time as this statement.

The report indicates that the shortfall in California has reached about 70,000 barrels of gasoline per day, relative to 1978 levels. Since demand has grown over the last year, the shortage is even greater than that, although restoration of supplies to 1978 levels would ease the situation considerably.

The reasons for this shortfall are several-fold. The worldwide crude oil shortage caused by the loss of production in Iran last winter has made petroleum

supplies tight throughout the world. The crude oil which did become available to partially offset the Iranian loss was lower quality, and therefore not as much gasoline could be produced. The gasoline allocation formula in effect prior to recent DOE changes was not able to reflect the rapid rate of growth in California and contributed to the shortage in the last month. Finally, the inability of the Congress to deal with the overall oil problem when I proposed my comprehensive energy program in April 1977 has left us as a nation, and California particularly, more vulnerable and less well prepared than we should be.

We have already taken steps to deal with this problem. At my direction, the Department of Energy has made two very important changes in the nationwide rules for allocating gasoline supplies between the States. On March 1, the Department brought the base period for gasoline allocation up to date from 1972 to 1978. This began the process of ensuring that rapidly growing States such as California are not penalized by basing gasoline allowances on out-of-date statistics. On May 1, an additional change was made to allow automatic growth adjustments for gasoline dealers who have experienced unusually high growth since the 1978 base period. This will give California added supplies to accommodate growth which has occurred over the last year.

Once they are fully established in the system, these changes should significantly ease the California situation. In addition, on May 11 of this year, the Department issued a rule which will assure adequate diesel fuel supplies for California's vast agricultural production.

In June 1978, the Department amended its entitlements program to provide refiners with additional incentives to use California-produced crude oil. This action has resulted in increased California crude oil production of over 60,000 barrels per day. The Department has also recently established incentive prices for enhanced oil recovery projects and newly discovered oil, both of which will be particularly beneficial to California crude oil production.

Earlier this month, I approved a Department of Transportation grant of $650 million to Los Angeles to improve its mass transit system. That was the largest Federal mass transit grant ever awarded. The funds will be used to purchase 1,200 new buses, to provide operating subsidies, and to develop a downtown "people mover" system. All of these projects should result in greater use of mass transit in Los Angeles and help provide an alternative to the automobile.

Today, I am directing that additional actions be taken to relieve the supply situation in California.

First, the DOE will increase from 3 percent to 5 percent the percentage of the State's total gasoline allocation that the Governor has authority to utilize, if requested by the Governor. While this action will not increase the total amount of gasoline available in California, it will give the Governor useful flexibility in directing gasoline to the areas where it is most needed.

Secondly, I am directing the Department of Energy, working with the Department of Defense, to change its regulations regarding the allocation of gasoline supplies to the Department of Defense to ensure that only direct, essential military and readiness oriented operations receive a 100-percent allocation of supply. Nonessential use of gasoline at military bases would be curtailed. This action should release some extra supplies of gasoline for the general population, especially in

States with major military installations such as California.

Third, I have instructed DOE to monitor the Western refineries' use of crude oil and gasoline stocks to make sure that they are not being unnecessarily cautious in releasing those stocks for immediate consumption. The Department will be prepared to use its regulatory authorities if necessary to assure proper use of stocks. In addition, DOE will work with the California refiners to ensure maximum production of gasoline, consistent with our overall national priority to rebuild home heating oil stocks for next winter.

Fourth, I have directed the Antitrust Division of the Department of Justice and the Department of Energy to establish a special auditing and investigative team to monitor the activities of oil companies, refiners, wholesalers, and distributors of gasoline to ensure that supplies of gasoline are not being withheld or manipulated in violation of Federal regulations or the antitrust laws of the United States. If we find any evidence of illegal conduct among refiners or distributors, we will take appropriate action.

Fifth, to gain additional reliable information on stocks held outside the primary oil distribution system, I have directed the Secretary of Energy to expedite collection of information on the quantities and location of selected petroleum products (for example, gasoline, distillate, and fuel oil) after these products are distributed by refiners and major wholesalers. The Department should be prepared to use all appropriate legal authority and penalties to make sure that this information is both accurate and submitted promptly.

Sixth, I have directed the Department of Energy to ensure that no gasoline is allocated away from California as a result of gasoline station closings within the State. Needed gasoline supplies should not be taken away from California just because a given retailer decides to discontinue his business.

Lastly, I am asking Charles Warren, who will be leaving shortly as Chairman of the Council on Environmental Quality, to oversee the implementation in California of the actions I am taking today. Mr. Warren will serve as my special Personal Representative for the California shortage problem. Before joining my administration, he served as chairman of the energy committee of the California State Assembly. He is intimately familiar with California's energy problems and will provide a central focus for the administration's efforts to ease the California shortage.

There are other possibilities for action which depend on joint Federal/State action for implementation.

First, enforcement of the 55-mile-per-hour speed limit could save up to 22,000 barrels of gasoline per day in California. I have directed the Secretary of Transportation to work with the Governors of all States to use the moneys which the Federal Government now has available to strengthen enforcement of the 55-mile-per-hour speed limit. I will also support legislative efforts which would strengthen sanctions and accelerate the schedule of penalties against States which fail to enforce this limit.

Second, my administration has identified several areas where current California environmental standards—which are more stringent than those required by Federal law—could yield additional gasoline supplies. Lowering the State's standards for the lead content and vapor pressures of gasoline during the immediate shortage could produce up to 25–35 thousand barrels of gasoline a day. However, in deciding whether to reduce standards, the State must balance the health and environmental effects against the additional gaso-

line available, with the decision resting with the State of California. Should California decide to change these standards, the Environmental Protection Agency stands ready to assist in any way possible to approve any such action by the State. In addition, the State might consider expediting the issuance of permits to increase thermal recovery operations to enhance crude oil production.

When all of these measures are implemented, California gasoline supplies for the remainder of this spring and summer should be brought into closer balance with demand. The specific environmental measures and enforcement of the 55-mile-per-hour speed limit would save a major share of the current supply shortfall. With the additional cooperation of California drivers, the long lines should then ease.

Continued and close cooperation between the Federal Government and the State of California will be essential to our success in alleviating the current shortages. We have taken an important step in establishing a strong partnership in a meeting which I had this morning with Governor Brown, California Speaker Leo McCarthy, Mayor Tom Bradley, and the California congressional delegation. We agreed to work together in a mutually supportive way to resolve this problem.

We must also bear in mind, as we work to solve the immediate difficulties in California, that our Nation has a serious, chronic, long-term energy problem. Decontrol of crude oil, which I have announced, will lead to additional production. Conservation will continue to be a key in dealing with the underlying energy situation which from time to time erupts in the kind of problem which California has faced over the last month. My windfall profits tax will generate the revenues for a massive effort to develop alternate energy technologies to reduce our dependence on uncertain foreign oil supplies.

These fundamental policies will help California and the Nation meet our energy challenge.

Alaska Public Lands Legislation

Statement on the House of Representatives Approval of the Legislation.   May 16, 1979

I am pleased and gratified by today's action on Alaska lands by the House of Representatives. The full House voted overwhelmingly to pass the Udall-Anderson bill, which I strongly supported.

This bill allows for development of most of Alaska's oil, gas, mineral, and timber resources, while preserving what is essential to Alaska's native cultures, scenic wonders, and abundant wildlife. Members of the House should feel justifiably proud of their historic vote for a truly superior bill.

Now that the House has acted firmly and properly to protect Alaska lands, I hope that the Senate will move promptly to take similar action. I have taken a number of steps to protect Alaska lands in the event acceptable legislation is not finally enacted by the Congress. However, I deeply hope that the Congress as a whole will take the opportunity to act in the interest of the entire Nation and pass an Alaska bill designed to serve future generations.

Tennessee Valley Authority

Nomination of Bob Clement To Be a Member of the Board of Directors.   May 16, 1979

The President today announced that he will nominate Bob Clement, of Knoxville,

Tenn., to be a member of the Board of Directors of the Tennessee Valley Authority for the remainder of the term expiring May 18, 1981. He would replace William Jenkins, who has resigned.

Clement was born September 23, 1943, in Nashville, Tenn. He received a B.S. from the University of Tennessee at Knoxville in 1967 and an M.B.A. from Memphis State University in 1968.

Clement served a 6-year term on the Tennessee Public Service Commission, including 2 years as chairman (from 1976 to 1978). He was previously employed with the Nashville brokerage insurance firm of Blair, Follin, Allen and Walker, and with the Bureau of Business Research in Memphis. He is currently with Bob Clement and Associates in Nashville. Clement has served as chairman of the National Association of Regulatory Commissioners' Presidential Advisory Committee and as vice president of the Southeast Association of Regulatory Commissioners.

Peace Corps

Executive Order 12137.   May 16, 1979

By virtue of the authority vested in me by the Peace Corps Act, as amended (22 U.S.C. 2501–2523) and Section 301 of Title 3 of the United States Code, and as President of the United States of America, it is hereby ordered as follows:

1–1. *Peace Corps.*

1–101. The Peace Corps, which was established as an agency in the Department of State pursuant to Executive Order No. 10924 of March 1, 1961 (26 FR 1789), which was continued in existence in that Department under the Peace Corps Act (the "Act") pursuant to Section 102 of

Executive Order No. 11041 of August 6, 1962 (27 FR 7859), and which was transferred to and continued as a component of ACTION by Executive Order No. 11603 of June 30, 1971 (36 FR 12675), shall be an agency within ACTION pursuant to the provisions of this Order.

1–102. All references to the "Director" in Part 1–1 of this Order shall refer to the Director of the Peace Corps for whom provision is made in Section 4(a) of the Act (22 U.S.C. 2503).

1–103. Exclusive of the functions otherwise delegated by or reserved to the President by this Order, and subject to the provisions of this Order, there are hereby delegated to the Director all functions conferred upon the President by the Act and by Section 2(b) of Reorganization Plan No. 1 of 1971.

1–104. The function of determining the portion of living allowances constituting basic compensation, conferred upon the President by Section 201(a) of Public Law 87–293 (26 U.S.C. 912(3)), is hereby delegated to the Director and shall be performed in consultation with the Secretary of the Treasury.

1–105. The functions of prescribing regulations and making determinations (relating to appointment of Peace Corps employees in the Foreign Service System), conferred upon the President by Section 5 of Public Law 89–135 (79 Stat. 551), are hereby delegated to the Director.

1–106. The functions of prescribing conditions, conferred upon the President by the second sentence of Section 5(e), as amended (22 U.S.C. 2504(e)), and the third proviso of Section 6 of the Act (22 U.S.C. 2505) (relating to providing health care in Government facilities) and hereinabove delegated to the Director, shall be exercised in consultation with the head of the United States Government agency responsible for the facility.

1–107. The reports required by Section 11 of the Act, as amended (22 U.S.C. 2510), shall be prepared by the Director and submitted to the Congress through the President.

1–108. Subject to applicable provisions of law, all funds appropriated or otherwise made available to the President for carrying out the provisions of the Act shall be deemed to be allocated without any further action of the President to the Director or to such subordinate officer as the Director may designate. The Director or such officer may allocate or transfer, as appropriate, any of such funds to any United States Government agency or part thereof for obligation or expenditures thereby consistent with applicable law.

1–109. Nothing in this Order shall be deemed to impair or limit the powers or functions vested in the Secretary of State by the Act.

1–110. The negotiation, conclusion, and termination of international agreements pursuant to the Act shall be under the direction of the Secretary of State.

1–111. Any substantial change in policies in effect on the date of this Order for the utilization of the Foreign Service Act of 1946, as amended, pursuant to Section 7 of the Act (22 U.S.C. 2506), shall be coordinated with the Secretary of State.

1–112. The Director shall consult and coordinate with the Director of ACTION to assure that the functions delegated to the Director by this Order are carried out consistently with the functions conferred upon the Director of ACTION by the Domestic Volunteer Service Act of 1973 (42 U.S.C. 4951 *et seq.*), ("Volunteer Service Act"), Reorganization Plan No. 1 of 1971 and this Order.

1–2. *The Peace Corps Advisory Council.*

1–201. In accordance with the provisions of the Federal Advisory Committee

Act (5 U.S.C. App. I), there is hereby established the Peace Corps Advisory Council.

1–202. The President shall appoint not more than 30 individuals to serve on the Council and shall designate one member as Chairperson. Members shall serve at the pleasure of the President.

1–203. The Council shall advise the President and the Director of the Peace Corps on initiatives needed to promote the purposes of the Peace Corps Act.

1–204. The Council shall submit annually to the President, through the Director of the Peace Corps, a report on its recommendations and activities.

1–205. The Council may request any agency of the United States Government to furnish it with such information as may be useful for the fulfillment of the Council's functions under this Order. Such agencies will, to the extent permitted by law, honor the Council's request.

1–206. The members of the Council shall receive no compensation for service on the Council. Each member of the Council may receive travel expenses, including per diem in lieu of subsistence (5 U.S.C. 5702 and 5703).

1–207. The functions of the President under the Federal Advisory Committee Act which are applicable to the Council, except that of reporting annually to the Congress, shall be performed by the Director of the Peace Corps in accordance with guidelines and procedures established by the Administrator of General Services.

1–208. In accord with the provisions of the Federal Advisory Committee Act (5 U.S.C. App. I), the Council shall terminate on December 31, 1980, unless extended.

1–3. *Reservation of functions to the President.*

1–301. There are hereby excluded from the delegations made by Section 1–1 of this Order the following powers and functions of the President:

(a) All authority conferred by Sections 4(b), 4(c) (2), 4(c) (3), 10(d), and 18 of the Act (22 U.S.C. 2503(b), (C) (2), (C) (3), 2509(d), and 2517).

(b) The authority conferred by Section 4(a) of the Act (22 U.S.C. 2503(a)) to appoint the Director and the Deputy Director of the Peace Corps.

(c) The authority conferred on the President by Section 5(f) (1) (B) of the Act (22 U.S.C. 2504(f) (1) (B)).

(d) The authority conferred by Section 10(f) of the Act (22 U.S.C. 2509(f)) to direct any agency of the United States Government to provide services, facilities, and commodities to officers carrying out functions under the Act.

(e) The authority conferred by Section 19 of the Act (22 U.S.C. 2518) to adopt and alter an official seal or emblem of the Peace Corps.

1–4. *Incidental Provisions.*

1–401. Persons appointed, employed, or assigned under Section 7(a) of the Act (22 U.S.C. 2506(a)) shall not, unless otherwise agreed by the agency in which such benefits may be exercised, be entitled to the benefits provided by Section 528 of the Foreign Service Act of 1946 (22 U.S.C. 928) in cases in which their service under the appointment, employment, or assignment exceeds thirty months.

1–402. Pursuant to Section 10(d) of the Act (22 U.S.C. 2509(d)), it is hereby determined to be in furtherance of the purposes of the Act that functions authorized thereby may be performed without regard to the applicable laws specified in Section 1 and 2 of Executive Order No. 11223 of May 12, 1965, and with or without consideration as specified in Section 3 of that Order, but subject to the limitations set forth in that Order.

1–403. As used in this Order, the words "Volunteers," "functions," "United States," and "United States Government agency" shall have the same meanings, respectively, as they have under the Act.

1–5. *National Voluntary Action Program.*

1–501. The National Voluntary Action Program to encourage and stimulate more widespread and effective voluntary action for solving public domestic problems, established in the Executive Branch of the Government by Section 1 of Executive Order No. 11470 of May 26, 1969, is continued in ACTION. That program shall supplement corresponding action by private and other non-Federal organizations such as the National Center for Voluntary Action. As used in this Order, the term "voluntary action" means the contribution or application of non-governmental resources of all kinds (time, money, goods, services, and skills) by private and other organizations of all types (profit and nonprofit, national and local, occupational, and altruistic) and by individual citizens.

1–6. *Director of ACTION.*

1–601. In addition to the functions vested in the Director of ACTION by the Domestic Volunteer Service Act of 1973 (42 U.S.C., Section 4951 *et seq.*), Reorganization Plan No. 1 of 1971, and Section 1–401 of this Order, the Director of ACTION shall:

(a) Encourage local, national and international voluntary activities directed toward the solution or mitigation of community problems.

(b) Provide for the development and operation of a clearinghouse for information on Government programs designed to foster voluntary action.

(c) Initiate proposals for the greater and more effective application of voluntary action in connection with Federal programs, and coordinate, as consistent with law, Federal activities involving such action.

(d) Make grants of seed money, as authorized by law, for stimulating the development or deployment of innovative voluntary action programs directed toward community problems.

1–602. The head of each Federal department and agency, or a designated representative, when so requested by the Director of ACTION or the Director of the Peace Corps, shall, to the extent permitted by law and funds available, furnish information and assistance, and participate in all ways appropriate to carry out the objectives of this Order, the Domestic Volunteer Service Act of 1973 and Reorganization Plan No. 1 of 1971.

1–603. The head of each Federal department or agency shall, when so requested by the Director of ACTION, designate a senior official to have primary and continuing responsibility for the participation and cooperation of that department or agency in matters concerning voluntary action.

1–604. The head of each Federal department or agency, or a designated representative, shall keep the Director of ACTION informed of proposed budgets, plans, and programs of that department or agency affecting voluntary action programs.

1–605. Under the direction of the President and subject to the responsibilities of the Secretary of State, the Director of ACTION shall be responsible for the general direction of those ACTION functions, which jointly serve ACTION domestic volunteer components and the Peace Corps, and for advising the Director of the Peace Corps to ensure that the functions delegated under this Order to the Director of the Peace Corps are carried out.

1–7. *General Provisions.*

1–701. Except to the extent that they may be inconsistent with this Order, all determinations, authorizations, regulations, rulings, certifications, orders, directives, contracts, agreements, and other actions made, issued or entered into with respect to any function affected by this Order and not revoked, superseded, or otherwise made inapplicable before the effective date of this Order shall continue in full force and effect until amended, modified, or terminated by appropriate authority.

1–702. Except as otherwise expressly provided herein, nothing in this Order shall be construed as subjecting any department, establishment, or other instrumentality of the Executive Branch of the Federal Government or the head thereof, or any function vested by law in or assigned pursuant to law to any such agency or head, to the authority of any other agency or head or as abrogating, modifying, or restricting any such function in any manner.

1–703. So much of the personnel, property, records, and unexpended balances or appropriations, allocations, and other funds employed, used, held, available, or to be made available in connection with the functions assigned to the Director of the Peace Corps or to the Director of ACTION by this Order as the Director of the Office of Management and Budget shall determine, shall be transferred to the Director of the Peace Corps or the Director of ACTION at such time or times as the Director of the Office of Management and Budget shall direct.

1–704. To the extent permitted by law, such further measures and dispositions as the Director of the Office of Management and Budget shall deem to be necessary in order to effectuate the provisions of this Order shall be carried out by such agencies as the Director of the Office of Management and Budget shall specify.

1–705. The authority conferred by Sections 1–703 and 1–704 of this Order shall supplement, not limit, the provisions of Section 1–108 of this Order.

1–706. Executive Order Nos. 11041, 11250, 11470 and 11603 are hereby superseded.

1–707. This Order shall become effective May 16, 1979.

JIMMY CARTER

The White House,
    May 16, 1979.

[Filed with the Office of the Federal Register,
    10:55 a.m., May 17, 1979]

Peace Corps

Memorandum From the President.
May 16, 1979

Memorandum for the Director of ACTION, the Director of Peace Corps, the Director of the Office of Management and Budget

Subject: Establishment of the Peace Corps as an Autonomous Agency within ACTION

I have today signed the attached Executive order to establish the Peace Corps as an autonomous agency within ACTION. The purpose of this order is to strengthen the vitality, visibility, and independence of the Peace Corps while preserving its position as a joint venture with our domestic volunteer service programs within the framework of ACTION.

This Executive order supersedes Executive Order 11603, issued in 1971. Executive Order 11603 assigned to the AC-

TION Director the authority to direct the Peace Corps. The attached order delegates that authority to the Peace Corps Director.

The order requires the Peace Corps Director to consult with the Director of ACTION and to coordinate Peace Corps activities with those of ACTION. It provides that the Director of ACTION will be responsible for the general direction of all ACTION functions which jointly serve ACTION's domestic volunteer components and the Peace Corps and for advising the Peace Corps Director to ensure the carrying out of the functions assigned to the Peace Corps Director. The order also incorporates those provisions of Executive Order 11603 which gave ACTION and its Director the responsibility for coordinating Federal voluntary ACTION activities. The order does not alter the existing relationship between the Peace Corps and other overseas programs of the United States Government, as set out in the Secretary of State's issuance of March 29, 1978, to the Chiefs of Mission.

The Directors of ACTION and the Peace Corps will agree within 30 days upon a plan implementing the changes required by the order. That plan and the resulting reorganization are to be developed and carried out by the Directors of ACTION and the Peace Corps according to the following principles:

• ACTION shall continue to be the principal agency within the Federal Government for administering volunteer service programs. The Director of ACTION shall be responsible for the coordination of programs under the Domestic Volunteer Service Act of 1973, the Peace Corps Act, and other Federal acts authorizing volunteer service programs.

• The Director of the Peace Corps shall have budgetary authority for the Peace Corps, to include responsibility for establishing and controlling a separate Peace Corps budget, subject only to ACTION policy guidance regarding coordination with domestic programs.

• The Director of Peace Corps shall direct and control the operations of the Peace Corps and such support functions as are necessary to carry out the responsibilities delegated by the Executive order. The Director of ACTION shall direct and control support functions which continue jointly to serve ACTION domestic volunteer components and Peace Corps. Decisions concerning the allocation of support functions are to be made jointly by the Peace Corps and ACTION Directors.

• Those support functions which should in the interests of economy, efficiency, and good management be carried out jointly, or by shared personnel, shall continue to be so carried out.

• Consistent with my August 11, 1977, memorandum, any transfers of functions or personnel from ACTION to the Peace Corps shall be carried out in a manner which minimizes disruption of programs and at the same time minimizes hardship to employees.

The Director of the Office of Management and Budget shall review the implementation agreement reached by the Peace Corps and ACTION Directors and shall sign such determination orders as may be necessary.

JIMMY CARTER

A. Philip Randolph

Statement on the Death of the Civil Rights Leader.   May 17, 1979

It can be said of few individuals in our time that they helped transform the face of the American Nation. A. Philip Randolph was one of those giants. His leadership in the trade union and civil rights movements has left an indelible mark on almost every area of our national life. A. Philip Randolph helped sweep away longstanding barriers of discrimination and segregation in industry and labor unions, in our schools and armed services, in politics and government.

For each new generation of civil rights leaders, he was an inspiration and an example. His dignity and integrity, his eloquence, his devotion to nonviolence, and his unshakable commitment to justice all helped shape the ideals and spirit of the civil rights movement.

His voice and inspiration will long be missed, but America will always be a more just, more humane, and more decent nation because A. Philip Randolph lived among us.

25th Anniversary of *Brown* v. *Board of Education*

Remarks at a White House Observance of the Supreme Court Decision.   May 17, 1979

I did not want to discriminate against Andy Young by interrupting his comments. [*Laughter*]

Although we meet today to remember a great civil rights victory, this is also a time of loss for the civil rights movement, because, as you know, A. Philip Randolph is no longer with us.

At a time when America was a completely segregated society, when there was hardly any civil rights movement that could be detected, Philip Randolph was a voice for justice and equal rights for all Americans.

His impact has been profound and far-reaching. It's staggering to think that one

man could have done so much to transform our Nation. I'm certain that there's no one in this room—certainly including the President—whose life has not been profoundly influenced by Philip Randolph's example.

His accomplishments are known to all of you. He organized the first black trade union in 1925. He organized and led the first march on Washington in 1941. He was probably the most instrumental figure during the Second World War in opening up industries, when our Nation was fighting for freedom, to give employment to black people.

But what he gave us most of all was the power of his example, his great personal dignity, his absolute integrity, his eloquence, his unshakable commitment to justice and equal rights, combined with a remarkable gentleness and humanity and commitment to nonviolence. His values and his ideals have been the guiding spirit of the modern civil rights movement. And even the equally famous leaders who have lived, I'm sure, would agree with that statement.

A. Philip Randolph is no longer with us, but his vision and his example, his inspiration still guides all of us today. Before I begin my own remarks, I would like for us to observe just a moment of silence in his memory.

Thank you very much.

I come today to meet with this distinguished group, with a sense of family, a sense of binding ourselves together as a family should, in times of celebration, in times of challenge, in times of achievement, in times of disappointment.

Twenty-five years ago, the legal basis for segregation was struck down in this Republic by the Supreme Court in *Brown* v. *Board of Education*. This was the most important of all civil rights cases, and there have been many important ones.

Twenty-five years later, today, the basis in reality for racial segregation still exists in our schools, and so does discrimination in housing and in other aspects of human life. But let us not be discouraged. Let us just be even more determined.

Three hundred and sixty years ago, the first enslaved people were unloaded from a ship on the shores of Virginia, and 1 year later, the pilgrims landed on Plymouth Rock to join with others later on in founding a free society. This, in a real sense, has been the story of America—a struggle to resolve this horrible contradiction between hopes and dreams of freedom and equality on one hand and the facts of life on the other.

A sad truce in this struggle was dictated, I believe, in 1896, when the Supreme Court—by a vote of 8 to 1—made the fraudulent Jim Crow concept of separate-but-equal the law of the land.

We know that there can be no lasting peace here or throughout the world without justice. And this fact was also known by thousands of organizers, teachers, lawyers, preachers, laborers, ordinary parents, students, who kept on clearing the way for May 17, 1954, when something changed at last.

Even as Chief Justice Warren began to read the decision, the wire service bells rang out, and every single newsroom in the United States became deathly silent.

First of all, it was black people themselves who were appearing before the courts in defense of their own rights. That was different. There had been change.

Second, the court was unanimous. All nine members spoke as one for the conscience of our country. That was different. There had been a change.

Third, there were thousands who now felt free to work side by side, in State by State, changing law after law. Many of you in this room helped to make those changes and to bring about those differences in the life of America.

I don't have to tell you that change is not easy. And you certainly don't have to tell me that change is difficult. The evidence is everywhere. Too many doors are still locked.

In one area significant legal action is still necessary. We have to realize that the promise of equal opportunity in housing, if we are to make the educational benefits of the *Brown* decision as available to the northern poor as they are becoming in the South. We need to amend the Fair Housing Act to remove the burden and the expense of enforcement of the law from the shoulders of the poor victims of housing discrimination. I've urged Congress to give HUD, Housing and Urban Development Department, the power to resolve complaints directly, and to provide Secretary Pat Harris with cease and desist authority.

This is not going to easy. But it's a very significant challenge to us, and your help—this group in this room—if inspired and motivated and organized, could get enough votes to pass it out of committee and to pass it easily in the Congress. But without your help, I'm afraid we still may not be successful. I propose that we do it now without delay, and that all of us join in together in this effort.

The first great campaign of the war for equality, I know you realize, was completed in this room—in this house, just above this room—with the Emancipation Proclamation to eliminate slavery. Second was the elimination of legalized social oppression, in which *Brown* was a decisive decision and a victory.

The third campaign for equal opportunity in the economic structure of our country may be the most difficult of all. Victory here will demand both determination and sensitivity. We all know that the final economic struggle will not be won tomorrow, even after 361 years since the first slaves came to our free country. But I believe that we can bring about the wisdom of history and the will of our time, and that once again we shall overcome, because in the long run, Americans are proudest of our Nation's progress toward world peace, but of social justice and a fair and an open and an equitable economic order.

Those are the goals of my administration and of this family gathered here today, to celebrate and to join with the unanimity of the nine Justices who spoke so clearly 25 years ago.

If you look around this reception, you'll see many of the 166 black Presidential appointments—appointees that I've been privileged to make. And there are also about the same number of black secretarial appointees here today. This is an unprecedented achievement, but we still have a long way to go together.

I'd like to announce today that we'll continue this process. I will nominate, for instance, Nat Jones, general counsel— [*applause*]—who's general counsel of the NAACP, to serve as a Federal judge in the sixth circuit of our judicial system.

And we are trying to continue the process of letting qualified and motivated black leaders serve in policymaking bodies, in addition to the judiciary and the executive branch of Government, the independent regulatory agencies. Marcus Alexis will be appointed as a new member of the Interstate Commerce Commission.

These men and others—the women who've been appointed and others—are making history today. But many of you were making history, I know, long before

Brown did. Some of you have been born since then.

Let's remember the words of the Court 25 years ago and let it join us together again, and I quote—these are the words of Chief Justice Warren—"We come then to the question presented, does segregation of children in public schools, solely on the basis of race, deprive children of the minority group of equal education opportunities?"

And the Court then said, as the world waited, "We believe that it does."

By the same principle, would not poor quality in education also deprive a child of equal opportunity to enter the mainstream of the American economy? All of us are working together in the Government because we believe that such deprivation does exist, and we are here to see that all American children will have the equal opportunity for quality education.

Is it not true that racial discrimination in housing also deprives our children of equal opportunity? We're joined here today because we believe that it does, and we are committed to equal opportunity in housing.

Finally, do not all practices of exclusion by race from employment or advancement also result in depriving our citizens of their rights to equal opportunities? We are all here today because we know that that deprivation still exists and it does prevent equality of opportunity in our Nation.

We are in this Government to see that there will be equal opportunity for all people in every aspect of American life. We will not be pushed back. We will not be turned away. We will fight to see that no one is left outside, that equality of opportunity and justice will prevail in our country, the land of the free.

Thank you very much.

885

How many of you all are serving in the Government in any capacity, would you just raise your hands way up? [*Laughter*] As soon as you get through—[*laughter*]—as soon as you get through celebrating, let's all go back to work.

NOTE: The President spoke at approximately 1:30 p.m. in the East Room at the White House.

Louis E. Martin, Special Assistant to the President, Mary Berry, Assistant Secretary for Education, and Joseph A. Califano, Secretary, Department of Health, Education, and Welfare, and Andrew Young, U.S. Representative to the United Nations, spoke prior to the President's remarks. Their remarks are included in the press release.

Advisory Commission on Intergovernmental Relations

Reappointment of Doris W. Dealaman as a Member.   May 17, 1979

The President today announced the reappointment of Doris W. Dealaman, of Bernardsville, N.J., as a member of the Advisory Commission on Intergovernmental Relations.

Dealaman is a member of the board of freeholders of Somerset County, N.J., and is active in the National Association of Counties.

Administrative Conference of the United States

Appointment of Michael N. Sohn as a Member of the Council.   May 17, 1979

The President today announced the appointment of Michael N. Sohn as a member of the Council of the Adminis-

trative Conference of the United States. Sohn is General Counsel of the Federal Trade Commission (FTC). He replaces FTC Chairman Michael Pertschuk as a member of this Council.

Interstate Commerce Commission

Nomination of Marcus Alexis To Be a Member.   May 17, 1979

The President today announced that he will nominate Marcus Alexis, of Evanston, Ill., to be a Commissioner of the Interstate Commerce Commission for a term expiring December 31, 1985.

Alexis is chairman of the economics department at Northwestern University.

He was born February 26, 1932, in New York City. He received a B.A. from Brooklyn College in 1953, an M.A. from Michigan State University in 1954, and a Ph. D. from the University of Minnesota in 1959.

From 1954 to 1957, Alexis was an instructor at the University of Minnesota, and from 1957 to 1960, he was an assistant professor at Macalester College. He was an associate professor at DePaul University from 1960 to 1962 and at the University of Rochester from 1962 to 1968. From 1968 to 1970, he was a professor at the University of Rochester. Alexis was a visiting professor at the University of California from 1969 to 1971. Since 1970 he has been a professor of economics at Northwestern, and since 1976 he has been chairman of the department.

Alexis is the author of numerous articles and books on marketing, particularly as it affects minorities and inner-city residents, and monetary policy. He is active in the American Economic Association and the American Marketing Association and is a member of the Caucus of Black Economists.

Clinch River Breeder Reactor

Statement on Action by the Senate Energy and Natural Resources Committee. May 17, 1979

I am very pleased by the action taken by the Senate Energy and Natural Resources Committee this morning approving Senator Bumpers' amendment on the Clinch River breeder reactor (CRBR). In adopting this amendment, the committee has endorsed a strong, technically sound research and development program that will not rush us unnecessarily toward a plutonium economy. The committee has acted in a fiscally responsible manner by voting against wasting an additional $1.5 billion of taxpayers' dollars on the CRBR.

We are currently compelled to spend $15 million per month on the Clinch River breeder reactor—a project which is premature, technically outmoded, and unnecessary. With all of the critical energy needs of our country competing for Federal resources, the CRBR's continued drain on the Federal Treasury is a shameful waste.

The committee has voted to approve a sound, well-structured program to ensure that breeder technology will be available to our country if and when it is needed.

I urge the full Senate and the House of Representatives to follow the lead of the Senate Energy and Natural Resources Committee to stop wasting Federal funds on this project and save our taxpayers $1.5 billion. Fiscal responsibility and sound energy policy demand that the committee's recommendations be enacted.

Women's Business Enterprise

Remarks on Signing Executive Order 12138 and a Memorandum Concerning Government Programs. May 18, 1979

THE PRESIDENT. I've gotten permission to say just a word before I sign the Executive order. [*Laughter*]

I consider this to be a very important and a very significant action on my part as President of our country.

One of the constant struggles in our society, ever since our Nation was formed, has been to eliminate discrimination, not only legal and overt discrimination but also a kind that's much more difficult to detect, to prove, and to correct. And today I think we're taking that kind of step.

There was a superb task force report, which many of you hold in your hands, called "The Bottom Line," pointing out in tangible form the discrimination that does exist in our free country against women who are involved directly in business.

I know many women—some who are married, some who are not—who have the full responsibility on their shoulders of supporting a family and providing a future life for children that might be acceptable. And almost invariably they have found it very difficult to achieve equal treatment in the business world. Part of this, I think, is a kind of oversight by American society; part of it is deliberate; part of it derives from intense competition, where newcomers are seldom welcomed to the entrepreneur field.

Government quite often mirrors almost exactly those attitudes in private business, and I think that we've addressed it in the proper fashion. Government can set an example. Unfortunately, it hasn't in the past.

I've seen many reports, long before I got

involved in politics, about the amount of national wealth, the actual holding of cash or reserves or bonds or stocks by women; I think perhaps more than 50 percent, even. But as far as the ownership and control of the business community, the active business opportunities in our Nation, women only hold about 4.6 percent of the businesses. And more than half those are tiny, having an annual income, gross income, of less than $5,000. So, we've only scratched the surface, really, in opening up legitimate opportunities for women who are equally competent, sometimes more competent than the men who are present or future competitors.

On my staff, Anne Wexler, Sarah Weddington are very eager to work with you. Pat Cloherty, as you know, headed up the previous study group. All of you have participated. Some of you, many of you I know personally as being extremely effective in politics, in government, in social service, in benevolent work. And many of you are at least equally as competent already, proven by your actions and achievements in the business world. Others among you who have a high profile, who are well recognized, who are intensely competitive, highly competent, knowledgeable, have not been as successful in business perhaps as you should have been.

Today, I'm signing an Executive order that has been very carefully prepared by highly interested people and approved by my legal staff in the Justice Department, Office of Management and Budget, that will direct—[*laughter*]—all of the agencies in the Federal Government to set a high priority for themselves of seeking in an innovative fashion to find opportunities for enhancing the achievements of women in the business field, in contracts directly with Federal Government agencies, to seek out an affirmative action attitude, op-

portunities to increase business or trade with women. Some agencies are already taking action. They are to be congratulated. But others will now be directed to take the first steps, and those that already have experience are encouraged or directed to take additional steps.

I would like to recruit all of you to join in with me in ensuring that this Executive order is carried out with enthusiasm. And I hope that you will bring to the attention of Anne or Sarah directly or me, if you see fit, Jack Watson, anyone else who works with me, any evidence of discrimination or any absence of enthusiastic compliance with this Executive order. Don't just take for granted that the signing of an Executive order is an accomplishment or an end in itself. It's the first tentative step toward what can be substantial achievement. We've experienced this already in the last 2 years.

We passed the first legislation that required, for instance, in local public works contracts, that 10 percent of those contracts should go to minority-owned businesses. Almost every one of my Cabinet officers, when they first saw that proposal from me, said this will be very difficult to achieve. Most of them have exceeded that requirement. We set as a goal for ourselves to triple purchases by the Government from minority-owned businesses, of file cabinets, paper, other things that the Government uses. And we set as a goal for ourselves in 1980, $3 billion worth of Government purchases from minority-owned businesses. Almost everyone said, "Can't do it." We will meet that goal.

I would like to make one final comment. It would be a mistake to think that the enhancement of women business opportunities will interfere in the enhancement of opportunities for minorities in our country, who also have the same problem. I think the two will be mutually supportive, because when you arouse the consciousness of the private world and the government world to the need to eliminate discrimination, and let minority women, for instance, join in with those who are not in the minority category, who are women, they can be mutually supportive. I hope that you will help me detect and root out the last remnants of racial or sex discrimination within our Government and within the private enterprise system of our country.

So, as I sign this document, I would like to assume that you will be partners with me in making sure that the provisions of the document are carried out with enthusiasm. I don't think you'll find my directors of agencies to be reluctant. But I know they would appreciate constructive advice and constructive criticism from you in how they can do a better job to make our Nation fairer and our whole system to be filled with simple justice, which, for many years, it has lacked.

[At this point, the President signed the Executive order.]

Now it's time for everybody to go to work. *[Laughter]*

Ms. HARVEY. Thank you, Mr. President.

This time last year, we welcomed your renewed personal support for the development of a national policy to assist women entrepreneurs. Today, your signature on this Executive order confirms your continuing support and that of your administration to this important objective.

This order establishes a landmark effort to welcome American women into the mainstream of our business and economic life.

On behalf of all my colleagues, I confirm our strong appreciation to you, to members of your administration, to our friends in the Congress, and to our colleagues in the private sector who have given us their sustained support and cooperation.

Ms. CLOHERTY. Mr. President?

THE PRESIDENT. Yes, ma'am? *[Laughter]*

Ms. CLOHERTY. I know this is a serious moment, but I want to tell you one funny thing. I thought you'd like to know that the taxidriver who brought me here from the airport asked if you were having a fashion show at the White House today. *[Laughter]*

THE PRESIDENT. What did you tell him?

Ms. CLOHERTY. I told him what was happening. And he sends his greetings. *[Laughter]*

Luckily for all of us, more and more women are choosing to use their talents in the private profitmaking sector. And business ownership, as you know, is a substantive undertaking in which negative sex stereotypes have no place, but accomplishments do.

The approach to Government assistance you have approved today is practical and realistic. It is a fine starting point for accelerating this important economic happening of women moving into the marketplace. In particular, its stress on providing skills and know-how, not on direct subsidies, responds to the requirements both of women entrepreneurs and of business. If well done, I think the Government effort should more than pay for itself in results from successful enterprises.

On behalf of businesswomen, may I thank you and your smart—that's these people—smart and dedicated team and all others in and outside government who have helped with this effort.

Thank you.

THE PRESIDENT. I might say that we are not doing women a favor today, I think we're doing our Nation a favor.

And I'd like to add one other comment. Within, I believe, every single agency in the Government now, there is a highly qualified, top executive who is a woman, and many women in most agencies. And I hope that you will contact them directly. Some of them, of course, are here, so they can kind of be a monitoring point for you. And I will tell all of my Cabinet the next meeting I have, Monday, to expect this and to look on it with favor, because you might find it easier to approach them or you may not. But I think that we need kind of a secret, inside analysis going on in addition to your monitoring, sometimes from the outside.

Thank you very much. I'm very proud of this.

NOTE: The President spoke at 11:48 a.m. at the ceremony in the Rose Garden at the White House. Patricia M. Harvey is Deputy Assistant Secretary of the Treasury for Administration, and Patricia M. Cloherty is Deputy Administrator of the Small Business Administration.

Women's Business Enterprise

Executive Order 12138. May 18, 1979

CREATING A NATIONAL WOMEN'S BUSINESS ENTERPRISE POLICY AND PRESCRIBING ARRANGEMENTS FOR DEVELOPING, COORDINATING AND IMPLEMENTING A NATIONAL PROGRAM FOR WOMEN'S BUSINESS ENTERPRISE

In response to the findings of the Interagency Task Force on Women Business Owners and congressional findings that recognize:

1. the significant role which small business and women entrepreneurs can play in promoting full employment and balanced growth in our economy;

2. the many obstacles facing women entrepreneurs; and

3. the need to aid and stimulate women's business enterprise;

By the authority vested in me as President of the United States of America, in order to create a National Women's Business Enterprise Policy and to prescribe arrangements for developing, coordinating and implementing a national program for women's business enterprise, it is ordered as follows:

1–1. *Responsibilities of the Federal Departments and Agencies.*

1–101. Within the constraints of statutory authority and as otherwise permitted by law:

(a) Each department and agency of the Executive Branch shall take appropriate action to facilitate, preserve and strengthen women's business enterprise and to ensure full participation by women in the free enterprise system.

(b) Each department and agency shall take affirmative action in support of women's business enterprise in appropriate programs and activities including, but not limited to:

(1) management, technical, financial and procurement assistance,

(2) business-related education, training, counseling and information dissemination, and

(3) procurement.

(c) Each department or agency empowered to extend Federal financial assistance to any program or activity shall issue regulations requiring the recipient of such assistance to take appropriate affirmative action in support of women's business enterprise and to prohibit actions or policies which discriminate against women's business enterprise on the ground of sex. For purposes of this subsection, Federal financial assistance means assistance extended by way of grant, cooperative agreement, loan or contract other than a contract of insurance or guaranty. These regulations shall prescribe sanctions for noncompliance. Unless otherwise specified by law, no agency sanctions shall be applied until the agency or department concerned has advised the appropriate person or persons of the failure to comply with its regulations and has determined that compliance cannot be secured by voluntary means.

1–102. For purposes of this Order, affirmative action may include, but is not limited to, creating or supporting new programs responsive to the special needs of women's business enterprise, establishing incentives to promote business or business-related opportunities for women's business enterprise, collecting and disseminating information in support of women's business enterprise, and insuring to women's business enterprise knowledge of and ready access to business-related services and resources. If, in implementing this Order, an agency undertakes to use or to require compliance with numerical set-asides, or similar measures, it shall state the purpose of such measure, and the measure shall be designed on the basis of pertinent factual findings of discrimination against women's business enterprise and the need for such measure.

1–103. In carrying out their responsibilities under Section 1–1, the departments and agencies shall consult the Department of Justice, and the Department of Justice shall provide legal guidance concerning these responsibilities.

1–2. *Establishment of the Interagency Committee on Women's Business Enterprise.*

1–201. To help insure that the actions ordered above are carried out in an effective manner, I hereby establish the Inter-agency Committee on Women's Business Enterprise (hereinafter called the Committee).

1–202. The Chairperson of the Committee (hereinafter called the Chairperson) shall be appointed by the President. The Chairperson shall be the presiding officer of the Committee and shall have such duties as prescribed in this Order or by the Committee in its rules of procedure. The Chairperson may also represent his or her department, agency or office on the Committee.

1–203. The Committee shall be composed of the Chairperson and other members appointed by the heads of departments and agencies from among high level policy-making officials. In making these appointments, the recommendations of the Chairperson shall be taken into consideration. The following departments and agencies and such other departments and agencies as the Chairperson shall select shall be members of the Committee: the Departments of Agriculture; Commerce; Defense; Energy; Health, Education, and Welfare; Housing and Urban Development; Interior; Justice; Labor; Transportation; Treasury; the Federal Trade Commission; General Services Administration; National Science Foundation; Office of Federal Procurement Policy; and the Small Business Administration. These members shall have a vote. Nonvoting members shall include the Executive Director of the Committee and at least one but no more than three representatives from the Executive Office of the President appointed by the President.

1–204. The Committee shall meet at least quarterly at the call of the Chairperson, and at such other times as may be determined to be useful according to the rules of procedure adopted by the Committee.

1–205. The Administrator of the Small

Business Administration shall provide an Executive Director and adequate staff and administrative support for the Committee. The staff shall be located in the Office of the Chief Counsel for Advocacy of the Small Business Administration, or in such other office as may be established specifically to further the policies expressed herein. Nothing in this Section prohibits the use of other properly available funds and resources in support of the Committee.

1–3. *Functions of the Committee.* The Committee shall in a manner consistent with law:

1–301. Promote, coordinate and monitor the plans, programs and operations of the departments and agencies of the Executive Branch which may contribute to the establishment, preservation and strengthening of women's business enterprise. It may, as appropriate, develop comprehensive interagency plans and specific program goals for women's business enterprise with the cooperation of the departments and agencies.

1–302. Establish such policies, definitions, procedures and guidelines to govern the implementation, interpretation and application of this order, and generally perform such functions and take such steps as the Committee may deem to be necessary or appropriate to achieve the purposes and carry out the provisions hereof.

1–303. Promote the mobilization of activities and resources of State and local governments, business and trade associations, private industry, colleges and universities, foundations, professional organizations, and volunteer and other groups toward the growth of women's business enterprise, and facilitate the coordination of the efforts of these groups with those of the departments and agencies.

1–304. Make an annual assessment of the progress made in the Federal Government toward assisting women's business enterprise to enter the mainstream of business ownership and to provide recommendations for future actions to the President.

1–305. Convene and consult as necessary with persons inside and outside government to develop and promote new ideas concerning the development of women's business enterprise.

1–306. Consider the findings and recommendations of government and private sector investigations and studies of the problems of women entrepreneurs, and promote further research into such problems.

1–307. Design a comprehensive and innovative plan for a joint Federal and private sector effort to develop increased numbers of new women-owned businesses and larger and more successful women-owned businesses. The plan should set specific reasonable targets which can be achieved at reasonable and identifiable costs and should provide for the measurement of progress towards these targets at the end of two and five years. Related outcomes such as income and tax revenues generated, jobs created, new products and services introduced or new domestic or foreign markets created should also be projected and measured in relation to costs wherever possible. The Committee should submit the plan to the President for approval within six months of the effective date of this Order.

1–4. *Other Responsibilities of the Federal Departments and Agencies.*

1–401. The head of each department and agency shall designate a high level official to have the responsibility for the participation and cooperation of that department or agency in carrying out this

Executive order. This person may be the same person who is the department or agency's representative to the Committee.

1–402. To the extent permitted by law, each department and agency upon request by the Chairperson shall furnish information, assistance and reports and otherwise cooperate with the Chairperson and the Committee in the performance of their functions hereunder. Each department or agency shall ensure that systematic data collection processes are capable of providing the Committee current data helpful in evaluating and promoting the efforts herein described.

1–403. The officials designated under Section 1–401, when so requested, shall review the policies and programs of the women's business enterprise program, and shall keep the Chairperson informed of proposed budget, plans and programs of their departments or agencies affecting women's business enterprise.

1–404. Each Federal department or agency, within constraints of law, shall continue current efforts to foster and promote women's business enterprise and to support the program herein set forth, and shall cooperate with the Chairperson and the Committee in increasing the total Federal effort.

1–5. *Reports.*

1–501. The Chairperson shall, promptly after the close of the fiscal year, submit to the President a full report of the activities of the Committee hereunder during the previous fiscal year. Further, the Chairperson shall, from time to time, submit to the President the Committee's recommendations for legislation or other action to promote the purposes of this Order.

1–502. Each Federal department and agency shall report to the Chairperson as hereinabove provided on a timely basis

so that the Chairperson and the Committee can consider such reports for the Committee report to the President.

1–6. *Definitions.* For the purposes of this Order, the following definitions shall apply:

1–601. "Women-owned business" means a business that is at least 51 percent owned by a woman or women who also control and operate it. "Control" in this context means exercising the power to make policy decisions. "Operate" in this context means being actively involved in the day-to-day management.

1–602. "Women's business enterprise" means a woman-owned business or businesses or the efforts of a woman or women to establish, maintain or develop such a business or businesses.

1–603. Nothing in subsections 1–601 or 1–602 of this Section (1–6) should be construed to prohibit the use of other definitions of a woman-owned business or women's business enterprise by departments and agencies of the Executive Branch where other definitions are deemed reasonable and useful for any purpose not inconsistent with the purposes of this Order. Wherever feasible, departments and agencies should use the definition of a woman-owned business in subsection 1–601 above for monitoring performance with respect to women's business enterprise in order to assure comparability of data throughout the Federal Government.

1–7. *Construction.* Nothing in this Order shall be construed as limiting the meaning or effect of any existing Executive order.

JIMMY CARTER

The White House,
    May 18, 1979.

[Filed with the Office of the Federal Register,
3:25 p.m., May 18, 1979]

Women's Business Enterprise

Memorandum From the President.
May 18, 1979

Memorandum for the Heads of Executive Departments and Agencies

The Task Force on Women Business Owners which began its work on August 4, 1977, presented me with its report, *The Bottom Line: Unequal Enterprise in America,* on June 28, 1978. I then directed the heads of all departments and agencies to analyze its recommendations and indicate what assistance they might provide women business owners.

The Task Force found many obstacles facing women entrepreneurs, including a lack of adequate capital, lack of marketing opportunities, and lack of management and technical skills. The Task Force concluded that these deficiencies result, at least in part, from discriminatory practices. The Task Force also recognized the significant contribution which small businesses and women entrepreneurs can make towards innovation, full employment and balanced growth in our economy.

To ensure that women can fully participate in our economic system I have today issued an Executive Order which establishes a national policy for expanding the opportunities for women's business enterprise. The Order creates an Interagency Committee on Women's Business Enterprise which will be the permanent structure for promoting, coordinating and monitoring greater efforts on behalf of women-owned businesses by the Federal Government.

The Order also directs Federal departments and agencies to cooperate with the Committee and to develop affirmative action plans for a greater role for women business owners in their business assistance and procurement activities.

There are many actions that agencies and departments could take to implement this policy. For instance, the Task Force noted that since women face special barriers in acquiring the capital necessary for creating or expanding their own businesses, they need greater access to Federal loan programs. As part of this new policy, the Small Business Administration (SBA) has agreed to take the following actions:

• Establish a goal of $50 million in FY 1980 for direct loans to women under Section 7(a) of the Small Business Act;

• Initiate a pilot 7(a) "mini-loan" program in FY 1980 for women whose needs for starting or expanding a business are for amounts under $20,000 and evaluate the usefulness of this pilot program in creating successful enterprises over a reasonable length of time.

• Encourage full participation of women in procurement activities by instructing SBA's Procurement Center Representatives to locate and assist women-owned businesses;

• Try to add 15,000 women-owned firms to SBA's new Procurement Automated Source System (PASS) by the end of FY 1980.

Recent data indicates that women-owned firms will receive only about $63 million in Federal procurement dollars in FY 1979. The Task Force found that efforts to encourage full participation of women in Federal procurement activity have been less than adequate. Therefore, the Office of Federal Procurement Policy has agreed to:

• Set the following overall goals for Federal prime contracts:

1) An approximate doubling of the dollar amount of Federal prime contracts to women-owned firms in FY 1980 to at least $150 million.

2) A redoubling of this amount in FY 1981 to $300 million.

• Develop and implement a process for collecting data on the numbers and amounts of Federal prime contracts and subcontracts under Federal prime contracts awarded women-owned business;

• Revise government-wide procurement regulations to assure that Federal prime contractors increase their use of women-owned firms as subcontractors. These revisions include:

1) Developing clauses for inclusion in prime contract solicitations and in prime contracts which encourage the use of women-owned firms as subcontractors to the maximum degree feasible.

2) Study the feasibility of developing an incentive clause for inclusion in appropriate prime contracts which offers a dollar award to a prime contractor for subcontracting with women-owned firms in excess of an agreed upon goal for such subcontracting.

The Task Force also found a serious lack of data about women entrepreneurs and the types of the businesses they own. In order to develop this needed information, the Department of Commerce has agreed to have the Census Bureau update its 1972 survey on women-owned businesses and conduct a special survey to gather additional essential demographic data on the woman business owner and her enterprise.

The Task Force stressed the importance of early education in encouraging women to have a free choice of all possible careers. Therefore, the Secretary of Health, Education, and Welfare has agreed to take the following actions:

• Develop and promote educational and counseling programs emphasizing entreprenurial skills and business enterprise as a career option for both males and females.

• Develop such programs for use in the Nation's public and private secondary schools, institutions of higher education and vocational education programs.

• Report to me at the end of FY 1980 on the progress of such efforts and on future plans.

This memo and the Executive Order express my personal commitment to a national women's business enterprise policy. I expect the heads of all departments and agencies with business assistance programs and activities such as those mentioned in Section 1 of the Executive Order, and those with procurement authority, to substantially improve the quality of this assistance and support to businesses owned by women. With your commitment and cooperation, we can greatly improve the opportunities for women who own businesses in our economic system.

JIMMY CARTER

Energy Management Partnership Legislation

Letter to the Speaker of the House and the President of the Senate Transmitting the Proposed Legislation. May 18, 1979

Dear Mr. Speaker: (Dear Mr. President:)

In furtherance of my energy program announced on April 5, 1979, I am transmitting herewith the proposed "Energy Management Partnership Act of 1979" (EMPA), a measure designed to assist the States in developing an ongoing energy planning and management capability and assist local governments in expanding their energy-related activities.

As you know, Congress in recent years has established a number of energy programs designed to assist States and local governments in achieving more efficient use of energy. Two State conservation planning programs were separately established by the Energy Policy and Conservation Act enacted in late 1975 and the Energy Conservation and Production Act adopted in 1976. With enactment of the National Energy Act (NEA), still other responsibilities must be assumed by States and local governments although Federal funding for some NEA programs is not provided.

Experience strongly suggests that these programs could be made more effective if they, as well as other State energy-related initiatives, were carried out as part of an overall State energy plan. The effectiveness of these programs could be increased by assisting States in establishing a mechanism for their integration at the State level.

This legislation addresses the concerns which Governors, local officials and others have raised regarding the need for better coordination in energy activities carried on at every level of government. Much more can be done if State and local energy agencies, working in partnership with the Federal government, are permitted to seek their own solutions to their energy problems.

The bill I am transmitting contains the following principal features:

1. *State energy plan.* Participation in the State energy plan program under EMPA would be voluntary. A participating State would receive an initial grant for planning activities in addition to assistance it receives to continue activities under existing Federal energy programs pending approval of the State energy plan. After the Secretary has approved the plan, these programs would be managed and monitored by the State according to the requirements and objectives of the State energy plan. The plan would provide a framework in which a State, working with local governments, would develop and implement its own strategies and programs.

2. *Energy emergency planning.* EMPA would provide support for State energy emergency planning. Some of the activities included in such planning are State plans for set-aside of petroleum products and other energy supplies, allocation of fuels in short supply during a period of supply disruption, monitoring of supply and consumption, and developing and implementing other emergency energy measures which are responsive to State needs.

3. *Special energy projects.* EMPA would authorize the Secretary of Energy to make grants to local governments and Indian tribes to develop and implement special energy projects. This feature of the bill would provide the flexibility necessary to support innovative projects which may not qualify under existing categorical programs but which are nevertheless worthy of Federal support. Projects having national applicability are given preference under this program.

4. *Funding for programs not now funded.* No Federal assistance to States is provided for some energy functions, including renewable resource development and removal of technical, economic and institutional barriers to energy production. EMPA would help fill these financial gaps.

5. *Coordination of Federal energy assistance.* EMPA would permit States to consolidate applications for assistance programs administered by the Department of Energy and would provide States flexibility in the use of administration funds under such programs.

I believe that to meet our national energy requirements requires concerted action with all levels of government working in partnership. Enactment of this bill would make a significant contribution toward that end. For these reasons, I urge prompt consideration of this proposed legislation.

Sincerely,

JIMMY CARTER

NOTE: This is the text of identical letters addressed to Thomas P. O'Neill, Jr., Speaker of the House of Representatives, and Walter F. Mondale, President of the Senate.

National Museum Day, 1979

Proclamation 4661.   May 18, 1979

By the President of the United States of America

A Proclamation

Museums are the custodians of a substantial part of humankind's heritage, whether produced by the skill of our ancestors or by our contemporaries.

Museums are centers of research for scholars, of education, of enlightenment for younger generations, and a source of enjoyment and cultural enhancement for all.

Museums enrich the quality of our communities and provide a sense of continuity and perspective which can enhance, in a unique way, the cultural opportunities which are provided by schools, colleges, universities, libraries and other institutions of learning.

In recognition of the contribution made by the museums of our Nation to the preservation of the heritage of the United States and to the furtherance and understanding of the peoples of the United States the 96th Congress, by House Joint Resolution 262, has designated May 18, 1979, as National Museum Day.

Now, THEREFORE, I, JIMMY CARTER, President of the United States of America,

do hereby proclaim May 18, 1979, as National Museum Day, and call upon the people of the United States, State and local government agencies, and interested organizations to observe that day with appropriate ceremonies, activities, and programs.

IN WITNESS WHEREOF, I have hereunto set my hand this 18th day of May, in the year of our Lord nineteen hundred seventy-nine, and of the Independence of the United States of America the two hundred and third.

JIMMY CARTER

[Filed with the Office of the Federal Register, 3:24 p.m., May 18, 1979]

Digest of Other White House Announcements

The following listing includes the President's public schedule and other items of general interest announced by the White House Press Office and not included elsewhere in this issue.

May 14

The President left Camp Hoover, Va., for Virginia Beach, where he spent the day on a deep sea fishing trip. He then returned to the White House.

The White House and the National Governors' Association announced that they will cosponsor a series of three regional seminars on foreign trade and export development during the month of June.

May 15

The President met at the White House with:

—Zbigniew Brzezinski, Assistant to the President for National Security Affairs;

—Frank B. Moore, Assistant to the President for Congressional Liaison;

—the Georgia Democratic congressional delegation;

—Senator and Mrs. Daniel Patrick Moynihan of New York and Mrs. Carter, for lunch;

—James T. McIntyre, Jr., Director of the Office of Management and Budget.

The President received the first Special Country Music Association Award in a ceremony in the Oval Office.

The President participated in a briefing by administration officials on the strategic arms limitation agreement given for a group of Senators in the East Room at the White House.

The President declared a major disaster for the State of Florida as a result of severe storms, tornadoes, and flooding, beginning on or about May 8, which caused extensive public and private property damage.

May 16

The President met at the White House with:

—Dr. Brzezinski;

—Mr. Moore, Danny C. Tate, Deputy Assistant for Congressional Liaison (Senate), William H. Cable, Deputy Assistant for Congressional Liaison (House), and James C. Free, Special Assistant for Congressional Liaison (House);

—Gov. Edmund G. Brown, Jr., and State and local officials from California, and members of the California congressional delegation, to discuss the gasoline shortages in California;

—Stansfield Turner, Director of Central Intelligence, Hamilton Jordan, Assistant to the President, and Dr. Brzezinski;

—Senator Edmund S. Muskie of Maine;

—administration officials to discuss the fiscal year 1981 Federal budget and economic overview.

The President participated in a briefing by administration officials on the strategic arms limitation agreement given for a group of community leaders in the East Room at the White House.

The President attended the Georgia State Society Fish Fry at the Longworth House Office Building.

The President transmitted to the Congress the annual report of the Commodity Credit Corporation.

May 17

The President met at the White House with:

—Dr. Brzezinski;

—Mr. Moore;

—Prime Minister Kalevi Sorsa of Finland, Chairman of the Socialist International Study Group on Disarmament;

—Senator John C. Stennis of Mississippi;

—Secretary of Health, Education, and Welfare Joseph A. Califano, Jr., Stuart E. Eizenstat, Assistant to the President for Domestic Affairs and Policy, Charles L. Schultze, Chairman of the Council of Economic Advisers, and Alfred E. Kahn, Advisor to the President on Inflation, to discuss national health insurance;

—Gov. Brendan T. Byrne, Senator Harrison A. Williams, Jr., and Representative James J. Howard, all of New Jersey.

May 18

The President met at the White House with:

—Vice President Mondale, Secretary

of State Cyrus R. Vance, Dr. Brzezinski, and Mr. Jordan;

—Mr. Moore and Mr. Tate;

—Mr. Schultze;

—a group of editors and news directors (transcript will be printed next week);

—Secretary of Transportation Brock Adams, Secretary of Energy James R. Schlesinger, Frank Press, Director of the Office of Science and Technology Policy, Mr. Eizenstat, Mr. Kahn, and representatives of the automobile industry and the academic community, to discuss new initiatives for basic research in automotive technology.

The President left the White House for a weekend stay at Camp David, Md.

NOMINATIONS SUBMITTED TO THE SENATE

The following list does not include promotions of members of the Uniformed Services, nominations to the Service Academies, or nominations of Foreign Service officers.

Submitted May 15, 1979

VICTOR GILINSKY, of Maryland, to be a member of the Nuclear Regulatory Commission for the term of 5 years expiring June 30, 1984 (reappointment).

A. LEE FRITSCHLER, of the District of Columbia, to be a Commissioner of the Postal Rate Commission for the term expiring October 14, 1982, vice Frank P. Saponaro, term expired.

Submitted May 16, 1979

DARIUS W. GASKINS, JR., of the District of Columbia, to be a member of the Interstate Commerce Commission for the term expiring December 31, 1984, vice Virginia Mae Brown, term expired.

THOMAS A. TRANTUM, of Connecticut, to be a member of the Interstate Commerce Commission for the term expiring December 31, 1985, vice Rupert L. Murphy, resigned.

NOMINATIONS—Continued

Submitted May 16—Continued

EMMETT JOHN RICE, of New York, to be a member of the Board of Governors of the Federal Reserve System for the unexpired term of 14 years from February 1, 1976, vice Stephen S. Gardner, deceased.

JAMES P. JONES, of Virginia, to be United States District Judge for the Western District of Virginia, vice a new position created by P.L. 95–486, approved October 20, 1978.

Withdrawn May 17, 1979

WILLIAM M. LANDAU, of New York, to be a member of the Board of Directors of the Overseas Private Investment Corporation for a term expiring December 17, 1980, vice Wallace F. Bennett, term expired, which was sent to the Senate on May 7, 1979.

Submitted May 17, 1979

WILLIAM M. LANDAU, of New York, to be a member of the Board of Directors of the Overseas Private Investment Corporation for a term expiring December 17, 1981, vice Donley L. Brady, term expired.

JOSEPH W. HATCHETT, of Florida, to be United States Circuit Judge for the Fifth Circuit, vice a new position created by P.L. 95–486, approved October 20, 1978.

THOMAS M. REAVLEY, of Texas, to be United States Circuit Judge for the Fifth Circuit, vice a new position created by P.L. 95–486, approved October 20, 1978.

WILLIAM L. HUNGATE, of Missouri, to be United States District Judge for the Eastern District of Missouri, vice a new position created by P.L. 95–486, approved October 20, 1978.

HOWARD F. SACHS, of Missouri, to be United States District Judge for the Western District of Missouri, vice a new position created by P.L. 95–486, approved October 20, 1978.

JOSE A. LOPEZ, of Puerto Rico, to be United States Marshal for the District of Puerto Rico for the term of 4 years (reappointment).

AVERN COHN, of Michigan, to be United States District Judge for the Eastern District of Michigan, vice a new position created by P.L. 95–486, approved October 20, 1978.

STEWART A. NEWBLATT, of Michigan, to be United States District Judge for the Eastern District of Michigan, vice a new position created by P.L. 95–486, approved October 20, 1978.

NOMINATIONS—Continued

Submitted May 17—Continued

ANNA DIGGS-TAYLOR, of Michigan, to be United States District Judge for the Eastern District of Michigan, vice a new position created by P.L. 95–486, approved October 20, 1978.

Submitted May 18, 1979

MARCUS ALEXIS, of Illinois, to be a member of the Interstate Commerce Commission for the term expiring December 31, 1985, vice Alfred Towson MacFarland, term expired.

CHECKLIST OF WHITE HOUSE PRESS RELEASES

The following listing contains releases of the White House Press Office which are not included in this issue.

Released May 14, 1979

Announcement: cosponsorship of regional seminars on foreign trade and export development by the White House and the National Governors' Association

Released May 15, 1979

Announcement: nomination of James P. Jones to be United States District Judge for the Western District of Virginia

Released May 16, 1979

Announcement: nomination of Avern Cohn to be United States District Judge for the Eastern District of Michigan

Announcement: nomination of Anna Diggs-Taylor to be United States District Judge for the Eastern District of Michigan

Announcement: nomination of Stewart A. Newblatt to be United States District Judge for the Eastern District of Michigan

News conference: on water policy cost-sharing legislation—by Secretary of the Interior Cecil D. Andrus

Fact sheet: water policy cost-sharing legislation

CHECKLIST—Continued

Released May 16—Continued

News conference: on administration measures taken to meet gasoline shortages in California—by Secretary of Energy James R. Schlesinger and Stuart E. Eizenstat, Assistant to the President for Domestic Affairs and Policy

Released May 17, 1979

Announcement: nomination of Joseph W. Hatchett to be United States Circuit Judge for the Fifth Circuit

Announcement: nomination of Thomas M. Reavley to be United States Circuit Judge for the Fifth Circuit

Announcement: nomination of William L. Hungate to be United States District Judge for the Eastern District of Missouri

Announcement: nomination of Howard F. Sachs to be United States District Judge for the Western District of Missouri

Announcement: nomination of Jose A. Lopez to be United States Marshal for the District of Puerto Rico

Released May 18, 1979

News conference: on basic research initiatives in automotive technology—by Secretary of Transportation Brock Adams, Frank Press, Director of the Office of Science and Technology Policy, and Philip Caldwell, vice chairman of Ford Motor Co. and president of the Automobile Manufacturers Association

Fact sheet: basic research initiatives in automotive technology

ACTS APPROVED BY THE PRESIDENT

Approved May 18, 1979

H.J. Res. 262_____ Public Law 96–11
A joint resolution to declare May 18, 1979 to be "National Museum Day".

Interview With the President

*Remarks and a Question-and-Answer Session
With Editors and News Directors.
May 18, 1979*

THE PRESIDENT. I'm very pleased to have all of you here. I see some old friends around the table from Georgia, and I'm very pleased.

I think this is one of the best things that we have done since I've been President, is to have in, on frequent occasions, distinguished leaders of the news media throughout the country. It gives me an opportunity to answer your questions, to learn about the interests around the Nation, and also to express in each case, at the beginning of the session, some particular point that illustrates the kind of difficulties or responsibilities that a President has to meet.

PANAMA CANAL TREATIES

Yesterday, there was a very disappointing vote in the House of Representatives on obtaining a rule for Panama Treaty implementation legislation. We only won the vote by two votes, which is very disturbing to me and, I'm sure, to the Nation. The fact is that the Panama treaties

have already been implemented. The President and three other Presidents before me negotiated the treaties. The Senate has now ratified the Panama treaties. They are the law of the land. They became effective the first day of April.

The Panama Canal Zone will become Panama territory on the first day of October 1979, no matter what the Congress does this year on implementation. The reason for the implementation legislation is to permit the United States to operate the Panama Canal between now and the year 2000 and also to defend the Canal Zone between now and the year 2000 with U.S. forces.

If the implementation legislation is not passed in a timely fashion and in compliance with the treaty, we would be faced with a very serious consequence.

We could not handle the problems or needs or obligations for and to American workers there. We could not transfer workers from one place to another. We couldn't deal effectively with the Panamanian workers who have been employed there for many years.

The citizenship status and basic rights of Americans in the Panama Canal Zone would be in doubt. We could not provide for the facilities and equipment to defend the canal. In fact, the operation of the canal itself might very well be interrupted.

I don't believe the Congress will put us, as a nation, in that posture. But there's a great deal of misinformation about this subject. Even some Members of the Congress feel that if they don't pass implementation legislation, they could somehow abrogate the treaties themselves.

As you know, the canal is very important to us. A substantial portion of oil, for instance, for the east coast is derived from wells in Alaska—comes down through the Panama Canal and up to this coast.

The gulf ports are dependent upon the Panama Canal in a very large way. About 6 or 7 percent of our total trade traffic goes through the Panama Canal with overseas destinations. Consumers would be adversely affected. Farm supplies, farm goods, grain, and other items use the Panama Canal in a very large and important fashion.

This is the kind of problem that a President does face in dealing with the Congress: to implement basic policy after that policy has been established.

ADMINISTRATION POLICIES

We will be facing the question in the future of how to deal with the SALT treaty, which will have been negotiated, I hope—if everything goes well—by the end of next month. And, of course, how to deal with the Rhodesian question, how to implement the Mideast peace treaty in an effective fashion—those are some of the foreign affairs problems that I have to face. Inflation, energy, and many other items on the domestic scene are of comparable importance and, I might say, of comparable difficulty.

I'd be glad to answer any questions that you all might have.

QUESTIONS

MEETING WITH PRESIDENT BREZHNEV

Q. Mr. President, when you meet with Secretary Brezhnev next month, what will be the priority items of discussion?— SALT, obviously, but there must be others. Can you talk about those a bit?

THE PRESIDENT. We've not yet agreed on an agenda, and it's a little bit difficult for me to answer your question definitively until we and the Soviets have concluded that discussion.

The conclusion of the SALT negotiations, which will be practically concluded then, and the signing of the documents would obviously be a major step. In arms control, we are dealing with the question of antisatellite capabilities, trying to restrain that. We'll proceed with further discussions of a comprehensive test ban on nuclear testing. The British are party to that, but we keep the British thoroughly informed. We will proceed also with discussions on the control of the transfer of conventional weapons to the developing countries and to others, as major arms suppliers. We've had several meetings on that subject.

We'll proceed with discussion of the mutual and balanced force reduction talks that have now been going on without much progress for the last 5 years in Vienna. We hope to make some progress there.

Prior to the time that I meet with President Brezhnev, I'll be meeting with Chancellor Schmidt in this room, I think the first week in June. And we are constantly consulting with our European allies on some of these subjects that affect them. Secretary Harold Brown, who's in Europe right now, has been involved with those subjects.

We'll also lay the groundwork, at least describe the parameters or a general outline of the SALT III discussions if everything goes well.

We'll have some discussion about trade, I'm sure, about refugee problems, about some potential improved ways for us to communicate with one another if regional altercations or disagreements should arise, so that we can have a stable and a more secure, more peaceful interrelationship with the Soviet Union; at the same time, meeting with the Soviets on a peacefully competitive basis and prevailing in those competitions as often as possible.

I'd say arms control, trade, better communications in the future would be the general outline. All of those items that I described to you, certainly with the exception of SALT, still have to be approved by the Soviets.

STRATEGIC ARMS LIMITATION

Q. Morris Wilkes from KRLB in Lubbock, Texas. What happens if the United States Senate does not ratify the SALT treaties? I was talking to some Senators on the Hill yesterday, and they said the votes are not there and they don't see them coming around. What happens if they do not ratify the treaty, Mr. President?

THE PRESIDENT. That's a terrible possibility to have to contemplate.

The SALT negotiations are a continuing process that were initiated as far back as President Eisenhower. And we've made steady, incremental progress—sometimes very slow, very tedious, very careful—with a limited test ban to protect the atmosphere, with SALT I, with Vladivostok, and now with SALT II. SALT II has been under negotiation for going on 7 years. I'm the third President who has participated in this process. It's a carefully balanced treaty. It's in our best interest. It protects our own Nation's security and will contribute to world peace and, I think, also is in the best interests of the Soviet Union.

Substantial amendments to the treaty—which would be an easy way out for a Senator, to say, "Well, we don't like what you've done, do it again"—would be, I think, unacceptable to the Soviet Union and to us, if there was any substantial change in the treaty terms. It would put me in a very difficult position.

And I think that a rejection of the treaty would interrupt—I wouldn't predict "terminate," but at least interrupt, with serious consequences, the process of controlling nuclear weapons over many years' time.

There would be no way to move to SALT III. It would be very difficult to reopen SALT II, because why should a President of the Soviet Union want to negotiate with the President of the United States if ultimate approval by the Senate of a carefully balanced treaty was extremely doubtful?

It would be a terrible blow to our own allies in Europe. I think it would shake the strength of NATO itself, because many of our allies in Europe feel that they are in the forefront of some possible confrontation between the two super powers, and they might be the first to suffer in case a nuclear war should take place. And for us to prove that we are not able to get along with the Soviet Union and control nuclear weapons, when we have thousands of nuclear weapons on both sides already, I think would cause many of our allies to look with doubt on the advisability of their having unilateral agreements with us.

I think they would start searching for some alternative to the NATO Alliance exclusively. I don't think they would abandon NATO, but they'd just have to start feelers to the East to see if they could have some insurance here to avoid a confrontation, when we ourselves have proven unable to lay the groundwork for nuclear arms control.

We would have a very serious problem, too, in trying to restrain other potential nuclear powers from coming into being. There are at least a dozen or more nations right now who have the technological capability of developing nuclear explosives. We have exerted a tremendous amount of effort, I and the Congress, in trying to restrain those nations and keep them from becoming nuclear explosive powers.

India, Pakistan, Iraq, South Africa, Argentina, Brazil, South Korea, Taiwan, and so forth, and others that I could name if I wanted to, have been restraining themselves, with a large part of their restraint predicated upon the anticipated voluntary control by the Soviet Union and the United States. If we should fail in this, it would be almost impossible for me to go to the President of Brazil or the Prime Minister of India and say, "Please do not develop a nuclear explosion." It would make me look ridiculous to try to continue that effort that I've been pursuing.

And the last thing that concerns me is—that I'll mention this afternoon because of the press of time—it would give the Soviets an enormous propaganda weapon to use against us. They would be identified, at least in their own mind and maybe in the minds of many nonaligned countries around the world as a peaceloving nation. They would certainly hammer this point—"We ourselves believe in nuclear arms control, but look what the United States has done."

In the peaceful competition that I described earlier with the Soviet Union, we would be at a decided disadvantage if we should reject this major move toward in-creased peace throughout the world, toward increased security for the United States, toward increased control of the world's most destructive weapon.

SENATOR EDWARD KENNEDY

Q. Mr. President, Herbert Kamm of the Cleveland Press, sir. Mr. President, I'd like to turn to a political question. As you no doubt are aware, the chairman of the Democratic Party in Cuyahoga County is leading an effort to encourage Senator Kennedy to run for President.

THE PRESIDENT. Yes, I've heard of that. [*Laughter*]

Q. Would you mind commenting, sir?

THE PRESIDENT. Well, what the local political organization does is something that I can't control. I've not talked to him about it. I would be glad to, if he has some particular concerns.

I think that this is the case in several instances around the country. It's certainly not an unprecedented political circumstance in the year prior to a Presidential election year. I'm not a candidate; I'm a President. I don't have any intention of announcing my own plans until late this year.

But Senator Kennedy is a very popular and attractive man. If he became a candidate, he would be a formidable opponent for anyone else who ran. If I decided to run, I wouldn't have any fear of meeting that kind of competition. It was there for me to face when I was an unknown Governor planning my campaign when Senator Kennedy was the prime potential opponent.

Senator Kennedy has announced repeatedly that he's not a candidate; he intends to support me; thinks I'll get the nomination. I think he's pleased with that. I take him at his word. But it doesn't cause me any deep concern. I would like to have the full and enthusiastic support of the Democratic leaders in the Cleveland area, Cuyahoga County, and also throughout Ohio, indeed, the entire Nation.

But I have to make difficult decisions. I'm responsible for them. I have no aversion to them. But people naturally get concerned about particular issues or ideas. And I don't know what the motivations of the county chairmen are, but I have confidence that eventually the Democrats will make the right decision—and the American people. [*Laughter*]

COAL

Q. Mr. President, Richard Grimes from West Virginia. There's a feeling in the State that your strong commitment in 1977 for coal has eased up somewhat, I think a lot of it having to do with the EPA regulations that are slowing our sale of coal. Is that true?

THE PRESIDENT. No. I doubt that any other administration has ever done as much to encourage the present and future production of coal as we have. It's been a top priority for us. We want to increase the production and use of coal tremendously in this country.

We've passed, by law, restraints on major stationary powerplants against the future, continued use of oil and natural gas and substitutes for coal. We've tried to encourage the use of coal in this respect. I think the new settlement between the United Mine Workers and the operators has provided a degree of stability and an absence of wildcat strikes and so forth that's encouraging.

I think that in the long run, the sure supply of coal, without unexpected interruption, is going to be helpful. Under the chairmanship of Governor Jay Rocke-

feller, a commission made up of all elements of the coal industry is now preparing a report for me that would give advice to me and the Nation on how we can increase the use and production of coal.

I've asked all the agencies who are interested—in the Federal Government, who have a responsibility in the Federal Government—to prepare advice for me on how we can increase the consumption of coal in our Nation. We are running out of oil and gas. Our basic energy proposal to the Congress in April of 1977 contemplated an enormous increase in the production and the use of coal.

We have tried to deal with the transportation problems that affect the coal industry, not only in West Virginia but throughout the Nation. And my guess is that when the environmental protection standards are promulgated, as is now required by Federal court order, that the need of our Nation for the use of coal will be a major factor in their decision.

I have met around this table within the last 2 weeks with the United States Senators, I think from 12 different coal-producing States, to get all of their ideas on the consequences of this decision. It's made by EPA, an independent agency, and the EPA Administrator was here. He's a sound person, and he's working with people who have a balanced view of the quality of our environment and the need to meet our energy requirements.

So, I don't think the people of West Virginia need to fear any deviation of my administration in enhancing the production and the use of coal.

The last thing is that we, if we get—if and when we get the windfall profits tax and the energy security fund, we'll have substantial, increased moneys for pilot plants for the liquefaction and gasification of coal and research and development on new ways to use coal that would be of tremendous benefit to West Virginia and to other States in the country.

MILITARY INSTALLATIONS

Q. Mr. President, I'm Ed Belkin, news director of KYW News Radio, Philadelphia. Citizens in the Northeast are increasingly disturbed with military facilities being closed or shifted to the so-called Sunbelt States from what is already an economically depressed area. I'm sure you know all too well the case of Frankford Arsenal. The battle of the aircraft carrier *Saratoga* is underway yet between Philadelphia and Newport News. And now, of course, there's the issue of basic training at Fort Dix. What are you doing to ensure that this apparent imbalance is corrected, so that all these facilities are not shifted out of the Northeast and that the thousands of jobs and millions and billions of dollars that would go with these facilities are not shifted elsewhere?

THE PRESIDENT. Economic factors and balance of military placement in the country are both factors in the ultimate decision. The primary factor, however, is how to enhance our Nation's security to an optimum degree within budgetary and personnel constraints.

I have never interfered in a very carefully evolved decision by the Department of Defense in deciding how to modify the base structure. I think that we have proven, since I've been in office, to have the best interests of Philadelphia at heart.

We recognize the adverse economic impact of the Frankford Arsenal decision. It was reassessed after I got into office, and again, after considering all the factors, the Defense Department felt that this change was advisable. I did not dispute that final decision. We assessed all the economic factors as well as the military factors.

On the *Saratoga,* we could save some money by having the repairs or the overhaul of *Saratoga* performed at Newport News. But I feel that it's very important for the shipyard not only at Newport News but also in Philadelphia—the Navy shipyards—to be kept available for future use in case of a national emergency.

And my administration, with the full knowledge of the Newport News people, went all out to assure that the major overhaul of the *Saratoga* would be carried out in Philadelphia. It was done on the basis of merit, and although it cost a little bit more to do the actual overhaul, it preserves the entity itself and the strength of the Philadelphia shipyard for future use in a balanced fashion.

These are very complicated decisions, and they have in the past been fraught with political interference. I don't believe that anybody could accuse me or my administration or the Defense Department, Charlie Duncan, the Deputy that makes the basic recommendation, of ever making one of these decisions on the basis of politics—not to get votes or anything else.

And sometimes we aggravate some extremely interested and dedicated and competent Members of Congress when those changes are made. But in balance, I can tell you that every decision has been made to the best of my ability, in the best interests of our Nation's security, within the budgetary and personnel limits.

On some occasions we make a decision, like in the Philadelphia shipyard overhaul case with the *Saratoga,* to preserve the ability of a defense establishment for future use in a case of emergency. That's the best answer I can give you.

UNDOCUMENTED ALIENS

Q. Mr. President, Raul Parra from the Spanish Television Network, Albuquerque. Are there any definite plans on how to deal with the illegal aliens influx from Mexico and the possibility of implementing the *bracero* program again?

THE PRESIDENT. We have no plans to use the *bracero* program again. As you know, I presented to the Congress my first year in office, after a great deal of study, a proposal on how to deal with the undocumented workers. There are many names for the same people—some, illegal aliens; some, undocumented aliens. I've lately been calling them undocumented workers. The other day someone suggested that we call them undocumented taxpayers. [*Laughter*]

But the Congress has not been willing to act on my recommendations. The Hispanic American community is sharply divided on the issue because the undocumented workers coming into our country compete in some areas for scarce jobs, as you know. In other cases, those very same American citizens who have Mexican heritage would like for their relatives to come here, and the pressures from economics in Mexico are quite severe now. But Mexico, with a large prospective improvement in their economy in the future because of the gas and oil discoveries, I think will help to assuage this problem.

I have met with López Portillo, President of Mexico, on this subject at length. I've sent Reubin Askew, former Governor of Florida and the chairman of my commission on immigration, down to meet several days with the President of Mexico, the Secretary of State—or the Foreign Minister, and others. We are trying to evolve a program that would be fair. And I think for the first time, at least in my historical memory, Mexico and the United States Governments are now working in harmony to try to hammer out a reasonable and fair approach to the problem. I don't say that we'll be together at the end, but we're working together.

The last thing is that I have pledged to all the minority groups in our country, and to the people of Mexico, that undoc-

umented workers who are in our Nation and who do not have a legal right to be here, will be treated fairly. They will not be abused, and their constitutional—or human rights will be preserved.

I'm sworn on my oath to uphold the law and the Constitution of my country, and there's no way that I can condone the illegal crossing of our border. But we're working the best we can to deal with the question that's been long in existence and to do it humanely and fairly and legally. Some modification of the law will be required.

The commission that has now been established will make those recommendations. I and the Congress are waiting for their recommendations to be made.

Ms. BARIO. Thank you, sir.

THE PRESIDENT. Thank you. I might take one other question.

PALESTINE LIBERATION ORGANIZATION

Q. Hal Rosen of Chicago. Earlier this week, on Monday, Joseph Sisco,[1] speaking before the Chicago Foreign Relations Council, said that while it's official U.S. policy that we don't recognize—or make contact, rather, with the PLO unless they recognize 242, that he sees modification in this in the future. While he's not an official Government spokesman, obviously, does his view reflect any change in our policy?

THE PRESIDENT. No, there's been no change. I don't contemplate any change. Our Nation is pledged, again, on its word of honor, which I have corroborated since I've been in office, that we will not deal with the PLO until they accept U.N. Resolution 242 as a basis for negotiations, which all the other Arab entities have done, and until they recognize the right of Israel to exist.

---

[1] Former Under Secretary of State for Political Affairs.

And I think that any such meeting as that, on any kind of an official basis, would be counterproductive. And we're not doing it surreptitiously. We're not cheating on our commitment. Obviously, as is well known by Israel, there are members* of the PLO, individual members* who are mayors of major cities, for instance, on the West Bank and in the Gaza Strip, and both we and the Israelis deal with them as Palestinians, not, however, in their capacity as members* of the PLO. So, there has been and will be no change in this policy.

I've got time, I think, if you would let me, to have either one more question or get an individual photograph with everybody here. And my preference would be to get a photograph. [*Laughter*]

We only have 3 or 4 minutes, so if you'd just come by, I'd like to just shake hands, and we'll have a photographer standing here. And then we'll send the photographs to you.

NOTE: The interview began at 1:15 p.m. in the Cabinet Room at the White House. Patricia Y. Bario is an Associate Press Secretary.

The transcript of the interview was released on May 19.

Cheyney State College

Address at the Commencement Exercises.
May 20, 1979

Dr. Wilson, Congressman Gray, Congressman Edgar, Senior Class President Shelton, Ms. Blango, members of the graduating class of 1979:

I'm glad to be here.

This is my third commencement address since I've been President. The first

---

*The President intended to say "supporters" of the PLO. [Printed in the transcript.]

one was to Notre Dame. Last year, I spoke to my own alma mater, the U.S. Naval Academy at Annapolis, and I'm continuing my very rare appearances at famous and great institutions of learning by coming here to Cheyney State.

I tried to think of a story that would illustrate some of the points I want to make. My staff this morning suggested that I tell the one about the surgeon and the architect and the politician who were arguing about which represented the oldest profession—since you are now getting ready to embark on new professions.

The surgeon said, "Surely it's mine, medicine, because the first woman was created with an operation when Adam's rib was removed." The architect said, "No, that's obviously not true, because the first act recorded was when order was created out of chaos, and that was certainly an architectural achievement." The politician said, "Well, who do you think created the chaos?" [*Laughter*]

I did not think that was a very good suggestion. [*Laughter*]

When I spoke at Notre Dame, I told a more appropriate story about the old gentleman who was arrested and taken before the judge for being drunk and setting a bed on fire. And the old gentleman, when asked by the judge if the charges were true, said, "Well, Your Honor, I plead guilty to being drunk, but the bed was on fire when I got in it." [*Laughter*]

I believe the latter is more appropriate to the occasion, because you and I have a lot in common. As President, I have a special opportunity to take part in the stream of history and also to study the course of history. Tonight, for instance, I will sleep in the same room where Abraham Lincoln slept when he was President, only a few steps from the place where he signed the Emancipation Proclamation.

Thursday, I met in the White House with several hundred black leaders, dozens of whom were instrumental in bringing about the Supreme Court decision, *Brown versus the Board of Education,* which occurred 25 years ago on that date, which struck down the separate but equal doctrine that had perpetuated segregation in the schools of a nation which has always claimed to be free and to provide equality of opportunity.

Not long ago, when I was in Memphis, I went with Mrs. Martin Luther King, Jr., to the balcony of a motel to visit the spot where her own husband was assassinated.

These events and others like them are profoundly moving, personal experiences. But I also feel a sense of history as I stand here today.

Many of you are the first in your family who ever had a chance to go to college. Neither my father nor any of his ancestors ever had a chance to finish high school or to go to college. So, I share the pride that you feel. And I also know the hardship that has gone into this achievement which is taking place today.

Ours, yours and mine, is a very special generation, the generation that Dr. Martin Luther King, Jr., was thinking of when he expressed his dream for America with an eloquence and a moral power that never will be forgotten.

One part of Dr. King's dream had a special meaning for me because of the State where he and I were born. He said, "I have a dream that one day on the red hills of Georgia, sons of former slaves and sons of former slaveholders will be able to sit down at the table of brotherhood."

And now when Andrew Young and I, two Georgians, sit down in the White House with other Cabinet members to hammer out foreign policy for the United States of America, it truly is a table of brotherhood.

I'm proud that we are working together for human rights around the world and for a majority rule, equality, and the end of racism and apartheid in southern Africa.

But I have not come to Cheyney State to boast about what my administration has done in foreign policy or civil rights or any other field. I'm not here to soothe you with promises that everything is going to be all right just because I happen to be in the White House or just because almost 200 superb black leaders now work with me to establish the policies of our Nation's Government. Instead, I'm here to talk to you very briefly today about some problems and to offer a challenge.

Our country does face extremely difficult problems—problems like inflation, energy shortages, inequality, discrimination, unemployment, and worldwide threats to peace. Each of these problems brings with it a tendency toward withdrawal from responsibility and sometimes crippling fears, fears that stand in the doorway between us and needed solutions. These fears of an uncertain future affect our daily lives. All of us, for instance—consumers, public officials, students, working people, business executives—hesitate to make individual sacrifices that we know are needed to fight inflation, because we are afraid that someone else may get a better deal.

We've seen the panic gasoline buying in California when everyone knows that this only makes our energy problems worse. Some people are afraid of losing their jobs. And this gives rise to racial bigotry and hatred.

All of us, if we are sane, are afraid of nuclear war, but the horror of the thought that mankind might actually be destroyed does not yet bring us together in a spirit of brotherhood and sisterhood to work for peace.

If our bellies are full and we are safe and secure, these fears, among others, contribute to our own sense of selfishness and the avoidance of responsibility. People are so concerned with getting ahead, with preserving what we have, with beating the system, that we refuse to become involved with anything outside our own personal lives. By taking refuge in either complacency or hopelessness, we mistakenly believe that we can grab and hold the best deal for ourselves in a difficult world.

Our problems are serious and they are real. They will not disappear if we ignore them. There are powerful special interests in our country which feed on the apathy of ordinary citizens. They enjoy the special privilege of power and influence, and they are determined to block positive change.

Those among you who believe in change—in improvement—those who are committed to making our country a greater country, must let your voices be heard if we are to defeat these special interests.

We know we need better programs in welfare, health care, education, and jobs. We know we need to control inflation, eliminate racial discrimination, have universal voter registration, control nuclear weapons, and help bring about majority rule in southern Africa.

The Congress of the United States can either make these decisions or block these decisions—decisions which affect every person in America.

I usually do not like polls. But I would like to take a little poll right here in the quadrangle. All of you who care about jobs, peace, eliminating racism, and ensuring justice for men and women, black and white, would you please raise your hand? Now, put your hands down. That's the easy part.

Tell the truth. Now all of you who voted in the last congressional election, 1978, in November, would you raise your hand? That's much better than the national average. [*Laughter*]

The question I would like to ask you is, why did the others not vote? Martin Luther King, Jr., was willing to risk and even give up his life so that you might have the right to vote—the right to shape the actions of your own Government. And he was not the only one. A lot of brave people have suffered and some have died to win that basic right. But that right is hollow, that right is empty, unless you use it.

When the *Brown* decision was handed down 25 years ago last Thursday, the school doors did not open up the following Monday. Do you know when they really began to let little black children into the schools that had been all white? I'll tell you when it began—when the voting rights bill was passed, that's when it began.

Both political candidates and incumbents have got to know that you will both vote and act. How are we going to have leadership to fight for equal opportunity and affirmative action in jobs, schools, and housing if even the act of voting is too great an effort?

Last November, two-thirds of the registered American adults did not vote. I ask you to join me in overcoming fear about the future, in battling apathy, and in fighting for change. One place to begin, for instance, is to keep the pressure on for equal opportunity in education and jobs.

Our economy has added 250,000 jobs for black and other minority teenagers since I became President. This year, we've committed $3.4 billion for youth employment and training—twice what we were spending 3 years ago. But we must do better. That's why I've asked Vice President Mondale to head a Cabinet-level task force to review everything both government and private industry is doing in youth employment and in training.

We're going to make sure these programs work. And we're going to look for ways to get private business to do its part as well.

As part of that review, we are taking another look at our summer job program which has been seriously troubled. The level of jobs in the future will depend on the effectiveness of this program. In the meantime, I'm going to make sure it's my business to assure that this summer we have the 1 million summer jobs for youth that have been promised.

The struggle for civil rights is not over. Talk to the members of the Congressional Black Caucus. They are deeply concerned about the attitude in the United States Congress toward civil rights.

We have made progress, but we've not achieved what we need to accomplish. The *Brown* decision and the voting rights act tore the mask of legality from the face of racism, and you and I are never going to let this mask of racism be put back on.

Before these legal actions, there were only a few thousand black students in State colleges all across the country. Now more than a million black students are going to colleges all over America, mostly in publicly supported colleges like this one.

These numbers do indicate that progress has been made. These numbers are important, because education leads to jobs—good jobs. And I was encouraged with what President Wilson told me on the way in from the airport about your success in getting jobs.

I'm going to tell it to you straight, because I care about the things you care

about, because you and others like you are the reason that I'm President, and because one day, one of you may have the job that I hold now. I don't know if you'll want it or not. [*Laughter*]

Change—change does not come easy. Changing the course of society is not like changing the channel on a television set.

In 1896, for example, the Supreme Court issued the evil principle of separate but equal. It took 58 years—more than one half a century—of losing court battles, marches, arrests, courage, sacrifice, before a new court finally killed the ghost of Jim Crow. But it happened because people like you, mostly blacks, many students, made it happen.

There were a lot of heroes. One of those heroes died last week, A. Philip Randolph. He was 90 years old. He spent his long life fighting against discrimination in jobs, in defense industries, in the Armed Forces of his own country. He fought more battles than he won, but he won enough to change the face of this Nation and the lives of all of us.

His fight, your fight, our fight, goes on. We've written the promise of equality into our laws. But we must have the means and the tools now to keep that promise.

There are still unlawful, documented racial discrimination practices in housing in our country, for instance, especially in our cities. That's why we are struggling in Congress now to give Patricia Harris, the Secretary of the Housing and Urban Development Department, cease-and-desist orders, so that the victims of discrimination in housing will no longer have to have the burden, very expensive burden, of enforcing the very laws designed to protect them.

We're not going to get this change into law through Congress without your political participation. The very least we need is your vote on election day. But we also need for every Member of the Congress to know that you are interested.

We have an energy crisis in our country. Yet too few of our people, and even fewer of our politicians, are willing to face that reality.

I proposed a windfall profits tax to develop very good programs for the poor, who bear the extra burdens of rising energy costs, to provide mass transit, to give us other forms of energy, and to keep the oil companies from pocketing billions of dollars in unearned, excess profits. When the time comes for a vote in Congress, you can be sure that the oil company lobbyists will still be there. And you can provide—and no one *but* you and other American citizens can provide—the counterveiling force that will curb the power of the lobbyists. If your voice is not heard, the oil companies will prevail again.

The most basic human right is the right of a person to live in peace. Today, as you march down this aisle to receive your diplomas, I'm thankful that none of you will have to march off to die in battle. I'm thankful that instead of fighting a war, we're debating a new step toward limiting the nuclear arms race. Peace and freedom are both precious gifts, and that's why the fight over ratification of the strategic arms limitation talks treaty is so important. As did Martin Luther King, Jr., you must make your voices heard in this battle for sanity and for peace.

Here at home, inflation threatens all the progress we have made. Again, I want to tell it to you straight, because inflation robs the poor, it robs minorities, and it robs those just starting out in life, like you, as surely as it robs old people who have to live on fixed incomes.

Inflation forces the Government to tighten the budget and to cut back on many programs that might help some of you. And inflation destroys some of the resources of business and industry needed to provide jobs for you and other Americans.

When Congress makes the tough choices on what has to be cut, who will stand with me to put people first unless you use your influence and your power?

I did not come here today to ask you to make my job easier. I came to urge you to help me make the job of every single elected officer in the United States tougher, more difficult, by insisting that government be more responsive, more compassionate, and more open to hear the voices of America.

That's why I'm proud to have people like Andrew Young working alongside me every day in my job of shaping foreign policy. And I have encouraged Andy not to be timid about speaking out.

And that's why I'm proud to have people like John Lewis and Eleanor Holmes Norton with me pressing the fight against fear and for justice here at home.

These are powerful people, and they are in powerful positions. But they cannot do it unless you back them up. Their effectiveness comes from the fact that they speak for you, just as my power as President comes from the fact that I speak for you and for other Americans.

I'm not here only to let you hear my voice, but so that we in government can be sure to hear your voice, and that together our voices will be too strong to be ignored; so that together we'll have the courage to win more victories which we can place alongside the great ones that we've won.

Most of the progress that has been initiated and achieved has not come from government. This progress has come from voices outside of government that slowly but surely were united in shouting for justice and equality in our own Nation, and slowly—often after many years, even generations—government finally listened.

The long struggle for civil rights, for equal rights, for human rights has been a cycle of action, and then reaction, of lash and then backlash, for the cancer of racial injustice has always been near the heart of America.

Three hundred and sixty years ago, the first slaves were unloaded on the east coast of this continent in chains. One year later, the pilgrims landed on Plymouth Rock searching for freedom. The story of America has been the struggle and agony of a people trying to heal that contradiction—and it's been painful, and it's not over.

A great victory still remains to be won where we are sure about our future, where we are sure about justice, sure about equality, sure about the morals and commitments of our Nation, sure that government accurately represents what our people are and what they would like to be. It can be done. Much has been done already. If it had not, you would not be here and I would not be here.

We must continue to fight our battles and to overcome our fears together, or we will not be able to stand together for these purposes tomorrow.

In his Nobel Prize acceptance speech, Dr. King said, "I have the audacity to believe that peoples everywhere can have three meals a day for their bodies, education and culture for their minds, and dignity, equality and freedom for their spirits."

I share that audacious dream. And I ask you to join each other, and to join with me, in the struggle to make that dream come true.

Thank you very much.

NOTE: The President spoke at 11:35 a.m. in the quadrangle at Cheyney State College, Cheyney, Pa. In his opening remarks, he referred to Dr. Wade Wilson, president of the college, Stephen Shelton, senior class president, and Antoinette Blango, class valedictorian.

Death of Ben Fortson

Statement by the President.   May 20, 1979

The death of Ben Fortson is a loss to all Georgians. He loved his State and its people and acted on that love through a lifetime of public service.

The people of Georgia shared his affection and repeatedly returned him to his post as secretary of state through an era of profound political, social, and economic change.

In my years in State government, particularly as Governor, I grew to know and greatly admire Ben Fortson. In one incident early in his career, he particularly demonstrated the courage and style that added dignity and integrity to State government for more than 40 years: All of State government was in turmoil over who was the legal Governor and, quietly, he kept the Great Seal of Georgia hidden in his wheelchair to prevent the contenders from using it to make their actions official until the controversy could be decided appropriately.

He was never too busy to stop and make history come alive for schoolchildren, and he consistently added a personal touch to the many activities of his office. The Georgia State Capitol will seem a far more lonely place without "Mr. Ben."

Rosalynn and I extend our deepest sympathies to his family.

White House Fellows

Appointment of 17 Fellows for the 1979–80 Program. May 21, 1979

The President today announced the appointments of the 1979–80 White House Fellows, the 15th group since the creation of the program.

The Fellows, who were chosen from among 1,346 applicants and screened by 11 regional panels, will begin their year of service with the Federal Government on September 1. The President's Commission interviewed 32 national finalists before recommending the 17 persons to the President.

The 1979–80 White House Fellows are:

MARI C. APONTE, 32, of Philadelphia, Pa., associate counsel, Blue Cross of Greater Philadelphia;

LINCOLN W. CAPLAN II, 28, of Cambridge, Mass., consultant, the Boston Consulting Group, Inc.;

FREDRICA P. CHALLANDES-ANGELINI, 29, of London, England, vice president, Amex Bank Ltd., London;

VICTORIA L. CHAN-PALAY, 33, of Concord, Mass., associate professor of neurobiology, Harvard Medical School, Boston;

ANNE H. COHN, 34, of Washington, D.C., Congressional Science Fellow, American Association for the Advancement of Science, in the office of the Honorable Albert Gore, Jr.;

ELIZABETH A. FETTER, 31, of Tyler, Tex., student/writer, Carpenter's Workshop, Pine Cove Conference Center, Tyler;

MARSHA ANNE JOHNSON, 31, of London, England, lieutenant commander, United States Navy, Mideast/CENTRO Plans and Policy Officer, United States Naval Forces, Europe;

KENNETH A. JONES, 32, of Pittsburgh, Pa., manager, functional analysis I, systems engineering department, pressurized water reactors division, Westinghouse Electric Corp., Pittsburgh;

JUDITH MERCADO, 28, of Chicago, Ill., director, corporate development, Northwest Industries, Chicago;

RICHARD NORTHERN, 30, of Louisville, Ky., partner, Jones, Rawlings, Keith & Northern, Louisville;

JAY A. REICH, 30, of Seattle, Wash., assistant chief criminal deputy, Juvenile Section, King County, Seattle;

R. GEORGE SARAUSKAS, 33, of Evanston, Ill., associate pastor, Saint Athanasius Church, Evanston;

KATHERINE A. SEBO, 34, of Greensboro, N.C., State senator, State of North Carolina, Raleigh, N.C.;

CARL G. SUHLER, 30, of Springfield, Colo., president, Baca Oil Co., Springfield; partner, Suhler Farmers, Springfield;

PAUL W. SWEENEY, JR., 28, of Chevy Chase, Md., attorney-associate, Arnold & Porter, Washington, D.C.;

GORDON TUCKER, 27, of Bronx, N.Y., assistant to the chancellor and assistant professor, the Jewish Theological Seminary of America, New York;

JUAN R. VIGIL, 35, of Albuquerque, N. Mex., manager, Bernalillo County, Albuquerque.

The White House Fellowship program was established in 1964 to provide outstanding Americans with firsthand experience in the process of governing the Nation. It is open to U.S. citizens, early in their careers, from all occupations and professions. Employees of the Federal Government are not eligible, with the exception of career Armed Forces personnel.

In addition to their job assignments with the Vice President, members of the Cabinet, and with the White House staff, the Fellows participate in an education program that includes off-the-record discussions with top-level Government officials, journalists, and leaders from various other segments of private life.

Leadership, intellectual and professional ability, and a commitment to community and Nation are broad criteria employed in the selection process.

Applications for the 1980–81 program will be available in August 1979. Application forms and additional information on the program may be obtained by sending a postcard to the Director, President's Commission on White House Fellowships, Washington, D.C. 20415, or by calling (202) 653–6263.

United States International Development Cooperation Agency

Message to the Congress Transmitting Amendments to Reorganization Plan No. 2 of 1979. May 21, 1979

To the Congress of the United States:

I herewith transmit amendments to Reorganization Plan No. 2 of 1979, which I transmitted to the Congress on April 10, 1979. Except as specifically amended hereby, Reorganization Plan No. 2 remains unmodified.

JIMMY CARTER

The White House,
May 21, 1979.

AMENDMENTS TO
REORGANIZATION PLAN No. 2 OF 1979

Prepared by the President and transmitted to the Senate and the House of Representatives in Congress assembled May 21, 1979, pursuant to the provisions of chapter 9 of title 5 of the United States Code.

Reorganization Plan No. 2 of 1979, which was transmitted to the Senate and the House of Representatives in Congress assembled on April 10, 1979, is hereby amended as follows:

A. Section 2 is amended to read:

"Section 2. *Director*

"The Agency shall be headed by the Director of the United States International Development Cooperation Agency (hereinafter referred to as the 'Director'), who shall be appointed by the President, by and with the advice and consent of the Senate, and shall receive compensation at the rate prescribed by law for Level II of the Executive Schedule. The Director shall have primary responsibility for establishing overall development assistance policy and coordinating international development activities supported by the United States. The Director shall serve as the principal advisor to the President and the Secretary of State on international development matters and also shall advise the President on all trade, science and technology, and other matters significantly affecting the developing nations. The Director shall report to the President and, on matters relating to foreign policy, to the Secretary of State. The Director shall designate the order in which other officials shall act for and exercise the powers of the Director during the absence or disability of the Director and the Deputy Director or in the event of vacancies in both such offices.".

B. Section 5 is amended to read:

"Section 5. *Performance of functions*

"The Director may from time to time establish, alter, consolidate, or discontinue organizational units within the Agency (other than units expressly established by statute or reorganization plan). The Director may from time to time delegate responsibility for carrying out any function or authority of the Director of the Agency to any officer, employee, or unit of the Agency, or any other officer or agency of the executive branch.".

C. Section 6 is amended to read:

"Section 6. *Transfers of functions*

"(a) There are hereby transferred to the Director all functions and authorities vested in the Agency for International Development or in its administrator pursuant to the following:

"(1) sections 233(b), 239(i), 296(e), 297(d), 298(c)(6), 299(d), 601(a) through (d), and 624(f)(2)(C) of the Foreign Assistance Act of 1961, as amended (22 U.S.C. 2193(b), 2199(i), 2220a (e), 2220b(d), 2220c(c)(6), 2220d(d), 2351(a) through (d), and 2384(f)(2) (C));

"(2) section 407 of the Agricultural Trade Development and Assistance Act of 1954, as amended (7 U.S.C. 1736a); and

"(3) section 706 of the Foreign Relations Authorization Act, Fiscal Year 1979 (49 U.S.C. 1518).

"(b) There are hereby transferred to the Director all functions and authorities vested in the agency primarily responsible for administering part I of the Foreign Assistance Act of 1961, as amended, or in its Administrator pursuant to the following:

"(1) sections 101(b), 119, 125, 531(a) (2), 601(e)(2), and 640B of such Act (22 U.S.C. 2151(b), 2151q, 2151w, 2346 (a)(2), 2351(e)(2), and 2399c); and

"(2) section 602 of the International Security Assistance and Arms Control Act of 1976 (22 U.S.C. 2352 note).

"(c) There are hereby transferred to the Director all functions and authorities vested in the Secretary of State pursuant to the following:

"(1) section 101(b) of the Foreign Assistance Act of 1961, as amended (22 U.S.C. 2151(b)), insofar as it relates to policy guidance other than foreign policy guidance, and section 622(c) of such Act (22 U.S.C. 2382(c)), insofar as it relates to development assistance; and

"(2) section 901 of Public Law 95–118 (22 U.S.C. 262g).".

Meeting With Federal Government Employees

Remarks and a Question-and-Answer Session With 13 Employees. May 21, 1979

THE PRESIDENT. First of all, I would like to welcome you here to the Cabinet Room. We had a meeting this morning with some of your bosses. We meet here every 2 weeks with the full Cabinet and the major agency leaders, and then, in between, I have important meetings like this, when we discuss matters of domestic and foreign consequence to our Nation.

Today, however, is a special occasion for me to have a chance to meet with a broader, representative group of career civil servants in our Government. You have been chosen, I think almost every one of you, perhaps everyone, because of outstanding achievement. And you've received awards for a special contribution to make our own Federal Government more effective and more efficient and a greater credit to me and to the country.

ADMINISTRATION POLICIES

I think it's accurate to point out that in the last 2½ years, I've been privileged to be part of the system which represents the American people in our Government, and I've recognized with a growing degree of appreciation the high quality and dedication of the overwhelming majority of people in the civil service system and in the administrative positions as well.

I know that you represent the Armed Forces, you represent the farmers, you represent the children in the schools, you represent people who are handicapped, you represent those who are looking for good housing, you represent the taxpayers, and you represent others who have perhaps only one contact with the Federal Government as a principal source of advice and counsel if they are in a profession, and that's the agencies like yourself and what you represent.

We are in a time, I believe, of concern, some troubled feeling on the part of the American people about energy, about inflation, about peace in the world, about taxation, about ethics. And you and I are partners in trying to address these troubled times, to meet the challenges and, also, take advantage of the exciting opportunities that we have to make a great nation's government even greater.

American people are concerned about some of the things in government. When I campaigned around the country for 2 years, most of the expressions of concern about waste, redtape, overregulation, often came up in townhall meeting-type formats from government employees themselves. And those who work for government out in the field, actually delivering services to the people of America, see in a much more vivid way than the average citizen in private life that any such defect in the Government ought to be rooted out.

And I have tried since I've been in this office to form a partnership with you. When there is waste, we want it to be eliminated. Almost all of you have contributed substantially and have been rewarded for your contributions to elimination of waste. We've tried to reduce the redtape, get rid of unnecessary regulations, and on the rare occasions when there is fraud in government, I've tried to form a partnership with you to root out that fraud.

We have now gotten the Congress to pass legislation authorizing Inspectors General in the different agencies. And they will not only be a constant source of investigation and improvement and inspiration, but they're also a place where you can go if you have a complaint or if you have a beneficial suggestion or if you

have a report to make about a defect in Government. And you will be protected from any sort of punishment.

I think we need to have some protection for whistleblowers, who come forward in a courageous way and say, "This is wrong in our Government. This is something that's been a defect for a long time and I want it rooted out." In the past, there have been cases where those kinds of people have been punished, and the example of that punishment has restrained others from coming forward in an effective way to improve the Government's structure itself.

I was very pleased when the Congress passed the civil service reform legislation. That legislation was evolved by people like you, working with Alan Campbell, and that legislation, after it was evolved, was put forward to the Congress, and I think it passed in a very fine form.

We are now seeking to let the volunteers who want to come forward to take advantage of a senior executive service do so, and the overwhelming portion of the senior executives do, indeed, want to participate in the kind of career opportunity that lets their initiative and lets their ability and lets their drive and their competence be recognized. And it's an inspiration to those who serve in government to do an even better job.

And I think that Alan has been very pleased at the vast percentage of those who do have that opportunity to want to leave the security which they formerly had when everybody moves in lockstep, no matter who does a good job and who doesn't, to the kind of competitive world where excellence will be indeed rewarded.

The suggestions that have been made last year by more than 42,000 Federal employees and saved our Nation over $350 million is a very good example of a new spirit of enthusiasm and dedication on

917

your part and on the part of the other thousands of people like you. Some of them are very tiny savings, a few hundred dollars or maybe a few thousand dollars at most. I remember one by a NASA employee that saved our Government, I think, $30 million, when they recommended that when a space shuttle was launched, it might be launched not with a carefully designed, new type of engine, but launched from the top of a modified 747. And this kind of a saving is a very good step in the right direction.

I know that you have some concerns that you want to express to me this afternoon. This program being taped for television will let the other Federal employees know about our interrelationship with one another. And, of course, we have members of the press who will be in the room throughout the session this afternoon.

I think it's good for me immediately to put your mind at ease about two or three rumors that have been floating throughout the civil service in the past.

There are absolutely no plans, for instance, to raise the minimum age at which Federal employees can be retired or can draw their retirement benefits. I don't know where the rumor came from. We have never considered it. I had never heard of it before it was publicized in the paper. And several of the civil servants have come to Alan Campbell and to my staff and said, "Why are you planning to raise the minimum retirement age?" We have no plans to raise the minimum retirement age.

Another question has been raised about the prospect of the combining of social security retirement with civil service retirement systems. I have taken no position at all on this. The Congress mandated that a commission study the feasibility or advisability of this step, and this commission is now doing the assessment work. They will make a recommendation, I think, just before Christmas, December 20 or something of that kind. And when that recommendation is made, all of you will have access to it. The Congress will have access to it. Alan Campbell will have access to it; so will I. And following that, then decisions can be made accordingly.

But in no case will the vested rights of civil servants who have contributed to a retirement fund be lost. I can't imagine any circumstance under which those vested retirement funds would be lost to you. This is a problem, I know, for many people who are concerned about security, to have the investigation going on. But I want to emphasize again that no decisions have been made. I have not taken a position on it. I do not intend to until I can very carefully study the report that will be concluded in December.

I might make two other points very quickly. We have established, and the Congress, as you know, has approved, the 5½-percent pay cap. This was done under the intense pressure of nationwide inflation. Including fringe benefits, which is included in the guidelines for private employees, it amounts to more than a 6-percent increase for Federal employees. This is not as much as many employees would like, but our Nation is faced with a very serious prospect of increasing inflation.

As you well know, the members of the Cabinet, my own senior staff in the White House, have taken zero increase—not 5½ or 6 percent, but zero increase. And I firmly believe, in spite of the fact some might not like the idea, that we in government ought to take the initiative in trying to constrain inflation. And a 1-percent difference between what the Federal employees get and the maximum limit under the voluntary wage guidelines, I don't think is too great a sacrifice to make to provide an example and also to let the people who support us with their tax moneys have confidence that we ourselves are willing to take action to control inflation in a time of trouble and challenge for our Nation.

The other point I'd like to make is that we have now under preparation—it has not been concluded and it has not yet come to my desk—a proposal to reform the compensation system. Alan Campbell will go over this in detail with you and the head of the unions and those who are interested. We must take action of this type in order to protect the comparability system. Otherwise, we're going to be back in a position which the Government witnessed many years ago, when every year the Congress would decide whether or not to give a certain salary increase. And to bring the Federal employees pay scale into an accurate, comparable situation with employees in the private business and industry is a very important challenge for us all.

I'm determined to bring this about so that there will be stability, credibility, and predictability in the establishment of pay levels for Federal employees in the future.

Let me close by saying that I'm grateful that you would come. I recognize among you superior achievement. And because you are here and because your own fellow workers know what an excellent job you have done, I know they'll look to you for advice and counsel and a report when you return back to your own jobs.

We've got an outstanding nation. The people look to us for leadership. In the past, and even now, they have sometimes been disappointed. I get my share of the criticism when the people are disturbed. You will have to share those criticisms with me. But that should just inspire us

to work in a closer spirit of harmony and partnership and do an even better job to correct the defects and the problems that we all know do exist at times in the Federal Government and set an example for the rest of the Nation and restore the credibility and the trust that's an integral part of strengthening our democratic system.

I'm very glad now, Alan, to hear from any of the people around the table. And I'd like to ask you to recognize them, if you don't mind.

MR. CAMPBELL. Yes. Who would like to make a comment or ask the President the first question?

QUESTIONS

POLICIES AFFECTING FEDERAL EMPLOYEES

MR. WILLIAMS. Mr. President, we appreciate very much this opportunity to meet with you and appreciate your encouraging statements about the Federal employees. I hope that this meeting can serve to better communicate your positions and your concerns to the Federal employees throughout the country.

I think the Federal employees, over 2 million of them, look to you as their leader and the developer of the policies and the programs that affect their very welfare. We do get feedback, and there are concerns and perhaps perceptions by a number of employees that perhaps a number of steps taken by the administration have indicated an "anti" attitude towards employees, such as the comparability pay concept, the rumors about retirement changes, payment for parking for Federal employees, the overall ceiling on executive salaries or restructuring of the pay system, and so forth.

So, I think all of those collectively have created a great deal of misconception, perhaps, on the part of our employees. I wish you could perhaps comment generally on this, and do you see new positive programs on the horizon that will be favorable to the Federal employee area?

THE PRESIDENT. I think many of the things that we've already done have been indeed favorable. I don't think anybody would deny that the new civil service legislation is favorable. It does provide more competition and it does provide, at the same time, a higher incentive for superb performance. But those are the kinds of characteristics that ought to pervade the feeling and the attitude of every employee, including the President of the United States. And it commensurately provides a higher degree of reward for those who are highly qualified and who are highly motivated and who do superior work. In my opinion, that is a major step in the right direction.

As I said before, I don't believe that the little more than 6-percent increase in pay, plus fringe benefits, is too great a sacrifice to ask among the civil servants who work with me in government. When I checked among my own Cabinet officers and within the White House staff, the top staff members, they were completely willing not to have any increase in their salaries during the time of very high inflation when we need to address this issue in a forceful fashion and also set an example for the rest of the country. And as I said, the 7-percent limit is the maximum limit. There have been many settlements around the country at a much lower level than this.

I can't do anything other than disavow the inaccurate reports that have been made about minimum age for retirement and so forth.

I forgot to mention a few minutes ago about the elimination of the right for free parking—as you know, this was a privilege that will be enjoyed until October, when it'll begin to be phased out—that has been enjoyed by just a very small portion of the Federal employees.

And in a time of energy shortages, in a time of need for the conservation of energy, in a time of very high air pollution, I believe it's a proper decision to have the Federal employees on the same basis as private employees, paying a very modest amount of parking fees, which will be an instigation to the sharing of an automobile by several employees, where most of them now come in, as you know, one person in an automobile. And also, it'll tend to make the use of the new rapid transit system more effective and more attractive. But I don't have any apology to make for that. It's something that's not highly popular, but I don't think it's an unwarranted sacrifice to ask.

MR. WILLIAMS. In the pay area, Mr. President, do you foresee that in the years ahead that Federal employees will be treated as well as employees in the private sector in terms of the cost of living?

THE PRESIDENT. Yes, I believe that if we can pass the reform compensation legislation that's now in preparation, the idea there is to have the Federal employees, in a very predictable way, have pay schedules that are accurately comparable to those paid in the private sector. It also permits some flexibility from one community in our Nation to another, so that the salaries are indeed comparable. I think that's the goal that we want to achieve.

MR. WILLIAMS. Thank you very much.

MR. CAMPBELL. Other questions? Mr. McDuffie.

GOVERNMENT CONTRACTS

MR. McDUFFIE. Last year, in January, my people extended you an invitation to visit our establishment at Fort Belvoir. As the boss, I'd like to renew that invitation to you.

My concern, and for my people, is concerning contracts. We hear continuously everything is going on contract—complete DIO, Director of Industrial Operations, and one fort, I think someplace in Georgia, is supposed to go on a trial basis, everything on a contract.

My concern is the people who work for me and look to me for leadership. They are all old; they're in the minority. When I say old—don't tell them I said this—but they're past 21. They are dedicated people, and most of them have over 20 years civil service behind them. Many of them are grandmothers who are working and striving to keep kids in college and keep homes together.

If things go on contract, my employees are the lowest paid in the wage rate system. They have no bumping rights to nobody. There's only one place to go, is home, and down to HEW for a handout. And I use this word "handout" deliberately, because that's what it amounts to when someone who has worked all of their life, their productive life, in civil service, and they go out.

Contract communications, I'm quite sure, is beneficial to the Government, and it should be. But if we are operating an installation where we are on a break-even basis, or close to break-even—in many cases in laundry, we aren't showing a profit. In my particular case, we are operating on a profit, paper profit, of course.

So, what's going to happen to these people? Now, short-term contracts, or contracts that can be bid on my operation—for example, he can lose money in the first year; the second year, he goes crazy, he becomes a millionaire. The seven laundries or the nine laundries in Europe are on contract at the present time, and the contracting cost has almost doubled in

the third year. It started out at a little over $6 million, and now it's almost $12 million for operating seven laundries. The loss in 1976, I believe it was, was just a little over $1½ million. It is currently projected to be over $6 million loss by going on contract.

But really, my concern, primarily, is the people in laundries throughout the United States and overseas. What's going to happen to these people when they don't have a job, no bumping rights, and most of them are too old to go out and train again? There's nothing there for them.

THE PRESIDENT. Well, I'm very concerned about the protection of the rights of employees of that kind, as you undoubtedly have known. When I was beginning our programs to reorganize the Government, to make it more efficient, more effective, I went into every agency, every major agency in the Washington area, personally, to answer questions. Sometimes five or six thousand people would come, and I would answer questions in the courtyards of the Pentagon and other places. And that was a frequent one asked: "Will you protect the jobs of people who might be affected when the Government is reorganized?" We have had six or seven or eight reorganization plans already approved. And I think that I can say that within the best of our ability, I think, successfully, we have protected the careers of those who might adversely have been affected.

The contracting part of decisions are made when the head of an agency is convinced, along with the Office of Management and Budget, that contracting itself can save indeed the taxpayers and the Federal Government substantial amounts of money. They make that recommendation then to me. And I have been extremely cautious in not putting forward my own approval of contracting outside, full-time employees, unless it is obvious that employees themselves will be protected and also that the Government will benefit by reduced cost for a given level of service.

If you have any information that would indicate that we have made a mistake in that respect, I wish you'd give it to me. I'll be glad to have it. And I'll discuss this with the Office of Management and Budget and also with Secretary of Defense Harold Brown and make sure that this does not ever occur anymore. And I'll read these papers myself, and thank you very much.

MR. CAMPBELL. I'll just add, if I might, Mr. President, that under the new guidelines that OMB has put out, which will go into effect May 30, any activity which currently is being done by the Government, there is a bias in favor of calculating the costs by giving a 10-percent advantage to continuing it in the Federal Government.

In addition to that, there are employee protections in situations where there is contracting out—I don't mean to suggest for a moment there aren't problems; there are indeed problems, and they're very human problems. But I can assure you that both the agency and the Office of Personnel Management do everything possible to protect the rights of employees and to go a step beyond that and do everything possible to find them employment elsewhere in the system.

MR. CRIBBINS. May I add something, sir?

THE PRESIDENT. Please do.

MR. CRIBBINS. I am in the Pentagon, and I do quite a lot of work with contracting. Every one of these contracts are treated very specifically on a case-by-case basis. And all of the very things that Mr. Campbell is talking about are considered—personal rights, environmental im-

pact, impact on a low-cost area or an area that's in trouble economically. And there are occasions when we go on contract to find out that maybe it wasn't the very best case, as Mr. McDuffie's. But I would say that that was rather an exception. In general, I would say the programs are being very well monitored, from where I sit.

THE PRESIDENT. My impression has been, maybe from a biased point of view, that we are much more cautious now with the new regulations that, Alan, you described, than was the case 3 or 4 years ago——

MR. CRIBBINS. That's correct, sir.

THE PRESIDENT. ——about protecting employees' rights.

MR. CRIBBINS. That is correct; much more so.

MR. CAMPBELL. Who's next?

CONFLICT-OF-INTEREST LAW

MR. CRIBBINS. I would like to try once more, while I have the floor. You mentioned the word "ethics." And I would solicit your support for this, and I know that you have given some support to it. I think that the new conflict-of-interest [law] [1] was needed. There wasn't any doubt about it. The perception was coming over that some people didn't care. But now I think maybe the pendulum has swung a bit far, and we are beginning to lose some really top-level people because of overly restrictive conflict-of-interest regulations.

And I would suggest, sir, that I am concerned that in the future—and, incidentally, I don't have that kind of future, so I'm not personally concerned—but in the future that we may deny ourselves some very good people, because these folk will be afraid that the very things they will do in government will preclude their fol-

----
[1] Printed in the transcript.

lowing through with a career outside of government.

THE PRESIDENT. This has been of concern to us. We've discussed it several times around this table when the full Cabinet was here. And as you know, there was one amendment added to the ethics legislation in the Senate that we did not support, that created a technical problem. And we are now working with the House and Senate to get those defects corrected, hopefully, before the first of July.

We have had a few people who have resigned from Government service because they felt that the new ethics legislation restricted them excessively in their future dealings with the Government, as it related to jobs that they were doing in the Government now. I think that it was necessary for some people to leave the Government because, in the past, there has been too much abuse by people who served in the Government for a limited period of time, got special knowledge or influence within the Government structure itself, went out and formed either a consulting firm or joined a legal firm, and came back and used improperly their former contacts in the Government. That kind of thing ought to be rooted out, and I'm determined to root it out.

MR. CRIBBIN. Great.

THE PRESIDENT. But the technical defect that was in the law, we are now trying to correct.

MR. CRIBBINS. Thank you, sir.

FEDERAL EMPLOYEE MORALE

MR. MULHERN. Mr. President, I have three points I'd like to make. First of all, I understand we're supposed to be here to give you feedback of how the Federal employees feel.

THE PRESIDENT. Exactly.

MR. MULHERN. The morale factor, I think, is a very significant one that we have to react to. And I don't think that some of the things that Bill Williams brought up about why they are concerned also gets over into this area of appreciation for the work being done by the majority. We always come out and we say to them, "We think all of you do a good job, *but* there are others," and then we dwell on those others.

THE PRESIDENT. Yes. That's true.

MR. MULHERN. I don't know of one situation where we have gotten favorable publicity other than—to the degree that I think they should—than when we got on the shot to the Moon. People got up and said, "My God, look what they did."

THE PRESIDENT. Yes.

MR. MULHERN. And we have all these other things that these other departments are doing. And somehow we've got to get it out, so that the Federal employee out there feels inside, "what a great government that we have here," and his part in it.

So, I think that in addition to these items that come up of concern to them, they are concerned about this other situation, as to how they fit socially within the cities and towns of our country with respect to people. And it's unfortunate we're not communicating to them the real good that this Government does for our people.

The second one is that——

THE PRESIDENT. Let me respond to that one very briefly.

MR. MULHERN. Yes, sir.

THE PRESIDENT. What you say also concerns me. I'm the representative of the employees of the Government, and I'm the top employee in the Government. I would say, not quite facetiously, that anybody who thinks they are being criticized as an employee ought to pick up the newspaper every day and compare the criticism they get to the criticism I get—every day. [*Laughter*] I don't object to it, because I know that constructive criticism can make us do a better job and correct errors in Government or defects in the Government that we might not otherwise have known about.

The thing that I have tried to do is to acknowledge freely that there has been excessive regulation, excessive redtape, excessive waste, excessive bureaucratic confusion and, on rare occasions, excessive fraud, and to point out that the rooting out of those things is not by me against the 2 million Federal employees, but it's me along with the overwhelming proportion of those Federal employees, all of us trying to improve the government mechanism together.

In other words, it's not me and the public against the Federal employees, it's me and the Federal employees, as partners, trying to make the Federal Government better.

And I very seldom make a speech anywhere in the agricultural area that I don't point out the improvements that have been made in agriculture. The year before last, last year, again this year, we're setting alltime records, for instance, in the export of agricultural products to foreign countries. This is something that everybody knows I didn't do. But this has been done by the superb professional economists and advisers and foreign sales experts within the Department of Agriculture.

So, I think there is a great deal of natural appreciation for what Federal employees do. And the thing I want to do is to make us all not be satisfied and not wince or cry out loud when we are criticized, but say we're trying to correct those defects and we're trying to make it so that we are not subject to legitimate criticism in the future.

But I'm very pleased at how we have been courageous enough to tackle some problems that have long existed in government. And I believe that we have begun to convince the American people now that we are trying to root out those few instances of fraud and that we don't try to cover up or hide those instances because we ourselves might be embarrassed.

It is somewhat of a reflection on me as President, having been in office for 2, 2½ years, to find that there's *a* person in the General Services Administration who is violating the law. But I would rather root that person out and let the public know we're rooting him out than to leave that person there. And if I get part of the blame, I'm just willing to accept that. And I'm sure that most of the civil servants are in the same category.

Go ahead and cover your next point.

PERSONNEL CEILINGS

MR. MULHERN. The second point was that personnel ceilings have been here in my own agency since '67.

THE PRESIDENT. Yes, I know.

MR. MULHERN. So, I know they're popular with the press and others, but sustained personnel ceilings gets down to a point of where it becomes detrimental. And we have to be careful when we say that, because it sounds good, but first you start contracting and signing cooperative agreements, and soon you start to get feedback: "Now, look, this is costing more money than if you did it the other way." And I'm sure the Government wants to do it where it's the most efficient. But sustained personnel ceilings is a real burden.

I think that that area needs to be examined very thoroughly to be sure that we're not overdoing it, or that there needs to be adjustments in different departments or sections of departments.

THE PRESIDENT. I agree to some extent. Let me give it to you from my perspective.

I have tried to restrain the growth in total Federal employment, but I've tried to do it in such a way as to eliminate excessive employees, when a normal attrition takes place in areas where they're not needed. In order to save time, just let me give you two quick examples.

Within the last 2 or 3 weeks, we've had two Ambassadors retire: one in Switzerland, one in Egypt. The one in Switzerland is a noncareer officer who's a top businessman, very successful. The other one is a career officer, Hermann Eilts, who has served in the Mideast for 30 years.

Both of them, when I asked them on retirement, "What is your major suggestion for improvement in the ambassadorial service?" they said, "We have entirely too many people in the foreign embassies of our country, in Egypt and in Switzerland. We could do a much better job if we had half as many people."

So, I have already contacted the Secretary of State and the Office of Management and Budget, and we're going to send a small team around to visit a representative number of embassies in foreign capitals. And if we can see there that we can do a better job with fewer people, that will be great. And then if we save 200 employees or 2,000 employees, if we can increase the number of agricultural experts who sell American grain overseas——

MR. MULHERN. Amen. Amen!

THE PRESIDENT. ——that's a good change, right? [*Laughter*]

MR. MULHERN. That's right.

THE PRESIDENT. That's the kind of thing we're trying to do. But we have not cut down overall levels of employment. We have tried to maintain them constant. But we've tried to focus the need and fill those needs, and we've tried to eliminate excessive employees where they are not needed.

MR. MULHERN. If the evaluation shows that it's excess, I think everybody is in agreement.

THE PRESIDENT. That's what we are trying to do.

MR. MULHERN. It's when the evaluation is not even made and the decisions are made, that's when we protest.

THE PRESIDENT. I can't deny that sometimes we make a mistake, and sometimes the impositions are arbitrary. But I have really tried to look at it personally. Obviously, I have to take the recommendations of the head of your agencies and also of the Office of Management and Budget, but I get involved in it personally and try to make the best judgment I can.

MR. MULHERN. I don't want to monopolize the time here.

MR. CAMPBELL. Since the President is allotted only a certain amount of time, we ought to at least get one question from one of the women.

THE PRESIDENT. Yes, I'd like that. [*Laughter*]

HEALTH INSURANCE COVERAGE

Ms. GIBSON. Well, Mr. President, I feel that many Federal employees are concerned about health insurance, health benefits. Specifically, will the new health insurance plan contain a clause to cover dentistry? The high cost of dentistry is not covered in most health insurances that we have in government. Has any provision been made for that?

MR. CAMPBELL. Should I respond to that, Mr. President?

THE PRESIDENT. I think I'd better let Alan respond. [*Laughter*] Please do.

MR. CAMPBELL. Yes. We are working with the carriers now about the possibility of including dental coverage in health plans. The difficulty is the dental coverage is very expensive, and health coverage in general is becoming much more expensive. We hope hospital cost containment will help in that regard.

But in order to include dental coverage, there would have to be a very substantial increase in cost of health insurance to both the employees and to the Government.

We are now looking very hard to see if there can be some cutback in some of the medical coverage in order to include dental, and then the employee can make a choice of the kind of package that he or she may want. We're very aware of it. We hope very much we will be able to accomplish it. But within what we think are reasonable costs, it's going to be very difficult.

THE PRESIDENT. And the choice would be made by the employee?

MR. CAMPBELL. Yes, the choice would be made by the employee.

MERIT PAY SYSTEM

MS. GARCIA. I'd like to get back to civil service reform, which I agree is an effective step forward. One major concern I've run into is the merit pay implementation. As a personnel director, I'm responsible for seeing that it's implemented effectively. But I don't think the employees feel that it can be done fair and equitably. I'd like to know your views. And following on that, do you plan to extend recommending merit pay to grade levels other than 13 through 15 supervisory and managerial levels?

THE PRESIDENT. Well, I'll let Scotty Campbell comment after I do.

The concept of the civil service reform laws was understood by me fairly well when we had the debates and when I met with congressional committees and when I went out and met with all the employees in different agencies. And I think that the idea was to try it at those particular pay levels first and make sure that we did have a smoothly functioning program before we extended it to other pay levels.

I think Scotty Campbell, again who sits in a biased position, might very well comment on what he sees as the problems in the implementation, in prospect and already discerned. And maybe you could meet with Scotty later to see if you have any particular cases where you don't think it has worked effectively. You could discuss them with him. Scotty, would you respond to that?

MR. CAMPBELL. Yes, very briefly. First, may I say, to reinforce what you said, Mr. President, about the Senior Executive Service, we are delighted that of the over 3,000 who already have agreed to join, only 7 had said no. This is in contrast to the predictions we got during the period of passage and, I think, speaks very well for the Federal employees at the top. They are willing to take risks. They are willing to be measured against their performance. And on the whole, I would argue that that is demonstration to the public and to all of us that we have a group of top managers in this Government that are willing to put their jobs on the line.

In relation to merit pay, there's no question that since we've not had performance appraisal in the Federal Government that amounted to anything, there is a great deal of concern among those at grades 13 through 15. My own judgment is that we are making good progress. Many of the agencies are now giving training in how you do performance appraisal. And my guess is that, like the Senior Executive Service, after people get through the first fear of change, that there will be a general acceptance of it.

But it is difficult. It's going to take time. The private sector people tell you how difficult it is. But none of the major companies are thinking of abandoning it, because if you don't have performance appraisal, what do you base decisions on? And that means you make automatic decisions, and you lose what we hope will be brought out of it.

I can just assure you, Mr. President, that we are working very hard to provide training in how you do performance appraisal. We're working with the employees in doing so. And I think a year and a half from now we will have the same kind of response to performance appraisal that we are now getting to the Senior Executive Service.

THE PRESIDENT. Scotty, how closely do you work with people like Ms. Garcia to make sure that the initial stages of it are working?

MR. CAMPBELL. We work very closely with the personnel directors across the Government, as well as with the Assistant Secretaries. And I must say, we learn as much from them as they learn from us as we attempt to put these systems into place.

THE PRESIDENT. Well, Scotty, our time has run out, but let me say this: As we get into the program on merit pay more thoroughly in the weeks and months ahead, I hope that if a problem does evolve where you and the personnel directors agree that we've got an unforeseen problem, that you will come to me and let me know about it. And we'll see what we can do to alleviate the problem.

MR. CAMPBELL. I certainly will.

THE PRESIDENT. I think that the principle, as you know, is very similar to the Senior Executive Service, that within a certain reservoir of funds, the ones who do superior work get a higher level of pay. And that, I think, will be an incentive for us all to try to do a better job, to let the

American people be truly proud of the outstanding work that we hope to continue to do in Federal Government service.

I'm part of you, and I'm very pleased today to have you representatives of the different agencies and also the different pay levels and also the different careers come and meet with me. I've learned a lot in preparing for this meeting, and I've also learned a lot from your comments and questions. I wish you well in the future, and I know you wish me the same. We'll do a good job for the taxpayers of our country.

Thank you very much.

MR. CAMPBELL. Thank you.

NOTE: The session began at 2:10 p.m. in the Cabinet Room at the White House.

Alan K. Campbell is Director of the Office of Personnel Management. Questioners were William E. Williams, Deputy Commissioner of the Internal Revenue Service; Rudolph F. McDuffie, manager of laundry for the Army Engineer Center at Fort Belvoir, Va.; Joseph P. Cribbins, a technical adviser on aviation logistics with the Department of the Army; Dr. Francis J. Mulhern, a veterinarian in the Bureau of Animal Industry, Department of Agriculture; Audrey N. Gibson, chief of the Secretary's Correspondence Unit at the Department of Housing and Urban Development; and Angelina Garcia, Director of Personnel Services at the International Communication Agency.

Basic Law of the Federal Republic of Germany

Message to President Walter Scheel on the 30th Anniversary of the Basic Law. May 22, 1979

Dear Mr. President:

On the occasion of the 30th anniversary of the Basic Law of the Federal Republic of Germany, adopted in Bonn on May 23, 1949, I wish to extend to you and to the people of the Federal Republic the very best wishes of the United States of America. The Basic Law has proved itself throughout a difficult and challenging generation of reconstruction and growth as the foundation of one of the most stable and flourishing democratic states in the world. The central place it provides for fundamental human rights and the democratic institutional framework it established have been translated into living practice by your government and people.

The relationship between the Federal Republic and the United States, resting in important part on the democratic vitality which your Basic Law provides, has gathered strength and dynamism over the years. Emerging from a period of turmoil and reconstruction, we entered more than 20 years ago into an alliance partnership which, though it has served its defensive purposes well, has proved to be far more than just a military pact. It has established a framework for mutual understanding and for recognition of the values we share and wish to preserve. In recent years our partnership has acquired a new dimension as a result of the impressive growth in strength and influence of the Federal Republic. My visit to Germany last year and the forthcoming visit of Chancellor Schmidt to the United States symbolize the warmth of German-American relations and the importance of our consultations on crucial international issues.

With congratulations and warm wishes,
Sincerely,

JIMMY CARTER

Financial Reform Legislation

Message to the Congress Proposing the Legislation. May 22, 1979

To the Congress of the United States:
For over a decade, the Federal government has limited the interest rates that savers can receive on their deposits in banks and savings institutions. In keeping with my commitment to eliminate inequitable and unnecessary regulations, I directed an Administration task force, chaired by the Treasury Department, to review the fairness, effectiveness and efficiency of these interest rate controls.

Based on the task force's findings, I am today recommending that the Congress enact comprehensive financial reform legislation. I am asking that the Congress permit an orderly transition to a system where the average depositor can receive market-level interest rates on his or her savings. I am also proposing measures to protect the long-term viability of savings institutions so that they can pay fair and competitive rates to depositors and continue their traditional role in meeting our nation's housing needs.

These actions will reform a system which has become increasingly unfair to the small saver. The present rate ceilings are costing the American people billions of dollars in lost interest annually. Our senior citizens, and others whose savings are concentrated in passbook accounts, have suffered the most. During a period of high inflation, it is particularly unconscionable for the Federal government to prohibit small savers from receiving the return on their deposits that is available to large and sophisticated investors.

The present ceilings have also contributed to sharp fluctuations in the flow of housing credit. Large cyclical swings in the availability of mortgage funds have increased housing costs and forced many prospective homebuyers out of the market during periods of high interest rates. The actions I am recommending today will help assure a steadier flow of mortgage credit for homebuyers.

Savings and loan associations exist to channel household savings into mortgages. Mutual savings banks are also major suppliers of housing credit. Because these institutions invest in long-term, fixed-rate mortgages, they are limited in their ability to meet competitive rates for savings when interest rates rise.

In 1966, interest rates rose sharply, and depositors fled many of these institutions to those able to pay higher interest rates. To prevent the failure of savings institutions and the disruption of the mortgage and housing markets, deposit rate ceilings covering commercial banks were temporarily extended to thrift institutions. The ceilings generally have been administered to permit thrift institutions to pay higher rates of interest than commercial banks.

Conditions have changed dramatically since these limitations were first imposed on thrift institutions. In the current economic and financial environment, the ceilings have the following effects:

• They discriminate against the small saver, who often lacks sufficient funds to purchase market-rate securities which are available to the large investor.

• They are increasingly ineffective in maintaining deposit flows to thrift institutions. The financial marketplace is becoming adept at creating new investment alternatives, such as the money market mutual funds, which induce the small saver to withdraw his funds to obtain benefits similar to those enjoyed by the large investor. While the six-month money market certificate has succeeded in maintaining the flow of housing credit since last year, it has imposed serious pressures on thrift institutions, and it is not a long-term solution.

• They avoid the discipline of competition and create inefficiencies in the financial marketplace. Financial institutions are limited to non-price competitive practices such as merchandising gifts, although the consumer might prefer a higher yield on his savings.

These problems cannot be solved overnight. They are rooted in the structure of our financial system, and their resolution will require a careful and deliberate approach which takes account of the realities facing our thrift institutions.

Our savings institutions have been required by law and influenced by tax incentives to invest primarily in residential mortgages. In most states, the law confines them to long-term fixed-rate mortgages. Their sources of funds—deposits—have considerably shorter maturities. When short-term interest rates rise sharply, revenues are limited by their earnings on the existing longer-term mortgages. Since their deposit liabilities are more volatile than their assets, they must pay depositors market rates or they start to lose their deposits.

While raising or removing the ceilings would give savings institutions the legal power to pay market rates to depositors, their economic ability to do so is still limited by the earnings from their mortgage investments. Savings institutions must be given new investment powers so that they can afford to pay higher rates and maintain the flow of mortgage credit. The transition to freer deposit rates and to new asset powers must be orderly, to avoid major shocks to the financial system.

The disparity between market rates and the ceilings is greatest during periods of high interest rates. Yet that is the time when it is most difficult for the regulatory agencies that set the ceilings to raise them substantially. These agencies are also responsible for the safety and soundness of financial institutions. If deposit interest rates rise sharply, the institutions' earnings come under great pressure unless, at the same time, their earnings are made more responsive to changing interest rates.

Accordingly, I shall ask the Congress to:

• provide that through an orderly transition period all deposit interest rates be permitted to rise to market-rate levels. This will be subject to emergency action on the part of the responsible regulators if the safety and soundness of financial institutions is threatened or the implementation of monetary policy so requires;

• grant the power to offer variable rate mortgages to all Federally-chartered savings institutions, subject to appropriate consumer safeguards. This authority, which would be phased in, would permit thrifts the earnings flexibility to pay competitive rates throughout the business cycle;

• permit all Federally-chartered savings institutions to invest up to 10% of their assets on consumer loans; and

• permit all Federally-insured institutions to offer interest-bearing transaction accounts to individuals.

These steps will bring the benefits of market rates to consumers, promote a steadier flow of mortgage credit and improve the efficiency of the financial markets.

In the interim, I support the efforts of the Federal Reserve, the FDIC, the Federal Home Loan Bank Board and the National Credit Union Administration to take steps to increase the interest rates payable to small savers. I urge them to pursue the direction begun with authorization of the six-month money market certificate, with the goal of increasing the responsiveness of the interest rate ceilings to market rates.

JIMMY CARTER

The White House,
May 22, 1979.

National Hispanic Heritage Week, 1979

Proclamation 4662. May 22, 1979

By the President of the United States of America

A Proclamation

From the earliest days of our Nation's history, Hispanics have played a central role in our country's development. First as explorers, then as settlers, and today as leaders in all segments of society, men and women of Hispanic ancestry have contributed greatly to our national heritage.

As a nation, we have not always properly appreciated these contributions. Too often, Hispanics have been the victim of stereotypes and prejudice. Even today, Hispanics endure a disproportionately high unemployment rate. As a nation, we must reaffirm our commitment to eliminate these residues of prejudice and bigotry.

Our Hispanic American communities continue to grow with our Nation. They share with our Nation a deep pride in their language and culture, and a sense of justice and compassion which nurtures our democratic system and keeps it progressing. It is important that we recognize these singular benefits and encourage their perpetuation.

This country must continue to provide its many ethnic groups with the opportunity to contribute their ideas, their experience, and their energies to the betterment of our society. We must be receptive to the richness of diverse cultures, but we also must work to assure that all Americans benefit in turn from the resulting improvements. With the assistance of our Hispanic citizens and through our own continued commitment, these goals will be achieved.

In 1968, our government formally acknowledged the value of our Hispanic heritage when Congress by joint resolution (82 Stat. 848) asked that the President issue an annual proclamation designating the week including September 15 and 16 as National Hispanic Heritage Week.

Now, THEREFORE, I, JIMMY CARTER, President of the United States of America, do hereby proclaim the week beginning Monday, September 10, 1979, as National Hispanic Heritage Week. I ask that all Americans reflect on the Hispanic heritage of our Nation and on the need to assure that all citizens share in the prosperity and abundance of our great country.

IN WITNESS WHEREOF, I have hereunto set my hand this twenty-second day of May, in the year of our Lord nineteen hundred seventy-nine, and of the Independence of the United States of America the two hundred and third.

JIMMY CARTER

[Filed with the Office of the Federal Register, 4 p.m., May 22, 1979]

Decontrol of Domestic Oil Prices

White House Statement on the House Democratic Caucus Vote Opposing Decontrol. May 22, 1979

The vote today, of course, was a procedural one, but any thoughts that such votes will change the President's policy are completely misdirected.

The President continues to seek a phased end to controls, coupled with a windfall profits tax to finance an energy security fund to help develop alternative energy forms.

The time for ducking the tough issues is past. Continued controls without comprehensive, fiscally responsible measures to encourage conservation, reduce imports, increase domestic production, and support alternatives to petroleum is not responsible policy, is a nonanswer to our Nation's energy problems, and is not acceptable to the administration.

President's Commission on White House Fellowships

Appointment of Three Members. May 23, 1979

The President today announced the appointment of three persons as members of the President's Commission on White House Fellowships. They are:

KENNETH T. BLAYLOCK, of Woodbridge, Va., national president of the American Federation of Government Employees;

J. T. DYKMAN, of Bethesda, Md., president of the White House Fellows Alumni Association and president of the Executive Group, Inc., an investment and real estate firm;

MARGARET BUSH WILSON, of St. Louis, Mo., chairman of the board of directors of the NAACP and chairman of the St. Louis Regional Panel on White House Fellowships.

Federal National Mortgage Association

Appointment of Five Public Members of the Board of Directors.   May 23, 1979

The President today announced the reappointment of four of the public members of the Board of Directors of the Federal National Mortgage Association and the appointment of a new member to replace Ruth Prokop, previously the fifth public member, who has left the Department of Housing and Urban Development to serve as Chairman of the Merit Systems

Protection Board. All these appointments are for terms expiring on the date of the annual meeting in 1980.

To replace Prokop, the President has appointed Henry A. Hubschman. Hubschman is an attorney with the Washington firm of Fried, Frank, Harris, Shriver & Kampelman. He is a former consultant and executive assistant to HUD Secretary Patricia Harris. Hubschman, 31, resides in Washington, D.C.

The four members reappointed today are:

MARVIN S. GILMAN, of Wilmington, Del., executive vice president of Leon N. Weiner & Associates and an associate professor of urban affairs and public policy at the University of Delaware;

JOHN G. HEIMANN, Comptroller of the Currency;

RAYMOND H. LAPIN, president and chairman of the board of R. H. Lapin Co. of San Francisco, a mortgage finance firm;

JOHN D. THOMPSON, president and treasurer of Vijon Realty Co. in Washington, D.C., and president of the National Association of Real Estate Brokers, Inc., which represents black realtors.

National Advisory Council on Indian Education

Appointment of John C. Rouillard as a Member. May 23, 1979

The President today announced the appointment of John C. Rouillard, of La Mesa, Calif., to be a member of the National Advisory Council on Indian Education for a term expiring September 29, 1981.

Rouillard is chairman of the department of American Indian studies at San Diego State University. He is a member of the Santee Sioux and a former high school teacher.

National Cable Television Association

Remarks and a Question-and-Answer Session by Satellite to the Annual Convention in Las Vegas, Nevada. May 23, 1979

THE PRESIDENT. Thank you, Bob. It's a real pleasure to join your meeting in Las Vegas this morning. In fact, I regret not being able to enjoy the city with you, especially as I'm sure that some of you who are riding a better streak at the casinos than I am in the Congress. There are consolations for you, of course. For one thing, the odds are obviously better where you are than they are with me in the Congress. For another, I can be sure that for every one of you who loses, I may gain a bigger supporter for my proposed improvements in the welfare system.

NATIONAL GOALS

However, even though I'm not able to take the day off to relax with you there, we have more serious risks to face together. Thanks to our cable and satellite technology, I'm able to meet with you here in the Map Room of the White House.

Best of all, I can do more than just speak to you. We can have a discussion together, something that cable televison can help make possible more often in the future throughout America, because our democracy is based on the premise that no matter how controversial and complex an issue may be, in the long run public discussion and debate will lead us to better decisions. That is what the founders of this Nation believed themselves 200 years ago. That's exactly how they hammered out the United States Constitution. They got together and they argued until they agreed.

Their example was never more important. Today we are at the same time a prosperous, democratic nation at peace and a divided nation confronting the serious and complicated problems of energy, inflation, and even the possible threat of nuclear war.

Your commitment and your help in making the discussion of these issues both wider and better focused is extremely important. As the technology relating to problems—all the way from oil production to the monitoring of nuclear missiles—becomes so difficult, yours is the kind of communicating technology that our Nation's founders would have welcomed to help us conduct important nationwide debates.

Cable television can help Americans understand that individual proposals such as the windfall profits tax, the wage and price standards, and even the SALT II treaty, are not final solutions to all our national problems, nor are they political spectator sports, nor are they points to be scored in some kind of game of playing the public opinion polls. But they are steps in the continuing search for common ground in our democracy's attempt to deal with the horrors that could come with war or depression or a lack of fuel before these crippling events can occur.

For example, we have an energy crisis in our country, a real energy crisis. Yet too few of our people and even fewer of our politicians are willing to face that reality. I proposed a windfall profits tax now on domestic oil production. It's designed not only to keep oil companies from pocketing billions of dollars in unearned, excess profits but also to begin to work on new scientific and technological solutions that can do for energy what satellites and cable are already doing for communications.

Inflation is even more difficult, because, unlike oil, we can't see it, we can't store it, we can only feel it as it robs all of us—business, people who work in fac-

tories, the elderly, the public. Who then is to blame if we are all victims? Discussion, as we're having this morning, can help us to realize that as each panicked sector tries to shove past another, tries to grab an advantage that's selfish; it's all of us who are robbing ourselves. This has to stop. We have to agree to stop it together.

Above all, I want the American people to discuss the strategic arms limitation treaty that I intend to sign in Vienna, Austria, next month, because it's essential to our responsibility as a force for peace in a nuclear age; because it will make our world safer and our country more secure; because I deeply believe it's the most vital step that we can take to preserve that most fundamental human right, the right that comes first in the Declaration of Independence, the right to live.

I'm not here this morning just to sell SALT or to sell wage and price standards or to sell a windfall profits tax. I'm here to open the discussion with you and among you to get you involved in the free exchange of ideas. That's the only way we can shape real solutions instead of just empty slogans for our complex problems.

And now I'll be glad to take your questions.

QUESTIONS

STRATEGIC ARMS LIMITATION

MR. SCHMIDT. Thank you, Mr. President. We have some cable operators here who would like to ask you a few questions. The first questioner is Bill Daniels of Denver, Colorado.

Q. Mr. President, I believe most Americans share with you a desire to end the threat of strategic weapons. My question is, however, how can we know with sufficient certainty that the Soviet Union is living up to its end of the bargain, especially after the loss of Iran as a listening post?

THE PRESIDENT. Well, in the first place, we've got 20 years' experience with the most advanced national technical means to discern accurately what the Soviets are doing in the design, the testing, the production, and the deployment of nuclear weapons that are controlled under the SALT II agreements. This is a multifaceted capability, depending on all kinds of intelligence, both technical electronics intelligence on the one hand and other forms as well.

We are very secure in our belief that we do have adequate technical means to confirm the SALT agreement, not based on mutual trust, but based on our own ability, with or without the Iran monitoring stations. They were important. We'd like to have them back, or an adequate replacement for them, but they're just one element in an all-inclusive, complex, adequate means by which we can assure compliance with SALT.

For instance, if the Soviets should decide to endanger the entire SALT process, to eliminate the advantages to them of the peaceful prospects to both nations brought about by détente and at the same time to endanger their own reputation in keeping the SALT process going and to go back to the cold war by trying to develop secretly a new missile, for instance, that's forbidden by SALT; not only would they have to go through the whole process of building it and getting a prototype model, but they would have to have at least 20 different test flights of that missile before it could possibly be placed into production and then deployed. It's inconceivable that they could go through this entire process without that process being detected. So, we are not relying upon the honesty of the

Soviets or trust in them, nor are they relying on us for that same assurance. We're relying on our own ability to monitor the Soviets' compliance, and I am convinced, the technicians are convinced, the Joint Chiefs of Staff are convinced, the Department of Defense is convinced that we do have adequate means to assure compliance by the Soviets with the SALT treaty that is proposed, as it has been for the last 15 to 20 years with previous agreements.

Q. Thank you, Mr. President.

INFLATION

MR. SCHMIDT. We have another question here, Mr. President. May I introduce Frank Scarpa of Vineland, New Jersey.

Q. Mr. President, it seems as if the old expression that the only thing certain in life is death and taxes needs to be expanded to add that inflation is another certainty. We've seen economic controls and guidelines come and go, and still inflation is at our throats. People point the finger of blame at Government spending, and the Government points a finger at private sector price increases. Sir, how do we stop blaming the other guy and stop this inflationary spiral?

THE PRESIDENT. Frank, one of the worst things that we can do is to look for a scapegoat or start blaming one another for a problem that's been with us for more than 10 years. The average inflation rate, as a matter of fact, before I became President, the last 3 years before I became President, was a little more than 8 percent. It's something that's been with us for a long time.

There are no trick answers. There are no easy answers. Inflation is a growing problem not only for ourselves but for our very stable, very strong, economically prosperous allies throughout the Western world. The best thing to do is to stick with the programs that we have initiated in the last 2½ years.

Let me give you a few quick examples. One is we are eliminating excess paperwork and redtape and regulation from Government. We've cut down the paperwork burden already by 15 percent. We're still working on it. We're trying to deregulate industries to let them be more intensely competitive.

Most of you flew to Las Vegas, and I think anyone who's been a constant air passenger, for instance, the last few years, will see the extreme advantages of the deregulation of the airline industry. We have saved air passengers about $2½ billion already by lowering prices, because there's more intense competition now in domestic and foreign flights.

I inherited, when I ran for President, for instance, a deficit in 1976 of $66 billion in the Federal budget. I have set as one of my major goals to work toward a balanced Federal budget. We will, this coming year, in the budget that Congress is presently considering, slash that deficit between 55 and 60 percent already. And we can have good momentum and a good support now from the American people to balance the budget actually.

In addition to that, we have established voluntary wage and price guidelines or standards. We are monitoring those compliance data very closely. We supervise with the greatest of attention the prices set, for instance, by the Fortune 500, the very largest corporations, and by an increasing number of middle-sized or even smaller corporations. There's been remarkably good compliance. Almost all of the labor settlements the last year have been within our 7-percent guidelines, a few exceptions, but almost all of them

have complied although this is a voluntary program. We've just got to stick to them.

I have tried the best I could to increase exports, a major cause in the past of very serious inflationary pressures. We are setting records every year. For instance, in agricultural exports, we set one in '77, another record last year. This year we'll have $27½ billion in exports, a new record this year in cutting down our trade deficit.

Eight or nine months ago, if you remember, the headlines almost every day were about the value of the American dollar going down in international monetary trade. We have stabilized the American dollar, beginning last November. And now some of our allies who were complaining in the past about it being too weak, like Germany and Japan, are now complaining that the dollar is too strong.

There are no magic answers. We're going to be faced with inflationary pressures for a long time. But the best thing that we can do is to stick to these programs that have begun and that are proven to be effective, to recognize that every American must contribute. It's not something that just business or just labor or just government can resolve. All of us are going to have to do our best, cut down waste and cooperate.

I don't want to paint an overly rosy picture. For the next 2 or 3 months, we are going to have some serious adverse data coming forward about the inflationary trends. Food looks a little better. I think the general economy is slowing down somewhat. It's going to get better in the near future, but we cannot abandon a permanent commitment to control inflation because we have a temporary disappointment for a few months after it was initiated. We're making good progress; we've got a lot more to go. Everybody's got to work together.

Q. Thank you, Mr. President.

ENERGY

MR. SCHMIDT. With the final question, Mr. President, is our newly elected chairman of the National Cable Television Association, Doug Dittrick, from Ridgewood, New Jersey.

Q. Mr. President, as you know, we are meeting in Las Vegas, an area particularly hard hit by the spreading shortage of gasoline that is now spreading throughout the country. Many of the attendees at our convention are now experiencing difficulty of easily and quickly being able to obtain gasoline. Why has this happened to us so suddenly? And what can we do as consumers, the oil companies, or government to help alleviate this problem?

THE PRESIDENT. Doug, it hasn't happened to us suddenly. I remember in 1973, 1974, when I was a Governor, we were faced with the same problem. And nothing was done. Our Nation didn't even attempt to develop a comprehensive energy policy to cut down on waste; to initiate conservation; to shift away from a heavy dependence on imported oil from the OPEC countries; to build up the use of American supplies of energy, particularly coal; and to shift toward new supplies of energy, like solar and other sources that would be more permanent.

Over 2 years ago, if you remember, after I'd only been in office for 90 days, we submitted to the Congress in April of 1977 a comprehensive energy proposal. This was a difficult issue for Congress to address, because we're not only the major consumers and the major wasters of oil in the whole world, we're also one of the major producers of oil in the whole world. It's a very narrowly divided issue in the

Congress and among the public. Although Congress did pass about 60 or 65 percent of the energy proposals that I put forward, the Congress did not pass a single act that dealt with oil.

More recently, as the shortages have become more apparent, as the OPEC prices have continued to go up, I have gone back to the Congress and said, "Would you please give me the authority to restrain purchases of gasoline, for instance, on certain days of the week, if the Governors in the individual States cannot handle it?" The Congress refused to give me this authority. I even asked for the right to restrain unnecessary lighting in buildings and billboards advertising. The Congress refused to give me this authority.

More recently, I asked the Congress to give me the authority to develop a standby gas rationing plan that would only be implemented in case we have a severe shortage, which I hope we won't have. And it could only be implemented if the Congress and the President both agreed, at that time in the future, that it ought to be implemented. Again, because of excessive timidity, the Congress refused to act.

The main problem is not just with the Congress. The American people have absolutely refused to accept a simple fact: We have an energy crisis. We have shortages of oil. The shortages are going to get worse in the future. We're going to have less oil to burn, and we're going to have to pay more for it.

Now, that is not a politically popular thing to say, but it's an actual fact. And the problem is that I'm afraid the American people are not going to be convinced and, therefore, convince the Congress to take action—and we can deal with this problem if we act together—unless there is such a severe crisis with shortages that the American people are shocked enough to finally say, "We have had enough, let's act courageously; let's start conserving; let's start taxing the oil companies with a windfall profits tax; let's put that money into an energy security fund to emphasize conservation, to develop solar power, to increase the production of coal, to have more research and development, and to deal with the energy crisis."

We can solve it, but I cannot solve it by myself. And I'm not trying to put the blame on other people. But until all of you there, representing the television cable industry, and other leaders in our country can convince the viewers and the listeners of our Nation that we really have an energy problem and they're going to have to induce Congress to act, until that happens, we're going to continue to have these shortages.

The last thing I want to say is this: We're doing the best we can to allot a reduced supply of oil in a fair and equitable way. We have got to build up reserve supplies of oil for the New England area, because 80 percent of the homes in New England are heated by oil. Over 80 percent of the oil they use up there is imported.

We've got to have enough diesel oil to meet the planting season and the cultivating season and the harvest season to produce food for us. The same thing goes for fishermen. They've got to produce fish for us to eat.

We have to have emergency supplies for defense needs—we are being very careful about that—and also for hospital, ambulances and police and fire trucks. That means that when we do have a reduced supply of, say, 5 percent, and those mandatory American users get their full allotment because all of us would suffer if they didn't, it means that we have a lower percentage of gasoline to go to the average

consumer going to and from work or going to and from a shopping trip.

When you go out on the streets either in Las Vegas or wherever you might have as a home, count the number of cars going to and from work that only have one person in them. Look at the trains going by that are almost empty, look at the rapid transit systems going by with buses almost empty, ask how many people eliminate completely unnecessary trips to the local supermarkets. And you'll see that so far, the American people have not faced a sheer fact that we have an energy shortage that is going to get worse in the future unless we act together.

In inflation and in energy, there's a tendency on the part of us to escape responsibility for taking our own actions by looking for someone else to blame for the problem.

I think your questions have been superb. I think they've emphasized three major challenges that I face—peace, the control of nuclear weapons, energy, and inflation. And there's no way that I can solve these problems as your elected President unless the American people are aroused enough and patriotic enough and unselfish enough to work together to solve them. Government can't do it. It has got to be done with the initiative coming and the support coming from the people of this country.

Thank you very much.

Q. Thank you, Mr. President.

MR. SCHMIDT. Mr. President, is there anything you'd like to say in closing?

THE PRESIDENT. Bob, I would like to say how much I appreciate this opportunity. And, as you pointed out, it's the first, so far as I know, in the history of our Nation whereby an opportunity is granted for a President to talk to a large and important group in our American societal structure and to have the response given back, both with applause and questions, where a President can learn at the same time with the full video coverage. And I hope that the listeners here will appreciate the technological advances that have been made in the cable television industry and also will see this as a means by which the American people can influence government, both the Congress and the President, to do an even better job. That's what we want to do, and with your help, I'm sure we can do that and make our great Nation an even greater Nation in the future.

Thank you very much.

NOTE: The President spoke at 12:30 p.m. from the Map Room at the White House. Bob Schmidt is president of the association.

Welfare Reform Legislation

Message to the Congress on the Proposed Legislation. May 23, 1979

To the Congress of the United States:

I am submitting today my Welfare Reform program in two bills: the Social Welfare Reform Amendments of 1979 and the Work and Training Opportunities Act of 1979. Enactment of these proposals will be an important step in addressing the key failings of the present welfare system—promoting efficiency, improving incentives and opportunities to work, and substantially improving the incomes of millions of poor people.

For too many years, we have lived with a welfare system universally recognized to be inadequate and ineffective. It is a crazy-quilt patchwork system stitched together over decades without direction or design. It should offer opportunity, but often breeds dependency. It should encourage and reward useful work, but often penalizes those who find jobs.

The guiding principles of my proposals are simple: those who can work should; and there should be adequate support for those who cannot.

The legislation I am submitting today will:

— redirect our welfare system towards employment wherever possible, and provide training and jobs to break the cycle of poverty;

— help secure stable employment with an adequate income for millions of low-income families;

— save hundreds of millions of dollars each year by reducing waste, fraud, and error through tightened and streamlined administration;

— remove major inequities in the present welfare system and redirect assistance to those most in need and least able to help themselves.

In my campaign I pledged to work for welfare reform. The need for reform is no less serious now. I urge Congress to act promptly on this critically important social legislation. The need for action is clear:

The present system is both inadequate and unacceptably unfair. Despite major efforts at all levels of government in the last twenty years, millions of American families throughout the U.S. still live in poverty. Moreover, under the present system assistance to needy households varies widely from state to state. Welfare benefits, including both food stamps and cash assistance, range from 49 percent to 96 percent of the poverty level. For example, current combined benefits in Mississippi for a family of four are $3,540 per year, while a poor family in Vermont receives $6,540. Twenty-four states have chosen not to provide Federally-supported cash benefits to two-parent families, while twenty-six do provide such assistance.

Many technical provisions of current law are inequitable or unnecessarily restrictive. For example:

—In those states which have adopted two-parent coverage, the family suddenly loses all benefits when the family breadwinner begins to work more than 100 hours a month. For a minimum wage earner that is only $290 per month. Yet a higher wage earner can earn more in 100 hours while retaining welfare benefits.

—A family which has been receiving public assistance and then starts to work, can continue receiving assistance even though their earnings may be higher than those of low-income families who are working but have never been on public assistance.

The present system is cumbersome and needlessly difficult to administer. For example:

—Recipients who work are required to submit detailed lists of work-related expenses—which must then be used to calculate benefits. This is burdensome to the recipient and the system, and invites errors and fraud.

—The basic Federal welfare program and the food stamp program currently have different definitions of income and assets, although the same state offices usually administer both programs, and although welfare recipients are almost always eligible for food stamps as well.

This new legislation makes a number of important program simplifications and adopts measures to reduce error and abuse. Savings from reduced errors in the first full year of implementation will be about $300 million. This is in addition to the Administration's present efforts in child support enforcement and error reduction, which will yield savings of over $800 million in the coming year.

The present system provides insufficient opportunities for families to move off cash assistance and into productive jobs. The great majority of family heads receiving cash assistance want to work.

Most of the poor who are able to work do in fact work, but usually in low paying and sporadic jobs. In 1977, more than three-fifths of the 3.8 million families with children with incomes below the official poverty line had either a part-time or a full-time worker. Over a million of these families were headed by women, most of whom supplemented their meager earnings with welfare. Yet, only one-fifth of these working poor families had a worker who was able to find a full-time, year-round job. In addition, almost three million other families with children live close to the poverty line despite the efforts of one or more family workers.

Even in a period of austerity and fiscal stringency, our Nation cannot afford to ignore its most pressing needs and its most needy. We must do what we can as soon as we can.

The legislation I am submitting today will help to meet the most pressing problems of our welfare system in the following ways:

• *increase employment and training* opportunities. Those who are expected to work will be required to do so if a suitable job is available. In addition, my proposed new legislation will assure participation in a structured job search effort, add resources for training and—for those for whom a private job cannot be found—seek to provide a public sector work opportunity. There will be over 620,000 work and training opportunities for welfare eligibles including 400,000 newly funded public service employment and training slots. The program is structured to assure that required work will always pay more than welfare. Subsidized public sector jobs will only be available to those who have completed a rigorous search for private work. Thus, individuals will have substantial opportunity and incentive as well as a requirement to move from welfare to work. And the legislation assures that states will have substantial incentives to join in the effort to move individuals from welfare to work.

• *improve the fairness and adequacy of welfare cash assistance* to needy families with children by:

—establishing a national minimum benefit (for AFDC and food stamp benefits combined) at 65% of poverty, raising benefits to 800,000 people in the 13 lowest benefit states; mandating coverage of two-parent families in the 24 states which now lack this coverage; and simplifying the benefit computation and eliminating several sources of inequity in the current system.

• *improve welfare administration* by aligning definitions in the Aid to Families with Dependent Children (AFDC) and food stamps programs, standardizing certain deductions that are now itemized, tightening eligibility determinations, and building upon HEW's program of anti-fraud, anti-waste efforts. Furthermore, food stamps will be cashed out for a portion of the needy aged, blind and disabled population receiving Supplemental Security Income (SSI). This step towards program consolidation will extend benefits to needy individuals who are eligible but do not currently participate in the food stamp program, and simplify the welfare system for recipients and administrators.

• *expand the earned income tax credit* to provide greater assistance to low-income working families and provide greater incentives to take private sector jobs.

• *provide fiscal relief* to state and local governments.

These two bills will increase the incomes of 2.3 million families, or nearly 6.5 million people. They will remove from poverty 800,000 families, or 2.2 million people. They will achieve important gains

in reducing error and waste. Their cost—$5.7 billion when fully implemented in FY 1982—is included in the Administration's budget projections submitted to Congress last January and fully consistent with a prudent budget policy.

It is rare that the President and Congress are given the opportunity to work together on legislation that does so much to benefit so many of the most needy.

I recognize that welfare reform is a difficult undertaking. No legislative struggle in the last decade has provided so much hopeful rhetoric or so much disappointment and frustration. We have spent several months in quiet, detailed consultations working to develop a package which I hope provides a basis for a legislative consensus.

I urge the Congress to cap a decade of debate on welfare reform with action. America's people, particularly her poor, have waited long enough for important progress in this area. A society like ours must be judged by what we do for the most needy in our midst. America must meet this challenge. Congress can make an important contribution by enacting the proposals I am making today.

JIMMY CARTER

The White House,
  May 23, 1979.

Foreign Intelligence Electronic Surveillance

Executive Order 12139.   May 23, 1979

By the authority vested in me as President by Sections 102 and 104 of the Foreign Intelligence Surveillance Act of 1978 (50 U.S.C. 1802 and 1804), in order to provide as set forth in that Act for the authorization of electronic surveillance for foreign intelligence purposes, it is hereby ordered as follows:

1–101.   Pursuant to Section 102(a)(1) of the Foreign Intelligence Surveillance Act of 1978 (50 U.S.C. 1802(a)), the Attorney General is authorized to approve electronic surveillance to acquire foreign intelligence information without a court order, but only if the Attorney General makes the certifications required by that Section.

1–102.   Pursuant to Section 102(b) of the Foreign Intelligence Act of 1978 (50 U.S.C. 1802(b)), the Attorney General is authorized to approve applications to the court having jurisdiction under Section 103 of that Act to obtain orders for electronic surveillance for the purpose of obtaining foreign intelligence information.

1–103.   Pursuant to Section 104(a) (7) of the Foreign Intelligence Surveillance Act of 1978 (50 U.S.C. 1804(a) (7)), the following officials, each of whom is employed in the area of national security or defense, is designated to make the certifications required by Section 104 (a)(7) of the Act in support of applications to conduct electronic surveillance:

(a) Secretary of State.
(b) Secretary of Defense.
(c) Director of Central Intelligence.
(d) Director of the Federal Bureau of Investigation.
(e) Deputy Secretary of State.
(f) Deputy Secretary of Defense.
(g) Deputy Director of Central Intelligence.

None of the above officials, nor anyone officially acting in that capacity, may exercise the authority to make the above certifications, unless that official has been appointed by the President with the advice and consent of the Senate.

1–104.   Section 2–202 of Executive Order No. 12036 is amended by inserting the following at the end of that section: "Any electronic surveillance, as defined in the Foreign Intelligence Surveillance Act of 1978, shall be conducted in accordance with that Act as well as this Order.".

1–105.   Section 2–203 of Executive Order No. 12036 is amended by inserting the following at the end of that section: "Any monitoring which constitutes electronic surveillance as defined in the Foreign Intelligence Surveillance Act of 1978 shall be conducted in accordance with that Act as well as this Order.".

JIMMY CARTER

The White House,
May 23, 1979.

[Filed with the Office of the Federal Register,
3:30 p.m., May 23, 1979]

Sunset Review Legislation

Statement by the President.   May 23, 1979

The House Rules Committee today holds important hearings on sunset legislation.

The leading sunset bill, H.R. 2, will double the proportion of the Federal budget that is subject to periodic review. It will ensure that we take a hard look at most Federal programs at least once a decade. Based on those reviews, inefficient and outmoded programs will be changed or eliminated. To assure that the process works, programs will be terminated unless affirmatively reenacted.

Too many Federal programs have been allowed to continue indefinitely without examining whether they are accomplishing what they were meant to do. The country's needs and priorities change, and we must assure that Government programs change with them. Along with civil service reform, reorganization, zero-based budgeting, and regulatory reform, sunset will help make the Government more efficient, more economical, and more responsive. That is why I have long supported the sunset approach.

In addition, H.R. 2 provides for sunset reviews for tax expenditures, and I support that provision. Tax expenditures total over $150 billion. These programs involve spending money for social goals, and they need regular reviews just as much as direct spending programs.

Sunset is a vital tool for controlling the Federal deficit. I congratulate Representatives Blanchard, Gephardt, and Mineta for sponsoring H.R. 2, and I congratulate Chairmen Bolling and Long and Congressman Derrick for the careful study they are giving to this bill and related proposals. I urge the Congress to move forward this year.

President's Export Council

Appointment of 27 Members.   May 24, 1979

The President today announced the appointment of 27 persons as members of the President's Export Council. They are:

JOHN W. BARRINGER, assistant to the president of L. T. Barringer & Co., a Memphis cotton merchant company, and owner of a cattle and cow-cropping farm in north Mississippi;

JOHN WOOD BROOKS, chairman of the board and chief executive officer of Celanese Corp. in New York City;

MORRIS M. BRYAN, JR., president of Jefferson Mills, Inc., in Jefferson, Ga.;

GEORGE D. BUSBEE, Governor of Georgia;

EMILE R. BUSSIERE, a Manchester, N.H., attorney and currently a member of this Council;

WILSON P. CANNON, JR., chairman of the board and chief executive officer of the Bank of Hawaii in Honolulu;

D. L. COMMONS, chief executive officer of Natomas Co. in San Francisco;

ROBERT DICKEY III, chairman and chief executive officer of Dravo Corp. in Pittsburgh;

JOHN NORMAN EFFERSON, chancellor of the Center for Agricultural Sciences and Rural Development at Louisiana State University;

KENNETH ALLEN GIBSON, mayor of Newark;

HARRY E. GOULD, JR., chairman of the board and chief executive officer of Gould Paper Corp. in New York City;

PAT GREATHOUSE, vice president of the United Auto Workers and cochairman of the UAW's International Affairs Department;

PAUL HALL, president of the Seafarers International Union of North America (also appointed Vice Chairman of the Council);

REGINALD H. JONES, chairman of the board and chief executive officer of General Electric (also appointed Chairman of the Council);

P. SCOTT LINDER, chief executive officer of Linder Industrial Machinery Co. in Lakeland, Fla.;

J. PAUL LYET, chairman and chief executive officer of Sperry Rand Corp. in New York City;

JOYCE DANNEN MILLER, vice president and director of social services of the Amalgamated Clothing & Textile Workers Union;

JUN MORI, a Los Angeles attorney and member of the Los Angeles Board of Harbor Commissioners;

HELEN EWING NELSON, of Mill Valley, Calif., president of the Consumer Research Foundation;

JAMES B. PEARSON, a Washington attorney and former U.S. Senator from Kansas;

TONY G. REYES, of Houston, Tex., president and chairman of the board of A–M Cargo, Inc.;

RUTH SCHUELER, president of Schueler & Co. in New York, an international supplier of medical and scientific products;

HERTA LANDE SEIDMAN, deputy commissioner of the New York State Department of Commerce;

MARK SHEPHERD, JR., of Dallas, Tex., chairman of the board and chief executive officer of Texas Instruments Inc.;

MAURICE SONNENBERG, of New York City, an investment consultant on industrial development and international trade;

ROSEMARY TOMICH, of Pasadena, Calif., owner of cattle feeding and livestock brokerage operations;

C. WILLIAM VERITY, JR., chairman of the board and chief executive officer of Armco, Inc.

The President's Export Council also includes:

—three Members of the Senate, appointed by the President of the Senate. They are Senators Jacob Javits, Harrison A. Williams, Jr., and Adlai E. Stevenson.

—three Members of the House of Representatives, appointed by the Speaker. They are Representatives Dan Rostenkowski, Thomas S. Foley, and Bill Alexander.

—the Department heads, or their representatives, of the Department of State, Treasury, Agriculture, Commerce, Labor, the Office of the Special Representative for Trade Negotiations, and the Export-Import Bank of the United States.

President's Export Council

Remarks at the Swearing In of the Chairman and Members. May 24, 1979

This morning I've spent probably 2 or 3 hours dealing with economic problems that face our Nation, primarily based upon international economic circumstances. I doubt if many Americans recognize the rapidly increasing importance of exports to the United States.

Just a few years ago we were almost independent of foreign trade, except for a few rare metals or other items which we were required to either import or to produce ourselves under very difficult circumstances. But that situation has changed dramatically. We've become much more heavily dependent upon imports. And we have seen, in a very beneficial way, a substantial portion of American productivity oriented toward the exporting of American products.

One out of every eight jobs in our country is now devoted to the manufacture and transportation of items to be exported. One out of every four acres of farmland

in our country is now devoted to the production of food and fiber which will be exported. So, this is a very important development in the history of our Nation, economically speaking, and the trend that I've just described so briefly is accelerating.

The challenge is going to be even greater in the future; and, commensurately, the opportunities are going to be even greater in the future.

This Export Council is a major step in the right direction. Under the chairmanship of Reg Jones, helped ably by Paul Hall, Seafarers Union, and with the broad representation, including Governor Busbee and distinguished members of both governments at all levels and the private industry, labor and business, consumers, I think I'll have an excellent avenue to make sure that we speak with a coherent voice and that plans are made productively for our country.

The Export Council can explain to interested private citizens and others, both here in our country and overseas, the policies of our Government, what we are trying to accomplish. At the same time, they will be a counsel for me, to give me advice and to let the Congress and all members of my own administration know how we can do a better job as we face this tremendous challenge in the future.

We've made some progress. This time last year, this time 8 or 9 months ago, the constant headline—almost every day, and I flinched when I read it—was that the American dollar was under attack when there was a problem with the Mideast or OPEC oil or a disturbance in Lebanon or when the Japanese trade agreements were in doubt, immediately the dollar went down. Every time gold went up, the dollar went down. Every time anything happened, the dollar went down. And I think that because we took strong action, the dollar has been very stable ever since the 1st of November.

This has helped us, and I think we are all grateful for this progress. But there can be no permanent stability for the dollar or for the international monetary system unless we are able to alleviate our very serious adverse trade balance. Because of various circumstances, which I won't try to outline this morning because of the press of time, we will reduce our negative trade balance this year about $10 billion compared to last year. It would be better than this if we weren't having an unanticipated sharp increase in OPEC oil prices.

But I think that one of the things we can do to compensate for this or other threatening developments is to dramatically increase the level of exports from our country to foreign nations. This will be a major factor in cutting down on inflation. It'll provide new jobs for our people; it'll give a new spirit of cooperation that might redound to our political benefit; it'll help to maintain peace around the world; it'll provide more harmony within our own country between labor and business, between the private sector and Government. The advantages are overwhelming, and the disadvantages are very few.

When I came into office, the so-called Tokyo Round of the Multilateral Trade Negotiations were in a dormant stage or worse. I think there was a sense of hopelessness when I met with the other Western democratic leaders in London 2 years ago and Bonn, Germany, a year ago, that nothing could be done. Under the superb leadership of Robert Strauss, we have now concluded agreements which are of great benefit to Americans.

The top legislative priority for me this year in international economics will be the early ratification of the Multilateral Trade Negotiations by the Congress. We're trying to work out agreements with the congressional leaders so that this will not be delayed. And I want to be sure that when this obvious advantage to American exporters is consummated into law, that our American producers are ready to take advantage of it.

Obstacles to American goods going overseas will be removed or drastically reduced, and some of the abuses that have been prevalent in imports from foreign countries will also be substantially eliminated. And we must be ready to take advantage of this good opportunity.

The last point I want to make to this group, who are so interested and so competent and who'll play such a major role in the future, is that the Export Administration Act will be renewed this year. There's been a great deal of controversy about this act. What we want to have is sure and prompt export licensing combined with an adequate reserve authority for the President to protect our national security. And the balancing of these two items is one that I feel sure can be better assured because of the new Export Council that's being established this morning.

I want to thank all the members who have expressed your willingness to serve. I think from my brief remarks you can see the breadth of responsibility which will now be on your shoulders. I welcome a chance to form this new partnership. It'll take part of the burdens off me, and I think it will eliminate future problems that we might otherwise have had to face because of a lack of planning and cooperation. It'll help to alleviate the problems that we now face, and it'll make it possible for us in the future to demonstrate, through vigorous action, that the free enterprise system of the United States is the best economic system on Earth.

Thank you very much.

NOTE: The President spoke at 11:28 a.m. at the ceremony in the Roosevelt Room at the White House.

Diesel Fuel Shortages

Announcement of Meeting on Federal-State Cooperation To Resolve Supply Problems. May 24, 1979

The President today announced that he is sending a team of top officials from several Federal agencies to Kansas City tomorrow to meet with Midwestern Governors and their representatives about diesel fuel shortage problems.

Agriculture is one of the sectors of the economy most seriously affected by the current energy shortage. It is particularly vulnerable to disruptions of supply because of its complex and far-ranging distribution system, and because of the critical importance of timing in its need for fuel, especially in the planting and harvesting of crops. Delays in planting due to an unusually wet spring in many parts of the country have further aggravated the situation by compressing the period of time during which plantings must be completed.

The President is strongly committed to meeting 100 percent of farmers' needs for diesel fuel. He has directed the Department of Energy to begin a mandatory allocation of diesel fuel to meet farmers' spring planting requirements. At the same time, the Department requested comments on establishing additional mandatory allocation priorities for mass transit systems.

The President has also instructed the Secretaries of Energy, Agriculture, and Transportation to work jointly with the States to meet farm diesel requirements with minimal disruptions. On Wednesday and Thursday of this week, these Departments sent a team to several Midwestern States to establish clear and explicit procedures for rapid implementation of the mandatory allocation program.

Yesterday the President met with Sen-ators from several farm States to get their viewpoints and suggestions and to outline the actions already underway. Following that meeting, the President directed Deputy Secretary of Agriculture Jim Williams and senior officials of DOE and DOT to meet Friday in Kansas City with Governors or their senior agriculture and energy advisers from a 10-State area to exchange information and to work out mutual problems in meeting the diesel fuel shortage during the critical planting period. The Federal interagency group will also meet with major fuel suppliers for the region while in Kansas City.

In addition, at the President's direction, DOE, USDA, and DOT are immediately assigning staff to the State energy offices, as needed, to assist in resolving diesel supply problems.

In his meeting with the farm State Senators, the President emphasized that middle distillate supplies are extremely tight. He also pointed out that, while we must immediately address the middle distillate requirements of agricultural production, we must also begin to increase inventories in order to meet diesel needs in transportation as well as home heating fuel requirements for next fall and winter.

The President also observed that we can avoid serious disruptions to our people and to the economy only if there is full realization of the energy problem and broad-based cooperation in dealing with it.

The President noted that the diesel allocation program will work only if everyone, including farmers, uses restraint to make it work. For example, the program should not be used to top off farm storage tanks. Unless farmers and suppliers resort to the program only to meet actual requirements, the system will be overloaded and unable to respond to immediate fuel needs.

Sugars, Sirups, and Molasses Imports

Proclamation 4663. May 24, 1979

AMENDMENT OF PROCLAMATION No. 4610 REGARDING THE ALLOCATION OF QUOTAS ON CERTAIN SUGARS, SIRUPS, AND MOLASSES

By the President of the United States of America

A Proclamation

1. By Proclamation No. 4610 of November 30, 1978, I modified Headnote 3 of Subpart A, Part 10, Schedule 1 of the Tariff Schedule of the United States (19 U.S.C. 1202, hereinafter referred to as "TSUS"). The proclamation was designed substantially to bring the United States into conformity with certain provisions of the International Sugar Agreement, 1977, which the United States is applying provisionally, by allocating a large portion of the sugar import quota to certain named countries which at the time of the issuance of the proclamation were parties or provisional parties to the International Sugar Agreement.

2. Taking into account the factors cited in Proclamation No. 4610, and in order to enable additional countries which have become or may decide to become parties or provisional parties to the International Sugar Agreement to share currently in the import quota set aside in Proclamation No. 4610 for the parties to the International Sugar Agreement, I find it appropriate to amend that proclamation by authorizing the Secretary of State to allocate the sugar quota among supplying countries or areas to the extent necessary to conform with the provisions of the International Sugar Agreement, 1977. I find

that the amendment hereinafter proclaimed is in conformity with the International Sugar Agreement, 1977, and that it gives, as provided for in Headnote 2, of Subpart A, Part 10, Schedule 1 of the TSUS, due consideration to the interests in the United States sugar market of domestic producers and materially affected contracting parties to the General Agreement on Tariffs and Trade.

Now, THEREFORE, I, JIMMY CARTER, President of the United States of America, acting under the authority vested in me by the Constitution and statutes, including section 201 of the Trade Expansion Act of 1962, and in conformity with Headnote 2 of Subpart A, Part 10, Schedule 1 of TSUS, do hereby proclaim:

A. The first paragraph of Headnote 3 of Subpart A, Part 10, Schedule 1 of the TSUS is modified by substituting for the second sentence of that paragraph the following:

"This quantity shall be allocated among supplying countries or areas to the extent necessary to conform with the provisions of the International Sugar Agreement, 1977, by the Secretary of State or his designee, after appropriate consultations with the Secretary of Agriculture and the Special Trade Representative. The Secretary of State or his designee shall inform the Commissioner of Customs of such allocation, which shall be published in the FEDERAL REGISTER.

B. The provisions of this proclamation shall become effective with respect to articles entered, or withdrawn from warehouse, for consumption on the day following the publication in the FEDERAL REGISTER of the first allocation made pursuant to this proclamation, except that articles which were released under the provisions of section 448(b) of the Tariff Act of 1931 (19 U.S.C. 1448(b)) prior to such date shall not be denied entry.

IN WITNESS WHEREOF, I have hereunto set my hand this twenty-fourth day of May, in the year of our Lord nineteen hundred seventy-nine, and of the Independence of the United States of America the two hundred and third.

JIMMY CARTER

[Filed with the Office of the Federal Register, 10:20 a.m., May 25, 1979]

The Federal Budget

Statement on Congressional Approval of the First Concurrent Resolution on the FY 1980 Budget. May 24, 1979

The budget I presented to Congress in January restricted Federal spending and reduced the deficit for fiscal year 1980 to less than $30 billion, well under half of what it was when I ran for election. At the time, I said: "This policy of restraint is not a casual one. It is an imperative if we are to overcome the threat of accelerating inflation."

The Congress, in approving the first budget resolution, has joined the administration in recognizing the urgency of fiscal restraint, while still providing for critical national needs. I congratulate the Congress and, in particular, Chairmen Muskie and Giaimo, who guided the resolution through their respective Houses.

National Commission on Employment Policy

Appointment of Nine Members. May 25, 1979

The President today announced the appointment of nine persons as members of the National Commission on Employment Policy.

This Commission was created last October by Public Law 95–524 to advise the President and Congress on national employment and training issues.

The members appointed today are:

MICHAEL J. DUKAKIS, of Brookline, Mass., director of intergovernmental studies at Harvard University's Kennedy School of Government and former Governor of Massachusetts;

ROY R. ESCARCEGA, of Hacienda Heights, Calif., vice president for the social services division of the East Los Angeles Community Union, where he is responsible for the implementation of a $1 million grant from the California Employment Development Department;

PATSY L. FRYMAN, of Fairfax, Va., assistant to the president of the Communications Workers of America, AFL–CIO;

ELI GINZBERG, the A. Barton Hepburn professor of economics at Columbia University's Graduate School of Business and director of the Conservation of Human Resources Project. Ginzberg was Chairman of the National Commission for Manpower Policy, the predecessor of this Commission. He has also been designated Chairman of this Commission;

GEORGE L. JENKINS, of Columbus, Ohio, an attorney and former assistant attorney general of Ohio;

SAM LENA, of Tucson, Ariz., owner of a retail package liquor store, and a former Arizona State senator and State representative;

RUTH LOVE, superintendent of the Oakland (California) Unified School District and former director of HEW's Right to Read Effort;

AUSTIN P. SULLIVAN, JR., of Wayzata, Minn., vice president for government and community relations of General Mills and chairman of the Minnesota Governor's Council on Employment and Training;

JULIUS B. THROWER, of Mobile, Ala., director of admissions and previously director of veterans affairs at S. D. Bishop State Junior College and vice chairman of the American Association of Minority Veterans Program Administrators.

Democratic National Committee

Remarks and a Question-and-Answer Session at the Committee's Spring Meeting.
May 25, 1979

THE PRESIDENT. Coleman said that was a good poll.

I would have been here a little earlier, but my carpool was late. [*Laughter*] When I arrived, I noticed that my free parking place had been taken away. [*Laughter*]

We have some problems in our country. One of them is energy. I told the Congress today—they're going home on recess, leaving Washington—that I could guarantee them enough gasoline to get home. [*Laughter*] Now, the trip back—[*laughter*]—we will have to look into that. Maybe John White, our great chairman, can assess the advisability of a nationwide application of the killer bee program. [*Laughter*]

I didn't come here to announce, and I didn't come here to outline past achievements. I want to speak to you this morning in kind of a rare way for a politician, for a President speaking to his own party leaders and his own personal friends.

I intend to answer questions in a few minutes, but first, I want to talk to you about the responsibility that we share as leaders of the Democratic Party. We won a great victory together in 1976, but the words which Adlai Stevenson used at the Democratic Convention still prey on my mind. He said, "Even more important than winning an election is governing the Nation. When the tumult and the shouting die," he said, "there is the stark reality of responsibility in an hour of history."

The responsibility for governing this Nation belongs to us Democrats. We fought for it, and we won this privilege.

And the American people now are looking closely to see how we discharge this responsibility. Some of that responsibility is very pleasant, very enjoyable, but some of it is very difficult.

You can inventory what we've already done—in cities, in jobs, world peace. But at times like these, it's not adequate, even when Democratic leaders assemble, just to inventory what we have done. The challenge is to look at now, and the challenge is to look to the future and not to sit here and congratulate one another when our Nation still faces troubled times.

In times like these, we must make decisions to deal with those problems, to answer those questions in a way that is not always easy and that's not always popular.

The founders of our Nation wondered whether a government of free people could rise above narrow, sectional interests in times of crisis and work for the good of the whole country. That is exactly the challenge that we face today.

The American people are disturbed, the American people are doubtful, the American people are uncertain about the future, the American people do not have automatic trust in you or me or other Democratic officials.

Too many Americans today are watching the spectacle of politicians grappling with the complex problems, for instance, of energy and inflation. They see the demagoguery and they see political timidity, and they wonder if we who are in office are equal to the challenge.

The American people are looking to us for honest answers—not false claims, not evasiveness, not politics as usual—but they look to us for clear leadership. What they often see here in Washington and elsewhere around the country is a system of government, which we love and which we are sworn to protect, which seems incapable of action. They see a Congress twisted and pulled in every direction by hundreds of well-financed and powerful special interests. They see every extreme position imaginable defended to the last breath, almost, to the last vote, by one unyielding, powerful group or another. They often see a balanced and fair approach that demands sacrifice, a little sacrifice from everyone, abandoned like an orphan without support and without friends. Often they see paralysis, stagnation, and drift. The American people don't like it and neither do I.

This country was not founded by people who said, "Me first, me last, and always." We've not prevailed as a free people in the face of challenge and crisis for more than two centuries by practicing the politics of selfishness. We've not continually enlarged individual liberty, freedom, responsibility, opportunity, human dignity for all the people by listening to the voices of those who say, "We must have 100 percent, now or nothing, and I will not listen to other voices who are seeking a common goal for our country."

The times we live in call for plain talk and call for political courage. Slogans will not do the job. Press conferences will not solve serious problems that we face in inflation, in energy, in maintaining peace in a troubled world.

We have already wasted years, as you know, under Republican leadership, looking for quick fixes, often just before a national election. This is a time to tell the American people the truth. The days of the quick fix and the painless solution, if they ever existed, are gone.

We can argue, we can debate, we can evade, we can duck, but one fact remains clear: So long as we spend our time searching for scapegoats or weeping or wringing our hands and just hoping for some kind of miraculous deliverance, our problems will get worse, the decisions will

get more difficult, the choices will diminish, our people will get more cynical, and the future for our great Nation will be less bright.

I'm not asking you to support verbatim every recommendation which I make. The question today is not whether government reaches solutions which any of us support 100 percent; the question is whether government, on these extremely difficult questions, can reach any acceptable solution at all.

The issue is not one of political philosophies, but a failure of will and a failure of the political process itself. The bottom line is clear. We need positive political solutions in America today, not just a sustained record of negative votes to appease some special, powerful political group back home. Whatever solutions we offer, there should be no illusions in the Democratic Party: No one in public office, in Detroit or in Washington, can escape having to make difficult decisions.

Every public official lives in Harry Truman's kitchen, and there is no way of avoiding the heat if we're going to meet the responsibilities of leadership which the American people have given to us.

As President, I've made mistakes, but I have made and I will continue to make decisions without fear which call for you and for your States to make some sacrifices. These decisions will not always be popular, but I didn't seek the Presidency for 2 or 3 or 4 years with my utmost capability because I wanted to live in some self-imposed comfort in the White House. I sought this office to lead our country, and I will never duck any decision which is vital to the welfare of this Nation just because the popularity polls might go down.

You, the leaders of our party—I need your help and support. And those of us— among those of us who are in positions of responsibility today, if we are unwilling to take the heat to make unpopular decisions, stick together in a semblance of unity to fight difficult battles without fear, to set our goals high, to be inspired, to recognize the potential greatness of our country, to stand up and fight when it's necessary, to offer answers to complicated and complex questions when we know there's no easy way—if we don't do these things, then we will have failed in our own hour of history.

The Democratic Party has a great history. Democrats have never been elected to office just because we wanted to avoid problems, to offer a timid course or a simple solution in difficult times. We are the party of the people not just because we most often win a majority of the votes, but because we believe in an America that's united by a common purpose and not united by a conglomeration of special interests.

Ours is a nation, ours is an America that lives on hope—hope based on a real expectation of fulfillment, not based on fear or cynicism or hatred or divisiveness or selfishness or despair, but based on justice, equality, optimism, and faith. If we are true to these principles, to these values, if we are true to that faith, then we will meet the challenge of leadership in the Democratic Party today. Together, we will succeed in our present task, and under those circumstances, I have absolutely no doubt that we will win again in 1980.

Thank you very much.

I'd like to answer a few questions. I think there are some microphones, and you'll have to go to the microphone, if you don't mind.

QUESTIONS

ADMINISTRATION'S ACCOMPLISHMENTS AND GOALS

Q. Mr. President, we are today the party in power, the dominant party. You are our public and party leader, and yet, Mr. President, it often appears that you may be reticent to fully exercise the entire prestige and power of those positions to bring about all these solutions which you espouse. Could you comment on that, please?

THE PRESIDENT. Yes, I'll try.

I didn't take this opportunity today to list the things we've done. The consummation of a Panama Canal Treaty after 14 years of fruitless effort; the bringing together of Israel and Egypt in a successful peace treaty after 30 years of warfare and hatred and death and destruction and divisiveness; or the conclusion of a SALT agreement after 7 years, when it had been unsuccessful; or the presentation to the Congress of these difficult issues which they have so far successfully resolved—and I didn't talk about civil service reform and the reduction in the unemployment rate by 25 percent and the rejuvenation of our cities, like Detroit—I haven't talked about those things.

But there are many areas of life that still prey on my mind, and I feel on my shoulders the responsibility that we have not successfully addressed and I need your help with them. And I'd like to respond to this question without blaming other people. There's enough blame to go around when we don't succeed. And I know that the President has that responsibility as the preeminent person, and I get my share of the blame, and I am not too weak to take it.

Now, energy is becoming *the* burning issue in our country. In 1980, I predict to you that how we handle the energy question is going to decide who wins and who loses, because the American people are interested in seeing can we work together.

Before I ever took oath of office, for the first time in the history of our Nation, in spite of devastating potential consequences because of an absence of an energy policy, we put one together in 90 days. And I have put more time on energy than I have SALT, the Mideast, Panama Canal Treaty, or any other foreign policy questions all put together.

And in April of 1977, I presented to the Congress a comprehensive, reasonable energy proposal. And I have been scorned and ridiculed by the press or others because I said this was the moral equivalent of war and that we actually have a very serious question. In many ways, I have been a lonely voice up until this moment. We've got a serious energy question, not only in the United States but around the world.

The Congress passed about 60, 65 percent of all of our energy proposals after almost 2 years of begging and pleading and threatening and hard work. They did not pass one sentence about oil. Now, I recognize that's a difficult proposition, because our Nation is not only one of the largest users and wasters of oil, but we are also one of the largest producers of oil. And the producers of oil have a powerful lobby, perhaps the most powerful lobby on Earth. And the Congress has not acted yet on a single issue that relates to oil.

Nobody here has forgotten about 1973, 1974 when we had gas lines. The situation has not improved. We're running now 2 or 3 million barrels a day less oil being produced than we are consuming on a worldwide basis, and American production of oil has been going down about 6 percent per year for the last 10 years.

It is obvious to anyone that looks at it that we've got a problem that's serious now. It's going to get more serious in the future. We're going to have less oil; we're going to have to pay more for it. Those are facts. They are unpleasant facts. And

so far, the American people, whom I do not want to condemn, and the Congress of the United States, who I do not want to condemn, have refused to accept that simple fact.

We are now using, for instance, in California, 7 percent more gasoline than we used a year ago. And we have less gasoline to go around. We're trying to plant crops in Iowa, Nebraska, Illinois, Ohio, and madly trying to move enough diesel fuel so the tractors won't stop, trying to build up reserve supplies of fuel in New England to heat homes this fall.

And the Congress has still not given me the authority that I have asked for. They rejected, including the Democrats, the proposals that I have made on rationing—not even willing to give me the authority to hold down waste of illumination on buildings and on billboards; not giving me the authority, if the Governors fail and request it, to reduce the sale of gasoline 1 day a week; not even willing to give me the authority to develop a standby rationing plan, just to develop one that could not go into effect unless a crisis existed and the President and the Congress agreed to put it into effect.

I'm not blaming the Congress, because the American people have not yet demanded this. They think that somehow or another a miracle is going to occur and a lot of oil is going to be released from secret hiding places, and if the Federal Government and the oil companies would just quit cheating everybody, the energy problem is going to blow over. That's not going to happen.

The Congress has got two proposals this year on inflation—real wage insurance, to tell the working people, whom you and I care about, "If you'll agree to hold down your wage demands and the inflation rate goes up, we'll give you a tax reduction so you won't lose by trying to be patriotic." I have not been able to get legislation out of committee. And the other bill that we have proposed to the Congress is on hospital cost containment. And I said a few minutes ago that the oil companies had the biggest and most powerful lobby. It's almost matched by hospital owners and doctors, many of whom are the same people, and you think, where is the competitive nature of health care? Who keeps the hospitals from putting people in the beds unnecessarily, performing operations that are not necessary? If somebody is going to be operated on Tuesday morning, put them in the bed on Friday so the hospitals can derive more profit, perform procedures that are not necessary—that's what we're trying to stamp out.

I'm having a terrible time getting that bill out of the Ways and Means Committee. I can't get it out of the commerce committee in the House, and I admit that this failure that I just described to you is, to a major degree, my fault. Maybe if I was a better politician, I would have gotten these bills through the Congress.

I've done the best I could. I have never backed down. I'm going to continue to fight. But I guarantee you, almost, this: that if everyone in this room would put 10 percent as much time trying to get hospital cost containment passed and to deal with our energy problem, I believe we could succeed. What Member of Congress, as a Democrat, could stand up against you? Very few.

We're coming up now with SALT. I have one life to live on this Earth. I've got one political career. And I will never face an issue—unless our country actually goes to war, God knows I hope it doesn't happen—but absent that, I will never face an issue so important as getting SALT ratified by the Senate. I won't tell you all the reasons now. But I need you to help me with it, not in a quiet way, saying, "I think

that's a great idea, I hope it passes," but in there fighting for it.

And I haven't made my announcement of what I'm going to do in 1980, but I've never backed down from a fight; I've never been afraid of the public opinion polls. And if and when I decide to run, it would be in every precinct in this country, no matter who else ran. And I have no doubt that it would be successful, because we've got a good record. And if we can prevail on these three issues—energy, inflation, and SALT—we'll have an even better record.

And I think with the courage that you asked me to exhibit—and I'll do the best I can to alleviate your concerns—if you will help me, we'll win, because we deserve to win, not because we're Democrats, but because we deserve to win.

OIL PRICE DECONTROLS

Q. Mr. President, first of all, I'm delighted to see that you have the sign behind you that you used in Virginia when you addressed our Jefferson-Jackson Day dinner. You addressed that group with the same courage and conviction that you have addressed us. I happen to be a Democrat. I've supported Democrats always from the courthouse to the White House. I started with Franklin Delano Roosevelt and moved right up to Jimmy Carter, and I've never regretted supporting the Democratic nominee and feel that we have offered the best the entire time.

I waited a while before I supported Jimmy Carter because, simply, I felt I was supporting one of the greatest men that I've ever had the privilege of supporting, and that was Hubert Humphrey. When I was assured that Hubert Humphrey was not going to be a Presidential candidate again, I've had the pleasure of supporting the man that I place in the same category that I placed Hubert Humphrey, a man of conviction and courage and vision, who has really led the Democratic Party, and one in which we can be proud.

And I want you to know that I feel that I speak for the majority of the group of the people here, as well as the majority of the group of people in America, that we want Jimmy Carter as our President again in 1980.

Mr. President, in World War II, I never saw controls bring about more of anything that we needed, and I simply support your theory of decontrol today, but we need some help in explaining that to the American people. Please give us that answer.

THE PRESIDENT. Thank you.

Well, you know, this is one of the— that's one of the best questions I've ever had, by the way. [*Laughter*] You know, I've sweated over this energy thing in the face of repetitive disappointments. We put forward a COET tax last year, you remember, a crude oil equalization tax that would have decontrolled oil, brought in to the Government a substantial amount of money—and we couldn't get it out of the Senate committee.

Now we've got a good package. Decontrol will be phased in over 28 months, slow, steady, and controllable. We can watch what goes on. We'll tax the oil companies heavily—and I don't care if the Congress makes it a little bit heavier—as the price of oil goes up, either because of OPEC or because of decontrol here, with a windfall profits tax. That profits tax is not a sure thing. It seems like a sure thing now. The day after I made my announcement, everybody said it didn't have a chance in the world to pass; now, everybody says it's going to pass whether we work or not. It's not.

Out of that windfall profits tax, which will grow year by year, we will create an energy security fund. That energy security fund will be a very important element of

dealing with the energy question. It will go, first of all, to help the very poor families, who cannot afford the rapidly increasing, inevitable prices of energy.

Secondly, it'll go to help us with mass transit, because a lot of people either don't have automobiles or, as is the case right now in California, for instance, people are beginning to see that it's better for them to go to and from a fixed destination, like a work place, on public transportation. That'll be a great boost.

And the third thing is to have a substantial amount of money growing every year for research and development, to let us have new sources of energy, like solar power, like liquefaction and gasification of coal, like geothermal power, the very things that all of you want. And it will leave the oil companies about 29 cents out of each dollar to put back into the exploration in the United States for increased supplies of oil and gas. To me it's a balanced program.

The Congress is wasting its time now passing resolutions about, "Are we or are we not going to decontrol?" That serves to cloud the issue so much on the windfall profits tax that it puts it in danger. And I hope that the Democrats and Republicans, the President and the Congress, all of you, and the American citizens will join in together and say, "Let's pass this package once and for all."

I would hate to see it fail. But it's going to require a concerted effort by all those who are interested in the future of our country. There is not a single vote, I guarantee you, in the energy question.

I have made many mistakes in my life. One of the worst mistakes I made was the evening in April of 1977 when I told the American public we've never had a comprehensive energy policy. When I propose this energy policy and fight for it, I said, to about 40 million people, my public opinion poll is going to go down 15 points.

The mistake I made was, it has gone down much more than that—[*laughter*]—and I think energy is one reason. But we can't back down. And I'm willing to fight this fight and to win it, and we will win it with your help.

1980 DEMOCRATIC NATIONAL CONVENTION

Q. Mr. President, my name is George Schwartz from Philadelphia, the birthplace of our Nation. And all I want is a little equal time with the mayor from Detroit. [*Laughter*]

I am presently the chairman of the host committee for the site selection committee when they come to Philadelphia June 7 and 8. I was also chairman of the delegation that came down here several weeks ago to make our presentation.

I merely want to bring to your attention the fact—and you mentioned Harry S. Truman and the heat in the kitchen, and I agree with you—in 1948, President Truman was under attack, was under criticism, very much like yourself, and what do you think he did? He came to Philadelphia. [*Laughter*] And it was a very successful convention for Mr. Truman, and he was reelected. Thank you very much, Mr. President. [*Laughter*]

THE PRESIDENT. I've got to go now, but let me say this, in closing, to you.

We talk about problems, and we talk about fears and doubts, we talk about divisiveness, we talk about concerns among the American people about government. I was facing about a thousand or so people in Portsmouth, New Hampshire, not too long ago. I hadn't planned to say it, but watching those people and their dreams and their hopes and their genuine concerns—I'm sure there were a lot of Republicans and Democrats in the audience—I felt that every one of them wanted their President to do a good job. I think a lot of them there, most of

them, were willing to give me help. And I closed my remarks by pointing out to them that in the news media, what we always see is the argument, the debate, the contention, the difference, the adverse vote, the criticism, the statistic that's not going well. But what we fail to remember—and I don't think that the news media ought to have to publicize this; I'm not saying that—what we fail to remember is our country is so strong economically, politically, militarily, morally, philosophically. We live in the strongest country on Earth, and we have a degree of freedom and a sense of individuality that lets us debate issues and lets us resolve those issues in a political context.

I can't dominate a single person in this Nation. I don't want to. That's not the role of a President. But the strength that we have can tide us over if we are threatened from overseas, or as we deal with a tiny nation looking to us for fairness, or as we reap the consequences of worldwide inflation, or as we acknowledge among ourselves, eventually, that we do waste too much energy. These kinds of things can be resolved, and that's why I'm so sure that the future for our Nation is going to be much greater than its past has been. And I'm very proud to be part of you and the leader of a party that has always espoused not fear, but hope; not divisiveness, although we're so different one from another, but cohesion and unity when it was critical for our Nation.

We have never failed our country—we Democrats—and I don't believe we'll fail in the future. So, in spite of our problems, I look forward to the future, including 1980.

Thank you very much.

NOTE: The President spoke at 11:53 a.m. in the Park Ballroom at the Sheraton-Park Hotel. He was introduced by Mayor Coleman Young of Detroit.

Department of Energy

Nomination of John Mark Deutch To Be
Under Secretary. May 25, 1979

The President today announced that he will nominate John Mark Deutch, of Lexington, Mass., to be Under Secretary of Energy. He would replace Dale Myers, who has resigned. Deutch is currently Director of the Office of Energy Research.

He was born July 29, 1938, in Brussels, Belgium, and became an American citizen in 1946. He received a B.A. in history and economics from Amherst College and a B.S. in chemical engineering from Massachusetts Institute of Technology in 1961, and a Ph. D. in physical chemistry from MIT in 1965. He was a postdoctoral fellow at the National Bureau of Standards.

From 1961 to 1965, Deutch worked on systems analysis in the Office of the Secretary of Defense. In 1965 and 1966, he was a consultant for program analysis in the Bureau of the Budget. From 1966 to 1969, Deutch was an assistant professor of chemistry at Princeton University. He was on the faculty at MIT from 1970 until he became director of the Office of Energy Research in 1977. He was chairman of the chemistry department from 1976 to 1977.

Deutch serves on the Defense Science Board and the Army Science Advisory Panel. He is the author of numerous publications.

Digest of Other White House Announcements

The following listing includes the President's public schedule and other items of general interest announced by the White House Press Office and not included elsewhere in this issue.

May 20

The President returned to the White House following his commencement address at Cheyney State College, Cheyney, Pa.

May 21

The President met at the White House with:

—Zbigniew Brzezinski, Assistant to the President for National Security Affairs;

—Frank B. Moore, Assistant to the President for Congressional Liaison;

—the Cabinet;

—U.S. Ambassador to Egypt Alfred L. Atherton, Jr., and Mrs. Atherton.

The President participated in a briefing by administration officials on the strategic arms limitation agreement given for a group of Senators in the East Room at the White House.

May 22

The President met at the White House with:

—Dr. Brzezinski;

—Mr. Moore;

—the Democratic congressional leadership;

—Mrs. Carter, for lunch;

—James T. McIntyre, Jr., Director of the Office of Management and Budget.

In a ceremony in the Oval Office, the President greeted Lisa Branchina, 15, of Hampton, Va., the 5 millionth winner of the Presidential Physical Fitness Award. Participants in the ceremony included officials of the President's Council on Physical Fitness and Sports, and the American Alliance for Health, Physical Education, Recreation and Dance, Minnie

Branchina, Lisa's mother, and George Nailor, Lisa's physical education teacher.

The President participated in a briefing by administration officials on the strategic arms limitation agreement given for a group of civic and community leaders in the East Room at the White House.

May 23

The President met at the White House with:

—Dr. Brzezinski;

—Mr. Moore, Danny C. Tate, Deputy Assistant for Congressional Liaison (Senate), and William B. Cable, Deputy Assistant for Congressional Liaison (House);

—Senators J. James Exon, Birch Bayh, John C. Culver, Gary W. Hart, Nancy Landon Kassebaum, George McGovern, and Edward Zorinsky, Secretary of Energy James R. Schlesinger, and White House staff members, to discuss the energy situation in the Midwest;

—Vice President Walter F. Mondale, Stansfield Turner, Director of Central Intelligence, Hamilton Jordan, Assistant to the President, and Dr. Brzezinski;

—Representative James R. Jones of Oklahoma, to discuss hospital cost containment legislation;

—Senator Donald W. Riegle, Jr., of Michigan;

—Representative William R. Cotter of Connecticut, to discuss hospital cost containment legislation.

The President has designated the Secretaries of Commerce, Housing and Urban Development, and Transportation, the Administrator of General Services, the Chairman of the National Museum Services Board, and the Director of the Institute of Museum Services, as members of the Federal Council on the Arts and the Humanities.

The President participated in the swearing-in ceremony for Richard F. Celeste as Director of the Peace Corps held in the East Room at the White House.

May 24

The President met at the White House with:

—Vice President Mondale, Secretary of the Treasury W. Michael Blumenthal, Charles L. Schultze, Chairman of the Council of Economic Advisers, Alfred E. Kahn, Advisor to the President on Inflation and Chairman of the Council on Wage and Price Stability, Barry P. Bosworth, Director of the Council on Wage and Price Stability, Stuart E. Eizenstat, Assistant to the President for Domestic Affairs and Policy, and Mr. McIntyre;

—Dr. Brzezinski;

—Mr. Moore, Mr. Cable, Mr. Tate, and Robert G. Beckel, Special Assistant for Congressional Liaison (House);

—Vice President Mondale;

—Peter Shapiro, chief executive of Essex County, N.J.

The President participated in a briefing by administration officials on the strategic arms limitation agreement given for a group of civic and community leaders in the East Room at the White House.

The President is sending Deputy Assistant to the President Bill Simpson on a followup tour of the flood disaster area in Mississippi. The President has directed Simpson to talk with State and local officials and with citizens in Jackson and smaller communities, and to provide him with an update on the progress of the recovery effort in all affected sections of the

State. Simpson will visit Columbia, Valley Park, Canton, and Jackson on Friday, May 25, to gather information for his report to the President.

May 25

The President met at the White House with:

—Vice President Mondale, Secretary of Defense Harold Brown, Deputy Secretary of State Warren Christopher, Dr. Brzezinski, and Mr. Jordan;

—Mr. Moore;

—Mr. Schultze;

—R. Heath Larry, president, and Forrest I. Rettgers, executive vice president, National Association of Manufacturers.

The President left the White House for Camp David, Md., where he spent the Memorial Day weekend.

NOMINATIONS SUBMITTED TO THE SENATE

The following list does not include promotions of members of the Uniformed Services, nominations to the Service Academies, or nominations of Foreign Service officers.

Submitted May 21, 1979

WILLIAM CORNET PRYOR, of the District of Columbia, to be an Associate Judge of the District of Columbia Court of Appeals for the term of 15 years, vice J. Walter Yeagley, retired.

Submitted May 22, 1979

ROBERT N. CLEMENT, of Tennessee, to be a member of the Board of Directors of the Tennessee Valley Authority for the remainder of the term expiring May 18, 1981, vice William Lewis Jenkins, resigned.

RICHARD D. CUDAHY, of Wisconsin, to be United States Circuit Judge for the Seventh Circuit, vice a new position created by P.L. 95–486, approved October 20, 1978.

SUSAN H. BLACK, of Florida, to be United States District Judge for the Middle District of Florida, vice a new position created by P.L. 95–486, approved October 20, 1978.

NOMINATIONS—Continued
Submitted May 22—Continued

JOSEPH C. HOWARD, SR., of Maryland, to be United States District Judge for the District of Maryland, vice a new position created by P.L. 95–486, approved October 20, 1978.

SHIRLEY B. JONES, of Maryland, to be United States District Judge for the District of Maryland, vice a new position created by P.L. 95–486, approved October 20, 1978.

JAMES B. MORAN, of Illinois, to be United States District Judge for the Northern District of Illinois, vice a new positon created by P.L. 95–486, approved October 20, 1978.

Submitted May 24, 1979

JOHN V. PARKER, of Louisiana, to be United States District Judge for the Middle District of Louisiana, vice a new position created by P.L. 95–486, approved October 20, 1978.

SCOTT O. WRIGHT, of Missouri, to be United States District Judge for the Western District of Missouri, vice a new position created by P.L. 95–486, approved October 20, 1978.

CHECKLIST OF WHITE HOUSE PRESS RELEASES

The following listing contains releases of the White House Press Office which are not included in this issue.

Released May 20, 1979

Advance text: remarks at the Cheyney State College commencement exercises

Released May 21, 1979

Announcement: nomination of William C. Pryor to be an Associate Judge of the District of Columbia Court of Appeals

Released May 22, 1979

Announcement: nomination of Richard D. Cudahy to be United States Circuit Judge for the Seventh Circuit

Announcement: nomination of Susan Black to be United States District Judge for the Middle District of Florida

Announcement: nomination of James B. Moran to be United States District Judge for the Northern District of Illinois

Announcement: nomination of Shirley B. Jones to be United States District Judge for the District of Maryland

CHECKLIST—Continued

Released May 22—Continued

Announcement: nomination of Joseph C. Howard, Sr., to be United States District Judge for the District of Maryland

Released May 23, 1979

News conference: on welfare reform legislation—by Secretary of Health, Education, and Welfare Joseph A. Califano, Jr., Secretary of Labor Ray Marshall, and Stuart E. Eizenstat, Assistant to the President for Domestic Affairs and Policy

Released May 24, 1979

Announcement: nomination of Scott O. Wright to be United States District Judge for the Western District of Missouri

Announcement: nomination of John V. Parker to be United States District Judge for the Middle District of Louisiana

Released May 25, 1979

Advance text: remarks at the Democratic National Committee spring meeting

Announcement: nomination of Sylvia H. Rambo to be United States District Judge for the Middle District of Pennsylvania

CHECKLIST—Continued

Released May 25—Continued

Announcement: nomination of Abner J. Mikva to be United States Circuit Judge for the District of Columbia Circuit

Announcement: nomination of Richard P. Conaboy to be United States District Judge for the Middle District of Pennsylvania

---

ACTS APPROVED BY THE PRESIDENT

Approved May 23, 1979

S. J. Res. 80_____ Public Law 96–12
A joint resolution to confer certain powers on the Presidential Commission appointed to investigate the Three Mile Island nuclear powerplant accident.

Approved May 24, 1979

S. J. Res. 71_____ Public Law 96–13
A joint resolution to authorize and request the President to proclaim the week of May 6 through 12, 1979, as "National Historic Preservation Week".

S. 532_____ Public Law 96–14
Pension Policy Commission Act.

PRESIDENTIAL DOCUMENTS

Week Ending Friday, June 1, 1979

Gold Medal for John Wayne

Statement on Signing S. 631 Into Law.
May 26, 1979

I have today approved S. 631, a bill to authorize the presentation of a specially struck gold medal to John Wayne. For nearly half a century, the Duke has symbolized the American ideals of integrity, courage, patriotism, and strength and has represented to the world many of the deepest values that this Nation respects. His conduct off the screen has been as exemplary as that of the characters he has portrayed. He has served, and will continue to serve, as a model for America's young people.

I ask all Americans to join with me in expressing our best wishes to John Wayne as he celebrates his 72d birthday this Saturday.

NOTE: As enacted, S. 631 is Public Law 96–15, approved May 26.

John H. Wood, Jr.

Statement on the Death of the U.S. District Judge. May 29, 1979

I am shocked and saddened by the death today of U.S. District Judge John H. Wood, Jr., in San Antonio, Tex. The killing of a Federal judge—or any judge—is an assault on our very system of justice. All Americans join me in condemning this heinous crime.

Judge Wood had a 30-year career in the private bar, followed by 8 years on the bench, where he served with distinction. A jurist who was courageous, hard-working, tough-minded, and fair, Judge Wood was admired by prosecutors and defense lawyers alike.

I have been assured by Attorney General Griffin Bell that Director William Webster and the Federal Bureau of Investigation have given top priority to bringing those responsible for Judge Wood's murder to justice. Deputy Assistant Director James Ingram of the FBI has been dispatched from FBI headquarters in Washington to take charge of the Federal investigation. Fifty special agents and two FBI specialists have been assigned to the investigation in Texas.

I know I speak on behalf of the American people in expressing outrage at the senseless death of Judge Wood. Rosalynn and I extend our deepest sympathies to his family and friends.

THE PRESIDENT'S NEWS CONFERENCE OF MAY 29, 1979

ENERGY

THE PRESIDENT. No matter how Americans may differ on energy, we are united on two basic goals: first, to provide every possible means to alleviate the current crisis at all levels of government and in the private sector of our economy; and, second, to get this country firmly on the way toward more lasting solutions for the energy question and to keep it there.

First things first: Today, by Executive order, I'm delegating to all the Nation's Governors the authority to help manage our gasoline supplies over the summer. Using these powers, which I have authority to delegate, the Governors will be able to require that at least some gasoline stations remain open on weekends, to establish minimum purchase requirements, to prevent tank topping, which can convert a scarce surplus into spot shortages, and to impose an odd-even day sales system to reduce crowding and confusion by enabling drivers to buy gasoline on alternate days according to their license plate numbers.

Some of this authority already exists in some of the States, but this action will assure that all Governors throughout the Nation have help in managing the kind of situation that existed this month in Nevada, California, and some other places in our country.

These steps will simply make it more convenient for drivers to purchase gasoline, but they do not save oil or gasoline. While some increased supply and better management may minimize inconvenience, continued care, planning, and conservation will be required throughout the summer if we are to avoid gasoline lines and spot shortages.

As I've said so often, our country faces a long-term, chronic problem in obtaining adequate energy supplies to meet our needs. We have not yet addressed this basic problem. Until we put in place policies that will cut back demand, reduce waste, ensure maximum production of oil here at home, and develop alternate supplies of energy—alternates to oil—we

will have to continue to live with the prospect of shortages.

It's necessary to stop aggravating the problem by blaming one another and by seeking out scapegoats. The fact is that the oil-producing countries are holding down supply while the rest of the world has increased demand. Our current difficulties have been made more severe by the stoppage of Iranian production this winter. Over 200 million barrels of oil which the world expected to have was simply not produced.

To meet demand over the winter and the spring, we had to draw down on our own supplies and also our own reserves, and reserve supplies of crude oil now are at very low levels. Since it takes 60 to 90 days for oil to be moved from a country like Iran across the ocean to our ports to be refined and then distributed, we are still feeling the loss of oil from that country even though Iran is producing oil again.

We now expect to see mild increases in oil supply, which should help to alleviate our present spot shortages. But in spite of this improvement, we will at best only have—at *best* we will only have about the same amount of oil during the summer that we had a year ago. In the meantime, Americans are expecting to use more than we had a year ago. Unless we are able to plan carefully and to conserve properly, spot shortages may exist.

As this Memorial Day has indicated, Americans are able to conserve energy if they are determined to do so. For example, Charles Warren, my Special Representative in California, reports that the use of trains and rapid transit in California was way up.

But I believe this country is capable of doing much more than just getting through the summer. Phased decontrol will begin June 1 to reduce our subsidy of imported oil and to increase domestic production of oil.

I've also proposed a windfall profits tax to capture, for public benefit, a substantial portion of the increased prices of oil resulting from decontrol. And I proposed an energy security fund to protect those who are least able to afford the rapidly increasing costs of energy, to improve mass transportation systems in our country, and to bring the full force of American science and technology to bear on this crucial problem.

These proposals, while not universally popular, are essential to get this country moving firmly on the way to a more lasting solution for our energy problem. I hope that I can have the support of the Congress and the American people for these energy proposals.

And now, I'd be glad to answer questions.

QUESTIONS

OIL SUPPLIES AND PRICES; PRESIDENT'S
USE OF HELICOPTERS

Q. Mr. President, I have a three-part question. What do you say to Members of Congress and the industry who say that decontrol will not lead to greater supplies? Also, what do you say to poor people who cannot afford the needed gas at these higher prices? And why did you use helicopters for two private fishing trips in recent days?

THE PRESIDENT. Can I take my choice of the questions? [*Laughter*]

Q. You can start from the beginning. [*Laughter*]

THE PRESIDENT. I'm convinced that the government control of oil prices has not worked. We presently have controls. Oil production in this country has continued to go down about 6 percent per year. Dependence on imported oil has gone up drastically, so that in spite of very rapid increases in the cost of foreign oil, our country has seen its imports now equal about one-half total consumption. This has robbed our Nation of valuable dollars. It's cut our country out of potential jobs. It's created very serious problems in our trade balance, and it's discouraged American production. It's also subsidized foreign oil and made energy seem to be much cheaper for consumers than it actually is.

I think it's better to reduce the Federal bureaucracy and to decontrol oil prices very slowly and steadily—oh, just 1 or 2 percent per month for 28 months—so that we can have increased domestic production and a reduction in imports.

As far as the poor people are concerned, we are only willing to let the oil companies keep, out of each dollar increased in price, about 29 cents. The rest goes to either local or State or Federal governments or to the owners of land where oil is produced.

The income for the Federal Government from the windfall profits tax, brought about by decontrol of oil, will go into an energy security fund. A substantial portion of this fund will be used to pay to poor families for the increased cost of oil and other energy. The rest of it will go, as I said, for rapid transit and to produce additional supplies of oil.

It's much less expensive for me, when I travel from one place to another, to go by helicopter. When I go by highway, because of security requirements, I have a very large entourage, including seven or eight carloads of press who follow me when I go by car. And at each intersection along the highways, the State Police have people there to guard the intersections to prevent my injury in case of an accident. So, it's much less expensive for me to go by helicopter.

TAX REDUCTIONS

Q. Mr. President, election year tax cuts are rather commonplace in this country, and I wonder if we can look forward to a Carter-proposed tax cut in 1980.

THE PRESIDENT. No, I doubt very seriously that we'll have any tax cut in 1980. My own major responsibility is to deal with the inflation question. Part of that, of course, is to be fiscally responsible in reducing the Federal deficit. If we have the option between substantial reductions in the deficit and controlling inflation on the one hand, and having tax reductions for the American people in an election year on the other, I would forgo the tax reduction and insist upon controlling inflation and cutting the deficit.

WAGE AND PRICE GUIDELINES

Q. Mr. President, United Airlines and the machinists union last week reached a contract settlement that was well over 30 percent, yet another assault on your 7-percent wage guidelines. How long can you expect the American people to sit tight and support a 7-percent guideline, when inflation is running at over 13 percent over the last 3 months and when the big unions are getting fat contracts?

THE PRESIDENT. Well, the problem is finding a suitable alternative. I don't maintain that every settlement in the last 6 or 8 months has been under the 7-percent guideline. There is absolutely no doubt in my mind, however, that the price constraints and the wage constraints that we have imposed on a voluntary basis have had very beneficial results. Eighty-five percent, at least, of all the wage settlements since we imposed the voluntary standards have been within the 7-percent guidelines. Even those that have exceeded the guidelines, in my opinion, have been

much lower than they would have been without the restraints.

We're trying to do three things, and we're going to stick with it: first of all, to have a fiscally responsible government, to cut down waste, and to reduce the Federal deficit; secondly, to eliminate the unwarranted regulations and redtape that's imposed by government on the private sector, which is highly inflationary; and, of course, the third thing is to stick with and to try to induce the American people to support the voluntary wage and price standards.

All of these factors working together will have a long-range, beneficial effect in controlling inflation. In my opinion, a deliberate recession, which is one alternative which would cause very high unemployment, is unacceptable. And mandatory wage and price controls, which have been tried in the past and have never worked, except during wartime, are also unacceptable.

So, we have a good, sound, anti-inflation program. It's going to require some time for it to be effective, but I intend to stick with it.

PRESIDENT'S LEADERSHIP RESPONSIBILITY

Q. Mr. President, many of your legislative initiatives have run into trouble on Capitol Hill this year—hospital cost control, the Panama Canal implementation legislation, oil price decontrol—legislation to extend that—and so forth. To what extent do you believe it is the President's responsibility to exert leadership over the Congress, and to what extent do you believe you've fulfilled that responsibility this year?

THE PRESIDENT. I think the President has a major responsibility not only to propose to the Congress legislation that's of benefit to the Nation, but also to fight for congressional approval of those proposals. The ones you mentioned as examples are very important to our Nation.

We have already signed, and the Senate has ratified, a Panama Canal agreement, two treaties. Those treaties became effective the first day of April. The Panama Canal Zone will become Panamanian territory on the 1st of October. If the Congress does not act to implement those treaties, then we would have no effective means by which we could adequately defend the Panama Canal between now and the year 2000, nor manage our personnel in keeping the canal open. I believe that the Congress will eventually be responsible and will pass the implementation legislation.

On oil decontrol, which I have proposed—and just described, I think, adequately—my belief is that the Congress will not change that law. The decontrol action that I have taken is in accordance with the law passed by Congress in 1975. There's a great deal of debate going on, and I believe that we will have decontrol, which is good for our country.

Hospital cost containment—here again, the Congress has a major responsibility to deal with this effectively. The lobbying pressure on the Members of Congress by the hospital lobby is extraordinary, but I believe that in the long run, the Congress will see that this is one of the tangible actions that they can take this year to help control inflation. Hospital costs have been going up twice as great in previous years as the inflation rate, a completely unwarranted, additional charge on the American people that ought to be stopped.

And so, I have not given up on any of these programs as far as getting them implemented by congressional action. But I'll bear my share of the responsibility if we fail.

My judgment is that the American people are beginning to feel that their own Government can't deal adequately with crucial issues to the country, like inflation and like energy and like having a peaceful world in which to live. And until the American public gets aroused, we're going to have difficulty in Washington getting action taken.

But I believe the public is becoming increasingly aroused as they see the need for this action, and I predict to you that the Congress will act favorably on these three items. I have no intent to back down. I'll fight for these three programs and others that I've proposed to the last vote in Congress, and I believe that we will win.

RELATIONS WITH CONGRESS

Q. Mr. President, even though it might not be your favorite way of doing things with Congress, why don't you get tough to the extent of saying to Members of Congress individually that, "If you won't help me on these major programs that I feel are important to the entire country, I won't go along with my administration providing the individual, district-by-district services that you are interested in as a Member of Congress"?

THE PRESIDENT. I represent those districts also. Every one of the people who lives in any congressional district is my constituent. And I don't think it's right to punish the people of our Nation who live in a particular farming community or city or congressional district because a particular Member of Congress does not comply with the proposals that I make that I believe to be in the best interest of our Nation.

The best approach that I have been able to make—and we've had a very good success in having the Congress approve my proposals in previous years—has been to deal, first of all, with the Congress directly, both as a body and also individual Members of the Congress.

When I do face a serious problem, like with the windfall profits tax when the prediction was we had no chance to get it passed, I take my case to the public as strongly and effectively as I can. I think that's the best way to induce the Congress Members to vote in the best interests of their constituents and mine, not to punish the constituents in a district.

ORGANIZATION OF PETROLEUM
EXPORTING COUNTRIES

Q. Mr. President, as you said before, decontrol begins Friday, and the OPEC Ministers meet next month. What do you expect the OPEC Ministers to do? What action do you expect them to take?

THE PRESIDENT. I don't know. I think OPEC has raised the price of oil excessively this year, and I hope they won't raise it any more.

I believe in the long run, they hurt not only our country but every nation on Earth, and especially the poor nations who are destitute to begin with. I think the OPEC nations in the long run hurt themselves by raising the price of oil excessively.

They have always demanded—and I give them credit by assuming that their demand was sincere—that countries, like our own, that use and waste so much energy cut back on consumption. That's one of the main thrusts of the energy proposals that I have made to the American people and to the Congress.

As you know, the major consuming nations in the International Energy Agency this spring have resolved, all of us, to cut back by 2 million barrels per day on our total worldwide consumption. This amounts to about a 5-percent reduction below our projected 1979 rate—reduction in consumption.

I'll be meeting with six leaders of other nations in Tokyo the last week in June and, there again, we'll try to deal with the question of consumption in the world being higher than present production.

I would like to see the OPEC nations level off their price, certainly not to exceed the rate of inflation; secondly, to increase production in return for which the consuming nations who waste a great deal of energy would impose and adhere to strict conservation measures.

Increased and sustained supply, a stable price, and reduced consumption is the best all-around approach, but I think there has to be some give-and-take, some recognition of mutual interest between us and OPEC, before we can succeed in stabilizing the energy supply and price situation.

PRESIDENT'S FISHING TRIPS

Q. This past Saturday, unbeknownst to anyone, you took off to Spruce Creek, Pennsylvania, and went fishing.

THE PRESIDENT. That's correct.

Q. Now, you told Helen Thomas [United Press International] at the beginning of the news conference that this saves energy by not having to drag along all the press people and not having us tail along. How many times previously have you been able to escape the news media and travel unbeknownst to anybody?

THE PRESIDENT. Not enough—[*laughter*]—and it wasn't unbeknownst to the press.

I have a rare opportunity to go fishing or to get out in the woods and swamps and in the fields and on the streams by myself. I really believe that it's not only good for me but for the country, to be able to do that on occasion. I wish I could do it more. But I don't intend to ignore any opportunity to take advantage of a fishing trip when my own work permits it, and I hope the press will understand and the people will understand that I, like the average American, need some recreation at times.

I enjoyed it. I didn't catch as many fish as my wife. It was one of the nicest days of my life, except for that fact—[*laughter*]—and I'm very proud that I had a chance.

RHODESIA

Q. Mr. President, the British, who've been our partners in formulating a policy towards Rhodesia, have recently ruled that the elections there were free and fair. Can you tell me now, does your administration intend to pursue a separate policy there, or will we now agree with the British conclusion?

THE PRESIDENT. We have been consulting closely with the British Government since the new administration under Mrs. Thatcher took over. Secretary Vance has just completed several days of discussions, both with her, with her Foreign Minister, and with other officials.

The new Rhodesian Zimbabwe Government will take office, I think, the 1st of June. Within 2 weeks after that date, I will make my decision about whether or not to lift the existing sanctions. I've given the Congress this assurance. And obviously, my decision would be made taking into consideration those consultations with Great Britain.

RELEASE OF SOVIET DISSIDENTS AND THEIR FAMILIES

Q. About a month ago, Mr. President, you brought about, helped bring about, a prisoner exchange with the Soviet Union. As part of that exchange, as I understand it, there was an agreement that the families of the Russian dissidents would be allowed immediate passage to the West.

However, many of those families have not been released, and there were reports that some of them have actually been harassed. Is that a breach of the agreement? What has the U.S. Government done about it? And secondly, do you have any information on another report that the Soviets are about to release 12 more prisoners, possibly including Anatoly Shcharanskiy?

THE PRESIDENT. I don't have any information about the second item except what I have read in the news. We have no direct information about that. I hope the report is true.

The Soviets did agree to release the families of the five dissidents, earlier, without delay and without harassment. My belief is that the families will be released. There have been delays. Whether they were brought about by an unwieldy democracy [bureaucracy],[1] or by actions of subordinates who weren't familiar with the government policy, or whether it was deliberate, I have no way to know.

There have been some delays. But I think in spite of this, the families will be reunited, and that's one reason that I'm very thankful about it.

Q. You do not see it as a breach of the agreement, then?

THE PRESIDENT. There was some delay, and there was some harassment of the families in my opinion. Whether that was imposed by the government officials or whether it was part of the unwieldy—the Soviet bureaucracy, I can't judge. But I'm thankful that the families will be released.

DEMOCRATIC PARTY SUPPORT FOR THE PRESIDENT

Q. Mr. President, John White, the party chairman, Democratic Party chairman, said the other day that he thought

---

[1] Printed in the transcript.

the activities of some of those Congressmen promoting Senator Kennedy were divisive and might turn the Presidency over to the Republicans in 1980. Now, do you agree with him? And would it be helpful if Senator Kennedy just today made a Sherman-like statement, as he did in 1974, take himself out of the race?

THE PRESIDENT. I don't have any quarrel to make with the statement that was issued by John White. No, I do not disagree with his statement.

I don't really have any comment to make about what Senator Kennedy does. He's made statements repeatedly about what he would do.

Let me make this point: No President can expect to have unanimous support, even within one's own party. This has been the case with every predecessor of mine who lived in the White House. But that's not my major concern. I'm not an announced candidate, and I don't intend to make every judgment about what ought to be done for this country on the basis of whether it would or would not lose support by nonpartisan Americans or officials in my own party for an upcoming election.

Some of the decisions that I have to make on inflation, on energy, on foreign affairs, are very difficult to make. I don't believe anyone can accuse me of trying to gain a vote, for instance, by my energy proposals. They've just lost votes, but they were necessary. And if I should ever modify my positions away from what's best for this country in order to pick up support, then I would not deserve to be President. So, I don't intend to do it.

If a few or even a large number of Democrats endorse someone else, that's their business. I'll continue to try to serve the country as best I can and deal with the political question when the election comes along.

STRATEGIC ARMS; MX MISSILE

Q. Mr. President, I know in your Inaugural Address, you dedicated your administration to eliminating atomic weapons from the Earth.

THE PRESIDENT. That's right.

Q. We're on the verge now of making the decision on the MX. I gather it has accuracy, it hits within 100 yards, and it has a doubling or a tripling of the atomic blast power. It could be a very destabilizing weapon in the strategic arms system, and also make SALT III very difficult to achieve. What's your decision on MX?

THE PRESIDENT. The most destabilizing thing that we could have in our strategic relationship with the Soviets would be acknowledged inferiority or a vulnerable strategic deployment of missiles. We have just completed almost 7 years of negotiations with the Soviets to actually reduce the present, permitted number of missiles on each side, to put constraints on the number of explosive warheads that could be on each missile, and to limit the improvement in quality of existing missiles. That is a major step toward my ultimate goal, which I believe is one shared by the Soviet Union leaders, of eliminating nuclear weapons from the face of the Earth in the future.

But while we do have heavy deployments of nuclear weapons by the Soviet Union—although now being constrained more severely than they were before—we must maintain an adequate level of armaments, and we must maintain the security from attack of the armaments we have.

So, when we do deploy new types of missiles to stay current and to keep our equivalency with the Soviet Union, that, in my opinion, contributes to peace, and this is completely permitted in the SALT

II agreement which we have just negotiated.

The agreement on new types of ICBM's is that each side can only have one new ICBM during the life of the treaty. And that was carefully planned in order to provide stability and to stop the enormous buildup which the Soviets have been demonstrating in recent years to catch up with us, since we were originally far ahead. And if we can maintain that rough equivalency with the Soviet Union, maintain an adequate defense, and maintain the security of our own missile systems, that is a major contributing factor to peace.

So, it is not destabilizing. I think it is stabilizing.

Q. Have you decided on the MX?

THE PRESIDENT. Not yet.

THE MIDDLE EAST

Q. Mr. President, on the Middle East, sir, is it feasible in your view to expect the Palestinians and other Arab nations to join the peace process as long as the United States does not put forward some of its own ideas in greater detail about what autonomy is going to look like on the West Bank and Gaza?

In other words, as long as the Israelis are continuing to say there will be no Palestinian homeland, there will be no entity linked or unlinked to Jordan, there will be no Palestinian state, is it not incumbent on the United States, again in this peace process, to come forward with some ideas of its own in order to encourage the Palestinians to join in?

THE PRESIDENT. We've never been reticent about putting forward our ideas both to the Israelis and the Egyptians and to others about what ought to be done in the West Bank, Gaza area. We've never espoused an independent Palestinian state. I think that would be a destabilizing factor there.

I believe the next step ought to be the exchange of views during the negotiations between Israel and Egypt. We will observe the different proposals that are inevitably going to be made; some of them have been described publicly. Then later on, after the negotiations proceed as far as they can do with any degree of momentum, we will reserve the right—requested, I might say, by both Israel and Egypt— to put forward United States proposals to break a deadlock or to provide a compromise solution.

We have been involved in that kind of process both at Camp David and when I went to the Middle East. I think that's one of the reasons that we've been as successful as we have so far.

But for us to preempt the negotiations by putting forward, to begin with, an American proposal, I think, would be counterproductive, and it would remove some of the reasonable responsibility that ought to be directly on the shoulders of Prime Minister Begin and his government and President Sadat and his government.

I might say that this past weekend, I talked personally to President Sadat and to Prime Minister Begin and, this morning, to Secretary Vance. And they were all very pleased and very excited not only at the progress made in El Arish and Beersheba but also at the attitude on both sides toward a constructive resolution of these very difficult issues.

So, at this point, I feel very hopeful that both sides are negotiating in good faith. We'll be there to help them when they need our help.

BERT LANCE

Q. Mr. President, last week an Atlanta grand jury indicted your former budget director, your friend, Mr. Lance, on criminal charges. I'm aware of the fact that the courts have enjoined discussion of this case and won't ask you to do that, sir, but in view of the confidence and friendship you have expressed publicly for Mr. Lance, I wonder if you could share with us your reaction to the indictment and your feeling about Mr. Lance at this time as a person?

THE PRESIDENT. Bert Lance is still my friend. I don't see any benefit to be derived from my commenting on the actions that are presently underway within the legal system of our country.

FRANK CORMIER [Associated Press]. Thank you, Mr. President.

THE PRESIDENT. Thank you. Thank you, everybody.

NOTE: President Carter's fiftieth news conference began at 4 p.m. in Room 450 of the Old Executive Office Building. It was broadcast live on radio and television.

Gasoline End-User Allocation

Executive Order 12140.   May 29, 1979

DELEGATION OF AUTHORITIES RELATING TO MOTOR GASOLINE END-USER ALLOCATION

By virtue of the authority vested in me by the Constitution and the statutes of the United States of America, including the Emergency Petroleum Allocation Act of 1973, as amended (P.L. 93–159), and as President of the United States of America, notwithstanding the delegations to the Secretary of Energy in Executive Order 11790 as amended by Executive Order 12038, it is hereby ordered:

SECTION 1–101. Each Governor is hereby delegated the authority to establish a system of end-user allocation for motor gasoline, subject to the terms and conditions as set forth below.

SEC. 1–102. When a Governor determines that his State, or any locality therein, is experiencing a shortage of motor gasoline available for retail distribution, such that the public health, safety, or welfare is endangered, he may require motor gasoline retail sales outlets in that State or locality to:

(a) Supply with gasoline (including gasohol) vehicles:

(1) which have a license plate number, the last digit of which is an even number, or where there are only letters on the license plate, the last letter of which is a letter in the first half of the alphabet (A–M), only on even days of the month;

(2) which have a license plate number, the last digit of which is an odd number, or where there are only letters on the license plate, the last letter of which is a letter in the last half of the alphabet (N–Z), only on odd days of the month; and

(3) which have individually or as a class been designated by the Governor of that State as eligible to purchase gasoline on any day in order to assure adequate supplies for such vehicles to protect the public health, safety, or welfare, or to assure necessary governmental services (including local, State and Federal).

(b) Require purchasers to purchase a specified minimum amount of gasoline (including gasohol), expressed in either gallons, fractions of gas tanks, or dollars, as determined by the Governor; and

(c) Supply gasoline at specified times of day or on specified days, as determined by the Governor to be necessary to reduce the length of or prevent lines of purchasers.

SEC. 1–103. A Governor may adopt such additional rules or regulations not inconsistent with Department of Energy policies and regulations and subdelegate this authority as he deems necessary to implement and enforce the provisions of section 1–102 above.

SEC. 1–104. For purposes of this Order, the term "Governor" includes the Governors of the 50 States, the Chief Executive Officer of the District of Columbia, Puerto Rico, and the territories and possessions of the United States, other than the Panama Canal Zone.

SEC. 1–105. This Order shall terminate, unless extended, at midnight on September 30, 1979. The Secretary of Energy may at any time revoke this delegation in whole or in part with respect to any State.

JIMMY CARTER

The White House,
May 29, 1979.

[Filed with the Office of the Federal Register, 10:28 a.m., May 30, 1979]

National Conference of Christians and Jews

Remarks at the 30th Annual Brotherhood Citation Dinner. May 29, 1979

Last September, I spent 13 days at Camp David with an Arab and a Jew. It was one of the most difficult times of my life; one of the most challenging, interesting and, ultimately, perhaps one of the most productive.

Both these leaders, President Sadat and Prime Minister Begin, were deeply religious. We were engaged in intense negotiation. But for 10 of those 13 days, they never saw or spoke to each other because the differences were so deep, and it was almost impossible for them to communicate even their most heartfelt beliefs and desires.

I had a chance to get to know those men very well, and we spent long hours speaking about death and war and hatred and bigotry and prejudice and division between one human being and another. And we spent a lot of time talking about hope and peace and brotherhood and love.

The men were quite different, and I had to orient my own schedule to accommodate theirs. President Sadat, highly disciplined, did not want to meet with anyone until about 10 o'clock in the morning, because he got up for his calisthenics, and then he took a long walk, and then he came back and rested for a while, and then he was ready to go to work.

So, one morning I saw him walk past my door, and I ran out and joined him. And for quite a while we walked in silence, and then we began a kind of fumbling conversation. I had an ulterior motive. I wanted to convince him to accept one of the propositions that had been relayed to me. But while we walked, President Sadat said, "I think that someone from the South in this country is especially qualified to recognize the damages of losing a war and of seeing people divided one from another by misunderstandings, even those who are brothers under God, and even in more recent times to see racial prejudice hold back progress among people."

He meant that as a compliment to me, and I instantaneously swelled with quiet pride. And then I recalled my own return to the South and my later service on the Sumter County School Board. I was a young ex-naval officer, idealistic, liberal for Sumter County, Georgia, living under a ruling by the U.S. Supreme Court known as separate-but-equal. I was somewhat proud of the fact that my own children went to an old and relatively dilapidated school, which I had attended and my wife attended, and her parents and my parents, and the black children in the other end of Plains went to a newer school.

I asked the other four school board members, all of whom were white men, to join with me in inspecting the school system of Sumter County. It had never been done. And we went to five or six schools which were attended by black students. There were 26 of them in the back room of old houses, in the basements of dilapidated churches; few school books, no blackboards.

I remember one where 14- or 15-year-old boys were sitting two to a chair, and the chair was designed for 4-year-olds. And we gave up our visits in embarrassment. I have to admit that I had served on the school board 3 months before it ever dawned on me clearly that white children were riding to school in buses and black children were walking to school.

We rationalized in those days that division of the races, because we attributed to blacks—because of their poverty and ancient discriminations—characteristics which we thought were inferior to those of white children. And we blanketly condemned or relegated to an inferior place many because of the faults of a few.

I'm not proud of this, but I think it illustrates the point I want to make tonight, because our Nation has been one of strength and dynamism and progress, inspired by the Government, by chamber of commerce attitudes, by a pioneer spirit, by a determination to excel, to explore new realms of achievement, to reach for and to grasp material progress, and we've been highly successful.

Our goals have been reached and then raised again. Our progress has been historically steady. Our per capita income in this Nation, all Americans, has doubled almost every generation. Our mean family income is now more than $16,000 a year. And the average income of an American in 3 days is equal to the annual income of many people who live in the less developed countries of our world.

We are now approaching a time when some sociologists name it a crisis of suc-cess or plenty, or perhaps even excess. Perhaps it's time now to reexamine our material achievements, because we might be faced with an era of scarcity or additional life simplicity.

Our social progress the last 200 years, however, has not been quite so steady. It has not been inspired always by government or by chambers of commerce or by organizational structures or by institutions. The social progress has been faltering, spasmodic, inspired by individual courageous human beings who rallied others with a cry of equality or justice or mercy.

Martin Luther King, Jr., forced this Nation, North and South, almost against its will, to recognize legal injustice and to do what was right. He was scorned, ignored, sometimes hated, imprisoned. But because he knew he was right and because Americans also knew he was right, he prevailed, and the laws were changed and black citizens were finally given a guaranteed right to vote. And our Nation took a major step forward and upward.

We now bask in the glory of his achievement, as a nation, assuming that perhaps our social progress has been adequate. But we cannot afford to be satisfied. In the last 2½ years, we have created 8 million net new jobs, but the unemployment rate among young people who speak foreign languages like Spanish, or who are black, is still 35 percent. And there is no more devastating blight on a human spirit than to have one life on this Earth, given by God, and not have a chance to use it; to feel worthless because one doesn't have a chance to prove worth.

Last year our budget for education was the highest in history, the biggest increase in history—$13 billion in aid for children to become better educated. But still many American Indians or other minority groups or the poor are alienated within the classrooms. There are still segregated schools—more in the North, ironically, than in the South these days. And racial discrimination, protected by law in housing, is still a burden for those who suffer from discrimination to attempt to correct through a complicated and highly expensive legal system.

Our Nation is at peace. No American has lost a life in battle since I've been in the White House. But we still live in a world which perhaps more than any other time in history is spending more of its resources on militarism, on weaponry, and we still have not yet been successful in controlling the threat of the ultimate weapon—nuclear explosives.

This past year the world was shocked by witnessing the television series about the Holocaust. Many of us searched our souls, but the thread of anti-Semitism still hangs like a dark cloud in our world. Our Nation, so wealthy, still has a lower and lower standard of morality. Families are disintegrating, the institution of marriage is scorned and ridiculed by many, the unity of our Nation, threatened, as each person becomes more self-sufficient and more doubtful about the efficacy of institutions which we in the past have held so dear.

But our Nation, in spite of these threats or these faults or these opportunities, is still almost unique. We have some advantages. We are a nation of refugees. We are the mixing pot of the world. We understand diversity and how to live in harmony when we are different. And this ability to contemplate others' problems, others' attitudes, others' languages, others' heritage, is an advantage.

Not too long ago I was meeting with the Prime Minister of Japan. We were talking about refugees from Indochina. Our Nation, in the last 2 or 3 years, has accepted 190,000 refugees, and we're now processing 30,000 more—not enough. But

I pointed out to Prime Minister Ohira that the Japanese have only received and processed three. And there was a general consensus around that table that the reason for that is that the Japanese are so homogeneous in their racial makeup, in an ancient island civilization, that there's an incapacity to receive aliens and to accommodate them successfully.

We still have a long way to go in our attitude toward the other nations, and we tend to adopt the ancient prejudice of the South by equating the faults or the sins of a few toward the many, and therefore rationalize a lack of action on our part to repair damage to the human spirit, to root out prejudice and bigotry and hatred and inequality.

We look at Rhodesia, and we see the acronyms ZAPU and ZANU, and we think about leaders there who have associated with socialist countries, and we say, "Well, it must be all right not to pursue majority rule with aggression and determination and idealism and commitment. Apartheid may not be so bad, because look at the political philosophy of the leaders of the blacks who seek equality." The same thing applies as an attitude in the Middle East—and affects you and me.

The most difficult single issue in the Middle East concerns Palestinians. And because some Arabs, some Palestinians, are filled with hatred and commit themselves publicly to boycotts and to terrorism, there's an unwillingness to address the basic problem of the Palestinian refugee in an open and compassionate and concerned way.

But we are a people who search for answers in spite of difficulties and who, over a period of years—sometimes, unfortunately, generations—have always made progress.

Paul Tillich said the search for the truth about our relationship with God and our fellow men is religion. And when we lose that desire to search for this truth, we lose our very religion.

The United States—and its people—is a searching nation. We are a free nation, not afraid to face defects, not afraid to expose problems, not afraid to debate differences, not afraid to correct mistakes. We want our Nation to be unified, strong, free, peaceful, with equality for our people. We want our Government to achieve greatness, to realize its ultimate potential. And we know that for a society, or for a government, the highest potential it can reach is to achieve simple justice.

That's not quite high enough. It's not the ultimate, because a single human being close to God can achieve not only simple justice but love. And perhaps that's the reason why individual human beings like Martin Luther King, Jr., have been able to reach higher and set a higher standard and achieve more in social progress and social justice than has a government. And it imposes an obligation on all of us in this room—leaders, blessed, influential—to set our standards high.

It would be a terrible day for us to awake and find that our inflation problems had been cured, we had plenty of energy, our material needs were met, poverty was eliminated, that we had then a nation with no purpose, without hope, exhausted in our struggle for material things, with the best of the American dream abandoned. Where would be our victory? What would be the measurement of our achievement?

I'm very grateful that your own slogan for this banquet, or perhaps this year, is "The Unfinished Task." Achievements have been great, but we should not ignore the challenges which face us, which are still great. I have no doubt that we, in a

spirit of love, can meet this challenge.

Thank you.

NOTE: The President spoke at 9:28 p.m. in the International Ballroom at the Washington Hilton Hotel. Prior to his remarks, he received the Brotherhood Award of the National Conference of Christians and Jews.

Vietnam Veterans Week, 1979

Remarks at a White House Reception.
May 30, 1979

MR. CONWAY. Mr. President, the Postmaster General and I would like you to accept on behalf of all Vietnam veterans this special Vietnam veterans stamp that will be issued on Armistice Day this year.

In the Postal Service, we like to think of stamps as minibillboards which tell the world what we Americans think is important. And although only a small gesture, this stamp is our way of honoring and thanking all the Vietnam veterans who answered their Nation's call to duty.

[*At this point, the President and James V. P. Conway, Deputy Postmaster General, unveiled the design of the new U.S. postage stamp.*]

THE PRESIDENT. You have honored me and my family, and you have honored this President's house by coming here this afternoon.

In March I signed a proclamation for Vietnam era veterans week. In that proclamation, I pointed out that the Vietnam war was the longest and most expensive in the history of our country. It resulted in the most costly gifts of human life and the greatest degree of human suffering. In addition, the war itself, the circumstances of it, were highly divisive in our country, perhaps more so than any other war except the War Between the States, more than 100 years ago.

Our Nation has a noble history, a history of patriotism and sacrifice, a history of courage in time of crisis. There is hardly a family here which has not experienced the suffering and the dedication of one's self in war. The first member of my family who moved to Georgia fought in the Revolution. My great-grandparents fought in the War Between the States. My father was a lieutenant in the First World War. I served in the Navy during the Second War and the Korean war. My oldest son volunteered to go to Vietnam and went there for a long time.

In almost every instance, our Nation has treated the participants and the veterans of war with honor and respect and appreciation and a sense of brotherhood and sharing. But as a father, and as the Governor of a State, as a candidate for President, I saw very clearly that the Vietnam war was different. There were no chamber of commerce proclamations, no bands that played martial music to welcome back most of the veterans of that war.

Although all service people have been heroic—as I said many times during the long campaign for President—veterans of Vietnam had to demonstrate an extra measure of heroism. It's easier to offer one's life, if necessary, for a country when you have assured knowledge that the people at home support you and appreciate what you are doing and share with you the commitment of our Nation. But to offer one's life in the most horrible possible circumstances, the most dangerous circumstances, with the realization that people back home do not give you that support, their prayers, their deep appreciation, and a sense of sharing, requires an extra measure of patriotism and sacrifice. As you well know, much more vividly than do I, that was the situation during the Vietnam war.

Many people opposed the war. That's a basic right in our country. But the unfortunate part of that opposition has been that many have seen our returning veterans, both during and since the war was concluded, as an unfortunate or embarrassing reminder of the divisiveness of the war itself. This has created additional hardship on those who are willing to serve.

In addition, there were special circumstances during those recent war years that were unprecedented to a remarkable degree. Those who were conscripted to go to Vietnam were those who were most unfortunate, who were deprived of political influence, who could not afford to be a student in college, who were relatively inarticulate, and who were disadvantaged to begin with. They were joined, obviously, by the extremely heroic volunteers who went to join them.

Most of those who have returned have almost miraculously been able to assimilate themselves back into civilian life and to further service of our country, even when the psychological or physical scars of war were still apparent. But those statistics which show that remarkable degree of success are no comfort to those who have not been able to overcome the psychic or physical damages of the war.

This factor has also been exacerbated or aggravated by the fact that those who went, being disadvantaged educationally or economically, still had those family problems when they returned. And our Nation has not done enough to respect and to honor and to recognize and to reward the special heroism that I have tried to describe in such fumbling ways.

There is obviously a need for better opportunities for education, for training, for housing, for jobs. When I was elected President, I searched for ways to demonstrate vividly that our Government would change its attitude of neglect toward the

Vietnam veterans. And the most significant action that I could take was to choose someone to head the Veterans Administration in whom I had the utmost confidence, who was strong, able, heroic, dedicated, and would be an effective spokesman to the Nation for those who served in the Vietnam war.

Three key aides in my administration are here on the stage with me—Max Cleland, our director; Dennis Wyant, Deputy Assistant Secretary of Labor, responsible for job programs; and Bill Lawson, who serves on my own White House staff.

There are slowly moving items of legislation before the Congress, and I hope that they can be expedited. We need to extend the time limit for GI rights for job training. We need substantially to expand the readjustment counseling service—obviously too long neglected.

Max Cleland reminds me that he testified for this legislation 10 years ago—is that right, Max?—and the special programs for vocational rehabilitation for those who are disabled. There are other actions, of course, which the Congress can take, and I urge the expeditious conclusion of these efforts. But perhaps more importantly for the future, even than these specific important pieces of legislation, is what might well be initiated this week.

I think the Nation is ready to change its heart and its mind and its attitude toward those whom you, assembled here, represent, and to recognize finally and with enthusiasm and concern, appreciation, and with love, the wisdom and the experience and the insight into the consciousness of America which you represent and the honor and valor and devotion and sacrifice and commitment that you have demonstrated during a time of crisis and of personal danger.

AUDIENCE MEMBER. What about Agent Orange victims, President Carter?

THE PRESIDENT. What about what?

Q. Twice as many men are dying here in the States as died in the war. Agent Orange contains dioxin, the most toxic substance known to mankind. Dow Chemical Company lied to this country, lied to the Government when it said it wasn't toxic.

THE PRESIDENT. I understand.

Q. Now thousands of our men are dying, President Carter. Max Cleland is implementing programs, but they're not sufficient enough.

THE PRESIDENT. I'll help Max with that, with the herbicide, you mean?

Q. Epidemiological studies done on the Vietnam veterans.

THE PRESIDENT. Max and I both agree.

Q. Thank you.

THE PRESIDENT. Let me say two things in conclusion. One is that your voice in my administration and in my consciousness and heart is Max Cleland. You could not possibly have a better representative than he. And secondly, that your contribution still is tremendously important in the consciousness of our Nation, because all of us agree that the best way to commemorate what you have accomplished in Vietnam is to build a world permanently at peace.

Is Philip Caputo here? Where? Do you mind if I read a quotation from your book?

MR. CAPUTO. No, sir.

The PRESIDENT. Fine. [*Laughter*]

I don't think I could close with a more appropriate remark than an excerpt from Philip Caputo's book, "A Rumor of War." Writing on the death of a friend and a classmate named Walter Levy, and I quote, "You were a part of us and a part of us died with you, the small part that was still young, that had not yet grown cynical, grown bitter and old with death. Your courage was an example to us, and whatever the rights or wrongs of the war, nothing can diminish the rightness of what you tried to do. Yours was the greater love. You died for the man you tried to save, and you died pro patria. As I write this 11 years after your death, the country for which you died wishes to forget the war in which you died. Its very name is a curse. There are no monuments to its heroes, for memorials are reminders and they would make it harder for your country to sink into the amnesia for which it longs. It wishes to forget, and it has forgotten, but there are a few of us who do remember, because of the small things that made us love you, your gestures, the words you spoke, and the way you looked. We loved you for what you were, and what you stood for."

And I would like to say, as President, on behalf of 220 million people of our country, we love you for what you were and what you stood for; and we love you for what you are and what you stand for.

Thank you very much.

Two things—I'm not in a hurry, and I would like to do——

AUDIENCE MEMBER. Mr. President.

THE PRESIDENT. Yes?

Q. I think that I do feel honored being here today. But I think there is a dishonor if we let this week just go by without trying to implement programs that realistically deal with a lot of the problems that the Vietnam combat veterans still suffer from.

You can say that most Vietnam era veterans have readjusted. But I would like to see a study done on the combat veterans, because those are the ones who are still having problems; those are the ones who are still coming into my office week after week after week at Swords to Plowshares in San Francisco.

And there are really no realistic programs to deal with their problems. So, I

think if you want to honor me as a Vietnam-disabled combat veteran, that you also have to implement realistic programs. And I think you have it going on the right track to do that. And I think that Max has. But I think there needs to be more, because I want to come home again. And unless I can come home again, there has to be programs to let me come home again.

THE PRESIDENT. What's your name?

Thank you very much, Jack. Jack McCloskey? Thank you.

I was going to say that you're welcome to look at this. It's your home, and I'm not in any hurry. I would like to stand just outside the door and shake hands with those of you who would like to meet the President personally. It would be an honor for me. And you've honored us by being here.

Thank you.

NOTE: The President spoke at 2:32 p.m. in the East Room at the White House.

Department of Justice

Nomination of Alan A. Parker To Be an Assistant Attorney General. May 31, 1979

The President today announced that he will nominate Alan A. Parker, of California, to be an Assistant Attorney General. He would replace Patricia M. Wald, who has resigned. Parker has been general counsel of the House Judiciary Committee since 1973.

He was born November 28, 1927, in New York City. He received an LL.B. from the University of Santa Clara Law School in 1964. He served in the U.S. Army from 1946 to 1947.

From 1948 to 1951 and from 1953 to 1960, Parker was a safety engineer and manager with Hale Hendlin Co. From

1951 to 1953, he was manager of Atwell, Vogel & Sterling, Inc., in Los Angeles. From 1960 to 1967, he was an inheritance tax appraiser in the office of the State controller on a part-time basis.

From 1965 to 1971, Parker was a partner with the firm of Chargin and Parker. From 1971 to 1973, he was legal assistant to Congressman Don Edwards.

Department of Justice

Nomination of Maurice Rosenberg To Be an Assistant Attorney General.   May 31, 1979

The President today announced that he will nominate Maurice Rosenberg, of New York, to be an Assistant Attorney General. He would replace Daniel J. Meador, who has resigned.

Rosenberg is a professor of law at Columbia Law School and is currently on leave of absence to work on a research project at the Center for Advanced Study in the Behavioral Sciences in Stanford, Calif.

Rosenberg was born September 3, 1919, in Oswego, N.Y. He received an A.B. from Syracuse University in 1940 and an LL.B. from Columbia School of Law in 1947. He served in the U.S. Army from 1941 to 1945.

From 1947 to 1949, Rosenberg was law clerk to Judge Stanley Fuld of the U.S. Court of Appeals for the Second Circuit. From 1949 to 1953, he practiced law with Cravath, Swaine & Moore in New York, and from 1953 to 1956, he practiced with Austrian, Lance & Stewart.

Rosenberg has been a professor at Columbia School of Law since 1956. He served as Special Assistant to the Attorney General from June 1976 to January 1977.

President's Commission on Executive Exchange

Appointment of 19 Public Members and 6 Government Representatives.   May 31, 1979

The President today announced the appointment of 19 public members and 6 Government representatives to the President's Commission on Executive Exchange. This Commission directs and monitors a program under which a small number of Federal employees take positions in the private sector for a year, and a small number of industry executives are placed in Government positions for the same period.

The 19 public members appointed today are:

JASON S. BERMAN, of Rockville, Md., president of Berman and Associates, a Washington public relations and public affairs consulting firm;

THOMAS HALE BOGGS, JR., a Washington attorney;

DONALD G. BRENNAN, of Irvington, N.Y., director of national security studies for the Hudson Institute;

ANDREW F. BRIMMER, president of Brimmer & Co. in Washington, D.C., and a former member of the Federal Reserve Board;

FRANCIS J. BRUZDA, of Doylestown, Pa., executive vice president of the Girard Bank in Philadelphia;

JOHN C. COLLET, of Blue Springs, Mo., president of Rupert Manufacturing Co.;

JOSEPH N. GOMEZ, of Chicago, a marketing executive with the Chicago Alliance of Businessmen's Manpower, Labor Relations, and On-the-job Training Program;

R. E. KIRBY, of Pittsburgh, Pa., chairman and chief executive officer of Westinghouse Electric Corp.;

MELINDA L. LLOYD, of New York City, director of corporate planning for the Sperry and Hutchinson Co.;

JAMES PATTERSON LOW, of McLean, Va., president of the American Society of Association Executives;

WILLIAM F. MCSWEENY, of Washington, D.C., president of Occidental International Corp.;

MARIANO J. MIER, of Guaynabo, P.R., chairman of the board of Bache P.R. Government Securities;

JACK S. PARKER, of Greenwich, Conn., vice chairman of the board, director, and executive officer of General Electric Co.;

MICHAEL V. ROGERS, of Manhattan, Kans., senior accountant with Varney, Mills and Hixson CPAs;

JAMES ROOSEVELT, of Newport Beach, Calif., president of James Roosevelt & Co. business and financial consultants, a former Congressman from California, and the son of President Franklin D. Roosevelt;

JAMES FRANKLIN SASSER, of Longwood, Fla., who was special assistant to the Administrator of AID until his retirement last year;

WILLIAM B. SCHWARTZ III, of Atlanta, an officer in the corporate division of the First National Bank of Atlanta;

HOBART TAYLOR, JR., of Washington, D.C., an attorney and former Director of the Export-Import Bank of the United States;

MARIETTA TREE, of New York City, a partner in the city planning firm of Llewelyn-Davies Associates.

The Government representatives appointed today are Tyrone Brown, a member of the Federal Communications Commission; Robert Carswell, Deputy Secretary of the Treasury; Charles William Duncan, Jr., Deputy Secretary of Defense; Jule M. Sugarman, Deputy Director of the Office of Personnel Management; John M. Sullivan, Administrator of the Federal Railroad Administration; and James H. Williams, Deputy Secretary of Agriculture.

Economic Policymaking

Memorandum From the President.
May 30, 1979

Memorandum for the Heads of Executive Departments and Agencies, the White House Staff

Subject: The Economic Policy Group and the Coordination of Economic Policymaking

To assure efficient coordination of economic policymaking, the following procedures shall be implemented immediately:

1. Under the direction of the President the Economic Policy Group (EPG) shall be the exclusive vehicle for coordinating the formulation, execution, and presentation of the Administration's domestic and international economic policies.

2. The EPG should normally operate through meetings of its Steering Group, consisting of the Secretary of the Treasury as the Chairman, the Chairman of the Council of Economic Advisers, the Director of the Office of Management and Budget, and the Advisor to the President on Inflation. The Vice President, the Assistant to the President for Domestic Affairs and Policy and a representative of the National Security Advisor shall participate *ex officio* in all meetings of the Steering Group. The Chairman of the EPG, consulting with the Steering Group, shall invite the participation of other Cabinet-level members of the Administration as appropriate to consider the issues under review. At the Chairman's call, the Steering Group should meet several times a week in the White House.

3. The Secretary of the Treasury, as Chairman of the EPG, is the Administration's chief economic spokesman, and major statements on economic policy by Administration officials should, whenever possible, be reviewed and coordinated by the EPG Steering Group.

4. The EPG Steering Group is responsible for advising the President so that all Presidential-decision memoranda reflect sound economic analysis and accurately relate the options presented to the Administration's overall economic program and priorities. For this purpose:

—The EPG Shall have an office in the White House.

—The EPG Steering Group shall have

access to decision memoranda—from agencies and from EOP and White House staff units—which involve policy issues having a significant impact on economic variables (e.g., inflation, employment, real growth, productivity, competition, international accounts, etc.).

—The departments, agencies, and Executive Office and White House staffs shall work closely with the EPG to assure the efficient coordination of economic policymaking.

5. These procedures should be implemented without modification of normal Executive Office, domestic policy and legislative clearance processes.

JIMMY CARTER

NOTE: The text of the memorandum was released on June 1.

Trade With Romania and Hungary

Message to the Congress. June 1, 1979

In accordance with subsection 402(d) (5) of the Trade Act of 1974, I transmit herewith my recommendation that the authority to waive subsections (a) and (b) of section 402 be extended for a further period of twelve months.

In accordance with subsections 402(d) (5)(B) and (C), this recommendation sets forth my reasons for recommending the extension of waiver authority and for my determination that continuation of the waivers applicable to the Socialist Republic of Romania and to the Hungarian People's Republic will substantially promote the objectives of section 402.

I include as part of my recommendation, my determination that further extension of the waiver authority, and continuation of the waivers applicable to the Socialist Republic of Romania and to the Hungarian People's Republic, will substantially promote the objectives of section 402.

JIMMY CARTER

The White House,
June 1, 1979.

RECOMMENDATION FOR EXTENSION OF WAIVER AUTHORITY

I recommend to the Congress that the waiver authority granted by subsection 402(c) of the Trade Act of 1974 (hereinafter referred to as "the Act") be further extended for twelve months. Pursuant to subsection 402(d)(5) of the Act I have today determined that further extension of the waiver authority granted by section 402(c) of the Act and continuation of the waivers currently applicable to the Socialist Republic of Romania and to the Hungarian People's Republic will substantially promote the objectives of section 402 of the Act. My determinations are attached to this recommendation, and are incorporated herein.

The general waiver authority conferred by section 402(c) of the Act has proved to be a useful instrument in permitting the expansion of relations between the United States and Eastern European countries. It permitted us to sign bilateral trade agreements with Romania and Hungary in April 1975 and March 1978, respectively, thereby laying the basis for growing trade and closer relations. Moreover, continuation of this authority will provide a basis for future steps to expand and improve our bilateral relations with other countries subject to subsections 402(a) and (b) of the Act, should circumstances permit. I believe that all of these considerations make extension of the general waiver authority in the national interest.

Extension of the waiver for Romania will permit us to continue to promote the objectives of section 402 of the Trade Act of 1974. Emigration from Romania to the United States has continued to increase during the period in which the waiver has been in effect, and 1978 saw a dramatic increase in overall emigration from Romania. The Administration has continued to advise Romanian officials periodically of our high interest in emigration both to the United States and to Israel. Most recently, we expressed our interest in improved emigration to the Government of Romania during high-level bilateral consultations held in Bucharest within the framework of the Final Act of the Conference on Security and Cooperation in Europe. Emigration to Israel and binational marriages were also discussed in detail during these consultations. This close dialogue with Romanian officials has led to the favorable resolution of many emigration and other humanitarian problems. In view of continuing progress in this respect, I recommend continuation of the waiver for Romania.

On April 7, 1978, when I issued a determination waiving the application of subsections (a) and (b) of section 402 of the Act with respect to Hungary, I noted that the Hungarian Government had stressed to the U.S. Government that it intended to continue dealing with emigration matters in a responsive and humanitarian way. Since that time the actions of the Hungarian authorities have remained consistent with this policy. The majority of Hungarians seeking to emigrate may do so without undue difficulty. Very few problem cases arise, and U.S. officials can discuss these constructively with the Hungarian Government. Most problem cases ultimately are favorably resolved. In view of the Hungarian record, I have determined that a continuation of the waiver for Hungary will substantially promote the objectives of section 402 of the Act.

Trade With Romania and Hungary

Memorandum From the President.
June 1, 1979

Presidential Determination No. 79–10

Memorandum for the Secretary of State

Subject: Determination under Subsections 402(d)(5) and (d)(5)(C) of the Trade Act of 1974—Continuation of Waiver Authority

Pursuant to the authority vested in me under the Trade Act of 1974, (Public Law 93–618, January 3, 1975; 88 Stat. 1978) (hereinafter "the Act"), I determine, pursuant to Subsections 402(d)(5) and (d)(5)(C) of the Act, that the further extension of the waiver authority granted by Subsection 402(c) of the Act will substantially promote the objectives of Section 402 of the Act. I further determine that continuation of the waivers applicable to the Socialist Republic of Romania and to the Hungarian People's Republic will substantially promote the objectives of Section 402 of the Act.

This determination shall be published in the FEDERAL REGISTER.

JIMMY CARTER

[Filed with the Office of the Federal Register, 3:51 p.m., June 12, 1979]

United States Ambassador to Niger

Nomination of James Keough Bishop.
June 1, 1979

The President today announced that he will nominate James Keough Bishop, of New Rochelle, N.Y., to be Ambassador

Extraordinary and Plenipotentiary of the United States to the Republic of Niger. He would replace Charles A. James, who has resigned. Bishop is currently Director of North African Affairs at the State Department.

He was born July 21, 1938, in New Rochelle. He received a B.S. from the College of the Holy Cross in 1960.

Bishop joined the Foreign Service in 1960 and served as a press officer at the State Department from 1961 to 1963. From 1963 to 1966, he was vice consul in Auckland, and from 1966 to 1968, he was economic officer in Beirut. From 1968 to 1970, he was economic officer in Yaounde.

From 1970 to 1974, Bishop was an international relations officer at the Bureau of African Affairs, and from 1974 to 1976, he was Deputy Director of the Office of West African Affairs. In 1976–77 he took the executive seminar in national and international affairs at the Foreign Service Institute. Since 1977 he has been Director of North African Affairs.

Department of Agriculture

Nomination of Daniel Marcus To Be General Counsel.   June 1, 1979

The President today announced that he will nominate Daniel Marcus, of Bethesda, Md., to be General Counsel of the Department of Agriculture. He would replace Sarah Weddington, who resigned to join the White House staff. Marcus is currently Deputy General Counsel at the Department of Health, Education, and Welfare.

He was born January 5, 1941, in Brooklyn, N.Y. He received a B.A. from Brandeis University in 1962 and an LL.B. from Yale Law School in 1965.

In 1965 and 1966, Marcus was law clerk to Judge Harold Leventhal of the U.S. Court of Appeals for the District of Columbia Circuit. From 1966 to 1977, he was an attorney with the Washington firm of Wilmer, Cutler & Pickering, as a partner from 1973 to 1977. He has been at HEW since 1977.

United States Special Representative to Antigua, Saint Christopher-Nevis-Anguilla, and Saint Vincent

Appointment of Sally Angela Shelton. June 1, 1979

The President today announced the appointment of Sally Angela Shelton as United States Special Representative to the States of Antigua, Saint Christopher-Nevis-Anguilla, and Saint Vincent. She will serve in this capacity concurrently with her positions as Ambassador to Barbados, to Grenada, and to Dominica, and as Minister to Saint Lucia.

Superior Court of the District of Columbia

Nomination of Truman A. Morrison III To Be an Associate Judge.   June 1, 1979

The President today announced that he will nominate Truman A. Morrison III to the vacancy on the District of Columbia Superior Court caused by the resignation of Judge John Penn. Penn was recently named to the United States District Court.

Morrison, 35, is Chief of the Trial Division of the Public Defender Service in Washington, D.C. He attended the University of Wisconsin Law School and clerked for Chief Judge John W. Reynolds of the Eastern District of Wisconsin following his graduation.

Morrison joined the Public Defender Service in 1971 and was named Chief of the Trial Division in 1975.

Director of the Census

Nomination of Vincent P. Barabba.
June 1, 1979

The President today announced that he will nominate Vincent P. Barabba, of Pittsford, N.Y., to be Director of the Bureau of the Census. He would replace Manuel Plotkin, who has resigned.

Barabba is currently manager of Xerox Corp.'s office of market research and is a former Director of the Bureau of the Census.

He was born September 6, 1934, in Chicago. He received a B.S. from California State University in 1962 and an MBA from the University of California at Los Angeles in 1965.

From 1966 to 1969, Barabba was with Datamatics, Inc., in Los Angeles, and from 1969 to 1973, he was with Decision Making Information in Santa Ana, Calif. He was Director of the Bureau of the Census from 1973 until 1976, when he joined Xerox.

Federal Home Loan Bank Board

Nomination of Andrew A. DiPrete To Be a Member. June 1, 1979

The President today announced that he will nominate Andrew A. DiPrete, of Providence, R.I., to be a member of the Federal Home Loan Bank Board. He would replace Garth Marston, who has resigned, for a term expiring June 30, 1979, and will also be nominated for an additional term expiring June 30, 1983.

DiPrete has been a partner in the Providence law firm of Tillinghast, Collins & Graham since 1965 and is a former director of the Rhode Island Department of Business Regulation.

He was born December 6, 1929, in Cranston, R.I. He received an A.B. from Harvard College in 1950 and an LL.B. from Yale Law School in 1953.

DiPrete was with the firm of Hinckley, Allen, Salisbury & Parsons from 1953 to 1961, as an associate until 1960, then as a partner, and then served as vice president of two real estate investment firms.

From 1963 to 1965, DiPrete was director of the Rhode Island Department of Business Regulation, with jurisdiction over all State-chartered financial institutions and all insurance companies doing business in Rhode Island. He also served as a member of the Rhode Island Board of Bank Incorporation and the Rhode Island Board of Building-Loan Association Incorporation.

DiPrete is a trustee of Butler Hospital and is active in civic affairs in Providence.

Decontrol of Domestic Oil Prices

Statement by the President. June 1, 1979

Today the first step in phased decontrol begins.

For too many years we have had little influence over our own energy future. The first step in phased decontrol is also the first step toward establishing that ability to influence our own future.

Phased decontrol will increase domestic production, reduce consumption, reduce our vulnerability to foreign supplies, and improve our balance of payments.

Phased decontrol will also mean a slight increase in prices over the next few years—although nothing like the large increases we have already seen in the first few months of this year, despite the old system of controls.

OPEC-induced increases are likely to continue whatever our decision on domestic controls. Indeed, attempts to block phased decontrol can only serve to encourge OPEC price increases and increase our vulnerability to them.

The facts are that we have no choice in the future but to use less energy and pay more for what we do use.

Next week, Chairman Ullman and the House Ways and Means Committee expect to begin work on the windfall tax bill, which will capture for public use a significant portion of the profits resulting from decontrol. The enactment of this tax is essential, because its revenues will be used to:

—Offset the increased prices due to decontrol for the poorest of our citizens;

—Increase our mass transit systems— both buses and rail service;

—Increase our investment in research and development for areas such as solar power, better ways to burn and use coal, substitutes for petroleum and oil shale production.

The time has come to face facts. Our energy problems are real. The time for dreaming of easy, painless answers is past. The time for rhetoric without responsibility is past.

The difficulties we face this summer could have been averted or substantially lessened had we faced facts in years gone by. If we fail to act responsibly now, our problems will certainly grow worse and our options fewer in the years to come.

Digest of Other White House Announcements

The following listing includes the President's public schedule and other items of general interest announced by the White House Press Office and not included elsewhere in this issue.

May 28

The President returned to the White House from Camp David, Md.

May 29

The President met at the White House with:

—Zbigniew Brzezinski, Assistant to the President for National Security Affairs;

—Frank B. Moore, Assistant to the President for Congressional Liaison;

—Kang Shi'en, Vice Premier of the State Council of the People's Republic of China.

The President transmitted to the Congress the 1978 annual report of the National Institute of Building Sciences.

May 30

The President met at the White House with:

—Dr. Brzezinski;

—Mr. Moore;

—Stansfield Turner, Director of Central Intelligence, Hamilton Jordan, Assistant to the President, and Dr. Brzezinski;

—Representative Charles Rose of North Carolina.

The President participated in a breakfast briefing by administration officials on the strategic arms limitation agreement given for community and civic leaders in the State Dining Room at the White House.

May 31

The President met at the White House with:

—Dr. Brzezinski;

—Mr. Moore;

—Representative Silvio O. Conte of Massachusetts;

—Mrs. Carter, for lunch;

—Secretary of Energy James R. Schlesinger, Stuart E. Eizenstat, Assistant to the President for Domestic Affairs and Policy, and representatives of the petroleum industy, to discuss current gasoline shortages and the long-term outlook.

The President received the 1979 Public Health Service Award from members of the National Association of Community Health Centers in a ceremony in the Oval Office.

The White House made available the following information on the President's financial affairs: the financial disclosure report for 1978; the net worth statement as of December 31, 1978; the 1978 joint income tax return; and the Internal Revenue Service final audit report for the 1977 joint income tax return.

The President has received the report of the Emergency Board which investigated the American Train Dispatchers Association labor dispute.

June 1

The President met at the White House with:

—Secretary of Defense Harold Brown, Deputy Secretary of State Warren M. Christopher, Dr. Brzezinski, and Mr. Jordan;

—Dr. Brzezinski;

—Mr. Moore;

—U.S. Ambassador to Saudi Arabia John C. West;

—Secretary Schlesinger, Mr. Eizenstat, and representatives of consumer and conservation groups, to discuss current gasoline shortages and the long-term outlook.

The President participated in a luncheon briefing by administration officials on the strategic arms limitation agreement given for community and civic leaders in the State Dining Room at the White House.

The President left the White House for a stay at Camp David, Md.

NOMINATIONS SUBMITTED TO THE SENATE

The following list does not include promotions of members of the Uniformed Services, nominations to the Service Academies, or nominations of Foreign Service officers.

Submitted May 29, 1979

JOHN MARK DEUTCH, of Massachusetts, to be Under Secretary of Energy, vice Dale D. Myers, resigned.

ABNER J. MIKVA, of Illinois, to be United States Circuit Judge for the District of Columbia Circuit, vice a new position created by P.L. 95–486, approved October 20, 1978.

RICHARD P. CONABOY, of Pennsylvania, to be United States District Judge for the Middle District of Pennsylvania, vice a new position created by P.L. 95–486, approved October 20, 1978.

SYLVIA H. RAMBO, of Pennsylvania, to be United States District Judge for the Middle District of Pennsylvania, vice a new position created by P.L. 95–486, approved October 20, 1978.

Submitted June 1, 1979

ALAN A. PARKER, of California, to be an Assistant Attorney General, vice Patricia M. Wald, resigning.

NOMINATIONS—Continued

Submitted June 1—Continued

MAURICE ROSENBERG, of New York, to be an Assistant Attorney General, vice Daniel J. Meador, resigning.

ZITA L. WEINSHIENK, of Colorado, to be United States District Judge for the District of Colorado, vice a new position created by P.L. 95–486, approved October 20, 1978.

DANIEL MARCUS, of Maryland, to be General Counsel of the Department of Agriculture, vice Sarah Weddington, resigned.

TRUMAN ALDRICH MORRISON III, of the District of Columbia, to be an Associate Judge of the Superior Court of the District of Columbia for a term of 15 years, vice John G. Penn, elevated.

JAMES KEOUGH BISHOP, of New York, a Foreign Service officer of Class two, to be Ambassador Extraordinary and Plenipotentiary of the United States of America to the Republic of Niger.

JIM R. CARRIGAN, of Colorado, to be United States District Judge for the District of Colorado, vice a new position created by P.L. 95–486, approved October 20, 1978.

ANDREW A. DIPRETE, of Rhode Island, to be a member of the Federal Home Loan Bank Board for the remainder of the term expiring June 30, 1979, vice Garth Marston, resigned.

ANDREW A. DIPRETE, of Rhode Island, to be a member of the Federal Home Loan Bank Board for the term of 4 years expiring June 30, 1983 (reappointment).

CHECKLIST OF WHITE HOUSE PRESS RELEASES

The following listing contains releases of the White House Press Office which are not included in this issue.

CHECKLIST—Continued

Released May 27, 1979

Advance text: remarks at Fordham University commencement exercises—by Zbigniew Brzezinski, Assistant to the President for National Security Affairs

Released May 29, 1979

Fact sheet: Executive Order 12140, delegation of authorities relating to motor gasoline end-user allocation

Released May 30, 1979

Fact sheet: Vietnam era veterans

Released May 31, 1979

Announcement: report of the Emergency Board to investigate the American Train Dispatchers Association labor dispute

Announcement: appointment of Lincoln P. Bloomfield to the National Security Council staff in charge of global issues

Released June 1, 1979

Announcement: nomination of Jim R. Carrigan to be United States District Judge for the District of Colorado

Announcement: nomination of Zita L. Weinshienk to be United States District Judge for District of Colorado

ACTS APPROVED BY THE PRESIDENT

Approved May 26, 1979

S. 631_____ Public Law 96–15

An act to authorize the President of the United States to present on behalf of the Congress a specially struck gold medal to John Wayne.

PRESIDENTIAL DOCUMENTS

Week Ending Friday, June 8, 1979

Energy

Interview With John Dancy of NBC News.
June 1, 1979

MR. DANCY. Mr. President, you've been meeting with oilmen this past week to get firsthand information from them on the shortages. I'd like to hear from you what we can expect in terms of supplies in June, July, and August.

THE PRESIDENT. I'm meeting with both the oil people and also consumers and other groups.

We have a permanent problem with oil supplies. We lost 200 million barrels of oil because of the problems in Iran. The last 2 weeks, oil imports have increased somewhat.

We believe that in the summer, we'll be better off than we were in May, which was perhaps our worst month, but even at best, in the summer, we're going to have no more oil or gasoline than we had a year ago. And demand for gasoline, because of more automobiles and a lack of conservation ethic or commitment, is going to cause some continued shortages.

We have relieved the spot shortages, I think, to some degree in California, primarily because of the small increase in supply and also because of strong conservation efforts made by the people of California.

MR. DANCY. Let's talk about that demand problem for just a moment. The latest NBC News-AP poll shows that 65 percent of the people in the country simply don't believe that there is a gasoline shortage. Is there a shortage in this country?

THE PRESIDENT. Yes. In April of 1977, more than 2 years ago, I proposed to the Congress a comprehensive energy policy for the first time in the history of our Nation. After 18 months of tough debate and argument, the Congress passed not one bit of legislation concerning oil. It's that difficult.

The Congress hears from the special interest groups, particularly the oil lobby. They very seldom hear from the American people. We have now come back to the Congress with a package that will work—slow, steady, carefully monitored decontrol of oil to get the Government out of it and to let the free enterprise system work, which will improve conservation, increase domestic exploration and production, and also open up an opportunity to decrease imports and dependence on foreign supplies. There will be some increase in the price of oil and gas inevitably, no matter what we do.

So, we're going to tax the oil companies very heavily—they can keep 29 cents out of every dollar—with a windfall profits tax. The windfall profits tax will go into an energy security fund. That fund will grow year by year because of increase in OPEC prices and because of increase in prices on domestic oil because of its shortage.

That energy reserve fund, or security fund, will be used to alleviate the heavy burden on the poor families of our country, to improve mass transit, which we need, and to provide a reservoir of money for research and development to develop other sources of energy—solar power, geothermal, gasification, liquefaction of coal.

The essence of it is this: If the American people will work together and accept the fact that we do have too much demand for limited supplies of energy, our country is strong enough to resolve the problem. We have the capability to resolve the problem. But we've got to face it frankly, and we've got to work together.

Mr. DANCY. But people are skeptical about this. And one reason seems to be that the crisis appears and disappears mysteriously. One week there's a gasoline shortage in California. The Governor of California comes here and talks to you, and you say that, "Well, the situation is going to get better." And the next day Jody Powell says, "Well, it's not going to get all that much better." How can people know what to believe?

THE PRESIDENT. Sometimes people don't want to face an unpleasant fact. That's a characteristic of my own, and it's a characteristic of the American people as well.

May was a very bad month. In the latter part of last month, May, we did have an increase in imports of oil. The California people helped a great deal, because they recognized the problem. Perhaps at first they overreacted to it, but eventually they began to use more rapid transit, they began to share automobiles, they began to observe the 55-mile-per-hour speed limit. The odd-even days imposed by Governor Brown helped to some degree, and the problem was partially alleviated.

The problem is not going away. Even at the best of circumstances in June or July, we are still going to have less gasoline available in California than they had a year ago. So, it won't be good. It will be better than it was in May.

Mr. DANCY. Mr. President, the poll also shows that 55 percent of the people don't believe that you or the Congress are doing a good job of managing this gasoline shortage. How do you restore, you and the Congress, restore some faith in your leadership?

THE PRESIDENT. That's a hard question to answer. I don't claim that the Government has done a good job with the energy problem; it hasn't. I would say last year, the Congress passed about 65 percent of the legislation that I had put forward 2 years ago on energy. We have not yet had the political courage or ability to deal with oil. We're not only the world's greatest consumer and waster of oil, we're also one of the world's largest producers of oil, and the oil lobby is extremely powerful in Washington. And it's been difficult to deal with this subject.

If the people ever get aroused enough to demand action, there's no doubt in my mind that the Congress will act. I think we have an excellent chance now to get the windfall profits tax passed, which will discourage waste, encourage production in America, and set up a reserve fund to explore other sources of energy. If this is done, it'll be a major step forward. And I think under those circumstances, the people will begin to see that the Government is doing its best.

We don't have a good record at all so far. But part of their need is for people to realize that we do indeed have a problem, that we can solve it if we work together, and that they will encourage the Congress to act.

MR. DANCY. Do you believe that the debate over energy has become so political, so highly emotional that when people vote against, say, the standby rationing plan, for example, they are, in effect, voting against you and against your leadership?

THE PRESIDENT. I don't interpret it as a personal attack on me or a rejection of leadership. It's an inability or unwillingness to deal with an unpleasant subject.

The problem is with us on a permanent basis. We're going to have to quit wasting oil; we're going to have to increase American production; we're going to have to decrease imports from foreign countries; we're going to have to shift toward more use of rapid transit; we're going to have to shift toward more research and development of other sources of energy to replace oil. Those are facts. You can't get away from them. And I think we've made a tremendous amount of progress in the last 2 years, because there's a growing awareness that we do indeed have a problem.

Now we're in a phase of trying to find an easy way out or trying to find a scapegoat to blame for the problem. But if we all work together, as I say, our country is strong enough and able enough to deal with this problem and not let it become a crisis.

MR. DANCY. You've been trying to build up supplies of home heating oil, I know.

THE PRESIDENT. Yes.

MR. DANCY. And one way that you have done that is the Government has offered the oil companies a $5-a-barrel subsidy in order to encourage them to go into the world market and buy that oil and import it so that we'll have enough heating oil in the wintertime. But our European Common Market allies now say that this is bad, because it is shifting the problem to them and it's raising the world price of heating oil.

How do you answer this criticism?

THE PRESIDENT. We've had two shortages identified recently, in addition to the one that you've described. One was tractor fuel to get our crops planted. I think we successfully weathered that potential crisis period. We were planting as much as 5 million acres of crops per day, and we didn't have any serious spot shortages, because the Governors—Republicans and Democrats—the Agriculture Department, the Energy Department, and the White House worked together on it.

We have another potential shortage next winter, and that is with home heating oil. I have committed myself to build up reserve supplies of home heating oil so that our people, in the Northeast, particularly, won't go cold this winter.

We were having a problem because some refineries that make home heating oil, say, in the Caribbean, because of high prices in Europe, were shifting that oil to Europe when we should have had access to buy it for American homeowners.

So, we did try to impose and did impose a difference in the price to make us competitive in that market. The Europeans didn't like part of what we did, but I think it'll help us to alleviate that potential crisis.

MR. DANCY. Gasoline prices were the leading cause last month of the big jump in the cost of living in the country. Isn't there a great danger in all of that for your anti-inflation program?

THE PRESIDENT. Yes. I might point out that this increase in price that we've experienced has been under so-called Government controls, and the slow, carefully monitored, phased out Government controls, I think, will help to alleviate the problem over the long run. We'll still have a problem; it'll help with it.

Obviously, the price of energy is something that I cannot control. We can do our best to alleviate the problem.

We have been asked by the OPEC nations, who have been the cause of the great increase in prices, to cut back on waste and consumption. Our European allies look at Americans using twice as much oil per person as they do, with the same standard of living, and say, "Please cut back on waste and on the consumption of oil."

I'll be meeting with the leaders of six major nations, democratic nations, in Tokyo, the last of this month, and that will be one of the high, important points on the agenda. How can the consuming nations reduce our demand for imported oil in return for which the OPEC nations would agree to stabilize supply and also to stabilize prices? This has to be a multinational approach. It's one of the greatest responsibilities on my shoulders, as a leader of a great nation, and also on the shoulders of others who represent the major consuming nations.

We've not yet successfully addressed it. We have to be courageous and tenacious, we have to tell the people the truth, the people have to believe the truth, and we have to work together. There is no magic answer to a very difficult question.

MR. DANCY. Finally, the poll does show that there is a rising awareness of the energy problem. When people were asked about it, they now place it number two behind inflation as one of their concerns.

I would assume that you find that encouraging.

THE PRESIDENT. Yes, I do find it encouraging, but also I think it illustrates vividly that the two are tied together. As long as we have excessive demand for a given level of supply of energy, it creates enormous increase in prices, and those prices for oil and for other sources of energy wind up increasing prices for almost every product that we use. So, successfully addressing the energy question will take us a great step down the road to successfully solving the chronic inflation problem.

MR. DANCY. Mr. President, thank you very much.

THE PRESIDENT. Thank you, John.

NOTE: The interview began at 11:35 a.m. in the Oval Office at the White House. It was taped for broadcast on the NBC television network on June 3.

The transcript of the interview was released on June 2.

Indianapolis, Indiana

Remarks at a Reception Prior to the Jefferson-Jackson Day Dinner.   June 2, 1979

THE PRESIDENT. Birch Bayh, come on up.

SENATOR BAYH. You know how proud we are to have the President of the United States right here in Indiana.

THE PRESIDENT. That's the shortest speech I've ever heard Birch Bayh make. And I'm going to make one almost as short, because you're the key people who have helped to hold the Democratic Party and its principles strong in Indiana.

Hearing about this event tonight has been a very thrilling thing for me. It's the biggest event you've ever had. I think it's a good, accurate indication of where the Democratic Party stands today, and it's a good preview of a tremendous victory for Democrats in 1980, right? [*Applause*]

I've got a personal note, also. I understand that I'm the first incumbent President ever to speak to the Jefferson-Jackson Day banquet in Indiana. And I would not be an incumbent President had it not been for many of you, and I want to thank you for that personal help.

Also, outside the Old South, with Birch Bayh's help, and many others, Indiana gave me the largest primary victory of any State in the Nation, and I thank you for that as well.

I rode in from the airport with Don Michael and Patty Evans. I think you know how lucky you are to have them heading up the party now. Democrats in Indiana have always had a majority in registration. The principles of the Democratic Party are accurately compatible with and represent the feeling of the people of Indiana. If we can maintain the spirit and the commitment and the partnership and the cooperation and the courage and the willingness to work that has been demonstrated here tonight, there's no doubt that the future for the Democratic Party will be even brighter than it has been in the past.

Birch Bayh is the kind of leader who sets the tone for our Nation's Government. He's kind of representing the spirit of the United States Senate. He's idealistic, he's a knowledgeable, competent, hard-working, and dedicated and effective United States Senator. And he's constantly exploring for ways in government to let our Nation accurately mirror the highest possible ideals which were dreamed about 200 years ago. He is the one who explores the cutting edge of new concepts involving our United States Constitution.

I'm going to say just a word in the other larger meeting about Marvella, but I know that everyone here shares my sorrow but also my appreciation and my pride in what Marvella Bayh meant not only to Indiana but to our entire country. She's an admirable example of true courage.

The last thing is, I need your help with the ratification of SALT, the SALT treaty with the Soviet Union; maintaining peace on Earth; dealing successfully with our energy problem; controlling inflation; restoring the confidence of the American people in our own Government; having strong, able farm families; keeping our people at work—these kinds of goals, which have exemplified the Democratic spirit ever since our Nation was formed, are still ever-present on my mind.

We've got the greatest nation on Earth. With your help, we can make it even greater in the future. That's what I'm determined to do. You help me.

Thank you very much. I'll see you inside.

NOTE: The President spoke at 6:25 p.m. to dinner guests in Convention Hall C at the Indianapolis Convention Center. In his remarks, he referred to Don Michael, chairman, and Patty Evans, vice chairman, Indiana Democratic Party.

Indianapolis, Indiana

Remarks at the State Democratic Party's Jefferson-Jackson Day Dinner. June 2, 1979

It is good to be back home in Indiana— and not just because of the kind of weeks I've had recently in Washington. [*Laughter*] It is like coming home for me because of the many wonderful friends that we made here during the long campaign, when you gave us a Hoosier welcome before the rest of the Nation knew me or cared about our campaign. You took me in, and my wife and my children, my mother, and made us part of you. And I thank you for it.

I remember Andy Jacobs was one of the first ones who ever recognized that I might be a future President, and I will always remember that in particular.

During my campaign, I often wondered why no matter where I started out, I always wound up in Indiana. I finally decided it was because of the Indiana mafia who was running my scheduling. [*Laughter*]

It still seems to me that sometimes we have more people working in the White House from Indiana even than we do from Georgia. But I know you're very proud of Terry and Tim and Fran.[1] Don't brag on them too much. With our fiscal austerity, we don't have enough money to increase their salaries. [*Laughter*] But I wish they would stand up just a moment. Tim, Fran, Terry.

As you know, we don't just have Hoosiers in the White House, we've got Bill Schreiber, who has helped us with the U.S.-Canada Boundary Commission. He's doing a good job. So far, we've only given up a small part of the territory of the United States to Canada. [*Laughter*] As you well know, we have Jim Joseph and Leo Krulitz in the Interior Department doing a superb job. And I think one of the stars of our administration has been Bob McKinney at the Federal Home Loan Bank Board. I thank you for letting them serve in Washington.

I rode in from the airport with Don Michael and Patty Evans. You don't know how it makes a Democratic President feel to see a tremendous demonstration of hard work and harmony and cooperation

and dedication and political courage that's been exemplified here tonight, with 3,500 strong Democrats all ready to continue to work, some in '79, and get some fine Indiana mayors elected this year; next year to change 7 Democratic Congressmen into 11 Democratic Congressmen from Indiana.

And I particularly would like to see Indiana follow the tradition of Henry Schricker and Roger Branigin and Matt Welsh and have a Democratic Governor from Indiana elected in 1980.

As I stood outside, I heard what Birch Bayh had to say about the Democratic delegation in Congress. You can really be proud of them. Lee Hamilton's support has been superb in foreign affairs. Phil Sharp has made sure that our energy resources are fairly shared. Floyd Fithian was talking to me on the way in from Washington today about the need of farmers and better energy supplies for them; Andy Jacobs, whom I already mentioned, Adam Benjamin helping us to keep the Federal budget deficit down.

As you know, the Republicans spent a lot of money last year to put a third Crane in Congress, but the people of Indiana wisely decided to keep Dave Evans. I thank you for that.

I spent last night and today with a few key Members of the House at Camp David. John Brademas was there, the superb Democratic whip, who's shown the kind of leadership that causes the American people to give us a strong Democratic majority in the Congress and who will keep it there. And I would like to say, in addition, how much I appreciate the kind of spirit that John Brademas has shown.

And, as you know, in the three terms that Birch Bayh has served, he's come to symbolize the kind of character and courageous action which molds and which shapes the character and the spirit of the

---

[1] Terrence D. Straub, Special Assistant for Congressional Liaison (House), Timothy E. Kraft, Assistant to the President, and Frances M. Voorde, Deputy Appointments Secretary to the President.

United States Senate with the same kind of ideals on which our Nation was founded 200 years ago. I thank you for your fine delegation.

I just want to add my voice to that of John Brademas and others, because we share the personal loss with Birch of Marvella Bayh. Her spirit and courage were well known here in Indiana, but they were equally well known throughout our Nation. She faced the prospects of an untimely death with courage and an inspirational attitude which sustained many others who faced sorrow and tragedy in their lives.

She was a personal friend of ours, and her deep faith in God and in our country have helped to sustain me and many others as we faced difficult times in our public life. We truly miss her radiant presence, but it lives among us without diminution.

I know that Birch, in the memorial service for her, pointed out that he did not want to see sorrowful faces as we talk about Marvella. And I do have a spirit of thanksgiving and happiness that she lived among us. And she still lives among us, as far as I'm concerned.

The last time I was in Indiana, I spoke at Notre Dame about our foreign policy and about our intention to support human rights around the world. In the 2 years since then, much has happened. It's been a time of rebuilding. We've accomplished a great deal. We have a lot to do. But when they write the history of these years, I hope that they'll say four things about what you and I have been able to do together.

First of all, I want them to say that we Democrats have made America prosperous again and that we believe as a party in hard work and that we have put our people back to work. That's one thing I want them to say.

And I want the historians also to say that we Democrats have not been afraid to tackle difficult and controversial issues, that we have never put temporary political gain ahead of the permanent benefit of the United States of America.

And I want them to say, after Vietnam and Watergate and CIA and other embarrassing circumstances, that we Democrats together have been able to restore the faith and the trust of the American people in their own Government.

And I think, as President, I want them to say, above everything else, that America has been at peace and that we have been instrumental in leading the rest of the world away from war.

That's a good, sound history lesson.

If we can build on this platform being carried out of peace, courage, prosperity, trust, we will have kept faith with our party, and we will have kept faith with the American people, and we will enter the 1980's as a proud, confident, strong, and united nation. We can bring our Nation and the world closer to a time when war, hunger, poverty, injustice, oppression, will be no more. This is what you and I can do; this is what you and I will do together.

It's sobering to think back just a few years and remember the cynicism and the distrust, a divided nation brought about by those in power during the previous administrations, to remember the disappointment and a sense of betrayal that clouded our land.

Great changes have taken place. We've demanded a government that does not need to cover up and which actually deserves the loyalty and the trust of the people. There are no more official government lies. There are no more enemies lists. There are no more sellouts to the special interest groups.

President Andrew Jackson summed up my own beliefs when he said, and I quote: "There are no necessary evils in government. Its evils exist only in its abuses."

We are eliminating abuses, and we are meeting head-on the problems that face our Nation. When I took office in January 1977, do you remember the number one problem of our country? Unemployment. In Gary, for instance, more than 1 worker in every 10 was out of a job. Republican economics said we had to tighten our belts, but you know whose belt got tightened—those least able to afford economic difficulty.

Democratic economics have taken people off the unemployment rolls by giving them jobs. We've had a net increase of more than 8 million jobs in the United States of America since I took office, with your help—a great achievement. Now, Republicans talk about the dignity of work, but Democrats create jobs so people can work.

Americans know that Republicans also talk a lot about balanced budgets. But in the 8 years of Republican administration, the budget deficit of the United States Government was greater than all the deficits combined of the other 192 years of our Nation's existence.

Republicans talk about cutting deficits; Democrats cut them. By 1980, we will have slashed the Federal deficit more than half, and at the same time—and this is important—we have substantially increased the aid going to the elderly, to the poor, to the young, to the sick.

We have made unprecedented commitments, even more than during the Johnson years, to teach young people basic skills and to help our young people go to college. Farm families have been strengthened, net farm income is up dramatically, and agricultural exports set new records every year. You have certainly not seen any grain embargoes during this administration, and you will not see them in the future.

Okay, we have accomplished a lot. But crucial problems still face us, and that's what I want to talk to you briefly about tonight: on energy, on inflation, on keeping peace in a dangerous world.

Recently a Senator, Gaylord Nelson, jokingly said that I had tackled every unpopular issue that was before our Nation, and when there were none left, that I went out and looked for one. Well, that's not exactly right, because there were always some left, as you know. I didn't have to go around looking for tough issues. They were around, I felt, looking for me long before I got to the White House, because the Republicans before me were too busy doing other things to face these issues frankly.

The Democratic Party is the party of the people, because the people trust us to make difficult choices, to provide answers for questions that are not easy, but they are questions that must be answered for the good of our whole Nation. They gave us a substantial majority in both Houses of Congress so we could find positive solutions. They did not give us majorities so that we could vote down every solution offered just because it was not absolutely perfect.

My experience in politics is that there are no absolutely perfect solutions. But I believe that our people are willing to support us Democrats if we meet the responsibilities courageously and devise best solutions within our power.

One of the most immobilizing fears among our people is the fear of being cheated and misled. As much as anything else, this keeps our people, for instance, from making a small, personal sacrifice to solve the problems of inflation and energy.

I believe Americans are willing to do their part on energy if they feel that others will join with them on an equal basis. But in the long run, we'll all suffer with a mistaken belief that somehow or another a problem does not exist, or if it does exist, that it will miraculously fade away. The choice is between some temporary inconvenience now or very real and severe hardships later on.

There are no magic cures. We cannot plant and harvest our crops any more with mules. We cannot fuel our factories with fireplaces. The times require plain talk and political courage from Democrats. The people have entrusted Democrats with governing this country, and I have said before that in 1980 they will again entrust Democrats with governing Indiana if we who are in office do a good job.

We are not elected to hide, nor to withdraw from a fight. We've got a fight going on now in the Congress concerning energy. Our present laws don't work, controlling the price of oil; our consumption and our waste is too high; American production is too low; we are importing an increasing amount of oil from foreign countries; and under the present law, you've seen what's happened to prices.

So, we've put forward a workable package. Maybe it's not perfect; I don't claim it's perfect. But it is absolutely necessary that the Congress act, with your support, on this difficult question.

The windfall profits tax which I proposed to the Congress will let the oil companies keep 29 cents on a dollar to be used to explore and to produce more American oil. Returns from that windfall profits tax will be used to construct a security fund for energy. Part of that money, a great deal of money, about $800 million, will go to help the poorest families in our Nation who are afflicted worst by increasing prices of energy.

Another part of that fund will go to improve rapid transit, rail transportation, and otherwise.

The other part, which will be increasing fairly rapidly, is to provide research and development to explore new kinds of energy—solar power, gasohol, the liquefaction and gasification of Indiana coal. If we do these things, then my judgment is that we can meet the tremendous challenge of worldwide energy shortages.

Early next week, I will appoint the members of a commission to study the potential for alcohol fuels, including gasohol, to be made from such things as agricultural products, forest wastes, garbage, even coal. Birch Bayh sponsored this legislation, and he will be chairman of this commission. I'll also appoint, by the way, Philip French of the Indiana Farm Bureau.

Now, let me tell you something very seriously, and I want you to remember this if nothing else from my speech. We have a great nation which can meet any challenge if we work together. We can solve the energy problem with the same courage, the same pioneer spirit, the same sense of partnership which has always been exemplified by the people of Indiana. Our economic strength, our military strength, our political strength, our ethical strength, our moral strength are unsurpassed by any other nation on Earth.

And the United States of America is at peace. The founder of our party, Thomas Jefferson, looked back on his long years of service to this Nation, and he said with pride, "During the period of my administration, not a drop of the blood of a single fellow citizen was shed by the sword of war." I'm also proud that not a single drop of American blood has been shed in war during my administration. And I pray to God every day that when my years as President are over, that I can still match that achievement of Thomas Jefferson.

Now, the SALT II treaty, which has been negotiated almost 7 years under three Presidents, is part of our efforts to wage peace. There is no doubt in my mind that the SALT II treaty, when ratified, will enhance the security of the United States. There is no doubt that the SALT treaty will contribute to world peace. There is no doubt that the SALT treaty will enhance détent and will leave our Nation stronger to compete peacefully but successfully with the Soviet Union. There is no doubt that the SALT treaty will contribute greatly to the prevention of a catastrophic nuclear war. There is no doubt that the SALT treaty goes a long way toward controlling present and future atomic weapons. There is no doubt that the SALT treaty helps us to prevent other nations who are presently not nuclear powers from developing atomic explosions of their own.

The SALT II treaty is part of a process that began way back when Eisenhower was President—SALT I, Vladivostok, antiballistic missiles, limited test ban. And now, after 7 more years, SALT II is part of a process.

If the SALT II treaty should be rejected by the United States Senate, that process would be interrupted. Our NATO Allies and others who look to us for leadership would be convinced that the United States could no longer be trusted to deal fairly and strongly and effectively with the Soviet Union to protect our interests on a peaceful basis. Those allies might very well have to look elsewhere for alliances and for leadership.

If the SALT II treaty is not ratified, that long process leading to the elimination of nuclear weapons might not be recommenced. The SALT II treaty does not depend on our trusting the Soviet Union. You've got sitting here on the stage Birch Bayh, the chairman of the Senate Intelligence Committee. It is a great honor to him and to Indiana that he occupies this position, because he is in control of receiving the most secret possible information to prove to him and to me and others who are willing to listen that our country can verify the terms of the SALT II treaty by our own means, by our own technical means.

Failure to ratify this treaty would contribute billions of more dollars to the purchase of weapons that are absolutely not needed. And if we don't have this treaty, every little incident around the world, every little disagreement will be magnified greatly in its importance, and the trust that must exist among nations will be severely threatened.

I hope that every one of you Democrats will let your other Senator from Indiana and others with whom you come in contact know how deeply you feel about peace and how deeply you feel about the control of nuclear weapons throughout the world. You could do nothing greater to benefit your Nation, your families, and your future families than to help me with this issue.

And finally, let me say that during my campaign, I promised you here in Indiana that we could have a government as good as our people. Some critics said this was just cheap political campaign talk, but you understood what I was trying to say.

Our foreign policy is as good as the American people when we speak out for human rights around the world. And we will continue to protect human rights as long as I'm your President. Our foreign policy is as good as the American people when we work to bring peace not just to our own shores but to ancient enemies.

And we will continue to work for peace around the world.

We won a victory of this kind when a peace treaty was signed recently, 2 months ago, between Egypt and Israel. We saw the first fruits of that just recently, and it thrilled my heart to see Israeli ships going through the Suez Canal, to see Israel returning occupied territory to Egypt, and to see open borders between Egyptians and Israelis, who have hated each other and killed each other's young men for decades, even for centuries, for almost 2,000 years.

That treaty was possible because of two courageous men, President Sadat and Prime Minister Begin. But we were able to help at some crucial points because of the moral strength and the moral leadership of our country. That treaty was not any personal accomplishment, though I was proud to be part of the process. Whatever I was able to contribute was possible only because both those nations, their leaders and their people, recognized that the American people—not just one administration, not just one particular President, but the American people—will always support those who seek freedom and justice and peace. That's what the United States Government must stand for in the world.

Freedom, justice, and peace—these are the sources of our true power on which all else must rest. These are the principles, as you know, which have made America great.

One of our finest rights in America is that we have the blessing to speak our minds, to complain, to debate, to argue, to study, and to resolve issues in the political arena.

In our eagerness to do that, sometimes we forget how much we have actually accomplished. We forget our enormous material abundance, and we forget the wonderful treasure of our freedom. We cannot afford to forget our blessings. To lose sight of our basic strength, just because we have some problems and differences and arguments and transient setbacks, would be even more unrealistic than to ignore those transient problems.

Our land is broad, our people are diverse, and many of our people, unfortunately, are frightened by a future which they see as very different from the past that we've known. It will be very different, just as our world now is very different from what it was in my boyhood or among our ancestors, but this should not be a cause of fear.

The problems are real and they are serious, but they are manageable if we have the courage and the will to face them together. There is no doubt that we have the strength. We have a degree of respect and freedom for individuals and a commitment to provide the finest possible opportunity for every American that's unmatched in human history. We do, indeed, live in the strongest country on Earth. We cannot let all that strength, all the innate power of our natural and human resources be frittered away by fear or by futility.

Franklin Roosevelt understood how fear itself could immobilize people, and in a much more desperate moment, he warned us of the power of fear to destroy us. We cannot let the fear of change, of uncertainty, or the fear of some manageable limits on material goods immobilize our mighty Nation.

I'm very proud to be part of you. I'm very proud to be the leader of our party and the leader of our Nation. In difficult times, we Democrats have always seen not doubt, but hope; not divisiveness, but unity, growing out of a respect and an understanding of our differences and of our human strength.

We have never failed our country, and we Democrats will certainly not fail our country now.

We do have problems. We can solve those problems. We can be strong and also at peace. We can make our economy work. But we cannot do it with slogans or gimmicks or magic or by trying to put the responsibility on someone else.

America must solve her problems the same way each of us solves our own problems—with hard work and persistence and courage and, occasionally, some pain and some sacrifice. But we must not confuse difficulty with defeat. The actions we take to get through our current problems will enhance our strength for a future that will be even brighter than our past.

I look forward to those years—next year, the next decade, the next century— because I know that the people of the United States have the will and the strength of character to make those years even better in the greatest nation on Earth.

Thank you very much.

NOTE: The President spoke at 8:15 p.m. in Convention Hall B at the Indianapolis Convention Center.

A. Philip Randolph

Remarks at Memorial Services for the Late Civil Rights Leader. June 3, 1979

The President of the United States has many invitations to speak, a thousand invitations for each one that I can accept. But when I heard about this memorial for A. Philip Randolph, I did not hesitate. I told my staff to cancel my other requests, and I wanted to be here personally.

I've had a chance to know some of the people who have already spoken. Bayard Rustin's words moved me deeply. And as I listened to him and thought about our country, I realized even more vividly that we are in a time of change, of doubt, of fear, of division, of uncertainty. When standards are transient and when we seek as individual human beings for some life which can inspire us, I doubt that there is a mother or a father in this Nation who, knowing A. Philip Randolph and what he was, would not want our sons and daughters to be like him.

It's not an accident that Mr. Rustin and the other members of his brotherhood called him "The Chief." That didn't mean that he was a domineering master, that he imposed his will on others, that he was an autocratic driver of those who worked under him and who looked to him for leadership. It meant that he was an object of admiration, of respect, even perhaps, of reverence.

When there was hardly any detectable civil rights movement in our country back in 1941, A. Philip Randolph led the march on Washington. As has been pointed out, he was scorned by those in power. And he was even feared somewhat by those who were oppressed, because his strong voice might create some disturbance in their own quiet lives if their own rights were pushed forward too loudly and too strongly. But he was not deterred.

He was a man of dignity; he was a man of tenacity; he was a man of eloquence; and he was a man of gentleness and of constant idealism. But the words "gentleness" and "idealism" don't quite describe what A. Philip Randolph was, because he was able to combine idealism with hard work and sweat.

He was a working man. His father was a tailor and a preacher. And he combined gentleness with kind of a brash courage in a time when it was not done. He stood up strongly, face to face, with four great Presidents: Woodrow Wilson, Franklin Roosevelt, Harry Truman, John Kennedy—not seeking publicity, not seeking a confrontation, but because he believed in a principle so deeply that he was not at all fearful or timid about a confrontation with the highest elected official of our country.

His struggle was not easy, but the victories he won were permanent, steps that seemed to be small. And one of the reasons for their permanence as building blocks for the future was that he did not leave behind him a battlefield of bitterness.

His own personal character assuaged the feelings of those who confronted him on the opposite side of an argument and lost. They accepted the judgment that was rendered when A. Philip Randolph won his important victories.

He was a man who studied Shakespeare—not to show that he was highly educated or erudite, not to learn how human beings can move like chameleons on and off the stage life with constantly changing principles and ideals and commitments, but he studied Shakespeare so that he could learn the constant truths of the human soul.

I found a passage from Shakespeare that I think might be appropriate, and I'd like to read it. It's just two lines. "Wherever the bright sun of heaven shall shine, his honor and the greatness of his name shall be"—and a very strange but pertinent ending—"and shall make new nations."

"Wherever the bright sun of heaven shall shine, his honor and the greatness of his name shall be and shall make new nations."

It would not be appropriate to take away from many others, some in this church, credit for the achievements of the last few years or decades. But I don't think there's any doubt that A. Philip Randolph contributed to the making of a new nation—not a perfect nation, not a

nation worthy of maintaining the status quo, but a nation of struggle which has observed progress and which recognizes that progress still remains to be made because we live in a society even here in the United States where inequality and hatred, deprivation and hunger, racism, still exist.

But I think that A. Philip Randolph and his life exemplified one additional truth that I'd like to say. Institutions, governments set as goals material progress: opening up the West, the expansion of our Nation, increase in gross national product, achievements of which chambers of commerce can be proud in individual cities. Those kinds of evidence of progress are supported by a wide range of institutions and organizations that mutually benefit from them. But social progress—equality, liberty, freedom, justice—that kind of progress comes rarely from government as the initiator; it almost invariably comes from a courageous human being whose fellow workers might call him the Chief.

We have a great nation. It can be much greater if we never forget the life and the times and the constant presence in our lives of the Chief.

NOTE: The President spoke at 2:45 p.m. at the Metropolitan African Methodist Episcopal Church.

The Cyprus Conflict

Letter to the Speaker of the House and the Chairman of the Senate Foreign Relations Committee. June 4, 1979

To Speaker Tip O'Neill: (To Chairman Frank Church:)

In accordance with the provisions of Public Law 95–384, I am submitting the following report on progress made during the past sixty days toward the conclusion of a negotiated solution of the Cyprus problem.

On May 18–19 Cyprus President Kyprianou and Turkish Cypriot leader Denktash met in Nicosia under the auspices of U.N. Secretary-General Waldheim. Following intensive discussions, the two Cypriot leaders agreed to resume full intercommunal negotiations in Nicosia on June 15. This is a significant decision, which holds open the promise that tangible progress can finally be made towards a just and lasting Cyprus settlement. The last round of negotiations was held more than two years ago, in the spring of 1977, and since that time the issue has virtually been stalemated.

In the course of their meeting the two Cypriot leaders concurred in a ten-point communique, issued by the Secretary-General on May 19, that will serve as a basis for the new round of negotiations. I am enclosing a copy of this communique for your information. As you will note, the two sides have agreed that the talks will be sustained and continuous, and that priority will be given to the resettlement of Varosha under United Nations auspices. Provision is made for initial practical measures by both sides to promote goodwill and mutual confidence.

In another significant step, President Kyprianou and Mr. Denktash also reached agreement on May 19 on a procedure for resolving the long-standing humanitarian problem of tracing and accounting for persons missing since the hostilities of 1974 and the intercommunal violence in Cyprus during the 1960's.

As I have noted in previous reports to the Congress, the Administration has long been actively engaged in promoting an early and effective resumption of Cyprus negotiations. Last November, in conjunction with the United Kingdom and Canada, we submitted to the two Cypriot

parties a series of suggestions for a substantive basis for renewed negotiations, and subsequently we strongly supported Secretary-General Waldheim's efforts to develop a negotiating agenda satisfactory to both sides. Through regular diplomatic channels and numerous high-level contacts, we have consistently urged a moderate, flexible and conciliatory approach. More recently, we actively encouraged all concerned to work for a successful outcome to the May 18–19 Kyprianou-Denktash meeting. I sent a message to the Secretary-General just prior to the meeting stressing the importance that we attach to a Cyprus settlement and pledging him our full and continuing support. Secretary Vance also sent messages to President Kyprianou and Mr. Denktash expressing our strong hope that their meeting would result in a productive resumption of intercommunal negotiations.

It is my firm hope that the new round of intercommunal negotiations will be both sustained and productive, and that concrete progress towards a Cyprus settlement will soon result. I assure you that we will continue as in past months to work closely with the United Nations, the Cypriot parties and our allies to help ensure the success of these talks.

Sincerely,

JIMMY CARTER

NOTE: This is the text of identical letters addressed to Thomas P. O'Neill, Jr., Speaker of the House of Representatives, and Frank Church, chairman of the Senate Foreign Relations Committee.

The text of the communique is included in the press release, and it reads as follows:

CYPRUS INTERCOMMUNAL NEGOTIATIONS

Communique agreed to by President Kyprianou and Turkish Cypriot Leader Denktash with United Nations Secretary General Waldheim, May 19, 1979.

1. It was agreed to resume the intercommunal talks on 15 June 1979.

2. The basis for the talks will be the Makarios/Denktash guidelines of 12 February 1977 and the U.N. resolutions relevant to the Cyprus question.

3. There should be respect for human rights and fundamental freedoms of all citizens of the Republic.

4. The talks will deal with all territorial and constitutional aspects.

5. Priority will be given to reaching agreement on the resettlement of Varosha under U.N. auspices simultaneously with the beginning of the consideration by the interlocutors of the constitutional and territorial aspects of a comprehensive settlement. After agreement on Varosha has been reached it will be implemented without awaiting the outcome of the discussion on other aspects of the Cyprus problem.

6. It was agreed to abstain from any action which might jeopardize the outcome of the talks, and special importance will be given to initial practical measures by both sides to promote goodwill, mutual confidence and the return to normal conditions.

7. The demilitarization of the Republic of Cyprus is envisaged, and matters relating thereto will be discussed.

8. The independence, sovereignty, territorial integrity and non-alignment of the Republic should be adequately guaranteed against union in whole or in part with any other country and against any form of partition or secession.

9. The intercommunal talks will be carried out in a continuing and sustained manner, avoiding any delay.

10. The intercommunal talks will take place in Nicosia.

National P.O.W.–M.I.A. Recognition Day, 1979

Proclamation 4664. June 4, 1979

By the President of the United States of America

A Proclamation

In each of America's past wars our prisoners of war have represented a special sacrifice. On them has fallen an added burden of loneliness, trauma, and hardship. Their burden becomes double when there is inhumane treatment by the enemy in violation of common human compassion, ethical standards, and international obligations.

The Congress has by Joint Resolution (Public Law 95–349) designated July 18, 1979, as "National P.O.W.–M.I.A. Recognition Day."

As we now enjoy the blessings of peace, it is appropriate that all Americans recognize the special debt owed those Americans held prisoner during wartime. It also is appropriate that we remember the unresolved casualties of war, our soldiers who are missing. The pain and bitterness of war endures for the families, relatives and friends of those whose fate is unknown. Our Nation will continue to seek answers to the questions that remain about their fate.

Now, THEREFORE, I, JIMMY CARTER, President of the United States of America, do hereby designate Wednesday, July 18, 1979, as National P.O.W.–M.I.A. Recognition Day, a day dedicated both to all former American prisoners of war as well as those still missing and to their families. I call on all Americans to join on this occasion in honoring those who made the special sacrifice of being captive in war, and their loved ones.

And I call on State and local officials and private organizations to observe this day with appropriate ceremonies and activities.

IN WITNESS WHEREOF, I have hereunto set my hand this fourth day of June, in the year of our Lord nineteen hundred seventy-nine, and of the Independence of the United States of America the two hundred and third.

JIMMY CARTER

[Filed with the Office of the Federal Register, 4:44 p.m., June 4, 1979]

Independent Water Project Review

Executive Order 12141.   June 5, 1979

By the authority vested in me as President by the Constitution and statutes of the United States of America, and in order to provide for an orderly implementation of the independent review of Federal water resource programs and projects, subsections (b) and (c) of Section 1–105 of Executive Order No. 12113 of January 4, 1979, are hereby amended to read as follows:

"(b) After October 1, 1979, an agency shall not submit to the Council, during any calendar quarter, more than one-third of the total reports, proposals, and plans scheduled for review during any one fiscal year.

"(c) The Chairman of the Council, or his designee, shall transmit the results of the impartial technical review to the appropriate agency head The transmittal shall include identification of any specific variations from Council approved procedures and manuals and the steps necessary to bring the plan into conformance. The results of the review shall be transmitted to the agency head within 60 days of the agency's submission of the report, proposal, or plan provided that funds and other resources have been made available for the review.".

JIMMY CARTER

The White House,
June 5, 1979.

[Filed with the Office of the Federal Register, 2:56 p.m., June 5, 1979]

Department of the Treasury

Nomination of Walter J. McDonald To Be an Assistant Secretary.   June 5, 1979

The President today announced that he will nominate Walter J. McDonald, of Washington, D.C., to be an Assistant Secretary of the Treasury. He would replace William Beckham, Jr., who has resigned, and his area of responsibility would be administration.

McDonald has been with the Treasury Department for 14 years, and is currently serving as Acting Assistant Secretary.

He was born December 21, 1926, in Staten Island, N.Y. He holds a degree in business administration from New York University and a masters degree in business from Southeastern University. He served in the U.S. Army during World War II and the Korean war.

Prior to joining the Treasury Department, McDonald was the Deputy Comptroller at Fort Irwin, Calif., for 4 years and served in a similar position with the Army in Europe for 6 years.

His initial assignment at Treasury was as a management analyst where he participated in a number of studies of the Department's activities. He has also served as the Chief of the Department's Emergency Planning Staff and as financial manager and EEO officer for the Office of the Secretary. Since 1974 he has been assigned as the Deputy Director of the Office of Management and Organization. In November 1978, he was assigned to the position of Acting Assistant Secretary.

Department of Health, Education, and Welfare

Nomination of Richard I. Beattie To Be General Counsel.   June 5, 1979

The President today announced that he will nominate Richard I. Beattie, of Washingon, D.C., to be General Counsel of the Department of Health, Education, and Welfare. He would replace F. Peter Libassi, who has resigned.

Beattie is currently executive assistant to HEW Secretary Joseph Califano, and is a former Deputy General Counsel at HEW.

He was born March 24, 1939, in New York City. He received a B.A. in economics from Dartmouth College in 1961 and an LL.B. from the University of Pennsylvania Law School in 1968. He served in the U.S. Marine Corps as a jet pilot from 1961 to 1965.

From 1968 to 1977, Beattie practiced law with the New York law firm of Simpson, Thacher & Bartlett, as an associate until 1975 and a partner from 1975 to 1977. He was Deputy General Counsel at HEW from 1977 until 1978, when he became executive assistant to Secretary Califano.

From 1970 to 1977, Beattie was also a trustee of Community Law Offices, a nonprofit corporation providing legal services to the poor in New York City. From 1975 to 1977, he was on the board of directors of City School News, a privately funded, nonprofit corporation organized as a public education information service for New York City.

Corporation for Public Broadcasting

Nomination of Michael R. Kelley To Be a Member of the Board of Directors. June 5, 1979

The President today announced that he will nominate Michael R. Kelley, of Fairfax, Va., to be a member of the Board of Directors of the Corporation for Public Broadcasting. He would replace Virginia Duncan, whose term has expired.

Kelley is a professor of English at George Mason University and a former broadcaster with several Washington radio stations.

He was born August 20, 1940, in Washington, D.C. He received a B.A. from Catholic University in 1962. He began his career in radio in 1961 as an announcer at WGAY, and worked at a number of stations, finally becoming news director of WASH–FM. During this time he also earned an M.F.A. degree in speech and drama from Catholic University.

In 1967 Kelley left broadcasting to accept an NDEA fellowship for doctoral study at Catholic University. He received a Ph. D. in English in 1970 and joined the faculty of George Mason University.

Kelley organized the first cooperative venture among Washington's three network-affiliated television stations, to produce "Time for English," 90 half-hour programs to teach conversational English to adults for whom it is a second language. He is the author of numerous articles and reviews on a variety of subjects.

International North Pacific Fisheries Commission

Appointment of Four Commissioners of the U.S. Section. June 5, 1979

The President today announced the appointment of four persons as Commissioners of the United States Section of the International North Pacific Fisheries Commission. They are:

ELMER E. RASMUSON, of Anchorage, Alaska, who was chairman of the board of the National Bank of Alaska until his retirement in 1974. He is a former mayor of Anchorage.

ROBERT M. THORSTENSON, of Petersburg, Alaska, president of Icicle Seafoods (formerly Petersburg Fisheries);

WILLIAM G. SALETIC, of Seattle, senior vice president of Peter Pan Seafoods, formerly executive manager of the Seiners Association and Purse Seine Vessel Owners Association of Seattle;

Harry L. Rietze, of Juneau, Alaska, Regional Director for the Alaska Region of the National Marine Fisheries Service.

Federal Pay System Reform

Message to the Congress Transmitting Proposed Legislation.   June 6, 1979

To the Congress of the United States:

I am transmitting to the Congress today legislation to reform the Federal civilian employee compensation system. The proposals I am making will insure that Federal employees are rewarded fairly for their work and that taxpayers' dollars for such compensation are well spent. This legislation is part of my continuing efforts to make the operation of the Federal government more efficient, effective and equitable.

The Federal pay system has been governed under the principle of comparability since 1962. The comparability principle requires that annual Federal employee pay increases be based upon a survey comparison with pay levels of employees with similar jobs in the non-Federal sector. By determining pay raises through an objective, annual survey, the pay setting process is depoliticized, employee expectations are stabilized, and the government is better able to plan the timing and approximate size of pay adjustments. This comparability principle is equitable to Federal employees and taxpayers alike.

Despite the soundness of the principle of comparability, significant problems have developed in the way the comparability principle is implemented. The existing comparability system, by excluding consideration of such factors as employee fringe benefits, has distorted the compari-

sons between the Federal and non-Federal sectors. In addition, other structural and procedural problems have developed with parts of our Federal employee compensation system. The blue-collar pay system, for example, has statutory requirements that result in unjustified salary levels for these workers.

The Federal Employees Compensation Reform Act of 1979 will remedy these problems. Its objectives are to:

—insure that Federal employees are paid fairly;

—make the comparability system more accurate;

—improve management flexibility in the compensation area so that needed employees can be better recruited and retained;

—make sure that taxpayers' money for Federal employee compensation is efficiently spent; and,

—eventually reduce the annual budgetary cost of the Federal payroll.

TOTAL COMPENSATION COMPARABILITY

At present, comparability between the the Federal and non-Federal sectors is measured only in terms of pay rates. However, a large part of compensation for both Federal and non-Federal employees consists of benefits aside from pay such as retirement and health plans. If we are to have a truly comparable Federal employee compensation system, such fringe benefits cannot be ignored. Under my proposal the value of benefits plus pay in the non-Federal sector would be compared with benefits plus pay in the Federal sector. This concept, known as total compensation comparability, would allow for a realistic assessment of whether the total compensation of Federal employees is ahead, comparable with, or behind that of their non-Federal counterparts.

At present, General Schedule employees of a given grade are paid the same rate regardless of where they work in the United States. However, pay rates in the non-Federal sector vary widely in different parts of our nation. As a result, Federal pay rates are significantly higher in some areas than local prevailing rates. In others, Federal rates are far below the local level. These differences either give the Federal government an unfair competitive advantage over other employers or hamper the government's ability to recruit and retain a qualified work force. My proposal would minimize this problem by requiring that the compensation of most white collar employees be comparable with compensation in the local area.

CHANGES IN THE BLUE-COLLAR PAY
SYSTEM

The system for paying blue-collar employees, known as the Federal Wage System, is already based upon the principle that Federal blue-collar pay rates should be comparable to prevailing local non-Federal rates. However, several features of the Federal Wage System law are inconsistent with this principle, such as one which requires the use of non-local wage data under certain circumstances and the distortion that results from applying average local pay rates to a designated step in the Federal grade structure. As a result, the Federal government pays many blue-collar workers well above local prevailing rates. My proposal would repeal these unjustified statutory provisions, and would allow the Office of Personnel Management to design provisions that reflect prevailing practices.

INCLUSION OF STATE AND LOCAL GOVERN-
MENTS IN COMPARABILITY SURVEYS

Under existing law, only private businesses are surveyed in the comparability process used to set Federal white and blue collar compensation rates. State and local government employment is excluded. This exclusion distorts true comparability. Today there are over 13 million State and local employees, almost 14 percent of the national work force. This is double the number employed in 1962 when comparability was first adopted. If compensation for Federal employees is to be truly comparable to what other Americans are paid, this large portion of the national work force should be included in the survey. In addition, there are a number of job categories in State and local government such as policeman, firefighter, and social worker which are analogous to certain Federal job categories but are not well represented in the private sector. This is a further reason why State and local government workers should be included in the comparability survey.

INCREASED MANAGEMENT FLEXIBILITY TO
RECRUIT AND RETAIN A QUALITY WORK
FORCE

This legislation would give Executive Branch managers needed flexibility to adopt more efficient and equitable industry pay practices. For example, premium pay such as overtime would be patterned after prevailing practices and the provisions of the Fair Labor Standards Act. Limited additional payments called "staffing differentials" would be authorized to aid in recruiting and retaining highly qualified individuals critically needed for the Federal work force. The Office of Personnel Management would be authorized to establish special pay and classification systems for those occupations that do not fit a standard pattern of the General Schedule and for which it is difficult to hire qualified employees. This would be similar to the authority the Office now has for special blue-collar schedules.

The reforms I am proposing today are based on the principle that comparability is the best long-term policy for determining compensation for Federal employees. It is not expected that any employee will suffer any actual reduction in current pay as a result of these proposals. However, in the long-run this legislation will create significant annual budget savings.

I ask the Congress to act promptly on these proposals to reform the Federal civilian compensation system. Federal employees will benefit from fairer compensation treatment. The American people will benefit from more efficient use of their tax dollars.

JIMMY CARTER

The White House,
June 6, 1979.

Meeting With Chancellor Helmut Schmidt of the Federal Republic of Germany

Remarks to Reporters Following the Meeting.
June 6, 1979

THE PRESIDENT. The Chancellor and I have had a very productive discussion of many items of importance to the Federal Republic of Germany and to the United States of America.

We discussed our plans for the economic summit conference in Tokyo, to be held the last part of this month. We spent, I would say, more of our time on the energy question than any other single issue, because it has become of crucial importance to our countries and to the entire world. We recognize the importance of our acting in concert to the extent that our own national interests permit.

We discussed the upcoming summit conference in Vienna between myself and President Brezhnev of the Soviet Union. As has been my custom ever since I've been in office, I sought the advice and counsel of Chancellor Schmidt. We recognize that our countries share a great responsibility as members of NATO, and we discussed how upcoming discussions on SALT III and theater-type weapons might be addressed after SALT II is concluded and ratified.

We had a general discussion about other regional areas of the world—southern Africa, Mideast, Persian Gulf area—and general relationships between our two countries and matters of mutual interest.

It's always a great honor for us to have the leader of Germany come here and consult on matters that are important, and we, I think, without question, consider these discussions both fruitful and they are held in a spirit of great frankness and mutual productivity.

I described to Chancellor Schmidt the elements of the SALT II agreement, and we have continued the discussion and consultations with our major allies, like the Federal Republic of Germany, as the SALT II negotiations have progressed.

Again, on behalf of the American people, I would like to say, Chancellor Schmidt, that we're delighted to have you here with us. This visit has been very helpful to me and to our people.

THE CHANCELLOR. Thank you.

Well, ladies and gentlemen, I would just like to add a very few words. Especially, I would like to stress what the President has said about the friendliness and the frankness, at the same time, and the productivity of the talks between the President and myself, and I would also like to include the talks I had earlier on with Secretaries Blumenthal and Schlesinger and Harold Brown.

It's almost now been a habit that there be at least one occasion in the course of

12 months that the President and I have a chance for private exchange of views, except of official conferences. We learn a lot from such private talks. We know that we depend heavily on the United States of America in many fields, not only in defense, also in economics and in international politics.

As you may have heard, I have a chance to make two or three public speeches today and tomorrow, day after tomorrow. And I will certainly not only publicly underline the strong feeling of indebtedness which my nation shares with me vis-a-vis the United States, vis-a-vis the United States Government, vis-a-vis the United States President, in principle and in general, but we'll especially take these opportunities in trying to emphasize towards the American public that we also, from a European and especially from a German point of interest, looking forward to a swift and positive ratification process as regards SALT II, that we are in agreement with the United States on the basic lines of our energy policies in particular and our economic policies in general.

Thank you very much, Jimmy, for your hospitality and for the frankness and friendliness of our talks.

THE PRESIDENT. Thank you, again.

NOTE: The President spoke at 2:55 p.m. on the South Grounds of the White House.

Meeting With Chancellor Schmidt of the Federal Republic of Germany

White House Statement. June 6, 1979

President Jimmy Carter and Federal Chancellor Helmut Schmidt met today for an extensive exchange of views. With their advisers they discussed the forthcoming Tokyo summit, and in particular the critical energy situation. They agreed on the need to reduce energy demand now and to increase energy supply over the longer term, including the use of alternatives to oil.

Later, the President and the Chancellor discussed privately a wide range of issues, including the forthcoming summit meeting in Vienna between Presidents Carter and Brezhnev, efforts to pursue the policy of détente, Western defense policy, Middle East, and southern Africa.

President Carter and Chancellor Schmidt agreed on the importance—for both Europe and America—of the SALT II agreement, and the Chancellor expressed strong support for the agreement. On Western defense policy, the two leaders reviewed the implications of Soviet military efforts, especially developments in theater nuclear forces. They agreed that these Soviet military efforts pose a challenge to the Alliance that requires a response. They discussed theater nuclear force modernization in particular, and agreed on the need for the NATO Alliance to move forward expeditiously with its deliberations on both force modernization and arms control, with a view to collective Alliance decisions in both areas.

They also reaffirmed their commitment to strengthen NATO's defenses as part of the Alliance's Long-Term Defense Program.

On the Middle East, the two leaders discussed the importance of the Egypt-Israel treaty and the need to move forward with the peace process, leading to a comprehensive peace throughout the region. They emphasized the importance of speedy progress in the negotiations concerning the West Bank and Gaza with a view to facilitating the exercise by the Palestinian people of their legitimate rights.

The two leaders discussed the situation in southern Africa. They reiterated the commitment of their two Governments to work together with Canada, France, and the United Kingdom for the implementation of Security Council Resolution 435 on Namibia. They exchanged views on developments in Zimbabwe-Rhodesia and their international implications, taking fully into account the special position of the United Kingdom in this regard.

During their talks, the two leaders also repeated their concern about the economic situation in Turkey, to which both of their countries are making significant contributions.

The two leaders will next meet at the Tokyo summit on June 28–29.

Air Quality Standards in Ohio

Statement on Actions by the Environmental Protection Agency To Preserve Coal-Related Jobs. June 6, 1979

Since the beginning of my administration, I have been concerned about the severe economic distress occurring in southeastern Ohio as a result of the steady loss of mining jobs in that area. At my direction, efforts have been undertaken within the administration to develop solutions to this problem. I am very pleased that today the Environmental Protection Agency has announced a series of actions which will not only preserve more than 7,000 jobs in southeastern Ohio, but will serve as the foundation for further action to solve this area's economic difficulties.

Senators Glenn and Metzenbaum and Congressman Applegate, as well as a number of State and local leaders in Ohio, are to be applauded by the citizens of Ohio for helping the administration focus its resources toward developing a solution to this serious problem.

The actions taken today by EPA will address the economic disruption problem in the following ways:

—EPA proposes to revise, after a 60-day comment period, the permissible emission levels at two Cleveland area coal-powered utilities. The revisions, which are based on new emissions data, would permit the plants to continue to burn Ohio high-sulfur coal if, as EPA now believes, this revision is proven to be consistent with all of the requirements of the Clean Air Act. This action would preserve 2,150 mining jobs and 3,225 jobs dependent on the mining jobs.

—EPA has reached an agreement—in principle—with another Ohio utility which would permit it to comply with clean air standards by using washed Ohio high-sulfur coal. This would preserve 670 mining jobs and 1,005 mine-dependent jobs.

—The CEI proposal and EPA's action in response is an example of the receptivity of the Agency to this problem. Other revisions will be proposed by EPA if warranted on their merits. EPA is currently reviewing proposed revisions.

As a result of these EPA actions, the administration will not proceed at this time with action under Section 125 of the Clean Air Act. The need for any action under that section will be evaluated at a later time, when the impact of the action taken today can be more fully assessed.

I am particularly gratified that the EPA has taken actions which, while preserving Ohio jobs, will neither sacrifice public health nor cause higher utility bills for Ohio's consumers. In my view, clean air must be preserved, and Ohio's consumers should not be forced at this time to bear unnecessary additional utility costs.

Finally, I recognize that the steps EPA is taking will not save every mining job which has been lost in recent times in southeastern Ohio. Under existing laws, there is no step that EPA or any Federal agency can take to accomplish that. But today's action is significant, for it represents the first major step taken by the Federal Government which will help preserve Ohio mining jobs.

It may be possible in the future to expand on today's action. Within the administration, we will continue our efforts in that direction. With the cooperation of State and local officials, those in the coal mining industry, and the Ohio utilities, I am hopeful that we can succeed.

National Transportation Safety Board

Nomination of G. H. Patrick Bursley To Be a Member. June 6, 1979

The President today announced that he will nominate G. H. Patrick Bursley, of Bethesda, Md., to be a member of the National Transportation Safety Board. He would replace Kay Bailey, who has resigned.

Bursley retired from the Coast Guard last year as Chief Counsel, with the rank of rear admiral, after 32 years of service.

He was born April 5, 1925, in Istanbul, Turkey. He received a B.S. from the U.S. Coast Guard Academy in 1946 and a J.D. from George Washington University Law School in 1953.

Bursley had various sea and shore assignments with the Coast Guard between 1946 and 1954. From 1954 to 1958, he was district legal officer in Seattle. From 1958 to 1960, he was Commanding Officer of the Coast Guard Cutter *Magnolia*. From 1960 to 1964, he was a district legal officer, first in San Francisco, then in Honolulu. From 1964 to 1966, he was Coast Guard liaison with the Treasury Department.

From 1966 to 1968, Bursley was assistant to the Deputy Under Secretary of Transportation. From 1968 to 1969, he was with the Office of Policy Review in the Office of the Secretary of Transportation, and from 1969 to 1972, he was Chief of the Maritime and International Law Division of the Coast Guard.

From 1972 to 1974, Bursley was captain of the port for the Coast Guard in Baltimore. From 1974 to 1976, he was Commander of the Second Coast Guard District. In 1976 he was Chief of the U.S. Delegation to the International Conference on Convention for the Limitation of Liability of Maritime Claims, held in London.

From 1976 until his retirement in 1978, Bursley was Chief Counsel to the Coast Guard and Chairman of the Marine Safety Council of the Coast Guard.

National Alcohol Fuels Commission

Appointment of the Seven Public Members. June 6, 1979

The President today announced the appointment of the seven public members of the National Alcohol Fuels Commission. The Commission also includes six Members of the Senate and six Members of the House of Representatives. The seven public members appointed today are:

CHARLENE M. BLOCK, of Terryville, Conn., an organizer for the United Auto Workers (UAW), who is active at the local and international levels. She is the UAW delegate to the New England Energy Congress, Connecticut UAW coordinator for Citizens Labor Energy Coalition, and chairperson of the UAW local consumer affairs committee.

JAMES B. CREAL, of Arlington, Va., president of the American Automobile Association (AAA).

PHILIP F. FRENCH, of Indianapolis, assistant executive vice president of the Indiana Farm Bureau, responsible for petroleum, crops, livestock and poultry, and farm and building supplies operations. He is also on the board of directors of CF Industries, Inc., a producer of nitrogen, phosphate, and potash fertilizers owned by 19 regional cooperatives.

SERGE GRATCH, of Birmingham, Mich., director of the Chemical Sciences Laboratory for the Ford Motor Co.

C. FRED JONES, of Auburndale, Fla., a farmer, cattleman, and citrus grower, and a member of the Florida House of Representatives, where he is chairman of the transportation committee.

SHARON L. PETERSON, of Winifred, Mont., secretary treasurer of her family's farm and ranch feedlot and trucking business. She is Montana legislative chairman and central Montana area spokeswoman for Women Involved in Farm Economics, and a founding member of the National Gasohol Commission, a citizens group gathering information on alcohol fuels.

THEODORE A. SCHWARTZ, of Livingston, N.J., an attorney specializing in environmental law, formerly deputy attorney general of New Jersey, in which capacity he represented all State agencies that had jurisdiction over health and environmental matters.

United Food and Commercial Workers International Union

*Remarks at the Union's Founding Convention.
June 7, 1979*

President Bill Wynn, United Food and Commercial Workers:

I want to thank you for that introduction and also that reception. I've always known that Bill Wynn was a man of great vision, but I never knew before that he was such an accurate analyst of recent history, and I thank you very much. [*Laughter*]

I'm honored in several ways to be introduced by one of the most decent, effective, and respected labor leaders in Amer-

ica, your president and my friend, Bill Wynn; to be able to join your secretary-treasurer, Sam Talarico, the members of the executive board, and the first delegates to the newest and now the largest union in the AFL–CIO, the United Food and Commercial Workers Union.

I'm honored to be with one of the most committed and the most caring men who've ever served on a President's Cabinet, Ray Marshall; and to be with the president emeritus of the Amalgamated Meatcutters, one of the fine leaders of the American labor movement, a man that I revere and respect, Paddy Gorman; and with a friend of yours and mine—who, coincidentally, joined me and my wife last night for supper at the White House with his wife—a great labor leader in America, Lane Kirkland.

I understand this is your inaugural convention. When I heard you were having an inauguration, I came right over. [*Laughter*] I had to walk all the way. As a matter of fact, I walk a lot these days. They've taken my parking place away, too. [*Laughter*]

I just left Fritz Mondale, who's meeting with the six New England Governors about the energy question. As I left, Fritz said, "Did you hear that Bill Wynn has endorsed you for reelection?" And I said, "Yes. And did you also hear that Bill Wynn has appointed 50 vice presidents in this new union?" And Fritz said, "Well, nobody's perfect, Mr. President." [*Laughter*]

I'm going to make kind of a different speech to you this afternoon, relatively brief, from my heart, as President of our great country. This historic merger of two unions, each with such a proud history, is a notable achievement not just for the labor movement itself but for our country. When this great new organization of working people speaks out for social justice and for improvements in the American way of life, your voice, the voice of the United Food and Commercial Workers, will be heard throughout the Nation. And I guarantee that your voice will always be heard in the office of the President of the United States.

I need the advice and the counsel of Bill Wynn, because I know that Bill Wynn believes in this country and he has shown over and over that he is never afraid to speak his own mind. And I'm sure that that's one of the major reasons that you chose him as your first leader.

Your new union was born out of a spirit of high principle and compromise. Each union could have jealously fought for every inch of territory, every office, every perk, every privilege, but instead you have pooled your strength and your resources in a common cause. And in the process, you have greatly magnified your strength and your resources.

Bill Wynn has outlined some of the achievements which you and I have realized together. There's no need for me to repeat them. This is not a time to rest on our laurels. We still have tough problems to face and tough problems to solve together. Today, all Americans face the same basic choice that you have just faced with such courage. Each of us can choose to be part of a stronger, more confident, and more prosperous nation, united through a sense of common purpose, or we can worry only about our own interests. We can be weakened and divided as a nation and be afraid of the future until all of us suffer in the end.

More than two centuries ago, the founders of our country expressed grave doubts whether a free people in a democracy like ours could ever rise above special personal or regional interests to deal with a crisis or a serious challenge with courage and in a sense of unity.

I see this concern every day in Washington. You see it on the evening news, the greatest democratic system of government which has ever existed on Earth, twisted and pulled in every direction by hundreds of well-financed, powerful, sometimes quite selfish special interest groups.

We see every extreme, one-sided political positions defended to the last vote by one unyielding, powerful group or another. We see every compromise, every evenhanded, fair solution that asks for just a little sacrifice from everyone abandoned like an orphan, without support and without friends.

We see our country facing serious problems in energy, inflation, and we see the threat of stagnation or paralysis and drift brought about by fear of the future and a lack of common purpose, courage, and unity.

I'm tired of seeing America pulled apart by selfishness, and I believe that you are tired of this prospect also.

But if we are united, I am not afraid of the future. I look forward to the challenges, and I look forward with you to the great victories ahead, if we work together.

Our country was not built, it has not prospered, by people who said, "Me first, me last, me always." We've not prevailed as a nation of free people for 200 years, continually enlarging freedom and dignity and opportunity, prosperity, hope for all Americans, by practicing the politics of selfishness. You know that. Neither the Retail Clerks nor the Amalgamated Meatcutters ever drew a line through the Nation and said, "We will look out for just our own dues-paying members, and the rest of America can take care of itself." You never said that, and as President, I thank you for it.

You've always used your influence and your power to fight for decency and to fight for opportunity for all Americans, for the working family, for the poor, the elderly, the black, the handicapped, those who don't speak English very well, disadvantaged kids who would never have a chance without your help. That's the spirit we need across our country. It's time to put first the interests of our Nation and our children in the United States of America.

Now, I'm not here to tell you that there are any cheap or easy or painless solutions to the serious problems that we do face. For too many years, our leaders have tried to postpone the hard decisions and to duck the unpopular choices. Now is the time for truth. The days of the quick fix and the painless cure, if they ever did exist, are gone.

The inflation which has been building in our Nation for more than 10 years will not recede overnight. Yet it can be controlled if we are determined, patient, persistent, fiscally responsible, and if each one of us, based on a belief that we're being treated fairly, is willing to sacrifice just a little.

There is no single stroke of the pen that can cure a 30-year growth of dependence by our own country on foreign oil. But we have the resources of our people, that God gave us, with our intelligence and our technology and our natural resources, to overcome the energy crisis if we have the will to face the challenge together.

Every generation of Americans has shown a willingness to sacrifice when necessary, through depressions and through war, to pass on to the next generation a freer, stronger, and more prosperous America. We must and we will do the same.

This is not a time for politics as usual. America was not built by political leaders who got up every morning and predicated the day's decisions on popularity polls. Harry Truman said, "America was not built on fear. America was built on courage, imagination, and an unbeatable determination to do the job."

I did not campaign across this country 2 or 3 years with all the members of my family just to sit in comfort at the White House or to read in some future history books that I was the 39th President of the United States. I sought this office to lead, to face problems frankly and without timidity, regardless of their difficulty. If the decisions that I have to make to safeguard the future of our country cost me some political support, then let the chips fall where they may.

I hope that God will never let me take the cheap and easy way around a difficult problem that faces the country that I lead. I will not slap mandatory Government controls on wages and prices just before the 1980 elections, as one of my predecessors did, and then later watch inflation skyrocket out of control. And I will never fight inflation by deliberately throwing millions of Americans out of work, as has been done in the past.

I tell you what I want. I want to build an economy in our country that is growing and producing so that my Amy and your children, in 5 years, 10 years from now, can look forward to a steady job. I want to see a country where every American can work and save and build for the future without fear that the dollar you earn this year will be worthless next year.

If we can join in a common purpose now, then the 1980's will be a time of hope, a time of rebuilding America, a time to fulfill some of the many dreams which we share: a dream of better cities, better education, health care, human rights, and peace.

No American should ever have to live in fear of bankruptcy because of a serious illness or a serious accident. No poor person should go without decent medical care in the richest nation on Earth. This is easy to talk about. We've heard speeches, we've heard testimony, we've had press conferences in support of national health insurance for 30 years. But not a single bill has passed either the Senate or the House. The time has come for us to quit talking and get down to work.

I'll send my national health program to the Congress next week. Together we can move towards—[*applause*]. Yesterday, I might add, I met with Russell Long, who is supportive. He had talked to Abe Ribicoff, who is supportive. Senator Kennedy shares the same goal I do. I met last week with Al Ullman, with Charlie Rangel. We've consulted very closely with leaders of the Congress, some of whom have not been willing to move in the past. But I think now, together, we can move towards the goal that we share: a comprehensive system of national health insurance to protect every American citizen.

Together, we can continue the civil rights revolution. We can offer jobs and training to minority teenagers who now grow up with no hope. We can rid the legacy of prejudice and discrimination from our society.

American women have waited 203 years for full equality. It's time to make the equal rights amendment the law of the land. If this great union would take as a major responsibility and goal the focusing of your own attention on individual members of the State legislatures in those four or five States that now face the final decision on the equal rights amendment, with my help and my wife's help, my fam-

ily's help, and many others, I believe that we can prevail.

Together we can continue the worldwide struggle for human rights. There are brave men and brave women in many nations striving against great odds to taste the kind of freedom which you and I take for granted. They look to America to hold high the lamp of freedom and liberty, and they must know that they are not alone. I pledge to you that as long as I am your President, our Nation will always stand up in defense of freedom and human rights in every nation on Earth.

Last week I welcomed several hundred Vietnam veterans to the White House. I told them that Americans feel love and respect and gratitude for the heroism and the sacrifice of every young American who served in Vietnam. You could see among that group of veterans, many of whom were in wheelchairs, the terrible cost of war. When I leave this office, I have no higher prayer than to be able to say that no young American has had to fight or die in combat and that all Americans have lived in peace.

Lasting peace in the Middle East and around the world can mean much more than just the absence of war. Together, we can begin to remove the specter of a nuclear holocaust from the world.

Next week I will go to Vienna to sign a treaty with the Soviet Union limiting nuclear arsenals on both sides. There is no doubt that SALT II will enhance the security of the United States. There is no doubt that the SALT treaty will leave our Nation stronger to compete peacefully and successfully with the Soviet Union. There is no doubt that the SALT treaty goes a long way toward controlling present and future nuclear weapons. There is no doubt that the SALT treaty helps us to prevent other nations who don't presently have nuclear weapons from developing those weapons for themselves. And there's no doubt that the SALT treaty will help prevent a nuclear war and will contribute to world peace.

And I want to make it very clear that verification of the SALT treaty is not based on trust of the Soviet Union. We can verify Soviet compliance with our own Nation's technical means.

SALT II is part of a long process that began with President Eisenhower. If SALT II is not ratified, if, after 7 long years of detailed, tedious negotiations under three Presidents, a carefully balanced agreement in our Nation's own interests, contributing to our Nation's strength, preserving world peace, if all that is lost, then the process of controlling nuclear weapons in future years would be very difficult to resurrect.

There is no decision that we face as a people more crucial to our Nation's security, our hopes for the future, or the chance of our children to live in a safe and secure and a livable world than to see the conclusion of the SALT II treaty and the commencement of a SALT III negotiating process with more drastic reductions in nuclear weapons. I hope you'll help me. Together, we must choose the side of peace.

In closing, let me say this: We have such enormous freedom as Americans— to debate, to criticize, to argue, to dispute, to complain, to resolve our problems openly—that we sometimes remember the transient problems and troubles and we forget how much we've accomplished together and the basic, tremendous inner strength of our country.

We live in the strongest, most open, most prosperous, most generous, most hopeful, most free nation on Earth. The problems we face are serious and they are real, but they are manageable. The challenge that we face is to use the basic spirit which is a characteristic of the American people.

We live in a time of rapid change. We must not permit the power of fear that Franklin Roosevelt warned us against— fear of the future, fear of uncertainty, fear of futility—to paralyze our will. We can make our economy work. We can be both strong and at peace. We can solve our problems as we always have, not through gimmicks or slogans, but through hard work and persistence and, occasionally, through pain and sacrifice.

John Gardner once wrote, and I'd like to quote, "A nation is never finished. You cannot build it and leave it standing like the pharaohs did with the pyramids. It has to be built and then rebuilt. It has to be recreated in each generation by believing and caring men and women."

It's our turn now. If we do not believe or do not care, nothing can save and preserve our Nation. If we believe and care, nothing can stop us.

We are a nation. You are a union of believing and caring men and women. I'm a working man, a farmer, a father, a President, and I look forward to the future, because I know that the people of the United States have the will and the strength of character to make those years still to come even better in the greatest nation on Earth.

Thank you very much.

NOTE: The President spoke at 2:40 p.m. in the Sheraton-Park Ballroom at the Sheraton-Park Hotel.

Trade Sanctions Against Rhodesia

Remarks Announcing Continuation of the U.S. Sanctions. June 7, 1979

After the most careful and thorough consideration, I have made a decision on the Zimbabwe-Rhodesian sanctions. First, I am absolutely convinced that the best interests of the United States would not be served by lifting the sanctions.

Secondly, I am equally convinced that the best interests of the people of Zimbabwe-Rhodesia would not be served by the lifting of the sanctions.

Finally, it's clear to me that although there has been some very encouraging progress made in that country, that the action taken has not been sufficient to satisfy the provision of the United States law described in the so-called Case-Javits amendment.

In reaching this decision, we have carefully assessed recent events in Zimbabwe-Rhodesia. We have consulted very closely with the British, who retain both legal and historic interests and responsibilities for that country.

The actual voting in the April elections appears to have been administered in a reasonably fair way under the circumstances. But the elections were held under a constitution that was drafted by and then submitted only to the white minority, only 60 percent of whom themselves supported the new constitution. The black citizens, who constitute 96 percent of the population of Zimbabwe-Rhodesia, never had a chance to consider nor to vote for or against the constitution under which the elections were held.

The constitution preserves extraordinary power for the 4-percent white minority. It gives this small minority vastly disproportionate numbers of votes in the country's parliament. It gives this 4 percent continued control over the army, the police, the system of justice, and the civil service, and it also lets the 4-percent majority [minority] [1] exercise a veto over any significant constitutional reform.

---

[1] Printed in the transcript.

Moreover, while the Case-Javits amendment called for free participation of all political factions or groups in the country in the recent election, the internal representatives of the opposing political parties were banned from the elections. They were unable to participate in the political process. They were prohibited from holding meetings, from having political rallies, from expressing their views against voting in the election, and even prevented from advertising their views in the news media.

For these reasons, I cannot conclude that the elections were either fair or free. Nor can I conclude that the other condition of the United States law has been fully met. The authorities in Zimbabwe-Rhodesia have expressed their willingness to attend an all-parties meeting, but they have not indicated that they are prepared to negotiate seriously about "all relevant issues." All relevant issues have to be considered in order to comply with the United States law.

We will, of course, continue to keep the question of the observance of sanctions under review. I sincerely hope that future progress can be made and made rapidly. Along with the British, we will particularly look for progress towards a wider political process and more legitimate and genuine majority rule. In so doing, we will report to the Congress and, obviously, consult with the Congress on a monthly basis on the progress being made in Zimbabwe-Rhodesia.

The position that I have outlined best serves not only American interests but the interests of our allies in a region of the world of increasing importance to us. It should preserve our diplomatic and ties of trade with friendly African Governments and also limit—and this is very important—limit the opportunity of outside powers to take advantage of the situation in southern Africa at the expense of the United States.

No other government on Earth has extended diplomatic relations or recognition to Zimbabwe-Rhodesian Government. However, these actions of the United States that I'm describing should help and encourage the newly elected authorities, including Mr. Muzorewa, to intensify their efforts to achieve genuine majority rule, an end to apartheid and racism, based on firm, reasonable, constitutional processes that exemplify the very principles on which the United States Government has been founded.

I consider this principle to be extremely important to represent in international affairs what our Nation stands for, what our people believe in.

I recognize, to be perfectly frank with you, that I do not have a majority of support in the United States Senate. My guess is that at the present time in the House we would have difficulty in this position prevailing. But because it is a matter of principle to me personally and to our country, because I see the prospect of our Nation being seriously damaged in its relationship with other countries, in southern Africa, and elsewhere, because to lift sanctions at this time would directly violate international law, our past agreements ever since President Johnson under the United Nations, and would not contribute to the best interests of either our country or the people in Zimbabwe-Rhodesia, I intend to do everything I can within my power to prevail on this decision.

It means a lot to our country to do what's right and what's decent and what's fair and what is principled. And in my opinion, the action that I've described fulfills these requirements.

Now Secretary Vance, who is with me on the platform, will be glad to answer any specific questions that you might have about this issue.

NOTE: The President spoke at 5:20 p.m. to reporters assembled in the Briefing Room at the White House.

Black Music Association

Remarks at a White House Dinner Honoring the Association.   June 7, 1979

How many of you know what month this is? Somebody said June. Right on! This is Black Music Month.

As you know, the purpose of the Black Music Association is to preserve, protect, and perpetuate black music on an international basis. And the time to do it on an international basis is right now at the White House, the center of your Government, and Rosalynn and I are very glad to have you here.

The Black Music Association is not an old organization, but it was one that was organized at the right time in the right place for the right reason. It's only a year old, but I understand it already has 2,000 members. And tomorrow in Philadelphia, you'll have your founders meeting in a very appropriate place.

As you know, our own Nation was founded in Philadelphia. And I was thinking this afternoon that if we had had the Black Music Association organized 203 years ago, so that Benjamin Franklin and Thomas Jefferson and George Washington could have just heard some of this music at the very beginning, our country could have avoided a lot of trouble and a lot of heartache and a lot of struggle and a lot of suffering and a lot of division, and would be even greater than it is now.

It's important, in my opinion, for our own Nation and the rest of the world to know the importance that the President of the United States and his family and friends attach to black music, because in many ways, the feelings of our own black citizens throughout the history of our country has been accurately expressed in the music. And it presents a kind of history of our Nation when you go back and see the evolution of black music. It's meant a lot to me as a young boy and a young man and adult in Georgia.

I won't make the other States feel inferior by naming all the black musicians that have come out of Georgia. I'll be nice to you this afternoon. But I think that it's accurate to say that in many ways, the deep feelings of pain and suffering, of alienation and a sense of being an outcast in one's own community, in one's own nation, a sense of hope and a sense of unity, a sense of deep religious faith, a sense of vision, sense of beauty has been expressed very deeply and in forceful terms in black music not only for me, from the South, but for all Americans, both black and white.

And it's obvious that this has not been limited to the United States of America. There's been a transcendent effect of black music that has never paid any attention to international borders. I think black music is a way to tie the black people of our country to their own ancestors and to tie the United States to other nations of the world. It's been an avenue for understanding and friendship that has been effective when politicians could not succeed.

In many ways, you've expressed the hopes of our country—life, even when slavery was characteristic of black people, liberty and a struggle for it, when it seemed to escape generation after generation of struggling people. And no one can

doubt that black music has always exemplified the pursuit of happiness.

So, in many ways I think that you have not only mirrored and described what was happening in our country, but you have presented a guide in times of despair and failure to what our country ought to be.

We are very deeply grateful tonight to have performers who in a very brief way can show the progress of black music during this historical time that I have just mentioned. There would be no possible way to choose enough different black musicians to give a total picture of what is meant by what you represent.

Sunday afternoon I went to a memorial service for A. Philip Randolph. I sat there and listened to Leontyne Price sing "The Lord's Prayer." When she approached the end of the song and hit a very high note, I said, "This is impossible for a human being to do." And then she raised about a half an octave and hit another note and cold chills went down my spine. And then she hit the final note and tears burst out of my eyes and flowed down my face; and I was not the only one. And although she hadn't quite finished the song, because she had to say "Amen," the entire audience, hundreds of people, broke out into simultaneous applause—just one type of music that is performed superbly.

And tonight we have four great artists. I'm not going to describe to you their biographies, because it's in your program. But we'll have Sara Jordan Powell, Chuck Berry, my long-time friend Billy Eckstine, Evelyn "Champagne" King, and Andrae Crouch to perform for us.

And I've learned one thing about black music, and that is that people who talk before the performance are not appreciated nearly so much as the performance itself. So, I'm ready now to join the audience, but to express on behalf of the 220 million people in our country my thanks to superb black musicians throughout the history of our country and my congratulations to the Black Music Association for spending your first birthday party here at the White House with us.

Thank you and congratulations.

NOTE: The President spoke at 7:45 p.m. on the South Grounds of the White House.

Deployment of the MX Missile

Remarks by the Deputy Press Secretary on the President's Decision. June 8, 1979

MR. GRANUM. After prolonged study and analysis, the President has decided that we will pursue a full-scale MX. Some of the key points on this are, of course, that the decision will continue the longstanding U.S. policy of maintaining a triad of three survivable strategic force components: intercontinental ballistic missiles, submarine-launched ballistic missiles, and heavy bombers.

In order to do this, we will deploy a new ICBM in a mobile basing mode that is both survivable and verifiable. The new ICBM, as I said, will be a full-scale MX, which is permitted under SALT II and is as capable as any missile the Soviets can deploy.

The final characteristics of the basing system will be worked out during the summer months. This decision will take into account costs, security, and environmental concerns, and the requirement that the system be adequately verifiable.

REPORTER. The President doesn't consider this a destabilizing weapon in the sense that you're now building a first-strike counterforce of your own?

MR. GRANUM. He does not. He believes very strongly that this decision will strengthen the possibilities of significant reductions and controls in SALT III. It stabilizes the strategic balance. And without that, of course, serious negotiations are not possible.

It also means that there can be no Soviet advantage in an arms race. Third, by stressing survivability through mobility and shelters, we can consider a significant reduction in strategic forces with no loss in security. And finally, the ultimate scale of this deployment can be adjusted to the progress that is made in the SALT III process.

NOTE: Deputy Press Secretary Rex Granum made the remarks in response to a question from a reporter at the regular news briefing which began at 11:44 a.m. in the Briefing Room at the White House.

Alaska Natural Gas Transportation System

Nomination of John T. Rhett To Be Federal Inspector. June 8, 1979

The President today announced that he will nominate John T. Rhett, of Arlington, Va., to be Federal Inspector for the Alaska Natural Gas Transportation System. This is a new position created by Reorganization Plan No. 1 of 1979. Rhett has been Deputy Assistant Administrator for Water Program Operations at the Environmental Protection Agency since 1973.

He was born February 20, 1925, in Ft. Benning, Ga. He received a B.S. from the U.S. Military Academy in 1945, a masters degree in engineering from the University of California in 1952, and a masters in international relations from George Washington University in 1965.

Rhett served with the U.S. Army Corps of Engineers from 1945 to 1973, starting as a second lieutenant and retiring as a colonel. From 1945 to 1965, he served in various troop, engineering, construction, school, and command positions.

From 1965 to 1967, he was with Land and Missile Infrastructure, Supreme Headquarters, Allied Powers Europe. He was commander of the 11th Engineer Group in Germany from 1967 to 1968 and chief of the Engineering Division of the U.S. Army Construction Agency in Vietnam from 1968 to 1969.

From 1969 to 1972, Rhett was district engineer for the Louisville Engineering District. From 1972 to 1973, he was resident member of the Board of Engineers for Rivers and Harbors.

Digest of Other White House Announcements

The following listing includes the President's public schedule and other items of general interest announced by the White House Press Office and not included elsewhere in this issue.

June 2

The President returned to the White House from a trip to Indianapolis, Indiana.

June 4

The President met at the White House with:

—Zbigniew Brzezinski, Assistant to the President for National Security Affairs;
—Frank B. Moore, Assistant to the President for Congressional Liaison;
—Jean François-Poncet, Minister of Foreign Affairs of France;

—Vice President Walter F. Mondale.

The President attended a reception for Armenian Americans held on the State Floor at the White House.

June 5

The President met at the White House with:

—Dr. Brzezinski;
—Mr. Moore;
—Representative Charles B. Rangel of New York;
—administration officials to discuss the fiscal year 1981 budget.

The President participated in a breakfast briefing by administration officials on the strategic arms limitation agreement given for scientists in the First Floor Private Dining Room at the White House.

The White House announced that Patricia Y. Bario has been named Deputy Press Secretary and James H. Purks III has been named as Assistant Press Secretary.

June 6

The President met at the White House with:

—Dr. Brzezinski;
—the Democratic congressional leadership;
—Mr. Moore;
—W. Averell Harriman;
—Vice President Mondale, Stansfield Turner, Director of Central Intelligence, Hamilton Jordan, Assistant to the President, and Dr. Brzezinski;
—Senator Russell B. Long of Louisiana.

The President has appointed John E. Menario, executive vice president of the Greater Portland (Maine) Chamber of Commerce, as a member of the Commerce Department's board to consider whether the Pittston Company's proposed oil refinery in Eastport, Maine, should be exempted from the Endangered Species Act of 1973.

June 7

The President met at the White House with:

—Dr. Brzezinski;

—the Republican congressional leadership;

—members of the Congressional Steel Caucus;

—Mr. Moore;

—administration officials to discuss the fiscal year 1981 budget;

—a group of Members of Congress to discuss U.S. trade sanctions against Rhodesia.

The President attended a portion of the meeting of administration officials with Governors of New England States held in the Cabinet Room.

June 8

The President met at the White House with:

—Secretary of State Cyrus R. Vance, Secretary of Defense Harold Brown, Dr. Brzezinski, and Mr. Jordan;

—Dr. Brzezinski;

—Mr. Moore;

—Charles L. Schultze, Chairman of the Council of Economic Advisers;

—members of the executive committee of the National School Board Association;

—Mrs. Carter, for lunch;

—administration officials to discuss the fiscal year 1981 budget.

The President left the White House for a weekend stay at Camp David, Md.

NOMINATIONS SUBMITTED TO THE SENATE

The following list does not include promotions of members of the Uniformed Services, nominations to the Service Academies, or nominations of Foreign Service officers.

NOMINATIONS—Continued

Submitted June 5, 1979

WALTER J. McDONALD, of the District of Columbia, to be an Assistant Secretary of the Treasury, vice William J. Beckham, Jr., resigned.

BOYCE F. MARTIN, JR., of Kentucky, to be United States Circuit Judge for the Sixth Circuit, vice a new position created by P.L. 95–486, approved October 20, 1978.

RICHARD M. BILBY, of Arizona, to be United States District Judge for the District of Arizona, vice William C. Frey, deceased.

LAWRENCE K. KARLTON, of California, to be United States District Judge for the Eastern District of California, vice Thomas J. Mac-Bride, retired.

WARREN W. EGINTON, of Connecticut, to be United States District Judge for the District of Connecticut, vice a new position created by P.L. 95–486, approved October 20, 1978.

WILLIAM J. CASTAGNA, of Florida, to be United States District Judge for the Middle District of Florida, vice a new position created by P.L. 95–486, approved October 20, 1978.

ORINDA D. EVANS, of Georgia, to be United States District Judge for the Northern District of Georgia, vice Albert J. Henderson, resigning.

MARVIN H. SHOOB, of Georgia, to be United States District Judge for the Northern District of Georgia, vice a new position created by P.L. 95–486, approved October 20, 1978.

G. ERNEST TIDWELL, of Georgia, to be United States District Judge for the Northern District of Georgia, vice a new position created by P.L. 95–486, approved October 20, 1978.

VERONICA D. WICKER, of Louisiana, to be United States District Judge for the Eastern District of Louisiana, vice a new position created by P.L. 95–486, approved October 20, 1978.

JOHN M. SHAW, of Louisiana, to be United States District Judge for the Western District of Louisiana, vice a new position created by P.L. 95–486, approved October 20, 1978.

FALCON B. HAWKINS, of South Carolina, to be United States District Judge for the District of South Carolina, vice a new position created by P.L. 95–486, approved October 20, 1978.

NOMINATIONS—Continued

Submitted June 5—Continued

C. WESTON HOUCK, of South Carolina, to be United States District Judge for the District of South Carolina, vice a new position created by P.L. 95–486, approved October 20, 1978.

VINCENT P. BARABBA, of New York, to be Director of the Census, vice Manuel D. Plotkin, resigned.

RICHARD I. BEATTIE, of the District of Columbia, to be General Counsel of the Department of Health, Education, and Welfare, vice Frank Peter S. Libassi, resigned.

MICHAEL R. KELLEY, of Virginia, to be a member of the Board of Directors of the Corporation for Public Broadcasting for a term expiring March 26, 1982, vice Virginia Bauer Duncan, term expired.

RUTH T. PROKOP, of the District of Columbia, to be a member of the Merit Systems Protection Board for the term of 7 years expiring March 1, 1986, vice Alan K. Campbell.

Withdrawn June 5, 1979

RUTH T. PROKOP, of the District of Columbia, to be a member of the Merit Systems Protection Board for the remainder of the term expiring March 1, 1981, which was sent to the Senate on January 18, 1979.

Submitted June 7, 1979

GEORGE HERBERT PATRICK BURSLEY, of Maryland, to be a member of the National Transportation Safety Board for the remainder of the term expiring December 31, 1979, vice Kay Bailey, resigned.

Submitted June 8, 1979

JOHN T. RHETT, of Virginia, to be Federal Inspector for the Alaska Natural Gas Transportation System (new position).

CHECKLIST OF WHITE HOUSE PRESS RELEASES

The following listing contains releases of the White House Press Office which are not included in this issue.

Released June 2, 1979

Advance text: remarks at the Jefferson-Jackson Day dinner in Indianapolis, Ind.

CHECKLIST—Continued

Released June 4, 1979

News conference: on actions to increase unleaded gasoline production—by Secretary of Energy James R. Schlesinger and Douglas M. Costle, Administrator of the Environmental Protection Agency

Fact sheet: actions to increase unleaded gasoline production

Announcement: nomination of Richard M. Bilby to be United States District Judge for the District of Arizona

Announcement: nomination of Lawrence K. Karlton to be United States District Judge for the Eastern District of California

Announcement: nomination of Warren W. Eginton to be United States District Judge for the District of Connecticut

Announcement: nomination of William J. Castagna to be United States District Judge for the Middle District of Florida

Announcement: nomination of Boyce F. Martin, Jr., to be United States Circuit Judge for the Sixth Circuit

Announcement: nomination of John M. Shaw to be United States District Judge for the Western District of Louisiana

Announcement: nomination of Veronica D. Wicker to be United States District Judge for the Eastern District of Louisiana

Announcement: nomination of C. Weston Houck to be United States District Judge for the District of South Carolina

Announcement: nomination of Falcon B. Hawkins to be United States District Judge for the District of South Carolina

Released June 5, 1979

Announcement: nomination of Orinda D. Evans to be United States District Judge for the Northern District of Georgia

Announcement: nomination of Marvin H. Shoob to be United States District Judge for the Northern District of Georgia

Announcement: nomination of G. Ernest Tidwell to be United States District Judge for the Northern District of Georgia

Released June 6, 1979

News conference: on Federal pay system reform—by Alan K. Campbell, Director of the Office of Personnel Management, and John P. White, Deputy Director of the Office of Management and Budget

Fact sheet: Federal pay system reform

CHECKLIST—Continued

Released June 7, 1979

Advance text: remarks at the founding convention of the United Food and Commercial Workers International Union

News conference: on continuation of U.S. trade sanctions against Rhodesia—by Secretary of State Cyrus R. Vance

ACTS APPROVED BY
THE PRESIDENT

Approved June 4, 1979

H.R. 1787_____ Public Law 96–16
An act to authorize a supplemental appropriation to the National Aeronautics and Space Administration for research and development.

ACTS APPROVED—Continued

Approved June 4—Continued

H.R. 2520_____ Public Law 96–17
An act to amend the National Ocean Pollution Research and Development and Monitoring Planning Act of 1978 to authorize appropriations to carry out the provisions of such Act for fiscal year 1980.

Approved June 8, 1979

H.R. 3404_____ Public Law 96–18
An act to amend the Federal Reserve Act to authorize Federal Reserve banks to lend certain obligations to the Secretary of the Treasury to meet the short-term cash requirements of the Treasury, and for other purposes.

PRESIDENTIAL DOCUMENTS

Week Ending Friday, June 15, 1979

Federal Communications Commission

Nomination of Tyrone Brown To Be a Member. June 11, 1979

The President today announced that he will nominate Tyrone Brown, of Washington, D.C., for reappointment as a member of the Federal Communications Commission for a 7-year term. Brown has been a member of the FCC since 1977.

He was born November 5, 1942, in Norfolk, Va. He received an A.B. from Hamilton College in 1964 and an LL.B. from Cornell Law School in 1967.

Brown was law clerk to Chief Justice Earl Warren in 1967 and an associate with a Washington law firm from 1968 to 1970. He was a special investigator for the President's Commission on Campus Unrest in 1970. From 1970 to 1971, he served as assistant to Senator Edmund S. Muskie, then as staff director of the Intergovernmental Relations Subcommittee of the Senate Government Operations Committee.

From 1971 to 1974, Brown was director and vice president for legal affairs of Post-Newsweek Stations, Inc., and its subsidiary companies. He was with the

Washington law firm of Caplin & Drysdale from 1974 until he was appointed to the FCC in 1977.

Securities and Exchange Commission

Nomination of John R. Evans To Be a Member. June 11, 1979

The President today announced that he will nominate John R. Evans, of Murray, Utah, for reappointment as a member of the Securities and Exchange Commission for a term expiring June 5, 1983. Evans has been a member of the Commission since 1973.

He was born June 1, 1932, in Bisbee, Ariz. He received a B.S. (1957) and an M.S. (1959) in economics from the University of Utah. He served as a research assistant in the University of Utah's Bureau of Economic and Business Research from 1960 to 1963, and was also an economics instructor in 1962–63. While he was at the University of Utah, Evans published numerous articles and studies in economics and business publications.

From 1963 to 1964, Evans was economics assistant to Senator Wallace F. Bennett of Utah, and from 1964 to 1971, he was minority staff director for the Senate Committee on Banking, Housing, and Urban Affairs. From 1971 to 1973, Evans was on the professional staff of that committee.

Securities and Exchange Commission

Nomination of Philip A. Loomis, Jr., To Be a Member.   June 11, 1979

The President today announced that he will nominate Philip A. Loomis, Jr., for reappointment as a member of the Securities and Exchange Commission (SEC) for a term expiring June 5, 1984. Loomis has been with the SEC since 1954 and has been a Commissioner since 1971.

He was born June 11, 1915, in Colorado Springs, Colo. He received an A.B. from Princeton University in 1938 and an LL.B. from Yale Law School in 1941. He was with the Office of Price Administration from 1942 to 1944 and served as associate counsel to Northrop Aircraft from 1944 to 1946.

From 1946 to 1954, Loomis practiced law in Los Angeles. He joined the SEC in 1954 and served as special consultant on the revision of SEC rules and regulations until 1955. From 1955 to 1963, he served as Associate Director, then Director, of the Division of Trading Exchanges (now Trading and Markets).

From 1955 to 1963, Loomis was General Counsel to the SEC. In that capacity, he drafted the 1960 amendments to the Investment Advisory Act of 1940 and had the primary staff responsibility for the legislation which became the Securities Acts Amendments of 1964. He also supervised the staff work on the legislation which became the Securities Investor Protection Act of 1970.

Securities Investor Protection Corporation

Nomination of Brenton H. Rupple To Be a Director.   June 11, 1979

The President today announced that he will nominate Brenton H. Rupple, of Milwaukee, Wis., for reappointment as a Director of the Securities Investor Protection Corporation.

Rupple is chairman and chief executive officer of Robert W. Baird & Co., a Milwaukee securities firm. He has been a member of the Securities Investor Protection Corporation since 1978.

Rupple, 55, has been with Baird & Co. and its predecessor company since 1948. He is a member of the Securities Industry Association and served on its executive committee from 1975 to 1978.

Overseas Private Investment Corporation

Nomination of Allie C. Felder, Jr., To Be a Member of the Board of Directors.   June 11, 1979

The President today announced that he will nominate Allie C. Felder, Jr., of Washington, D.C., for reappointment as a member of the Board of Directors of the Overseas Private Investment Corporation (OPIC).

Felder is director of the Outreach Division of the Cooperative League of the U.S.A. and executive vice president of the Cooperative League Fund. He has been a member of the OPIC Board of Directors since 1971.

He was born August 12, 1921, in Durham, N.C. He received a B.A. in agriculture from Hampton Institute, an M.S.C. in agricultural economics and rural sociology from the University of Illinois, and a Ph. D. in the same area from Ohio State University.

Felder taught at the International Cooperative Training Center at the University of Wisconsin and was an associate professor of agricultural economics at Hampton Institute. He spent 13 years in India as a consultant to the American International Association and for the Cooperative League of the U.S.A. For 8 years, he was director of the Cooperative League's office there.

National Advisory Council on Extension and Continuing Education

Appointment of Four Members.
June 11, 1979

The President today announced the appointment of four persons as members of the National Advisory Council on Extension and Continuing Education. They are:

FRANCES M. DAVIN, of Brandon, Fla., Hillsborough County Commissioner for District 4, chairman of the social services committee of the State Association of County Commissioners, and former personnel director for an electronic engineering company.

LEO C. DONAHUE, of Somerville, Mass., now retired and active in community affairs, formerly superintendent of schools for Somerville. He served on the Massachusetts Board of Education and State Board of Vocational Education and on the Massachusetts State Board of Collegiate Authority for 16 years.

LOWELL EKLUND, of Bloomfield Hills, Mich., dean and professor of continuing education at Oakland University in Rochester, Mich., since its establishment in 1958.

RUPERT TRUJILLO, of Albuquerque, N. Mex., dean of the division of continuing education and community services of the University of New Mexico.

Meeting With Vice President Muhammad Husni Mubarak of Egypt

White House Statement. June 11, 1979

President Carter and Egyptian Vice President Husni Mubarak met in the Oval Office for 50 minutes. Also attending the session on the American side were Vice President Mondale, Secretary of State Vance, Dr. Zbigniew Brzezinski, Assistant to the President for National Security Affairs, Assistant Secretary of State Harold Saunders, William Quandt, NSC staff member, and Robert Hunter, NSC staff member. Ambassador Ashraf Ghorbal and Under Secretary of State for Foreign Affairs Usoma al-Baz accompanied Vice President Mubarak.

In accepting the special message that Vice President Mubarak conveyed on behalf of President Sadat, President Carter expressed his personal pleasure at being able to welcome Vice President Mubarak again to the White House. He reiterated his warm personal regard and high esteem for President Sadat and welcomed the opportunity to continue close consultations with Egyptian leaders.

President Carter and Vice President Mubarak reviewed the status of Egyptian-American cooperation in a number of fields. The President expressed great interest in Egypt's priority efforts to expand its economic and social development. Bilateral military relations were also discussed. Citing the administration's proposal for $1.5 billion in foreign military sales credits over the next 3 years, the President reaffirmed his intention to assist Egypt in meeting its legitimate defense needs. He also said that they discussed how the United States might help to meet Egypt's longer term defense needs and the desirability of regular and systematic consultations towards this end. Referring to the Middle East peace negotiations, the President stressed the administration's determination to help resolve the difficult issues that must be addressed so as to achieve a comprehensive peace.

In addition to his meeting with President Carter, Vice President Mubarak today met separately with Secretary Vance, Secretary of Defense Brown, and Ambassador Strauss. Vice President Mubarak will meet with Members of Congress before he departs for London on the evening of June 13.

National Health Plan

Remarks Announcing Proposed Legislation. June 12, 1979

THE PRESIDENT. Today I'm proposing to the Congress a National Health Plan. This major initiative will meet the most urgent needs in health care of the American people in a practical, cost-efficient, and fiscally responsible manner. It will provide health care for millions of Americans and protect our people against the overwhelming financial burdens of major illness.

It's been 30 years since President Harry Truman proposed access to quality health care as a basic right for Americans, and it's been nearly 15 years since the Congress enacted legislation establishing Medicaid and Medicare. Now is the time to move forward again.

I challenge all those who are concerned about health and financial security of the American people to rise above the differences that have created stalemate for the last 30 years, and act now, this year. No American should live in fear that serious illness or accident will bring bankruptcy or a lifetime of debt. Yet today 80 million

Americans are unprotected against catastrophic medical costs. Millions more may lose their health insurance through unemployment or because of the death of a parent or a spouse. The National Health Plan will rid this Nation of the fear of financial ruin from catastrophic illness.

No American should be deprived of a right for health services or be discouraged about obtaining medical treatment because of poverty. The National Health Plan will extend comprehensive coverage, a full range of medical and hospital care, to almost 16 million low-income Americans for the first time. No elderly American should be forced to depend on charity when Medicare hospital coverage reaches its limits or face unlimited out-of-pocket expenses for medical care. The National Health Plan guarantees adequate hospital coverage for the elderly and for the disabled, caps their out-of-pocket expenses, and requires physicians to accept Medicare payments as full payment for coverage of covered services.

No newborn child in America should be denied a chance for a full and productive life because of a lack of needed health service care. Our infant mortality rate is one of the highest in the industrialized world. My plan will provide prenatal, delivery, and infant care to all pregnant women and newborn children up to the age of 1 year.

And no American taxpayer should be forced to foot the bill for waste, fraud, and inefficient administration. The National Health Plan will establish Healthcare, a new Federal program consolidating Medicare and Medicaid into a single administrative unit. Through good management practices, the National Health Plan will curb waste, will eliminate duplication and abuse, and encourage competition.

A strong and effective health system absolutely requires establishment of cost containment measures far more effective than we have today. The American people now spend more than 9 percent of our gross national product on health services, $200 billion a year. Hospital costs are rising $1 million per hour, 24 hours a day, 365 days a year. It's time to draw the line on skyrocketing hospital costs.

For 2 years, now, I've asked Congress for hospital cost containment legislation. That bill alone will save Americans $53 billion over the next 5 years. I've had the support of key congressional leaders, including those here today. Congress must enact a strong hospital cost containment bill if the National Health Plan is to become a reality.

A truly comprehensive health program is among the great unfinished items on our Nation's social agenda. The National Health Plan I'm submitting today establishes the framework and creates the momentum for reaching that long-sought goal. This plan meets urgent national needs. No longer will the elderly find the benefits of Medicare illusory when they are most needed. No longer will working families live in fear of catastrophic medical expenses. No longer will millions of the poor be forced to depend only on emergency rooms or outpatient clinics or charity hospitals for basic care, or do without health care altogther. No longer will low-income women be forced to bring their children into the world with inadequate medical care or help.

There are those who sincerely believe that we must insist upon a full-scale, comprehensive plan enacted all at once. The idea of all or nothing has been pursued now for almost three decades. But I must say in all candor that no child of poverty, no elderly American, no middle-class family has yet benefited from a rigid and

unswerving commitment to this principle of all or nothing. The National Health Plan that I proposed will provide millions of our people—men, women, and children—with better health, greater economic security, and more productive, dignified, and hopeful lives. The American people have waited long enough. I call on the Congress to act without delay.

I might say that the Healthcare plan has been evolved through careful consultation with key congressional leaders and with representatives of American organizations and groups over the last few months. Today we have many of those congressional leaders represented here, with the leadership of crucial committees, and I'd like to call on a few of them to say a word at this time.

First, in the House, I'd like to ask Jim Corman and Chairman Charlie Rangel to say a word, and then I'll call on others after them.

Jim?

REPRESENTATIVE CORMAN. Thank you, Mr. President.

As you know, some of us have worked long and hard for a national health security program. This is a very constructive first step. For the first time, it acknowledges the fact that regardless of whether they're rich or poor, women expecting children and babies, and hopefully in later years, older children, will have universal coverage. We'll see if that works. If it does, we have something to build on. And I'm delighted and honored to support the program.

THE PRESIDENT. Thank you, Jim.

REPRESENTATIVE RANGEL. Thank you, Mr. President.

I'm pleased to be here with such distinguished colleagues in government. It is true that we have been rather stubborn in trying to get our way for bills that we thought were in the best interests of the

American people. But I think by seeing the leadership and the sponsors of your legislation here today, that it means that we can no longer afford the purity of our position at the expense of our aged and our youngsters, and we're looking forward in the Subcommittee on Health in Ways and Means in getting this before our committee as soon as possible.

And I personally am pleased that my colleague on that subcommittee, Jim Corman, that has a constituency of his own, will be joining with me in the sponsorship of the bill.

THE PRESIDENT. Now Congressman Harley Staggers, the chairman of the commerce committee in the House.

REPRESENTATIVE STAGGERS. *Mr. President, my colleagues, ladies and gentlemen:*

I'm happy to be here on this really momentous occasion, and to congratulate you, Mr. President, for having the courage to bring forth a bill now, because it's been, as you said, proposed back in Harry Truman's time. And each President since that time has talked about it. This is the first instrument that I've seen that a President has brought to the Hill. And I congratulate you on your vision and your courage for doing it.

And I would say that in this bill is something that I've believed in and talked so much about, is the fact of prevention of disease. I've said that so many times we wait until somebody gets sick, and then we want to get the cure. Let's try to keep them, as you do in this bill, try to keep them from getting sick.

I think prevention is the greatest thing that we've missed all down through the centuries, instead of healing. We need healing, this is true; people are bound to get sick. And this is an instrument of healing and of mercy to the people of the land, and I congratulate you again.

THE PRESIDENT. I think you know that in both the House and Senate, there is a duality or more of responsibility for health care. The commerce committee and the Ways and Means Committee in the House will be the instrumental ones in actually getting legislation passed. In the Senate, of course, the Finance Committee and the health care committee will have the same responsibility.

We are fortunate to have Senator Russell Long here, who will be holding hearings very shortly. He can outline his exact schedule for you. But I think the fact that we have a broad range of support, as exhibited here on the platform with me, is a good indication that we mean business. We intend to have the health care plan passed and implemented for the benefit of the American people after so many decades of delay.

I'd like to ask Senator Russell Long to comment, if you will.

SENATOR LONG. Thank you, Mr. President.

It was my privilege to be the committee chairman and the Senate floor manager for the last big breakthrough in the health area. I refer to the bill that gave us Medicare and Medicaid. I applaud the President for the breakthrough that is implicit in what he has done here in providing leadership from the White House to move us a very long stride forward in better health legislation.

We on the Finance Committee will study the President's recommendations. We'll add some of our own. We'll try to take the best that he has to offer and the best that we can offer and bring the Senate a bill.

He's familiar with my views, and I think I'm familiar with the President's views. I would hope that we can join together in bringing better health care to the people even more rapidly than the President has in mind. It's my hope that we can move some of those dates forward, that some of the most urgent care that we'd like to see provided for the American people, that they're not now getting, will start next year, in 1980.

Of course, all these things are negotiable. We want to work with the President. I'm confident he'll work with us, and we're very happy about this day.

THE PRESIDENT. Russell, when do you think hearings might be starting?

SENATOR LONG. Well, we're already meeting on some parts of what you're recommending, Mr. President. We called off a meeting today to come here and talk to you. [*Laughter*] We were going to be meeting on cost containment this morning, but we'll be back at it tomorrow morning.

THE PRESIDENT. Very good. We'll let you hurry back and go to work.

SENATOR LONG. You can't ask for much more prompt service than that. [*Laughter*]

THE PRESIDENT. Senator Abe Ribicoff, who's worked for many years in the Senate for better health care.

SENATOR RIBICOFF. Mr. President, I think this is doable this year. It can only be done if the main actors will cooperate. And the main actors are the President of the United States, Senator Long, and Senator Kennedy. As I analyze the three proposals, there are so many similarities that there is no reason why the main parties involved—the President, Senator Long, and Senator Kennedy—can't compromise their difference and work this out.

In a speech on the Senate floor, I pointed out the similarities. There is rhetoric, there is controversy, there is politics in this issue that affects every person in the United States. But when you consider the similarities, the controversy can be submerged. And I believe the controversy will be submerged and we should be able to pass national health insurance this year.

THE PRESIDENT. Thank you very much. That's a good statement, and I agree with you.

Gaylord Nelson, who's helped us so much with hospital cost containment, and also with the broader aspects of health care.

SENATOR NELSON. Mr. President, as so often has been my fate throughout history in politics, I'm called upon to say something when everything else has been said. [*Laughter*]

Let me say, Mr. President, I wish to join the others here in commending you for moving forward with a health insurance plan. I think it is absolutely necessary that we have Presidential leadership in order to get moving, because there are as many plans as there are Members of Congress.

We're going to have to seek to reach a common agreement on proceeding to bring to the people of this country a sound and efficient health care insurance program, and you have taken a major step in the leadership position of coming forward with a proposal. And I join the chairman of the Finance Committee in saying that I know that we are prepared in that committee to proceed expeditiously to give consideration to the pending legislation, this one and others that are before the committee, and, I would hope, report legislation yet this year.

THE PRESIDENT. I think Senator Ribicoff expressed my feelings very clearly. For many years, the obstacle to progress was the wide disparity in concepts of what health care should be. But now there's a broad range of consensus.

I'm determined to see this legislation passed and to have it be advantageous for the poor people who are presently deprived of health care at all; the elderly, who have a genuine fear of dependence upon Medicare because benefits run out or because their costs are too high; mothers, or prospective mothers, who have the great responsibility of bringing a child into the world without adequate prenatal or postnatal care; and the average American family who can be wiped out financially by a catastrophic illness—these categories of Americans have waited too long for action. And now with a concerted effort by myself and my whole administration, the leaders in the House and Senate who have been long impatient about inaction, and the full support of the American people, we will have success this year.

Now Secretary Joe Califano and Stu Eizenstat will be glad to answer questions on the specific nature of the proposal for the press. And we will now ask the Senators to go back to the Finance Committee and pass hospital cost containment—[*laughter*]—to clear the decks for this broader coverage consideration in the very near future.

Thank you very much.

NOTE: The President spoke at 11:06 a.m. to reporters assembled in Room 450 of the Old Executive Office Building. Following his remarks, Secretary of Health, Education, and Welfare Joseph A. Califano, Jr., and Stuart E. Eizenstat, Assistant to the President for Domestic Affairs and Policy, held a news conference on the proposed legislation.

National Health Plan

Message to the Congress on Proposed Legislation. June 12, 1979

To the Congress of the United States:

Today I am proposing to the Congress a National Health Plan. This major new initiative will improve health care for millions of Americans and protect all our people against the overwhelming financial burdens of serious illness.

It has been 30 years since President Truman challenged Congress to secure for all Americans access to quality health care as a matter of right. It has been nearly 15 years since the Congress, responding to the leadership of Presidents Kennedy and Johnson, finally enacted Medicare and Medicaid. Now, after a decade and a half of inaction, it is time to move forward once again.

I have consulted with the Congress, with consumers, with leaders of labor, management, and the health care industry, and have carefully weighed every option. My proposal is practical, premised on effective cost controls, and consistent with sound budget practices. It will:

—protect all Americans from the cost of catastrophic illness or accident

—extend comprehensive health coverage to almost 16 million low-income Americans

—provide coverage for prenatal, delivery, postnatal, and infant care, without cost-sharing

—establish Healthcare, which will provide more efficient Federal administration of health coverage for the poor and the elderly

—reform the health care system to promote competition and contain costs

—create both the framework and the momentum for a universal, comprehensive national health plan.

PROTECTION FROM CATASTROPHIC
EXPENSES

No American should live in fear that a serious illness or accident will mean bankruptcy or a lifetime of debt. Yet today over 80 million Americans are unprotected against devastating medical costs, and millions more can lose the protection they now have because of unemployment or the death of a working spouse.

This National Health Plan will protect every American from the serious financial burden caused by major illness and injury. All employers will provide catastrophic coverage for full-time employees and their families, with subsidies to ease the burden on small businesses. No family will be required to pay more than $2500 for medical expenses in a single year. Americans who are not covered elsewhere can obtain affordable catastrophic coverage from a special Federal program. Under this special program, no one will be denied coverage because he or she is labelled a "bad medical risk."

EXPANDED BENEFITS FOR THE ELDERLY

The cost of health care falls most cruelly on America's older citizens who, with reduced incomes, have the highest medical expenses. Because Medicare places limits on hospital days and places no ceiling on out-of-pocket expenses, serious illness threatens senior citizens with loss of their homes and their life savings. Under the National Health Plan, the elderly will have unlimited hospital coverage and will be required to pay no more than $1250 for medical expenses in a single year.

Today, the elderly also face heavy financial burdens because physicians increasingly charge more than the Medicare fee. Under the National Health Plan, physicians would be prohibited from charging elderly patients more than the allowable fee.

IMPROVED PROGRAM FOR THE POOR

The National Health Plan also provides expanded benefits for the poor. The Plan will extend comprehensive coverage—full physician, hospital and related services—to all Americans with incomes below 55% of poverty ($4200 for a family of four). In addition, persons with incomes above 55% of poverty will be able to "spend-down" into comprehensive coverage if their medical expenses in a given year reduce their income to the eligibility level. A family of four with an income of $4500, for example, will be covered after $300 of medical expenses. Under these provisions, 15.7 million poor people, including 1.2 million elderly, will receive comprehensive coverage for the first time.

Today the existence of 53 separate State and territorial Medicaid programs impedes efficient management. Under the National Health Plan, the administration of programs for the poor and the elderly will be significantly upgraded by the creation of a single new Federal program—Healthcare. Healthcare will improve claims processing, reduce error rates in eligibility determination, and facilitate detection of fraud and abuse.

HEALTH SERVICES FOR MOTHERS AND INFANTS

Prevention is the best way to eliminate the suffering and cost of illness, and one of the most effective preventive health measures we can take is to assure health care for expectant mothers and infants. We have been far too slow to learn this lesson. Our infant mortality rates are higher than those of eleven other nations. This inexcusable record can and will be corrected.

Under the National Health Plan, employers will provide employees and their families with coverage for prenatal care, delivery, and infant care to age one, without any cost-sharing. A high priority in future years must be to expand this coverage to include children up to age six. The employer provisions of the Plan, combined with the Child Health Assurance Plan I have already proposed for low-income expectant mothers and children, will assure that no newborn child in this country will be denied the chance for a full and productive life by the high costs of health care.

EXTENDED INSURANCE COVERAGE

Today, many employees and their families suddenly lose all health coverage when the employee is laid off or is between jobs. Under the National Health Plan, employer-based insurance policies will be required to maintain coverage for 90 days after employment ends. In addition, employer-based policies will be required to maintain family coverage for 90 days after an employee's death, and to cover dependents until age 26.

COST CONTAINMENT

A renewed emphasis on cost containment must accompany new health benefits. The American people now spend over 9% of the Gross National Product on health services—$200 billion a year. Hospital costs in America are rising $1 million an hour, 24 hours a day. It is time to draw the line.

The National Health Plan is premised on passage of strong hospital cost containment legislation, which will save the American people $53 billion over the next five years, including $28 billion in Federal, State, and local expenditures. The Nation cannot afford expanded coverage without hospital cost containment legislation. In addition, my National Health Plan proposes a $3 billion annual limit on hospital capital expenditures. This Nation cannot support more duplicative

facilities and more unnecessary equipment. We must not add to the 130,000 excess hospital beds we now have. We must and we will insure that needed extensions in coverage do not become the excuse for further waste.

This Plan will also provide for a mandatory fee schedule for physicians who serve Healthcare patients. The fee schedule will curb excessive inflation in physician fees and will reduce the disparities in fees paid to rural physicians as compared to urban physicians, and primary care physicians as compared to specialists. Over time, the new fee schedule will help produce a better geographic distribution of physicians and increase the availability of primary care services.

The Healthcare fee schedule will provide a model for private health insurance plans. Private plans will publish the names of physicians who agree to adhere to the Healthcare fee schedule for all their patients. To assure that Blue Shield and similar organizations reexamine their physician reimbursement policies, the Plan will prohibit physician domination of the governing boards of these organizations.

INCREASED COMPETITION

Competition has been weak in the health care industry because a very high percentage of costs are paid by third parties, and because patients generally cannot determine or shop for the services they need. In recent years, however, health maintenance organizations (HMOs) have injected important competitive forces into the health care system. The National Health Plan will encourage further competition by giving employees and Healthcare beneficiaries new financial incentives to enroll in HMOs or other cost-effective health plans.

Employers will be required to make equal contributions to the various health plans they offer their employees. Employees who choose more cost-effective plans will either pay lower premiums, receive additional compensation, or receive expanded health benefits.

The Healthcare program will pay a fixed amount on behalf of elderly beneficiaries who choose to enroll in HMOs. If the HMO can provide the standard Healthcare benefit package for less than the fixed amount, it must offer additional health benefits to the patient.

The Plan also promotes competition by requiring Healthcare to use competitive bidding to select private companies to perform claims processing and related functions. Demonstration projects by the Department of Health, Education, and Welfare have shown that this change will produce significant administrative savings.

FRAMEWORK FOR A COMPREHENSIVE
PLAN

A universal, comprehensive national health insurance program is one of the major unfinished items on America's social agenda. The National Health Plan I am proposing today creates both the framework and the momentum to reach that long-sought goal. In future years, the Plan can be expanded to include all low-income persons. Employer coverage can be made more fully comprehensive, with subsidies to ease the burden on small businesses. First-dollar coverage for preventive services can be extended throughout early childhood. I am today sending to the Congress an outline of a fully comprehensive plan which builds upon the significant health care improvements that I am asking the Congress to enact this session.

Consistent with current budgetary constraints, new Federal spending for the National Health Plan will not begin until FY '83. When the Plan is fully implemented, the Federal budget cost in 1980 dollars will be 18 billion and the premium cost to employers and employees will be $8 billion. A substantial portion of these expenditures reflect reduced out-of-pocket expenses for individuals and reduced spending by State and local governments for their health programs. These expenditures are a social investment in the future of our children, the economic security of our elderly, and the well-being and peace of mind of all Americans. They are an investment in a more effective and efficient health care system. Over time, the Plan's emphasis on prevention, competition, and cost containment will reap important dividends for our Nation and its people.

I urge the Congress not to lose this precious opportunity for progress. The real needs of our people are not served by waiting and hoping for a better tomorrow. That tomorrow will never come unless we act today. The National Health Plan I propose will provide millions of our citizens with better health, greater economic security, and more productive, dignified, and hopeful lives. The American people have waited long enough. I call on the Congress to act without delay.

JIMMY CARTER

The White House,
June 12, 1979.

John Wayne

*Statement on the Death of the
Film Actor. June 12, 1979*

John Wayne was bigger than life. In an age of few heroes, he was the genuine article. But he was more than just a hero—he was a symbol of many of the most basic qualities that made America great. The ruggedness, the tough independence, the sense of personal conviction and courage—on and off the screen—reflected the best of our national character.

It was because of what John Wayne said about what we are and what we can be that his great and deep love of America was returned in full measure.

Rosalynn and I extend our deepest sympathies to his family.

Energy Emergency in Florida

Memorandum From the President.
June 12, 1979

Memorandum for the Administrator of the Environmental Protection Agency

Based on a request submitted to me by the Governor of the State of Florida to extend my May 5, 1979 determination that a regional energy emergency continues to exist in the State of Florida of such severity that a temporary suspension of certain particulate and opacity control regulations which apply to fossil-fuel fired electric generating plants under the Florida Air Quality Implementation Plan may be necessary, and that other means of responding to the energy emergency may be inadequate, I hereby extend that determination for thirty days from June 5 to and including July 4, 1979. This extension is limited by the same conditions as my original determination.

If, during the extension, I find that a regional energy emergency no longer exists in Florida, I will direct that this extension be rescinded, and that all suspension orders issued by the Governor be terminated on the day of that rescission. Please continue to work with State officials to monitor carefully the residual oil supply in Florida, and to inform me if the emergency should cease to exist. You will continue to retain full authority to disapprove temporary suspension of regulations in Florida and to exercise your emergency powers authority under Section 303 of the Clean Air Act, when and if necessary. It is important to keep suspensions to an absolute minimum since Section 110(f) of the Clean Air Act limits each suspension to a maximum duration of 120 days.

I commend Governor Graham for his continued efforts in energy conservation and his commitment that no extension of any suspension will be granted if the result would be a violation of any national ambient primary or secondary air quality standard.

This determination shall be published in the FEDERAL REGISTER.

JIMMY CARTER

[Filed with the Office of the Federal Register, 2:56 p.m., June 12, 1979]

Steel Imports

Proclamation 4665.   June 12, 1979

EXTENSION OF TEMPORARY QUANTITATIVE LIMITATION ON THE IMPORTATION INTO THE UNITED STATES OF CERTAIN ARTICLES OF STAINLESS STEEL OR ALLOY TOOL STEEL

By the President of the United States of America

A Proclamation

1. On June 11, 1976, by Proclamation 4445, the President proclaimed, pursuant

to the Constitution and the statutes of the United States (including section 203 of the Trade Act of 1974 (19 U.S.C. 2253) (the Trade Act)), the imposition of temporary quantitative limitations on the importation into the United States of certain articles of stainless steel or alloy tool steel. These limitations were effective as to those articles entered, or withdrawn from warehouse, for consumption on or after June 14, 1976, and were to continue for a period of three years from that date unless earlier modified, or terminated. Proclamation 4445 was subsequently modified by Proclamation 4477 of November 16, 1976, Proclamation 4509 of June 15, 1977, and Proclamation 4559 of April 5, 1978. Import relief currently in effect under Proclamation 4445, as amended, with respect to articles provided for in items 923.20 through 923.26, inclusive, of the Tariff Schedules of the United States (TSUS) (19 U.S.C. 1202), is scheduled to terminate at the close of June 13, 1979, unless extended by the President pursuant to section 203(h)(3) of the Trade Act (19 U.S.C. 2253(h) (3)).

2. Pursuant to sections 203(i)(2) and (i)(3) of the Trade Act (19 U.S.C. 2253(i)(2) and (i)(3)), the United States International Trade Commission (USITC), on April 24, 1979, reported to the President (USITC Report 203–5) the results of its investigation under section 203(i) of the Trade Act (19 U.S.C. 2253(i)). The USITC advised that it was evenly divided on the question of the probable economic effect on the domestic industry concerned of the termination of the import relief provided for in items 923.20 through 923.26, inclusive, of the TSUS.

3. Section 203(h)(3) of the Trade Act (19 U.S.C. 2253(h)(3)) provides that

any import relief provided pursuant to section 203 may be extended by the President, at a level of relief no greater than the level in effect immediately before such extension, if the President determines, after taking into account the advice received from the USITC under section 203(i)(2) of the Trade Act (19 U.S.C. 2253(i)(2)) and after taking into account the considerations described in section 202(c) of the Trade Act (19 U.S.C. 2252 (c)), that such extension is in the national interest.

4. In accordance with section 203(h) (3) of the Trade Act (19 U.S.C. 2253 (h)(3)), having taken into account the advice received from the USITC under section 203(i)(2) of the Trade Act (19 U.S.C. 2253(i)(2)), and the considerations described in section 202(c) of the Trade Act (19 U.S.C. 2252(c)), I have determined that the extension of the import relief provided for in items 923.20 through 923.26, inclusive, of the TSUS is in the national interest.

Now, THEREFORE, I, JIMMY CARTER, President of the United States of America, acting under the authority vested in me by the Constitution and the statutes of the United States, including section 203 of the Trade Act (19 U.S.C. 2253), and in accordance with Article XIX of the General Agreement on Tariffs and Trade (GATT) (61 Stat. (pt. 5) A58; 8 UST (pt. 2) 1786), do proclaim that—

(1) Items 608.52, 608.76, 608.78, 608.85, 608.88, 609.06, 609.07 and 609.08, in Part I of Schedule XX to the GATT are modified to conform with the Quantitative restrictions set forth in the Annex to this proclamation.

(2) Subpart A, part 2 of the Appendix to the TSUS is modified as set forth in the Annex to this proclamation.

(3) The authority to make changes in the quantitative restrictions provided for in this proclamation, as set forth in the Annex to this proclamation, is hereby delegated to the Special Representative for Trade Negotiations.

(4) This proclamation shall be effective as to those articles entered, or withdrawn from warehouse, for consumption on or after June 14, 1979, and before the close of February 13, 1980, unless the period of its effectiveness is earlier expressly modified or terminated.

IN WITNESS WHEREOF, I have hereunto set my hand this twelfth day of June in the year of our Lord nineteen hundred and seventy-nine, and of the Independence of the United States of America the two hundred and third.

JIMMY CARTER

[Filed with the Office of the Federal Register, 2:55 p.m., June 12, 1979]

NOTE: The annex is printed in the FEDERAL REGISTER of June 14, 1979.

Advisory Commission on Intergovernmental Relations

Appointment of Two Members.
June 12, 1979

The President today announced the appointment of two persons as members of the Advisory Commission on Intergovernmental Relations for 2-year terms. They are:

JOHN DALTON, Governor of Virginia, to replace Otis Bowen, Governor of Indiana, whose term on the Commission has expired;

LEO McCARTHY, speaker of the California State Assembly, to replace Martin Sabo, who has retired as a State legislator.

Commission on Presidential Scholars

Appointment of Three Members.
June 12, 1979

The President today announced the appointment of three persons as members of the Commission on Presidential Scholars. They are:

REBECCA BARNHILL HUNDLEY, of Thomasville, N.C., a former claims manager and assistant secretary of the Occidental Life Insurance Co. of North Carolina in Raleigh. She is active in civic affairs and serves on the North Carolina State Judicial Standards Commission and the State Banking Laws Study Commission.

JOANNE RAJOPPI, of Springfield, N.J., a freelance writer, editor of the New Jersey Carpenters Funds' publication, and former newspaper writer. She is active in local politics and serves as Union County freeholder vice chairperson.

CECILE C. WARONKER, of Atlanta, Ga., a teacher of remedial mathematics and reading in the Atlanta public school system.

Hazardous Waste Disposal

Letter to the Speaker of the House and the President of the Senate Transmitting Proposed Legislation. June 13, 1979

Dear Mr. Speaker: (Dear Mr. President:)

Today I am transmitting legislation to address some of the most significant environmental and public health problems facing our Nation. The problems which the legislation is designed to address are extremely serious. Recent months have focused public attention on a series of past improper hazardous waste disposal incidents such as the tragedy of Love Canal, New York. This case clearly demonstrates the unacceptable costs of improper hazardous waste disposal which may accrue from other incidents such as:

- contamination of surface and ground waters including drinking water supplies;
- staggering financial costs of cleaning up and containing wastes; and
- acute poisoning, carcinogenicity, mutagenicity, and promotion of miscarriages and birth defects.

The proposed legislation is a comprehensive program with the financial responsibility shared by Federal, State and local governments as well as industry. For spills of oil or hazardous substances, the legislation establishes a comprehensive and uniform system of notification, emergency response, enforcement, liability and limited economic compensation for such incidents. For uncontrolled sites, the proposed legislation would establish essentially the same program but without economic compensation. This comprehensive program would be implemented by:

- requiring notification of spills and the presence of uncontrolled hazardous waste disposal sites;
- empowering the Federal Government to clean up and mitigate pollution in those incidents where the liable parties do not respond adequately or cannot be quickly identified;
- enforcing higher standards of care in the handling of oil, hazardous substances and hazardous wastes including recovery from liable parties of governmental response costs and economic compensation;
- providing compensation for the economic damages sustained by innocent victims of spills.

The States have a significant role in implementing this legislation. Although the proposed legislation authorizes Federal action in emergency situations, the States are expected to provide financing for both the short-term and long-term containment of releases from hazardous dumpsites.

The legislation provides a major innovation in the manner we approach environmental rehabilitation. In particular, those elements of the private sector which produce hazardous chemicals will share, along with the Federal and State governments, in the financial responsibility for meeting the goals of the legislation through a system of fees.

The legislation provides for a mid-term evaluation. Within three years of enactment a report will be submitted to the Congress which would include experience to date in implementing the legislation; the extent, if any, of the critical uncontrolled sites problem; projected funds required for spill response; extent of State participation; and recommendations for statutory modification in such areas as fee structure, fund operation, liability limits, and financial responsibility limits.

It has become abundantly clear over the past several months that exposure of humans and the environment to dangers from spills of oil, hazardous substances and hazardous wastes and from releases at uncontrolled hazardous waste disposal sites are two of the most pressing environmental problems facing the Nation. I believe that the proposed legislation represents a comprehensive and effective approach for protecting people and the environment from such incidents. I am hopeful that this proposal will receive prompt consideration and speedy enactment. The health of the public and the environment cannot afford less.

Sincerely,

JIMMY CARTER

NOTE: This is the text of identical letters addressed to Thomas P. O'Neill, Jr., Speaker of the House of Representatives, and Walter F. Mondale, President of the Senate.

Gold Medal for Hubert H. Humphrey

Statement on Signing S. 613 Into Law.
June 13, 1979

I have approved S. 613, a bill authorizing that a special gold medal be struck in recognition of Hubert Humphrey's distinguished career, and that as President I present it to Mrs. Humphrey on behalf of the Congress.

Hubert Humphrey's unyielding dedication to the principles of equality and social justice will forever remind us that one person can make a difference in the life and well-being of a whole nation. We have a long road to travel before we fully achieve the goals he sought, but few men or women have paved as much of that road as Hubert Humphrey did. Let us dedicate ourselves to finishing his work.

It is an honor and privilege for me as President to join with the Congress in tribute to this great American.

NOTE: As enacted, S. 613 is Public Law 96-21, approved June 13.

Department of Defense

Nomination of John Howard Moxley III
To Be an Assistant Secretary.   June 13, 1979

The President today announced that he will nominate John Howard Moxley III, of La Jolla, Calif., to be Assistant Secretary of Defense. His area of responsibility would be health affairs, and he would replace Robert N. Smith, who has resigned.

Moxley is currently vice chancellor for health sciences and dean of the School of Medicine of the University of California at San Diego.

He was born January 10, 1935, in Elizabeth, N.J. He received an A.B. from Williams College in 1957 and an M.D. from the University of Colorado School of Medicine in 1961.

Moxley was at Peter Bent Brigham Hospital in Boston from 1961 to 1963 as medical house officer, then assistant resident physician. From 1963 to 1965, he was a clinical associate at the National Cancer Institute. From 1965 to 1966, he was a senior resident at Peter Bent Brigham Hospital.

From 1966 to 1969, Moxley was an instructor in medicine and assistant to the dean of Harvard Medical School. From 1969 to 1973, he was dean of the University of Maryland School of Medicine and associate professor of medicine. Since 1973 he has been at the University of California at San Diego.

Moxley is the author of numerous articles. He has served as a member of the President's National Advisory Commission on Health Manpower and as a clinical associate and consultant at veterans hospitals.

Department of Commerce

Nomination of Samuel B. Nemirow To Be
Assistant Secretary for Maritime Affairs.
June 13, 1979

The President today announced that he will nominate Samuel B. Nemirow, of Fairfax, Va., to be Assistant Secretary of Commerce for Maritime Affairs. He would replace Robert Blackwell, who has resigned.

Nemirow has been Deputy Assistant Secretary for Maritime Affairs since 1972. He was born October 23, 1940, in Hartford, Conn. He received a B.A. from the University of Connecticut in 1958 and an LL.B. from Boston University in 1962.

From 1965 to 1969, Nemirow was assistant to the Chairman of the Federal Maritime Commission. From 1969 to 1970, he practiced law with the Washington firm of Galland, Kharasch, Calkins & Brown. From 1970 to 1972, he was Chief of the Regulation Division at the Transportation Department.

Railroad Retirement Board

Nomination of Charles J. Chamberlain To Be a Member. June 13, 1979

The President today announced that he will nominate Charles J. Chamberlain, of Des Plaines, Ill., for reappointment as a member of the Railroad Retirement Board.

Chamberlain has been the labor member of this Board since 1977. The Board administers retirement-survivor and unemployment-sickness benefit programs provided by Federal laws for the Nation's railroad workers and their families.

Chamberlain was born August 7, 1921. From 1938 to 1956, he worked for the Chicago and North Western Railroad as a signalman and signal maintainer. From 1941 to 1977, he held various posts in the Brotherhood of Railroad Signalmen, beginning as recording secretary for Local 108 and finally serving as president of the union.

Chamberlain also served as chairman of the Railway Labor Executives' Association from 1970 to 1977. He was an alderman in De Kalb, Ill., from 1954 to 1958.

United States Advisory Commission on International Communication, Cultural and Educational Affairs

Nomination of Jean McKee To Be a Member. June 13, 1979

The President today announced that he will nominate Jean McKee, of New York City, to be a member of the United States Advisory Commission on International Communication, Cultural and Educational Affairs for a 3-year term.

McKee was chief of staff for the minority leader of the New York State Assembly, Perry B. Duryea, until last December.

She was born June 20, 1929, in New Haven, Conn. She received a degree in political science from Vassar College. She worked for the New York Republican State Committee from 1953 to 1955, and as a researcher for a private research organization from 1957 to 1959. She was also active in a number of Republican political campaigns between 1952 and 1962.

From 1962 to 1966, McKee was a partner and treasurer of a public relations and public opinion polling firm, Consensus, Inc., leaving the firm in 1964 to work on then-Governor Nelson Rockefeller's national campaign committee and the New York Republican State Committee, and in 1965 to work on former Senator Kenneth Keating's campaign for judge of the court of appeals.

In 1966 McKee worked for the New York Republican State Committee and the Republican State campaign committee. In 1967 she joined the staff of Senator Jacob K. Javits. She worked in his New York and Washington offices until 1975, and was named administrative assistant in 1973.

In 1976 and 1977, McKee served as Deputy Administrator, then Acting Administrator, of the American Revolution Bicentennial Administration. She was chief of staff to Minority Leader Duryea and operations director of his campaign during 1978.

The President's Trip to Vienna, Austria

Remarks on Departure From the White House. June 14, 1979

Mr. Vice President and citizens of our great country:

Thiry-five years ago during another summit meeting in Potsdam, a brief message was brought to President Truman. Just before dawn on the desert of Alamogordo the first atomic bomb had been exploded—man had unleased the power of matter itself, and world events have never been the same.

Since then, the unchanging duty of of every American President has been to avoid nuclear war while maintaining and even enhancing the security of the United States of America. That is exactly the purpose of my mission to Vienna. We know that progress in this search is most often measured in inches and not in miles. And we know that the only way to have peace in the end is to wage peace constantly from a position of constant and sustained national strength.

The summit in Vienna will be the 10th such summit between American Presidents and the leaders of the Soviet Union since World War II. We do have significant differences between the Soviet Union. They are important, and they require the most careful discussion.

We will make clear to the Soviet Union our views and our purposes throughout the world, so that no misunderstanding on their part might provide a dangerous prospect for the people of our two nations and the rest of the world.

We will try to broaden our communications with the Soviets and to create new channels of understanding between our two countries for these purposes.

We will seek new areas where more cooperation might be forthcoming and also less competition. The arms limitation treaty which President Brezhnev and I will sign next Monday embodies that spirit, and it gives us enhanced national security and an increased hope for a peaceful future.

And with SALT II, we continue the 30-year search for ways to avoid nuclear war. That was the goal of the Limited Test Ban Treaty; that was the goal of the Anti-Ballistic Missile Treaty; that was the goal of SALT I. It has been the goal with SALT II of three Presidents negotiating over the last 7 years on behalf of the American people to make this agreement which we will sign next week fair, equitable, a stabilizing force, and verifiable. That will be our goal as we begin to discuss further limitations on SALT III.

No one treaty can take us back to the time that we enjoyed before nuclear weapons became a potential destructive force, just as no one summit conference can end the sharp competition between ourselves and the Soviet Union. But we and the Soviet Union can agree that the security of both nations and the stability of the world depends upon the avoiding of a nuclear conflict which some few may survive, but which certainly no one could win.

I approach this summit in Vienna with hope, but without any false expectations.

The goals which lie at the heart of my mission today—improving our own Nation's security and enhancing the prospects for world peace and the avoidance of nuclear war—transcend all other issues that I will ever face in my own life in public service.

I'm grateful for the guidance of members of my Cabinet, my administration, the Congress, and the American people, and for the good wishes of our Nation as I go on this mission.

I go to Vienna with a confidence which can only come from representing the greatest, the most powerful, and the most free society on Earth.

Thank you all very much. I'll certainly do the best I can.

NOTE: The President spoke at approximately 8 a.m. on the South Lawn of the White House.

Veterans' Health Care Amendments of 1979

Statement on Signing S. 7 Into Law.
June 14, 1979

Out of a deep sense of commitment, Congress by resolution, and I by proclamation, called upon the Nation this year to honor the sacrifice and contributions of the 9.9 million Vietnam era veterans during Vietnam Veterans Week, from May 28 through June 3, 1979. The veterans of Vietnam had to demonstrate an extra measure of heroism because of the divisiveness of the war. We as a nation are finally ready to recognize and appreciate their valor and patriotism.

The statistics that show that the overwhelming majority of returned Vietnam veterans have readjusted successfully are a tribute to their courage, but no comfort to those who have not been able to overcome the psychic or physical damages of the war. In declaring Vietnam Veterans Week, I spoke of our Nation's moral debt to these veterans. In signing S. 7, we begin today to repay that debt.

S. 7 will enable the VA to provide special readjustment counseling for Vietnam era veterans and their families. This is an extremely important feature. The burden and pain of the war and its recurring trauma are shared fully by the veterans' families. Their well-being is essential for successful rehabilitation. The counseling provision includes important mental health followup services as well. The VA will make every attempt to provide services for eligible veterans and, when necessary, avail itself of the services of community mental health centers and other facilities where VA readjustment counseling centers are inaccessible or unable to provide necessary services.

S. 7 will also permit the VA to establish a 5-year pilot program for the treatment and rehabilitation of veterans with alcohol or drug dependence or abuse problems. While drug problems are on the decline among Vietnam veterans, alcohol problems are rising. This important pilot program will enable veterans to receive appropriate treatment and counseling for these special problems in their own communities where such treatment is most effective.

I am concerned about the hospital construction provision of S. 7 which may delay or impair important hospital construction projects undertaken by the VA system. Our commitment to the health needs of our veteran population must come first; I believe that VA recommendations on future construction sites have been based on that commitment. I hope that this new authority in S. 7 will not politicize nor

unnecessarily delay future VA construc-
tions.

The special provisions of S. 7 which
are the key initiatives of my legislative
program will permit the VA to more fully
and flexibly respond to special needs, particularly those of Vietnam era veterans
which have not until now been fully and
adequately addressed. Max Cleland, my
VA Administrator, testified 10 years ago
on behalf of psychological readjustment
counseling. I congratulate Senator Alan
Cranston, who has been a tireless champion for psychological readjustment
counseling legislation for many years and
deserves great credit for final passage of
this legislation.

The Nation has shown its appreciation
to veterans over the years. With this act
we demonstrate again our recognition of
those contributions. We also give special
tribute to Vietnam era veterans and
demonstrate forcefully that this country
has opened its eyes and its heart to their
unique experience and sacrifice.

NOTE: As enacted, S. 7 is Public Law 96–22,
approved June 13.

United States Ambassador to New Zealand and Western Samoa

Nomination of Anne Clark Martindell.
June 14, 1979

The President today announced that
he will nominate Anne Clark Martindell,
of Princeton, N.J., to be Ambassador
Extraordinary and Plenipotentiary of the
United States to New Zealand and to
Western Samoa. She would replace Armi-
stead I. Selden, Jr., resigned.

Martindell is Director of the Office of
United States Foreign Disaster Assistance.

She was born July 18, 1914, in New
York City. She attended Smith College
and Sir George Williams College.

From 1963 to 1967, Martindell was a
teacher, then reading supervisor, at Miss
Mason's School in Princeton. She was a
New Jersey State senator from 1973 to
1977. Since 1977 she has been Director
of the Office of Foreign Disaster Assistance. She is a member of the Advisory
Council of the Department of Politics at
Princeton University.

Department of Energy

Nomination of Louis F. Moret To Be Director
of the Office of Minority Economic Impact.
June 14, 1979

The President today announced that he
is nominating Louis F. Moret, of Los
Angeles, Calif., to be Director of the
Office of Minority Economic Impact at
the Energy Department. The President
announced his intention to nominate
Moret for this position on May 5, 1979, in
Los Angeles.

Moret has been Director of the Office
of Minority Business Enterprise at the
Commerce Department since 1977.

He was born October 18, 1944, in Los
Angeles. He received a B.A. in sociology
from Whittier College in 1972 and an
M.P.A. from the University of Southern
California in 1976.

In 1972 Moret was southern California
Chicano coordinator for Hubert H.
Humphrey's Presidential campaign, and
campaign manager for Richard Alatorre's campaign for the assembly. In 1975
he was campaign manager for Edward
Avila's campaign for councilman, and
served as vice president for public affairs
for the National Economic Development
Association.

From 1975 to 1976, Moret was affirmative action officer for the Montebello Unified School District in Montebello, Calif. In 1976 and 1977, he was chief of staff for California Assemblyman Richard Alatorre.

sumer concerns. He has worked with business and consumer groups on legislation to create an agency for consumer advocacy.

Consumer Product Safety Commission

Nomination of Stuart M. Statler To Be a Commissioner. June 14, 1979

The President today announced that he will nominate Stuart M. Statler, of Washington, D.C., to be a Commissioner of the Consumer Product Safety Commission for a term expiring October 26, 1986.

Statler has been chief counsel to the minority for the Senate Permanent Subcommittee on Investigations since 1973, and counsel to Senator Charles Percy since 1971.

He was born June 15, 1943, in New York City. He received a B.A. from Amherst College in 1965 and a J.D. from Harvard Law School in 1968.

From 1968 to 1970, Statler was special assistant to the Chairman of the National Commission on Product Safety, the Commission whose recommendations led to the creation of the Consumer Product Safety Commission.

From 1970 to 1971, Statler was senior staff associate of the President's Advisory Council on Executive Organization, where he served on the Task Force on Independent Regulatory Commissions. From 1971 to 1973, he was minority counsel to the Senate Subcommittee on Executive Reorganization.

As chief counsel to the minority of the Investigations Subcommittee, Statler has been involved in a wide range of investigations of fraud, corruption, or misfeasance, many of which are related to con-

National Credit Union Administration Board

Nomination of P. A. Mack, Jr., To Be a Member. June 14, 1979

The President today announced that he will nominate P. A. Mack, Jr., of Indianapolis, Ind., to be a member of the National Credit Union Administration Board for a 4-year term. Mack has been administrative assistant to Senator Birch Bayh since 1971.

He was born September 8, 1930, in Chicago, Ill. He received a B.S. in agriculture from Purdue University in 1952 and an M.B.A. in management, finance, and marketing from Indiana University in 1955.

From 1953 to 1955, Mack taught courses in personnel relations at Indiana University. From 1955 to 1957, he was a quality control superviser for Quaker Oats Co. In 1958–59 he taught management at DePaul University.

From 1958 to 1968, Mack was an agricultural lending officer and consultant with the Harris Trust and Savings Bank in Chicago. From 1960 to 1971, he also served on the board of directors of the Tazewell County National Bank in Delavan, Ill., where he was responsible for the management of the entire securities portfolio.

From 1968 to 1971, he was vice president of the Continental Illinois National Bank in Chicago.

Since 1955 he has also been owner and manager of Mack Farms, in Delavan, Ill.

1041

Community Services Administration

Nomination of Frankie M. Freeman To Be Inspector General. June 14, 1979

The President today announced that he will nominate Frankie M. Freeman, of St. Louis, Mo., to be Inspector General of the Community Services Administration. Freeman is a senior partner in the St. Louis law firm of Freeman, Whitfield, Montgomery & Walton.

She was born November 24, 1916, in Danville, Va. She attended Hampton Institute, Hampton, Va., and received her law degree from the Howard University School of Law in 1947. She taught business law for 2 years, and began her law practice in St. Louis in 1949.

Ms. Freeman has a strong investigative background. She has been a member of the U.S. Commission on Civil Rights since 1964 and served as the general counsel of the St. Louis Housing Authority from 1969 to 1970. She also served as assistant attorney general of Missouri from 1955 to 1956. From 1956 to 1970, she was a full-time staff attorney for the St. Louis Housing and Land Clearance Authorities, serving in the position of associate general counsel from 1956 to 1969. In 1970 she returned to her law practice.

Digest of Other White House Announcements

The following listing includes the President's public schedule and other items of general interest announced by the White House Press Office and not included elsewhere in this issue.

June 11

The President left Camp David, Md., for a fishing trip at Leetown, W. Va. While he was in Leetown, the President toured the National Fish Health Research Laboratory. He then returned to the White House.

The President participated in a briefing by administration officials on the Panama Canal treaties implementing legislation given for Members of the House of Representatives on the State Floor at the White House.

June 12

The President met at the White House with:

—Zbigniew Brzezinski, Assistant to the President for National Security Affairs;

—Rev. Leon Sullivan;

—Frank B. Moore, Assistant to the President for Congressional Liaison;

—William J. Green, Democratic candidate for mayor of Philadelphia;

—Prime Minister Odvar Nordli of Norway and Vice President Walter F. Mondale;

—former Ambassador John J. McCloy.

The President participated in a briefing by administration officials on the strategic arms limitation agreement given for civic and community leaders in the East Room at the White House.

The President has accorded the personal rank of Ambassador to William A. Hayne, Deputy Assistant Secretary of State for International Environmental Affairs, while he serves as head of the U.S. delegation to the diplomatic conference on the protection of migratory species being held in Bonn, Federal Republic of Germany.

June 13

The President met at the White House with:

—Dr. Brzezinski;

—Mr. Moore;

—Stansfield Turner, Director of Central Intelligence, Hamilton Jordan, Assistant to the President, and Dr. Brzezinski;

—the Joint Chiefs of Staff;

—Vice President Mondale;

—Gen. Bernard W. Rogers, appointed as Supreme Allied Commander, Europe, and Commander in Chief of U.S. Forces in Europe.

The White House announced that President Carter has invited President-elect Jaime Roldós of Ecuador to meet with him in July.

The President today announced that he will nominate Frederick H. Schultz, of Jacksonville, Fla., to be Vice Chairman of the Board of Governors of the Federal Reserve System. The President announced his intention to nominate Schultz as a member of the Board on April 12, 1979.

June 14

The President today declared a major disaster for the State of Texas as a result of severe storms and flooding, beginning on or about May 30, which caused extensive public and private property damage.

June 15

The President today declared a major disaster for the State of Kansas as a result of severe storms and flooding, beginning on or about June 7, which caused extensive public and private property damage.

NOMINATIONS SUBMITTED TO THE SENATE

The following list does not include promotions of members of the Uniformed Services, nominations to the Service Academies, or nominations of Foreign Service officers.

Submitted June 12, 1979

GEORGE ARCENEAUX, JR., of Louisiana, to be United States District Judge for the Eastern District of Louisiana, vice a new position created by P.L. 95–486, approved October 20, 1978.

TYRONE BROWN, of the District of Columbia, to be a member of the Federal Communications Commission for a term of 7 years from July 1, 1979 (reappointment).

ALLIE C. FELDER, JR., of the District of Columbia, to be a member of the Board of Directors of the Overseas Private Investment Corporation for a term expiring December 17, 1981 (reappointment).

BRENTON H. RUPPLE, of Wisconsin, to be a Director of the Securities Investor Protection Corporation for a term expiring December 31, 1981 (reappointment).

Submitted June 14, 1979

ANNE CLARK MARTINDELL, of New Jersey, to be Ambassador Extraordinary and Plenipotentiary of the United States of America to New Zealand, and to serve concurrently and without additional compensation as Ambassador Extraordinary and Plenipotentiary of the United States of America to Western Samoa.

JOHN HOWARD MOXLEY III, of California, to be an Assistant Secretary of Defense, vice Robert Nelson Smith, resigned.

OTTO R. SKOPIL, JR., of Oregon, to be United States Circuit Judge for the Ninth Circuit, vice a new position created by P.L. 95–486, approved October 20, 1978.

LYNN C. HIGBY, of Florida, to be United States District Judge for the Northern District of Florida, vice a new position created by P.L. 95–486, approved October 20, 1978.

ROBERT L. VINING, JR., of Georgia, to be United States District Judge for the Northern District of Georgia, vice a new position created by P.L. 95–486, approved October 20, 1978.

1043

NOMINATIONS—Continued

Submitted June 14—Continued

PATRICK E. CARR, of Louisiana, to be United States District Judge for the Eastern District of Louisiana, vice a new position created by P.L. 95–486, approved October 20, 1978.

ROBERT J. STAKER, of West Virginia, to be United States District Judge for the Southern District of West Virginia, vice a new position created by P.L. 95–486, approved October 20, 1978.

SAMUEL B. NEMIROW, of Virginia, to be Assistant Secretary of Commerce for Maritime Affairs, vice Robert J. Blackwell, resigned.

LOUIS F. MORET, of California, to be Director of the Office of Minority Economic Impact (new position).

FRANKIE MUSE FREEMAN, of Missouri, to be Inspector General, Community Services Administration (new position).

STUART M. STATLER, of the District of Columbia, to be a Commissioner of the Consumer Product Safety Commission for the remainder of the term expiring October 26, 1979, vice Barbara H. Franklin, resigned.

STUART M. STATLER, of the District of Columbia, to be a Commissioner of the Consumer Product Safety Commission for a term of 7 years from October 27, 1979 (reappointment).

JOHN W. MACY, JR., of Virginia, to be Director of the Federal Emergency Management Agency (new position).

FREDERICK H. SCHULTZ, of Florida, to be a member of the Board of Governors of the Federal Reserve System for the unexpired term of 14 years from February 1, 1968, vice Philip C. Jackson, Jr., resigned.

FREDERICK H. SCHULTZ, of Florida, to be Vice Chairman of the Board of Governors of the Federal Reserve System for a term of 4 years (new position).

P. A. MACK, JR., of Indiana, to be a member of the National Credit Union Administration Board for the term of 4 years (new position).

CHARLES J. CHAMBERLAIN, of Illinois, to be a member of the Railroad Retirement Board for the term of 5 years from August 29, 1979 (reappointment).

JEAN McKEE, of New York, to be a member of the United States Advisory Commission on International Communication, Cultural and Educational Affairs for a term of 3 years (new position).

CHECKLIST OF WHITE HOUSE PRESS RELEASES

The following listing contains releases of the White House Press Office which are not included in this issue.

Released June 11, 1979

News conference: on changes in the Federal timber policy as an anti-inflation measure—by Alfred E. Kahn, Advisor to the President on Inflation, Secretary of Agriculture Bob Bergland, and John R. McGuire, Chief of the Forest Service, Department of Agriculture

Fact sheet: departure from even-flow timber harvest on Federal lands

Announcement: nomination of George Arceneaux, Jr., to be United States District Judge for the Eastern District of Louisiana

Released June 12, 1979

News conference: on the National Health Plan—by Stuart E. Eizenstat, Assistant to the President for Domestic Affairs and Policy, and Secretary of Health, Education, and Welfare Joseph A. Califano, Jr.

Released June 13, 1979

News conference: on proposed hazardous waste disposal legislation—by Douglas M. Costle, Administrator, and Thomas C. Jorling, Assistant Administrator for Water and Hazardous Materials, Environmental Protection Agency, James W. Moorman, Assistant Attorney General, Land and Natural Resources Division, and Mr. Eizenstat

Announcement: nomination of Otto R. Skopil, Jr., to be United States Circuit Judge for the Ninth Circuit

Announcement: nomination of Patrick E. Carr to be United States District Judge for the Eastern District of Louisiana

Announcement: nomination of Lynn C. Higby to be United States District Judge for the Northern District of Florida

Announcement: nomination of Robert L. Vining, Jr., to be United States District Judge for the Northern District of Georgia

Announcement: nomination of Robert J. Staker to be United States District Judge for the Southern District of West Virginia

Announcement: visit of President-elect Jaime Roldós of Ecuador

CHECKLIST—Continued

Released June 13—Continued

Announcement: appointment of Marshall Brement to the National Security Council staff in charge of Soviet-Eastern European affairs and East-West relations

Announcement: appointment of Gerald G. Oplinger to the National Security Council staff in charge of nuclear nonproliferation issues

Released June 14, 1979

Advance text: remarks on departure from the White House for a trip to Vienna, Austria

ACTS APPROVED BY THE PRESIDENT

Approved June 13, 1979

H.R. 2805_____ Public Law 96–19

An act to make technical and conforming changes to the financial disclosure provisions in the Ethics in Government Act of 1978.

ACTS APPROVED—Continued

Approved June 13—Continued

S. 348_____ Public Law 96–20

An act to authorize the President of the United States to present on behalf of the Congress a specially struck gold medal to Ben Abruzzo, Maxie Anderson, and Larry Newman.

S. 613_____ Public Law 96–21

An act authorizing the President of the United States to present a gold medal to the widow of Hubert H. Humphrey.

S. 7_____ Public Law 96–22

Veterans' Health Care Amendments of 1979.

S. 709_____ Public Law 96–23

An act to authorize appropriations for the Coast Guard for fiscal years 1980 and 1981, and for other purposes.

Editor's Note

The President's Trip to Vienna, Austria

The President was in Vienna on Friday, June 15. Releases and announcements issued on the trip will be printed in next week's issue.

Vienna Summit Meeting

Remarks of President Rudolph Kirchschläger of Austria and President Carter at the Welcoming Ceremony. June 14, 1979

PRESIDENT KIRCHSCHLÄGER. Mr. President of the United States of America, on behalf of the people of Austria, I bid you, Mr. President, your distinguished wife, Mrs. Carter, and your distinguished party, a very cordial welcome on Austrian soil.

We Austrians are delighted and profoundly gratified at the fact that your meeting with the Chairman of the Presidium of the Supreme Soviet of the Soviet Union takes place in Vienna, the capital of the Republic of Austria. We hope sincerely that we will be able to offer you for your encounter an environment and an atmosphere which will facilitate your highly responsible talks.

I am well aware of the fact that we have no right and that we have no wish to influence your deliberations. But, Mr. President, let me add one more word to this welcome, speaking not only as the Federal President of the Republic of Austria but also as one of the about 4,000 million human beings in this world.

We hope and we wish and we trust from the depth of our hearts that the meeting between you, Mr. President, and the Chairman of the Presidium of the Supreme Soviet will lead not only to the signing of SALT II but will also help to develop the relations and the relations of trust between the world powers and ·will contribute towards the further process of détente and thus towards a reduction of armaments.

Mr. President, once again, a very cordial welcome to you in Austria.

PRESIDENT CARTER. We are all delighted to visit the beautiful and historic city of Vienna. And on behalf of the American people, I want to express my appreciation to President Kirchschläger, Chancellor Kreisky, and the Government and the people of Austria for hosting this summit meeting.

The good wishes expressed by your President have been very important to me and accurately express the purpose of our meeting.

The United States and Austria are united by strong bonds of friendship, mutual respect, and shared devotion to democratic ideals. The people of my nation unequivocally support and appreciate the freedom, the independence, and the neutrality of Austria.

I've come to meet with President Brezhnev on a mission of peace—to strengthen and to enlarge cooperation and understanding between the United States of America and the Soviet Union, to reduce the dangers of nuclear war, and to move towards a more stable and a more secure world.

This summit involves the United States and the Soviet Union directly. But all people have an urgent stake in these talks. No human being can rest secure in a world of unrestrained nuclear weapons. All nations and all people share an overriding interest in maintaining peace in the nuclear age.

This city is especially appropriate as a setting to pursue the goals of understanding. Historically, Vienna has been a crossroads where different cultures and political systems meet. The United States and the Soviet Union, for instance, concluded the first major cooperative agreement of the postwar period 24 years ago in this city in 1955, helping to move both nations beyond the hostilities and suspicions of the cold war era towards stability in Europe and greater cooperation in the pursuit of peace.

Vienna is the headquarters of the International Atomic Energy Agency, on which all nations rely to provide safeguards for the peaceful use of atomic power. And along with New York and Geneva, Vienna is the third city of the United Nations.

For nearly three decades, the United States and the Soviet Union have sought to limit and to control the momentum of the nuclear arms race. This week we continue in that process with the signing of SALT II. We have no illusion that this agreement will rid the world once and for all of danger, nor will it end all the differences that exist between our two countries. But we are confident that SALT II will widen the areas of cooperation and

reduce substantially the dangers of nuclear holocaust.

The people of Vienna, the people of Europe, and the peoples of many other nations have known the bitter price of war twice in this century. With the success of this summit meeting, all people will take another step towards security and lasting peace.

Mr. President, thank you for your good wishes. We'll do our best to make them come true.

NOTE: The exchange began at 9:50 p.m. at the Vienna Airport.

Following his remarks, President Carter went to the residence of the U.S. Ambassador to Austria, where he stayed during the summit meeting.

Vienna Summit Meeting

Toast at a Working Dinner Hosted by the United States Delegation.   June 16, 1979

I have a brief toast, with your permission, Mr. President.

Mr. President, we have come to Vienna in search of common understanding in a spirit of common sense. We have come to explore, to clarify, and to attempt to resolve all our differences. We have come to take one more step towards avoiding a nuclear conflict in which some few might survive, but which no one can win.

Mr. President, if I had one thing to mention in my toast tonight, it would be to propose our two nations' success in holding a steady course towards control of weapons and then halting any drift towards uncertainty that might come from our failure to control and to regulate the arms competition.

We must consider the wider possibilities of SALT II. As we worked to conclude our agreement on strategic arms, we have found that we could work together for other positive change. In fact, our new SALT II treaty could provide the basic framework that we seek to reduce tension and conflict around the world.

The world is moving quickly towards more varied forms of government. Young nations are asserting a new independent place for themselves. We are seeing the decline of racism, the end of colonialism, and there is a worldwide movement against poverty and social injustice. At the same time, we face dangers that create combat in some regions of the world, trouble [in] international relations on a global scale, and encourage the spread of nuclear and conventional arms in many nations.

Very briefly, Mr. President, let me say that we believe in restraining conflicts that could undermine the goals that we have established for ourselves. We are working for cooperation among nations, for the peaceful settlement of disputes, for economic development with social justice and for human rights around the world. These are the ideas we would like to explore with you as we discuss the unique responsibilities of the relationship between the United States and the Soviet Union.

And, finally, Mr. President, I believe that our successful effort to limit nuclear weapons can be a framework for guidance toward new areas of cooperation and for facing peacefully those areas in which we still compete.

Mr. President, we raise our glasses to toast our success for SALT II. Let us pledge to seek new areas of common understanding in the same spirit of common sense. Let us pledge our continuing cooperation and honesty in our discussions, enhanced security of both nations, and, above all, a peaceful world.

Mr. President, I would like to propose a toast to you, Mr. President, and to the heroic people of the Soviet Union, our present and future friends.

NOTE: President Carter spoke at 9:15 p.m. at the residence of the U.S. Ambassador to Austria.

Earlier in the day, President Carter, President Brezhnev, and their delegations held morning and afternoon meetings at the U.S. Embassy.

As printed above, the item follows the press release.

Vienna Summit Meeting

Toast at a Working Dinner Hosted by the Soviet Delegation. June 17, 1979

Today, Mr. President, we discussed a range of issues important not only to each of us but to the entire world. On some of the issues, particularly in the arms control field, we were able to further our joint efforts to develop rules curbing the military competition between us and to lay the groundwork for further progress on the control and the regulation of nuclear weapons.

On some other issues, particularly international problems in troubled areas of the world, we did not always agree. And we were not able to develop a common approach. We did agree, however, to continue searching for a peaceful solution of these differences.

Both our countries face risks that stem from the changes sweeping many parts of the world today. As the two major nuclear powers, we have a special responsibility to deal with that change.

I believe that two possible roads lie before us. There is a road of competition and even confrontation. Any effort by either of our nations to exploit the turbulence that exists in various parts of the world pushes us towards that road. The United States can and will protect its vital interests if this becomes the route we must follow.

But there is another way, Mr. President—the path of restraint and, where possible, cooperation. This is the path we prefer.

I hope, Mr. President, that détente, which has been growing in Europe because of your great work, can now encompass other regions of the world. I hope that we can work together so that the rules of restraint, the mutual respect accorded each other's interests, and the recognition of the danger of unbridled competition will lead to an even more stable peace in Europe and can progressively be applied to other troubled regions of our planet.

In southern Africa there is a struggle for racial justice. We Americans know that violence is not the solution, and so we seek peaceful resolution of the conflicts there.

In Southeast Asia war continues, with national territories being invaded and occupied by foreign troops. We believe the war in Kampuchea can only be ended by the withdrawal of foreign forces and the honoring of national independence and international borders.

We must all show compassion, Mr. President, for the tens of thousands of suffering people who have been driven from their homes and their homelands. The callous indifference with which the world ignored refugees in Europe in the 1930's must not be repeated in the Asia of the 1970's.

In the Middle East, Israel and Egypt have taken an historic step toward a comprehensive peace. Thirty years of hatred had brought only war and terrorism. Only the courage of Egyptian and Israeli leaders has now enabled us to start down the road of a comprehensive peace.

On all these major international questions the United States stands for the peaceful reconciliation of differences and against the use of force. So, too, we stand for measures to control the instruments of war.

The SALT agreement which we will sign here tomorrow provides a good foundation, one that will be strengthened by the other arms control initiatives that we are pursuing together.

Let us build on that foundation so that we can narrow our differences in a spirit of respect for the independence of all nations and the value of every human being.

Let us both agree never to use offensive weapons against any nation in an act of aggression.

Let us discourage the use of foreign forces in troubled regions of the world and encourage the peaceful settlement of disputes among the people who are directly involved.

Mr. President, in all the world's history, no two nations have ever had a greater responsibility to act with restraint and to seek mutual accommodation than do the United States and the Soviet Union. We do have many differences of history, ideology, and economic and social systems.

Mr. President, we are both concerned about the future, and I am sure that with honesty and good will we can make progress toward a safer and more peaceful world.

Now, Mr. President, I would like to propose a toast: First of all, to my friend, President Brezhnev; secondly, to the heroic people of the Soviet Union; and thirdly, to our strong, determined, constant, unswerving commitment toward peace in the world and a control of all weapons.

Thank you, Mr. President.

NOTE: President Carter spoke at 8:10 p.m. at the Soviet Embassy.

Earlier in the day, President Carter, President Brezhnev, and their delegations held morning and afternoon meetings at the Soviet Embassy.

As printed above, the item follows the press release.

Vienna Summit Meeting

United States-Soviet Union Treaty on the Limitation of Strategic Offensive Arms and Related Documents. June 18, 1979

TREATY BETWEEN THE UNITED STATES OF AMERICA AND THE UNION OF SOVIET SOCIALIST REPUBLICS ON THE LIMITATION OF STRATEGIC OFFENSIVE ARMS

The United States of America and the Union of Soviet Socialist Republics, hereinafter referred to as the Parties,

Conscious that nuclear war would have devastating consequences for all mankind,

Proceeding from the Basic Principles of Relations Between the United States of America and the Union of Soviet Socialist Republics of May 29, 1972,

Attaching particular significance to the limitation of strategic arms and determined to continue their efforts begun with the Treaty on the Limitation of Anti-Ballistic Missile Systems and the Interim Agreement on Certain Measures with Respect to the Limitation of Strategic Offensive Arms, of May 26, 1972,

Convinced that the additional measures limiting strategic offensive arms provided for in this Treaty will contribute to the improvement of relations between the Parties, help to reduce the risk of out-

break of nuclear war and strengthen international peace and security,

Mindful of their obligations under Article VI of the Treaty on the Non-Proliferation of Nuclear Weapons,

Guided by the principle of equality and equal security,

Recognizing that the strengthening of strategic stability meets the interests of the Parties and the interests of international security,

Reaffirming their desire to take measures for the further limitation and for the further reduction of strategic arms, having in mind the goal of achieving general and complete disarmament,

Declaring their intention to undertake in the near future negotiations further to limit and further to reduce strategic offensive arms,

Have agreed as follows:

ARTICLE I

Each Party undertakes, in accordance with the provisions of this Treaty, to limit strategic offensive arms quantitatively and qualitatively, to exercise restraint in the development of new types of strategic offensive arms, and to adopt other measures provided for in this Treaty.

ARTICLE II

For the purposes of this Treaty:

1. Intercontinental ballistic missile (ICBM) launchers are land-based launchers of ballistic missiles capable of a range in excess of the shortest distance between the northeastern border of the continental part of the territory of the United States of America and the northwestern border of the continental part of the territory of the Union of Soviet Socialist Republics, that is, a range in excess of 5,500 kilometers.

2. Submarine-launched ballistic missile (SLBM) launchers are launchers of ballistic missiles installed on any nuclear-powered submarine or launchers of modern ballistic missiles installed on any submarine, regardless of its type.

3. Heavy bombers are considered to be:
(a) currently, for the United States of America, bombers of the B–52 and B–1 types, and for the Union of Soviet Socialist Republics, bombers of the Tupolev–95 and Myasishchev types;
(b) in the future, types of bombers which can carry out the mission of a heavy bomber in a manner similar or superior to that of bombers listed in subparagraph (a) above;
(c) types of bombers equipped for cruise missiles capable of a range in excess of 600 kilometers; and
(d) types of bombers equipped for ASBMs.

4. Air-to-surface ballistic missiles (ASBMs) are any such missiles capable of a range in excess of 600 kilometers and installed in an aircraft or on its external mountings.

5. Launchers of ICBMs and SLBMs equipped with multiple independently targetable reentry vehicles (MIRVs) are launchers of the types developed and tested for launching ICBMs or SLBMs equipped with MIRVs.

6. ASBMs equipped with MIRVs are ASBMs of the types which have been flight-tested with MIRVs.

7. Heavy ICBMs are ICBMs which have a launch-weight greater or a throw-weight greater than that of the heaviest, in terms of either launch-weight or throw-weight, respectively, of the light ICBMs deployed by either Party as of the date of signature of this Treaty.

8. Cruise missiles are unmanned, self-propelled, guided, weapon-delivery vehicles which sustain flight through the use of aerodynamic lift over most of their flight path and which are flight-tested from or deployed on aircraft, that is, air-launched cruise missiles, or such vehicles which are referred to as cruise missiles in subparagraph 1(b) of Article IX.

ARTICLE III

1. Upon entry into force of this Treaty, each Party undertakes to limit ICBM launchers, SLBM launchers, heavy bombers, and ASBMs to an aggregate number not to exceed 2,400.

2. Each Party undertakes to limit, from January 1, 1981, strategic offensive arms referred to in paragraph 1 of this Article to an aggregate number not to exceed 2,250, and to initiate reductions of those arms which as of that date would be in excess of this aggregate number.

3. Within the aggregate numbers provided for in paragraphs 1 and 2 of this Article and subject to the provisions of this Treaty, each Party has the right to determine the composition of these aggregates.

4. For each bomber of a type equipped for ASBMs, the aggregate numbers provided for in paragraphs 1 and 2 of this Article shall include the maximum number of such missiles for which a bomber of that type is equipped for one operational mission.

5. A heavy bomber equipped only for ASBMs shall not itself be included in the aggregate numbers provided for in paragraphs 1 and 2 of this Article.

6. Reductions of the numbers of strategic offensive arms required to comply with the provisions of paragraphs 1 and 2 of this Article shall be carried out as provided for in Article XI.

ARTICLE IV

1. Each Party undertakes not to start construction of additional fixed ICBM launchers.

2. Each Party undertakes not to relocate fixed ICBM launchers.

3. Each Party undertakes not to convert launchers of light ICBMs, or of ICBMs of older types deployed prior to 1964, into launchers of heavy ICBMs of types deployed after that time.

4. Each Party undertakes in the process of modernization and replacement of ICBM silo launchers not to increase the original internal volume of an ICBM silo launcher by more than thirty-two percent. Within this limit each Party has the right to determine whether such an increase will be made through an increase in the original diameter or in the original depth of an ICBM silo launcher, or in both of these dimensions.

5. Each Party undertakes:

(a) not to supply ICBM launcher deployment areas with intercontinental ballistic missiles in excess of a number consistent with normal deployment, maintenance, training, and replacement requirements;

(b) not to provide storage facilities for or to store ICBMs in excess of normal deployment requirements at launch sites of ICBM launchers;

(c) not to develop, test, or deploy systems for rapid reload of ICBM launchers.

6. Subject to the provisions of this Treaty, each Party undertakes not to have under construction at any time strategic offensive arms referred to in paragraph 1 of Article III in excess of numbers consistent with a normal construction schedule.

7. Each Party undertakes not to develop, test, or deploy ICBMs which have a launch-weight greater or a throw-weight greater than that of the heaviest, in terms of either launch-weight or throw-weight, respectively, of the heavy ICBMs deployed by either Party as of the date of signature of this Treaty.

8. Each Party undertakes not to convert land-based launchers of ballistic missiles which are not ICBMs into launchers for launching ICBMs, and not to test them for this purpose.

9. Each Party undertakes not to flight-test or deploy new types of ICBMs, that is, types of ICBMs not flight-tested as of May 1, 1979, except that each Party may flight-test and deploy one new type of light ICBM.

10. Each Party undertakes not to flight-test or deploy ICBMs of a type flight-tested as of May 1, 1979 with a number of reentry vehicles greater than the maximum number of reentry vehicles with which an ICBM of that type has been flight-tested as of that date.

11. Each Party undertakes not to flight-test or deploy ICBMs of the one new type permitted pursuant to paragraph 9 of this Article with a number of reentry vehicles greater than the maximum number of reentry vehicles with which an ICBM of either Party has been flight-tested as of May 1, 1979, that is, ten.

12. Each Party undertakes not to flight-test or deploy SLBMs with a number of reentry vehicles greater than the maximum number of reentry vehicles with which an SLBM of either Party has been flight-tested as of May 1, 1979, that is, fourteen.

13. Each Party undertakes not to flight-test or deploy ASBMs with a number of reentry vehicles greater than the maximum number of reentry vehicles with which an ICBM of either Party has

1053

been flight-tested as of May 1, 1979, that is, ten.

14. Each Party undertakes not to deploy at any one time on heavy bombers equipped for cruise missiles capable of a range in excess of 600 kilometers a number of such cruise missiles which exceeds the product of 28 and the number of such heavy bombers.

ARTICLE V

1. Within the aggregate numbers provided for in paragraphs 1 and 2 of Article III, each Party undertakes to limit launchers of ICBMs and SLBMs equipped with MIRVs, ASBMs equipped with MIRVs, and heavy bombers equipped for cruise missiles capable of a range in excess of 600 kilometers to an aggregate number not to exceed 1,320.

2. Within the aggregate number provided for in paragraph 1 of this Article, each Party undertakes to limit launchers of ICBMs and SLBMs equipped with MIRVs, and ASBMs equipped with MIRVs to an aggregate number not to exceed 1,200.

3. Within the aggregate number provided for in paragraph 2 of this Article, each Party undertakes to limit launchers of ICBMs equipped with MIRVs to an aggregate number not to exceed 820.

4. For each bomber of a type equipped for ASBMs equipped with MIRVs, the aggregate numbers provided for in paragraphs 1 and 2 of this Article shall include the maximum number of ASBMs for which a bomber of that type is equipped for one operational mission.

5. Within the aggregate numbers provided for in paragraphs 1, 2, and 3 of this Article and subject to the provisions of this Treaty, each Party has the right to determine the composition of these aggregates.

ARTICLE VI

1. The limitations provided for in this Treaty shall apply to those arms which are:

(a) operational;

(b) in the final stage of construction;

(c) in reserve, in storage, or mothballed;

(d) undergoing overhaul, repair, modernization, or conversion.

2. Those arms in the final stage of construction are:

(a) SLBM launchers on submarines which have begun sea trials;

(b) ASBMs after a bomber of a type equipped for such missiles has been brought out of the shop, plant, or other facility where its final assembly or conversion for the purpose of equipping it for such missiles has been performed;

(c) other strategic offensive arms which are finally assembled in a shop, plant, or other facility after they have been brought out of the shop, plant, or other facility where their final assembly has been performed.

3. ICBM and SLBM launchers of a type not subject to the limitation provided for in Article V, which undergo conversion into launchers of a type subject to that limitation, shall become subject to that limitation as follows:

(a) fixed ICBM launchers when work on their conversion reaches the stage which first definitely indicates that they are being so converted;

(b) SLBM launchers on a submarine when that submarine first goes to sea after their conversion has been performed.

4. ASBMs on a bomber which undergoes conversion from a bomber of a type

equipped for ASBMs which are not subject to the limitation provided for in Article V into a bomber of a type equipped for ASBMs which are subject to that limitation shall become subject to that limitation when the bomber is brought out of the shop, plant, or other facility where such conversion has been performed.

5. A heavy bomber of a type not subject to the limitation provided for in paragraph 1 of Article V shall become subject to that limitation when it is brought out of the shop, plant, or other facility where it has been converted into a heavy bomber of a type equipped for cruise missiles capable of a range in excess of 600 kilometers. A bomber of a type not subject to the limitation provided for in paragraph 1 or 2 of Article III shall become subject to that limitation and to the limitation provided for in paragraph 1 of Article V when it is brought out of the shop, plant, or other facility where it has been converted into a bomber of a type equipped for cruise missiles capable of a range in excess of 600 kilometers.

6. The arms subject to the limitations provided for in this Treaty shall continue to be subject to these limitations until they are dismantled, are destroyed, or otherwise cease to be subject to these limitations under procedures to be agreed upon.

7. In accordance with the provisions of Article XVII, the Parties will agree in the Standing Consultative Commission upon procedures to implement the provisions of this Article.

ARTICLE VII

1. The limitations provided for in Article III shall not apply to ICBM and SLBM test and training launchers or to space vehicle launchers for exploration and use of outer space. ICBM and SLBM test and training launchers are ICBM and SLBM launchers used only for testing or training.

2. The parties agree that:

(a) there shall be no significant increase in the number of ICBM or SLBM test and training launchers or in the number of such launchers of heavy ICBMs;

(b) construction or conversion of ICBM launchers at test ranges shall be undertaken only for purposes of testing and training;

(c) there shall be no conversion of ICBM test and training launchers or of space vehicle launchers into ICBM launchers subject to the limitations provided for in Article III.

ARTICLE VIII

1. Each Party undertakes not to flight-test cruise missiles capable of a range in excess of 600 kilometers or ASBMs from aircraft other than bombers or to convert such aircraft into aircraft equipped for such missiles.

2. Each Party undertakes not to convert aircraft other than bombers into aircraft which can carry out the mission of a heavy bomber as referred to in subparagraph 3(b) of Article II.

ARTICLE IX

1. Each Party undertakes not to develop, test, or deploy:

(a) ballistic missiles capable of a range in excess of 600 kilometers for installation on waterborne vehicles other than submarines, or launchers of such missiles;

(b) fixed ballistic or cruise missile launchers for emplacement on the ocean floor, on the seabed, or on the beds of internal waters and inland waters, or in the subsoil thereof, or mobile launchers of such missiles, which move only in contact with the ocean floor, the seabed, or the beds of internal waters and inland waters, or missiles for such launchers;

(c) systems for placing into Earth orbit nuclear weapons or any other kind of weapons of mass destruction, including fractional orbital missiles;

(d) mobile launchers of heavy ICBMs;

(e) SLBMs which have a launch-weight greater or a throw-weight greater than that of the heaviest, in terms of either launch-weight or throw-weight, respectively, of the light ICBMs deployed by either Party as of the date of signature of this Treaty, or launchers of such SLBMs; or

(f) ASBMs which have a launch-weight greater or a throw-weight greater than that of the heaviest, in terms of either launch-weight or throw-weight, respectively, of the light ICBMs deployed by either Party as of the date of signature of this Treaty.

2. Each Party undertakes not to flight-test from aircraft cruise missiles capable of a range in excess of 600 kilometers which are equipped with multiple independently targetable warheads and not to deploy such cruise missiles on aircraft.

ARTICLE X

Subject to the provisions of this Treaty, modernization and replacement of strategic offensive arms may be carried out.

ARTICLE XI

1. Strategic offensive arms which would be in excess of the aggregate numbers provided for in this Treaty as well as strategic offensive arms prohibited by this Treaty shall be dismantled or destroyed under procedures to be agreed upon in the Standing Consultative Commission.

2. Dismantling or destruction of strategic offensive arms which would be in excess of the aggregate number provided for in paragraph 1 of Article III shall begin on the date of the entry into force of this Treaty and shall be completed within the following periods from that date: four months for ICBM launchers; six months for SLBM launchers; and three months for heavy bombers.

3. Dismantling or destruction of strategic offensive arms which would be in excess of the aggregate number provided for in paragraph 2 of Article III shall be initiated no later than January 1, 1981, shall be carried out throughout the ensuing twelve-month period, and shall be completed no later than December 31, 1981.

4. Dismantling or destruction of strategic offensive arms prohibited by this Treaty shall be completed within the shortest possible agreed period of time, but not later than six months after the entry into force of this Treaty.

ARTICLE XII

In order to ensure the viability and effectiveness of this Treaty, each Party undertakes not to circumvent the provisions of this Treaty, through any other state or states, or in any other manner.

ARTICLE XIII

Each Party undertakes not to assume any international obligations which would conflict with this Treaty.

ARTICLE XIV

The Parties undertake to begin, promptly after the entry into force of this Treaty, active negotiations with the objective of achieving, as soon as possible, agreement on further measures for the limitation and reduction of strategic arms. It is also the objective of the Parties to conclude well in advance of 1985 an agreement limiting strategic offensive arms to replace this Treaty upon its expiration.

ARTICLE XV

1. For the purpose of providing assurance of compliance with the provisions of this Treaty, each Party shall use national technical means of verification at its disposal in a manner consistent with generally recognized principles of international law.

2. Each Party undertakes not to interfere with the national technical means of verification of the other Party operating in accordance with paragraph 1 of this Article.

3. Each Party undertakes not to use deliberate concealment measures which impede verification by national technical means of compliance with the provisions of this Treaty. This obligation shall not require changes in current construction, assembly, conversion, or overhaul practices.

ARTICLE XVI

1. Each Party undertakes, before conducting each planned ICBM launch, to notify the other Party well in advance on a case-by-case basis that such a launch will occur, except for single ICBM launches from test ranges or from ICBM launcher deployment areas, which are not planned to extend beyond its national territory.

2. The Parties shall agree in the Standing Consultative Commission upon procedures to implement the provisions of this Article.

ARTICLE XVII

1. To promote the objectives and implementation of the provisions of this Treaty, the Parties shall use the Standing Consultative Commission established by the Memorandum of Understanding Between the Government of the United States of America and the Government of the Union of Soviet Socialist Republics Regarding the Establishment of a Standing Consultative Commission of December 21, 1972.

2. Within the framework of the Standing Consultative Commission, with respect to this Treaty, the Parties will:

(a) consider questions concerning compliance with the obligations assumed and related situations which may be considered ambiguous;

(b) provide on a voluntary basis such information as either Party considers necessary to assure confidence in compliance with the obligations assumed;

(c) consider questions involving unintended interference with national technical means of verification, and questions involving unintended impeding of verification by national technical means of compliance with the provisions of this Treaty;

(d) consider possible changes in the strategic situation which have a bearing on the provisions of this Treaty;

(e) agree upon procedures for replacement, conversion, and dismantling or destruction, of strategic offensive arms in cases provided for in the provisions of this Treaty and upon procedures for removal of such arms from the aggregate numbers when they otherwise cease to be subject to the limitations provided for in this Treaty, and at regular sessions of the Standing Consultative Commission, notify each other in accordance with the aforementioned procedures, at least twice annually, of actions completed and those in process;

(f) consider, as appropriate, possible proposals for further increasing the viability of this Treaty, including proposals for amendments in accordance with the provisions of this Treaty;

(g) consider, as appropriate, proposals for further measures limiting strategic offensive arms.

3. In the Standing Consultative Commission the Parties shall maintain by category the agreed data base on the numbers of strategic offensive arms established by the Memorandum of Understanding Between the United States of America and the Union of Soviet Socialist Republics Regarding the Establishment of a Data Base on the Numbers of Strategic Offensive Arms of June 18, 1979.

ARTICLE XVIII

Each Party may propose amendments to this Treaty. Agreed amendments shall enter into force in accordance with the procedures governing the entry into force of this Treaty.

ARTICLE XIX

1. This Treaty shall be subject to ratification in accordance with the constitutional procedures of each Party. This Treaty shall enter into force on the day of the exchange of instruments of ratification and shall remain in force through December 31, 1985, unless replaced earlier by an agreement further limiting strategic offensive arms.

2. This Treaty shall be registered pursuant to Article 102 of the Charter of the United Nations.

3. Each Party shall, in exercising its national sovereignty, have the right to withdraw from this Treaty if it decides that extraordinary events related to the subject matter of this Treaty have jeopardized its supreme interests. It shall give notice of its decision to the other Party six months prior to withdrawal from the Treaty. Such notice shall include a statement of the extraordinary events the notifying Party regards as having jeopardized its supreme interests.

Done at Vienna on June 18, 1979, in two copies, each in the English and Russian languages, both texts being equally authentic.

For the United States of America
JIMMY CARTER
President of the United States of America

For the Union of Soviet Socialist Republics
L. BREZHNEV
General Secretary of the CPSU, Chairman of the Presidium of the Supreme Soviet of the USSR

PROTOCOL TO THE TREATY BETWEEN THE UNITED STATES OF AMERICA AND THE UNION OF SOVIET SOCIALIST REPUBLICS ON THE LIMITATION OF STRATEGIC OFFENSIVE ARMS

The United States of America and the Union of Soviet Socialist Republics, hereinafter referred to as the Parties,

Having agreed on limitations on strategic offensive arms in the Treaty,

Have agreed on additional limitations for the period during which this Protocol remains in force, as follows:

ARTICLE I

Each Party undertakes not to deploy mobile ICBM launchers or to flight-test ICBMs from such launchers.

ARTICLE II

1. Each Party undertakes not to deploy cruise missiles capable of a range in excess of 600 kilometers on sea-based launchers or on land-based launchers.

2. Each Party undertakes not to flight-test cruise missiles capable of a range in excess of 600 kilometers which are equipped with multiple independently targetable warheads from sea-based launchers or on land-based launchers.

3. For the purposes of this Protocol, cruise missiles are unmanned, self-propelled, guided, weapon-delivery vehicles which sustain flight through the use of aerodynamic lift over most of their flight path and which are flight-tested from or deployed on sea-based or land-based launchers, that is, sea-launched cruise missiles and ground-launched cruise missiles, respectively.

ARTICLE III

Each Party undertakes not to flight-test or deploy ASBMs.

ARTICLE IV

This Protocol shall be considered an integral part of the Treaty. It shall enter into force on the day of the entry into force of the Treaty and shall remain in force through December 31, 1981, unless replaced earlier by an agreement on further measures limiting strategic offensive arms.

Done at Vienna on June 18, 1979, in two copies, each in the English and Russian languages, both texts being equally authentic.

For the United States of America

JIMMY CARTER
President of the United States of America

For the Union of Soviet Socialist Republics

L. BREZHNEV
General Secretary of the CPSU, Chairman of the Presidium of the Supreme Soviet of the USSR

AGREED STATEMENTS AND COMMON UNDERSTANDINGS REGARDING THE TREATY BETWEEN THE UNITED STATES OF AMERICA AND THE UNION OF SOVIET SOCIALIST REPUBLICS ON THE LIMITATION OF STRATEGIC OFFENSIVE ARMS

In connection with the Treaty Between the United States of America and the Union of Soviet Socialist Republics on the Limitation of Strategic Offensive Arms, the Parties have agreed on the following Agreed Statements and Common Understandings undertaken on behalf of the Government of the United States of America and the Government of the Union of Soviet Socialist Republics:

To paragraph 1 of Article II of the Treaty

First Agreed Statement. The term "intercontinental ballistic missile launchers," as defined in paragraph 1 of Article II of the Treaty, includes all launchers which have been developed and tested for launching ICBMs. If a launcher has been developed and tested for launching an ICBM, all launchers of that type shall be considered to have been developed and tested for launching ICBMs.

First Common Understanding. If a launcher contains or launches an ICBM, that launcher shall be considered to have been developed and tested for launching ICBMs.

Second Common Understanding. If a launcher has been developed and tested for launching an ICBM, all launchers of that type, except for ICBM test and training launchers, shall be included in the aggregate numbers of strategic offensive arms provided for in Article III of the Treaty, pursuant to the provisions of Article VI of the Treaty.

Third Common Understanding. The one hundred and seventy-seven former Atlas and Titan I ICBM launchers of the United States of America, which are no longer operational and are partially dismantled, shall not be considered as subject to the limitations provided for in the Treaty.

Second Agreed Statement. After the date on which the Protocol ceases to be in force, mobile ICBM launchers shall be subject to the relevant limitations provided for in the Treaty which are applicable to ICBM launchers, unless the Parties agree that mobile ICBM launchers shall not be deployed after that date.

To Paragraph 2 of Article II of the Treaty

Agreed Statement. Modern submarine-launched ballistic missiles are: for the United States of America, missiles installed in all nuclear-powered submarines; for the Union of Soviet Socialist Republics, missiles of the type installed in nuclear-powered submarines made operational since 1965; and for both Parties,

submarine-launched ballistic missiles first flight-tested since 1965 and installed in any submarine, regardless of its type.

To Paragraph 3 of Article II of the Treaty

First Agreed Statement. The term "bombers," as used in paragraph 3 of Article II and other provisions of the Treaty, means airplanes of types initially constructed to be equipped for bombs or missiles.

Second Agreed Statement. The Parties shall notify each other on a case-by-case basis in the Standing Consultative Commission of inclusion of types of bombers as heavy bombers pursuant to the provisions of paragraph 3 of Article II of the Treaty; in this connection the Parties shall hold consultations, as appropriate, consistent with the provisions of paragraph 2 of Article XVII of the Treaty.

Third Agreed Statement. The criteria the Parties shall use to make case-by-case determinations of which types of bombers in the future can carry out the mission of a heavy bomber in a manner similar or superior to that of current heavy bombers, as referred to in subparagraph 3(b) of Article II of the Treaty, shall be agreed upon in the Standing Consultative Commission.

Fourth Agreed Statement. Having agreed that every bomber of a type included in paragraph 3 of Article II of the Treaty is to be considered a heavy bomber, the Parties further agree that:

(a) airplanes which otherwise would be bombers of a heavy bomber type shall not be considered to be bombers of a heavy bomber type if they have functionally related observable differences which indicate that they cannot perform the mission of a heavy bomber;

(b) airplanes which otherwise would be bombers of a type equipped for cruise missiles capable of a range in excess of 600 kilometers shall not be considered to be bombers of a type equipped for cruise missiles capable of a range in excess of 600 kilometers if they have functionally related observable differences which indicate that they cannot perform the mission of a bomber equipped for cruise missiles capable of a range in excess of 600 kilometers, except that heavy bombers of current types, as designated in subparagraph 3(a) of Article II of the Treaty, which otherwise would be of a type equipped for cruise missiles capable of a range in excess of 600 kilometers shall not be considered to be heavy bombers of a type equipped for cruise missiles capable of a range in excess of 600 kilometers if they are distinguishable on the basis of externally observable differences from heavy bombers of a type equipped for cruise missiles capable of a range in excess of 600 kilometers; and

(c) airplanes which otherwise would be bombers of a type equipped for ASBMs shall not be considered to be bombers of a type equipped for ASBMs if they have functionally related observable differences which indicate that they cannot perform the mission of a bomber equipped for ASBMs, except that heavy bombers of current types, as designated in subparagraph 3 (a) of Article II of the Treaty, which otherwise would be of a type equipped for ASBMs shall not be considered to be heavy bombers of a type equipped for ASBMs if they are distinguishable on the basis of externally observable differences from heavy bombers of a type equipped for ASBMs.

First Common Understanding. Functionally related observable differences are differences in the observable features of airplanes which indicate whether or not these airplanes can perform the mission of a heavy bomber, or whether or not they can perform the mission of a bomber equipped for cruise missiles capable of a range in excess of 600 kilometers or whether or not they can perform the mission of a bomber equipped for ASBMs. Functionally related observable differences shall be verifiable by national technical means. To this end, the Parties may take, as appropriate, cooperative measures contributing to the effectiveness of verification by national technical means.

Fifth Agreed Statement. Tupolev–142 airplanes in their current configuration, that is, in the configuration for anti-submarine warfare, are considered to be airplanes of a type different from types of heavy bombers referred to in subparagraph 3(a) of Article II of the Treaty and not subject to the Fourth Agreed Statement to paragraph 3 of Article II of the Treaty. This Agreed Statement does not preclude improvement of Tupolev-142 airplanes as an anti-submarine system, and does not prejudice or set a precedent for designation in the future of types of airplanes as heavy bombers pursuant to subparagraph 3(b) of Article II of the Treaty or for application of the Fourth Agreed Statement to paragraph 3 of Article II of the Treaty to such airplanes.

Second Common Understanding. Not later than six months after entry into force of the Treaty the Union of Soviet Socialist Republics will give its thirty-one Myasishchev airplanes used as tankers in

1061

existence as of the date of signature of the Treaty functionally related observable differences which indicate that they cannot perform the mission of a heavy bomber.

Third Common Understanding. The designations by the United States of America and by the Union of Soviet Socialist Republics for heavy bombers referred to in subparagraph 3(a) of Article II of the Treaty correspond in the following manner:

Heavy bombers of the types designated by the United States of America as the B-52 and the B-1 are known to the Union of Soviet Socialist Republics by the same designations;

Heavy bombers of the type designated by the Union of Soviet Socialist Republics as the Tupolev-95 are known to the United States of America as heavy bombers of the Bear type; and

Heavy bombers of the type designated by the Union of Soviet Socialist Republics as the Myasishchev are known to the United States of America as heavy bombers of the Bison type.

To Paragraph 5 of Article II of the Treaty

First Agreed Statement. If a launcher has been developed and tested for launching an ICBM or an SLBM equipped with MIRVs, all launchers of that type shall be considered to have been developed and tested for launching ICBMs or SLBMs equipped with MIRVs.

First Common Understanding. If a launcher contains or launches an ICBM or an SLBM equipped with MIRVs, that launcher shall be considered to have been developed and tested for launching ICBMs or SLBMs equipped with MIRVs.

Second Common Understanding. If a launcher has been developed and tested for launching an ICBM or an SLBM equipped with MIRVs, all launchers of that type, except for ICBM and SLBM test and training launchers, shall be included in the corresponding aggregate numbers provided for in Article V of the Treaty, pursuant to the provisions of Article VI of the Treaty.

Second Agreed Statement. ICBMs and SLBMs equipped with MIRVs are ICBMs and SLBMs of the types which have been flight-tested with two or more independently targetable reentry vehicles, regardless of whether or not they have also been flight-tested with a single reentry vehicle or with multiple reentry vehicles which are not independently targetable. As of the date of signature of the Treaty, such ICBMs and SLBMs are: for the United States of America, Minuteman III ICBMs, Poseidon C-3 SLBMs, and Trident C-4 SLBMs; and for the Union of Soviet Socialist Republics, RS-16, RS-18, RS-20 ICBMs and RSM-50 SLBMs.

Each Party will notify the other Party in the Standing Consultative Commission on a case-by-case basis of the designation of the one new type of light ICBM, if equipped with MIRVs, permitted pursuant to paragraph 9 of Article IV of the Treaty when first flight-tested; of designations of additional types of SLBMs equipped with MIRVs when first installed on a submarine; and of designations of types of ASBMs equipped with MIRVs when first flight-tested.

Third Common Understanding. The designations by the United States of America and by the Union of Soviet Socialist Republics for ICBMs and SLBMs equipped with MIRVs correspond in the following manner:

Missiles of the type designated by the United States of America as the Minuteman III and known to the Union of Soviet Socialist Republics by the same designation, a light ICBM that has been flight-tested with multiple independently targetable reentry vehicles;

Missiles of the type designated by the United States of America as the Poseidon C–3 and known to the Union of Soviet Socialist Republics by the same designation, an SLBM that was first flight-tested in 1968 and that has been flight-tested with multiple independently targetable reentry vehicles;

Missiles of the type designated by the United States of America as the Trident C–4 and known to the Union of Soviet Socialist Republics by the same designation, an SLBM that was first flight-tested in 1977 and that has been flight-tested with multiple independently targetable reentry vehicles;

Missiles of the type designated by the Union of Soviet Socialist Republics as the RS–16 and known to the United States of America as the SS–17, a light ICBM that has been flight-tested with a single reentry vehicle and with multiple independently targetable reentry vehicles;

Missiles of the type designated by the Union of Soviet Socialist Republics as the RS–18 and known to the United States of America as the SS–19, the heaviest in terms of launch-weight and throw-weight of light ICBMs, which has been flight-tested with a single reentry vehicle and with multiple independently targetable reentry vehicles;

Missiles of the type designated by the Union of Soviet Socialist Republics as the RS–20 and known to the United States of America as the SS–18, the heaviest in terms of launch-weight and throw-weight of heavy ICBMs, which has been flight-tested with a single reentry vehicle and with multiple independently targetable reentry vehicles;

Missiles of the type designated by the Union of Soviet Socialist Republics as the RSM–50 and known to the United States of America as the SS–N–18, an SLBM that has been flight-tested with a single reentry vehicle and with multiple independently targetable reentry vehicles.

Third Agreed Statement. Reentry vehicles are independently targetable:

(a) if, after separation from the booster, maneuvering and targeting of the reentry vehicles to separate aim points along trajectories which are unrelated to each other are accomplished by means of devices which are installed in a self-contained dispensing mechanism or on the reentry vehicles, and which are based on the use of electronic or other computers in combination with devices using jet engines, including rocket engines, or aerodynamic systems;

(b) if maneuvering and targeting of the reentry vehicles to separate aim points along trajectories which are unrelated to each other are accomplished by means of other devices which may be developed in the future.

Fourth Common Understanding. For the purposes of this Treaty, all ICBM launchers in the Derazhnya and Pervomaysk areas in the Union of Soviet Socialist Republics are included in the aggregate numbers provided for in Article V of the Treaty.

Fifth Common Understanding. If ICBM or SLBM launchers are converted, constructed or undergo significant changes to their principal observable structural design features after entry into force of the Treaty, any such launchers which are launchers of missiles equipped with MIRVs shall be distinguishable from launchers of missiles not equipped with MIRVs, and any such launchers which are launchers of missiles not equipped with MIRVs shall be distinguishable from launchers of missiles equipped with MIRVs, on the basis of externally observable design features of the launchers. Submarines with launchers of SLBMs equipped with MIRVs shall be distinguishable from submarines with launchers of SLBMs not equipped with MIRVs on the basis of externally observable design features of the submarines.

This Common Understanding does not require changes to launcher conversion or construction programs, or to programs including significant changes to the principal observable structural design features of launchers, underway as of the date of signature of the Treaty.

To Paragraph 6 of Article II of the Treaty

First Agreed Statement. ASBMs of the types which have been flight-tested with MIRVs are all ASBMs of the types which have been flight-tested with two or more independently targetable reentry vehicles, regardless of whether or not they have also been flight-tested with a single reentry vehicle or with multiple reentry vehicles which are not independently targetable.

Second Agreed Statement. Reentry vehicles are independently targetable:

(a) if, after separation from the booster, maneuvering and targeting of the reentry vehicles to separate aim points along trajectories which are unrelated to each other

are accomplished by means of devices which are installed in a self-contained dispensing mechanism or on the reentry vehicles, and which are based on the use of electronic or other computers in combination with devices using jet engines, including rocket engines, or aerodynamic systems;

(b) if maneuvering and targeting of the reentry vehicles to separate aim points along trajectories which are unrelated to each other are accomplished by means of other devices which may be developed in the future.

To Paragraph 7 of Article II of the Treaty

First Agreed Statement. The launch-weight of an ICBM is the weight of the fully loaded missile itself at the time of launch.

Second Agreed Statement. The throw-weight of an ICBM is the sum of the weight of:

(a) its reentry vehicle or reentry vehicles;

(b) any self-contained dispensing mechanisms or other appropriate devices for targeting one reentry vehicle, or for releasing or for dispensing and targeting two or more reentry vehicles; and

(c) its penetration aids, including devices for their release.

Common Understanding. The term "other appropriate devices," as used in the definition of the throw-weight of an ICBM in the Second Agreed Statement to paragraph 7 of Article II of the Treaty, means any devices for dispensing and targeting two or more reentry vehicles; and any devices for releasing two or more reentry vehicles or for targeting one reentry vehicle, which cannot provide their reentry vehicles or reentry vehicle with additional velocity of more than 1,000 meters per second.

To Paragraph 8 of Article II of the Treaty

First Agreed Statement. If a cruise missile is capable of a range in excess of 600 kilometers, all cruise missiles of that type shall be considered to be cruise missiles capable of a range in excess of 600 kilometers.

First Common Understanding. If a cruise missile has been flight-tested to a range in excess of 600 kilometers, it shall be considered to be a cruise missile capable of a range in excess of 600 kilometers.

Second Common Understanding. Cruise missiles not capable of a range in excess of 600 kilometers shall not be considered to be of a type capable of a range in excess of 600 kilometers if they are distinguishable on the basis of externally observable design features from cruise missiles of types capable of a range in excess of 600 kilometers.

Second Agreed Statement. The range of which a cruise missile is capable is the maximum distance which can be covered by the missile in its standard design mode flying until fuel exhaustion, determined by projecting its flight path onto the Earth's sphere from the point of launch to the point of impact.

Third Agreed Statement. If an unmanned, self-propelled, guided vehicle which sustains flight through the use of aerodynamic lift over most of its flight path has been flight-tested or deployed for weapon delivery, all vehicles of that type shall be considered to be weapon-delivery vehicles.

Third Common Understanding. Unmanned, self-propelled, guided vehicles which sustain flight through the use of aerodynamic lift over most of their flight path and are not weapon-delivery vehicles, that is, unarmed, pilotless, guided vehicles, shall not be considered to be cruise missiles if such vehicles are distinguishable from cruise missiles on the basis of externally observable design features.

Fourth Common Understanding. Neither Party shall convert unarmed, pilotless, guided vehicles into cruise missiles capable of a range in excess of 600 kilometers, nor shall either Party convert cruise missiles capable of a range in excess of 600 kilometers into unarmed, pilotless, guided vehicles.

Fifth Common Understanding. Neither Party has plans during the term of the Treaty to flight-test from or deploy on aircraft unarmed, pilotless, guided vehicles which are capable of a range in excess of 600 kilometers. In the future, should a Party have such plans, that Party will provide notification thereof to the other Party well in advance of such flight-testing or deployment. This Common Understanding does not apply to target drones.

To Paragraph 4 of Article IV of the Treaty

Agreed Statement. The word "original" in paragraph 4 of Article IV of the Treaty refers to the internal dimensions of an ICBM silo launcher, including its internal volume, as of May 26, 1972, or as of the date on which such launcher becomes operational, whichever is later.

Common Understanding. The obligations provided for in paragraph 4 of Article IV of the Treaty and in the Agreed Statement thereto mean that the original diameter or the original depth of an ICBM silo launcher may not be increased by an amount greater than that which would result in an increase in the original internal volume of the ICBM silo launcher by thirty-two percent solely through an increase in one of these dimensions.

To Paragraph 5 of Article IV of the Treaty

Agreed Statement. The term "normal deployment requirements," as used in paragraph 5 of Article IV of the Treaty, means the deployment of one missile at each ICBM launcher.

To Paragraph 6 of Article IV of the Treaty

Common Understanding. A normal construction schedule, in paragraph 6 of Article IV of the Treaty, is understood to be one consistent with the past or present construction practices of each Party.

To Paragraph 7 of Article IV of the Treaty

First Agreed Statement. The launch-weight of an ICBM is the weight of the fully loaded missile itself at the time of launch.

Second Agreed Statement. The throw-weight of an ICBM is the sum of the weight of:

(a) its reentry vehicle or reentry vehicles;

(b) any self-contained dispensing mechanisms or other appropriate devices for targeting one reentry vehicle, or for releasing or for dispensing and targeting two or more reentry vehicles; and

(c) its penetration aids, including devices for their release.

Common Understanding. The term

"other appropriate devices," as used in the definition of the throw-weight of an ICBM in the Second Agreed Statement to paragraph 7 of Article IV of the Treaty, means any devices for dispensing and targeting two or more reentry vehicles; and any devices for releasing two or more reentry vehicles or for targeting one reentry vehicle, which cannot provide their reentry vehicles or reentry vehicle with additional velocity of more than 1,000 meters per second.

To Paragraph 8 of Article IV of the Treaty

Common Understanding. During the term of the Treaty, the Union of Soviet Socialist Republics will not produce, test, or deploy ICBMs of the type designated by the Union of Soviet Socialist Republics as the RS–14 and known to the United States of America as the SS–16, a light ICBM first flight-tested after 1970 and flight-tested only with a single reentry vehicle; this Common Understanding also means that the Union of Soviet Socialist Republics will not produce the third stage of that missile, the reentry vehicle of that missile, or the appropriate device for targeting the reentry vehicle of that missile.

To Paragraph 9 of Article IV of the Treaty

First Agreed Statement. The term "new types of ICBMs," as used in paragraph 9 of Article IV of the Treaty, refers to any ICBM which is different from those ICBMs flight-tested as of May 1, 1979 in any one or more of the following respects:

(a) the number of stages, the length, the largest diameter, the launch-weight, or the throw-weight, of the missile;

(b) the type of propellant (that is, liquid or solid) of any of its stages.

First Common Understanding. As used in the First Agreed Statement to paragraph 9 of Article IV of the Treaty, the term "different," referring to the length, the diameter, the launch-weight, and the throw-weight, of the missile, means a difference in excess of five percent.

Second Agreed Statement. Every ICBM of the one new type of light ICBM permitted to each Party pursuant to paragraph 9 of Article IV of the Treaty shall have the same number of stages and the same type of propellant (that is, liquid or solid) of each stage as the first ICBM of the one new type of light ICBM launched by that Party. In addition, after the twenty-fifth launch of an ICBM of that type, or after the last launch before deployment begins of ICBMs of that type, whichever occurs earlier, ICBMs of the one new type of light ICBM permitted to that Party shall not be different in any one or more of the following respects: the length, the largest diameter, the launch-weight, or the throw-weight, of the missile.

A Party which launches ICBMs of the one new type of light ICBM permitted pursuant to paragraph 9 of Article IV of the Treaty shall promptly notify the other Party of the date of the first launch and of the date of either the twenty-fifth or the last launch before deployment begins of ICBMs of that type, whichever occurs earlier.

Second Common Understanding. As used in the Second Agreed Statement to paragraph 9 of Article IV of the Treaty, the term "different," referring to the length, the diameter, the launch-weight, and the throw-weight, of the missile, means a

difference in excess of five percent from the value established for each of the above parameters as of the twenty-fifth launch or as of the last launch before deployment begins, whichever occurs earlier. The values demonstrated in each of the above parameters during the last twelve of the twenty-five launches or during the last twelve launches before deployment begins, whichever twelve launches occur earlier, shall not vary by more than ten percent from any other of the corresponding values demonstrated during those twelve launches.

Third Common Understanding. The limitations with respect to launch-weight and throw-weight, provided for in the First Agreed Statement and the First Common Understanding to paragraph 9 of Article IV of the Treaty, do not preclude the flight-testing or the deployment of ICBMs with fewer reentry vehicles, or fewer penetration aids, or both, than the maximum number of reentry vehicles and the maximum number of penetration aids with which ICBMs of that type have been flight-tested as of May 1, 1979, even if this results in a decrease in launch-weight or in throw-weight in excess of five percent.

In addition to the aforementioned cases, those limitations do not preclude a decrease in launch-weight or in throw-weight in excess of five percent, in the case of the flight-testing or the deployment of ICBMs with a lesser quantity of propellant, including the propellant of a self-contained dispensing mechanism or other appropriate device, than the maximum quantity of propellant, including the propellant of a self-contained dispensing mechanism or other appropriate device, with which ICBMs of that type have been flight-tested as of May 1, 1979, provided that such an ICBM is at the same time flight-tested or deployed with fewer reentry vehicles, or fewer penetration aids, or both, than the maximum number of reentry vehicles and the maximum number of penetration aids with which ICBMs of that type have been flight-tested as of May 1, 1979, and the decrease in launch-weight and throw-weight in such cases results only from the reduction in the number of reentry vehicles, or penetration aids, or both, and the reduction in the quantity of propellant.

Fourth Common Understanding. The limitations with respect to launch-weight and throw-weight, provided for in the Second Agreed Statement and the Second Common Understanding to paragraph 9 of Article IV of the Treaty, do not preclude the flight-testing or the deployment of ICBMs of the one new type of light ICBM permitted to each Party pursuant to paragraph 9 of Article IV of the Treaty with fewer reentry vehicles, or fewer penetration aids, or both, than the maximum number of reentry vehicles and the maximum number of penetration aids with which ICBMs of that type have been flight-tested, even if this results in a decrease in launch-weight or in throw-weight in excess of five percent.

In addition to the aforementioned cases, those limitations do not preclude a decrease in launch-weight or in throw-weight in excess of five percent, in the case of the flight-testing or the deployment of ICBMs of that type with a lesser quantity of propellant, including the propellant of a self-contained dispensing mechanism or other appropriate device, than the maximum quantity of propellant, including the propellant of a self-contained dispensing mechanism or other appropriate device, with which ICBMs of that type have been flight-tested, provided that such an ICBM is at the same time flight-tested or deployed with fewer

reentry vehicles, or fewer penetration aids, or both, than the maximum number of reentry vehicles and the maximum number of penetration aids with which ICBMs of that type have been flight-tested, and the decrease in launch-weight and throw-weight in such cases results only from the reduction in the number of reentry vehicles, or penetration aids, or both, and the reduction in the quantity of propellant.

To Paragraph 10 of Article IV of the Treaty

First Agreed Statement. The following types of ICBMs and SLBMs equipped with MIRVs have been flight-tested with the maximum number of reentry vehicles set forth below:

For the United States of America

ICBMs of the Minuteman III type—seven reentry vehicles;

SLBMs of the Poseidon C–3 type—fourteen reentry vehicles;

SLBMs of the Trident C–4 type—seven reentry vehicles;

For the Union of Soviet Socialist Republics

ICBMs of the RS–16 type—four reentry vehicles;

ICBMs of the RS–18 type—six reentry vehicles;

ICBMs of the RS–20 type—ten reentry vehicles;

SLBMs of the RSM–50 type—seven reentry vehicles.

Common Understanding. Minuteman III ICBMs of the United States of America have been deployed with no more than three reentry vehicles. During the term of the Treaty, the United States of America has no plans to and will not flight-test or deploy missiles of this type with more than three reentry vehicles.

Second Agreed Statement. During the flight-testing of any ICBM, SLBM, or ASBM after May 1, 1979 the number of procedures for releasing or for dispensing may not exceed the maximum number of reentry vehicles established for missiles of corresponding types as provided for in paragraphs 10, 11, 12, and 13 of Article IV of the Treaty. In this Agreed Statement "procedures for releasing or for dispensing" are understood to mean maneuvers of a missile associated with targeting and releasing or dispensing its reentry vehicles to aim points, whether or not a reentry vehicle is actually released or dispensed. Procedures for releasing anti-missile defense penetration aids will not be considered to be procedures for releasing or for dispensing a reentry vehicle so long as the procedures for releasing anti-missile defense penetration aids differ from those for releasing or for dispensing reentry vehicles.

Third Agreed Statement. Each Party undertakes:

(a) not to flight-test or deploy ICBMs equipped with multiple reentry vehicles, of a type flight-tested as of May 1, 1979, with reentry vehicles the weight of any of which is less than the weight of the lightest of those reentry vehicles with which an ICBM of that type has been flight-tested as of that date;

(b) not to flight-test or deploy ICBMs equipped with a single reentry vehicle and without an appropriate device for targeting a reentry vehicle, of a type flight-tested as of May 1, 1979, with a reentry vehicle the weight of which is less than the weight of the lightest reentry vehicle on an ICBM of a type equipped with MIRVs and flight-tested by that Party as of May 1, 1979; and

(c) not to flight-test or deploy ICBMs equipped with a single reentry vehicle and with an appropriate device for targeting a reentry vehicle, of a type flight-tested as of May 1, 1979, with a reentry vehicle the weight of which is less than fifty percent of the throw-weight of that ICBM.

To Paragraph 11 of Article IV of the Treaty

First Agreed Statement. Each Party undertakes not to flight-test or deploy the one new type of light ICBM permitted to each Party pursuant to paragraph 9 of Article IV of the Treaty with a number of reentry vehicles greater than the maximum number of reentry vehicles with which an ICBM of that type has been flight-tested as of the twenty-fifth launch or the last launch before deployment begins of ICBMs of that type, whichever occurs earlier.

Second Agreed Statement. During the flight-testing of any ICBM, SLBM, or ASBM after May 1, 1979 the number of procedures for releasing or for dispensing may not exceed the maximum number of reentry vehicles established for missiles of corresponding types as provided for in paragraphs 10, 11, 12, and 13 of Article IV of the Treaty. In this Agreed Statement "procedures for releasing or for dispensing" are understood to mean maneuvers of a missile associated with targeting and releasing or dispensing its reentry vehicles to aim points, whether or not a reentry vehicle is actually released or dispensed. Procedures for releasing anti-missile defense penetration aids will not be considered to be procedures for releasing or for dispensing a reentry vehicle so long as the procedures for releasing anti-missile defense penetration aids differ from those for releasing or for dispensing reentry vehicles.

To Paragraph 12 of Article IV of the Treaty

First Agreed Statement. The following types of ICBMs and SLBMs equipped with MIRVs have been flight-tested with the maximum number of reentry vehicles set forth below:

For the United States of America

ICBMs of the Minuteman III type—seven reentry vehicles;

SLBMs of the Poseidon C–3 type—fourteen reentry vehicles;

SLBMs of the Trident C–4 type—seven reentry vehicles;

For the Union of Soviet Socialist Republics

ICBMs of the RS–16 type—four reentry vehicles;

ICBMs of the RS–18 type—six reentry vehicles;

ICBMs of the RS–20 type—ten reentry vehicles;

SLBMs of the RSM–50 type—seven reentry vehicles.

Second Agreed Statement. During the flight-testing of any ICBM, SLBM, or ASBM after May 1, 1979 the number of procedures for releasing or for dispensing may not exceed the maximum number of reentry vehicles established for missiles of corresponding types as provided for in paragraphs 10, 11, 12, and 13 of Article IV of the Treaty. In this Agreed Statement "procedures for releasing or for dispensing" are understood to mean maneuvers of a missile associated with targeting and releasing or dispensing its reentry vehicles to aim points, whether or not a reentry vehicle is actually released or dispensed. Procedures for releasing anti-missile defense penetration aids differ be considered to be procedures for releasing or for dispensing a reentry vehicle so long as the procedures for releasing anti-missile defense penetration aids differ from those for releasing or for dispensing reentry vehicles.

To Paragraph 13 of Article IV of the Treaty

Agreed Statement. During the flight-testing of any ICBM, SLBM, or ASBM after May 1, 1979 the number of procedures for releasing or for dispensing may not exceed the maximum number of reentry vehicles established for missiles of corresponding types as provided for in paragraphs 10, 11, 12, and 13 of Article IV of the Treaty. In this Agreed Statement "procedures for releasing or for dispensing" are understood to mean maneuvers of a missile associated with targeting and releasing or dispensing its reentry vehicles to aim points, whether or not a reentry vehicle is actually released or dispensed. Procedures for releasing anti-missile defense penetration aids will not be considered to be procedures for releasing or for dispensing a reentry vehicle so long as the procedures for releasing anti-missile defense penetration aids differ from those for releasing or for dispensing reentry vehicles.

To Paragraph 14 of Article IV of the Treaty

First Agreed Statement. For the purposes of the limitation provided for in paragraph 14 of Article IV of the Treaty, there shall be considered to be deployed on each heavy bomber of a type equipped for cruise missiles capable of a range in excess of 600 kilometers the maximum number of such missiles for which any bomber of that type is equipped for one operational mission.

Second Agreed Statement. During the term of the Treaty no bomber of the B–52 or B–1 types of the United States of America and no bomber of the Tupolev–95 or Myasishchev types of the Union of Soviet Socialist Republics will be equipped for more than twenty cruise missiles capable of a range in excess of 600 kilometers.

To Paragraph 4 of Article V of the Treaty

Agreed Statement. If a bomber is equipped for ASBMs equipped with MIRVs, all bombers of that type shall be considered to be equipped for ASBMs equipped with MIRVs.

To Paragraph 3 of Article VI of the Treaty

Agreed Statement. The procedures referred to in paragraph 7 of Article VI of the Treaty shall include procedures determining the manner in which mobile ICBM launchers of a type not subject to the limitation provided for in Article V of the Treaty, which undergo conversion into launchers of a type subject to that limitation, shall become subject to that limitation, unless the Parties agree that mobile ICBM launchers shall not be deployed after the date on which the Protocol ceases to be in force.

To Paragraph 6 of Article VI of the Treaty

Agreed Statement. The procedures for removal of strategic offensive arms from the aggregate numbers provided for in the Treaty, which are referred to in paragraph 6 of Article VI of the Treaty, and which are to be agreed upon in the Standing Consultative Commission, shall include:

(a) procedures for removal from the aggregate numbers, provided for in Article V of the Treaty, of ICBM and SLBM launchers which are being converted from launchers of a type subject to the limitation provided for in Article V of the Treaty, into launchers of a type not subject to that limitation;

(b) procedures for removal from the aggregate numbers, provided for in Articles III and V of the Treaty, of bombers which are being converted from bombers of a type subject to the limitations provided for in Article III of the Treaty or in Articles III and V of the Treaty into airplanes or bombers of a type not so subject.

Common Understanding. The procedures referred to in subparagraph (b) of the Agreed Statement to paragraph 6 of Article VI of the Treaty for removal of bombers from the aggregate numbers provided for in Articles III and V of the Treaty shall be based upon the existence of functionally related observable differences which indicate whether or not they can perform the mission of a heavy bomber, or whether or not they can perform the mission of a bomber equipped for cruise missiles capable of a range in excess of 600 kilometers.

To Paragraph 1 of Article VII of the Treaty

Common Understanding. The term "testing," as used in Article VII of the Treaty, includes research and development.

To Paragraph 2 of Article VII of the Treaty

First Agreed Statement. The term "significant increase," as used in subparagraph 2(a) of Article VII of the Treaty, means an increase of fifteen percent or more. Any new ICBM test and training launchers which replace ICBM test and training launchers at test ranges will be located only at test ranges.

Second Agreed Statement. Current test ranges where ICBMs are tested are located: for the United States of America, near Santa Maria, California, and at Cape Canaveral, Florida; and for the Union of Soviet Socialist Republics, in the areas of Tyura-Tam and Plesetskaya. In the future, each Party shall provide notification in the Standing Consultative Commission of the location of any other test range used by that Party to test ICBMs.

First Common Understanding. At test ranges where ICBMs are tested, other arms, including those not limited by the Treaty, may also be tested.

Second Common Understanding. Of the eighteen launchers of fractional orbital missiles at the test range where ICBMs are tested in the area of Tyura-Tam, twelve launchers shall be dismantled or destroyed and six launchers may be converted to launchers for testing missiles undergoing modernization.

Dismantling or destruction of the twelve launchers shall begin upon entry into force of the Treaty and shall be completed within eight months, under procedures for dismantling or destruction of these launchers to be agreed upon in the Standing Consultative Commission. These twelve launchers shall not be replaced.

Conversion of the six launchers may be carried out after entry into force of the Treaty. After entry into force of the Treaty, fractional orbital missiles shall be removed and shall be destroyed pursuant to the provisions of subparagraph 1(c) of Article IX and of Article XI of the Treaty and shall not be replaced by other missiles, except in the case of conversion of these six launchers for testing missiles undergoing modernization. After removal of the fractional orbital missiles, and prior to such conversion, any activities associated with these launchers shall be limited to normal maintenance requirements for launchers in which missiles are not deployed. These six launchers shall be subject to the provisions of Article VII of the Treaty and, if converted, to the provisions of the Fifth Common Understanding to paragraph 5 of Article II of the Treaty.

To Paragraph 1 of Article VIII of the Treaty

Agreed Statement. For purposes of testing only, each Party has the right, through initial construction or, as an exception to the provisions of paragraph 1 of Article VIII of the Treaty, by conversion, to equip for cruise missiles capable of a range in excess of 600 kilometers or for ASBMs no more than sixteen airplanes, including airplanes which are prototypes of bombers equipped for such missiles. Each Party also has the right, as an exception to the provisions of paragraph 1 of Article VIII of the Treaty, to flight-test from such airplanes cruise missiles capable of a range in excess of 600 kilometers and, after the date on which the Protocol ceases to be in force, to flight-test ASBMs from such airplanes as well, unless the Parties agree that they will not flight-test ASBMs after that date.

The limitations provided for in Article III of the Treaty shall not apply to such airplanes.

The aforementioned airplanes may include only:

(a) airplanes other than bombers which, as an exception to the provisions of paragraph 1 of Article VIII of the Treaty, have been converted into airplanes equipped for cruise missiles capable of a range in excess of 600 kilometers or for ASBMs;

(b) airplanes considered to be heavy bombers pursuant to subparagraph 3(c) or 3(d) of Article II of the Treaty; and

(c) airplanes other than heavy bombers which, prior to March 7, 1979, were used for testing cruise missiles capable of a range in excess of 600 kilometers.

The airplanes referred to in subparagraphs (a) and (b) of this Agreed Statement shall be distinguishable on the basis of functionally related observable differences from airplanes which otherwise would be of the same type but cannot perform the mission of a bomber equipped for cruise missiles capable of a range in excess of 600 kilometers or for ASBMs.

The airplanes referred to in subparagraph (c) of this Agreed Statement shall not be used for testing cruise missiles capable of a range in excess of 600 kilometers after the expiration of a six-month period from the date of entry into force of the Treaty, unless by the expiration of that period they are distinguishable on the basis of functionally related observable differences from airplanes which otherwise would be of the same type but cannot perform the mission of a bomber equipped for cruise missiles capable of a range in excess of 600 kilometers.

First Common Understanding. The term "testing," as used in the Agreed Statement to paragraph 1 of Article VIII of the Treaty, includes research and development.

Second Common Understanding. The Parties shall notify each other in the Standing Consultative Commission of the number of airplanes, according to type, used for testing pursuant to the Agreed Statement to paragraph 1 of Article VIII of the Treaty. Such notification shall be provided at the first regular session of the Standing Consultative Commission held after an airplane has been used for such testing.

Third Common Understanding. None of the sixteen airplanes referred to in the Agreed Statement to paragraph 1 of Article VIII of the Treaty may be replaced, except in the event of the involuntary destruction of any such airplane or in the case of the dismantling or destruction of any such airplane. The procedures for such replacement and for removal of any such airplane from that number, in case of its conversion, shall be agreed upon in the Standing Consultative Commission.

To Paragraph 1 of Article IX of the Treaty

Common Understanding to subparagraph (a). The obligations provided for in subparagraph 1(a) of Article IX of the Treaty do not affect current practices for transporting ballistic missiles.

Agreed Statement to subparagraph (b). The obligations provided for in subparagraph 1(b) of Article IX of the Treaty shall apply to all areas of the ocean floor and the seabed, including the seabed zone referred to in Articles I and II of the 1971 Treaty on the Prohibition of the

Emplacement of Nuclear Weapons and Other Weapons of Mass Destruction on the Seabed and the Ocean Floor and in the Subsoil Thereof.

Common Understanding to subparagraph (c). The provisions of subparagraph 1(c) of Article IX of the Treaty do not require the dismantling or destruction of any existing launchers of either Party.

First Agreed Statement to subparagraphs (e) *and* (f). The launch-weight of an SLBM or of an ASBM is the weight of the fully loaded missile itself at the time of launch.

Second Agreed Statement to subparagraphs (e) *and* (f). The throw-weight of an SLBM or of an ASBM is the sum of the weight of:

(a) its reentry vehicle or reentry vehicles;

(b) any self-contained dispensing mechanisms or other appropriate devices for targeting one reentry vehicle, or for releasing or for dispensing and targeting two or more reentry vehicles; and

(c) its penetration aids, including devices for their release.

Common Understanding to subparagraphs (e) *and* (f). The term "other appropriate devices," as used in the definition of the throw-weight of an SLBM or of an ASBM in the Second Agreed Statement to subparagraphs 1(e) and 1(f) of Article IX of the Treaty, means any devices for dispensing and targeting two or more reentry vehicles; and any devices for releasing two or more reentry vehicles or for targeting one reentry vehicle, which cannot provide their reentry vehicles or reentry vehicle with additional velocity of more than 1,000 meters per second.

To Paragraph 2 of Article IX of the Treaty

Agreed Statement. Warheads of a cruise missile are independently targetable if maneuvering or targeting of the warheads to separate aim points along ballistic trajectories or any other flight paths, which are unrelated to each other, is accomplished during a flight of a cruise missile.

To Paragraph 3 of Article XV of the Treaty

First Agreed Statement. Deliberate concealment measures, as referred to in paragraph 3 of Article XV of the Treaty, are measures carried out deliberately to hinder or deliberately to impede verification by national technical means of compliance with the provisions of the Treaty.

Second Agreed Statement. The obligation not to use deliberate concealment measures, provided for in paragraph 3 of Article XV of the Treaty, does not preclude the testing of anti-missile defense penetration aids.

First Common Understanding. The provisions of paragraph 3 of Article XV of the Treaty and the First Agreed Statement thereto apply to all provisions of the Treaty, including provisions associated with testing. In this connection, the obligation not to use deliberate concealment measures includes the obligation not to use deliberate concealment measures associated with testing, including those measures aimed at concealing the association between ICBMs and launchers during testing.

Second Common Understanding. Each Party is free to use various methods of transmitting telemetric information during testing, including its encryption, except that, in accordance with the provisions of paragraph 3 of Article XV of the Treaty, neither Party shall engage in deliberate denial of telemetric information, such as through the use of telemetry encryption, whenever such denial impedes verification of compliance with the provisions of the Treaty.

Third Common Understanding. In addition to the obligations provided for in paragraph 3 of Article XV of the Treaty, no shelters which impede verification by national technical means of compliance with the provisions of the Treaty shall be used over ICBM silo launchers.

To Paragraph 1 of Article XVI of the Treaty

First Common Understanding. ICBM launches to which the obligations provided for in Article XVI of the Treaty apply, include, among others, those ICBM launches for which advance notification is required pursuant to the provisions of the Agreement on Measures to Reduce the Risk of Outbreak of Nuclear War Between the United States of America and the Union of Soviet Socialist Republics, signed September 30, 1971, and the Agreement Between the Government of the United States of America and the Government of the Union of Soviet Socialist Republics on the Prevention of Incidents On and Over the High Seas, signed May 25, 1972. Nothing in Article XVI of the Treaty is intended to inhibit advance notification, on a voluntary basis, of any ICBM launches not subject to its provisions, the advance notification of which would enhance confidence between the Parties.

Second Common Understanding. A multiple ICBM launch conducted by a Party, as distinct from single ICBM launches referred to in Article XVI of the Treaty, is a launch which would result in two or more of its ICBMs being in flight at the same time.

Third Common Understanding. The test ranges referred to in Article XVI of the Treaty are those covered by the Second Agreed Statement to paragraph 2 of Article VII of the Treaty.

To Paragraph 3 of Article XVII of the Treaty

Agreed Statement. In order to maintain the agreed data base on the numbers of strategic offensive arms subject to the limitations provided for in the Treaty in accordance with paragraph 3 of Article XVII of the Treaty, at each regular session of the Standing Consultative Commission the Parties will notify each other of and consider changes in those numbers in the following categories: launchers of ICBMs; fixed launchers of ICBMs; launchers of ICBMs equipped with MIRVs; launchers of SLBMs; launchers of SLBMs equipped with MIRVs; heavy bombers; heavy bombers equipped for cruise missiles capable of a range in excess of 600 kilometers; heavy bombers equipped only for ASBMs; ASBMs; and ASBMs equipped with MIRVs.

To Paragraph 2 of Article II of the Protocol

Agreed Statement. Warheads of a cruise missile are independently targetable if maneuvering or targeting of the warheads to separate aim points along ballistic trajectories or any other flight paths, which are unrelated to each other, is accomplished during a flight of a cruise missile.

To Paragraph 3 of Article II of the Protocol

First Agreed Statement. If a cruise missile is capable of a range in excess of 600 kilometers, all cruise missiles of that type shall be considered to be cruise missiles capable of a range in excess of 600 kilometers.

First Common Understanding. If a cruise missile has been flight-tested to a range in excess of 600 kilometers, it shall be considered to be a cruise missile capable of a range in excess of 600 kilometers.

Second Common Understanding. Cruise missiles not capable of a range in excess of 600 kilometers shall not be considered to be of a type capable of a range in excess of 600 kilometers if they are distinguishable on the basis of externally observable design features from cruise missiles of types capable of a range in excess of 600 kilometers.

Second Agreed Statement. The range of which a cruise missile is capable is the maximum distance which can be covered by the missile in its standard design mode flying until fuel exhaustion, determined by projecting its flight path onto the Earth's sphere from the point of launch to the point of impact.

Third Agreed Statement. If an unmanned, self-propelled, guided vehicle which sustains flight through the use of aerodynamic lift over most of its flight path has been flight-tested or deployed for weapon delivery, all vehicles of that type shall be considered to be weapon-delivery vehicles.

Third Common Understanding. Unmanned, self-propelled, guided vehicles which sustain flight through the use of aerodynamic lift over most of their flight path and are not weapon-delivery vehicles, that is, unarmed, pilotless, guided vehicles, shall not be considered to be cruise missiles if such vehicles are distinguishable from cruise missiles on the basis of externally observable design features.

Fourth Common Understanding. Neither Party shall convert unarmed, pilotless, guided vehicles into cruise missiles capable of a range in excess of 600 kilometers, nor shall either Party convert cruise mis-

siles capable of a range in excess of 600 kilometers into unarmed, pilotless, guided vehicles.

Fifth Common Understanding. Neither Party has plans during the term of the Protocol to flight-test from or deploy on sea-based or land-based launchers unarmed, pilotless, guided vehicles which are capable of a range in excess of 600 kilometers. In the future, should a Party have such plans, that Party will provide notification thereof to the other Party well in advance of such flight-testing or deployment. This Common Understanding does not apply to target drones.

Done at Vienna, on June 18, 1979, in two copies, each in the English and Russian languages, both texts being equally authentic.

For the United States of America

> JIMMY CARTER
> *President of the United States of America*

For the Union of Soviet Socialist Republics

> L. BREZHNEV
> *General Secretary of the CPSU, Chairman of the Presidium of the Supreme Soviet of the USSR*

MEMORANDUM OF UNDERSTANDING BETWEEN THE UNITED STATES OF AMERICA AND THE UNION OF SOVIET SOCIALIST REPUBLICS REGARDING THE ESTABLISHMENT OF A DATA BASE ON THE NUMBERS OF STRATEGIC OFFENSIVE ARMS

For the purposes of the Treaty Between the United States of America and the Union of Soviet Socialist Republics on the Limitation of Strategic Offensive Arms, the Parties have considered data on numbers of strategic offensive arms and agree that as of November 1, 1978 there existed the following numbers of strategic offensive arms subject to the limitations provided for in the Treaty which is being signed today.

	U.S.A.	U.S.S.R.
Launchers of ICBMs	1,054	1,398
Fixed launchers of ICBMs	1,054	1,398
Launchers of ICBMs equipped with MIRVs	550	576
Launchers of SLBMs	656	950
Launchers of SLBMs equipped with MIRVs	496	128
Heavy bombers	574	156
Heavy bombers equipped for cruise missiles capable of a range in excess of 600 kilometers	0	0
Heavy bombers equipped only for ASBMs	0	0
ASBMs	0	0
ASBMs equipped with MIRVs	0	0

At the time of entry into force of the Treaty the Parties will update the above agreed data in the categories listed in this Memorandum.

Done at Vienna on June 18, 1979, in two copies, each in the English and Russian languages, both texts being equally authentic.

For the United States of America

RALPH EARLE II
*Chief of the United States
Delegation to the Strategic
Arms Limitation Talks*

For the Union of Soviet Socialist Republics

V. KARPOV
*Chief of the USSR
Delegation to the Strategic
Arms Limitation Talks*

———

STATEMENT OF DATA ON THE NUMBERS OF STRATEGIC OFFENSIVE ARMS AS OF THE DATE OF SIGNATURE OF THE TREATY

The United States of America declares that as of June 18, 1979 it possesses the following numbers of strategic offensive arms subject to the limitations provided for in the Treaty which is being signed today:

Launchers of ICBMs	1,054
Fixed launchers of ICBMs	1,054
Launchers of ICBMs equipped with MIRVs	550
Launchers of SLBMs	656
Launchers of SLBMs equipped with MIRVs	496
Heavy bombers	573
Heavy bombers equipped for cruise missiles capable of a range in excess of 600 kilometers	3
Heavy bombers equipped only for ASBMs	0
ASBMs	0
ASBMs equipped with MIRVs	0

June 18, 1979

RALPH EARLE II
*Chief of the United States
Delegation to the Strategic
Arms Limitation Talks*

I certify that this is a true copy of the document signed by Ambassador Ralph Earle II entitled "Statement of Data on the Numbers of Strategic Offensive Arms as of the Date of Signature of the Treaty" and given to Ambassador V. Karpov on June 18, 1979 in Vienna, Austria.

THOMAS GRAHAM, JR.
*General Counsel,
United States Arms Control and Disarmament Agency*

———

STATEMENT OF DATA ON THE NUMBERS OF STRATEGIC OFFENSIVE ARMS AS OF THE DATE OF SIGNATURE OF THE TREATY

The Union of Soviet Socialist Republics declares that as of June 18, 1979 it possesses the following numbers of strategic offensive arms subject to the limitations provided for in the Treaty which is being signed today:

Launchers of ICBMs	1,398
Fixed launchers of ICBMs	1,398
Launchers of ICBMs equipped with MIRVs	608
Launchers of SLBMs	950
Launchers of SLBMs equipped with MIRVs	144
Heavy bombers	156
Heavy bombers equipped for cruise missiles capable of a range in excess of 600 kilometers	0
Heavy bombers equiped only for ASBMs	0
ASBMs	0
ASBMs equipped with MIRVs	0

June 18, 1979

V. KARPOV
*Chief of the USSR
Delegation to the Strategic
Arms Limitation Talks*

JOINT STATEMENT OF PRINCIPLES AND BASIC GUIDELINES FOR SUBSEQUENT NEGOTIATIONS ON THE LIMITATION OF STRATEGIC ARMS

The United States of America and the Union of Soviet Socialist Republics, hereinafter referred to as the Parties,

Having concluded the Treaty on the Limitation of Strategic Offensive Arms,

Reaffirming that the strengthening of strategic stability meets the interests of the Parties and the interests of international security,

Convinced that early agreement on the further limitation and further reduction of strategic arms would serve to strengthen international peace and security and to reduce the risk of outbreak of nuclear war,

Have agreed as follows:

First. The Parties will continue to pursue negotiations, in accordance with the principle of equality and equal security, on measures for the further limitation and reduction in the numbers of strategic arms, as well as for their further qualitative limitation.

In furtherance of existing agreements between the Parties on the limitation and reduction of strategic arms, the Parties will continue, for the purposes of reducing and averting the risk of outbreak of nuclear war, to seek measures to strengthen strategic stability by, among other things, limitations on strategic offensive arms most destabilizing to the strategic balance and by measures to reduce and to avert the risk of surprise attack.

Second. Further limitations and reductions of strategic arms must be subject to adequate verification by national technical means, using additionally, as appropriate, cooperative measures contributing to the effectiveness of verification by national technical means. The Parties will seek to strengthen verification and to perfect the operation of the Standing Consultative Commission in order to promote assurance of compliance with the obligations assumed by the Parties.

Third. The Parties shall pursue in the course of these negotiations, taking into consideration factors that determine the strategic situation, the following objectives:

1) significant and substantial reductions in the numbers of strategic offensive arms;

2) qualitative limitations on strategic offensive arms, including restrictions on the development, testing, and deployment of new types of strategic offensive arms and on the modernization of existing strategic offensive arms;

3) resolution of the issues included in the Protocol to the Treaty Between the United States of America and the Union of Soviet Socialist Re-

publics on the Limitation of Strategic Offensive Arms in the context of the negotiations relating to the implementation of the principles and objectives set out herein.

Fourth. The Parties will consider other steps to ensure and enhance strategic stability, to ensure the equality and equal security of the Parties, and to implement the above principles and objectives. Each Party will be free to raise any issue relative to the further limitation of strategic arms. The Parties will also consider further joint measures, as appropriate, to strengthen international peace and security and to reduce the risk of outbreak of nuclear war.

Vienna, June 18, 1979

For the United States of America

> JIMMY CARTER
> *President of the United States of America*

For the Union of Soviet Socialist Republics

> L. BREZHNEV
> *General Secretary of the CPSU, Chairman of the Presidium of the Supreme Soviet of the USSR*

SOVIET BACKFIRE STATEMENT

On June 16, 1979, President Brezhnev handed President Carter the following written statement:

"The Soviet side informs the U.S. side that the Soviet 'Tu–22M' airplane, called 'Backfire' in the U.S.A., is a medium-range bomber and that it does not intend to give this airplane the capability of operating at intercontinental distances. In this connection, the Soviet side states that it will not increase the radius of action of this airplane in such a way as to enable it to strike targets on the territory of the U.S.A. Nor does it intend to give it such a capability in any other manner, including by in-flight refueling. At the same time, the Soviet side states that it will not increase the production rate of this airplane as compared to the present rate."

President Brezhnev confirmed that the Soviet Backfire production rate would not exceed 30 per year.

President Carter stated that the United States enters into the SALT II agreement on the basis of the commitments contained in the Soviet statement and that it considers the carrying out of these commitments to be essential to the obligations assumed under the Treaty.

CYRUS VANCE

Vienna Summit Meeting

Remarks of President Brezhnev and President Carter on Signing the Treaty on the Limitation of Strategic Offensive Arms. June 18, 1979

PRESIDENT BREZHNEV. President Carter and I have just affixed our signatures to the Treaty on the Limitation of Strategic Offensive Arms and related documents. This has been an event long awaited by the Soviet and American peoples, by the peoples of other countries, by all those who desire a durable peace and realize the danger of a further buildup of nuclear arsenals.

In signing this treaty, we are helping to defend the most sacred right of every individual—the right to live. Many representatives of our two countries have worked long and hard to draft the treaty. I think it will be fair to specially mention the contributions made by Secretary Vance and Minister Gromyko, Secretary Brown and Minister Ustinov. President

Carter and I have also had to do a good deal of work.

To act in such a way as to prevent an outbreak of nuclear war is an obligation that the Soviet Union and the United States have jointly assumed. The treaty that has been signed today reaffirms our desire to fulfill that obligation. In terms of both quantitative and qualitative limitations of strategic arms, it goes far beyond the SALT I agreement.

The entry into force of this treaty opens up the possibility to begin elaborating subsequent measures to not only limit but also reduce strategic arms. By concluding the SALT II treaty, we are making a major step forward along the road of an overall improvement of Soviet-American relations and, consequently, of the entire international climate.

For the Soviet Union, this is a logical continuation of the peaceful foreign policy line defined by our Party Congresses, a line that we intend to go on following.

The signing of the treaty has appropriately crowned the Soviet-American summit meeting here in Vienna. On this auspicious occasion, we express our sincere gratitude to the President, the Chancellor and the Government of the Austrian Republic, and to the people of Austria for the warm hospitality and cordiality extended to us.

PRESIDENT CARTER. *Mr. President, fellow citizens of the world:*

Unfortunately, in the past the most powerful currents of history have often been the ones which swept nations to war. Yet as we look back on the causes of so many wars, we can see times when a more watchful course, even a small careful shift, might have guided nations that much better, that much further in the ways of peace. That is the purpose of what we have done here today in Vienna in signing this treaty.

Today, the threat of nuclear holocaust still hangs over us, as it has for more than 30 years. Our two nations are now armed with thousands of nuclear weapons, each capable of causing devastation beyond measure and beyond imagination. Several other nations now have nuclear arms, and even more have the ability to develop the same destructive weapons. Weapons technology has continued to advance and so have the dangers and the obvious need to control and to regulate this arms competition.

The strategic arms limitation talks, which have gone on for nearly 10 years without interruption, represent the realization that a nuclear arms competition without shared rules and without verifiable limits and without a continuing dialog would be an invitation to disaster. Such an unrestrained competition would tempt fate in the future and would insult our intelligence and threaten the very existence of humanity.

This prospect is a challenge to our courage and to our creativity. If we cannot control the power to destroy, we can neither guide our own fate nor preserve our own future.

Like SALT I, the Anti-Ballistic Missile Treaty, and the Limited Test Ban before it, this SALT II treaty is based on the real security needs of our two nations. It will not end the continuing need for military strength and for readiness on both sides. But SALT II does place important, new limits on both the number and the quality of nuclear arms. And it has allowed us to continue on course toward a safer world with even more substantial limitations and reductions in SALT III. We cannot interrupt nor endanger this process.

I, as President, am entrusted with the security of the United States of America. I would never take any action that would jeopardize that sacred trust. President Brezhnev, you and I both have children and grandchildren, and we want them to live and to live in peace. We have both worked hard to give our own and our own nations' children that security.

We realize that no one treaty, no one meeting can guarantee the future safety of our nations. In the end, peace can be won only if we have pursued it and struggled tenaciously to keep the peace all along. Yet, this fight for peace has often seemed the most difficult victory to win.

Here today, as we set very careful limits on our power, we draw boundaries around our fears of one another. As we begin to control our fears, we can better ensure our future.

We can now continue to explore the planets. We can discover the essence of matter. We can find the power to preserve ourselves and to preserve our Earth.

Each of us has only one nation. We both share the same world. Not one nation on this Earth, not one people, not one single human being is harmed or threatened or deprived by this victory in the battle for peace. Indeed, a victory is here today for all.

In our lifetime, we have learned to make war by unlocking the atom—the power of creation itself. To make peace, we must limit our use of that power by sharing our courage, our wisdom, and our faith. These fundamental strengths of humankind have brought us to this very table today.

In setting our hands to this treaty, we set our nations on a safer course. We've labored long to make SALT II a safe and useful chart toward the future. Let us

pledge now, all together, to use this treaty as we continue our passage to peace.

NOTE: The exchange began at 1:02 p.m. in the Redoutensäle at the Hofburg, the imperial palace. President Brezhnev spoke in Russian, and his remarks were translated by an interpreter.

Earlier in the day, President Carter and President Brezhnev met privately at the U.S. Embassy. They then went to the Soviet Embassy for a meeting with their delegations.

Following the signing ceremony, President Carter went to the Vienna Airport for departure ceremonies.

Vienna Summit Meeting

Joint U.S.-U.S.S.R. Communique.
June 18, 1979

By mutual agreement, President of the United States of America Jimmy Carter and General Secretary of the CPSU Central Committee and President of the Presidium of the USSR Supreme Soviet Leonid I. Brezhnev held meetings in Vienna, Austria, from June 15 to June 18, 1979. President Carter and President Brezhnev conducted their discussions with the participation of:

On the American side, Cyrus Vance, Secretary of State of the United States of America; Harold Brown, Secretary of Defense of the United States of America; Zbigniew Brzezinski, Assistant to the President for National Security Affairs; and General David Jones, Chairman of the Joint Chiefs of Staff.

On the Soviet side, A. A. Gromyko, Member of the Politburo of the CPSU and Minister of Foreign Affairs; D. F. Ustinov, Member of the Politburo of the CPSU and Minister of Defense; K. U. Chernenko, Member of the Politburo of the CPSU and Secretary of the Central Committee of the CPSU; and Marshal

N. V. Ogarkov, First Deputy Minister of Defense of the USSR and Chief of the General Staff of the Armed Forces of the USSR.

Also participating in the talks were:

On the American side, George Seignious, Director of the Arms Control and Disarmament Agency; Hamilton Jordan, Assistant to the President; Jody Powell, Assistant to the President; Malcolm Toon, Ambassador of the United States of America to the USSR; and Ralph Earle, Chief of the US Delegation at the Strategic Arms Limitation Talks.

On the Soviet side, A. M. Aleksandrov, Assistant to the General Secretary of the Central Committee of the CPSU; L. M. Zamyatin, Section Chief of the Central Committee of the CPSU; G. M. Korniyenko, First Deputy Minister of Foreign Affairs of the USSR; A. F. Dobrynin, Ambassador of the USSR to the United States of America; V. G. Komplektov, Member of the Collegium of the Ministry of Foreign Affairs of the USSR; and V. P. Karpov, Chief of the USSR Delegation at the Strategic Arms Limitation Talks.

President Carter and President Brezhnev signed the Treaty on the Limitation of Strategic Offensive Arms. Basic issues of US-Soviet relations and pressing international problems were also discussed. The exchange of views was characterized by the desire to expand mutual understanding and to find mutually acceptable solutions to problems of interest to both sides. In their discussions they devoted special attention to reducing the risk of war through further limits on strategic arms and through other endeavors in arms limitation and disarmament.

The two sides expressed their appreciation to the Government of Austria for its hospitality and for providing all necessary facilities for the success of the meetings.

I. GENERAL ASPECTS OF US-SOVIET RELATIONS

There is agreement between the sides that the state of relations between the United States and the Soviet Union is of great importance for the fundamental interests of the peoples of both countries and that it significantly affects the development of the international situation as a whole. Recognizing the great responsibility connected with this, the sides have expressed their firm intent to continue working toward the establishment of a more stable and constructive foundation for US-Soviet relations. To this end, the two sides acknowledged the necessity of expanding areas of cooperation between them.

Such cooperation should be based on the principles of complete equality, equal security, respect for sovereignty and nonintervention in each other's internal affairs, and should facilitate the relaxation of international tension and the peaceful conduct of mutually beneficial relations between states, and thereby enhance international stability and world peace.

The sides reaffirmed their conviction that full implementation of each of the provisions of the "Basic Principles of Relations between the United States of America and the Union of Soviet Socialist Republics" as well as other treaties and agreements concluded between them would contribute to a more stable relationship between the two countries.

The two sides stressed the importance of peaceful resolution of disputes, respect for the sovereignty and territorial integrity of states, and of efforts so that conflicts or situations would not arise which could serve to increase international tensions. They recognize the right of the peoples of all states to determine their future without outside interference.

Recognizing that an armed world conflict can and must be avoided, the sides believe that at the present time there is no more important and urgent task for mankind than ending the arms race and preventing war. They expressed their intention to make every effort to attain that goal. To that end, they also recognized the value of consultation between themselves and with other governments, at the United Nations and elsewhere, in order to prevent and eliminate conflict in various regions of the world.

The sides note with satisfaction the growing practice of contacts between government officials of the USA and the USSR in the course of which key questions of US-Soviet relations and pressing international issues are discussed. The process of developing useful ties between the US Congress and the Supreme Soviet of the USSR and of exchanges between non-governmental organizations is continuing.

The talks again confirmed the specific significance of personal meetings between the leaders of the USA and the USSR in resolving the basic questions in the relations between the two states. In principle, it has been agreed that such meetings will be held in the future on a regular basis, with the understanding that the specific timing will be determined by mutual agreement.

Agreement has also been reached on broadening the practice of consultations and exchanges of opinion between representatives of the sides on other levels.

II. LIMITATIONS OF NUCLEAR AND CONVENTIONAL ARMS

The two sides reaffirmed their deep conviction that special importance should be attached to the problems of the preven-

tion of nuclear war and to curbing the competition in strategic arms. Both sides recognized that nuclear war would be a disaster for all mankind. Each stated that it is not striving and will not strive for military superiority, since that can only result in dangerous instability, generating higher levels of armaments with no benefit to the security of either side.

Recognizing that the USA and the USSR have a special responsibility to reduce the risk of nuclear war and contribute to world peace, President Carter and President Brezhnev committed themselves to take major steps to limit nuclear weapons with the objective of ultimately eliminating them, and to complete successfully other arms limitation and disarmament negotiations.

SALT. In the course of the meeting, President Carter and President Brezhnev confirmed and signed the Treaty Between the USA and the USSR on the Limitation of Strategic Offensive Arms, the Protocol thereto, the Joint Statement of Principles and Basic Guidelines for Subsequent Negotiations on the Limitation of Strategic Arms and the document entitled Agreed Statements and Common Understandings Regarding the Treaty Between the USA and USSR on the Limitation of Strategic Offensive Arms.

At the same time, the sides again stressed the great significance of the Treaty on the Limitation of Anti-Ballistic Missile Systems and strict compliance with its provisions and of other agreements previously concluded between them in the field of strategic arms limitation and reducing the danger of nuclear war.

Both sides express their deep satisfaction with the process of the negotiations on strategic arms limitations and the fact that their persistent efforts for many years to conclude a new treaty have been crowned with success. This treaty sets equal ceilings on the nuclear delivery systems of both sides; to begin the process of reductions it requires the reduction of existing nuclear arms; to begin to limit the threat represented by the qualitative arms race it also places substantial constraints on the modernization of strategic offensive systems and the development of new ones.

The new Treaty on the Limitation of Strategic Offensive Arms and the Protocol thereto represent a mutually acceptable balance between the interests of the sides based on the principles of equality and equal security. These documents are a substantial contribution to the prevention of nuclear war and the deepening of détente, and thus serve the interests not only of the American and Soviet peoples, but the aspirations of mankind for peace.

The two sides reaffirmed their commitment strictly to observe every provision in the treaty.

President Carter and President Brezhnev discussed questions relating to the SALT III negotiations and in this connection expressed the firm intention of the sides to act in accordance with the Joint Statement of Principles and Basic Guidelines for Subsequent Negotiations on the Limitation of Strategic Arms.

Comprehensive Test Ban Treaty. It was noted that there has been definite progress at the negotiations, in which the UK is also participating, on an international treaty comprehensively banning test explosions of nuclear weapons in any environment and an associated protocol. They confirmed the intention of the USA and the USSR to work, together with the UK, to complete preparation of this treaty as soon as possible.

Non-proliferation. The two sides reaffirmed the importance they attach to nuclear non-proliferation. They consist-

ently advocate the further strengthening of the regime of non-proliferation of nuclear weapons and confirm their resolve to continue to comply strictly with the obligations they have assumed under the Treaty on the Non-Proliferation of Nuclear Weapons. They stressed the importance of applying comprehensive international safeguards under the International Atomic Energy Agency and pledged to continue their efforts to strengthen these safeguards.

They noted the profound threat posed to world security by the proliferation of nuclear weapons, and agreed that the states already possessing nuclear weapons bear a special responsibility to demonstrate restraint. To this end, they affirmed their joint conviction that further efforts are needed, including on a regional basis, and expressed the hope that the conclusion of the SALT II Treaty will make an important contribution toward non-proliferation objectives.

Both sides further committed themselves to close cooperation, along with other countries, to insure a successful conclusion to the Non-Proliferation Treaty Review Conference in 1980, and called upon all states which have not already done so to sign and ratify the Non-Proliferation Treaty.

Vienna Negotiations. President Carter and President Brezhnev emphasized the great importance the sides attached to the negotiations on the mutual reduction of forces and armaments and associated measures in Central Europe in which they are participating with other states. A reduction of the military forces of both sides and the implementation of associated measures in Central Europe would be a major contribution to stability and security.

ASAT. It was also agreed to continue actively searching for mutually acceptable agreement in the ongoing negotiations on anti-satellite systems.

Conventional Arms Transfers. The two sides agreed that their respective representatives will meet promptly to discuss questions related to the next round of negotiations on limiting conventional arms transfers.

Chemical Weapons. The two sides reaffirmed the importance of a general, complete and verifiable prohibition of chemical weapons and agreed to intensify their efforts to prepare an agreed joint proposal for presentation to the Committee on Disarmament.

Radiological Weapons. President Carter and President Brezhnev were pleased to be able to confirm that bilateral agreement on major elements of a treaty banning the development, production, stockpiling and use of radiological weapons has been reached. An agreed joint proposal will be presented to the Committee on Disarmament this year.

Indian Ocean. The two sides agreed that their respective representatives will meet promptly to discuss the resumption of the talks on questions concerning arms limitation measures in the Indian Ocean.

Other Questions of Arms Limitations and General Disarmament. In discussing other questions connected with solving the problems of limiting the arms race and of disarmament, the sides expressed their support for the Final Document adopted at the Special Session of the UN General Assembly on Disarmament. The sides noted their support for a second special session of the UN General Assembly devoted to disarmament and for that session to be followed by the convocation of a World Disarmament Conference with universal participation, adequately prepared and at an appropriate time.

The USA and the USSR will continue to cooperate between themselves and with other member states of the Committee on Disarmament with its enlarged membership for the purpose of working out effective steps in the field of disarmament in that forum.

In summing up the exchange of views on the state of negotiations being conducted between the USA and the USSR, or with their participation, on a number of questions connected with arms limitation and disarmament, the sides agreed to give new impetus to the joint efforts to achieve practical results at these negotiations.

III. INTERNATIONAL ISSUES

There was a broad exchange of views on major international issues. The sides expressed their support for the process of international détente which in their view should become increasingly specific in nature and spread to all areas of the globe, thus helping to promote increased international stability.

President Carter and President Brezhnev devoted particular attention to situations of tension which complicate the international situation and interfere with positive developments in other areas. The two sides believe that all states must conduct themselves with particular responsibility and restraint in order to contribute to the elimination of present situations of tension and to prevent new ones from arising.

The two sides noted the importance of increasing international cooperation on such global issues as the promotion of worldwide economic development, the protection of the environment, and the peaceful use of space and the world ocean for the benefit of all mankind. They expressed their support for the efforts of the developing countries to deal with the problems they face.

Noting the important role of the UN as an instrument for maintaining peace, security and the development of international cooperation, the USA and the USSR confirm their intention to promote the improvement of the effectiveness of this organization on the basis of the UN Charter.

The sides noted with satisfaction the positive developments which have taken place in recent years with respect to the situation on the European continent. They underscored the significance of the Final Act of the Conference on Security and Cooperation in Europe. The two sides agreed that continuation of the CSCE process is important to promote security and cooperation in Europe. They called attention to the need for full implementation of all the provisions of the Helsinki Final Act. The USA and the USSR will work to facilitate a constructive meeting of the representatives of the participating states of the All-European Conference, which is scheduled to take place in 1980 in Madrid.

Each side reaffirmed its interest in a just, comprehensive and lasting peace in the Middle East and set forth its position on ways and means of resolving the Middle East problem.

There was an exchange of views concerning developments in Africa. They noted some normalization of the situation in certain areas of that continent, and the efforts of the independent states of Africa toward cooperation, economic development and peaceful relations and the positive role in this respect of the Organization of African Unity. They also indicated their respective views regarding the situation in Southern Africa.

The sides recognized the importance to world peace of peace and stability in Asia. They agreed that the independence, sov-

ereignty and territorial integrity of all nations in the area must be fully respected. They also indicated their respective views regarding the situation in Southeast Asia.

IV. COOPERATION IN BILATERAL MATTERS

The importance of cooperation between the USA and the USSR on the basis of mutual benefit, in accordance with the agreements which exist between the two countries, was emphasized. The sides took note of positive developments in the wide range of cultural, academic, scientific and technical exchange programs, which are continuing between the two countries.

Proceeding on the established principles of equality, reciprocity and mutual benefit as the basis for the conduct of such programs, the sides reaffirmed their commitment to continue and intensify cooperation in these areas.

The two sides confirmed that economic and commercial relations represent an important element in the development of improved bilateral ties. Both sides stated their position in favor of strengthening these relations, and recognized the necessity of working toward the elimination of obstacles to mutually beneficial trade and financial relations. The two sides expressed their determination to encourage the relevant organizations and enterprises in their respective countries to enter into mutually beneficial commercial agreements and contracts on a long-term basis.

President Carter and President Brezhnev expressed mutual satisfaction with the results of the talks which were held. They are convinced that the deepening of mutual understanding between the sides on several issues as a result of the meeting and the consistent implementation of the agreements which have been reached will facilitate the development of US-Soviet relations and represents a joint contribution of the two countries to strengthening détente, international security and peace.

JIMMY CARTER
President of the United States of America

L. BREZHNEV
General Secretary of the CPSU, Chairman of the Presidium of the Supreme Soviet of the USSR

June 18, 1979

Vienna Summit Meeting

Address Delivered Before a Joint Session of the Congress. June 18, 1979

Mr. President, Mr. Speaker, Members of the Congress of the United States of America, and my fellow citizens:

The truth of the nuclear age is that the United States and the Soviet Union must live in peace, or we may not live at all.

From the beginning of history, the fortunes of men and nations were made and unmade in unending cycles of war and peace. Combat was often the measure of human courage. Willingness to risk war was the mark of statecraft. My fellow Americans, that pattern of war must now be broken forever.

Between nations armed with thousands of thermonuclear weapons—each one capable of causing unimaginable destruction—there can be no more cycles of both war and peace. There can only be peace.

About 2 hours ago, I returned from 3 days of intensive talks with President Leonid Brezhnev of the Soviet Union. I come here tonight to meet with you in a spirit of patience, of hope, and of reason and responsibility.

Patience—because the way is long and hard, and the obstacles ahead are at least as great as those that have been overcome in the last 30 years of diligent and dedicated work.

Hope—because I'm thankful to be able to report to you tonight that real progress has been made.

Reason and responsibility—because both will be needed in full measure if the promise which has been awakened in Vienna is to be fulfilled and the way is to be opened for the next phase in the struggle for a safe and a sane Earth.

Nothing will more strongly affect the outcome of that struggle than the relationship between the two predominant military powers in the world, the United States of America and the Soviet Union.

The talks in Vienna were important in themselves. But their truest significance was as a part of a process—a process that, as you well know, began long before I became President.

This is the 10th time since the end of World War II when the leader of the United States and the leader of the Soviet Union have met at a summit conference. During these past 3 days, we've moved closer to a goal of stability and security in Soviet-American relationships.

That has been the purpose of American policy ever since the rivalry between the United States and the Soviet Union became a central fact in international relations more than a generation ago at the end of World War II.

With the support of the Congress of the United States and with the support of the people of this Nation, every President throughout this period has sought to reduce the most dangerous elements of the Soviet-American competition.

While the United States still had an absolute nuclear monopoly, President Truman sought to place control of the atomic bomb under international authority. President Eisenhower made the first efforts to control nuclear testing. President Kennedy negotiated with the Soviet Union prohibition against atmospheric testing of nuclear explosives. President Johnson broadened the area of negotiations for the first time to include atomic weapons themselves. President Nixon concluded the first strategic arms limitation agreement, SALT I. President Ford negotiated the Vladivostok accords. You can see that this is a vital and a continuing process.

Later this week I will deliver to the United States Senate the complete and signed text of the second strategic arms limitation agreement, SALT II.

This treaty is the product of 7 long years of tough, painstaking negotiation under the leadership of three different Presidents. When ratified, it will be a truly national achievement—an achievement of the Executive and of the Congress, an achievement of civilians and of our military leaders, of liberals and conservatives, of Democrats and Republicans.

Of course, SALT II will not end the competition between the United States and the Soviet Union. That competition is based on fundamentally different visions of human society and human destiny. As long as that basic difference persists, there will always be some degree of tension in the relationship between our two countries. The United States has no fear of this rivalry. But we want it to be peaceful.

In any age, such rivalry risks degeneration into war. But our age is unique, for the terrible power of nuclear weapons has created an incentive that never existed before for avoiding war. This tendency transcends even the very deep differences of politics and philosophy. In the age of the hydrogen bomb, there is no longer any meaningful distinction between global war and global suicide.

Our shared understanding of these realities has given the world an interval of peace—a kind of a strange peace—marked by tension, marked by danger, marked even sometimes by regional conflict, but a kind of peace nonetheless. In the 27 years before Hiroshima, the leading powers of the world were twice engulfed in total war. In the 34 years since Hiroshima, humanity has by no means been free of armed conflict. Yet, at least we have avoided a world war.

Yet this kind of twilight peace carries the ever-present danger of a catastrophic nuclear war, a war that in horror and destruction and massive death would dwarf all the combined wars of man's long and bloody history.

We must prevent such a war. We absolutely must prevent such a war.

To keep the peace, to prevent the war, we must have strong military forces, we must have strong alliances, we must have a strong national resolve—so strong that no potential adversary would dare be tempted to attack our country. We have that strength. And the strength of the United States is not diminishing; the strength of our great country is growing, and I thank God for it.

Yet, for these same reasons—in order to keep the peace—we must prevent an uncontrolled and pointless nuclear arms race that would damage the security of all countries, including our own, by exposing the world to an ever greater risk of war through instability and through tension and through uncertainty about the future. That's why the new strategic arms limitation treaty is so important.

SALT II will undoubtedly become the most exhaustively discussed and debated treaty of our time, perhaps of all times. The Secretary of State, the Secretary of Defense, the members of the Joint Chiefs of Staff, the Director of the Arms Control and Disarmament Agency, and many others who hammered out this treaty will testify for it before the Senate, in detail and in public. As President of our country, I will explain it throughout our Nation to every American who will listen. This treaty will withstand the most severe scrutiny because it is so clearly in the interest of American security and of world peace.

SALT II is the most detailed, far-reaching, comprehensive treaty in the history of arms control. Its provisions are interwoven by the give-and-take of the long negotiating process. Neither side obtained everything it sought. But the package that did emerge is a carefully balanced whole, and it will make the world a safer place for both sides.

The restrictions on strategic nuclear weapons are complex, because these weapons represent the highest development of the complicated technical skills of two great nations. But the basic realities underlying this treaty and the thrust of the treaty itself are not so complex. When all is said and done, SALT II is a matter of common sense.

The SALT II treaty reduces the danger of nuclear war. For the first time, it places equal ceilings on the strategic arsenals of both sides, ending a previous numerical imbalance in favor of the Soviet Union.

SALT II preserves our options to build the forces we need to maintain that strategic balance. The treaty enhances our own ability to monitor what the Soviet Union is doing. And it leads directly to the next step in more effectively controlling nuclear weapons.

Again, SALT II does not end the arms competition. But it does make that competition safer and more predictable, with clear rules and verifiable limits, where

otherwise there would be no rules and there would be no limits.

It's in our interest because it slows down—it even reverses—the momentum of the Soviet arms buildup that has been of such great concern to all of us. Under this new treaty, the Soviet Union will be held to a third fewer strategic missile launchers and bombers by 1985 than they would have simply by continuing to build at their present rate.

With SALT II, the numbers of warheads on missiles, their throw-weight, and the qualitative development of new missiles will all be limited. The Soviet Union will have to destroy or dismantle some 250 strategic missile systems—systems such as nuclear submarines armed with relatively new missiles, built in the early 1970's, and aircraft will have to be destroyed by the Soviet Union carrying their largest multimegaton bomb. Once dismantled, under the provisions of SALT II, these systems cannot be replaced.

By contrast, no operational United States forces will have to be reduced.

For one Soviet missile alone—the SS–18—the SALT II limits will mean that some 6,000 fewer Soviet nuclear warheads can be built and aimed at our country. SALT II limits severely for the first time the number of warheads that can be mounted on these very large missiles of the Soviet Union, cutting down their actual potential by 6,000.

With or without SALT II, we must modernize and strengthen our own strategic forces—and we are doing so—but SALT II will make this task easier, surer, and less expensive.

The agreement constrains none of the reasonable programs we've planned to improve our own defenses. Moreover, it helps us to respond more effectively to our most pressing strategic problem—the prospective vulnerability in the 1980's of our land-based silo missiles. The MX missile, which has been so highly publicized, is permitted under SALT II. Yet its verifiable mobile development system will enhance stability as it deprives an attacker of the confidence that a successful first strike could be launched against the United States ICBM's, or intercontinental ballistic missiles.

Without the SALT II limits, the Soviet Union could build so many warheads that any land-based system, fixed or mobile, could be jeopardized.

With SALT II, we can concentrate more effort on preserving the balance in our own conventional and NATO forces. Without the SALT II treaty, we would be forced to spend extra billions and billions of dollars each year in a dangerous, destabilizing, unnecessary nuclear arms race.

As I have said many times, SALT II is not based on trust. Compliance will be assured by our own Nation's means of verification, including extremely sophisticated ·satellites, powerful electronic systems, and a vast intelligence network. Were the Soviet Union to take enormous risk of trying to violate this treaty in any way that might affect the strategic balance, there is no doubt that we would discover it in time to respond fully and effectively.

It's the SALT II agreement itself which forbids concealment measures—many of them for the first time—forbids interference with our monitoring, and forbids the encryption or the encoding of crucial missile-test information. A violation of this part of the agreement—which we would quickly detect—would be just as serious as a violation of the limits on strategic weapons themselves.

Consider these prospects for a moment. Suppose the Soviet leaders build a thousand additional missiles, above and beyond the ones they have now, many new, advanced, and of a formidable design. This can happen only if the SALT II treaty is defeated.

Suppose the Soviet leaders wanted to double the number of warheads on all their existing missiles; suppose they wanted to triple the annual production rate of the Backfire bomber and greatly improve its characteristics in range and payload. These kinds of things can happen only if the SALT II treaty is defeated.

Suppose the Soviet Union leaders encrypt all data on their missile tests; suppose they conceal their nuclear launcher deployment rate and hide all their existing missile systems. Those things can happen only if the SALT II treaty is defeated.

SALT II is very important. But it's more than a single arms control agreement; it's part of a long, historical process of gradually reducing the danger of nuclear war—a process that we in this room must not undermine.

The SALT II treaty must be judged on its own merits. And on its own merits, it is a substantial gain for national security for us and the people whom we represent, and it's a gain for international stability. But it would be the height of irresponsibility to ignore other possible consequences of a failure to ratify this treaty.

These consequences would include: greatly increased spending for strategic nuclear arms which we do not need; greater uncertainty about the strategic balance between ourselves and the Soviet Union; vastly increased danger of nuclear proliferation among other nations of the world who do not presently have nuclear explosives; increased political tension between the East and the West, with greater likelihood that other inevitable problems would escalate into serious super power confrontations.

Rejection would also be a damaging blow to the Western Alliance. All of our European and other allies, including especially those who are most directly and courageously facing Soviet power, all of them strongly support SALT II. If the Senate were to reject the treaty, America's leadership of this alliance would be compromised, and the alliance itself would be severely shaken.

In short, SALT II is not a favor we are doing for the Soviet Union. It's a deliberate, calculated move that we are making as a matter of self-interest for the United States—a move that happens to serve the goals of both security and survival, that strengthens both the military position of our own country and the cause of world peace.

And, of course, SALT II is the absolutely indispensable precondition for moving on to much deeper and more significant cuts under SALT III.

Although we will not begin negotiations on SALT III until SALT II goes into effect, I discussed other nuclear control issues with President Brezhnev, such as much deeper mutual reductions in nuclear weapon inventories, stricter limit on the production of nuclear warheads and launchers, enhanced survivability and stability of missile systems that are authorized under existing SALT agreement, prenotification about missile tests and mass use or exercises of strategic bombers, and limits and controls on types of missiles which are not presently covered under any SALT agreement

Though SALT is the most important single part of the complex relationship between the United States and the Soviet Union, it is only a part. The U.S.-Soviet relationship covers a broad range of issues, some of which bear directly on our joint

responsibility to reduce the possibility of war. President Brezhnev and I discussed these issues in Vienna this morning in a long private session with only the interpreters present.

I undertook all these discussions with a firm confidence in the strength of America. Militarily, our power is second to none. I'm determined that it will remain so. We will continue to have military power to deter any possible aggression, to maintain security of our country, and to permit the continuing search for peace and for the control of arms from a position of strength. We must have that strength so that we will never be afraid to negotiate for peace.

Economically, despite serious problems of energy and inflation, we are by far the most productive nation on Earth. Along with our allies, our economic strength is three times greater than that of the Soviet Union and all its allies.

Diplomatically, we've strengthened our friendships with Western Europe and Japan, with China and India, with Israel and Egypt, and with the countries of the Third World. Our alliances are stronger because they are based not on force, but on common interests and often on common values.

Politically, our democratic system is an enormous advantage, not only to each of us as individuals who enjoy freedom but to all of us together because our Nation is stronger. Our support of human rights, backed by the concrete example of the American society, has aligned us with peoples all over the world who yearn for freedom.

These strengths are such that we need fear no other country. This confidence in our Nation helped me in Vienna as we discussed specific areas of potential, either direct or indirect, confrontation around the world, including places like southern Africa or the Middle East.

For instance, I made it clear to President Brezhnev that Cuban military activities in Africa, sponsored by or supported by the Soviet Union, and also the growing Cuban involvement in the problems of Central America and the Caribbean can only have a negative impact on U.S.-Soviet relations.

Our strength, our resolve, our determination, our willingness to protect our own interests, our willingness to discuss these problems with others are the best means by which we can resolve these differences and alleviate these tests successfully for our people.

Despite disagreements, our exchange in Vienna was useful, because it enabled us to clarify our positions directly to each other, face-to-face, and, thus, to reduce the chances of future miscalculations on both sides.

And, finally, I would like to say to you that President Brezhnev and I developed a better sense of each other as leaders and as men. The responsibility for many decisions involving the very future of the world rests on me as the leader of this great country, and it's vital that my judgments be based on as much firsthand knowledge and experience as possible.

In these conversations, I was careful to leave no doubt about either my desire for peace or my determination to defend the interests of the United States and of our allies. I believe that together we laid a foundation on which we can build a more stable relationship between our two countries.

We will seek to broaden the areas of cooperation, and we will compete where and when we must. We know how determined the Soviet leaders are to secure their interests, and we are equally determined to protect and to advance our own.

We look to the future—all of us Americans look to the future—with anticipation and with confidence, not only because of the vast material powers of our Nation but because of the power of our Nation's ideas and ideals and principles. The ultimate future of the human race lies not with tyranny, but with freedom; not with war, but with peace.

With that kind of vision to sustain us, we must now complete the work of ratifying this treaty, a major step in the limitation of nuclear weapons and a major step toward world peace. And then we may turn our energies not only to further progress along that path but also more urgently to our own domestic agenda in the knowledge that we have strengthened the security of a nation which we love and also strengthened peace for all the world.

Thank you very much.

NOTE: The President spoke at 9:03 p.m. in the House Chamber at the Capitol. He was introduced by Thomas P. O'Neill, Jr., Speaker of the House of Representatives. The address was broadcast live on radio and television.

Multilateral Trade Negotiations

Message to the Congress Transmitting Trade Agreements and Proposed Implementing Legislation. June 19, 1979

To the Congress of the United States:

I am today transmitting to the Congress, pursuant to Section 102 of the Trade Act of 1974, the texts of the trade agreements negotiated in the Tokyo Round of the Multilateral Trade Negotiations and entered into in Geneva on April 12, 1979.

With these agreements, I am submitting the proposed Trade Agreements Act of 1979, which will revise domestic law as required or appropriate to implement the Geneva agreements, and fulfill our international commitment.

These agreements offer new opportunities for all Americans.

—For American farmers the agreements expand world markets for American farm products.

—For American workers, the agreements offer more jobs, higher incomes, and more effective responses to unfair foreign competition.

—For American businesses, the agreements will open major new markets overseas for American products.

—For American consumers, the agreements will make available a wider choice of goods at better prices.

In short, the agreements mean a stronger, more prosperous, more competitive American economy. They mean lower inflation rates and a more favorable balance of trade.

These agreements bring to a successful conclusion the most ambitious and comprehensive effort undertaken by the international community since World War II to revise the rules of international trade and to achieve a fairer, more open, world trading system. They come at a time when intense pressures around the world threaten to disrupt the international trading system.

Representatives of ninety-nine nations worked for five years to reduce or remove thousands of specific barriers to trade—including both tariff and nontariff barriers—and to develop new rules which will govern the international trading system in the coming decades.

Since World War II, a period of remarkable trade expansion, our experience teaches us that international trade brings strength and growth to economies throughout the world. It serves the cause

of peace by enriching the lives of people everywhere.

By responding to the needs of today's rapidly changing world economy, these agreements ensure that growing prosperity and growing interdependence through increased trade will continue to benefit all nations.

World trade has expanded more than six-fold since completion of the Kennedy Round of trade negotiations in 1967, and now exceeds $1.3 trillion annually.

Our nation is much more heavily dependent on trade than in the past. Today, one of every three acres in America produces food or fiber for export. One of every seven manufacturing jobs in our country depends on exports.

Economic interdependence will continue to increase in the future—and so will our opportunities.

Approval and implementation by the Congress of the Tokyo Round Agreements will be the first important step toward realizing those opportunities by building a solid foundation for continued strong growth of trade. The package assembled under the direction of Robert Strauss, my Special Trade Representative, is an achievement which represents vast potential for the American economy.

The most important achievement of the Tokyo Round is a series of codes of conduct regulating nontariff barriers to trade. The code agreements are described more fully in the attachments to this Message. Also attached is a statement of administrative action detailing executive branch implementation of these laws. These agreements will accomplish the following:

—Codes on subsidies and countervailing duties and on anti-dumping will limit trade distortions arising from such practices, and will give signatories to the agreements the right to challenge and counteract such practices when they cause material injury or breach agreed rules.

—An agreement on technical barriers to trade will require countries to use fair and open procedures in adopting product standards.

—An agreement on government procurement will open purchases by all signatory governments to bids from foreign producers.

—An agreement on customs valuation will encourage predictable and uniform practices for appraising imports for the purpose of assessing import duties.

—An agreement on import licensing will reduce unnecessary or unduly complicated licensing requirements.

—An agreement on civil aircraft will provide a basis for fairer trade in this important U.S. export sector.

—In the agricultural sector, specific product concessions from our trading partners and international commodity arrangements will enhance export opportunities. An agreement on a multilateral agricultural framework will provide a forum for future consultations on problems arising in agricultural trade.

—Tariff reductions have been carefully negotiated in close consultation with American industry and labor, and will be phased in over the next eight years.

Agreements on the international trading framework will accomplish the following:

—tighten procedures for handling international trade disputes,

—respond to the needs of developing countries in a fair and balanced manner, while increasing their level of responsible participation in the trading system,

—modernize the international rules applicable to trade measures that can be taken in response to balance-of-payments emergencies,

—provide a basis for examining the existing international rules on export and import restraints.

The agreements meet the major objectives and directives of the Trade Act of 1974. They provide new opportunities for U.S. exports. They help fight inflation by assuring access to lower-cost goods for both U.S. consumers and U.S. industries. They strengthen our ability to meet unfair foreign trade practices, and assure that U.S trade concessions are matched by reciprocal trade benefits for U.S. goods.

Throughout the negotiating process, these talks were conducted with an unprecedented degree of participation and advice from Congress, American industrial and agricultural communities, labor, and consumers alike.

Through continued cooperation and aggressive application and enforcement of the provisions of these agreements, we can ensure a fair and open international trading system, and usher in a new era of effective joint efforts by business, labor and government.

These agreements will make it possible for us to demonstrate, through vigorous and peaceful action, that the free enterprise system of the United States is the best economic system in the world now and in the future. They are also a central element in my program to stimulate domestic economic growth, to control inflation, and to expand our exports.

Therefore, in the interest of strengthening our economy and the international trading system, I urge immediate approval and implementation of the Tokyo Round Agreements by the Congress.

JIMMY CARTER

The White House,
June 19, 1979.

Solar Energy

Remarks Announcing Administration
Proposals. June 20, 1979

In 1891, during the Presidency of William Henry Harrison [Benjamin Harrison], electric lights were first installed in the White House, the residence of the leaders of our country. At that time, commercial electricity was not economically feasible, but President Harrison wanted to affirm his confidence in the technological capability of our country.

This afternoon, I've arranged for this ceremony to be illuminated by solar power. [*Laughter*] And I think we've done an excellent job in utilizing that tremendous, sometimes untapped resource.

Unfortunately, in the last few years, that confidence that President Harrison expressed in our Nation's ability to meet new challenges has not always been evident. Lately, as we have begun to see the first signs of inevitable shortages of fossil fuels, our country has been disconcerted, sometimes discouraged. Some few Americans have almost reached a state of panic.

We import now about half of all the oil we use from overseas. And this dependence on foreign sources of oil is of great concern to all of us.

America was not built on timidity or panic or uncertainty about the future or a lack of confidence in our own technology or our own will or ability. America was built with vision, with faith, and also with hard work. It's time for us to recognize once again, with the surest degree of confidence, the great natural resources which God has given us and to seize the opportunities that we have to build a more prosperous, self-reliant, enjoyable, confident future in which all Americans can share.

Today, in directly harnessing the power of the Sun, we're taking the energy that God gave us, the most renewable energy that we will ever see, and using it to replace our dwindling supplies of fossil fuels.

There is no longer any question that solar energy is both feasible and also cost-effective. In those homes now using electricity, a typical solar hot water heating system, such as the one behind me, can pay for itself in 7 to 10 years. As energy costs increase, which is an almost inevitable prospect, that period for paying for this investment will be substantially reduced. Solar energy will not pollute our air or water. We will not run short of it. No one can ever embargo the Sun or interrupt its delivery to us. But we must work together to turn our vision and our dream into a solar reality.

Today, I am sending to the Congress legislative recommendations for a new solar strategy that will move our Nation toward true energy security and abundant, readily available energy supplies.

This effort to analyze where we are and where our tremendous opportunities might be was originated by a meeting between myself and congressional leaders known as the Solar Energy Caucus and by many private groups. In May of 1978, on Sun Day, I went out to Colorado to make a speech there. And beginning on that date, we began to put forward, from many sources, the recommendation submitted to Congress this day.

This solar strategy will not be easy to accomplish. It will be a tremendous, exciting challenge to the American people, a challenge as important as exploring our first frontiers or building the greatest industrial society on Earth. By the end of this century, I want our Nation to derive 20 percent of all the energy we use from the Sun—direct solar energy in radiation and also renewable forms of energy derived more indirectly from the Sun. This is a bold proposal, and it's an ambitious goal. But it is attainable if we have the will to achieve it.

Government action alone cannot make this goal come true. It will require a concerted effort of all of us—government at all levels, industry, labor, business, inventors, entrepreneurs, architects, builders, homeowners, concerned citizens, all working together.

If we do not learn to eliminate waste and to be more productive and more efficient in the ways we use energy, then we will fall short of this goal. But if we use our technological imagination, if we can work together to harness the light of the Sun, the power of the wind, and the strength of rushing streams, then we will succeed.

In this as in all major national programs, of course, the Federal Government can be a catalyst for change. I'm proposing a coordinated governmentwide effort, using all the tools at our disposal, to spend more than $1 billion in fiscal year 1980 to stimulate solar and other renewable forms of energy. I'm directing the Tennessee Valley Authority, our Nation's largest utility, to become a solar showcase. I'm proposing major tax credits to speed the development and the commercialization of solar energy.

This strong Federal commitment to solar energy will be sustained year after year after year after year. It will not be a temporary program.

An important new program in the solar strategy is the creation of a solar bank, which will be funded out of the energy security fund, the money to be derived from the windfall profits tax now making its way through Congress. This will allow us to encourage the use of solar energy in residential and commercial buildings and in many other uses.

In the year 2000, the solar water heater behind me, which is being dedicated today, will still be here supplying cheap, efficient energy. A generation from now, this solar heater can either be a curiosity, a museum piece, an example of a road not taken, or it can be just a small part of one of the greatest and most exciting adventures ever undertaken by the American people: harnessing the power of the Sun to enrich our lives as we move away from our crippling dependence on foreign oil.

As President, I am determined that America will move toward the solar age with effectiveness and determination, with excitement, high spirits, and with confidence. Therefore, I dedicate, this afternoon, this solar heater, harnessing the rays of the Sun to the benefit of those who serve our country at the White House, with the faith that American technology will meet challenges that lie ahead and that we will build a more self-reliant and a more secure nation for the generations to come.

On behalf of the people of our country, I want to thank the Members of Congress who are assembled here this afternoon, the members of my own administration, dozens of private citizens groups who have long worked with dedication and sometimes disappointment in increasing the interest in and the dedication to solar power. I think all of us working together can assure the success of what is being initiated this afternoon—a national program supported and enjoyed by all Americans to make solar energy a clean, sure, economical, exciting part of Americans' lives.

Thank you very much.

NOTE: The President spoke at 1:31 p.m. at the dedication ceremony, which was held on the West Terrace at the White House.

Solar Energy

Message to the Congress. June 20, 1979

To the Congress of the United States:

On Sun Day, May 3, 1978 we began a national mobilization in our country toward the time when our major sources of energy will be derived from the sun. On that day, I committed our Nation and our government to developing an aggressive policy to harness solar and renewable sources of energy. I ordered a major government-wide review to determine how best to marshal the tools of the government to hasten the day when solar and renewable sources of energy become our primary energy resources. As a result of that study, we are now able to set an ambitious goal for the use of solar energy and to make a long term commitment to a society based largely on renewable sources of energy.

In this Message I will outline the major elements of a national solar strategy. It relies not only on the Federal government, both Executive and Congress, but also on State and local governments, and on private industry, entrepreneurs, and inventors who have already given us significant progress in the availability of solar technologies. Ultimately, this strategy depends on the strength of the American people's commitment to finding and using substitutes for our diminishing supplies of traditional fossil fuels.

Events of the last year—the more than 30% increase in the price of oil we import and the supply shortage caused by the interruption of oil production in Iran—have made the task of developing a national solar strategy all the more urgent, and all the more imperative.

More than ever before, we can see clearly the dangers of continued excessive reliance on oil for our long-term future

security. Our energy problem demands that we act forcefully to diversify our energy supplies, to make maximum use of the resources we have, and to develop alternatives to conventional fuels.

Past governmental policies to control the prices of oil and natural gas at levels below their real market value have impeded development and use of solar and renewable resource alternatives. Both price controls and direct subsidies that the government has provided to various existing energy technologies have made it much more difficult for solar and renewable resource technologies to compete.

In April of this year I announced my decision to begin the process of decontrolling domestic oil prices. Last November, I signed into law the Natural Gas Policy Act which will bring the price of that premium fuel to its true market level over the next five years. Together, these steps will provide much-needed incentives to encourage maximum exploration and production of our domestic resources. They provide strong incentives to curb waste of our precious energy resources. Equally important, these steps will help solar and renewable resource technologies compete as the prices of oil and natural gas begin to reflect their real market value. Consumers will see more clearly the benefits of investing in energy systems for which fuel costs will not escalate each year. Industry can plan and invest with more certainty, knowing the market terms under which their products will compete.

We must further strengthen America's commitment to conservation. We must learn to use energy more efficiently and productively in our homes, our transportation systems and our industries. Sound conservation practices go hand in hand with a strong solar and renewable resource policy. For example, a well-designed and well-insulated home is better able to make use of solar power effectively than one which is energy inefficient.

We must also find better ways to burn and use coal—a fossil fuel which we have in abundance. Coal must and will be a key part of a successful transition away from oil. We must and will do more to utilize that resource. Solar energy and an increased use of coal will help in the near and mid-term to accelerate our transition away from crude oil.

But it is clear that in the years ahead we must increasingly rely on those sources of power which are renewable. The transition to widespread use of solar energy has already begun. Our task is to speed it along. True energy security—in both price and supply—can come only from the development of solar and renewable technologies.

In addition to fundamental security, solar and renewable sources of energy provide numerous social and environmental benefits.

Energy from the sun is clean and safe. It will not pollute the air we breathe or the water we drink. It does not run the risk of an accident which may threaten the health or life of our citizens. There are no toxic wastes to cause disposal problems.

Increased use of solar and renewable sources of energy is an important hedge against inflation in the long run. Unlike the costs of depletable resources, which rise exponentially as reserves are consumed, the cost of power from the sun will go down as we develop better and cheaper ways of applying it to everyday needs. For everyone in our society—especially our low-income or fixed-income families—solar energy provides an important way to avoid rising fuel costs.

No foreign cartel can set the price of sun power; no one can embargo it. Every solar collector in this country, every in-

vestment in using wind or biomass energy, every advance in making electricity directly from the sun decreases our reliance on uncertain sources of imported oil, bolsters our international trade position, and enhances the security of our Nation.

Solar energy can put hundreds of thousands of Americans to work. Because solar applications tend to be dispersed and decentralized, jobs created will be spread fairly evenly around the Nation. Job potentials span the ranges of our employment spectrum, from relatively unskilled labor to advanced engineers, from plumbers and metal workers to architects and contractors, from scientists and inventors to factory workers, from the small businessman to the large industrialist. Every investment in solar and renewable energy systems keeps American dollars working for us here at home, creating new jobs and opportunities, rather than sending precious funds to a foreign cartel.

Increased reliance on solar and renewable technologies can also increase the amount of control each one of us as individuals and each of our local communities has over our energy supplies. Instead of relying on large, centralized energy installations, many solar and renewable technologies are smaller and manageable by the homeowner, the farmer, or the individual factory or plant. By their very nature, renewable technologies are less likely to engage the kind of tension and conflict we have seen in other energy areas, such as the problems posed by siting a very large energy facility, or trading off between surface uses of land and development of the energy minerals that might lie below that land.

Finally, solar and renewable technologies provide great international opportunities, both in foreign trade, and in the ability to work with developing nations to permit them to harness their own, indigenous resources rather than become dependent on fuels imported from other nations.

It is a mistake to think of solar energy as exotic or unconventional. Much of the technology for applying the sun's power to everyday tasks has been in use for hundreds of years. There were windmills on our great plains long before there were high tension wires. There were factories in New England using waterpower long before the internal combustion engine was invented. In Florida, before World War II, there were more than 60,000 homes and buildings using solar hot water heaters. The Native Americans who built the great cliff dwellings of the West understood and applied solar heating principles that we have neglected in recent years, but which are available for us to use today.

These traditional and benign sources of energy fell into disuse because of a brief glut of cheap crude oil. These years are over. That inescapable fact is not a cause for despondency or a threat to our standard of living. On the contrary, it presents us with an opportunity to improve the quality of our lives, add dynamism to our economy and clean up our environment. We can meet this challenge by applying the time-tested technologies of solar power, and by developing and deploying new devices to harness the rays of the sun.

The government-wide survey I commissioned concluded that many solar technologies are available and economical today. These are here and now technologies ready for use in our homes, schools, factories, and farms. Solar hot water heating is competitive economically today against electric power in virtually every region of the country. Application of passive design principles that take into ac-

count energy efficiency and make maximum use of the direct power of the sun in the intrinsic design of the structure is both good economics and good common sense. Burning of wood, some uses of biomass for electricity generation, and low head hydropower have repeatedly been shown to be cost competitive.

Numerous other solar and renewable resources applications are close to economic competitiveness, among them solar space heating, solar industrial process heat, wind-generated electricity, many biomass conversion systems, and some photovoltaic applications.

We have a great potential and a great opportunity to expand dramatically the contribution of solar energy between now and the end of this century. I am today establishing for our country an ambitious and very important goal for solar and renewable sources of energy. It is a challenge to our country and to our ingenuity.

We should commit ourselves to a national goal of meeting one fifth—20%— of our energy needs with solar and renewable resources by the end of this century. This goal sets a high standard against which we can collectively measure our progress in reducing our dependence on oil imports and securing our country's energy future. It will require that all of us examine carefully the potential solar and renewable technologies hold for our country and invest in these systems wherever we can.

In setting this goal, we must all recognize that the Federal government cannot achieve it alone. Nor is the Federal budget the only tool that should be considered in determining the courses we set to reach this goal. The extent to which solar and renewable technologies become more competitive will depend upon the cost of existing sources of energy, especially oil and natural gas. The degree to which existing solar technologies achieve widespread use in the near term will be as much if not more a function of the commitment on the part of energy users in this country to consider these technologies as it will be a function of the incentives the government is able to provide.

State and local governments must make an all-out effort to promote the use of solar and renewable resources if the barriers now found at those levels are to be overcome. Zoning ordinances, laws governing access to the sun, housing codes, and state public utility commission policies are not Federal responsibilities. Although the Federal government should provide leadership, whether or not these tools are used to hinder or to help solar and renewable energy use ultimately depends upon decisions by each city, county and state. The potential for success in each of these areas is great; the responsibility is likewise. I call on our Governors, our Mayors, and our county officials to join with me in helping to make our goal a reality.

American industry must also be willing to make investments of its own if we are to reach our solar goal. We are setting a goal for which industry can plan. We are providing strong and certain incentives that it can count on. Industry, in turn, must accelerate and expand its research, development, demonstration, and promotional activities. The manufacturing, construction, financing, marketing, and service skills of American business and labor are essential. Banks and financial institutions will need to examine and strengthen their lending policies to assure that solar technologies are offered a fair chance in the marketplace. Universities and the academic community must mobilize to find ways of bringing those solar and renewable technologies that are still not ready for commercial introduction closer to the marketplace. Small businesses and family

farmers also have opportunities for significant use of solar and renewable resources. They, too, must join in this effort.

Finally, each one of us in our daily lives needs to examine our own uses of energy and to learn how we can make solar and renewable resources meet our own needs. What kind of house we buy, or whether we are willing to work in our own communities to accelerate the use of solar energy, will be essential in determining whether we reach our goal.

The Federal government also has a responsibility in providing incentives, information, and the impetus for meeting our 20% solar goal by the year 2000. Almost every agency of the Federal government has responsibilities which touch in one way or another on solar energy. Government agencies helped finance over one million U.S. homes in 1978. By their lending policies and their willingness to assist solar investments, these agencies have significant leverage.

The Tennessee Valley Authority is the Nation's largest utility and producer of power. It has a far-reaching opportunity to become a solar showcase—to set an example for all utilities, whether public or privately owned, of how to accelerate the use of solar technologies. The Department of Defense (DOD) is a major consumer of energy and a major provider of housing. A multitude of opportunities exist for DOD to demonstrate the use of solar. The Agency for International Development (AID) works full time in helping other countries to meet their essential needs, including energy. Solar and renewable resources hold significant potential for these countries and, through AID, we can assist in promoting the worldwide application of these technologies.

The Department of Energy has a particularly significant responsibility in aiding the development and encouraging the use of solar energy technologies, in providing back-up information and training for users of solar, and, generally, in directing our government-funded research and development program to ensure that future solar and renewable technologies are given the resources and institutional support that they need.

As a government-wide study, the Domestic Policy Review of Solar Energy has provided a unique opportunity to draw together the disparate functions of government and determine how best to marshal all of the government's tools to accelerate the use of solar and renewable resources. As a result of that study, the set of programs and funding recommendations that I have already made and am adding to today will provide more than $1 billion for solar energy in FY 1980, with a sustained Federal commitment to solar energy in the years beyond. The FY 1980 budget will be the highest ever recommended by any President for solar energy. It is a significant milestone for our country.

This $1 billion of Federal expenditures—divided between incentives for current use of solar and renewable resources such as tax credits, loans and grants, support activities to develop standards, model building codes, and information programs, and longer term research and development—launches our Nation well on the way toward our solar goal. It is a commitment we will sustain in the years ahead.

I am today proposing the establishment of a national Solar Bank as a government corporation to be located within the Department of Housing and Urban Development (HUD). It will provide a major impetus toward use of today's solar technologies by increasing the availability of financing at reasonable terms for solar investments in residential and commercial buildings.

The Solar Bank will be funded at $100 million annually out of the Energy Security Trust Fund from revenues generated by the windfall profits tax. The Bank will be authorized to provide interest subsidies for home improvement loans and mortgages for residential and commercial buildings. It will pay up front subsidies to banks and other lending institutions which, in turn, will offer loans and mortgages for solar investments at interest rates below the prevailing market rate. Ceilings on the amount of the loan or portion of a loan which can be subsidized will be set.

The Solar Bank will be governed by a Board of Directors including the Secretary of HUD, the Secretary of Energy, and the Secretary of the Treasury. The Board of Directors will be empowered to set the specific level of interest subsidy at rates which will best serve the purposes of accelerating the use of solar systems in residential and commercial buildings. Standards of eligibility for systems receiving Solar Bank assistance will be set by the Secretary of HUD in consultation with the Secretary of Energy.

The Solar Bank I have proposed is similar in many respects to that introduced by Congressman Stephen Neal of North Carolina. A companion bill has been introduced in the Senate by Senator Robert Morgan of North Carolina. To them, and to the co-sponsors of this legislation, we owe our gratitude for the hard work and sound conceptual thinking that has been done on how a Solar Bank should be designed.

The Solar Bank will complement the residential and commercial tax credits that I originally proposed in April 1977 and that were signed into law with the National Energy Act last November. To provide full and effective coverage for all solar and renewable resource technologies which can be used in residential and commercial buildings, I have recently proposed two additional tax credits, to be funded out of the Energy Security Trust Fund.

I am directing the Department of the Treasury to send to the Congress legislation which will provide a 20% tax credit up to a total of $2,000 for passive solar systems in new homes. Credits will also be proposed for passive solar in commercial buildings. Passive solar applications are competitive today, but we need to provide incentives to owners, builders, architects, and contractors to ensure early and widespread use.

I am also directing the Treasury to prepare and transmit legislation to provide a tax credit for purchasers of airtight woodburning stoves for use in principal residences. This credit would equal 15% of the cost of the stove, and will be available through December 1982. There is a great potential to expand significantly the use of wood for home heating. It can help lower residential fuel bills, particularly as oil and natural gas prices increase.

With these levels of assistance, hot water heating can be made fully competitive with electricity. In many instances, complete passive solar home designs, including solar heating and cooling, will be economically attractive alternatives.

A strong Federal program to provide accurate and up-to-date solar information to homeowners, builders, architects and contractors will be coupled with these financial incentives. The Department of Energy has established a National Solar User Information Program to collect, evaluate and publish information on the performance of solar systems throughout the country. Expanding the government's information dissemination systems through seminars, technical journals, state

energy offices, and the Solar Energy Research Institute will be a major thrust of DOE's program in 1980. The four Regional Solar Energy Centers will become fully operational in 1980, providing information to the general public and to groups such as builders, contractors, and architects who will play key roles in the acceleration of solar technologies.

To be fully effective, however, these incentives must be combined with a determined effort by the architects, engineers, and builders who design and construct our homes and offices, schools, hotels, restaurants, and other buildings we live and work in. I am calling upon the deans of our schools of architecture and engineering to do their part by making the teaching of solar energy principles an essential part of their curricula. The young men and women being trained today must learn to regard the solar energy and overall energy efficiency of the buildings they design as no less important than their structural integrity. I call as well on America's builders to build and market homes which offer the buyer freedom from escalating utility bills.

In the end, it will be consumers of this country who will make the purchasing decisions that will dictate the future of this industry. They must have confidence in the industry and in the products which it produces before they will be willing to make necessary investments. To this end, both industry and government must be ever vigilant to assure that consumers are well protected from fraud and abuse.

———

Significant opportunities for use of existing solar technologies are also available in the agricultural and industrial sectors of our economy. Industrial process heat can be generated using solar technologies. Critical agricultural activities—fueling tractors, running irrigation pumps and drying crops—provide numerous opportunities for the use of solar and other renewable resources.

Biomass, gasohol, wind energy, low head hydro, and various direct solar technologies hold significant promise in the agricultural and industrial sectors. I will soon be forwarding legislation to the Congress which will:

• Provide a 25% investment tax credit for agricultural and industrial process heat uses of solar energy. This is a 15% addition to the existing investment tax credit and it will remain available through 1989. This responds directly to the concern expressed in the Domestic Policy Review that the tax credit currently provided in the National Energy Act is set at too low a level and expires too early to provide needed incentives. These uses now account for about 25% of our energy demand. Substitution of solar and other renewable resources for a portion of this energy would significantly reduce our dependence on foreign oil.

• Permanently exempt gasohol from the Federal gasoline excise tax. More and more Americans are learning that a gasohol blend of 90% gasoline and 10% alcohol—which is made from various agricultural products or wastes—is an efficient octane-boosting fuel for automobiles and other gasoline engines.

The existing tax incentives of the National Energy Act will continue to stimulate the uses of these technologies in the industrial and agricultural sectors.

The Department of Agriculture will have a significant responsibility for informing farmers and other agricultural users of energy about how solar and other renewable sources can begin to help meet their needs. The Farmers Home Administration and other agencies within the Agriculture Department will continue to provide financial and technical assistance to farmers in using solar and other renewable technologies.

The TVA is demonstrating what can be done by utilities in helping private industries, farmers, and residential customers apply existing solar technologies. The goal of the TVA's "Solar Memphis" program is to install 1,000 solar water heaters this year by offering long-term, low-interest loans, by inspecting solar installations, and by backing manufacturers' warranties. In addition, the TVA's 1.75 million square foot passive solar office complex in Chattanooga, Tennessee will be designed to be completely energy self-sufficient and will be a model for the nation in the use of renewable technologies in office buildings.

The Small Business Administration is now operating a solar loan program for small manufacturers and purchasers of solar technologies. Next year, the SBA aims to triple the amount of funds available to small businesses under this program over the amount originally appropriated. We will also marshal the efforts of agencies such as the Economic Development Administration to include solar and other renewable resources within their assistance programs.

These activities, along with the basic information dissemination programs of the Department of Energy, will help increase the use of solar and other renewable resource technologies in residential, commercial, agricultural, and industrial buildings.

Finally, we will strive to increase use of solar energy by the Federal government itself. An estimated 350 solar systems will be placed in government facilities and buildings over the next fifteen months. Energy audits of all large federal buildings will be completed in 1979. DOE will continue to develop guidelines which take into account the lifetime energy costs of various systems. The Department of Defense, which accounts for about 72% of all government-owned buildings, is playing a major role in the federal solar buildings program. To date, DOD has over 100 solar projects in various stages of completion, ranging in size from solar hot water heaters in residences to solar heating and air conditioning of Naval, Air Force and Army base facilities. When all of the presently planned solar projects are complete, DOD estimates that they will be providing more than 20 billion Btu's of energy. The Federal government must set an example, and I call upon the states to do likewise.

———

The Domestic Policy Review recommended several important changes in the direction and nature of the Federal research and development program for future solar and renewable resource technologies. It found that solar demonstration programs for active hot water systems and high-cost centralized solar electric technologies had been overemphasized at the expense of those systems which hold wider potential to displace the use of oil and natural gas.

As a result of the Domestic Policy Review, the FY 1980 budget for DOE's research and development program for solar and renewable energy sources was redirected toward technologies such as photovoltaics, biomass, wind energy, and systems for generation of process heat. To respond to these new priorities, over $130 million in increased funding was provided in the R&D program, an increase of 40% over FY 1979 levels.

While solar heating and cooling units are already being used to meet the energy requirements of buildings throughout the country, the DOE is supporting continued advances in these products, by providing funds to industry, small business, Federal laboratories, and the research community to reduce the cost of solar systems and to improve performance. Improved system design, analysis, and system-integration activities are being carried out for active heating and cooling systems, passive systems, and agricultural and industrial process heating systems. The program also supports product improvements for such key components as solar collectors, energy storage units, and controls.

Photovoltaics, which permit the direct conversion of sunlight into electricity, hold significant promise as a solar technology for the future. Research and development efforts are directed at reducing the cost of photovoltaic systems. In addition, new systems which produce hydrogen through an electrochemical reaction can be used to produce electricity. There is no question about our technical ability to use photovoltaics to generate electricity. These systems are already used extensively to meet remote energy needs in our space program. The main issue now is how to reduce the costs of photovoltaics for grid-related applications such as providing electricity to residential buildings over the next five to ten years. The photovoltaic program involves all aspects of research and development, from hardware components to materials, marketing and distribution systems. The Federal government has already made commitments to purchase $30 million of photovoltaic systems at a specified cost per watt as a means of stimulating private efforts to reduce the cost of this technology.

DOE's research and development program has also emphasized wind energy. Our objective is the development of wind systems which will compete cost-effectively with conventional technologies. There will also be efforts to develop wind technologies for small units suitable for farm and rural use and for large utility units.

Biomass conversion holds significant promise as a major source of renewable energy over the coming decades. Liquid and gaseous fuels produced from organic wastes and crops can displace oil and natural gas both as direct combustion fuels and as chemical feedstocks. Some biomass fuels, such as gasohol, are in use today. Others, such as liquid fuels from organic wastes, require additional research and development.

In the coming fiscal year, DOE will complete construction of the solar power tower in Barstow, California. Such systems could potentially displace some oil- and gas-fired generators. The DOE solar thermal program is also concentrating on reducing to near commercial levels the costs of distributed receiver systems by 1983 and similarly reducing the future costs of central receiver systems. This program supports R&D efforts in advanced space heating and cooling, photovoltaic concentration, and high temperature industrial heat applications.

The oceans are another potential source of solar energy. We will pursue research and development efforts directed toward ocean thermal energy conversion, and other concepts such as the use of salinity gradients, waves, and ocean currents.

DOE is working with the National Aeronautics and Space Administration to evaluate the concept of a solar power satellite system (SPS) which would capture solar energy in space for transmission to earth. A determination will be made in January 1981 on whether this system should proceed to the exploratory research stage.

DOE will undertake intensified efforts involving solar energy storage and basic solar energy research. In the basic research area, emphasis is being placed on the development of new materials to better use or convert the sun's energy, solar photochemistry (including the possibility of using electrochemical cells to convert the energy of sunlight into electricity and/or fuels) and research on artificial photosynthesis.

In Fiscal Year 1980 we will begin building a new 300-acre solar research facility for the Solar Energy Research Institute at Golden, Colorado. This institute, along with four regional solar centers established across the country, will help provide a focus for research and development activities and will become information centers for individuals and firms who market or install solar equipment.

In addition to DOE's research and development activities, several other agencies will continue to support commercial introduction of solar technologies as they become available. AID, TVA and the Department of Agriculture now have and will continue to have significant responsibilities in the demonstration of new solar and renewable resource systems.

The Domestic Policy Review identified numerous specific program suggestions, many of which I believe can and should be implemented. Over the course of the coming weeks, I will be issuing a series of detailed directives to the appropriate agencies to implement or consider recommendations in accordance with my instructions.

Some of these suggestions involve detailed budget issues which should be taken up in our normal budget planning process. In order to provide much-needed flexibility to DOE to respond to these— and other—suggestions, I am directing the

Office of Management and Budget to provide an additional $100 million to DOE for use on solar programs beyond that which had previously been identified for the FY 1981 base program.

An essential element of a successful national solar strategy must be a clear central means of coordinating the many programs administered by the numerous agencies of government which have a role in accelerating the development and use of these energy sources. I am today directing that the Secretary of Energy establish a permanent, standing Subcommittee of the Energy Coordinating Committee (ECC) to monitor and direct the implementation of our national solar program. The ECC membership includes the major agencies which have responsibilities for solar and renewable resource use. By using this existing mechanism, but strengthening its focus on solar and renewable activities, we can provide an immediate and direct means to coordinate the Federal solar effort. The Subcommittee will report on a regular basis to the ECC, and through it directly to me, on the progress of our many and varied solar activities. The Subcommittee will be able to identify quickly any problems that arise and the ECC will provide a forum to resolve them. Since the membership of the ECC includes key agencies of the Executive Office of the President, especially the Office of Management and Budget, the Special Assistant to the President for Consumer Affairs, the Council on Environmental Quality, and the Domestic Policy Staff, direct and easy access to my staff and Members of the Cabinet is assured.

The Standing Subcommittee of the ECC has an extremely important responsibility. I am expecting it to provide the leadership and the day-to-day coordinating function which will be essential as we strive to meet our national solar goal.

We are today taking an historic step. We are making a commitment to as important a goal as we can set for our Nation—the provision of 20% of our energy needs from solar and renewable sources of energy by the year 2000.

We are launching a major program—one which requires and has received a significant commitment from the Federal government to accelerate the development and use of solar technologies.

We are marshalling the best that the agencies of government can provide and asking for the commitment of each of them, in their diverse and numerous functions, to assist our country in meeting our solar goal.

The stakes for which we are playing are very high. When we speak of energy security, we are in fact talking about how we can assure the future economic and military security of our country—how we can maintain the liberties and freedoms which make our Nation great.

In developing and implementing a national solar strategy we are taking yet another critical step toward a future which will not be plagued by the kinds of energy problems we are now experiencing, and which will increase the prospects of avoiding worse difficulties.

We have set a challenge for ourselves. I have set a challenge for my Presidency. It will require the best that American ingenuity can offer, and all the determination which our society can muster. Although government will lead, inspire, and encourage, our goal can be achieved only if each American citizen, each business, and each community takes our solar goal to heart.

Whether our energy future will be bright—with the power of the sun—or whether it will be dim, as our fossil resources decline, is the choice that is now before us. We must take the path I have outlined today.

JIMMY CARTER

The White House,
    June 20, 1979.

Interview With the President

Question-and-Answer Session With Yoshio Hori and Yoshiki Hidaka of the Japan Broadcasting Corporation (NHK). June 20, 1979

MR. HORI. I'm most grateful to you for giving us this opportunity to make an interview with you as part of the very tight schedule between Vienna talks and Tokyo summit.

THE PRESIDENT. Well, it's a great opportunity for me to be able to talk to the Japanese people, and I look forward to the interview.

STRATEGIC ARMS LIMITATION

MR. HORI. Thank you. Anyway, first of all, please accept our congratulations on the successful culmination of the SALT II talks. And the signing of the accord is a tribute to many years of your effort. We Japanese wish to express deep satisfaction and thanks to you, Mr. President.

THE PRESIDENT. We believe that this new agreement between ourselves and the Soviet Union will not only help our own two nations to have a more peaceful future, but also will be a great contribution to the entire world to limit armaments and to lead towards peace.

MR. HORI. And this question: Could you tell me a little more completely the future image of the world peace and prospect of disarmament?

THE PRESIDENT. There is no doubt that both we and the Soviet Union are determined to control armaments in the future. Both nations will stay strong. My most important responsibility is to guarantee the security of the United States of America and also the security of our allies and to protect our interests. So, within a realm of strength, we will reduce armaments on both sides, particularly nuclear weapons, and we hope that other nations will join us in this commitment in years to come.

MR. HIDAKA. How is your feeling right now, after returning from meeting with Mr. Brezhnev down there?

THE PRESIDENT. Well, I'm very pleased with the results of the Vienna talks, but now I'm thinking almost exclusively about the happy prospect of being in Japan. This is a very exciting thing for me. I don't think there's any doubt that our close relations with the people of Japan and the prospect for the economic summit there is one of the most important and exciting responsibilities that I have.

U.S.-JAPANESE RELATIONS

MR. HORI. For keeping world peace, Japanese people are more concerned with the elimination of the causes of war rather than the maintenance of the balance of powers. What kind of role do you expect for Japanese involving world peace?

THE PRESIDENT. The close relationship between the United States and Japan is important not only for the economic prosperity of the people of both countries, but it's also a great stabilizing factor in maintaining world peace. For any other nation to look upon this close friendship and close alliance in trade, commerce, culture, security, science, education, tourism, between the United States and Japan, it gives the accurate feeling of mutual strength and mutual confidence, and, I think, tends to provide peaceful relationships throughout Asia and, indeed, throughout the world.

So, the sharing of all these experiences and all these prospects for the future between the United States and Japan is certainly a major contributing factor to peace.

PRESIDENT'S VISIT TO JAPAN

MR. HIDAKA. Now you completed two historical things—one in the Mideast, now talks with the leader of Soviet Russia. And Japanese people now expecting your coming to Japan. What do you now have in mind to accomplish when you come to Japan, sir?

THE PRESIDENT. I think the highlight of my visit will be personally to meet the Emperor. I'm excited about this, and have long had a great admiration for him as a center of the Japanese nation, and as the image of the preservation of the beautiful culture of Japan and the dynamic growth of Japan in meeting modern challenges and modern opportunities. He's an admirable person from the viewpoint of Americans, because he's a beautiful poet and also, of course, because of his superb accomplishments as a marine biologist and because of what he represents accurately in the character of the Japanese people.

So, I would say meeting the Emperor is something that I look forward to with great anticipation; also, to renew my friendship with Prime Minister Ohira, whom I've met on my one brief visit to Japan in 1975, and who came here in May to explore possibilities for alleviating all the problems between us and for shaping a more firm future between Japan and the United States. And I think one of the most enjoyable prospects is just to get to know the Japanese people. I will be bringing my wife, Rosalynn, and my daughter, Amy, to Japan, and we hope to take every opportunity to have personal contact and establish personal friendship with the people of Japan.

Obviously, the economic summit is a great tribute to Japan and is a recognition of the economic and social and political leadership of Japan in the councils of world governments. And this is a great tribute to the present and past leaders of Japan that the economic summit is being conducted there.

We will be exploring the problems of energy, the monetary system, trade, commerce, security. I think the most important single issue to be resolved in Japan at the economic summit is probably that of energy. And we look forward to exploring new ways to deal with this challenge for us all.

ENERGY

MR. HORI. At the talks in Tokyo, you will introduce a proposal for the solution of the energy problem?

THE PRESIDENT. Yes. I have a great advantage in being there 2 days before the economic summit begins. So, Prime Minister Ohira and I will be discussing a common program to present to the other leaders.

Obviously, we will have to explore new ways to conserve energy, to cut down on waste, and to reduce our dependence in the future on imported oil. We'll also have to evolve a common approach to the oil-exporting countries, so that they will provide a stable supply of oil and minimize the increase in prices in the future.

There's a wonderful opportunity for us to explore other forms of energy—coal, solar power, and technological advances in which Japan and the United States and others can cooperate in the future.

What we want is predictability, conservation, new sources of energy, and closer consultation and cooperation between our countries. And these are some of the ideas that I will be exploring first with Prime Minister Ohira and then with the other leaders of the nations who will be at the economic summit.

MR. HIDAKA. You said joint proposal with Prime Minister Ohira?

THE PRESIDENT. Yes.

MR. HIDAKA. You have all the makeup, concrete proposal, or you are in planning session? Can you elaborate on that a little before your coming to our country, sir?

THE PRESIDENT. Well, we have obviously explored many of these ideas in preparation for the economic summit. But I'm sure that he and I will make them more firm and more concrete during the 2 or 3 days immediately before the summit conference. And I will look forward to learning from him as a great leader, and I'm sure that the Japanese leaders will want to know the American position also before the economic summit commences. But all the nations involved in this summit will be sharing these proposals and decisions, and I believe that the Tokyo meeting will go down in history as the first multinational conference at which the energy question has been explored so deeply. It's long overdue. This is a wonderful opportunity for us all.

MR. HIDAKA. Any kind of the binding of the proposal for the conference—I mean, just in binding——

THE PRESIDENT. Yes, obviously, no nation can impose its will on the other. But we have already made a decision during 1979 to reduce our dependence on imported oil by 2 million barrels per day, all of us nations put together. And we will then be exploring in Tokyo how to extend this conservation effort to 1980 and to subsequent years and, most importantly,

how we can cooperate with each other in building up the supplies of alternative sources of energy in addition to the fossil fuels.

MR. HORI. What about nuclear energy?

THE PRESIDENT. Our country derives about 12 percent of all electricity from atomic power. And we will obviously have to rely upon atomic power in the future years as well. In nuclear power and in the use of coal, we obviously will want to increase the safety of both sources of energy and also to reduce any damage to the quality of air and water.

So, as we explore additional sources of energy—nuclear, coal, solar—we will want to have more efficiency, more safety, and a cleaner environment.

U.S.-JAPANESE RELATIONS

MR. HORI. Next, Mr. President, I would like to ask your opinion about the relationship between the United States and Japan——

THE PRESIDENT. Yes.

MR. HORI.——particularly in the time of economic problems.

THE PRESIDENT. Never in the history of the world have two nations had such massive economic relations as the United States and Japan, separated by an ocean; we're not contiguous one to another. We look upon the Pacific Ocean not as an obstacle to trade, but as a tremendous highway to let us transfer goods back and forth.

Because of the enormous trade that we have between us, obviously, on occasion, some problems do arise, because we're both highly technological nations, we have advanced science, we have hardworking people, we have innovations, and sometimes we sell the same products and we compete with one another. But in a democracy, when people are free, as is the case with Japan and the United States, we don't conceal problems; we put them on the table, and we discuss them openly and we resolve them.

In a totalitarian country, these problems would never be known, they would fester like a sore. But between us and Japan, we address them without fear and they become highly publicized. But we should never forget that we have tremendous areas of agreement and tremendous areas of common benefit.

So, compared to the benefits and the agreements, the problems are very minor. But the problems are the issues which get publicized.

I think in Prime Minister Ohira's visit to Washington in May, we made great progress in trying to resolve the few differences between us, and we'll continue to make progress on my visit to Japan. But no one should ever forget how close we are together and how many agreements we have. And no one should ever be fearful about our publicly discussing the problems, because that's the way to resolve problems between friends.

MR. HIDAKA. Now many Japanese have been very encouraged by your remarks in talks with Mr. Ohira. And the people notice an upsurge of protectionism in your country, but your administration trying to be nice to us and encouraging us to have good relationship. Do you have ideas much farther to develop a good relationship—I mean, what we can do to promote or to maintain this relationship for both countries?

THE PRESIDENT. Yes. Yesterday, I presented to the Congress of the United States the results of the so-called Tokyo Round of discussions, the Multilateral Trade Negotiations. And I have confidence that the Congress will adopt this proposal without delay. This is a guarantee that now and in the future years that

protectionist barriers will not be raised around our country or around Japan and other nations.

We want to have maximum openness and freedom of trade, because we can not only compete with one another successfully, but we derive enormous benefits from one another. I think that the trade imbalance has been a problem in the past. There is still some problem there. We buy much more from Japan than we sell to you. But I think that we have recognized this problem. And without disturbing the economy of either nation, we are addressing the problem successfully.

There is still a need for us to continue to explore ways of increased trade. From my part of the country, we produce agricultural products—citrus, beef, timber, plywood, coal—and we export these kinds of products to Japan, along with many others. And, of course, we buy great quantities from you as well. But in both cases, we see our consumers benefiting from a plentiful supply of goods at low cost. We have to protect our own industry, as do you. And this is sometimes creating conflict. But those conflicts are being resolved successfully, and the Tokyo Round of reducing barriers of protectionism is a major step forward in the right direction.

U.S. POLICY TOWARDS THE FAR EAST

MR. HORI. U.S. policy, foreign policy, on the Far East, from my point of view, has been so practical and flexible since the end of Vietnam war. For us, therefore, it's rather difficult to understand what is the goal of your policy for those in Far East. And in connection with this, could you tell me your policy on China?

THE PRESIDENT. Yes. Our ultimate goal is peace in the Far East. We share this goal with Japan. Our second goal is better relationships among the nations involved—our country and all those who occupy the Far East area of the world. Again, we share the same goal with Japan. We want increased trade, more attention given to basic human rights, to freedom, to democracy, to openness, to the exchange of goods and people. We share all these goals with Japan. We want security for our people. We share this goal also with Japan. The American military presence in the Far East will be sustained, and this is good for our people and good for the people of Japan.

We want to share experiences and share ideas and share information with the people and the leaders of Japan.

I've been very pleased that we have improved our relationships since I've been in the White House, with India, with the Southeast Asian nations, with the Philippines, obviously with the People's Republic of China. We have tried to strengthen the ASEAN nations, as well as an organization, recognizing their independence, and strengthen our ties with New Zealand and Australia. We will maintain the stability of the Korean peninsula.

My own judgment is that history will show the great benefits of normalized relationships with China. We have not let the well-being of the people of Taiwan suffer. My belief is that those citizens of Taiwan will still be secure. We'll still have trade with them, recognizing the People's Republic of China, however, as the Government of China.

I think that our new relationship with China can be a stabilizing factor, and not only between China and Japan, China and the other Asian nations, but also between China and the Soviet Union. We want to see peaceful relationships between countries who have in the past been potential adversaries.

So, in every way, I think that our place in the Far East is sound and firm and more stabilizing, more peaceful, and will give a better life to the people in that region of the world.

MR. HIDAKA. In connection with that, some people, particularly in the Congress, encourage us to build up much more military power to assist you. Can I ask you on that point, do you encourage us to do it or is it completely our business, so you have no interest in commenting on that, sir?

THE PRESIDENT. We enjoy the alliance and the sharing of responsibility for security with the people of Japan. But the level of your defense commitments is a domestic matter, a decision to be made by the Japanese people. We trust your judgment, and we have full confidence in you.

PRESIDENT'S VISIT TO KOREA

MR. HORI. After the summit in Tokyo, you are going to visit Korea.

THE PRESIDENT. Yes.

MR. HORI. Have you any schedule to meet with Mr. Kim Dae-jung in Korea?

THE PRESIDENT. I will be meeting not only with President Park but also the leaders of the opposition, both within the government, the religious leaders, and others. This has been my custom whenever I visit a foreign country, and I look forward to continuing this custom in Korea.

MR. HIDAKA. It mean opposition party people in Korea, you are going to meet them?

THE PRESIDENT. Yes, I will.

MR. HIDAKA. It might be a very popular action in Japan and other countries in Asia, I think.

THE PRESIDENT. Well, we are committed, as we have been for the last quarter century, to peace and stability in the Korean peninsula, and we have no intention of abandoning this responsibility. What we would ultimately like to see are

1111

the leaders of North and South Korea negotiating directly with one another, either with or without our own presence, to reach an accommodation with one another. But until that happy event can come to be, we will continue to maintain an American presence there to keep the balance of power intact within the Korean peninsula to ensure peace.

PEOPLE'S REPUBLIC OF CHINA

MR. HIDAKA. Do you have at this time any desire to visit China soon?

THE PRESIDENT. Yes, I would like to visit China within the next 12 months or so. I will not go this year. Our Vice President will go to China this year. But I have received an invitation to visit China from Chairman Hua and Vice Premier Deng Xiaoping, and I have told them that when the occasion permits, hopefully within the next 12 months, I would like to visit China.

U.S.-JAPANESE RELATIONS

MR. HIDAKA. On general terms, you are optimistic on the relationship between Japan and the United States.

THE PRESIDENT. Very much so, yes.

MR. HORI. No future danger or any trouble, anything you do not foresee or anticipate?

THE PRESIDENT. No. We are independent countries, each making its own decisions. But we have so many things in common, and we have such an easy ability to communicate with each other and to address any disputes or differences immediately, before they become a crisis, that I can see no possibility in the future of serious differences arising between our two countries.

MR. HIDAKA. Personally, I got surprised so much you know about Japan and the Emperor. How did you learn that? Did you know before? Did you make a quick study, sir?

THE PRESIDENT. No. I have been interested in Japan and have studied about Japan for many years. I was in Japan briefly in 1975. And because of my own responsibilities as President of the United States, I've long recognized the importance to us of Japan. We have many visitors here from Japan, and we have many Americans who go to Japan. So, because of our common interests, this has aroused my own study of Japan.

I have been interested in the Emperor's poems—not only himself, but his grandfather and others—and how simple and beautiful they are as expressions of the basic philosophy of the Japanese people— a quiet dignity, a reverence for the historical characteristics of the nation, a willingness to accommodate change with assurance and confidence and hard work and dedication, a peaceful inclination toward one another, a calmness and grace, an awareness and an appreciation for the natural beauty of the Earth. These kinds of expressions in the Emperor's poems have been very interesting to me.

In addition, his accomplishments as a scientist have been of great interest. I have a scientific background myself, and so that's one reason that I'm very excited about having a chance to meet him personally.

MR. HORI. Mr. President, could you convey directly to the viewers your message on this occasion?

THE PRESIDENT. Yes, I'd be glad to. I think I'll look at the people directly.

On behalf of the 220 million people who live in the United States of America, I want to express to the people of Japan. first of all, our great and unswerving friendship, a recognition that we share common commitments, common goals, common problems, common ideals, and a common future. In the area of common security, trade, commerce, education, culture, tourism, science—in all these areas of life, we have much in common. In addition, we share a belief in the worth of individual human beings, in democratic principles, in a search for peace, in the worth of each person.

I am very grateful for a chance to come to your great country, to bring my own wife and my daughter. We look forward to seeing as much of you individually as possible, to learning about your beautiful country, so that we can bring back to the United States an even fuller realization of what you have been down through history, what you are today, and the glorious future that I know is in store for the people of the great country of Japan.

The economic summit conference which will be held in Tokyo is indeed a tribute to you, to the great accomplishments of your leaders now and in the past, and of the recognition of Japan's role of leadership in the world. And I'm very grateful to be part of this recognition of your glorious achievements, now and in the future.

So, as a friend, I tell you that we are looking forward to being with you in the next few days. And I believe that both my Nation and yours might very well benefit from the exchange of views between the leaders of our two countries.

Thank you very much.

MR. HORI. On behalf of NHK and its viewers, I'm very thankful to you for taking time to interview with me. And also we extend our best wishes for the successful visit to our country.

THE PRESIDENT. Thank you very much. I've enjoyed the interview very much.

MR. HIDAKA. We are going to cover entirely live your meeting with Japanese people in Shimoda——

THE PRESIDENT. Oh, good, good.

MR. HIDAKA. ——completely live.

THE PRESIDENT. Well, we look forward to that.

MR. HIDAKA. Yes, sir. And I myself am going down there to comment on that. Japanese press quite well received your advance team down there.

THE PRESIDENT. You think it's a good place for me to go and visit? [*Laughter*]

MR. HIDAKA. Yes, sir. Thank you, sir.

THE PRESIDENT. I think we're going to have time for some quiet time to eat a meal and to visit with some of the people there. And this is a very exciting prospect for us. I look forward to seeing you there.

MR. HORI. Thank you, sir.

NOTE: The interview began at 2:07 p.m. in the Map Room at the White House. It was taped for later broadcast on Japanese television.

Bill Stewart

Statement on the Death of the ABC News Correspondent. June 21, 1979

The murder of American newsman Bill Stewart in Nicaragua was an act of barbarism that all civilized people condemn.

Journalists seeking to report the news and inform the public are soldiers in no nation's army. When they are made innocent victims of violence and war, all people who cherish the truth and believe in free debate pay a terrible price.

I know the American people share my sense of outrage and loss at the death of this gifted, dedicated young man. On behalf of all Americans, I want to express my deepest sympathy to Bill Stewart's wife and family for their suffering and loss.

NOTE: The correspondent was killed by a member of the National Guard after he approached a government maintained street barricade in Managua. He was in Nicaragua to cover the fighting between the government forces and members of the Sandinista National Liberation Front.

Trucking Industry Deregulation
Remarks Announcing Proposed Legislation.
June 21, 1979

THE PRESIDENT. The importance of this announcement is vividly demonstrated by those who have assembled here to initiate a major objective in the Congress.

When I ran for President, I promised to work vigorously to lift the heavy hand of Government regulation from the American free enterprise economy whenever possible and whenever consistent with the national interests and whenever consistent with the best interests of the American people.

Today I am proposing legislation that will reduce the redtape and the excess regulations that have strangled and strait-jacketed the trucking industry of America for the last 40 years.

Unnecessary and sometimes absolutely nonsensical regulations issued by the Federal Government concerning the trucking industry of our country are costing American consumers billions of dollars every year in higher transportation costs and on almost every food item and manufactured item and raw material that we use.

There is a gross waste of energy, a duplication of effort, a high degree of inefficiency in one of the most crucial industries of our country. Too many trucks are rattling back and forth empty on the road today, burning up precious diesel fuel because the ICC rules prohibit two-way hauling. Some trucking firms can deliver all the ingredients necessary to make soup to a factory, but are forbidden from hauling soup away from the factory.

Other rules defy human imagination. Some truckers can haul milk; they can't haul butter. They can haul cream; they can't haul cheese. Others can transport paint in 2-gallon cans; they can't haul paint in 5-gallon cans. Some truckers are allowed to haul bananas; they can't haul pineapple. They can haul pineapple and bananas if they are mixed. [*Laughter*]

Our highways are filled with truckers driving miles out of their way, because the ICC requires for them to follow specific routes that defy rhyme or reason. One trucking firm, for instance, must go from Denver to Albuquerque by way of Salt Lake City, an unnecessary detour of 300 miles.

The ICC regulations strangle competition. Trucking companies are allowed to meet together in secret to set rates, a practice that would be absolutely illegal price-fixing in almost any other business.

It's difficult, if not impossible, for new trucking firms to enter the industry. This is one reason why minorities own less than 1 percent of all interstate moving companies. ICC requirements also short-change small towns and small cities by forbidding truckers to make intermediate stops along their assigned routes, even though they pass through the small town in question.

Restrictions like these are symbols of Government regulations gone wild. They do not make economic sense. They waste millions of gallons of fuel. They breed a climate of disrespect for the law. They exclude Americans from entering one of the country's most important major industries.

Today I'm sending to the Congress the Trucking Competition and Safety Act of 1979, which will end all the abuses that I've described to you and at long last bring sensible Federal regulation to the trucking industry.

This bill will immediately remove all certificate restrictions on two-way trips and intermediate stops. It will gradually remove all other route restrictions by the year 1983. It will end price-fixing. It will encourage price competition, the formation of new trucking firms, and other forms of competitive behavior. It will improve service to our small communities. It will strengthen the Department of Transportation's ability to improve truck safety on our Nation's highways. And it will help all Americans in the battle against inflation by reducing the cost of shipping throughout the United States, which touches almost every single item that Americans use.

Soon I will send to the Congress proposals which will ensure that consumers receive increased protection in the household goods moving industry.

The best anti-inflation medicine, in my opinion, is real competition under the American free enterprise system. Airline deregulation has already saved American travelers over $2½ billion in reduced air fares. Air travel has increased; the profits of the American airline companies has also increased. According to the Council on Wage and Price Stability, this trucking deregulation bill will save American consumers $5 billion.

America's free economy has provided the greatest material blessing to us of any nation on Earth. I'm determined to bring common sense, equity, and efficiency to the entire regulatory process, so that the strength of our economy can be realized and the public good can be served and protected. These proposals are a major step toward that goal.

Who is for this legislation? There are organizations represented here which indicate an answer to that question: farm families who produce grain, cattle, other livestock; processors of food; retail merchants; small business leaders; consumers; manufacturers; independent business people; representatives of State government, city government, county government; those who are interested in improved highway safety; those who are interested

in the conservation of energy; those who are interested in controlling inflation. Those are some of the people who are for this legislation.

Who's against it? Some truckers who now have a noncompetitive advantage and who want to perpetuate a Government bureaucracy to protect such interests.

Many Members of the Congress have played a major role in pursuing the concept of deregulation for many years quite effectively. The House Members, as you may know, are now involved in a very important series of votes and debates on the Panama implementation legislation. But I would like to mention Chairman Bizz Johnson, who cannot be here now because of that vote, but who was instrumental in passing, insofar as the House is concerned, the airline deregulation bill; Chairman Jim Howard, head of the Subcommittee on Highway Transportation, who will be holding hearings on this legislation throughout the country and who's pledged to me personally a fair hearing on this legislation; Senator Howard Cannon, who is here, chairman of the Senate Commerce Committee—he was one of the leaders in putting forward the airline deregulation bill through the Senate last year—Senator Charles Percy, who drafted the trucking safety bill, extracts from which have been incorporated in this new 1979 legislation; and Senator Ted Kennedy, who has been in the forefront of all phases of regulatory reform in a very effective way for many years. He will be sponsoring this legislation, working closely with the other men that I have mentioned here. He was the first to suggest a comprehensive approach to trucking deregulation.

I consider this legislation to be one of the most important proposals that I have ever made to the Congress, and I want to express again this afternoon my deep appreciation to the leaders in Congress, whom I've named, along with many others who have been instrumental in bringing us this far.

And I would like to ask all those organizations represented here this afternoon, speaking for millions of Americans who will be benefited, not to rest with the introduction of this legislation. The issue will be in doubt. But if we work together, remember the best interests of our country and the best interests of Americans who look to us for leadership and fairness, and who believe in the free enterprise system of our country, this legislation will pass.

I'd like now to call on Senator Kennedy to make some remarks, after which Senator Howard Cannon will comment.

SENATOR KENNEDY. Thank you very much, Mr. President.

I want to congratulate President Carter and the administration for the preparation of this legislation. Just a little over 8 months ago, Mr. President, as you reminded all of us, we met here in the White House when you signed your airline deregulation bill, and that has made such a difference to consumers and to the battles of inflation, which this country is concerned about, under the leadership of Howard Cannon and the other Members which you've identified.

This legislation, as the President has mentioned, makes sense from an inflation point of view, saving consumers and business men and women $5 billion, makes sense from an energy point of view—more than 20 percent of the trucks that travel on the roads of this country travel empty. It makes sense from a regulatory reform point of view. Just about half of the trucking industry is deregulated and works and functions effectively for consumers as well as for truckers and shippers. And it makes sense for all Americans, for the American consumer.

I look forward to working with the President, my colleagues in the Congress, and particularly Senator Cannon and the members of the Commerce Committee in getting early action on this legislation.

SENATOR CANNON. Mr. President, the Commerce Committee has actively been concerned about Federal regulation for a number of years: airlines, air freight, railroads, communications, maritime, motor carriers. We've not avoided controversy in these particular areas. The trucking hearings are well under way in our committee.

We've already heard from a number of very responsible witnesses expressing concerns. We held hearings in March. We held a hearing on the household moving industry this week. We have two more next week on general trucking and more to follow this summer, both in Washington and other parts of the country.

Next week we'll be hearing from Secretary Adams, Senator Kennedy, Representative Fenwick, Chairman O'Neal,[1] and others. As a comprehensive legislative proposal, this bill will be very useful to our committee in the inquiry that is now well under way.

I can assure you and all of the people here that the committee's consideration of this legislation will be thorough and fair, and we look forward to working with you in developing a good comprehensive legislative program.

Thank you.

SENATOR PERCY. Mr. President, it's an honor to be with you.

When I first introduced the 55-mile-per-hour speed limit, the first bill that was put in on that, it was about as popular in southern Illinois and Western States as my bill that charged Senators parking fees for the Senate garage. [*Laughter*] But

---

[1] A. Daniel O'Neal, Chairman of the Interstate Commerce Commission.

today I think we have a momentous step forward, because 3 years ago, we did say that we could save 75 million barrels of oil a year and 12,000 lives. Now, 3 years later, we have saved 40,000 lives and over a quarter of a million barrels of oil by that program.

What we can accomplish here in energy savings alone can be tremendous. With that aspect of this bill of your own that I'm addressing myself to today— and Senator Kennedy and I are introducing today, with Senators Packwood and Magnuson's cosponsorship, the truck safety act, which will be a complement to this—we're grateful for what you have included in this bill on truck safety.

I think the promise for the future can be just as great. We slaughter more people on the highway just through unsafe trucks today as we did at any time in the Vietnam war: 17,500 fatalities caused by trucks and buses nationally last year; deaths caused by heavy trucks, over 26,000 pounds, are up 53 percent since 1975, over 5,000 deaths. Truckdriving is one of the most hazardous occupations in America today. Truckdriver fatalities: up 41 percent since 1975, over a thousand slaughtered every single year.

If there isn't universal support by truckers and Teamsters for the regulatory aspects of this, there is in truck safety. They both stand united in supporting this legislation. Forty-two percent of 26,000 trucks inspected by Federal spotchecks were declared imminently hazardous and ordered immediately off the road, mainly because of faulty brakes. Heavy trucks caused 11 percent of fatal accidents, yet make up only 1 percent of vehicles. Ninety-seven percent, however, of all deaths caused by truck-car accidents are to occupants of cars. They are the ones that ought to support this legislation vigorously, and I commend your administra-

tion and you, Mr. President, for your leadership in this area.

Thank you.

SECRETARY OF TRANSPORTATION ADAMS. *Mr. President, Members of the Congress:*

This represents many years of effort by many people, and, Mr. President, we are proud to have participated with you in developing it, in a course of almost 2 years of having come into the administration, people from every walk of life, including truckers, shippers, consumers, and those who are most involved in trying to see that we have a reasonable type of truck regulation in the United States and that we save energy, that we do away with these unnecessary backhauls and we modernize a system that has needed work on it for over 20 years.

I'm pleased we've all been able to be a part of this effort. And we are looking forward to going to Capitol Hill and passing legislation that will truly make this an energy-efficient, noninflationary industry.

Thank you, Mr. President.

NOTE: The President spoke at 1:30 p.m. in the State Dining Room at the White House.

Trucking Industry Deregulation

Message to the Congress Transmitting Proposed Legislation. June 21, 1979

To the Congress of the United States:

I am today transmitting to the Congress legislation to reduce substantially Federal economic regulation over the trucking industry.

The trucking industry today is subject to perhaps more complex, detailed, and burdensome Federal regulation than any other industry in our Nation.

1117

Not only does the Interstate Commerce Commission control who may enter the trucking industry, the ICC must also approve the application of an existing carrier seeking to offer new services or improve its old ones.

But ICC regulation merely begins when a certificate is awarded. The ICC, not the trucking company, decides what cities and towns a carrier may serve. The ICC, not the trucking company, decides in detail what commodities the carrier may haul—and whether any commodities can be carried on the return trip. The ICC, not the trucking company, often decides the actual highway the trucker must use, whether stops may be made to serve points along the way, and whether the trucker may take the most direct route to its destination.

This system of detailed regulation was imposed in 1935 when the trucking industry was in its infancy, and when the Nation was in the midst of its most serious depression. At that time, competition was blamed for the Nation's economic woes. Many believed that extensive government control was needed to protect the newly developing trucking industry.

In the 44 years since regulation was first imposed, conditions have changed dramatically. The trucking industry has matured and prospered, and our economy has become strong. But our system of regulation has remained basically the same.

ICC-regulated carriers are also sheltered from price competition. In 1948, Congress overrode President Truman's veto and enacted a special immunity from the antitrust laws that permits regulated trucking companies to meet together and decide upon rates. This conduct, which would be a felony in nearly every other industry, stifles competition, discourages innovative pricing, and forces the prices of consumer products higher than they otherwise would be.

Our current regulatory system contributes to three of our Nation's most pressing problems—inflation, excessive government regulation and the shortage of energy. Since regulation permits price-fixing and stifles price competition, consumers are unnecessarily paying billions of dollars a year in higher transportation prices. During these inflationary times, government policies that needlessly raise costs cannot be tolerated.

Regulation also subjects one of our Nation's most important industries to a mindless scheme of unnecessary government interference and control. Rather than putting their talents and energies to the task of providing the prices and services customers want, trucking companies are forced to concentrate on proposing measures that government regulators will permit.

Finally, regulation needlessly wastes our Nation's precious fuel by preventing carriers from making the most productive use of their equipment, and by requiring empty backhauls and circuitous routings.

The legislation I am proposing will restore the competitive spirit to the trucking industry, reduce inflation, minimize government regulation and save energy.

The major provisions in the legislation are summarized below.

NEW, COMPETITIVE POLICY STATEMENT

The bill I propose establishes a new policy statement to govern all aspects of ICC regulation of the trucking industry. The policy statement emphasizes reliance on competition rather than government regulation to the maximum extent possible to reduce rates, improve service, attract capital, increase efficiency and offer the opportunity to earn fair profits.

The policy statement also emphasizes the need to reduce existing regulations which contribute to concentration of market power, waste energy, restrict entry and services to smaller and other communities, protect larger carriers at the expense of smaller carriers, and adversely affect the long-term maintenance of fair wages and working conditions.

The policy statement also emphasizes the need for fairer and more expeditious regulatory procedures and the need for more effective safety regulation.

REMOVAL OF CERTIFICATE RESTRICTIONS

ICC certificates today are subject to a variety of restrictions that control every aspect of a motor carrier's operations. For example:

Backhaul Restrictions. Many certificates award only one-way authority, or specify that a carrier may haul commodities to a point, but with "no transportation for compensation upon return unless otherwise authorized." As recently as 1975, only half the operating certificates awarded contained authority to haul goods on a return trip.

Prohibition on Intermediate Stops. Many certificates prohibit carriers from making intermediate stops between authorized points. This prevents carriers from maximizing their loads, increases costs, and keeps many towns, especially smaller ones, from receiving the best possible service.

Route Restrictions. Most certificates authorizing the carriage of general commodities specify the actual highway the truck must use.

In addition to restricting operating flexibility, these restrictions harm service to small towns. A carrier cannot leave the highway to serve a town off the beaten track without violating the law.

Circuitous Routings. In some instances, carriers are required to take an indirect route or travel through a designated "gateway city" to reach their destination. For example:

—Denver, Colorado and Albuquerque, New Mexico, are connected to each other via Interstate 25, a distance of 442 miles. Garrett Freight Lines is permitted to haul freight from Denver to Albuquerque—but only if it goes by way of Salt Lake City, a distance of 730 miles.

—In 1974, during the height of the energy crisis, Consolidated Freightways was denied a request to travel directly between Minneapolis-St. Paul and Dallas. The carrier's route authority required it to travel 37% extra miles on trips between the two points. Despite the company's desire to eliminate excessive mileage and save fuel, the ICC denied the request because the new service would harm carriers already serving the route.

Circuitous routings, like regulations which require trucks to travel empty, waste precious fuel and increase costs and prices.

Commodity Restrictions. ICC certificates specify in detail the commodities a carrier is authorized to haul. These restrictions often follow no logical pattern and serve no apparent purpose. Some certificates, for example, authorize the carrier to haul crated, but not uncrated machinery; or allow paint hauled in 2-gallon cans, but not paint in 5-gallon cans. One recent certificate permits a carrier to haul bananas. The carrier may also haul pineapples, but only if mixed with loads of bananas.

In another case, a regulated trucker whose certificate authorizes him to haul "foodstuffs" recently wanted to haul beer. Permission was denied by the ICC. Although "wine" falls into the category of "foodstuffs," "beer" does not. If this trucker persists in his desire to haul beer, he must go through the burdensome, costly and time-consuming process of obtaining a certificate to haul "malt beverages."

As a result of backhaul and other regulatory restrictions, enormous amounts of fuel are wasted each year. This waste needlessly raises prices and significantly aggravates the energy shortage.

The legislation I am proposing provides that:

—All backhaul restrictions are removed immediately.

—All prohibitions on making intermediate stops between authorized points are removed immediately.

—All route restrictions, including requirements that a carrier take a circuitous route or pass through a designated gateway city, must be removed no later than December 31, 1981.

—All restrictions limiting the types of commodities a carrier may haul must be removed no later than December 31, 1982.

—All other restrictions must be removed no later than December 31, 1983.

—The ICC is directed to adopt liberal standards and expedited procedures for carrier petitions for removal of individual restrictions prior to the statutory deadlines. Opponents to carriers' petitions have the burden of proof to show why a restriction should not be removed.

—The ICC is directed to develop a program allowing existing carriers to increase each year their operating authority by a limited amount without ICC approval. The ICC program shall emphasize increased opportunities to serve small towns.

ENTRY AND PROCEDURAL REFORM

Before a carrier can haul regulated commodities, and before an existing carrier can expand or rationalize its operations, it must obtain authority from the ICC. Obtaining new authority has been difficult. The applicant has the burden of proving that the new competition is "required" by the public convenience and necessity. Carriers already serving the route have been able to block new entry if they could provide the service themselves, or if the new competition might impair their profitability. Although the ICC has begun to grant a larger percentage of these applications, the existing statute still requires carriers to meet an excessive burden. The ICC needs new statutory authority to carry forward the liberalization that it has begun.

This regulatory maze is particularly burdensome to small businesses. Large businesses may be able to afford experts to go through complicated regulations and wait the long months or years to obtain decisions, but this is not true for the small entrepreneur.

The legislation I propose liberalizes these restrictive entry standards. The bill substantially reduces regulation over time, and places increasing reliance upon the competitive marketplace. The bill:

—Retains the requirement that the applicant prove it meets financial, safety and insurance requirements (i.e, that it is "fit, willing, and able").

—Reverses the burden of proof and requires *opponents* of new competition to show that the transportation applied for would be inconsistent with the public convenience and necessity.

—Applies new standards for the "public convenience and necessity" test. The ICC must give substantial weight in favor of the application where it finds that the service would lower operating costs, improve fuel efficiency, meet consumer or user preference for service or lower rates, improve service to small communities; or generally improve the competitive climate. The ICC shall not consider possible diversion of revenues or traffic from other carriers.

—Requires the ICC to make a final decision on entry applications within 90 days.

—Grants the application of any fit, willing and able carrier to enter a point which an authorized carrier does not serve, or which a railroad has abandoned.

EXEMPTIONS FROM ICC REGULATION

From the start, major farm organizations opposed Federal economic regulation of the trucking industry. Farmers believed regulation would raise prices and limit the operating flexibility needed for distribution of agricultural products, many of which are perishable. Congress responded in 1935 by granting an exemption from ICC regulation for unprocessed agricultural commodities.

The agricultural exemption has served our Nation's farmers and consumers well. The exemption is too restrictive, however, and should be expanded. For example:

—raisins are exempt, if they are coated with honey, cinnamon, or sugar but not if they are coated with chocolate;

—wood chips for making wood pulp are not exempt, but wood cut into short crosswise lengths for firewood (not sawed lengthwise) are;

—frozen dinners are exempt, unless they are frozen chicken or seafood dinners;

—crab shells are exempt, but oyster shells are not;

—an owner-operator has stated, "I carry all the ingredients to the cannery to make the soup, but I cannot carry the canned soup back."

These narrow restrictions have resulted in significantly more empty backhauls for exempt truckers than for regulated truckers. The transportation costs for food, and hence food prices to consumers, are consequently higher.

The bill I propose expands the agricultural exemption to include livestock; agricultural, horticultural or aquacultural commodities; food and any edible products; and farm implements and supplies, including seed, fertilizer, and chemicals.

These provisions will allow better utilization of trucks and fewer empty backhauls. The result will be better trucking services and, most important, lower rates for farmers and lower food prices for consumers.

The bill also gives the ICC authority to grant exemptions from regulation, and expands the authority of agricultural cooperatives to haul regulated commodities for non-farmers.

CONTRACT CARRIERS AND FREIGHT FORWARDERS

CONTRACT CARRIERS

Contract carriers are ICC-regulated carriers who give specialized service to a limited number of shippers. They differ from common carriers in that they do not hold themselves out as serving the general public.

Although regulation of contract carriers has been less severe, this segment of the industry has been subject to two major restrictions: (1) they have been prohibited from applying for common carrier authority; and (2) they have been prohibited from entering into contracts to serve more than eight shippers. This second restriction has been particularly harmful to small shippers because contract carriers naturally arrange to serve only the eight largest shippers they can find.

Although the ICC has recently decided to reverse these two restrictions, their decision is being challenged in the courts by the trucking industry, and the outcome remains uncertain.

The bill I propose permits contract carriers to hold common carrier authority, and states that the ICC may not limit the number of shippers that a contract carrier may serve.

FREIGHT FORWARDERS

Freight forwarders are regulated companies who consolidate small shipments, pay a common carrier (railroad, motor carrier or airline) to transport the shipments to the forwarder's terminal in another area, and then deliver the shipments to their ultimate destination.

The bill removes unnecessary restrictions on freight forwarders. Freight forwarders will be permitted to negotiate rates and enter into contracts with rail and motor carriers. The removal of these restrictions will enable freight forwarders to compete more effectively, and will afford shippers of small shipments a greater variety of price and service options.

RATES AND RATE BUREAUS

Collective ratemaking, commonly known as price-fixing, is normally a felony, punishable by fines up to $100,000 and three years imprisonment for individuals, and up to $1 million for corporations.

Since 1948, however, the regulated trucking industry has enjoyed a special exemption from the antitrust laws. This immunity allows trucking companies to meet in secret and decide the prices they will charge for truck transportation. Although rate agreements are theoretically subject to ICC review, the ICC has been inclined to rubber stamp rate agreements rather than subject them to an independent and thorough review. This lack of effective oversight is due in part to the

sheer volume of processing, some 5,000 pages of rate tariffs are filed before the ICC each day.

Legalized price-fixing and the lack of rate flexibility have cost consumers billions of dollars in higher prices. There is considerable evidence that rates are significantly higher today than they would be if set by the competitive marketplace.

—The Director of the Council on Wage and Price Stability has stated that consumers pay some $5 billion a year in extra costs because of the current regulatory system.

—Rates for the transportation of exempt agricultural commodities are lower than they would be under regulation. A representative of the American Farm Bureau Federation has estimated that: ". . . if agriculture had been saddled with a totally regulated motor carrier and barge transportation system for the past 35 years, the cost of transportation, which now accounts for nearly 10% of the nation's food bill, *would be a third greater.*"

—In the mid-1950's, fresh and frozen dressed poultry and frozen fruits and vegetables were declared exempt from ICC regulation. The U.S. Department of Agriculture estimates that as a result of deregulation, trucking rates dropped substantially for those commodities.

—A recent study concludes that unregulated household mover rates within Maryland are 27–87% lower than rates for comparable interstate shipments.

—The trucking industry is highly profitable. Last year the largest eight trucking companies earned an average return on equity of 28.8%. These returns far exceed the average 14% return on equity earned by unregulated manufacturing companies, as well as the return on equity for the top firms in any other major industry.

Because regulation permits such high profits and makes operating certificates so scarce, ICC certificates are bought and sold for enormous sums. When Associated Transport went bankrupt in 1976, the operating rights carried on its balance sheet at $976,000 sold for over $20 million. Eastern Freightway, Inc., recently sold rights for about $3.8 million. Ultimately, of course, the buyer must recover the certificate's price from its customers in the form of higher prices.

The bill I propose:

—repeals the special antitrust immunity, making the trucking industry subject to the same antitrust laws that govern most other industries. Although carriers would be prohibited from discussing and voting on rates, rate bureaus may continue to publish rates. Carriers may also continue to interline and set joint line rates so that a shipper can pay one rate even though more than one carrier hauls the shipment to its final destination;

—encourages price competition by preventing the ICC from disapproving rates within a zone. For the first two years, carriers may lower their rates 20%, or raise their rates 5% per year, without ICC interference. At the end of two years, the ICC may not disapprove a rate reduction unless the rate would be predatory, and carriers may raise their rates 7% per year.

MERGERS

The bill requires the ICC to weigh possible anticompetitive effects of the proposed mergers.

The ICC may not approve or authorize any merger or acquisition if there is likely to be a substantial lessening of competition, creation of a monopoly, or a restraint of trade—unless the ICC finds that the anticompetitive effects of the transaction are outweighed by significant transportation needs that could not be satisfied by a reasonably available alternative having materially less anticompetitive effects.

After five years, the ICC's authority over mergers is eliminated, and jurisdiction is transferred to the FTC and the Department of Justice.

PRIVATE CARRIAGE

Under existing law, non-transportation companies (such as Montgomery Ward and Pet Milk) may transport their own goods free from ICC regulation. Although these "private carriers" are not directly regulated by the ICC, their operations have been severely restricted. As a result, private carriers are plagued with an unusually high rate of empty backhauls. The bill I propose would allow private carriers to apply for authority to carry non-company commodities, to provide transportation for corporate subsidiaries, and to permit private carriers to "trip-lease" with certificated carriers for single trips.

TRUCKLOAD TRANSPORTATION

"Truckload" motor carriers of property, who concentrate on hauling specialized commodities in full truckload lots, are already a relatively competitive sector of the trucking industry. The ICC has been more liberal in granting entry, and rates are often negotiated between the shipper and carrier. Truckload carriers compete with railroads and with private carriers. The Commission has recently announced plans to deregulate several types of these "special commodity" carriers of truckload traffic.

The bill builds on this trend toward less regulation of this segment of the industry. After two years, entry and rate controls over truckload transportation are removed.

After two years, any trucking company that meets safety, financial, and insurance requirements may haul truckload lots to any point. Rates are subject only to the antitrust law's prohibition on predatory pricing. "Truckload" transportation is defined as carriage (a) by specialized commodity carriers, as categorized by the Commission; (b) in lots over 10,000 pounds; or (c) in lots under a single bill of lading.

PROPOSAL FOR FURTHER CHANGE

The legislative changes I am proposing in this bill will make the trucking industry substantially more efficient, competitive, and responsive to consumers. It will also greatly reduce government interference with the economic decisions of trucking companies. However, there will remain a greater degree of regulation over trucking than exists for any industry of comparable size and competitive potential. After increased competition in this industry has had a chance to take hold, we should consider whether ICC regulation over the trucking industry should continue.

The bill requires the Secretary of Transportation, in cooperation with the ICC and the Department of Justice, to report to the Congress by January 1, 1983, on the effects of this legislation, and whether ICC regulation over the trucking industry should be continued.

Finally, I will soon send to Congress proposals which assure that consumers receive increased protection in the household moving industry.

IMPROVEMENT OF SERVICE TO SMALL COMMUNITIES

The bill I propose contains the following provisions that will improve trucking service to small communities:

1. The general policy statement that governs ICC decisions specifically directs the ICC to improve small town service. There is no such provision in existing law.

2. In determining whether applications for entry meet the "public convenience and necessity" standard, the ICC is directed to emphasize increased service to small communities. There is no such requirement in existing law.

3. Certificate restrictions are liberalized to improve service to small communities. For example, many certificates today specify the actual highway a trucking company must use. If a truck leaves the designated highway to serve a town off the beaten track, it is violating the law. The proposed legislation liberalizes these certificate restrictions, and makes it easier for trucking companies to obtain authority to serve small towns.

Many existing certificates do not allow trucks to make intermediate stops and serve towns between authorized points. These restrictions are particularly harmful to towns that are so small that trucking companies are unwilling to undergo the costly and often unsuccessful process of obtaining authority to serve them. The proposed legislation would remove these restrictions and permit carriers to stop at intermediate points immediately.

4. The program for phased route expansion without ICC approval will emphasize increased service to small communities. There is no such program under existing law.

5. The agricultural commodity and agricultural co-op exemptions are substantially broadened. This will give carriers serving small towns increased opportunities to fill their trucks with commodities they cannot now carry.

6. Increased pricing flexibility will allow lower backhaul rates to small communities.

7. Any carrier that meets financial, safety, and insurance requirements (a "fit, willing, and able" carrier) may enter a point which an authorized carrier no longer serves, or which a railroad aban-

dons. There is no such provision in existing law.

SAFETY

Reforms in safety enforcement are necessary because present levels of safety are unsatisfactory, and because authority to monitor safety practices and to sanction safety violations should be strengthened. These provisions are distinct from the economic reforms and are not made necessary by them.

The bill I propose places new emphasis on the existing fitness test which guarantees that all new entrants into the industry are safe. It also consolidates the safety authority in the Department of Transportation, and gives the Secretary of Transportation broader and more effective authority to deal with safety violations.

These reform proposals for the trucking industry, together with airline deregulation and my recently proposed rail reforms, fundamentally reshape Federal regulatory policies toward the transportation industries. These new policies recognize that our national interest in a more productive, fuel-efficient and responsive transportation system can be best achieved with less Federal regulation and more reliance on private initiative.

JIMMY CARTER

The White House,
June 21, 1979.

Vice President's Trip to the People's Republic of China

Statement by the President. June 21, 1979

At the invitation of the Government of the People's Republic of China, Vice President Walter F. Mondale will make an official visit to the People's Republic of China in August 1979.

The Vice President will be visiting the P.R.C. as my personal representative to continue the important process of high-level consultations on both bilateral and multilateral issues of major importance to the United States and the People's Republic of China. His visit will also permit a review of the broad range of significant developments in U.S.–P.R.C. relations that have taken place since normalization of relations on January 1, 1979.

Panama Canal Treaties

Statement on House of Representatives Approval of Legislation To Implement the Treaties. June 21, 1979

The House of Representatives today passed vital legislation providing for our management and defense of the Panama Canal. I deeply appreciate both the courage of all those Members who recognized the national interests by voting for this legislation and the effective leadership of Jim Wright, Jack Murphy, John Brademas, David Bowen, and the statesmanship of Ed Derwinski, who shepherded the bill to passage.

Improvements in the bill are still needed to make certain that the legislation is fully consistent with our commitments under the Panama Canal Treaty. We will be seeking those improvements as the legislative process continues. I am looking forward to early Senate action and a quick conference that will ensure our ability to maintain and defend the canal.

NOTE: Press Secretary Jody Powell read the statement at 3:05 p.m. to reporters assembled in the Briefing Room at the White House.

Also included in the press release is a question-and-answer session with reporters.

Alaska Natural Gas Transportation System

Executive Order 12142. June 21, 1979

By the authority vested in me as President by the Constitution and laws of the United States of America, including Section 301 of Title 3 of the United States Code and Sections 201 and 205 of Reorganization Plan No. 1 of 1979, it is hereby ordered as follows:

1–101. Reorganization Plan No. 1 of 1979, not having been disapproved by Congress (S. Res. 126, 125 Cong. Rec. S 6563–64 (May 23, 1979); H. Res. 199, 125 Cong. Rec. H 3950–51 (May 31, 1979)), shall be effective on July 1, 1979.

1–102. In accord with Section 201 of that Plan, there is hereby established the Executive Policy Board for the system for the transportation of Alaska natural gas ("the System") as such system is defined in the Alaska Natural Gas Transportation Act of 1976 (15 U.S.C. 719 *et seq.*).

1–103. The Board shall consist of the Secretaries of the Departments of Agriculture, Energy, Labor, Transportation, and the Interior, the Administrator of the Environmental Protection Agency, the Chief of Engineers of the United States Army, and the Chairman of the Federal Energy Regulatory Commission. Additional members may be elected to the Board by vote of a majority of the members. The Board will by majority vote elect a Chairman to serve for a one-year term.

1–104. The Board shall perform the following functions:

(a) Advise the Federal Inspector for the Alaska Natural Gas Transportation System (the "Federal Inspector") established by Reorganization Plan No. 1 of 1979, on policy issues in accord with applicable law and existing Departmental or Agency policies.

(b) Provide advice, through the Federal Inspector, to the officers representing and exercising the functions of the Federal Departments and Agencies that concern the System ("Agency Authorized Officers").

(c) Advise the Federal Inspector and the Agency Authorized Officers on matters concerning enforcement actions.

(d) At least every six months, assess the progress made and problems encountered in constructing the System and make necessary recommendations to the Federal Inspector.

1–105. The Federal Inspector shall keep the Board informed of the progress made and problems encountered in the course of construction of the System.

1–106. Whenever the Federal Inspector determines that implementation of Departmental or Agency enforcement policies and procedures would require action inconsistent with Section 9 of the Alaska Natural Gas Transportation Act of 1976, the Federal Inspector shall issue a written statement of such determination including a complete factual and legal basis for the determination. A copy of each statement shall be forwarded promptly to the Board and made available to the public by the Federal Inspector.

1–107. After written notice of a proposed enforcement action is given by the Federal Inspector, the Federal Inspector will be subject to the rules of procedure for *ex parte* contacts as reflected in the guidelines and policies of Departments and Agencies from which the specific enforcement authority is transferred.

1–108. The Federal Inspector and all employees of the Office of the Federal Inspector shall be subject to the provisions of Executive Order No. 11222, concerning standards of conduct for Federal employees. The Federal Inspector shall issue standards of conduct, pursuant to the

Order, for the Office of the Federal Inspector.

1–109. To the extent permitted by law, each Department and Agency shall cooperate with and furnish necessary information and assistance to the Board in the performance of its functions.

1–110. This Order shall be effective on July 1, 1979.

JIMMY CARTER

The White House,
June 21, 1979.

[Filed with the Office of the Federal Register, 9:13 a.m., June 22, 1979]

Independence Day, 1979

Message of the President. June 21, 1979

We celebrate the Fourth of July as our Independence Day, not because we had achieved our independence on that day— years of suffering and sacrifice would pass before that was finally achieved— but because it was the day when we declared our irrevocable will for freedom.

Freedom and justice cannot be secured permanently. They must be constantly re-won in a thousand daily battles. The great heritage we received from our forefathers was not a perfected nation, but the dream of a nation dedicated to the fulfillment of the highest human ideals and aspirations and the evidence of their will and progress in making that dream a reality.

That dream has caught fire in the hearts of succeeding generations of Americans and in the hearts of people throughout the world. It is the strength behind our power, the force that unites and energizes us in the continuing struggle to bring freedom and justice to all people.

JIMMY CARTER

Department of the Air Force

Nomination of Hans M. Mark To Be Secretary. June 21, 1979

The President today announced that he will nominate Hans M. Mark, of Alexandria, Va., to be Secretary of the Air Force. He would replace John C. Stetson, who has resigned. Mark is currently Under Secretary of the Air Force.

He was born June 17, 1929, in Mannheim, Germany. He came to the United States in 1940 and became a citizen in 1945. He received an A.B. in physics from the University of California at Berkeley in 1951 and a Ph. D. in physics from Massachusetts Institute of Technology in 1954.

In 1954–55 Mark was a research associate at M.I.T. and acting head of the Neutron Physics Group at the Laboratory for Nuclear Science there. In 1955–56 he was a research physicist at the University of California at Berkeley, and from 1956 to 1958, he did research at the university's Lawrence Radiation Laboratory. In 1957–58 he was also a lecturer in physics at Berkeley.

From 1958 to 1960, Mark was an assistant professor of physics at M.I.T. From 1960 to 1969, he was at Berkeley, serving on the faculty in nuclear engineering, doing research at the Lawrence Radiation Laboratory, and administering the Berkeley research reactor.

From 1969 until his appointment as Under Secretary in 1977, Mark was Director of the Ames Research Center of the National Aeronautics and Space Administration. He also served as a lecturer in applied science at the University of California at Davis from 1969 to 1973 and as a consulting professor of engineering at Stanford University from 1973 to 1977.

Department of the Air Force

Nomination of Antonia Handler Chayes To Be Under Secretary. June 21, 1979

The President today announced that he will nominate Antonia Handler Chayes, of Cambridge, Mass., to be Under Secretary of the Air Force. She would replace Hans M. Mark, who is being nominated today to be Secretary of the Air Force. Chayes is currently Assistant Secretary of the Air Force for Manpower and Reserve Affairs.

She was born July 21, 1929, in New York City. She received a B.A. from Radcliffe College in 1949 and an LL.B. from George Washington University Law School in 1953.

From 1959 to 1961, Chayes was executive assistant to the dean of Harvard Law School, and from 1961 to 1962, she worked on the White House staff drafting correspondence. She was a consultant to a Baltimore community development firm in 1963 and 1964 and a social science adviser to the National Institute of Mental Health in 1964 and 1965.

From 1966 to 1968, Chayes was director of education and urban development for the Model Cities Administration's Action for Boston Community Development program. She was dean of Tufts University's Jackson College from 1968 to 1970 and an associate professor of political science at Tufts from 1970 to 1972.

From 1972 to 1973, Chayes was law clerk to Judge Charles E. Wyzanski, Jr., of the U.S. District Court for the District of Massachusetts. She was a partner in the Boston firm of Csaplar & Bok from 1974 until her appointment in 1977 as Assistant Secretary of the Air Force.

Department of the Air Force

Nomination of Robert J. Hermann To Be an Assistant Secretary. June 21, 1979

The President today announced that he will nominate Robert J. Hermann, of Columbia, Md., to be Assistant Secretary of the Air Force. He would replace John J. Martin, who has resigned, and his area of responsibility would be research, development, and logistics. Hermann is currently Deputy Under Secretary of Defense for Communications, Command, Control, and Intelligence.

He was born April 6, 1933, in Sheldahl, Iowa. He received a B.S. (1954), M.S. (1959), and Ph. D. (1963) in electrical engineering from Iowa State University. He served in the U.S. Air Force from 1955 to 1957.

From 1959 to 1962, Hermann served with the National Security Agency in Europe as head of a research and development laboratory. After receiving his Ph. D. in 1963, Hermann served for a year as an electrical engineer in the NSA Office of Research and Equipment Development.

In 1964–65 Hermann was a staff assistant for special intelligence in the Office of the Director of Defense Research and Engineering. He returned to NSA from 1965 to 1975, and served as Chief of the Office of Systems Engineering (1965–69); Deputy Assistant Director of NSA for Science and Technology; Acting Chief of the Office of Systems Management; Chief of the Electronic Intelligence & Systems Engineering Group (1970–73); and Deputy Director of NSA for Research and Engineering (1973–75).

In 1975 Hermann was assigned as a special assistant to Gen. Alexander Haig, Supreme Allied Commander, Europe, for strategic warning and combat information systems. In 1977 he was appointed Deputy Assistant Secretary of Defense. In that capacity, he has represented the United States on the NATO Command and Control and Data Processing Committee and the NATO Joint Communications and Electronic Committee.

Comprehensive Test Ban Negotiations

Nomination of Herbert F. York for the Rank of Ambassador While Serving as U.S. Representative. June 21, 1979

The President today announced that he will nominate Herbert F. York, of La Jolla, Calif., for the rank of Ambassador during his assignment as the United States Representative to the Comprehensive Test Ban negotiations.

York was accorded the personal rank of Ambassador on February 1, 1979. The validity of personal ranks of Ambassador, accorded without Senate confirmation, is limited to 6 months.

York, 57, has been head of the U.S. Delegation to the CTB negotiations since earlier this year. Previously, he was a professor of physics at the University of California at San Diego. He has also served as Director of Defense Research and Engineering in the Office of the Secretary of Defense and as director of the Lawrence Radiation Laboratory, Livermore.

Mississippi River Commission

Nomination of Sam Epstein Angel To Be a Member. June 21, 1979

The President today announced that he will nominate Sam Epstein Angel, of Lake Village, Ark., to be a member of the Mississippi River Commission for a 9-year term. He would replace the late James Yancey.

Angel, 40, is manager of Sam Epstein Estate, Gin and Farm. He is a commissioner of the Southeast Arkansas Levee District and the Chicot County Watershed District. He also serves as a member of the Chicot County Rural Development Authority.

Independent Truckers' Strikes

Remarks to Reporters on the Situation. June 21, 1979

In recent days, we've seen truckers' strikes throughout our Nation. We all know that independent truckers do play a vital role in the economy of our country, and my administration is trying to work with them to meet their legitimate grievances. Some action has already been announced. Other decisions will be announced soon. At that time, the striking truckers should go back to work and end the interruption of delivery of food and fuel and other goods to American citizens.

Most important, however, I want to stress in the strongest possible terms that violence and lawlessness will not be tolerated under any circumstances. Murder, vandalism, and physical intimidation are criminal acts, and they will be treated as such.

I've asked for and received from Director William Webster of the Federal Bureau of Investigation a report on the death of the young trucker in Alabama. And I have also instructed the FBI to provide all appropriate assistance for local and State officials who are enforcing the law and controlling any violence on or near the Nation's highways.

The full resources of the Department of Justice will be used to ensure that order is preserved, that violators are apprehended, and that individual rights of American citizens are protected. As necessary, the Federal Government will also coordinate the protection of truckdrivers who are moving in interstate commerce. We will do whatever is necessary to see that those truckers who want to work are not threatened by either violence or intimidation.

I want to commend the Governors who have acted swiftly and effectively to stop violence in their States. They have my full support and the support of the Federal Government for their efforts to put an immediate end to strike-related violence and lawlessness.

Director Webster is here with me, and he will be glad to answer any questions that you might have about how the Federal Government is and will cooperate with local and State officials in eliminating violence in this strike, and he's here now for that purpose.

NOTE: The President spoke at 4:03 p.m. in the Briefing Room at the White House.

Defense Sales to Barbados

Memorandum From the President.
June 21, 1979

Presidential Determination No. 79–11

Memorandum for the Secretary of State

Subject: Eligibility of Barbados to Make Purchases of Defense Articles and Defense Services Under the Arms Export Control Act

Pursuant to the authority vested in me by Section 3(a)(1) of the Arms Export Control Act, I hereby find that the sale of defense articles and defense services to the Government of Barbados will strengthen the security of the United States and promote world peace.

You are directed on my behalf to report this finding to the Congress.

This finding, which amends Presidential Determination No. 73–10 of January 2, 1973 (38 FR 7211), as amended by Presidential Determinations No. 73–12 of April 26, 1973 (38 FR 12799), No. 74–9 of December 13, 1973 (39 FR 3537), No. 75–2 of October 29, 1974 (39 FR 39863), No. 75–21 of May 20, 1975 (40 FR 24889), No. 76–1 of August 5, 1975 (40 FR 37205), No. 76–11 of March 25, 1976 (41 FR 14163), No. 76–12 of April 14, 1976 (41 FR 18281), No. 77–5 of November 5, 1976 (41 FR 50625), No. 77–17 of August 1, 1977 (42 FR 40169), and No. 77–20 of September 1, 1977 (42 FR 48867), and No. 79–5 of February 6, 1979 (44 FR 12153), shall be published in the FEDERAL REGISTER.

JIMMY CARTER

[Filed with the Office of the Federal Register, 4:27 p.m. June 28, 1979]

JUSTIFICATION FOR PRESIDENTIAL DETERMINATION ON THE ELIGIBILITY OF BARBADOS TO MAKE PURCHASES OF DEFENSE ARTICLES AND DEFENSE SERVICES UNDER THE ARMS EXPORT CONTROL ACT

Section 3(a)(1) of the Arms Export Control Act requires, as a condition of eligibility for the purchase of defense articles and defense services from the United States under the Act, that the President find that the furnishing of defense articles and services to the country concerned "will strengthen the security of the United States and promote world peace."

Presidential Determination No. 73–10, dated January 2, 1973, established a consolidated list of countries eligible to make purchases of defense articles and services on a Foreign Military Sales (FMS) basis under the Arms Export Control Act. Because of changing international circumstances, new countries are added to this list from time to time. It is my judgment that circumstances now merit the addition of Barbados to the list of countries so eligible.

The island of Barbados lies in the southeast approach to the Caribbean, an area of strategic importance to the U.S. Stability in this area will promote world peace. The small Barbados defense force is inadequately equipped to patrol its coast and territorial waters against smugglers, narcotics traffickers, and arms runners. The states of the area have come to feel increasingly vulnerable, and they have discussed regional security cooperation, including the possibility of forming a regional coast guard. My finding, enabling Barbados to purchase defense articles and services under the Arms Export Control Act, will enable the United States to respond quickly to justified requests for support for modest national or regional defense forces. In view of the limitations of section 4 of the Act on the purposes for which FMS sales may be made, no sale would be made to or for the police or other forces engaged in ongoing civil law enforcement.

I have concluded that the provision of modest amounts of defense articles to Barbados would be in the interest of the United States and will reduce the potential for instability in an area of particular concern to this country. For the foregoing reasons, I have found that the sale under the Act of defense articles and defense services to Barbados will strengthen the security of the United States and promote world peace.

NOTE: The texts of the memorandum and the justification were released on June 22.

Amendments to the Ethics in Government Act of 1978

Statement on Signing S. 869 Into Law.
June 22, 1979

I have signed into law S. 869, a bill amending title V of the Ethics in Government Act of 1978, which strengthened safeguards against abuse of the "revolving door" between high-level Federal service and subsequent employment on behalf of private interests. As amended, these new safeguards will be effective July 1, 1979.

Since the enactment of the law, which I proposed in March 1977, the Office of Government Ethics was established in the Office of Personnel Management and developed regulations to implement the postemployment restrictions. During the course of its work, the operation of title V was examined very closely, and it was determined by the Office of Government Ethics and the Department of Justice, in conjunction with other executive agencies, that a literal reading of the law allowed for certain unintended results and might have unnecessarily restrictive effects in certain cases. I therefore decided to support adjustments in the language of the act to address these problems.

The process is now completed, and I am pleased to say that the amendments, together with the regulations which have been issued, have produced a balanced, effective package.

The amendments preserve the central protections of the law against misuse of influence acquired through public service while eliminating some ambiguities in the statute and providing reasonable adjustments where the effects of the original provisions might have been undesirable.

Enactment of this legislation would not have been possible without the outstanding leadership of Congressman George Danielson, floor manager of the bill in the House, and Senator Abe Ribicoff, floor manager in the Senate. The legislation received excellent cooperation on both sides of the aisle in the House and the Senate.

Congress responded promptly on my recommendation to clarify and refine the act, and because the Attorney General and the Office of Government Ethics have implemented the law with vigor and common sense, the foundation has been laid for a sound program fulfilling my commitment to assure that Federal officials are of the highest professional caliber and meet the highest standards of integrity, openness, and efficiency.

NOTE: As enacted, S. 869 is Public Law 96–28, approved June 22.

United States Ambassador to Uruguay

Nomination of Lyle Franklin Lane.
June 22, 1979

The President today announced that he will nominate Lyle Franklin Lane, of Tacoma, Wash., to be Ambassador Extraordinary and Plenipotentiary of the United States to Uruguay. He would replace Lawrence A. Pezzullo, who has been appointed Ambassador to Nicaragua. Lane has been principal officer of the United States Interest Section in Havana since 1977.

He was born September 19, 1926, in Tacoma, Wash. He received a B.A. from the University of Washington in 1950 and an M.S. from George Washington University in 1969. He served in the U.S. Army from 1946 to 1947.

Lane joined the State Department in 1950 as an organizational methods examiner, and then served as consular and administrative officer in Guayaquil, then political officer in Madrid. From 1959 to 1961, he was international relations officer at the State Department.

In 1961–62 Lane took advanced economic studies at Berkeley, and from 1962 to 1966, he was principal officer in Cebu. From 1966 to 1968, he was detailed to AID in Guatemala. In 1968–69 he attended the National War College.

From 1969 to 1971, Lane was administrative officer in the Bureau of Inter-American Affairs at State. From 1971 to 1972, he was Deputy Director, then Acting Director of the National Security Council Interdepartmental Group for Inter-American Affairs. From 1972 to 1973, he was Deputy Executive Director of the Office of Management, Bureau of Inter-American Affairs.

From 1973 to 1976, Lane was Deputy Chief of Mission in San José. From 1976 to 1977, he was Deputy Chief of Mission in Lima.

Relations With the People on Taiwan

Executive Order 12143.   June 22, 1979

MAINTAINING UNOFFICIAL RELATIONS
WITH THE PEOPLE ON TAIWAN

In light of the recognition of the People's Republic of China by the United States of America as the sole legal government of China, and by the authority vested in me as President of the United States of America, by the Taiwan Relations Act (Public Law 96–8, 93 Stat. 14, 22 U.S.C. 3301 *et seq.,* hereinafter referred to as "the Act"), and Section 301 of Title 3 of the United States Code, in order to facilitate the maintenance of commercial, cultural and other relations between the people of the United States and the people on Taiwan without official representation or diplomatic relations, it is hereby ordered as follows:

1–1. *Delegation and Reservation of Functions.*

1–101. Exclusive of the functions otherwise delegated, or reserved to the President, by this Order, there are delegated to the Secretary of State all functions conferred upon the President by the Act. In carrying out these functions, the Secretary of State shall consult with other departments and agencies as appropriate.

1–102. There are delegated to the Director of the Office of Personnel Management the functions conferred upon the President by paragraphs (1) and (2) of Section 11(a) of the Act. These functions shall be exercised in consultation with the Secretary of State.

1–103. There are reserved to the President the functions conferred upon the President by Section 3, Section 7(a)(3), and the second sentence of Section 9(b), and the determination specified in Section 10(a) of the Act.

1–2. *Specification of Laws and Determinations.*

1–201. Pursuant to Section 7(a) of the Act, I specify the following provisions of law:

(a) Section 4082 of the Revised Statutes (22 U.S.C. 1172);

(b) Section 1707 of the Revised Statutes (22 U.S.C. 1173);

(c) Section 1708 of the Revised Statutes (22 U.S.C. 1174);

(d) Section 1709 of the Revised Statutes, as amended (22 U.S.C. 1175);

(e) Section 1710 of the Revised Statutes, as amended (22 U.S.C. 1176);

(f) Section 1711 of the Revised Statutes, as amended (22 U.S.C. 1177);

(g) Section 1718 of the Revised Statutes (22 U.S.C. 1185); and

(h) Section 7 of the Act of April 5, 1906 (22 U.S.C. 1195).

1–202. Pursuant to Section 9(b) of the Act, and in furtherance of the purposes of the Act, the procurement of services may be effected without regard to the following provisions of law and limitations of authority:

(a) Section 3648 of the Revised Statutes, as amended (31 U.S.C. 529);

(b) Section 9 of the Act of June 30, 1906 (31 U.S.C. 627), and Sections 3679 and 3732 of the Revised Statutes (31 U.S.C. 665; 41 U.S.C. 11), to the extent necessary to permit the indemnification of contractors against unusually hazardous risks, as defined in Institute contracts, consistent, to the extent practicable, with regulations prescribed by the Department of Defense pursuant to the provisions of the Act of August 28, 1958 (50 U.S.C. 1431 *et seq.*), and Executive Order No. 10789 of November 14, 1958, as amended;

(c) Section 3709 of the Revised Statutes and Section 302 of the Federal Property and Administrative Services Act of 1949 (41 U.S.C. 5, 252);

(d) Section 3710 of the Revised Statutes (41 U.S.C. 8);

(e) Section 2 of Title III of the Act of March 3, 1933 (41 U.S.C. 10a);

(f) Section 3735 of the Revised Statutes (41 U.S.C. 13);

(g) Section 304(b) of the Federal Property and Administrative Services Act of 1949 (41 U.S.C. 254(b)), so as to permit the payment of fees in excess of the prescribed fee limitations, but nothing herein shall be construed as authorizing the use of the cost-plus-a-percentage-of-cost system of contracting;

(h) Section 305 of the Federal Property and Administrative Services Act of 1949 (41 U.S.C. 255);

(i) Sections 2 through 16 of the Contract Disputes Act of 1978 (41 U.S.C. 601–613);

(j) Sections 2304, 2305 and 2306(a) through (f) of Title 10 of the United States Code, but nothing herein shall be construed as authorizing the use of the cost-plus-a-percentage-of-cost system of contracting; and

(k) Section 719 of the Defense Production Act of 1950 (50 U.S.C. App. 2168).

1–203. (a) With respect to cost-type contracts with the American Institute in Taiwan under which no fee is charged or paid, amendments and modifications of such contracts may be made with or without consideration and may be utilized to accomplish the same things as any original contract could have accomplished, irrespective of the time or circumstances of the making, or the form of the contract amended or modified, or of the amending or modifying contract and irrespective of rights which may have accrued under the contract or the amendments or modifications thereof.

(b) With respect to contracts heretofore or hereafter made under the Act, other than those described in subsection (a) of this Section, amendments and modifications of such contracts may be made with or without consideration and may be utilized to accomplish the same things as any original contract could have accomplished, irrespective of the time or circumstances of the making, or the form of the contract amended or modified, or of the amending or modifying contract, and irrespective of rights which may have accrued under the contract or the amendments or modifications thereof, if

the Secretary of State determines in each case that such action is necessary to protect the foreign policy interests of the United States.

1–204. Pursuant to Section 10(a) of the Act, the Coordination Council for North American Affairs is determined to be the unofficial instrumentality established by the people on Taiwan having the necessary authority under the laws applied by the people on Taiwan to provide assurances and take other actions on behalf of Taiwan in accordance with the Act.

1–3. *President's Memorandum of December 30, 1978.*

1–301. This Order supersedes my memorandum of December 30, 1978 for all departments and agencies entitled "Relations With the People on Taiwan" (44 FR 1075). Agreements and arrangements referred to in paragraph (B) of that memorandum shall continue in force and shall be performed in accordance with the Act and this Order.

JIMMY CARTER

The White House,
June 22, 1979.

[Filed with the Office of the Federal Register,
4:35 p.m., June 22, 1979]

Ambassador at Large and Coordinator for Mexican Affairs

Nomination of Robert Krueger.
June 22, 1979

The President today announced that he will nominate Robert Krueger, of New Braunfels, Tex., to be Ambassador at Large and Coordinator for Mexican Affairs. Krueger is a former U.S. Representative from the 21st District of Texas.

He was born September 19, 1935, in New Braunfels, Tex. He received a B.S. from Southern Methodist University in

1957, an M.A. from Duke University in 1958, and a B.Litt. (1963) and D. Phil. (1965) from Oxford University.

From 1961 to 1973, Krueger was a professor and dean of the College of Arts and Sciences at Duke University. From 1973 to 1975, he was chairman of the board of Comal Hosiery Mills. From 1975 to 1979, he was U.S. Representative from the 21st District. Since leaving the Congress, he has been a businessman and rancher in New Braunfels.

Independent Truckers' Strikes

White House Statement. June 22, 1979

Over the past few days the actions of the Nation's independent truckers have had a serious impact on the country's transportation system. The White House staff has met with a number of trucking industry representatives to learn firsthand of their concerns and has kept the President closely informed of developments. The truckers have many legitimate concerns. Some can be remedied speedily, some will take time and much hard work to improve.

The key problems that face the truckers are the same as those that face all of us: too little fuel at too high price. Because of OPEC price increases and the cutback in Iranian oil production, our Nation's long-term energy problem has become a critical shortage of diesel fuel both for truckers and for other transportation industries.

While the steps the administration intends to take to address the truckers concerns are important, the President wishes to underscore the statement he made yesterday deploring the acts of violence that have accompanied the truckers' strike.

None of the problems faced by the independents can justify the lawlessness that has occurred in some parts of the country. We will not tolerate shootings, vandalism, or violations of individual rights. Law enforcement is primarily a State responsibility, but the Federal Government will provide every assistance to the States to help them preserve order.

To help increase supplies of diesel fuel, a number of steps have already been taken. Two weeks ago, incentive entitlement payments for importation of middle distillates, which includes diesel, were increased by $5 per barrel. Since then these imports have increased substantially. In addition, every effort is being made to increase refinery output of diesel, gasoline, and other products. With rising crude oil imports, additional supplies of diesel and gasoline should be refined as quickly as possible. This administration will not tolerate any withholding of available supplies. A major audit of the Nation's refineries is now underway as part of the administration's efforts to ensure maximum refinery utilization.

Besides increasing overall diesel supplies, we must ensure that available fuel is distributed where it is most needed.

To accomplish this the Department of Energy recently instituted a special program, Special Rule #9, to provide farmers and others with 100 percent of their needs. This allocation was based on the critical importance of timely planting to ensure adequate national food supplies. Because of weather problems, farmers were far behind in their planting schedules earlier this year. Each day of delay due to fuel shortages could have cost the Nation millions of dollars in lower crop yields and higher food prices.

As Secretary Bergland indicated this morning, Rule #9 has succeeded well in solving that potential problem. Despite weather problems, planting is now complete in most areas. The danger of severe crop loss is now past.

But the special allocation to farmers has forced other diesel users to cut back sharply. Truckers, rail and barge companies, and other users have experienced severe reductions.

Because Rule #9 has succeeded in its initial purpose, and may now be creating significant supply dislocations, Secretary Schlesinger, after consultation with Secretary Bergland and the President, has suspended Rule #9 effective immediately. This action will allow the normal distribution system for diesel distribution to operate. This does not mean that farmers will lack supplies necessary for their operations. Farmers' needs continue to be critical, and the President intends to ensure that they will be adequately supplied. To ensure that farmers' needs are provided for, the President has asked Secretary Bergland, in coordination with Secretary Schlesinger, to monitor the farm situation on a daily basis and to report to him immediately if the situation changes.

The President also urges the Governors to use their State set-aside allocations to protect farmers against fuel shortages. We will continue to monitor the situation closely so that we can make adjustments later if necessary.

In suspending Rule #9 only one allocation has been retained. This involves the priority for mass transit operations. During a period of shortages of both gasoline and diesel fuel it would be self-defeating to allow diesel shortages to divert commuters from energy-efficient buses to automobiles. Because transit utilizes only 2 percent of the Nation's diesel, this allocation should not significantly impact on other diesel users.

Increased supplies and more efficient distribution should do much to help ease supply shortages and to slow the recent price spiral.

To help ease the price squeeze caused by rising fuel prices, the ICC last week implemented a new system to allow an automatic, 100-percent pass-through of fuel cost increases. This system will provide independent truckers leasing to regulated carriers with significant immediate revenue increases. This index will be adjusted weekly to cover any further price increases, and the surcharge *must* be passed through to independent operators. The President fully supports this change in ICC procedures which will benefit the majority of independent truckers.

For exempt haulers who are not regulated by the ICC, this fuel price surcharge published by the ICC should form one basis for negotiations concerning a fair price for hauling exempt commodities. In addition to this standard the President has asked the Departments of Agriculture and Transportation, working with the ICC, to develop plans for publishing an index of prices charged for hauling various exempt commodities. Updated in a timely fashion, this index could provide another basis for negotiations between brokers and exempt haulers, helping to ensure fair prices.

In addition to the critical issues of price and availability of diesel fuel, the independent truckers have raised a number of other concerns.

For many independents one of the most aggravating problems is the wide variety of taxes, permits, and standards under which they must operate in the different States. The President will immediately call together a number of the Nation's Governors to discuss with them ways in which we can bring about greater uniformity, simplicity, and reciprocity in State and Federal regulation and taxation of the trucking industry.

At the Federal level the President has asked Secretary Adams to speed up the implementation of several programs to develop systems to allow truckers to stop only once during any one trip to file fuel, registration, and licensing fees. This program would allow for computerized figuring of State tax shares and would allow truckers to make only one payment, greatly simplifying the paperwork and administrative burdens that independent operators must deal with. The program will be implemented in six States by December of 1980.

One aspect of the differing State regulatory requirements is the variation in allowable truck weights and lengths permitted on the Nation's highways. Although Federal law sets maximum truck weights, it allows the States the right to set limits below these levels. Obviously in each State the question of truck weights involves complex issues of road capacity, cost allocation, and safety. The President believes that the States should continue to make the final judgments on these difficult issues.

However, there could be substantial benefits to the Nation's transportation system if allowable truck weights were standardized nationwide. The President urges the Governors and State legislatures of those States below the Federal minimum to consider these potential benefits and to review carefully their decisions on truck weight and size limits in light of the current situation.

There are other problems that plague the Nation's truckers. For example, there are many reports of illegal and unfair overcharges of truckers at loading and unloading docks. One approach to the problem has been suggested by Congressman

Neal Smith of Iowa in his bill, H.R. 753. This bill, or a measure designed to accomplish its goals, deserves early and favorable consideration by the Congress and has the administration's full support.

Also, as part of the Department of Transportation's program to develop a "new automobile," DOT will support research to improve diesel engine efficiency.

On these and other longer term problems the President is prepared to work with the Congress, the Governors, and the truckers to devise sound solutions. The Federal Government in Washington cannot solve every problem with a law or a ruling. But working together we can accomplish a great deal.

While this work goes forward, all independent truckers should return to work to provide the Nation with vitally needed transportation services. Those who choose not to work should know that unlawful interference with the rights of their fellow citizens will not be tolerated.

White House Management Task Force on Energy Shortages

Announcement of Establishment of the Task Force. June 22, 1979

The President has established a White House Management Task Force on Energy Shortages. The Task Force will be chaired by Jack Watson, Assistant to the President for Intergovernmental Affairs and Secretary to the Cabinet, and directed by Gene Eidenberg, Deputy Assistant to the President for Intergovernmental Affairs and Deputy Secretary to the Cabinet, of the White House staff.

Working with representatives of the appropriate departments and White House staff, the Task Force will be the central point for managing the Federal

Government's response to various energy shortage problems as they occur.

The President has said repeatedly that the energy problems facing the Nation will not be easily alleviated. While the Nation embarks on initiatives to develop alternative and increased domestic energy supplies, the U.S. will continue to be dependent on imported oil. The President believes it is essential that there be a governmentwide mechanism charged with anticipating and responding to the periodic energy shortages such as the Nation is presently experiencing.

It is clear that gasoline, diesel, and home heating supplies cannot be managed separately. It is equally clear that the special problems and needs of American agriculture, the elderly, the poor, independent truckers, mass transit riders, and many others cannot be handled separately from each other. The Departments of Energy, Agriculture, Justice, Transportation, the Environmental Protection Agency, and a number of other key Federal agencies must work in full cooperation with each other, under Presidential direction. The White House Task Force will provide the necessary coordination and direction.

The Task Force's initial agenda will include the following topics:

—middle distillates and related problems (truckers, home heating fuel, agriculture, mass transit, etc.) ;
—gasoline (shortages, etc.) ;
—electrical power requirements and capabilities in major cities this summer;
—public information efforts to ensure the public is informed of current and prospective energy shortage situations in a timely way.

Because every level of government has a critical role to play in managing scarce energy resources, the Task Force will work closely with the Nation's Governors and other local elected officials.

Stuart Eizenstat will continue to chair the Energy Task Force, responsible for the development of energy policy options for the President.

Independent Truckers' Strikes
Letter to State Governors. June 22, 1979

I am writing to summarize for you the steps I have taken, or am prepared to take, to assist in assuring that the disruptions by independent truck operators in service is brought to an end. In reaching these decisions, my staff has consulted constantly and closely with the leadership and staff of the National Governors' Association and with individual governors all over the country.

The seriousness of the problem facing our nation's economy, if these disruptions continue, cannot be overstated. We must assure all our citizens that transport of agricultural and manufactured products will take place without harrassment, violence and other illegal acts. None of the problems faced by the independents can justify the lawlessness that has occurred in some parts of the country. Shootings, vandalism and murder are senseless criminal acts that serve only to undermine support for the truckers' demands. We will not tolerate lawbreaking or violations of individual rights in any form. Although law enforcement is primarily a state responsibility, the federal government will provide every assistance to the states to help them preserve order. I want to stress in the strongest possible terms that violence and lawlessness will not be tolerated under any circumstances. Murder, vandalism and physical intimidation are criminal acts, and they will be treated as such.

The full resources of the Department of Justice will be used to ensure that order is preserved, that violators are apprehended, and that individual rights of American citizens are protected. As necessary, the Federal government will also coordinate the protection of truck drivers who are moving in interstate commerce. We will do whatever is necessary to see that those truckers who want to work are not threatened by either violence or intimidation.

We all recognize that there are concerns that the independent owner-operators have which must be addressed. Those concerns fall into several categories. I want you to know what has been done in each area so that you will be fully informed as you respond to the situation in your state.

MANAGEMENT OF THE PROBLEM

Jack Watson and Gene Eidenberg of my staff will direct a special White House Management Task Force on Energy Shortages. This Task Force will be responsible for coordinating and directing the federal response to all energy shortage situations that develop. I have charged Messrs. Watson and Eidenberg with handling the federal response to the independent truckers' strike as a first priority.

THE PRICE OF DIESEL FUEL

As is true of all petroleum products, the price of diesel is going up. The independent owner-operators have had to absorb cost increases since January totalling more than 35%. On June 15th, the ICC issued a major change in its regulations that provides as follows:

—All owner-operators handling freight to compensate for escalating fuel costs for regulated carriers are given an automatic pass-through of fuel cost increases, irrespective of whether or not the regulated carrier for whom they work files for an increase in rates with the ICC.

—The surcharge amount guaranteed will be adjusted every week and will *be announced by noon on Tuesday.* It will be based on weekly surveys of fuel costs at truck stops throughout the country.

—The new system requires no paperwork by the owner-operator.

—Owner-operators can receive higher compensation for fuel costs based on higher surcharges if actual costs are higher, and the carrier for whom they operate files for higher rates. The higher surcharge would automatically pass through to the owner-operator. This tariff filing can be done on a simple expedited basis and ICC is ready to help the carrier in that publication action.

For exempt haulers who are not regulated by the ICC, this fuel price surcharge published by the ICC should form one basis for negotiations concerning a fair price for hauling exempt commodities. In addition to this standard, I have asked the Departments of Agriculture and Transportation, working with the ICC, to develop plans for an index of prices charged for hauling various exempt commodities. If updated in a timely fashion, such an index could provide another basis for negotiations between brokers and exempt haulers, helping to insure fair prices.

ALLOCATION PRIORITIES

The DOE is lifting Special Rule #9 effective immediately. As you know, Rule #9 was promulgated to insure that 100% of farmers' diesel needs were met during the spring planting season. Planting is now completed in all but a few scattered areas, and field work will be in those areas within the next few days.

The USDA will, of course, continue to monitor the needs of farmers throughout the nation who face different planting and harvesting cycles. Farmers' needs will be met through the regular supply channels. In suspending Rule #9, only the priority allocation for mass transit operations will be retained. During a period of shortages of both gasoline and diesel fuel, it would be self-defeating to allow diesel shortages to divert commuters from energy efficient buses to automobiles. Because transit utilizes only 2% of the nation's diesel, this allocation should not significantly impact on other diesel users.

STANDARD NATIONAL LENGTH AND WEIGHT
REQUIREMENTS

One particularly important aspect of differing state regulatory requirements is the inconsistency in allowable truck weights and lengths permitted on the nation's highways. Although federal law sets maximum truck weights, it allows the states the right to set limits below these levels. Obviously, in different states the question of truck weights involves complex issues of road capacity, cost allocation, and safety. I believe that the states should continue to make the final judgments on these difficult issues.

There would be, however, a substantial benefit to the nation's transportation system if allowable truck weights were standardized nationwide. I am urging all the governors and state legislatures to consider this potential benefit and to review carefully their decisions on truck weight and size limits in light of the current situation.

On these and other longer-term problems I intend to work with the Congress, the governors, the truckers, and others to devise sound solutions. The Federal government in Washington cannot solve every problem with a law or a ruling but working together we can accomplish a great deal.

While all these efforts go forward, I am calling upon independent truckers to continue to provide the nation with vitally needed transportation services. These are times for cooperation and sharing, not confrontation. Only by acting together with common sense and persistence will we be able to solve the nation's serious and pressing energy problems.

Sincerely,

JIMMY CARTER

Equal Employment Opportunity Commission

Executive Order 12144. June 22, 1979

TRANSFER OF CERTAIN EQUAL PAY AND
AGE DISCRIMINATION IN EMPLOYMENT
ENFORCEMENT FUNCTIONS

By the authority vested in me as President of the United States of America by the Constitution and laws of the United States, including Section 9 of Reorganization Plan No. 1 of 1978 (43 FR 19807), in order to effectuate the transfer of certain functions relating to the enforcement of equal pay and age discrimination in employment programs from the Department of Labor to the Equal Employment Opportunity Commission, it is hereby ordered as follows:

1–101. Sections 1 and 2 of Reorganization Plan No. 1 of 1978 (43 FR 19807) shall become effective on July 1, 1979, with the exception of the transfer of functions from the Civil Service Commission, already effective January 1, 1979 (Executive Order No. 12106).

1–102. The records, property, personnel and positions, and unexpended balances of appropriations or funds, available or to be made available, which relate to the functions transferred as provided in this Order are hereby transferred from the Department of Labor to the Equal Employment Opportunity Commission.

1–103. The Director of the Office of Management and Budget shall make such determinations, issue such Orders, and take all actions necessary or appropriate to effectuate the transfers provided in this Order, including the transfer of funds, records, property, and personnel.

1–104. This Order shall be effective July 1, 1979.

JIMMY CARTER

The White House,
   June 22, 1979.

[Filed with the Office of the Federal Register,
     10:08 a.m., June 25, 1979]

Captive Nations Week, 1979

Proclamation 4666. June 22, 1979

*By the President of the United States
           of America*

A Proclamation

Twenty years ago, by a joint resolution approved July 17, 1959 (73 Stat. 212), the Eighty-Sixth Congress authorized and requested the President to proclaim the third week in July of each year as Captive Nations Week.

However greatly the world has changed in the past generation, our country's fundamental faith in human freedom remains constant. Americans now, as at all times in our history, remain steadfast in our belief that liberty and national independence are among the universal birthrights of mankind.

Remembering our democratic heritage and our commitment to human rights, let us take this occasion to reaffirm our admiration for all the men and women around the world who are committed to the cause of freedom.

And mindful of our own rich and diverse heritage, let us express our compassion and respect for persons around the world still seeking the realization of these ideals in their own lands.

Now, THEREFORE, I, JIMMY CARTER, President of the United States of America, do hereby designate the week beginning July 15, 1979, as Captive Nations Week.

I invite the people of the United States to observe this week with appropriate ceremonies and activities and to reaffirm their dedication to the ideals which unite us and serve as inspiration to others.

IN WITNESS WHEREOF, I have hereunto set my hand this twenty-second day of June, in the year of our Lord nineteen hundred seventy-nine, and of the Independence of the United States of America the two hundred and third.

JIMMY CARTER

[Filed with the Office of the Federal Register,
   ·   10:09 a.m., June 25, 1979]

Digest of Other
White House Announcements

The following listing includes the President's public schedule and other items of general interest announced by the White House Press Office and not included elsewhere in this issue.

June 15

President Carter and President L. I. Brezhnev met with Austrian President Rudolph Kirchschläger and Chancellor Bruno Kreisky in the afternoon at the Hofburg, the imperial palace.

In the evening, President Carter and President Brezhnev were the guests of President Kirchschläger at a performance of the opera "The Abduction from the Seraglio" at the Staatsoper.

June 20

The President met at the White House with:

—Zbigniew Brzezinski, Assistant to the President for National Security Affairs;
—the Democratic congressional leadership;
—Frank B. Moore, Assistant to the President for Congressional Liaison, Danny C. Tate, Deputy Assistant for Congressional Liaison (House), and William H. Cable, Deputy Assistant for Congressional Liaison (Senate);
—Vice President Walter F. Mondale, Stansfield Turner, Director of Central Intelligence, Hamilton Jordan, Assistant to the President, and Dr. Brzezinski;
—Vice President Mondale.

June 21

The President met at the White House with:

—Vice President Mondale, Secretary of the Treasury W. Michael Blumenthal, Stuart E. Eizenstat, Assistant to the President for Domestic Affairs and Policy, James T. McIntyre, Jr., Director, and John P. White, Deputy Director, Office of Management and Budget, Charles L. Schultze, Chairman of the Council of Economic Advisers, Alfred E. Kahn, Ad-

visor to the President on Inflation and Chairman of the Council on Wage and Price Stability, and Barry P. Bosworth, Director of the Council on Wage and Price Stability;
—Dr. Brzezinski;
—Mr. Moore.

June 22

The President met at the White House with:

—Vice President Mondale, Secretary of State Cyrus R. Vance, Secretary of Defense Harold Brown, Dr. Brzezinski, and Mr. Jordan;
—Dr. Brzezinski;
—Mr. Moore;
—Ambassador Dick Clark, U.S. Coordinator for Refugee Affairs.

The White House announced that during the President's trip to East Asia, he has asked the Vice President to closely monitor developments in the energy area, including shortages and other short-term problems that arise, as well as the policy process and legislative actions. The Vice President will keep the President apprised of major developments and will continue the management of the energy situation on behalf of the President.

NOMINATIONS SUBMITTED TO THE SENATE

The following list does not include promotions of members of the Uniformed Services, nominations to the Service Academies, or nominations of Foreign Service officers.

Submitted June 21, 1979

HANS MICHAEL MARK, of Virginia, to be Secretary of the Air Force, vice John C. Stetson, resigned.

ANTONIA HANDLER CHAYES, of Massachusetts, to be Under Secretary of the Air Force, vice Hans Michael Mark.

ROBERT JAY HERMANN, of Maryland, to be an Assistant Secretary of the Air Force, vice John J. Martin, resigned.

NOMINATIONS—Continued

Submitted June 21—Continued

SAM EPSTEIN ANGEL, of Arkansas, to be a member of the Mississippi River Commission for a term of 9 years, vice James Williams Yancey, deceased.

HERBERT F. YORK, of California, for the rank of Ambassador during the tenure of his assignment as the United States Representative to the Comprehensive Test Ban negotiations.

Submitted June 22, 1979

LYLE FRANKLIN LANE, of Washington, a Foreign Service officer of Class one, to be Ambassador Extraordinary and Plenipotentiary of the United States of America to Uruguay.

ROBERT KRUEGER, of Texas, to be Ambassador at Large and Coordinator for Mexican Affairs.

CHECKLIST OF WHITE HOUSE PRESS RELEASES

The following listing contains releases of the White House Press Office which are not included in this issue.

Released June 14, 1979

Advance text: remarks on arrival in Vienna, Austria

Released June 16, 1979

News conference: on the U.S.-Soviet bilateral meetings—by Jody Powell, Press Secretary to the President, and Leonid Zamyatin, Chief, International Information Section, Central Committee, Communist Party of the Soviet Union

Advance text: toast at a working dinner at the U.S. Ambassador's residence

Released June 17, 1979

News conference: on the U.S.-Soviet bilateral meetings—by Mr. Powell and Mr. Zamyatin

Advance text: toast at a working dinner at the Soviet Embassy

Released June 18, 1979

Advance text: remarks at the signing ceremony for the strategic arms limitation treaty

News conference: on the strategic arms limitation treaty—by Mr. Powell, Ambassador Ralph Earle, chief negotiator for SALT II, Deputy Assistant Secretary of State Robert Barry, Mark Ramee, assistant to Ambassador Earle, and Jerrold Schecter, Associate Press Secretary

CHECKLIST—Continued

Released June 18—Continued

Advance text: address on the strategic arms limitation treaty before a joint session of Congress

Released June 19, 1979

News conference: on rural transportation initiatives—by Jack H. Watson, Jr., Assistant to the President for Intergovernmental Affairs, Secretary of Agriculture Bob Bergland, Secretary of Labor Ray Marshall, Secretary of Transportation Brock Adams, Assistant Secretary of Health, Education, and Welfare Arabella Martinez, Senator Patrick J. Leahy of Vermont, and Representative Gillis W. Long of Louisiana

Fact sheet: rural transportation initiatives

News conference: on Multilateral Trade Negotiations legislation—by Ambassador Robert S. Strauss, Special Representative for Trade Negotiations

Released June 20, 1979

News conference: on the President's message to Congress on solar energy—by Stuart E. Eizenstat, Assistant to the President for Domestic Affairs and Policy, and Secretary of Energy James R. Schlesinger

Fact sheet: the President's message to Congress on solar energy

Fact sheet: White House solar system

Released June 21, 1979

Statements: support for the proposed trucking deregulation legislation by government, business, and civic leaders

News conference: on the proposed trucking deregulation legislation—by Senators Howard W. Cannon of Nevada and Charles H. Percy of Illinois, Secretary Adams, and Alfred E. Kahn, Advisor to the President on Inflation

News conference: on the independent truckers' strikes—by William H. Webster, Director of the Federal Bureau of Investigation, and Philip Heymann, Assistant Attorney General, Department of Justice

Released June 22, 1979

News conference: on the U.S. Court of Appeals decision on Federal procurement policy measures as part of the anti-inflation program—by Mr. Kahn

CHECKLIST—Continued

Released June 22—Continued

News conference: on the independent truckers' strikes—by Mr. Eizenstat

---

ACTS APPROVED BY
THE PRESIDENT

Approved June 19, 1979

H.R. 3915_____ Public Law 96–24
An act to amend title IV of the Employee Retirement Income Security Act of 1974 to postpone for 10 months the date on which the corporation must pay benefits under terminated multiemployer plans.

S. 199_____ Public Law 96–25
Shipping Act Amendments of 1979.

ACTS APPROVED—Continued

Approved June 21, 1979

H.R. 3577_____ Public Law 96–26
An act to amend section 8 of the National Advisory Committee on Oceans and Atmosphere Act of 1977 to authorize appropriations to carry out the provisions of such Act for fiscal year 1980, and for other purposes.

H.R. 3879_____ Public Law 96–27
An act to authorize additional appropriations for the Temporary Commission on Financial Oversight of the District of Columbia, and for other purposes.

Approved June 22, 1979

S. 869_____ Public Law 96–28
An act to amend section 207 of title 18, United States Code.

INDEX

Aamodt, Gary Jay Northrop_____ 464
Aaron, David L_____ 327, 401, 467, 841
Abortion _____ 478
Abzug, Bella S_____ 26, 52
Accident Compensation and Insurance
Issues, Interagency Council on_____ 339
ACTION
   See also Peace Corps
   Associate Director_____ 666, 667
   Director _____ 878, 881
   National Voluntary Action Program__ 880
   Programs, organizational review_____ 396
Adams, Brock. *See* Transportation, Sec-
retary of

Addresses to the Nation

   Energy _____ 609
   SALT II treaty_____ 1087
   State of the Union_____ 103

Addresses and Remarks

   See also News Conferences
   Alaska public lands briefing_____ 773
   American Newspaper Publishers Asso-
ciation, New York, N.Y_____ 693
   American Retail Federation_____ 832
   Anti-inflation program briefing_____ 306
   Austria, President's visit_____ 1038,
                   1047–1049, 1079
   Awards and citations
      Conservationist of the Year Award_ 443
      Martin Luther King, Jr. Nonviolent
Peace Awards, Atlanta, Ga_____ 27
      National Caucus on the Black
Aged Living Legacy awards____ 317
      National Small Business Person of
the Year Award_____ 868
   Black Music Association_____ 1014
   Brown v. *Board of Education,* anniver-
sary observance_____ 883
   Budget message signing ceremony____ 95
   Cheyney State College, Pa., commence-
ment address_____ 908
   Cinco de Mayo celebration, Los An-
geles, Calif_____ 810
   Democratic Party activities
      Congressional campaign dinner____ 827
      Dinners and receptions
         Bedford, N.H_____ 714
         Des Moines, Iowa_____ 804
         Los Angeles, Calif_____ 372
         Manchester, N.H_____ 713
         Wausau, Wis_____ 567

Addresses and Remarks—**Continued**

   Democratic Party activities—Continued
      Jefferson-Jackson Day dinners
         Indianapolis, Ind_____ 988, 989
         Milwaukee, Wis_____ 573
         Richmond, Va_____ 630
      National Committee spring meeting_ 948
   Dubs, Adolph, memorial ceremony___ 295
   Egypt, President's trip_____ 395,
        405, 407, 410, 412, 415, 430
   Egypt-U.S. Business Council, dinner
honoring President Sadat_____ 546
   Egyptian-Israeli peace treaty signing
ceremonies _____ 517, 522
   Elk City, Okla., town meeting_____ 469
   Energy briefing_____ 862
   Federal civil justice system legisla-
tion _____ 340
   Federal employees, question-and-an-
swer session_____ 916
   Foreign leaders, U.S. visits
      Canada, Prime Minister Trudeau__ 379
      China, Vice Premier Deng_____ 189,
             192, 195, 198, 211
      Germany, Federal Republic of,
Chancellor Schmidt_____ 1004
      Japan, Prime Minister Ohira___ 761, 768
      Thailand, Prime Minister Kriang-
sak _____ 221, 225
   Gasoline shortages in California_____ 872
   Georgia General Assembly, Atlanta__ 297,
                      328
   Georgia Institute of Technology,
Atlanta _____ 300, 328
   Guadeloupe, meeting with Western
European leaders_____ 17
   Holocaust commemorative ceremony at
the Capitol_____ 684
   Hospital cost containment legislation_ 383,
                      603
   House-Senate bipartisan senior citizen
intern program_____ 837
   Interviews with the news media
      American Press Institute_____ 557
      Black media representatives_____ 33
      China, People's Republic of, Cen-
tral TV_____ 163
      Editors and news directors_____ 181,
         243, 621, 845, 901
      Egyptian television_____ 455
      Foreign Policy Conference for edi-
tors and broadcasters_____ 310

Addresses and Remarks—Continued

Interviews with the news media—Con.
Israeli television_____ 453
Japanese Broadcasting Corporation_ 1107
Mexican television_____ 235, 252
NBC News_____ 47, 985
United Press International News-
paper Advisory Board_____ 735
Iowa State Association of Counties,
Des Moines_____ 789
Israel, President's trip_____ 394,
415, 417, 419, 424, 428, 430
Law Day, White House reception___ 757
League of Women Voters of the
United States_____ 771
Mental health systems legislation_____ 857
Mexico, President's trip_____ 272,
273, 277, 280, 281, 284
Middle East peace talks, role of Robert
Strauss _____ 687
Moscone, George, memorial tribute,
San Francisco, Calif_____ 807
National Academy of Sciences_____ 677
National Association for Equal Oppor-
tunity in Higher Education_____ 742
National Cable Television Association_ 932
National Conference of Christians and
Jews _____ 969
National Governors' Association_____ 330
National health plan_____ 1024
National prayer breakfast_____ 58
Placita de Dolores dedication, Los An-
geles, Calif_____ 809
Portsmouth, N.H., town meeting_____ 699
President's Commission on the Acci-
dent at Three Mile Island
Establishment _____ 657
Members, meeting with the Presi-
dent _____ 691
President's portrait unveiling, Atlanta,
Ga _____ 296
Randolph, A. Philip, memorial serv-
ices _____ 996
Recording Industry Association of
America _____ 446
Sapelo Island, Ga., exchange with re-
porters _____ 669
Solar energy_____ 1095
Standby gasoline rationing plan_____ 840
Swearing-in ceremonies
President's Export Council, mem-
bers _____ 943
Small Business Conference Commis-
sion, members_____ 368
Three Mile Island nuclear plant, Pa.,
President's visit_____ 578
Truckers' strikes, independent_____ 1129
Trucking industry deregulation_____ 1114
United Food and Commercial Work-
ers International Union_____ 1008

Addresses and Remarks—Continued

Vice President's trip to Nordic coun-
tries and Netherlands_____ 639
Vienna Summit Meeting. *See* Vienna
Summit Meeting
Vietnam veterans reception_____ 972
White House Conference on Balanced
National Growth and Economic
Development _____ 65
White House Correspondents Associa-
tion _____ 743
Windfall profits tax and energy secu-
rity trust fund, message signing
ceremony _____ 728
Women's business enterprise_____ 887
Zablocki, Repr. Clement J., reception
in Milwaukee, Wis_____ 572
Zimbabwe-Rhodesia, trade sanctions_ 1012

Adler, Kurt _____ 807 ftn.
Administration. *See other part of title*
Administration, Office of_____ 3, 337, 824
Administrative Conference of the United
States _____ 494, 886
Admiralty Island National Monument,
Alaska _____ 855
Advertising Council_____ 786
Advertising lighting restrictions_____ 370
Advisor to the President on Inflation.
See Kahn, Alfred E.
Advisory Commission on Intergovern-
mental Relations_____ 463, 886, 1034
Advisory Committee on Federal Pay____ 64
Advisory committees, Federal_____ 463, 468
Afghanistan
Alignment with Soviet Union____ 316, 565
U.S. Ambassador_____ 271, 295
U.S. development and military assist-
ance programs_____ 310
AFL–CIO _____ 26, 732, 1008
Africa
See also specific country
International Exchange-of-Persons pro-
gram _____ 324
Presidential travel, possibility of_____ 39
U.S. relations_____ 39, 565, 1013
Africa, southern
Racial situation, U.S. policy_____ 39,
157, 160, 357, 576, 909, 910, 1013,
1050
Soviet and Cuban involvement___ 160, 1092
African Methodist Episcopal Zion
Church _____ 618
Agency. *See other part of title*
Aging, Administration on_____ 441
Agreement on International Carriage of
Perishable Foodstuffs_____ 83
Agricultural agreement with China_____ 204
Agricultural areas. *See* Rural areas
Agricultural commodities
See also Food; *specific commodity*
Transportation costs_____ 1122

Agricultural Development, International
  Fund for_____ 63
Agricultural research and development__ 533
Agricultural trade
  International negotiations and agree-
    ments _____ 6, 152, 438, 946
  U.S. and
    China _____ 152, 205
    Japan _____ 152, 767
    Mexico _____ 791
    OPEC nations_____ 802
  U.S. exports
    See also specific commodity
    Balance of trade, effect on_____ 152
    Embargoes _____ 570, 805
    Farm income, effect on_____ 152
    Levels increase_____ 66,
        152, 307, 534, 570, 802, 806, 924
    Revenues pay for farmers' energy
      use _____ 791
  U.S. imports
    Meat _____ 336
    Sugar, sirup, molasses_____ 153, 946
Agriculture, Department of
  See also specific constituent agencies
  Agricultural exchange agreement with
    China _____ 206
  Alaska Natural Gas Transportation
    System, transfer of functions_____ 595
  Budget deferrals_____ 200
  Deputy Secretary. *See* Agriculture, De-
    puty Secretary of
  Diesel fuel shortages_____ 945, 987, 1140
  Employees, President's assessment____ 924
  Gasohol research_____ 792
  General Counsel_____ 980, 984
  Inspector General_____ 366, 377
  National Forest System, roadless areas
    evaluation _____ 151, 671
  Rural development activities_____ 75, 77
  Secretary. *See* Agriculture, Secretary of
  Solar energy demonstration_____ 1105
  Trucking rates for transportation of
    exempt commodities___ 1122, 1136, 1139
  Under Secretary_____ 218
Agriculture, Deputy Secretary of (James
    H. Williams)
  Commodity   Credit   Corporation,
    Board of Directors member____ 110, 179
  Diesel fuel allocations for farmers___ 945
  Nomination _____ 42, 91
  President's Commission on Executive
    Exchange, member_____ 977
Agriculture, energy use and needs
  Development of alternatives to oil____ 534,
        792–794, 1102, 1103, 1105
  Fuel requirements guarantee_____ 791,
        803, 846, 937, 945, 951, 987
    Rule No. 9_____ 1135, 1136, 1139,1140
Agriculture, farm sector and farmers
  Controls over harvests, future____ 307, 806
  Demonstrations in Washington, D.C.__ 186,
        249, 353

Agriculture, farm sector and farmers—Con.
  Economic distress programs_____ 74, 153
  Elk City, Okla., farmers invitation to
    visit President_____ 473
  Energy use and needs. *See* Agriculture,
    energy use and needs
  Exports. *See under* Agricultural trade
  Income _____ 152, 186, 307, 570, 806
  1977 farm bill_____ 186, 249, 570
  Parity demands_____ 249, 353
  Productivity _____ 152, 307, 534
  Progress during administration_____ 152,
        570, 805
Agriculture, National Association of State
  Departments of_____ 239 (Digest)
Agriculture, Secretary of (Bob Bergland)
  *For functions of the Department in
    general, see* Agriculture, Depart-
    ment of
  Agricultural import decisions_____ 336, 946
  Alaska Natural Gas Transportation
    System, Executive Policy Board
    member _____ 1126
  China, People's Republic of, visit to__ 205
  Fuel supplies for farmers_____ 791,
        803, 945, 1135, 1136
  National Forest System functions____ 672
  National Wilderness Preservation Sys-
    tem, report preparation____ 240 (Digest)
  News conference _____ 1044 (Checklist)
  Relations with farmers_____ 353, 805
Ahlberg, Clark D_____ 464
Ahmadou Sallah, Ousman_____ 842
Aid to Families With Dependent Chil-
  dren _____ 940
Air Force, Department of the
  Assistant Secretary_____ 1128, 1142
  Secretary _____ 1127, 1142
  Under Secretary_____ 1128, 1142
Air Force Academy, United States_____ 435
Air Line Pilots Association_____ 293
Air Quality Planning Grant program___ 74
Aircraft and aviation
  Hijacking _____ 63
  Industry deregulation results
    Competition increase_____ 130, 935
    Consumer prices reduction_____ 127,
        484, 719, 834, 935, 1115
    Industry profits increase__ 105,484, 1115
  U.S. exports, international agree-
    ment _____ 6
Airline labor dispute, Emergency Board
  to investigate an_____ 89 (Digest), 293
Alabama
  Civic and community leaders, meet-
    ing with the President_____ 842
  Disaster declaration_____ 675 (Digest)
Alaska
  Land preservation_____ 444, 773, 855, 877
  National monuments_____ 151, 766, 855
  North Slope oil_____ 185, 723, 725

Alaska Natural Gas Transportation
System _____ 591, 1016, 1019, 1126
Alaska Pipeline Company, Northwest___ 591
Alcohol Fuels Commission, National____ 1007
Alexander, Repr. Bill_____ 943
Alexander, Clifford_____ 837
Alexander, Lee_____ 402
Alexander, Margaret Walker_____ 318
Alexis, Marcus_____ 885, 886, 900
Alien Property, Office of_____ 217
Aliens, undocumented
    Consultations with Mexico_____ 145,
        184, 185, 236, 253, 306, 907
    Legislative proposals_____ 185,
        236, 253, 864, 907
    Letter to State Governors_____ 806
    Living conditions in U.S_____ 811
    President's commitment to enforce im-
        migration laws_____ 236, 253, 260, 564
    Select Commission on Immigration
        and Refugee Policy, permanent
        solution recommendation_____ 564, 812
Allara, Michael A_____ 842
Allen, Richard R_____ 215, 241
Alm, Alvin L_____ 733
Alston, Philip H_____ 46, 91
Altman, Roger C_____ 240
Altmayer, Jay P_____ 782
Ambassadorial Appointments, Presiden-
    tial Advisory Board on_____ 552
Ambassadors
    Foreign, presentation of credentials___ 25,
        376, 377, 554, 842
    United States
        See also Appointments and Nomina-
            tions; *country to which assigned*
        Ambassadors at Large_____ 42,
            91, 364, 377, 687, 1134, 1143
American Alliance for Health, Physical
    Education, Recreation and Dance____ 955
American Bar Association_____ 760
American Battle Monuments Commis-
    sion _____ 81
American Cancer Society_____ 553
American Federation of Labor and Con-
    gress of Industrial Organizations. *See*
    AFL–CIO
American Heart Month (Proc. 4633)___ 21
American Hellenic Educational Progres-
    sive Association_____ 618
American National Red Cross_____ 376, 552
American Newspaper Publishers Asso-
    ciation _____ 693, 733
American Press Institute_____ 557
American Public Gas Association_____ 793
American Retail Federation_____ 832
American Society of Newspaper Editors_ 788
American States, Organization of___ 279, 644
American Train Dispatchers Association_ 818,
    984
Amiar, Jose-Joseph_____ 25
Amin Dada, Idi_____ 867
Amiotte, Arthur D_____ 464

Anderson, Repr. John B_____ 776
Anderson, R. Lanier, III_____ 675
Andrawes, Adib_____ 455
Andrews Air Force Base, Md_____ 842
Andrus, Cecil D. *See* Interior, Secretary
    of the
Andrus, Mrs. Cecil D_____ 554
Andrus, Tracy_____ 554
Angel, Sam Epstein_____ 1129, 1143
Angola, alignment with Soviet Union___ 316
Anti-Ballistic Missile Treaty_____ 1038
Antigua, U.S. Special Representative___ 980
Anti-inflation program
    See also Inflation
    Competition policy___ 234, 242 (Checklist)
    Congressional actions_____ 105
    Consumer involvement____ 620 (Checklist)
    Consumer prices monitoring_____ 635
    Control and reduction policies
        Antitrust laws enforcement_____ 105, 234
        Deregulation of energy prices___ 611, 622
        Federal budget restraint_____ 55,
            95, 97, 104, 111, 114, 123, 255, 300,
            471, 487, 489, 650, 701, 704, 790, 796,
            833, 935
        Hospital cost containment_____ 105,
            123, 256, 383, 386, 569, 603, 838, 846,
            951
        Real wage insurance__ 115, 124, 256, 951
        Regulatory reform____ 115, 650, 701, 935
        U.S. exports increase_____ 650,
            736, 796, 935, 944
    Mentions _____ 741, 902
    Partnership with American people to
        control ____ 576, 650, 796, 933, 934, 1010
    State and local government coopera-
        tion _____ 124
    Voluntary wage and price guidelines.
        See under Wages and prices
    White House briefing for State and
        local officials_____ 306, 378 (Checklist)
Antitrust Laws and Procedures, National
    Commission for the Review of_____ 132,
        178, 875
Aponte, Mari C_____ 914
Appalachian Regional Commission_____ 79, 81
Appleby, Tom_____ 270
Applegate, Repr. Douglas_____ 1006
Applewhaite, Leon B_____ 784, 843

Appointments and Nominations
    ACTION
        Associate Director_____ 666, 667
        Peace Corps, Director_____ 551, 554
    Administrative Conference of the
        United States, Council of the, mem-
        ber _____ 886
    Advisory Commission on Intergovern-
        mental Relations, members_____ 463,
            886, 1034
    Agriculture Department
        Commodity Credit Corporation,
            Board of Directors, member__ 110, 179

Appointments and Nominations—Continued

Agriculture Department—Continued
Deputy Secretary_____ 43, 91
General Counsel_____ 980, 984
Inspector General_____ 366, 377
Under Secretary_____ 218
Air Force Department
Assistant Secretary_____ 1128, 1142
Secretary _____ 1127, 1142
Under Secretary_____ 1128, 1142
Alaska Natural Gas Transportation
System, Federal Inspector___ 1016, 1019
Ambassadors, U.S.
Ambassadors at Large_____ 42,
91, 364, 377, 1134, 1143
Bahrain _____ 101, 179
Barbados _____ 664, 667
China. People's Republic of_____ 41, 91
Congo _____ 580, 619
Czechoslovakia _____ 383, 402
Dominica _____ 664, 667
Egypt _____ 819, 843
Grenada _____ 664, 667
Guatemala _____ 783, 842
Iran _____ 685, 732
Jamaica _____ 220, 241
Liberia _____ 579, 619
Malta _____ 215, 241
Nauru _____ 46, 91
New Zealand_____ 1040, 1043
Nicaragua _____ 686, 733
Niger _____ 979, 984
Tunisia _____ 101, 179
Uruguay _____ 1132, 1143
Western Samoa_____ 1040, 1043
American National Red Cross
Board of Directors, member_____ 376
Board of Governors, Chairman____ 552
Antigua, U.S. Special Representative_ 980
Army Department
Assistant Secretary_____ 109, 179
Chief of Staff, U.S. Army_____ 763
Board for International Food and Agri-
cultural Development, member____ 437
California Debris Commission, mem-
ber _____ 43, 91
Commerce Department
Assistant Secretary_____ 1036, 1044
Bureau of the Census, Director____ 981,
1019
Inspector General_____ 398, 402
Patent and Trademark Office, As-
sistant Commissioner_____ 196, 218
Under Secretary_____ 782, 842
United States Fire Administration,
Administrator _____ 22, 91
Commission on Civil Rights, Staff Di-
rector _____ 91
Commission on Presidential Scholars,
members _____ 598, 1034
Committee for the Preservation of the
White House, member_____ 782

Appointments and Nominations—Continued

Committee for Purchase From the
Blind and Other Severely Handi-
capped, member_____ 163, 437
Commodity Futures Trading Com-
mission
Chairman _____ 41, 93
Commissioner _____ 598, 619
Communications Satellite Corporation,
Board of Directors, members_ 91, 271, 294
Community Services Administration,
Inspector General_____ 1042, 1044
Comprehensive Test Ban Negotiations
U.S. delegation head, rank of Am-
bassador _____ 215
U.S. Representative_____ 1129, 1143
Consumer Product Safety Commission,
Commissioner _____ 1041, 1044
Corporation for Public Broadcasting,
Board of Directors, members_____ 46,
91, 435, 441, 1001, 1019
Council of Economic Advisers, mem-
ber _____ 599, 619
Defense Department, Assistant Secre-
taries _____ 269, 294, 1036, 1043
District of Columbia
Court of Appeals, Associate Judge__ 957
Superior Court, Associate Judges__ 46,
91, 665, 667, 980, 984
Emergency Board to investigate a rail-
way labor dispute, Chairman and
members _____ 819
Endangered Species Committee, mem-
bers _____ 23, 376
Energy Department
Office of Minority Economic Impact,
Director _____ 1040, 1044
Under Secretary_____ 955, 983
Federal Communications Commission,
members _____ 46, 91, 1021, 1043
Federal Deposit Insurance Corpora-
tion, Board of Directors, member___ 91
Federal Election Commission, mem-
bers _____ 45, 46, 90, 91, 757, 788
Federal Emergency Management
Agency
Acting Associate Director_____ 599
Acting Director_____ 567
Director _____ 781
Federal Home Loan Bank Board,
member _____ 981, 984
Federal Labor Relations Authority
General Counsel_____ 528, 554
Members _____24, 46, 90, 784, 843
Federal National Mortgage Associa-
tion, Board of Directors, members_ 931
Federal Regional Councils, Chairper-
sons _____ 269
Federal Reserve System, Board of Gov-
ernors
Members _____ 663, 664, 899, 1044
Vice Chairman_____ 1043, 1044

Appointments and Nominations—Continued

General Services Administration
Administrator _____ 458, 619
Inspector General_____ 198, 378
Health, Education, and Welfare Department
Assistant Secretaries_____ 339, 377
Deputy Inspector General_____ 616, 667
General Counsel_____ 1000, 1019
Housing and Urban Development Department
Assistant Secretaries_____ 42, 61, 93
Inspector General_____ 365, 377
Interior Department
Assistant Secretary_____ 46, 91
Inspector General_____ 365, 377
International Commission for the Conservation of Atlantic Tunas, U.S.
Commissioner _____ 436
International Monetary Fund, U.S.
Alternate Executive Director___ 446, 468
International North Pacific Fisheries Commission, U.S. Section, Commissioners _____ 1001
Interstate Commerce Commission, members _____ 871, 886, 899, 900
Interstate Commission on the Potomac River Basin, member_____ 399
John F. Kennedy Center for the Performing Arts
Advisory Committee on the Arts, members _____ 464
Board of Trustees, members_____ 23
Justice Department
Assistant Attorneys General_____ 975, 976, 983, 984
Law Enforcement Assistance Administration, Administrator_____ 268, 294
Labor Department
Commissioner of Labor Statistics___ 527, 554
Deputy Assistant Secretary____ 339, 377
Inspector General_____ 365, 377
Legal Services Corporation, Board of Directors, members_____ 46, 91, 92
Merit Systems Protection Board
Chairman _____ 46, 90
Members _____ 2, 46, 90, 1019
Special Counsel_____ 46
Middle East peace negotiations
Deputy to the Personal Representative _____ 852
Personal Representative of the President _____ 687
Mississippi River Commission, members _____ 44, 92, 1129, 1143
Mutual and Balanced Force Reductions negotiations, U.S. Representative _____ 110, 179
National Advisory Council on Extension and Continuing Education, members _____ 1023

Appointments and Nominations—Continued

National Advisory Council on Indian Education, members_____ 446, 932
National Advisory Council on Women's Educational Programs, members___ 339, 377
National Aeronautics and Space Administration, Inspector General_ 398, 402
National Alcohol Fuels Commission, members _____ 1007
National Cancer Advisory Board, Chairman and members_____ 686
National Capital Planning Commission, member_____ 687
National Commission on Employment Policy, members_____ 947
National Commission on the International Year of the Child, member__ 229
National Commission on Libraries and Information Science, members___ 196, 218
National Commission on Social Security, members_____ 23, 45, 46, 90, 92
National Council on the Arts, members _____ 45, 92, 435, 441
National Council on Educational Research, member_____ 44, 91
National Council on the Humanities, members _____ 45, 46, 90, 91, 231, 241
National Credit Union Administration, National Credit Union Board, members _____ 397, 402, 1041, 1044
National Institute of Building Sciences, Board of Directors, members_____ 44, 92, 607, 619
National Museum Services Board, members _____ 269
National Railroad Passenger Corporation, Board of Directors, members____ 92, 397, 402
National Science Foundation, National Science Board, members_____ 46, 92, 93, 196, 218, 528, 554
National Security Council, staff members _____ 984, 1045
National Transportation Safety Board, members _____ 437, 441, 1007, 1019
Non-Proliferation Treaty Review Conference, U.S. delegation head, rank of Ambassador_____ 685
North Atlantic Treaty Organization, Supreme Allied Commander, Europe, and Commander in Chief of U.S. Forces in Europe_____ 363
Nuclear Regulatory Commission, member _____ 855, 899
Occupational Safety and Health Review Commission
Chairman _____ 552
Members _____ 552, 619
Office of Personnel Management
Deputy Director_____ 2, 46, 90
Director _____ 2, 46, 90

Appointments and Nominations—Continued

Office of Personnel Management—Con.
Office of Government Ethics, Director _____ 41
Ohio River Basin Commission, Chairman _____ 607
Organization for Economic Cooperation and Development, Development Assistance Committee, Chairman__ 224, 241
Overseas Private Investment Corporation, Board of Directors, members__ 783, 842, 899, 1022, 1043
Pension Benefit Guaranty Corporation, Advisory Committee, member_____ 781
Permanent Committee for the Oliver Wendell Holmes Devise, member__ 746
Postal Rate Commission
Chairman _____ 856
Commissioners _____ 373, 378, 856, 899
Presidential Advisory Board on Ambassadorial Appointments, members___ 552
Presidential Commission on World Hunger, member_____ 213
President's Advisory Committee for Women, Chair, Vice-Chairs, and members _____ 826
President's Commission on the Accident at Three Mile Island, members _____ 660, 856
President's Commission on Executive Exchange, members and representatives _____ 976
President's Commission on Pension Policy, members_____ 271
President's Commission on White House Fellowships, members_____ 931
President's Committee on Employment of the Handicapped, members_____ 463
President's Committee on the National Medal of Science, members_____ 448
President's Export Council, members_ 942
Railroad Retirement Board, member__ 1037, 1044
Renegotiation Board, member____ 375, 402
Saint Christopher-Nevis-Anguilla, U.S. Special Representative_____ 980
Saint Lucia, U.S. Minister_____ 664, 667
Saint Vincent, U.S. Special Representative _____ 980
Securities and Exchange Commission, members _____ 1021, 1022
Securities Investor Protection Corporation, Director_____ 1022, 1043
Select Commission on Immigration and Refugee Policy, members_____ 450
Small Business Administration, Inspector General_____ 399, 402
Small Business Conference Commission, members_____ 229

Appointments and Nominations—Continued

State Department
Assistant Secretary_____ 21, 91
Coordinator for Mexican Affairs___ 1134, 1143
Coordinator for Population Affairs_ 377, 378
Coordinator for Refugee Affairs__ 364, 377
Tennessee Valley Authority, Board of Directors, member_____ 877, 957
Transportation Department, Inspector General _____ 398, 402
Treasury Department, Assistant Secretary _____ 1000, 1018
United States Advisory Commission on International Communication, Cultural and Educational Affairs, members _____ 729, 787
United States Air Force Academy, Board of Visitors, members_____ 435
United States Arms Control and Disarmament Agency, Director_____ 45, 90
U.S. attorneys
Florida _____ 241, 242
Louisiana _____ 667, 668
Pennsylvania _____ 93
U.S. circuit judges
District of Columbia_____ 733, 787, 958, 983
2d circuit_____ 733, 787, 788
3d circuit_____ 619
4th circuit_____ 843
5th circuit_____ 93, 555, 619, 675, 733, 787, 899, 900
6th circuit____ 441, 620, 667, 1018, 1019
7th circuit_____ 957
9th circuit_____ 788, 1043, 1044
U.S. district judges
Arizona _____ 733, 787, 1018, 1019
Arkansas _____ 402, 403
California _____ 1018, 1019
Colorado _____ 984
Connecticut _____ 1018, 1019
District of Columbia_____ 93, 378, 402
Florida _____ 957, 1018, 1019
Georgia _____ 1018, 1019, 1043, 1044
Illinois _____ 733, 787, 957
Iowa _____ 441
Louisiana _____ 957, 958, 1018, 1019, 1043, 1044
Maryland _____ 957, 958
Massachusetts _____ 179, 180
Michigan _____ 899, 900
Missouri _____ 899, 900, 957, 958
Montana _____ 441
Nevada _____ 667, 668
New Hampshire_____ 241, 242
New York_____ 93
North Carolina_____ 554, 555
Pennsylvania _____ 958, 983
South Carolina_____ 1018, 1019
South Dakota_____ 441

Appointments and Nominations—Continued

U.S. district judges—Continued
Texas _____ 241,
294, 327, 328, 377, 378, 402, 403
Virginia _____ 667, 668, 899, 900
West Virginia_____ 1044
United States Foreign Claims Settle-
ment Commission, member_____ 46, 90
United States Marine Corps, Com-
mandant _____ 672
U.S. marshals
Illinois _____ 788
Nebraska _____ 468
Pennsylvania _____ 733, 787
Puerto Rico_____ 899, 900
United States Military Academy,
Board of Visitors, members_____ 687
United States Naval Academy, Board
of Visitors, members_____ 730
United States Postal Service, Board
of Governors, members_____ 24,
46, 90, 215, 241
United States Railway Association,
Board of Directors, member_____ 43, 93
United States Tax Court, judge__ 820, 843
Veterans Administration, Inspector
General _____ 367, 377
White House Conference on Families,
Chairperson _____ 667
White House Conference on Library
and Information Services, Advisory
Committee, members_____ 400, 746
White House Fellows_____ 914
White House staff
Assistant Press Secretary_____ 1017
Deputy Assistant to the President_ 7
Deputy Press Secretary_____ 1017
Special Assistant to the President for
Congressional Liaison_____ 377, 378
Arce Alvarez, Roberto_____ 554
Arceneaux, George, Jr_____ 1043, 1044
Archer, Repr. William R_____ 666
Architectural Barrier Awareness Week,
National _____ 641
Arctic National Wildlife Range, Alaska_ 855
Arias-Schreiber, Alfonso_____ 554
Arizona, U.S. district judges_____ 733,
787, 1018, 1019
Arkansas
Disaster declaration (Digest) _____ 667, 674
U.S. district judge_____ 402, 403
Arky, Marlin_____ 464
Armed Forces, United States
Draft registration and reinstatement__ 249,
472
East Asia, military capability in_____ 764
Mention _____ 311
Military Award program_____ 363
Military installations_____ 906
Military personnel, taxation of_____ 479
Pay increases_____ 64

Armed Forces, United States—Continued
South Korea, withdrawal of troops___ 247
Armenian Americans_____ 1017
Arms Control and Disarmament Agency,
United States. *See* United States Arms
Control and Disarmament Agency
Arms and weapons systems
See also specific weapons system;
Nuclear weapons
Control and disarmament_____ 108, 158
Sales to foreign countries_____ 51,
53, 106, 184, 563, 902, 1023, 1130
Science and technology development_ 542
Army, Department of the
See also specific constituent agencies
Assistant Secretary_____ 109, 179
Chief of Engineers_____ 1126
Chief of Staff, U.S. Army_____ 763
Secretary _____ 83
Arntz, Bill_____ 270
Art awards, Women's Caucus for_____ 217
Arts, National Council on the_ 45, 92, 435, 441
Arts and Humanities, Federal Council on
the _____ 956
Arts and Humanities, National Endow-
ment for the_____ 142
Asad, Hafiz al-_____ 456
Asian/Pacific American Heritage Week
(Proc. 4650)_____ 549
Asian/Pacific Americans_____ 786
Askew, Reubin O'D. *See* Select Com-
mission on Immigration and Refugee
Policy, Chairman
Aspen, Marvin E_____ 733, 787
Assassination investigations_____ 37
Association of Southeast Asian Nations
(ASEAN) _____ 303, 304, 765
Astin, Helen S_____ 44, 91
Atherton, Alfred L., Jr____ 669, 819, 843, 955
Atherton, Mrs. Alfred L., Jr_____ 955
Atkins, Chet_____ 447
Atkinson, Richard C_____ 205
Atlanta, Ga_____ 296–306
Atmospheric Research Project, Global__ 538
Atomic Energy Agency, International___ 159,
452, 1048
Attorney General (Griffin B. Bell)
Electronic surveillance orders re-
view _____ 585
Federal civil justice system proposals__ 340
Meetings with the President (Di-
gest) _____ 25, 178
Mention _____ 760n.
News conference_____ 378 (Checklist)
Offshore oil spill pollution, study re-
sponsibilities _____ 339
Spanish-speaking Americans civil
rights violations, corrective program
establishment _____ 847
Standby gasoline rationing plan recom-
mendations _____ 814, 821
Weber case position_____ 847

Attorney General—Continued
Wood, Judge John H., Jr., investigation of murder_____ 959
Attorneys, U.S. *See* U.S. attorneys *under* Appointments and Nominations
Attorneys General, National Association of State_____ 618
Australia
Australian-American Week celebrations _____ 376
Prime Minister J. Malcolm Fraser____ 2
Australian-American Association_____ 376
Austria
Chancellor Bruno Kreisky_____ 1047, 1142
President Rudolph Kirchschläger____ 1047, 1142
U.S. Ambassador_____ 1048
Vienna Summit Meeting. *See* Vienna Summit Meeting
Automobile Manufacturers Association__ 900
Automobiles
Air pollution control_____ 183
Industry employees' health care costs_ 838
No-fault insurance_____ 131
Representatives, meeting with the President _____ 899 (Digest)
Research initiatives technology, news conference _____ 900 (Checklist)
Technical developments for fuel efficiency _____ 797
Automotive Products Trade Act of 1965, Operation of the_____ 178
Aviation. *See* Aircraft and aviation
Aviation, Convention on International Civil _____ 449
Aviation Organization, International Civil _____ 449
Awards and citations
American Cancer Society Courage Award _____ 554
Cancer Research Foundation awards__ 786 (Digest)
Conservationist of the Year Award___ 443
Martin Luther King, Jr. Nonviolent Peace Award_____ 27
National Caucus on the Black Aged Living Legacy awards_____ 317
National Security Medal_____ 179
National Small Business Person of the Year _____ 868
Presidential Medal of Freedom_____ 87
Presidential Physical Fitness Award__ 955
Public Health Service Award_____ 983
Special Country Music Association Award _____ 898 (Digest)
Teacher of the Year Award_____ 598
Women's Caucus for Art awards_____ 217

B-1 _____ 1052, 1062
B-52 _____ 1052, 1062
Babbitt, Bruce E_____ 660
Babione, Dale R_____ 437
Backfire bomber_____ 1079, 1090
Bahrain, U.S. Ambassador_____ 101, 179

Bakhtiar, Shahpour_____ 50, 259
Bakke case_____ 847
Bank, National Development_____ 99, 137
Banks and banking
Federal access to bank records_____ 583
Federal institutions deregulation__ 132, 928
Baptista de Oliveira Figueiredo, João___239 (Digest), 401
Barabba, Vincent P_____ 981, 1019
Barbados
U.S. Ambassador_____ 293, 664
U.S. arms sales_____ 1130
Bario, Patricia Y___ 252n., 852n., 908n., 1017
Barringer, John W_____ 942
Barrow, Gen. Robert H_____ 672
Barry, Marion S., Jr_____ 25, 144
Barry, Robert_____ 1143
Bartlett, Sen. Dewey_____ 374
Baryshnikov, Mikhail_____ 376 (Digest)
Bass, Mary P_____ 398, 402
Battle Monuments Commission, American _____ 81
Bauman, Repr. Robert E_____ 667
Bayh, Sen. Birch
Gasohol production legislation sponsorship _____ 993
Jefferson-Jackson Day dinner, Indianapolis, Ind., remarks_____ 988
Meeting with the President___ 956 (Digest)
Mention _____ 990
President's assessment_____ 989
SALT II treaty consideration_____ 994
Bayh, Marvella_____ 691, 989, 991
Bazargan, Mehdi_____ 257, 259, 352
Beall, C. E. Campbell_____ 400
Beall, Donald R_____ 241 (Checklist)
Beattie, Richard I_____ 1000, 1019
Beaumont, Dina G_____ 552
Beckel, Robert G., meetings with the President (Digest)_____ 618, 666, 731, 842, 956
Beckman, Aldo B_____ 746n.
Bedford, N. H_____ 714, 733
Beef prices and price controls_____ 475, 705, 754, 796, 849, 850
Begin, Menahem. *See* Israel, Prime Minister
Begin, Mrs. Menahem____ 417n., 430n., 522n.
Belew, David O., Jr_____ 241, 242
Bell, Griffin B. *See* Attorney General
Benedick, Richard Elliot_____ 377, 378
Benjamin, Repr. Adam, Jr_____ 990
Benoit, Joan_____ 770
Bentsen, Sen. Lloyd M_____ 376
Bergin, Thomas P_____ 435, 441
Bergland, Bob. *See* Agriculture, Secretary of
Berman, Jason S_____ 293, 976
Bermudez-Milla, Jose Antonio_____ 25
Bernstein, Irving_____ 23
Bernstein, Leonard_____ 281, 282ftn.
Berry, Chuck_____ 1015
Berry, Mary_____ 742, 886n.
Better Way Club_____ 568

Betz, Gary Louis_____ 241, 242
Biden, Sen. Joseph R_____ 293
Bilby, Richard M_____ 1018, 1019

Bill Signings

*See also last page of text in each issue
for acts approved*
Ethics in Government Act of 1978
amendments, statement_____ 1131
Humphrey, Hubert H., gold medal,
statement _____ 1036
Taiwan Relations Act, statement____ 640
Veterans' Health Care Amendments,
statement _____ 1039
Wayne, John, gold medal, statement__ 959

Billings, K. LeMoyne_____ 24
Bingham, Rebecca T_____ 400
Biomass energy_____ 1105
Bishop, Isabel_____ 217
Bishop, James Keough_____ 979, 984
Black, Marilyn W_____ 598
Black, Norman W_____ 327, 328
Black, Susan H_____ 957
Black Aged, National Caucus on the____ 317
Black Caucus, Congressional_____ 911
Black Music Association_____ 1014
Black Press Week_____ 440
Blacks
See also Minorities
Business assistance_____ 847
Civil rights_____ 884, 970
Employment _____ 126
Higher education___ 48, 140, 173, 743, 911
Judicial appointments_____ 36,
131, 759, 847, 885
Leaders, meetings with the President__ 810,
841
Media representatives, interview with
the President_____ 33
Blanchard, Repr. James J_____ 942
Blango, Antoinette_____ 913
Blass, Elizabeth W_____ 464
Blatnik, John_____ 293
Blaylock, Kenneth T_____ 931
Bleicher, Michael M_____ 578n.
Blind and Other Severely Handicapped,
Committee for Purchase From the_ 163, 437
Block, Charlene M_____ 1007
Bloomfield, Lincoln P_____ 984
Blumenfeld, Michael_____ 109, 179
Blumenthal, W. Michael. *See* Treasury,
Secretary of the
Board. *See other part of title*
Boggs, Thomas Hale_____ 976
Bolivia, Ambassador to U.S_____ 554
Bolling, Repr. Richard_____ 840, 942
Bolt, nut, and large screw industry_____ 3
Bonker, Repr. Don_____ 867
Bonn Economic Summit Conference____ 160
Bonyun, William L_____ 464
Borkowski, Francis T_____ 464

Bosworth, Barry P. *See* Wage and Price
Stability, Council on, Director
Bosworth, Stephen W_____ 101, 179
Boucher, Paul R_____ 399, 402
Bouna Ould Sidi, Sidi_____ 376
Bowden, Henry L_____ 271
Bowen, Repr. David R_____ 1125
Bowers, Shellie F_____ 665, 667
Bowie, Robert R_____ 25
Boy Scouts of America_____ 240
Boyer, Neil A_____ 815
Brademas, Repr. John_____ 1125
Bradley, Thomas_____ 872, 876
Bragg, John T_____ 271
Branch Line Railroad Investments_____ 76
Branchina, Lisa_____ 955
Branchina, Minnie_____ 955, 956
Branigin, Roger_____ 990
Branscomb, Lewis M_____ 528, 554
Brazil, inaugural ceremonies, U.S. dele-
gation _ 239 (Digest), 241 (Checklist), 401
Breathitt, Frances H_____ 24
Breeder reactors
Clinch River breeder reactor plant.
See Clinch River breeder reactor
plant
Federal research and development pro-
grams _____ 149
Brement, Marshall_____ 1045
Brennan, Donald G_____ 976
Brezhnev, L. I. *See* Union of Soviet So-
cialist Republics, President
Brimmer, Andrew F_____ 976
Broadcast System, Emergency_____ 567
Broadcasters, National Association of___ 482,
490
Broadcasting, Corporation for Public
Annual report_____ 609
Board of Directors, members_____ 46,
91, 435, 441, 1001, 1019
Brooks, Repr. Jack_____ 217, 240, 666
Brooks, John Wood_____ 942
Brown, Bailey_____ 441
Brown, Gov. Edmund G.
Balanced Federal budget, proposed
constitutional amendment_____ 562
California gasoline shortages actions__ 800,
872, 876, 898, 986
Mention _____ 350
Brown, Harold. *See* Defense, Secretary of
Brown, June Gibbs_____ 365, 377
Brown, Tyrone_____ 977, 1021, 1043
*Brown v. Board of Education*__ 883, 909–911
Bruzda, Francis J_____ 976
Bryan, Morris M., Jr_____ 942
Bryant, John H_____ 815
Bryant, Tom_____ 857, 858
Brzezinski, Zbigniew
Chicago Council on Foreign Relations,
remarks _____ 619
Fordham University commencement
address _____ 944 (Checklist)

Brzezinski, Zbigniew—Continued
  Meetings with the President (Digest) _ 14,
    25, 26, 89, 177–179, 217, 239–241,
    293, 327, 329, 375–377, 400, 440,
    467, 468, 553, 554, 617, 618, 666, 667,
    731, 732, 786–788, 841, 842, 897–899,
    955–957, 982, 983, 1017, 1018, 1042,
    1043, 1142
  Mentions _____ 329n., 744
  Middle East, visit to__ 436, 468 (Checklist)
  Vienna Summit statement_____ 839
Budget
  Constitutional amendment for bal-
    anced budget_____ 57, 562
  Deficit reduction_____ 114,
    307, 571, 577, 635, 653, 704, 716, 790,
    830, 833, 935
  Fiscal 1980
    Deficit figure decision_____ 54
    Eximbank allocation_____ 331
    First resolution, congressional ap-
      proval _____ 947
    Mentions _____ 40, 104, 111, 123, 306
    Message to Congress_____ 95, 96
    News conference statement_____ 50
    Social programs allocations_____ 34,
      116, 123, 177, 187
  Fiscal 1981, administration officials,
    meetings with the President
    (Digest) _____ 898, 1017, 1018
  Rescissions and deferrals_____ 200,
    272, 433, 603, 720
  Zero-base budgeting. *See* Zero-base
    budgeting
Bugotu, Francis _____ 554
Building Sciences, National Institute
  of _____ 44, 92, 607, 619, 982
Building temperature restrictions, emer-
  gency _____ 370, 690, 797
Bumpers, Sen. Dale_____ 887
Bureau. *See other part of title*
Burger, Warren E_____ 760n.
Burke, Selma_____ 217
Burkhalter, William M_____ 375, 402
Bursley, G. H. Patrick_____ 1007, 1019
Burton, Repr. John_____ 667
Busbee, Gov. George D_ 66, 330, 334, 942, 943
Business and industry, U.S.
  See also Corporations; *specific busi-
    ness or industry*
  Administration's accomplishments and
    goals _____ 561, 634
  Forest products development_____ 670
  Innovation, Federal Government
    policy on_____ 680
  Investment growth_____ 112
  Minority-owned businesses_____ 847
  Privacy rights_____ 582
  Science and technology develop-
    ment _____ 530, 545

Business and industry, U.S.—Continued
  Voluntary wage and price guidelines.
    See under Wages and prices
  Wage rate comparability surveys_____ 1003
  Women's enterprises_____ 888, 890, 894
Bussiere, Emile R_____ 942
Byrd, Sen. Harry F., Jr_____ 36
Byrd, Sen. Robert C.
  Legislation passage leadership
    Department of education_____ 756
    Standby gasoline rationing plan____ 840
  Meetings with the President (Digest) _ 178,
    293
  President's assessment_____ 829
Byrne, Gov. Brendan T_____ 402, 898

Cabinet, meetings with the President
  (Digest) __ 89, 239, 617, 731, 841, 842, 955
Cable, William H., meetings with the
  President (Digest)_____ 467,
    553, 618, 731, 732, 786, 842, 898,
    956, 1142
Cable television_____ 932, 933, 938
Cable Television Association, National__ 932
Cafferty, Pastora San Juan_____ 730
Caldwell, Philip_____ 900
Calhoun, Ga_____ 731
Califano, Joseph A., Jr. *See* Health, Edu-
  cation, and Welfare, Secretary of
California
  Crude oil production_____ 874
  Gasoline shortages_____ 800,
    808, 862, 872, 875, 898, 900, 985, 986
  President's visit_____ 787,
    807, 809, 810, 841, 843
  U.S. district judge_____ 1018, 1019
California Chicano Caucus_____ 810
California Debris Commission_____ 43, 91
Callaghan, James_____ 17,
    20n., 25 (Digest), 26 (Checklist)
Callaghan, Mrs. James_____ 25 (Digest)
Camacho, Ernest M_____ 229, 811
Cambodia, Vietnamese invasion_____ 303,
    348, 765
Camp, George W_____ 215, 241
Camp David, Md.
  Middle East peace negotiations, meet-
    ings of Egyptian and Israeli
    Ministers _____ 303, 329, 346
  President's visits (Digest)
    Departures _____ 89,
      179, 217, 241, 440, 619, 899, 957, 982
    Returns _____ 14,
      177, 216, 239, 292, 327, 467, 666, 983
Camp Hoover, Va_____ 842, 897
Campaign, 1980 Presidential. *See* Presi-
  dential campaign, 1980
Campbell, Alan K. *See* Personnel Man-
  agement, Office of, Director
Campbell, Ed_____ 804 ftn.
Canada
  Cyprus conflict actions_____ 191
  Energy project with U.S_____ 591
  Joint statement_____ 381

Canada—Continued
Prime Minister Pierre Trudeau_____ 327, 376, 379
Tokyo Summit attendance announce-
  ment _____ 550
Treaties with U.S.
  Fishery _____ 776
  Maritime boundary_____ 776
U.S. border States, relationship with__ 335
Canal Zone Government_____ 102
Cancer Advisory Board, National___ 675, 686
Cancer Control Month (Proc. 4643)___ 389
Cancer Courage award_____ 554
Cancer Program, National_____ 675 (Digest)
Cancer Research Foundation awards,
  General Motors_____ 786
Cancer Society, American_____ 553
Candidacy plans, President's 1980. *See*
  Presidential campaign, 1980
Cannon, Sen. Howard W___ 1115, 1116, 1143
Cannon, Wilson P., Jr_____ 942
Capital Planning Commission, National_ 687
Capp, Lincoln W., II_____ 914
Captive Nations Week (Proc. 4666)____ 1141
Caputo, Philip_____ 974
Carey, Gov. Hugh_____ 240
Carlucci, Frank C_____ 553
Carnegie Commission on the Future of
  Public Broadcasting_____ 199
Carr, Patrick E_____ 1044
Carrigan, Jim R_____ 984
Carroll, Gov. Julian____ 330, 334, 360, 362n.
Carswell, Robert_____ 977
Carter, Amy_____ 240, 710, 745, 1108
Carter, Billy_____ 47, 348
Carter, Chip_____ 436, 804
Carter, Jack and Judy_____ 731
Carter, Lillian_____ 804, 839
Carter, Lisle C., Jr_____ 271
Carter, Rosalynn
  Israeli Prime Minister Begin, dinner
    with _____ 400 (Digest)
  Luncheons with the President (Di-
    gest) _____ 25,
      89, 179, 217, 240, 241, 327, 377, 467,
      553, 787, 898, 955, 983
  Mental health systems legislation,
    remarks _____ 858
  Mentions _____ 745, 842
  Middle East, visit to_____ 417, 428
  U.S. Embassy in Mexico, remarks___ 278
Carter, Sarah Rosemary_____ 731
Carter, W. Beverly, Jr_____ 42, 91
Carter's Warehouse_____ 652
Cary, Harold F_____ 436
Castagna, William J_____ 1018, 1019
Castillo, Leonel J_____ 812
Cedano, Blanca_____ 44, 92
Celeste, Richard F. *See* Peace Corps,
  Director
Census, Bureau of the_____ 239 (Digest),
      981, 1019
Central Intelligence Agency_____ 179, 553

Central Intelligence Agency, Director
  (Stansfield Turner)
  Meetings with the President (Digest)_ 25,
      89, 178, 217, 241, 293, 327, 401, 467,
      618, 666, 732, 787, 842, 898, 956, 982,
      1017, 1043, 1142
  Mention _____ 37
  SALT II treaty role_____ 753
Cerda, Maria B_____ 229
CETA. *See* Comprehensive Employment
  and Training Act programs
Chai Zemin_____ 377, 787
Challandes-Angelini, Frederica P_____ 914
Chamberlain, Charles J_____ 1037, 1044
Chambers, Marjorie Bell_____ 88, 217, 827
Champ, Norman B_____ 45, 92
Chan, Tom_____ 229
Chancellor, John_____ 47, 410n.
Chaney, Mary Louise_____ 464
Chan-Palay, Victoria L_____ 914
Chartrand, Robert Lee_____ 400
Chayes, Antonia Handler_____ 1128, 1142
Chernyayev, Rudolf_____ 731
Cherry Blossom princesses_____ 618
Cheyney State College, Pa_ 742, 908, 913, 957
Chicago Council on Foreign Relations_ 619
Chicano Caucus, California_____ 810
Child, National Commission on the Inter-
  national Year of the_____ 229
Children, Aid to Families With Depend-
  ent _____ 940
Children, National Center of Economic
  Education for_____ 842
Children and youth
  Child welfare reform_____ 138
  Employment _____ 126, 187, 836, 910
  Health programs_____ 117, 134, 862, 1030
Chile, whaling operations_____ 266–268
China, People's Republic of
  Agreements with U.S.
    Consular relations and Consulates
      General _____ 209
    Culture _____ 207
    High energy physics_____ 205
    Science and technology_____ 200, 539
    Space, agriculture, and education__ 202
  Ambassador to U.S_____ 377
  Central TV, interview with the Presi-
    dent _____ 163
  Clothespin exports_____ 233
  Congressional visit_____ 666
  Foreign Minister Huang Hua_____ 14,
      209, 210n., 248
  International Exchange-of-Persons pro-
    gram _____ 324
  Japan, relationship with_____ 764
  Joint statement_____ 212
  Mention _____ 576
  Premier Hua Guofeng_____ 1, 1112
  Science and technology programs with
    U.S _____ 539
  Secretary of the Treasury's visit_____ 348
  Taiwan, agreement to peacefully re-
    solve differences with_____ 52, 257

China, People's Republic of—Continued
  Trade with U.S_____ 331–334, 358, 749
  U.S. Ambassador_____ 41, 91
  U.S. arms sales_____ 184
  U.S. relations_____ 2,
    107, 157, 248, 257, 356, 640, 1111
    Congressional resolutions_____ 170, 257
    Soviet reaction to normalization___ 57,
        173, 259
  Vice Premier of the State Council____ 982
  Vice President's visit_____ 1125
China, People's Republic of, Vice Premier
    (Deng Xiaoping)
  Mentions _____ 53, 248, 359
  New Year's message from the Presi-
    dent _____ 2
  Visit to U.S.
    Agreements with U.S_____ 200,
        202, 205, 207, 209, 212
    Announcement _____ 88
    Joint statement_____ 213
    Kennedy Center for the Performing
      Arts _____ 195
    Meetings with the President_____ 191,
        198, 218
    Postvisit comments_____ 259, 356, 540
    Previsit comments_____ 54,
        107, 164, 165, 172, 174, 181, 186
    State dinner_____ 192
    Welcoming ceremony_____ 189
China, Republic of. *See* Taiwan
Chinese New Year_____ 109
Chou Pei-yuan_____ 205
Christians and Jews, National Confer-
    ence of_____ 969
Christopher, Warren M. *See* State, Dep-
    uty Secretary of
Church, Sen. Frank_____ 191,
        240 (Digest), 462, 997
Church, Mrs. Frank_____ 240 (Digest)
Cinco de Mayo celebration_____ 810, 843
Circuit judges, U.S. *See* U.S. circuit
    judges *under* Appointments and Nomi-
    nations
Cire, George E_____ 294
Civil Aeronautics Board_____ 235, 843
Civil justice system, Federal____ 340–346, 378
Civil rights. *See* Human rights, domestic
Civil Rights, Commission on_____ 91
Civil Service Commission, United States_ 8, 64
Civil service reform. *See* Federal civil
    service reform
Civil Service Reform Act_____ 462
Clark, Carolyn G_____ 464
Clark, Dick. *See* Coordinator for Refugee
    Affairs *under* State, Department of
Clark, James, Jr_____ 271
Clark, Joan M_____ 215, 241
Clark, Kenneth B_____ 401
Clark, Septima Poinsettia_____ 318
Clean Water Act of 1977_____ 702
Cleary, Timothy F_____ 552, 619
Cleland, Max_____ 974

Clement, Robert N_____ 877, 957
Clifford, Clark M_____ 553
Clifford, Maurice C_____ 464
Clinch River breeder reactor plant
  Congressional actions
    House Science and Technology
      Committee _____ 730, 795
    Senate Energy and Natural Re-
      sources Committee_____ 887
    President's opposition to project____ 149,
        741, 795
Cloherty, Patricia M_____ 888–890
Clothespin industry_____ 232–234, 325
Clough, Susan S_____ 751
Coal
  Emission standards_____ 841 (Digest), 905
  Federal mine health activities_____ 103
  Increased production_____ 864, 905, 1098
  Industry revitalization_____ 633
  Natural gas extraction from_____ 793
  New technologies development_____ 553,
        622, 905
  Strip mining_____ 150
Coal Industry, President's Commission
    on the_____ 649, 905
Coastal Zone Management_____ 178
Cobb, Montague_____ 319
Cohen, Kelley_____ 464
Cohen, Marvin S_____ 843
Cohen, Sen. William S_____ 178 (Digest)
Cohn, Anne H_____ 914
Cohn, Avern_____ 899, 900
Coker, Ed_____ 270
Colleges and universities
  See also Education
  Black institutions___ 48, 140, 173, 742, 911
  Developing institutions program_____ 140
  Science and technology programs____ 544
  Student loans_____ 140, 711
  Tuition tax credit_____ 625
Collet, John C_____ 976
Collins, Repr. Cardiss_____ 666
Collins, Paul_____ 464
Colorado, U.S. district judge_____ 984
Commerce, Department of
  See also specific constituent agencies
  Assistant Secretary_____ 619
  Board to consider Pittston Company's
    proposed oil refinery_____ 1017 (Digest)
  Budget deferral_____ 200
  Counselor on Labor Management
    Relations _____ 3
  Economic development plan require-
    ments _____ 75
  Federal emergency management, trans-
    fer of functions_____ 566
  Inspector General_____ 398, 402
  Science and technology programs___ 140
  Secretary. *See* Commerce, Secretary of
  State and regional development pro-
    grams _____ 78
  Title V Regional Commissions_____ 78–80
  Under Secretary_____ 782, 842

Commerce, international
See also Multilateral trade negotia-
tions; Tokyo Economic Summit
Conference
Administration's accomplishments and
goals _____ 118, 160
Exports
Agricultural. See Agricultural trade
International credit negotiations___ 125,
438
Technology controls_____ 543
Imports
Bolts, nuts, and large screws_____ 3
Clothespins _____ 232–234, 325
Meat _____ 336
Natural gas_____ 58, 182, 183, 236, 737
Oil. See Oil imports
Steel _____ 1032
Sugar, sirup, and molasses_____ 153, 946
Television receivers, color_____ 166
Multilateral trade negotiations. See
Multilateral trade negotiations
National Governors' Association, com-
mittee on international trade and
foreign relations, question-and-
answer session_____ 330
Trade, U.S.
Balance of payments_____ 330, 736, 944
China _____ 331–334, 358, 749
Countervailing duties' waiver_____ 46, 125
Foreign boycotts, U.S. position on_ 146
Generalized System of Preferences_ 367
International agreements_____ 6, 7
Japan _____ 766
Soviet Union_____ 358, 749
Uganda _____ 224, 225
Zimbabwe-Rhodesia___ 1012, 1018, 1020
Commerce, Secretary of (Juanita M.
Kreps)
For functions of the Department in
general, see Commerce, Department
of
China, People's Republic of, visit to___ 174,
213, 331
Federal emergency management func-
tions (EO 12127) _____ 566
Industrial innovation initiatives ac-
tions _____ 531, 680
International trade study_____ 332–334
Meetings with the President_____ 467, 666
Mentions _____ 96, 548
Offshore oil spill pollution functions
(EO 12123)_____ 338
President's Export Council, adminis-
trative responsibilities (EO 12131)_ 785
Ugandan trade actions_____ 867
Whale protection, investigation of
foreign violations_____ 265, 1435
White House Conference on Economic
Development, executive agency rep-
resentative _____ 65, 68

Commerce Commission, Interstate. See
Interstate Commerce Commission
Commission. See other part of title
Committee. See other part of title
Commodity Credit Corporation_ 110, 179, 898
Commodity Futures Trading Commis-
sion _____ 41, 93, 598, 619
Commons, D. L_____ 942
Communication Agency, International__ 142,
272, 324
Communications Commission, Federal__ 46,
91, 1021, 1043
Communications Satellite Corporation__ 91,
271, 294
Communications and telecommunications
Cable television_____ 932, 933, 938
Electromagnetic spectrum_____ 541
Public broadcasting system_____ 482
Rural areas systems_____ 270
U.S. international policy_____ 240
Community Development Block Grant
program _____ 136
Community Health Centers, National As-
sociation of_____ 983
Community Mental Health System_____ 134,
135, 860
Community Services Administration___ 337,
1042, 1044
Compensation reform act, Federal em-
ployees, proposed_____ 1002
Comprehensive Employment and Train-
ing Act programs
Administration's accomplishments and
goals _____ 126
Private Sector Initiatives program____ 73,
99, 126, 601
Comprehensive Test Ban negotiations___ 215,
1129, 1143
Compton, W. Dale_____ 448
Conaboy, Richard P_____ 958, 983
Conference. See other part of title
Congo
Ambassador to U.S_____ 25
U.S. Ambassador_____ 580, 619
Congress
See also Congress, Communications to
Action on administration's proposals
Alaska public lands_____ 877
Budget _____ 947
Clinch River breeder reactor_____ 730,
795, 887
Education, department of_____ 711, 756
Energy. See Energy legislation
Hospital cost containment_____ 952, 963
Panama Canal treaties_____ 963, 1125
Real wage insurance_____ 951
Bipartisan senior citizen intern pro-
gram _____ 837
Budget process_____ 100
China, People's Republic of, bipartisan
delegation's visit_____ 666

Congress—Continued
  Members, meeting with the President.
    See Digest of White House An-
    nouncements *at the end of each
    issue*
  Members' term of office, President's
    assessment _____ 739
  Relationship with the President_____ 121,
                                      963, 1014

Congress, Communications to

ADDRESSES
  SALT II treaty_____ 1087
  State of the Union_____ 103

LETTERS TO MEMBERS
  Alaska public lands legislation_____ 855
  Clothespin industry_____ 232, 233
  Cyprus conflict_____ 191, 461, 997
  Egyptian-Israeli peace treaty____ 590, 638
  Energy management legislation_____ 895
  Hazardous waste disposal_____ 1034
  Panama Canal treaties_____ 102
  Turkey, U.S. economic assistance____ 647

MESSAGES
  Agency for International Develop-
    ment, personnel system_____ 760
  Budget, 1980_____ 96
  Budget rescissions and deferrals_____ 200,
                             272, 433, 603, 720
  District of Columbia budget_____ 217
  Education, department of, proposed__ 264
  Emergency weekend gasoline sales
    restrictions _____ 608
  Energy conservation contingency
    plans _____ 370–372
  Energy security trust fund_____ 721
  Federal civil justice system_____ 342
  Federal civilian and military pay in-
    creases _____ 64
  Federal pay system reform_____ 1002
  Financial reform legislation_____ 928
  Freight rail industry deregulation legis-
    lation _____ 459
  Hospital cost containment legislation_ 386
  Intergovernmental fiscal assistance
    legislation _____ 391
  International development cooperation
    agency, proposed_____ 395
  Mental health systems legislation_____ 859
  Multilateral trade negotiations___ 46, 1092
  National energy plan_____ 816
  National health plan_____ 1028
  National privacy policy_____ 581
  Public works and economic develop-
    ment legislation_____ 599
  Regulatory reform_____ 491
  Romania and Hungary, U.S. trade
    with _____ 978
  Science and technology policy_____ 528
  Solar energy_____ 1097
  Standby gasoline rationing plan_____ 371
    Amendment _____ 813, 820

Congress, Communications to—Continued

MESSAGES—Continued
  State of the Union_____ 121
  Taiwan-U.S. relations_____ 165
  Trucking industry deregulation legis-
    lation _____ 1117
  Welfare reform legislation_____ 938
  Windfall profits tax_____ 721
  Wiretapping and electronic surveil-
    lance _____ 587

REORGANIZATION PLANS
  Alaska Natural Gas Transportation
    System (No. 1 of 1979) _____ 591
  United States International Develop-
    ment Cooperation Agency (No. 2
    of 1979) _____ 642
    Amendments _____ 915

REPORTS
  Administration on Aging_____ 441
  Coal mine health activities, Federal__ 103
  Coastal Zone Management_____ 178
  Corporation for Public Broadcasting_ 609
  Council on Environmental Quality___ 119
  Council on Wage and Price Stability_ 178,
                                   393, 815
  Cuba, U.S. policy_____ 240 (Digest)
  Defense Department's Military Award
    program _____ 363
  Economic Report of the President____ 110
  Export financing negotiations_____ 438
  Federal advisory committees_____ 463
  Fuel assurances, initial_____ 326
  Hazardous materials control_____ 178
  Health information and promotion___ 467
  International communications policy__ 240
  International Exchange-of-Persons pro-
    gram _____ 324
  International export credit negotia-
    tions _____ 438
  International journalistic freedom_____ 240
  International Whaling Commission__ 265
  Japan-U.S. Cooperative Medical Sci-
    ence program_____ 732
  National Cancer Advisory Board_____ 675
                                   (Digest)
  National Cancer Program____ 675 (Digest)
  National Heart, Lung, and Blood In-
    stitute _____ 178
  National Wilderness Preservation Sys-
    tem _____ 240
  Nuclear Non-Proliferation Act of 1978_ 452
  Office of Alien Property_____ 217
  Operation of the Automotive Products
    Trade Act of 1965_____ 178
  Transportation Department's Military
    Award program_____ 363
  United Nations, U.S. participation in_ 62
  United States Arms Control and Dis-
    armament Agency_____ 683
  United States Sinai Support Mission_ 64,
                                     756

Congress, Communications to—Continued

REPORTS—Continued

White House Conference on Balanced
National Growth and Economic Development _____ 69

TREATIES AND OTHER INTERNATIONAL
AGREEMENTS

Agreement on International Carriage
of Perishable Foodstuffs_____ 83

Canada
Fishery treaty_____ 776
Maritime boundary treaty_____ 776

Convention on the Intergovernmental
Martime Consultative Organization, amendments_____ 778

Convention on International Civil
Aviation _____ 449

Convention on Pollution from Ships__ 85

Convention on the Prevention of Marine Pollution_____ 223

Convention for the Safety of Life at
Sea _____ 86

France
Income and property taxes_____ 238
Taxation and fiscal evasion_____ 238

Germany, Federal Republic of
Extradition treaty_____ 85
Social security agreement_____ 362

Hungary, taxation and fiscal evasion
convention _____ 822

International Wheat Agreement,
1971 _____ 434

Japan, extradition treaty_____ 598

Maritime boundary treaties with
Mexico, Venezuela, and Cuba_____ 86

Mexico, extradition treaty_____ 450

Nice Agreement on International
Trademarks _____ 84

Northwest Atlantic Fisheries Convention _____ 777

Tuvalu, friendship treaty_____ 822

United Kingdom, taxation and fiscal
evasion convention_____ 663, 778

Congressional Black Caucus_____ 911

Congressional Liaison, Office of_____ 179

Congressional Steel Caucus_____ 1018

Connally, John_____ 744, 1147

Connecticut, U.S. district judge__ 1018, 1019

Connell, Lawrence, Jr_____ 397, 402

Conservation
Energy. *See* Energy conservation
Water _____ 150

Conservationist of the Year Award_____ 443

Considine, Frank W_____ 548

Constitutional Convention for balanced
Federal budget, proposed_____ 350, 562

Consular relations and Consulates General agreement with China_____ 209

Consumer interests
Anti-inflation competition policy_____ 234

Consumer interests—Continued
Public representation in Federal Government _____ 131

Consumer Product Safety Commission__ 1041,
1044

Consumers Cooperative Banks, National _____ 136

Conte, Repr. Silvio O_____ 983

Convention. *See other part of title*

Conway, James V. P_____ 972

Cooke, John W_____ 631

Coopersmith, Esther Lipsen_____ 464

Coordination Council for North American Affairs_____ 640, 1134

Cordova, Valdemar A_____ 733, 787

Corman, Repr. James C_____ 666, 1025

Corporation. *See other part of title*

Corporations
Profits _____ 473
Voluntary wage and price guidelines.
See under Wages and prices

Corps of Engineers_____ 594, 793

Costle, Douglas M. *See* Environmental
Protection Agency, Administrator

Cota-Robles, Eugene H_____ 46, 92

Cotter, Repr. William R_____ 956

Cotton program, upland_____ 786

Council. *See other part of title*

Country Music Association Award,
Special _____ 898

Courts, United States
Appointments and nominations. *See
specific groups under* Appointments
and Nominations

Federal civil justice system_____ 340

Federal judgeships, merit selection____ 131,
171, 759

Minority appointments_____ 36,
131, 759, 772, 847, 885

Cowan, Geoffrey_____ 46, 91

Coyne, Marshall B_____ 24

Craig, Lois A_____ 44, 92

Craig, Sara_____ 270

Cranston, Sen. Alan_____ 1040

Creal, James B_____ 1007

Credit Union Administration, National.
See National Credit Union Administration

Cribbins, Joseph P_____ 922, 927

Criminal code, Federal_____ 146

Critical energy facility program (EO
12129) _____ 614

Cronkite, Walter_____ 410n.

Crouch, Andrae_____ 1015

Cruise missiles_____ 155, 156, 695

Cuba
Maritime boundary treaty with U.S__ 86
Soviet-U.S. relations, effect on_ 316, 1092
U.S. policy, report_____ 240 (Digest)

Cudahy, Richard D_____ 957

Cultural agreement with China_____ 207

Culver, Sen. John C_____ 804, 956

Current, Gloster_____ 319

Curry, Susanne Shutz_____ 464
Cutler, Elliot R_____ 733
Cutler, Henry_____ 464
Cutler, Lynn_____ 789, 794, 795n.
Cutler, Mitchell S_____ 464
Cutler, Walter L_____ 685, 732
Cyprus
Conflict settlement
Progress reports for negotiated
solution _____ 191, 461, 997
U.S. support of U.N. negotiating
efforts _____ 648
Mention _____ 357
President Spyros Kyprianou_____ 998
Czechoslovakia, U.S. Ambassador___ 383, 402

Dallas, Tex_____ 482
Dalton, John_____ 1034
D'Amours, Repr. Norman E_____ 700,
713, 715, 718
Dancy, John_____ 985–987
Danielson, Repr. George E_____ 1130
Danks, Dale_____ 672
Davin, Frances M_____ 1023
Davis, Richard J_____ 637n.
Day, Clarence C_____ 464
Dayan, Moshe_____ 251, 263, 329
Days, Drew S., III_____ 1159
Dealaman, Doris W_____ 886
Dean, Jonathan_____ 110, 179
Dean, Paul R_____ 271
DeAnda, James_____ 294
DeConcini, Sen. Dennis_____ 432
Defense, Department of
See also specific constituent agencies
Assistant Secretaries__ 269, 294, 1036, 1043
Budget deferrals_____ 200, 603
Contractors indemnification regula-
tions _____ 1132
Deputy Secretary_____ 906
Gasoline allocations for military opera-
tions _____ 875
Land-based missiles development_____ 696
Military Award program_____ 363
Military facilities placement decisions_ 906
Solar energy programs_____ 1100, 1104
University research and development
programs _____ 543
Defense, Secretary of (Harold Brown)
*For functions of the Department in
general, see* Defense, Department
of
Draft registration support_____ 249
Government contracts decision_____ 922
Meetings with the President (Digest)_ 26,
89, 179, 217, 239, 240, 327, 377, 400,
468, 554, 618, 732, 787, 842, 957,
983, 1018, 1142
Mentions _____ 831, 902, 1024, 1079
Middle East, visit to_____ 302, 312, 350
News conferences (Checklist)_____ 843
Permanent American cemetery in Pan-
ama responsibilities_____ 82
SALT II treaty verification_____ 749

Defense, Secretary of—Continued
Security assistance programs admin-
istration (EO 12118)_____ 224
Defense and national security
See also Arms and weapons systems;
Armed Forces, United States
Administration's accomplishments and
goals _____ 561, 719, 836
Defense spending_____ 98,
116, 176, 299, 304, 695
Military facilities_____ 906
National security information_____ 170
Oil emergency supplies_____ 937
President's commitment to American
strength _____ 106, 155, 636
Science and technology development_ 541
Security assistance program_____ 225
Defense Program, Long-Term_____ 156
Defense Transportation Day, National__ 237
Delbridge, Brig. Gen. Norman G_____ 43, 91
Democratic National Committee
Chairman
Meetings with the President
(Digest) _____ 89, 376
Mentions _____ 571n., 948
1980 Presidential campaign state-
ment _____ 966
Spring meeting_____ 948, 958
Democratic Party
Congressional campaign dinner_____ 827
Dinners and receptions
Bedford, N.H_____ 714
Des Moines, Iowa_____ 804
Los Angeles, Calif_____ 372
Manchester, N.H_____ 713
Wausau, Wis_____ 567
Jefferson-Jackson Day dinners
Indianapolis, Ind_____ 988, 989
Milwaukee, Wis_____ 573
Richmond, Va_____ 630
New Governors, meeting with the
President _____ 376
State chairmen, meeting with the
President _____ 666
Support for the President_____ 966
Dempsey, Charles L_____ 365, 377
Deng Xiaoping. *See* China, Vice Premier
Denktash, Rauf_____ 998
Denmark, Vice President's visit____ 220, 639
Denton, Harold R_____ 579, 617, 618
Denver, Colo_____ 183
Deposit Insurance Corporation, Fed-
eral _____ 91, 930
Derrick, Repr. Butler_____ 942
Derwinski, Repr. Edward_____ 1125
Des Moines, Iowa_____ 789, 804, 843
Desai, Morarji_____ 316, 560, 732, 851
Deutch, John Mark_____ 955, 983
Developing countries
Generalized System of Preferences___ 367
Science and technology assistance pro-
grams _____540, 681

Developing countries—Continued
U.S. foreign assistance program reorga-
nization _____ 279, 395, 642, 915
U.S. policy_____ 355
Diamond, Sidney A_____ 196, 218
Diaz, Patricia O'Reilly_____ 464
Diaz Ordaz, Gustavo_____ 809
Dickey, Robert, III_____ 942
Diesel fuel
Allocations
Farmers _____ 803,
846, 937, 945, 951, 987, 1135, 1139
Fishermen _____ 846, 937
Mass transit_____ 1136
Truckers _____ 1135, 1139
1978 farmers consumption_____ 791
Prices _____ 1139
Diggs-Taylor, Anna_____ 900
Dillman, James J_____ 23, 46, 90
Dillon, Douglas_____ 269, 294
Dingell, Repr. John D_____ 840
DiPrete, Andrew A_____ 981, 984
Dirks, Leslie C_____ 179
Disability insurance system_____ 138
Disadvantaged persons
Federal assistance for energy price
increases _____ 864, 953
Health coverage_____ 1029
Welfare reform legislation_____ 938
Disarmament, Socialist International
Study Group on_____ 898
Disaster assistance
Domestic
Mississippi _____ 672, 674
Texas _____ 665
Foreign, Yugoslavia_____ 669
Disaster declarations (Digest)
Alabama _____ 675
Arkansas _____ 667, 674
Florida _____ 898
Hawaii _____ 402
Illinois _____ 786
Kansas _____ 1043
Louisiana _____ 787
Marshall Islands_____ 293
Minnesota _____ 786
Mississippi _____ 675
New Mexico_____ 217
North Dakota_____ 732
Oklahoma _____ 674
Tennessee _____ 841
Texas _____ 667, 732, 1043
District of Columbia
Court of Appeals, Associate Judge____ 957
1980 budget_____ 217
Superior Court, Associate Judges_____ 46,
91, 665, 667, 980, 984
U.S. circuit judges_____ 733, 787, 958, 983
U.S. district judges_____ 93, 378, 402
Voting rights amendment_=__ 143, 144, 298
District judges, U.S. *See* U.S. district
judges *under* Appoinntments and
Nominations

Djerassi, Carl_____ 448
Dobrynin, A. F_____ 356
Dogin, Henry S_____ 268, 294
Dogoloff, Lee I_____ 618
Dollar, U.S., value of
Mentions _____ 113, 736, 935
Stabilization measures_____ 119, 160
U.S. trade imbalance, effects on_____ 953
Domestic Policy Review of Solar
Energy _____ 1101, 1103–1105
Domestic Policy Staff_____ 619, 824
Domestic Violence, Interdepartmental
Committee on_____ 729
Dominica, U.S. Ambassador_____ 664
Dominican Republic, Ambassador to
U.S _____ 25
Donahue, Leo C_____ 1023
Donaldson, Sam_____ 744
Dorval, Romeo_____ 720n.
Douglas, Cathleen_____ 773, 774
Draft reinstatement_____ 249, 472, 654
Dreher, Jennie Taber Clarkson_____ 464
Drinan, Repr. Robert F_____ 666
Drug Abuse, Strategy Council on_____ 618
Drug Abuse and Drug Traffic Prevention,
Federal Strategy for_____ 618, 619
Drug Abuse and Policy, Office of_____ 824
Drugs and narcotics
Illegal trafficking _____ 135, 236
Policy functions_____ 824
Dubs, Adolph
Day honoring (EO 12120)_____ 271
Death statement_____ 269
Memorial ceremonies_____ 295
President's remarks_____ 297, 302
Dudley, Dudley_____ 700, 720n.
Duffy, James H_____ 373, 378
Dukakis, Michael J_____ 947
Duncan, Charles W., Jr_____ 906, 977
Dunfey, Walter J_____ 465
Dunn, Read P., Jr_____ 598, 619
Dupuis, Sylvia L_____ 687
Durkin, Sen. John A_____ 700, 714, 715, 718
Duskin, Elizabeth_____ 45, 92
Dykman, J. T_____ 931
Dymshits, Mark_____ 731
Dyson, Earl Eugene_____ 465

Eads, George C_____ 599, 619
Eagleburger, Lawrence S_____ 670
Earle, Ralph, II_____ 1077, 1143
Earthquake Hazards Reduction program,
National _____ 537
Easter Seal Campaign_____ 377
Easter Seal Poster Child_____ 377
Easter vacation, President's_____ 669
Eastport, Maine_____ 1017
Eaton, Cyrus_____ 837
Ecevit, Bulent_____ 192
Echelman, Shirley_____ 400
Eckstine, Billy_____ 1015
Economic Advisers, Council of__ 467, 599, 619

Economic Advisers, Council of, Chairman
(Charles L. Schultze)
Economic Policy Group member_____ 977
Meetings with the President (Digest)_ 14,
  25, 89, 178, 240, 327, 401, 553, 554,
  666, 732, 841, 898, 956, 957, 1018,
  1142
Mention _____ 96
News conference (Checklist)_____ 179
Economic Community, European_ 83, 539, 550
Economic Cooperation and Development,
  Organization for_____ 7, 224, 241, 787
Economic Development, White House
  Conference on Balanced National
  Growth and_____ 65, 69
Economic Development Administration_ 75,
  77, 601, 1103
Economic Policy Group_____ 977
Economic Report of the President__ 110, 179
Economy, international. *See* Commerce,
  international
Economy, national
  Development programs_ 74, 378 (Checklist)
  Impact of
    Antitrust laws enforcement_____ 132
    Federal budget_____ 96
    International trade agreements____ 161
    Oil imports_____ 351
    Regulatory reform_____ 105
  Inflation. *See* Inflation
  Intergovernmental fiscal assistance___ 391
  Mentions _____ 300, 736
  Productivity growth____ 103, 111, 113, 935
  Public works and economic develop-
    ment legislation_____ 600
Ecuador, President-elect Jaime Roldós__ 1043,
  1044
Edelman, Edmund_____ 813n.
Edington, Patricia G_____ 465
Edison, Thomas_____ 528
Edison and the Centennial of Light,
  Thomas _____ 197
Education
  See also Colleges and universities
  Equal opportunity_____ 884, 885, 909
  Exchange programs with Japan_____ 767
  Federal assistance_____ 708, 848, 970
  Federal programs_____ 139, 709
  International Exchange-of-Persons pro-
    gram _____ 324
  Prayer in public schools_____ 625, 655
  Private schools_____ 848
  Spanish-speaking Americans_____ 813
  Student loans_____ 140, 711
Education, department of
  Advantages of separation from HEW_ 127,
    246, 849
  Congressmen, meeting with the Presi-
    dent _____ 786 (Digest)
  Fact sheet_____ 242 (Checklist)
  Legislation
    Congressional consideration____ 711, 756
    Message to Congress transmitting
      proposal _____ 264

Education, department of—Continued
  Legislation—Continued
    President's promise to resubmit
      proposal in 1979_____ 100, 127
    Science and technology programs
      emphasis _____ 545
Education, Federal Interagency Commit-
  tee on_____ 49
Education, National Advisory Council on
  Extension and Continuing_____ 1023
Education, National Association for
  Equal Opportunity in Higher_____ 742
Education, Office of_____ 139
Educational, space, and agricultural
  agreement with China_____ 202
Educational Research, National Council
  on _____ 44, 91
Efferson, John Norman_____ 942
Eginton, Warren W_____ 1018, 1019
Egypt
  See also Middle East
  Peace negotiations and treaty. *See*
    under Middle East
  President's visit_____ 383,
    394, 405–415, 430, 440, 441
  Prime Minister Mustafa Khalil. *See*
    Egypt, Prime Minister
  U.S. Ambassador_____ 819, 843, 855
  U.S. trade mission_____ 640
  Vice President_____ 1023
Egypt, President (Anwar al-Sadat)
  Comprehensive peace negotiations
    Commitment to settlement_____ 751
    Mentions _____ 688, 703, 967
  Egyptian-Israeli peace negotiations
    Mentions _____ 32,
      263, 315, 346, 360, 394, 400, 425, 427,
      431, 432, 436, 457, 488, 969
    Palestinian position_____ 455
  President's trip to Egypt
    Announcement _____ 383
    Meetings _____ 405,
      407, 410, 412, 415, 430
  Egyptian-Israeli peace treaty
    Joint statement_____ 490
    Letters of agreement_____ 515, 516
    Prime Minister Begin's trip to
      Egypt _____ 618
  Visit to U.S.
    Announcement _____ 467
    Dinner honoring_____ 546
    Mentions _____ 471, 720, 831
    Signing ceremonies_____ 517, 522, 554
Egypt, Prime Minister (Mustafa Khalil)
  Egypt-U.S. Business Council, dinner
    attendance _____ 547, 548n.
  Meeting with the President___ 553 (Digest)
  Middle East peace negotiations
    Meetings with Israeli Foreign
      Minister Dayan_____ 251, 263, 329
    Mentions _____ 347, 408
Eidenberg, Gene_____ 1137, 1139

Eilts, Herman_____ 925
Einstein, Albert_____ 528, 678, 681, 682
Einstein Centennial, Albert_____ 390
Eisenhower, Dwight D_____ 994, 1012, 1088
Eizenstat, Stuart E.
  Economic Policy Group member_____ 977
  Meetings with the President (Digest)_ 14,
    25, 178, 240, 241, 327, 467, 553, 554,
    666, 732, 842, 898, 899, 956, 983, 1142
  Mentions _____ 708, 865, 1028n., 1138
  News conferences (Checklist)_____ 378,
    402, 468, 619, 733, 900, 958, 1028,
    1044, 1143, 1144
Eklund, Lowell_____ 1023
Election Commission, Federal. *See* Federal Election Commission
Elections, public financing_____ 106, 129
Electromagnetic spectrum_____ 541
Electronic surveillance_____ 587, 940
Elisburg, Donald S_____ 1159
Elk City, Okla_____ 469, 841
Elkins, Paul H_____ 465
Emergency Board to investigate an airline labor dispute_____ 89 (Digest), 293
Emergency Board to investigate a railway labor dispute_____ 818, 983, 984
Emergency Broadcast System_____ 567
Emergency building temperature restrictions _____ 370, 690, 797
Emergency declarations (Digest)
  Florida _____ 553
  Georgia _____ 440
  Illinois _____ 89
  Iowa _____ 619
  Mississippi _____ 674
  Missouri _____ 440
  New Hampshire_____ 440
  Washington _____ 440
  Wisconsin _____ 89
Emergency Management Agency, Federal. *See* Federal Emergency Management Agency
Emergency weekend gasoline sales restrictions _____ 370, 608
Employee Management Relations Commission _____ 606
Employment Opportunity Commission, Equal _____ 142, 1140
Employment Policy, National Commission on_____ 947
Employment and unemployment
  Administration's accomplishments and goals _____ 122,
    561, 568, 632, 634, 716, 829, 991
  Employment tax credits_____ 77
  Federal programs_____ 99, 126, 836
  Mining jobs in southeastern Ohio___ 1006
  Minority opportunities_____ 34, 116, 813
  Relationship with inflation_____ 70, 73
  Solar energy systems, new job creation _____ 1098
  Statistics _____ 104,
    112, 117, 126, 299, 568, 716, 829, 970

Employment and unemployment—Continued
  Welfare reform, effect on_____ 939
Endangered Species Committee_____ 23, 376
Energy
  See also Alcohol fuels; Biomass energy; Coal; Gasohol; Gasoline; Geothermal energy; Hydroelectric power; Natural gas; Nuclear energy; Oil; Solar energy; Synthetic fuels
  Administration's accomplishments and goals _____ 122, 632, 717, 830, 946
  Canadian-U.S. relations_____ 381
  Congressional leaders, meeting with the President_____ 554 (Digest)
  Conservation. *See* Energy conservation
  Critical facility program_____ 614
  Energy crisis solution
    Cooperation of all Americans_____ 873,
      937, 951, 993, 1010
    Public recognition of crisis_____ 912,
      933, 936, 993, 1010
  Federal resources management_____ 150
  Florida emergency_____ 637, 817, 1032
  Forest land resources_____ 670
  Fuel companies. *See* Fuel companies
  Industrial consumption, relationship with production growth_____ 148
  Initial fuel assurances_____ 326
  Japan-U.S. development and research programs ___ 767, 1108, 1145, 1149, 1150
  Legislation. *See* Energy legislation
  Mentions _____ 902, 948
  Midwest situation, Congressmen and administration officials, meeting with the President (Digest)_____ 956
  1980 Presidential election issue_____ 951
  Prices. *See* Energy prices
  Research and development. *See* Energy research and development
  Rural areas_____ 791, 843
  Supplies. *See* Energy supplies
  White House briefing for community and civic leaders_____ 862 (Digest)
Energy, Department of
  See also specific constituent agencies
  Alaska Natural Gas Transportation System, transfer of functions_____ 594
  Annual report_____ 842
  Assistant Secretary_____ 733
  Budget rescission and deferrals___ 200, 720
  California gasoline shortages actions_ 808,
    874, 875
  Diesel fuel allocations for farmers____ 945,
    987, 1135, 1139
  Energy conservation contingency plan responsibilities _____ 370, 371
  Energy Extension Service program__ 1492
  Energy security trust fund, initiatives development for_____ 727
  Federal energy use reduction responsibilities _____ 216, 647
  Fossil fuels construction program___ 720

Energy, Department of—Continued
Gasoline allocations responsibilities___ 968, 2084
High energy physics agreement with China _____ 205
Natural gas recovery funding_____ 793
Office of Minority Economic Impact, Director _____ 1040, 1044
Oil
   Decontrol program_____ 721–724
   Imports responsibilities_____ 629, 630
   Industry monitoring_____ 872
President's Commission on the Accident at Three Mile Island, support services (EO 12130)_____ 659
Radioactivity exposure analysis_____ 182
Solar energy programs___ 1110, 1102–1105
Under Secretary_____ 955, 983
Energy, Secretary of (James R. Schlesinger)
Alaska natural gas pipeline construction actions_____ 1245
Alaska Natural Gas Transportation System, Executive Policy Board member _____ 1126
Diesel fuel allocations for farmers_ 803, 1136
Energy Coordinating Committee, subcommittee establishment_____ 1106
High energy physics agreement with China _____ 207
Meetings with the President (Digest)_ 14, 553, 554, 899, 956, 983
Mention _____ 255
Mexican energy supplies purchase__ 58, 185
National energy supply shortage analysis _____ 1227
National Security Award_____ 1515
New England home heating oil inventories _____ 700, 705
News conferences (Checklist) _____ 900, 1019, 1143
Petroleum imports recommendation__ 628
President's Commission on the Accident at Three Mile Island, report reception _____ 691
President's letter to Sen. DeConcini in support of_____ 432
Solar energy development bank, board of directors member_____ 1101
State energy projects management___ 896
Energy Act of 1978, National_____ 1103
Energy Agency, International. *See* International Energy Agency
Energy conservation
Domestic oil prices, effect on_____ 611
Japanese support_____ 1109
Mandatory measures
   Automobile fuel efficiency improvement _____ 797
   Contingency plans_____ 370, 608, 612, 689, 797
   Federal use reduction_____ 216, 613

Energy conservation—Continued
Mandatory measures—Continued
   55 mile-per-hour speed limit enforcement _____ 613, 864, 876
   Standby gasoline rationing. *See* Standby gasoline rationing plan
Mentions _____ 679, 700, 805, 808, 1097
Rural areas_____ 623
Science and technology development__ 533
State planning programs_____ 896
Voluntary measures
Homes
   Temperature restrictions_____ 255, 262, 562, 864
   Weatherization _____ 262, 562
Mass transit use increase__ 255, 613, 960
Mention _____ 258
Unnecessary driving reduction____ 255, 262, 612, 864
Woodburning stoves_____ 797
Energy Coordinating Committee____ 337, 1106
Energy Impact Assistance program___ 77, 150
Energy legislation
See also Energy security trust fund; Standby gasoline rationing plan; Windfall profits tax
Congressional inaction_____ 557, 577, 632, 873, 951
First national plan, 1977_____ 245, 255, 262, 830
Second national plan, message transmittal to Congress_____ 816
Energy management partnership act, proposed _____ 895
Energy physics agreement with China___ 205
Energy prices
Future increases inevitability_____ 577
Impact on
   American conservation_____ 262
   Disadvantaged persons. *See under* Disadvantaged persons
New England_____ 700, 718, 739
Energy research and development
Administration's policy_____ 532
Agricultural research centers_____ 793
Budget allocations_____ 98, 148, 149, 484
U.S. programs size_____ 679
Energy security trust fund
Announcement _____ 610
Appeal for congressional and public support_ 612, 613, 633, 679, 790, 830, 865
Legislative priority of administration_ 649
Mention _____ 739
Message transmitting proposal to Congress _____ 721, 728
News conference_____ 733 (Checklist)

Energy security trust fund—Continued
Purposes
Energy technologies research and development _____ 613,
633, 649, 679, 700, 718, 735, 816,
848, 865, 905, 953, 961, 986, 993,
1102
Low-income assistance for price
increases _____ 624,
632, 649, 680, 700, 718, 735, 816,
848, 865, 953, 961, 986, 993
Mass transit improvement_____ 613,
633, 649, 679, 816, 848, 865, 953,
961, 986, 993
Energy Shortages, White House Manage-
ment Task Force on_____ 1137, 1139
Enger, Valdik_____ 731
Engineers, Corps of_____ 594
Environment
Alaska lands_____ 775, 855, 877
Federal actions, effects abroad_____ 10,
14 (Checklist)
Federal programs_____ 75, 147, 150
Hazardous waste disposal_____ 1034, 1044
Leaders, meeting with the President__ 400
Science and technology development__ 537
Wilderness resource enlargement_____ 670
Environmental Policy Act of 1978, Na-
tional _____ 121
Environmental Protection Agency
Air pollution standards_____ 183, 349
Assistant Administrator_____ 1044
Coal industry emission standards__ 841, 905
Gasoline emission standards_____ 876
Ohio mining jobs preservation_____ 1006
Regulatory process streamlining__ 151, 535
Rural areas programs_____ 75
Environmental Protection Agency, Ad-
ministrator (Douglas M. Costle)
Alaska Natural Gas Transportation
System
Executive Policy Board member____ 1126
Transfer of functions_____ 594, 1126
Energy emergency monitoring_____ 637,
817, 1032
Meeting with the President__ 327 (Digest)
Mention _____ 905
News conferences (Checklist)___1019, 1044
Environmental Quality, Council on
Annual report_____ 119
Chairman _____ 872, 876, 960
Environmental information exchange
with foreign nations_____ 10–13
Equal employment opportunity_____ 847
Equal Employment Opportunity Com-
mission _____ 142, 1140
Equal Opportunity in Higher Education,
National Association for_____ 742
Equal rights amendment
Administration's efforts to secure rati-
fication _____ 144, 1011
Biblical basis for_____ 472
Deadline extension for ratification___ 143
President's appeal for public support_ 298

Ertel, Repr. Allen E_____ 667
Escarcega, Roy R_____ 947
Ethics, Office of Government_____ 1131
Ethics in Government Act of 1978
amendments _____ 1131
Europe, Conference on Security and
Cooperation in_____ 979
Europe
See also specific country
U.S. delegation's visit_____ 436
European Economic Community_ 83, 539, 550
European Space Organization_____ 538
Evans, Repr. David W_____ 990
Evans, John R_____ 1021
Evans, Orinda D_____ 1018, 1019
Evans, Patty_____ 989, 990
Evron, Ephraim_____ 25
Executive Exchange, President's Commis-
sion on_____ 866, 976
Executive group to combat fraud and
waste in government, proposed_____ 780
Executive Office of the President_____ 824

Executive Orders

Alaska Natural Gas Transportation
System (EO 12142)_____ 1126
Competitive status for handicapped
Federal employees (EO 12125)___ 434
Critical energy facility program (EO
12129) _____ 614
Drug policy functions (EO 12133)___ 824
Dubs, Adolph (EO 12120)_____ 271
Emergency Board to investigate a rail-
way labor dispute (EO 12132)____ 818
Energy Coordinating Committee (EO
12121) _____ 337
Environmental effects abroad of major
Federal actions (EO 12114)_____ 10
Equal Employment Opportunity Com-
mission (EO 12144)_____1140
Executive Office of the President,
printing services (EO 12134)_____ 824
Executive Schedule
(EO 12111)_____ 3
(EO 12119)_____ 270
Federal civil service reorganization
(EO 12126)_____ 550
Federal Emergency Management
Agency (EO 12127)_____ 566
Food stamps issuance by United States
Postal Service (EO 12116)_____ 83
Foreign intelligence electronic surveil-
lance (EO 12139)_____ 940
Foreign Service employee-manage-
ment relations (EO 12128)_____ 606
Gasoline end-user allocation (EO
12140) _____ 968
Generalized System of Preferences for
developing countries (EO 12124)__ 367
Independent water project review
(EO 12113)_____ 8
(EO 12141)_____ 1000

Executive Orders—Continued

Office of Administration
(EO 12112)_____ 3
(EO 12122)_____ 337
Offshore oil spill pollution (EO
12123) _____ 338
Panama, permanent American cemetery in (EO 12115)_____ 81
Peace Corps (EO 12137)_____ 877
President's Advisory Committee for
Women (EO 12135)_____ 825
President's Commission on the Accident at Three Mile Island (EO
12130) _____ 659
President's Commission on Executive
Exchange (EO 12136)_____ 866
President's Export Council (EO
12131) _____ 784
Security assistance programs, administration of (EO 12118)_____ 224
Taiwan-U.S. relations (EO 12143)__ 1132
Ugandan imports (EO 12117)_____ 224
Women's business enterprise (EO
12138) _____ 890
Executive Schedule_____ 3, 270
Exon, Sen. J. James_____ 956
Export Administration Act_____ 146, 333, 944
Export Council, President's_____ 784, 942, 943
Export Credits, International Arrangement on_____ 439
Export-Import Bank of the United
States _____ 331, 332, 439
Exports. *See under* Commerce, international

Fahd Bin Abd al-Aziz al-Sa'ud_____ 182,
240, 242, 456
Fair Housing Act_____ 884
Falco, K. Mathea_____ 21, 91
Faletau, 'Inoke_____ 554
Falk, Peter_____ 770
Fallows, James M_____ 744, 751
Families, White House Conference on__ 667,
668
Families With Dependent Children, Aid
to _____ 940
Family, American_____ 138
Family Grant program, Individual_____ 553
Fang Yi_____ 203, 205n., 207
Far East, U.S. policy_____ 1110
Farm Safety Week, National_____ 433
Farmers Home Administration
Business and industry loans___ 74, 601–603
Rural development services_____ 75, 77
Solar energy programs_____ 1103
Farms and farming. *See* Agriculture, farm
sector and farmers
Fascell, Repr. Dante B_____ 666
Father's Day (Proc. 4659)_____ 747
Federal advisory committees_____ 463, 468
Federal Bureau of Investigation
Deputy Assistant Director_____ 37, 959
Director _____ 959, 1130, 1143

Federal civil justice system_____ 340–346, 378
Federal civil service reform
EO 12126_____ 550
Federal employee performance, effect
on _____ 634, 917, 920
Management improvement program__ 779
Mentions _____ 75, 128, 719
Federal Communications Commission
Broadcasting regulatory reform___ 482, 483
Members _____ 46, 91, 1021, 1043
Federal Contract Compliance Programs,
Office of_____ 142
Federal Council on the Arts and Humanities _____ 956
Federal departments and agencies
See also Memorandums to Federal
Agencies; *specific department or
agency*
Administration's accomplishments and
goals _____ 122, 569, 632, 718, 830
Anti-inflation program_____ 308
Economic growth policy_____ 76
Energy use reduction_____ 216
Government regulations, public participation programs_____ 867
Government integrity, restoration of__ 561,
569, 715, 829, 991
Inspectors General offices. *See* Federal Inspectors General offices
Nuclear nonproliferation activities___ 452
Privacy rights policy_____ 582, 585, 586
Regional commissions_____ 79, 80
Regulatory management_____ 491
Science and technology activities__ 531, 544
Solar energy programs_____ 1100
Waste energy programs_____ 1100
Federal Deposit Insurance Corporation__ 91,
930
Federal Election Commission, members__ 45,
46, 90, 91, 757, 788
Federal Emergency Management Agency
Acting Associate Director_____ 599
Acting Director_____ 567
Activation _____ 566
Director _____ 781, 1044
Purposes of creation_____ 537
Federal employees
Free parking elimination_____ 613
Handicapped, competitive status for__ 434,
441
Pay increases_____ 7, 64, 115
Pay reform legislation_____ 128, 1002, 1019
Question-and-answer session with the
President _____ 916
Federal Energy Regulatory Commission_ 594,
1126
Federal Highway Administration_____ 75
Federal Home Loan Bank Board_____ 930,
981, 984, 990
Federal inspector for the Alaska natural
gas transportation system, office of,
proposed _____ 591–593, 596, 597

Federal Inspectors General offices
Coordination of Federal investiga-
tive activities_____ 779
Executive Group to Combat Fraud
and Waste in Government, member-
ship _____ 780
Federal fraud and abuse investigations_ 300,
308, 462, 719, 917
Federal Interagency Committee on Edu-
cation _____ 49
Federal Labor Relations Authority
General Counsel_____ 528, 554
Members _____ 24, 46, 90, 784, 843
Federal Maritime Commission_____ 338, 339
Federal National Mortgage Association_ 931
Federal Pay, Advisory Committee on___ 64
Federal pipeline inspector, office of the,
proposed _____ 381
Federal Procurement Policy, Office of___ 241
(Checklist)
Federal Regional Councils_____ 81, 269
Federal Reserve System
Anti-inflation program_____ 114
Board of Governors
Chairman _____ 401
Members _____ 663, 664, 899, 1044
Vice Chairman_____ 1043, 1044
Interest rate control____ 132, 707, 930
Federal Service Impasses Panel_____ 23
Federal and State Laws Relating to Wire-
tapping and Electronic Surveillance,
National Commission for the Review
of _____ 585, 587–590
Federal Strategy for Drug Abuse and
Drug Traffic Prevention_____ 618, 619
Federal Trade Commission_ 234, 235, 242, 339
Federal Wage System_____ 1003
Feinstein, Dianne_____ 808 ftn.
Felder, Allie C., Jr_____ 1022, 1043
Ferre, Sister M. Isolina_____ 340, 377
Ferre, Maurice_____ 401
Ferris, Charles D_____ 483, 485
Fetter, Elizabeth A_____ 914
Fettig, Lester A_____ 241 (Checklist)
Financial Management Improvement
Program, Joint_____ 462
Financial reports, President's_____ 983
Finch, Gov. Cliff_____ 672, 674, 731
Finland
Prime Minister Kalevi Sorsa_____ 898
Vice President's visit_____ 220, 639
Fire Administration, United States_ 22, 91, 566
Fire Prevention and Control, National
Academy for_____ 566
Fiscal assistance legislation, intergovern-
mental _____ 391, 401–403
Fish Fry, Georgia State Society_____ 898
Fish Health Research Laboratory, Na-
tional _____ 1042
Fisheries Commission, International
North Pacific_____ 1001
Fishing industry
Diesel fuel guarantees_____ 846, 937
Legislation _____ 855

Fishing industry—Continued
Production increase_____ 754
Fishing trips, President's_____ 964, 1042
Fithian, Repr. Floyd J_____ 990
Flag Day and Week (Proc. 4660) _____ 817
Fleener, Terre_____ 798
Flores, Batuel_____ 281n.
Florida
Disaster declaration_____ 898
Emergency declaration_____ 553
Energy emergency_____ 637, 817, 1032
U.S. attorney_____ 241
U.S. district judges_____ 242,
957, 1018, 1019, 1043, 1044
Florio, Repr. James J_____ 468
Floyd, Sloppy_____ 300
Foley, Repr. Thomas S_____ 943
Food
Federal programs_____ 135
Mention _____ 935
Prices _____ 717, 754, 796, 850
Stamps _____ 83, 188, 480
U.S. exports exchange for foreign oil,
possibility _____ 791, 802
Food and Agricultural Development,
Board for International_____ 437
Food Aid Committee_____ 434
Food Aid Convention_____ 434
Food and Commercial Workers Interna-
tional Union, United_____ 1008, 1020
Foodstuffs, Agreement on International
Carriage of Perishable_____ 83
Ford, Gerald R_____ 695, 786
Ford Motor Company_____ 900
Fordham University, N.Y_____ 984
Foreign assistance
See also Developing countries; *specific
country or region*
Program reorganization_____ 279,
294, 395, 643, 915
Security assistance programs adminis-
tration _____ 225
Foreign Claims Settlement Commission
of the United States_____ 46, 90, 720
Foreign policy
See also specific country or region
Administration's accomplishments and
goals _____ 155,
561, 569, 636, 720, 830, 845, 950
Noninvolvement in other countries' in-
ternal affairs_____ 347
Reflection of American ideals_____ 355,
494, 636, 720, 830
Senators, meeting with the President__ 240
(Digest)
U.S. relations with former Soviet
allies _____ 564
U.S. security responsibilities_____ 301
Foreign Policy Conference_____ 310
Foreign Service_____ 606, 760
Forest Service_____ 775
Forest System, National_____ 151, 671
Forests, New England energy source____ 701

Fortson, Ben_____ 913
Foundation for International Tech-
    nological Cooperation_____ 141, 161
Fowler, Frank E_____ 465
France
    Conventions with U.S.
        Income and property taxes_____ 238
        Taxation and fiscal evasion_____ 238
    Minister of Foreign Affairs_____ 1017
    President Valéry Giscard d'Estaing___ 17,
        20n., 25 (Digest), 26 (Checklist)
    Tokyo Summit attendance announce-
        ment _____ 550
Francisco Otero, Joaquin_____ 450
François-Poncet, Jean_____ 1017
Frankford Arsenal, Pa_____ 906
Franklin, Benjamin_____ 677
Franklin, John Hope_____ 729, 787
Fraser, J. Malcolm_____ 2
Fraud and waste in government, execu-
    tive group to combat, proposed_____ 780
Frazier, A. D., Jr_____ 231, 241
Frazier, Henry B., III_____ 24, 46, 90
Fred, Matthew_____ 773
Free, James C_____ 732, 898
Freeman, Frankie M_____ 1042, 1044
Freeman, Orville L_____ 213
Freeman, Rowland G., III_____ 458, 619
Freight rail industry. *See* Railroads
French, Philip_____ 993, 1008
Friedersdorf, Max L_____ 46, 91
Friedl, Ernestine_____ 46, 92
Friedlander, Paul S_____ 46, 91
Friedman, Martin_____ 45, 92
Fritschler, A. Lee_____ 856, 899
Frosch, Robert A_____ 206
Frydenlund, Knut_____ 33n.
Fryman, Patsy L_____ 947
Fuel assurances, initial_____ 326
Fuel companies
    Collusion investigations of gasoline
        shortages _____ 872
    Divestiture and nationalization, possi-
        bility _____ 654
    Representatives, meeting with the
        President _____ 983
    Windfall profits tax. *See* Windfall prof-
        its tax
Full Employment and Balanced Growth
    Act _____ 116, 126
Fuqua, Repr. Don_____ 730

Gabonese Republic, Ambassador to U.S_ 25
Gallen, Gov. Hugh_____ 700, 713, 715
Gambia, Ambassador to U.S_____ 842
Gambling, legalized_____ 246
Gammino, Michael A., Jr_____ 435, 441
Gamser, Howard G_____ 23
Gandy, Lt. Gov. Evelyn_____ 731
Garcia, Angelina_____ 926, 927
Gardner, John_____ 1012
Gardner, Richard N_____ 618
Garza, Reynaldo G_____ 733, 787
Gas, natural. *See* Natural gas

Gas Pipeline, Northern_____ 381
Gaskins, Darius W., Jr_____ 871, 899
Gasohol
    Budget allocations increase_____ 484
    Excise tax exemption_____ 1103
    Forest products and crops conver-
        sion to_____ 614, 792, 799
    Legislation _____ 484
    Production plants construction_____ 792
Gasoline
    California shortages_____ 808,
        872, 873, 898, 900, 985
    Consumer and conservation represent-
        atives, meeting with the President_ 983
    Emergency sales restrictions_____ 370
        608, 689
    End-user allocation (EO 12140)_____ 968,
        984 (Checklist)
    National and State ration reserves____ 814,
        821, 960
    Standby rationing plan. *See* Standby
        gasoline rationing plan
    Supplies _____ 705
    Unleaded production____ 1019 (Checklist)
Geller, Henry_____ 619
General Accounting Office_____ 462
General Motors Corporation_____ 740, 786
General Schedule_____ 1003
General Services Administration
    Inspector General_____ 198, 378
    Misconduct investigations_____ 719, 924
    President's Commission on the Acci-
        dent at Three Mile Island, support
        services _____ 659
General Services Administration, Admin-
        istrator (Joel W. Solomon)
    Meetings with the President (Di-
        gest) _____ 178, 467
    Resignation _____ 448
General Services Administration, Admin-
        istrator (Rowland G. Freeman III)
    Federal Council on the Arts and the
        Humanities, member_____ 956
    Nomination _____ 458, 619
Generalized System of Preferences_____ 367
Genocide, Convention on the Prevention
    and Punishment of the Crime of_____ 162
Genocide, International Treaty on the
    Prevention and the Punishment of___ 684
Gentry, John N_____ 25, 467
Geological Survey_____ 374
Georgia
    Emergency declaration_____ 440
    1976 campaign volunteers, meeting
        with the President_____ 618
    President's visit_____ 296–306,
        667, 669, 675 (Digest) 731
    U.S. district judges_ 1018, 1019, 1043, 1044
Georgia Institute of Technology_____ 300
Georgia Lions International_____ 617
Georgia State Society Fish Fry_____ 898
Gephardt, Repr. Richard A_____ 942

Germany, Federal Republic of
Basic Law_____ 927
Coal development project with U.S.
and Japan_____ 1150
Extradition treaty with U.S._____ 85
Social security agreement with U.S.___ 362
Tokyo Summit attendance announce-
ment _____ 550
Germany, Federal Republic of, Chancel-
lor (Helmut Schmidt)
Guadeloupe Conference
Conclusion remarks_____ 19
Meetings with the President and
Western European leaders_____ 20n.,
25 (Digest), 26 (Digest)
Turkey, economic aid actions for____ 653
Visit to U.S.
Announcement _____ 666 (Digest)
Meetings with the President__ 1004, 1005
Mention _____ 902
Giaimo, Repr. Robert N_____ 179, 591n.
Giant Foods_____ 850
Gibson, Audrey N_____ 925, 927
Gibson, Kenneth A_____ 402, 942
Gilinsky, Victor_____ 855, 899
Gilligan, John J_____ 294
Gilman, Marvin S_____ 932
Ginzberg, Eli_____ 947
Ginzburg, Alexander_____ 731
Giscard d'Estaing, Valéry_____ 17,
20n., 25 (Digest), 26 (Checklist)
Gitlin, Christine Miles_____ 465
Glenn, Sen. John H., Jr_____ 178, 617, 1006
Gleysteen, Mr. and Mrs. William H____ 1155
Global Atmospheric Research Project___ 538
GNP. *See* Gross national product
Goldhammer, Robert F_____ 465
Goldman, Patricia A_____ 437, 441
Gomez, Joseph N_____ 976
Gonzales, Arnold_____ 401
Good, Mary Lowe_____ 448
Goode, Malvin_____ 319
Gordon, H. Stephan_____ 528, 554
Gorman, Paddy_____ 1008
Gould, Harry E., Jr_____ 942
Government reform and reorganization
Federal pay system_____ 919, 1002
1979 proposals_____ 127, 378 (Checklist)
Progress during administration_____ 74, 127
Governors' Association, National. *See*
National Governors' Association
Gowdy, Sharon Kaye_____ 465
Graham, Gov. Robert___ 328, 637, 638, 1032
Graham, Thomas, Jr_____ 1077
Gramley, Lyle E_____ 467
Grandmaison, Joe_____ 270
Granum, Rex_____ 1016n.
Gratch, Serge_____ 1008
Gray, Hanna Holborn_____ 553
Gray, Repr. William H., III_____ 787
Greathouse, Pat_____ 942

Greece
Cyprus conflict_____ 191
Mention _____ 846
U.S. policy_____ 156
Green, Joyce Hens_____ 378, 402
Green, William J_____ 1042
Greenough, William C_____ 271
Grenada, U.S. Ambassador_____ 664
Griffiths, Martha W_____ 271
Gromyko, A. A_____ 1079
Gross national product_____ 307,
736, 1025, 1030
Grunitzky, Yao_____ 842
Guadeloupe, President's visit___ 14, 17, 25, 26
Guatemala, Ambassador to U.S_ 376, 783, 842
Guinea, Ambassador to U.S_____ 842
Gun control_____ 652
Guyette, Curtis W_____ 733, 787
Gwirtzman, Milton S_____ 23, 46, 90

Hackler, Lloyd_____ 832
Haffenreffer, Carolyn B_____ 465
Haggerty, Patrick E_____ 660
Hahn, Kenneth_____ 813n.
Hall, Paul_____ 942, 943
Halpern, Paul_____ 465
Hamilton, Charles V_____ 46, 90
Hamilton, Repr. Lee H_____ 666, 990
Handicapped, Committee for Purchase
From the Blind and Other Severely__ 163,
437
Handicapped, President's Committee on
Employment of the_____ 463
Handicapped persons
Competitive status for Federal em-
ployees (EO 12125)_____ 434,
441 (Checklist)
Federal programs_____ 144
Handler, Philip_____ 683n.
Hanley, Joy J_____ 446
Harkin, Repr. Thomas R_____ 789, 795n., 805
Harriman, W. Averell_____ 293, 1017
Harriman, Mrs. W. Averell_____ 293
Harris, Neil_____ 269, 294
Harris, Ralph_____ 746n.
Harris, Maj. Gen. Richard L_____ 44, 92
Harris, Thomas E_____ 757, 788
Harrison, Benjamin_____ 1095
Harrison, Edythe C_____ 465
Hart, Sen. Gary W_____ 178 (Digest), 956
Hartigan, Neil_____ 401
Hartman, Hermene D_____ 465
Harvey, Patricia M_____ 889, 890n.
Hatch Act_____ 147
Hatcher, Richard_____ 402
Hatchett, Joseph W_____ 899, 900
Hatfield, Sen. Paul G_____ 441, 867
Hathaway, Dale Ernest_____ 218
Haughton, Ronald W_____ 24, 46, 90
Hawaii, disaster declaration_____ 402
Hawkins, Repr. Augustus_____ 318
Hawkins, Falcon B_____ 1018, 1019
Hayes, Robert M_____ 400

Hayne, William A_____ 1042
Hazardous Materials Control, Annual
  Report on_____ 178 (Digest)
Health, Education, and Welfare, Depart-
  ment of
  See also specific constituent agencies
  Assistant Secretaries_____ 339,
                        377, 742, 886n., 1143
  Black colleges and institutions
    strengthening _____ 49
  Budget rescission_____ 200
  Department of education, advantages
    of separation from_____ 849
  Deputy Inspector General_____ 616, 667
  Federal paperwork reduction_____ 869
  General Counsel_____ 1000, 1019
  Health research strategy_____ 535
  Healthcare program promotion_____ 1031
  Mental health demonstration projects_ 862
  President's Commission on the Acci-
    dent at Three Mile Island, support
    services _____ 659
  Radioactivity exposure analysis_____ 182
  Reports preparation_____ 103,
        362, 1604, 1704, 1705, 1966, 2035,
        2105
  Rural development programs_____ 75
  Welfare program administration_____ 940
Health, Education, and Welfare, Secre-
  tary of (Joseph A. Califano, Jr.)
  *For functions of the Department in
    general, see* Health, Education, and
    Welfare, Department of
  Black colleges and institutions respon-
    sibilities _____ 49
  Health information and promotion, re-
    port preparation_____ 467 (Digest)
  Interdepartmental Committee on Do-
    mestic Violence, Chairman_____ 729
  Meetings with the President (Digest)_ 240,
                                        898
  Mentions _____ 246, 386ftn., 691, 886n.
  National health plan legislation brief-
    ing _____ 65
  News conferences (Checklist)_____ 402,
                        859, 958, 1028, 1044
  Women's educational programs ac-
    tions _____ 895
  World Health Organization, U.S.
    Chief Delegate_____ 815
Health, National Institutes of_____ 544
Health, Physical Education, Recreation
  and Dance, American Alliance for____ 955
Health Assembly, World_____ 815
Health Maintenance Organizations____ 134
Health and medical care
  Federal coal mine activities_____ 103
  Federal programs_____ 117, 135, 534
  Hazardous waste disposal_____ 1034, 1044
  Health costs review_____ 74
  Health insurance_____ 898, 925
  Hospital cost containment. *See* Hos-
    pital cost containment

Health and medical care—Continued
  Information and promotion status, re-
    port _____ 467 (Digest)
  Mental health. *See* Mental health
  National plan
    Briefing by HEW Secretary Cali-
      fano _____ 65
    Budget allocation_____ 98
    Congressional leaders, meeting with
      the President_____ 1011
    Mentions _____ 104, 137
    News conference_____ 1044 (Checklist)
    Proposed legislation_____ 1024, 1028
  Older persons_____ 673, 838
  Regulatory reform_____ 475
  Rural initiatives_____ 794
Health Service Award, Public_____ 983
Health Service Corps, National_____ 134
Healthcare program, Federal_____ 1024,
                        1025, 1028–1031
Hearst, Patricia Campbell__ 217 (Digest), 218
Heart, Lung, and Blood Institute, Na-
  tional _____ 178
Heart Month, American_____ 21
Hector, Louis J_____ 46, 90
Hedemann, Knut_____ 377
Heineman, Benjamin W_____ 339, 377
Helicopters, President's use of_____ 961
Hemingway, Ernest_____ 670
Henderson, Albert J_____ 675
Henderson, Maureen M_____ 686
Henry, Aaron_____ 317, 323n.
Hermann, Robert J_____ 1128, 1142
Hernandez, Richard_____ 811
Herrera Campins, Luis_____ 239 (Digest), 401
Herschler, Gov. Ed_____ 23
Hesburgh, Theodore M_____ 540
Heumann, Judith E_____ 464
Heymann, Philip_____ 619, 1143
Hidaka, Yoshiki_____ 1107
Hidalgo y Castilla, Father Miguel_____ 809
Higby, Lynn C_____ 1043, 1044
Higginbotham, A. Leon, Jr_____ 742
High Energy Physics, Committee on____ 206
Highways, 55-mile speed limit__ 480, 613, 876
Hill, Jesse, Jr_____ 33n., 91, 271, 294
Hill, Kenneth_____ 665
Hill, Warren G_____ 400
Hinerfeld, Ruth_____ 773 ftn.
Hirohito, Emperor_____ 1108, 1112
Hispanic Americans. *See* Spanish-speak-
  ing Americans
Hispanic Heritage Week, National (Proc.
  4662) _____ 930
Hodges, Luther H., Jr_____ 782, 842
Holland, Jerome H_____ 552
Holman, M. Carl_____ 46, 90
Holmes Devise, Permanent Committee
  for the Oliver Wendell_____ 746
Holocaust, Days of Remembrance of
  Victims of the_____ 580, 684, 733
Holocaust, President's Commission on
  the _____ 147, 293, 685

Home Administration, Farmers_____ 601–603
Home Builders, National Association of_ 732
Home Loan Bank Board, Federal_____ 930,
                  981, 984, 990
Home Ownership Assistance Plan_____ 74
Honduras, Ambassador to U.S_____ 25
Hooks, Benjamin_____ 38
Hori, Yoshio_____ 1107
Horvitz, Wayne_____ 752
Hospital cost containment legislation
  Appeal for public support____ 37, 838, 952
  Congressional inaction_____ 952, 963, 1025
  Inflation control measure_____ 37,
      99, 105, 123, 569, 576, 963, 1025
  Mentions _____ 111, 134, 926
  Message transmitting proposals to Con-
    gress _____ 383, 386
  National health plan, relationship
    with _____ 1030
  News conference_____ 402 (Checklist)
  Public comments received by White
    House (Checklist)_____ 402, 441
  Repr. James R. Jones of Oklahoma,
    meeting with the President (Di-
    gest) _____ 956
  White House briefing for civic and
    community leaders_____ 603
Houck, C. Weston_____ 1019
Housing
  Discriminatory practices_____ 884, 911
  Federal mortgage programs_____ 709, 928
  Heating oil supplies. *See* Home heating
    under Oil supplies
  New homes construction_ 117, 136, 704, 754
Housing and Urban Development, De-
  partment of
  See also specific constituent agencies
  Assistant Secretaries_____ 42, 61, 93
  Budget rescission_____ 200
  Federal paperwork reduction actions_ 75
  Housing discrimination enforcement__ 143,
                  884
  Housing rehabilitation program_____ 77
  Inspector General_____ 365, 377
  Mental health demonstration proj-
    ects _____ 862
  Solar energy development bank_____ 1101
  Urban Development Action Grant
    program _____ 74, 600, 601
Housing and Urban Development, Sec-
  retary of (Patricia Roberts Harris)__ 566,
                 884, 911, 956
Howard, Repr. James J___ 89, 666, 898, 1115
Howard, Joseph C., Sr_____ 957, 958
Howard, Lee M_____ 815
Howe, Kay_____ 46, 90
Hua Guofeng_____ 1, 1112
Huang Hua__ 14 (Checklist), 209, 210n., 248
Hubert H. Humphrey Fellowship pro-
  gram _____ 324
Huckel, Claire_____ 377
Hull, Ron_____ 465

Human rights
  Administration's accomplishments and
    goals _____ 122, 569, 636, 720, 830
  Domestic
    Blacks _____ 142, 883, 911, 970
    District of Columbia voting rights__ 143,
                  144
    Freedom of the press_____ 693
    Handicapped _____ 145, 858
    Indians _____ 145
    Labor laws_____ 108, 146
    Privacy rights_____ 145
    Undocumented aliens_____ 145, 810
    Women _____ 108, 143, 1011
  Foreign
    Panama _____ 575
    Philippines _____ 867
    Uganda _____ 867
    U.S. efforts through United Na-
      tions _____ 63
  Mentions _____ 684, 830
  Progress during administration_____ 162
  Reflection of American ideals_____ 108,
          161, 357, 720, 1011
  U.S. foreign policy, relationship with_ 162,
                  627
Human Rights, Inter-American Conven-
  tion on_____ 162
Humanities, National Council on the.
  See National Council on the Humani-
  ties
Humphrey, Hubert H_____ 1036
Humphrey, Hubert H., Fellowship pro-
  gram _____ 324
Hundley, Rebecca B_____ 1034
Hungary
  Taxation and fiscal evasion convention
    with U.S_____ 822
  Trade with U.S_____ 978, 979
Hungate, William L_____ 899, 900
Hunger, Presidential Commission on
  World _____ 147, 213
Hunt, Gov. James_____ 544
Hunt, Pierre_____ 26
Hussein I, King_____ 454, 456
Huyser, Gen. Robert E_____ 239 (Digest)
Hydroelectric power, New England
  small-scale production plants_____ 701, 792

ICBMs
  See also MX missile
  Mobile basing mode_____ 696, 1016
  Research and development_____ 155
  SALT II treaty provisions_ 967, 1051, 1059
Iceland, Vice President's visit_____ 220, 639
Illinois
  Disaster declaration_____ 786
  Emergency declaration_____ 89
  U.S. district judges_____ 733, 787, 957
  U.S. marshal_____ 788
Immigration and Naturalization Serv-
  ice _____ 806
Immigration and Refugee Policy, Select
  Commission on_____ 450, 564, 812, 907

Imports. *See under* Commerce, international
Independence Day_____ 1127
India
   Alignment with Soviet Union_____ 316
   Minister of External Affairs__ 731 (Digest)
   Nuclear materials exports from U.S__ 559
   Prime Minister Morarji Desai_____ 851
Indian Education, National Advisory
   Council on_____ 446, 932
Indiana, President's visit_____ 988, 989, 1017
Indianapolis, Ind_____ 988, 989, 1017
Indians, American, administration's pol-
   icy _____ 144
Individual Family Grant program_____ 553
Indo-U.S. Joint Commission___ 731 (Digest)
Indochina
   See also specific countries
   Refugees
     Mention _____ 1050
     Resettlement in United States and
      Japan _____ 765, 971
   U.S. policy_____ 303, 765
Industry. *See* Business and industry, U.S.
Inflation
   See also Anti-inflation program
   Causes
     Foreign exchange market prices___ 125,
      474, 487, 736
     Oil imports. *See under* Oil imports
     Severe winter weather_ 635, 705, 736, 796
     Small beef herds_____ 635, 705, 736
   Impact on
     Elderly ____ 111, 113, 122, 796, 838, 912
     Employment _____ 70, 73
     Federal taxation_____ 116, 247
     Interest rates_____ 113, 122, 707
     Poor _____ 111, 113, 122, 188, 912
     Public confidence_____ 113, 123
   1978 increases in inflation rate,
     President's assessment_____ 112
Ingram, James_____ 959
Inspectors General offices, Federal. *See*
   Federal Inspectors General offices
Institute of Museum Services_____ 956
Institute for Scientific and Technologi-
   cal Cooperation
   Congressional consideration_____ 681
   Reorganization Plan No. 2 of 1979___ 643,
     644
   Research and technological innovation
     in foreign countries_____ 279, 396, 540
Intelligence community
   Foreign electronic surveillance_____ 940
   Statutory charters_____ 146
Interagency Committee on Women's
   Business Enterprise_____ 891, 892, 894
Interagency Coordinating Council_____ 75,
     77–80, 668
Interagency Council on Accident Com-
   pensation and Insurance Issues_____ 339
Interagency Regulatory Liaison Group__ 535

Interagency Task Force on Women Busi-
   ness Owners_____ 890
Inter-American Convention on Human
   Rights _____ 162
Intercontinental ballistic missiles. *See*
   ICBMs
Interdepartmental Committee on Domes-
   tic Violence_____ 729
Interdepartmental task force for women_ 826
Interest rates
   Federal Reserve Board control_____ 707
   Reform legislation_____ 132, 928, 930
Intergovernmental fiscal assistance leg-
   islation _____ 391, 401–403
Intergovernmental Maritime Consulta-
   tive Organization, Convention on the_ 778
Intergovernmental Relations, Advisory
   Commission on_____ 463, 886, 1034
Intergovernmental Science, Engineering,
   and Technology Advisory Panel_____ 544
Interior, Department of the
   See also specific constituent agencies
   Alaska Natural Gas Transportation
     System, transfer of functions_____ 594
   Assistant Secretary_____ 46, 91
   Budget rescission and deferrals___ 200, 603
   Inspector General_____ 365, 377
   Solicitor _____ 990
   Under Secretary_____ 990
Interior, Secretary of the (Cecil D. An-
   drus)
   *For functions of the Department in
   general, see* Interior, Department of
   the
   Alaska Natural Gas Transportation
     System, Executive Policy Board
     member _____ 1126
   Meeting with the President__ 240 (Digest)
   Mentions _____ 246, 386, 773
   News conferences (Checklist)_____ 402, 900
International Arrangement on Export
   Credits _____ 438
International Atomic Energy Agency___ 159,
     452, 1048
International Boundary Commission,
   United States and Canada_____ 990
International Civil Aviation Organiza-
   tion _____ 449
International Commission for the Con-
   servation of Atlantic Tunas_____ 436
International Commission for the North-
   west Atlantic Fisheries_____ 777
International Committee on Telecom-
   munications _____ 270
International Communication, Cultural
   and Educational Affairs, United States
   Advisory Commission on_____ 729,
     787, 1037, 1044
International Communication Agency__ 142,
     208, 272, 324
International communications policy___ 240

International Development, Agency for
Administrator _____ 294
Personnel system_____ 760
Reorganization ____ 396, 643, 644, 646, 915
Science and technology programs____ 540
Solar energy programs_____ 1100, 1105
International Development Cooperation
Agency, United States_____ 279,
395, 642, 915
International Energy Agency
Energy conservation commitment____ 381,
647, 767, 816, 964
Energy research and development____ 538
International Exchange-of-Persons pro-
gram _____ 324
International Fund for Agricultural De-
velopment _____ 63
International Holocaust Commemora-
tion Day (Proc. 4652)_____ 581
International journalistic freedom_____ 240
International Labor Organization_____ 63
International Monetary Fund_____ 446, 468
International North Pacific Fisheries
Commission _____ 1001
International Nuclear Fuel Cycle Evalua-
tion _____ 159, 452, 541, 767
International Steel Agreement_____ 7
International Sugar Agreement_____ 153, 161
International Telecommunications Con-
vention _____ 541
International Tin Agreement_____ 161
International Trade Commission, United
States. *See* United States International
Trade Commission
International Trademarks, Nice Agree-
ment on_____ 84
International Treaty on the Prevention
and the Punishment of Genocide____ 684
International Whaling Commission_____ 265
International Wheat Agreement, 1971__ 434
International Wheat Council_____ 434
Interstate Commerce Commission
Chairman _____ 217
Fuel price surcharge_____ 1136, 1139
Members _____ 871, 886, 899, 900
Mention _____ 235
Rail industry deregulation_____ 460
Trucking industry deregulation_ 1114, 1118
Interstate Commission on the Potomac
River Basin_____ 399
Inventors' Day, National_____ 196
Investor Protection Corporation, Secu-
rities _____ 1022, 1043
Ionatana Ionatana_____ 842
Iowa
Emergency declaration_____ 619 (Digest)
Farmers, fuel supplies for____ 791, 803, 862
President's visit____ 787, 789, 804, 841, 843
U.S. district judge_____ 441
Iowa State Association of Counties__ 789, 843
Iowa State University_____ 794
Iran
Ayatullah Ruhollah Khomeini____ 51, 352

Iran—Continued
Israel, relationship with_____ 359
Mentions _____ 239 (Digest), 301
Oil supplies to U.S_____ 51,
171, 255, 347, 352, 661, 704, 808, 961,
985
Prime Minister Mehdi Bazargan_____ 257,
259, 352
Shah Mohammed Reza Pahlavi_____ 50,
259, 313, 565
U.S. Ambassador_____ 732
U.S. arms sales_____ 51
U.S. kerosene sales_____ 51, 171
U.S. monitoring stations for SALT
II verification_____ 56, 934
U.S. relations
American citizens' safety_____ 257
Bahktiar government_____ 50, 259
Khomeini government_____ 352
Noninterference in internal conflict_ 159,
171, 255, 302, 312, 313, 565
Israel
Ambassador to U.S_____ 25
American prisoner release_____ 798
Foreign Minister Moshe Dayan_____ 251,
263, 329
Iran, relationship with_____ 359
Peace negotiations and treaty. *See*
under Middle East
President's visit_____ 383,
394, 415–430, 440, 441
Romanian emigration_____ 979
U.S. oil supplies_____ 352
U.S. trade mission_____ 640
Israel, Prime Minister (Menahem
Begin)
Comprehensive peace negotiations
Commitment to settlement_____ 251
Mentions _____ 688, 703, 967
Egyptian-Israeli peace negotiations
Mentions _____ 32,
263, 329, 352, 394, 406, 408, 413, 416,
425, 427, 432, 436, 457, 969, 995
Palestinian position_____ 455
President's trip to Israel
Announcement _____ 383
Meetings _____ 417, 419, 420, 428, 430
Visit to U.S.
Announcement _____ 346
Meetings with the President____ 372,
374, 382, 400
Mentions _____ 360, 375
Joint statement_____ 440
Letters of agreement_____ 515, 516
Trip to Egypt_____ 618
Visit to U.S.
Announcement _____ 467
Mentions _____ 471, 548, 720, 831
Signing ceremonies_____ 517, 522, 554
Italy
Tokyo Summit attendance announce-
ment _____ 550
U.S. Ambassador_____ 618

Jackson, Andrew_____ 992
Jackson, Sen. Henry M_____ 178, 840, 865
Jackson, Jesse_____ 618
Jackson, Miss_____ 670, 673
Jacobs, Repr. Andrew, Jr_____ 990
Jacobson, Lele G_____ 465
Jadwin, Linda J_____ 465
Jamaica, U.S. Ambassador_____ 220, 241
James, Gov. Fob_____ 842
Japan
　Diet members, meeting with the President _____ 786
　Energy development and research programs with U.S._____ 539
　Extradition treaty with U.S._____ 598
　Indochinese refugees_____ 971
　Japanese Broadcasting Corporation, interview with the President_____ 1107
　Joint statement_____ 763
　President's visit_____ 1108–1110
　Television receivers exports_____ 167, 168
　Tokyo Summit. *See* Tokyo Economic Summit Conference
　Trade with China_____ 334
　U.S. relations_____ 156
Japan, Prime Minister (Masayoshi Ohira)
　Mentions _____ 745, 1108–1110
　Visit to U.S.
　　Announcement _____ 468
　　Meetings with the President_____ 761, 763, 768
Japan-U.S. Cooperative Medical Science program _____ 732
Javits, Sen. Jacob K_____ 240, 385, 386, 943
Jefferson, Thomas_____ 677, 759, 832, 993
Jefferson-Jackson Day dinners__ 573, 630, 988
Jen Hsin-min_____ 206
Jenkins, Repr. Ed_____ 841
Jenkins, George L_____ 947
Jennings, Peter_____ 410n
Jimenez, Gloria C_____ 599
Jogging habits, President's_____ 737
John F. Kennedy Center for the Performing Arts_____ 23, 464
Johnson, Daniel, Sr_____ 774
Johnson, Frank M., Jr_____ 555, 619
Johnson, Repr. Harold T_____ 1115
Johnson, Mrs. Harold T_____ 376
Johnson, Lyndon B_____ 694, 828, 1028, 1088
Johnson, Marsha A_____ 914
Johnson, Nicholas_____ 400
Joint Chiefs of Staff_____ 553, 1043
Joint Financial Management Improvement program_____ 462

Joint Statements

Canada _____ 381
China, People's Republic of_____ 212
Egyptian-Israeli peace treaty_____ 490
Japan _____ 763
Mexico _____ 287

Joint Statements—Continued

　Thailand _____ 230
　Union of Soviet Socialist Republics__ 1081

Jones, Anne P_____ 46, 91
Jones, C. Fred_____ 1008
Jones, Gen. David C_____ 436
Jones, James E., Jr_____ 23
Jones, James P_____ 899, 900
Jones, Repr. James R_____ 956
Jones, Kenneth A_____ 914
Jones, Milton_____ 306n.
Jones, Nat_____ 885
Jones, Reginald H_____ 942, 943
Jones, Shirley B_____ 957
Jordan, Barbara_____ 553
Jordan, Hamilton, meetings with the President (Digest)_____ 26, 89, 178, 179, 217, 240, 293, 327, 401, 467, 468, 553, 618, 666, 732, 787, 842, 898, 899, 956, 957, 982, 983, 1017, 1018, 1043, 1142
Jordan
　Middle East peace settlement position_ 350
　Secretary of Defense's visit___ 453, 454, 456
　U.S. delegation's visit__ 436, 468 (Checklist)
Jorling, Thomas C_____ 1044
Joseph, James A_____ 990
Journalistic freedom, international_____ 240
Junior Achievement Program_____ 179
Justice, Department of
　See also specific constituent agencies
　Assistant Attorneys General_____ 234, 235, 242, 619, 975, 976, 983, 984, 1044, 1143, 1159
　Attorney General. *See* Attorney General
　Budget deferral_____ 200
　Competition policy for fighting inflation _____ 234, 235
　Ethics in Government Act of 1978, amendment recommendation_____ 1130
　Federal civil justice system_____ 344–346
　Government regulations, public participation funding programs authority _____ 868
　Hearst, Patricia, sentence commutation recommendation_____ 217 (Digest)
　Independent truckers' strike actions__ 1130, 1139
　Oil industry monitoring_____ 1130, 1139
　Railroad merger jurisdiction_____ 460
　Trucking industry deregulation report responsibilities _____ 1124
　Undocumented aliens, fair treatment investigations _____ 807
　Wiretapping and electronic surveillance review system_____ 587, 589
　Women's business enterprises_____ 888, 891
Justice, National Institute of_____ 131
Justice system, Federal civil____ 340–346, 378

Kahn, Alfred E.
Anti-inflation program actions_____ 234,
309n., 621, 752
Meetings with the President (Digest)_ 14,
25, 178, 240, 327, 467, 554, 732, 842,
898, 899, 956
Mentions _____ 657n., 745
News conferences (Checklist)_____ 241,
620, 668, 843
President's assessment_____ 651
Voluntary energy conservation, com-
ments on_____ 561
Kang Shi'en_____ 982
Kansas, disaster declaration_____ 1043
Kantor, Michael_____ 46, 91
Kapnick, Harvey_____ 271
Kardelj, Edvard_____ 293
Karlton, Lawrence K_____ 1018, 1019
Kasha, Michael_____ 196, 218
Kassebaum, Sen. Nancy Landon_____ 956
Katz, Nancy_____ 842
Kazen, George P_____ 402, 403
Kearse, Amalya L_____ 788
Kee, Esther G_____ 553
Keefe, Robert_____ 401
Keene, Joseph Ransdell_____ 667, 668
Keeton, Robert E_____ 179, 180
Kelley, James F_____ 465
Kelley, Michael R_____ 1001, 1019
Kelly, Bernard_____ 270
Kelm, Doug_____ 270
Kemeny, John G. *See* President's Com-
mission on the Accident at Three Mile
Island, Chairman
Kemp, John_____ 270
Kennedy, Cornelia G_____ 620, 667
Kennedy, Sen. Edward M.
Federal civil justice system, reform
proposals _____ 341
Hospital cost containment legislation
support _____ 385
Mental health systems legislation spon-
sorship _____ 857
Mention _____ 170
National health plan legislation sup-
port _____ 1011
1980 budget recommendation_____ 187
1980 Presidential candidate, possi-
bility _____ 848, 904, 966
Trucking industry deregulation legis-
lation support_____ 1116
Windfall profits tax position_____ 753, 865
Kennedy, John F.
Mention _____ 828
President's comments on
Medicare and Medicaid enactment_ 1028
Nuclear explosives test ban agree-
ment with Soviet Union___ 695, 1088
Quoted _____ 678, 694
Kennedy Center for the Performing Arts,
John F_____ 23, 464
Keppel, Francis_____ 196, 218
Kester, John G_____ 435

Khalid Bin Abdul Aziz_____ 456
Khalil, Mustafa. *See* Egypt, Prime Min-
ister
Khan, Sultan Muhammad_____ 376 (Digest)
Khomeini, Ayatullah Ruhollah_____ 51, 352
Khorshed, Omar_____ 526
Killeen, James R_____ 687
Kimball, Tom_____ 444
Kimche, Lee_____ 956
Kimelman, Henry L_____ 465
King, Coretta Scott_____ 33n., 909
King, Evelyn (Champagne)_____ 1015
King, Martin Luther, Jr.
Birthday, message of the President___ 22
Mention _____ 912
National holiday for, President's sup-
port _____ 34, 145
President's comments on
Civil rights efforts_____ 970, 972
Dream for America_____ 909
Quoted _____ 913
King, Martin Luther, Jr. Center for
Social Change_____ 33n.
King, Martin Luther, Jr. Nonviolent
Peace Award_____ 27
King, Martin Luther, Sr_____ 33n., 319
Kirby, R. E_____ 976
Kirchschläger, Rudolph_____ 1047, 1142
Kirk, Elise Kuhl_____ 465
Kirkland, Lane_____ 1008
Kiwanis International_____ 467
Klaus, Ida_____ 819
Kling, S. Lee_____ 92
Knowles, Marjorie Fine_____ 365, 377
Koch, Edward I_____ 240
Koger, Ira McKissick_____ 465
Kollek, Teddy_____ 417n.
Koontz, Elizabeth_____ 827
Korea, People's Democratic Republic of,
influence of China_____ 187
Korea, Republic of
American troops, withdrawal_____ 247, 764
Mention _____ 187
President Park Chung Hee__ 675 (Digest),
1111
Television receivers exports_____ 167, 168
U.S. relations_____ 156
Whaling operations_____ 266–268
Kraft, Timothy E_____ 245, 990
Kravitch, Phyllis A_____ 93
Kreisky, Bruno_____ 1047, 1142
Kreps, Juanita M. *See* Commerce, Secre-
tary of
Kriangsak Chomanan. *See* Thailand,
Prime Minister
Kroll, Bernard_____ 306n.
Krueger, Robert_____ 1134, 1143
Krulitz, Leo M_____ 990
Krumholtz, Fred J_____ 607
Kutak, Robert J_____ 46, 92
Kuznetsov, Edward_____ 731
Kyprianou, Spyros_____ 998

Labor
   See also specific union
   Labor law reform legislation_____ 146
   Occupational safety and health_____ 135
   Voluntary wage and price compliance_ 48,
                            307, 935
Labor, Department of
   See also specific constituent agencies
   Assistant Secretary_____ 1159
   Budget deferral_____ 200
   Commissioner of Labor Statistics__ 527, 554
   Deputy Assistant Secretary__ 339, 377, 974
   Equal employment enforcement, trans-
     fer of functions (EO 12144)_____ 1140
   Inspector General_____ 365, 377
   Rural wastewater treatment training
     programs _____ 75
   Undocumented aliens investigations__ 806
Labor, Secretary of (Ray Marshall)
   *For functions of the Department in
     general, see* Labor, Department of
   Alaska Natural Gas Transportation
     System, Executive Policy Board
     member _____ 1126
   Federal civilian and military pay in-
     crease recommendations_____ 64
   Meeting with the President___ 467 (Digest)
   Mentions _____ 752, 1008
   News conference_____ 1143 (Checklist)
   Venezuela inauguration ceremonies,
     U.S. delegation head_____ 401
Labor Organization, International_____ 63
Labor Relations Authority, Federal. *See*
   Federal Labor Relations Authority
Laise, Carol C_____ 553
Lamine Conde, Mamady_____ 842
Lance, Thomas Bertram_____ 968
Landau, William M_____ 783, 842, 899
Lane, Lyle Franklin_____ 1132, 1143
Lapin, Raymond H_____ 932
Larry, R. Heath_____ 957
Las Vegas, Nev_____ 932
Latin America, U.S. policy_____ 160
Lauder, Ronald S_____ 465
Lauredo, Luis_____ 401
Law Day, U.S.A. (Proc. 4649)_____ 527, 757
Law Enforcement Assistance Adminis-
   tration _____ 131, 268, 344
Law enforcement and crime
   Federal criminal code_____ 146
   Wiretapping and electronic surveil-
     lance _____ 587
Lawrence, Loren E_____ 220, 241
Lawson, Marjorie M_____ 24
Lawson, William_____ 974
League of Women Voters of the United
   States _____ 771
Leahy, Sen. Patrick J_____ 1143
Lecht, Daniel_____ 465
Lederman, Leon M_____ 448
Lee, Linda J_____ 827
Leetown, W. Va_____ 1042
Leffall, Ruth McWilliams_____ 465

Legal Services Corporation_____ 46, 91, 92
LeGrand, Keech_____ 473ftn.
Lena, Sam_____ 947
Leon Bejarano, Armando_____ 281n.
Leonard, James_____ 852
Leonard, Walter J_____ 730
Lesher, Richard L_____ 548n.
Lesotho, Ambassador to U.S_____ 554

Letters, Messages, Telegrams

   See also Resignations and Retirements
   Albert Einstein Centennial, message__ 390
   Aliens, undocumented, letter to State
     Governors _____ 806
   China, People's Republic of-U.S. rela-
     tions, messages_____ 1, 2
   Chinese New Year, message_____ 109
   Germany, Federal Republic of, Basic
     Law, message to President Walter
     Scheel _____ 927
   Independence Day, message_____ 1127
   King, Martin Luther, Jr., birthday
     message _____ 22
   Mississippi disaster emergency, tele-
     grams to Gov. Finch and Mayor
     Danks of Jackson_____ 672, 674
   National Nursing Home Week, mes-
     sage _____ 549
   Neave, Airey, death, message to Brit-
     ish Prime Minister Callaghan_____ 567
   St. Patrick's Day, message_____ 432
   Secretary of Energy, letter to Sen.
     Dennis DeConcini_____ 432
   Thomas Edison and the Centennial of
     Light, message_____ 197
   Truckers' strikes, independent, letter to
     State Governors_____ 1138
   Wichita Falls, Tex., tornado disaster,
     telegram to Mayor Hill_____ 665
   Yugoslavia, earthquake, letter to Presi-
     dent Tito_____ 670

Letters to Members of Congress. *See un-
   der* Congress, Communications to
Levesque, Anna Doyle_____ 340, 377
Levitas, Repr. Elliott H_____ 33n.
Lewis, Carolyn_____ 856
Lewis, Gabriel_____ 837
Lewis, John_____ 912
Lewis, John P_____ 224, 241
Liberia, U.S. Ambassador_____ 579, 619
Libraries and Information Science, Na-
   tional Commission on_____ 196, 218
Library and Information Services, White
   House Conference on_____ 400, 746
Lighting restrictions, advertising_____ 370
Limited Test Ban Treaty_____ 1038
Lincoln, Abraham_____ 677, 728, 908
Linder, P. Scott_____ 942
Linowes, David_____ 619
Linowitz, Sol M_____ 147
Linton, Ron M_____ 465
Lions Club International_____ 240

Livable Cities and Neighborhood Self-
  Help Development programs_____ 136
Lizarraga, David_____ 401
Lloyd, Melinda L_____ 976
Lobby law reform_____ 129
Lomax, Charles_____ 293
Long, Repr. Gillis W_____ 942, 1143
Long, Sen. Russell B____ 217, 1011, 1017, 1026
Long-Term Defense program_____ 156
Loomis, Philip A., Jr_____ 1022
Lopez, Alfredo_____ 837
López, Bernard B_____ 45, 92
Lopez, Franklin Delano_____ 401
Lopez, Jose A_____ 899, 900
Lopez, Rose Marie_____ 400
Lopez-Doriga, Joaquin_____ 252
Lopez Guevara, Carlos Alfredo_____ 377
López Portillo, Mrs. Carmen_____ 281ftn.
López Portillo, José. *See* Mexico, Presi-
  dent
Lora Gonzales, Francisco Augusto_____ 25
Los Angeles, Calif____ 372, 809, 810, 843, 875
Los Angeles Times_____ 813
Loughlin, Martin F_____ 241, 242
Louisiana
  Black leaders, meeting with the Presi-
    dent _____ 841
  Disaster declaration_____ 787 (Digest)
  U.S. attorney_____ 667, 668
  U.S. district judges_____ 957,
    958, 1018, 1019, 1043, 1044
Loutfi, Ali_____ 548n.
Love, Ruth_____ 947
Love Canal, N.Y_____ 1034
Lovelace, Alan M_____ 241 (Checklist)
Low, James Patterson_____ 976
Lowe, Richard B., III_____ 616, 667
Loyalty Day (Proc. 4657)_____ 662
Lubar, Sheldon B_____ 229
Lubick, Donald C_____ 733
Lucey, Patrick J_____ 278, 574
Ludwig, Ruby B_____ 446
Lukash, Rear Adm. William M_ 618 (Digest)
Lumber industry_____ 1044
Lusk, Robert F_____ 465
Lyet, J. Paul_____ 942
Lyman, Ralph A_____ 240
Lyons, John H_____ 271

Mabry, Guy O_____ 44, 92
Mack, P. A., Jr_____ 1041, 1044
MacNaughton, Donald S_____ 23, 46, 90
Macy, John W., Jr_____ 781, 1044
Madison, James_____ 759
Magnuson, Sen. Warren G_____ 591n.
Maher, Robert W_____ 377, 378, 842
Maier, Henry W_____ 402, 573
Maloney, Tom_____ 270
Malta, U.S. Ambassador_____ 215, 241
Management and Budget, Office of
  Assistant Director_____ 378, 733
  Federal energy use reduction monitor-
    ing _____ 647

Management and Budget, Office of—Con.
  Energy security trust fund responsibili-
    ties _____ 727
  Federal personnel ceilings_____ 925
  Government contract decisions_____ 922
  Independent water project review____ 9
  Joint Financial Management Improve-
    ment program_____ 462
  1980 fiscal budget preparation_____ 95
  Paperwork reduction_____ 494
  Privacy rights policy implementation_ 586
  United States International Develop-
    ment Cooperation Agency, budget
    submittal reception_____ 395, 644, 646
  Women's business enterprises_____ 888
Management and Budget, Office of,
  Deputy Director (John P. White)
  American Red Cross, Board of Gov-
    ernors member_____ 376 (Digest)
  Meetings with the President_ 1142 (Digest)
  News conferences (Checklist)___ 294, 1019
  Nomination _____ 46, 89
Management and Budget, Office of,
  Director (James T. McIntyre, Jr.)
  *For functions of the Office in general,
    see* Management and Budget, Office
  of
  Alaska Natural Gas Transportation
    System, transfer of functions_____ 597
  Budget message remarks_____ 96
  Critical energy facility program estab-
    lishment (EO 12129)_____ 614
  Economic growth policy for State and
    local governments_____ 77, 80
  Economic Policy Group member_____ 917
  Equal employment enforcement, trans-
    fer of functions (EO 12144)_____ 1141
  Federal civilian and military pay in-
    crease recommendation_____ 64
  Federal emergency management func-
    tions (EO 12127)_____ 566
  Management improvement and waste
    and fraud elimination_____ 779
  Meetings with the President (Digest)_ 14,
    25, 89, 178, 217, 239, 240, 327, 376,
    401, 467, 553, 554, 618, 666, 732, 786,
    841, 842, 898, 955, 956, 1142
  News conferences (Checklist)____ 241, 378
  Peace Corps functions (EO 12137)___ 881,
    882
  Printing services functions (EO
    12134) _____ 825
Management improvement council,
  Presidential, proposed_____ 780
Manchester, N.H_____ 713
Manilow, Lewis_____ 729, 787
Mansfield, Mike_____ 316
Manufacturers, National Association of__ 957
Marcus, Daniel_____ 980, 984
Marine Corps, United States_____ 672
Marine Pollution, Convention on the Pre-
  vention of_____ 223

Maritime Commission, Federal_____ 338, 339
Maritime Consultative Organization, Convention on the Intergovernmental_ 778
Maritime Day, National_____ 606
Maritime industry. *See* Ships and shipping
Mark, Hans M_____ 1127, 1142
Marks, Paul A_____ 660
Marlin, Fred_____ 670
Marquette University, Wis_____ 572, 573
Marrett, Cora B_____ 661
Marshall, Ray. *See* Labor, Secretary of
Marshall Islands, disaster declaration___ 293 (Digest)
Marshals, U.S. *See* U.S. Marshals *under* Appointments and Nominations
Martin, Boyce F., Jr_____ 1018, 1019
Martin, Louis E_____ 39, 49, 886n.
Martin Luther King, Jr. Center for Social Change _____ 33n.
Martin Luther King, Jr. Nonviolent Peace Award_____ 27
Martindell, Anne Clark_____ 1040, 1043
Martinez, Arabella_____ 1143
Maryland, U.S. district judges_____ 957, 958
Mass transit
Energy conservation measure_ 255, 613, 960
Energy security trust fund allocations. *See under* Energy security trust fund
Los Angeles use increase_____ 875, 953
Massachusetts
Civic and community leaders, meeting with the President_____ 468
U.S. district judges_____ 179, 180
Massey, Alyne Queener_____ 465
Massey, Walter E_____ 46, 92
Matsunaga, Sen. and Mrs. Spark M____ 1155
Mauritania, Ambassador to U.S_____ 376
Maynard, Libby_____ 401
Maynor, Dorothy_____ 320
Mays, Benjamin_____ 33n., 60, 320, 553
McBride, Lloyd_____ 661
McBride, Thomas F_____ 366, 377
McCalpin, F. William_____ 46, 92
McCarthy, Leo_____ 876, 1034
McCloy, John J_____ 1042
McClure, Dorothy Watson_____ 465
McCowan, Alec_____ 60
McDaniel, Gary L_____ 868, 870
McDaniel, Virginia_____ 870
McDevitt, Justin H_____ 400
McDonald, Alice_____ 827
McDonald, Gabrielle Anne Kirk_____ 377, 378
McDonald, Walter J_____ 1000, 1018
McDuffie, Rudolph_____ 920, 927
McGarry, John W_____ 45, 90
McGill, William J_____ 200
McGovern, Sen. George_____ 956
McGuire, John R_____ 1044
McIntyre, James T., Jr. *See* Management and Budget, Office of, Director

McIntyre, Thomas J_____ 700, 714, 715
McKee, Jean_____ 1037, 1044
McKelvey, Jean T_____ 23
McKinney, Alice Greene_____ 465
McKinney, Robert H_____ 990
McNamara, Margaret C_____ 400
McNaught, John J_____ 179, 180
McNichols, William H_____ 328
McPherson, Harry C., Jr_____ 661
McSweeney, Dorothy Pierce_____ 465
McSweeney, William F_____ 976
Mead, Margaret_____ 87
Meade, Edward J., Jr_____ 400
Meador, Daniel J_____ 340–342
Meany, George_____ 26
Meat industry_____ 336
Meatcutters, Amalgamated_____ 1008
Medal of Freedom, Presidential_____ 87
Medicaid and Medicare
Child health programs_____ 117, 134, 862
Consolidation under national health plan _____ 1024
Hospital costs coverage_____ 838
Mentally ill outpatient services_____ 857
Mention _____ 1028
Older persons coverage_____ 1029
Medical information act, privacy of, proposed _____ 583
Meehan, Francis J_____ 383, 402
Meetings with foreign leaders
Australia, Prime Minister J. Malcolm Fraser _____ 2
Austria, President Rudolph Kirchschläger _____ 1047, 1142
Canada, Prime Minister Pierre Elliott Trudeau _____ 379, 381
China, People's Republic of, Vice Premier Deng Xiaoping_____ 189, 192, 195, 198, 211, 212, 218 (Checklist)
Egypt, President Anwar al-Sadat____ 405, 407, 410, 412, 415, 430, 518, 522n., 523, 548n.
Finland, Prime Minister Kalevi Sorsa_ 898
France, President Valéry Giscard d'Estaing _____ 17, 25 (Digest)
Germany, Federal Republic of, Chancellor Helmut Schmidt_____ 17, 25 (Digest), 1004, 1005
Israel, Prime Minister Menahem Begin _____ 372, 374, 382, 400, 417n., 417, 419, 428, 430n., 518, 522n., 523
Japan, Prime Minister Masayoshi Ohira _____ 761, 763, 768
Mexico, President José López Portillo_ 272, 273, 280, 281, 284, 287
Norway, Prime Minister Odvar Nordli _____ 1042 (Digest)
Panama, President Aristides Royo___ 836
Sweden, Prime Minister Ola Ullsten__ 89
Thailand, Prime Minister Kriangsak Chomanan _____ 221, 225, 229

Meetings with foreign leaders—Continued
Union of Soviet Socialist Republics,
President L. I. Brezhnev_____ 1048,
1049, 1051, 1079, 1081, 1143
United Kingdom, Prime Minister
James Callaghan_____ 17, 25 (Digest)
Meguid, Abdel_____ 548n.
Meierotto, Larry E_____ 46, 91

Memorandums to Federal Agencies

Barbados, U.S. defense sales to_____ 1130
Black colleges and universities, histor-
ically _____ 48
Clothespin industry_____ 232–234
Economic policymaking_____ 977
Energy use reduction_____ 219, 647
Federal pay and the anti-inflation pro-
gram _____ 7
Florida energy emergency_____ 817, 1032
Government regulations, public par-
ticipation _____ 867
Independent water project review___ 10
Interdepartmental Committee on
Domestic Violence_____ 729
International trade agreements_____ 5
Joint Financial Management Improve-
ment program_____ 462
Management improvement and waste
and fraud elimination_____ 779
Offshore oil spill pollution_____ 338
Peace Corps_____ 881
Red Cross Month_____ 214
Regional commissions_____ 79
Romania and Hungary, trade withU.S_ 979
Senior Executive Service
Conversion rights_____ 392
Pay schedule_____ 393
Ugandan trade_____ 867
United States Savings Bonds program_ 309
Women's business enterprise_____ 894
Youth summer employment program_ 836

Memorial Day (Proc. 4651)_____ 550
Menario, John E_____ 376, 1017
Mendez, Jose F_____ 465
Mental health legislation_____ 135,
857, 859, 861, 862
Mental Health, President's Commis-
sion on_____ 857, 859–861
Mental Health Centers, Community____ 860
Mental Health System, Community_____ 135
Mercado, Judith_____ 914
Merino Rabago, Francisco_____ 281n.
Merit Systems Protection Board_____ 2,
46, 90, 1019
Messages to Congress. *See under* Con-
gress, Communications to
Mestre, Luis E_____ 465
Metzenbaum, Howard M_____ 1006
Mexico
Aliens, undocumented. *See* Aliens,
undocumented
Foreign Minister_____ 791, 802

Mexico—Continued
Illegal drug trafficking_____ 564
Mention _____ 809
Mexican television, interviews with
the President_____ 235, 252
Oil and natural gas supplies to U.S.___ 58,
612, 736, 791, 813
President's visit
Dinner honoring President López
Portillo _____ 281, 294 (Checklist)
Ixtlilco el Grande, town square
remarks _____ 280
Joint communique_____ 287
Luncheon honoring President
Carter _____ 273
Mexican Congress address_____ 284,
294 (Checklist)
Postvisit comments_____ 331
Previsit comments____ 181, 243, 256, 260
Return _____ 293 (Digest)
U.S. Embassy visit_____ 277
Welcoming ceremony_____ 272
Science and technological cooperation
with U.S_____ 539
Treaties with U.S.
Extradition _____ 450
Maritime boundary_____ 86
U.S. border States, relationship with__ 335
U.S. grain exchange for Mexican
oil _____ 791, 802
U.S.-Mexican border fence_____ 563
Mexico, President (José López Portillo)
President's visit to Mexico
Meetings with the President_____ 272,
273, 277, 279n., 280, 281, 284, 287,
294
Previsit comments_____ 58, 237
Relationship with the President_____ 181,
235, 243, 252, 253, 736
Undocumented aliens, negotiations
with U.S_____ 184,
185, 236, 253, 564, 806, 812, 907
Meyer, Lt. Gen. Edward C_____ 763
Meyer, Helen_____ 746
Mica, Repr. Dan_____ 667
Michael, Don_____ 989, 990
Michigan, U.S. district judges_____ 899, 900
Middle East
American military bases_____ 350
Comprehensive peace negotiations
Mentions _____ 1005, 1024, 1050
U.S. role_____ 703, 967
Egyptian-Israeli peace negotiations
Deputy to the Personal Represent-
ative of the President_____ 852
Egyptian Prime Minister Khalil and
Israeli Foreign Minister Dayan,
visit to U.S_____ 263, 303, 329, 331
Israeli television, interview with the
President _____ 453
Personal Representative of the Presi-
dent _____ 687, 703, 852

Middle East—Continued
Egyptian-Israeli peace negotiations—Con.
President's trip to Egypt
Announcement _____ 383
Departure from U.S._____ 394,
                    402 (Checklist)
Dinner honoring President Car-
ter _____ 410
Meetings with President Sa-
dat _____ 407, 410, 415, 430
People's Assembly address_____ 412
Return to U.S._____ 430
Trip from Cairo to Alexandria,
exchange with reporters_____ 407
Welcoming ceremony_____ 405
President's trip to Israel
Announcement _____ 383
Cabinet action approving negotia-
tions proposals_____ 432
Departure from Israel_____ 428
Dinner honoring President Car-
ter _____ 419
Knesset address_____ 424
Meeting with Prime Minister
Begin _____ 417
Welcoming ceremony_____ 415
Prime Minister Begin's visit to U.S.
Meetings with the President_____ 372,
                    373, 382, 400
Mentions _____ 346, 360, 375
Secretary of Defense's visit_____ 302, 312
U.S. delegation's visit to Saudi
Arabia and Jordan_____ 436
U.S. role_____ 107,
159, 251, 302, 313, 315, 357, 360
Egyptian-Israeli peace treaty
Egyptian Cabinet approval_____ 436
Israeli Knesset approval_____ 439
Israeli settlement policy_____ 755
Japanese support_____ 765
Joint letter of agreement_____ 515
Mention _____ 490
Prime Minister Begin's visit to
Egypt _____ 1005
Texts of treaty and related docu-
ments _____ 495
U.S. financial assistance, authoriz-
ing legislation_____ 471, 590, 638
U.S. monitoring of Sinai area_____ 756
International Exchange-of-Persons____ 324
Palestinians. *See* Palestinians
Terrorist attacks_____ 656
U.S. arms sales_____ 656
United States Sinai Support Mission__ 64
Middle Income Student Assistance pro-
gram _____ 264
Middletown, Pa._____ 578
Mier, Mariano J._____ 977
Migratory species, diplomatic conference
on the protection of_____ 1042
Mikva, Abner J._____ 958, 983
Milativic, Veljko_____ 670
Military Academy, United States_____ 687

Military aircraft, White House passen-
ger lists_____ 240
Miller, Betty_____ 270
Miller, G. William_____ 401
Miller, Joyce Dannen_____ 942
Miller, Leonard_____ 44, 92
Millhone, John P_____ 44, 92, 607, 619
Millonzi, Robert I_____ 465
Milwaukee, Wis_____ 572, 573
Mine Workers, United_____ 905
Mineta, Repr. Norman Y_____ 942
Mining and minerals
Alaska claims_____ 855
Nonfuel energy sources_____ 533
Ohio jobs preservation_____ 1006
Minnesota, disaster declaration_____ 786
                            (Digest)
Minorities
See also specific group
Administration's accomplishments_ 561, 888
Business assistance_____ 145, 847, 888
Economic development programs____ 77
Equal employment opportunities_____ 847
Judicial appointments_____ 36,
131, 759, 772, 847, 885
Publishing firms, Government loans__ 35
Minority Economic Impact, Office of__ 1040,
                            1044
Minuteman missiles_____ 696
MIRVs _____ 1052, 1062
Mishkin, Chase Mitchell_____ 465
Mishkin, Paul J_____ 746
Mississippi, flood disaster_____ 672,
674, 675 (Digest), 956
Mississippi River Commission_____ 44,
92, 1129, 1143
Missouri
Emergency declaration_____ 440 (Digest)
U.S. district judges_____ 899, 900, 957, 958
Misty Fiords National Monument,
Alaska _____ 855
Mitchell, Clarence M., Jr._____ 377
Mmahat, Arlene Montgomery_____ 465
Momjian, Joan Reed_____ 465
Mondale, Joan_____ 220n., 401
Mondale, Walter F. *See* Vice President
Mondjo, Nicolas_____ 25
Monetary and Fiscal Policy, National Ad-
visory Council on International_____ 439
Monetary Fund, International_____ 446, 468
Montana, U.S. district judge_____ 441
Monterroso Miranda, Felipe Doroteo___ 376
Moore, Bessie B_____ 196, 218
Moore, Calvin C_____ 448
Moore, Frank B., meetings with the Presi-
dent (Digest)_____ 89,
179, 217, 239–241, 293, 327, 376, 377,
401, 440, 467, 468, 553, 554, 617, 618,
666, 731, 732, 786, 787, 841, 842, 898,
899, 955–957, 982, 983, 1017, 1018,
1042, 1043, 1142
Moorman, James W_____ 1044
Morales, Ana Marta_____ 466

Moran, James B_____ 957
Moret, Louis F_____ 811, 1040, 1044
Morgan, Sen. Robert_____ 1101
Mori, Jun_____ 942
Moroz, Valentyn_____ 731
Morris, Charles J_____ 23
Morrison, Truman A., III_____ 980, 984
Mortgage Association, Federal National_ 931
Mortgage programs, Federal_____ 709
Morton, Rogers C. B_____ 674
Moscone, George_____ 807, 808 ftn., 843
Moss, Ambler_____ 837
Most Favored Nations legislation_____ 358, 359
Mother's Day (Proc. 4646)_____ 438
Moxley, John Howard, III_____ 1036, 1043
Moynihan, Sen. Daniel P_____ 240, 898
Mozambique, relationship with Western
    nations _____ 316
Mubarak, Muhammad Husni_____ 1023
Muellenberg, Kurt W_____ 198, 378
Muftic, Michael_____ 293
Mulhern, Francis J_____ 923, 924, 927
Multilateral Development Banks_____ 279, 396
Multilateral trade negotiations (MTN)
    Canadian support_____ 382
    Congressional support, President's ap-
       peal for_____ 107, 118, 125, 331
    Countervailing duties' waiver_____ 46
Multilateral trade negotiations agree-
    ments
    Administration's legislative priority___ 944
    Mentions _____ 1100, 1147
    Message transmittal to Congress of
       agreements and implementing legis-
       lation _____ 1092
       lation _____ 1092, 1143 (Checklist)
    Purposes of agreements_____ 125, 331
    Statement by the President_____ 662
Multiple Sclerosis Society, National_____ 842
Multi-State Regional Action Planning
    Commissions _____ 602
Murnaghan, Francis D., Jr_____ 843
Murphy, Christopher Jay, III_____ 466
Murphy, Repr. John M_____ 89, 1125
Murphy, Mrs. John M_____ 89
Murphy, Thomas_____ 786
Museum Day, National (Proc. 4661)_ 897
Museum Services, Institute of_____ 956
Museum Services Board, National_____ 269,
    294, 956
Music Corporation of America, Inc_____ 373n.
Muskie, Sen. Edmund S__179, 590n., 591, 898
Mutual and Balanced Force Reductions
    Negotiations _____ 110, 179
Muzorewa, Bishop Abel Tendekai_____ 1014
MX missile_____ 967, 1016, 1090

NAACP. *See* National Association for the
    Advancement of Colored People
Nailor, George_____ 956
Namibia, majority government rule__ 39, 357
NASA. *See* National Aeronautics and
    Space Administration

National Academy for Fire Prevention
    and Control_____ 566
National Academy of Sciences_____ 677, 733
National Advisory Committee for Women
    Acting Chairperson_____ 88, 217 (Digest)
    Chairperson _____ 26
    Relationship with the President_____ 52
    White House statement_____ 27
National Advisory Council on Extension
    and Continuing Education_____ 1023
National Advisory Council on Indian
    Education _____ 446, 932
National Advisory Council on Interna-
    tional Monetary and Fiscal Policy__ 439
National Advisory Council on Women's
    Educational Programs_____ 339, 377
National Aeronautics and Space Admin-
    istration
    Inspector General_____ 398, 402
    Rockwell International, contract with_ 241
       (Checklist)
    Solar energy programs_____ 1105
    U.S.-China science and technology
       agreements _____ 204, 211
National Alcohol Fuels Commission____ 1007
National Architectural Barriers Aware-
    ness Week (Proc. 4656)_____ 641
National Association for the Advance-
    ment of Colored People_____ 38
National Association of Broadcasters___ 482,
    490
National Association of Community
    Health Centers_____ 983
National Association for Equal Oppor-
    tunity in Higher Education_____ 742
National Association of Home Builders__ 732
National Association of Manufacturers__ 957
National Association of State Attorneys
    General _____ 618
National Association of State Depart-
    ments of Agriculture_____ 239 (Digest)
National Cable Television Association__ 932
National Cancer Advisory Board_____ 675
    (Digest), 686
National Cancer Program_____ 675 (Digest)
National Capital Planning Commission_ 687
National Caucus on the Black Aged____ 317
National Center of Economic Education
    for Children_____ 842
National Championship Chess Team___ 787
National Commission on Employment
    Policy _____ 947
National Commission on the Interna-
    tional Year of the Child_____ 229
National Commission on Libraries and
    Information Science_____ 196, 218
National Commission on Neighborhoods_ 618
National Commission for the Review of
    Antitrust Laws and Procedures_132, 178, 875
National Commission for the Review of
    Federal and State Laws Relating to
    Wiretapping and Electronic Surveil-
    lance _____ 585, 587–590

National Commission on Social Security, members _____ 23, 45, 46, 90, 92
National Conference of Christians and Jews _____ 969
National Consumer Cooperative Bank__ 136
National Council on the Arts_ 45, 92, 435, 441
National Council on Educational Research _____ 44, 91
National Council on the Humanities, members _____ 45, 46, 90, 91, 231, 241
National Credit Union Administration
Interest rate increase for small savers__ 930
National Credit Union Board, members _____ 397, 402, 1041, 1044
National Defense Transportation Day (Proc. 4639) _____ 237
National Development Bank____ 99, 117, 137
National Earthquake Hazards Reduction program _____ 537
National Endowment for the Arts and Humanities _____ 142
National Energy Act of 1978_____ 1103
National Environmental Policy Act of 1978 _____ 121
National Farm Safety Week (Proc. 4345) _____ 433
National Fish Health Research Laboratory _____ 1042
National Forest System_____ 151, 671
National Governors' Association
Committee on international trade and foreign relations, question-and-answer session with the President___ 330
Foreign trade and export development seminars, sponsorship_____ 897 (Digest), 900 (Checklist)
Independent truckers' strikes recommendations _____ 1138
Winter session meeting, White House dinner for members attending_____ 354
National Health Service Corps_____ 134
National Heart, Lung, and Blood Institute _____ 178
National Hispanic Heritage Week (Proc. 4662) _____ 930
National Institute of Building Sciences
Annual report_____ 982 (Digest)
Board of Directors, members_____ 44, 92, 607, 619
National Institute of Justice_____ 131
National Institutes of Health_____ 544
National Inventors' Day (Proc. 4635)___ 196
National Maritime Day (Proc. 4653)___ 606
National Multiple Sclerosis Society_____ 842
National Museum Day (Proc. 4661)_____ 897
National Museum Services Board_____ 269, 294, 956
National Newspapers Publishers Association _____ 440
National Nursing Home Week_____ 549
National Poison Prevention Week (Proc. 4638) _____ 231

National P.O.W.–M.I.A. Recognition Day (Proc. 4664)_____ 999
National prayer breakfast_____ 58
National Productivity Council_____ 531
National public works and economic development act, proposed_____ 599, 601, 602
National Railroad Passenger Corporation _____ 92, 397, 402
National Railway Labor Conference__ 818, 819
National School Board Association_____ 1018
National Science Foundation
Director _____ 205
National Science Board, members_____ 46, 92, 93, 196, 218, 528, 554
Science and technology programs_____ 530, 544, 545
National security. *See* Defense and national security
National Security Council_____ 189, 670, 984, 1045
National security information_____ 170, 585
National Security Medal_____ 179
National Small Business Person of the Year _____ 868
National Solar User Information Program _____ 1102
National Telecommunications and Information Administration_____ 586
National Toxicology program_____ 536
National Transportation Safety Board___ 437, 441, 1007, 1019
National Transportation Week (Proc. 4639) _____ 237
National Voluntary Action program____ 880
National Wilderness Preservation System _____ 240, 671
National Wildlife Federation_____ 443
NATO. *See* North Atlantic Treaty Organization
Natural gas
Extraction from coal and shale_____ 793
Imports _____ 236
Mexican supplies to U.S_____ 58, 182, 185, 612, 737, 791, 813
Production _____ 175
Natural Gas Policy Act of 1978_____ 1097
Natural Gas Transportation System, Alaska _____ 592, 1016, 1019, 1126
Natural resources, department of, proposed _____ 378, 444, 534
Naturalization Service, Immigration and _____ 806
Nauru, U.S. Ambassador_____ 46, 91
Naval Academy, United States_____ 730
Navon, Yitzhak_____ 415, 419n.
Navy, Department of the, printing services functions_____ 824
Neal, Repr. Stephen L_____ 1101
Neave, Airey_____ 567
Nebraska, U.S. marshal_____ 468
Neel, Alice_____ 217
Neighborhood Self-Help Development programs, Livable Cities and_____ 136

Neighborhoods, National Commission on_ 618
Nelson, David S_____ 179, 180
Nelson, Dorothy W_____ 271
Nelson, Sen. Gaylord
  Hospital cost containment legislation
    support _____ 384, 385, 569, 576
  Mention _____ 992
  National health plan support_____ 1027
  White House Conference on Small
    Business sponsorship_____ 369
Nelson, Helen Ewing_____ 942
Nemirow, Samuel B_____ 1036, 1044
Netherlands, Vice President's visit___ 220, 639
Neuharth, Allen H_____ 699n.
Neusner, Jacob_____ 46, 90
Neustadt, Richard_____ 619
Nevada
  Radioactivity exposure_____ 182
  U.S. district judge_____ 667, 668
Nevelson, Louise_____ 217
"New Foundation"_____ 172
New Hampshire
  Emergency declaration_____ 440 (Digest)
  President's visit_____ 699–720, 733
  U.S. district judge_____ 241, 242
New Mexico, disaster declaration_____ 217
                         (Digest)
New York, U.S. district judge_____ 93
New York City, N.Y., President's visits_ 189n.,
                       328, 693, 788
New York City Ballet Company_ 376 (Digest)
New Zealand, U.S. Ambassador___ 1040, 1043
Newblatt, Stewart A_____ 899, 900
Newell, Wayne A_____ 446
Newman, Jon O_____ 733, 787
Newman, Joseph H_____ 44, 92
Newport News, Va_____ 906

News Conferences

January 17 (No. 42)_____ 50
January 26 (No. 43)_____ 170
February 12 (No. 44)_____ 255
February 27 (No. 45)_____ 346
March 25 (No. 46)_____ 482
April 10 (No. 47)_____ 648
April 30 (No. 48)_____ 747
May 4 (No. 49)_____ 795
May 29 (No. 50)_____ 959

News media
  See also Addresses and Remarks, inter-
    views with the news media
  Federal access to files_____ 585
  First amendment privileges_____ 485
  Journalists' overseas trips_____ 628
Newspaper Editors, American Society of_ 788
Newspaper Publishers Association, Amer-
  ican _____ 440, 693, 733
Nicaragua
  U.S. Ambassador_____ 686, 733
  U.S. policy_____ 160
Nice Agreement on International Trade-
  marks _____ 84
Niger, U.S. Ambassador_____ 979, 984

Nigeria, U.S. relations_____ 355
Nigh, Gov. and Mrs. George_____ 217
Nims, Arthur L., III_____ 820, 843
Nixon, Richard M.
  Chinese Vice Premier Deng, White
    House invitation to dinner for___ 54, 175
  President's comments on
    Mandatory wage and price controls_ 849
    SALT negotiations_____ 695, 1088
Nolan, Kathleen_____ 46, 91
Non-Proliferation Treaty Review Confer-
  ence _____ 685
Nordli, Odvar_____ 1042
North American Affairs, Coordination
  Council for_____ 640, 1134
North Atlantic Treaty Organization
  Military capabilities improvement____ 156,
                         314, 316
  SALT II treaty rejection, effect on_ 695, 903
  Supreme Allied Commander, Europe,
    and Commander in Chief of U.S.
    Forces in Europe_____ 363, 1043
  Turkish economic strengthening re-
    sponsibilities _____ 845
  U.S. defense spending_____ 98, 106
  West German support_____ 1005
North Carolina, U.S. district judge__ 554, 555
North Dakota, disaster declaration_____ 732
                         (Digest)
North Pacific Fisheries Commission, In-
  ternational _____ 1001
Northern, Richard_____ 914
Northern Gas Pipeline_____ 381
Northwest Alaska Pipeline Company___ 591
Northwest Atlantic Fisheries, Interna-
  tional Commission for_____ 777
Northwest Atlantic Fisheries Convention_ 777
Norton, Eleanor Holmes_____ 912
Norton, Mary Beth_____ 46, 90
Norway
  Ambassador to U.S_____ 377
  Foreign Minister_____ 33n.
  Prime Minister Odvar Nordli_____ 1042
  Vice President's visit_____ 220, 639
Norwood, Janet L_____ 527, 554
Nuclear energy
  See also Nuclear weapons; Clinch
    River breeder reactor plant
  Federal programs_____ 149
  Fuel transfers to foreign countries____ 559
  Meetings with the President (Digest)
    Administration officials and environ-
      mental and community leaders__ 841
    Energy Secretary Schlesinger and
      Congressmen _____ 553
  Powerplants. *See* Nuclear powerplants
  President's position on future use_ 799, 1109
  Three Mile Island nuclear plant, Pa.
    See Three Mile Island nuclear
    plant, Pa.
  Waste disposal_____ 558, 706
  Weapons. *See* Nuclear weapons
Nuclear Fuel Cycle Evaluation, Interna-
  tional _____ 159, 452, 541, 767

Nuclear Non-Proliferation Act of 1978__ 452
Nuclear powerplants
Construction _____ 712, 741
Safety
Federal Government role_____ 702
Public concern, effect on_____ 706
Three Mile Island, Pa., accident,
reassessment due to_____ 558,
577, 681, 702, 712, 798
Nuclear Regulatory Commission
India, U.S. nuclear materials export
to _____ 559
Member _____ 855, 899
Office of Nuclear Reactor Regulation,
Director _____ 579, 617, 618
Three Mile Island, Pa., accident
study _____ 702, 741, 798
Nuclear weapons
See also specific weapons system
Nonproliferation
Indian Ocean deployment limits___ 158
Japanese support_____ 767
Mentions _____ 106, 541, 681, 719, 795
Transfer limit of conventional arms_ 158,
171, 357
U.S. leadership role_____ 590, 694, 835
Production _____ 559
Strategic arms limitation. *See* Stra-
tegic arms limitation
Test ban treaty___ 176, 216, 543, 902, 1038
Nuñez, Louis_____ 91
Nunn, Sen. Sam_____ 178
Nursing Home Week, National_____ 549

Oberstar, Repr. James L_____ 293
Obey, Repr. David R_____ 567, 666
O'Callaghan, Michael_____ 435
Occupational Safety and Health Review
Commission
Annual report_____ 841
Chairman _____ 552
Federal paperwork reduction_____ 795, 869
Member _____ 552, 619
Ochenrider, Elizabeth R_____ 466
Ochi, Rose Matsui_____ 450
O'Connor, Patrick J_____ 466
Odom, Col. William_____ 436
Office. *See other part of title*
Ohio, mining jobs_____ 1006
Ohio River Basin Commission_____ 607
Ohira, Masayoshi. *See* Japan, Prime
Minister
Ohrt, Alvin_____ 795n.
Oil
See also OPEC; Fuel companies
Canadian production_____ 381
Imports. *See* Oil imports
Israel, supplies to_____ 352, 427, 428
Legislation, congressional inaction_ 611, 632
Offshore pollution_____ 338, 1035
Prices. *See* Oil prices
Production _____ 175, 951
Supplies. *See* Oil supplies

Oil imports
Iranian supplies. *See under* Iran
Mention _____ 796
Mexican supplies_____ 58,
612, 736, 791, 802, 813
Reduction, relationship with
Balance of payments deficit_____ 118
Increased domestic production_ 245, 1095
Saudi Arabian supplies___ 1226, 1246, 1766
Tariff suspension_____ 628
Threat to national security_____ 678
U.S. food exchange for, possibility_ 791, 802
Oil prices decontrol
Base period control level_____ 722
Congress, consultations with the Presi-
dent _____ 56, 149
Legislation extending controls_____ 801,
931, 963
Mentions _____ 236, 700, 1586
Purposes
Conservation measure_____ 721, 873, 985
Domestic production increase_____ 600,
721, 748, 816, 873, 876, 961, 985,
1097
Import reduction_____ 622,
649, 816, 873, 960, 985
Inflation control measure_____ 988
Statement by the President_____ 981
Windfall profits tax, relationship
with _____ 721,
735, 748, 801, 816, 864, 953, 961
Oil supplies
Defense emergency allocations_____ 937
Home heating
New England_____ 739, 862
Reserve stocks buildup_____ 848,
937, 951, 987
O'Keeffe, Georgia_____ 217
Oklahoma
Black leaders, meeting with the Presi-
dent _____ 841 (Digest)
Disaster declaration_____ 674 (Digest)
President's visit_____ 469
State legislature and officials, meetings
with the President_____ 217, 841
Older Americans Month (Proc. 4658)__ 673
Older persons
Food stamps_____ 480
Hospital costs_____ 387
House-Senate bipartisan intern pro-
gram _____ 837
Interest rates, effect on_____ 928
Legislation _____ 139
Mental health services funding_____ 862
National health plan provisions_____ 1029
Rural housing program_____ 843
Oliver Wendell Holmes Devise, Perma-
nent Committee for the_____ 746
O'Malley, Carlon M_____ 93
O'Neal, A. Daniel_____ 217
O'Neill, Repr. Thomas P., Jr. *See* Speaker
of the House of Representatives

OPEC (Organization of Petroleum Exporting Countries)
Decontrol of U.S. oil prices, effect of_ 982
Mentions _____ 721, 736
Past price increases_____ 611, 717, 944, 964
Price structure_____ 245
U.S. agricultural products exchange for oil, possibility_____ 802
Operation of the Automotive Products Trade Act of 1965_____ 178
Oplinger, Gerald G_____ 1045
O'Reilly, Jacqueline D_____ 466
Organization. *See other part of title*
Ortique, Revius O., Jr_____ 46, 92
Ortiz, Frank V., Jr_____ 293, 783, 842
Ortiz, Mrs. Frank V., Jr_____ 293
Otero, Joaquin_____ 812
Overseas Private Investment Corporation
Board of Directors, members_____ 783, 842, 899, 1022, 1043
Reorganization _____ 279, 396, 643
Overton, William Ray_____ 402, 403
Owen, Henry D_____ 294
Owens, Jesse_____ 322
Oxman, Stephan A_____ 436
Ozar, I. I_____ 293
Ozores, Carlos_____ 837

Padron, Eduardo J_____ 466
Pahlavi, Mohammed Reza_____ 50, 259, 313, 565
Pakistan, Ambassador to U.S_____ 376
Palestine Liberation Organization
Israel, refusal to recognize autonomy of _____ 454, 456, 623, 907
Mention _____ 453
Palestinians
Camp David agreement to resolve settlement of_____ 455
Mentions _____ 427, 488, 703, 911, 1005
Right to autonomy_ 408, 413, 455, 623, 967
Pan American Day and Week (Proc. 4644) _____ 390
Panama
Ambassador to U.S_____ 377
Permanent American cemetery_____ 81
President Aristides Royo_____ 683, 836, 837
Panama Canal Company_____ 102
Panama Canal treaties
Implementing legislation
Congressional consideration_____ 901, 963, 1125
Congressmen, administration briefings for (Digest)_____ 841, 1042
1977 treaty and related agreements__ 102, 160, 836
U.S. human rights policy, effect on___ 585
Paperwork reduction
Broadcasting industry_____ 483
Federal Government_____ 129, 494, 869, 935
HEW forms_____ 864
OSHA regulations_____ 868
Pappas, Jographia_____ 466

Park Chung Hee_____ 675 (Digest), 1111
Parker, Alan A_____ 975, 983
Parker, Jack S_____ 977
Parker, John V_____ 957, 958
Parker, Robert M_____ 241
Parks, Rosa_____ 321
Pastor, Robert A_____ 189, 837
Patent and Trademark Office_____ 196, 218
Peace Corps
See also ACTION
EO 12137_____ 877
Establishment as autonomous agency within ACTION_____ 881
Programs, organizational review_____ 396
Peace Corps, Director (Richard F. Celeste)
Functions _____ 877, 881
Nomination _____ 551, 554
Swearing in_____ 956 (Digest)
Peace Corps Advisory Council_____ 878, 879
Pearson, James B_____ 942
Pease, Repr. Donald J_____ 867
Peek, Linda K_____ 742n.
Pelletreau, Robert H., Jr_____ 101, 179
Penn, John G_____ 93
Pennsylvania
President's visit_____ 578
U.S. attorney_____ 93
U.S. district judges_____ 958, 983
U.S. marshal_____ 733, 787
Pension Benefit Guaranty Corporation__ 781
Pension Policy, President's Commission on _____ 138, 271
People's Temple _____ 35
Percy, Sen. Charles_____ 1115, 1116, 1143
Perlman, Itzhak_____ 526
Permanent Committee for the Oliver Wendell Holmes Devise_____ 746
Personal Representative of the President. *See under* Middle East, Egyptian-Israeli peace negotiations
Personnel Interchange, President's Commission on_____ 866
Personnel Management, Office of
Deputy Director_____ 2, 46, 90
Federal employees protection_____ 922
Federal pay system reform actions____ 1003
Office of Government Ethics, Director_ 41
President's Commission on Executive Exchange, staff services_____ 867
Senior Executive Service review_____ 393
Personnel Management, Office of, Director (Alan K. Campbell)
Appointment and nomination____ 2, 46, 90
Federal Government employees, question-and-answer session_____ 917
Federal pay increase compliance responsibilities _____ 8
Investigative and audit training improvement responsibilities_____ 779
News conference (Checklist) _____ 1019
Summer youth employment program__ 836

Personnel Management, Office of, Director—Continued
Taiwan relations functions (EO 12143) _____ 1133
Pertschuk, Michael_____ 234, 235, 242
Peru
　Ambassador to U.S_____ 554
　Whaling operations_____ 266–268
Peterson, Esther
　Anti-inflation program actions_____ 234
　Mentions _____ 621, 838
　News conferences (Checklist)____ 242, 620
　Public participation in Federal agency proceedings _____ 867
Peterson, Russell_____ 661
Peterson, Sharon L_____ 1008
Petrie, Elizabeth_____ 466
Petroleum Exporting Countries, Organization of. *See* OPEC
Petroleum Reserve program, Strategic__ 147, 720
Pettigrew, Richard A_____ 378
Pettit, Joseph M_____ 306n.
Pezzullo, Lawrence A_____ 686, 733
Philadelphia, Pa_____ 787, 906
Philippines
　U.S. naval bases_____ 626
　U.S. policy_____ 156
Photovoltaic cells_____ 712, 1104
Physical Fitness Award, Presidential____ 955
Physical Fitness and Sports, President's Council on_____ 955
Pigford, Thomas_____ 661
Pipeline inspector, office of the Federal, proposed _____ 381
Pippert, Wes_____ 748
Pirie, Robert B., Jr_____ 269, 294
Pitot, Henry C_____ 686
Pittston Company_____ 376, 1017
Placita de Dolores, Los Angeles, Calif___ 809, 843
Plains, Ga_____ 675 (Digest)
Plotkin, Manuel D_____ 239 (Digest)
Poison Prevention Week, National_____ 231
Poland, clothespin exports_____ 233
Politz, Henry A_____ 788
Polland, Rebecca R_____ 437
Pollution
　Air _____ 183, 349, 539
　Oil spills_____ 338
　Water _____ 224, 349
Pollution from Ships, Convention on____ 85
Pork industry_____ 754
Porter, Donald James_____ 441
Porter, Paul C_____ 466
Portsmouth, N.H_____ 699, 733
Portugal, U.S. policy_____ 156
Poseidon submarines_____ 108
Postal Rate Commission___ 373, 378, 856, 899
Postal Service, United States. *See* United States Postal Service
Potomac River Basin, Interstate Commission on the_____ 399

P.O.W.–M.I.A. Recognition Day, National _____ 999
Powell, Jody
　Announcements to the press_____ 218, 383
　Mentions _____ 621, 743, 744
　News conferences_____ 658n., 843, 1143
　White House statements reading___ 310, 609, 731, 1125
Powell, Sara Jordan_____ 1015
Powerplants. *See* Nuclear powerplants
Prayer breakfast, national_____ 58
Prayer for Peace, Memorial Day (Proc. 4651) _____ 550
Prayer in public schools_____ 625, 655
Prentiss, Maj. Gen. Louis W_____ 44, 92
Presidency, views on
　Controversial issues management____ 789, 949, 1010
　Responsibilities of position_____ 475, 962
　State legislature experience, relationship with_____ 296
President of the Senate. *See* Vice President
Presidential Advisory Board on Ambassadorial Appointments_____ 552
Presidential campaign, 1980, President's candidacy, possibility of_____ 40, 172, 563, 738, 798, 952
Presidential Commission on World Hunger _____ 147, 213
Presidential management improvement council, proposed_____ 780
Presidential Medal of Freedom_____ 87
Presidential Physical Fitness Award___ 955
Presidential Scholars_____ 852
Presidential Scholars, Commission on___ 598, 853, 1034
Presidential term of office, President's assessment _____ 738
President's Advisory Committee for Women (EO 12135)_____ 825, 826
President's Commission on the Accident at Three Mile Island
　Chairman _____ 658, 660, 701
　Establishment _____ 657, 659
　Meetings with the President_____ 691, 702
　Members _____ 660, 856
　Mentions _____ 713, 798
President's Commission on the Coal Industry _____ 649, 905
President's Commission on Executive Exchange _____ 866, 976
President's Commission on the Holocaust _____ 147, 293, 684
President's Commission on Mental Health _____ 857, 859–861
President's Commission on Pension Policy _____ 138, 271
President's Commission on Personnel Interchange _____ 866
President's Commission on White House Fellowships _____ 931

President's Committee on Employment
of the Handicapped_____ 463
President's Committee on the National
Medal of Science_____ 448
President's Council on Physical Fitness
and Sports_____ 955
President's Export Council____ 784, 942, 943
President's financial reports_____ 983
President's policymaking procedures___ 261
President's religious convictions_____ 472
President's travel
Domestic
California __ 787, 807, 809, 810, 841, 843
Georgia _____ 296–
306, 669, 675 (Digest), 731
Indiana _____ 988, 989, 1017
Iowa _____ 787, 789, 804, 841, 843
New Hampshire _____ 699–720, 733
New York_____ 217, 327, 328, 693
Oklahoma _____ 469
Pennsylvania _____ 578
Texas _____ 482
Virginia _____ 630
Wisconsin _____ 567, 572, 573
Foreign
Austria _____ 1038, 1045, 1047–1081
Egypt _____ 394, 405–415, 430
Guadeloupe _____ 14, 17, 25, 26
Israel _____ 394, 415–430
Mexico ____ 272, 273, 277, 280, 281, 284
Press, Frank. *See* Science and Technol-
ogy Policy, Office of, Director
Preston, Robert F_____ 720n.
Price, Leontyne_____ 526, 1015
Privacy Act of 1974_____ 586
Privacy of medical information act, pro-
posed _____ 583
Privacy policy, national_____ 581, 619
Privacy Protection Study Commission_ 582,
619
Privacy of research records act, pro-
posed _____ 584
Private Industry Councils_____ 126
Private schools_____ 848
Private Sector Initiative program_____ 73,
99, 126, 601

Proclamations

American Heart Month (Proc.
4633) _____ 21
Asian/Pacific American Heritage Week
(Proc. 4650)_____ 549
Bolt, nut, and large screw industry
(Proc. 4632)_____ 3
Cancer Control Month (Proc. 4643)_ 389
Captive Nations Week (Proc. 4666)_ 1141
Clothespin imports (Proc. 4640)_____ 325
Days of remembrance of victims of the
Holocaust (Proc. 4652)_____ 580
Father's Day (Proc. 4659)_____ 747
Flag Day and National Flag Week
(Proc. 4660)_____ 817
Law Day, U.S.A. (Proc. 4649)_____ 527

Proclamations—Continued
Loyalty Day (Proc. 4657)_____ 662
Meat imports (Proc. 4642)_____ 336
Mother's Day (Proc. 4646)_____ 438
National Architectural Barrier Aware-
ness Week (Proc. 4656)_____ 641
National Defense Transportation Day
and National Transportation Week
(Proc. 4639)_____ 237
National Farm Safety Week (Proc.
4645) _____ 433
National Hispanic Heritage Week
(Proc. 4662)_____ 930
National Inventors' Day (Proc. 4635)_ 196
National Maritime Day (Proc. 4653)_ 606
National Museum Day (Proc. 4661)__ 897
National Poison Prevention Week
(Proc. 4638)_____ 231
National P.O.W.–M.I.A. Recognition
Day (Proc. 4664)_____ 999
North Atlantic Treaty Organization,
30th anniversary (Proc. 4648)_____ 451
Older Americans Month (Proc.
4658) _____ 673
Pan American Day and Pan American
Week (Proc. 4644)_____ 390
Petroleum imports and products
(Proc. 4655)_____ 628
Prayer for Peace, Memorial Day (Proc.
4651) _____ 550
Red Cross Month (Proc. 4636)_____ 213
Save Your Vision Week (Proc. 4637)_ 219
Small Business Week (Proc. 4641)___ 335
Steel imports (Proc. 4665)_____ 1032
Sugars, sirups, and molasses imports
(Proc. 4663) _____ 946
Television receiver imports (Proc.
4634) _____ 166
Vietnam Veterans Week (Proc.
4647) _____ 445
World Trade Week (Proc. 4654)____ 616
Procurement practices, Federal_____ 308
Producer Price Index_____ 717
Productivity Council, National_____ 531
Prokop, Ruth T_____ 2, 46, 90, 1019
Pryor, William Cornet_____ 957
Public broadcasting
Administration's priorities_____ 141
First amendment privileges_____ 486
Industry deregulation_____ 483, 485
Legislation _____ 488
Worldwide impact_____ 482
Public Broadcasting, Carnegie Com-
mission on the Future of_____ 199
Public Broadcasting, Corporation for___ 609,
1001, 1019
Public Health Service Award_____ 983
Public lands, roadless area review and
evaluation _____ 669, 670
Public works and economic development
act, national, proposed_____ 599, 601, 602
Publishing firms, minority_____ 35
Puerto Rico, U.S. marshal_____ 899, 900

Purks, James H., III_____ 1017
Racial Discrimination, Convention on__ 162
Radio Conference, Worldwide Adminis-
trative _____ 541
Radioactivity exposure_____ 182
Ragone, David V_____ 46, 92
Railroad Investments, Branch Line_____ 76
Railroad Passenger Corporation, Na-
tional _____ 92, 397, 402
Railroad Retirement Board_____ 1037, 1044
Railroads, industry deregulation_____ 105,
114, 128, 130, 459
Railway Association, United States____ 43, 93
Railway Labor Conference, National_ 818, 819
Railway labor dispute, Emergency Board
to investigate a
EO 12132_____ 818, 819
Report _____ 983, 984
Rajoppi, Joanne_____ 1034
Rambo, Sylvia H_____ 958, 983
Ramee, Mark_____ 1143
Ramsay, Ann S_____ 827
Randall, Carolyn D_____ 733 (Checklist), 787
Randolph, A. Philip
Death statement_____ 882
Living Legacy Awards recipient_____ 321
Memorial services_____ 996, 1015
President's assessment_____ 883, 911
Randolph, Sen. Jennings_____ 65, 68, 293
Range, M. Athalie_____ 397, 402
Rangel, Repr. Charles B.
Hospital cost containment legislation
support _____ 384–386
Meetings with the President (Digest)_ 293,
1017
National health plan support___ 1011, 1025
Rasmuson, Elmer E_____ 1001
Rau, Violet E_____ 446
Raynor, Rev. John P_____ 573n.
Read, Sister Joel_____ 46, 90
Real wage insurance
Anti-inflation policy_____ 74, 105, 951
Mention _____ 111
President's appeal for congressional
support _____ 256, 951
Tax credit feature__ 74, 115, 124, 307, 951
Reavley, Thomas M_____ 899, 900
Recording Industry Association of
America _____ 446
Recreation, forest land allocation_____ 671
Red Cross, American National_____ 376, 552
Red Cross Month (Proc. 4636)____ 213, 214
Reddy, N. S_____ 732
Redstone, Sumner Murray_____ 466
Reed, Edward C., Jr_____ 667, 668
Regional Action Planning Commissions,
Multi-State _____ 602
Regional Commissions, Title V. See Title
V Regional Commissions
Regional Councils, Federal_____ 81
Regulatory Analyses Review Group____ 74,
128, 492
Regulatory Calendar_____ 128, 492, 535

Regulatory Council_____ 74, 128, 492, 535
Regulatory Liaison Group, Interagency_ 536
Regulatory reform
Administration's program proposals to
Congress _____ 491
Airline industry. See under Aircraft
and aviation
Bus industry_____ 105, 128
Drug laws_____ 135
Federal regulatory system_____ 111,
114, 127, 482, 719, 834
Financial institutions_____ 928
Medical care_____ 475
Railroad industry_____ 105,
114, 128, 130, 459
Safety and health regulations_____ 634, 834
Science and technology programs_____ 537
State and local government regula-
tions _____72, 100
Trucking industry___ 105, 114, 128, 130, 459
Regulatory reform act of 1979, pro-
posed _____ 493
Reich, Jay A_____ 914
Reiche, Frank P_____ 757, 788
Religion, President's views on_____ 472
Renegotiation Board_____ 375, 402
Reorganization Plans. See under Con-
gress, Communications to
Reports to Congress. See under Congress,
Communications to
Reports to the President
Emergency Board to investigate an air-
line industry dispute_____ 293
Federal Strategy for Drug Abuse and
Drug Traffic Prevention_____ 618
National Commission on Neighbor-
hoods _____ 618
National Commission for the Review
of Antitrust Laws and Procedures__ 178
Research and development
Energy. See Energy research and de-
velopment
Federal funding_____ 99, 678
Science and technology. See Science
and technology
Research records acts, privacy of, pro-
posed _____ 584

Resignations and Retirements

Commerce Department, Bureau of the
Census, Director_____ 239 (Digest)
General Services Administrator_____ 448
Law Enforcement Assistance Adminis-
trator _____ 294

Retail Federation, American_____ 832
Rettgers, Forrest I_____ 957
Revenue sharing_____ 250
Reyes, Tony G_____ 942
Reynolds, Allan L_____ 367, 377
Reynolds, James J_____ 819
Reynoso, Cruz_____ 450, 812
Rhett, John T_____ 1016, 1019
Rhodesia. See Zimbabwe-Rhodesia

Ribicoff, Sen. Abraham
  Legislation passage leadership
    Department of education _____ 756
    Ethics in Government Act of 1978
      amendments _____ 1132
    Meeting with the President__ 178 (Digest)
    National health plan support___ 1011, 1027
    Reelection, decision not to seek_____ 782
Ribicoff, Lois M_____ 24
Rice, Emmett J_____ 663, 899
Richmond, Julius B_____ 815
Richmond, Va_____ 630
Riegle, Sen. Donald W., Jr_____ 956
Rietze, Harry L_____ 1002
Riley, Richard W_____ 463
Rivera, José A_____ 435, 441
Roadless area review and evaluation
  lands _____ 151, 671
Robb, Lt. Gov. Charles S_____ 631
Robb, Lynda Johnson_____ 826
Roberts, Joseph L., Jr_____ 33n.
Robinson, Mary Lou_____ 327, 328
Robison, Olin C_____ 730, 787
Rockefeller, Gov. John D., IV_____ 65,
                              67, 648, 905
Rockefeller, Nelson A_____ 189
Rockwell International_____ 241 (Checklist)
Rodgers, David H_____ 23, 46, 90
Rodino, Repr. Peter W., Jr_____ 340, 341
Rodriguez, Mr. and Mrs. Stephen_____ 808n.
Roe, Repr. Robert A_____ 666
Roel, Santiago_____ 281n., 791, 802, 812
Rogers, Barbara B_____ 466
Rogers, Gen. Bernard W_____ 363, 378, 1043
Rogers, Bill_____ 738, 770
Rogers, Michael V_____ 977
Rogers, Repr. Paul G_____ 385
Roldós, Jaime_____ 1043, 1044
Romania
  Clothespin exports_____ 233
  Emigration to Israel and U.S_____ 979
  Trade with U.S_____ 978, 979
Romanian Orthodox Church, Patriarch
  Justin, meeting with the President___ 842
Ronstadt, Linda_____ 745
Roosevelt, Franklin D_____ 995, 1012
Roosevelt, Franklin D., Jr_____ 24
Roosevelt, James_____ 977
Roosevelt, Theodore_____ 775
Roosevelt, Theodore, IV_____ 774
Rose, Repr. Charles_____ 982
Rosenberg, Maurice_____ 976, 984
Rosenquist, James A_____ 435, 441
Rosenthal, Repr. Benjamin_____ 666
Ross, Diana_____ 373
Rostenkowski, Repr. Dan_____ 943
Rouillard, John C_____ 932
Rousakis, John_____ 402
Rowley, Janet D_____ 686
Royo, Aristides_____ 683, 836, 837
Rubal, Marina_____ 466
Rubber industry_____ 161, 752
Rudolph, Wilma_____ 25

Runnion, Marjorie B_____ 466
Rupple, Brenton H_____ 1022, 1043
Rural areas
  See also Agriculture
  Federal policy
    Comprehensive program_____ 154, 794
    Review _____ 73, 77
  Income _____ 600, 602
    See also under Agriculture, farm
      sector and farmers
  Legislation _____ 77, 153, 599
  President's comments on attitudes,
    values _____ 792
  Private investment_____ 600, 602
  Progress during administration____ 154, 570
Rural Development, Working Group on_ 75
Rural development policies and programs
  Communications systems_____ 270
  Energy
    Conservation _____ 623
    Development initiative__ 843 (Checklist)
    See also Agriculture, energy use and
      needs
  Health care_____ 75, 77, 154, 794
  Housing _____ 74,
    77, 136, 154, 218, 794, 843 (Checklist)
  Loans and grants_____ 74, 75, 600–602
  Training and employment_____ 75,
                        154, 600, 602
  Transportation _____ 75,
           77, 154, 1143 (Checklist)
  Water and sewer services_____ 75,
         77, 154, 675 (Checklist), 795
Russell, Harold J_____ 464
Russo, Repr. Martin A_____ 667, 731
Rustin, Bayard_____ 321, 996
Rzepca, Fred_____ 466

Sachs, Howard F_____ 899, 900
Sacks, Howard R_____ 46, 92
Sadat, Anwar al-. *See* Egypt, President
Sadat, Mrs. Anwar al-_____ 522n.
Saint Christopher-Nevis-Anguilla, U.S.
  Special Representative_____ 980
Saint Lucia
  Independence celebrations, U.S. dele-
    gation _____ 293
  U.S. Minister_____ 664
Saint Patrick's Day_____ 432
Saint Vincent, U.S. Special Representa-
  tive _____ 980
Saletic, William G_____ 1001
Salmon, Thomas P_____ 43, 93
Salpeter, Edwin E_____ 46, 93
SALT. *See* Strategic arms limitation
Samoa, Western, U.S. Ambassador_ 1040, 1043
Sampson, Robert G_____ 464
Samuels, Sheldon W_____ 686
San Francisco, Calif_____ 807
Sanchez, Manuel_____ 466
Sanders, Harold Barefoot, Jr_____ 241
Sapelo Island, Ga_____ 669
Saratoga, U.S.S_____ 906
Sarauskas, R. George_____ 914

Sasser, James Franklin_____ 977
Satellite Corporation, Communications_ 271
Sato, Frank S_____ 398, 402
Saudi Arabia
    Crown Prince Fahd Bin Abd al-Aziz
        al-Sa'ud _____ 182, 240, 242, 456
    Middle East peace settlement position_ 456
    U.S. Ambassador_____ 983
    U.S. delegation's visit_ 436, 468 (Checklist)
    U.S. military bases_____ 350
Saunders, Louise H_____ 229
Save Your Vision Week (Proc. 4637) ___ 218
Savings Bonds, United States_____ 309
Savings and loan associations, interest
    rates _____ 929
Sayed, Ali al-_____ 548n.
Schaeffer, Milton T_____ 466
Scharf, Helen M_____ 687
Schaffer, Beverly K_____ 23
Schecter, Jerrold_____ 436, 768, 1143
Scheel, Walter_____ 927
Schlesinger, James R. *See* Energy, Sec-
    retary of
Schmidt, Bob_____ 937, 938n.
Schmidt, Helmut. *See* Germany, Federal
    Republic of, Chancellor
School Board Association, National_____ 1018
Schools. *See* Education
Schreiber, William M_____ 990
Schricker, Henry_____ 990
Schrier, Morris M_____ 686
Schroeder, Mary M_____ 788
Schropp, Jill L_____ 827
Schueler, Ruth_____ 942
Schultz, Frederick H_____ 664, 1043, 1044
Schultze, Charles L. *See* Economic Ad-
    visers, Council of, Chairman
Schwartz, Theodore A_____ 1008
Schwartz, William B., III_____ 977
Scianna, Kerin Rodgers_____ 466
Science, Engineering, and Technology
    Advisory Panel, Intergovernmental___ 544
Science, President's Committee on the
    National Medal of_____ 448
Science Foundation, National. *See* Na-
    tional Science Foundation
Science and technology
    Administration's policy, message to
        Congress _____ 528
    Research and development_____ 140,
        141, 529, 678
Science and Technology, United States-
    Soviet Joint Commission on_____ 539
Science and technology agreement with
    China _____ 200, 540
Science and Technology for Develop-
    ment, United Nations Conference on_ 540
Science and Technology Policy, Office
    of _____ 204, 207, 545
Science and Technology Policy, Office of,
    Director (Frank Press)
    Meeting with the President___ 899 (Digest)
    Mention _____ 544

Science and Technology Policy, Office of,
    Director—Continued
    News conference_____ 900 (Checklist)
    Science and technology regulatory
        reform responsibilities_____ 536
    Space, agriculture, and education
        agreement with China_____ 202, 205n.
    Water research responsibilities_____ 534
Sciences, National Academy of_____ 677, 733
Scientific and Technological Coopera-
    tion, Institute for. *See* Institute for
    Scientific and Technological Coopera-
    tion
Scientific and Technological Coopera-
    tion, United States-People's Republic
    of China Joint Commission on_____ 202
Scroggin, Fred_____ 443
Sea, Convention for the Safety of Life
    at _____ 86
Seafarers Union_____ 943
Sears Roebuck and Co_____ 850
Sebo, Katherine A_____ 914
Securities and Exchange Commission___ 339,
        1021, 1022
Securities Investor Protection Corpora-
    tion _____ 1022, 1043
Security, national. *See* Defense and na-
    tional security
Security Council, National_____ 984
Security Medal, National_____ 179
Segovia, Andres_____ 447
Seidman, Herta Lande_____ 942
Seignious, George M., II_____ 45, 90
Select Commission on Immigration and
    Refugee Policy_____ 450, 564, 812, 907
Selikoff, Irving J_____ 686
Senior citizens. *See* Older persons
Senior Executive Service_____ 392,
        393, 917, 926
Seybolt, George_____ 956
Shakespeare, William_____ 997
Shamir, Yitzhak_____ 428n.
Shapiro, Peter_____ 956
Sharp, Repr. Philip R_____ 990
Sharpe, Lois K_____ 399
Shaw, John M_____ 1018, 1019
Shaw, Robert L_____ 45, 92
Sheen, Bishop Fulton_____ 58
Shelton, Sally Angela_____ 665, 667, 980
Shelton, Stephen_____ 913
Shenefield, John H_____ 178, 234, 242
Shepherd, Mark, Jr_____ 942
Sherburne, Neil C_____ 730, 787
Shilon, Dan_____ 453
Ships, Convention on Pollution from___ 85
Ships and shipping, administration's pro-
    posals _____ 130
Shoob, Marvin H_____ 1018, 1019
Shorenstein, Carole J_____ 466
Short, D. Clive_____ 468
Shump, Ramona_____ 46, 92
Sick, Gary_____ 436
Sights, Dale_____ 229

Sills, Beverly_____ 447
Silverstein, Leonard L_____ 730, 787
Simon, Dorothy M_____ 448
Simon, Ted_____ 466
Simpson, George L., Jr_____ 306n.
Simpson, William
  Deputy Assistant to the President, ap-
    pointment _____ 7
  Mississippi flood disaster actions_____ 672,
    674, 675 (Checklist), 956 (Digest)
Sinai Support Mission, United States_ 64, 756
Sisco, Joseph_____ 907ftn.
Skopil, Otto R., Jr_____ 1043, 1044
Slaughter, John B_____ 448
Slichter, Charles Pence_____ 46, 93
Sloviter, Dolores K_____ 619
Small Business, White House Conference
  on. *See* White House Conference on
  Small Business
Small Business Administration
  Administrator _____ 369, 868, 891
  Budget rescission_____ 453
  Businesswomen loan programs_____ 894
  Deputy Administrator_____ 890
  Inspector General_____ 399, 402
  Legislation _____ 141
  Mention _____ 35
  Procurement Automated Source Sys-
    tem _____ 894
  Public works and economic develop-
    ment programs_____ 601–603
  Solar energy programs_____ 1103
Small Business Conference Commission_ 229,
                                        368
Small Business Person of the Year, Na-
  tional _____ 868
Small Business Week (Proc. 4641)_____ 335
Small businesses_____ 141, 1029
Smith, Repr. Neal
  Mentions _____ 789, 795n., 805
  Mexican oil, proposal to exchange U.S.
    corn for_____ 791, 802
  Trucking industry deregulation legis-
    lation sponsorship_____ 1137
  White House Conference on Small
    Business sponsorship_____ 369
Smith, Robert P_____ 579, 619
Smoking, Surgeon General's report on___ 55
Snowden, Judy Glissen_____ 466
Snyder, Paul W_____ 23
Social Security, National Commission on.
  See National Commission on Social
  Security
Social security system
  Administration's accomplishments_ 122, 569
  Civil service retirement system_____ 918
  Federal Republic of Germany-U.S.
    agreement _____ 362
  Payments increase_____ 796, 838
  Reform _____ 99, 137, 173
Social welfare reform amendments, pro-
  posed _____ 938

Socialist International Study Group on
  Disarmament _____ 898
Sofaer, Abraham D_____ 93
Sohn, Michael N_____ 886
Solar energy
  Administration's proposals_____ 148,
    1095, 1097, 1143 (Checklist)
  Congressmen and solar groups repre-
    sentatives, meetings with the Presi-
    dent (Digest)_____ 327, 553
  Energy security trust fund, future
    development allocations from_____ 614
  Mention _____ 792
  Photovoltaic cells_____ 712, 1104
  Swine and poultry houses heating____ 194
  Water heating_____ 533
Solar Energy, Domestic Policy Review
  of _____ 1101, 1103–1105
Solar Energy Caucus_____ 1095
Solar Energy Centers, Regional_____ 1102
Solar energy development bank___ 1096, 1101
Solar Energy Research Institute_____ 148,
                                    149, 1102, 1105
"Solar Memphis" program_____ 1103
Solar User Information Program, Na-
  tional _____ 1102
Solberg, Hilmar L_____ 467
Solomon, Joel W. (Jay)_____ 178, 448, 467
Solomon Islands, Ambassador to U.S___ 554
Sonnenberg, Maurice_____ 942
Sorsa, Kalevi_____ 898
South Africa, majority rule government_ 38,
                                        357
South Carolina, U.S. district judge_____ 1018,
                                        1019
South Dakota, U.S. district judge_____ 441
Southeast Asian Nations, Association
  of _____ 303, 304
Soviet Union. *See* Union of Soviet Soci-
  alist Republics
So-Whon Hyon_____ 1154
Space, agricultural, and educational
  agreement with China_____ 204
Space Organization, European_____ 538
Space program
  National policy_____ 536
  1980 budget allocations_____ 141
  Private industries research and de-
    velopment _____ 712
  Purposes of program_____ 681
  Space Shuttle_____ 141, 536, 681, 712
Spanish-speaking Americans
  Discrimination _____ 237, 813
  Employment _____ 813
  Federal Government representation___ 811,
                                        847
  Judicial appointments_____ 131, 759, 847
  Mexican immigration_____ 812, 907
Spaulding, Asa_____ 322
Speaker of the House of Representatives
  (Thomas P. O'Neill, Jr.)
  Communications from the President__ 102,
    232, 461, 895, 997, 1034

Speaker of the House—Continued
Mentions _____ 103, 109n., 745, 1092n.
President's assessment_____ 829
Standby gasoline rationing plan support _____ 840
Special Country Music Association award _____ 898
Special Representative for Trade Negotiations (Robert S. Strauss)
Import functions
Steel _____ 1034
Sugar _____ 946
Television receivers_____ 167–169
Meeting with the President___ 467 (Digest)
Mentions _____ 490n., 746, 768, 827, 1024
Multilateral trade negotiations, Tokyo Round negotiator_____ 6, 47, 331, 834, 944, 1093
U.S. trade mission to Egypt and Israel, delegation head_____ 640
Spielman, Phyllis R_____ 781
Spirou, Christos C_____ 700, 720n.
Sprague, Irvine Henry_____ 91
Sprague, Philip A_____ 196, 218
Staggers, Repr. Harley O_____ 293, 385, 1026
Staker, Robert J_____ 1044
Standby gasoline rationing plan
Conditions necessary for implementation _____ 748, 797, 863
President's plan
Congressional actions_____ 705, 748, 823, 840, 846, 936, 951
Message transmitting proposals to Congress _____ 371, 402
Amendments _____ 813, 820
President's appeal for congressional approval _____ 655, 689
Stark, Arthur_____ 23
State, Department of
See also specific constituent agencies
Ambassadors at Large_____ 42, 91, 364, 377, 687, 1134, 1143
Assistant Secretary_____ 21, 91
Coordinator for Mexican Affairs_____ 1134, 1143
Coordinator for Population Affairs____ 377, 378
Coordinator for Refugee Affairs (Dick Clark)
Meeting with the President_____ 1142 (Digest)
Mentions _____ 789, 795n.
Nomination _____ 364, 377
President's assessment_____ 804
Coordinator for State and Local Governments _____ 2083
Cyprus conflict settlement actions___ 461
Deputy Assistant Secretary_____ 1042, 1143
Deputy Secretary. *See* State, Deputy Secretary of
Environmental effects abroad of Federal actions, responsibilities for_ 10–13

State, Department of—Continued
Foreign assistance programs reorganization _____ 279, 395, 643, 976
Mention _____ 362
Treaty and international agreement reports _____ 84–87, 223, 238, 239, 434, 449, 450, 776, 778, 822, 1155
Whale conservation programs_____ 267
State, Deputy Secretary of (Warren M. Christopher)
Cyprus conflict negotiations_____ 192
Meetings with the President (Digest)_ 957, 983
Middle East and European leaders, discussions with_____ 436
Panama, meeting with President Royo_ 837
State, Secretary of (Cyrus R. Vance)
For functions of the Department in general, see State, Department of
British Government, consultations with new administration_____ 803, 965
China, People's Republic of
Consular Relations and Consulates General agreement_____ 212
New Year's message to Huang Hua_ 15
Cyprus conflict settlement actions____ 998
Dubs, Adolph, commemorative service remarks _____ 295
Egyptian-Israeli peace negotiations__ 251, 263, 303, 329n., 408, 688, 852, 969
Environmental effects abroad of Federal actions, responsibilities for____ 11
Foreign Service review_____ 925
Hungary and Romania, visit to_____ 157
Iran, meeting with emissaries of the Khomeini government_____ 352
Meetings with the President (Digest)_ 26, 89, 179, 217, 239, 240, 293, 327, 377, 400, 468, 554, 618, 732, 787, 842, 899, 1018, 1142
Mentions _____ 332, 333, 670, 768, 798, 831, 837n., 847, 1014, 1024
News conferences (Checklist)___ 843, 1020
Panama, permanent American cemetery negotiations_____ 81
Security assistance program administration _____ 224
Soviet backfire bomber statement____ 1079
Sugar imports actions_____ 946
Taiwan relations responsibilities_____ 1131
Ugandan trade actions_____ 225, 867
United Nations role_____ 62
State and local governments
Anti-inflation program_____ 124, 308
Economic growth and development activities _____ 66, 70, 71, 78
Federal aid_____ 250
Hazardous waste disposal_____ 1035
Health programs_____ 1031
Hospital cost expenditures_____ 387

State and local governments—Continued
Intergovernmental fiscal assistance leg-
islation _____ 391, 401
Privacy rights policy_____ 583
Regional commissions_____ 79
Relationship with Federal Govern-
ment _____ 130
Science and technology programs_____ 544
Solar energy programs_____ 1100
Truck weights and lengths regula-
tions _____ 1137, 1140
Wage rate comparability surveys_____ 1003
Welfare reform programs_____ 117
State of the Union
Address _____ 103, 179
Message to the Congress_____ 121

Statements by the President
See also Bill Signings
Air quality standards in Ohio_____ 1006
Alaska public lands_____ 877
Carnegie Commission on the Future of
Public Broadcasting_____ 199
Clinch River breeder reactor_____ 730,
795, 887
Deaths
Bartlett, Sen. Dewey_____ 374
Bayh, Marvella_____ 691
Dubs, Adolph_____ 269
Eaton, Cyrus_____ 837
Fortson, Ben_____ 913
Morton, Rogers C. B_____ 674
Randolph, A. Philip_____ 882
Rockefeller, Nelson A_____ 189
Stewart, Bill_____ 1113
Wayne, John_____ 1031
Wood, John H., Jr_____ 959
Education, department of, proposed__ 756
Egyptian-Israeli peace negotiations___ 346,
432, 436, 449
Energy conservation contingency
plans _____ 690
Energy crisis_____ 648, 747, 959
Gasoline shortages in California___ 808, 873
Geological Survey, 100th anniversary__ 374
Inflation _____ 255
Multilateral trade negotiations agree-
ments _____ 662
National Forest System_____ 671
1980 fiscal year budget_____ 50, 947
North Atlantic Treaty Organization__ 363
Oil prices, phased decontrol of do-
mestic _____ 981
Panama Canal treaties, implementing
legislation _____ 1125
Regulatory reform_____ 482
Ribicoff, Sen. Abraham, reelection de-
cision _____ 782
Standby gasoline rationing plan__ 690, 823
Sunset review legislation_____ 941
Trucking industry labor dispute_____ 657
Uganda, human rights_____ 867

Statements by the President—Continued
Vice President's visits
China _____ 1125
Nordic countries and the Nether-
lands _____ 220
Statements Other Than Presidential
See also White House Statements
Afghanistan, development and military
assistance programs, White House
Press Secretary_____ 310
MX missile deployment, White House
Deputy Press Secretary_____ 1016
Urban aid program funds, White
House Press Secretary_____ 609
Statler, Stuart M_____ 1041, 1044
Steel Agreement, International_____ 7
Steel Caucus, Congressional_____ 1018
Steel imports (Proc. 4665)_____ 1032
Steering Committee of the Economic
Policy Group_____ 977
Stein, Leon_____ 46, 90
Stennis, Sen. John C_____ 89, 786, 898
Stephens, Betty J_____ 466
Sterner, Michael_____ 436
Stevens, Paul_____ 490n.
Stevenson, Sen. Adlai E_____ 943, 948
Stewart, Bill_____ 1113
Stone, James M_____ 41, 93
Stone, Patsy S_____ 466
Stone, Sen. Richard_____ 217
Strategic arms limitation
Administration's policy statement_ 694–699
International support_ 382, 764, 1004, 1005
MX missile deployment_____ 1016
SALT II negotiations
Chief negotiator_____ 1077
Mentions _____ 158,
356, 543, 637, 652, 683, 772, 902, 966
News conference_____ 843 (Checklist)
Soviets negotiating in good faith_ 170
Strengths of U.S. position_____ 1091
White House statement_____ 329
SALT II treaty
Address to Congress_____ 1087
Appeal for public support_____ 637,
719, 805, 831, 839, 952, 1012
Briefings by administration officials
(Digest) _____ 898,
995, 956, 982, 983, 1017, 1042
New missile systems development
terms _____ 966
Purposes of treaty
Alliances, strengthening of_____ 32,
845, 851, 903
Developing nations, example of
peaceful intentions of U.S____ 32,
559, 845, 851, 994
National security enhancement__ 107,
694, 835, 994
Soviet-U.S. relations improve-
ment _____ 32, 845, 851, 903, 944

Strategic arms limitation—Continued
  SALT II treaty—Continued
    Purposes of treaty—Continued
      World peace contributor_____ 32,
        107, 576, 694, 835, 851, 903, 966,
        994
    Senate ratification
      Final vote in 1979, possibility of__ 751
      President's appeal for_____ 750,
        831, 845, 852
    Treaty amendments, possibility
      of _____ 903
    Soviet military capability, effect on
      ratification _____ 56
    Text of treaty and related docu-
      ments _____ 1051
    Verification of terms_____ 107,
      305, 749, 934, 994
  SALT III negotiations_ 682, 683, 903, 1091
  U.S.-Soviet relations, effect on_____ 300,
    305, 317, 348, 851, 1091
  Vienna Summit Meeting. *See* Vienna
    Summit Meeting
Strategic Offensive Arms, United States-
  Soviet Union Treaty on the Limita-
  tion of_____ 1051
Strategic Petroleum Reserve program____ 147,
  720
Strategy Council on Drug Abuse_____ 618
Straub, Terrence D_____ 990
Strauss, Robert S. *See* Special Repre-
  sentative for Trade Negotiations; Mid-
  dle East, Egyptian-Israeli peace nego-
  tiations, Personal Representative of the
  President
Student Assistance program, Middle In-
  come _____ 264
Submarines _____ 558, 695
Sugar Agreement, International____ 153, 161
Sugar industry
  Domestic programs_____ 153
  Imports _____ 153, 946
Sugarman, Jule M_____ 2, 46, 90, 977
Suhler, Carl G_____ 914
Sullivan, Austin P., Jr_____ 947
Sullivan, John M_____ 977
Sullivan, Rev. Leon_____ 1042
Sullivan, William J_____ 24, 46, 90
Sulsona, Herman_____ 466
Sun Day_____ 1097
Sunset review legislation_____ 129, 494, 941
Supplementary Security Income_____ 940
Swan, Robert J_____ 446
Swearing-in ceremonies. *See under* Ad-
  dresses and Remarks
Sweden
  Prime Minister Ola Ullsten_____ 33, 89
  Vice President's visit_____ 220, 639
Sweeney, Paul W., Jr_____ 914
Swing, William L_____ 580, 619
Swygert, H. Patrick_____ 3, 46
Syria, Middle East peace settlement role_ 453,
  456

Syvrud, Donald E_____ 446, 468
Szanton, Peter L_____ 294
Tabenken, Gerald M_____ 293, 466
Taiwan
  China, People's Republic of, agreement
    to peacefully resolve differences
    with _____ 52,
    257
  EO 12143_____ 1132
  Television receivers exports_____ 167, 168
  Trade with U.S_____ 158, 331, 334, 1111
  U.S. relations
    Continuation of commercial and cul-
      tural relations_____ 1,
      170, 257, 356, 576, 1111
    Legislation _____ 165, 170
    Memorandum to Federal agencies__ 1
Taiwan Relations Act_____ 640
Talarico, Sam_____ 1008
Talley, Mae Sue_____ 730, 787
Talmadge, Sen. Herman E_____ 33n., 384
Tanzania, alignment with the Soviet
  Union _____ 316
Task Force on Women Business Owners_ 894,
  895
Tate, Danny C., meetings with the Presi-
  dent (Digest) _____ 467,
  553, 618, 666, 732, 786, 842, 898, 899,
  956, 1142
Tate, S. Shepherd_____ 760n.
Tax Court, United States_____ 820, 843
Taxation
  See also Windfall profits tax
  Business investment credit_____ 601
  Carryover basis reform_____ 132
  Employment tax credit_____ 99, 601
  Energy credits
    Gasohol investment_____ 792
    Solar installation_____ 1102, 1103
    Woodburning stoves installation___ 1102
  Federal expenditures review_____ 942
  France, conventions with U.S.
    Income and property taxes_____ 238
    Taxation and fiscal evasion_____ 238
  Hungary-U.S. taxation and fiscal eva-
    sion convention_____ 822
  Income tax surcharge_____ 651
  Reduction and reform_____ 188, 962
  Relationship with inflation_____ 247
  United Kingdom-U.S. taxation and
    fiscal evasion convention_____ 663, 778
Taylor, Eldon D_____ 398, 402
Taylor, Harriett R_____ 665, 667
Taylor, Hobart, Jr_____ 977
Taylor, Susanne Dabney_____ 466
Taylor, Theodore B_____ 661
Teamsters Union__ 48, 560, 740, 745, 752, 850
Technological Cooperation, Foundation
  for International_____ 141, 161
Technological Cooperation, Institute for
  Scientific and. *See* Institute for Scien-
  tific and Technological Cooperation
Telecommunications, International Com-
  mittee on_____ 270

Telecommunications Convention, International _____ 541
Telecommunications and Information Administration, National _____ 586
Television receivers, color _____ 166
Templeton, Robert _____ 297
Teng Hsiao-p'ing. *See* Deng Xiaoping
Tennessee, disaster declaration _____ 841
Tennessee Valley Authority
  Board of Directors, member _____ 877, 957
  Budget deferral _____ 200
  Solar energy programs _____ 1096, 1100, 1103, 1105
Test Ban Negotiations, Comprehensive _____ 216, 1129, 1143
Test Ban Treaty, Limited _____ 1038
Texas
  Black leaders, meeting with the President _____ 841
  Disaster declaration _____ 667, 732
  President's visit _____ 482
  U.S. district judges _____ 241, 294, 327, 328, 377, 378, 402, 403
Textile industry representatives, meeting with the President _____ 467
Thahane, Timothy _____ 554
Thailand
  Joint statement _____ 230–232
  U.S. relations _____ 53
Thailand, Prime Minister (Kriangsak Chomanan), visit to U.S.
  Announcement _____ 178 (Digest), 179 (Checklist)
  Meetings with the President _____ 221, 226, 242 (Checklist)
  President's previsit comments _____ 54, 182
Thatcher, Margaret _____ 803, 965
Thaxton, Carlton J _____ 400
Thompson, John D _____ 932
Thompson, Brig. Gen. Nathaniel R., Jr _____ 163
Thomson, Meldrim _____ 720n.
Thomson, Robert _____ 467, 732
Thornburgh, Gov. Richard _____ 578, 579
Thorstenson, Robert M _____ 1001
Three Mile Island, President's Commission on the Accident at. *See* President's Commission on the Accident at Three Mile Island
Three Mile Island, Pa., nuclear plant accident
  See also President's Commission on the Accident at Three Mile Island
  Federal monitoring _____ 558, 577, 625
  Mention _____ 795
  President's meetings with Federal officials (Digest) _____ 617, 618
  Results of accident
    Federal administration investigations _____ 741
    Nuclear energy reassessment _____ 558, 577, 624, 681, 702, 712, 798
  White House statement _____ 617
Thrower, Julius B _____ 947
Thurston, Don _____ 482

Tidwell, G. Ernest _____ 1018, 1019
Tillich, Paul _____ 972
Tin Agreement, International _____ 161
Tin industry _____ 161
Title V Regional Commissions
  Federal and regional growth policy implementation _____ 72, 79, 81
  Proposed legislation _____ 78
  State cooperation efforts _____ 66
Tito, Josip Broz _____ 670
Tlatelolco, Treaty of _____ 159, 835
Tobacco industry _____ 55
Tobin, Joan Fleischmann _____ 91
Todd, Brig. Gen. Harold _____ 436
Togo, Ambassador to U.S. _____ 842
Tokyo Economic Summit Conference _____ 550, 1004, 1108, 1109
Tomich, Rosemary _____ 942
Toner, Joseph _____ 402
Tonga, Ambassador to U.S. _____ 554
Torres, Julio _____ 466
Toxicology program, national _____ 536
Trade, U.S. *See under* Commerce, international
Trade agreements act, proposed _____ 1092
Trade Commission, Federal _____ 234, 235, 242, 339
Trade Commission, United States International. *See* United States International Trade Commission
Trade Negotiations, Special Representative for. *See* Special Representative for Trade Negotiations
Trade Policy Staff Committee _____ 168, 169
Trade Week, World _____ 616
Trademarks, Nice Agreement on International _____ 84
Train Dispatchers Association, American _____ 818, 984
Trans-Alaska Oil Pipeline _____ 592
Transportation
  See also Aircraft and aviation; Mass transit; Railroads; Ships and shipping; Trucking industry
  Industries deregulation _____ 128, 130, 459
Transportation, Department of
  See also specific constituent agencies
  Air quality and transportation planning _____ 75
  Alaska Natural Gas Transportation System, transfer of functions _____ 594
  Annual report, 1977 _____ 786
  Budget deferrals _____ 200, 272
  Diesel fuel shortages _____ 945
  55-mile per hour speed limit enforcement _____ 876
  Inspector General _____ 398, 402
  Mass transit assistance _____ 727, 875
  Military Awards program _____ 363
  Offshore oil spill pollution _____ 338
  Prices index for hauling exempt commodities _____ 1136, 1139
  Railroad industry study _____ 459

Transportation, Secretary of (Brock Adams)
For functions of the Department in general, see Transportation, Department of
Alaska Natural Gas Transportation System, Executive Policy Board member _____ 1126
Federal Council on the Arts and the Humanities, member_____ 956
Meetings with the President (Digest) _____ 786, 899
News conferences (Checklist)_____ 468, 900, 1143
Trucking industry deregulation actions _____ 1117, 1124, 1125, 1137
Transportation Day and National Transportation Week, National Defense___ 237
Transportation Safety Board, National_ 437, 441, 1007, 1019
Trantum, Thomas A_____ 871, 899
Treasury, Department of the
See also specific constituent agencies
Alaska Natural Gas Transportation System, transfer of functions_____ 596
Assistant Secretaries__ 240, 733, 1000, 1018
Budget deferrals_____ 200, 272
Cash management policies review_____ 462
Counselor on Legislative and Intergovernmental Policy_____ 270
Deputy Assistant Secretary_____ 890
Energy security trust fund responsibilities _____ 727
Energy tax credit legislation_____ 1102
Interest rate controls review_____ 928
Tax courts reform responsibilities_____ 345
Treasury, Secretary of the (W. Michael Blumenthal)
For functions of the Department in general, see Treasury, Department of the
Alaska Natural Gas Transportation System, transfer of functions_____ 596
China, People's Republic of, visit to__ 174, 213, 331, 348
Color television receiver imports functions (Proc. 4634)_____ 168
Countervailing duties' waiver_____ 46
Economic Policy Group, Chairman__ 977
Electronic surveillance orders review_ 585, 589
Export financing negotiations_____ 439
Hungary and Romania, visit to_____ 157
Investigative and audit training program improvement_____ 779
Meetings with the President (Digest)_ 25, 178, 240, 327, 401, 467, 554, 732, 841, 956, 1142
Mentions _____ 96, 157, 865, 1155
Multilateral development banks arrangements _____ 396
1980 budget preparation_____ 96
Oil price decontrol adjustments___ 724, 725

Treasury, Secretary of the—Continued
Solar energy development bank, board of directors member_____ 1101
Ugandan import actions_____ 224, 867
Treaties and other international agreements. *See under* Congress, Communications to
Tree, Marietta_____ 977
Trident submarine_____ 155, 696
Trucking competition and safety act, proposed _____ 1114
Trucking industry
Deregulation
President's commitment to reform in 1979 _____ 105, 114, 128, 130, 459
Proposed legislation_____ 1114, 1117, 1143 (Checklist)
Independent truckers' strikes_____ 1129, 1135, 1143, 1144, 1159
Labor dispute_____ 657, 668
Representatives, meeting with the President _____ 178
Trudeau, Pierre Elliott_____ 327, 376, 379, 381
Trujillo, Rupert_____ 1023
Truman, Harry S.
Mentions _____ 1038
President's comments on
Health care program_____ 1024, 1028
Nuclear control efforts_____ 1087
Quoted _____ 1010
Trunk, Ann_____ 662
Tucker, Benjamin M_____ 466
Tucker, Gordon_____ 914
Tucker, Repr. James (Jim) Guy_____ 667, 668
Tucker, Sterling_____ 61, 93
Tunas, International Commission for the Conservation of Atlantic_____ 436
Tunisia, U.S. Ambassador_____ 101, 179
Turkey
Cyprus conflict_____ 191, 461, 998
Mentions _____ 845, 1006
U.S. economic assistance_____ 647, 653
U.S. relations_____ 156
Turner, Stansfield. *See* Central Intelligence Agency, Director
Tuvalu
Ambassador to U.S_____ 842
Friendship treaty with U.S_____ 822
Udall, Repr. Morris K_____ 776
Udall-Anderson act, proposed_____ 855, 877
Uganda
Human rights violations_____ 867
Trade with U.S_____ 224, 867
Ullman, Repr. Al_____ 217, 982, 1011
Ullsten, Ola_____ 33, 89
Union of Soviet Socialist Republics
Ambassador to U.S_____ 356
Arms sales from U.S_____ 184
Convention on International Civil Aviation _____ 449
Exchange of Soviet citizens with U.S__ 731, 751, 965
Foreign Minister_____ 1079

Union of Soviet Socialist Republics—Con.
  Foreign relations
    China _____ 57, 289
    Former allies_____ 565
    Japan _____ 764
    United States
      Détente maintenance_____ 158
      Impact of
        Chinese-U.S. normalization___ 172
        SALT II treaty_____ 300,
          305, 317, 348, 851, 1091
        Peaceful competition policy_____ 260,
          693, 903
    Strategic arms limitation. *See* Strategic
      arms limitation
    Trade with U.S_____ 331, 358, 359, 749
    Vienna Summit Meeting. *See* Vienna
      Summit Meeting
Union of Soviet Socialist Republics,
  President (L. I. Brezhnev)
    Invitation to visit U.S_____ 158
    Soviet dissidents' exchange approval__ 751
    Trade with U.S., position on_____ 331, 356
    U.S. arms sales to China, warning
      against _____ 184
    Vienna Summit Meeting. *See* Vienna
      Summit Meeting
United Automobile Workers_____ 740, 752
United Food and Commercial Workers
  International Union_____ 1008, 1020
United Kingdom
  Cyprus conflict settlement actions_ 191, 998
  Elections _____ 803
  Nuclear test ban_____ 902
  Prime Minister James Callaghan_____ 17,
    20n., 25 (Digest), 26 (Checklist)
  Prime Minister Margaret Thatcher___ 803,
    965
  Taxation and fiscal evasion convention
    with U.S_____ 663, 778
  Tokyo Summit attendance announce-
    ment _____ 550
  Zimbabwe-Rhodesia settlement ac-
    tions _____ 357, 755, 1013
United Mine Workers_____ 905
United Nations
  Cyprus conflict settlement actions____ 191,
    461, 648
  Egyptian-Israeli peace treaty imple-
    mentation _____ 497,
    499, 501, 502, 505, 516, 517
  High Commissioner for Refugees____ 765
  International covenants on human
    rights _____ 162
  Secretary-General _____ 62, 191, 461, 998
  Security Council_____ 192
  U.S. foreign assistance programs_____ 279,
    396, 644
  U.S. participation_____ 62

United Nations, U.S. Representative
  (Andrew J. Young)
  African nations, relationship with____ 38
  Australian-American Week, U.S. Rep-
    resentative _____ 376
  Meeting with the President____ 14 (Digest)
  Mentions _____883, 886n., 909, 912
  President's assessment_____ 31, 62
United Nations Conference on Science
  and Technology for Development____ 540
United Nations Decade for Women,
  Equality, Development and Peace____ 825
United Press International Newspaper
  Advisory Board_____ 735
United States Advisory Commission on
  International Communication, Cul-
  tural and Educational Affairs_____ 729,
    787, 1037, 1044
United States Air Force Academy_____ 435
United States Arms Control and Dis-
  armament Agency
  Annual report_____ 683
  Assistant Director_____ 685
  General Counsel_____ 1077
  Member _____ 45, 90
United States Civil Service Commission_ 8,
    64
United States Fire Administration_____ 22,
    91, 566
United States Foreign Claims Settlement
  Commission _____ 46, 90
United States International Development
  Cooperation Agency____ 279, 395, 642, 915
United States International Trade Com-
  mission
  Bolt, nut, and large screw imports____ 4
  Clothespin imports_____ 232, 233, 325
  Steel imports_____ 1033
  Television receiver imports_____ 166, 167
United States Marine Corps_____ 672
United States Military Academy_____ 687
United States Naval Academy_____ 730
United States-People's Republic of China
  Joint Commission on Scientific and
  Technological Cooperation_____ 202
United States Postal Service
  Board of Governors, members_____ 24,
    46, 90, 215, 241
  Deputy Postmaster General_____ 972
  Food stamps issuance_____ 83
United States Railway Association_____ 43, 93
United States Savings Bonds_____ 309
U.S.S. *Saratoga*_____ 906
United States Sinai Support Mission_ 64, 756
United States-Soviet Joint Commission
  on Science and Technology_____ 539
United States-Soviet Union Standing
  Consultative Commission_____ 1056, 1057
United States-Soviet Union Treaty on
  the Limitation of Strategic Offensive
  Arms _____ 1051
United States Tax Court_____ 820, 843
Upland cotton program_____ 786

Urban areas
Alternate transportation methods____ 864
Federal assistance programs___ 72, 77, 609
Public works and economic develop-
ment _____ 600, 668
Urban Development Action Grant pro-
gram _____ 74, 136, 600, 601
Urban Mass Transportation Administra-
tion _____ 75
Uruguay, U.S. Ambassador_____ 1132, 1143
Utah, radioactivity exposure_____ 182
Utility costs_____ 479

Vajpayee, Atal Bihari_____ 731 (Digest)
Vaky, Viron P_____ 837
Valuchek, Andrew_____ 293
Van Derzee, James_____ 322
Van Doren, Charles N_____ 685
Van Lennep, Emile_____ 787
Vance, Cyrus R. *See* State, Secretary of
Vance, Susan Margaret_____ 340, 377
Vanden Heuvel, William J_____ 815
Vaux Junior High School, Pa_____ 787
Vega, Marta Moreno_____ 466
Velde, Richard W_____ 294
Venezuela
Inaugural ceremonies, U.S. delega-
tion _____ 239, 241
Maritime boundary treaty with U.S__ 86
Verity, C. William, Jr_____ 942
Veterans
Legislation _____ 139
Vietnam. *See* Vietnam veterans
Veterans Administration_____ 367,
377, 974, 1040
Veterans' Federal Coordinating Commit-
tee _____ 974
Veterans' Health Care Amendments____ 1039
Vice President (Walter F. Mondale)
Economic Policy Group, *ex officio*
member _____ 977
Energy situation management in Presi-
dent's absence_____ 1142
Inauguration ceremonies in Brazil and
Venezuela, U.S. delegation head___ 239
(Digest)
Meetings with the President (Digest)_ 14,
25, 26, 89, 178, 179, 217, 239, 240,
242, 293, 327, 376, 377, 400, 401, 467,
553, 554, 731, 732, 786, 787, 841, 842,
898, 956, 957, 1017, 1042, 1043, 1142
Mentions ____ 370n., 373, 548n., 827, 1008
News conference_____ 378 (Checklist)
President of Senate, communications
from the President___ 102, 232, 897, 1035
President's trip to Egypt and Israel,
departure and return remarks___ 394, 430
Trips to foreign countries
China, People's Republic of_____ 1112
Nordic countries and Netherlands_ 220,
691
Youth employment and training task
force, chairman_____ 911
Vickery, Gordon_____ 22, 91, 567

Vienna Summit Meeting
Announcement _____ 839
Departure _____ 1038
Meetings with Soviet President Brezh-
nev__ 1048, 1049, 1051, 1079, 1081, 1143
Presummit comments_____ 772,
805, 831, 902, 1002
SALT II treaty
Signing ceremony_____ 1079, 1143
Soviet backfire bomber statement___ 1079
Texts of treaty and related docu-
ments _____ 1051
U.S.S.R.-U.S. joint statement_____ 1081
Welcoming ceremony_____ 1047, 1143
Working dinners
Soviet Embassy_____ 1049, 1143
U.S. Ambassador's residence_ 1048, 1143
Vietnam
Invasion of Cambodia__ 303, 314, 348, 765
Refugees _____ 1149
Vietnam veterans_____ 973–975, 984, 1011
Vietnam Veterans Week (Proc. 4647)__ 445,
972
Vietor, Harold Duane_____ 441
Vigil, Juan R_____ 914
Vining, Robert L., Jr_____ 1043, 1044
Vins, Georgi_____ 731, 758n.
Violence, Interdepartmental Committee
on Domestic_____ 729
Virginia
President's visit_____ 630
U.S. district judge_____ 667, 668, 899, 900
Virginia Beach, Va_____ 897
Vision Week, Save Your_____ 219
Voluntary Action program, National___ 880
Voorde, Frances M_____ 990n.
Voting rights_____ 911

Wade, Larry_____ 481n.
Wade, Mrs. Paul R_____ 481n.
Wage insurance, real. *See* Real wage in-
surance
Wage and Price Stability, Council on
Anti-inflation program_____ 125
Reports _____ 178, 393, 815
Wage and price monitoring_____ 256,
471, 560, 752, 850
Wage and Price Stability, Council on,
Chairman. *See* Kahn, Alfred E.
Wage and Price Stability, Council on, Di-
rector (Barry Bosworth)
Meetings with the President (Digest)_ 14,
25, 240, 327, 467, 554, 732, 842, 956,
1142
Mentions _____ 252, 752, 1122
Wage System, Federal_____ 1003
Wages and prices
Mandatory controls_____ 849
Real wage insurance. *See* Real wage
insurance
Voluntary guidelines
Corporations _____ 124,
256, 486, 560, 622, 635, 650, 740, 752,
833, 850, 935

Wages and prices—Continued
  Voluntary guidelines—Continued
    Labor _____ 477, 635, 752, 850
    Mentions _____ 74,
        115, 307, 650, 704, 714, 736, 962
    Violation of guidelines_____ 471,
        560, 740, 752
Wahl, Constance_____ 466
Wald, Patricia M_____ 733, 787
Walden, Phil_____ 447
Waldheim, Kurt_____ 62, 191, 461, 998
Walker, A. Maceo, Sr_____ 229
Waronker, Cecile C_____ 1034
Warren, Charles_____ 872, 876, 960
Warren, Dave_____ 45, 91
Warren, Earl_____ 884, 885
Washington, emergency declaration____ 440
Wasilewski, Vincent T_____ 490n.
Wasserman, Lew R_____ 373
Watanabe, Ruth K_____ 293
Water Resources Council_____ 8–10
Water and waterways
  EO 12141_____ 1000
  Legislation _____ 150, 900
  Project review_____ 8–10
  Rural areas programs_____ 75,
      675 (Checklist), 733, 794, 795
  Science and technology development_ 534
Watson, Jack H., Jr.
  Meetings with the President (Digest)_ 178,
      240
  Mentions _____ 67, 658n., 794, 888
  News conference_____ 1154 (Checklist)
  President's representative to Witchita
      Falls, Tex., tornado disaster___ 665, 668
  White House Management Task Force
      on Energy Shortages, Chairman___ 1137,
      1139
Wausau, Wis_____ 567
Waxman, Repr. Henry A_ 293, 384, 385, 857
Wayne, John_____ 813n., 959, 1031
Weaver, A. Vernon, Jr_____ 369, 868, 891
Weaver, Robert_____ 322
Webb, Marcia_____ 466
Weber case_____ 847
Webster, William_____ 959, 1130, 1143
Weddington, Sarah___ 553, 772 ftn., 773, 888
Weicker, Sen. Lowell P., Jr_____ 867
Weinberg, Steven_____ 448
Weinshienk, Zita L_____ 984
Weisman, Marcia Simon_____ 466
Welfare reform amendments, social, pro-
    posed _____ 938
Welfare system
  Administration's accomplishments____ 122
  Reform legislation_____ 76,
      117, 138, 258, 939, 950
Wellford, W. Harrison_____ 378
Welsh, Matt_____ 990
Welsh, William B_____ 42
Wesley, Charles_____ 322
West, John C_____ 983
West Virginia, U.S. district judges_____ 1044

Wexler, Anne_____ 245, 554, 666, 888
Whaling Commission, International____ 265
Wheat Agreement, 1971, International__ 434
Wheat Council, International_____ 434
Wheat reserves_____ 153
Wheat Trade Convention_____ 434
Whinnery, John R_____ 448
Whistle-blowers, Federal Government__ 917
White, Howard_____ 46, 91
White, John. *See* Chairman *under* Demo-
    cratic National Committee
White, John P. *See* Management and
    Budget, Deputy Director
White House, Committee for the Preser-
    vation of the_____ 782
White House Conference on Balanced
    National Growth and Economic Devel-
    opment _____ 65, 69
White House Conference on Families_ 667, 668
White House Conference on Library and
    Information Services_____ 400, 746
White House Conference on Small Busi-
    ness
  Advisory group_____ 369
  Chairman _____ 811
  Mentions _____ 370
  Preconference preparation_____ 142, 335
White House Correspondents Associa-
    tion _____ 743
White House Fellows_____ 914
White House Fellowships, President's
    Commission on_____ 931
White House Management Task Force
    on Energy Shortages_____ 1137, 1139
White House Military Office_____ 170
White House passenger lists for military
    aircraft _____ 240
White House Rural Development Initia-
    tives program_____ 270
White House solar system_____ 1143
White House staff
  Advisor to the President on Inflation.
      See Kahn, Alfred E.
  Assistant Press Secretary_____ 1017
  Assistants to the President
    Congressional Liaison. *See* Moore,
        Frank B.
    Domestic Affairs and Policy. *See*
        Eizenstat, Stuart E.
    Intergovernmental Affairs. *See*
        Watson, Jack H., Jr.
    Jordan, Hamilton. *See* Jordan,
        Hamilton
    Kraft, Timothy E_____ 245, 990
    National Security Affairs. *See* Brze-
        zinski, Zbigniew
    Reorganization _____ 378
  Associate Press Secretaries
    Bario, Patricia Y____ 252n., 852n., 908n.
    Schecter, Jerrold_____ 768, 1143
  Deputy Advisor on Inflation and Coun-
      selor on Labor-Management Rela-
      tions _____ 25, 467

White House staff—Continued
Deputy Appointments Secretary_____ 990n.
Deputy Assistants
Congressional Liaison (House). *See*
Cable, William H.
Congressional Liaison (Senate). *See*
Tate, Danny C.
Eidenberg, Gene_____ 1137, 1139
National Security Affairs_____ 327,
401, 467, 841
Simpson, William. *See* Simpson,
William
Deputy Press Secretaries
Bario, Patricia Y_____ 1017
Granum, Rex_____ 1016n.
Wurfel, Walter W_____ 189, 566, 628
Physician to the President____ 618 (Digest)
Press Secretary to the President. *See*
Powell, Jody
Special Assistants
Congressional Liaisons (House)
Beckel, Robert G. *See* Beckel,
Robert G.
Free, James C_____ 732, 898
Maher, Robert W_____ 377, 378, 842
Straub, Terrence D_____ 990
Congressional Liaison (Senate)____ 467,
732
Consumer Affairs. *See* Peterson,
Esther
Martin, Louis E_____ 39, 49, 886n.
Weddington, Sarah_____ 553,
772 ftn., 773, 888

White House Statements

Australia, meeting with Primer Minister Fraser_____ 3
Egypt
President Sadat, meetings with__ 407, 410
Vice President Mubarak, meeting
with _____ 1023
Germany, Federal Republic of, meeting with Chancellor Schmidt_____ 1005
Israel, meeting with Prime Minister
Begin _____ 372, 374, 382
National Advisory Committee for
Women _____ 27
National health plan legislation_____ 65
Oil prices decontrol_____ 931
Soviet citizens' exchange with U.S.___ 731
Strategic arms limitation_____ 329
Three Mile Island nuclear plant, Pa__ 617
Truckers' strike, independent_____ 1135

Whitten, Repr. Jamie L_____ 240, 591n.
Wichita Falls, Tex_____ 665, 668
Wicker, Veronica D_____ 1018, 1019
Wien Air Alaska_____ 89, 293
Wiesel, Elie_____ 293, 685
Wilderness areas_____ 151
Wilderness Preservation System, National _____ 240, 671
Wilkes, Peter J_____ 788

Wilkins, Roy_____ 323
Williams, Sen. Harrison A., Jr_____ 385,
386, 898, 943
Williams, James H. *See* Agriculture,
Deputy Secretary of
Williams, Richard L_____ 667, 668
Williams, William E_____ 919, 927
Willis, William_____ 23
Wilson, Margaret Bush_____ 931
Wilson, Rosine McFaddin_____ 466
Wilson, Wade_____ 742, 911, 913
Wilson, Woodrow_____ 832
Wimer, Connie_____ 466
Winberry, Charles B., Jr_____ 554, 555
Wind energy systems_____ 1104
Windfall profits tax
See also Energy security trust fund
Announcement _____ 610, 611
Appeal for congressional and public
support _____ 653,
718, 753, 790, 801, 830, 912, 982
Congressional amendments to President's proposal, possibility_ 749, 753, 790
Congressmen, meeting with the President _____ 732
Mentions _____ 802, 805, 848, 873, 905, 933
Message to Congress transmitting proposals _____ 721, 728
News conference_____ 733 (Checklist)
Wiretapping _____ 585, 587
Wiretapping and Electronic Surveillance,
National Commission for the Review
of Federal and State Laws Relating to_ 585,
587–590
Wisconsin
Emergency declaration_____ 89
President's visit_____ 567, 572, 573
Wogan, Gerald N_____ 686
Wolf, Peter H_____ 46, 91
Women
Administration's accomplishments and
goals _____ 888
Business enterprises_____ 887, 890, 894
Employment _____ 126, 890
Equal rights amendment. *See* Equal
rights amendment
Judicial appointments___ 131, 759, 772, 847
Women, Equality, Development and
Peace, United Nations Decade for____ 825
Women, National Advisory Committee
for. *See* National Advisory Committee
for Women
Women, President's Advisory Committee
for _____ 825, 826
Women Business Owners, Interagency
Task Force on_____ 890, 894, 895
Women Voters of the United States,
League of_____ 771
Women's Business Enterprise, Interagency Committee on_____ 891, 892, 894
Women's Caucus for Art awards_____ 217
Women's Educational Programs, National Advisory Council on_____ 339, 377
Wood, John H., Jr_____ 959

Woodburning stoves
  Installation tax credit_____ 701, 1102
  New designs_____ 793
  White House installation_____ 793, 801
Woodcock, Leonard_____ 41, 88, 91, 348
Woods, Jessie A_____ 45, 92
Work and training opportunities act, pro-
  posed _____ 938
Working Group on Rural Development___ 75
World Health Assembly_____ 815
World Hunger, Presidential Commission
  on _____ 147, 213
World Trade Week (Proc. 4654)_____ 616
Worldwide Administrative Radio Con-
  ference _____ 541
Wright, Repr. Jim_____ 1125
Wright, Martha Sinnard_____ 466
Wright, Scott O_____ 957, 958
Wruble, Bernhardt K_____ 41
Wurfel, Walter W_____ 189, 566, 628
Wyant, Dennis R_____ 339, 377, 974
Wyman, Rosalind W_____ 45, 92
Wynn, William H_____ 1008, 1009

Yarborough, Richard W_____ 46, 90
Yidan, Yigael_____ 428n.
York, Herbert F_____ 215, 1129, 1143

Young, Andrew J. *See* United Nations,
  U.S. Representative
Young, Mrs. Andrew J_____ 376
Young, Coleman_____ 948, 954n.
Yugoslavia, earthquake in_____ 670

Zablocki, Repr. Clement J___ 572, 591n., 643
Zabludovsky, Jacobo_____ 235
Zamyatin, Leonid_____ 1143
Zero-base budgeting_____ 75, 97, 100
Zhao Zhongxiang_____ 163
Zimbabwe-Rhodesia
  Elections
    Comments on_____ 737, 755
    President's assessment_____ 1013
  Majority rule, U.S. policy____ 39, 357, 755
  Mentions _____ 902, 1006
  Trade sanctions
    Comments on_____ 755, 847, 965
    Meeting with congressional leaders_ 1018
      (Digest)
    News conference_____ 1020 (Checklist)
    President's decision_____ 1013
Zimmerman, Harriet M_____ 46, 90
Zobel, Rya W_____ 179, 180
Zorinsky, Sen. Edward_____ 956
Zukerman, Pinchas_____ 526
Zumas, Nicholas H_____ 819

U.S. GOVERNMENT PRINTING OFFICE : 1980—O-44-000